Landmark Supreme Court Cases

The Most Influential Decisions
of the Supreme Court of the United States

Gary Hartman

Roy M. Mersky

Cindy L. Tate

Facts On File, Inc.

Landmark Supreme Court Cases: The Most Influential Decisions of the Supreme Court of the United States

Copyright © 2004 by Gary Hartman and Roy M. Mersky

Facts On File, Inc.
132 West 31st Street
New York NY 10001

Library of Congress Cataloging-in-Publication Data

Hartman, Gary R.
    Landmark Supreme Court cases : the most influential decisions of the Supreme Court of the United States / Gary Hartman and Roy M. Mersky
        p. cm.
    Includes bibliographical references and index.
    ISBN 0-8160-2452-9 (alk. paper)
    1. United States. Supreme Court. 2. Law—United States—Cases. I. Mersky, Roy M. II. Tate, Cindy L. III. United States. Supreme Court. IV. Title.
KF8742.H37 2003
347.73'26—dc222003057776

Facts On File books are available at special discounts when purchased in bulk quantities for businesses, associations, institutions, or sales promotions. Please call our Special Sales Department in New York at (212) 967-8800 or (800) 322-8755.

You can find Facts On File on the World Wide Web at http://www.factsonfile.com

Text design by Erika K. Arroyo
Cover design by Cathy Rincon

Printed in the United States of America

VB Hermitage 10 9 8 7 6 5 4 3 2 1

This book is printed on acid-free paper.

CONTENTS

LIST OF ENTRIES BY SUBJECT

PREFACE

Landmark Supreme Court Cases is a reference guide that summarizes some of the most important decisions of the U.S. Supreme Court. This book provides a snapshot of the issues, history, and arguments leading to the significant decisions of our highest court. Information on the results of the cases and their effect on legal, social, and political positions in our nation is also provided. The authors hope that these brief summaries will pique your interest and lead you to seek out and read the related cases and recommended readings found at the end of each summary. As you use this book, you will encounter many legal citations, which are references to where the complete decision of the Supreme Court can be found for a particular case. These citations begin with the case name, printed in italics. The first number following the case name is the volume number of the publication in which the decision may be found. This number is followed by an abbreviation of the name of the publication, called a report or reporter. The publication abbreviation is followed by a page number on which the decision may be found within the publication. Finally, the citation concludes with the year in which the case was decided.

INTRODUCTION

The U.S. Supreme Court was created by Article III of the U.S. Constitution as the third branch of the federal government. Unlike the constitutional provisions for the executive and legislative branches of the federal government, the constitutional provision for the judicial branch was written in broad, general terms. This generality has given the Court and Congress the flexibility to make some adjustments to the Court as American government and society changed while still adhering to the Court's constitutionally designated role of interpreting the Constitution. Congress initially supplemented the constitutional provisions for the federal judiciary by enacting the Judiciary Act of 1789, which set up the structure of our federal court system and set the number of justices that would sit on the Supreme Court, among other things. However, the number of justices sitting on the Supreme Court was repeatedly adjusted, ranging in number from six to ten, with Congress finally settling on nine, the current number, in 1869. In 1803, the Court itself supplemented the constitutional provisions with its decision in *Marbury v. Madison*, giving itself the power to review the constitutionality of congressional legislation.

While the constitutional provisions for the Supreme Court are written broadly, they are not without their limitations. Justices of the Supreme Court are appointed for life by the president, but must be confirmed by a majority of the Senate. The Supreme Court is limited to hearing and reviewing actual cases and controversies. Therefore, an actual disagreement over an issue must exist. Moreover, the Supreme Court does not give advisory opinions, advice on whether a law or action would be constitutional given a hypothetical situation.

The Supreme Court has two types of jurisdiction: original jurisdiction, which allows the Court to act as a trial court, and appellate jurisdiction, which allows the Court to review the decisions of lower federal or state courts. Further, the Court has two types of appellate jurisdiction, mandatory and discretionary. The cases in this book that refer to the parties as Appellant and Appellee are cases of mandatory appellate jurisdiction. The cases that refer to Petitioner and Respondent are cases of discretionary jurisdiction. The Court's discretionary jurisdiction is invoked by parties through the filing of a "petition for certiorari," which requests review. The Court reviews these petitions and if four justices vote in favor of review, the case will come before the Court. Each year approximately 7,000 cases are filed in the Supreme Court. During its term, which begins in October and ends in June or July, the Court actually hears about 150 cases and writes approximately 90 opinions.

During the Court sessions, the Court hears oral arguments on the issues. After the oral arguments, the Court votes to come to a decision. After a decision, the opinions are written with the senior justice of the majority assigning the writing of the majority opinion and the senior justice of the minority assigning the writing of the minority opinion. Other justices may write separate opinions to express their individual views.

The Supreme Court's decisions initially had little impact on the shaping of our nation as the Court's early decisions focused on small issues such as whether to wear wigs during the Court sessions and on organizational issues. Additionally, the early Court had no home of its own. The Court borrowed space in other government buildings and many of the justices wrote their opinions at home. As the Court has evolved it found a permanent home across from the Capitol in Washington, D.C., and its opinions have shaped American government and society because, not only do the opinions address the specific dispute at hand, but they also interpret legal issues and answer policy questions that have a much broader effect than just the specific dispute at hand. Issues in the form of legal questions have allowed the Court to make policy affecting abortion, capital punishment, criminal procedure, and other policy issues you will find throughout this book.

This book will give you a glimpse of our highest court and its evolution through changing times and changing justices, an evolution that reflects its importance as the interpreter of the U.S. Constitution.

SOURCES

Barnum, David G. *The Supreme Court & American Democracy.* New York: St. Martin's Press, 1993.

Baum, Lawrence. *The Supreme Court.* 2d ed. Washington, D.C.: Congressional Quarterly, Inc., 1985.

Schwartz, Bernard. *A History of the Supreme Court.* New York: Oxford University Press, 1993.

Wasby, Stephen L. *The Supreme Court in the Federal Judicial System.* New York: Holt, Rinehart and Winston, 1984.

Witt, Elder, ed. *The Supreme Court and Its Work.* Washington, D.C.: Congressional Quarterly, Inc., 1981.

LANDMARK SUPREME COURT CASES

ABORTION

Case Title: *Harris v. McRae*

Legal Citation: 448 U.S. 297

Year of Decision: 1980

KEY ISSUES

Does it violate the equal protection clause of the Fifth Amendment or the establishment clause of the First Amendment to limit federal funds to reimburse for the cost of an abortion under a Medicaid program?

HISTORY OF THE CASE

In 1965 Title XIX of the Social Security Act established the Medicaid program. The program provides federal financial assistance to states that reimburse the costs for medical treatment for needy persons. In 1976, Congress passed the Hyde Amendment that banned the use of federal funds to reimburse the costs of an abortion under a Medicaid program. Later versions of the Hyde Amendment allowed some exceptions. Actions were brought in federal district court by indigent women who sued on behalf of similarly situated women; the New York City Health and Hospitals Corporation, which provided abortion services; Officers of the Women's Division of the Board of Global Ministries of the United Methodist Church, which sought to enjoin enforcement of the Hyde Amendment on the grounds that it violated the due process clause of the Fifth Amendment, the free exercise clause of the First Amendment, and the obligation under Title XIX to provide funds for all medically necessary abortions.

SUMMARY OF ARGUMENTS

The plaintiffs argued that the Hyde Amendment was unconstitutional in that it severely limited the rights of poor women to gain access to an abortion, in violation of the due process clause of the Fifth Amendment and the free exercise and establishment clauses of the First Amendment.

DECISION

Justice Stewart wrote the opinion. He held that Title XIX of the Social Security Act does not require a state to pay for a medically necessary abortion. He noted that nothing in the legislative history revealed that Congress intended to require participating states to assume the full costs of providing any medical service in its plan. The purpose of Congress in enacting Title XIX was to provide federal assistance for all legitimate state expenditures under an approved Medicaid plan. In addition, the legislative history of the Hyde Amendment does not reveal that Congress intended the states to continue to fund medically necessary abortion even when federal funding was withdrawn.

In addition, he wrote that the funding restrictions in the Hyde Amendment do not violate the "liberty" interest identified in *ROE V. WADE* as including the freedom to decide whether to terminate a pregnancy. The reasons for this are that the Hyde Amendment does not place a government obstacle in the path of women who choose to terminate a pregnancy; there is no constitutional entitlement to funds for the full range of protected reproductive choices; to read such a requirement into the Constitution would require that Congress subsidize such procedures even when it had not enacted a medical program such as Medicaid to subsidize other medically necessary services.

He continued that although the amendment may coincide with the tenets of the Roman Catholic Church, this fact does not indicate the government's aid of or preference for the Catholic religion and make the amendment a violation of the establishment clause. He also held that the petitioners lacked standing to assert the challenge to the Hyde Amendment. The named parties for the indigent women did not allege or prove that they "sought an abortion under compulsion of religious belief." The officers of the Women's Division of the Board of Global Ministries of the United Methodist Church failed to allege that they are or expect to be pregnant, or that they are eligible for Medicaid. They therefore lacked a personal interest in the complaint that is needed to confer standing. The Women's Division as an organization fails to meet the requirement of standing because the claim is of the type "that required participation of the individual members for a proper understanding and resolution of their free exercise claims."

According to the opinion, the Hyde Amendment did not violate the Fifth Amendment equal protection provision because the government neither invaded a substantive constitutional right or freedom, nor acted with the purpose of treating a suspect class in a detrimental manner. The requirement of the equal protection provision is that a purposefully detrimental action be directed at a suspect class. The Court held that the amendment was rationally related to the legitimate state interest of protecting potential life by encouraging childbirth.

Justice White wrote a concurring opinion in which he noted that in MAHER V. ROE (1977) the Court held that allowing costs for childbirth and defraying costs for nontherapeutic abortions violated the equal protection provision of the Fifth Amendment. He argued that the *Maher* case was indistinguishable from the one at issue. He reasoned that the Court in *Maher* held that the government is not required to fund nontherapeutic abortions if doing so furthered the legitimate state interest in normal childbirth.

Justice Brennan wrote a dissenting opinion in which Justices Blackmun and Marshall joined. He reasoned that through its refusal to subsidize abortions, the Hyde Amendment effectively removed an indigent woman's right to choose abortion over childbirth.

Justice Marshall wrote a dissenting opinion in which he argued that the case was different from the case in *Maher*. He reasoned that the petitioners in *Harris* were seeking a benefit that was available to nonindigent women in a similar situation. In *Maher* the Court held that the denial of funding for nontherapeutic abortions was not a denial of equal protection because the Medicaid funding was available only for medically necessary procedures.

Justice Stevens wrote a dissenting opinion in which he argued, similar to Justice Marshall, that the petitioners in this case were not in the same situation as those in *Maher*. They were objecting to their exclusion from a benefit that was available to all other women who had the means to pay for an abortion. In addition, he argued that in *Roe v. Wade* it was decided that even after the fetus was viable, a state could not prohibit an abortion to protect the health of the mother. Conceding this, he said the exercise of the right to protect one's own health could not be the basis for denying an abortion to which she would otherwise be entitled were she not indi-gent. He said it was misleading of the Court to focus on the legitimate state interest, when in cases where that interest conflicts with the health of the mother the Court has conceded that the state's interest must yield.

Aftermath

In *Poelker v. Doe* (1977), the Court upheld a policy that prohibited abortions in public hospitals except in cases in which there was a threat of grave physiological injury or death. In *Beal v. Doe* (1977), the Court held that the Social Security Act does not require states to fund nontherapeutic abortions for participation in the Medicaid program. In WEBSTER V. REPRODUCTIVE HEALTH SERVICES (1989), the Court sustained a Missouri law that made it unlawful for any public facility to perform abortions other than to save the life of the mother. In abandoning the trimester approach to determining viability, it strengthened the anti-abortion position on the Court. In later decisions the Court has upheld the constitutionality of parental notification requirements.

Significance

This case addresses direct payment to a woman or her doctor to subsidize abortion. Together with *Maher* it has provided the Court with the power to prohibit abortions in public hospitals, even in cases in which a woman does not seek state aid. In providing that the state may legitimately withhold funds to poor women seeking nontherapeutic abortions, the Court restricted the availability of choice provided by Roe and set the stage for further restrictions on the right to an abortion. It set the stage for such cases as *Webster,* which further restricted the right provided by *Roe*.

Related Cases

Beal v. Doe, 432 U.S. 438 (1977)

Belloti v. Baird, 443 U.S. 622 (1979)

City of Akron. Akron Center for Reproductive Health, Inc., 462 U.S. 416 (1983)

Maher, Commissioner of Social Services v. Roe, 432 U.S. 464 (1977)

Planned Parenthood of Central Missouri v. Danforth, 428 U.S. 52 (1976)

Poelker v. Doe, 432 U.S. 519 (1977)

Roe v. Wade, 410 U.S. 113 (1973)

Webster v. Reproductive Health Services, 492 U.S. 490 (1989)

RECOMMENDED READING

M. Perry, *Why the Supreme Court Was Plainly Wrong in the Hyde Amendment Case: A Brief Comment on Harris v. McRae,* 32 Stanford Law Review 1113 (1980).

Tribe, Laurence. *Constitutional Choices.* Cambridge, Mass.: Harvard University Press, 1985.

Peter Westen, *Correspondence,* 33 Stanford Law Review 1187 (1981).

Case Title: *Maher, Commissioner of Social Services v. Roe*

Legal Citations: 432 U.S. 464; 97 S.Ct. 2376; 53 L.Ed. 2d 484

Year of Decision: 1977

KEY ISSUES

Does a Connecticut statute prohibiting the use of Medicaid funds in payment of abortions that are not medically necessary violate the equal protection clause of the Fourteenth Amendment?

HISTORY OF THE CASE

Under the Connecticut statute, for a patient to have an abortion in the first three months of pregnancy (first trimester) paid for with public funds (Medicaid), the medical facility must submit a certificate from the patient's physician stating that the abortion is medically necessary. The two persons involved in this case were unable to obtain certification and brought this suit in federal district court claiming violation of the due process and equal protection clauses of the Fourteenth Amendment. The district court held that the Fourteenth Amendment forbids exclusion of nontherapeutic abortions from a state welfare program that covers medical expenses that are part of pregnancy and childbirth.

SUMMARY OF ARGUMENTS

Maher, the commissioner of social services of Connecticut, argued that the Connecticut statute did not violate the equal protection and due process clauses of the Fourteenth Amendment.

Susan Roe argued that the Connecticut statute violated the equal protection and due process clauses of the Fourteenth Amendment. Roe argued that Connecticut must treat abortion and childbirth equally.

DECISION

States are not required by the Constitution to fund abortions, whether or not medically necessary. There is no explicit right to health care.

Justice Powell delivered the opinion: A state is under no obligation to provide medical care, but when it does, it is subject to constitutional limits. The fact that the impact of the regulation falls on the poor does not unduly burden such a person, because Connecticut funds childbirth. The woman's position remains the same.

Justice Brennan wrote a dissent saying that the majority is allowing states to interfere indirectly with the privacy right, thereby protecting the rich but not the poor.

AFTERMATH

This decision has its major impact on persons dependent on public health care who seek reimbursement for abortion, while funding at greater expense the persons who carry their pregnancies to term.

SIGNIFICANCE

This case shows the evolution of the concept of medical privacy. Several other states also have restricted the use of public funds for elective abortions.

RELATED CASES

Harris v. McRae, 448 U.S. 297 (1980)

Poelker v. Doe, 432 U.S. 438 (1977)

Williams v. Zbaraz, 448 U.S. 358 (1980)

RECOMMENDED READING

Bobbitt, Philip. *Constitutional Fate: Theory of the Constitution.* New York: Oxford University Press, 1982.

Samuel Estreicher, *Congressional Power and Congressional Rights: Reflections on Proposed "Human Life" Legislation,* 68 Virginia Law Review 333 (1982).

Case Title: *Planned Parenthood of Central Missouri v. Danforth*

Legal Citations: 428 U.S. 52; 49 L.Ed. 2d. 788; 96 S.Ct. 2831

Year of Decision: 1976

KEY ISSUES

Were certain provisions of a Missouri statute regulating abortion unconstitutional?

HISTORY OF THE CASE

Litigation instituted in the U.S. District Court for the Eastern District of Missouri challenged the validity, under the U.S. Constitution, of a Missouri statute setting forth conditions and limitations on abortions and establishing criminal offenses for noncompliance with the various conditions and limitations. The specific provisions of the statute attacked were (1) a provision defining "viability," for purposes that any abortion not necessary to preserve the life or health of the mother should not be performed unless the attending physician would certify with reasonable medical certainty that the fetus is not viable, as that stage of fetal development when the life of the unborn child may be continued indefinitely outside the womb by natural or artificial life-supportive systems, (2) a provision requiring that a woman, prior to submitting to an abortion during the first 12 weeks of pregnancy, must certify in writing her consent to the procedure and that her consent is informed, freely given, and not the result of coercion, (3) a provision requiring the prior written consent of the spouse of a woman seeking an abortion during the first 12 weeks of pregnancy, unless the abortion were certified by a physician to be necessary for preservation of the mother's life, (4) a provision, with respect to the first 12 weeks of pregnancy when the pregnant woman is unmarried and under 18 years of age, for the written consent of a parent or legal guardian unless the abortion were certified by a physician as necessary for preservation of the mother's life, (5) a provision

prohibiting the saline amniocentesis technique of abortion, in which the amniotic fluid is withdrawn and a saline or other fluid is inserted into the amniotic sac, after the first 12 weeks of pregnancy, (6) recordkeeping and reporting provisions, imposing requirements upon health facilities and physicians concerned with abortions, irrespective of the pregnancy stage, and (7) a standard of care provision, declaring, in its first sentence, that no person who performs or induces an abortion shall fail to exercise that degree of professional skill, care, and diligence to preserve the life and health of the fetus that such person would be required to exercise in order to preserve the life and health of any fetus intended to be born and not aborted, and providing, in its second sentence, that any physician or person assisting in an abortion who failed to take such measures to encourage or sustain the life of the child would be deemed guilty of manslaughter if the child's death resulted. The district court upheld the constitutionality of the several challenged provisions of the statute with the exception of the first sentence of the standard of care provision.

SUMMARY OF ARGUMENTS

The complaint charged that certain provisions of the bill were invalid in that they deprived the plaintiffs and their patients of various alleged constitutional rights, including the privacy of the doctor-patient relationship, the physician's right to the free exercise of medical practice, the right of a woman to determine whether to bear children, the right to life of their patients, and the right to receive adequate medical treatment, all in violation of the First, Fourth, Fifth, Eighth, Ninth, and Fourteenth Amendments to the U.S. Constitution. The petition further alleges that the legislation violates the rights of due process and equal protection guaranteed plaintiffs and their patients under the Constitution, and that it imposes a cruel and unusual punishment upon women for forcing them to bear pregnancies that they conceive.

DECISION

On direct appeals from the decision of the three-judge district court, the U.S. Supreme Court affirmed in part, reversed in part, and remanded. In an opinion by Justice Blackmun, it was held, expressing the unanimous view of the Court, that (1) the viability definition provision, which reflected the fact that the determination of viability, varying with each pregnancy, was a matter for the judgment of the responsible attending physician, was not unconstitutional, since it did not circumvent the permissible limitations on state regulation of abortions, (2) the pregnant woman's consent provision was not unconstitutional since the state could validly require a pregnant woman's prior written consent for an abortion to assure awareness of the abortion decision and its significance, and (3) the recordkeeping and reporting provisions were not constitutionally offensive in themselves and imposed no legally significant impact or consequence on the abortion decision or on the physician-patient relationship; expressing the view of six members of the Court, that (4) the spousal consent provision was unconstitutional, since the state, being unable to regulate or proscribe abortions during the first stage of pregnancy when a physician and patient make such decision, could not delegate authority to any particular person, even a pregnant woman's spouse, to prevent abortion during the first stage of pregnancy, (5) the first sentence of the standard of care provision was unconstitutional, since it impermissibly required a physician to preserve the life and health of a fetus, whatever the stage of the pregnancy, and this provision was not severable from the rest of the standard of care provision and, expressing the view of five members of the Court, that (6) the parental consent provision was unconstitutional, since the state did not have the constitutional authority to give a third party an absolute, and possibly arbitrary, veto over the decision of a physician and his patient to terminate the patient's pregnancy, regardless of the reason for withholding the consent, and (7) the saline amniocentesis prohibition provision was unconstitutional since it failed as a reasonable regulation for the protection of maternal health, being instead an unreasonable or arbitrary regulation designed to inhibit the vast majority of abortions after the first 12 weeks of pregnancy.

AFTERMATH

The ad hoc nature of the strict scrutiny test used to examine governmental regulations of abortion procedures was well demonstrated on a single day in 1983 when the Supreme Court decided three separate cases involving several different types of abortion regulations (*Akron v. Akron Center for Reproductive Health, Inc.,* 462 U.S. 416; *Planned Parenthood v. Ashcroft,* 462 U.S. 476; *Simopoulos v. Virginia,* 462 U.S. 506). Six justices required that government regulations of previability abortions comply with the principles set forth in ROE V. WADE; these regulations must be reasonably related to the "compelling" interest in protecting the health of the woman. These justices wished to use this approach to protect the *Roe v. Wade* principle that a woman has a fundamental right to choose to have an abortion free from interference by the state with her decision or the professional judgment of her attending physician. In contrast three justices called into question the legitimacy of judicial control of abortion regulations (although they did not advocate, at this time, a direct overruling of *Roe*) because they believed that courts should uphold any government regulation of abortion that was not totally arbitrary.

A majority of the justices on the Supreme Court, throughout the 1980s, believed that the right of privacy only protected a woman's ability to choose to have an abortion without certain types of government interference and did not give women a right to have an abortion at government expense. Thus, in WEBSTER V. REPRODUCTIVE HEALTH SERVICES (492 U.S. 490), the Supreme Court upheld a state law prohibition against the use of public facilities or public funds for abortion services.

SIGNIFICANCE

The decision in *Danforth* further refines *Roe* by allowing and disallowing certain medical and procedural restrictions on the woman's right to receive an abortion.

RELATED CASES

Ohio v. Akron Center for Reproductive Health, 497 U.S. 502 (1990)

Planned Parenthood of Southeastern Pennsylvania v. Casey, 505 U.S. 833 (1992)

Rust v. Sullivan, 500 U.S. 173 (1991)

RECOMMENDED READING

Keynes, Edward, with Randall K. Miller. *The Courts vs. Congress: Prayer, Busing and Abortion.* Durham, N.C.: Duke University Press, 1989.

David A. J. Richard, *The Individual, the Family and the Constitution: A Jurisprudential Perspective*, 55 New York University Law Review 1 (April 1980).

John Siliciano, *The Minor's Right to Privacy: Limitations on State Action after Danforth and Carey*, 77 Columbia Law Review 1216 (December 1977).

Case Title: *Roe v. Wade*

Legal Citations: 410 U.S. 113; 35 L.Ed. 2d. 147; 93 S.Ct. 705

Year of Decision: 1973

KEY ISSUES

May a state constitutionally make it a crime to procure an abortion except to save the mother's life?

HISTORY OF THE CASE

Three reasons have been advanced to explain historically the enactment of criminal abortion laws in the 19th century and to justify their continued existence. (1) It has been argued that these laws were the product of a Victorian social concern to discourage illicit sexual conduct. (2) Concern with abortion as a medical procedure. When most criminal abortion laws were first enacted, the procedure was hazardous to the woman. (3) The state's interest in protecting prenatal life.

An unmarried pregnant woman who wished to terminate her pregnancy by abortion instituted an action in the U.S. District Court for the Northern District of Texas, seeking a judgment that the Texas criminal abortion statutes, which prohibited abortions except for the medical purpose of saving the mother's life, were unconstitutional. She also sought an injunction against their continued enforcement. A physician, who alleged that he had been previously arrested for violations of the Texas statutes and that two prosecutions were presently pending against him in the state courts, sought and was granted permission to intervene. A separate action, similar to that filed by the

unmarried, pregnant woman, was filed by a married, childless couple, who alleged that should the wife become pregnant at some future date, they would wish to terminate the pregnancy by abortion. The two actions were consolidated and heard together by a three-judge district court, which held that (1) the unmarried, pregnant woman and the physician had standing to sue, (2) the married, childless couple's complaint should be dismissed because they lacked standing to sue, (3) abstention was not warranted with respect to a declaratory judgment, (4) the right to choose whether to have children was protected by the Ninth Amendment through the 14th Amendment, (5) the Texas criminal abortion statutes were unconstitutionally vague and overbroad, and (6) the application for injunctive relief should be denied under the abstention doctrine. All parties appealed to the U.S. Court of Appeals for the Fifth Circuit to preserve their arguments, which court ordered the appeals be suspended pending decision on the appeal taken by all parties to the U.S. Supreme Court from the district court's denial of injunctive relief.

SUMMARY OF ARGUMENTS

Roe alleged that she was unmarried and pregnant; that she wished to terminate her pregnancy by an abortion "performed by a competent, licensed physician, under safe, clinical conditions"; that she was unable to get a "legal" abortion in Texas because her life did not appear to be threatened by the continuation of her pregnancy; and that she could not afford to travel to another jurisdiction in order to secure a legal abortion under safe conditions. She claimed that the Texas statutes were unconstitutionally vague and that they abridged her right of personal privacy, protected by the First, Fourth, Fifth, Ninth, and Fourteenth Amendments. By an amendment to her complaint, Roe purported to sue "on behalf of herself and all other women" in her situation.

James Hubert Hallford, a licensed physician, alleged that he had been arrested previously for violations of the Texas abortion statutes. He described conditions of patients who came to him seeking abortions, and he claimed that for many cases he, as a physician, was unable to determine whether they fell within or outside the exception recognized by the state law—to save the life of the mother. He alleged that, as a consequence, the statutes were vague and uncertain, in violation of the Fourteenth Amendment, and that they violated his own and his patients' rights to privacy in the doctor-patient relationship and his own right to practice medicine, rights he claimed were guaranteed by the First, Fourth, Fifth, Ninth, and Fourteenth Amendments.

John and Mary Doe, a married couple, filed a companion complaint. The Does alleged that they were a childless couple; that Mrs. Doe was suffering from a "neural-chemical" disorder; that her physician had "advised her to avoid pregnancy until such time as her condition has materially improved" (although a pregnancy at the present time would not present "a serious risk" to her life); that, following medical advice, she had discontinued use of birth control pills; and that if she should become pregnant, she would want to terminate the pregnancy by an abortion performed by a competent, licensed physician under safe, clinical conditions. By an amendment to their complaint, the Does purported to sue "on behalf of themselves and all couples similarly situated."

DECISION

On appeal, the U.S. Supreme Court dismissed the physician's complaint, but affirmed the district court's judgment in all other respects. In an opinion by Justice Blackmun, expressing the views of seven members of the Court, it was held that (1) the pregnant, unmarried woman had standing to sue, (2) the complaint of the childless, married couple presented no actual justiciable case or controversy, and had been properly dismissed, (3) states have legitimate interests in seeing that abortions are performed under circumstances that insure maximum safety for the patient, (4) the right to privacy encompasses a woman's decision whether or not to terminate her pregnancy, (5) a woman's right to terminate her pregnancy is not absolute, and may to some extent be limited by the state's legitimate interests in safeguarding the woman's health, in maintaining proper medical standards, and in protecting potential human life, (6) the unborn are not included within the definition of "person" as used in the Fourteenth Amendment, (7) prior to the end of the first trimester of pregnancy, the state may not interfere with or regulate an attending physician's decision, reached in consultation with his patient, that the patient's pregnancy should be terminated, (8) from and after the end of the first trimester, and

until the time when the fetus becomes viable (able to survive outside the mother's body), the state may regulate the abortion procedure only to the extent that such regulation relates to the preservation and protection of maternal health, (9) from and after the time when the fetus becomes viable, the state may prohibit abortions altogether, except those necessary to preserve the life or health of the mother, and (10) the state may proscribe the performance of all abortions except those performed by physicians currently licensed by the state; and expressing the view of six members of the Court, it was held that the physician's complaint should be dismissed and he should return to the pending state court proceeding and the remedies available there.

AFTERMATH

The *Roe v. Wade* majority opinion appeared to establish a rigid "trimester" structure for the judicial examination of abortion regulations. Virtually no regulations would be upheld that related to first trimester abortions; any regulation of abortions performed between the end of the first trimester and the time when the fetus was viable (as determined by an attending physician) would be upheld only if the regulation was narrowly tailored to protect the health of the woman. Abortions could be outlawed after the fetus was viable, although the ban on postviability abortions, and all other abortion regulations, would have to include an exception for abortions performed to protect the life or health of the woman. In the late 1970s and throughout the 1980s the Supreme Court's rulings, though not its opinions, appeared to adopt a test of "reasonableness" for abortion regulations. State abortion regulations that were reasonably related to protecting the pregnant woman, or were reasonably related to protecting the health or existence of a viable fetus, would be upheld. An abortion regulation would be invalidated if a majority of justices believed that the regulation merely deterred abortions and was not a reasonable means of protecting a pregnant woman or a viable fetus. In 1989, in *Webster v. Reproductive Health Services,* a majority of justices on the Supreme Court appeared to reject the *Roe v. Wade* formal "trimester" analytical structure although they did not at that time replace the *Roe* analysis with any new test for the judicial review of abortion regulations.

In *Planned Parenthood v. Casey* (1992), the Court reviewed Pennsylvania abortion law. This required informed consent and a 24-hour waiting period prior to the procedure. A minor seeking an abortion required the consent of one parent (the law allowed for a judicial bypass procedure which would allow the minor to get court approval instead of parental consent). A married woman seeking an abortion had to indicate that she notified her husband of her intention to abort the fetus. In a bitter, 5-4 decision, the Court again reaffirmed *Roe*, but it upheld most of the Pennsylvania provisions. For the first time, the justices imposed a new standard to determine the validity of laws restricting abortions. The new standard asks whether a state abortion regulation has the purpose or effect of imposing an "undue burden," which is defined as a "substantial obstacle in the path of a woman seeking an abortion before the fetus attains viability." Under this standard, the only provision to fail the undue-burden test was the husband notification requirement.

SIGNIFICANCE

The Court held that a woman's right to an abortion fell within the right to privacy (recognized in *Griswold v. Connecticut*) protected by the Fourteenth Amendment. The decision gave a woman total autonomy over the pregnancy during the first trimester and defined different levels of state interest for the second and third trimesters. As a result, the laws of 46 states were affected by the Court's ruling.

RELATED CASES

Baker v. Carr, 396 U.S. 186, 204 (1962)

Bray v. Alexandria Women's Health Clinic, 506 U.S. 263 (1993)

Griswold v. Connecticut, 381 U.S. 479 (1965)

Planned Parenthood of Southeastern Pennsylvania v. Casey, 505 U.S. 833 (1992)

Republic National Bank of Miami v. United States, 506 U.S. 80 (1992)

RECOMMENDED READING

John Hart Ely, *The Wages of Crying Wolf: A Comment on* Roe v. Wade, 82 Yale Law Journal 920 (April–July 1973).

Faux, Marian. *Roe v. Wade.* New York: Macmillan, 1980.

Glendon, Mary Ann. *Abortion and Divorce in Western Law.* Cambridge, Mass.: Harvard University Press, 1987.

Horan, Dennis, et al., eds. *Abortion and the Constitution: Reversing* Roe v. Wade *through the Courts.* Washington, D.C.: Georgetown University Press, 1987.

Keynes, Edward, with Randall K. Miller. *The Court vs. Congress: Prayer, Busing and Abortion.* Durham, N.C.: Duke University Press, 1989.

Rabin, Eva R. *Abortion, Politics and the Courts:* Roe v. Wade *and Its Aftermath.* New York: Greenwood Press, 1987.

Schwartz, Bernard. *The Ascent of Pragmatism: The Burger Court in Action.* New York: Addison-Wesley, 1990.

Case Title: *Thornburgh v. American College of Obstetricians and Gynecologists*

Legal Citations: 476 U.S. 747; 106 S.Ct. 2169; 90 L.Ed. 2d 779

Year of Decision: 1986

KEY ISSUES

Does a Pennsylvania statute aimed toward restricting abortions unconstitutionally restrict the fundamental right to privacy?

HISTORY OF THE CASE

In 1974, the Pennsylvania General Assembly enacted the state's first Abortion Control Act. The Abortion Control Act contained provisions regarding the information a woman was required to receive prior to consenting to an abortion, the reporting requirements imposed upon physicians, and the procedures to be followed when faced with postviability abortions. After five years of litigation, many provisions of this act were struck down as unconstitutional. In 1978 and 1981, the legislature revised the law and imposed restrictions upon both the physician performing and the woman seeking an abortion. Before the law took effect, the American College of Obstetricians and Gynecologists (ACOG) and others sued, alleging the act remained unconstitutional and seeking a preliminary injunction. The federal district court denied the motion almost entirely.

ACOG appealed, and the U.S. Court of Appeals eventually held in favor of ACOG. The court found numerous provisions that unconstitutionally invaded a woman's fundamental right to privacy and remanded the case to the trial court. Pennsylvania attorney general Richard Thornburgh appealed to the Supreme Court.

SUMMARY OF ARGUMENTS

The parties contested three points. First, Attorney General Thornburgh argued that the Court is allowed to review a nonfinal appellate court decision holding a state statute unconstitutional. However, the ACOG argued that U.S. law prevented review by the Supreme Court. Second, Thornburgh asserted that the appellate court exceeded its proper scope of review in considering the matter. ACOG countered that the review standard was appropriate and that the court of appeals properly reversed the district court's injunction denial. Third, and most relevant to the privacy issue, Thornburgh maintained the Pennsylvania abortion act was constitutional, contrary to the appellate court's decision. Furthermore, he claimed that it was consistent with prior Supreme Court decisions. Appellee ACOG argued the opposite: that the court of appeals applied the correct principles when assessing the state law's constitutionality.

DECISION

In the 5-4 decision written by Justice Blackmun, the Court ruled on the three points described above. The Court seemed to equivocate about the procedural issue. The justices agreed with ACOG that a federal statute precluded Supreme Court appellate jurisdiction before a court of appeals final decision; nevertheless, the Supreme Court accepted the case for review, choosing to decide the case on its merits.

With regard to whether the appellate court exceeded its authority in deciding the issues before it on appeal from the trial level, the Court ruled it did not. The Blackmun opinion noted that appropriate review standards typically limit appellate review, as Thornburgh argued. This approach is not an inflexible one, however, and proceedings deviating from the stated norm are allowable given the proper legal and factual circumstances. Here, the Court decided those circumstances existed.

On the privacy issue questions, the Supreme Court invalidated six portions of the Pennsylvania abortion law. The Court ruled that six provisions in the statute unconstitutionally burdened the fundamental right to privacy. One invalidated section, which prescribed in detail the method for securing "informed consent" from the woman, was seen as an "outright attempt to . . . discourag[e] abortion in the privacy of the informed consent dialogue between the woman and her physician." The Court considered the information required by law to be communicated from doctor to patient "intimidating," "overinclusive," and "serv[ing] only to confuse and punish [the woman] and to heighten her anxiety, contrary to accepted medical practice." Other stricken provisions mandated extensive record-keeping by physicians performing abortions, allowed public inspection of the potentially revealing records, and various regulations on post-viability abortions.

AFTERMATH

The *Thornburgh* case represents a deep doctrinal division in the Court. As Justice White wrote in his dissent, when the Supreme Court defines "fundamental" liberties mentioned nowhere in the Constitution, it must act cautiously. How to define the nature, provenance, and legitimacy of the constitutional right to privacy continues to bedevil the Court, and, on a broader level, society at large.

SIGNIFICANCE

Our constitutional right to privacy may be our most cherished civil guarantee as citizens of the United States. Public discussion on the extent of this right continues with respect to abortion, as well as other politically and socially charged issues such as homosexual privacy rights.

RELATED CASES

Akron Center for Reproductive Health, Inc. v. City of Akron, 462 U.S. 416 (1983)

Bowers v. Hardwick, 478 U.S. 186 (1986)

Planned Parenthood Ass'n of Kansas City v. Ashcroft, 462 U.S. 476 (1983)

Planned Parenthood of Central Mo. v. Danforth, 428 U.S. 52 (1976)

Planned Parenthood of S.E. Pa. v. Casey, 505 U.S. 833 (1992)

Roe v. Wade, 410 U.S. 113 (1973)

Webster v. Reproductive Health Services, 492 U.S. 490 (1989)

RECOMMENDED READING

Dworkin, Ronald. *Life's Dominion: An Argument About Abortion, Euthanasia, and Individual Freedom.* New York: Knopf, 1993.

David A. J. Richards, *Constitutional Legitimacy and Constitutional Privacy,* 61 New York University Law Review 800 (1986).

Reva Siegel, *Reasoning from the Body: A Historical Perspective on Abortion Regulation and Questions of Equal Protection,* 44 Stanford Law Review 261 (1992).

Tribe, Laurence H. *Abortion: The Clash of Absolutes.* New York: Norton, 1992.

Wardle, Lynn D. *The Abortion Privacy Doctrine: A Compendium and Critique of Federal Court Abortion Cases.* Buffalo, N.Y.: W. S. Hein, 1980.

Case Title: *Webster v. Reproductive Health Services*

Alternate Case Title: Missouri Abortion Case

Legal Citations: 492 U.S. 490; 109 S.Ct. 3040; 106 L.Ed. 2d 410

Year of Decision: 1989

KEY ISSUES

Did a state law regulating and restricting abortion deprive women of the right to privacy as found in the concept of personal liberty in the Fourteenth Amendment to the U.S. Constitution?

HISTORY OF THE CASE

Webster v. Reproductive Health Services is part of a continuing line of cases considering the individual's constitutional right to privacy first articulated by the Supreme Court in GRISWOLD V. CONNECTICUT (1965). The stormy impact of the right to privacy is the result of its use as the constitutional basis for the most controversial of the Court's decisions, those dealing with abortion. It is also a constitutional right for which the Court has had difficulty finding an encompassing provision. The justices have, therefore, relied on a combination of express and implied constitutional language.

In *Griswold,* a Planned Parenthood group challenged Connecticut state law that made the use of contraceptives illegal. The Supreme Court found the statute invalid under the right to privacy granted by the due process clause of the Fourteenth Amendment. Justice Goldberg in his concurring opinion also relied on the Ninth Amendment, which provides that "enumeration in the constitution of certain rights shall not be construed to deny . . . others retained by the people." His interpretation substantiated his view that any right not reserved to the federal government is reserved to the people and can only be restricted for a compelling state interest.

It was against this background that ROE V. WADE (1973) came before the Court. This controversial decision, written by Justice Blackmun for a 7-2 majority, held that women have a constitutionally protected right to terminate their pregnancies in the early stages. The Fourteenth Amendment encompasses this in the right to privacy, which a government cannot restrict without a compelling state interest. Compelling state interest was defined to include the need to protect the mother after the first trimester, or when the mother's body is no longer essential to continued gestation—that is, the point of viability of the fetus. *Roe v. Wade* further set out a trimester schedule for this compelling state interest. It provided that a woman can make her own decision to terminate her pregnancy during the first 12 weeks. In the second trimester the state may regulate abortion to protect the mother's health, and during the third the state may prohibit abortion at the point of viability.

The unexpected decision in *Roe v. Wade* sparked a surge in anti-abortion activism. Abortion opponents, previously poorly organized, regrouped and within a short period became a political force. They initially sought a constitutional amendment to reverse *Roe* but failed both on the congressional level and later on the state level, where their efforts to organize a constitutional convention encountered fatal opposition. Legislative attempts to curb the jurisdiction of the Supreme Court and to establish that "human life begins at conception" also failed.

Abortion opponents were more successful on the local level in cutting off public funds for abortion. Such action set the stage for a series of cases in which the Court was urged to overrule or limit the decision. Between 1976 and 1985 the Court heard 10 abortion cases. MAHER V. ROE (1977) dealt with the constitutionality of a Connecticut Welfare Department regulation that limited Medicaid benefits to only first trimester therapeutic abortions. *Beal v. Doe* (1977) concerned similar Pennsylvania regulations, and *Poelker v. Doe* (1977) challenged a St. Louis city policy of prohibiting abortions in city hospitals. In *Planned Parenthood v. Danforth* (1976), a Missouri statute required spousal and parental consent before an abortion was considered. In all of these cases, the Court found the regulations unconstitutional in light of the holding.

Again in 1983, in *Akron v. Akron Center for Reproductive Health, Roe* was reaffirmed when the Court declared that a woman had a "fundamental right to abortion" that the city of Akron could not restrict by requiring that all second and third trimester abortions be performed in a hospital. Other cases followed, as did federal and state legislation attempting to restrict *Roe v. Wade.* Only in HARRIS V. McRAE (1980) was federal legislation prohibiting the use of federal funds to perform abortions upheld.

The controversy intensified as the composition of the Supreme Court changed. With appointments by two Republican administrations, abortion opponents felt confident that *Roe v. Wade* could be reversed. It is against this background that the *Webster* case was heard.

In June 1986, the Missouri legislature enacted a statute dealing with unborn children and abortions. The statute's preamble stated that life begins at conception and that this constituted an interest that must be protected by the state. Other statutory provisions required doctors to perform tests on women more than 20 weeks pregnant to ascertain the viability of the fetus before performing an abortion. Public hospitals and public employees were further prohibited from performing nontherapeutic abortions and from providing abortion counseling.

Five health professionals employed by the state and two nonprofit corporations brought a class action in the U.S. District Court for the Western District of Missouri challenging the constitutionality of the statute. The district court struck down each of the provisions discussed above, among others; and the court of appeals affirmed, declaring all challenged provisions unconstitutional under *Roe v. Wade.* Missouri appealed to the Supreme Court to reverse or to otherwise limit the lower court decision.

SUMMARY OF ARGUMENTS

The fever pitch of interest in the case was reflected in the record number of amicus (friend of the court) briefs filed with the Supreme Court. Seventy-eight individuals, groups, and organizations—including law professors, members of Congress, health professionals, and interest groups on both sides of the issue—submitted such briefs.

On April 26, 1989, the Supreme Court convened to hear the oral arguments on the case. The case for Missouri was argued by William L. Webster, attorney general of Missouri, facing Frank Susman, an attorney for Planned Parenthood. Susman argued to uphold the right to abortion under the Fourteenth Amendment's due process clause protecting personal liberty; he also advocated that the right of contraception and the right of abortion are not distinct and separate and that if abortion was illegal then contraception should be illegal.

Webster argued the constitutionality of the provisions of the Missouri statute. Charles Fried, a Harvard Law School professor and formerly solicitor general under the Ronald Reagan administration, argued for the United States as a friend of the court, supporting Missouri and claiming that there is no constitutional right to abortion and that *Roe v. Wade* should be overruled. Fried's brief and that of Missouri proposed that the constitution be interpreted to contain only "rights explicitly mentioned in the text."

The Court began its deliberations and on July 3, 1989, it handed down its decision.

DECISION

Chief Justice Rehnquist announced the 5-4 judgment of the Court. He stated that it was not necessary to pass judgment on the constitutionality of the statute's preamble, which stated that life begins at conception, as it merely reflected the legislature's value judgment favoring childbirth over abortion. Until the provision was used to restrict abortion activities, it need not be addressed. Rehnquist went on to say that state restrictions on the use of public facilities and employees to perform nontherapeutic abortions (but allowing for payment for medical services connected to childbirth) did not conflict with previous court decisions nor with the due process clause, as the Fourteenth Amendment does not grant a right to government aid even when necessary to secure "life, liberty or property interest."

The provision requiring tests by doctors to determine the viability of the fetus of 20 or more weeks was upheld because it furthered the state's interest in protecting potential human life. Such tests were found to be permissive and to be used only to make viability findings based on the physician's reasonable professional judgment.

Justice Rehnquist noted that this point conflicts with the prescription in *Roe v. Wade,* which limited state involvement in second trimester abortions to those necessary to save the mother's life. This was a major flaw in *Roe v. Wade's* trimester analysis, and this framework was now to be abandoned: "The framework's key elements, trimester and viability, are not found in the Constitution's text or in any place else one would expect to find a constitutional principle." The state's interest in potential future life was found to be equally compelling throughout pregnancy and not restricted to viability.

The chief justice concluded the court's opinion by stating that *Roe v. Wade* would not be overruled because its facts differed from those presented in *Webster. Roe v. Wade* dealt with a Texas statute that made illegal all nontherapeutic abortions. Missouri, on the other hand, sought only to limit abortions after the point of viability. *Roe* was therefore modified and limited by a new standard for review of abortion restrictions based on furthering "the state's interest in protecting potential human life.

AFTERMATH

The *Webster* decision limited abortion rights without clearly defining those limits. As a result, state legislators were left with the task of drafting statutes that would pass constitutional scrutiny in future cases. For at least the near future, however, *Webster*'s legacy appears to be a renewal of abortion as a political issue on the state and local levels.

SIGNIFICANCE

In legalizing abortion under many circumstances, *Roe v. Wade* had a profound impact on American society, and served as a rallying point for those who view life as beginning at the moment of conception. Motivated by the desire to overturn *Roe v. Wade,* opponents of abortion became unprecedentedly active in the legislative and judicial arenas. *Webster* also has inspired similar activism on the part of those who favor less stringent regulation of abortion. The *Webster* ruling left the door open to a variety of legislative approaches to the problem, which continue to be the focus of electoral and lobbying efforts.

In refusing the opportunity to overrule *Roe v. Wade,* the Court in *Webster* reaffirmed the broader constitutional concept of the right of privacy. The precise contours of that right are likely to be among the important questions deliberated by the Court well into the 21st century.

RELATED CASES

Akron v. Akron Center for Reproductive Health, Inc., 462 U.S. 416, 103 S.Ct. 2481, 76 L.Ed. 2d 687 (1983)

Colautti v. Franklin, 439 U.S. 379, 99 S.Ct. 675, 58L.Ed. 2d 596 (1979)

Griswold v. Connecticut, 381 U.S. 479, 85 S.Ct. 1678, 14 L.Ed. 2d 596 (1965)

Harris v. McRae, 448 U.S. 297, 100 S.Ct. 2671, 65 L.Ed. 2d 784 (1980)

Maher v. Roe, 432 U.S. 464, 97 S.Ct. 2376, 53 L.Ed. 2d 484 (1977)

Planned Parenthood of Southeastern Pennsylvania v. Casey, 505 U.S. 833, 112 S.Ct. 2791, 120 L.Ed. 2d 674 (1992)

Planned Parenthood of Central Missouri v. Danforth, 428 U.S. 52, 96 S.Ct. 2831, 49 L.Ed. 2d 528 (1976)

Roe v. Wade, 410 U.S. 113, 93 S.Ct. 705, 35 L.Ed. 2d 147 (1973)

Thornburgh v. American College of Obstetricians and Gynecologists, 476 U.S. 747, 106 S.Ct. 2169, 90 L.Ed. 2d 779 (1985)

RECOMMENDED READING

Faux, Marian. *Roe v. Wade.* New York: Macmillan, 1988.

Glendon, Mary Ann. *Abortion and Divorce in Western Law.* Cambridge, Mass.: Harvard University Press, 1987.

Horan, Dennis, Edward R. Grant, and Paige C. Cunningham, eds. *Abortion and the Constitution: Reversing* Roe v. Wade *through the Courts.* Washington, D.C.: Georgetown University Press, 1987.

Joffee, Frederick S., Barbara L. Lindheim and Philip R. Lee. *Abortion Politics: Private Morality and Public Policy.* New York: McGraw Hill, 1987.

Petchesky, Rosalind. *Abortion and Women's Choice: The State, Sexuality and Reproductive Freedom.* New York: Longman, 1984.

Rabin, Eva R. *Abortion, Politics and the Courts:* Roe v. Wade *and Its Aftermath.* Rev. ed. New York: Greenwood Press, 1987.

Sarvis, Betty, and Hyman Rodman. *The Abortion Controversy.* 2d ed. New York: Columbia University Press, 1974.

ANTITRUST AND COMPETITION

Case Title: *The Butcher's Benevolent Association of New Orleans v. The Crescent City Live-Stock Landing and Slaughter-House Company; Paul Esteben, L. Ruch, J. P. Rouede, W. Maylie, S. Firmberg, B. Beaubay, William Fagan, J. D. Broderick, N. Seibel, M. Lannes, J. Gitzinger, J. P. Aycock, D. Verges, The Live-Stock Dealers' and Butchers' Association of New Orleans, and Charles Cavaroc v. The State of Louisiana, ex. rel. S. Belden, Attorney-General; The Butchers' Benevolent Association of New Orleans v. The Crescent City Live-Stock and Slaughter-House Company*

Alternate Case Title: The Slaughter-House Cases

Legal Citations: 83 U.S. 36; 21 L.Ed. 394

Year of Decision: 1872

KEY ISSUES

Do the Civil War amendments grant U.S. citizens broad protection against the actions of state governments?

HISTORY OF THE CASE

The state of Louisiana granted a state corporation the exclusive right to operate facilities in New Orleans for the landing, keeping, and slaughter of livestock. The Butchers' Benevolent Association, a group of excluded butchers, sought an injunction against the monopoly on the grounds that they were prevented from practicing their trade unless they worked at the monopolist corporation and paid its fees. The state courts upheld the law.

SUMMARY OF ARGUMENTS

The plaintiffs' appeal was based on four grounds: (1) that the statute created an involuntary servitude forbidden by the Thirteenth Amendment; (2) that it abridged the privileges and immunities of citizens of the United States; (3) that it denied plaintiffs the equal protection of the laws; and (4) that it deprived them of their property without due process of law, all under the Fourteenth Amendment.

DECISION

The Court ruled that the state of Louisiana could act as it did, for the following reasons: (1) The proper interpretation of the Civil War amendments must reflect their historical setting. Thus, the meaning of "involuntary servitude" as used in the Thirteenth Amendment is restricted to personal servitude, not a servitude attached to property, as the plaintiffs claimed. (2) The Fourteenth Amendment clearly distinguishes between citizenship of the states and citizenship of the United States. Only those privileges and immunities of U.S. citizens are protected by the Fourteenth Amendment. Privileges and immunities of state citizens upon which the plaintiffs relied here are unaffected, and rest for their security and protection in the power of the several states as recognized in Article IV of the U.S. Constitution. The Constitution does not control the power of the state governments over the right of their own citizens except to require that a state grant equal rights to its own citizens and citizens of other states within its jurisdiction. Therefore, the plaintiffs, as citizens of the United States, had no privilege or immunity that has been infringed by the state law. (3) The equal protection clause of the Fourteenth Amendment is intended primarily to prevent state discrimination against blacks, although Congress may extend its scope to other areas. But the plaintiffs did not claim a denial of equal justice in the state courts, and therefore had no reason to have a remedy under the equal protection clause. (4) The restraint imposed by Louisiana upon the exercise of the plaintiffs' trade simply cannot be held to be a deprivation of property within the meaning of the Fourteenth Amendment. That clause should not be construed to cover such state restraint upon trade.

AFTERMATH

Justice Field in his dissent stated his belief that the Fourteenth Amendment protected those privileges and immunities "which of right belong to the citizens of all free governments." Among these privileges was the right to pursue lawful employment. The Supreme Court never did accept Justice Field's views of the Fourteenth Amendment's privileges and immunities clause, and the majority's interpretation in the Slaughter-House Cases is still the accepted reading of that provision, rendering the clause inoperative as a check on state laws.

SIGNIFICANCE

This case, the first requiring interpretation of these amendments, rendered the privileges and immunities clause of the Fourteenth Amendment, which sought to equalize the advantages of citizenship among the states, ineffective in protecting individual rights against invasion by state governments. Instead, the Court looked to the due process and equal protection clauses. The plaintiffs in this case were not attacking the procedure used, but instead the actual fairness of the state-approved monopoly. Although the Court rejected the notion of substantive due process in this case, the scope of the clause was unclear for many years. Gradually the Court began to examine the substance of state legislation to determine whether it was reasonable.

RELATED CASES

Morgan v. Illinois, 504 U.S. 719 (1992)

Richmond v. J. A. Croson Co., 488 U.S. 469 (1989)

United States v. Kozminski, 487 U.S. 931 (1988)

RECOMMENDED READING

Normand G. Benoit, *The Privileges or Immunities Clause of the Fourteenth Amendment: Can There Be Life after Death?*, Suffolk University Law Review 61 (1976).

Philip B. Kurland, *The Privileges or Immunities Clause: "Its Hour Come Round at Last"?*, Washington University Law Quarterly (1972).

Case Title: *Nebbia v. New York*

Legal Citation: 291 U.S. 502

Year of Decision: 1934

KEY ISSUES

May a state fix the cost at which a product is sold?

HISTORY OF THE CASE

The New York legislature passed an act that established a Milk Control Board for setting the price of milk. The board set the price for milk sold in stores at nine cents a quart. Nebbia, a store owner, sold two quarts of milk and a five-cent loaf of bread for eighteen cents and was convicted for violating the board's order. Two appeals confirmed the conviction. Nebbia then appealed to the U.S. Supreme Court.

SUMMARY OF ARGUMENTS

Nebbia argued that the order of the Milk Control Board denied him equal protection of the laws and denied him due process. He showed that the order required him, if he purchased from a dealer, to pay eight cents per quart and to resell at no less than nine cents per quart. The same dealer, however, could buy his supply from a farmer at lower prices and deliver the milk to consumers for ten cents a quart.

The state argued that the regulation would stabilize the industry for an essential food product.

DECISION

Justice Roberts wrote the majority opinion in a 5-4 decision that affirmed the conviction. He concluded that Nebbia was neither compelled to buy from dealers nor to sell at the minimum price. As a result, the difference in price on its face was not arbitrary or unreasonable as required of equal protection challenges.

Regarding the due process challenge, Justice Roberts held that the legislative means employed by the state had a real and substantial relation to the health and stability of the dairy industry. He concluded that as far as due process is concerned, a state is free to adopt whatever economic policy that reasonably may be deemed to promote public welfare, in the absence of constitutional restriction.

The dissenting justices felt that the statute constituted an arbitrary interference with the rights of the "little" grocer to conduct his business in an open market. They did not believe that the legislature could destroy the rights of one group while enriching the other, even if it seems advantageous to the public.

AFTERMATH

Nebbia was the first case that indicated the Court's reluctance to accept total economic freedom for individuals in the wake of the New Deal, the social and economic reforms enacted to alleviate the effects of the Great Depression. In the years following this decision, the Court widely enforced economic regulation by the states.

SIGNIFICANCE

Nebbia required that economic regulation be substantially related to the objective sought to be attained. The test was essentially that of an earlier opinion but the Court refused to impose its own views about correct economic policy on the states.

RELATED CASES

U.S. v. Carolene Products Co., 304 U.S. 144 (1938)

West Coast Hotel Co. v. Parrish, 300 U.S. 379 (1937)

Williamson v. Lee Optical, 348 U.S. 483 (1955)

RECOMMENDED READING

Bork, Robert H. *The Tempting of America: The Political Seduction of the Law.* New York: Free Press, 1990.

Schwartz, Bernard. *A Commentary on the Constitution of the United States.* Part II. *The Rights of Property.* New York: Macmillan, 1985, 104–111.

Case Title: *Standard Oil Company of New Jersey v. United States*

Legal Citations: 221 U.S. 1; 31 S.Ct. 502; 55 L.Ed. 619

Year of Decision: 1911

KEY ISSUES

Did Standard Oil of New Jersey violated the Sherman Antitrust Act by conspiring "to restrain the trade and commerce in petroleum, refined oil" and other products with the intent to monopolize this commerce?

HISTORY OF THE CASE

From 1870 to 1882 Standard Oil of Ohio, a subsidiary of Standard Oil of New Jersey, entered into agreements with some 60 other companies engaged in the oil business to fix the price of oil products, limiting their production and controlling their transportation. The participating companies obtained preferential rates over their competitors from railroads, forcing competitors to either become members or be driven out of business.

This case was brought to the Supreme Court on appeal from the U.S. District Court for the Eastern District of Missouri.

SUMMARY OF ARGUMENTS

Standard Oil argued that the development of its business resulted from the exercise of lawful competitive methods. Standard Oil also argued that the antitrust act was inapplicable as it extended congressional power beyond that which was granted by the Commerce Clause.

The United States argued that Standard Oil and others engaged in a conspiracy to restrain trade and commerce in petroleum, petroleum products, and oil.

DECISION

The Court held that Standard Oil Company of New Jersey and its subsidiaries constituted a monopoly in violation of the Sherman Antitrust Act of 1890. Therefore, it was ordered to dissolve and to discontinue the illegal combination between that corporation and its subsidiaries.

Chief Justice White delivered the majority opinion of the Court, saying that the statute was written because of the need to combat restraint of trade and all contracts that attempt to monopolize. Freedom to contract was "the essence of freedom from undue restraint on the right to contract." He set out a rule of reason balancing private rights with governmental rights.

Justice Harlan wrote for the dissent, saying that the Court's interpretation of the Antitrust Act had usurped the legislative function.

AFTERMATH

This represents the first case of trust-busting. The Supreme Court's adoption of the "rule of reason," a rule that requires review of the circumstances of a case to determine whether acts unreasonably restrain trade, represents the emergence of modern antitrust law. At first, the business community was afraid that the rule would lead to rampant involuntary dissolution; however, it was later found that other oil companies were still engaged in predatory pricing and other forms of unfair competition.

SIGNIFICANCE

The rule of reason was based on facts, using a case-by-case approach, not common law and constitutional arguments. Some felt that this new approach made little impact, and the market essentially remained the same.

RELATED CASES

Indiana Farmer's Guide Publishing Co. v. Prairie Farmer Publishing Co., 293 U.S. 268 (1934)

United States v. E.C. Knight Co., 156 U.S. 1 (1895)

United States v. Reading, 226 U.S. 324 (1912)

RECOMMENDED READING

Milton Handler, *Reforming the Antitrust Laws,* 82 Columbia Law Review 1287 (1982).

Rudolph J. Peritz, *The "Rule of Reason" in Antitrust Law: Property Logic in Restraint of Competition,* 40 Hastings Law Journal 285 (1989).

Case Title: *Swift & Company v. United States*

Legal Citations: 196 U.S. 375; 25 S.Ct. 276; 49 L.Ed. 518

Year of Decision: 1905

KEY ISSUES

Does appellants' method of trade in fresh meat violate the act of July 2, 1890, "to protect trade and commerce against unlawful restraints and monopolies"?

HISTORY OF THE CASE

Swift & Co. bought livestock in Chicago, which they slaughtered in their respective states, creating meat for human consumption. They also sold meat to buyers in different states, shipping it by rail. Swift slaughterhouses controlled the majority of the trade in fresh meats. They did not compete with themselves. They did not bid against each other, and from time to time they fixed prices at secret meetings. They also received a lower rate for transportation than others.

This case was an appeal from the circuit court granting an injunction against Swift for violations of the act of July 2, 1890, a law designed to protect commerce from monopolies.

SUMMARY OF ARGUMENTS

The United States argued that Swift and others were buying, selling, and shipping meat in a manner and with the intention to gain an economic advantage through control of the market. The government argued that through these acts the companies had gained control of over half of the trade of fresh meat.

Swift & Company argued that all of its acts were conducted in a lawful manner and therefore, its intent was irrelevant.

DECISION

The federal government could regulate stockyards because they were acting in the stream of commerce. Justice Holmes wrote the opinion for the Court, holding that the activities of the packers involved interstate commerce: "Commerce among the States is not a technical legal conception, but a practical one, drawn from the course of business. When cattle are sent for sale from a place in one State, with the expectation that they will end their transit, after purchase, in another, and when in effect they do so, with only the interruption necessary to find a purchaser at the stockyards, and when this is a typical, constantly recurring course, the current thus existing is an arbitrary control to which the public might be subjected without regulation."

Justice Holmes also proposed that a business with the capacity to affect public interest affected commerce directly. A private business did not. Also, by accepting the concept of a "current of commerce," he hinted at bringing local business activities under the federal commerce power.

AFTERMATH

This ruling incorporated into the congressional power to regulate commerce the concept of business and the public interest. Conventional thinking would also classify this case as overruling UNITED STATES V. E.C. KNIGHT CO., 156 U.S. 1 (1895).

SIGNIFICANCE

Holmes's solution of melding two concepts, a current of commerce and business affected with a public interest, was to last until the 1930s. After this case, a narrow interpretation of the commerce clause in which it was determined whether goods were in the stream of commerce was no longer used and the Court merely looked at whether an activity had an effect on commerce.

RELATED CASES

Munn v. Illinois, 94 U.S. 113 (1877)

United States v. E.C. Knight Co., 156 U.S. 1 (1895)

RECOMMENDED READING

Barry Cushman, *A Stream of Legal Consciousness: The Current of Commerce Doctrine from Swift to Jones and Laughlin,* 61 Fordham Law Review 105 (1992).

Marc I. Steinberg, *SEC and Other Permanent Injunctions: Standards for their Imposition, Modification and Dissolution,* 66 Cornell Law Review 41 (1980).

Case Title: *United States v. E.C. Knight Co.*

Alternate Case Title: The Sugar Case

Legal Citation: 156 U.S. 1

Year of Decision: 1895

KEY ISSUES

May Congress regulate the wholly intrastate manufacturing of sugar under its constitutional power to regulate commerce among the states?

HISTORY OF THE CASE

The American Sugar Refining Company acquired ownership of four other sugar refineries. These acquisitions created a virtual monopoly, with American Sugar in control of 98 percent of the U.S. refined-sugar market. The federal government then filed suit against American Sugar, alleging that it had violated the act of 1890, also known as the Sherman Antitrust Act, which provides that "every contract, combination . . . or conspiracy in restraint of trade and commerce among the several States is illegal . . . and that persons who monopolize trade among the several States shall be guilty of a misdemeanor." The government sought an injunction to set aside the acquisitions of the four refineries, but the U.S. Court of Appeals for the Third Circuit found no Sherman Act violation.

SUMMARY OF ARGUMENTS

American Sugar argued that the refining of sugar was not part of interstate commerce and not subject to the Sherman Act. It also contended it had not engaged in any monopoly actions that would have constituted a restraint of trade.

The government argued that sugar was a daily necessity in American life, that interstate commerce was indispensable to the nationwide consumption of sugar, and that Congress therefore had the power to eliminate the refining monopoly due to its effects on that commerce.

DECISION

The Supreme Court, in an opinion written by Chief Justice Fuller, held that the Sherman Act was inapplicable because Congress lacked the power to regulate "manufacturing." Chief Justice Fuller assumed for the sake of argument that American Sugar had a true monopoly, although he noted that the price of sugar had not risen significantly since the acquisitions. He argued that the regulation of wholly intrastate monopolies was part of each state's police power, whereas the power to control interstate commerce belonged exclusively to Congress. American Sugar had obtained a monopoly only in the manufacture of sugar; Chief Justice Fuller found this monopoly beyond Congress's power: "Commerce succeeds to manufacture, and is not a part of it." In his opinion, to find such indirect effects within the commerce power would strike a great blow to the federal system. He asserted that in many forms of manufacture "the instrumentality of commerce [is] necessarily invoked," but only a monopoly that bore a direct relation to commerce between the states was within the reach of Congress through the Sherman Act.

Justice Harlan wrote alone in dissent. He took a much less formal view of the distinction between manufacture and commerce, which he saw as only a difference of degree. Since Congress clearly had the power to prohibit the interstate transportation of products produced by a monopoly, it must also have the power to regulate "in advance of transportation." In Justice Harlan's view, the Constitution was not intended to render the federal government powerless in a time of "national emergency."

AFTERMATH

The formalistic analysis conducted by Chief Justice Fuller soon gave way to Justice Harlan's "realist" approach, and by the 1940s Congress had the power to regulate almost any business activity through the commerce clause.

SIGNIFICANCE

This decision marked the beginning of the Court's attempt to define what activities and items were included in commerce and could be regulated. The Court focused on the activity itself and not the activity's effect.

RELATED CASES

Gibbons v. Ogden, 22 U.S. (9 Wheat.) 1 (1824)

United States v. Darby, 312 U.S. 100 (1941)

RECOMMENDED READING

Richard A. Epstein, *The Proper Scope of the Commerce Power,* 73 Virginia Law Review 1387 (1987).

Kilgore, Carrol D. *Judicial Tyranny.* Chicago: Thomas Nelson, 1977.

Case Title: *Virginia Pharmacy Board v. Virginia Consumer Council*

Alternate Case Title: The Drug Advertising Case

Legal Citation: 425 U.S. 748

Year of Decision: 1976

KEY ISSUES

May a state completely prohibit the advertising of prescription drug prices?

HISTORY OF THE CASE

Virginia law prohibited anyone other than licensed pharmacists from dispensing prescription drugs. The state then enacted a statute making it unprofessional conduct for a licensed pharmacist to advertise the prices of prescription drugs; thus, the state effectively prohibited all advertising of prescription drug prices in any form. The Consumer Council, as consumers of prescription drugs, then brought suit in the Federal District Court for the Eastern District of Virginia. They alleged that the prohibition on advertising violated their right to free speech under the First and Fourteenth Amendments of the U.S. Constitution. The council prevailed in the district court, and the state of Virginia appealed to the U.S. Supreme Court.

SUMMARY OF ARGUMENTS

The council argued that they had a constitutional right, as recipients of prescription drug advertising, to hear this form of speech free from government interference. They noted that prices for prescription drugs varied by as much as 1,000 percent even within the same city; thus, price advertisements would save them money because they could compare prices before purchasing.

Virginia argued that the statute involved a constitutional use of its police power because the widespread advertising of prescription medication might lead to a bargain hunting mentality that would eliminate the valuable pharmacist-customer relationship. The state also asserted an interest in protecting the reputation of the pharmacist as a professional rather than a "mere retailer of drugs."

DECISION

The Supreme Court, in an opinion written by Justice Powell, held that the Virginia statute was an unconstitutional interference with the freedom of speech. Justice Powell disagreed with Virginia's contention that the council, as recipient of the speech rather than the speaker, had no First Amendment interest: "Where a speaker exists . . .

the protection accorded is to the communication, to its source and to its recipients both." He then proclaimed that "commercial speech," which previously had not been considered speech for First Amendment purposes, was indeed entitled to constitutional protection. In Justice Powell's opinion, the sentence "I will sell you X drug at Y price" was not "so removed from the exposition of ideas" that it lacked First Amendment protection. He argued that the consumer's interest in the price of a prescription drug might be greater than his interest in any constitutionally protected political debate. Furthermore, Justice Powell found a strong societal interest in the free flow of commercial information because that information was "indispensable to the proper allocation of resources in [our] free enterprise system."

Justice Powell argued that the state's paternalistic reasons for the statute were contrary to the best interests of its citizens, who would be best served by full access to price information. He stated, "It is precisely this kind of choice, between the dangers of suppressing information and the dangers of its misuse if it is freely available, that the First Amendment makes for us." Thus, while Virginia remained free to regulate deceptive advertising or advertising of illegal products, it could not completely prohibit any form of valid product advertisement. In a footnote, Justice Powell contended that the Court's holding did not necessarily suggest that the state could not prohibit advertising by professionals such as doctors or lawyers. He argued that the state might have a different regulatory interest where the advertising involved services rather than products because the rendering of professional services involved an "enhanced possibility for confusion and deception."

Justice Rehnquist delivered the lone dissent. His argument in many ways echoed that of Justice Holmes in the infamous case of LOCHNER V. NEW YORK. He noted that Virginia did not prohibit the dissemination of drug prices over the phone, so this case did not concern access to price information. In Justice Rehnquist's opinion, the Court had simply determined that pharmacists had a right to advertise that could not be overridden by the Virginia legislature. He found this approach repugnant insofar as "there is certainly nothing in the United States Constitution which requires the Virginia Legislature to hew to the teachings of Adam Smith in its legislative decisions regulating the pharmacy profession." Justice Rehnquist did not believe that the First Amendment had been intended to protect "the decision of a particular individual as to whether to purchase one or another kind of shampoo." He argued that the Court was using the First Amendment as a tool to achieve its preferred result in much the same way it had once used economic due process for the same purpose.

AFTERMATH

Soon after the Court determined that the Constitution protected commercial speech, it ruled that laws prohibiting advertising of professional services were unconstitutional.

SIGNIFICANCE

The decision indicated that commercial speech, specifically price advertising, may find some protection under the First and Fourteenth Amendments.

RELATED CASES

Bates v. State Bar of Arizona, 433 U.S. 350 (1977)

Central Hudson Gas v. Public Service Commission of New York, 447 U.S. 557 (1980)

RECOMMENDED READING

Ronald Coase, *Advertising and Free Speech*, 6 Journal of Legal Studies 1 (1977).

Thomas H. Jackson, and John C. Jeffries, Jr., *Commercial Speech: Economic Due Process and the First Amendment*, 65 Virginia Law Review 1 (1979).

CIVIL RIGHTS AND
EQUAL PROTECTION

Case Title: *Baker v. Carr*

Alternate Case Titles: The Reapportionment Case, The Political Thicket Case

Legal Citations: 369 U.S. 186; 82 S.Ct. 691; 7 L.Ed. 2d 663

Year of Decision: 1962

KEY ISSUES

Do federal courts have the power to hear claims by voters challenging the constitutionality of the distribution of legislative seats in a state legislature, or is this a matter that can be decided only by the voters through their elected representatives?

HISTORY OF THE CASE

The Tennessee constitution required that both houses of the state legislature be apportioned among districts "according to the number of qualified electors in each." The legislature had been reapportioned only three times: in 1881, 1891, and 1901.

By 1960, the legislative districts were grossly unequal. Rural areas had a disproportionate number of representatives in relation to their population. Senate district populations ranged from 25,000 to 132,000, thus 20 of the 33 members of the Senate were elected by barely one-third of the state's population. Though urban areas had grown significantly in the 60 years since the last reapportionment, the rural areas managed to retain their political power and control of the state legislature.

Charles Baker was the mayor of Millington, Tennessee. This Memphis suburb had grown rapidly since the end of World War II. With this growth came increased financial needs. Little money, however, was forthcoming from the rural-dominated legislature.

Baker and voters in the urban counties brought suit in federal district court to compel the state legislature to reapportion the legislative districts so that the urban areas would have representation in proportion to their population. They alleged that the 1901 apportionment statute still in effect denied voters in urban areas equal protection under the Fourteenth Amendment "by virtue of the debasement of their votes." A three-judge federal court dismissed their claim, holding that the court lacked jurisdiction to hear the case and that no claim was stated upon which relief could be granted. The voters appealed.

SUMMARY OF ARGUMENTS

The appellants, who included the mayor of Nashville, argued that the state of Tennessee arbitrarily apportioned the legislative seats among the counties and subsequently failed to reapportion the seats in light of substantial population growth and redistribution in violation of the Fourteenth Amendment. The appellees, including Joe C. Carr, the Secretary of State, argued that the court lacked jurisdiction to hear the case and that the appellants failed to state a claim for which relief could be granted.

DECISION

The Supreme Court did not rule on the merits of the voters' claims, but instead only grappled with the procedural issues of whether a federal court had the power to decide an issues such as this. Specifically, the Court ruled on the legal issues of jurisdiction, standing, and justiciability.

Justice William J. Brennan, Jr., writing for a six-member majority, quickly determined that the federal court had jurisdiction (had the power) to rule on the voters' claim. Justice Brennan wrote that if a claim arises under the Constitution, federal laws, or treaties, a federal court has jurisdiction over the claim, provided that the claim is not "so attenuated and unsubstantial as to be absolutely devoid of merit." Since this was not a meritless claim, the district court possessed jurisdiction.

Justice Brennan also quickly resolved the standing question, which asked whether the individuals who brought the suit had had their rights violated. Brennan considered whether they had "such a personal stake in the outcome." The Court held that "voters who allege facts showing disadvantage to themselves as individuals have standing to sue."

The question of whether the challenge to the state legislature's apportionment was a justiciable claim was the most difficult of the three issues addressed in *Baker v. Carr*. The state argued that the federal court could not hear a claim that challenged the apportionment of the legislature because it was a nonjusticiable "political question." The state relied on the case of *Luther v. Borden. Luther* involved a simple trespass, complicated by the fact that Rhode Island, the state where the case arose, was in the midst of a civil dispute. Two groups claimed to be the rightful government of the state.

The defendants in *Luther* responded to the claim of trespass by arguing that they were the agents of Rhode Island's government. The Supreme Court declined to rule on the case, noting that to do so would require a finding of which of the two competing groups had the rightful claim to the state's government. One hundred years later, Tennessee argued that the makeup of its legislature involved a similar "political question" that could not be resolved by federal courts.

In the lengthiest part of *Baker v. Carr,* Justice Brennan explained: "the mere fact that the suit seeks protection of a political right does not mean it presents a political question." Instead, the political question doctrine is "primarily a function of the separation of powers." A case is a "nonjusticiable political question" when it concerns "a textually demonstrable constitutional commitment of the issue to a coordinate political department." Some general categories of political question cases were those involving foreign relations, dates of the duration of military hostilities, the validity of legislative enactments under congressional procedural formalities, and whether Indians are recognized as a tribe under federal law. In each of these broad categories, the Court had declined to hear the case because one of the other two branches of the federal government had, by necessity, exclusive control.

Tennessee's apportionment of its legislature did not present a political question because as a state, it was not a "co-equal branch" of the federal government. Justice Brennan explained that in *Luther v. Borden* the Court had not deferred to the state of Rhode Island, but instead had declined to rule to avoid conflict with the executive branch and Congress. Brennan explained that the Court in *Luther* had recognized "the commitment to the other two branches of the decision as to which is the lawful state government." The Supreme Court therefore directed the district court to conduct a full trial to decide the constitutionality of the apportionment of the Tennessee legislature.

Three justices wrote separate decisions concurring in the Court's decision. Justice Douglas defended the Court's decision against charges that this matter was "beyond the competence of courts." It made no difference that legislative apportionment involved complicated issues. Justice Douglas explained: "Adjudication is often perplexing and complicated."

Justice Tom C. Clark also joined in the Court's opinion, but he was unhappy that the Court had not gone ahead and ruled on the merits: "The Court holds that the appellants have alleged a cause of action. However, it refuses to award relief here—although the facts are undisputed—and fails to give the District Court any guidance whatever." Justice Clark affirmed "that an appropriate remedy may be formulated." Also of interest, Justice Clark stated that he believed it was constitutional for state legislatures to have one house whose representation is not exclusively based on population, as in the U.S. Senate.

Justice Stewart wrote his concurrence to emphasize the narrowness of the majority's holding. He criticized his fellow justices: "The separate writings of my dissenting and concurring Brothers stray so far from the subject of today's decision as to convey, I think, a distressingly inaccurate impression of what the Court decides." He explained that the Court decided "three things and no more: '(a) that the Court possessed jurisdiction of the subject matter; (b) that a justiciable cause of action is stated upon which appellants would be entitled to relief; and (c) that the appellants have standing to challenge the Tennessee apportionment statutes.'"

Justices Felix Frankfurter and John Marshall Harlan each wrote lengthy dissenting opinions. Justice Frankfurter warned of the dire consequences of the Court's decision. He described the holding as "a massive repudiation of the experience of our whole past." Justice Frankfurter believed the ruling, by involving itself in the political arena, would undermine the legitimacy of the U.S. Supreme Court:

> The Court's authority—possessed of neither the purse nor the sword—ultimately rests on sustained public confidence in its moral sanction. Such feeling must be nourished by the Court's complete detachment, in fact and in appearance, from political entangle-

ments and by abstention from injecting itself into the clash of political settlements.

Justice Frankfurter then spent the next 63 pages explaining why the Court's holding involved a break with past decisions in outlining the history of the judiciary's attempts to avoid involvement in the political arena.

While Justice Frankfurter criticized the majority's opinion for ignoring the broad issues of the Court's involving itself in the political arena, Justice Harlan focused on what he perceived as a lack of harm from the abridgment of a federal right. Justice Harlan accused the majority of ignoring a simple and basic question: "Does the complaint disclose a violation of a federal constitutional right . . .?" Justice Harlan's opinion provided a negative response to this question: "I can find nothing in the Equal Protection Clause or elsewhere in the Federal Constitution which expressly or impliedly supports the view that state legislatures must be so structured as to reflect with approximate equality the voice of every voter."

AFTERMATH

On remand, the district court gave the legislature an additional year to reformulate a different apportionment plan. The district court implied that Tennessee possibly could have one house not based exclusively on population, as suggested by Justice Clark. However, this was held not to be constitutionally permissible in the 1964 Supreme Court case, REYNOLDS V. SIMS.

SIGNIFICANCE

The Court's ruling in *Baker* opened the door for numerous challenges to the apportionment of state legislatures. Even though the *Baker* decision did not rule on the merits of the case, the majority's opinion was interpreted by lower courts as requiring at least one house of state legislatures to be apportioned on the basis of districts of equal population. As subsequent Supreme Court cases would hold, however, this was a narrow reading of *Baker v. Carr.*

RELATED CASES

Gray v. Sanders, 372 U.S. 368 (1963)

Reynolds v. Sims, 377 U.S. 533 (1964)

Wesberry v. Sanders, 376 U.S. 1 (1964)

RECOMMENDED READING

Cortner, Richard C. *The Apportionment Cases.* Knoxville: University of Tennessee Press, 1970.

Dixon, Robert G., Jr. *Democratic Representation: Reapportionment in Law and Politics.* New York: Oxford University Press, 1968.

Graham, Gene S. *One Man, One Vote:* Baker v. Carr *and the American Levellers.* Boston: Little, Brown, 1972.

Hanson, Royce. *The Political Thicket.* Englewood Cliffs, N.J.: Prentice Hall, 1966.

Case Title: *Batson v. Kentucky*

Alternate Case Title: The "Excluded Black Jurors" Case

Legal Citations: 476 U.S. 79; 106 S.Ct. 1712; 90 L.Ed. 2d 69

Year of Decision: 1986

KEY ISSUES

Does a state deny an African-American defendant equal protection in violation of the Fourteenth Amendment, and a right to a fair trial under the Sixth Amendment, by using peremptory challenges, challenges not requiring explanation, to exclude all African Americans from a trial by jury?

HISTORY OF THE CASE

Mr. Batson, a black man, was indicted in Kentucky on charges of second-degree burglary and receipt of stolen goods. On the first day of trial, the prosecutor used his peremptory challenges, those not requiring explanation, to strike all four black persons on the venire, the group of citizens from which the trial jury was to be selected. A jury composed of only white persons was selected. Defense counsel moved to discharge the jury before it was sworn. Counsel requested a hearing on his motion. The trial judge denied Batson's motion, stating that the parties could use their peremptories to "strike anybody they wanted to."

He reasoned that the cross-section requirement of the Sixth Amendment applied only to the selection of the venire, not the selection of the trial jury itself.

The jury convicted Batson on both counts. On appeal, Batson argued that although *Swain v. Alabama*, 380 U.S. 202, a prior decision requiring a demonstration of the systematic exclusion of African Americans as jurors to sustain an equal protection action, foreclosed on any equal protection claims based solely on the prosecutor's conduct, he was still entitled to a jury drawn from a cross section of the community and that the prosecutor's use of peremptories violated his rights under the Sixth Amendment and § 11 of the Kentucky Constitution. The Supreme Court of Kentucky affirmed the convictions. It relied on *Swain* and held that a defendant alleging lack of a fair cross section must demonstrate systematic exclusion of a group of jurors from the venire. The U.S. Supreme Court granted certiorari, 471 U.S. 1052 (1985) and reversed.

SUMMARY OF ARGUMENTS

Defense counsel argued that the prosecutor's removal of the black veniremen violated petitioner's rights under the Sixth Amendment to a jury drawn from a cross section of the community.

The state argued that the privilege of unfettered exercise of the peremptory challenge is of vital importance to the criminal justice system, and should remain unchanged from the standards set out in *Swain*. They also argued that changing the current standards would cause serious administrative difficulties.

DECISION

Justice Powell wrote the opinion for the Court in which Justices Brennan, White, Marshall, Blackmun, Stevens, and O'Conner joined. Justice Powell held that a state denies a black defendant equal protection when it puts him on trial before a jury from which members of his race have been purposefully excluded, reaffirming the principle announced in *Strauder v. West Virginia*, 100 U.S. 303. Powell believed that the resolution of petitioner's claims turned on the application of equal protection principles and did not express a view on the merits of petitioner's Sixth Amendment claims (although Batson raised only a Sixth Amendment claim, not an equal protection claim).

Justice Powell found that a defendant does not have a right to a petit jury composed in whole or in part of members of his own race. The equal protection clause guarantees the defendant only that the state will not exclude members of his race from the jury venire on account of race, or on the false assumption that members of his race as a group are not qualified to serve as jurors. Justice Powell urged that such discrimination not only discriminated against the defendant but also discriminated against the excluded juror, and undermined public confidence in the fairness of the judicial system. He also stated that although these principles concern the selection of the venire, they also apply to the selection of the petit jury.

Justice Powell rejected the portion of *Swain v. Alabama* concerning the evidentiary burden placed on a defendant who claims that he has been denied equal protection through the state's discriminatory use of peremptory challenges. *Swain* required a defendant to show proof of repeated striking of blacks over a number of cases to establish a violation of the equal protection clause—a very difficult burden of proof. Justice Powell found that a defendant may make a prima facie showing, a presentation of evidence sufficient for the case to move forward, of purposeful racial discrimination in the selection of the venire by relying solely on the facts concerning its selection at defendant's own trial. A defendant no longer had to show that the peremptory challenge system as a whole was being perverted.

Justice Powell even devised a method by which a defendant can make a prima facie showing of purposeful discrimination. First, he had to show that he is a member of a cognizable racial group and that the prosecutor has exercised peremptory challenges to remove from the venire members of the defendant's race. Then he had to show that such facts and any circumstances raise an inference that the prosecutor used peremptory challenges to exclude the veniremen from the petit jury on account of their race. Once this was shown, the burden shifted to the prosecutor to come up with a neutral reason for challenging the black jurors. Justice Powell also directed that a prosecutor cannot rebut the defendant's case by merely denying that he had a discriminatory motive or good faith in making the individual selections. He did not believe that his decision would undermine the contribution the challenge generally makes to the administration of justice, nor would it create serious administrative difficulties.

In Justice White's concurring opinion, he stated that the practice of peremptorily eliminating blacks from petit juries in cases with black defendants remains widespread. Therefore, he agreed that an opportunity to overcome the peremptory's presumption of legitimacy should be afforded when this occurs. Justice White added that he would adhere to the rule announced in *De Stefano v. Woods*, 392 U.S. 145 (1968) that decisions by the Court should not be applied retroactively.

In a concurring opinion, Justice Marshall stated that the Court's decision in this case would not end the racial discrimination that peremptories inject into the jury-selection process. He argued that any prosecutor could easily assert a neutral reason for striking a juror, making the Court's protection in the instant case illusory. He feared that a prosecutor's own conscious or unconscious racism might lead him to lie to himself in an effort to convince himself that his motives are legal. Justice Marshall stressed that this could lead to more racial prejudice. He believed that the only way to eliminate racial prejudice in the use of peremptories was to eliminate peremptory challenges entirely. He noted that they were not required by the Constitution, and their elimination would not impair the constitutional guarantee of impartial jury and fair trial. However, he was able to view the majority decision as a step toward eliminating that practice.

Justice Stevens was joined by Justice Brennan in his concurring opinion. He believed that the Court correctly decided the issues regarding peremptories and their use in violation of the equal protection clause, even though petitioner did not raise these issues. Justice Stevens based his conclusion on respondent's reliance on an equal protection argument in defense of the judgment, and on the several amici curiae, persons who are not parties to the case but have an interest in the matters at issue, which also addressed the equal protection argument. He supported his findings with specific quotes from the respondent's arguments identifying the Fourteenth Amendment as the controlling issue.

Justice O' Connor's concurrence stated that in addition to agreeing with the majority's opinion, she also believed that the decision should not apply retroactively.

Chief Justice Burger wrote a long and spirited dissent, which was joined by Justice Rehnquist. He urged that review of an equal protection argument is improper when a petitioner has not made an equal protection claim at the lower courts or the U.S. Supreme Court, and can show no reason why he did not make those claims. Justice Burger criticized the reversal of the 21-year-old unanimous decision and constitutional holding in *Swain* on the basis of arguments disclaimed by petitioner arguing that this was a departure from the Court's usual procedure, and without explanation. Justice Burger stated that there should have been a reargument on the equal protection question, the Court should have directed the parties to brief that issue in addition to the Sixth Amendment question, or the Court should have dismissed the petition for certiorari as improvidently granted due to the lack of argument regarding equal protection.

Justice Burger then gave examples of the importance of the peremptory challenge by quoting Justice White, who traced the development of the peremptory challenge in *Swain*. This historical account highlighted the long and venerable tradition of peremptory challenges in England and the United States. He stated that the "peremptory challenge is 'one of the most important of the rights' in our justice system," and should not require inquiry into a party's use of it. Justice Burger stated that the majority should have paid more attention to the history of the peremptory challenge, instead of recounting the well-established principle that intentional exclusion of racial groups from jury venires violates the equal protection clause. He criticized the Court's silence on applying the conventional equal protection framework, and on its failure to state whether there were limits to the exercise of peremptory challenges by defense counsel. He did not like the majority's middle ground requirement of a "neutral" explanation, and he believed that it would not further the ends of justice. Justice Burger believed that either a challenge has to be explained or it does not. He insisted that the likely results of *Batson*'s holding was to diminish confidence in the jury system and to interject racial matters into the jury selection process. Justice Burger also saw the Court's holding as developing a newly created constitutional right. He ended by assenting to Justice White's conclusion that the decision not apply retroactively. However, he still urged that this case be set for reargument.

Justice Rehnquist wrote the final dissenting opinion in which Chief Justice Burger joined. He began by questioning whether the majority did what they set out to do: merely to reexamine the portion of *Swain* concerning the evidentiary burden placed on a criminal defendant who claims he has been denied equal protection through the state's use of peremptory challenges to exclude members of his race from the petit jury. He then showed two circumstances in which a state might use its peremptories to exclude blacks from juries in criminal cases.

He quoted *Swain,* which held that when a state uses the peremptory to exclude a black person from a particular jury based on the belief that that person would be more likely to favor a black defendant, it is not a violation of equal protection. Justice Rehnquist reiterated that peremptory challenge should be used, as was done historically, upon the instincts, beliefs, and "unaccountable prejudices" of the prosecutor or defense counsel. He believed that in light of these considerations, it is not a denial of equal protection to strike black people in a particular case.

He further argued the fairness of such peremptory challenges, which state that everyone is subject to being challenged without cause. Justice Rehnquist saw nothing "unequal" about the state using its peremptories to strike blacks from the jury in cases involving black defendants—as long as the challenges were also used to strike white jurors in cases involving white defendants, and the same with Asians, Hispanics, or any other racial or ethnic group. If applied across the board, he did not see an equal protection violation.

Additionally, Justice Rehnquist did not see a violation of any other constitutional interest, nor any harm to the remainder of the community or the excluded jurors. He backed the use of group affiliations as a legitimate basis for a state's use of peremptory challenges, and he felt they were helpful in eliminating persons who may be biased. He did not agree with any substantive departure from *Swain,* and he argued that the petitioner in this case did not make an appropriate showing to overcome the presumption announced in *Swain* that the state's use of peremptory challenges was related to the context of the case.

AFTERMATH

The Court overruled the part of *Swain* that precluded a criminal defendant from making out an equal protection violation based on the exclusion by peremptory challenges for black jurors in the defendant's particular case. As a result, *Batson* took a significant step toward eliminating racial discrimination in the selection of criminal juries.

SIGNIFICANCE

Since *Batson,* the Court has extended its doctrine to prohibit the use of racially discriminatory peremptories by criminal defendants, civil litigants, defendants of a different race from the excluded juror, and in cases of sex-based discriminatory peremptory strikes.

RELATED CASES

Edmonson v. Leesville Concrete (1991)

J.E.B. v. Alabama, 114 S.Ct. 1419 (1994)

Powers v. Ohio, 499 U.S. 400 (1991)

Swain v. Alabama, 380 U.S. 202 (1965)

RECOMMENDED READING

Albert W. Alschuler, *The Supreme Court and the Jury: Voir Dire, Peremptory Challenges, and the Review of Jury Verdicts,* 56 University of Chicago Law Review 153, 196–198 (1989).

Leonard Mandell, *Extending* Batson v. Kentucky: *Do Gender-Based Peremptory Challenges Violate the Constitutional Guarantee of Equal Protection?,* 2 ABA Preview of United States Supreme Court Cases, 57, 57 (1993).

Case Title: *Brown v. Board of Education of Topeka, Kansas*

Alternate Case Titles: Brown School Admissions Case, School Desegregation Cases

Legal Citations: First Brown: 347 U.S. 483; 74 S.Ct. 686; 98 L.Ed. 873 (1954). Second Brown: 349 U.S. 294; 75 S.Ct. 753; 99 L.Ed. 1083 (1955)

Years of Decision: 1954, 1955

~ ◟

KEY ISSUES

Did the practice of segregating schools by race—almost universal in southern and border states prior to the decision—deprive black children of equal protection of the law, guaranteed to all Americans regardless of race under the Fourteenth Amendment to the U.S. Constitution?

HISTORY OF THE CASE

In the states where slavery was practiced prior to the passage of the Thirteenth Amendment outlawing slavery in 1865, a variety of laws had prohibited the education of slaves based on the theory that education might make them less tractable and encourage rebelliousness. In all parts of the country, public education was far from universal in the mid-19th century for children of any color, but tax-supported education was rare indeed in the agrarian South.

The federal government, during the Reconstruction period immediately following the Civil War, tried to establish a minimal system of schools for blacks in the former slave states under the auspices of the Freedmen's Bureau. When the bureau was shut down in 1870, this rudimentary system of education was largely abandoned. Reconstruction drew to a close in the South in the mid-1870s as federal troops were withdrawn and state governments fell back under the control of the local white population. Southern whites were determined to use both the law and extralegal intimidation to restore their domination over former slaves by establishing a rigid economic, political, and social caste system. By 1900, southern blacks had been effectively denied the right to vote, reduced to a condition of quasi serfdom in most rural areas, and subjected to a system of legally mandated segregation that barred social interaction between whites and blacks in almost every arena of life, including education.

In the late 19th and early 20th centuries, state and local governments gradually accepted the responsibility of offering all children at least several years of free public education, but educational standards in the South lagged far behind the rest of the nation, for whites as well as blacks. The education provided southern black children was even more inferior and totally separate. In 1910, expenditures per pupil for black schools averaged less than a third of those spent on white pupils.

Black plaintiffs challenged legally imposed segregation in the courts, contending that state laws imposing segregation violated the rights to equal protection of the laws guaranteed them under the Fourteenth Amendment to the Constitution. In 1896, the Supreme Court by an 8-1 decision upheld a Louisiana law mandating separate but equal accommodations on passenger trains (PLESSY V. FERGUSON). Three years later, in *Cumming v. Richmond County Board of Education,* the Court unanimously upheld segregation in the public schools, declaring that education was a matter left to state jurisdiction and that federal interference could not be justified. In 1908, the Court gave further sanction to Jim Crow education when it upheld, in *Berea College v. Kentucky,* a state law requiring segregation in private educational institutions.

The National Association for the Advancement of Colored People (NAACP) formulated in the early and mid-1930s a strategy for legally challenging school segregation on the ground that, in practice, separate education was never equal. The organization began by challenging state universities in border states such as Missouri and Maryland that maintained law schools for whites but not for blacks. In a critical 1938 decision (MISSOURI EX REL. GAINES V. CANADA), the Court ruled that the state of Missouri had to admit a black applicant to the state-supported law school since it had failed to provide a law school for black residents of the state.

The NAACP's goal was to abolish all forms of segregation in public education, but initially its legal drive focused on obtaining support in federal courts for "absolute equality," rather than challenging the courts to reverse the separate but equal doctrine laid down in *Plessy v. Ferguson.* The organization's legal strategists believed that the South would find the support of two absolutely equal parallel educational systems too expensive to sustain. Pursuing this strategy, the NAACP won case after case: forcing school districts to pay teachers in black schools exactly what they paid teachers in white schools, state law schools to admit black students, and state universities to admit black undergraduates.

This strategy, while successful in individual cases, was painstakingly slow. In each case, the plaintiffs had to establish that separate educational facilities offered blacks were inferior in some way to those offered whites. Without a direct reversal of the *Plessy* doctrine ruling segregation inherently unequal, it would take generations to equalize the thousands of school districts in the South.

By 1950, the NAACP decided that it would have to develop cases that would force the Supreme Court to address the issue of whether segregated schools were inherently unequal and, therefore, a violation of the equal protection of the laws guaranteed all Americans regardless of race or color.

The decision known as *Brown v. Board of Education* dealt with not one case but five separate cases that raised similar issues and that the Court, therefore, decided to hear together and decide together.

Briggs v. Elliot was a challenge to the segregated schools of Clarendon County, South Carolina, carefully crafted by the NAACP to challenge segregation per se. In arguing the case before a special three-judge panel in federal district court in Charleston, the plaintiffs presented evidence from social scientists that segregation in the schools reduced the self-esteem of black children. Resting on the *Plessy* doctrine, two of the judges rejected this argument but ordered the defendants to "promptly" provide equal educational facilities to black pupils. Judge J. Waites Waring dissented, accepted the NAACP's argument that a child attending a segregated school was "poisoned by prejudice" and that segregation in education was "an evil that must be eradicated."

Brown v. Board of Education of Topeka, Kansas was a case challenging the very concept of segregation, since the facilities provided to black and white students were essentially comparable. The case was heard by a three-judge panel of district judges who decided unanimously against the plaintiffs on the basis that the Supreme Court had yet to overturn the separate-but-equal doctrine. In the "Findings of Fact" attached to the opinion, however, the judges declared: "Segregation with the sanction of law . . . has a tendency to retard the educational and mental development of Negro children and to deprive them of some of the benefits they would receive in a racially integrated school system." This statement, as one NAACP lawyer remarked, would clearly put the Supreme Court "on the spot."

Gebhart et al. v. Belton et al. was a Delaware case seeking to overturn a decision by the state's chancery court that segregation in the schools created inequality and, therefore, violated the constitutional rights of the plaintiffs.

Davis et al. v. County School Board of Prince Edward County, Virginia et al. framed the issue of whether segregation had to be eliminated despite rapid and substantial efforts by the school district to improve the quality of black schools. A three-judge district court decision declaring that segregation had "for generations been a part of the mores of her people" ruled in favor of the state of Virginia and simply ordered the Prince Edward School Board to continue to equalize its facilities for black students "with diligence and dispatch."

The fifth case, *Bolling v. Sharp*, challenged school segregation in the District of Columbia. The plaintiffs' arguments were based entirely on the issue of segregation per se, intentionally avoiding the question of inferior facilities. The U.S. District Court judge who heard the case ruled that no claim of inequality had been made and, given that the constitutionality of segregation had been upheld, there was no basis upon which relief could be granted.

During the spring and summer of 1952, the Supreme Court accepted jurisdiction by granting writs of certiorari (which require transference of certified records from an inferior to a superior court) in the Kansas, South Carolina, and Virginia cases. Deciding that it should settle all the pending segregation cases together, the Court directed that the Delaware and District of Columbia cases also be argued at the same time.

SUMMARY OF ARGUMENTS

On December 9, 1952, the Supreme Court convened to hear the arguments on the five cases.

Each of the cases was argued separately. Thurgood Marshall, who in 1967 would become the first black justice appointed to the court, represented the NAACP. He faced John W. Davis, the 1924 Democratic Party candidate for the presidency, who represented South Carolina in the Briggs case. The thrust of the arguments presented by Marshall and the other lawyers demanding an end to school desegregation was that there was overwhelming psychological and sociological evidence demonstrating that school segregation did irreparable harm to black school children by stigmatizing them as inferior. The plaintiffs argued that "segregated schools are not equal and cannot be made equal, and that hence they [the plaintiffs] are deprived of the equal protection of the laws."

The defendants contended that segregation of the schools on an equal basis was in the best interests of the children and that as long as equal facilities were provided for black children there was no infringement of the plaintiffs' due process rights under the Fourteenth Amendment. The U.S. Justice Department filed an amicus curiae (friend of the court) brief supporting the plaintiffs.

The arguments were concluded on December 11, 1952, and the court began its own deliberations. After considerable internal discussion during which it became apparent that the justices were deeply divided over many questions, the Court on June 8, 1953, unanimously restored all five cases to the docket for reargument October 12 and posed a series of questions to the litigants; two of the questions required the plaintiffs and defendants to review the historical evidence on the intentions of Congress, the Fourteenth Amendment; two other questions asked, assuming the Court did find school segregation unlawful, how both plaintiffs and defendants would propose the Court go about ending it.

As both sides were preparing to reargue the cases, Chief Justice Fred Vinson died of a heart attack on September 8, 1953. President Dwight Eisenhower appointed California governor Earl Warren to replace Vinson. With Warren presiding as acting chief justice, as he was still awaiting Senate confirmation, the Court convened for three days of reargument on December 7. The NAACP's basic argument was that the Fourteenth Amendment involved a flat prohibition on discriminatory actions by the states.

Davis argued that the framers of the amendment had not regarded segregation per se as a denial of due process and that the Supreme Court had ruled seven times in favor of the separate-but-equal doctrine, making it a matter of settled law that should not be disturbed. Assistant Attorney General J. Lee Rankin, appearing to present the Justice Department's brief as a friend of the Court, declared that "segregation in public schools cannot be maintained under the 14th Amendment" and that the Court should send the cases back down to the district courts with the instruction that the lower courts oversee a desegregation process to be carried out "with deliberate speed."

DECISION

In the deliberations that followed the arguments, Warren convinced his colleagues that the sensitivity of the issue almost demanded that the Court speak with a single, resolute voice and settle the issue once and forever. Warren assigned himself the responsibility of writing a majority opinion. It would express the compromise formula the justices had agreed to in order to overturn *Plessy v. Ferguson*—that is, to rule segregation in the schools an unconstitutional denial of equal protection of the laws, but to hold over the cases for reargument during the next term as to how the decision should be implemented.

Warren read the Court's firm but brief and low-key opinion on May 17, 1954. He began by stating that the Court found the circumstances surrounding the adoption of the Fourteenth Amendment as "at best . . . inconclusive." He then traced the Court's interpretation of the amendment, noting that the "separate but equal" doctrine developed 20 years after the Court's first rulings. Declaring that public education had become "perhaps the most important function of state and local government," he said that the critical issue raised by the cases was: "Does segregation of children in public schools solely on the basis of race . . . deprive the children of the minority group of equal educational opportunities?" Warren answered the question in his next sentence: "We believe that it does."

"Segregation," he went on, quoting from the findings of fact in the *Brown* case, "of white and colored children in public schools has a detrimental effect upon the colored children. The impact is greater when it has the sanction of the law; for the policy of segregating the races is usually interpreted as denoting the inferiority of the Negro group. A sense of inferiority affects the motivation of a child to learn." Warren then declared that this "finding is amply supported by modern authority. Any language in *Plessy v. Ferguson* contrary to this finding is rejected." To this paragraph, Warren added a footnote citing a number of scholarly sources, concluding the footnote by saying: "And see generally Myrdal, *An American Dilemma*." This reference to Gunnar Myrdal provoked considerable outrage in the South since Myrdal, a

Swedish socialist, had castigated the region for its ubiquitous racism. Warren continued:

> We conclude that in the field of education the doctrine of "separate but equal" has no place. Separate educational facilities are inherently unequal. Therefore, we hold that the plaintiffs and others similarly situated . . . are, by reason of the segregation complained of, deprived of the equal protection of the laws guaranteed by the Fourteenth Amendment.

Warren concluded by requesting the parties to present further arguments in the fall of 1954 on how the Court's decision should be implemented.

The Court postponed arguments until April 11, 1955. Marshall argued strenuously for decisive action to end segregation by setting a fixed date by which segregation would have to end throughout the South. The defendants argued, for the most part, that no fixed timetable should be imposed and that too rapid desegregation might destroy the system of public education in many areas of the South. Speaking as a friend of the Court for the government of the United States, Solicitor General Simon E. Sobeloff urged the justices to instruct the district courts to direct the segregated school districts to make a prompt start on the process of integration and complete it "as speedily as feasible."

Finally, on May 31, 1955, Warren delivered a unanimous seven-paragraph opinion on the implementation of the Brown decision directing the district courts to monitor the "good faith" of local school boards in planning and implementing desegregation plans. The lower courts, Warren said, should be guided by "equitable principles" and "a practical flexibility." In the most famous phrase of the case, Warren said that the district courts should see that the parties to the cases be admitted "to public schools on a racially nondiscriminatory basis with all deliberate speed."

AFTERMATH

The phrase "all deliberate speed" proved subject to varying interpretations. It would take nearly a quarter century and hundreds of lower-court decisions before the Supreme Court's edict in Brown had been fully implemented throughout the South. Even then, in both North and South, pat-

terns of residential segregation and concentration of blacks in urban areas and whites in suburban areas were reflected in school enrollments.

In the immediate aftermath of the second Brown decision, the South sought to use tokenism to meet the letter of the law while negating the spirit. District courts frequently granted school boards long delays and accepted the enrollment of handfuls of black school children in formerly white schools as adequate compliance. The first major crisis in the desegregation process came in Little Rock in 1957 when Arkansas governor Orval Faubus used National Guardsmen to prevent the enrollment of a few blacks in the city's Central High School. After talks with Faubus led nowhere, President Eisenhower reluctantly sent U.S. Army paratroopers to enforce court orders. Some 750 school districts were desegregated—at least on a token basis—in the first four years after the Brown decision, but only an additional 49 were desegregated during the period 1958 to 1960. The process of desegregation picked up speed in the early 1960s and, after the passage of the 1964 Civil Rights Act, federal authorities had more weapons in the legal battle. In 1969 Chief Justice Warren Burger wrote a short and unanimous opinion in *Alexander v. Holmes County (Mississippi) Board of Education* declaring, "the obligation of every school district is to terminate dual school systems at once." By 1972 over 46 percent of black children in the South were attending schools in which the majority of students were white, a higher percentage than could be found in other sections of the nation.

SIGNIFICANCE

Brown v. Board of Education would be ranked by most historians as among the two or three most far-reaching and significant decisions ever handed down by an American court. Over the next decade additional decisions wiped out legally sanctioned segregation in almost every aspect of American life, even outlawing in 1967 state laws barring interracial marriage. The decision also sparked a mass movement among blacks demanding their civil rights. Starting with the bus boycott in Montgomery, Alabama, led by Martin Luther King, Jr., it quickly spread across the nation, transforming the nation's political life. Although still beset by economic problems, American blacks were freed from the system of legally sanctioned discrimination within two decades of the Brown decision.

RELATED CASES

Bolling v. Sharpe, 347 U.S. 497, 74 S.Ct. 693, 98 L.Ed. 884 (1954)

McLaurin v. Oklahoma State Regents, 339 U.S. 637, 70 S.Ct. 851, 94 L.Ed. 1149 (1950)

Plessy v. Ferguson, 163 U.S. 537, 16 S.Ct. 1138, 41 L.Ed. 256 (1896)

Sweatt v. Painter, 339 U.S. 629, 70 S.Ct. 848, 94 L.Ed. 1114 (1950)

RECOMMENDED READING

Bell, Derrick. *Race, Racism and American Law.* Boston: Little, Brown, 1980.

Brown v. Board of Education *and Its Legacy,* 61 Fordham Law Review 1 (October 1992).

Friedman, Leon. *Argument: The Oral Argument Before the Supreme Court in* Brown v. Board of Education, *1952–1955.* New York: Chelsea House, 1969.

Graglia, Lino. *Disaster by Decree: The Supreme Court Decisions on Race and the Schools.* Ithaca, N.Y.: Cornell University Press, 1976.

Kluger, Richard. *Simple Justice: The History of* Brown v. Board of Education *and Black America's Struggle for Equality.* New York: Knopf, 1976.

Speer, Hugh. *The Case of the Century: A Historical and Social Perspective on* Brown v. Board of Education. Kansas City, Mo.: University of Missouri Press, 1968.

Case Title: *Burlington Industries, Inc. v. Ellerth*

Alternate Case Title: Employer Liability for Sexual Harassment Case

Legal Citation: 118 S.Ct. 2257

Year of Decision: 1998

KEY ISSUES

Can an employer be liable for the sexual harassment of an employee when the employee suffers no adverse tangible job consequences and there is a lack of evidence indicating the employer is negligent or otherwise at fault?

HISTORY OF THE CASE

Title VII of the Civil Rights Act of 1964 makes it "an unlawful employment practice for an employer . . . to discriminate against any individual with respect to his compensation, terms, conditions, or privileges of employment, because of such individual's race, color, religion, sex, or national origin." Earlier cases held that the Title VII language "is not limited to 'economic' or 'tangible' discrimination" (*Meritor Savings Bank, FSB v. Vinson,* U.S. 57, 64 [1986]), and that abusive conduct may be actionable even if it does not seriously affect the employee's psychological well-being or lead the employee to suffer injury (*Harris v. Forklift Systems, Inc.,* 510 U.S. 17 [1993]). At the time Ellerth brought her suit against Burlington Industries, however, the courts had developed no consistent standard for holding employers liable for abusive conduct on the part of supervisors.

Kimberly Ellerth worked for more than one year as a salesperson in one of Burlington's divisions in Chicago. During her employment, Ellerth was subjected to constant sexual harassment by one of her supervisors but did not inform anyone in authority about the supervisor's offensive conduct, despite knowing that Burlington had a policy against sexual harassment. Some months after quitting her job, Ellerth sued, alleging that Burlington engaged in sexual harassment and forced her resignation, in violation of Title VII.

The trial court found the supervisor's behavior severe and pervasive enough to create a hostile work environment, but found that Burlington neither knew nor should have known about the conduct. Accordingly, the trial court dismissed Ellerth's claim. On appeal, however, Ellerth succeeded in having her claim reinstated. The appellate judges wrote eight separate opinions, reflecting no consensus for a controlling rationale. These judges were able to agree that the issue they confronted was vicarious liability—that is, whether Burlington has liability for the supervisor's misconduct, rather than liability limited to its own negligence—but they were unable to agree whether Burlington could be held responsible for the supervisor's actions even though Burlington was not negligent. The Supreme Court decided to hear the case to resolve whether an employer has vicarious liability when a supervisor creates a hostile work environment by making explicit threats to alter a subordinate's terms or conditions of employment, based on sex, but does not fulfill the threat.

SUMMARY OF ARGUMENTS

The Supreme Court stated the issue of real concern as vicarious liability. Thus, the parties argued principles of agency law, since Title VII defines the term "employer" to include "agents" of the employer. Ellerth argued that, under the common law of agency, Burlington should be held liable for harm caused by the misuse of supervisory authority. Burlington argued that its own lack of negligence or of knowledge of the supervisor's actions should shield Burlington from liability.

DECISION

The Supreme Court, in its decision favoring Ellerth, held that an employer is subject to vicarious liability to a victimized employee for a hostile environment created by a supervisor with authority over the employee. The effect on employers was somewhat softened in that the Court also crafted a defense for cases where a supervisor takes no tangible employment action such as denying a promotion or raise. In such cases, the employer can avoid liability if it can prove (a) that the employer exercised reasonable care to prevent and correct promptly any sexually harassing behavior and (b) that the plaintiff employee unreasonably failed to take advantage of any preventive or corrective opportunities provided by the employer or to avoid harm otherwise.

This was not an easy case, as demonstrated by the complicated reasoning in the opinion written by Justice Kennedy for the majority. Despite the opinion's detailed discussion of agency law, the outcome ultimately flowed from Title VII's strong policy stance against sexual harassment in the workplace.

The dissent, written by Justice Thomas and joined by Justice Scalia, argued that the majority took the policy too far. Justice Thomas objected that, under the rule stated by the majority, employer liability now would be judged by different standards depending upon whether a sexually or racially hostile work environment were alleged. The standard, according to Justice Thomas, should be the same in both instances: An employer should be liable if, and only if, the plaintiff proves that the employer was negligent in permitting the

supervisor's conduct to occur. Because sexual harassment is a form of employment discrimination, Justice Thomas would restore parallel treatment of employer liability for racial and sexual harassment, rather than holding employers to a higher standard of liability for a sexually hostile work environment. The dissent also argued that the defense for employers is poorly articulated by the majority and provides little guidance for how employers can actually avoid vicarious liability.

AFTERMATH

Kimberly Ellerth's suit had been dismissed at trial because Burlington, neither knowing nor having reason to know of the hostile work environment created by Ellerth's supervisor, was not legally negligent. In light of the Supreme Court's decision, plaintiffs in Ellerth's position now are able to proceed to trial, and the burden shifts to the employer to prove (a) reasonable care to prevent and correct promptly any sexually harassing behavior and (b) the plaintiff employee failed to take advantage of the preventive or corrective opportunities or otherwise to avoid harm.

SIGNIFICANCE

Much like *Harris v. Forklift Systems, Inc.* (1993), *Burlington Industries* demonstrates the vitality of Title VII in the workplace sexual harassment context. Even a relatively conservative Supreme Court continues to expand the scope of Title VII protection against sexually motivated harassment. It is too early to assess the degree to which the holding will further "Congress' intention to promote conciliation rather than litigation in the Title VII context." In the short run, in fact, there is likely to be more litigation to clarify the applicable legal rules broadly described by the Court.

RELATED CASES

Faragher v. City of Boca Raton, 118 S.Ct. 2275 (1998)

Harris v. Forklift Systems, Inc., 510 U.S. 17 (1993)

Meritor Savings Bank, FSB v. Vinson, 477 U.S. 57 (1986)

RECOMMENDED READING

Elizabeth M. Brama, *The Changing Burden of Employer Liability for Workplace Discrimination,* 83 Minnesota Law Review 1481 (1999).

Misty L. Gill, *The Changed Face of Liability for Hostile Work Environment Sexual Harassment: The Supreme Court Imposes Strict Liability in* Faragher v. City of Boca Raton *and* Burlington Industries, Inc. v. Ellerth, 32 Creighton Law Review 1651 (1999).

Tara Kaesebier, *Employer Liability in Supervisor Sexual Harassment Cases: The Supreme Court Finally Speaks,* 31 Arizona State Law Journal 203 (1999).

Joy Sabino Mullane, *Employer Liability for Hostile Environment Sexual Harassment Created by Supervisors under Title VII: Toward a Clearer Standard?,* 51 Florida Law Review 559 (1999).

Case Title: *Bush v. Gore*

Alternate Case Title: The Hanging Chad Case

Legal Citation: 531 U.S. 98

Year of Decision: 2000

KEY ISSUES

Is it unconstitutional for a state supreme court to create new standards for addressing presidential election conflicts and to order a manual recount of votes without providing a uniform standard for the procedure?

HISTORY OF THE CASE

During the 2000 presidential election between George W. Bush and Albert Gore, Jr., the state of Florida encountered difficulty with its election process. After the votes had been tabulated in the various counties of the state of Florida, Bush had received more votes, but his margin of victory was less than one-half of 1 percent. Because of the small margin of victory, the Florida election rules provided for an automatic machine recount. The result of the machine recount still indicated victory for Bush, but by an even smaller margin. Gore then sought manual recounts in several counties. Due to these recounts, the Florida Supreme Court extended the deadline by which the counties had to submit their election returns

to the Florida secretary of state. The U.S. Supreme Court reviewed this decision and vacated it, but upon return of the case to the Florida Supreme Court, the extended deadline was reinstated.

Bush was declared the winner of Florida's 25 electoral votes. However, Gore filed a lawsuit contesting the certification of the election results. Upon appeal, the Florida Supreme Court ordered a manual recount of all undervotes, votes that when counted by the machines did not register a vote for president.

Bush and Richard Cheney filed an application in the U.S. Supreme Court seeking to have the Florida Supreme Court's order to recount stopped. The Supreme Court granted the application and granted review of the issues.

SUMMARY OF ARGUMENTS

George W. Bush and Richard Cheney argued that the Florida Supreme Court's decision to have a manual recount violated Article II of the U.S. Constitution and conflicted with 3 U.S.C. § 5. Bush also argued that the Florida Supreme Court's decision violated the equal protection clause and the due process clause.

Albert Gore, Jr., argued that Article II of the U.S. Constitution did not give the Supreme Court a basis to override the Florida Supreme Court's decision. Gore also argued that the Florida Supreme Court's decision was consistent with 3 U.S.C. § 5. Finally, Gore argued that the Fourteenth Amendment provided no basis for the Supreme Court to disregard Florida's statutory rules and proceedings for determining the outcome of the presidential election.

DECISION

The Court indicated that individual U.S. citizens do not have a "constitutional right to vote for electors for the President of the United States unless and until the state legislature chooses a statewide election" as the way in which it will appoint the Electoral College members. Article II of the Constitution provides that the state legislatures will select how electors are appointed. However, the states have selected that the individual citizens will vote for the electors, making the right to vote a fundamental right.

The Court found that the Florida Supreme Court had ordered the recount to determine the intent of the voters with respect to undervotes;

however, the Court found the procedures used to perform the Florida Supreme Court ordered recount were not uniform. For example, some counties counted a punch ballot where a chad, a piece of the ballot, was merely dimpled, whereas other counties required the chad to be separated from the ballot on several corners to be counted. Therefore, an unequal evaluation of the ballots occurred in violation of the equal protection clause. The Court also found that the manual recount in some counties was extended to overvotes, ballots that contained more than one vote for president, and the Florida Supreme Court's order did not specify who was to recount the ballots. The Court found the whole recount process to be inconsistent and unable to be conducted so as to comply with equal protection and due process standards without additional standards. The Court found that any recount able to meet the December 12 deadline for appointing electors to the Electoral College would not be conducted in a constitutional manner, thus the Court reversed the Florida Supreme Court's order to recount.

Chief Justice Rehnquist, joined by Justices Scalia and Thomas, wrote a concurrence finding additional grounds on which to reverse the judgment of the Florida Supreme Court. The chief justice acknowledged that in most cases, the Supreme Court deferred to state court decisions on state law. However, the chief justice found that a federal question existed when a state departs from the legislative scheme for appointing presidential electors. Chief Justice Rehnquist found that the Florida Supreme Court's interpretation of the state's election laws, allowing the extension of the deadline for certification of votes and requiring late vote tallies to be included in the certification, violated Article II.

Justice Stevens, joined by Justices Ginsburg and Breyer, dissented. Justice Stevens found that there was not a substantial federal question at issue in this case to be resolved by the Court. Justice Souter found the Florida Supreme Court's decision to be consistent with Article II's grant of authority. Further, Justice Stevens did not think the Florida Supreme Court's failure to specify uniform standards for the recount constituted a constitutional violation. Rather, he found unconstitutional the majority's decision to disenfranchise those voters whose ballots were legal votes, but were rejected during the machine count. Finally, Justice Stevens found that the Florida Supreme Court had made no substantive changes to Florida election law.

Justice Souter, joined by Justice Breyer and joined in part by Justices Stevens and Ginsburg, dissented, finding that no issue presented required the U.S. Supreme Court's review. Specifically, Justice Souter found that the interpretations of Florida law by the Florida Supreme Court, such as what constituted a legal vote, raised no substantial question under Article II. Justice Souter did find evidence of an equal protection violation in the various standards used to recount ballots and determine a voter's intent; however, he thought the majority should have remanded the case to the Florida Supreme Court and given them a chance to remedy the standard inequities and try to count the ballots before the deadline.

Justice Ginsburg wrote a separate dissent joined by Justice Stevens and joined in part by Justices Souter and Breyer. Justice Ginsburg found no reason to reverse the Florida Supreme Court's interpretation of Florida law, stating that rarely did the Court reject an interpretation of a state's highest court; rather, federal courts deferred to state supreme court interpretations of their state law. Further, Justice Ginsburg found that Bush did not present a substantial equal protection claim and that any concern about the December 12 deadline was irrelevant.

Justice Breyer, joined in part by Justices Stevens, Ginsburg, and Souter, dissented finding it was wrong for the Court to review the decision of the Florida Supreme Court as the federal questions were insubstantial, except for the lack of uniform standards for the recount that implicated equal protection concerns. Justice Breyer found no justification for halting the recount as there was no evidence that the recount could not have been completed by the established deadline.

Aftermath

George W. Bush ultimately was declared the winner of the 2000 presidential election.

Significance

The significance of this case resides in the media attention the election received and the worldwide pause that ensued as all waited for the outcome of the election. Given the economic and foreign policy whirlwinds the current presidency was thrust into almost immediately, one might wonder if the election fiasco was a sign of times to come. The Supreme Court's decision to insert itself into this dispute was unexpected and suggests that when an issue is of national importance, the Court will find a federal question so that it may control the outcome.

RELATED CASE

Bush v. Palm Beach County Canvassing Board, 531 U.S. 70 (2000)

RECOMMENDED READING

Florida State Law Review, Volume 29 (2001) (entire volume consists of articles on *Bush v. Gore*).

Spencer Overton, *Rules, Standards, and* Bush v. Gore: *Form and the Law of Democracy,* 37 Harvard Civil Rights–Civil Liberties Law Review 65 (2002).

Case Title: *Bush v. Vera*

Alternate Case Title: Racial Gerrymandering Two

Legal Citation: 517 U.S. 952

Year of Decision: 1996

KEY ISSUES

Does a state redistricting plan motivated by race consciousness, incumbency protection, and compliance with the Voting Rights Act that creates two new majority-minority districts with extremely irregular boundaries and reconfigures a third to create a majority-minority district with extremely irregular boundaries violate the Fourteenth Amendment?

HISTORY OF THE CASE

The results of the 1990 census indicated that Texas experienced a rise in population and was entitled to three additional congressional seats in the House of Representatives. Therefore, Texas adopted a redistricting plan that, among other things, created two new congressional districts

and reconfigured a third congressional district. One of the new districts was a majority black district, another was a majority Hispanic district, and the reconfigured district was a majority black district. Six Texas voters filed a lawsuit alleging that 24 of the 30 congressional districts in the state constituted racial gerrymanders in violation of the Fourteenth Amendment. The district court found the two new congressional districts and the reconfigured district to be unconstitutional. The governor of Texas, George W. Bush, and others appealed the decision.

SUMMARY OF ARGUMENTS

George W. Bush and the other appellants argued that the strange shape of the districts was the result of efforts to protect incumbents and unite "communities of interest." Further, appellants contended that the districts were justified as the state's attempt to comply with the Voting Rights Act, specifically section 2, which prohibits any electoral procedure that results in hindering a person's right to vote on account of race or color. Finally, appellants argued that the districts were justified by the state's interest in remedying past racial discrimination, conceding that the districts were created to enhance the opportunity for the election of minority representatives.

Appellees, Al Vera and other Texas voters, argued that the districts constituted racial gerrymanders that were not narrowly tailored to further a compelling state interest in violation of the Fourteenth Amendment.

DECISION

The Supreme Court found the districts at issue to be unconstitutional. The Court found that the districts were subject to strict scrutiny because strict scrutiny is applied when race is a predominant factor in drawing district lines and the traditional districting principles are subordinated to the race factor. Further, the Court found that the districts were not narrowly tailored to serve a compelling state interest.

Justice O'Connor wrote the opinion for the Court, which was joined by Chief Justice Rehnquist and Justice Kennedy. Justice O'Connor first addressed whether the districts were subject to strict scrutiny. Justice O'Connor stated that strict scrutiny applied when redistricting on its face was so irregular that it could be viewed only as a segregation of the races for voting purposes or when race was the dominant factor in drawing the district lines. While Justice O'Connor acknowledged that Texas had mixed motives for the way the district lines were drawn, she found that race was the predominant factor as there was substantial direct evidence of Texas's racial motivations. Justice O'Connor found that the creation of majority-minority districts in and of itself was not objectionable, but became objectionable when traditional districting principles were subordinated to race. If the traditional districting principles had outweighed race, then strict scrutiny would have been inapplicable. Justice O'Connor reviewed each district individually, but determined that no reason existed to reverse the district court's findings.

Next, Justice O'Connor looked at whether the racial classifications had been narrowly tailored to further a compelling interest of the state. While Justice O'Connor indicated that compliance with the Voting Rights Act could be a compelling state interest, it could not be a compelling interest in this situation as traditional principles of districting were subordinated to race substantially more than necessary. Further, Justice O'Connor stated that a state interest in remedying past discrimination could also be a compelling interest when the discrimination sought to be remedied was specific, identified discrimination, and a strong evidentiary basis indicated remedial action was necessary. However, Justice O'Connor found that the racial classifications were not narrowly tailored in this case.

Justice O'Connor wrote a separate concurrence in an attempt to give guidance to states on the issue of simultaneous compliance with the Court's decisions in this case, the *Shaw* decisions, and the Voting Rights Act. Justice O'Connor clearly stated that the Voting Rights Act could coexist both in principle and in practice with *Shaw* and its progeny.

Justice Kennedy also concurred, reiterating that strict scrutiny should apply to this case and that the racial classifications were not narrowly tailored to further a compelling state interest. However, Justice Kennedy indicated that he did not want to extend these determinations in a general manner so as to require this result despite varying facts of future cases.

Justice Thomas was joined by Justice Scalia in a separate concurrence indicating his view that

the application of strict scrutiny to the redistricting plan was not a close question. Justice Thomas also stated his disagreement with Justice O'Connor that strict scrutiny was not automatically applicable to the intentional creation of majority-minority districts. Rather, Justice Thomas found that strict scrutiny applies to all government classifications based on race with no exception.

Justice Stevens, joined by Justices Ginsberg and Breyer, dissented. Justice Stevens found that the Court erred in finding the districts unconstitutional, stating that the Court erred in applying strict scrutiny to all the districts at issue and concluding that none met this standard. Further, Justice Stevens found that the Court had improperly focused on the role the race factor played in redistricting decisions. However, even if strict scrutiny were applicable, Justice Stevens would have found the districts constitutional as race was only considered to the extent necessary to comply with the Voting Rights Act. Justice Stevens would have classified this case as political, not racial, gerrymandering and cautioned that states would find it difficult to avoid litigation in future redistricting. Further, Justice Stevens stated that the Court has guaranteed it will have a hand in drawing voting district lines.

Finally, Justice Souter, joined by Justices Ginsburg and Breyer, also dissented. Justice Souter found the Court had failed to describe the necessary elements for this new cause of action for racial gerrymanders; thus potential litigants were not adequately on notice, nor did courts have standards to enforce the Court's decision. Justice Souter felt the Court had failed to adequately distinguish between lawful and unlawful uses of race in redistricting. Justice Souter pointed out what he considered to be the problems associated with this lack of standards, only to find that any effort by the Court to define the applicable standards created more questions and confusion.

AFTERMATH

Texas continued to have problems with its voting districts after the decision in *Bush v. Vera*. After the decision, the courts provided an interim districting map that was used for elections in 1998. After the 2000 census, Texas was entitled to two additional congressional seats; however, the legislature still did not enact a redistricting plan. Because of difficulty reaching a compromise on a districting map, Texas has continued to use court-drawn maps.

SIGNIFICANCE

The decision in *Bush v. Vera* confirmed that the Court was not going to back away from its decision in the *Shaw* cases to apply strict scrutiny to cases alleging racial gerrymandering and to find redistricting plans unconstitutional if race was a predominant consideration in drawing district lines. However, *Bush v. Vera* did provide some clarification as to how states might comply with *Shaw's* standards and the Voting Rights Act. Unfortunately, questions still remain as to how to avoid redistricting litigation and create a constitutional redistricting plan.

RELATED CASES

Shaw v. Reno, 509 U.S. 630 (1993)

Shaw v. Hunt, 517 U.S. 899 (1996)

RECOMMENDED READING

Burke, Christopher M. *The Appearance of Equality: Racial Gerrymandering, Redistricting, and the Supreme Court.* Westport, Conn.: Greenwood Press, 1999.

Kousser, J. Morgan. *Colorblind Justice: Minority Voting Rights and the Undoing of the Second Reconstruction.* Chapel Hill: University of North Carolina Press, 1999.

Peacock, Anthony A. *Affirmative Action and Representation:* Shaw v. Reno *and the Future of Voting Rights.* Durham, N.C.: Carolina Academic Press, 1997.

Case Title: *Caban v. Mohammed*

Alternate Case Title: The "Parental Rights for Fathers" Case

Legal Citations: 441 U.S. 380; 99 S.Ct. 1760; 60 L.Ed. 2d 297

Year of Decision: 1979

KEY ISSUES

Is a New York statute constitutional that required the consent of the mother, but not the father, for the adoption of a child born out of wedlock?

HISTORY OF THE CASE

Appellant Abdiel Caban and appellee Maria Mohammed lived together in New York out of wedlock from 1968 until the end of 1973. They had two children. Caban was identified as the father on the birth certificates. The couple separated; Mohammed took the children and married another man. During the next two years, Caban frequently saw or otherwise maintained contact with the children.

Mohammed and her husband subsequently petitioned for adoption of the children and appellant Caban filed a cross-petition for adoption. Under New York law, a natural mother has parental rights without having to adopt her child born out of wedlock. However, a mother may adopt her illegitimate child. Mohammed's petition was granted under § 111 of the New York Domestic Relations Law, which permits an unwed mother, but not an unwed father, to block an adoption of their child by withholding consent. The New York Supreme Court, Appellate Division, affirmed. The New York Court of Appeals dismissed the appeal in a memorandum decision. Caban appealed to the Supreme Court.

SUMMARY OF ARGUMENTS

Caban claimed that the distinction drawn under New York law between the adoption rights of an unwed father and those of other parents violates the equal protection clause of the Fourteenth Amendment. He further argued that the Supreme Court's decision in *Quilloin v. Walcott* (1978) recognized the due process right of natural fathers to maintain a parental relationship with their children unless a court finds that they are unfit as parents.

Mohammed and her husband argued that the statute was justified by a fundamental difference between maternal and paternal relations. They also argued that the statute served the end of promoting the adoption of illegitimate children and that unwed fathers were not treated differently under § 111 from other parents.

DECISION

Justice Powell wrote the decision for the Court joined by Justices Marshall, Brennan, White and Blackmun. He held that the New York statute was unconstitutional because the distinction it made between the rights of unmarried mothers and the rights of unmarried fathers was not shown to be substantially related to an important state interest.

Justice Powell believed that section 111 treated unmarried parents differently according to their sex because Mohammed could block adoption of her children by withholding her consent; however, Caban could block Mohammed's adoption only by showing that it was not in the best interest of the children. When Justice Powell was unable to find a substantial relation to any important state interest, he found the sex-based distinction in section 111 between unmarried mothers and unmarried fathers in violation of the equal protection clause of the Fourteenth Amendment.

Justice Powell did not believe that maternal and paternal roles were invariably different in importance. He also did not believe that unwed fathers were more likely to oppose adoption of their children than unwed mothers. However, he stated that when the father did not participate in the childrearing, the equal protection clause did not preclude the state from withholding the privilege of blocking the adoption of that child.

Justice Stewart wrote a dissenting opinion stating that the New York Domestic Relations Law did not violate the Constitution. He reasoned that the Court underestimated the state's interest in promoting the welfare of illegitimate children. He felt that children born out of wedlock were born with certain handicaps that adoption could have removed. He saw major differences in the roles of parents concerning illegitimate children, and he believed that only the mother was an indispensable party.

Justice Stewart disregarded Caban's contention that the statute violated the equal protection clause by granting rights to the unwed mother that it did not give to the unwed father. He believed that it was enough for Caban to be given the opportunity to participate in the adoption proceedings and to present evidence on whether the adoption would be in the best interest of the children. He challenged whether unwed mothers and fathers were similarly situated with respect to adoptions of newborn children and infants, because only the mother carried and gave birth to the child. The mother also is always an identifiable parent. Stewart also found the contention troublesome that the statute, in withholding from the unwed father certain rights granted to all other classes of parents, violated the equal protec-

tion and due process clauses. Justice Stewart believed that the State's interest in facilitating adoptions that were in the best interests of illegitimate children was an important state interest, and the gender-based statute fully served this goal.

Justice Stevens also wrote a dissenting opinion joined by Chief Justice Burger and Justice Rehnquist. He believed that the state's interest in facilitating adoption was strong, maybe even "compelling" when one considered the large number of children born out of wedlock and the benefits of legitimacy and life's basic necessities that adoption could provide. He further believed that the differences between natural mothers and natural fathers provided justification for treating them differently. He observed that the mother carried and had the final decision whether to bear the child. He also stressed that after birth, the mother's identity is certain while the father's may not be, and that the mother inevitably must make decisions regarding child care while the father may take no part. He argued that the differences between males and females through pregnancy and infancy were important and have a large impact on a child's destiny. Finally, Justice Stevens regarded the Court's holding as very narrow because it would not be applied retroactively, and applied to only future adoptions for older children with whom the father has established a relationship.

AFTERMATH

The Court left open the question of whether the unwed father of a newborn, with whom the father has not had the opportunity to develop a relationship, had a legal interest in and the right to veto the adoption of his child. However, the New York Court of Appeals answered this question in *In re Raquel Marie X*, 76 N.Y.2d at 405, 1. It held that an unwed father has such a right if he is willing to assume custody of the child and promptly manifests parental responsibility using all possible means.

SIGNIFICANCE

With *Caban*, the Supreme Court expanded the sphere of fundamental rights to include an unmarried father's, granting a father some power to block the adoption of his children by others. This case was championed as giving all fathers, regardless of their past or present marital status, the ability to enjoy a fundamental right to sustain a relationship with their children.

RELATED CASES

Lehr v. Robertson, 463 U.S. 248 (1983)

Quilloin v. Walcott, 434 U.S. 246 (1978)

Stanley v. Illinois, 405 U.S. 645 (1972)

RECOMMENDED READING

Ann Freedman, *Sex Equality, Sex Differences, and the Supreme Court,* 92 Yale Law Journal 913 (1983).

Sylvia Law, *Rethinking Sex and the Constitution,* 132 University of Pennsylvania Law Review 955 (1984).

Christine Littleton, *Reconstructing Sexual Equality,* 75 California Law Review 1279 (1987).

Case Title: *Colegrove v. Green*

Alternate Case Title: The "Political Thicket" Case

Legal Citation: 328 U.S. 549

Year of Decision: 1946

KEY ISSUES

Can the courts, through judicial decisions, reapportion state legislative districts?

HISTORY OF THE CASE

Illinois had a redistricting plan that contained an unequal distribution of population among voting districts. It had not changed the boundaries of congressional districts in the state since 1901, and great discrepancies existed among the districts. Some voters brought suit for a decree declaring Illinois law governing congressional districts invalid. They wanted to compel a reapportionment under the guarantee clause regarding a state's apportionment of voters for seats in the federal House of Representatives. The district court dismissed the bill and the voters appealed.

SUMMARY OF ARGUMENTS

Plaintiffs claimed that the districts lacked approximate equality of population and were not spatially proportionate, and therefore violated Article One and the Fourteenth Amendment of the U.S. Constitution. They also argued that the reduction in the effectiveness of their vote was the result of willful legislative discrimination against them and therefore amounted to a denial of the equal protection of the laws guaranteed by the Fourteenth Amendment.

DECISION

Justice Frankfurter wrote the opinion for the Court holding that reapportionment and voting dilution were political questions and therefore not justiciable. He declared that a suit to compel a reapportionment presented a political question and warned against involving the judiciary in the politics of the people. He also stated that the Court could not itself redistrict the state and that "it is hostile to a democratic system to involve the judiciary in the politics of the people. . . . Courts ought not to enter this political thicket." He believed that reapportioning and redistricting were the exclusive domain of the legislative branch of government.

Justice Rutledge wrote a concurring opinion stating the issue more bluntly: "There is not, and could not be except abstractly, a right of absolute equality in voting." He believed that the right to equal voting was not an absolute right and that trying to remedy it might have rendered worse results than the unequal voting itself. Justice Jackson took no part in the consideration or decision of the case.

Justice Black wrote a dissenting opinion stating that the district court had jurisdiction and that the complaint presented a justiciable case and controversy, since the facts as alleged by petitioners showed that they had been injured as individuals. He also believed that there was no adequate remedy at law for depriving them of their right to vote and thus could have and should have granted relief. He believed that since no supervision over the elections was asked for, the Court could have declared the state apportionment bill invalid and enjoined state officials from enforcing it.

AFTERMATH

Until *BAKER V. CARR* (1962), in which the Court rejected the rule of *Colegrove* and held that the judiciary was competent to decide issues of malapportionment, it was widely believed that even gross disparities in the populations of the legislative districts did not present justiciable controversies. The Court squarely overturned *Colegrove* in *Wesberry v. Sanders,* holding that challenges to congressional apportionment plans were justiciable and that such plans must be consistent with the principle of one person, one vote.

SIGNIFICANCE

Colegrove was the first important apportionment decision in which there was a one man–one vote constitutional challenge. It showed the Court's reluctance to enter into disputes over redistricting and reapportionment, since it refused to adjudicate the constitutional claim.

RELATED CASES

Baker v. Carr, 369 U.S. 186 (1962)

Gomillion v. Lightfoot, 364 U.S. 339 (1960)

Reynolds v. Sims, 377 U.S. 533 (1964)

RECOMMENDED READING

Larry Alexander, *Lost in the Political Thicket,* 41 Florida Law Review 563 (1989).

Bork, Robert H. *The Tempting of America: The Political Seduction of the Law.* New York: Free Press, 1990.

Hanson, Royce. *The Political Thicket.* Englewood Cliffs, N.J.: Prentice Hall, 1966.

Case Title: *Cooper v. Aaron*

Alternate Case Title: Little Rock School Crisis

Legal Citations: 358 U.S. 1; 78 S.Ct. 1401; 3 L.Ed. 2d 5

Year of Decision: 1958

KEY ISSUES

How much speed is appropriate in an effort to desegregate public schools?

HISTORY OF THE CASE

In compliance with the case of *BROWN V. BOARD OF EDUCATION,* 349 U.S. 294 (1954), public schools were ordered to begin the process of racial desegregation. William G. Cooper was the president of the school board of Little Rock, Arkansas. After the *Brown* decision, the Little Rock District School Board began to prepare a plan to gradually desegregate their public schools. The first school to be integrated was Central High School. Superintendent Virgil Blossom's plan was to start in 1957 at Central High School and ultimately complete desegregation by 1963. The school board adopted the plan, in spite of their recognition that there would be many objections. There was a challenge by a group of black plaintiffs desiring a more rapid completion, also known as *Aaron v. Cooper* in the U.S. District Court for the Eastern District of Arkansas and in the Eighth Circuit. In that case, the school board's plan was upheld. (See 143 F. Sup. 855 and 243 F. 2d. 361.) John Aaron represented a class of 32 other students who tried to enroll in another public high school. While the school district began plans to implement the Blossom plan, Governor Orval Faubus, who was running for reelection, attempted to use the Arkansas state legislature to prevent desegregation. To that end, the Arkansas state constitution was amended, commanding the Arkansas general assembly to oppose the desegregation decisions of the U.S. Supreme Court and, further, a statute was passed relieving all school children from compulsory attendance at racially mixed schools. Additionally, a state sovereignty commission was created to encourage segregationist attitudes.

The day before school desegregation was to begin, Governor Faubus ordered the Arkansas National Guard to prevent the entrance of nine black students into Central High School. President Dwight D. Eisenhower, Governor Faubus, the Little Rock School Board, and many members of the community fought for several weeks before a federal district court found that the governor had no grounds to mobilize the National Guard. President Eisenhower dispatched paratroopers to enforce desegregation. After a school year filled with tension, the Little Rock School Board asked the district court for and received a two and one-half year delay with regard to their desegregation plan. The NAACP appealed the case to the Eighth

Circuit, which reversed the decision of the district court.

SUMMARY OF ARGUMENTS

In a highly unusual move, the Court convened a special summer term beginning August 28, 1958, and heard arguments on September 11. Thurgood Marshall, later to become the first black member of the Court, argued for John Aaron and the respondents. Richard Butler represented the Little Rock School Board. The arguments of Mr. Butler raised sympathy for the school board and conditioned their request for delay on the interference of the governor and state officials with the operations of the board in the governance of their district. Marshall urged that the Court not compromise or yield to the delaying tactics of Governor Faubus or the Arkansas legislature.

DECISION

In another highly unusual action, the Court issued an unsigned order on September 12, unanimously affirming the judgment of the Eighth Circuit Court of Appeals. On September 29, the Court issued its formal opinion, written by Chief Justice Earl Warren and personally signed by all nine justices of the Court.

Because of the imminent beginning of the new school year at Central High School, the Supreme Court declared that there must be a prompt reaction to the actions of the legislators and governor of Arkansas. The Court found that the school board had acted in entirely good faith in dealing with the unfortunate events, but that, in spite of the frustrating conditions facing the board, there was no good legal excuse for delaying desegregation. The Court found that the constitutional rights of the students were not to be sacrificed or yielded to violence and disorder, nor were they subject to being nullified by state legislators or others, whether directly or indirectly, through evasive schemes to maintain segregation. Chief Justice Warren stated that the unanimous decision of the Court in *Brown v. Board of Education* was briefed and argued twice and that the Court had again examined the decision and it again unanimously reaffirmed the correctness of *Brown*:

The principles announced in that decision and the obedience of the States to them, according to the command of the Constitu-

tion, are indispensable for the protection of the freedoms guaranteed by our fundamental charter for all of us. Our constitutional ideal of equal justice under law is thus made a living truth.

AFTERMATH

In spite of the Supreme Court's order, Governor Faubus and the Arkansas legislature closed all four Little Rock high schools during the entire 1958–59 school year. Finally, in the fall of 1959, the Little Rock high schools opened to black and white students.

SIGNIFICANCE

In the *Cooper* decision, the Supreme Court recognized that the federal courts were facing massive resistance. Not until the passage of the Civil Rights Act of 1964 was there federal legislation that authorized the attorney general to intervene directly in school desegregation suits.

RELATED CASES

Brown v. Board of Education, 347 U.S. 483 (1954), 349 U.S. 294 (1955)

Faubus v. Aaron, 361 U.S. 197 (1959)

Green v. County School Board of New Kent County, Virginia, 391 U.S. 430 (1968)

Swann v. Charlotte-Mecklenburg Board of Education, 402 U.S. 1 (1971)

RECOMMENDED READING

Freyer, Tony. *The Little Rock Crisis: A Constitutional Interpretation.* Westport, Conn.: Greenwood Press, 1984.

Huckaby, Elizabeth. *Crisis at Central High: Little Rock, 1957–58.* Baton Rouge: Louisiana State University Press, 1980.

Spitzberg, Irving. *Racial Politics in Little Rock 1954–1964.* New York: Garland Publishing, 1987.

Case Title: *Craig v. Boren*

Alternate Case Title: The "Gender-Based Discrimination" Case

Legal Citations: 429 U.S. 190; 97 S.Ct. 451

Year of Decision: 1976

~

KEY ISSUES

Is an Oklahoma statute that prohibits the sale of "nonintoxicating" 3.2 percent beer to males under the age of 21 and to females under the age of 18 a denial of equal protection of the laws to males between the ages of 18 and 20 in violation of the Fourteenth Amendment? The case was an appeal of an action that challenged the constitutionality of a state law.

HISTORY OF THE CASE

This was the third case involving the issue of gender classification to come before the Supreme Court in five years. Beginning in 1971 with *Reed v. Reed*, the Court had struggled with the issue of when it is appropriate to treat men and women differently under the Constitution.

Appellant Craig was a male between 18 and 21 years old, and appellant Whitener was a licensed vendor of 3.2 percent beer. Both brought the action against the governor of Oklahoma to challenge the Oklahoma statute prohibiting the sale of "nonintoxicating" 3.2 percent beer to males under 21 and females under 18 in the District Court of the Western District of Oklahoma. The complaint sought a determination of the rights and status of Craig and Whitener, declaratory relief, and injunctive relief in the form of a court order preventing the enforcement of the statute. A three-judge district court held that appellee's statistical evidence regarding young males' drunk-driving arrests and traffic injuries demonstrated that the gender-based discrimination was substantially related to the achievement of traffic safety on Oklahoma roads. The district court sustained the constitutionality of the different age limits for males and females and dismissed the action. The appellants appealed to the U.S. Supreme Court.

SUMMARY OF ARGUMENTS

The appellants argued that the Oklahoma statute constituted a gender-based discrimination that denied to males 18 to 20 years of age the equal protection of the laws.

The appellees argued that the difference between males and females warranted the differential in age drawn by the Oklahoma statute. They also argued that the Oklahoma statutory provisions enforced state policies concerning the sale and distribution of alcohol and by force of the Twenty-first Amendment, which repealed the total prohibition of the manufacture and sale of intoxicating liquor and only prohibited such sale or manufacture in violation of state law, should therefore be held to withstand the equal protection challenge.

DECISION

Justice Brennan wrote the opinion for the Court holding that under *Reed*, Oklahoma's 3.2 percent beer statute invidiously discriminated against males 18 to 20 years of age. He struck down the Oklahoma statute, finding that the evidence the state presented to justify the gender discrimination did not substantially advance Oklahoma's purpose of preventing traffic accidents.

Justice Brennan began his analysis referring to *Reed v. Reed*, which emphasized that statutory classifications that distinguished between males and females were "subject to scrutiny under Equal Protection Clause." Classifications by gender could withstand constitutional challenge only if they served important governmental objectives and were substantially related to the achievement of those objectives. Justice Brennan then stated two examples of objectives that were insufficient to sustain the use of an overt gender classifications: in the appointment of administrators of intestate decedents. These objectives were "reducing the workload on probate courts," and "avoiding intrafamily controversy."

Justice Brennan then turned to the alleged necessity of the age differential between males and females with respect to the purchase of 3.2 percent beer. Justice Brennan concluded that the gender-based distinction did not closely serve the objective of enhancing traffic safety as the state purported. He believed that the statistics presented by the appellees were unpersuasive and unhelpful to the equal protection analysis. He concluded that sex did not represent a legitimate, accurate substitute for the regulation of drinking and driving.

Justice Powell wrote a concurring opinion expressing reservations about the appropriate standard for equal protection analysis and the relevance of the statistical evidence. He believed that the case turned on whether the state legislature had adopted a means that bore a "fair and substantial relation" to the state's objective. He concluded that the gender-based classification did not bear a fair and substantial relation to the state objectives of promoting highway safety.

Justice Stevens also wrote a concurring opinion arguing against a two-tiered analysis of equal protection claims. He did not see the classification as totally irrational, but he felt that its justification was unacceptable because it restrained 100 percent of the class (all males 18 to 20) for the actions of about 2 percent without any indication that the law would have a deterrence effect on that 2 percent, or on the other 98 percent.

Justice Rehnquist wrote a dissenting opinion objecting to the majority opinion on two grounds: (1) the Court's conclusion that men may invoke a more stringent standard of judicial review than pertains to most types of classifications by challenging a gender-based statute that treats them less favorably than women; and (2) the Court's enunciation of that standard without citation to any source. He also criticized the Court's rejection of the appellee's statistics, believing that they created reasonable inferences that incidences of drunk driving were much higher than actual arrests. He believed that the statistics were valuable and were improperly "denigrated to misconceive the nature of the equal protection analysis." Justice Rehnquist felt that the Court's analysis was not relevant to equal protection but to due process, asking whether there were enough persons in the category who drove while drunk to justify the application of such a prohibition against all members of that group.

Justice Stewart and Blackmun wrote concurring opinions, and Chief Justice Burger wrote a dissenting opinion.

AFTERMATH

After *Craig,* discrimination based on gender was neither suspect nor subject to the less exacting rational basis standard; rather, it was "quasi-suspect," judged by a more flexible intermediate level of scrutiny. The test articulated in *Craig* has been employed in other areas of constitutional adjudication, such as in cases of regulations based on illegitimacy and alienage.

SIGNIFICANCE

Craig was the first case in which the Court held that equal protection challenges based on gender classifications would be subject to an intermediate level of scrutiny. It marked the third standard concerning gender classification announced by the Court in a five-year period, and it constituted a retreat from the Court's strict level scrutiny employed three years earlier in FRONTIERO V. RICHARDSON.

RELATED CASES

Frontiero v. Richardson, 411 U.S. 677 (1973)

Mississippi Univ. for Women v. Hogan, 458 U.S. 718 (1982)

Reed v. Reed, 404 U.S. 71 (1971)

RECOMMENDED READING

Ruth Ginsburg, *Sexual Equality under the Fourteenth and Equal Rights Amendment,* 1979 Washington University Law Quarterly 161 (1979).

Kenneth Karst, *Forward: Equal Citizenship under the Fourteenth Amendment,* 91 Harvard Law Review 1 (1977).

Case Title: *Dandridge v. Williams*

Legal Citation: 397 U.S. 471

Year of Decision: 1970

KEY ISSUES

Does imposition of a ceiling on welfare benefits deny equal protection to large families, which receive less assistance per family member than do smaller families?

HISTORY OF THE CASE

In a series of decisions in the 1960s concerning rights to fair treatment in the criminal process, voting rights, and ability to engage in interstate travel, opinions of the Supreme Court had indicated classifications that burden the poor were to be reviewed under an increased standard of review as suspect classifications, classifications based upon traits that seem to go against constitutional principles and therefore are subject to strict scrutiny. The Court had not yet squarely faced a law, however, that burdened a class of persons who lacked financial resources for the allocation of benefits that had no other constitutional recognition. The Court has never recognized the interest of an individual in government subsistence benefits as a fundamental constitutional interest.

The state of Maryland had a welfare scheme that implemented the Aid to Families with Dependent Children (AFDC) program, jointly financed by the state and federal governments. Maryland granted most eligible families their "standard of need," but Annapolis imposed a "maximum grant" limit of $250 per month per family, regardless of the family size or computed standard of need.

SUMMARY OF ARGUMENTS

Maryland argued that its maximum grant regulation was wholly free of any invidiously discriminatory purpose or effect, and that the regulation was rationally supportable because it encouraged gainful employment; maintained an equitable balance in economic status between welfare families and those supported by a wage earner; provided incentives for family planning; and allocated available public funds in such a way as fully to meet the needs of the largest possible number of families. Williams, the plaintiff, challenged the Maryland scheme as denying equal protection since large families received less aid per child than small families.

DECISION

A majority of the Court upheld the law under a rational relationship test, which requires a rational basis for enactment and a reasonable relationship to the achievement of a legitimate government objective. The Court found that the state had a legitimate interest in the economy and the provision of certain families. The majority found no basis for distinguishing this law from any other economic regulation, since all such measures to some extent involved the reallocation of resources or wealth. The majority found that the regulations constituted "economic and social welfare" legislation, which merited only the tradi-

tional standard of review. The Maryland scheme satisfied this deferential standard since it bore a rational relation to several legitimate state objectives (e.g., encouraging employment by prohibiting payments that might compare favorably with what a job would provide).

Specifically, Justice Stewart's majority opinion stated:

> [Here] we deal with state regulation in the social and economic field, not affecting freedoms guaranteed by the Bill of Rights, and claimed to violate the 14th Amendment only because the regulation results in some disparity in grants of welfare payments to the largest AFDC families. For this Court to approve the invalidation of state economic or social regulation would be far too reminiscent of an era when the Court thought the 14th Amendment gave it power to strike down state laws "because they might be unwise, improvident, or out of harmony with a particular school of thought." That era long ago passed into history.
>
> In the area of economics and social welfare, a State does not violate the Equal Protection Clause merely because the classifications made by its laws are imperfect. If the classification has some "reasonable basis," it does not offend the Constitution.
>
> The Constitution may impose certain procedural safeguards upon systems of welfare administration. But the Constitution does not empower this Court to second-guess state officials charged with the difficult responsibility of allocating limited public welfare funds among the myriad of potential recipients.

This result was reached over the strong dissent of Justice Marshall, who argued that classifications that burden poor persons in the ability to obtain the basic necessities for functioning in society should be judged by some meaningful standard of review, even if they were not subjected to the compelling interest test. Marshall conceded that strict scrutiny was not appropriate, but he also disagreed with the majority's finding that the traditional, deferential, "mere rationality" test was the correct one. Instead, he gave the first major exposition of his "sliding scale" theory: Rather than a rigid "two-tier" standard, by which all statutes are given either extreme deference or strict scrutiny, the degree of review should be adjusted along a spectrum, depending on (1) the type of classification; (2) the "relative importance to individuals in the class discriminated against of the governmental benefits that they do not receive"; and (3) the strength of the interests asserted by the state in support of the classification.

When this analysis was applied to the facts of *Dandridge,* Marshall concluded that a significant degree of scrutiny should be given, since the welfare recipients' interest in the benefits was large, and, in his view, the state's asserted interest in its scheme relatively weak. The scheme was not sufficient to withstand this significant scrutiny, he contended.

AFTERMATH

This position has been followed consistently by the Court; it has held that there was no basis for using any form of strict scrutiny, or increased standard of review, to test legislation that burdens classifications of poor persons in the receipt of other forms of welfare benefits, public housing, or access to the judicial process when no fundamental right is involved.

SIGNIFICANCE

Dandridge falls squarely in line with a series of cases in which the Court rejected claims that various "necessities of life" were fundamental interests whose impairment should trigger strict scrutiny.

RELATED CASES

James v. Valtierra, 402 U.S. 137 (1971)

San Antonio Independent School District v. Rodriguez, 411 U.S. 1 (1973)

RECOMMENDED READING

Cox, Archibald. *The Court and the Constitution.* Boston: Houghton Mifflin, 1987.

Schwartz, Bernard. *The Ascent of Pragmatism: The Burger Court in Action.* Reading, Mass.: Addison-Wesley, 1990.

The Equal Protection Clause and Exclusionary Zoning after Valtierra *and* Dandridge, 81 Yale Law Journal 61 (1971).

Case Title: *Davis v. Monroe County Board of Education*

Alternate Case Title: Peer Sexual Harassment in Schools Case

Legal Citation: 119 S.Ct. 1661

Year of Decision: 1999

KEY ISSUES

In the case of "student-on-student," or peer, sexual harassment, may the parents of the victim successfully sue the school board for damages?

HISTORY OF THE CASE

Aurelia Davis filed suit against the county school board and school officials seeking damages for the sexual harassment of her daughter LaShonda by a fifth-grade classmate. Among other things, Davis alleged that the school board's deliberate indifference to the persistent sexual advances created an intimidating, hostile, offensive, and abusive school environment. Title IX of the Educational Amendments of 1972 prohibits a student from being "excluded from participation in, be[ing] denied the benefits of, or be[ing] subjected to discrimination under any education program or activity receiving Federal financial assistance." The lower federal courts dismissed Davis's suit, finding that student-on-student harassment provides no ground for a private cause of action under Title IX.

SUMMARY OF ARGUMENTS

Davis argued that the plain language of Title IX compels the conclusion that the statute is intended to recipients of federal funding from permitting this form of discrimination in their programs or activities. Because the statute has its focus on the benefited class of students rather than the perpetrator of the discrimination, argues Davis, the statute must work to protect students from the discriminatory misconduct of their peers.

The school board argued that Title IX only proscribes misconduct by grant recipients (schools), not third parties (students). Moreover, contended the school board, it would be contrary to the purpose of the legislation to impose liability on a funding recipient for the misconduct of third parties, over whom recipients exercise little control.

DECISION

The Supreme Court held that a private Title IX damages action may lie against a school board in cases of student-on-student harassment, but only where the school board is deliberately indifferent to the sexual harassment of which it has actual knowledge. Additionally, the harassment must be so severe, pervasive, and objectively offensive that it can be said to deprive the victims of access to the educational opportunities or benefits provided by the school.

In her opinion for a narrow 5-4 majority, Justice O'Connor agreed with the school board that a recipient of federal funds is liable under Title IX only for its own misconduct, not for that of third parties. However, pointing to the prolonged pattern of sexual harassment documented in the case history, Justice O'Connor concluded that the school board should be held liable for its *own* decision to remain idle in the face of known student-on-student harassment in its schools.

AFTERMATH

The immediate result of the decision merely allows Davis her day in court. Originally, the lower courts had dismissed her suit without trial. Now, she will be allowed to present evidence that her daughter was subjected to harassment that was severe, pervasive, and objectively offensive; that the school board had actual knowledge of the misconduct and was deliberately indifferent; and that the harassment had a concrete, negative effect on LaShonda Davis's ability to receive an education. The outcome of Davis's case will now be determined by a jury.

SIGNIFICANCE

As with recent sexual harassment decisions in the employment context, this decision reflects the continuing strength of gender discrimination laws and the degree to which their values have been absorbed into American society over the last 30 years. Time will determine, however, the accuracy of the dissent's prediction that the decision will create a flood of litigation, will cripple school disciplinary powers and bankrupt school districts, and will further involve the federal government in matters better left to local control.

RELATED CASES

Gebser v. Lago Vista Independent School Dist., 524 U.S. 274 (1998)

Pennhurst State School and Hospital v. Halderman, 451 U.S. 1 (1981)

RECOMMENDED READING

Daniel G. McBride, *Guidance for Student Peer Sexual Harassment? Not!* 50 Stanford Law Review 523 (1998).

Michael W. McClain, *New Standards for Peer Sexual Harassment in the Schools: Title IX Liability under* Davis v. Monroe County Board of Education, 28 Journal of Law and Education 611 (1999).

Joanna L. Routh, *The $100,000 Kiss: What Constitutes Peer Sexual Harassment for Schoolchildren under the* Davis v. Monroe County Board of Education *Holding?,* 28 Journal of Law and Education 619 (1999).

Case Title: *Dred Scott v. Sanford*

Alternate Case Titles: Missouri Compromise Decision; Citizenship for Blacks

Legal Citations: 19 Howard 393; 60 L.Ed. 691

Year of Decision: 1856

KEY ISSUES

Did the black inhabitants of the United States have the right of citizenship, and was the Missouri Compromise a legal means of attempting to extend freedom to the black inhabitants of those territories north of latitude 36° 30'?

HISTORY OF THE CASE

Dred Scott and his wife, Harriet, were slaves of Dr. John Emerson, an army physician who was stationed in various western posts. Dr. Emerson was billeted to Fort Snelling in what is now Minnesota and also to the military post at Rock Island in the state of Illinois. Both of these military posts are north of the Missouri Compromise Line. The Missouri Compromise Line was so named because during the negotiations for Missouri's statehood, it was decided that, with the exception of Missouri, no new slave states could be admitted to the United States north of the latitude line 36° 30'N. Harriet Scott was formerly owned by a Major Taliaferro, who sold her in 1835 to Dr. Emerson. In 1836, Dred and Harriet were married with the consent of Dr. Emerson. The Scotts had two children, Eliza and Lizzie. Eliza was born on the steamboat *Gipsey* on the Mississippi River above the boundary of Missouri. Lizzie was born in the state of Missouri at the military post called Jefferson Barracks.

After Dr. Emerson left military service, he returned to Missouri. After Dr. Emerson's death, Emerson's widow subsequently hired out the Scotts for labor and at some point the Scotts acquired sufficient money to attempt to purchase their freedom. Mrs. Emerson refused, and the Scotts brought a suit to the circuit court of the state of Missouri for their freedom. The circuit judge granted them permission to sue.

In 1850, the jury found in favor of the Scotts. Counsel for Mrs. Emerson appealed to the Missouri Supreme Court. In March 1852 that Court ruled 2 to 1 against Dred Scott and his family in the case of *Scott, A Man of Color v. Emerson* (15 Mo. 576), which argued that the hiring of a slave for two days in a free state would entitle the slave to sue for freedom. Former cases held that the act of setting foot upon free soil was sufficient for freedom, and intent had no impact upon the freedom issue.

In a decision that clearly recognized the political climate, Justice William Scott wrote that it was "a humiliating spectacle to see a court of a state confiscate the property of her own citizens by the command of a foreign law." Justice Scott acknowledged the political climate and declared that it was time to end the "black vomit" that was becoming an epidemic in the Missouri territory. Justices Scott and Ryland determined that they would not suffer to have the old laws enforced, and that it was entirely unreasonable to liberate slaves under the argument that the mere touching of soil of a free state entitled them to freedom.

The court further argued that the consequences of slavery are "more hurtful to the master than to the slaves. There is no comparison between the slave in the United States and the cruel, uncivilized Negro in Africa. When the condition of our slaves is contrasted with the state of their miserable race in Africa; when their civilization, intelligence, and instruction is considered, and the means now employed to restore them to the country from which they have been torn, bearing with them the blessings of civilized life, we are almost persuaded that their introduction amongst us was in the providence of God who makes the evil passions of men subservient to his own glory, a means of placing that unhappy race within the pale of civilized nations."

Justice Campbell in his dissent departed from the opinion of the majority of the court with regard to the freedom of Dred Scott and family. He felt that a review of the case law of Missouri and of the neighboring slave states clearly held that a slave held in servitude was entitled to freedom when setting foot upon free territory. Justice Campbell, however, objected to the taking of property, for example, the slave, by action of Congress. He felt that people outside of the state of Missouri had no right to interfere with the institution of slavery or the domestic laws of the state. He agreed with the other two justices on the invalidity of the Missouri Compromise.

Thus, the state court departed from the commonly accepted principle that slaves who move to free states become free. This shift in favor of the slaveowners put strong pressure on the political moderates of both parties and served to entrench the differences between slave and free states.

Rather than appealing the state court decision directly to the Supreme Court, Scott's attorneys took a new direction. In 1851, the Supreme Court had decided the case of *Strader v. Graham,* which involved the case of slave musicians from Kentucky taken into Ohio for performances. To the Kentucky Court of Appeals, the persons who helped the slaves escape were guilty of theft of property, and the U.S. Supreme Court unanimously agreed. Chief Justice Roger B. Taney wrote the opinion in the *Strader* case. Thus, a federal suit for freedom was brought in the Circuit Court for St. Louis County, Missouri, alleging that Scott was a citizen of Missouri and that Sanford, the son-in-law of Dr. Emerson, a resident of New York, was now the owner of the Scotts. Because of the question of diversity of citizenship, federal jurisdiction was alleged. As for whether a slave could be a free citizen, the court below ruled against Scott and held that once he returned to slave soil, Scott remained a slave.

SUMMARY OF ARGUMENTS

The *Dred Scott* case was argued twice before the Supreme Court. In February 1856, Sanford's attorney dropped the bombshell argument that Scott was not free because the Missouri Compromise was unconstitutional. The Court was bitterly divided about how to deal with the case and agreed to stall for time. The case was reargued in December 1856, and four days were devoted to the proceedings. Justice Benjamin Curtis's brother, George T. Curtis, argued with Montgomery Blair for Scott. Sanford employed Henry S. Geyer and Reverdy Johnson. Blair and Geyer dominated the second argument, with Blair claiming that case law declared Scott free and Geyer arguing that Congress had no authority to keep a slaveholder from taking his property with him, and since Scott had never been a citizen, he could not sue his owner in federal court.

DECISION

The case was appealed to the Supreme Court on the basis of an improper charge to the jury. Chief Justice Taney stated the question of Dred Scott's citizenship simply: "Can a Negro whose ancestors were imported into this country and sold as slaves become a member of the political community which was formed and brought into existence by the Constitution of the United States?" In the opinion of the chief justice, each state could determine who could be a citizen within its boundaries. Citizenship of a state is not coextensive with citizenship of the United States. Each state was allowed to determine, as deemed proper, the class or description of persons within its boundaries entitled to citizenship. The chief justice stated that the authors of the Declaration of Independence and the U.S. Constitution did not feel that slaves were fit to associate with the white race, that all of the 13 original colonies recognized slavery, and that the African race was a distinct form of property expressly recognized in the Constitution. The chief justice went on to review various state decisions with regard to property rights of slaves and concluded that it was not for the federal government to go against the wishes of the states who abrogated the Articles of Confederation in forming the United States of America: such an act would involve the taking of property without compensation. The chief justice held that there was no authority in the Constitution for Congress to draw a line such as in the Missouri Compromise, and that whether they had or had not the authority to do so, Congress had no right to determine freedom for the citizens of any state. The matters were to be left solely to the determination of the state courts.

The effect of Taney's opinion, which was joined by six other justices, was to conclude as a matter of law that slaves and free blacks were not citizens. They were consigned to an inferior legal position.

All of the justices wrote separate opinions. Justice Daniel wrote that "the African Negro race never have been acknowledged as belonging to the family of nations . . . that this race has been by all the nations of Europe regarded as subjects of capture or purchase; as subjects of commerce or traffic." The tenor of the seven members of the Court in the majority was extremely similar.

Only Justices Curtis and McLean dissented. Justice McLean wrote that all slavery has its origin in power and is against right: "A slave is not a mere chattel. He bears the impress of his Maker, and is amenable to the laws of God and man; and he is destined to an endless existence."

Justice McLean held that the prior cases of the state and English common law clearly held that the removal of a slave to a free state entitled the slave to freedom. He further found that it was appropriate for Congress to enact the Missouri Compromise Act in 1820 as a condition for acquiring land from the government of France. His opinion reflects the fact that some form of law was necessary to create the territories and implement the wishes of the United States, which had paid for the land. Thus a public act of the Congress is entitled to be noticed and respected as much as any other law. Justice Curtis was offended by the idea that "the Creator of all men had endowed the White race exclusively with the great natural rights which the Declaration of Independence asserts." He agreed that the states may exclude numerous people from the right to vote or hold office or other franchises on the basis of their age or sex or marital condition, but he found nothing to prevent a person of color from being a citizen of the United States and thus having the right to access the courts created by the Constitution.

Curtis further found that the act of Dr. Emerson in consenting to the marriage of Dred and Harriet Scott in the free state of Illinois was an effectual abandonment of his right over the Scotts as a master. Curtis was not persuaded that the Missouri Compromise was invalid. Rather, he noted that the first seven presidents of the United States had all signed the Constitution and were all involved in the purchase of this Missouri Territory from the government of France.

AFTERMATH

In the Dred Scott decision, the Supreme Court judicially protected slavery. Dred Scott remained a slave, and it became apparent that the judicial process would do nothing to remove his condition of bondage. Scott died of tuberculosis less than two years later.

SIGNIFICANCE

The Fourteenth Amendment, adopted in 1868, provided citizenship to the newly freed slaves and overturned the Dred Scott decision. The "Black Codes" of the southern states, passed after Reconstruction ended, kept African Americans in a state only minimally above that of slavery. Not until the Civil Rights Act of 1963 was any significant effort made to give full citizenship to black Americans.

RELATED CASES

U.S. v. Reese, 92 U.S. 214 (1876)

Civil Rights Cases, 109 U.S. 3 (1883)

Plessy v. Ferguson, 163 U.S. 537 (1896)

RECOMMENDED READING

Ehrlich, W. *They Have No Rights: Dred Scott's Struggle for Freedom.* Westport, Conn.: Greenwood Press, 1979.

Fehrenbacher, D. E. *The Dred Scott Case: Its Significance in American Law and Politics.* New York: Oxford University Press, 1978.

Case Title: *Equal Employment Opportunity Commission (EEOC) v. Wyoming et al.*

Alternate Case Title: Age Discrimination in Employment Case

Legal Citation: 460 U.S. 226

Year of Decision: 1983

KEY ISSUES

Is the exercise by Congress of its commerce power, extending application of the Age Discrimination in Employment Act to state and local governments, an unconstitutional intrusion into an area of state sovereignty reserved by the Tenth Amendment?

HISTORY OF THE CASE

The ADEA makes it unlawful for an employer to discriminate against an employee between the ages of 40 and 70 on the basis of age except where age is a "bona fide occupational qualification reasonably necessary to the normal operation of the particular business." In 1974 the definition was extended to apply to state and local governments. A Wyoming supervisor of the Game and Fish Department was asked to retire at age 55 under Wyoming law. He filed a complaint with the EEOC, which then filed a suit in federal district court. The court dismissed the suit.

SUMMARY OF ARGUMENTS

The appellant, the EEOC, argued that the extension of the ADEA to state and local governments did not intrude upon Wyoming's state sovereignty, as reserved by the Tenth Amendment.

The appellee, the state of Wyoming, argued that the application of the ADEA to the states was precluded by the Tenth Amendment constraints on the commerce powers of Congress.

DECISION

Justice Brennan wrote for the majority that the ADEA was a valid exercise of congressional power under the commerce clause. Congress and the executive branch agreed at its passage that age discrimination was harmful to the economy to both business and the employee.

Chief Justice Burger wrote for the dissent disagreeing that the commerce clause provided a valid basis for congressional authority, which in turn would invalidate the act under the Fourteenth Amendment.

Justice Burger concluded that the act of defining the qualifications of employees was an essential of sovereignty. He also concluded that neither the Constitution nor any of the amendments transferred the function of establishing these employment qualifications from the states to the federal government. Further, this amendment to the ADEA violated the Tenth Amendment, which states that Congress may not exercise power not delegated to it.

AFTERMATH

The courts continue to resolve issues of state autonomy on the basis of balancing the merits of congressional policy. The courts at times are reluctant to strike down an act of Congress on Congress's own authority.

SIGNIFICANCE

This decision settled the conflict between state sovereignty under the Tenth Amendment and the commerce power of Congress. The jurisdiction of the commerce clause was extended, which had a major impact on early retirement laws. Further, this ruling was crucial because employment in the state and local government sector had been on the rise.

RELATED CASES

Hodel v. Virginia Mining and Reclamation Association, 452 U.S. 264 (1981)

National League of Cities v. Usery, 426 U.S. 833 (1976)

RECOMMENDED READING

Dean Alfange, Jr., *Congressional Regulation of the States Qua States: From National League of Cities to EEOC v. Wyoming,* Supreme Court Review 215 (1983).

Keyes, Edward, and Randall K. Miller. *The Court vs. Congress: Prayer, Busing and Abortion.* Durham, N.C.: Duke University Press, 1989.

❧

Case Title: *Foley v. Connelie, Superintendent of New York State Police, et al.*

Legal Citation: 435 U.S. 291

Year of Decision: 1977

❧

KEY ISSUES

Does a New York statute limiting appointment of state police officers to citizens of the United States violate the equal protection clause of the Fourteenth Amendment?

HISTORY OF THE CASE

This case was an appeal from the U.S. District Court for the Southern District of New York, where Edmund Foley, an alien lawfully in the United States as a permanent resident, applied for a position as a New York State trooper, for which an examination is required. Foley was denied the right to take the examination. He brought this action for declaratory judgment that state's exclusion of aliens from its police force violated the equal protection clause of the Fourteenth Amendment. The district court held the statute constitutional.

Foley was an Irish citizen who had lived in the United States for four years. When he applied for a position as a New York State trooper, the state police commissioner refused to allow him to take a qualification test because noncitizens were prohibited by statute from becoming members of the state police force. Foley was not currently eligible for American citizenship due to the waiting period imposed by Congress.

SUMMARY OF ARGUMENTS

Appellant, Edmund Foley, argued that the New York statute precluding aliens from being members of the state police force violated the equal protection clause of the Fourteenth Amendment.

Appellee, Connelie, the superintendent of the New York State Police, argued that police officers were state officers who participated directly in the execution of broad public policy. Therefore, the state was entitled to limit the position to persons who were U.S. citizens.

Chief Justice Warren Burger wrote for the majority, stating that a trooper in New York is a member of the police force charged with law enforcement for the benefit of the people of New York; strict scrutiny of the law is not required because it would erase all distinction between citizen and alien. An alien cannot vote and has other restrictions. A state only needs to justify its exclusionary classifications by showing a relationship between "the interest sought to be protected and the limiting classification. . . . The right to govern is reserved to citizens." The enforcement and execution of the police function bears a rational relationship to citizenship.

Justices Marshall and Stevens, in their dissents, opposed the rational basis tests. Justice Marshall favored strict scrutiny of a compelling state interest; Justice Stevens favored an individual determination of the alien's employment skills, instead of prejudgment based on characteristics that aliens as a group are supposed to have.

DECISION

A New York statute limiting appointment of members of the state police force to U.S. citizens does not violate the equal protection clause of the Fourteenth Amendment.

AFTERMATH

States have the power to exclude aliens from certain jobs in the public sector. A stricter standard of review will be applied when reviewing the exclusion of aliens from private positions, whereas as rational basis standard will apply to review of alien exclusion from positions involving democratic decisionmaking.

SIGNIFICANCE

Foley gave meaning to the exception carved out of the application of strict scrutiny to alienage in *Sugarman v. Dougall* (1973). In *Sugarman*, the Court found that in certain circumstances, states may require citizenship as a qualification for holding a public position. The decision in Foley gave substance to this ruling by determining that the position of police officer could require citizenship as an employment qualification.

RELATED CASES

Graham v. Richardson, 403 U.S. 365 (1971)

Sugarman v. Dougall, 413 U.S. 634 (1973)

Ambach v. Norwick, 414 U.S. 68 (1979)

RECOMMENDED READING

A Dual Standard for State Discrimination against Aliens, 92 Harvard Law Review 1516 (1979).

Steven J. Casad, *Alienage and Public Employment: The Need for an Intermediate Standard in Equal Protection*, 32 Hastings Law Journal 163 (1980).

Schwartz, Bernard. *The Ascent of Pragmatism: The Burger Court in Action*. New York: Addison-Wesley, 1990.

Case Title: *Furman v. Georgia*

Alternate Case Title: Death Penalty Case

Legal Citation: 408 U.S. 238

Year of Decision: 1972

KEY ISSUES

Does the death penalty constitute cruel and unusual punishment within the meaning of the Eighth Amendment as applied to the states by the Fourteenth Amendment of the U.S. Constitution?

HISTORY OF THE CASE

The U.S. Supreme Court agreed to review the decision of the Georgia Supreme Court affirming the decision of the death penalty in the cases of the two defendants convicted of murder and rape, and the judgment of the Texas Court of Criminal Appeals affirming the death penalty on one defendant.

The issue of whether the death penalty was imposed was decided according to the discretion of the judge or jury under Georgia state law. At issue was whether this discretion constituted cruel and unusual punishment.

SUMMARY OF ARGUMENTS

The petitioner, William Henry Furman, argued that his sentence of death violated the Eighth

Amendment because the death penalty violated the standards of decency and failed to properly account for his mental impairment.

The state of Georgia, respondent, argued that the death penalty was not cruel and unusual punishment and did not deprive Furman of his life without due process of law. Further, Georgia argued that the death penalty was an appropriate maximum punishment for murder.

Justice Douglas wrote one of the majority opinions saying that current systems of criminal justice in the United States operate in an unpredictable and arbitrary manner and do not serve as a deterrent.

DECISION

Standardless, discretionary jury sentencing in capital cases violates the Eighth Amendment because arbitrary imposition of the death penalty is cruel and unusual punishment as is punishment that is too severe for the crime.

AFTERMATH

This is the first Supreme Court case to hold unconstitutional a state capital punishment law, but state legislatures did not do away with capital punishment. Instead, they devised ways to administer it in a more consistent fashion. Over 600 prisoners on death row had their death sentences lifted by the *Furman* decision.

SIGNIFICANCE

The Court recognized important new rights in capital punishment law without abolishing it. The decision required that capital punishment be administered in a more organized fashion so there is some assurance that jury findings justify the imposition of the death sentence. Most states enacted death penalty statutes to avoid arbitrariness.

RELATED CASES

Gardner v. Florida, 430 U.S. 349 (1977)

Gregg v. Georgia, 428 U.S. 280 (1976)

RECOMMENDED READING

David C. Baldus et al., *Identifying Comparatively Excessive Standards of Death: A Quantitative Approach,* 33 Stanford Law Review 1 (1980).

Sheleff, Leon Shaskolsky. *Ultimate Penalties.* Columbus: Ohio State University Press, 1987, 82–87.

White, Welsh S. *Life in a Balance.* Ann Arbor: University of Michigan Press, 1984.

Case Title: *Gomillion v. Lightfoot*

Alternate Case Title: Tuskegee Gerrymander Case

Legal Citation: 364 U.S. 339

Year of Decision: 1960

KEY ISSUES

Does a state legislative act, which redefines a city's boundaries in such a way as to exclude almost all black citizens from the city, violate the due process and equal protection clauses of the Fourteenth Amendment and the right to vote as guaranteed in the Fifteenth Amendment?

HISTORY OF THE CASE

A state redistricting measure altered the shape of Tuskegee, Alabama, from a square to a 28-sided figure removing all but four or five of its 400 black voters and not a single white voter. The results deprived blacks of residence in Tuskegee and the right to vote in municipal elections.

SUMMARY OF ARGUMENTS

Appellants, black citizens of Tuskegee, Alabama, argued that the state redistricting act violated the due process and equal protection clauses of the Fourteenth Amendment and denied their right to vote in violation of the Fifteenth Amendment.

Appellees, the mayor of Tuskegee and others, argued the state had unrestricted power to define its political subdivisions and therefore did not violate the Fourteenth and Fifteenth Amendments.

Justice Frankfurter delivered the opinion of the Court, saying the act constitutes discrimination against blacks in violation of the due process and equal protection clauses of the Fourteenth Amendment. It also violates the right to vote guaranteed by the Fifteenth Amendment. The Court would not sanction a law that singles out a minority for discriminatory purposes, and federal courts have jurisdiction over a local municipal act "when state power is used as an instrument for circumventing a federally protected right" (346).

AFTERMATH

Courts look at the intent of legislation and apply the strict scrutiny test in cases involving gerrymandering the redistricting of political divisions with an ulterior motive, if race is the predominant factor in drawing a district, thereby making the gerrymandering unconstitutional.

SIGNIFICANCE

This case limited state power when discrimination was the goal of state redistricting.

RELATED CASES

Miller v. Johnson, 115 S.Ct. 2475 (1995)

Reynolds v. Sims, 377 U.S. 533 (1964)

Shaw v. Reno, 509 U.S. 630 (1993)

RECOMMENDED READING

Elliot, Ward E.Y. *The Rise of the Guardian Democracy.* Cambridge, Mass.: Harvard University Press, 1974.
J. D. Lucas, *Dragon in the Thicket: A Perusal of* Gomillion v. Lightfoot, 1961 Supreme Court Review 194.
The Supreme Court, 1960 Term, 75 Harvard Law Review 136 (1961).

Case Title: *Graham v. Richardson*

Legal Citation: 403 U.S. 365

Year of Decision: 1971

KEY ISSUES

Does the equal protection clause of the Fourteenth Amendment prevent a state from conditioning welfare benefits on whether the beneficiary is a U.S. citizen or upon the number of years a noncitizen beneficiary has resided in the United States?

HISTORY OF THE CASE

This case was brought as a class action suit: There were three named plaintiffs in the action. One case arose in Arizona. The plaintiff in that case questioned the constitutionality of a state statute that restricted the benefits of general assistance to citizens of the United States and those who resided in the United States for a total of 15 years. The plaintiff in that case, Richardson, was a legal resident alien. She met all of the requirements for conferring benefits under this program except for the 15-year residency requirement. She instituted her claim in the District Court of Arizona against the commissioner of the state's Department of Public Welfare seeking declaratory relief, an injunction against the enforcement of the statute, and an award in the amount allegedly due her. She claimed that the alien residency requirement violated the equal protection clause of the Fourteenth Amendment and the constitutional right to travel. A three-judge court upheld Richardson's motion for summary judgment.

The second claim arose in Pennsylvania. The statute challenged in that case restricted the provision of general assistance to needy persons who qualified under the federally supported assistance programs originating with the Social Security Act and partly supported by federal grants and other needy persons who are citizens of the United States. The plaintiff in that case, Leger, was a legal resident alien. She resided continually in Pennsylvania for four years, where she worked and paid taxes. Her husband, a U.S. citizen, became ill, forcing them both to give up their employment. They both applied for public assistance. They were both ineligible under federal programs. Her husband qualified under a state program, but she was denied the state benefits because of her alienage. Leger instituted her class action in the District Court of Pennsylvania against the executive director of the Philadelphia County Board of Assistance and the Department of Public Welfare. She sought declaratory relief, an injunction against the enforcement of the statute, and a money award for back payments that had been withheld. She obtained a temporary restraining order preventing the state agents from continuing to deny her assistance.

The third claim was brought by Jervis, a legal resident alien living in Pennsylvania who after five years of working and paying taxes became unable to work due to illness. She applied for aid and was denied because of alienage. Her motion for immediate relief through a temporary restraining order was denied. A three-judge court ruled that the statute violated the equal protection clause of the U.S. Constitution and prevented its further enforcement.

SUMMARY OF ARGUMENTS

The plaintiffs argued on behalf of the class that restricting benefits based on alien status effects invidious discrimination in violation of the equal protection clause of the Fourteenth Amendment.

The state agents argued that consistent with the equal protection clause of the Fourteenth Amendment, a state may favor U.S. citizens over aliens in the distribution of welfare benefits. They offered that this distinction was not invidious discrimination because the states were not discriminating with respect to race or national origin.

DECISION

Justice Blackmun, writing for eight justices, held that the Fourteenth Amendment prohibition against denying equal protection of the laws encompasses resident aliens as well as citizens. He concluded that the challenged statutes thus were unconstitutional. Using traditional equal protection analysis, a state retains broad discretion to classify as long as it does so on a reasonable basis. He noted the previous decisions of the Court established that classifications based on alienage, like those based on nationality or race, are suspect classifications and subject to close judicial scrutiny. He noted that aliens as a group represent a discrete and insular minority for whom heightened judicial solicitude is appropriate.

Blackmun concluded that under this standard the state's proffered reason of preferring U.S. citizens in the assignment of benefits was insufficient: "We conclude that a State's desire to preserve limited welfare benefits for its own citizens is inadequate to justify Pennsylvania's making noncitizens ineligible for public assistance, and Arizona's restricting benefits to citizens and longtime resident aliens." He offered two reasons for this conclusion. The first reason was that special public interest doctrine upon which the state agencies grounded their argument had been refuted by the Court. The second reason was that a state may

not accomplish the legitimate purpose of preserving fiscal integrity by creating invidious distinctions between classes of citizens. For equal protection purposes, both legal aliens and citizens are "persons"; therefore, the concern for fiscal integrity is not a compelling justification.

Justice Harlan concurred in the judgment and the part of the opinion that discussed federal and state relations regarding aliens and the terms of their occupancy in the United States and the refutation of Arizona's argument that the classification based on years of residency is allowed under the Social Security Act.

AFTERMATH

Shortly after this decision the Court began to retreat from its characterization of alienage as a suspect classification. The political community exception to treating alienage classifications as inherently suspect was articulated in *Foley v. Connelie* and *Ambach v. Norwick*. This exception adopted a rational basis standard in circumstances in which the classification involved a participation in the processes of democratic decision making. This political community exception has been broadened to encompass not only those positions involving extensive discretionary powers but also all functions important to the concept of self-government. Since *Graham,* the Court had addressed claims distinguishing the economic and sovereign function of the state; *Graham* addressed only the economic function of the state. This distinction supports the political community exception, which allows a state to limit participation in state government to those persons who are citizens.

In *Cabell v. Chavez-Salido,* the Court established a two-part test to gauge which standard of review is appropriate in cases involving classifications based on alienage. Part one of the test requires the Court to gauge the inclusiveness of the restrictive classification. Once the Court determines whether the classification is overinclusive or underinclusive, it will determine whether the classification involves a state political function. If the Court determines that the state classification is narrowly written and involves a state political function, the rational relation test is applied. Critics of the current approach by the Court argue that the political community exception, which applies the rational basis standard, threatens to swallow the rule that classifications based on alienage are inherently suspect and subject to close judicial scrutiny.

SIGNIFICANCE

Though the Court had acknowledged in previous cases the legislation that discriminated against aliens was illegitimate, it did so on grounds that the legislation was based on an illegitimate state purpose or constituted an unjustified means to a legitimate end. *Graham* was the first time that the Court recognized aliens as a "discrete and insular" minority for the purpose of applying an equal protection standard and review to challenged legislation. This case was the first to establish that classifications based on alienage were inherently suspect and subject to close judicial scrutiny.

The Court reasoned that resident aliens contribute equally as citizens to the tax revenues, and thus the state justification of preserving tax revenues for citizens could not alone constitute a compelling state interest. This case constituted a clear rejection of the right-privilege distinction, under which government benefits were a privilege that could be taken away by the government, unlike rights. This distinction had been the basis for the special public interest doctrine used by states to justify such classifications.

RELATED CASES

Ambach v. Norwick, 441 U.S. 68 (1979)

Cabell v. Chavez-Salido, 102 S.Ct. 735 (1982)

Foley v. Connelie, 435 U.S. 291 (1978)

Mathews v. Diaz, 426 U.S. 67 (1976)

Sugarman v. Dougall, 413 U.S. 634 (1973)

Yick Wo v. Hopkins, 118 U.S. 356, 369 (1886)

RECOMMENDED READING

Linda S. Bosniak, *Membership, Equality, and the Difference that Alienage Makes,* 69 New York University Law Review 1047 (1994).

Developments in the Law—Immigration Policy and the Rights of Aliens VI. Discrimination against Documented Aliens, 96 Harvard Law Review 1400 (1983).

Gerald Rosberg, *The Protection of Aliens from Discriminatory Treatment by the National Government,* Supreme Court Review 275 (1977).

Case Title: *Gratz v. Bollinger*

Alternate Case Title: Case of Racial Preferences in Undergraduate Admissions

Legal Citation: Not yet available

Year of Decision: 2003

KEY ISSUES

Does a state university's use of racial preferences in its undergraduate admissions process violate the equal protection clause of the Fourteenth Amendment; Title VI of the Civil Rights Act, which states that no person may be discriminated against by a program receiving federal funding; and 42 U.S.C. § 1981, which states all persons shall be entitled to the "full and equal benefit of all laws"?

HISTORY OF THE CASE

The admissions policy for the University of Michigan changed over the years. In 1995 and 1996, the policy was to consider in the admissions process combined grade-point averages with factors including strength of high school curriculum, residency, alumni connections, and unusual circumstances pertaining to the applicant. The resulting combined score was coupled with an applicant's ACT or SAT score to determine admission. During those years, the admission of students with identical scores varied based on the racial and ethnic status of the applicant. In 1997, additional points were added to applicants' scores if they were in an underrepresented minority or attended a high school populated predominantly by minorities underrepresented at the university. Beginning in 1998, the university changed to a points system that awarded an applicant a certain number of points for each admission factor considered and then set the admission decision at various numerical levels. For example, if an applicant scored between 100 and 150 points, the applicant was automatically admitted. In 1999 and 2000, an applicant from an underrepresented minority or racial group was automatically given 20 points.

However, during those years, the university also had a review committee that individually considered certain applicants who met minimum scores but who may have had qualities important to the university, including race or ethnicity.

Petitioners Jennifer Gratz and Patrick Hamacher were white Michigan residents who had applied for admission to the University of Michigan's College of Literature Science and the Arts in 1995 and 1997, respectively. Both petitioners were denied admission despite being qualified applicants. In 1997, the petitioners brought a class-action suit in the District Court for the Eastern District of Michigan alleging racial discrimination in violation of the Fourteenth Amendment, Title VI of the Civil Rights Act of 1964, and 42 U.S.C. § 1981. The district court certified the class of petitioners who had applied for admission to the university but had not been admitted and who were members of racial and ethnic groups treated less favorably by the university. Hamacher was designated as the class representative. The district court found in favor of the petitioners with regard to the admissions procedures for the years 1995 through 1998 but found for the respondents with regard to the years 1999 and 2000. Appeals were made to the Sixth Circuit Court of Appeals, but before the case was heard, Gratz and Hamacher petitioned the U.S. Supreme Court for review so the case could be heard together with *Grutter v. Bollinger,* a case challenging the admissions procedures of the university's law school.

The last time the U.S. Supreme Court had considered racial preferences in university admissions programs was in *Regents of the University of California v. Bakke* in 1978. The parties and the Court in *Gratz* relied on Justice Powell's opinion in *Bakke* that the consideration of race as a factor in admissions may in some situations serve a compelling government interest. However, the parties' interpretation of what met or violated Justice Powell's guidelines was significantly different.

SUMMARY OF ARGUMENTS

Petitioners argued that the university's use of race as an admissions factor violated the equal protection clause of the Fourteenth Amendment, Title VI of the Civil Rights Act of 1964, and 42 U.S.C. § 1981. They further argued that the use of racial classifications could only be used to remedy iden-

tified discrimination, and, moreover, diversity was not a compelling interest to be furthered by racial preferences. Even if diversity was a compelling interest, the petitioners argued that the university had not narrowly tailored its use of race to achieve this interest.

The respondents, who included Lee Bollinger, the university's president when Hamacher applied for admission, argued that the admissions program was narrowly tailored to further the university's interest in educational diversity and provided the individualized consideration found constitutionally permissible in *Bakke*.

DECISION

The Court found that the undergraduate admissions procedures of the University of Michigan violated the equal protection clause of the Fourteenth Amendment, Title VI, and § 1981. Chief Justice Rehnquist gave the opinion of the Court. Although no party addressed the issue of standing, the chief justice addressed this issue because Justice Stevens raised it in his dissent. The chief justice found that the petitioners had standing because Hamacher was able and willing to apply as transfer student if race was no longer used in the admissions process. The use of race in transfer admissions and freshmen admissions did not differ significantly; thus Hamacher had a personal stake in the litigation, considering his past injury of admission denial, and a potential future injury, if he reapplied to the university.

The strict scrutiny standard was applied in arriving at a decision, as all racial classifications reviewed under equal protection analysis are subject to strict scrutiny. The Court found that the procedure of awarding an automatic 20 points to every underrepresented minority applicant was not narrowly tailored to achieve the university's diversity interest. The chief justice reviewed Justice Powell's opinion in *Bakke* and determined that the university's policy did not give the individualized consideration to applicants, a process found to be constitutional by Justice Powell.

Justice O'Connor concurred, also stating that the admissions process did not give applicants a meaningful individualized review. Justice O'Connor also pointed out that the points awarded for other diversity variables besides race, such as leadership and personal achievement, are significantly lower than those awarded for race.

Justice Thomas also concurred, indicating that he found the Court's decision to be a correct application of precedent, and Justice Breyer concurred with the Court's decision as well.

Justice Stevens, joined by Justice Souter, dissented, finding that the petitioners lacked standing because they were not in the process of reapplying to the university through the undergraduate admissions process at the time the suit was filed. Thus, he found the action should be dismissed. Justice Stevens sought to differentiate between the freshman admissions process and the transfer admissions process, stating that the freshman policy was at issue and only the transfer policy, which was not challenged, would have applied to Hamacher, the class representative. Justice Stevens found that the petitioners did not have a personal stake in the suit and therefore lacked standing.

Justice Souter, joined by Justice Ginsburg, also dissented. Justice Souter agreed with Justice Stevens that Hamacher had no standing to seek relief regarding the freshman admissions policy because he would not be harmed by it. Justice Souter also indicated that he would not find the admissions policy unconstitutional because the process was not a "quota" system, one that set a certain number of minority applicants that must be admitted, like the system struck down in *Bakke*. He found that a nonminority applicant could achieve a score that exceeded that of a minority applicant who received the automatic 20 points through points earned on other factors, such as leadership, curriculum, and test scores, and that race was not set apart from the other point-assessed considerations. Moreover, Justice Souter did not find that the automatic 20 points "convert race into a decisive factor comparable to reserving minority places in *Bakke*." Justice Souter found the undergraduate process to accomplish the same objective, achieving a "critical mass" of minority students, as the law school process upheld in *Grutter v. Bollinger*.

Justice Ginsburg wrote a separate dissent along with Justice Souter, finding that the undergraduate admissions policy did not violate the Constitution. Justice Ginsburg reflected on the racial oppression of the past and still existing in society at large and concluded that in implementing policies of equality, there was a distinction between a policy of inclusion and one of exclusion. Specifically, denial of a benefit or imposition of a burden based on race is violative of the Constitution, but consideration of race to undo the effects of past discrimination and prevent future discrimination may not be. Justice Ginsburg clarified that any "race-conscious" measuring system should be carefully reviewed. She found no evidence that the university's policy was meant to be an exclusionary policy, one that limited a particular race's enrollment. Moreover, Justice Ginsburg praised the university's forthrightness as favorable compared to other programs that seek to accomplish the same goal but achieve it through "winks, nods and disguises."

AFTERMATH

The Court's decision was met with mixed reactions. Overall, the university was pleased that the Court found that affirmative action could be used in admissions, but acknowledged it would be adjusting its admissions policy for more individualized review. While the Court's decision technically only affects public university admissions, it will likely impact admissions decisions at private institutions and hiring decisions in the business world. Additionally, the decision will likely make affirmative action a significant issue in future presidential elections.

SIGNIFICANCE

The decisions in this case and *Grutter v. Bollinger* marked the most significant decision on affirmative action in admissions policies in 25 years. Based on the decision, race may be considered in the admissions process, but institutions of higher education will have to replace numerically indexed systems of admissions with systems of individual review if they plan to include race as a factor.

RELATED CASES

Grutter v. Bollinger, 288 F.3d 732 (2003)

Regents of the University of California v. Bakke, 438 U.S. 265 (1978)

Richmond v. J. A. Croson Co., 488 U.S. 469 (1989)

RECOMMENDED READING

Goodwin Liu, *The Causation Fallacy: Bakke and the Basic Arithmetic of Selective Admissions*, 100 Michigan Law Review 1045 (2002).

Orfield, Gary, and Edward Miller. *Chilling Admissions: The Affirmative Action Crisis and the Search for Alternatives.* Cambridge, Mass.: Harvard Education Publishing Group, 1998.

Orfield, Gary, ed. *Diversity Challenged: Evidence on the Impact of Affirmative Action.* Cambridge, Mass.: Harvard Education Publishing Group, 2001.

Case Title: *Grutter v. Bollinger*

Alternate Case Title: Law School Admissions Case

Legal Citation: 288 F.3d 732

Year of Decision: 2003

KEY ISSUES

Is the use of race as a factor in a university's law school admissions process unlawful?

HISTORY OF THE CASE

The law school at the University of Michigan is ranked as one of the top law schools in the United States. The law school's admissions process consisted of an evaluation of each applicant, considering his or her undergraduate grade-point average, LSAT (Law School Admissions Test) score, personal statement, letters of recommendation, and essay, as well as other criteria important to the law school's objectives, one of which is to achieve diversity. The law school did not define this diversity as only racial or ethnic diversity, although it did seek to enroll a "critical mass" of minority students.

The petitioner, Barbara Grutter, applied to the school in 1996. Grutter was a white Michigan resident with a grade point average of 3.8 and an LSAT score of 161. While Grutter was initially put on the school's waiting list, she ultimately was denied admission. Grutter brought suit in the District Court for the Eastern District of Michigan. Her motion to certify a class action was granted, and it was ultimately decided that the use of race

as a factor in the law school's admissions process was unlawful. The court of appeals reversed the decision, finding the law school's use of race to be narrowly tailored. The U.S. Supreme Court granted certiorari.

SUMMARY OF ARGUMENTS

The petitioner, Grutter, argued that the law school discriminated against her on the basis of race, violating the equal protection clause of the Fourteenth Amendment, Title VI of the Civil Rights Act of 1964, and 42 U.S.C. § 1981. Grutter argued that race was used as a "predominant" factor in making admissions decisions, and that the use of such a factor was not justified by any compelling interest.

The respondents, one of whom was Lee Bollinger, the university's president at the time of Grutter's application, argued that the consideration of race in the admissions process was justified because it assisted the school in attaining a diverse student body.

DECISION

Justice O'Connor wrote the opinion of the Court, which found that the law school had a "compelling interest in obtaining a diverse student body" and that its use of race was narrowly tailored to achieve this objective. She noted that the Court only had one significant holding in the decision of *Regents of the University of California v. Bakke* (1978), which was that the consideration of race in a university's admissions process could serve a substantial interest, and that Justice Powell had approved only one such interest, attaining diversity in the student body. Justice O'Connor indicated that the Court endorsed this view held by Justice Powell. The Court applied a strict scrutiny analysis, stating that all governmentally imposed racial classifications must be reviewed under this standard.

Justice O'Connor deferred to the law school's judgment that it was essential for the university to have a diverse student body and to its determination that a "critical mass" of underrepresented minority students was necessary to achieve this diverse student body. She determined that the law school's admissions program was not a quota system, a system which would not have been considered "narrowly tailored," because it did not give "bonuses" for certain races or ethnicities, but, rather, had an individualized review of each applicant's information. Moreover, Justice O'Connor found that the law school gave significant weight to diversity factors other than race. Finally, Justice O'Connor noted that all admissions programs that were conscious of race must have time limitations and indicated that the Court believed the law school's promise that it would terminate the "race-conscious" admissions procedures as soon as possible.

Justice Ginsburg, joined by Justice Breyer, concurred with the opinion of the Court, citing the perpetuation of racial bias as impeding realization of the goal of diversity and predicting progress towards nondiscrimination, which would end the need for affirmative action.

Justice Rehnquist dissented, joined by Justices Scalia, Kennedy, and Thomas, finding that the law school's consideration of race was not narrowly tailored to achieve the interest of diversity in education. Justice Rehnquist found the "critical mass" requirement to amount to racial balancing at the law school. Justice Rehnquist pointed out that the percentage of students from underrepresented minority groups admitted was closely correlated to the percentage of applicants from that same minority group. For example, if 9.7 percent of the applicants were black, approximately 9.7 percent of the students admitted were black. Justice Rehnquist also found the admissions process failed the strict scrutiny analysis because the use of race as a factor in admissions did not have a precise time limitation.

Justice Kennedy wrote a separate dissent, finding that the Court failed to apply the strict scrutiny analysis required of a governmentally imposed racial classification. He pointed to the Court's deference to the law school's definition of its diversity objective as constituting such failure. Justice Kennedy found the law school's administration of the admission process to constitute a quota system.

Justice Scalia also dissented, joined by Justice Thomas. Justice Scalia found that the statistics proved that the law school's admissions program sought to achieve a class racially proportionate to the pool of applicants. He found racial understanding not "uniquely relevant" to law school or public education, concluding that if universities could use racial discrimination to achieve this understanding then public and private employers could also use racial discrimination to achieve racial understanding.

Finally, Justice Thomas, joined by Justice Scalia, dissented, indicating his belief that blacks did not need the interference of university administrations to succeed. Justice Thomas focused on the diversity interest the law school sought to further through its admissions process. He found that educational benefits were the interest sought by the law school, not diversity, and that in achieving this interest the law school did not want to sacrifice its status as one of the nation's top institutions. Justice Thomas indicated that maintenance of a public law school was not a necessity and, therefore, the state of Michigan had no compelling interest in having a law school in general or an elite law school. He also found the deference by the Court to the law school to be violative of the strict scrutiny analysis.

AFTERMATH

While the decision permits the use of race as a factor in the admissions process, the challenge will be to create a policy that is narrowly tailored. Further, the decision will likely affect the hiring processes for both public and private companies.

SIGNIFICANCE

This was the first time in 25 years that the Court had reviewed the use of race in the public university admissions process. The decision affirms that race may be considered as part of the admissions process for public universities. Many public groups and individuals, including the Bush administration and a number of Fortune 500 companies, voiced their opinions on the affirmative action issue by filing briefs in the case.

RELATED CASES

Gratz v. Bollinger, No. 02-516 (2003)

Regents of the University of California v. Bakke, 438 U.S. 265 (1978)

Sheet Metal Workers v. EEOC, 478 U.S. 421 (1986)

RECOMMENDED READING

Kathleen A. Graves, *Affirmative Action in Law School Admissions: an Analysis of Why Affirmative Action Is No Longer the Answer . . . Or Is It?,* 23 Southern Illinois University Law Journal 149 (1998).

Linda F. Wightman, *The Threat to Diversity in Legal Education: An Empirical Analysis of the Consequences of Abandoning Race as a Factor in Law School Admission Decisions,* 72 New York University Law Review 1 (1997).

Case Title: *Hampton v. Mow Sun Wong*

Legal Citation: 426 U.S. 88

Year of Decision: 1976

KEY ISSUES

Does a federal regulation that bars noncitizens from employment in the federal competitive civil service violate the due process of the law as set out in the Fifth Amendment?

HISTORY OF THE CASE

The Civil Service Commission had regulations barring noncitizens from employment in positions with certain federal agencies that were filled based on the results of a competitive examination. Five resident aliens brought the action to challenge the policy. Each of the aliens was denied federal employment on the sole basis that he or she was not an American citizen or native of American Samoa. All were Chinese residents who qualified in all other respects for an available job.

One of the plaintiffs was terminated after 10 days of satisfactory work at the post office because his personnel record revealed that he was not a citizen. Two of the plaintiffs were denied access to the positions of janitor and file clerk, even though they had participated in the California Supplemental Training and Education Program and had other work experience that demonstrated their capabilities as workers. One plaintiff was not permitted to take an examination although she had adequate work and education experience. The last plaintiff sought a position as a clerk-typist, but because of her alienage was not allowed to take the typing test.

The plaintiffs brought this class action on behalf of all aliens living in the United States.

They named as defendants the chairman and the commissioners of the Civil Service Commission and the heads of the three agencies that denied them employment. The complaint alleged that aliens face special problems in seeking employment because of language barriers. The plaintiffs noted that although 300,000 federal jobs become available each year, noncitizens are not eligible to compete for them except when these jobs are exempted from the competitive civil service. They contended that the advantage given to citizens seeking such employment is arbitrary and violates the due process clause of the Fifth Amendment and Executive Order No. 11,478, 3 CFR 803, which forbids discrimination in federal employment on the basis of "national origin." They sought declaratory and injunctive relief.

The defendants sought to have the complaint dismissed. The district court reasoned that the prohibition against discrimination on the basis of "national origin" in the executive order prohibited discrimination among citizens on that basis, not between citizens and noncitizens. In addition, the court rejected the Civil Service Commission's argument that the regulation was inconsistent with Section 502 of the Public Works for Water Pollution Control, and Power Development and Atomic Energy Commission Appropriation Act, which permitted payment to classes of persons who are made ineligible by the Civil Service Regulation. Lastly, the district court held that discrimination against aliens was constitutional.

Four of the plaintiffs appealed this decision. During the time the appeal was pending, the Supreme Court decided two cases, *SUGARMAN V. DOUGALL* and *In re Griffiths,* in which the Court recognized the importance of protecting the employment opportunities of aliens.

The court of appeals reversed the decision. It agreed with the analysis of the nonconstitutional issues, but held that the regulations violated the due process clause of the Fifth Amendment. The court concluded that the commission regulation could not be justified considering that it protected only a small fraction of the positions covered by the rule. The court accepted the conclusion that exclusion was constitutional in positions involving policymaking or national security, but the court was unwilling to support the broad exclusion fostered by the regulation at issue.

The Supreme Court agreed to hear the case to resolve the question of "whether a regulation of the United States Civil Service Commission that bars resident aliens from employment in the federal competitive civil service is constitutional."

SUMMARY OF ARGUMENTS

The plaintiffs argued that by excluding all persons except American citizens and native American Samoans, the regulation adopted and enforced by the Civil Service Commission violated the due process clause of the Fifth Amendment and Executive Order No. 11,478, which prohibited discrimination in employment based on "national origin."

The Civil Service Commission argued that discrimination on the basis of alienage was not unconstitutional. The Public Works for Water Pollution Control and Power Development and Atomic Energy Commission Appropriations Act provided that "no part of any appropriation shall be used to pay compensation of any officer or employee of the Government . . . unless such person (1) is a citizen of the United States, (2) is a person in the service of the United States on the date of enactment of this Act, who, being eligible for citizenship, had filed a declaration of intention to become a citizen of the United States prior to such date, (3) is a person who owed allegiance to the United States." Based on this regulation the commission contended that it acted permissibly in not opening up the civil service to all those whom Congress had indicated it would be willing to pay for their work. The commission additionally argued that the equal protection element of the due process clause of the Fifth Amendment did not apply to federal actions related to aliens. Therefore there was no need to justify the regulation. In the alternative they contended that the Fifth Amendment imposes a slight burden on the federal government to justify the exclusion of aliens and that this burden was met by several factors not considered by the lower courts.

DECISION

Justice Stevens wrote for the plurality and affirmed the opinion of the court of appeals. In refuting the contention of the commission, Justice Stevens argued that the federal government is compelled, as are the states, to govern impartially. While agreeing with the defendant's position that

a justification for citizenship requirement may have importance in certain contexts, Justice Stevens did not agree with the argument that the power of the federal government in this area was so complete that it may subject arbitrarily all aliens to rules substantially different from those applied to citizens.

He went on to note that the rule adopted and enforced by the commission subjected this already disadvantaged group to disparate treatment based solely on their alienage. He noted that this deprivation infringed on the interest in liberty protected by the due process clause of the Constitution: "The added disadvantage resulting from the enforcement of the rule—ineligibility for employment in a major sector of the economy—is of sufficient significance to be characterized as a deprivation of an interest in liberty." Because the regulation had the effect of disadvantaging this group, which constituted a discreet and insular minority, they must be afforded due process of law.

In subjecting the rule to scrutiny the Court noted that the commission identified several interests that Congress or the president might deem sufficient to justify the exclusion of noncitizens from federal service. A broad exclusion, for example, might help the president in negotiating treaties with foreign powers by enabling him to offer employment opportunities to citizens of a given foreign country in exchange for reciprocal concessions. Excluding aliens also provides an adequate incentive to qualify for naturalization.

Justice Stevens held that the problem with the cited interests was that they could not be reasonably assumed to have influenced the Civil Service Commission, the U.S. Postal Service, the General Service Administration, or the Department of Health, Education, and Welfare in the administration of their responsibilities, and particularly in relation to this case. He went on to note that neither the Congress nor the president required the commission to adopt a citizenship requirement as a condition of eligibility for employment in the civil service. The policy had been in place since the commission's inception in 1883 and both the Congress and the president were aware of it; therefore, Justice Stevens felt that the appropriate question was whether they acquiesced to this rule and whether this acquiescence should be given the same support as an express statutory of presidential command.

The last interest cited by the commission was that in certain positions there is a need for undivided loyalty to the federal government. The citizenship requirement served that end while eliminating the need for the commission to specifically delineate those positions that required such loyalty. The Court held that this is a valid interest and that in situations in which the government has such an interest it may limit access to those positions to citizens.

Justice Stevens then went on to recount the history of the Civil Service Commission. He felt that this history revealed that there was a trend to establish standards with respect to citizenship, but that this was not demonstrative of whether the president would act in such a manner. He felt that this trend merely gave the commission discretion in how to formulate its standard rather than set in place obligatory commands.

It is the business of the commission to adopt regulations that will best promote the efficiency of the federal civil service. The commission's function is limited and specific: to promote an efficient federal service. Justice Stevens noted that, in general, removing unnecessary restrictions fostered this end. He continued that, with the exception of the interest served by having citizens in positions that require loyalty to the U.S. government, the interests cited by the commission are not matters properly the business of the commission.

Justice Stevens went on to note that even in light of the cited and acceptable interest of securing citizens in positions that require loyalty, the commission had a responsibility to perform its responsibilities with a level of expertise that demanded it make known the reasons for its important decisions. The commission had not made any attempt to evaluate the desirability of a general exclusionary rule and the value of enlarging the eligible applicant pool. Justice Stevens continued that the Court had no basis on which to infer that setting up categories in which citizenship would be required was an onerous task that justified such a broad exclusionary policy. He therefore rejected their argument of administrative convenience.

He concluded the impact of the rule adopted by the commission was the same as those state regulations rejected in the *Sugarman* case, which rejected a large group of people, all of whom were not the target of the legislation. Since the decision to admit these aliens was made by the Congress and the president, the decision to exclude them from an area traditionally noted as part of an individual's liberty—economic opportunity—must be made at that same level of government. He concluded that the regulation at issue denied the class of liberty without due process of law and was therefore invalid.

Justice Brennan wrote a concurring opinion in which Justice Marshall joined. He noted that there are equal protection questions that would be raised if the Congress or president were the relevant actors barring employment of aliens by the government.

Justice Rehnquist wrote a dissenting opinion in which the chief justice, Justice White, and Justice Blackmun joined. He reasoned that the Court's holding enunciated a concept of procedural due process guaranteed by the Fifth Amendment that is out of line with the doctrine established by the previous court decisions.

He first noted that in the areas of immigration and regulation of aliens, the power of the deferral courts is severely limited. He continued that though Congress wields broad power to prescribe the terms and conditions of entry of aliens, this power is curtailed by the requirements of complying with the due process clause of the Constitution. However, this requirement of due process does not mean that aliens have protected liberty interest in securing federal employment. He noted that in reaching their decision the plurality overlooked this limitation.

He continued that the *Sugarman* case to which the Court referred specifically did not apply its holding to the federal government. The Court, instead of applying traditional equal protection analysis, melded together the concepts of equal protection and procedural due process. "What the Court seem to do is to engraft notions of due process onto the case law from this Court dealing with the delegation by Congress of its legislative authority to administrative agencies."

Justice Rehnquist noted that the only grounds on which the procedure may be challenged is to argue that it was an improper delegation of authority. Yet, he felt that under traditional standards governing the delegation of authority the commission was empowered to act as it did. Congress delegated to the president the power to prescribe regulations for admission of individuals to the Civil Service and to ascertain the fitness of applicants as to age health, character, knowledge, and ability for employment as set down in the Civil Service Act. The president, acting under this authority, promulgated Executive Order 10, 577 in which he authorized the Civil Service Commission to establish standards with respect to citizenship, age, education, residency, or other requirements that must be met before an individual may be eligible to compete for civil service employment. Under this authority the Civil Service Commission promulgated regulations to exclude aliens from examination for or appointment to the civil service. Thus, concluded Justice Rehnquist, Congress and the president took power they possessed and delegated it to the commission. "This is the process by which all federal regulations are promulgated, and to forbid it would be to necessarily dismantle the entire structure of the Executive Branch."

Justice Stevens then noted that the decision to exclude aliens is a political question reserved to Congress. Once it is determined that the power has been delegated appropriately then the reasons why this power is exercised is foreclosed from consideration by the judiciary. This is because the delegation is subject to the same scrutiny as if Congress had itself exercised such authority. For the Court to exercise authority in this area would transcend the bounds of its jurisdiction. He concluded that the regulation does not infringe upon any constitutional right of the class members. "I conclude therefor the Congress, in the exercise of its political judgment, could have excluded aliens from the civil service. The fact that it chose, in a separate political decision, to allow the Civil Service Commission to make this determination does not render the governmental policy any less 'political' and consequently, does not render it any more subject to judicial scrutiny."

AFTERMATH

To determine whether a federal statute is constitutionally valid, courts review the statute for congressional violations of the equal protection clause of the Fifth Amendment. For state classifications involving alienage, the Court analyzes whether the appropriate entity is making the relevant decision. This question often turns on whether the entity is authorized to act in such a manner and whether the action is congressionally sanctioned.

Following this decision, President Ford issued an executive order making citizenship a condition for federal employment.

SIGNIFICANCE

The original position of the Court stated in *Detroit Bank v. United States* was that the Fifth Amendment does not contain an equal protection clause. In BOLLING V. SHARPE, the Court held that discrimination may be of such a degree as to be unjustifiable and, as such, violative of due process protected by the Fifth Amendment. In invalidating a gender classification in *Weinberger v. Weisenfeld,* the Court later held that "this Court's approach to Fifth Amendment equal protection claims has always been the same as to equal protection claims under the Fourteenth Amendment."

On the same day as this decision *Mathews v. Diaz* was decided. In *Mathews* the Court reached a seemingly opposite conclusion. The Court held that a federal statute that limited participation in a federal medical insurance program to citizens and aliens who had resided continuously in the United States for five years was valid. The Court reasoned that Congress may legitimately determine that a resident's ties to the United States grow stronger the longer the residency and may condition the receipt of benefits of the stronger tie. It further reasoned that the business of regulating the conditions of entry and residence of aliens is exclusively within the dominion of the political branches of the federal government.

The basis of the reasoning in *Hampton* is that the decision to impose a deprivation of an important liberty must be made by either the Congress or the executive branch, which made the decisions under which the aliens were admitted. This reasoning implies the nondelegation doctrine. The nondelegation doctrine is grounded in the separation of powers. It allocates power to perform functions by branch and views the delegation of these functions to another branch or an administrative person as invalid. The rationale for this approach includes (1) to ensure policy choices are made by the legislature and not by the executive branch; (2) to promote reliability for those affected by regulation; and (3) to work against arbitrariness or caprice on the part of administrators because the discretion is limited. The nondelegation doctrine serves to promote the rule of law.

RELATED CASES

Bolling v. Sharpe, 347 U.S. 497 (1954)

Detroit Bank v. United States, 317 U.S. 329 (1943)

In re Griffiths, 413 U.S. 717 (1973)

Mathews v. Diaz, 426 U.S. 67 (1976)

Sugarman v. Dougall, 413 U.S. 634 (1973)

Vance v. Bradley, 440 U.S. 93 (1979)

Weinberg v. Wiesenfeld, 420 U.S. 636 (1975)

RECOMMENDED READING

David F. Levi, *The Equal Treatment of Aliens: Preemption or Equal Protection?,* 31 Stanford Law Review 1069 (1979).

Richard A. Posner, *The DeFunis Case and the Constitutionality of Preferential Treatment of Racial Minorities,* Supreme Court Review 1 (1974).

Gerald M. Rosberg, *The Protection of Aliens from Discriminatory Treatment by the National Government,* Supreme Court Review 275 (1977).

State Burdens on Resident Aliens: A New Preemption Analysis, 89 Yale Law Journal 940 (1980).

Case Title: *Harper v. Virginia State Board of Elections*

Legal Citation: 383 U.S. 663

Year of Decision: 1966

KEY ISSUES

Do poll taxes violate the equal protection clause of the Fourteenth Amendment?

HISTORY OF THE CASE

Virginia residents brought suits to have the Virginia poll tax declared unconstitutional. A three-judge district court dismissed the complaint based on the holding in *Breedlove v. Suttles,* which upheld a poll tax in Georgia. The plaintiffs appealed this dismissal to the Supreme Court.

The Virginia Constitution directed the General Assembly to levy an annual poll tax not to exceed $1.50 on every resident of the state over the age of 21. Payment of the poll tax was a precondition to voting. The poll tax was to be paid for three years preceding the year in which a voter registered. Those who did not pay the poll tax were disenfranchised.

SUMMARY OF ARGUMENTS

The plaintiffs argued that the poll tax worked to disenfranchise in a discriminatory manner and thus violated the equal protection clause of the Fourteenth Amendment.

The Virginia State Board of Elections argued that voting was not a First Amendment right and the Fourteenth Amendment did not place a limit on the state's power to prescribe the qualifications of voters. The board also argued that the poll tax did not violate the equal protection clause.

DECISION

Justice Douglas, writing for six judges, held that the poll tax was unconstitutional because it was inconsistent with the equal protection clause of the Fourteenth Amendment. He noted that the right to vote in state elections is nowhere expressly protected in the Constitution and that the right to vote is implicit in the First Amendment. As a result this right may not be conditioned upon payment of a tax or fee. In addition, he noted that once the right of suffrage was granted it could not be made conditional on requirements inconsistent with the equal protection clause: "That is to say, the right of suffrage is subject to the imposition of state standards which are not discriminatory and which do not contravene any restriction that Congress, acting pursuant to its constitutional powers, has imposed."

He concluded that a state violates the equal protection clause when it makes affluence or a payment of any fee an electoral standard. He reasoned that, unlike literacy tests, poll taxes bear no relation to the ability of the voter to exercise his right. He continued that the case history demonstrated that the equal protection clause of the Fourteenth Amendment prohibits the state from adopting voter qualifications that work inviduously to discriminate.

Justice Black dissented on the ground that in *Breedlove v. Suttles* (1937) the Court held that a state poll tax in Georgia, which was a prerequisite to voting in state elections, was valid. The Court explicitly rejected the reasoning that the equal protection clause was violated by placing an undue burden on different groups of people according to age, sex, or the ability to pay. In addition, he noted that in *Butler v. Thompson* (1951) the Court upheld a Virginia state poll tax also challenged on equal protection grounds. He argued that the Court should adhere to the holding in those cases. By doing the opposite, he argued that the majority had given the clause a new meaning; the fact that a law has the result of treating groups differently does not by itself make the law invalid. He also felt that the Court used "the old natural-law-due-process formula" as the basis for invalidating the poll tax as a violation of the equal protection clause. This formula uses the equal protection clause to write into the Constitution what the Court feels is good government policy.

Justice Harlan joined by Justice Stewart dissented on the ground that the Court's invalidation of the poll tax was an infringement on the right of the state and the federal political process. They argued that the Court, in using the equal protection clause to invalidate the Virginia state poll tax, departed from the established standard regarding the application of the clause. He reasoned that the equal protection clause prohibits the state from arbitrarily treating people differently, but that the clause does not require equal treatment of all people.

He continued that poll taxes and property qualifications have been a traditional part of the political structure, and though they may not be in accord with modern notions of equity, it is not the job of the Court to invalidate these provisions. If these provisions truly do not square with the modern notion of equity, then the legislature should address this by invalidating these taxes.

Aftermath

In *Bullock v. Carter* (1972) the Court invalidated a Texas scheme that imposed filing fees on political candidates for state and local office. The Court reasoned that the scheme was invalid because the Texas filing fees had an impact on voters by limiting their candidate choices due to the candidate's or voters' lack of financial resources to support a campaign; therefore, the law must be "closely

scrutinized and found reasonably necessary to the accomplishment of legitimate state objectives in order to pass constitutional muster." In *Lubin v. Panish* (1974) the Court invalidated a similar scheme in California.

Significance

The decision in *Harper* was an extension of the holding in *Edward v. California* (1941), in which the Court invalidated a law that prohibited bringing a nonresident indigent into the state. The Court reasoned that the state may not qualify or limit one's right as an American citizen based on his wealth.

This decision came two years after the passage of the Twenty-fourth Amendment, which prohibits states from imposing poll taxes as a requirement for voting in federal elections. This decision in applying strict scrutiny to the classification gauged whether wealth is a suspect classification. The decision reaffirmed a basic underpinning of the American political system: that all citizens, regardless of wealth, should be able to participate in decision making of the government.

The case also came in the aftermath of other cases in which the Court addressed other infringements on the exercise of one's right to vote. In *Reynolds v. Sims,* a seminal case in the area of reapportionment, the Court held that the equal protection clause required state legislatures to be apportioned on a one man/one vote basis. In *Carrington v. Rash* the Court invalidated a Texas statute that prohibited a member of the armed services who moved into the state during active duty from voting in state elections. In *Kramer v. Union Free School District No. 15,* the Court invalidated a New York educational law that made otherwise eligible voters in state and federal elections ineligible to vote in school district elections if they did not meet one of the following three requirements: (1) that they were the owner or lessee of taxable real property located in the district; (2) that the person was the spouse of one who owned or leased property in the district; or (3) that the person was the parent or guardian of a child enrolled for a specific time period in the school district during the preceding year. The Court held that the law was not narrowly tailored enough to capture only the target group of persons primarily interested in school affairs.

In *Cipriano v. City of Houma*, the Court invalidated a Louisiana law that permitted only property-owning taxpayers to vote in municipal elections. A similar provision was invalidated by the Court in *City of Phoenix v. Kolodziejski*. However, in *Salyer Land Co. v. Tulare Lake Basin Water Storage District*, the Court held that *Kramer, Cipriano,* and *Kolodziejski* did not prevent California from limiting participation in a water district election to persons and corporations that owned land in the district, or from apportioning votes to the assessed value of the land. The justices reasoned that the representation afforded was in proportion to the land possessed and therefore the plural election requirement of *Reynold* and its progeny were inapplicable.

RELATED CASES

Ball v. James, 451 U.S. 355 (1981)

Breedlove v. Suttles, 302 U.S. 277 (1937)

Bullock v. Carter, 405 U.S. 134 (1972)

Carrington v. Rash, 380 U.S. 89 (1965)

Cipriani v. City of Jouma, 395 U.S. 701 (1969)

City of Phoenix v. Kolodziejski, 399 U.S. 204 (1969)

Edwards v. California, 314 U.S. 160 (1941)

Kramer v. Union Free School District No. 15, 395 U.S. 621 (1969)

Lassiter v. Northampton County Board of Elections, 360 U.S. 45 (1959)

Reynolds v. Sims, 377 U.S. 533 (1964)

Salyer Land Co. v. Tulare Lake Bason Water Storage District, 410 U.S. 719 (1973)

RECOMMENDED READING

Berger, Raoul. *Government by Judiciary: The Transformation of the Fourteenth Amendment*. Cambridge, Mass.: Harvard University Press, 1977.

Sandford Levinson, *Suffrage and Community: Who Should Vote?*, Florida Law Review 545 (1989).

Gerald L. Neuman, *We Are the People*, 13 Michigan Law Review 259 (1992).

William Van Alstyne, *The Fourteenth Amendment, the "Right" to Vote, and the Understanding of the Thirty-ninth Congress*, Supreme Court Review 33 (1965).

Case Title: *Harris v. Forklift Systems, Inc.*

Alternate Case Title: Abusive Work Environment Case

Legal Citation: 510 U.S. 17

Year of Decision: 1993

KEY ISSUES

To be legally actionable as "abusive (or hostile) work environment" harassment, must an employer's conduct seriously affect an employee's psychological well-being or lead the employee to suffer injury?

HISTORY OF THE CASE

Title VII of the Civil Rights Act of 1964 makes it "an unlawful employment practice for an employer . . . to discriminate against any individual with respect to his compensation, terms, conditions, or privileges of employment, because of such individual's race, color, religion, sex, or national origin." In the earlier case of *Meritor Savings Bank, FSB v. Vinson* (1986), the U.S. Supreme Court held that the Title VII language "is not limited to 'economic' or 'tangible' discrimination." But, in the aftermath of *Meritor*, the various federal courts of appeals had failed to agree on a definition of conduct that would constitute an abusive or hostile work environment.

Teresa Harris worked as a manager at Forklift Systems, Inc., an equipment rental company, where throughout her time of employment her supervisor insulted her because of her gender and often made her the target of unwanted sexual innuendo. After two years of such treatment, Harris quit and then sued Forklift, claiming that the employer's conduct had created an abusive work environment for her because of her gender. The trial court found this treatment to be close to an abusive environment but held that the work environment was not intimidating or abusive to Harris, in part because the employer's conduct was not so severe as to be expected to seriously affect Harris's psychological well-being.

SUMMARY OF ARGUMENTS

Harris argued that her employer's behavior offended her and would have offended any reasonable woman. The trial court erred, according to Harris, in considering whether she had suffered concrete psychological harm.

The employer argued that the trial court correctly applied the *Meritor* standard in concluding that the work environment was not intimidating or abusive to Harris.

DECISION

The Court unanimously held in favor of Harris that, to be actionable as abusive work environment harassment, conduct need not seriously affect an employees's psychological well-being or lead the employee to suffer injury. In her opinion for the Court, Justice O'Connor emphasized that whether an environment is hostile or abusive can be determined only by looking at all the circumstances. Factors to be considered may include the frequency of the discriminatory conduct; its severity; whether it is physically threatening or humiliating, or a mere offensive utterance; and whether it unreasonably interferes with an employee's work performance. The effect on the employee's psychological well-being is relevant to determining whether she actually found the environment abusive. But while psychological harm may be taken into account, neither psychological harm nor any other single factor is required.

AFTERMATH

In addressing a conflict among the lower courts, the Court in the *Harris* case attempted to clarify the standard by which abusiveness in the workplace would be determined. The complaining employee is now required to prove neither psychological harm nor injury resulting from the employer's offensive conduct. Rather, juries must look at all the circumstances to decide whether sex-related conduct engaged in (or permitted by) an employer is egregious enough to warrant an award of damages.

SIGNIFICANCE

The decision in *Harris* reflected the strength of Title VII and the extent to which its values had been woven into the fabric of society over a 30-year span. Even a relatively conservative Court had little difficulty in reaching the unanimous pro-plaintiff conclusion. Yet, in crafting a resolution, the Court failed to confront some other issues lurking in the sexual harassment context. Even though the objectionable conduct in *Harris* consisted mostly of speech, the Court did not address the interplay between Title VII and the First Amendment—why speech presumably protected by the First Amendment is nevertheless actionable under Title VII. Nor did the Court explain why the burden is on the victim of sexual harassment to prove that the offensive conduct is so pervasive and unreasonable as to constitute an abusive environment—why disparate treatment of male and female employees is not itself sufficient proof of a Title VII violation. Such issues are bound to arise in future cases as the Court responds to modern workplace relationships.

RELATED CASES

Meritor Savings Bank, FSB v. Vinson, 477 U.S. (1986)

RECOMMENDED READING

Cynthia L. Estlund, *The Architecture of the First Amendment and the Case of Workplace Harassment*, 72 Notre Dame Law Review 1361 (1997).

Jeffrey M. Lipman and Hugh J. Cain, *Evolution in Hostile Environment Claims since Harris v. Forklift Systems, Inc.*, 47 Drake Law Review 585 (1999).

Miranda Oshige, *What's Sex Got to Do with It?*, 47 Stanford Law Review 565 (1995).

Case Title: *James v. Valtierra*

Alternate Case Title: *Shaffer v. Valtierra*

Legal Citation: 402 U.S. 137

Year of Decision: 1971

KEY ISSUES

Does a California law, which requires that low-rent housing projects be approved by a majority vote at a community election, violate the equal protection clause of the Fourteenth Amendment?

HISTORY OF THE CASE

Citizens of San Jose, California, and San Mateo County filed suit in federal district court seeking a declaration that the referendum requirement for low-income housing projects (Article 34) in the California Constitution violated the equal protection clause of the U.S. Constitution. As a result of a local vote, the housing authorities in their area could not apply for federal funds. A three-judge court held that Article 34 denied the plaintiffs equal protection of the laws and enjoined its enforcement. Two appeals were taken from the judgment, one by the San Jose City Council, and the other by a single member of the council.

SUMMARY OF ARGUMENTS

Ronald James argued that the justification for the referendum requirement was reasonable and that the equal protection clause of the Fourteenth Amendment was incorrectly applied by the trial court.

Anita Valtierra, one of the citizens opposing the referendum, argued that the referendum requirement violated the equal protection clause of the Fourteenth Amendment because it denied poor people the use of ordinary lawmaking procedures and because it encouraged a racial veto of the federal fund distribution for public housing. Valtierra also argued that the referendum requirement violated the supremacy clause because it was inconsistent with federal public housing provisions.

DECISION

The Court held that the California law requiring a local referendum on low-income housing projects did not violate the equal protection clause of the Fourteenth Amendment. The Court found no racial bias in "a law seemingly neutral on its face."

Justice Black delivered the opinion of the Court. He held that Article 34 does not make any "distinctions based on race," and that "a lawmaking procedure that 'disadvantages' a particular group does not always deny equal protection." The referendum provision, Justice Black argued, demonstrates a "devotion to democracy, not to bias, discrimination, or prejudice."

Justice Thurgood Marshall disagreed. In his dissenting opinion he stated: "The article explic-

itly singles out low-income persons to bear its burden. Publicly assisted housing developments designed to accommodate the aged, veterans, state employees, persons of moderate income, or any class of citizens other than the poor, need not be approved by prior referenda."

AFTERMATH

Courts have consistently refused to require local communities to construct affordable housing, even in the face of an enduring pattern of racial discrimination.

Nevertheless, where a court finds a constitutional violation in a given municipality that is aggravated by the discriminatory practices of neighboring communities, a court may conceivably order area-wide relief under *Hills v. Gautreaux,* 425 U.S. 284 (1976). In *Hills,* a tenant of Chicago's public housing system brought suit against the Chicago Housing Authority (CHA) and the Department of Housing and Urban Development (HUD). The complaint alleged that the CHA deliberately selected housing sites in predominantly black areas to avoid placing black families in white neighborhoods. The federal district court ordered both agencies to take corrective action limited to the city of Chicago. The Supreme Court held that a remedial order beyond Chicago's geographic boundary was warranted in view of HUD's constitutional and statutory violations. Such relief is justified when there is evidence of discrimination by neighboring communities and where the disturbance to government operations caused by the order would be minimal, especially in a suit against HUD.

SIGNIFICANCE

Although local housing authorities may not discriminate on the basis of race, communities have no statutory or constitutional obligation to construct affordable housing.

RELATED CASES

Dandrige v. Williams, 397 U.S. 471 (1970)

Hunter v. Erickson, 393 U.S. 385 (1969)

RECOMMENDED READING

Mark J. Powell, *Fair Housing in the United States: A Legal Response to Municipal Intransigence,* University of Illinois Law Review 279 (1997).

The Equal Protection Clause and Exclusionary Zoning after Valtierra *and* Dandridge, 81 Yale Law Journal 61–86 (1971).

The Supreme Court, 1970 Term, 85 Harvard Law Review 122–134 (November 1971).

Case Title: *Johnson v. Transportation Agency, Santa Clara County*

Legal Citation: 480 U.S. 616

Year of Decision: 1987

KEY ISSUES

Was a male employee of a county transportation agency discriminated against when he was passed over for promotion in favor of a female employee?

HISTORY OF THE CASE

In December 1978, the Santa Clara County Transit District Board of Supervisors adopted an affirmative action plan for the county Transportation Agency. The plan was adopted because "mere prohibition of discriminatory practices is not enough to remedy the effects of past practices and to permit attainment of an equitable representation of minorities, women and handicapped persons." The plan intended to achieve "a statistically measurable yearly improvement in hiring, training and promotion of minorities and women throughout the Agency in all major job classifications where they are underrepresented." As a benchmark to evaluate progress, the agency stated its long-term goal was to attain a workforce whose composition reflected the proportion of minorities and women in the area labor force. The agency's plan set aside no specific number of positions for minorities or women, but it authorized the consideration of ethnicity or sex as a factor when evaluating qualified candidates for jobs in which members of such groups were poorly represented. One such job was the road dispatcher position, the subject of the dispute in this case.

On December 12, 1979, the agency announced a vacancy for the promotional position of road dispatcher in the agency's Roads Division. Dispatchers assign road crews, equipment, and materials, and they maintain records pertaining to road maintenance jobs. Twelve employees applied for the promotion, including Joyce, a woman, and Johnson, the petitioner in this case. Joyce had worked for the county since 1970, serving as an account clerk until 1975. She had applied for a road dispatcher position in 1974 but was deemed ineligible because she had not served as a road maintenance worker. In 1975, Joyce transferred from a senior account clerk position to a road maintenance worker position, becoming the first woman to fill such a job. During her four years in that position, she occasionally worked as a road dispatcher.

Petitioner Johnson began with the county in 1967 as a road yard clerk, after private employment that included working as a supervisor and dispatcher. He had also unsuccessfully applied for the road dispatcher opening in 1974. In 1977, his clerical position was downgraded, and he sought and received a transfer to the position of road maintenance worker. He also occasionally worked as a dispatcher while performing that job.

Nine of the applicants, including Joyce and Johnson, were deemed qualified for the job, and they were interviewed by a two-person board. Seven of the applicants scored above 70 on this interview, which meant that they were certified as eligible for selection by the appointing authority. The scores awarded ranged from 70 to 80. Johnson was tied for second with a score of 75 while Joyce ranked next with a score of 73. A second interview was conducted by three agency supervisors, who ultimately recommended that Johnson be promoted. Prior to the second interview, Joyce had contacted the county's Affirmative Action Office because she feared that her application might not receive disinterested review. The office in turn contacted the agency's affirmative action coordinator, whom the agency's plan makes responsible for, among other things, keeping the director informed of opportunities for the agency to accomplish its objectives under the plan. At the time, the agency had never employed a woman as a road dispatcher. The coordinator recommended to the director of the agency, James Graebner, that Joyce be promoted.

Graebner, authorized to choose any of the seven persons deemed eligible, thus had the benefit of suggestions by the second interview panel and by the agency coordinator in arriving at his decision. After deliberation, Graebner concluded that the promotion should be given to Joyce. As he testified: "I tried to look at the whole picture, the combination of her qualifications and Mr. Johnson's qualifications, their test scores, their expertise, their background, affirmative action matters, things like that . . . I believe it was a combination of all those."

Johnson filed suit in the U.S. District Court for the Northern District of California alleging that he had been denied promotion on the basis of sex in violation of Title VII of the 1964 Civil Rights Act, which makes it an unlawful employment practice to discriminate in the hiring, firing, and treatment of employees based on "race, color, religion, sex or national origin." The district court found that Johnson was more qualified for the dispatcher position than Joyce, and that the sex of Joyce was the "determining factor in her selection." The court found the agency's plan invalid on the ground that the evidence did not satisfy the criterion of *Steelworkers v. Weber* (1979) that the plan be temporary. In *Weber,* the Court upheld an affirmative action plan because, among other things, it did not seek to maintain a racial balance, but to eliminate a racial imbalance.

The Court of Appeals for the Ninth Circuit reversed, holding that the absence of an express termination date in the plan was not conclusive as to the plan's validity, since the plan repeatedly expressed its objective as the attainment, rather than the maintenance, of a workforce mirroring the labor force in the county. The court of appeals added that because the plan established no fixed percentage of positions for minorities or women, a relatively explicit deadline was less essential. The court held further that the agency's consideration of Joyce's sex in filling the road dispatcher position was lawful. The agency plan had been adopted, the court said, to address a conspicuous imbalance in the agency's workforce, and neither unnecessarily trammeled the rights of other employees nor created an absolute bar to their advancement. After the Ninth Circuit decision denying his Title VII claim of sexual discrimination, Johnson sought review in the U.S. Supreme Court.

SUMMARY OF ARGUMENTS

Johnson argued that he had been denied promotion on the basis of sex in violation of Title VII of the 1964 Civil Rights Act.

Johnson argued that the plan could not be justified as remedial because the agency had not been guilty of past sexual discrimination and, even if the plan could be justified as remedial, it was not narrowly tailored.

The agency argued that gender was only one of the considerations taken into account when promoting a qualified person to a job in which women had not been previously employed. The agency also argued that the plan was narrowly tailored and Johnson's Title VII rights had not been violated.

DECISION

Justice Brennan delivered the opinion of the Court. Following the Court's precedent in *Steelworkers v. Weber,* Justice Brennan used a two-part analysis to address Johnson's claim of employment discrimination. The first question in this case was whether the consideration of the sex of applicants for particular types of jobs was justified by the existence of a "manifest imbalance" that reflected underrepresentation of women in "traditionally segregated job categories." By comparing the percentage of women in the employer's workforce with the percentage in the area labor market, the Court concluded that such a "manifest imbalance" did exist. The Court also pointed out that the plan did not establish quotas and that sex was only one factor to be considered of many. The Court held that "[t]he promotion of Joyce thus satisfies the first requirement enunciated in *Weber,* since it was undertaken to further an affirmative action plan designed to eliminate Agency work force imbalances in traditionally segregated job categories."

The next question the Court considered was whether the plan violated the rights of male employees. The Court reiterated that the plan enforced no quotas: "[T]he plan sets aside no positions for women." The Court again noted that sex was only one factor of many: "The Plan . . . resembles the 'Harvard Plan' approvingly noted by Justice Powell in *Regents of the University of California v. Blake,* . . . which considers race along with other criteria in determining admission to college." The Court also pointed out that "the Agency Plan requires women to compete with all other qualified applicants" and that Johnson "had no absolute entitlement to the road dispatcher position." Finally, the Court found that the goal of the plan to "attain" a balanced workforce was aspirational, not mandatory. For all of these reasons, the Court held that the plan did not violate the rights of male employees.

The Court concluded that "the Agency has sought to take a moderate, gradual approach to eliminating the imbalance in its work force, one which establishes realistic guidance for employment decisions, and which visits minimal intrusion on the legitimate expectations of other employees." The Court held that "the Agency appropriately took into account as one factor the sex of Diane Joyce in determining that she should be promoted to the road dispatcher position . . . Such a plan is fully consistent with Title VII, for it embodies the contribution that voluntary employer action can make in eliminating the vestiges of discrimination in the workplace."

AFTERMATH

According to one commentator, employers have been unable to institute broad remedial affirmative action plans because of the focus on job skills and the difficulty of determining the existence of a manifest imbalance in job categories.

SIGNIFICANCE

This case established a two-part test for determining whether voluntary affirmative action programs are in compliance with Title VII of the 1964 Civil Rights Act. This case laid down the general rule that an employer need not suggest that it is guilty of past illegal discrimination in order to employ voluntary affirmative remedies.

The Johnson decision made it possible for public employers to institute affirmative action plans. Criticism of the decision or the lack of criticism depended on a person's view of affirmative action. In the end, Johnson retired early and Joyce continued her work with the agency.

RELATED CASES

Firefighters v. Cleveland, 478 U.S. 501 (1986)

McDonnell Douglas Corp. v. Green, 411 U.S. 792 (1973)

Regents of University of California v. Bakke, 438 U.S. 265 (1978)

Steelworkers v. Weber, 443 U.S. 193 (1979)

Wygant v. Jackson Board of Education, 476 U.S. 267 (1986)

RECOMMENDED READING

Bork, Robert H. *The Tempting of America: The Political Seduction of the Law.* New York: Free Press, 1990.

David D. Meyer, *Finding a "Manifest Imbalance": The Case for a Unified Statistical Test for Voluntary Affirmative Action under Title VII*, 87 Michigan Law Review 1986–2025 (June 1989).

Case Title: *Katzenbach v. Morgan*

Legal Citation: 384 U.S. 641

Year of Decision: 1966

KEY ISSUES

Did Congress exceed its constitutional powers, thereby violating the Tenth Amendment, through the enactment of Section 4(e) of the Voting Rights Act of 1965, which provided that the right to vote could not be denied to a person who successfully completed the sixth grade in a public or accredited private school in Puerto Rico, even if the classes were not taught in English?

HISTORY OF THE CASE

State laws in New York conditioned the right to vote on an ability to read and write English. The Supreme Court had previously held that English literacy requirements did not violate the Fourteenth and Fifteenth Amendments. In 1965 Congress enacted the Voting Rights Act pursuant to its enforcement power under Section 5 of the Fourteenth Amendment. Section 4(e) gave the right to vote to Puerto Ricans who had completed the sixth grade in an accredited public school and were unable to read or write English. Under Section 4(e), voting could not be conditioned on English literacy.

SUMMARY OF ARGUMENTS

Appellant Katzenbach, the U.S. attorney general, argued that Section 4(e) was a proper exercise of congressional power.

Appellees, registered voters in New York City, including Morgan, argued that Section 4(e) could be upheld only if the judiciary first determined that the state law was prohibited by the Fourteenth Amendment. Appellees also argued that Section 4(e) was inconsistent with the letter and spirit of the Constitution.

DECISION

Justice Brennan delivered the opinion of the Court. Brennan found that Congress could enact appropriate legislation prohibiting certain actions to enforce the equal protection clause without a prior determination by the Court that the act sought to be prohibited violated the Fourteenth Amendment. Brennan found that it was within Congress's grant of legislative power to exercise its discretion in determining what legislation was necessary to protect Fourteenth Amendment guarantees. The Court restricted its determination to whether Section 4(e) was a permissible enactment to enforce the equal protection clause. Specifically, Brennan found that Section 4(e) constituted legislation to enforce the equal protection clause and was within congressional authority as the Court could perceive a basis for the action.

Justice Douglas joined the Court's opinion, but he reserved judgment on whether Section 4(e) was consistent with the letter and spirit of the Constitution.

Justices Harlan and Stewart dissented, defining the relevant issue as whether New York's literacy test was reasonably designed to further a legitimate state interest. The justices found voting to essentially be a matter of state concern and believed it was the place of the judiciary to determine whether a state practice violated the equal protection clause. The justices would have upheld the New York literacy test. They believed that allowing Congress to override New York's literacy test allowed the Fourteenth Amendment to eclipse state authority regarding voting.

AFTERMATH

The decision enabled many New York City residents, who had migrated from Puerto Rico, to vote.

SIGNIFICANCE

The Court's decision in *Katzenbach v. Morgan* allowed Congress to find certain actions unconstitutional and enact legislation to remedy the violations.

RELATED CASES

Oregon v. Mitchell, 400 U.S. 112 (1970)

Rome v. United States, 446 U.S. 156 (1980)

South Carolina v. Katzenbach, 383 U.S. 301 (1966)

RECOMMENDED READING

Alexander M. Bickel, *The Voting Rights Cases,* Supreme Court Review 79–102 (1966).

Robert A. Burt, *Miranda and Title II: A Morganatic Marriage,* Supreme Court Review 81–134 (1969).

Stephen L. Carter, *The Morgan "Power" and the Forced Reconsideration of Constitutional Decisions,* 53 University of Chicago Law Review 819–863 (1986).

Keynes, Edward, with Randall K. Miller. *The Courts vs. Congress.* Durham, N.C.: Duke University Press, 1989.

Daniel J. Leffell, *Congressional Power to Enforce Due Process Rights,* 80 Columbia Law Review 1265–1295 (October 1980).

Case Title: *Kirchberg v. Feenstra*

Alternate Case Title: Sex Discrimination Case

Legal Citations: 450 U.S. 455; 101 S.Ct. 1195; 67 L.Ed. 2d 428

Year of Decision: 1981

KEY ISSUES

Does a superseded Louisiana statute that gave the husband the right to dispose of property without the wife's consent violate the equal protection clause of the Fourteenth Amendment?

HISTORY OF THE CASE

In 1974, Joan Feenstra filed a criminal charge against her husband. He hired an attorney to represent him and signed a $3,000 promissory note secured by a mortgage on the home Feenstra owned jointly with his wife. She had no knowledge of this mortgage, nor need she have based on Article 2404 of the Louisiana Civil Code, which gave a husband exclusive control over the community property. Mrs. Feenstra learned of the mortgage in 1976 when Karl Kirchberg, her husband's attorney, threatened to foreclose. She refused to pay. This action was filed in the U.S. District Court for the Eastern District of Louisiana. While Mrs. Feenstra's appeal was pending before the Fifth Circuit Court of Appeals the Louisiana legislature revised its code relating to community property and granted spouses equal control over community property. The provisions became effective in 1980 so that the court of appeals was required to deal with the old provisions and decide whether they violated the Fourteenth Amendment.

SUMMARY OF ARGUMENTS

Kirchberg argued that Mrs. Feenstra could have prohibited her husband from executing a mortgage without her consent using state statutory provisions. He also argued that the mortgage was valid because of the decision of the court of appeals that the state statute was prospective, not retroactive.

Mrs. Feenstra argued that the mortgage was invalid because Article 2404 violated the equal protection clause of the Fourteenth Amendment and, therefore, was unconstitutional.

Justice Marshall wrote the opinion for the Court. The court of appeals found that the old code discriminated on the basis of gender and that in order for it to be valid there must be a strong state interest; otherwise, the statute violated the equal protection clause. The Court held that its finding was not retroactive. The Court affirmed the judgment because Kirchberg focused on what Mrs. Feenstra could do to avoid the situation and not on an important government interest. Also, Mrs. Feenstra did not appeal from the decision below and so avoided any claim that an important government objective was served by the statute. The mortgage executed on the Feenstra home by the husband without the wife's consent under an unconstitutional statute is void.

DECISION

The gender allocation of managerial rights to the husband allowing him to sell or exchange community property without the wife's consent violates the equal protection clause of the Fourteenth Amendment.

SIGNIFICANCE

The Supreme Court has accepted the view that the negative stereotype of a woman does not provide constitutional grounds that denies women access to positions of power in the public sphere. A claim of citizenship is to be treated with respect and equality. In the years that followed, more and more women would serve in Congress, in the Attorney General's Office, and as heads of large corporations.

RELATED CASES

Califano v. Westcott, 443 U.S. 76 (1979)

Frontiero v. Richardson, 411 U.S. 677 (1973)

Reed v. Reed, 404 U.S. 71 (1971)

RECOMMENDED READING

Kirp, Donald. *Gender Justice.* Chicago: University of Chicago Press, 1986.

Case Title: *Korematsu v. United States*

Alternate Case Title: The Japanese Exclusion Case

Legal Citations: 323 U.S. 214; 65 S.Ct. 193; 89 L.Ed. 194

Year of Decision: 1944

KEY ISSUES

Can the dangers of war justify excluding people from their homes during wartime on the basis of race?

HISTORY OF THE CASE

On December 7, 1941, Japan bombed Pearl Harbor, which caused the United States to enter World War II. On February 19, 1942, President Franklin Roosevelt issued Executive Order No. 9066, designed to prevent espionage and sabotage aimed at American defense installations. The executive order provided that military commanders might, in their discretion, "prescribe military areas" and define their extent, "from which any or all persons may be excluded, and with respect to which the right of any person to enter, remain in, or leave shall be subject to whatever restrictions" the "Military Commander may impose in his discretion."

Lt. Gen. John DeWitt was designated as the military commander of the Western Defense Command on February 20, 1942. In his capacity as military commander, Lieutenant General DeWitt issued a series of public proclamations. Public Proclamation No. 1, issued on March 2, 1942, stated that the entire Pacific Coast was "particularly subject to attack, to attempted invasion . . . and, in connection therewith, is subject to espionage and acts of sabotage." Proclamations that followed included establishment of Military Areas Nos. 1 and 2, which encompassed all of California, Washington, Oregon, Idaho, Montana, Nevada, Utah, and part of Arizona.

Later that month, on March 18, President Roosevelt issued Executive Order No. 9102, establishing the War Relocation Authority. On March 21, 1942, Congress passed a law making it a misdemeanor for anyone to "enter, remain in, leave, or commit any act in any military area or military zone proscribed . . . by any military commander . . . contrary to the restrictions applicable to any such area." On March 24, Lieutenant General DeWitt instituted a curfew in the military areas. Three days later, the general proclaimed that it was necessary "to provide for the welfare and to insure the orderly evacuation and resettlement of Japanese." A March 29 order prohibited "all alien Japanese and persons of Japanese ancestry" from leaving Military Area No. 1 until otherwise directed. General DeWitt directed otherwise on May 3, excluding those of Japanese ancestry from part of Military Area No. 1.

Fred Korematsu was an American citizen of Japanese ancestry. He had lived in Alameda County, California, his entire life. Soon after the Japanese bombed Pearl Harbor, Mr. Korematsu volunteered for military service, but was rejected for health reasons. When the relocation orders were issued, Mr. Korematsu chose not to leave his home. On June 12, he was arrested, then tried and convicted for violating the exclusion order. A federal court sentenced him to five years imprisonment, but immediately paroled him. Mr. Korematsu was taken to an assembly center, and then to an internment camp in Topaz, Utah.

Mr. Korematsu appealed his conviction. He argued that the exclusion order violated his constitutional rights by discriminating against him and other Japanese Americans on the basis of their race. He argued that while the courts, in an earlier case, had upheld the constitutionality of a curfew order imposed only on Japanese Americans, excluding citizens from their homes was a much more drastic measure that could not be justified on the same grounds as a mere curfew. Additionally, he urged the Court to consider the entire military program directed at Japanese Americans, because as a practical matter, the program as a whole planned for the relocation of all Japanese Americans to concentration camps.

The U.S. government argued that Mr. Korematsu had been convicted only for remaining in the area contrary to the exclusion order, and that the Court therefore should not consider any other aspects of the military's program. Additionally, the United States argued that the exclusion order was justified because of the potential of an imminent Japanese invasion and the inability of the government to separate loyal Japanese Americans from potential saboteurs. The Ninth Circuit Court of Appeals rejected Mr. Korematsu's arguments and affirmed his conviction. Mr. Korematsu sought relief from the U.S. Supreme Court.

DECISION

The Supreme Court, in an opinion written by Justice Hugo L. Black, upheld the constitutionality of the exclusion order "[i]n the light of the principles . . . announced in the *Hirabayashi* case," 323 U.S. at 217, in which the Court had upheld the constitutionality of a curfew order imposed on Japanese Americans. The Court rejected Mr. Korematsu's argument that the rationale of *Hirabayashi* did not apply because to exclude a person from one's home was a much greater deprivation of liberty than a simple curfew:

> True, exclusion from the area in which one's home is located is a far greater deprivation than constant confinement to the home from 8 p.m. to 6 a.m. Nothing short of apprehension by the proper military authorities of the gravest imminent danger to the public safety can constitutionally justify either. But exclusion from a threatened

area, no less than curfew, has a definite and close relationship to the prevention of espionage and sabotage.

The perceived possibility of a Japanese invasion of the West Coast was enough for the Court's majority to justify ordering American citizens to abandon their homes and surrender to military authorities.

Similarly, the Court believed that Japanese Americans alone could be singled out as a group by the exclusion order: "Like curfew, exclusion of those of Japanese origin was deemed necessary because of the presence of an unascertained number of disloyal members of the group, most of whom we have no doubt were loyal to this country." Unfortunately for Fred Korematsu and the other American citizens of Japanese descent, the "war-making branches of the Government" believed that what disloyal Japanese Americans there were "could not readily be isolated and separately dealt with." Justice Black and his fellow justices in the majority refused to question this belief.

The Court also refused to consider the exclusion order together with the order that Japanese Americans were to report to assembly or relocation centers, and then be sent to internment camps. To do so "would be to go beyond the issues raised." The Court claimed that they could not "say either as a matter of fact or law that his presence in that center would have resulted in his detention in a relocation center." This was a separate issue that the Court deemed to be beyond the scope of Mr. Korematsu's conviction.

Justice Black ended his opinion defensively, responding to attacks by the dissenting justices. On behalf of the Court's majority, he claimed that this was "military urgency," and "[t]o cast this case into outlines of racial prejudice, without reference to the real military dangers which were presented, merely confuses the issue." The Court also was unhappy with the dissenting justices' charges as to the nature of the assembly and relocation centers: "We deem it unjustifiable to call them concentration camps with all the ugly connotations that term implies."

Justice Felix Frankfurter concurred, emphasizing the military nature of the exclusion order. He added "the war power of the Government is 'the power to wage war successfully.'" That action

is not to be stigmatized as lawless because like action in times of peace would be lawless." Justice Frankfurter ended by noting that "[t]o find that the Constitution does not forbid the military measure now complained of does not carry with it approval of that which Congress and the Executive did. This is their business, not ours."

Three Supreme Court justices spoke out against forced removal of groups of American citizens from their homes. The first of these, Justice Owen J. Roberts, did not mince words:

> This is not a case of keeping people off the streets at night as was *Kiyoshi Hirabayashi v. United States,* . . . nor a case of temporary exclusion of a citizen from an area for his own safety or that of the community, nor a case of offering him an opportunity to go temporarily out of an area where his presence might cause danger to himself or to his fellows. On the contrary, it is the case of convicting a citizen as a punishment for not submitting to imprisonment in a concentration camp, based on his ancestry, and solely because of his ancestry, without evidence or inquiry concerning his loyalty and good disposition towards the United States. If this be a correct statement of the facts disclosed by this record, and facts of which we take judicial notice, I need hardly labor the conclusion that Constitutional rights have been violated.

Justice Roberts expressed similar contempt for the Court's refusal to confront the conflicting orders to which Mr. Korematsu was subjected:

> The two conflicting orders, one which commanded him to stay and the other which commanded him to go, were nothing but a cleverly devised trap to accomplish the real purpose of the military authority, which was to lock him up in a concentration camp. . . . Why should we set up a figmentary and artificial situation instead of addressing ourselves to the actualities of the case?

The second dissenter, Justice Frank Murphy, agreed with the Court's majority that the test for determining the constitutionality of military action was "whether the deprivation is reasonably related to a public danger that is so 'immediate, imminent, and impending' as not to admit of delay and not to permit the intervention of ordinary constitutional processes to alleviate the danger." Justice Murphy did not believe, however, that the threat posed by Japanese Americans was sufficient to support "one of the most sweeping and complete deprivations of constitutional rights in the history of this nation in the absence of martial law." Justice Murphy recognized the need to allow the military to protect the country in time of war: "[W]e must not erect too high or too meticulous standards; it is necessary only that the action have some reasonable relation to the removal of the dangers of invasion, sabotage and espionage." The exclusion, however, was inherently not reasonably related to national security demands. "[T]hat relation is lacking because the exclusion order necessarily must rely for its reasonableness upon the assumption that *all* persons of Japanese ancestry may have dangerous tendency to commit sabotage and espionage and to aid our Japanese enemy in other ways. It is difficult to believe that reason, logic or experience could be marshalled in support of such an assumption."

Justice Murphy thought that the exclusion order was based not on military dangers but on racial prejudices. He cited as evidence of this language used by General DeWitt in reports on the exclusion. For example, General DeWitt had referred to Japanese Americans as "'an enemy race' whose 'racial strains are undiluted.'" Justice Murphy thus viewed the general's supposed rationale "to be largely an accumulation of much of the misinformation, half-truths and insinuations that for years have been directed against Japanese Americans by people with racial and economic prejudices." Murphy concluded bluntly: "I dissent, therefore, from this legalization of racism. Racial discrimination in any form and in any degree has no justifiable part whatever in our democratic way of life."

The third dissenter, Justice Robert H. Jackson, argued that the military order of General DeWitt "ha[d] no place under the Constitution." However, while the exclusion order should not be required to "conform to conventional tests of constitutionality," neither should courts of law be required to enforce military expedients.

Justice Jackson began by focusing on the crime for which Mr. Korematsu was convicted and its tension with the U.S. Constitution. Mr. Korematsu was convicted of "being present in the state whereof he is a citizen, near the place where he was born, and where all his life he has lived." Jackson emphasized the arbitrary nature of the exclusion order's application: "[H]ere is an attempt to make an otherwise innocent act a crime merely because this prisoner is the son of parents as to whom he had no choice, and belongs to a race from which there is no way to resign." He noted that the order was contrary to the important constitutional principle that guilt is personal and not inheritable because Mr. Korematsu's act was made criminal based on the status of his parents.

Jackson, too, recognized that it was more important that military operations "be successful, rather than legal." Wartime measures cannot be made to fit peacetime notions of constitutionality: "Defense measures will not, and often should not, be held within the limits that bind civil authority in peace." Still, Justice Jackson would not "distort the Constitution to approve all that the military may deem expedient." He felt that the judiciary had no way by which to judge the constitutionality of the exclusion order:

> How does the Court know that these orders have a reasonable basis in necessity? No evidence whatsoever on that subject has been taken by this or any other court. . . . So the Court, having no real evidence before it, has no choice but to accept General DeWitt's own unsworn, self-serving statement, untested by any cross-examination, that what he did was reasonable. And thus it will always be when courts try to look into the reasonableness of a military order.

In Justice Jackson's eyes, courts, with their rules of evidence and procedure, were ill equipped to review military decisions such as the exclusion order. Additionally, purporting to test the constitutionality of a military order could potentially be more harmful than the order itself:

> [O]nce a judicial opinion rationalizes such an order to show that it conforms to the

Constitution, or rather rationalizes the Constitution to show that the Constitution sanctions such an order, the Court for all time has validated the principle of racial discrimination in criminal procedure and of transplanting American citizens.

Thus, while Justice Jackson conceded that the military might reasonably execute an exclusion order, the courts could not be asked to enforce a military order that was unconstitutional: "The courts can exercise only the judicial power, can apply only law, and must abide by the Constitution, or they cease to be civil courts and become instruments of military policy." Because the exclusion order "ha[d] no place in law under the Constitution," Justice Jackson would have reversed Mr. Korematsu's conviction and ordered him released.

AFTERMATH

Fred Korematsu had to wait 40 years for justice. In January 1983, his case was reopened in federal district court in San Francisco. His conviction was overturned that November. In 1988, Congress passed legislation to help all victims of the internment program. Those interned were to be paid $20,000 each. *See Restitution for World War II Internment of Japanese-Americans and Aleuts,* PL 100–383, August 10, 1988, 50 U.S.C. App. 1989b–4.

SIGNIFICANCE

Ironically, *Korematsu v. United States* was the first case in which the Supreme Court used the "strict scrutiny" test to review a law that classified people on the basis of race. Since *Korematsu*, "strict scrutiny" review has afforded racial minorities significantly more protection than it did Fred Korematsu in 1944.

RELATED CASES

Ex parte Endo, 323 U.S. 283 (1944)

Hirabayashi v. United States, 320 U.S. 81 (1943)

Yasui v. United States, 320 U.S. 115 (1943)

RECOMMENDED READING

Daniels, Roger. *Concentration Camps USA: Japanese Americans and World War II.* New York: Holt, Rinehart, 1971.

Grodzins, Morton. *Americans Betrayed: Politics and the Japanese Evacuation.* Chicago: University of Chicago Press, 1949.

Irons, Peter., ed. *Justice Delayed: The Record of the Japanese American Internment Cases.* New York: Oxford University Press, 1989.

Tateishi, John. *And Justice for All: An Oral History of the Japanese American Detention Camps.* New York: Random House, 1984.

Case Title: *Kramer v. Union Free School District*

Legal Citations: 395 U.S. 621; 89 S.Ct. 1886; 23 L.Ed. 2d 583

Year of Decision: 1969

KEY ISSUES

The New York state legislature passed a law that limited the right to vote in school board elections to the parents of school-age children or to persons who owned or leased real property. The question before the Court was whether a state law that limits the right to vote in school board elections should be subjected to "strict scrutiny" analysis.

HISTORY OF THE CASE

In 1965, Morris Kramer had no children and did not own or lease any real property. He attempted to register to vote in a local school district election. His application was rejected for the above reasons, even though he was a U.S. citizen and registered to vote in New York state and federal elections. Kramer filed a class action suit in the U.S. district court. This court, after some procedural wrangling and an appeal to the court of appeals, dismissed his complaint. Kramer appealed directly to the Supreme Court, which accepted his case.

SUMMARY OF ARGUMENTS

The state of New York argued for the Union Free School District. The state claimed that it had the right to limit "franchise" to those primarily interested in school district elections. *Franchise* means any constitutional or statutory right or privilege; here, it involves the right to vote. The state claimed that because Kramer had no children and paid no real property taxes (monies that partly fund state schools), the often complex school system operations had little, if any, relevance to him. It argued that the law was "rationally related" to the state's legitimate goal of streamlining the electoral process by involving only those "directly affected" by school system matters.

Kramer asserted that by excluding him from participating in the district elections, the state denied him equal protection of the laws. He claimed that all members of the community have an interest in the quality of public education and that decisions taken by local school boards affect the entire population. He also pointed out that property taxes affect everyone through their impact on the prices of goods and services in the community. Because voting is such a fundamental right in our country, he argued that strict scrutiny should be given the statute.

DECISION

The Court struck down the New York law as unconstitutional. Chief Justice Warren wrote the Court's 5-3 majority opinion. The majority used strict scrutiny analysis to determine that the state law violates the equal protection clause of the Fourteenth Amendment.

The Court determined that the rational basis standard should not be used when reviewing statutes that deny some residents the right to vote. The general presumption of constitutionality afforded this type of state law and the traditional approval courts give them is not applicable in this situation.

Instead, strict scrutiny must be used when any fundamental right may be infringed by a law or regulation. The test requires the state to establish that it has a compelling interest justifying the law. Distinctions created by the law must be essential to further some governmental purpose, and the law must be "narrowly tailored" to meet the state's objective. Chief Justice Warren justified this careful examination, instead of a lesser standard, because the right to vote is a foundation of our representative society.

Using strict scrutiny, the Court did not address the compelling-interest question. It sidestepped the issue of whether a state could limit the franchise to those "primarily interested" or "primarily affected" by these school district elections. Instead, the Court said the distinctions drawn by the law did not meet the exacting precision required of statutes. The Court announced that the restrictions imposed by the law did not select for "interest" with sufficient precision to meet the strict standard of review that the Court concluded should apply when the right to vote is denied. The Supreme Court reversed the judgment of the district court and found the law unconstitutional.

AFTERMATH

In this and other similar cases, the Warren Court established the strict scrutiny standard as the correct test of legislation denying the right to vote. It used the equal protection clause to invalidate these denials of the right to vote. When the Court invokes this test, it virtually always condemns the classification.

SIGNIFICANCE

As odd as it may seem, the right to vote has no direct textual support in the Constitution. True, the Fifteenth Amendment forbids denying the right on the basis of race, and the Nineteenth Amendment forbids denial on the basis of sex; however, the Constitution itself grants no positive right to vote in general. The Supreme Court nevertheless interprets the Constitution to grant the right, using the equal protection clause as the vehicle for creation and ultimate subsidy of that particular right.

RELATED CASES

Ball v. James, 451 U.S. 355, 101 S.Ct., 68 L.Ed. 2d 150 (1981)

Cipriano v. City of Houman, 395 U.S. 701, 89 S.Ct. 1897, 23 L.Ed. 2d 647 (1969)

Hill v. Stone, 421 U.S. 289, 95 S.Ct. 1637, 44 L.Ed. 2d 172 (1975)

McDonald v. Board of Election Commissioners, 394 U.S. 802, 89 S.Ct. 1404, 22 L.Ed. 2d 739 (1969)

Phoenix v. Kolodziejski, 399 U.S. 204, 90 S.Ct. 1990, 26 L.Ed. 2d 523 (1970)

RECOMMENDED READING

The Supreme Court, 1968 Term, 83 Harvard Law Review 77 (1969).

Case Title: *Lane v. Wilson*

Legal Citations: 307 U.S. 268; 59 S.Ct. 872; 83 L.Ed 1281

Year of Decision: 1939

KEY ISSUES

Does a voting rights statute that makes registration contingent on voting in 1914 or registering within a two-week period violate the Fifteenth Amendment by denying qualified citizens the right to vote?

HISTORY OF THE CASE

This case came to the Supreme Court after the Tenth Circuit Court of Appeals affirmed the holding for the state of Oklahoma. Lane, a black citizen, brought the action claiming discriminatory treatment by a voting provision. The provision made registration a prerequisite to voting, but stated that those who had voted in the 1914 election would be exempt from the requirement. All citizens qualified to vote in 1916 who did not register during a two-week period were disenfranchised (deprived of the right to vote).

SUMMARY OF ARGUMENTS

Lane argued that the Oklahoma statute violated his constitutional right to vote.

The county election officials, which included Wilson, argued that the Oklahoma statute was constitutional and that the proper forum for Lane's complaint was the Oklahoma state court system. The election officials also argued that Lane's assumption of the statute's invalidity meant there was no statute under which he could register and, therefore, no denial of any right existed.

DECISION

Justice Frankfurter delivered the opinion of the Court. He held that the Oklahoma registration system that prevented blacks from registering was unconstitutional because it effectively denied black citizens the right to vote, a right guaranteed by the Fifteenth Amendment against all state attempts to deny it: "The Amendment nullifies sophisticated as well as simple-minded modes of discrimination." The Oklahoma statute gave black citizens too short a time to register to vote, making the law too confined to comply with the Fifteenth Amendment. The Court also found the "grandfather clause" of the 1914 election discriminatory because it covered mainly white voters. The amendment "secures freedom from discrimination on account of race in matters affecting the franchise."

AFTERMATH

Racial discrimination and political ambivalence were prevalent before the passage of the Fifteenth Amendment, and only grew stronger. Each state statute that was found unconstitutional came back to the courts more invidiously. This resulted in little progress for black citizens in voting rights.

SIGNIFICANCE

The use of litigation to eliminate voting discrimination was not effective. The judiciary was unable to enforce the Fifteenth Amendment right to vote. For more than 75 years, there was no effective statutory protection. Not until the passage of the Voting Rights Act in 1965 did Congress finally do what the courts were unable to do.

RELATED CASES

Guinn v. United States, 238 U.S. 347 (1915)

Nixon v. Herndon, 273 U.S. 536 (1927)

Smith v. Allbright, 321 U.S. 649 (1944)

RECOMMENDED READING

Scott Gluck, *Congressional Reaction to Judicial Construction of Section 5 of the Voting Rights Act of 1965,* 29 Columbia Journal of Law and Social Problems 337 (1996).

Eric Schnapper, *Perpetuation of Past Discrimination,* 96 Harvard Law Review 828 (1983).

Case Title: *Lau v. Nichols*

Legal Citation: 414 U.S. 563

Year of Decision: 1974

◆∼

KEY ISSUES

Does the failure of a school system to provide English language instruction to approximately 1,800 students of Chinese ancestry who do not speak English violate the equal protection clause of the Fourteenth Amendment or section 601 of the Civil Rights Act of 1964?

HISTORY OF THE CASE

Non-English-speaking Chinese students brought a class action against officials of the San Francisco Unified School District because the school district did not teach English to all Chinese-speaking students. The petitioners did not seek any specific relief. Both the district court and the court of appeals denied relief, holding that there was no violation of the equal protection clause of the Fourteenth Amendment or of section 601 of the Civil Rights Act of 1964. The Supreme Court agreed to hear the case because of the public importance of the question presented.

SUMMARY OF ARGUMENTS

Lau argued that the exclusionary policy that denied teaching English to the Chinese-speaking students and the failure to provide for alternate instructional procedures was an outright denial of equal protection as guaranteed by the Fourteenth Amendment as well as a violation of section 601 of the Civil Rights Act of 1964, which bans discrimination based on race, color, or national origin in any program or activity receiving federal financial assistance.

The school district argued that under the California Educational Code it could determine when and under what circumstances instruction was to be given bilingually. Since not all Chinese-speaking students were denied the opportunity for bilingual instruction, the school system held that it was not denying equal protection to those students based on their race, color, or national origin.

DECISION

Justice Douglas delivered the unanimous opinion of the Court that the denial of bilingual teaching to the 1,800 students was a violation of section 601 of the Civil Rights Act of 1964. He did not feel the need to address the issue of the equal protection argument. The statute governed the issue because the school district involved in the litigation received large amounts of federal financial assistance. The Court held that the Chinese-speaking minority received fewer benefits from the school system that denied them a meaningful opportunity to participate in the educational program of the state than the English-speaking majority. Quoting President John F. Kennedy's address to Congress on June 19, 1963, the Court concluded that simple justice requires that public funds, to which all taxpayers of all races contribute, should not be spent in any way that would encourage, entrench, subsidize, or result in racial discrimination.

Justice Blackmun stressed in a concurring opinion, joined by Chief Justice Burger, that the opinion of the Court should not be taken too broadly, as it relates to a large number of children and not merely one or two or even a small group. He did not regard the decision as conclusive on the issue of whether school districts would be required to provide special instruction to minority students. To him, numbers were at the heart of the case.

AFTERMATH

Following the *Lau* decision, the Department of Health, Education and Welfare appointed a task force consisting primarily of professional educators to advise the department on implementing the decision throughout the country. A system of guidelines was developed that came to be known as the "Lau Remedies." These remedies required instruction in students' native language where it was practical to do so. Although there were no uniform standards for school districts to follow, the Department of Health, Education and Welfare had begun to treat the remedies as regulations. Between 1975 and 1980 nearly 500 compliance agreements were negotiated in deficient school districts. The Reagan administration withdrew a proposal to formalize the *Lau* Remedies.

SIGNIFICANCE

Since *Lau,* a number of lower courts have enforced the *Lau* Remedies and have found the requirements of the task force to be essential components of educational programs providing meaningful access to education for non-English-speaking children.

RELATED CASES

Cintron v. Brentwood Union Free School District, 455 F. Supp. 57 (E.D.N.Y. 1978)

Guadalupe Organization, Inc. v. Tempe Elementary School District, 587 F. 2d 1022 (9th Cir. 1978)

Otero v. Mesa County School District Number 51, 568 F. 2d 1312 (10th Cir. 1977)

Rios v. Read, 480 F. Supp. 14 (E.D.N.Y. 1978)

RECOMMENDED READING

Jonathan D. Haft, *Assuring Equal Educational Opportunities for Language Minority Students: Bilingual Education and the Equal Educational Opportunity Act of 1974,* 18 Columbia Journal of Law and Social Problems 209 (1983).

Betsy Levin, *An Analysis of the Federal Attempt to Regulate Bilingual Education: Protecting Civil Rights or Controlling Curriculum?,* 12 Journal of Law and Education 29 (1983).

Case Title: *Loving v. Virginia*

Legal Citations: 388 U.S. 1; 87 S.Ct. 1817; 18 L.Ed. 2d 1010

Year of Decision: 1967

KEY ISSUES

The essential issue in this case was whether a state antimiscegenation statute, that is, one that prohibited marriage between persons of different races, violated the equal protection clause of the Fourteenth Amendment.

HISTORY OF THE CASE

In 1967, 16 states had laws prohibiting interracial marriage: Alabama, Arkansas, Delaware, Florida, Georgia, Kentucky, Louisiana, Mississippi, Missouri, North Carolina, Oklahoma, South Carolina, Tennessee, Texas, Virginia, and West Virginia. Section 20-54 of the Virginia Code prohibited white people from marrying "colored" persons. Section 20-57 declared interracial marriages void. Section 20-58 prohibited interracial couples from leaving the state to marry and then return to the state to cohabit as spouses. Section 20-59 declared violations of the previous sections as felonies punishable by one to five years in prison.

In 1958, Richard Loving, a white man, married Mildred Jeter, a black woman, in Washington, D.C. After the couple moved to Virginia, a grand jury indicted the Lovings for violating Virginia's ban on interracial marriages. The Lovings pleaded guilty of violating Section 20-58 of the Virginia Code. The trial judge suspended a one-year jail sentence for a 25-year period upon the condition that the Lovings leave the state and not return together for 25 years. The Lovings moved to Washington, D.C. In 1963, the Lovings moved for the state trial court to vacate the judgment and set aside the sentence on the grounds that it violated the Fourteenth Amendment to the U.S. Constitution. The trial judge denied the motion, and the Lovings appealed. The Supreme Court of Appeals of Virginia upheld the convictions.

SUMMARY OF ARGUMENTS

The Lovings argued that the Virginia statute violated the equal protection and due process clauses of the Fourteenth Amendment.

Virginia argued that equal protection merely demands that penal laws be applied equally to members of different races. Moreover, Virginia argued that the antimiscegenation statutes were applied equally among the races and were therefore not racially discriminatory.

DECISION

The Supreme Court rejected Virginia's argument, finding that "equal application" of a penal statute composed of racial classifications does not necessarily remove that statute from the Fourteenth Amendment's prohibition of invidious racial discrimination, discrimination unrelated to a legitimate purpose. Consequently, the Court employed a strict scrutiny analysis of the antimiscegenation statutes. Finding no legitimate state purpose that could justify the racial classifications, the Court declared Virginia's antimiscegenation statutes in violation of the equal protection clause of the Fourteenth Amendment.

AFTERMATH

After initiation of the litigation, Maryland repealed its prohibition against interracial marriage.

The Court's decision in *Loving* had the effect of invalidating other states' similar miscegenation statutes. Unfortunately, only eight years after the Court's decision, Richard Loving died.

SIGNIFICANCE

As the Court aptly stated, "[t]here can be no doubt that restricting the freedom to marry solely because of racial classifications violates the central meaning of [equal protection]."

RELATED CASES

Maynard v. Hill, 125 U.S. 190 (1888)

Skinner v. Oklahoma, 316 U.S. 535 (1942)

Zablocki v. Redhail, 434 U.S. 374 (1978)

RECOMMENDED READING

Robert A. Pratt, *Crossing the Color Line: A Historical Assessment and Personal Narrative of* Loving v. Virginia, 41 Howard Law Journal 229 (1998).

W. Wadlington, *The Loving Case: Virginia's Anti-Miscegenation Statute in Historical Perspective*, 52 Virginia Law Review 1189 (1966).

Lynn D. Wardle, Loving v. Virginia *and the Constitutional Right to Marry, 1790–1990*, 41 Howard Law Journal 289 (1998).

Case Title: *Michael M. v. Superior Court of Sonoma County*

Legal Citations: 450 U.S. 464; 101 S.Ct. 1200; 67 L.Ed. 2d 437

Year of Decision: 1981

KEY ISSUES

Does California's statutory rape law violate the equal protection clause of the Fourteenth Amendment?

HISTORY OF THE CASE

A complaint filed in the summer of 1978 in the municipal court of Sonoma County, California, alleged that a 17-year-old male had unlawful sexual intercourse with a female under the age of 18. Unlawful sexual intercourse defined under California law is "an act of sexual intercourse accomplished with a female not the wife of the perpetrator, where the female is under the age of 18." The trial court and the California court of appeals denied the request for relief and the California Supreme Court reviewed the case.

The California Supreme Court held the law to be discriminatory on the basis of sex because only females may be victims and only males may violate this law. The court further stated that the state had a compelling interest in preventing pregnancies that resulted from rape. The gender classification was necessary to identify the offender and victim. The U.S. Supreme Court agreed to hear the case.

SUMMARY OF ARGUMENTS

The petitioner argued that the California law discriminated on the basis of gender in violation of the equal protection clause of the Constitution because only men were held criminally liable under the statute. Petitioner also argued that the California statute was both over- and underinclusive and that a gender neutral statute would have served the state's goals equally as well.

California argued that the statute was justified because it sought to prevent illegitimate teenage pregnancies and the statute did not violate the equal protection clause of the Fourteenth Amendment. California also argued that a gender neutral statute would hinder effective enforcement of the statute.

DECISION

Justice Rehnquist delivered the opinion of the Court affirming the California Supreme Court's decision. The California statutory rape law, in which only the male participant in the sexual act is criminally liable, was upheld because it is designed to prevent illegitimate adolescent pregnancies. The statute does not violate the equal protection clause. Gender-based classifications are not inherently suspect so as to compel "strict scrutiny" but they must further the state interest.

Because all significant consequences of teenage pregnancy fall on the female, the legislature is within its rights to punish the male who suffers few consequences of his conduct. For the female also to be criminally liable would frustrate the state's interest because she would be less likely to report the rape if she would be subject to criminal prosecution. This statute protects women from sexual intercourse at a young age when the consequences are more severe. The statute is an additional deterrent for men.

Justice Brennan dissented, saying that the Court put too much emphasis on the prevention of teenage pregnancy and not enough on whether the sex-based discrimination is related to the achievement of that goal. He argued that California had not met the burden of proving there were fewer teenage pregnancies under the gender-based rape law than there would be if the law were gender neutral. California must show that it deters females more effectively than males from having sexual intercourse.

AFTERMATH

The holding reflects the "traditional attitudes toward male-female relationships by making males more guilty."

SIGNIFICANCE

This case illustrated the intermediate scrutiny the Court uses to review cases of gender discrimination. Here, the state's interest in preventing unwanted teenage pregnancy outweighed the interests of male defendants to be treated equally under the law.

RELATED CASES

Califano v. Webster, 430 U.S. 313 (1977)

Craig v. Boren, 429 U.S. 190 (1976)

Reed v. Reed, 404 U.S. 71 (1971)

RECOMMENDED READING

Kirp, Donald L. *Gender Justice.* Chicago: University of Chicago Press, 1986.

Leslie Landau, *Gender Based Statutory Rape Law Does Not Violate the Equal Protection Clause,* 67 Cornell Law Review 1109 (1982).

Frances Olsen, *Statutory Rape: A Feminist Critique of Rights Analysis,* 63 Texas Law Review 387 (1982).

Case Title: *Milliken v. Bradley*

Legal Citations: 418 U.S. 717; 94 S.Ct. 3112; 41 L.Ed. 2d 1069

Year of Decision: 1974

KEY ISSUES

Does the district court have the power to fashion a remedy encompassing both a segregated urban school district and independent suburban school districts?

HISTORY OF THE CASE

In BROWN V. BOARD OF EDUCATION (1954), the Court held racial segregation in public schools unconstitutional, but in the early 1970s, the Supreme Court began to permit racial school assignments. These resulted in racial quotas (SWANN V. CHARLOTTE-MECKLENBURG BOARD OF EDUCATION [1971]). Quotas did not improve education. More recent cases have encouraged a color-blind interpretation of the Constitution.

A federal district court in 1971 held that the Detroit Board of Education maintained a racially segregated system. The findings showed that meaningful desegregation was impossible within the predominantly black Detroit school system, so the district court devised a new remedy. It ordered Detroit and surrounding suburbs to become one school district, and ordered racial busing with the goal of eliminating the predominantly black schools.

SUMMARY OF ARGUMENTS

William G. Milliken, governor of the state of Michigan, argued that the decision of the court of appeals finding de jure segregation was without basis in fact or law and the decision of the court of appeals that a Detroit-only desegregation plan was insufficient to remedy segregation was clearly erroneous.

Bradley argued that an interdistrict desegregation plan was proper and no constitutionally guaranteed rights of the suburban school districts had been violated.

DECISION

Chief Justice Burger, who wrote for the majority, decided that federal district courts have limited power to impose interdistrict desegregation orders, and that this issue belonged to the local school boards. Justice Burger worried about the district court's intervention into local affairs and the massive impact of its remedy. Although the district court had not found evidence of a violation in the suburban schools, its remedy included not only Detroit but 53 suburban school districts. The Court rejected the busing plan because there was no interdistrict violation. It went on to affirm the historical importance of local control over public schools. Limits for school busing were set for the first time.

Justice Douglas, in dissent, felt that the district court plan should be affirmed; in that manner there would be no violation of the equal protection clause even if the schools were segregated and black schools were not only "separate but inferior." He thought that state actions such as choosing sites for building schools had brought about black schools and white schools, and that the majority was recommending a return to local control of school systems.

AFTERMATH

This case represented a defeat for busing in Detroit. School systems remained separate and unequal.

SIGNIFICANCE

Interdistrict remedies for segregation will not be allowed if intentional segregation only exists in one district.

RELATED CASES

Brown v. Board of Education, 347 U.S. 483 (1954)

Green v. School Board of New Kent County, 391 U.S. 432 (1968)

Swann v. Charlotte-Mecklenburg Board of Education, 402 U.S. 1 (1971)

RECOMMENDED READING

Paul Gewirtz, *Remedies and Resistance,* 92 Yale Law Journal 585 (1983).

Graglia, Lino A. *Disaster by Decree.* Ithaca, N.Y.: Cornell University Press, 1976.

Case Title: *Mississippi University for Women v. Hogan*

Legal Citations: 458 U.S. 718; 102 S.Ct. 3331; 73 L.Ed. 2d 1090

Year of Decision: 1982

KEY ISSUES

Does a state university's provision that reserves certain educational opportunities solely for women violate the equal protection clause of the Fourteenth Amendment?

HISTORY OF THE CASE

In 1884 the Mississippi University for Women was founded by the state legislature as the Mississippi Industrial Institute. From its beginnings, its enrollment was limited to women. In 1971 a School of Nursing was established, offering a two-year degree. Three years later the school offered a baccalaureate program in nursing. Joe Hogan, a registered nurse, applied for admission in 1979. Although otherwise qualified, he was denied admission solely because of his sex. He filed an action in the U.S. District Court for the Northern District of Mississippi based on the single-sex admission of the school. He sought injunctive and declaratory relief and compensatory damages. Injunctive relief orders someone to reverse an injury inflicted and declaratory relief gives a determination of the rights and status of the parties.

The district court denied the injunctive relief, saying that the same-sex policy bears a rational relationship to the state's legitimate interest in giving women an education and affording them unique benefits. The court entered summary judgment, a decision that determines a question of law and disposes of an action without a trial. The Court of Appeals for the Fifth Circuit reversed. It stated that the district court used the wrong test, and that the proper test was the state interest in providing an education for all its citizens. The state failed to show that providing a unique educational opportunity for females but not for males bears an important relationship to that interest. The Supreme Court agreed to hear the case.

SUMMARY OF ARGUMENTS

Hogan argued that the single-sex admissions policy violated his Fourteenth Amendment right to equal protection. He noted that the opportunity to study at other state-supported institutions was not equivocally the same, since he would have to give up his job to attend those schools.

Mississippi argued that the single-sex admissions policy was justified as a remedial program for prior discrimination against women in educational opportunities.

DECISION

Justice O'Connor delivered the opinion of the Court, which held that the state's policy of excluding males from the Mississippi University of Women School of Nursing violated the equal protection clause. She noted that the party seeking to uphold a statute that classifies the individual on the basis of gender has the burden of showing "exceedingly persuasive justification" for the classification. This burden is met when the classification serves "important governmental objectives and the discrimination means employed are substantially related to the achievement of those objectives."

Single-sex admission cannot be upheld on the grounds that it compensates for discrimination against women. Rather than compensating for discrimination, the school's policy tends to perpetuate a stereotype view that nursing is a woman's job. This case is inconsistent with the claim that excluding men from the School of Nursing is necessary to educational goals.

Chief Justice Burger dissented to emphasize that this finding is limited to a professional nursing school.

AFTERMATH

The case brought about intermediate scrutiny as a standard of review for gender-based classifications, a lesser standard than strict scrutiny and a higher standard than the rational basis test. Care is necessary in ascertaining whether a statute reflects stereotyped images. The Virginia Military Institute and the Citadel resisted desegregation of their all-male facilities; however, the Court's deci-

sion in *United States v. Virginia* (1996) forced the schools to admit women upon the Court's order.

SIGNIFICANCE

Prior to *Mississippi University,* the Court's focus regarding the equal protection clause had been on racial inequality. *Mississippi University* expanded the Court's focus regarding the equal protection clause to include gender. This was the Court's first ruling on education segregated by sex.

RELATED CASES

Frontiero v. Richardson, 411 U.S. 677 (1973)

Kirchberg v. Feenstra, 450 U.S. 455 (1981)

Reed v. Reed, 404 U.S. 71 (1971)

RECOMMENDED READING

Keynes, Edward, with Randall Miller. *The Court versus Congress: Prayer, Busing and Abortion.* Durham, N.C.: Duke University Press, 1989.

Kirp, Donald L. *Gender Justice.* Chicago: University of Chicago Press, 1986.

Mary Ellen Shull, *Reinforcement of Middle Level Review Regarding Gender Classification,* 11 Pepperdine Law Review 421 (1984).

Case Title: *Missouri ex rel. Gaines v. Canada*

Legal Citations: 305 U.S. 337; 59 S.Ct. 232; 83 L.Ed. 208

Year of Decision: 1938

KEY ISSUES

Does a state deny equal protection, in violation of the Fourteenth Amendment, when it requires a black citizen to pursue a legal education in another state, with any necessary funding provided by the home state, because no program within the state will admit black students?

HISTORY OF THE CASE

Lloyd Gaines, a citizen of Missouri, applied to attend the School of Law of the University of Missouri and was refused admission because he was black. Gaines had graduated in 1935 from Lincoln University, Missouri's state-sponsored school for the higher education of blacks. Upon rejection for admission at the University of Missouri, Gaines was directed to a state statute that allowed him to apply for aid from the state superintendent of schools so that he could attend a law school in an adjacent state.

Instead of applying to attend a law school in an adjacent state, Gaines brought an action to compel the curators of the University of Missouri to admit him. The circuit court ruled against him. The Missouri Supreme Court affirmed the circuit court's decision. Gaines then appealed to the U.S. Supreme Court.

SUMMARY OF ARGUMENTS

Gaines argued that forced attendance at a law school in an adjacent state denied him the equal protection privileges of a Missouri citizen who intends to practice law within the state. Gaines specifically noted the privileges of opportunities for the particular study of Missouri law, for the observation of the local courts, and for the prestige of the Missouri law school among the citizens of the state.

The state first argued that a separate state statute gave the curators of Lincoln University the power to organize a law school that would provide a substantially equal opportunity for African Americans as the University of Missouri gave to students of other races. The state also argued that Gaines's action was unwarranted because, pending the establishment of such a school, the provision for the education of African Americans at schools in adjacent states, with Missouri funding, was sufficient to provide a substantially equal educational opportunity.

DECISION

Chief Justice Hughes wrote the opinion for the Court in which Justices Brandeis, Stone, Roberts, Cardozo, Black, and Reed joined. The Court held that Missouri was itself to provide for the right to a legal education of its citizens, and that its failure to do so within the boundaries of the state violated the Fourteenth Amendment.

The Court responded to Missouri's first argument—that state law provided for the organization of a law school at Lincoln University—by noting that the statute gave the curators of Lin-

coln University the power to establish a law school "whenever necessary and practicable in their opinion." The Court deemed this power too speculative, especially considering that Gaines had instead been counseled to obtain his legal training outside Missouri at the point of his inquiry. In response to the state's suggestion that the provision for attendance outside Missouri was a temporary condition, the Court remarked that the discretion granted to the curator of Lincoln University created the possibility that the condition could continue indefinitely, which was insufficient to rectify the violation of Gaines's rights.

With regard to Missouri's provision for legal education outside the state, the Court observed that the U.S. system of federalism required each state to be responsible for the rights of its citizens within its own sphere of authority. The Court held that requiring an African American to attend school elsewhere "may mitigate the inconvenience of the discrimination but cannot serve to validate it." Moreover, the Court noted that evidence of limited demand for such an educational opportunity within the state of Missouri constituted an insufficient basis for the denial of Gaines's personal constitutional right to equal protection.

Justice McReynolds wrote in dissent an opinion that was joined by Justice Butler. Justice McReynolds noted that federal interference with Missouri's public policy in separating the races was not warranted since Missouri adequately provided for Gaines's right through the option of attendance at an adjacent state law school.

AFTERMATH

Although *Gaines* fits within the "separate but equal" list of equal protection cases, the case began the Supreme Court's examination of the "equality" of separate state-sponsored graduate and professional educational opportunities. Twelve years later the Court would hold in *SWEATT V. PAINTER* that separate provisions for legal education were, by themselves, not equal protection, and four years after that held, in *BROWN V. BOARD OF EDUCATION*, that supplying separate public education opportunities was inherently unequal protection.

SIGNIFICANCE

The Court ruled that a device used by several states in observance of "Jim Crow" laws was insufficient to provide equal protection to African-American citizens. As a result, *Gaines* represents one of the earliest cases in which the Court upheld an African American's personal constitutional rights as a barrier to the imposition of segregationist policies.

RELATED CASES

Brown v. Board of Education of Topeka, Kansas, 349 U.S. 294 (1954)

McLaurin v. Oklahoma State Regents, 339 U.S. 637 (1950)

Pearson v. Murray, 169 Md. 478, 182 A. 590 (1936)

Plessy v. Ferguson, 163 U.S. 537 (1896)

Sweatt v. Painter, 339 U.S. 629 (1950)

RECOMMENDED READING

Lusky, Louis. *By What Right?* Charlottesville, Va.: The Michie Co., 1975.

———, *Minority Rights and the Public Interest,* 52 Yale Law Journal 1 (1942).

Case Title: *City of Mobile, Alabama v. Bolden*

Legal Citations: 446 U.S. 55; 100 S.Ct. 1490; 64 L.Ed. 2d 47

Year of Decision: 1980

KEY ISSUES

Does a city's system of municipal elections violate the constitutional rights of the city's black voters under the Fifteenth Amendment right to vote and the equal protection clause of the Fourteenth Amendment to be free of discrimination?

HISTORY OF THE CASE

Mobile, Alabama, was governed by a commission of three members elected at-large, which means the city was not divided into districts and the whole city voted on all members, who exercise all executive, legislative, and administrative

power for the city. A class action brought by black residents of Mobile, including Bolden, in federal district court alleged on behalf of the black constituents of the city that this at-large election process diluted their voting strength in violation of the Fifteenth Amendment and the Fourteenth Amendment, preventing the election of a black commissioner who probably would have been elected if the city was divided into election districts. The blacks had "registered to vote without hindrance." The district court held the at-large elections to be in violation of the Fifteenth Amendment and to have "invidiously discriminated" against blacks and ordered the commission to disband and be replaced with single-member districts. The court of appeals affirmed.

SUMMARY OF ARGUMENTS

The black residents of Mobile argued that the at-large election process violated their Fifteenth Amendment rights. The city and the three incumbent commissioners argued that to violate the Fifteenth Amendment there had to be a discriminatory motive and none existed; therefore, there was no violation of the Fifteenth Amendment.

Justice Stewart wrote for the Court, holding that Mobile's at-large electoral system did not violate the rights of black voters according to the Fifteenth Amendment. "Racially discriminatory motivation" is necessary for a violation of that amendment. The amendment prohibits only premeditated discriminatory practices related to the right to vote. Here the blacks registered without any problems.

The Court held that the at-large voting system does not violate the Fourteenth Amendment because the amendment does not require proportional representation. Blacks can participate, but there is no constitutional guarantee of electoral victory.

Justice Blackmun wrote that the district court should have considered an alternative governing system to convert Mobile to a mayor-council system instead of doing away with the at-large elections. This would have given black voters equal footing with others.

Justice Stevens wrote that the standard adopted by the Court in *GOMILLION V. LIGHTFOOT* (1960) should be followed, which entails:

1. whether the political structure is traditional;
2. whether it has an adverse impact on a minority;
3. whether there is any support for the system or whether it was motivated to curtail the strength of a minority.

Under this standard it is necessary to retain Mobile's government.

Justice White wrote a dissenting opinion saying that the majority looked only at the invidious aspect while past decisions under these fact patterns looked at whether the electoral plan excluded the black vote.

DECISION

Mobile's at-large voting system does not violate the right to vote under the Fifteenth Amendment because there was no discriminatory activities. The blacks voted without any problems. There was no violation under the Fourteenth Amendment because there was no premeditated discrimination.

AFTERMATH

Two years later Congress amended Section 2 of the Voting Rights Act, overruling *Bolden* and making at-large elections illegal where they cause discrimination or result in discrimination.

SIGNIFICANCE

For a violation of the Fifteenth Amendment to be found, there must be a showing of discriminatory motivation.

RELATED CASES

Gomillion v. Lightfoot, 364 U.S. 339 (1960)

Lane v. Wilson, 307 U.S. 268 (1939)

Smith v. Allwright, 321 U.S. 649 (1944)

RECOMMENDED READING

Gayle Binion, *Intent and Equal Protection: A Reconsideration,* Supreme Court Review 397 (1983).

Making the Violation Fit the Remedy: The Intent Standard and Equal Protection Law, 92 Yale Law Journal 328 (1982).

Therstrom, Abigail M. *Whose Vote Counts?* Cambridge, Mass.: Harvard University Press, 1987.

Case Title: *Moose Lodge No. 107 v. Irvis*

Legal Citations: 407 U.S. 163; 92 S.Ct. 1965; 32 L.Ed. 2d 627

Year of Decision: 1972

KEY ISSUES

Is a state, by virtue of the power to dispense liquor licenses, significantly involved in discrimination so as to violate the equal protection clause of the Fourteenth Amendment of the U.S. Constitution?

HISTORY OF THE CASE

Moose Lodge, a private club, refused to serve the black guest of a member. The guest contended that since the state of Pennsylvania had given the club one of a limited number of liquor licenses, the act was sufficient to render the club's discrimination attributable to state action. In *Burton v. Wilmington* (1961), a similar situation existed, but that case involved a public restaurant and a public building; Moose Lodge was a private club in a private building.

SUMMARY OF ARGUMENTS

K. Leroy Irvis argued that the club's refusal to serve him violated the equal protection clause of the Fourteenth Amendment.

The Moose Lodge argued that it was not acting under the authority of the state in its refusal; therefore, no state action and no violation existed.

DECISION

Justice Rehnquist wrote the opinion for the Court, holding that the mere fact that a state grants a license to an entity does not transform it into an action by the state for which a citizen may recover, "even where the number of licenses is limited." There was a suggestion that if the licenses were so limited that those who had them had a monopoly in dispensing liquor, the result would be different.

Justice Douglas wrote one of the dissenting opinions. He conceded that, as a general rule, activities of a private club were beyond the reach of the Constitution, but the situation here was different because there was a state-enforced scarcity of licenses that restricted the ability of blacks to obtain liquor. If someone wanted to form a club to serve blacks, he or she would have to buy an existing club license and pay a monopoly price attributable to the state.

AFTERMATH

The difference between the theories of "state action" and "under color of state law" are still unclear after *Moose Lodge*. The Court has yet to settle on one of these theories so it refers to it as the state action theory, an uncertain area of the law. Further, even though no state action was found in *Moose Lodge,* several states attempted to use their regulation of alcoholic beverages to fight racial discrimination.

SIGNIFICANCE

State regulation of an activity does not automatically constitute "state action" that may be reviewed on constitutional grounds.

RELATED CASES

Burton v. Wilmington Parking Authority, 365 U.S. 715 (1961)

Flagg Brothers v. Brooks, 436 U.S. 149 (1978)

RECOMMENDED READING

Michael M. Burns, *The Exclusion of Women from Influential Men's Clubs and the Inner Sanctum and the Myth of Full Equality,* 16 Harvard Civil Rights and Civil Liberties Law Review 321 (1983).

Lucretia I. Hollingsworth, *Sex Discrimination in Private Clubs,* 29 Hastings Law Journal 421 (1977).

The Supreme Court, 1971 Term, 86 Supreme Court Review 70 (1972).

Case Title: *Orr v. Orr*

Legal Citations: 440 U.S. 268; 99 S.Ct. 1102; 59 L.Ed. 2d 306

Year of Decision: 1979

KEY ISSUES

Do the Alabama alimony statutes under which only husbands may be required to pay alimony violate the equal protection clause of the Fourteenth Amendment to the U.S. Constitution?

HISTORY OF THE CASE

William and Lillian Orr were divorced in 1974. The divorce decree provided that Mr. Orr would pay Mrs. Orr alimony each month. Two years later, Mrs. Orr initiated a contempt proceeding in circuit court alleging that Mr. Orr was not obeying the decree and paying alimony. Mr. Orr defended himself with a motion that Alabama's alimony statues be declared unconstitutional because they authorize courts to obligate husbands to pay alimony but not wives.

SUMMARY OF ARGUMENTS

The appellant, William Herbert Orr, argued that Alabama's alimony statute was based on "archaic notions" of gender roles, rather than any real difference between men and women and the distinction in the statute did not serve any important governmental purpose.

The appellee, Lillian M. Orr, argued that the alimony law gave economic preference to women to compensate for past discrimination.

Justice Brennan wrote the opinion for the Court. Declaring sex and gender a quasi-suspect classification, he held that the alimony statutes had to be in furtherance of an important government objective. Although it is important to remedy past discrimination against women who cannot support themselves, the courts should do so on a case-by-case basis and not make the generalization that all men can support themselves. The Court emphasized that this was a statute that perpetuated a negative stereotype against women and was based on the idea that a woman's place was in the home.

The dissent emphasized that Mr. Orr did not have standing to bring this suit. As the gender issue was not brought before a lower court, Mr. Orr should still have to pay alimony.

DECISION

The Alabama alimony statutes that provide that husbands, but not wives, may be required to pay alimony on divorce violates the equal protection clause of the Fourteenth Amendment.

AFTERMATH

States are forced to amend their alimony statutes to be gender neutral in response to the decision in Orr.

SIGNIFICANCE

The Court analyzed the gender-based classification found in the Alabama statute by applying an intermediate standard of review that required the classification serve an important governmental objective and be substantially related to achieving that objective.

RELATED CASES

Craig v. Boren, 429 U.S. 190 (1976)

Reed v. Reed, 404 U.S. 71 (1971)

Stanton v. Stanton, 471 U.S. 7 (1975)

RECOMMENDED READING

Mary E. Becker, *Prince Charming: Abstract Equality,* Supreme Court Review 201 (1987).

Gary D. Gilson, *Alimony Awards and Middle-Tier Equal Protection Scrutiny,* 59 Nebraska Law Review 172 (1980).

Diane M. Signoracci, *A Husband's Constitutional Right Not to Pay Alimony,* 41 Ohio State Law Journal 1061 (1980).

Case Title: *Personnel Administrator of Mass. v. Feeney*

Legal Citations: 442 U.S. 256; 99 S.Ct. 2282; 60 L.Ed. 2d 870

Year of Decision: 1979

KEY ISSUES

Does a state statute that grants absolute, lifetime preference for state civil service employment to veterans of American military service deny equal protection to women?

HISTORY OF THE CASE

While working for 12 years as a state employee, Helen B. Feeney had passed numerous competitive civil service examinations for better jobs. Because a Massachusetts law granted absolute preference to military veterans, however, Feeney was ranked below male veterans who had achieved lower test scores than she had. In addition, since more than 98 percent of the veterans in Massachusetts were men, the statute overwhelmingly benefited males to the detriment of females.

Feeney brought suit in federal district court, claiming the statute discriminated against women and denied her equal protection under the Fourteenth Amendment to the U.S. Constitution. The Fourteenth Amendment provides, in part, that no state shall "deny to any person within its jurisdiction equal protection of the laws." The federal court invalidated the law because of its severe, exclusionary impact upon women. The personnel administrator of Massachusetts appealed to the U.S. Supreme Court.

SUMMARY OF ARGUMENTS

Feeney argued that the Massachusetts legislators were aware of the natural and probable consequences of the law. She maintained that when they passed the law, they knew that the absolute preference would produce an enormous statistical impact to discriminate against women. Thus, she reasoned that the legislators intentionally discriminated against women in violation of the Fourteenth Amendment.

Massachusetts contended that the purpose of the preference for veterans was to benefit veterans and not to discriminate against women. Also, because the policy on its face did not purposefully discriminate against women, the state argued the statute should not be subject to the sort of special scrutiny the Court gives to such laws.

DECISION

Justice Stewart delivered the 7-2 majority opinion of the Court, which held that the statute was not purposefully gender-based. Stewart reasoned that because a significant number of men were also nonveterans, they were equally affected by the law, so the statute does not intentionally prefer men over women. The Court also stressed that only when the legislature passes a law "because of" and not "in spite of" its adverse effects upon women could there be said to have been purposeful discrimination. The majority concluded that there was no proof that the Massachusetts legislature sought to disadvantage women by the policy; the fact that 50 times as many veterans were men was just one of the incidental consequences of the statute. Therefore, the statute did not violate the equal protection clause.

The dissenters believed that the state did not meet its burden of proving that sex-based considerations played no part in the adoption of the scheme. They saw no difference in previous Court decisions that invalidated laws reflecting "archaic assumptions about women's roles."

AFTERMATH

The *Feeney* requirement that the plaintiff must prove an actual discriminatory purpose has been a roadblock for pregnancy-based discrimination. The Court also has upheld seniority systems even though employers had for years excluded minorities from certain jobs: even though the seniority system had a foreseeable, discriminatory effect upon a minority's ability to obtain future promotions, it was upheld because no purposeful discrimination was proven. After losing her Supreme Court battle, Feeney later obtained a degree in gerontology.

SIGNIFICANCE

The Fourteenth Amendment's guarantee that no person shall be denied the equal protection of the laws must coexist with the practical necessity that most legislation classifies for one purpose or another. Such classifications inevitably result in disadvantages to various groups or persons. The Court has come to grips with this reality by stating that, if a law neither burdens a fundamental right nor targets a class based on race, sex, national origin, alienage, or other similar trait, it will uphold the legislative classification so long as it bears a rational relation to some legitimate end. In *Feeney*, because the Court believed that women were not being targeted by the veterans preference scheme, the legislation was upheld.

RELATED CASES

Bray v. Alexandria's Women's Health Clinic, 506 U.S. 263 (1993)

International Brotherhood of Teamsters v. United States, 431 U.S. 324 (1977)

Washington v. Davis, 426 U.S. 229 (1976)

RECOMMENDED READING

Gayle Binion, *"Intent" and Equal Protection: A Reconsideration*, Supreme Court Review 397–457 (1983).

Leo Kanowitz, *"Benign" Sex Discrimination: Its Troubles and Their Cure*, 31 Hastings Law Review 1379–1431 (July 1980).

Bruce E. Rosenblum, *Discriminatory Purpose and Disproportionate Impact: An Assessment after Feeney*, 79 Columbia Law Review 1376–1413 (1979).

Case Title: *Plessy v. Ferguson*

Alternate Case Title: The Separate but Equal Case

Legal Citations: 163 U.S. 537; 16 S.Ct. 1138; 41 L.Ed. 256

Year of Decision: 1896

KEY ISSUES

Do the states have the right to require separate accommodations in interstate commerce based on race?

HISTORY OF THE CASE

In the late 19th century, the legislatures of many southern states passed laws imposing racial segregation. These laws, called "Jim Crow" laws, created two separate societies, one for whites and one for blacks.

Homer Plessy, a light-skinned black man, bought a first-class ticket to travel from New Orleans to Covington, Louisiana, on the East Louisiana Railroad. At this time, trains segregated their passengers, having cars specifically for whites and cars specifically designated for blacks. On June 7, 1892, he entered a car for white passengers, where he took a vacant seat. A police officer was summoned, and Mr. Plessy was forced to leave the coach. He was imprisoned in the jail of New Orleans for having violated the "Jim Crow" law of Louisiana, which separated blacks from whites on trains. Plessy was tried before the criminal district court of Orleans Parish, but before he could be fined or sentenced, he filed a petition for a writ of prohibition against Judge John H. Ferguson, the judge of the criminal district court. The Louisiana Supreme Court reviewed the petition of Mr. Plessy and found that the statute was constitutional and that Mr. Plessy, being one-eighth black, was "a member of the colored race." Plessy petitioned to the U.S. Supreme Court and the Court accepted jurisdiction.

SUMMARY OF ARGUMENTS

Mr. Plessy's case was argued by Albion Tourgee, who affirmed that the concept of separate but equal was in theory equal and impartial, but that its object was to debase and to distinguish one race as inferior to the other. Regardless of the intent of the law, black citizens were constantly reminded of white superiority and supremacy. Tourgee uttered the famous words, "Justice is pictured blind and her daughter, the law, ought at least to be colorblind."

Alexander Morse represented Judge Ferguson. Morse argued that the Louisiana legislature was at liberty to act with reference to the usage, custom, and traditions of their people, with a view to promoting their comfort and preserving the public peace in good order.

DECISION

Justice Henry Brown wrote the majority opinion. By a vote of 8-1, the Court ruled that laws permitting, and even requiring, the separation of persons by race do not imply the inferiority of either race to the other. Justice Brown further found that the distinction based on skin color has no tendency to destroy the legal equality of the races. Justice Brown also stated that laws requiring the separation of races commonly have been upheld, especially with regard to separate schools for white and for black children. Brown ruled that there was a distinction between laws that interfere with political equality for "the negro" and those that require the separation of races in schools, theaters, and railroad cars:

We consider the underlying fallacy of the plaintiff's [Plessy's] argument to consist in the assumption that the enforced separation of the two races stamps the colored race with a badge of inferiority. If this be so, it is not by reason of anything found in the act, but solely because the colored race chooses to put that construction upon it.

Justice John M. Harlan of Kentucky wrote a thundering dissent. Harlan, a former slaveowner, argued that the Thirteenth and Fourteenth Amendments to the Constitution added to the dignity and glory of American citizenship by securing personal liberty to all persons born or naturalized in the United States. To that end, they "removed the race line" from our government. Justice Harlan had no trouble recognizing that the intent of this law was to interfere with the personal liberties of black citizens of Louisiana. Justice Harlan continued:

The white race deems itself to be the dominant race in this country. And so it is, in prestige, in achievements, in education, in wealth, and in power. So, I doubt not, it will continue to be for all time, if it remains true to its great heritage, and holds fast to the principles of constitutional liberty. But in view of the constitution, in the eye of the law, there is in this country no superior, dominant, ruling class of citizens. There is no caste here. Our constitution is colorblind, and neither knows nor tolerates classes among citizens. In respect of civil rights, all citizens are equal before the law. The humblest is the peer of the most powerful. The law regards man as man, and takes no account of his surroundings or his color when his civil rights as guaranteed by the supreme law of the land are involved. It is therefore to be regretted that this high tribunal, the final expositor of the fundamental law of the land, has reached the conclusion that it is competent for the state to regulate the enjoyment by citizens of their civil rights solely upon the basis of color.

In my opinion, the judgment this day rendered will, in time, prove to be quite as pernicious as the decision made by this tribunal in the Dred Scott Case.

AFTERMATH

For more than 60 years, the Supreme Court regarded "separate but equal" as an appropriate interpretation of the law with regard to the civil rights of black citizens.

SIGNIFICANCE

Plessy v. Ferguson encouraged legislators in the South to pass "Jim Crow" laws, which intensified the segregation of blacks and whites, the disenfranchisement of black voters, and other violations of the civil rights of blacks.

RELATED CASES

Muir v. Louisville Park Theatrical Assn., 347 U.S. 971 (1954)

Watson v. Memphis, 373 U.S. 526 (1963)

RECOMMENDED READING

Carmichael, Peter A. *The South and Segregation.* Washington, D.C.: Public Affairs Press, 1965.

Fischer, Roger A. *The Segregation Struggle in Louisiana, 1862–1877.* Urbana: University of Illinois Press, 1974.

Woodward, C. Vann. *The Strange Career of Jim Crow.* 3d ed. New York: Oxford University Press, 1974.

Case Title: *Reed v. Reed*

Legal Citations: 404 U.S. 71; 92 S.Ct. 251; 30 L.Ed. 2d 225

Year of Decision: 1971

KEY ISSUES

Is a statute preferring men over women as administrators of estates constitutional?

HISTORY OF THE CASE

Richard Reed died without a will. His adoptive parents, then separated, filed competing petitions seeking to administer their son's estate. An Idaho statute established a scheme for the selection of the administrator of such an estate, where eligible persons were grouped into 11 categories by their relationship to the decedent. The statute further provided that when more than one person in the same category are claiming and are "equally entitled" to administer, males must be preferred to females.

Based on this portion of the statute, the probate court held in favor of the father. Sally Reed, the mother of the deceased, appealed to the U.S. District Court of the Fourth Judicial District of Idaho. The district court held that the challenged section violated the equal protection clause under the Fourteenth Amendment and was, therefore, void. However, Cecil Reed, the father of the deceased, took a further appeal to the Idaho Supreme Court, which reversed the district court's holding.

SUMMARY OF ARGUMENTS

The state, on behalf of Cecil Reed, argued that the statute's preference of males over females simply reduced the work load of probate courts by eliminating hearings on the merits. Therefore, the state contended that the statute was intended as "benign" legislation.

Sally Reed argued that the section of the Idaho Code violated the equal protection clause of the Fourteenth Amendment because the selection of males over equally qualified females was arbitrary. She also challenged the section as a violation of the Idaho Constitution.

DECISION

The Supreme Court reversed the judgment of the Idaho Supreme Court. Chief Justice Burger delivered the unanimous decision of the Court, holding that the arbitrary preference of males could not withstand constitutional attack. He reasoned that the equal protection clause forbids the states from legislating that different persons be placed into separate classes on the basis of criteria wholly unrelated to the objective of that legislation. He stated that such gender-based classifications must be reasonable, not arbitrary. Most important, Burger decided that the scheme's mandatory preference of males was not reasonably related to the state's objective of reducing the workload by eliminating one class of contests.

AFTERMATH

Before *Reed,* the Court had easily found that a sex-based statute was rationally related to some legitimate state objective, usually the preservation of women's "proper role." The Court, in *Reed*, overcame this traditionally weak rational basis test in holding that the state's objective was not legitimate. However, after *Reed*, the Court began to develop a higher, intermediate standard of review for gender classifications. By this level of scrutiny, the Court analyzes whether the classifications by gender serve important governmental objectives that are substantially related to the achievement of those objectives. Today, this intermediate level of review is difficult to overcome in cases involving gender-based classifications. In 1996 the Court seemed to heighten this intermediate standard of review in determining that a state must show an "exceedingly persuasive justification" for a gender-based scheme, and that the courts must give "skeptical scrutiny" to that scheme. The justification given must be genuine and not created after the fact or in response to litigation. This is a demanding burden that rests on the state.

SIGNIFICANCE

For the first time in its history, the Court rejected a sex-based legislation under the equal protection clause. Although the Court declined to make gender a "suspect" classification entitling it to greater scrutiny than a "mere rationality" review, it did pave the way for later cases to elevate the standard of review.

RELATED CASES

Craig v. Boren, 429 U.S. 190 (1976)

Frontiero v. Richardson, 411 U.S. 677 (1973)

Michael M. v. Superior Court, 450 U.S. 464 (1981)

Mississippi University for Women v. Hogan, 458 U.S. 718 (1982)

U.S. v. Virginia, 116 S.Ct. 2264 (1996)

RECOMMENDED READING

John D. Johnson, Jr., *Sex Discrimination and the Supreme Court, 1971–1974*, 49 New York University Law Review 617 (1974).

Kirp, David L., et al. *Gender Justice*. Chicago: University of Chicago Press, 1986.

Schwartz, Bernard. *The Ascent of Pragmatism: The Burger Court in Action*. New York: Addison-Wesley, 1990.

Case Title: *Regents of the University of California v. Bakke*

Alternate Case Title: The Reverse Discrimination Case

Legal Citations: 438 U.S. 265; 98 S.Ct. 2733; 57 L.Ed. 2d 750

Year of Decision: 1977

KEY ISSUES

Was a white male applicant denied admission to the University of California at Davis Medical School discriminated against when the admissions process held open spaces in each year's class for less qualified minority applicants?

HISTORY OF THE CASE

In 1973, the Medical School of the University of California at Davis had a class size of 100 students. The medical school had a dual admissions process. In addition to the general admissions program, a special admissions program operated with a separate committee that chose students for 16 of the 100 spaces in each class. Applicants who wished to be considered in the special admissions process indicated on the 1973 application form that they were "economically and/or educationally disadvantaged" applicants. On the 1974 application, applicants checked a box to indicate they were members of a "minority group," which the medical school considered to be "Blacks," "Chicanos," "Asians," and "American Indians." Students considered under the special admissions program were also considered under the general program for the remaining 84 spaces, but at no point did they compete with the applicants in the general program for the 16 reserved seats. Although many disadvantaged whites sought consideration under the admissions program, none received an offer for admission under the special program. Thus, under the Davis Medical School admissions process, whites competed for 84 spaces in each entering class, whereas members of the preferred "minority groups" were considered for all 100 spaces.

Allan Bakke was a white male who applied to the Davis Medical School in 1973 and in 1974. He was a graduate of the University of Minnesota, where he had received a mechanical engineering degree and earned a 3.50 GPA. Bakke had served in the Naval Reserve Officers Training Corps to pay for his education, and after college, from 1963 to 1967, served in the U.S. Marine Corps in Vietnam. During his military service, he had developed an interest in becoming a doctor. After leaving the Marine Corps, Bakke took the required prerequisites for medical school while working full-time as a NASA research engineer. Bakke was twice denied admission under the general program, whereas students were admitted under the special program with lower entrance exam scores, grade point averages, and interview scores.

After Bakke's second rejection, he filed suit in the Superior Court of California, the trial court level, to compel the medical school to admit him. He argued that the special admissions program excluded him on the basis of his race, violating his rights under the equal protection clause, Title VI of the Civil Rights Act of 1964, and under the California Constitution. The university in response asked the court to determine that their admissions process was lawful. They defended the admissions process, arguing it was necessary to overcome the substantial, chronic minority underrepresentation in the medical profession. The Superior Court found that the special program operated as a racial quota because the minority applicants were rated only against one another. The trial court also declared that taking race into account when making admissions decisions violated the U.S. Constitution, the California Constitution, and Title VI of the Civil Rights Act of 1964, which prohibits discrimination on the basis of race, color, or national origin under federally funded programs.

The California Supreme Court heard the case directly on appeal from the trial court "because of the importance of the issues involved." The California high court determined that, while the aims of the Medical School's special admissions program were legitimate, the program was unconstitutional because it did not use the least intrusive means of achieving those goals.

Additionally, the California Supreme Court held that the equal protection clause of the Four-

teenth Amendment required that "no applicant may be rejected because of his race, in favor of another who is less qualified, as measured by standards applied without regard to race."

SUMMARY OF ARGUMENTS

The petitioner, the university, argued that its special admissions program was lawful and did not violate the equal protection clause of the Fourteenth Amendment. The university also argued that no private right of action existed under Title VI of the Civil Rights Act of 1964.

Bakke, the respondent, argued that the admissions program excluded him based on his race in violation of the equal protection clause of the Fourteenth Amendment. Bakke also argued that he had a private right of action under Title VI of the Civil Rights Act of 1964.

DECISION

The U.S. Supreme Court both affirmed and reversed the ruling of the California Supreme Court. In the Court's confusing ruling, the California Supreme Court's decision ordering the Davis Medical School to admit Bakke was upheld. Only a single justice, Justice Powell, supported the opinion of the Court in its entirety. Four of the remaining nine justices agreed with the ordering of the medical school to admit Bakke, but disagreed with Justice Powell's reasoning. The other four justices disagreed with compelling the medical school to admit Bakke, but agreed with part of Justice Powell's opinion. While finally resolving the case at the personal level, the *Bakke* decision left the issue of the constitutionality of racial preferences in college admissions processes unsettled.

Justice Powell's opinion, which "announced the Court's judgment" and "express[ed] his views of the case," began by stating that Title VI of the Civil Rights Act of 1964, which prohibited discrimination "on the ground of race, color, or national origin" in the administering of programs funded by the federal government, prohibited the same sort of discrimination as the equal protection clause of the U.S. Constitution. Powell then analyzed the degree of constitutional protections accorded Bakke. He first concluded that "[r]acial and ethnic distinctions of any sort are inherently suspect and thus call for the most exacting judicial examination." He also rejected the argument made by the medical school that "discrimination against members of the white 'majority' cannot be suspect if its purpose can be characterized as 'benign.'"

Justice Powell continued by stating that the university's racial criteria would only pass constitutional scrutiny if they were "'necessary . . . to the accomplishment' of its purpose or the safeguarding of its interest." The university gave four purposes for the racial classifications: (1) "reducing the historic deficit of traditionally disfavored minorities in medical schools and in the medical profession," (2) "countering the effects of societal discrimination," (3) "increasing the number of physicians who will practice in communities currently underserved," and (4) "obtaining the educational benefits that flow from an ethnically diverse student body."

Justice Powell rejected the first three of these purposes. First, Powell rejected the goal of having a certain percentage of minorities in the student body because "[p]referring members of any one group for no reason other than race or ethnic origin is discrimination for its own sake." Second, countering the effects of societal discrimination was not the university's job: "Its broad mission is education, not the formulation of any legislative policy or the adjudication of particular claims of illegality." Third, though Powell agreed that increasing the number of physicians serving in areas currently underserved was a laudable goal, "there is virtually no evidence in the record indicating that petitioner's special admissions program is either needed or geared to promote that goal."

Justice Powell did recognize that attaining a diverse student body was a constitutionally permissive goal. Such diversity, however, "encompasses a far broader array of qualifications and characteristics of which racial or ethnic origin is but a single though important element. Petitioner's special admissions program, focused solely on ethnic diversity, would hinder rather than further attainment of genuine diversity." Because the medical school's special admissions program focused solely on race, Bakke's constitutional rights were violated and he was therefore entitled to be admitted to the Davis Medical School. The California Supreme Court's order to admit Bakke was thus affirmed. The part of the state high court's opinion that prohibited the school from ever taking race into account in their admissions process, however, reversed. Justice

Powell wrote that "the courts below failed to recognize that the State has a substantial interest that legitimately may be served by a properly devised admissions program involving the competitive consideration of ethnic origin."

Justice Stevens wrote an opinion, joined by Chief Justice Burger, Justice Stewart, and Justice Rehnquist, that agreed with the judgment to uphold the order to admit Bakke, but on the narrow grounds of Title VI. Because Stevens and the justices who joined his opinion believed that the case could be resolved completely under the statute, it was unnecessary to reach the constitutional issues. "[T]he question whether race can ever be used as a factor in an admissions decision is not an issue in this case, and that discussion of that issue is inappropriate."

Justices Brennan, White, Marshall, and Blackmun jointly wrote an opinion that dissented from the order to admit Bakke, but agreed with part of Justice Powell's reasoning. These four justices agreed with Justice Powell that "Title VI goes no further in prohibiting the use of race than the Equal Protection Clause" and agreed "that some uses of race in university admissions are permissible." They disagreed, however, with Powell that the specific use of race in the admissions process was unconstitutional. Justices Brennan, White, Marshall, and Blackmun believed that the medical school's consideration of race was constitutional because it did not act "to demean or insult any racial group, but to remedy disadvantages cast on minorities by past racial prejudice."

Justices White, Marshall, and Blackmun also wrote their own separate opinions. Justice White wrote separately to state his belief that Bakke did not have a "private cause of action under Title VI." Justice Marshall wrote to state his strong conviction that the university could constitutionally "remedy the effects of [the] legacy of discrimination." Justice Blackmun expressed his hope that a policy of affirmative action, such as the one used by the medical school, could soon be halted: "I yield to no one in my earnest hope that the time will come when an 'affirmative action' program is unnecessary and is, in truth, only a relic of the past. . . . At some time, however, beyond any period of what some would claim is only a transitory inequality, the United States must and will reach a stage of maturity where action along this line is no longer necessary."

AFTERMATH

Allan Bakke was admitted to the University of California at Davis Medical School and graduated in 1982. He interned at the Mayo Clinic in Rochester, Minnesota, where he later served as a resident in anesthesiology.

SIGNIFICANCE

The significance of the *Bakke* decision stems from what it did not do. It did not finally resolve the constitutionality of affirmative action programs. It was a complex compromise that strictly held only that Allan Bakke was to be admitted to the Davis Medical School. The U.S. Supreme Court to this day has not established a firm rule explaining how race can constitutionally be taken into account in school admissions and hiring decisions.

In 1997, California passed a law outlawing state affirmative action programs. In 2002, the U.S. Supreme Court agreed to hear two affirmative action lawsuits involving the University of Michigan, *GRUTTER V. BOLLINGER* and *GRATZ V. BOLLINGER*, which will give the Court the opportunity to revisit its decision in *Bakke*.

RELATED CASE

Kaiser Aluminum & Chem. Corp. v. Weber, 443 U.S. 193 (1979)

RECOMMENDED READING

Dreyfus, Joel, and Charles Lawrence III. *The Bakke Case: The Politics of Inequality.* New York: Harcourt Brace Jovanovich, 1979.

Wilkenson, J. Harvie. *From* Brown *to* Bakke: *The Supreme Court and School Integration: 1954–78.* New York: Oxford University Press, 1979.

~~~

Case Title: *Reynolds v. Sims*

Alternate Case Titles: The Reapportionment Case; the State Legislature Apportionment Case; the "One Person, One Vote" Case

Legal Citations: 377 U.S. 533; 84 S.Ct. 1362; 12 L.Ed. 2d 506

Year of Decision: 1964

KEY ISSUES

Does the equal protection clause of the Fourteenth Amendment require representatives in state legislatures to be elected from districts with the same population?

HISTORY OF THE CASE

As with many southern states in the early 1960s, the Alabama legislature gave greater representation to voters living in rural areas. The Alabama legislature consisted of a Senate with 35 members and a House of Representatives with 106 members. The 35 senators were divided among districts composed of one or more of the state's 67 counties, with no counties split between separate districts. Each of the 67 counties elected at least one member of the House of Representatives, with the remaining 39 members allocated among the counties on the basis of their population. Because the rural counties had much smaller populations than their urban counterparts, rural voters were represented disproportionately. The apportionment of seats in the Alabama legislature had been unchanged since 1903.

On August 26, 1961, voters from Jefferson County, an urban county, challenged the apportionment of the Alabama legislature in federal district court. The voters argued that "since the population growth in the state from 1900 to 1960 had been uneven, Jefferson and other counties were now the victims of serious discrimination with respect to the allocation of legislative representation."

Encouraged by the holding of *BAKER V. CARR,* the voters from Jefferson County urged the federal court to enjoin the upcoming primary election, scheduled for the following month. The district court refused to stop the election. The federal court urged the legislature to take action in reapportioning its body. If the legislature failed to act, the court warned it would be under a "clear duty" to take some sort of action before the November 1962 general election.

The Alabama legislature responded to the federal court's suggestion half-heartedly. In July, the Alabama legislature adopted two reapportionment plans to take effect for the 1966 elections. One plan was a proposed constitutional amendment and the other plan was a statutory measure, enacted as standby legislation in case the proposed amendment failed.

The proposed constitutional amendment provided for the House of Representatives to consist of 106 members, "apportioned by giving one seat to each of Alabama's counties and distributing the others according to population using an 'equal proportions' method. . . . The Senate was to be composed of 67 members, one from each county." In the statutory reapportionment plan, the Senate would have 35 members, "representing 35 senatorial districts established along county lines, and altered only a few of the former districts." The House of Representatives would have 106 members, with each county receiving one member and the remaining 39 apportioned "on a rough population basis, requiring increasingly more population to be accorded additional seats."

On July 21, 1962, the federal district court held that both the current composition of the Alabama legislature and the two proposed plans violated the equal protection clause of the Fourteenth Amendment of the U.S. Constitution. The court cited the great disparity in the size of the legislative districts: "[O]nly 25.1 percent of Alabama's population resided in districts represented by a majority of the members of the Senate, and only 25.7 percent lived in counties which could elect a majority of the members of the House of Representatives. Population-variance ratios of up to about 41-to-1 existed in the Senate, and up to about 16-to-1 in the House." For example, Bullock County, with a population of 13,462, had two seats in the House of Representatives, whereas Mobile County, with a population of 314,301, had only three representatives.

The district court held that the proposed plans did not adequately improve the existing disparities, but they actually made representation more unfair. The court pointed out that under the proposed constitutional amendment, "[t]he present control of the Senate by members representing 25.1 percent of the people of Alabama would be reduced to control by members representing 19.4 percent of the people of the State." The court also rejected an argument that the allocation of at least one representative to each county in the upper house was analogous to the representation of the states in the U.S. Senate, in which each state receives two senators regardless of the state's population: "The analogy cannot survive the most

superficial examination into the history of the Federal Constitution . . . [n]or can it survive a comparison of the different political natures of states and counties."

The district court issued an order for a temporary apportionment plan for the general election in November. In the temporary plan, the House of Representatives would follow the state's constitutional amendment plan, with 106 members, one for each county, and the remainder allocated to the counties by population, and the Senate would follow the statutory plan, with 35 senators from districts established along county lines. The district court made it clear that this was only a "'moderate action' . . . designed to break the strangle hold by the smaller counties on the Alabama Legislature and would not suffice as a permanent reapportionment."

Both the voters and the state appealed the district court's decision, and the U.S. Supreme Court agreed to resolve the issue.

DECISION

The U.S. Supreme Court agreed with the district court that both the existing and proposed apportionments of the Alabama legislature were unconstitutional. Chief Justice Earl Warren, in his opinion for the Court, began by explaining the constitutional right to vote: "[T]he Constitution protects the right of all qualified citizens to vote, in state as well as in federal elections." The right to vote is one of the most important of rights protected by the Constitution. "[A]ny alleged infringement of the right of citizens to vote must be carefully and meticulously scrutinized."

Chief Justice Warren then looked to the Court's decisions involving statewide primary elections and congressional elections. The Court stated that these cases held that "one person's vote must be counted equally with those of all other voters in a State." This concept applied equally to state legislatures. The argument that the apportionment respected the boundaries of counties did not excuse the unconstitutionality of Alabama from not giving equal weight to all votes. Chief Justice Warren stated it simply: "Legislators represent people, not trees or acres. Legislators are elected by voters, not farms or cities or economic interests." Thus, Alabama's legislative apportionment, based upon county lines, amounted to discrimination: "Diluting the weight of votes because of place of residence impairs basic constitutional rights under the Fourteenth Amendment just as much as invidious discriminations based upon factors such as race . . . or economic status."

In the Court's view, the allocation of two senators to each state in the U.S. Senate was "inapposite" to the composition of state legislatures. "Arising from unique historical circumstances, [the U.S. Senate's apportionment] is based on the consideration that in establishing our type of federalism a group of formerly independent States bound together under one national government." Alabama, therefore, was bound to provide equal representation for rural and urban voters alike because the Constitution required "that the seats in both houses of a bicameral state legislature must be apportioned on a population basis."

Justice Tom Clark concurred in the Court's opinion, but he would have decided the case on narrower grounds. He believed that the "federal analogy" was applicable at the state level: "[I]n my view, if one house of the state Legislature meets the population standard, representation in the other house might include some departure from it so as to take into account, on a rational basis, other factors in order to afford some representation to the various elements of the State." Justice Potter Stewart also concurred in the majority opinion. He would have affirmed the district court's opinion based on somewhat narrower grounds.

Justice Harlan strongly dissented from the Court's majority opinion, as he had done in *Baker v. Carr*. He raised many compelling scholarly constitutional arguments in his lengthy dissenting opinion. Justice Harlan focused primarily on the wording and history of the Fourteenth Amendment, issues not discussed in Chief Justice Warren's opinion for the majority.

Justice Harlan began by making the unpopular statement that the Fourteenth Amendment *permits* the states to deny its citizens the right to vote. He cited the following language from Section Two of the Fourteenth Amendment:

> But when the right to vote at any election for the choice of electors for President and Vice President of the United States, Representatives in Congress, the Executive and

Judicial officers of a state, or the members of the Legislature thereof, is denied to any of the male inhabitants of such State, . . .

The wording of the amendment then continued, explaining that the state's representation in Congress would be reduced if the right to vote was denied. Justice Harlan concluded from the amendment's wording that if the denial of the right to vote was permitted, then so, too, would be a "dilution" of the right.

Justice Harlan further argued that because most of the states that ratified the Fourteenth Amendment had state legislatures in which representation was not based entirely on population, it was unlikely that they intended the Fourteenth Amendment to prohibit such legislative apportionment. Justice Harlan queried: "Can it be seriously contended that the legislatures of these states, almost two-thirds of those concerned, would have ratified an amendment which might render their own States' constitutions unconstitutional?"

Lastly, Justice Harlan was concerned about the ramifications of the Court's decision. He saw no end to the Court's involvement in supervising legislative apportionment.

> It should by now be obvious that these cases do not mark the end of reapportionment problems in the courts. Predictions once made that the courts would never have to face the problem of actually working out an apportionment have proved false. . . .
>
> Generalities cannot obscure the cold truth that cases of this type are not amenable to the development of judicial standards.

Harlan was concerned that the majority's decision did not provide a workable standard for the lower courts to test the constitutionality of legislative apportionment. Whatever the merit of his arguments, they did not persuade his fellow justices; he was but one of nine justices on the Supreme Court who opposed the Court's holding.

AFTERMATH

Although the case was remanded to the district court, there were no further proceedings. The Alabama legislature was accordingly reapportioned so that both houses had equal population districts.

SIGNIFICANCE

With the Court's decision in *Reynolds v. Sims,* there was no longer any ambiguity that both houses of state legislatures had to be apportioned according to population. This case thus required the majority of state legislatures to be reapportioned, since most had at least one house that was not based exclusively on equal population districts.

RELATED CASES

Baker v. Carr, 369 U.S. 186 (1962)

Gray v. Sanders, 372 U.S. 368 (1963)

Wesberry v. Sanders, 376 U.S. 1 (1964)

RECOMMENDED READING

Cortner, Richard C. *The Apportionment Cases.* Knoxville: University of Tennessee Press, 1970.

Dixon, Robert G., Jr. *Democratic Representation: Reapportionment in Law and Politics.* New York: Oxford University Press, 1968.

Hanson, Royce. *The Political Thicket.* Englewood Cliffs, N.J.: Prentice Hall, 1966.

Case Title: *Rogers v. Lodge*

Legal Citation: 458 U.S. 613

Year of Decision: 1982

KEY ISSUES

Does an at-large election system that has the mere effect of excluding blacks from county offices violate the Fourteenth Amendment's guarantee of equal protection?

HISTORY OF THE CASE

Generally speaking, in order for a party to succeed on a claim of denial of equal protection, it must show that the unequal treatment was intentional. Upon showing this intentional or purposeful discrimination, the Court will raise its level of

scrutiny in examining the facts of the case. The higher the level of scrutiny, the more likely the offended party is to succeed. The mere fact that a law is less favorable to one group over another, however, is generally not enough to warrant a finding of a denial of equal protection.

Burke County, Georgia, elected its five county commissioners in an at-large election system, one where voters are not divided into districts but all vote on all candidates. White voters constituted a marginal majority of eligible voters and no black candidate had ever been elected to office. A class action suit was brought on behalf of all black residents of the county. The federal district court found the election system denied blacks equal protection and ordered the county divided into districts. The Court of Appeals for the Fifth Circuit affirmed. The Supreme Court agreed to hear the case because of the importance of the issues raised.

SUMMARY OF ARGUMENTS

The county argued that the election procedure was neither discriminatory in purpose nor in effect, as only 38 percent of registered voters were black. As a result, the fact that no black had ever won any election was merely a reflection of the county demographics among registered voters. The county further argued that the election procedure as adopted in 1911 was not adopted for discriminatory purposes.

The class members argued that the system diluted the power of the black vote because they were in a minority. They also maintained that past discrimination had restricted the opportunity of blacks to effectively participate in the elections.

DECISION

Justice White delivered the opinion of the Court in the 6-3 decision affirming the lower courts' findings. The Court decided that the discriminatory purpose of the election scheme could be shown by circumstantial evidence. The Court noted that the system was indeed neutral and adopted with no malignant intent. Given the discriminatory impact on black citizens, however, as well as the history of discrimination in the county, the unresponsiveness of county officials to the needs of the black community, and the fact that the state legislature maintained the system, enough circumstantial evidence was provided to support an inference of intentional discrimination.

AFTERMATH

The Court has followed a generally uniform approach to equal protection challenges. The Court does not believe that an otherwise neutral law should be struck down simply because it adversely affects a certain group. The law must still be shown to have a discriminatory purpose. Discriminatory purpose has been dealt with in a number of ways, none of which are exclusive. The Court's focus on vote dilution issues remained on the effect on the black population. The Court's concern for its effect on other minority groups was not as prevalent.

SIGNIFICANCE

Rogers effectively widened the route that may be taken in challenges based on discrimination and equal protection grounds. Circumstantial evidence is not widely looked upon as the most favorable evidence to support any given conclusion. However, the accumulation of circumstantial evidence may secure a position well enough to prove purposeful discrimination.

RELATED CASES

Arlington Heights v. Metropolitan Housing Corporation, 429 U.S. 252 (1977)

Personnel Administrator of Massachusetts v. Feeney, 445 U.S. 901 (1980)

Yick Wo v. Hopkins, 118 U.S. 356 (1886)

RECOMMENDED READING

Timothy G. O'Rourke, *Constitutional and Statutory Challenges to Local At-Large Elections,* 17 University of Richmond Law Review 39 (1982).

The Supreme Court, 1981 Term, 96 Harvard Law Review 106 (1982).

Case Title: *Romer v. Evans*

Alternate Case Title: Gay Rights Case

Legal Citation: 517 U.S. 620

Year of Decision: 1996

KEY ISSUES

Did a Colorado state constitutional amendment, titled "No Protected Status Based on Homosexual, Lesbian or Bisexual Orientation," discriminate against gays and lesbians in violation of the equal protection clause of the Fourteenth Amendment to the U.S. Constitution?

HISTORY OF THE CASE

Various municipalities in Colorado had passed local ordinances that banned discrimination in many transactions and activities, including housing, employment, education, public accommodations, and health and welfare services. Statewide controversy arose because of the protection these ordinances gave to persons discriminated against by reason of their sexual orientation. Against this backdrop, in a 1992 statewide referendum, Colorado voters enacted "Amendment 2" to the state constitution. Amendment 2 repealed the local ordinances to the extent they prohibited discrimination on the basis of "homosexual, lesbian or bisexual orientation, conduct, practices or relationships." Beyond repealing those provisions, Amendment 2 prohibited all legislative, executive, or judicial action at any level of state or local government designed to protect gays and lesbians.

Soon after Amendment 2 was adopted, litigation to declare its invalidity and stop its enforcement was begun by individual plaintiffs, three municipalities, and certain other government employees. Although Governor Romer had opposed Amendment 2 on record, he was named in his official capacity as a defendant, along with the Colorado attorney general and the state of Colorado.

The trial court granted a preliminary injunction to temporarily halt enforcement of Amendment 2, and the defendants appealed to the state supreme court. The Colorado Supreme Court upheld the interim injunction and referred the case back to the trial court with the further holding that Amendment 2 was subject to strict scrutiny under the federal Fourteenth Amendment because it infringed the fundamental right of gays and lesbians to participate in the political process. The trial court permanently enjoined enforcement of Amendment 2, and the Colorado Supreme Court, in a second opinion, affirmed that ruling.

SUMMARY OF ARGUMENTS

In the U.S. Supreme Court, the state's principal argument in defense of Amendment 2 was that it put gays and lesbians in the same position as all other persons. So, the state said, the measure did no more than deny homosexuals special rights. Moreover, argued the state, Amendment 2 embodied respect for citizens' freedom of association, in particular the liberties of landlords or employers who have personal or religious objections to homosexuality.

The plaintiffs argued that the amendment put gays and lesbians in a solitary class with respect to transactions and relations in both the private and the governmental spheres. The amendment withdrew from homosexuals, but no others, specific legal protection from the injuries caused by discrimination, and it prohibited the reinstatement of those laws and policies.

DECISION

The U.S. Supreme Court held that Amendment 2 violates the equal protection clause. In his opinion on behalf of the 6-3 majority, Justice Kennedy pointed to the detrimental change in legal status of gays and lesbians caused by the amendment. As interpreted by the state supreme court, Amendment 2 would repeal all existing statutes, regulations, ordinances, and policies of state and local entities barring discrimination based on sexual orientation, and its ultimate effect would be to prohibit any governmental entity from adopting similar, or more protective, measures in the future. Thus, according to the majority, the amendment goes well beyond merely depriving homosexuals of special rights; rather, it imposes a broad disability upon those persons alone, forbidding them, but no other people, to seek specific legal protection from injuries caused by discrimination in a wide range of public and private transactions.

A large portion of the majority opinion consists of traditional equal protection analysis, which seeks to balance the Fourteenth Amendment's promise that no person shall be denied equal protection with the practical reality that most legislation classifies people for one purpose or another. Under this analysis, the majority found that the effect of the amendment was so far-reaching that it could not be satisfactorily explained by its ostensible purposes—that is, respect for other citizens' freedom of association, particularly landlords or employers who have personal or religious objections to homosexuality. Thus, the majority found that Amendment 2 was not directed to an identifiable legitimate purpose or discrete objective. In simple terms, the Court held that the purpose of Amendment 2 was to discriminate against lesbians and gays. It was a classification of persons, based solely on their sexual orientation, undertaken for its own sake, something the equal protection clause does not permit.

Justice Scalia wrote a minority opinion, joined by Chief Justice Rehnquist and Justice Thomas. Justice Scalia vehemently disagreed with the majority's conclusion that Amendment 2 was based on a "bare . . . desire to harm" homosexuals. Rather, according to the minority, the amendment was a modest attempt to preserve traditional sexual values against the efforts of a politically powerful minority to revise those values through use of the laws. Justice Scalia was particularly critical of the majority for its unacknowledged contradiction of the Court's decision, in *Bowers v. Hardwick*, (1986), that the Constitution does not prohibit making homosexual behavior a crime. If it is constitutionally permissible for a state to make homosexual conduct criminal, asserted Justice Scalia, surely it is constitutionally permissible for a state to enact other laws, such as Amendment 2, merely disfavoring homosexual conduct.

AFTERMATH

The immediate effect of the decision in *Romer* was to reinstate the local ordinances protecting the rights of gays and lesbians and to permit other communities to adopt similar measures.

SIGNIFICANCE

The *Romer* opinion may prove significant not so much for its legal holding as for its tone. Ten years earlier, the Court's opinion in *Bowers* had reflected nothing short of scorn in its attitude toward homosexuality. Consequently, lower courts read Bowers far beyond its immediate context to uphold, for instance, laws prohibiting same-sex couples from adopting children and decisions removing children from the custody of gay parents. By the same token, the much more respectful tone of language in *Romer* may be expected to influence courts—and, for that matter, citizens—to treat lesbians and gays in a more accepting manner.

Even more broadly, *Romer* could signal a greater willingness on the part of the Court to be an actor in America's "culture wars," to use a term invoked in Justice Scalia's dissent. Traditionally, the Court has tended to defer such issues to the political branches of government, and its greater exercise of moral leadership on questions of cultural values would constitute a profound shift in the legal landscape.

RELATED CASE

Bowers v. Hardwick, 478 U.S. 186 (1986)

RECOMMENDED READING

Robert D. Dodson, *Homosexual Discrimination and Gender: Was* Romer v. Evans *Really a Victory for Gay Rights?* 35 California Western Law Review 271 (1999).

William N. Eskridge, Jr., Hardwick *and Historiography,* University of Illinois Law Review 631 (1999).

Andrew Koppelman, Romer v. Evans *and Invidious Intent*, 6 William and Mary Bill of Rights Journal 89 (1997).

H. Jefferson Powell, *The Lawfulness of* Romer v. Evans, 77 North Carolina Law Review 241 (1998).

S. I. Strong, Romer v. Evans *and the Permissibility of Morality Legislation*, 39 Arizona Law Review 1259 (1997).

Case Title: *Rostker v. Goldberg*

Legal Citation: 453 U.S. 57

Year of Decision: 1981

KEY ISSUES

Does mandatory draft registration for men, but not women, violate equal protection?

HISTORY OF THE CASE

This case started in 1971, when several men subject to registration for the draft filed a claim in district court stating that the registration violated due process and equal protection rights, among other things. In 1975, registration for the draft was discontinued, and the case was in limbo. The case was never dismissed, and it was resurrected in 1980 when an act providing for the registration for the draft was about to go into effect. The district court found that the act violated the due process clause of the Fifth Amendment as well as the equal protection clause of the Fourteenth Amendment. This decision was appealed to the Third Circuit, which stayed the district court's order. The U.S. Supreme Court decided to review the case.

SUMMARY OF ARGUMENTS

The young men who were subject to draft registration contended that the act took away property without due process, imposed involuntary servitude, violated rights of free expression and assembly, and discriminated between males and females (equal protection).

Congress argued that there was no military need to draft women. Women were excluded from combat through statutes and military policy, so drafting them was unnecessary.

DECISION

Justice Rehnquist delivered the opinion of the Court, which held that the act did not violate the due process clause or the equal protection clause. The Court used a middle-level, heightened scrutiny (between strict scrutiny and rational basis) standard of *CRAIG V. BOREN*. The Court stated that great deference should be given to Congress when it comes to military affairs, and that Congress weighed this decision carefully by conducting studies and holding hearings on the subject. Because women were unavailable for combat, Congress was justified in exempting them from the draft; it did not violate the equal protection clause. Additionally, volunteers could fill noncombat posts, so the distinction between drafting for combat versus noncombat posts was irrelevant.

Justice White dissented, stating that women could be drafted for noncombat purposes. He doubted that all of the noncombat positions could be filled by volunteers.

Justices Marshall and Brennan dissented, contending that women should be required to register for the draft even if they were not actually drafted when the time came. This would enable the military to decide at the time whether men only were needed. They believed that the need to maintain an adequate army was important, but that the male-only registration was not substantially related to that objective.

AFTERMATH

The Court has continued to give great deference to Congress in assuming the constitutionality of its decisions, especially in matters of military affairs.

SIGNIFICANCE

This case showed that the Court will give Congress the benefit of the doubt regarding the constitutionality of its legislation, and that men and women must be "similarly situated" to overcome the heightened scrutiny test in an equal opportunity challenge.

RELATED CASES

Craig v. Boren, 429 U.S. 190 (1976)

Michael M. v. Superior Court, 450 U.S. 464 (1981)

Orr v. Orr, 440 U.S. 268 (1979)

Reed v. Reed, 404 U.S. 71 (1971)

RECOMMENDED READING

Equal Protection, the Supreme Court, 1980 Term, 95 Harvard Law Review 162–181 (November 1981).

Kirp, Donald L., et al. *Gender Justice*. Chicago: University of Chicago Press, 1986.

S. E. H., *Males Only Draft Registration Does Not Violate Equal Protection Component of the Fifth Amendment*, 59 Washington University Law Quarterly 1371–1392 (winter 1982).

Case Title: *Runyon v. McCrary*

Legal Citation: 427 U.S. 160

Year of Decision: 1976

KEY ISSUES

Are private schools prohibited from denying admission to qualified black applicants solely on account of their race?

HISTORY OF THE CASE

Two Virginia private schools, supported entirely by tuition payments, denied admission to blacks. Two black students who had been denied admission brought an action in federal district court under 42 U.S.C. § 1981, which guarantees all persons the right to make and enforce contracts. Congress passed the act to forbid discrimination by private parties in making contracts. The district court found that the schools violated the act by summarily rejecting non-Caucasians. The court of appeals affirmed the district court's decision. Because of the importance of the issues presented by the case, the Supreme Court agreed to a review.

SUMMARY OF ARGUMENTS

The school district argued that the power of Congress to enact legislation under the Thirteenth Amendment is limited to ending slavery. The schools believed that even if Congress had the authority to remove "badges and incidents" of slavery, it does not have the power to regulate private citizens in their associational choices, for example, who will be allowed to attend their school. The schools maintained that the relationships between the schools and the students were not commercial contracts but merely associational relationships that had the utmost protection from governmental intrusion.

McCrary argued that the act of Congress does not compel individuals to make contracts, but it does prohibit someone who makes an offer to contract from making a condition based on race. Since the schools held themselves open to public enrollment, with the exception of blacks, they were generally within the scope of governmental regulation.

DECISION

Justice Stevens wrote for the majority in the 7-2 decision affirming the lower courts. The Court held that the Constitution has never provided affirmative protection for outright discrimination. The Court maintained that the enabling clause of the Thirteenth Amendment gives Congress the ability to rationally determine the badges and incidents of slavery. The consequence of this ability is that any determination must be rationally translated into effective legislation. The Court believed that the act of Congress regarding contractual obligations was a rational exercise of its ability to enact such laws and was therefore valid.

The Court rejected the questions concerning associational freedoms because the conduct was not merely associational but commercially public in nature. The schools solicited by mailers, and one posted an advertisement in the Yellow Pages. As a result, the schools could not reasonably claim to be private in nature. The conduct prohibited by the act was related to discrimination affecting the public interest. Since the schools held themselves out to the general public and excluded blacks, the conduct was within the regulatory powers of Congress.

AFTERMATH

The Court later narrowed its view concerning the right to enter contracts under 42 U.S.C. § 1981. Private associational concerns and freedom of contract notions seem to have risen to the surface of the issue. The Court now looks to the literal meaning of the statute rather than enlarging it. As a result, discrimination after a contract is formed is not actionable under the statute because it does not affect the right to enter the contract.

SIGNIFICANCE

The Court's decision in *Runyon* prohibited race discrimination in the private sector and was viewed as an important step toward eliminating race discrimination.

This case opened the doors to private schools for black students, but had minimal long-range effects. The case is limited, yet has the potential for great expansion in the area of contractual discrimination. Since it has never been expressly overruled, it is still good law. The contract questions answered by the Court may yet prove to affect other types of contacts and associations.

RELATED CASES

Johnson v. Railway Express Agency, 421 U.S. 454 (1975)

Jones v. Alfred H. Mayer Co., 392 U.S. 409 (1968)

Patterson v. McLean Credit Union, 491 U.S. 164 (1989)

RECOMMENDED READING

Robert J. Kaczorowski, *The Enforcement Provisions of the Civil Rights Act of 1866: A Legislative History in Light of* Runyon v. McCrary, 98 Yale Law Journal 565 (1989).

Samuel A. Marcosson, *The Court at the Cross Roads:* Runyon, *Section 1981, and the Meaning of Precedent,* 37 Emory Law Journal 949 (1988).

James McClellan, *The Foibles and Fables of* Runyon, 67 Washington University Law Quarterly 13 (1989).

Bernard Schwartz, *Rehnquist,* Runyon, *and* Jones—*The Chief Justice, Civil Rights, and Stare Decisis,* 31 Tulsa Law Journal 251 (1995).

Case Title: *Schlesinger v. Ballard*

Legal Citation: 419 U.S. 498

Year of Decision: 1975

KEY ISSUES

Does a federal statute treat male and female naval officers differently for purposes of pension retirement benefits?

HISTORY OF THE CASE

The Fourteenth Amendment directs the government to treat similarly situated persons equally. This "equal protection" guarantee governs all state actions that classify individuals for different benefits or burdens under the law. The Fifth Amendment's due process clause prohibits the federal government from engaging in unjustifiable discrimination.

Navy lieutenant Robert C. Ballard failed twice to be selected for promotion to lieutenant commander. A federal statute (10 U.S.C. § 6382 [a]) made male officers subject to mandatory discharge if they failed to be selected for promotion after 9 or more years of active service. A similar statute, 10 U.S.C. § 6401, on the other hand, allowed female officers 13 years of commissioned service before a mandatory discharge for want of promotion. Ballard filed suit claiming that the difference in the two statutes unconstitutionally discriminated against him based on sex in violation of his Fifth Amendment due process rights. A California federal district court upheld his claim, and the government appealed. Neither contending party challenged the preceding discrimination against women officers that barred their being assigned to positions likely to lead to promotion.

SUMMARY OF ARGUMENTS

Ballard contended that the dueling statutes treated male and female officers differently, existed for mere administrative and fiscal convenience purposes, and therefore were impermissibly unconstitutional. The government argued that the differing treatment accorded male and female naval officers reflected not an overboard generalization, but instead the demonstrable fact that male and female officers are not similarly situated.

DECISION

The severely divided Court analyzed the issues using "rational relationship" scrutiny, as opposed to the "strict scrutiny" criterion used by the lower court. The rational relationship standard is traditionally lenient and used by courts in equal protection cases involving nonsuspect classes. The strict scrutiny test requires a narrowly tailored compelling state interest showing that the governmental classification is necessary.

The Supreme Court held Congress's motivation in enacting the two statutes legitimate under the "rational relationship" standard. The Court found that certain social policies and the fact that there were fewer positions to which women could be assigned affecting military promotional opportunities guided the legislation. Additionally, the majority decided that the statutes were nonarbitrary and did not exist for mere administrative and fiscal convenience. The 5-4 majority reversed the trial court and held that Ballard suffered no constitutional injury in that the statute did not violate the Fifth Amendment's due process guarantee.

AFTERMATH

The *Ballard* decision reviewed in isolation a single aspect of a large case involving pension benefits in a complicated military retirement situation. In one respect, it illustrated the problem courts encounter when asked to decide such discrete issues.

The Court's decision was viewed by some as an indication that the Court wanted to protect legislation favoring opportunities for women. Others saw the decision as emphasizing the view that women were inferior and thus needed special treatment.

SIGNIFICANCE

Prior to *Ballard*, the Supreme Court analyzed equal protection claims under one of two tiers: either a rational relationship or strict scrutiny test. As the 1970s progressed, the courts began to apply broader levels of scrutiny to the same cases. The *Ballard* case helped pave the way to an "intermediate-level" scrutiny applied to equal protection issues. This "intermediate-level" standard is widely used in gender classification litigation today.

RELATED CASES

Craig v. Boren, 404 U.S. 76 (1972)

Davis v. Passman, 442 U.S. 228 (1979)

Frontiero v. Richardson, 411 U.S. 677 (1973)

Owens v. Brown, 455 F. Supp. 291 (D.D.C. 1978)

Reed v. Reed, 404 U.S. 71 (1971)

RECOMMENDED READING

The Supreme Court, 1974 Term, 89 Harvard Law Review (1975): 59–67.

Case Title: *Shapiro v. Thompson*

Legal Citations: 394 U.S. 618; 89 S.Ct. 1322; 22 L.Ed. 2d 600

Year of Decision: 1969

KEY ISSUES

Does a state that creates a one-year residency requirement as a condition for receiving state welfare assistance violate the Fourteenth Amendment's guarantee of equal protection?

HISTORY OF THE CASE

Vivian Thompson, a pregnant, unmarried woman with one child, was denied welfare benefits solely because she and her child had not been residents of Connecticut for a full year prior to their applications. Two similar cases were joined before the Supreme Court. In all three instances, the district courts found that the state's denial of benefits to otherwise eligible residents of less than a year constituted an invidious discrimination denying all the petitioners equal protection of the laws. Shapiro, representing Connecticut, appealed.

SUMMARY OF ARGUMENTS

Bernard Shapiro, the welfare commissioner of the state of Connecticut, argued that Connecticut had a historical right to legislate for the public welfare and that there was a legislative purpose for passing the provisions in question.

Vivian Thompson and others argued that the Connecticut statute violated the privileges and immunities clause of the Fourteenth Amendment because it infringed upon the right to travel. Thompson also argued that the statute violated the equal protection clause because it discriminated against certain persons based on their wealth and created an unreasonable classification of persons.

States may not withhold welfare benefits anymore than they may withhold state services from short-term residents. Because a fundamental constitutional right is involved, the strict standard of compelling state interest must be applied. State statues must be examined without regard to federal law and Congress cannot authorize the states to deny equal protection.

Justice Stewart wrote a concurring opinion in which he stated that the Court has recognized an established constitutional right.

Justices Warren and Black wrote dissenting opinions, pointing out that Congress has imposed residence requirements, and, since the state here acted pursuant to congressional authority, the statutes should be upheld.

Justice Harlan also wrote a rather lengthy dissent, saying that the compelling interest doctrine should be applied only in racial discrimination cases and not expanded to include recent interstate travelers. Harlan also said that when a statute affects matters not in the Constitution, they should not be defined as affecting fundamental rights to which the stringent equal protection test is applied.

DECISION

The Court held that a state's denial of welfare benefits to residents of less than a year constitutes discrimination and violates the equal protection clause.

Justice Brennan delivered the opinion of the Court. He agreed that the statute preserves the fiscal integrity of state public assistance programs, but he noted that it does this only by discouraging the influx of poor families needing assistance. He held that a state purpose of inhibiting immigration by needy persons violates the Constitution as a burden on the right to travel. Any law whose "sole purpose is the chilling of the exercise of a constitutional right" is invalid. It is obvious that the statute's intent is to keep needy people from coming into the state to obtain larger benefits, which infringes on the right to travel.

AFTERMATH

The fundamental rights approach as applied to residency requirements is limited and not expanded into other areas, such as in-state tuition or state mineral royalties. *Shapiro* was distinguishable from subsequent residency requirement cases because it involved the "basic necessities of life."

SIGNIFICANCE

Since this case, the Court has held that there is no constitutional right to receive welfare benefits.

RELATED CASES

Plyler v. Doe, 457 U.S. 202 (1982)

San Antonio Independent School District v. Rodriquez, 411 U.S. 1 (1969)

RECOMMENDED READING

Keynes, Edward with Randall K. Miller. *The Court v. Congress.* Durham, N.C.: Duke University Press, 1989.

Lusky, Louis. *By What Right.* Charlottesville, Va.: The Michie Co., 1975.

Margaret K. Rosenheim, Shapiro v. Thompson: *The Beggars Are Coming to Town,* Supreme Court Review 303 (1969).

Schwartz, Bernard. *The Ascent of Pragmatism: The Burger Court in Action.* New York: Addison-Wesley, 1990.

Case Title: *Shaw v. Reno*

Alternate Case Title: The Racial Gerrymandering Case

Legal Citation: 509 U.S. 630

Year of Decision: 1993

KEY ISSUES

Does an allegation of irregularly drawn boundary lines in a voting district reapportionment plan state an equal protection claim without proof of a discriminatory effect?

HISTORY OF THE CASE

Because of the results of the 1990 census, North Carolina was entitled to one more representative in the House of Representatives. Therefore, North Carolina had to create an additional voting district in the state. North Carolina created a reapportionment plan that included one district in which the majority of the voters were black. Under the Voting Rights Act of 1965, North Carolina had to have federal authorization to change its voting districts, so North Carolina submitted its reapportionment plan to the attorney general of the United States, Janet Reno, for approval. Reno objected to the reapportionment plan finding that North Carolina could have created a second "majority black" district. Subsequently, North Carolina revised its reapportionment plan and created a second majority black district that had extremely irregularly shaped boundaries. As a result, five white North Carolina residents, including Shaw, filed a lawsuit against the state and federal officers, including Reno, alleging that the reapportionment plan constituted unconstitutional racial gerrymandering in violation of the Fourteenth Amendment.

The district court dismissed the suit against the federal officers finding it lacked subject matter jurisdiction. The district court also dismissed the claim against the state for failure to state an equal protection claim upon which relief could be granted. The Supreme Court noted that it had probable jurisdiction and reviewed the claims.

SUMMARY OF ARGUMENTS

Shaw and the other North Carolina residents argued that the state had created an unconstitutional racial gerrymander that violated the equal protection clause of the Fourteenth Amendment. However, the residents did not argue that the plan unconstitutionally dilated white voting strength. Rather, the segregation of a majority of black voters into two districts violated the white residents' right to participate in a "color blind electoral process." The residents argued that the redistricting was so irregular on its face that it could only be viewed as racial segregation unjustified by a compelling state interest.

The state of North Carolina argued that it had a compelling interest in creating majority black districts to comply with the Voting Rights Act and that the plan advanced the state's compelling interest in eradicating the effects of past discrimination.

DECISION

Justice O'Connor wrote the opinion for the majority that was joined by Chief Justice Rehnquist and Justices Scalia, Kennedy, and Thomas. Justice O'Connor indicated that the district court had properly dismissed the residents' claims against the federal officers, but she found that the residents had stated an equal protection claim upon which relief could be granted.

First, Justice O'Connor found that if a racial classification appears on the face of a statute, it is not necessary to question the legislative purpose of the statute. Second, if a statute does make a distinction based upon race, the statute must be narrowly tailored to further a compelling government interest. Justice O'Connor found this strict scrutiny standard to apply to statutes, such as the North Carolina reapportionment plan, that cannot be explained on grounds other than race and that the difficulty of proof does not reduce the amount of scrutiny such statutes should receive as compared to other statutes that make racial classifications. Therefore, Justice O'Connor found that appearances are important when analyzing reapportionment. Moreover, Justice O'Connor found that it was more likely that elected officials would believe that their primary obligation was to represent only members of the majority group in the district rather than their whole constituency. Justice O'Connor also took issue with some of the dissenters, finding that nothing in the Court's case law indicated that racial and political gerrymandering had to be subjected to the same level of judicial scrutiny, nor was equal protection analysis dependent upon whether the racially segregated group was benefited or burdened by the statute.

Justice White dissented, joined by Justices Blackmun and Stevens. Justice White found the Court's decision in *United Jewish Organizations of Williamsburgh, Inc. v. Carey* (1977) to be controlling. That decision rejected a claim that creation of majority-minority districts violated the Constitution because the Court found that the white majority's influence over the political process had not been affected. Therefore, Justice White held that the appropriate question was whether the residents had been unconstitutionally denied their chance to effectively influence the political process. To prove this denial of effective influence, a group must show a "strong indicia of lack of political power" and "denial of fair representation." Justice White concluded that the residents had not stated an equal protection claim upon which relief could be granted.

Justice Blackmun wrote a separate dissent stating that consciously using race in a reapportionment plan was not a violation of the equal protection clause unless the effect of such use denied a group equal access to the political process or reduced the group's voting strength.

Justice Stevens also wrote a separate dissent finding that it is not a violation of the equal protection clause to reapportion voting districts in a manner to facilitate the election of a minority group member. Justice Stevens thought the issue should be whether the purpose of the reapportionment was to enhance the majority's power at the expense of the minority group. If the reapportionment was to benefit the minority, no constitutional violation would exist.

Finally, Justice Souter dissented, finding that the majority's decision had created an entirely new cause of action subject to strict scrutiny. Justice Souter distinguished electoral districting from other governmental conduct stating that electoral districting always involves the consideration of race whereas other governmental conduct typically considers race at the expense of a member of another race. Further, Justice Souter found that the decision of what district a voter was placed in did not deny a right of one voter to the benefit of another—both were still entitled to vote. Moreover, no constitutional violation exists when the candidate a voter supports loses the election. Therefore, Justice Souter held that to state a claim for equal protection relief, the purpose and effect of the reapportionment must be to reduce the effectiveness of a voter.

AFTERMATH

After the decision in *Shaw,* the case was returned to the district court. The district court upheld the reapportionment plan as constitutional under the *Shaw* standard. However, the decision was appealed again to the Supreme Court. In 1996, in *Shaw v. Hunt* (1996), the Supreme Court found one of the majority black districts unconstitutional.

SIGNIFICANCE

Future reapportionment plans will be subject to the *Shaw* standard. However, the states will still be subject to the Voting Rights Act as well. Compliance with both of these laws may prove to be difficult, if not impossible, as race must be a consideration under the Voting Rights Act, yet *Shaw* essentially precludes consideration of race as the only factor in reapportioning voting districts.

RELATED CASES

Mobile v. Bolden, 446 U.S. 55 (1980)

Rogers v. Lodge, 458 U.S. 613 (1982)

United Jewish Organizations of Williamsburgh, Inc. v. Carey, 430 U.S. 144 (1977)

Whitcomb v. Chavis, 403 U.S. 124 (1971)

RECOMMENDED READING

Richard H. Pildes, *The Supreme Court, Racial Politics, and the Right to Vote:* Shaw v. Reno *and the Future of the Voting Rights Act,* 44 American Law Review 1 (1994).

Yarbrough, Tinsley E. *Race and Redistricting: The* Shaw-Cromartie *cases.* Lawrence: University Press of Kansas, 2002.

Case Title: *Shelley v. Kraemer*

Legal Citations: 334 U.S. 1; 68 S.Ct. 836; 92 L.Ed. 1161

Year of Decision: 1948

KEY ISSUES

Does the Fourteenth Amendment equal protection clause prohibit judicial enforcement by state courts of restrictive covenants based on race or color?

HISTORY OF THE CASE

Shelley, a black person, bought property without knowledge that it was encumbered by a restrictive agreement at the time of purchase. The covenant stated that "no part of this property shall be occupied by any person not of the Caucasian race." Shelley brought an action in state court. The court held that the covenant never became final because it was not signed by all the owners. The state supreme court reversed, holding that the agreement was effective and violated none of Shelley's constitutional rights. The Supreme Court agreed to hear the case.

SUMMARY OF ARGUMENTS

J. D. and Ethel Lee Shelley argued that restrictive covenants based on race or color were illegal and unenforceable and that state enforcement of such covenants was a violation of the Fourteenth Amendment.

Louis W. and Fern E. Kraemer argued that the restrictive covenant did not violate the Fourteenth Amendment nor did the state's enforcement of the covenant violate the Fourteenth Amendment. The Kraemers also argued that the Shelleys were accorded due process and were not deprived of any property or civil rights.

DECISION

Chief Justice Vinson wrote the opinion, saying that private agreements to exclude persons of designated race or color from the occupancy of a residence does not violate the Fourteenth Amendment, but it does violate the equal protection clause for state courts to enforce them. Thus, in granting judi-

cial enforcement of these agreements, the state denied Shelley the equal protection of the laws.

Participation of the state in the enforcement of restrictive covenants operates as a denial of equal protection; therefore, the action of the state courts cannot be valid. The difference between judicial enforcement and nonenforcement of a restrictive covenant "is the difference to Shelley between being denied rights of property available to other members of the community and being accorded full enjoyment of those rights on equal footing."

AFTERMATH

What is essentially a private act of discrimination may become illegal state action if the state is in any way involved in carrying out that action.

SIGNIFICANCE

Any private action that goes into court may become state action. This case became the basis for several civil rights actions.

RELATED CASES

Barrows v. Jackson, 346 U.S. 249 (1953)

Bell v. Maryland, 378 U.S. 226 (1964)

Pennsylvania v. Board of Trusts, 353 U.S. 230 (1957)

RECOMMENDED READING

Louis Henkin, Shelley v. Kraemer, 110 University of Pennsylvania 473 (1962).

Lusky, Louis. *By What Right.* Charlottesville, Va.: The Michie Co., 1975.

Maimon Schwarzschild, *Value Pluralism and the Constitution: In Defense of the State Action Doctrine,* Supreme Court Review 129 (1988).

Case Title: *Skinner v. State of Oklahoma ex. rel. Williamson, Atty. Gen. of Oklahoma*

Legal Citation: 316 U.S. 535

Year of Decision: 1942

KEY ISSUES

Does a state statute that provides for discretionary sterilization of repeat criminal offenders violate the Constitution's guarantees of equal protection and due process?

HISTORY OF THE CASE

Skinner was convicted of stealing chickens and sentenced to time in an Oklahoma reformatory. Three years later he was convicted of robbery with a firearm, and again sentenced to time in an Oklahoma reformatory. Five years later he was again convicted of robbery with a firearm and again sentenced to time in a reformatory. A year later, the Oklahoma legislature passed a law that allowed for proceedings to be brought by the state attorney general for sterilization of habitual criminals involved in crimes of moral turpitude.

The purpose of the statute was to eradicate undesirable genetic propensity for criminal activity. While Skinner was incarcerated for his third conviction, the attorney general brought proceedings to have him sterilized as an habitual offender. A judgment was entered directing that a vasectomy be performed on Skinner. The judgment was affirmed by the Oklahoma Supreme Court. The U.S. Supreme Court agreed to hear the case after the Oklahoma Supreme Court decision.

SUMMARY OF ARGUMENTS

Skinner challenged the procedure as cruel and unusual punishment, a violation of his right to due process, and a denial of equal protection of the law. Since the statute did not provide the defendant (petitioner) an opportunity as to be heard whether he was the potential parent of socially undesirable offspring, he argued that it could not afford him the due process and equal protection that the Constitution requires.

Oklahoma argued that the statute was an appropriate use of the police power traditionally reserved to the states. The state contended that all due process requirements were in effect under the statute and that the discretionary proceedings were constitutionally permissible because state legislatures have the right to recognize "degrees of evil."

DECISION

Justice Douglas wrote the majority opinion that the Oklahoma sterilization statute constituted a denial of equal protection. His opinion quickly dismissed Skinner's other arguments concerning cruel and unusual punishment and due process. The Court found that under the statute, some offenses of equal magnitude and otherwise identi-

cal punishments were omitted from the statute. For example, a criminal convicted of embezzling three times would not be sterilized, whereas a criminal convicted of larceny three times could be sterilized. The Court concluded that such an inconsistency in the operation of the law constituted a denial of equal protection and reversed the decision of the Oklahoma Supreme Court.

AFTERMATH

No state had attempted to provide for involuntary sterilization of criminals since the decision. Recent developments in Texas and California concerning *voluntary* chemical castration, however, raise issues very similar to those presented in *Skinner*.

SIGNIFICANCE

The decision in *Skinner v. Oklahoma ex rel. Williamson* made involuntary sterilization of criminals illegal. In recent years, however, states have begun to develop measures for criminals who wish to voluntarily terminate their reproductive capabilities. The Supreme Court has not decided a case on this new alternative sentencing concept. Should the opportunity arise, it may look to *Skinner* for answers.

RELATED CASES

State v. Feilen, 126 P. 75 (1912)

Zablocki v. Redhail, 434 U.S. 374 (1978)

RECOMMENDED READING

Bork, Robert H. *The Tempting of America: The Political Seduction of the Law.* New York: Free Press, 1990.

Stacy Russell, *Castration of Repeat Sexual Offenders: An International Comparative Analysis,* 19 Houston Journal of International Law 425 (1997).

Elizabeth S. Scott, *Sterilization of Mentally Retarded Persons: Reproductive Rights and Family Privacy,* Duke Law Journal 806 (1986).

Case Title: *Smith v. Allwright*

Alternate Case Title: White Primary Case

Legal Citations: 321 U.S. 649; 64 S.Ct. 757; 88 L.Ed. 987

Year of Decision: 1944

~

KEY ISSUES

Does a private political party's exclusion of citizens from the right to vote in a primary election because of their skin color violate the Fifteenth and Fourteenth Amendments?

HISTORY OF THE CASE

This case came before the Supreme Court from the Fifth Circuit Court of Appeals to review a claim for damages brought by a black citizen of Houston, Texas. The citizen claimed that he was refused a ballot in a primary election for the nomination of Democratic Party candidates to the U.S. House and Senate, governor of Texas, and other state officers. The refusal was based solely on the skin color of the proposed voter pursuant to a resolution adopted at a Democratic convention.

SUMMARY OF ARGUMENTS

Lonnie E. Smith argued that, by denying him the right to vote in the Democratic primary elections, the Democratic Party of Texas violated Sections 31 and 43 of Title 8 of the United States Code (8 U.S.C.A. §§ 31 and 43) and deprived him of rights secured by Sections 2 and 4 of Article I and the Fourteenth, Fifteenth, and Seventeenth Amendments to the U.S. Constitution.

DECISION

Justice Reed wrote the opinion for the Court. He stated that the resolution of the Democratic Party of Texas is invalid because "[t]he Fourteenth Amendment forbids a state from making or enforcing any law which abridges the privileges or immunities of citizens of the United States and the Fifteenth Amendment specifically interdicts any denial or abridgement by a state of the right of citizens to vote on account of color." The Court found that the running of primaries is a governmental function, even when the task is delegated by the state to a private political party. Thus, in this case, the Democratic Party was a "state actor" for purposes of the Fourteenth and Fifteenth Amendments.

Justice Reed cast a critical light on the discriminatory actions of the Democratic Party of Texas:

> The United States is a constitutional democracy. Its organic law grants to all citizens a right to participate in the choice of elected officials without restriction by any state because of race. This grant to the people of the opportunity for choice is not to be nullified by a state through casting its electoral process in a form which permits a private organization to practice racial discrimination in the election. Constitutional rights would be of little value if they could be thus indirectly denied.

Justice Roberts wrote the Court's dissenting opinion. He was concerned that overruling *Grovey v. Townsend*, a case upholding a rule barring blacks from the Texas Democratic primary, would start a trend of "good for this day and train only."

AFTERMATH

Black voter registration increased in the 1940s but stalled in the 1950s as states used other disenfranchising techniques, such as poll taxes and literacy tests.

SIGNIFICANCE

While the case may have ended "whites only" primaries, the number of black voters did not significantly increase as states scrambled to come up with new ideas to keep black citizens from voting. Five years after the decision, 80 percent of eligible black voters remained unregistered.

RELATED CASES

Grovey v. Townsend, 295 U.S. 45 (1935)

Nixon v. Herndon, 273 U.S. 536 (1927)

Terry v. Adams, 345 U.S. 461 (1953)

RECOMMENDED READING

Elliott, Ward E. Y. *The Rise of Guardian Democracy*. Cambridge, Mass.: Harvard University Press, 1974.

Schwartz, Bernard. *Civil Rights*. Statutory History of the United States. New York: Chelsea House Publishers, 1970.

Case Title: *Sosna v. Iowa*

Legal Citation: 419 U.S. 393

Year of Decision: 1975

KEY ISSUES

Does an Iowa provision that requires people to be a state resident for one year before they sue for divorce violate the equal protection or due process clauses of the U.S. Constitution?

HISTORY OF THE CASE

Sosna and her husband were married in Michigan in 1964. They lived together in New York from October 1967 until August 1971, when they separated. They both continued to live in New York. In August 1972, Sosna moved to Iowa and petitioned for a divorce the following month. The court dismissed the petition for lack of jurisdiction, because, according to Iowa Code provisions, one must be a resident of Iowa for one year before suing for divorce. She then took the case to the district court of Jackson County Iowa, claiming that the Code provision was unconstitutional. The district court found that the provision was constitutional, and the U.S. Supreme Court took the case. Even though Sosna met the Iowa residency requirement by the time the case reached the Supreme Court, the issue was not moot because a class of persons that did not meet the residency requirements still existed.

SUMMARY OF ARGUMENTS

Sosna contended that the provision created two classes of persons and discriminated against those who had recently traveled to Iowa, thereby violating the equal protection clause. Additionally, Sosna claimed that the provision violated the due process clause because it denies one the opportunity to prove residency by means other than the time in the state and therefore denies the only means of divorce.

Iowa argued that the provision merely delayed the divorce process. Iowa also contended that it had the right to regulate divorces so as to protect its judgments from collateral attacks by other states, actions with another purpose that have the effect of overturning the judgment.

DECISION

Justice Rehnquist delivered the opinion of the Court, which held that Iowa's provision requiring one year of residence in order to sue for divorce was constitutional. The Court stated that the provision delayed divorce, but it did not prevent it. Also, the residency requirement required a showing of more than just physical presence with the intent to remain in the state. Therefore, Sosna's due process rights were not violated.

Additionally, the Court found that Iowa has an interest in assuring that those seeking a divorce be attached to the state to avoid mingling in other state's affairs. This was also found to avoid collateral attacks from other states. The state had a stronger interest in not becoming a forum for countless divorces, which, combined with the fact that divorces would eventually be granted after a year of residency, was enough for the Court to hold that it did not violate the equal protection clause.

Justice White dissented on the grounds that he believed the case to be moot because Sosna had already obtained her divorce by the time the Supreme Court heard the case.

Justice Marshall and Justice Brennan dissented, stating that the provision interfered with the right to travel. They believed that strict scrutiny should be applied, not the balancing test that the majority applied. Applying the strict scrutiny test, the dissent found that Iowa did not have a compelling interest in keeping the one-year residency provision. Therefore, they believed the equal protection clause was violated.

AFTERMATH

The Court continues to follow *Sosna*, but it is quick to distinguish cases in which residency requirements penalize aliens seeking benefits available to residents. The Court also distinguishes cases in which the freedom to travel is severely impaired.

SIGNIFICANCE

Interference with the freedom to travel usually triggers strict scrutiny because it is a fundamental right. Strict scrutiny is applied to cases in which residency requirements constitute a penalty or a deterrent because that impairs the freedom to travel, but in cases where what is sought will eventually be given, the Court has applied a lesser standard. Here, the Court determined that the state's interest was stronger and that it was not penalizing Sosna, so equal protection was not violated.

RELATED CASES

Dunn v. Blumstein, 405 U.S. 330 (1972)

Martinez v. Bynum, 461 U.S. 321 (1983)

Shapiro v. Thompson, 394 U.S. 618 (1969)

RECOMMENDED READING

Radcliffe, James E. *The Case or Controversy Provision.* University Park: Pennsylvania State University Press, 1978.

The Supreme Court, 1974 Term, 89 Harvard Law Review 87–95 (November 1975).

Case Title: *Strauder v. West Virginia*

Legal Citation: 100 U.S. 303

Year of Decision: 1880

KEY ISSUES

Does the Fourteenth Amendment prohibit discrimination in jury selection?

HISTORY OF THE CASE

Under West Virginia law, only white males could serve on juries. An all-white West Virginia jury convicted Taylor Strauder, a black man, of murder. The state supreme court affirmed the conviction. The U.S. Supreme Court agreed to hear the case because of the importance of the issues involved.

SUMMARY OF ARGUMENTS

Taylor Strauder argued that jury selection is a right that should be enjoyed without discrimination based on race.

West Virginia argued that the jury provision did not discriminate against Strauder as it nevertheless provided him with a trial by jury.

DECISION

Justice Strong wrote the majority opinion in the 7-2 decision reversing the state's conviction. The Court looked to the recently enacted Fourteenth Amendment and declared West Virginia's jury statute, which stated only white men were eligible to serve on a jury, a denial of equal protection. The Court limited the opinion to apply only to blacks, however, and not other "suspect" classes.

AFTERMATH

Since *Strauder,* the Supreme Court has dealt repeatedly with the issue of discrimination in the courtroom. The equal protection clause has come to protect not only blacks but all races. The Court in more recent years has also applied the Fourteenth Amendment to cases of gender exclusion. The enormous growth of the amendment's protection has virtually eliminated discrimination in the legal process.

SIGNIFICANCE

Strauder was the first case to confront racial discrimination in the courts. The Court's decision limited the application of the Fourteenth Amendment only to blacks rather than all citizens. While this interpretation was true to legislative intent, this view has been abandoned by subsequent decisions.

RELATED CASES

Batson v. Kentucky, 476 U.S. 79 (1986)

Georgia v. McCollum, 505 U.S. 42 (1992)

J. E. B. v. Alabama ex rel. T.B., 511 U.S. 127 (1994)

Taylor v. Louisiana, 419 U.S. 522 (1975)

RECOMMENDED READING

Currie, David P. *The Constitution in the Supreme Court, 1789–1888.* Chicago: University of Chicago Press, 1985.

Graglia, Lino A. *Disaster by Decree.* Ithaca, N.Y.: Cornell University Press, 1976.

William T. Pizzi, Batson v. Kentucky: *Curing the Disease but Killing the Patient,* Supreme Court Review 97 (1987).

Case Title: *Sugarman v. Dougall*

Legal Citation: 413 U.S. 634

Year of Decision: 1973

KEY ISSUES

Does a state statute violate the equal protection clause of the Fourteenth Amendment because it provides that only citizens may hold permanent positions in the competitive class of the state civil service?

HISTORY OF THE CASE

Nonprofit organizations that received funds through the Human Resources Administration of New York City employed Patrick McDougall, a registered resident alien, and other registered resident aliens. The organizations merged with a state agency. After the merger, all employees became employees of the city. A state law provided that only citizens could hold permanent positions in the competitive sector of the civil service. The city dismissed all alien employees from permanent positions in the competitive sector. The aliens brought a class action against Sugarman, the administrator of the New York City Human Resources Administration, and others alleging that the statute denied them equal protection. The district court agreed and declared the statute unconstitutional. The Supreme Court agreed to hear the case because of the importance of the issue presented.

SUMMARY OF ARGUMENTS

The city argued that civil servants participate directly in the formulation and execution of government policy and should therefore be free from competing obligations to another power. The city believed that having loyal employees was a substantially important enough interest to warrant the citizenship requirement.

The aliens maintained that the law swept indiscriminately and was not narrowly tailored to achieve the government interest.

DECISION

Justice Blackmum wrote for the majority in the 8-1 decision invalidating the citizenship requirement. The level of scrutiny the Court applied required the city to show a "substantial state interest" in requiring citizenship for civil service workers. In addition, the challenged law must be "narrowly and precisely drawn" to achieve that end. When the Court applies this approach, the government almost always loses. This case is no exception. The Court reasoned that a resident alien may lawfully reside in New York for a long period of time, pay taxes, and serve in the armed forces. In view of the breadth and imprecision of the law in the context of strict scrutiny, the Court struck it down as a violation of equal protection.

AFTERMATH

The Court has continued to examine the rights of aliens under various state and federal laws. The level of scrutiny has not diminished, yet there have been instances in which a state has a compelling enough interest in regulating aliens as such. As a result, citizenship may be important in some circumstances.

SIGNIFICANCE

Sugarman mandates that the states are constitutionally required to allow aliens to represent government entities. Aliens enjoy a vast array of privileges that U.S. citizens enjoy.

RELATED CASES

Examining Board of Engineers v. Flores de Otero, 426 U.S. 572 (1976)

Graham v. Richardson, 403 U.S. 365 (1971)

Toll v. Moreno, 458 U.S. 1 (1982)

Yick Wo v. Hopkins, 118 U.S. 356 (1886)

RECOMMENDED READING

Earl M. Maltz, *Citizenship and the Constitution: A History and Critique of the Supreme Court's Alienage Jurisprudence,* 28 Arizona State Law Journal 1135 (1996).

John E. Richards, *Public Employment Rights of Aliens,* 34 Baylor Law Review 371 (1982).

Schwartz, Bernard. *The Ascent of Pragmatism: The Burger Court in Action.* New York: Addison-Wesley, 1990.

Case Title: *Swann v. Charlotte-Mecklenburg Board of Education*

Alternate Case Title: School Busing Case

Legal Citations: 402 U.S. 1; 28 L.Ed. 2d. 554; 91 S.Ct. 1267

Year of Decision: 1971

KEY ISSUES

Are district courts justified in ordering compliance with their own desegregation plans when the local school authorities fail to desegregate voluntarily?

HISTORY OF THE CASE

In the U.S. District Court for the Western District of North Carolina, an action was brought for the purpose of requiring the defendant, a North Carolina county school board, to cease maintaining a racially segregated, dual public school system. The district court approved a desegregation plan, but several years later the school system, which included approximately 29 percent black students and 71 percent white students, remained substantially segregated. The district court found the school board's further proposals for desegregation inadequate and appointed an expert who provided additional desegregation proposals. The district court ordered, among other things, (1) that faculty members be reassigned so that the ratio of black and white faculty members in each school was approximately the same as the ratio of black and white faculty members throughout the school system; (2) that new attendance zones be created for secondary schools, and some inner-city black students be transported to outlying, predominantly white schools, so that the percentage of blacks would range from about 17 percent to less than 36 percent in each high school and would range from about 9 percent to about 33 percent in each junior high school; and (3) that new attendance zones and pairing and grouping of schools be used for elementary schools, and the amount of busing of elementary school students be substantially increased, so that the percentage of blacks in

each elementary school would range from about 9 percent to about 38 percent. The Court of Appeals for the Fifth Circuit affirmed the orders pertaining to faculty desegregation and secondary school rezoning and busing, but vacated the order pertaining to elementary school students on the ground that the amount of additional busing would be unnecessarily extensive. On remand from the court of appeals, the district court requested the school board to adopt a new plan for elementary school students, but after the school board failed to do so, the district court reinstated the expert's plan.

SUMMARY OF ARGUMENTS

The petitioners argued that the Charlotte-Mecklenburg Board of Education was not in compliance with the constitutional requirement of the desegregation of public schools as a remedy for the inherently unequal status among schools resulting from racial segregation. Therefore, they argued that the district court's plan of affirmative action to remedy the problem was a permissible exercise of its remedial power under the Constitution.

Respondents argued that if a desegregation plan promised to accomplish a system in which no child was excluded from any school because of race, the plan was constitutional regardless of whether predominantly black or predominantly white schools remained. Respondents also argued that the Constitution did not require racial balancing in schools.

DECISION

The U.S. Supreme Court affirmed the district court's order reinstating the expert's plan for elementary school students. In an opinion by Chief Justice Burger, expressing the unanimous views of the Court, it was held that (1) in default by school authorities of their obligation to proffer acceptable remedies, the district court had broad power to fashion a remedy that would assure a unitary school system, and such power was not restricted by public education provisions of the Federal Civil Rights Act of 1964; (2) the district court's order reassigning teachers in order to achieve faculty desegregation was proper; (3) although the constitutional command to desegregate schools did not mean that the number of students in every school in every community always had to reflect the racial composition of the school system as a whole, the use of racial ratios as a starting point in the process of shaping a remedy was within the district court's equitable discretion; (4) in order to achieve truly nondiscriminatory assignments of students, the district court could properly take affirmative action in the form of remedial altering of attendance zones, including pairing or grouping of schools and use of noncompact or noncontiguous zones; and (5) under the circumstances of the instant case, the district court's orders requiring additional busing of elementary and secondary school students as a means of school desegregation were within the Court's power to provide equitable relief.

AFTERMATH

After *Swann,* congressional members sought to introduce legislation limiting the Court's authority with respect to cases involving school desegregation.

The final, and most important, limit on federal court remedial powers arose in MILLIKEN V. BRADLEY (1974). A majority in that case prohibited district courts from fashioning remedies that included more than one school district, absent any finding that other school districts have failed to operate unitary, integrated school systems or that the boundary lines of the affected school districts were established with the purpose of fostering racial segregation.

In *Dayton Bd. of Education v. Brinkman* 433 U.S. 406 (1977), the Court unanimously held that, if the evidence in the record supported a finding of segregation throughout the school system, the judge might be able to order systemwide busing if it did not impair educational interests. If the segregation in fact occurred only in a part of the system, the remedy must be limited to that area.

SIGNIFICANCE

In this case, the Court discussed in more precise terms the scope of the duty of school authorities and district courts to fashion an end to racially segregated school systems. A federal court is not empowered to take any action or to require the school authorities to take any action until there has been a showing of de jure segregation. The Court has preserved the de jure–de facto distinction. De jure segregation is that required by law, whereas de facto segregation is that which is caused not by state action, but by socioeconomic factors. Only if there is a showing of purposeful discrimination in a substantial portion of a school district is there a presumption of intentional discrimination in the rest of the district. The presumption can be rebutted only by showing that no such intent existed.

Even when the Court finds there has been purposeful discrimination, school authorities are given the opportunity to submit a plan for desegregation. Only when the school authorities are found to be engaged in de jure segregation and also fail to submit an adequate desegregation plan does the district court have the authority to order specific steps to desegregate the schools.

RELATED CASES

Freeman v. Pitts, 503 U.S. 467 (1992)

Rufo v. Inmates of the Suffolk County Jail, 502 U.S. 367 (1992)

United States v. Fordice, 505 U.S. 717 (1992)

RECOMMENDED READING

Paul Gewirtz, *Remedies and Resistance,* 92 Yale Law Journal 585 (March 1983).

Graglia, Lino A. *Disaster by Decree.* Ithaca, N.Y.: Cornell University Press, 1976.

Kempner, Edward, and Randall K. Miller. *The Court vs. Congress.* Durham, N.C.: Duke University Press, 1989.

Schwartz, Bernard. *Swann's Way: The School Busing Case and North Carolina.* New York: Oxford University Press, 1986.

Case Title: *Sweatt v. Painter*

Legal Citations: 339 U.S. 629; 70 S.Ct. 848; 94 L.Ed. 114

Year of Decision: 1950

KEY ISSUES

Does a state deny equal protection, as prescribed by the Fourteenth Amendment, when it provides separate and unequal opportunities for professional and graduate education in a state university to members of different races?

HISTORY OF THE CASE

Heman Marion Sweatt applied for admission to the University of Texas Law School in 1946, but his application was rejected solely on the basis that he was black. State law mandated the race restriction for the study of law at the school and, at the time, no law school in Texas admitted blacks. Sweatt brought suit against the appropriate school officials to compel his admission.

The state trial court recognized the equal protection violation but continued the case for six months to allow the state to supply substantially equal facilities. Thereafter, in December 1946, the court denied Sweatt's writ on the basis of an adopted order by the authorized university officials calling for the opening of a law school for blacks in February 1947. Sweatt appealed the decision and refused to register in the new school.

Upon remand from the Texas Court of Civil Appeals the trial court found that the new school offered opportunities for the study of law that were substantially equivalent to those offered white students at the University of Texas. The new school, however, possessed no independent faculty or library and lacked accreditation. Nevertheless, the court of civil appeals subsequently affirmed the trial court's decision, and Sweatt's petition for a writ of error was denied by the Texas Supreme Court.

SUMMARY OF ARGUMENTS

Sweatt argued that the opportunities made available to him as a black man violated his right to equal protection of the laws.

The state argued that the new law school at the Texas State University for Negroes, established in the interim between the trial in the case and the Supreme Court briefings, provided the substantial equivalent of a white student's opportunities at the University of Texas Law School. The state noted that since the trial the new law school was "on the road to full accreditation . . . has a faculty of five full-time professors . . . a library of some 16,500 volumes serviced by a full-time staff . . . a practice court and legal aid association . . . and one alumnus who has become a member of the Texas Bar."

DECISION

Chief Justice Vinson delivered the opinion of the Court. The Court held that the facilities available to Sweatt, either under the prior physical description of the proposed new school or the realized beginnings of the law school at the Texas State University for Negroes, were insufficient to constitute substantial equality with the facilities available to white students at the University of Texas Law School. The Court not only noted the differences in facilities but also pointed to distinctions in the reputation of the faculty, experience of the administration, position and influence of the alumni, standing in the community, traditions, and prestige as grounds for finding that substantial equality between the two schools did not exist. In this regard, the Court noted the University of Texas Law School's status as one of the nation's ranking law schools as a factor that was not offered in the new law school.

Furthermore, the Court recognized that opportunities of a legal career are also connected to the practice of the profession. The Court noted that the new law school excluded, on the basis of race, 85 percent of the population of the state. The Court also observed that "most of the lawyers, witnesses, jurors, judges and other officials with whom [Sweatt] will inevitably be dealing when he becomes a member of the Texas Bar" would be excluded from the permissible student body at the new law school. The Court held that exclusion of a white majority from the new law school did not equate with the exclusion of blacks from the University of Texas Law School because such supposition ignored the reality of the differences in prestige in the two institutions.

The Court held that the state violated Sweatt's personal right to equal protection under the Fourteenth Amendment, but limited its holding by refusing to overturn the raced-based rights analysis of *PLESSY V. FERGUSON* (the separate-but-equal doctrine).

AFTERMATH

Four years later, the Court extended the *Sweatt* rationale beyond state-sponsored professional and graduate education programs to prohibit separate facilities in all public education in *BROWN V. BOARD OF EDUCATION*. This holding has been extended so that all states must provide nonseparate opportunities, even in fields other than education, for all races.

SIGNIFICANCE

Sweatt represented one of several cases that chipped away at the "separate, but equal" doctrine of *Plessy v. Ferguson.* The Court's concern with the prestige of the law schools at issue in *Sweatt* provided the basis for its recognition in *Brown v. Board of Education* that the pejorative status placed upon a minority by maintaining separate facilities is inherently unequal and therefore violates the equal protection guarantees of the Fourteenth Amendment.

RELATED CASES

Brown v. Board of Education of Topeka, Kansas, 349 U.S. 294 (1954)

McLaurin v. Oklahoma State Regents, 339 U.S. 637 (1950)

Missouri ex rel. Gaines v. Canada, 305 U.S. 337 (1938)

Plessy v. Ferguson, 163 U.S. 537 (1896)

RECOMMENDED READING

Dworkin, Ronald. *Taking Rights Seriously.* Cambridge, Mass.: Harvard University Press, 1977.

Meyer, Howard N. *The Amendment That Refused to Die.* Radnor, Pa.: Chilton Book Co., 1973.

Peter Westen, *The Empty Idea of Equality,* 95 Harvard Law Review 537 (1982).

❦

Case Title: *Terry v. Adams*

Alternate Case Title: The White Primary Cases

Legal Citation: 345 U.S. 461

Year of Decision: 1953

∾

KEY ISSUES

Is a private political association that excludes blacks from its pre-primary in county elections a "state actor, one acting under authorization of the state," and therefore subject to constitutional prohibitions against discrimination in voting rights?

HISTORY OF THE CASE

In order for a party to succeed on an allegation that its constitutional rights have been violated, the offending party must be acting under the authority of the state or government. There are very few exceptions to this basic tenet of constitutional law. The right to vote is not one of the exceptions.

The Jaybird Democratic Association was a private group of citizens that endorsed candidates for political office in Fort Bend County, Texas, elections. Before the Democratic Party primary, the association would decide which candidates to endorse by means of a "pre-primary" in which only members of the association could vote. Blacks were excluded from membership in the association and were therefore ineligible to vote in the pre-primary. The association's elections were not governed by state laws and did not use state elective machinery or funds. Candidates elected by the association were not certified by the association as its candidates in the Democratic primary, but filed their own names as candidates. For more than 60 years, however, the association's candidates had nearly always been nominated in the Democratic Party primary and subsequently had nearly always been elected to county office. A group of black voters sued in district court to determine the legality of their being excluded from voting in the association pre-primaries. The district court held that the combined election machinery of the association and the Democratic Party deprived the petitioners of their right to vote on account of their race and color, contrary to the Fifteenth Amendment of the U.S. Constitution. It did not, however, issue an injunction, prohibiting the association's activities and forcing the inclusion of blacks, but instead retained jurisdiction or power over the case, to grant further appropriate relief. The Court of Appeals for the Fifth Circuit reversed the decision of the district court, and the case went to the U.S. Supreme Court.

SUMMARY OF ARGUMENTS

The petitioners argued that they were effectively denied a voice in county elections because of the dominance of the Jaybird Democratic Association's pre-primary in the Democratic primary and sub-sequent general election. As a result, they believed that their Fifteenth Amendment rights were being circumvented by the association.

The respondent argued that it was nothing more than an association that merely put its "stamp of approval" on political candidates, much like religious groups or social action groups have done.

DECISION

Although there was no majority opinion, the Court held that the Jaybird Democratic Association was a state actor and was therefore subject to constitutional restraints. Justice Black, joined by Justice Douglas and Justice Burton, found that the qualifications prescribed by Texas entitling electors to vote at county-operated primaries were the sole qualifications entitling electors to vote at the countywide Jaybird primaries, except that blacks were excluded. As a result, the three justices believed that the county and Jaybird elections were so closely linked that they were virtually indistinguishable. The justices held that for a state to permit the duplication of its election process is to permit a flagrant abuse of those processes to defeat the purposes of the Fifteenth Amendment. Although the state did not have any control or input in the Jaybird process, the mere effect of its existence was enough to justify placing the association in the category of a state actor.

Justice Frankfurter found that through the comprehensive "scheme" of regulation of political primaries in Texas, the county election officials were "clothed" with the authority of the state to secure its interest in "fair methods and a fair expression" of preferences in the selection of nominees for political office. By allowing the Jaybird pre-primary to exclude blacks, the state had a hand in the exclusionary practices. Although the Court could not directly tell the state to participate in and regulate the "pre-primary," it could nevertheless eliminate the unlawful tactic of circumscribing the regular channels of the democratic process to which all qualified citizens are a part.

Justices Clark, Reed, and Jackson concurred, finding that the Jaybird Democratic Association operated as "part and parcel" of the Democratic Party, which existed under the auspices of Texas law. They held that the association's mechanism for selecting candidates struck to the core of the electoral process in Fort Bend County, Texas. The association had taken on the attributes of government by its long-standing success in endorsing winning candidates. As a result, the Constitution's safeguards came into play.

Justice Minton was the sole dissenter. In his opinion, for there to have been state action, the wrong must have been committed by the state. He found that the record did not show any compliance by the organization with state standards or any cooperation by or with the state in any other manner. He saw the association's primary as the "concerted action of individuals" and not state action. Participation in the association was voluntary and secondary to the Democratic primary. The mere success rate of the candidates endorsed was not enough to bridge the gap between individual, lawful activity and state-endorsed, state-condoned, state-sanctioned activity. Justice Minton saw the Jaybirds as a "pressure" group similar to other special interest groups at the time that were not subject to constitutional scrutiny. Although he did not agree with the objectives of the group, he certainly did not feel that the federal government could prohibit its electoral actions under the auspices of state action.

AFTERMATH

The Court opened an otherwise closed door on equal protection challenges concerning private associations. Although the Court later withdrew from its activist role, it nevertheless has remained open to constitutional challenges brought by groups affected by private associations and clubs.

SIGNIFICANCE

Through this decision and other related decisions the Court expanded the concept of state action to include private conduct. Some commentators have concluded that the Court could label a state actor as such because of the tenuous and scant relationships between the actors and the state. The result of such an approach could be the virtual privatization of the Constitution resting upon unconvincingly drawn lines.

RELATED CASES

Civil Rights Cases, 109 U.S. 3 (1883)

Grovey v. Townsend, 295 U.S. 45 (1935)

Nixon v. Herndon, 273 U.S. 536 (1927)

Smith v. Allwright, 321 U.S. 649 (1944)

RECOMMENDED READING

Michael M. Burns, *The Exclusion of Women from Influential Men's Clubs: The Inner Sanctum and the Myth of Full Equality,* 18 Harvard Civil Rights–Civil Liberties Law Review 321 (1983).

Elliot, Ward E. Y. *The Rise of Guardian Democracy.* Cambridge, Mass.; Harvard University Press, 1974.

Case Title: *Trop v. Dulles*

Alternate Case Title: The Denationalization Case

Legal Citation: 356 U.S. 86

Year of Decision: 1958

KEY ISSUES

May Congress denationalize soldiers who receive dishonorable discharges for desertion?

HISTORY OF THE CASE

Trop was dishonorably discharged from the U.S. Army in 1944 after he was convicted of desertion. He later sought to obtain a passport, but he was denied on the grounds that his dishonorable discharge for desertion had deprived him of his citizenship under the Nationality Act of 1940. Trop sued to stop enforcement of the act, but he was unsuccessful in both the district court and the Court of Appeals for the Second Circuit.

SUMMARY OF ARGUMENTS

Trop argued that denationalization was a punishment for desertion, and that it was unconstitutional because it was cruel and unusual in violation of the Eighth Amendment.

The government argued that the act was a reasonable exercise of Congress's war powers; that it was not "punishment" in the traditional criminal sense; and even if it were deemed punishment it was not cruel or unusual.

DECISION

The Court, in a narrow 5-4 decision written by Chief Justice Warren, held that the relevant portion of the act was unconstitutional. Chief Justice Warren argued that citizenship could be voluntarily relinquished or abandoned, but it could not be divested by the exercise of the powers of the national government. He contended that while desertion or failure to pay taxes certainly "deals a dangerous blow to this country," it was not punishable by denationalization. Chief Justice Warren argued that while the death penalty would have been a constitutional form of punishment, it was cruel and unusual to denationalize a deserter. In Chief Justice Warren's opinion, denationalization was a penalty "forbidden by the principle of civilized treatment guaranteed by the Eighth Amendment." He argued that the state of perpetual uncertainty that followed denationalization was worse than execution: "It is a form of punishment more primitive than torture, for it destroys for the individual the political existence that was centuries in the development."

Justice Frankfurter, joined by three other justices, wrote a vigorous dissent. He argued that the Court's untenable view of what was cruel and unusual evinced a lack of judicial self-restraint. Justice Frankfurter acknowledged that one might disagree with the act, but "the Constitution has not authorized the judges to sit in judgment on the wisdom of what Congress and the Executive Branch do." Because desertion was a refusal to perform the "ultimate duty of citizenship," Congress had a reasonable basis for punishing deserters with the withdrawal of that citizenship. Justice Frankfurter, assailing the decision of the majority, vehemently disagreed that denationalization was unconstitutional: "Is constitutional dialectic so empty of reason that it can be seriously urged that loss of citizenship is a fate worse than death?"

AFTERMATH

In 1963, the Court held that persons who left the country to avoid military service during wartime could not be punished by banishment from the United States.

SIGNIFICANCE

Denationalizing a U.S. citizen is not an acceptable type of punishment for the crime of desertion during wartime.

RELATED CASES

Nishikawa v. Dulles, 356 U.S. 129 (1958)

Perez v. Brownwell, 356 U.S. 44 (1958)

RECOMMENDED READING

Cable, John L. *Decisive Decisions of United States Citizenship.* Charlottesville, Va.: The Michie Co., 1967.

Meltsner, Michael. *Cruel and Unusual.* New York: Random House, 1973.

Case Title: *Washington v. Davis*

Alternate Case Title: The Police Admission Test Case

Legal Citation: 426 U.S. 229

Year of Decision: 1976

KEY ISSUES

May a police department base hiring decisions on written test scores when a greater percentage of black applicants than whites fail the test?

HISTORY OF THE CASE

The District of Columbia Metropolitan Police Department used a written examination, created by the U.S. Civil Service Commission for use by government agencies, as one of the standards for admission to its police training program. The exam, known as "Test 21," tested verbal ability, vocabulary, reading, and comprehension. Along with other requirements, applicants needed to answer 40 of the test's 80 questions correctly in order to gain admission to the program. Test 21 had been a useful tool in predicting training school performance, although it was not necessarily a predictor of future job performance. A higher percentage of blacks failed the test than whites. Alfred E. Davis, a black applicant who had failed the test, filed a suit against the police department and Walter E. Washington, who was then the mayor of the District of Columbia, alleging that the test deprived him of the equal protection of the law guaranteed by the Fifth Amendment. Washington prevailed in the district Court, but the Court of Appeals for the District of Columbia Circuit reversed and directed judgment for Davis.

SUMMARY OF ARGUMENTS

Davis argued that the test was unconstitutional because (1) it did not predict job performance, (2) the number of black police officers was not proportionate to the population mix of the city, and (3) a disproportionate percentage of blacks failed the test.

Washington argued that because Davis had not alleged that the police department had a discriminatory purpose in administering the test, the test was constitutional under rational basis review.

DECISION

The Supreme Court, in an opinion written by Justice White, held that the police department's use of Test 21 had been constitutional. Under the Court's equal protection analysis, the police department's action would be subject to rational basis review unless Davis could demonstrate that the use of Test 21 had both a racially discriminatory impact and some underlying discriminatory purpose. Justice White began by noting that there was no evidence of discriminatory purpose; in fact, 44 percent of new police recruits were black, and the "Department had systematically and affirmatively sought to enroll black officers, many of whom passed the test but failed to report for duty." Justice White argued that these factors also distinguished this case from those in which discrimination was impossible to explain on nonracial grounds. In the absence of a showing of discriminatory purpose, the Court would not subject the police department's actions to strict scrutiny. As Justice White stated: "Disproportionate impact is not irrelevant, but it is not the sole touchstone of an invidious racial discrimination forbidden by the Constitution."

Justice White then proceeded to inquire whether the police department had a rational basis for concluding that the test served a constitutionally permissible purpose. The police department had contended that the test provided insight into the applicant's oral and written communication skills, both of which are required for the job. In Justice White's view, it was "untenable that the Constitution prevents the Government from seeking modestly to upgrade the communicative abilities of its employees rather than to be satisfied with some lower level of competence." He argued that Davis's position might invalidate "a whole range of tax, welfare, public service, regulatory, and licensing statutes that may be more burdensome to the poor and to the average black than to the more affluent white." Given these considerations, the Court was unable to say that Davis's misfortune required a constitutional remedy.

AFTERMATH

This decision forced civil rights groups to work harder because it compelled them to prove the discriminatory intent behind challenged rules and practices thought to have a racially disproportionate effect.

SIGNIFICANCE

A racially disproportionate impact by itself does not automatically render a practice or rule unconstitutional.

RELATED CASE

Yick Wo v. Hopkins, 118 U.S. 351 (1886)

RECOMMENDED READING

Robert W. Bennett, *"Mere" Rationality in Constitutional Law: Judicial Review and Democratic Theory,* 67 California Law Review 1049 (1977).
John Hart Ely, *Legislative and Administrative Motivation in Constitutional Law,* 79 Yale Law Journal 1205 (1970).

Case Title: *Whitcomb v. Chavis*

Legal Citations: 403 U.S. 124; 29 L.Ed. 2d. 363; 91 S.Ct. 1858

Year of Decision: 1971

KEY ISSUES

Did an Indiana county's multimember district illegally minimize and cancel out the voting power of the resident black community? Multimember districts are represented by two or more legislators whereas a single-member district is represented only by one legislator.

HISTORY OF THE CASE

A lawsuit was filed in the U.S. District Court for the Southern District of Indiana attacking Indiana's state legislative apportionment for creating a single district of Marion County for the election of eight state senators and 15 state assemblymen. The District Court, after withholding judgment for two months to allow the state legislature to correct the malapportionment according to the principles enumerated by the court, (1) redistricted Marion County into single-member districts on the ground that the multimember Marion County district illegally minimized and canceled out the voting power of the cognizable racial minority in the Marion County ghetto, as evidenced by fewer legislators' having resided in the ghetto than the ghetto's proportion of the county population; and (2) redistricted the entire state into single-member districts on the ground that the state was malapportioned by population-per-senator variations of 80,496 to 106,790 and population-per-assemblyman variations of 41,449 to 53,003.

SUMMARY OF ARGUMENTS

Plaintiffs attacked the constitutionality of two statutes of the state of Indiana that provided for multimember districting-at-large of General Assembly seats in Marion County, Indiana. They also alleged that the two statutes invidiously diluted the force and effect of the vote of black citizens and poor persons living within certain Marion County census tracts constituting what was termed "the ghetto area." Residents of the area were alleged to have particular demographic characteristics rendering them a minority interest group with distinctive interests in specific areas of the substantive law. With single-member districting, it was said, the ghetto area would elect three members of the house and one senator; whereas, under the present districting voters in the area "have almost no political force or control over legislators because the effect of their vote is cancelled out by other contrary interest groups" in Marion County. The mechanism of political party organization and the influence of party chairmen in nominating candidates were additional factors alleged to frustrate the exercise of power by residents of the ghetto area.

DECISION

On appeal, the U.S. Supreme Court reversed. Justice White announced the Court's judgment. In Parts I through VI of his opinion, expressing the view of five members of the Court, he held that evidence that the ghetto has fewer resident legislators than its proportion of the county population did not prove invidious discrimination against ghetto residents. In Part VII of his opinion, Justice White, joined by Chief Justice Burger and Justices Black and Blackmun, held that the district court properly ordered statewide reapportionment.

AFTERMATH

Voting districts that were purposefully created to continue racial discrimination were found unconstitutional. In *White v. Regester* 412 U.S. 755 (1973), the Court upheld a judgment of a district court that invalidated two multimember districts, one found to discriminate against blacks, the other against Hispanic Americans. The Court found that plaintiffs had proven that "the political processes leading to nomination and election were not equally open to participation by the group in question—that its members had less opportunity than did other residents in the district to participate in the political processes and to elect legislators of their choice."

SIGNIFICANCE

The Court has refused to overturn legislative districting that complies with the one-person, one-vote principle because the particular districting plan has a disproportionate effect on racial minorities.

RELATED CASES

Chisom v. Roemer, 501 U.S. 380 (1991)

Missouri v. Jenkins, 495 U.S. 33 (1990)

Spallone v. United States, 493 U.S. 265 (1990)

RECOMMENDED READING

Thernstrom, Abigail M. *Whose Votes Count?* Cambridge, Mass.: Harvard University Press, 1987.

Case Title: *Wygant v. Jackson Board of Education*

Alternate Case Title: The Teacher Seniority Case

Legal Citation: 476 U.S. 267

Year of Decision: 1986

KEY ISSUES

May a school board lay off nonminority teachers while retaining minority teachers with less seniority in order to prevent a reduction in the total percentage of minority teachers?

HISTORY OF THE CASE

The collective bargaining agreement between the school board of Jackson County, Michigan, and the local teachers union provided that in laying off teachers, those with the most seniority would be retained. However, it also contained a clause providing that at no time would there be a greater percentage of minorities laid off than the current percentage of minorities employed at the time of the layoff. The plaintiffs, including Wendy Wygant, were nonminority teachers who had been laid off. In some cases, those who had been laid off were tenured teachers while certain minority teachers retained had been in a trial period of employment and under review to determine whether they would become permanent employees. The plaintiffs filed suit in federal district court alleging that the minority clause violated their right to the equal protection of the laws under the Fourteenth Amendment. The district court held that the clause was constitutional as an attempt to remedy societal discrimination by providing role models for minority schoolchildren. The Court of Appeals for the Sixth Circuit affirmed the decision.

SUMMARY OF ARGUMENTS

The plaintiffs argued that the minority retention provision was a racial classification that required strict scrutiny under the equal protection clause of the Fourteenth Amendment. They claimed that strict scrutiny would require proof that the provision constituted an attempt to remedy past discrimination by the school board, and none had been shown in this case.

The board, supported by briefs filed by the attorneys general of numerous states, argued that the provision was a narrowly tailored attempt to remedy societal discrimination by providing minority teachers as role models for children. It also claimed that it had engaged in past hiring discrimination against minorities; thus, the provision was an appropriate remedial response.

DECISION

Justice Powell announced the judgment of a narrowly divided Court. Five justices agreed that the provision violated the Fourteenth Amendment, although they differed over the reason for this decision. Traditional equal protection analysis requires that race-based classifications be justified by a "compelling government interest," and the means chosen must be "narrowly tailored" to fulfill that purpose. Justice Powell argued that only an attempt to remedy past discrimination by the school board, and not societal discrimination in general, would serve as a compelling government interest. Justice Powell argued that the district court's role model theory, if taken to its logical conclusion, could lead to exactly the type of segregated schools rejected by the Court in its historic BROWN V. BOARD OF EDUCATION decision. He acknowledged the difficulties facing public school officials who were constitutionally required to take race into account in order to remedy the vestiges of discrimination while at the same time facing a duty to avoid discrimination on the basis of race. He then noted that even if the board were able to demonstrate past discrimination, the provision was unconstitutional because it was not a narrowly tailored means of fulfilling the government interest in question.

Justice Powell held that because layoffs "impose the entire burden of achieving racial equality on particular [innocent] individuals," they cannot serve as a narrowly tailored means of fulfilling even legitimate purposes. He referred to the use of hiring goals as a more acceptable means of remedying past discrimination.

Justice O'Connor's concurrence differed from the plurality in two respects. First, she did not believe that the relevant government actor—in this case, the school board—should be required to make particularized findings of past discrimination in order to enact a remedy. Justice O'Connor would have left it to the plaintiffs in any given case to prove that there had been no past discrimination by the government. Second, she did not address the general question of whether layoffs were a constitutional means to remedy past discrimination. Because the minority layoff provision in this case was tied to the number of minority students in the school district, not the number of qualified minority applicants in the relevant labor pool, it was clearly not narrowly tailored to remedy past discrimination.

Justice Marshall wrote a dissent joined by Justices Blackmun and Brennan. He argued that the Court had applied an overly stringent form of analysis; in his opinion the provision constituted a constitutional attempt to preserve the benefits of a legitimate affirmative action hiring program. Justice Marshall also argued that eliminating the layoff provision would eviscerate the benefits of that hiring program. He asserted that while layoffs clearly impose a burden on any group, their effect is similar to minority hiring preferences, which are clearly constitutional.

AFTERMATH

Less than a year after the decision in *Wygant*, the Court indicated that proper uses of affirmative action were a remedy for past discrimination permitted by the Constitution.

SIGNIFICANCE

Unless past discrimination can be shown, the preference of one person over another based on race is unconstitutional as an equal protection violation.

RELATED CASES

Fullilove v. Klutznick, 448 U.S. 448 (1980)

Swann v. Charlotte-Mecklenburg Board of Education, 402 U.S. 1 (1971)

RECOMMENDED READING

Cox, Archibald. *The Court and the Constitution.* Boston: Houghton Mifflin, 1987.

Joel L. Selig, *Affirmative Action in Employment: The Legacy of a Supreme Court Majority,* 63 Indiana Law Review 301 (1988).

Case Title: *Yick Wo v. Hopkins*

Legal Citation: 118 U.S. 356

Year of Decision: 1886

KEY ISSUES

How far can a city or government go to use its police power without being discriminatory?

HISTORY OF THE CASE

Prior to the first Chinese Exclusion Act in 1882, free immigration of Chinese aliens led to a substantial increase in their concentration in California. By 1880, for example, the Chinese population constituted 10 percent of the population of the state of California. Moreover, almost half of them were concentrated in the San Francisco area. This concentration quickly became a concern for California lawmakers, who passed several restrictive laws that were clearly discriminatory against Chinese residents and aliens alike. For example, in 1876 the "Queue Ordinance" was passed in San Francisco, which specifically denied Chinese residents police protection for their homes and businesses. Three years later, the California Constitution was amended to prohibit Chinese aliens from working for any government entity in the state. Soon after, the California legislature made employing Chinese workers by any corporation chartered in California a misdemeanor.

Although these measures were overtly unfair, they were less controversial than the seemingly nondiscriminatory ordinance regulating persons operating a laundry within the San Francisco city limits. Passed in 1880, this ordinance gave the Board of Supervisors authority to grant and renew licenses for operating wooden laundry facilities. Because the regulation dealt only with wooden facilities, the city claimed that its purpose of preventing fire was an appropriate exercise of its police power. Violation of the ordinance carried a penalty of a misdemeanor conviction with a jail sentence of up to six months and a fine of up to $1,000.

Although the purpose of the ordinance was legitimate, its application by the Board of Supervisors was clearly discriminatory. In 1880, 240 out of 310 wooden laundries in San Francisco had Chinese owners. Over 200 Chinese owners applied for the license, but only a single permit out of the 80 licenses granted was issued to a Chinese owner, Mary Meagles. Yick Wo, a resident alien, continued to operate his laundry. He was arrested and fined $10. Because he refused to pay, he was jailed for 10 days. Upon his release, Yick Wo petitioned the California Supreme Court and was denied a writ of habeas corpus. He then appealed to the U.S. Supreme Court, naming Sheriff Hopkins in the suit and claiming that the city of San Francisco violated his due process rights under the Fourteenth Amendment.

SUMMARY OF ARGUMENTS

Yick Wo claimed that the ordinance violated his due process rights under the Fourteenth Amendment because of its unfair application by the Board of Supervisors. He supported this claim by using statistical information, stated above, that showed that only 1 out of over 200 Chinese owners received a laundry license.

The city of San Francisco argued in response that it was exercising its "indestructible and inalienable" police power granted under the Constitution. The city also asserted that its police power could not be infringed upon even by the Fourteenth Amendment.

DECISION

Justice Matthews, in a unanimous opinion for the Court, held that the San Francisco fire prevention ordinance violated the due process clause of the Fourteenth Amendment and was therefore unconstitutional. The Court held that the guarantees given by the Fourteenth Amendment, under which the right to earn a living is included, applies to all persons, citizens and aliens alike. Specifically, San Francisco's arbitrary enforcement of the fire prevention ordinance discriminated against Chinese wooden laundry owners and violated their equal protection rights under the Fourteenth Amendment. The test used by Justice Matthews was the following: the legislation satisfied the constitutional requirements of the Fourteenth Amendment if it (1) specifically regulated health and safety practices and (2) was applied fairly. In this case, the power granted by the ordinance to the Board of Supervisors was broader than that which is given under police power. The ordinance allowed the board to use the fire prevention ordinance to arbitrarily regulate both the health and safety practices of wooden facilities and persons such as Yick Wo who operated wooden laundry facilities. This regulation was not only discriminatory but also was outside the police power of the city of San Francisco. Therefore, the Court held that the San Francisco ordinance was unconstitutional, limiting the police power of local governments by expanding the Fourteenth Amendment to prevent discriminatory actions by these municipalities against all persons.

AFTERMATH

The Matthews opinion revolutionized constitutional law by limiting the police power of local and state governments, prohibiting discrimination using the due process clause, and defining the coverage of the Fourteenth Amendment to include aliens. Although this opinion did not put an end to discrimination, the Supreme Court's classification of alienage as a "suspect" class 85 years later required proof of a compelling government interest for alienage discrimination to be upheld.

SIGNIFICANCE

The application of the Fourteenth Amendment outside the context of the Civil War and slavery had consequential implications. After this decision, public officials were put on notice that blatant discrimination against Chinese persons would no longer be acceptable to the legal system. The anti-Chinese movement across the country subsided somewhat. The Supreme Court's composition changed shortly after 1886, however. Afterward, the Fourteenth Amendment was used mainly to prevent restrictions against property rights up until the mid-20th century, when the due process clause was used to fight the persecution of blacks in the form of the "Jim Crow" laws.

RELATED CASES

Civil Rights Cases, 109 U.S. 3 (1883)

Plessy v. Ferguson, 163 U.S. 537 (1896)

Slaughterhouse Cases, 83 U.S. 36 (1873)

RECOMMENDED READING

Cheng-Tsu, W. *"Chink": A Documentary History of Anti-Chinese Prejudice in America.* New York: World Publishing, 1972.

Konuitz, M. R. *The Alien and the Asiatic in American Law.* Ithaca, N.Y.: Cornell University Press, 1946.

Saxton, A. *The Indispensible Enemy: Labor and the Anti-Chinese Movement in California.* Berkeley: University of California Press, 1971.

CONTRACTS

Case Title: *Calder v. Bull*

Alternate Case Title: The "Natural Rights" Case

Legal Citation: 3 U.S. (3 Dall.) 386

Year of Decision: 1798

KEY ISSUES

Is state legislation that invalidates a prior court decision disposing of property under a will an ex post facto law that violates the Constitution?

HISTORY OF THE CASE

This case originated in a Connecticut probate court after the death of Norman Morrison. Caleb Bull and his wife and Calder and his wife were engaged in a dispute over Morrison's will, which affected how Morrison's property would be distributed.

The Court of Probate for Hartford, Connecticut, passed a decree against the will of Norman Morrison and vested a right to recover certain property in appellants Calder and his wife. The Connecticut legislature then passed a resolution of law that set aside the decree of the Court of Probate for Hartford. The effect of the resolution or law was to revise that decision of the Court of Probate for Hartford, one of its inferior courts, and to direct a new hearing of the case by the James Court of Probate. The James Court of Probate then approved the will of Norman Morrison, divested appellant Calder and his wife of the property, and declared the right of that property to be in appellees Bull and his wife. Appellants Calder and his wife claim the premises in question, in right of his wife, as heiress of N. Morrison, physician. Appellee Bull and wife claimed the property under the will of N. Morrison, the grandson.

SUMMARY OF ARGUMENTS

Appellants, Calder and his wife, contended that the above named resolution or law of the legislature of Connecticut was an ex post facto law, prohibited by the Constitution of the United States.

They further claimed that any law of the federal government, or of any of the state governments, contrary to the Constitution of the United States, was void. Therefore, the appellants asserted that the Connecticut legislature had no power to issue the resolution granting a new hearing.

The appellees, Bull and his wife, argued that the resolution was not an ex post facto law and the Connecticut legislature had acted within the scope of its authority.

DECISION

The Court unanimously held that the legislature's action was not an "ex post facto Law" forbidden the states by Article I, section 10. Justice Chase, writing the opinion for the Court, believed that the legislation did not impair a vested right and therefore was consistent with natural justice, the rules and principles that guide human conduct and are enforceable against the states even though they are not contained in the Constitution. However, the Court disagreed over the role of "natural law" in constitutional interpretation.

Justice Chase did not believe that the "omnipotence" of the legislature was absolute or without control, but he felt that its authority should not be expressly restrained by the Constitution or the fundamental law of the state. He argued that the reasons the people of the United States instituted the Constitution was for the establishment of justice, promotion of the general welfare, liberty, and the protection of their persons and property from violence. He believed that these purposes dictated the nature and terms of the social compact and legislative power and that an act of the legislature contrary to the principles in the social compact was not a rightful exercise of legislative authority. For example, Justice Chase maintained that "natural law" prohibits "a law that destroys or impairs the lawful private contracts of citizens [or] that takes property from A. and gives it to B." He argued that private property must be protected from legislative intrusion even if the legislature were not "expressly restrained by the Constitution."

Justice Paterson wrote a concurring opinion finding that the Connecticut legislature did nothing more than exercise its power of granting new trials as it had done from the beginning. He believed that the resolution of the Connecticut legislature was not an ex post facto law within the meaning of the Constitution because the words "ex post facto," when applied to law, referred to crimes and nothing else. Thus, he believed that it referred only to penal statutes, and not this case.

Justice Iredell wrote a dissenting opinion against the belief that a legislative act against natural justice in itself must be void. He felt that no court should have the power to declare it so. He argued that it has been the policy of the states and the people of the United States to precisely define legislative power, and to set limitations within those confines. He argued that if the federal legislature passed a law within the general scope of their constitutional power, the Court could not pronounce it void just because it believed that the law was contrary to natural justice. He asserted that at most, the Court could state that the act was "inconsistent with natural justice." Justice Iredell stated that if an act of Congress or of a state legislature violated the Constitution's provisions, then it was definitely void. However, he maintained that as long as the legislature pursued the authority delegated to them, their acts would be valid since they were exercising the discretion vested in them by the people—and it is only the people to whom the legislature is responsible for the discharge of their trust.

AFTERMATH

Because the Supreme Court affirmed the actions of the probate court, Morrison's will was approved and the property went to the Bulls. Justice Iredell disagreed with Justice Chase's proposition that legislation might be held invalid under natural law even if the legislation did not violate any specific constitutional principles or provisions, and his views have prevailed. Since the 1800s, courts have used their power to invalidate legislation, usually where specific constitutional provisions supplied the principle of invalidity.

SIGNIFICANCE

Calder demonstrated a classic debate between Justice Chase and Justice Iredell over the scope and nature of judicial power. It has proved fundamental to constitutional law. Justice Chase's opinion illustrated the belief that there is an "unwritten" Constitution consisting of principles of natural law that is enforceable against the states. Justice Iredell believed that the very existence of a written

Constitution was authority against the proposition that courts can call on principles of natural justice.

RELATED CASE

Fletcher v. Peck, 10 U.S. 87 (1810)

RECOMMENDED READING

Bailyn, Bernard. *The Ideological Origins of the American Revolution.* Cambridge, Mass.: Belknap Press of Harvard University Press, 1967.

Edwin S. Corwin, *The "Higher Law" Background of American Constitutional Law,* 42 Harvard Law Review (1928).

Suzanna Sherry, *The Founder's Unwritten Constitution,* 54 University of Chicago Law Review (1987).

Case Title: *Proprietors of the Charles River Bridge v. Proprietors of the Warren Bridge*

Alternate Case Title: The Warren Bridge Case

Legal Citations: 36 U.S. (11 Pet.) 420; 9 L.Ed. 773

Year of Decision: 1837

KEY ISSUES

Does the contracts clause distinguish between public and private contracts and, if so, should ambiguities in public contracts be interpreted in favor of the private party or the state?

HISTORY OF THE CASE

The state of Massachusetts had granted a charter to the Charles River Bridge Co. to build a toll bridge between Boston and Charleston. The charter implied, but did not expressly say, that the state would not grant any charters for competing bridges. Later the legislature granted a charter to another company to construct a free bridge.

The owners of the Charles River Bridge filed a bill seeking an injunction to prevent the erection of the Warren Bridge and for general relief. The Massachusetts Supreme Court dismissed the bill and the owners of the Charles River Bridge appealed to the U.S. Supreme Court.

Early decisions of the Supreme Court interpreted the contracts clause as giving broad protection against state interference in all contracts, both private and public. In *Fletcher v. Peck,* 10 U.S. 87 (1910), the Court noted that the language of the Constitution does not distinguish between public and private contracts.

SUMMARY OF ARGUMENTS

The Court addressed the issue of whether a charter granted by the state should be interpreted as exclusive when the charter did not explicitly state that it was exclusive. Chief Justice Taney noted earlier cases that had established that a charter is a contract binding on the state. Previous cases also established to the Court's satisfaction that a state law could work retroactively to divest vested rights so long as the law did not "impair the obligation of a contract." Taney stated that this case called for the Court to decide whether a contract to which the state was a party should be interpreted strictly according to the language it contained, or whether a court could recognize implied promises on the part of the state.

The Court was faced with a conflict between the need for stability of contracts involving the state and the need for flexibility in cases where changing circumstances cause state contracts to result in harm to the public. If the Court decided that it would enforce the implied grant of an exclusive right to build a bridge, then the stability of public contracts would be bolstered; private parties would be able to rely on the understanding they reached with the state. If the Court ruled that implied promises would not be enforced, the state could conceivably alter bargains it had made whenever they proved inconvenient or unprofitable.

DECISION

The Court said that "any ambiguity in the terms of the contract must operate against the adventurers, and in favor of the public, and the plaintiffs can claim nothing that is not clearly given them by the act." Thus, the Court affirmed the Massachusetts Supreme Court's dismissal of the Charles River Bridge Company's claim. The decision favored flexibility over stability in public contracts.

AFTERMATH

The decision reflected the Court's intent to support a state's power over an individual's property right. The obligation of the state would now be strictly interpreted according to the language of the contract in favor of the state. The Court did not say that contracts between private parties were subject to the rule established by this decision.

SIGNIFICANCE

There developed as a result of this case a double standard for reviewing contracts. Private contracts enjoyed broader interpretation, which allowed for the enforcement of implied promises. Public contracts were interpreted narrowly with a bias in favor of the state.

RELATED CASES

Fletcher v. Peck, 10 U.S. (6 Cranch) 87; 3 L.Ed. 162 (1810)

Trustees of Dartmouth College v. Woodword, 17 U.S. (4 Wheat) 518, 4 L.Ed. 629 (1819)

RECOMMENDED READING

Currie, David P. *The Constitution in the Supreme Court 1789–1888.* Chicago: University of Chicago Press, 1985.

———. *The Constitution in the Supreme Court: Article IV and Federal Powers 1836–1864,* 1983 Duke Law Journal 695 (1983).

Horwitz, Morton J. *The Transformation of American Law 1780–1860.* Cambridge, Mass.: Harvard University Press, 1977.

Thomas W. Merrill, *Public Contracts and the Transformation of the Constitutional Order,* 37 Case Western Reserve Law Review 597 (1987).

Case Title: *The Trustees of Dartmouth College v. Woodward*

Alternate Case Title: Dartmouth College Case

Legal Citation: 17 U.S. 518

Year of Decision: 1819

∽

KEY ISSUES

Is the charter of a privately funded institution a contract and, if so, is it protected by the contracts clause of the U.S. Constitution?

HISTORY OF THE CASE

This action brought in state court requested Dartmouth College, a corporation, to turn over certain records. The case went to the Superior Court of the state of New Hampshire and then to the U.S. Supreme Court.

Prior to the American Revolution, Eleazar Wheelock sought and was granted a charter from the king of England for Dartmouth College. Under the college charter, Wheelock, as founder and president of Dartmouth, could nominate his successor. After the American Revolution, Wheelock's son John was the president of Dartmouth and John's administration was challenged by the trustees. The dispute was taken to the state's politicians and the New Hampshire legislature enacted several acts that purported to change the name of the college and its governing structure, among other things. However, the trustees refused to accept the charter as amended by the state legislature and brought suit. Daniel Webster argued the case for the trustees of Dartmouth College.

Under the college charter, the founder and president of Dartmouth, Eleazar Wheelock, could nominate his successor. His son John was president and his administration was challenged by the trustees. Wheelock took the dispute to the state's politicians, but the trustees would not accept a charter amended by the state legislature. The trustees brought suit. Daniel Webster argued for Dartmouth College.

SUMMARY OF ARGUMENTS

The appellants, the trustees, argued that the acts enacted by the New Hampshire legislature altering the name and governing structure of Dartmouth College violated the contracts clause of the U.S. Constitution. The contracts clause states that "no state shall pass any . . . law impairing the obligation of contracts." In support of this contention, the trustees argued that the grant of corporate powers and privileges through the charter was a contract for a private purpose and the acts of the New Hampshire legislature impaired the

contract by essentially abolishing the old entity and establishing a new one.

The appellee, William H. Woodward, the secretary and treasurer of the trustees of Dartmouth, the entity established by the New Hampshire legislature, argued that the occurrence of the American Revolution changed the circumstances under which the charter was originally granted and, therefore, the original charter had become unfit for use. Woodward also argued that the charter was not the type of contract that was contemplated by the contracts clause and, even if it was, the acts did not impair the contract. Woodward also argued that Dartmouth College was a public institution, not a private charity.

Chief Justice Marshall stated that private corporations were free from legislative interference; this included business corporations while public corporations did not get this protection; private corporations were protected under the contracts clause, so legislatures were prohibited from revising or repealing their charters. Although Dartmouth had public purposes, it was a private charitable entity because private individuals founded the corporation. A public corporation was created by public institutions for the public advantage.

DECISION

The charter of a private corporation is a contract protected by the Constitution from legislative interference. The state of New Hampshire could not put its own trustees on the college's Board of Trustees to increase its size through legislation since its charter gave it the right to fill vacancies.

AFTERMATH

This was the first time the Court had held a corporate charter to be a contract. The decision brought corporate charters under the protection of the contracts clause. This interpretation of the contracts clause kept legislative interference from state economic affairs. The practical effect of the case was lessened by the state legislature's adoption of approving a charter only with the right to amend.

SIGNIFICANCE

The case strengthened the power of business by giving businesses a constitutional base. Corporations could not be subject to arbitrary interference; it was to be regarded as a state function providing goods and services that the state could not. This posed a threat to states that had no way to curb corporate abuse. Corporations used the contract clause to challenge taxation and rate regulation.

RELATED CASE

Fletcher v. Peck, 10 U.S. 87 (1810)

RECOMMENDED READING

B. A. Campbell, *John Marshall, the Virginia Political Economy, and the Dartmouth College Decision,* 19 American Journal of Legal History 40 (1975).

Friendly, Henry J. *The Dartmouth College Case and the Public-Private Penumbra.* Austin: University of Texas at Austin, 1968.

Hunting, Warren B. *The Obligations of the Contract Clause of the United States Constitution.* Westport, Conn.: Greenwood Press, 1919.

Stites, Francis N. *Private Interest and Public Gain: The Dartmouth College Case, 1819.* Amherst: University of Massachusetts Press, 1972.

Case Title: *Fletcher v. Peck*

Legal Citation: 10 U.S. 87

Year of Decision: 1810

KEY ISSUES

Is a contract to convey land protected from state law by the contracts clause of the U.S. Constitution?

HISTORY OF THE CASE

This case was brought in federal Circuit Court for the District of Massachusetts as a contract action. Peck was a Boston land speculator. The court ruled for the defendant and the case was then heard by the U.S. Supreme Court, enabling it to apply both state and federal law since the case originated in federal court.

Pursuant to a Georgia legislative land grant, the original grantees of the land in question sold a portion of their land. The new buyer then resold a portion. After an election, the grant was revoked but in the meanwhile the land was again resold; Peck then bought it and sold it to Fletcher, who had no notice of the revocation.

SUMMARY OF ARGUMENTS

Appellant, Robert Fletcher, argued that the title to the land sold to him by appellee, John Peck, was impaired because the state of Georgia had no authority to sell the land. Fletcher argued that Georgia lacked authority to sell the land because the legislative act granting this power to sell was fraudulently procured and the United States, not Georgia, held legal title.

Peck argued that the state constitution gave Georgia title to the land conveyed and a legislative act gave Georgia all jurisdictional and territorial rights. Therefore, Georgia was legally empowered to sell the land.

Chief Justice Marshall wrote for the majority that Georgia could not revoke its grant because of the contracts clause. A contract contains binding obligations. Under the Constitution, a law that annuls a contract between individuals violates the contracts clause. This reasoning also allows a state statute to be declared unconstitutional as part of litigation between private parties.

Justice Johnson wrote for the dissent, saying that the interpretation of the contracts clause espoused by Chief Justice Marshall deprived states of the power of eminent domain, the power to take private property for public use.

DECISION

A contract to convey land was protected from state law by the contracts clause of the Constitution.

AFTERMATH

This was the first Supreme Court case to be decided on the obligations of the contracts clause; it was the first to declare a state statute unconstitutional under federal law.

SIGNIFICANCE

This case altered 19th-century constitutional law by applying the contracts provision to property. It became a major tool for state legislation to be struck down in federal courts.

RELATED CASES

Charles River Bridge v. Warren Bridge, 36 U.S. 420 (1837)

Home Building and Loan Association v. Braisdell, 290 U.S. 415 (1935)

Trustees of Dartmouth College v. Woodward, 17 U.S. 517 (1819)

RECOMMENDED READING

Magrath, Peter C. *Yazoo: Law and Politics in the New Republic: The Case of* Fletcher v. Peck. Providence, R.I.: Brown University Press, 1966.

McCloskey, Robert C. *The American Supreme Court.* Chicago: University of Chicago Press, 1960.

Robert C. Palmer, *Obligations of Contracts: Intent and Distortion,* 37 Case Western Reserve Law Review 631 (1987).

Wiecek, William M. *The Guarantee Clause of the United States Constitution.* Ithaca, N.Y.: Cornell University Press, 1972.

Case Title: *Home Building & Loan Association v. Blaisdell*

Legal Citation: 290 U.S. 398

Year of Decision: 1934

KEY ISSUES

May the government alter existing contractual obligations in order to respond to emergency situations?

HISTORY OF THE CASE

Article I, section 10 of the U.S. Constitution states that "no state shall pass any law impairing the obligation of contracts." The Supreme Court held that the due process clause of the Fifth Amendment extended this provision to the federal government.

During the Great Depression, the Minnesota legislature passed a statute allowing local courts to give relief from mortgage foreclosures. The severe financial and economic depression of the

time had resulted in high unemployment, which created hardships for property owners who were not able to pay their mortgage. The statute allowed local courts to grant extensions to homeowners so that the banks could not foreclose on their homes. Before a court could approve an extension for a homeowner, it had to order the mortgagor to pay a reasonable part of the payment due on the property. The local courts had the power to change the contracts between the home owners and the banks in order to create a reasonable payment schedule for the homeowner. The statute was designed only to last until the end of the depression.

SUMMARY OF ARGUMENTS

Home Building & Loan argued that the statute allowing courts to interfere with private contracts violated the Constitution's statement that "no state shall pass any law impairing the obligation of contracts."

The state asserted that interference with the mortgage contracts was necessary to deal with the depression and to protect society as a whole.

DECISION

The Supreme Court upheld the Minnesota statute in order to protect vital public interests. Because the depression had created an economic emergency, modifications to such contracts were allowed as long as they were reasonable. The Court stressed that the statute would end when the economic emergency was over, and that a state had a power to protect the security of its citizens in emergency situations.

AFTERMATH

This case has not been overruled, and subsequent decisions have affirmed the idea that governments are not absolutely prohibited from modifying public or private contracts. Subsequent decisions have rendered the contracts clause ("no state shall pass any law impairing the obligation of contracts") mostly dead.

SIGNIFICANCE

This case is often regarded as a major starting point for reading the contracts clause out of the Constitution. A government is able to modify contracts in order to protect the health, welfare, and safety of its citizens.

RELATED CASES

Allied Structural Steel Co. v. Spannaus, 438 U.S. 234 (1978)

Energy Reserves Group, Inc. v. Kansas Power and Light Co., 459 U.S. 400 (1983)

U.S. Trust Co. v. New Jersey, 431 U.S. 1 (1977)

RECOMMENDED READING

Keynes, Edward, with Randall K. Miller. *The Court vs. Congress: Prayer, Busing and Abortion.* Durham, N.C.: Duke University Press, 1989.

Robert C. Palmer, *Obligations of Contracts: Intent and Distortion,* 37 Case Western Reserve Law Review 631–673 (summer 1987).

Case Title: *Lochner v. New York*

Alternate Case Title: The Bakeshop Case

Legal Citations: 198 U.S. 45; 25 S.Ct. 539; 49 L.Ed. 937

Year of Decision: 1905

KEY ISSUES

Does a state law that prohibits employees from working in bakeries more than 10 hours a day or 60 hours a week unconstitutionally infringe on the Fourteenth Amendment right to sell and purchase labor?

HISTORY OF THE CASE

The late 19th and early 20th centuries saw the height of the Progressive movement, which worked for reformist state legislation to improve the dismal working conditions that were a by-product of America's industrial revolution. The reforms included statutes regulating wages and hours, the employment of women and children, and conditions of the workplace.

The state law at issue in *Lochner v. New York* was such a reformist law. Section 110 of the labor law of the state of New York provided that no employees could be required or permitted to work in bakeries more than 60 hours in a week, or 10 hours a day.

Joseph Lochner owned a "biscuit, bread and cake bakery and confectionery establishment" in Utica, New York. Lochner was convicted in county court of violating the New York labor law by requiring employee Aman Schmitter to work more than 60 hours a week. Lochner appealed his conviction to the Appellate Division of the Supreme Court, which affirmed his conviction by a vote of three to two. Lochner then appealed to the New York Court of Appeals, the highest court of the state, which also affirmed the conviction, albeit by a court divided 4-3.

Lochner then sought relief from the U.S. Supreme Court.

SUMMARY OF ARGUMENTS

Lochner argued that the statute's classification violated the equal protection clause of the Fourteenth Amendment. Lochner's attorneys, Frank H. Field and Henry Weissmann, argued that the law "singles out a certain number of men employing bakers, and permits all others similarly situated, including many who are competitors in business, to work their employés as long as they choose." Lochner's attorneys argued that the law was an improper exercise of state police power because it abridged the "fundamental right to pursue occupations." The statute was not intended to protect public health, as contended by the state. Lochner's attorneys contended that the statute could not reasonably be construed as benefiting public health because "there is no danger to the employé in a first-class bakery and so far as unsanitary conditions are concerned the employé is protected by other sections of the law."

The state of New York countered by claiming that Lochner had not met his "burden of demonstrating that the statute is repugnant to the provisions of the Federal Constitution." Julius M. Mayer, the New York attorney general, argued before the Court that the statute "was a proper exercise of the police power of the State." "The unhealthful character of the baker's occupation" made necessary a statute that restricted the employees as well as the employer.

> The State . . . has a right to safeguard the citizen against his own lack of knowledge. In dealing with certain classes of men the

State may properly say that . . . it shall not permit these men, when engaged in dangerous or unhealthful occupations, to work for a longer period of time each day than is found to be in the interest of the health of the person.

The state of New York simply argued that it had determined that those working as bakers needed to be protected from being forced to work potentially dangerously long hours.

DECISION

The Supreme Court held, in an opinion written by Justice Rufus W. Peckham, that the New York law was unconstitutional. "The statute necessarily interferes with the right of contract between the employer and employés, concerning the number of hours in which the latter may labor in the bakery of the employer. The general right to make a contract in relation to his business is part of the liberty of the individual protected by the Fourteenth Amendment of the Federal Constitution." The court explained that this liberty encompasses "[t]he right to purchase or to sell labor."

The Court distinguished other cases that had been upheld as valid exercises of state police power. Justice Peckman explained that when deciding whether state laws impermissibly infringed on the liberty of contract, or were valid exercises of the police power, the Court made the following inquiry:

Is this a fair, reasonable and appropriate exercise of the police power of the State, or is it an unreasonable, unnecessary and arbitrary interference with the right of the individual to his personal liberty or to enter into those contracts in relation to labor which may seem to him appropriate or necessary for the support of himself and his family?

The Court found that the New York law did not meet this test: "There is, in our judgment, no reasonable foundation for holding this to be necessary or appropriate as a health law to safeguard the public health or the health of individuals who are following the trade of a baker." The Court did not believe that a baker's occupation was unhealthy. Just because a law relates "in a remote

degree to the public health does not necessarily render the enforcement valid." Indeed, if they were to uphold this as a valid public health law, there would be no end to the degree the liberty of contract of employees and employers could be limited: "Some occupations are more healthy than others, but we think there are none which might not come under the power of the legislature to supervise and control the hours working therein, if the mere fact that the occupation is not absolutely and perfectly healthy is to confer that right upon the legislative department of the Government." In short, from the majority's perspective, the law was not a "health law," but merely "an illegal interference with the rights of individuals, both employers and employés, to make contracts regarding labor upon such terms as they may think best."

Justice John Marshall Harlan dissented from the majority decision, and wrote an opinion that was joined by Justice Edward White and Justice William Day. Justice Harlan recognized "that there is a liberty of contract which cannot be violated," but explained "that such liberty of contract is subject to such regulations as the State may reasonably prescribe for the common good and well-being of society." Harlan believed that the test of the constitutionality of such state statutes was much more lenient than the standard used by the Court's majority. "[T]he rule is universal that a legislative enactment, Federal or state, is never to be disregarded or held invalid unless it be, beyond question, plainly and palpably in excess of legislative power."

Justice Harlan found that the New York law, "enacted in order to protect the physical well-being of those who work in bakery and confectionery establishments," did not exceed the state's legislative power. He believed that the New York legislature could have reasonably concluded that working in bakeries more than 10 hours a day was dangerous. Justice Harlan cited contemporary treatises as authority that working conditions in bakeries were potentially unhealthy. One commentator had written that a baker's work "is among the hardest and most laborious imaginable," and another explained that the "constant inhaling of flour dust causes inflammation of the lungs and of the bronchial tubes." These hardships took a heavy toll; bakers "seldom live[d] over their fiftieth year, most of them dying between the ages of forty and fifty." Because Justice Harlan believed that the New York statute was a reasonable measure responding to potential health problems, he would have upheld its constitutionality.

Justice Oliver Wendell Holmes wrote a separate dissent, which filled fewer than two full pages in the United States *Reports*. While brief, the opinion is perhaps one of the most frequently cited dissenting opinions in the history of the Court. Holmes described a Constitution superior to individual ideologies and defined the proper role of the Supreme Court as primarily deferring to the choices of the majority, as expressed by state laws. The following excerpts are the most notable:

[A] constitution is not intended to embody a particular economic theory, whether of paternalism and the organic relation of the citizen to the State or of *laissez faire*. It is made for people of fundamentally differing views, and the accident of our finding certain opinions natural and familiar or novel and even shocking ought not to conclude our judgment upon the question whether statutes embodying them conflict with the Constitution of the United States. . . .

I think that the word liberty in the Fourteenth Amendment is perverted when it is held to prevent the natural outcome of a dominant opinion, unless it can be said that a rational and fair man necessarily would admit that the statute proposed would infringe fundamental principles as they have been understood by the traditions of our people and our law.

Justice Holmes would not have overturned the law that the democratically elected New York legislature deemed reasonable.

AFTERMATH

The *Lochner* decision was met by reports in the press of threatened strikes, but these never occurred. Actually, the 10-hour workday was soon achieved by many in the baking industry with unionization.

SIGNIFICANCE

The *Lochner* decision marked the peak of the Supreme Court's protection of "the liberty of contract" at the expense of state-enacted economic regulations. The Court has since abdicated its role of reviewing economic legislation, instead deferring to the judgment of state legislatures.

RELATED CASES

Bunting v. Oregon, 243 U.S. 426 (1917)

Holden v. Hardy, 169 U.S. 366 (1898)

Muller v. Oregon, 208 U.S. 412 (1908)

West Coast Hotel Co. v. Parrish, 300 U.S. 379 (1937)

RECOMMENDED READING

Kens, Paul. *Judicial Power and Reform Politics: The Anatomy of* Lochner v. New York. Lawrence: University Press of Kansas, 1990.

———. Lochner v. New York: *A Case of Economics, Philosophy, Politics, and the Supreme Court.* Ph.D. diss., University of Texas at Austin, 1987.

Semonche, John E. *Charting the Future: The Supreme Court Responds to a Changing Society, 1890–1920.* Westport, Conn.: Greenwood Press, 1978.

Siegan, Bernard H. *Economic Liberties and the Constitution.* Chicago: University of Chicago Press, 1980.

Case Title: *Muller v. Oregon*

Legal Citation: 208 U.S. 412

Year of Decision: 1908

KEY ISSUES

Do laws that limit the work hours for women violate the U.S. Constitution?

HISTORY OF THE CASE

On February 9, 1903, the Oregon legislature passed an act that prohibited women from working in "any mechanical establishment, or factory, or laundry" for more than 10 hours a day. Curt Muller, owner of Grand Laundry in Portland, brought this suit to the Supreme Court because he was fined for allowing one of his female employees to work more than 10 hours. He was found guilty at trial, fined $10.00, and the decision was affirmed by the Oregon Supreme Court. It went to the U.S. Supreme Court by writ of error, which indicated an error in law of the lower courts, and sought review.

SUMMARY OF ARGUMENTS

Muller contended that the statute prevented people from making their own contracts, thereby violating the Fourteenth Amendment, which says that no state shall abridge the privileges and immunities of citizens or deny them due process. He also argued that the law did not apply equally to all people, and that it had no reasonable relationship to public health, safety, or welfare.

Oregon, represented by Louis Brandeis (later Justice Brandeis), did not present per se legal arguments, but rather presented scientific evidence regarding the physiology of women and the detrimental effect of long hours on women.

DECISION

Justice Brewer delivered the opinion of the Court, which first recognized that women had equal rights of contract with men under Oregon law. It also recognized that working hour limits as applied to men were previously held unconstitutional in LOCHNER V. NEW YORK, (1905), because they interfered with contractual rights. However, the Court affirmed the conviction, citing the differences between men and women as the reason. The Court held that the physical strength and reproductive role of women, as well as their dependency on men, required protection from long working hours for their own health as well as the health of future generations.

AFTERMATH

At the time, this case sent the message that women were more important for the promulgation of the human race than as laborers, especially considering that a minimum wage law for women was turned down in *Adkins v. Children's Hosp.* (1923).

SIGNIFICANCE

The limitation on maximum working hours was a signal for things to come for men as well as women with the New Deal legislation, social and economic reform measures used to ease the effects of the Great Depression. Sex-specific labor statutes were abolished with the Civil Rights Act of 1964, which banned discrimination in the workplace based on sex or pregnancy. However, *Muller* set a precedent for court recognition of the effect laws had on people's lives and the impact its decisions would have on working people.

RELATED CASES

Adkins v. Children's Hosp., 261 U.S. 525 (1923)

Bunting v. Oregon, 243 U.S. 412 (1908)

Lochner v. New York, 198 U.S. 45 (1905)

Nebbia v. New York, 291 U.S. 502 (1934)

West Coast Hotel Co. v. Parrish, 300 U.S. 379 (1937)

RECOMMENDED READING

Ronald K. L. Collins II and Jennifer Frieser, *Looking Back on* Muller v. Oregon. Part I, 69 American Bar Association Journal 294 (1983).

———, *Looking Back on* Muller v. Oregon. Part II, 69 American Bar Association Journal 472 (1983).

Semonche, John E. *Charting the Future: The Supreme Court Responds to a Changing Society, 1890–1920.* Westport, Conn.: Greenwood Press, 1978.

Case Title: *Stone v. Mississippi*

Alternate Case Title: Police Powers Case

Legal Citations: 101 U.S. 814; 11 Otto 814; 25 L.Ed. 1079

Year of Decision: 1879

KEY ISSUES

Does a state legislature have the right to revoke the charter of a lottery company through exercise of its police powers against popular sentiment?

HISTORY OF THE CASE

In 1867, the Mississippi legislature granted a charter to a lottery company that was to be valid for 25 years. In 1869, the legislature passed a law that "the legislature shall never authorize any lottery," which was ratified by the people. The attorney general of Mississippi filed suit to declare the 25-year charter repealed.

SUMMARY OF ARGUMENTS

Stone argued that he was exercising his rights under his corporation's charter to operate a lottery and these rights were not extinguished by the passage of the constitutional provision.

Mississippi agreed that Stone was complying with his charter, but argued that the charter was repealed by the passage of the constitutional provision.

Chief Justice Waite delivered the Court's opinion that state police powers create an implied term in all contracts. A legislature may not "bargain away" the ability to provide for public health, safety, and morals or "divest itself of the power to provide for them." By reading into every contract a police powers escape clause, a provision that would essentially void the contract if it impaired the public health, safety, and morals, the Court exempted state statutes affecting the public health, safety, and morals from the contracts clause prohibition. The Court considered lotteries and gambling to be included with and subject to the police powers. When determining whether a contract had been entered through the granting of a corporate charter, the court found the state legislature had granted the company the right to conduct lotteries in return for revenue, but this alone was not enough. Rather, "whether the alleged contract exists depends on the authority of the legislature to bind the state and the people of the state in that way."

DECISION

The legislation prohibiting lotteries and gambling does not conflict with the contracts clause of the Constitution. The lottery company has nothing more than a license to enjoy the privilege for the time agreed, subject to future legislation or constitutional control.

AFTERMATH

This case points out that there is a difference between traditional lotteries, gift enterprises, and casino gambling. Common gambling is tolerated partly because it requires skill. Lotteries infest whole communities, while gambling only involves a few individuals. But excluding gambling from the definition of lottery, the Supreme Court gave Congress guidance when it passed anti-lottery bills.

SIGNIFICANCE

Beginning in the 1940s, the Court's contract clause interpretations demonstrated a reluctance to strike down social and economic legislation under other constitutional provisions. The Court denied every contracts clause claim presented to it between 1941 and 1977.

RELATED CASES

City of El Paso v. Simmons, 379 U.S. 497 (1965)

Federal Communications Commission v. American Broadcasting Co. 347 U.S. 284 (1954)

Manigault v. Springs, 199 U.S. 473 (1905)

RECOMMENDED READING

Robert A. Graham, *The Constitution, the Legislature, and Unfair Surprise: Toward a Reliance-Based Approach to the Contract Clause,* 92 Michigan Law Review 398 (1993).

Richard Shawn Oliphant, *Prohibiting Casinos from Advertising: The Irrational Application of 18 USC 1304,* 38 Arizona Law Review 1373 (1996).

David B. Toscano, *Forbearance Agreements: Invalid Contracts for the Surrender of Sovereignty,* 92 Columbia Law Review 426 (1992).

DUE PROCESS

Case Title: *Adamson v. California*

Alternate Case Title: The State Due Process Case

Legal Citation: 332 U.S. 46

Year of Decision: 1947

KEY ISSUES

Does the Fourteenth Amendment to the U.S. Constitution require the states to apply the Fifth Amendment with regard to the privilege against self-incrimination in state criminal trials?

HISTORY OF THE CASE

Admiral Dewey N. Adamson was tried and convicted for first-degree murder in Los Angeles County, California. The conviction was based partly on the admission into evidence at trial of a portion of a pair of women's stockings found in his bedroom. The stockings found did not belong to the dead victim; however, a piece of women's stockings was found under the victim's body. The tops of the victim's stockings were not found, and the corpse was bare-legged. The California court held that the tops of the stockings were admissible in evidence because they showed Adamson's interest in women's stocking tops. This was such strong circumstantial evidence that it tended to identify the defendant as the person responsible for the crime at issue. Adamson's death sentence was affirmed by the California Supreme Court, and it was that judgment which was under review by the U.S. Supreme Court.

SUMMARY OF ARGUMENTS

Adamson's counsel argued that the California law permitting opposing counsel to comment on a defendant's failure to explain or deny evidence or facts in the case against him inherently violated due process guaranteed by the Fourteenth Amendment of the Constitution in that the burden of proof was shifted to the defendant, who no longer had the presumption of innocence. Such a law as California's removes from the accused any procedural safeguards against self-incrimination.

The use of the stockings in evidence at trial was not only irrelevant but was used to excite and prejudice the jury and served to deny the defendant a fair trial.

The attorney general of California claimed that the state had made no shift in the burden of proof from the state to the defendant by the admission of the evidence. The right given by the statute to the court to comment upon a defendant's failure to explain or deny evidence against him violated neither the Fourteenth Amendment nor the Fifth Amendment. The attorney general also argued that the admission of the stockings found in Adamson's room was admissible evidence and the fact that it may have been a poor reflection upon him did not mean that it was not appropriate evidence in a criminal trial.

DECISION

In a 5-4 vote, Justice Stanley Reed opposed the application of the Fifth Amendment's guarantee against self-incrimination to the states. In an opinion notable for judicial restraint, Reed spoke for a majority of the Court in continuing the view that there was a limited incorporation of federal rights in state criminal trials. He noted that the Fifth Amendment's protection from self-incrimination was not incorporated into the Fourteenth Amendment for application to state action. Thus the states were free to abridge the privileges and immunities flowing from state citizenship. Only those rights that are so fundamental that they are "implicit in the concept of ordered liberty" (332 U.S. 46 at 54) are secure from state interference. Reed further argued that the courts of the states may have their own ideas as to the most efficient administration of criminal justice:

> The purpose of due process is not to protect an accused against a proper conviction but against an unfair conviction. When evidence is before a jury that threatens conviction, it does not seem unfair to require him to choose between leaving the adverse evidence unexplained and subjecting himself to impeachment through disclosure of former crimes.

Justice Felix Frankfurter wrote a concurring opinion that noted that in the period of 70 years between the incorporation of the Fourteenth

Amendment into the Constitution and the beginning of the then-current membership of the Supreme Court, 43 judges reviewed that amendment, and of those 43 judges only one ever indicated belief that the Fourteenth Amendment was a shorthand summary of the first eight amendments.

Justice Hugo Black wrote the dissent, which was joined by Justices Douglas, Murphy, and Rutledge. Justice Black refused to reaffirm the TWINING V. NEW JERSEY decision, which concluded that the Fourteenth Amendment protection of privileges and immunities of national citizenship did not include protection against self-incrimination, because he felt that the authors of that decision had failed to notice the intent of the framers of the Fourteenth Amendment to overturn the 1833 case of *Barron v. Baltimore* (7 Peter. [U.S.] 243, 8 L.Ed. 672), which also held that the Fifth Amendment was inapplicable to the states. Black found that the Supreme Court had never given "full consideration or exposition to this purpose." He further argued that "history conclusively demonstrates that the language of the first section of the Fourteenth Amendment, taken as a whole, was thought by those responsible for its submission to the people, and by those who opposed its submission, sufficiently explicit to guarantee that thereafter no state could deprive its citizens of the privileges and protections of the Bill of Rights." Justice Black attached 30 pages of debate and legislative history as an appendix to his dissent.

AFTERMATH

The Court has never adopted Justice Black's total incorporation approach, but rather has taken a selective incorporation approach in applying nearly all the individual components of the Bill of Rights to the states. *Adamson* therefore served to keep the door of the federal courts closed to many convicted in state trials.

SIGNIFICANCE

Of the four dissenting justices—Hugo Black, Frank Murphy, William O. Douglas, Wiley Rutledge—Justices Black and Douglas continued to serve on the Court until the 1960s and were at last able to see their view prevail. In the 1964 and 1965 cases of MALLOY V. HOGAN and GRIFFIN V. CALIFORNIA, the Supreme Court finally extended the privilege against self-incrimination to virtually every situation.

RELATED CASES

Griffin v. California, 380 U.S. 609 (1965)

Malloy v. Hogan, 378 U.S. 1 (1964)

Palko v. Connecticut, 302 U.S. 319 (1937)

Twining v. New Jersey, 211 U.S. 78 (1908)

RECOMMENDED READING

Berger, Raoul. *Government by Judiciary: The Transformation of the Fourteenth Amendment.* Cambridge, Mass.: Harvard University Press, 1977.

Cortner, Richard C. *The Supreme Court and the Second Bill of Rights: The Fourteenth Amendment and the Nationalization of Civil Liberties.* Madison: University of Wisconsin Press, 1981.

Levy, Leonard, Charles Farrman, and Stanley Morrison. *The Fourteenth Amendment and the Bill of Rights: The Incorporation Theory.* New York: Da Capo Press, 1970.

Case Title: *Betts v. Brady*

Alternate Case Title: The "Right to Counsel" Case

Legal Citations: 316 U.S. 455; 62 S.Ct. 1252

Year of Decision: 1942

KEY ISSUES

Is a petitioner's conviction and sentence a deprivation of his liberty without due process of law, in violation of the Sixth Amendment and incorporated into the Fourteenth Amendment to the U.S. Constitution, because of the court's refusal to appoint counsel at his request?

HISTORY OF THE CASE

Smith Betts was indicted for robbery in the Circuit Court of Carroll County, Maryland. He was unable to afford counsel. Betts told the judge of his situation and requested counsel be appointed for him. The judge refused his request, stating that this was not the practice in Carroll County unless the charge was rape or murder. Betts pleaded not guilty without waiving his right to counsel. He elected for trial without a jury. The judge found Betts guilty and imposed a sentence of eight years.

Betts filed a petition for a writ of habeas corpus with a judge of the circuit court for Washington County while serving his sentence. The writ was issued, the case was heard, and his contention was rejected. He filed another petition for a writ of habeas corpus, based on the same grounds as the earlier petition, with Carroll T. Bond, chief judge of the Court of Appeals of Maryland. A hearing was afforded, evidence at Betts's trial was incorporated into the record, and the cause was argued. Judge Bond granted the writ, but remanded Betts to the custody of the respondent, prison warden Patrick J. Brady. The petitioner then applied to the U.S. Supreme Court.

SUMMARY OF ARGUMENTS

Betts argued that the Fourteenth Amendment required the appointment of counsel for indigent persons accused of crimes in state courts. He also argued that if counsel is not appointed, the prisoner is entitled to release because the court's failure to appoint counsel deprives the court of jurisdiction and renders the judgment void.

Brady argued that the appointment of counsel to an indigent person was only necessary for due process to the extent that without such appointment the indigent defendant would not receive a fair and just hearing.

DECISION

Justice Roberts wrote the opinion for the Court holding that the Supreme Court has jurisdiction to review the decision of the state court since it is a final disposition by the highest court of Maryland in which a judgment could be had, and that Betts's conviction and sentence was not a deprivation of his liberty without due process of law merely due to the court's refusal to appoint counsel at his request. Justice Roberts found that appointment of counsel is not a fundamental right essential to a fair trial.

He stated that section 237 of the Judicial Code declares the Supreme Court competent to review, upon certiorari, "any cause wherein a final judgment . . . has been rendered . . . by the highest court" of a state "in which a decision could be had" on a federal question. Justice Roberts stated

that as long as a petitioner has exhausted all of his state remedies, he could appeal to the Supreme Court.

Justice Roberts found that the judgment entered by Judge Bond, the chief justice of the Court of Appeals of Maryland, complied with the requirements of section 237. Justice Roberts also found it an impermissible denial of all recourse to the Supreme Court to hold that the ability to make successive applications to courts and judges of Maryland—which is a right prisoners have—was not a final judgment. He would have held differently had the court not been the highest court of Maryland in which a judgment could be had.

Justice Roberts began his analysis of the due process by distinguishing between the Sixth Amendment due process guarantees, which apply only to trials in the federal court, and those guaranteed by the Fifth Amendment, which secure due process against invasion by the federal government, and apply to state actions through the Fourteenth Amendment. He stated that the due process rules were not to be applied as a set of hard and fast rules, but should be applied in light of other circumstances. Justice Roberts used the following test to determine when due process had been denied: if a trial was conducted in such manner that it was "shocking to the universal sense of justice" or "offensive to the common and fundamental ideas of fairness and right."

Distinguishing other cases that Betts relied on, namely *Powell v. Alabama,* (1932) Justice Roberts found the issue here to be whether in every criminal case, regardless of the circumstances, due process of law requires the state to appoint counsel. Justice Roberts decided this issue beginning with a reference to constitutional and statutory provisions existing in the colonies and states prior to the inclusion of the Bill of Rights, and in the constitutional, legislative, and judicial history of the states to the present date. He found various constitutional provisions among the original 13 colonies regarding the right to counsel. Justice Roberts said this background showed an attempt to do away with rules that denied representation, in whole or in part, by counsel in criminal prosecutions. In addition, he showed that the statutes in force at the time of the adoption of the Bill of Rights, the great majority of states, the people, their representatives, and their courts did not consider the appointment of counsel a fundamental right, essential to a fair trial.

Justice Roberts used this evidence to conclude that the concept of due process incorporated in the Fourteenth Amendment did not obligate the states to furnish counsel in every such case. Instead, he argued that each court had the power, if it deemed, to appoint counsel where needed in the interest of fairness. Justice Roberts added that in Maryland, if the situation had been different—if Betts had not been an able man of ordinary intelligence with a little familiarity with criminal procedure—then a refusal to appoint counsel would have resulted in a reversal of a judgment of conviction. He closed stating that although lack of counsel in a particular case may result in a conviction lacking such fundamental fairness guaranteed by the Fourteenth Amendment, that amendment does not embody an inexonerable command that no trial for any offense can be fairly conducted and justice accorded a defendant who is not represented by counsel.

Justice Black wrote a dissenting opinion joined by Justice Murphy and Justice Douglas. Justice Black determined petitioner's right to counsel based on a narrower question than the majority proposed. He asked whether in view of the nature of the offense and the circumstances of his trial and conviction, Betts was denied the procedural protection that is his right under the federal Constitution. He noted that Betts was a farm hand, too poor to afford counsel, and was a man of little education, perhaps not of ordinary intelligence as the majority stated.

Justice Black felt that the majority's view gave the Supreme Court too much supervisory power. He stated that earlier decisions declared the right to counsel in criminal proceedings a fundamental right, guarded from invasion by the Sixth Amendment, whose purpose was to guard against arbitrary or unjust deprivation of liberty by the federal government. Justice Black also believed that denial to the poor the request of counsel was shocking to the "universal sense of justice" throughout this country. He insisted that no man should be deprived of counsel merely because of his poverty—otherwise it defeated the promise of our democratic society to provide equal justice under the law.

Aftermath

The standard established in *Betts* was overruled by *GIDEON V. WAINWRIGHT* (1963), which held

that indigent defendants in state felony prosecutions have a right to the assistance of counsel. *Gideon* replaces the *Betts* balancing test with an absolute requirement declaring that no matter what the substance of the crime, a defendant is entitled to a lawyer in state and federal court.

The exception to the *Betts* decision, which required counsel to be appointed in noncapital cases when the absence of counsel would deprive the defendant of a fair hearing, was seldom used.

Significance

The Fourteenth Amendment incorporation cases greatly extended the degree of supervision the Court could give to the practices of state governments, especially in the area of criminal procedure. Formerly, the Court could exercise only general oversight, but now close scrutiny became possible. *Betts* fixed the "special circumstances" test as the trigger for the provision of appointed counsel.

Related Cases

Argesinger v. Hamlin, 407 U.S. 25 (1972)

Gideon v. Wainwright, 372 U.S. 335 (1963)

In re Gault, 387 U.S. 1 (1967)

Recommended Reading

Yale Kamisar, Betts v. Brady *Twenty Years Later: The Right to Counsel and Due Process*, 61 Michigan Law Review 219 (1962).

Case Title: *Bolling v. Sharpe*

Alternate Case Title: The District of Columbia Desegregation Case

Legal Citations: 347 U.S. 497; 74 S.Ct. 693

Year of Decision: 1954

Key Issues

Is racial segregation in the public schools of the District of Columbia a denial to black children of the due process of law guaranteed by the Fifth Amendment?

HISTORY OF THE CASE

In BROWN V. BOARD OF EDUCATION (1954), the Supreme Court held that the Constitution prohibits the states from maintaining racially segregated public schools. *Bolling* challenged the validity of segregation in the public schools of the District of Columbia. Petitioners, black children, were refused admission to a public school attended by white children solely because they were black. They looked to the District Court of the District of Columbia to gain admission to the school. That court dismissed their complaint. The U.S. Supreme Court agreed to hear the case before judgment in the court of appeals because of the importance of the constitutional question presented.

SUMMARY OF ARGUMENTS

Petitioners alleged that racial segregation in the public schools of the District of Columbia deprived them of due process of law under the Fifth Amendment.

Respondents argued that no provision in the Constitution prohibited the federal government from discriminating on the basis of race.

DECISION

Chief Justice Warren wrote the opinion for the Court. He held that racial segregation in the public schools of the District of Columbia was a denial of the due process of law guaranteed by the Fifth Amendment. Previously, the Court held that the Fourteenth Amendment prohibits the states from maintaining racially segregated public schools. The Fifth Amendment, which applies to the District of Columbia, did not contain an equal protection clause; however, it contained a due process clause. Justice Warren stated that the equal protection clause and the due process clause are not always interchangeable, but that discrimination may be so unjustifiable as to violate due process.

Chief Justice Warren looked to the language of the Constitution to declare that it prohibited discrimination by the general government, or by the states, against any citizen because of his race. He added that liberty under law extended to the full range of conduct that an individual is free to pursue. The government cannot restrict this liberty unless it has a proper governmental objective. Justice Warren then reasoned that segregation in public education is not related to any proper governmental objective; therefore, it constituted an arbitrary deprivation of their liberty in violation of the due process clause.

He concluded stating that in light of the Court's decision in *Brown*, which held that the Constitution prohibits states from maintaining racially segregated schools, the same Constitution should not impose a lesser standard on the federal government.

AFTERMATH

The Court remained wedded to the existence and centrality of the antidiscrimination principle in its pursuit to end segregation throughout the South and the rest of the country. President Eisenhower ordered the desegregation of the schools in Washington, D.C., after this decision.

SIGNIFICANCE

Bolling has meant that even though the Fifth Amendment does not have equal protection language, nor can the Fifth be read to incorporate the Fourteenth Amendment's equal protection language for states, the due process clause of the Fifth Amendment served a corresponding, though not identical, function for the federal government.

RELATED CASES

Baker v. Carr, 369 U.S. 186 (1992)

Brown v. Board of Education, 347 U.S. 483 (1954)

Plessy v. Ferguson, 163 U.S. 537 (1896)

Smuck v. Hobson, 408 F.2d 175 (D.C. Cir. 1969)

RECOMMENDED READING

Charles L. Black, *The Lawfulness of the Segregation Decisions*, 69 Yale Law Journal 421 (1960).

John P. Frank and Robert F. Munro, *The Original Understanding of "Equal Protection of the Laws"*, Washington University Law Quarterly 421 (1972).

Kluger, R. *Simple Justice: The History of* Brown v. Board of Education *and Black America's Struggle for Equality*. New York: Knopf, 1976.

Case Title: *Duncan v. Louisiana*

Alternate Case Title: The "Right to Jury Trial" Case

Legal Citation: 391 U.S. 145

Year of Decision: 1968

KEY ISSUES

Does a defendant convicted of simple battery—a misdemeanor punishable by a maximum of two years' imprisonment and a $300 fine—have the right to a jury trial?

HISTORY OF THE CASE

Appellant Duncan was convicted of simple battery in the Twenty-fifth Judicial District Court of Louisiana. Under Louisiana law, simple battery is a misdemeanor, punishable by a maximum of two years' imprisonment and a $300 fine. Duncan sought trial by jury, but because the Louisiana Constitution granted jury trials only in cases involving capital punishment or imprisonment at hard labor, the trial judge denied the request. Duncan was convicted and sentenced to 60 days in prison and a $150 fine. He sought review from the Louisiana Supreme Court, which denied his requests, failing to find an error of law. Duncan then sought the review of the U.S. Supreme Court.

SUMMARY OF ARGUMENTS

Duncan's attorney argued that the Sixth and Fourteenth Amendments to the U.S. Constitution secured the right to jury trial in state criminal prosecutions where a sentence as long as two years may be imposed.

The state of Louisiana argued that the Constitution imposed no duty upon the states to have a jury trial in any criminal case. Louisiana also argued that if the Court held that the Fourteenth Amendment ensured a right to jury trial, the integrity of nonjury trials would be questioned. Finally, Louisiana contended that the appellant's crime did not reach the level of seriousness necessary for a jury trial.

DECISION

Justice White wrote the opinion for the Court, holding that the Sixth Amendment right to a jury trial was applicable to the states via the Fourteenth Amendment due process clause of the U.S. Constitution. He stated the varied protections that fall under the due process clause, which include the right to be compensated for property taken by the state, the rights of speech, press and religion under the First Amendment, the right to be free from unreasonable searches and seizures under the Fourth Amendment, and various other rights guaranteed by the first eight amendments that were held to be protected against state action. To determine whether a right extended by the Fifth and Sixth Amendments with respect to federal criminal proceedings was protected against state action by the Fourteenth Amendment, he insisted on asking whether the particular criminal procedure was fundamental or necessary to the "Anglo-American regime of ordered liberty" that had developed in the United States at that time.

He answered the question of whether the state could impose criminal punishment without granting a jury trial by first analyzing the importance of the jury trial in America. He began with a review of the history of the jury trial going back to England and Colonial times. He found the "structure and style" of the criminal process in America developed with and relied upon the jury trial. He concluded that "we believe that trial by jury in criminal cases is fundamental to the American scheme of justice." Thus, he maintained that the Fourteenth Amendment guaranteed a right of jury trial in all criminal cases that would come under the protection of the Sixth Amendment were they tried in federal court.

Justice White also suggested that jury trials were required where the potential penalty was more than six months imprisonment. He looked to the maximum authorized legislative penalty for simple battery in order to determine its level of seriousness because he recognized the need for more "objective" criteria to aid in jury trial determinations.

Justice Fortas filed a concurring opinion in which he stated that the application of the due process clause guaranteed to states would inflict "a serious blow upon the principle of federalism." Justice Black also wrote a concurring opinion joined by Justice Douglas. Justice Harlan dissented, joined by Justice Stewart. He disagreed with the majority's approach to the case and interpretation of the due process clause, disagreeing with the entire incorporation view of the Fourteenth Amendment. He did not see jury trials as the only fair means of trying criminal cases.

AFTERMATH

The Court subsequently added the Fifth Amendment prohibition on "double jeopardy," and the Eight Amendment prohibition on "excessive" bail to the enumerations set out in *Duncan,* which the Court held applicable to the states through incorporation into the Fourteenth Amendment. After *Duncan,* the potential sentence exposure, and not the sentence actually imposed, became the proper measure of an offense's seriousness.

SIGNIFICANCE

The Court decided in *Duncan* that the guarantees of the Bill of Rights "selectively" incorporated in the due process clause of the Fourteenth Amendment should apply to states in precisely the same manner as they applied to the federal government. *Duncan* redefined the test of PALKO V. CONNECTI-CUT (1937), which asked whether the right was so fundamental as to be ranked "implicit in the concept of ordered liberty," to whether the right was "fundamental to the American scheme of justice."

RELATED CASES

Baldwin v. New York, 399 U.S. 66 (1970)

Palko v. Connecticut, 302 U.S. 319 (1937)

Williams v. Florida, 399 U.S. 78 (1970)

RECOMMENDED READING

Jerold Israel, *Selective Incorporation Revisited,* 71 Georgetown Law Journal 253 (1982).

Case Title: *Escobedo v. State of Illinois*

Legal Citation: 378 U.S. 478

Year of Decision: 1964

KEY ISSUES

Is it a violation of the Sixth Amendment of the Constitution for the police to refuse to honor a person's request for an attorney during an interrogation, and is the statement elicited from that interrogation rendered inadmissible by this refusal?

HISTORY OF THE CASE

Escobedo, the appellant in this case, argued that the Illinois Police Department violated his Sixth Amendment right to "the assistance of Counsel" when they refused to honor his request to speak with his attorney. The Sixth Amendment guarantee, to this point, had been interpreted as operative only after the person became a suspect and became subject to judicial proceedings. In this case, the appellant was being questioned about his possible involvement in the murder of his brother-in-law. While in police custody he requested several times to speak with his attorney; all of these requests were denied. In addition, Escobedo's attorney requested to speak with his client at the station house; all of his requests were denied. The trial court allowed Escobedo's self-incriminating statement made during this interrogation into evidence. Escobedo was convicted of murder. The Illinois Supreme Court in its original opinion held that the statement was inadmissible and reversed the conviction. At a rehearing the Illinois Supreme Court affirmed the conviction.

SUMMARY OF ARGUMENTS

Escobedo's attorney argued that the police acted in violation of the Sixth and Fourteenth Amendments by refusing to let him speak with his attorney. At the time of his interrogation Escobedo was "in fact" the suspect, even though he had not yet been charged with a crime. The state supreme court found that "the petitioner had become the accused, and the purpose of his interrogation was to 'get him' to confess his guilt despite his constitutional right not to do so." The state supreme court also held that the statement illicited from the defendant during this interrogation was inadmissible because "'the guiding hand of counsel' was essential to advise the petitioner of his rights in this delicate situation."

The state argued that case history supported the legitimacy of the police officers' actions in refusing to provide Escobedo with counsel. The right to an attorney was not guaranteed until the person had been formally indicted. To require legal representation at an early stage of the investigative process would impede the ability of the police to obtain information that would be helpful in resolving the situation.

DECISION

Justice Goldberg, writing for five of the justices, found that the right to counsel begins before the defendant has been indicted. It begins when the investigation is no longer a general inquiry and focuses on a particular suspect. At that time the adversarial process begins, and the suspect should be allowed, if he wishes, to consult with a legal representative. Dismissing the argument that this would make the investigative process ineffective, Justice Goldberg argued that an investigative process of any merit would not have to rely on the "citizens' abdication through unawareness of their constitutional rights."

There were three dissents in this case. Two, one by Justice Harlan and one by Justice Stewart, relied on the *Cicenia v. La Gay* decision (1958) as binding precedent. In that case the Court ruled the defendant did not have a constitutional right to be advised by counsel before being indicted. Justice White's dissent, which was joined by Justice Clark and Stewart, relied on *Massiah v. U.S.* (1964) to support the argument of the state that the right to counsel begins only after indictment. He argued that the Court had made inadmissible all statements except those on which the accused expressly waives the right to counsel.

AFTERMATH

In changing the standard by which confessions were analyzed for admissibility, this decision affected the policy of police departments and district attorney's offices across the nation. This is one of a series of cases in which the Court replaced the due process analysis in determining the admissibility of confessions with an objective standard based on the Sixth Amendment right to counsel. This case extended the time at which a suspect may invoke his or her Sixth Amendment right to before the indictment stage. Escobedo found himself in trouble with the law numerous times after this decision and ultimately went to prison several years later.

SIGNIFICANCE

This case set the stage for *MIRANDA V. ARIZONA*, in which the Court adopted a per se rule regarding confessions to protect suspects from the coercive atmosphere of police investigation and to protect the suspect's right against self-incrimination.

RELATED CASES

Miranda v. Arizona, 384 U.S. 436 (1966)

Brown v. Mississippi, 297 U.S. 278 (1936)

Malloy v. Hogan, 378 U.S. 1 (1964)

RECOMMENDED READING

Mark S. Bransdorfer, *Miranda Right-to-Counsel and the Fruit of the Poisonous Tree Doctrine*, 62 Indiana Law Journal 1061 (fall 1987).

Lawrence Herman, *The Supreme Court, The Attorney General, and the Good Old Days of Police Interrogation*, 48 Ohio State Law Journal 733.

W. Brian Stack, *Criminal Procedure—Confessions—Waiver of Privilege against Self-Incrimination Held Invalid Due to Police Failure to Inform Suspect of Attorney's Attempt to Contact Him—State v. Reed*, 25 Seton Hall Law Review 353 (1994).

Case Title: *Fay v. Noia*

Legal Citation: 372 U.S. 391

Year of Decision: 1963

KEY ISSUES

May a person obtain habeas corpus relief from an imprisonment for a conviction procured by a coerced confession obtained in violation of the Fourteenth Amendment when he/she has not availed him/herself of the available remedies within the state judicial system?

HISTORY OF THE CASE

Noia was convicted of felony murder in state court. His conviction rested on a coerced confession obtained by the police. Noia allowed the time to appeal directly to elapse and then requested federal habeas corpus review. The Supreme Court granted Noia's petition for review. Fay, the prison warden, and the government objected to this; they argued that by failing to avail himself of the opportunity to appeal within the state system, Noia relinquished his right to appeal to the Supreme Court.

SUMMARY OF ARGUMENTS

Noia argued that the nature of the petition was such that the Supreme Court should grant jurisdiction. He felt the circumstances that led to his conviction were such that the Court should, in the interest of justice, review his case.

The government argued that the doctrine of abstention (in which a state is allowed to first complete its administration of the case without prejudice to federal rights interwoven in the state proceedings), which was codified in 28 U.S.C. 2254, prevented the Court from issuing the writ of habeas corpus: Noia purposefully allowed the statute of limitation to run out and destroyed for himself the possibility of seeking remedy in the lower courts. The state argued that federal courts should not issue the writ in a circumstance in which the defendant purposefully circumvented the state judicial system. In doing so, Fay waived his right to apply for the writ of habeas corpus.

DECISION

Justice Brennan, in writing the opinion of the Court, held that the federal courts have the power to grant relief when the state judicial system has not provided it. Noia's failure to seek state remedies did not validate the unconstitutional conduct by which the conviction was obtained. Justice Brennan relied on the notion of federal habeas corpus review as independent. He noted that rarely "has the Court predicated its deference to state procedural rules on a want of power to entertain a habeas application where a procedural default was committed by the defendant in the state courts. Typically, the Court like the District Court in the instant case, has approached the problem as an aspect of the rule requiring exhaus-

tion of the state remedies, which is not a rule distributing power as between the state and federal courts."

He also emphasized the notion that federal courts could deny relief if a petitioner deliberately failed to fully adjudicate his claims in state courts, deliberately by passing the state court appellate procedures to be heard by the federal court.

In his dissent, Justice Harlan argued that if the habeas petitioner has violated a reasonable state rule and is therefore barred from state judicial review, the federal courts do not have statutory or constitutional authority to release the petitioner from detention.

AFTERMATH

This decision overruled *Darr v. Burford*, in which the Court held that a state prisoner must ordinarily seek certiorari in the Supreme Court as a precondition of applying for federal habeas corpus. *Fay v. Noia* ruled that state prisoners are no longer barred from petitioning the Supreme Court after failing to file a petition in the state court system within the allotted time. The Court's rationale was that the requirement imposed by *Darr*—that the defendant proceed through the state court system and file for certiorari in the allotted time—was an unnecessary step in the processing of federal claims of those convicted of state crimes.

This case was itself overruled in 1992 by *Keeney v. Tamayo-Reyes*. In that opinion, written by Justice White, it was held that the *Fay* standard must be overruled in favor of a cause and prejudice standard. Justice White reasoned that in light of the decisions in the *Fay* progeny, such as *Wainright v. Sykes* and *Coleman v. Thompson,* which narrowed the ruling in *Fay*, "it was necessary to implement a new, more uniform standard for petitioners seeking habeas corpus." Justice White went on to reason that the new standard served to allow state courts to correct their own errors, to allow good use of judicial economy by preventing duplicative fact finding, and to allow the use of the appropriate judicial forum.

SIGNIFICANCE

This decision empowered the federal courts to issue writs of habeas corpus regardless of what had occurred in prior state court proceedings. The sweeping language of the decision opened up to the federal court an avenue of jurisdiction in cases that were previously precluded from jurisdiction because of state procedural requirements. As noted in the decision, it marked "a return to the common-law principle that restricts contrary to fundamental law, by whatever authority imposed, could be redressed by writ of habeas corpus."

Later decisions such as *Davis v. U.S.* (1973) and *Wainright v. Sykes* (1977) limited the power of the federal court to issue writs of habeas corpus without respect to what occurred in prior state court proceedings; a defendant is now required to show cause and prejudice, meaning give reasons for the actions taken and indicate the harm done, before the federal courts will assert jurisdiction.

Fay narrowed the scope of the requirement that a petitioner exhaust his state court remedies and refused to apply independent and adequate state ground doctrine to review in another proceeding. It also limited jurisdiction to lower courts where there was a deliberate bypass of state court procedures. This decision put the burden on the federal courts to determine whether the petitioner purposefully avoided the procedure of state courts—which would disentitle him or her to federal court review—or whether the defendant, because of harmless error, did not avail himself of the available state remedies, in which case federal jurisdiction could be asserted.

RELATED CASES

Coleman v. Thompson, 111 S.Ct. 546 (1991)

Davis v. U.S., 411 U.S. 233 (1973)

Keeney v. Tamayo-Reyes, 504 U.S. 1 (1992)

Reed v. Ross, 104 S.Ct. 2901 (1984)

Wainright v. Sykes, 433 U.S. 72 (1977)

RECOMMENDED READING

Jack A. Guttenberg, *Federal Habeas Corpus, Constitutional Rights, and Procedural Forfeitures: The Delicate Balance*, 12 Hofstra Law Review 617 (1984).

Rae K. Inafuku, *Coleman v. Thompson—Sacrificing Fundamental Rights in Deference to the States: The Supreme Court's 1991 Interpretation of the Writ of Habeas Corpus*, 34 Santa Clara Law Review 625 (1994).

Maria L. Marcus, *Federal Habeas Corpus after State Court Default: A Definition of Cause and Prejudice*, 53 Fordham Law Review 663 (1985).

Kathleen Patchel, *The New Habeas*, 42 Hastings Law Journal 939 (1991).

Curtis Reitz, *Federal Habeas Corpus: Postconviction Remedy for State Prisoners*, 108 University of Pennsylvania Law Review 461 (1960).

Judith Resnik, *Tiers*, 57 Southern California Law Review 837 (1984).

Case Title: *Ferguson v. Skrupa*

Legal Citation: 372 U.S. 726

Year of Decision: 1963

KEY ISSUES

Does a state legislature violate the due process clause of the U.S. Constitution if it enacts a statute that regulates who may engage in certain business practices within the state?

HISTORY OF THE CASE

The Kansas legislature enacted a statute that made it a misdemeanor offense to engage in the practice of debt adjusting except as it related to the practice of law. Debt adjusting was the practice of contracting with debtors to distribute payments to creditors for a fee. The district court held that the statute was unconstitutional and enjoined its enforcement. The court reasoned that the statute violated the due process clause of the U.S. Constitution because it was an "unreasonable regulation of a lawful business." In support of its finding the district court relied on *Commonwealth v. Stone*, in which the Superior Court of Pennsylvania struck down a statute similar to the Kansas statute on the grounds that "the State could regulate, but could not prohibit," a "legitimate" business. Finding debt adjusting not to be "against the public interest" and concluding that it could "see no justification for such interference" with this business, the Pennsylvania court relied heavily on *Adams v. Tanner*. In that case the Court held that the due process clause forbids a state to prohibit a business that is "useful" and not "inherently immoral or dangerous to public welfare." The decision of the district court was appealed to the U.S. Supreme Court.

SUMMARY OF ARGUMENTS

Skrupa alleged in his complaint that he was engaged in the debt adjusting business, that his business was useful and desirable, that he did not engage in inherently immoral or dangerous business practices, and therefore the legislature could not "absolutely prohibit" his business activities.

Ferguson, attorney general for the state of Kansas, argued that the Court should adopt the approach originally intended by the framers of the Constitution, which is to leave to the state legislatures to decide the wisdom and propriety of certain statutes, unless they clearly violated a constitutional maxim. He argued that the Court should allow Kansas the discretion to develop policies within the state without judicial monitoring.

DECISION

Justice Black, in writing the opinion for eight justices, held that the district court erred in applying the philosophy of *Adams v. Tanner* and its progeny to "draw on their own view of morality, legitimacy and usefulness of a particular business in order to decide whether the statute bears too heavily upon that business and by so doing violates due process." The Court reasoned that the structure of government originally intended by the U.S. Constitution was not one in which the decisions of state legislatures were subject to judicial review and approval, but rather one where the Court would interfere with the decisions of state legislatures only when the statute at issue violated a provision of the U.S. Constitution. The Court cited Justice Holmes as the original proponent of the idea that unless a state legislature is expressly prohibited by the U.S. Constitution from acting in a certain way, the state legislature is free to act in whatever way it wishes.

The Court stated that this decision would mark the return of the Court to the "doctrine that prevailed in *Lochner, Adkins, Burns,* and like cases. . . . We have returned to the original constitutional proposition that courts do not substitute their social and economic beliefs for the judgment of legislative bodies, who are elected to pass laws." The Court went on to support the contention that the states have broad scope in designing legislation that is appropriate for the

state. More specifically, the Court held that it is within this broad scope for the state legislature to regulate commercial and business affairs that tend to be accompanied by injurious practices.

The Court also stated that in coming to this decision it turned away from the days when it used the due process clause "to strike down state laws, regulatory or business and industrial conditions, because they may be unwise, improvident, or out of harmony with a particular school of thought."

Justice Harlan wrote a concurring opinion in which he agreed with the opinion of the Court but felt that the decision should have rested on the fact that the statute at issue was valid because it bore a rational relation to a constitutionally permissible objective.

AFTERMATH

The period following 1937 signified a new approach by the Court to substantive due process questions. The Court adopted a more deferential, anti-interventionist attitude toward economic regulation challenged on those grounds. The *Ferguson* decision changed the modern interpretation of substantive economic due process. In the post-1937 decisions, the Court would no longer use due process to substitute its own policy for those of the legislature.

The post-1937 Court decisions exemplify the Court's aversion to the *Lochner*-era approach to substantive economic due process issues wherein the Court made determinations whether legislation was fair and reasonable in its content and in its application. The Court in this and subsequent decisions presumed the constitutionality of an act unless it contravened a constitutional provision. The Court proceeded on the assumption that economic consequences don't matter.

SIGNIFICANCE

This decision, one of the progeny of the *Williamson v. Lee Optical Co.* (1955), reinforced the doctrine established in that case and the standard of review employed by the Court. *Williamson* established the rational relationship test or doctrine: in resolving constitutional questions about state statutes that regulated economic rights, the Court was to determine if there was a rational relationship between the statute at issue and a legitimate government end. If there were, the statute would pass constitutional muster. This approach involved a lower standard of scrutiny than the Court usually employed in gauging the constitutionality of other substantive due process issues. The Court no longer addressed the effect of the act on the persons involved; the only question was whether the challenged statute or regulation was rationally related to a government interest. The progeny of *Williamson* and *Ferguson* revealed that this new, relaxed scrutiny allowed for regulations to be upheld in cases in which the government interest was far from substantial.

This decision marked a departure from the *Lochner*-era approach to substantive economic due process interpretation; the Court no longer used the due process clause as a vehicle to hold laws unconstitutional when it was felt that the law was unwise. The new approach gave the state legislators autonomy in determining the social and economic perspective it felt was appropriate for its constituency.

RELATED CASES

Lochner v. New York, 198 U.S. 45 (1905)

Slaughterhouse Cases, 83 U.S. (16 Wall.) 36 (1873)

Williamson v. Lee Optical Co., 348 U.S. 483 (1955)

RECOMMENDED READING

Michael J. Phillips, *Entry Restrictions in the Lochner Court*, 4 George Mason Law Review 39 (1996).

———, *Another Look at Economic Substantive Due Process*, Wisconsin Law Review 265 (1987).

Stephen F. Ross, *Legislative Enforcement of Equal Protection*, 72 Minnesota Law Review 311 (1987).

Case Title: *Frontiero v. Richardson*

Legal Citation: 411 U.S. 677

Year of Decision: 1978

KEY ISSUES

May the government grant different benefits to men and women in the military?

HISTORY OF THE CASE

In an effort to encourage enlisted military personnel to reenlist and attract career personnel, Congress established a fringe benefit scheme for military personnel competitive with that of other businesses and industries. Part of the scheme was to provide for increased basic allowance for housing and the entitlement of a military member's dependents to comprehensive dental and medical care. Under the adopted statute a serviceman was entitled to claim his wife as dependent whether or not she was in fact dependent on him for support. A servicewoman, however, was not able to do the same for her husband unless she could prove that he was dependent on her for more than half of his support.

Sharon Frontiero sought housing and medical benefits for her husband on the ground that he was dependent. Her application was denied because she failed to demonstrate that her husband was dependent on her for more than half of his support, even though a man in a similar situation would have been able to receive such increased benefits for his wife without supplying supporting documentation.

SUMMARY OF ARGUMENTS

Frontiero argued that the difference in treatment constituted unconstitutional discrimination against servicewomen in violation of the due process clause of the Fifth Amendment. She argued that the discriminatory impact was twofold: (1) the additional burden of demonstrating that the spouse is in fact dependent for more than half of his support on the serviceperson is placed solely on female servicepersons; and (2) males who do not in fact provide more than half of the support for their spouse are granted these increased benefits while women who are similarly situated are denied such benefits. Frontiero argued that classifications based on sex, like those based on race, are inherently suspect and therefore must be subject to strict judicial scrutiny.

The government argued that the classification served as an administrative convenience because more men than women had spouses who were dependent on them for more than half of their support. The government contended that legislating to provide for administrative convenience was within Congress's power if it reasonably felt that such actions would serve a government interest because it was cheaper and easier to administer. The government offered no evidence to support this contention.

DECISION

Justice Brennan wrote the plurality opinion and reasoned that the statute was constitutionally invalid because it was based solely upon sex. Brennan argued that sex, like race, was an inherently suspect classification and that it was subject to strict judicial scrutiny. Under this standard, for the statute to pass constitutional muster it must serve a compelling state interest. The Court held that inconvenience was not a compelling enough reason to justify classifying on the basis of race, and invalidated the statute.

In addition, Brennan held that the case of REED V. REED (1971) supported the contention that the statute was invalid. In *Reed* the Court, in resolving a dispute over an Idaho statute that gave preference to males in assigning administrators of estates when there was a woman similarly situated, held that classifications based on sex were subject to equal protection analysis.

Justice Stewart concurred in judgment and argued that, based on *Reed v. Reed,* the statute works an invidious discrimination as it was arbitrary and did not serve a legitimate interest.

Justice Powell, writing for Justice Burger and Blackmun, concurred in judgment but disagreed with the portion of the opinion that elevated sex classifications to the level of race classifications and subjected them to strict scrutiny. He argued that the Court could have reached the same decision by relying on *Reed* for the proposition that sex classifications are subject to equal protection analysis and therefore must be sustained unless "it is 'patently arbitrary' and bears no rational relationship to a legitimate governmental interest." He argued that the Court's invalidation of the statute because it treated similarly situated persons differently was sufficient justification to invalidate the statute at issue.

Justice Rehnquist dissented based on the reasoning of *Frontiero v. Laird,* in which the district court stated that the classification was based on the nature of the relationship between a service member and a dependent and was not based on sex. Therefore, the district court applied the rational basis test and found that different treatment of males and females was reasonable under these circumstances.

AFTERMATH

Although the holding of this case was that sex classifications were to be judged by the same standard of review—strict scrutiny—as applied to racial classifications, the Court in the later decision of CRAIG V. BOREN (1976) established intermediate scrutiny as the appropriate standard to be applied to classifications based on gender differences. Intermediate scrutiny is a level between rational basis review and strict scrutiny/suspect classifications. Currently, to pass constitutional muster a gender classification "must serve important governmental objectives and must be substantially related to achievements of those objectives." (*Craig v. Boren* [1976]).

SIGNIFICANCE

Though later lessened, this decision thrust gender classifications into the same category of racial classifications and made classifications based solely on gender suspect. This decision was a product of *Reed v. Reed,* in which the stereotypes that had been supported by the Court were challenged and classifications based solely on gender were seen as illegitimate. *Reed* established minimum rationality as the standard by which classification based solely on gender would be judged, which required a reasonable classification relating to a legitimate government interest. The decision in *Frontiero* required the higher standard of strict scrutiny. These decisions explicitly overrule previous Supreme Court cases such as *Minor v. Happerset* (1875) and *Bradwell v. Illinois* (1873), which not only upheld classifications based on gender but also supported these decisions with reasoning based on stereotypes about the role women should play in society.

RELATED CASES

Craig v. Boren, 429 U.S. 190 (1976)

Dothard v. Rawlinson, 433 U.S. 321 (1971)

Michael M. v. Superior Court of Sonoma County, 450 U.S. 464 (1981)

Mississippi University for Women v. Hogan, 458 U.S. 718 (1982)

Personnel Administrator of Massachusetts v. Feeney, 442 U.S. 256 (1979)

Reed v. Reed, 404 U.S. 71 (1971)

United States v. Virginia, 116 S.Ct. 2264 (1996)

RECOMMENDED READING

Deborah L. Brake, *Sex as a Suspect Class: An Argument for Applying Strict Scrutiny to Gender Discrimination Re-examining Gender Scrutiny: A Symposium Discussion,* Seton Hall Constitutional Law Journal 953 (summer 1996).

Maureen B. Cavanaugh, *Towards a New Equal Protection: Two Kinds of Equality,* 12 Law & Inequality Journal 381 (June 1994).

William A. DeVan, *Toward a New Standard in Gender Discrimination: The Case of Virginia Military Institute,* 33 William and Mary Law Review 489 (winter 1992).

Eugene Doherty, *Equal Protection under the Fifth and Fourteenth Amendments: Patterns of Congruence, Divergence and Judicial Deference,* 16 Ohio Northern University Law Review 591 (1989).

William R. Engles, *The "Substantial Relation" Question in Gender Discrimination Cases,* 52 University of Chicago Law Review 149 (winter 1985).

Case Title: *In re Gault et al.*

Legal Citations: 387 U.S. 1; 18 L.Ed. 2d 527; 87 S.Ct. 1428

Year of Decision: 1967

KEY ISSUES

Do juveniles have the right to an attorney?

HISTORY OF THE CASE

Fifteen-year-old Gerald Gault was taken into custody by the police in Arizona for allegedly having made obscene phone calls. At the time, Gerald was under a six-month probation order as the result of having been with another boy who had stolen a lady's purse. Gerald was taken into custody at 10:00 A.M. on June 8, 1964, and no steps

were taken to advise either his father or mother of his detention in the county children's home. When his mother arrived home from work at 6:00 P.M., Gerald was not there. (School was not in session.) Gerald's older brother was sent to look for Gerald at the home of a friend. He then learned that his brother was in custody.

Mrs. Gault went to the detention home and found out that the juvenile court would hold a hearing at 3:00 P.M. on the following day. The police filed a petition requesting a hearing and order regarding the care and custody of Gerald with the court on the day of the hearing. The Gaults did not receive this petition. (Indeed, although it was filed June 9, the Gaults never saw it until August 17.) At the hearing, Gerald, his mother, his older brother, and two probation officers appeared. (Gerald's father was out of town on business.) The woman who had complained of receiving the obscene phone calls was not present. No one was under oath, and there was no record made of what occurred during the hearing. Later, the juvenile judge testified that Gerald was questioned about the telephone call and that there was some conflict about what he said. After being kept in the detention home for three days, Gerald was released and given a plain piece of paper on which one of the detention officers had written the following note:

Mrs. Gault:

Judge McGhee has set Monday June 15, 1964 at 11 A.M. as the date and time for further Hearings on Gerald's delinquency

/s/Flagg

On June 15, Gerald, his father and mother, and the detention officers were present before Judge McGhee. At no time did Mrs. Cook, the woman who had allegedly received the obscene phone calls, ever testify or present an affidavit to the court. One of the probation officers testified that he had talked to Mrs. Cook once over the telephone.

At the hearing, the judge referred Gerald to a juvenile delinquents' school for the period until he turned 21, until or unless he was discharged sooner. Thus, following a brief hearing, Gerald was sentenced to spend six years in the state industrial school. Had he been an adult, the maximum punishment would have been a 50-dollar fine or two months in the county jail. There was no requirement under Arizona law that, as a juvenile, he receive any notice of the hearings or that he could obtain an attorney. He had no right to confront or examine the woman who complained about the phone calls. Further, there was no protection against admissions of his guilt.

Arizona law does not permit appeals in juvenile cases. Therefore, the Gaults filed a petition for a writ of habeas corpus with the Arizona Supreme Court. The writ was referred to a superior court, and on August 17, the juvenile judge was cross-examined about the basis for his actions. The superior court dismissed the writ, and the Gaults asked for a review by the Arizona Supreme Court. The Arizona Supreme Court upheld the dismissal of the writ of habeas corpus and concluded that the state juvenile system was adequate.

Summary of Arguments

The attorneys for the Gaults argued that the sentence was unconstitutional because there was no requirement for a notice of hearings, there was no requirement that the parent or child be informed of the specific charges being brought, there was no right to an appeal, and the proceedings themselves were conducted without basic constitutional rights for the juvenile, including the right to an attorney, the right to confront his accuser, and the privilege against self-incrimination. The Gaults' attorneys also argued that the use of unsworn hearsay testimony and the failure to make a record of the hearing made the juvenile court hearing defective.

The state and a variety of associations representing juvenile judges and juvenile courts opposed the Gaults. They argued that the nature of the juvenile justice system was intended to be informal, and that the state's intervention was based on a paternalistic regard for the best interests of a wayward or disturbed child.

Decision

Justice Abe Fortas wrote the majority opinion for Chief Justice Warren and Justices Douglas, Clark, and Brennan. Justices Black and White filed a separate concurring opinion. Justice Harlan filed an opinion that concurred in part and dissented in part. Only Justice Stewart dissented. Justice Fortas began with his decision in *Kent v. U.S.* (1966) and traced the history of the juvenile courts in the United States. In 1899, Illinois became the first state to create a juvenile court system. The idea quickly spread to every state, as well as the District of Columbia and Puerto Rico. The movement toward establishing a juvenile court system was based on the assumption that society was not concerned with whether the child was guilty or innocent, but with what could be done in his best interests and in the best interests of the state to prevent him from continuing on a downward slide. The child was to be treated as essentially good and to be the object of the state's care, and not treated as if he was under arrest or on trial.

While very high motives and enlightened impulses created the juvenile justice system, according to Justice Fortas, the results had given the justices unbridled discretion and arbitrary power. Loose procedures, heavy-handed methods, and crowded calendars often resulted in depriving juveniles of many fundamental rights to which they were entitled. Justice Fortas found that "[u]nder our Constitution, the condition of being a boy does not justify a kangaroo court." Justice Fortas was appalled that the judge made no inquiry of either Gerald's mother and father, his older brother, or of his school. Had Gerald been over 18, the punishment would have been a fine ranging from five dollars to 50 dollars or a jail sentence of not more than two months. Instead, he was sentenced to six years in a juvenile home. The idea of reaching such a tremendous decision without any ceremony, without a hearing, without the assistance of counsel, or without any legal reasoning in no way measured up to the essential standards of due process and fair treatment.

Justice Fortas noted that the parents had no time to obtain an attorney and that they had no idea of the charges against their son. He found it particularly repugnant that under the law of Arizona, the very same juvenile officer who arrested Gerald, initiated the proceedings against him, and then testified against him, was then charged with being the superintendent of the detention center if Gerald were sentenced. The detention officer was the only court officer present, other than the judge. There was no one present who could be said to represent the interests of the child. Further, Gerald was denied the right to confront and cross-examine his accuser. Gerald or his parents were never told that he did not have to testify or make a statement or that his statements might be used to commit him to the home for delinquent children.

The Supreme Court devoted a serious amount of time to the question of whether Gerald was capable of making an informed confession. His statement was made in front of the police officer who arrested him, away from his parents, without the assistance of counsel, and without any notification that he had a right to be silent. This confession was never written down, signed, or submitted to the court. Justice Fortas found that there was no reason at all to find a different rule with regard to juveniles than adults. Absent a valid confession, the court must have sworn testimony by witnesses available by cross-examination in order to make any finding of guilt.

In his dissent, Justice Stewart noted that the practical consequence of this ruling was to substantially overhaul the entire system of juvenile justice in the United States.

AFTERMATH

Gerald's case was reversed, and the argument over extending due process requirements to the states continued.

SIGNIFICANCE

The *Gault* case placed new emphasis on due process for juveniles, which greatly increased the requirements to adequately manage juvenile court cases. Much debate continues over whether the *Gault* decision prompted an overemphasis on due process rather than on the issue of remedies for juvenile delinquency.

RELATED CASES

Kent v. U.S., 383 U.S. 541 (1966)

McKeiver v. Pennsylvania, 403 U.S. 528 (1971)

RECOMMENDED READING

George, B. James. *Gault and the Juvenile Court Revolution.* Ann Arbor: Michigan Institute of Continuing Legal Education, 1968.

Michigan Institute of Continuing Legal Education. *Gault: The Question of Representation.* Ann Arbor: Michigan Institute of Continuing Legal Education, 1967.

Nordin, Virginia Davis, ed. *Gault: What Now for the Juvenile Court?* Ann Arbor: Michigan Institute of Continuing Legal Education, 1968.

Case Title: *Gideon v. Wainwright*

Legal Citation: 372 U.S. 335

Year of Decision: 1963

KEY ISSUES

Do the Sixth and Fourteenth Amendments to the U.S. Constitution require a state to provide counsel to indigent defendants in criminal prosecutions?

HISTORY OF THE CASE

Gideon was charged in Florida state court with the felony offense of breaking and entering with the intent to commit a misdemeanor. When he requested a lawyer at his trial he was denied. The judge, in denying his request, said the state was required only to provide legal representation to those defendants charged with capital offenses. The jury at his trial convicted him and he was sentenced to five years in state prison. Gideon then filed a habeas corpus petition challenging the validity of his conviction and sentence. He grounded his challenge on the trial court's refusal to provide him with counsel, a right he argued was guaranteed by the Bill of Rights in the Constitution. The state supreme court denied all relief to Gideon.

SUMMARY OF ARGUMENTS

Gideon argued that the Bill of Rights as applied to the states through the Fourteenth Amendment provided him the right to counsel, which the state violated by refusing to provide him with legal representation. He thus felt that the conviction that resulted from him representing himself, in a trial that was inherently unfair, should be vacated.

Wainwright, the director of the Division of Corrections, argued that there was no recognized constitutional right to counsel in noncapital criminal trials and that there were no special circumstances that would justify abandoning the state's public policy on this issue for Gideon's case.

DECISION

Justice Black, writing for the majority, overruled BETTS V. BRADY (1942) and held that the states are required by the Sixth Amendment, made applicable to the states through the Fourteenth Amendment, to provide counsel for indigent criminal defendants. In addition, he held that the state's refusal to appoint a lawyer, upon Gideon's request, violated the due process clause of the Fourteenth Amendment. The Court noted that the facts of the Betts case were substantially similar to those at issue in Gideon's case. Both men were indigent criminal defendants denied the right to representation by the trial judge on the grounds that their crimes were not of the type that the state's policy allowed for representation. The Court overruled the conclusion in Betts that the Sixth Amendment right to counsel did not qualify as fundamental to a fair trial and therefore was not obligatory on the states.

Justice Black noted that 10 years before the decision in Betts, the Court in POWELL V. ALABAMA declared that the "right to the aid of counsel is this fundamental character." Noting that although the holding of that case was limited to the facts of the case, he argued that "its conclusions about the fundamental nature of the right to counsel are unmistakable." He also noted that in Grosjean v. American Press Co. (1936) the Court upheld the principle that fundamental rights should be safeguarded against state action: "We concluded that certain fundamental rights, safeguarded by the first eight amendments against federal action were also safeguarded against state action by the due process of law clause of the Fourteenth Amendment, and among them the fundamental right of the accused to the aid of counsel in criminal prosecutions."

He argued that in light of the case history, even the Court in Betts had to concede that "one charged with crime, who is unable to obtain counsel, must be furnished counsel by the state." He contended that the ruling in this case constituted a return to old precedents that were more sound than the newly adopted ones. He said it is an obvious truth that one cannot receive a fair criminal trial without counsel. In addition, the history of the Constitution supports the need for counsel

for those tried for crimes: "from the very beginning, our state and national constitutions and laws have laid great emphasis on procedural and substantive safeguards designed to assure fair trials before impartial tribunals in which every defendant stands equal before the law."

Justice Douglas joined the Court and provided a brief history of the connection between the Bill of Rights and the Fourteenth Amendment.

Justice Clark concurred with the result of the Court. He argued the Court's holding did no more than erase an illogical distinction between capital and noncapital offenses for the purpose of providing counsel by the state.

Justice Harlan concurred in the result, but felt that Betts should be viewed in a light more accurate than that portrayed by the Court. He argued that Betts in fact was not a break in precedent, but an extension of precedent. Harlan pointed to the specific factual circumstances in Powell v. Alabama and their importance to the decision that a state court had a duty to assign counsel for a capital case. Harlan contended Betts extended the possibility of the existence of "special circumstances" to noncapital trials.

AFTERMATH

The Court has extended the right of counsel of defendants charged with only misdemeanor offenses, on the grounds that the brevity of sentence that a defendant faces does not negate the right of counsel. In later decisions the Court went on to note that the nature of the charge is not the determining factor for the right of counsel, but rather the character of the possible punishment—most important, the loss of liberty. These adaptations are based on the notion that the defendant who faces criminal prosecution should be on equal footing with the state that prosecutes him.

SIGNIFICANCE

In Gideon the Court abandoned the arbitrary distinction between capital and noncapital crimes and fully incorporated the Sixth Amendment right to counsel into the Fourteenth Amendment. By designating due process as the appropriate standard by which to view abridgment of the Sixth Amendment right, the Court created a new theoretical and constitutional basis for a defendant's right to counsel in state criminal trials. Once the defendant presented the preliminary evidence of the denial of his right to counsel, the relationship with due process was presumed.

In addition, this decision acknowledged the adversarial nature of criminal proceedings. Gideon offers the ideal that both parties are on equal footing and the result reached can be counted on to be accurate. Though the reality of equality among the parties in the adversarial process has not been realized, this decision creates an ideal that fairness within the criminal justice system is not a function of one's financial ability.

RELATED CASES

Argersinger v. Hamlin, 407 U.S. 25 (1972)

Betts v. Brady, 316 U.S. 455 (1942)

Grosjean v. American Press Co., 297 U.S. 233 (1936)

Patterson v. Warden, 372 U.S. 776 (1963)

Powell v. Alabama, 287 U.S. 45 (1932)

RECOMMENDED READING

Robert S. Catz and Nancy Lee Firak, *The Right to Appointed Counsel in Quasi-Criminal Cases: Towards an Effective Assistance of Counsel Standard,* 19 Harvard Civil Rights–Civil Liberties Law Review 397.

Alfredo Garcia, *The Right to Counsel under Siege: Requiem for an Endangered Right?,* 29 American Criminal Law Review 35.

Richard Klein, *The Emperor Gideon Has No Clothes: The Empty Promise of the Constitutional Right to Effective Assistance of Counsel,* 13 Hastings Constitutional Law Quarterly 625.

Case Title: *Goss v. Lopez*

Legal Citation: 419 U.S. 565

Year of Decision: 1975

KEY ISSUES

Is it a violation of the due process clause of the Fourteenth Amendment for a public high school administrator to temporarily suspend a student from high school without providing him or her with a hearing or notice?

HISTORY OF THE CASE

Ohio law provided for free education to all children between 6 and 21. In addition it provided administrative procedures and recourse for students who were expelled. There were no similar procedures for temporarily suspended students.

In this case a group of students, of which Lopez was one, sued on behalf of all students who had been suspended from their school in the Columbus Public School System. There were nine named plaintiffs in the class action. Six of the plaintiffs were suspended because of disruptive conduct at the school. None of them was given a hearing, but they were offered a conference to discuss their future with their parents and the principal. One of the named plaintiffs was suspended for her involvement in a demonstration at another school. Two plaintiffs were suspended for their alleged involvement in a disturbance in the school lunchroom and the damage that resulted from the incident.

The students sought to enjoin the public administrators from issuing suspensions as a disciplinary measure without a hearing. They also sought to have the past suspensions removed from the records of the named plaintiffs.

A three-judge court declared that the plaintiffs had been denied due process of law because they were suspended without a hearing before the suspension or a reasonable time thereafter. The district court held that there are minimum requirements of due process such as notice and a hearing that the Columbus Public School System failed to meet.

SUMMARY OF ARGUMENTS

Goss argued on behalf of the Columbus Public School System that there is no constitutional right to an education at the public expense and therefore the due process clause does not protect against expulsion from public school. In addition, he argued that even if this right is protected by the due process clause generally, the clause comes into play only in those situations in which the state subjects the student to a severe detriment or loss.

Lopez argued, on behalf of the class, that section 3313.66 of the Ohio law is unconstitutional.

The law empowered the principal to suspend for up to 10 days or to expel a student. Lopez argued that because this law allowed public school administrators to deprive students of their right to an education without a hearing, it violated the procedural due process requirement of the Fourteenth Amendment.

DECISION

Justice White, writing for the majority, affirmed the decision of the district court. He refuted the assertion of Goss that the right to an education was not an interest protected by the due process clause of the Constitution. To think so would be to misconceive the nature of due process rights. Due process encompasses those rights defined by state statutes and rules. He concluded that, based on state law creating the public school system and making attendance in school mandatory, the class clearly had a legitimate claim. Once the right to an education was extended to all children, the right may not be withdrawn without fair procedure to determine whether there is legitimate cause for the action. He stated that this was true even though Ohio was not under a constitutional requirement to provide such a service: "Although Ohio may not be constitutionally obligated to establish and maintain a public school system, it has nevertheless done so and has required its children to attend. Those young people do not 'shed their constitutional rights' at the schoolhouse door." The Fourteenth Amendment applies to all the agents of the state, including the Board of Education.

Justice White noted the due process clause forbids arbitrary deprivations of liberty by the state. Previous cases had established that "where a person's good name, reputation, honor, or integrity is at stake because of what the government is doing to him, the minimal requirements of the Clause must be satisfied." Justice White found the temporary suspension to be of such a nature as to require due process. He felt that the threat of damaged standing within the school community and the higher education community was sufficient to justify requiring the state to meet the minimum requirements of due process: "It is apparent that the claimed right of the State to determine unilaterally and without process whether that misconduct has occurred immediately collides with the requirements of the Constitution."

Justice White also rejected the argument of the administrators that the interest at stake was not of such a degree as to warrant judicial intervention. He noted that the Court must look to the nature, not the relative weight, of the state infringement. In so doing, he found that though the students were only temporarily expelled from school, the right to a hearing was still required: "Neither the property interest in educational benefits temporarily denied nor the liberty interest in reputation, which is also implicated, is so insubstantial that suspensions may constitutionally be imposed by any procedure the school chooses, no matter how arbitrary."

He noted that the practical meaning of the majority for school administrators was that they are required to protect the student's property interest in their education by providing for a hearing before or relatively soon after the suspension takes place. At that hearing the student should be given the opportunity to explain his version of the facts and provide background information about what led up to the events in question. He stopped short, however, of requiring an adversarial hearing in which the student would have the right to cross-examine witnesses and verify his version of the event in question. Justice White felt that the requirements of effective notice and an informal hearing were enough to minimize the probability of erroneous action being taken on the part of the school official.

Justice Powell dissented, joined by Justices Blackmun and Rehnquist. Powell dissented on the grounds that the Court's act of judicial intervention would impede the functioning of the school system and diminish the quality of education provided. The dissenters argued that the alleged infringements were too speculative and that the suspension, because it was only temporary, did not pose a substantial threat to the property interest of the student in his or her education. These combined reasons led Justice Powell to conclude that the imposition of a constitutional rule was not justified.

Justice Powell argued that the Court's past decisions make clear that interests are created, and their dimension are defined by state law. The challenged legislation provided for an education that was not free of discipline. The right to an education was a part of a total package, which allows the state authority control over the direction of the school and choosing appropriate discipline regulations and methodologies: "Thus the very legislation that 'defines' the dimension of the student's entitlement, while providing a right to education generally, does not establish this right free of discipline imposed in accord with Ohio law. Rather, the right is encompassed in the entire package of statutory provisions governing education in Ohio—of which the power to suspend is one."

He continued that however the right is defined, the temporary nature of the deprivation is nothing more than a routine disciplinary measure that does not take on constitutional dimensions. He went on to note that the named plaintiffs had not shown any educational injury as a result of their suspensions.

Justice Powell continued that previous decisions by the Court allowed schools broad discretion in development and execution of their policies. He noted that this broad area of discretion included the area of discipline. This approach recognized the limited role of the judiciary in monitoring the unique structure of a public education system. He concluded that the effect of the majority's decision was to impede the operation of daily functions by school administrators then not obliged to follow and provide hearings to disciplined students: "Few rulings would interfere more extensively in the daily functioning of schools than subjecting routine discipline to the formalities and judicial oversight of due process." The effect would be to constitutionalize routine classroom decisions, of which suspension is one.

AFTERMATH

Though the Court set out that notice and a hearing must be afforded to students punished by suspension for 10 days or less, it was vague about the specifics of what was sufficient to meet these requirements. The lower courts have had to grapple with these issues. Many of the questions that the issue of procedural due process for students raise in this context are how specific the notice must be; whether the student must be notified of the type of behavior punished by expulsion; whether a school must comply with local policies that afford more procedural due process than required by *Goss;* and what the qualities under the emergency exception in *Goss* are.

Practically, the courts have shown great deference to school administrators in suits challenging the procedural due process afforded students in suspension proceedings. In general the courts have found that oral notice is sufficient to meet the notice requirement of *Goss;* parents do not have the right of notice and a hearing when the child is excluded, but the child has the right to both; and rules do not have to be written to be enforced. The exception language in *Goss* has been given broad interpretation; adversarial hearings are not required for short-term hearings; and as long as a jurisdiction meets the minimum requirement of *Goss* it may afford more procedural due process rights to students.

Though these decisions stripped a significant amount of discretion from the school in terms of disciplining students, problems with the use of discretion by school administrators still exist. Many cases have involved the discrepancy in the rates and types of punishment given to minorities, particularly African Americans, with those given to nonminorities. These suits have alleged that even with the procedural due process protections in place, school administrators have disproportionately used disciplinary measures on minorities. Minorities represent a disproportionate percentage of school expulsions and suspensions, compared with their number in the school population.

In *Board of Curators of the University of Missouri v. Horowitz,* the Court held that the *Goss* due process requirements were limited to dismissals for misconduct and suspensions. This decision limited the due process rights accorded to students to disciplinary matters, rather than extending them to academic matters.

SIGNIFICANCE

Goss gave constitutional dimension to matters that had been traditionally considered matters of local concern. It is a seminal case in the area of substantive due process right of public school students. In addition, the Court implied that the use of disciplinary actions that result in greater than 10-day suspensions should be accorded greater due process protections than required by *Goss.'* Courts have used the 10-day limit in *Goss* to differentiate between procedures required for short-term suspension and those required for longer periods.

RELATED CASES

Board of Curators of University of Missouri v. Horowitz, 435 U.S. 78 (1978)

Dixon v. Alabama State Board of Education, 294
    F.2d 150, 158 (5th Cir. 1961), cert. denied,
    368 U.S. 930 (1961)

Mathews v. Eldridge, 424 U.S. 319 (1976)

New Jersey v. T.L.O., 469 U.S. 325 (1985)

*Tinker v. Des Moines Independent Community
    School District,* 393 U.S. 503 (1969)

RECOMMENDED READING

Dolores Cooper and John L. Strope, Jr., *Short-Term
    Suspensions Fourteen Years Later,* 58 Education
    Law Reporter 871 (1990).

Frank Easterbrook, *Substance and Due Process,*
    Supreme Court Review 85 (1982).

Henry Monaghan, *Of "Liberty" and "Property,"* 62
    Cornell Law Review 405 (1977).

Jacqueline A. Stefkovich, *Students' Fourth and Four-
    teenth Amendment Rights after Tinker: A Half Full
    Glass?,* 69 St. John's Law Review 481 (1995).

Case Title: *Griffin v. Breckenridge*

Legal Citation: 403 U.S. 88

Year of Decision: 1971

KEY ISSUES

Does the Ku Klux Klan Act, a federal statute,
apply to private conspiracies? If so, is this application consistent with the Thirteenth Amendment
and the right of Congress to protect the right of
interstate travel?

HISTORY OF THE CASE

The petitioners filed a complaint in the District
Court for the Southern District of Mississippi seeking compensatory and punitive damages. Their
complaint stated they were African-American citizens who resided in Mississippi. On July 2, 1966,
they were passengers in an automobile belonging
to and driven by R. G. Grady, a resident of Tennessee. The defendants acted under a mistaken
belief that R. G. Grady was a worker in the civil
rights movement. They conspired, planned, and

agreed to block passage of the plaintiffs in the
automobile. They stopped, detained, assaulted,
beat, and injured them with deadly weapons.

As part of this conspiracy, the defendants
drove their truck into the path of Grady's automobile and blocked its passage over the public
road. The defendants then forced the plaintiffs to
get out of Grady's automobile and prevented the
plaintiffs from escaping. James Breckenridge
clubbed Grady; in addition, he pointed firearms at
the plaintiffs and threatened to kill or injure them
if he was not obeyed. As a result, the plaintiffs
were terrorized to such a degree as to deprive
them of their liberty. In addition, the plaintiffs suffered extreme terror, mental anguish, and emotional and physical distress because of these
menacing acts that caused them to be stricken
with immediate fear of death. They further
alleged that James Calvin Breckenridge willfully,
intentionally, and maliciously clubbed each of the
plaintiffs on the head, severely injuring them,
while he and his brother continued to assault
them and prevent their escape by pointing
firearms at them.

As a result of this conspiracy and the consequent acts, the defendants prevented the plaintiffs
and other African Americans from enjoying their
rights, privileges, and immunities as citizens of the
United States and the state of Mississippi. These
rights included freedom of speech, movement,
association, and assembly; the right to petition
their government for redress of grievances; the
right not to be enslaved nor deprived of life, liberty, or property other than by due process of law,
and their rights to travel the public highways
without restraint in the same manner as similarly
situated white citizens in Mississippi.

The plaintiffs asserted federal court jurisdiction under Title 18, section 1985 (3) of the United
States Code, which provides that:

> If two or more persons in any State or Ter-
> ritory conspire or go in disguise on the
> highway or on the premises of another, for
> the purpose of depriving either directly and
> indirectly, any person or class of persons of
> the equal protection of the laws or of equal
> privileges and immunities under the laws
> (and) in any case of conspiracy set forth in
> this section, if one or more persons engaged
> therein do, or cause to be done, any act in

furtherance of the object of such conspiracy, whereby another is injured in his person or property, or deprived of having and exercising any right or privilege of a citizen of the United States, the party so injured or deprived may have an action for the recovery of damages, occasioned by such injury or deprivation, against any one or more of the conspirators.

The district court dismissed the complaint on the grounds that the plaintiffs had failed to state a cause of action. It relied on *Collins v. Hardyman* to hold that only conspiracies under the color of state law are covered by the statute that the plaintiffs sought to invoke. The court of appeals affirmed the district court's opinion.

SUMMARY OF ARGUMENTS

The petitioners argued that the respondents conspired to assault them as they traveled upon the federal, state and, local highways in an automobile driven by Grady, a citizen of Tennessee, for the purpose of preventing them and other African Americans through force, violence, and intimidation from seeking the equal protection of the laws and from enjoying the equal rights, privileges, and immunities of citizens under the laws of the United States and of Mississippi. They argued that in so doing they were liable under Title 18, section 1985 (3) of the United States Code for the damages that resulted from their acts.

The defendants argued that the claim should be dismissed because the statute the plaintiffs sought to invoke was not applicable to private actions. They relied on the opinion of *Collins v. Hardyman*, in which the Court held that the language of the statute applied only to actions performed under the color of state law.

DECISION

Justice Stewart, in writing the opinion of the Court, held that the statute encompassed the actions of private persons. He reasoned that the type of behavior addressed by the statute is rarely carried out under the color of state law and therefore to read the statute as encompassing only that behavior would render it meaningless and make it artificially restrictive: "On their face, the words of the statute fully encompass the conduct of private

persons. The provisions speak simply of 'two or more persons in any State or Territory' who 'conspire or go in disguise on the highway or on the premises of another.' Going in disguise, in particular, is in this context an activity so little associated with official action and so commonly connected with private marauders that this clause could almost never be applicable under the artificially restrictive construction of Collins." He went on to note that the legislative history of the statute and its companion statutory provisions made clear that Congress intended the statute to encompass private as well as state-sponsored actions. In addition, he noted that the plain meaning of the statute was to cover actions motivated by racial, class-based, or other invidious discrimination to deny the target the equal protection of the law or equal protection or equal privileges—action not likely to be taken by a state agent.

When analyzing the complaint in light of this reasoning, Justice Stewart found that the alleged acts were intended to be covered by the statute: "Indeed, the conduct here alleged lies so close to the core of the coverage intended by Congress that it is hard to conceive of wholly private conduct that would come within the statute if this does not." In addressing the issue of whether Congress had the power to act in such a manner he concluded that the power to regulate private action such as addressed by the statute was within Congress's power and in this instance the power was exercised legitimately to secure the equal enjoyment of right to all citizens.

Rev. Statute § 1985 (3) is not limited to state action, but "was framed to protect from invasion by private persons, the equal privileges and immunities under the laws, of all persons and classes of persons." Its companion statutory provisions prohibited three forms of state action. These forms are action under the authority of state law, interference with or influence upon state authority, and a private conspiracy of such a magnitude that it supplants government authorities and satisfies the state action requirement. Stewart concluded that given the forms that the related statutes cover, it is impossible to believe that Congress intended that statute at issue merely to duplicate the scope and prohibitions of these statutes.

He next noted that though the statute was intended to reach private action, Congress did not intend to create a general federal tort law or: "The language requiring intent to deprive of equal protection, or equal privileges and immunities, means that there must be some racial, or perhaps otherwise class-based, invidiously discriminatory animus behind the conspirators' action. The conspiracy, in other words, must aim at a deprivation of the equal enjoyment of rights secured by the law to all."

Stewart concluded that for a complaint to come within the legislation it must allege that the defendants (1) conspired or went in disguise on the highway or premises of another (2) for the purpose of depriving, directly or indirectly, any person or class of persons of the equal protection of laws or equal privileges and immunities under the law; (3) one or more of the conspirators caused or caused to be done an act in furtherance of the conspiracy in which (4a) another person or property was injured or (4b) deprived of having and exercising any rights and privileges as a U.S. citizen. The complaint at issue met all of these requirements and as a result a cause of action under statute.

Lastly, Justice Stewart concluded that Congress had the power to restrict private action. In this case the power is derived from section 2 of the Thirteenth Amendment. The Thirteenth Amendment gives Congress the power to deter and address through legislation badges and incidents of slavery. The incidents alleged in the petitioners' complaint were of this kind. He noted that the right to interstate travel is constitutionally protected. One of the results of this conspiracy was to interfere with the petitioners' right to travel through Mississippi.

Justice Harlan concurred. He took exception to the Court's reliance on the right to interstate travel. He found it to be an unnecessary premise upon which to justify federal jurisdiction under the statute.

AFTERMATH

The task of translating the guidelines set in *Griffin* proved a monumental task for state courts. For 10 years after the decision, lower courts grappled with shaping a body of law around 1985 (3). The three major areas of controversy were (1) whether the section was limited to discrimination against racial groups, (2) whether the section in any way was still limited by a requirement that the state

have a connection to the complained of action, (3) the source of congressional power to reach private conspiracies. As to the first area, the list of classes that would not qualify for protection under the act grew to enormous proportions, and the courts have had difficulty defining exactly how far the section should extend. The courts have split around how liberally to interpret the section. Lower courts range from giving broad reading to *Griffin* and therefore addressing purely private conspiracies to requiring some degree of intrusion by the state to invoke the statute.

Since *Griffin,* the Court has increasingly adopted a more formal treatment of the statute. The Court has become increasingly reluctant to apply section 1985 (3). In 1993, a call was made for its application to prevent and find liable anti-abortion protesters who assault and intimidate employees and patients at a women's health clinic. Though factually very similar to the *Griffin* case, in *Bray v. Alexandria* the Court refused to apply section 1985 (3) to a case involving the assault and intimidation of patients at a women's health clinic by abortion protesters. The demise in the use of this statute has left a gap in the enforcement of civil rights. As a result a patchwork of efforts has been developed to fill the gap.

The scope of the kind and degree of actions that may be proscribed and assigned liability under section 1985 (3) is still unclear. The Court has extended the holding of *Griffin* to gender discrimination in employment. The Court in *Great American Federal Savings & Loan Ass'n v. Novotny* (1979) held that the statute was remedial only. In *United Brotherhood of Carpenters & Joiners v. Scott* (1983), the Court found that discriminatory intentions based on classification as a union member was insufficient to invoke the statute as it was not intended to reach that type of class-based discrimination. The Court has also held that economically motivated animus was not the type envisioned by the Court when it adopted 1985 (3) in the Reconstruction era.

SIGNIFICANCE

Griffin recognized a right to substantial equality of citizenship. For the first 100 years after its enactment, section 1985 (3) remained nearly dormant. The decision of *Griffin* marked the rebirth of section 1985 (3)'s use after the Reconstruction period, when it was enacted. Since its original enactment the statute was given meaning. *Griffin* overruled the holding in *Collins v. Hardyman* that the statute was invoked only in conspiracies that involved state action.

Griffin imposed two requirements on a § 1985 (3) action. First, the court must hold that the defendant's conduct falls within the statute. Second, the court must hold that Congress has the power to address the alleged action. These requirements were designed to address the concern that the statute would be interpreted as "general federal tort law," which would punish all actions against the person or property of another.

Section 1985 (3) was recognized by commentators as a response to rampant violence in the South by the Ku Klux Klan. It was enacted to curb the violence directed at African Americans, Republicans, and northern "carpetbaggers." The violence threatened to eliminate the ability of the state authorities to maintain a civil society and administer equal protection of the laws. Congress in enacting this statute felt that the Fourteenth Amendment authorized legislation against private discrimination.

RELATED CASES

Collins v. Hardyman, 341 U.S. 651 (1951)

Great American Federal Savings & Loan Ass'n v. Novotny, 442 U.S. 366 (1979)

Monell v. NYS Dept. of Soc. Servs., 436 U.S. 658 (1978)

Monroe v. Pape, 365 U.S. 167 (1961)

United Brotherhood of Carpenters & Joiners v. Scott, 463 U.S. 825 (1983)

RECOMMENDED READING

Daniel E. Durden, *Republicans as a Protected Class?: Harrison v. Kvat Food Management, Inc. and the Scope of Section 1985 (3)*, 36 American University Law Review 193 (1986).

Ken Gormley, *Private Conspiracies and the Constitution: A Modern Vision of 42 U.S.C. Section 1985 (3)*, 64 Texas Law Review 527 (1985).

John Valery White, *Vindicating Rights in a Federal System: Rediscovering 42 U.S.C. 1985 (3)'s Equality Right*, 69 Temple Law Review 145 (1996).

Case Title: *Griffin v. California*

Legal Citations: 380 U.S. 609; 85 S.Ct. 1229; 14 L.Ed. 2d. 106

Year of Decision: 1965

KEY ISSUES

Does the Fifth Amendment against self-incrimination apply to the states?

HISTORY OF THE CASE

Eddie Dean Griffin was convicted of the murder and attempted rape of Essie Mae Hodson and sentenced to death. He had been arrested in Mexicali, Mexico, and admitted to the police officers that on December 2, 1961, he was drinking wine and beer in a club in Los Angeles, where he met Hodson, Eddie Seay, her common law husband, and some other people. During the evening, Eddie Griffin gave Eddie Seay a ten-dollar bill to buy more wine. Seay disappeared with the money, and Griffin followed Hodson home to the apartment she shared with Seay. Hodson let Griffin in and, according to Seay's account, told him she would make up the missing change by allowing Griffin to have intercourse with her. Seay came into the room and started a fight, which continued down the back staircase and into the alley. Seay ran off, and Hodson, even though she had been hit several times during the fight, did engage in sexual intercourse with Griffin in a "trashbox." Hodson was found in the alley next morning bleeding from her head. She was taken to the hospital and treated for extensive injuries, including a skull fracture. She died the next day.

In the course of his statement to the investigating police officers, defendant Griffin admitted that he had left the trashbox when he heard who he thought was a night watchman pass by. Additionally, he admitted that he had gonorrhea and syphilis, both of which would have destroyed his ability to produce sperm, hence the inability of the coroner to find the presence of sperm during his autopsy of Ms. Hodson. Griffin was arrested on December 19, 1961, in Mexico for the rape and assault of Amanda Encinas, and this evidence was presented to the jury in his trial in Los Angeles even though the arrest and trial took place in Mexico. Griffin refused to testify during the trial and his failure to testify was commented upon by the prosecuting attorney and by the court in its instructions to the jury.

SUMMARY OF ARGUMENTS

The attorney for Griffin argued that the failure of the accused to testify at a state criminal trial is his constitutional right. Permitting the prosecution to attack that right violates the Fifth Amendment privilege against self-incrimination and the Fourteenth Amendment guarantee of due process. Griffin's attorney also argued that it was a violation of due process for the prosecutor to comment upon the evidence from the trial in Mexico, where the defendant had been, in effect, acquitted. The introduction of the extraneous matter of the trial in Mexico clearly prejudiced the jury.

The state of California argued that the provisions of California law permitting comment upon the defendant's failure to explain or deny evidence did not violate the Fifth Amendment because no federal rule was imposed upon the states. The state further argued that the evidence should be admissible to show guilt because it showed a common plan, scheme, or design in the committing of a prior offense. Additionally, the state argued that the jury should be afforded wide latitude concerning the background and history of an offender with regard to aggravating circumstances that should properly be considered.

DECISION

Justice William Douglas wrote the opinion of the Court. In a 7-2 vote, the Court rejected the ADAM-SON V. CALIFORNIA (1947) decision. Justice Black found that if this were a federal trial, reversible error would have been committed, and found that it was entirely wrong for the Court to make any inference about the silence of the accused. Adverse comments by prosecutors and judges were strictly forbidden, and the Fifth Amendment was now incorporated into the laws of the states through the due process clause of the Fourteenth Amendment.

Justices Potter Stewart and Byron White dissented, finding that Griffin had not been compelled to be a witness against himself. They felt that the California law permitting comment on silence was not coercive, but "rather a means of

articulating and bringing into the light of rational discussion of fact inescapably impressed on the jury's consciousness."

AFTERMATH

During the Reagan administration, Attorney General Edwin Meese and others attacked the incorporation doctrine as inconsistent with the original intent of the authors of the Constitution. *Griffin* has withstood these attacks.

SIGNIFICANCE

With the *Griffin* decision, the incorporation doctrine, which makes certain portions of the Bill of Rights applicable to the states, came to its high-water mark. By virtue of this decision, almost all of the guarantees of the Bill of Rights have been applied to the states.

RELATED CASES

Adamson v. California, 322 U.S. 46 (1947)

Malloy v. Hogan, 378 U.S. 1 (1964)

Palko v. Connecticut, 302 U.S. 319 (1937)

Twining v. New Jersey, 211 U.S. 78 (1908)

RECOMMENDED READING

Craig M. Bradley, Griffin v. California: *Still Viable after All These Years,* 79 Michigan Law Review 1290 (1981).

Curtis, Michael K. *No State Shall Abridge: The Fourteenth Amendment and the Bill of Rights.* Durham, N.C.: Duke University Press, 1986.

Nelson, William F. *The Fourteenth Amendment: From Political Principle to Judicial Doctrine.* Cambridge, Mass.: Harvard University Press, 1988.

Case Title: *Harris v. New York*

Legal Citation: 401 U.S. 222

Year of Decision: 1971

KEY ISSUES

May a statement that is inadmissible for the prosecutor's case be used to attack the credibility of the defendant's trial testimony?

HISTORY OF THE CASE

Harris was charged with selling heroin to an undercover police officer on two separate occasions. During the trial Harris was questioned regarding statements he made after his arrest. On direct examination he denied selling the undercover officers heroin. On cross-examination he was questioned regarding statements he made to the officers after his arrest, which partially contradicted his direct testimony. He responded that he could not remember any of the questions or responses recited by the prosecutor. The statement containing the questions Harris was allegedly asked after arrest was placed in evidence by Harris's counsel for use on appeal. The trial judge instructed the jury to consider the information regarding Harris's post-arrest statement only in the context of determining his credibility. Harris's post-arrest statements were inadmissible as evidence because Harris was not informed of his right to have counsel appointed. The jury found Harris guilt on one of the counts of selling heroin.

SUMMARY OF ARGUMENTS

Harris argued that statements inadmissible under *Miranda* (because a defendant was not informed of his right to remain silent, that anything he said could be used against him in a court of law, his right to counsel and his right to have counsel appointed prior to interrogation) cannot be used to impeach the defendant.

The state argued that the prosecutor was not using the statement for its case in chief and this had not contravened the holding in *Miranda*. The state reasoned the holding in *Miranda* extended only to the use of such statements in the case and for limited uses, such as impeachment contradicting or pointing out flaws in defendant's testimony.

DECISION

Justice Blackmun, writing for the majority of the Court, held that an otherwise inadmissible statement could be used for impeachment purposes. The Court interpreted the holding in MIRANDA V. ARIZONA (1966) narrowly, as barring the prosecution from using statements "of an accused made while in custody prior to having or effectively waiving counsel." He continued that it does not follow from this that a statement inadmissible

against the defendant in the prosecution's case is barred for all purposes.

In *Walder v. United States*, the Court allowed physical evidence that was inadmissible in the case in chief to be used for impeachment purposes. Though the defendant in *Walder* was impeached over collateral matters, that difference did not justify a different response. In that the testimony that Harris provided at trial was different from the statements he gave the undercover officers after his arrest, the impeachment process provided a valuable aid to the jury in assessing the petitioner's credibility. He concluded that the benefits of impeaching the defendant should not be lost to protect against the possibility that allowing these statements to be used would encourage police misconduct. The exclusion of evidence obtained by police misconduct is sufficient to deter this type of abuse.

The privilege of the defendant to testify or refuse to testify on his own behalf is not inclusive of the right to commit perjury. Justice Burger held that a defendant who voluntarily takes the stand cannot disregard his or her obligation to speak truthfully and accurately: "The shield provided by *Miranda* cannot be perverted into a license to use perjury by way of a defense, free from the risk of confrontation with prior inconsistent utterances." Therefore, the use of the conflicting statements was appropriate in impeaching the defendant.

Justice Black dissented.

Justice Brennan wrote a dissenting opinion in which Justice Douglas and Justice Marshall joined. He reasoned that evidence that cannot be used in the case in chief should not be used to impeach the witness. The statements in this case were used to impeach Harris's testimony on a matter directly related to the crime he was on trial for; unlike *Walder* the defendant was not impeached on a collateral matter. Citing *Walder*, Justice Brennan noted that the Court in that case had recognized that in a situation such as Harris's, in which the defendant's testimony denies complicity in the crimes for which he is charged, the Constitution guarantees the defendant the opportunity to deny all elements of the case against him: "Of course, the constitution guarantees a defendant the fullest opportunity to meet the accusation against him. He must be free to deny all the elements of the case against him without thereby giving leave to the Government to introduce by way of rebuttal evidence illegally secured by it, and therefore not available for its case in chief" (*Walder v. United States*, 347 U.S. 65). In *Walder* the defendant denied not only the charges against him, but made a sweeping claim that he had never been involved in any activity like that for which he was charged. It was then that the government was allowed to rebut that statement with evidence of the prior commission of the act of which he was accused.

He noted that the Court in *Walder* did not identify the constitutional provisions that guarantee a defendant the right to meet the accusations against him. He felt that *Miranda* addressed that issue and held that the Fifth Amendment's provision against self-incrimination was one of the provisions that supported this guarantee. The privilege against self-incrimination is protected fully when the defendant's right to remain silent is the unfettered exercise of his own will. To allow the prosecutor to use tainted statement cuts down on the privilege by making its assertion costly: "Thus, the accused is denied an unfettered choice when the decision whether to take the stand is burdened by the risk that an illegally obtained prior statement may be introduced to impeach his direct testimony complicity in the crime charged against him." The privilege established in *Miranda* protects against self-incrimination in any manner.

He continued that deterring police brutality was only one of the motivations behind excluding improperly obtained statements. The larger objective is to safeguard the integrity of the adversarial process. Once again relying on *Miranda*, he reasoned that the privilege against self-incrimination is a mainstay in the adversarial system.

AFTERMATH

In later cases the Court continued to retreat from the broad privilege provided by the *Miranda* decision. By shifting the emphasis to the deterrence of police brutality the Court has been able to limit the exclusionary privilege to only those situations in which police brutality would be deterred. In *Michigan v. Tucker* (1974), the Court held that Miranda warnings were not a constitutional requirement of the Fifth Amendment but rather a safeguard created by the judiciary. The Court has redefined the Miranda privilege to exclude only such statements attained through direct, inten-

tional questioning while the police have held the defendant in custody without advising him of his rights. In *New York v. Quarles* (1984), the Court created the "public safety" exception to the *Miranda* exclusionary rule. The Court held that statements obtained before *Miranda* warning were given are not automatically excluded, because *Miranda* rights are not constitutional rights, but rather procedural safeguards to enforce the Fifth Amendment. The Court thus rejected the presumption of coercion that *Miranda* adopted in its absolute exclusion of statements obtained during custodial interrogation before *Miranda* warnings were given.

SIGNIFICANCE

In adopting a narrow reading of *Miranda* the Court limited the privilege established by the case. After *Harris,* the privilege against self-incrimination was limited to the case in chief.

Prior to 1966 the Supreme Court excluded incriminating statements obtained through brutal or unofficial police tactics through the due process clause of the Fourteenth Amendment. This became known as the "coerced-confession" doctrine and was administered on a case-by-case basis. The Court directly addressed the issue of coerced confessions in *Miranda v. Arizona.* In that case the Court established an absolute rule of exclusion of such confession based on the Fifth Amendment. In 1970 the Court began to modify this decision. *Harris* represents the first case in which the Court retreated from the broad reading of Miranda.

RELATED CASES

Michigan v. Tucker, 417 U.S. 433 (1974)

Miranda v. Arizona, 384 U.S. 436 (1966)

New York v. Quarles, 104 S.Ct. 2626 (1984)

RECOMMENDED READING

Alan Dershowitz and John Hart Ely, Harris v. New York: *Some Anxious Observations on the Candor and Logic of the Emerging Nixon Majority,* 80 Yale Law Journal 1198 (1971).

Martin Gardner, *The Emerging Good Faith Exception to the Miranda Rule—A Critique,* 35 Hastings Law Journal 429 (1984).

Stephen S. Goodman IV, *Criminal Law—Fifth Amendment Miranda Warnings—An Exception to Admin-*

istering Miranda Warnings Exists Where Police Questioning Is Prompted by Concern for Public Safety, 16 St. Mary's Law Journal 489 (1985).

Thomas Schrock, Robert Welch, and Ronald Collins, *Interrogational Rights: Reflections on Miranda v. Arizona,* 52 Southern California Law Review 1 (1978).

David Sonenshein, *Miranda and the Burger Court: Trends and Countertrends,* 13 Loyola University Chicago Law Journal 405 (1982).

Case Title: *Hurtado v. People of the State of California*

Legal Citation: 110 U.S. 516

Year of Decision: 1884

KEY ISSUES

Does the due process clause of the Fourteenth Amendment of the Constitution require an indictment by a grand jury in a state prosecution for murder?

HISTORY OF THE CASE

In February 1882, the district attorney of Sacramento County, California, charged Joseph Hurtado with murder. The district attorney brought the charge without any previous investigation by a grand jury. Hurtado was arraigned in March 1882 and pleaded not guilty. A trial ensued, and the jury found Hurtado guilty of murder in the first degree. In June 1882, the Superior Court of Sacramento County rendered its judgment on the verdict, that Hurtado be punished by death. Hurtado appealed to the California Supreme Court, which affirmed the judgment. From this judgment, Hurtado appealed to the U.S. Supreme Court.

SUMMARY OF ARGUMENTS

Hurtado argued that his constitutional right to due process was violated because he was never indicted by a grand jury. The Fifth Amendment states that "no person shall be held to answer for

a capital or otherwise infamous crime, unless on a presentment or indictment of a grand jury . . . nor be deprived of life, liberty, or property without due process of law." Hurtado argued that this provision of the Fifth Amendment is incorporated under the due process clause of the Fourteenth Amendment and is therefore applicable to the states—in this case, California.

DECISION

Justice Matthews delivered the opinion of the Court, which held that the Fifth Amendment's requirement of a grand jury indictment applies only to the federal government, not the states. The Fourteenth Amendment says that no state "shall . . . deprive any person of life, liberty, or property without due process of law," but it does not say anything about grand jury indictments. If the Fourteenth Amendment made indictments a requirement of due process, "it would have embodied, as did the Fifth Amendment, express declarations to that effect." One of the "fundamental principles of liberty and justice . . . resides in the right of the people to make their own laws, and alter them at their pleasure." Thus, the state of California had a right to bring a charge of murder without a grand jury indictment. The judgment of the California Supreme Court, that Hurtado be punished by death, was affirmed.

AFTERMATH

Prior to the date of his scheduled execution, Hurtado died in prison. This case has not been overturned. Courts have upheld the right of states to bring initial accusations against alleged criminals in a manner and form they may devise. The Fifth Amendment right to a grand jury still does not apply to state prosecutions.

In the landmark case of *POWELL V. STATE OF ALABAMA* (1932), the Court concluded that certain fundamental rights, safeguarded by the first eight amendments against federal action, were also safeguarded against state action by the due process of law clause of the Fourteenth Amendment. This meant that certain provisions of the Bill of Rights were incorporated into the Fourteenth Amendment and protected citizens against state action. Even so, the Court has not included the right to a grand jury indictment as one of these fundamental rights.

One should also note that the decision in *Powell* was foreshadowed by Justice Harlan's dissenting opinion in *Hurtado*. In *Hurtado*, Harlan stated that "'[d]ue process of law,' within the meaning of the national constitution, does not import one thing with reference to the powers of the states and another with reference to the powers of the general government." Justice Harlan was ahead of his time on this issue.

SIGNIFICANCE

This case demonstrates the significance of state sovereignty. Each state has a right to make its own laws, as long as certain fundamental rights are not violated. Arguably, the right to a grand jury indictment is not a fundamental right.

RELATED CASES

Beavers v. Henkel, 194 U.S. 73 (1904)

Dowdell v. United States, 221 U.S. 325 (1911)

Powell v. State of Alabama, 287 U.S. 45 (1932)

State v. Fulton, Ohio, 566 N.E.2d 1195, *cert. denied,* 502 U.S. 828 (1991)

RECOMMENDED READING

James R. Acker, *Grand Jury and Capital Punishment,* 21 Pacific Law Journal 31–118 (1989).

Case Title: *Irvin v. Dowd*

Legal Citation: 366 U.S. 717

Year of Decision: 1961

KEY ISSUES

How does a court know when a jury is sufficiently impartial?

HISTORY OF THE CASE

Six murders were committed near Evansville, Indiana, between 1954 and 1955. The crimes, extensively covered by the local news media, aroused great excitement and indignation throughout Vanderburgh County, where Evansville is located, and adjoining Gibson County. A suspect, Leslie Irvin, was arrested on April 8, 1995. Shortly thereafter, the prosecutor and police officials issued press releases that Irvin had confessed to the six murders. The Vanderburgh County Grand Jury indicted Irvin for murder. This indictment resulted in Irvin's conviction for the murder of Whitney Wesley Kerr allegedly committed in Vanderburgh County on December 23, 1954.

After the indictment, counsel appointed to defend Irvin immediately sought a change of venue from Vanderburgh County, which was granted, but to adjoining Gibson County. Alleging that the widespread and inflammatory publicity had also highly prejudiced the inhabitants of Gibson County, Irvin's counsel, on October 29, 1955, sought another change of venue. Counsel sought to remove the case from Gibson County to a county sufficiently removed from the Evansville locality that a fair trial would not be prejudiced. The motion was denied because the pertinent Indiana statute allowed only a single change of venue.

Irvin brought a habeas corpus proceeding, a proceeding brought to determine whether a person is being deprived of liberty through unlawful imprisonment, to test the validity of his murder conviction and sentence of death. The Indiana Supreme Court affirmed the conviction, and the U.S. Supreme Court denied direct review. Irvin immediately sought habeas relief in the U.S. District Court for the Northern District of Indiana, claiming that he did not receive a fair trial. On appeal, Irvin's claim of an unfair trial was denied. The Supreme Court decided to review the case.

SUMMARY OF ARGUMENTS

Irvin argued that forcing him to be tried by a jury with preconceived opinions about his guilt violated his constitutional rights. He also argued that the denial of his motion for change of venue, the Indiana statute allowing only one change of venue, the overruling of his motions for continuance, and the denial of a hearing on these motions violated his due process rights.

A. F. Dowd, the warden of the Indiana State Prison at Michigan City, Indiana, argued that the trial court had afforded Irvin every constitutional right available under the Fourteenth Amendment.

DECISION

He claimed the Indiana statute limiting him to only one change of venue was unconstitutional. On this issue, the Court cited a case that interpreted the Indiana statute to mean that the necessity of transfer depends on the totality of the surrounding facts. Under this construction of the statute, the Court found that it was not unconstitutional. However, when the Court considered the particular facts of the case, it found that the jurors were unfairly prejudiced, and thus that Irvin was not given a fair trial.

Justice Clark delivered the opinion of the Court. He noted that "findings of impartiality should be set aside only where prejudice is manifest." He quoted *United States v. Wood* (1936) to emphasize that no fixed rule exists to guide the Court in determining the mind-set of the jurors: "Impartiality is not a technical conception. It is a state of mind. For the ascertainment of this mental attitude of appropriate indifference, the Constitution lays down no particular test and procedure is not chained to any ancient formula."

On the widespread effects of the news media's coverage of the case, the Court found that "the force of this continued adverse publicity caused such excitement and fostered a strong prejudice among the people of Gibson County." Then, upon examining the 2,783-page record of the jury selection process, the Court found that 370 prospective jurors (or almost 90 percent of those examined on the point) entertained some opinion as to Irvin's guilt—ranging from mere suspicion to absolute certainty. The Court found a "pattern of deep and bitter prejudice" throughout the community and noted that eight out of the 12 jurors thought Irvin was guilty before the trial began. Based on these findings, the Court vacated Irvin's conviction for murder and sentence of death.

AFTERMATH

The Court noted that Irvin was still subject to custody under the indictment filed by the state of Indiana in the Circuit Court of Gibson County charging him with murder in the first degree, and he could be tried on this or any other indictment.

The Court's ruling on the scope of judicial inquiry into the impartiality of jurors is still good law. The Court may vacate a conviction as a violation of due process in cases in which the prejudice of the jurors is manifest.

SIGNIFICANCE

In a highly publicized murder trial, more than one change of venue may be necessary to ensure a fair trial by a panel of impartial jurors.

RELATED CASES

Gaskins v. McKellar, 916 F.2d 941, 949 (4th Cir. 1990)

U.S. v. McCarthy, 961 F.2d 972, 976 (1st Cir. 1992)

U.S. v. Polan, 970 F.2d 1280, 1284 (3rd Cir. 1992)

U.S. v. Flores, 63 F.3d 1342 1357-58 (5th Cir. 1995)

U.S. v. Amerson, 938 F.2d 116, 117-18 (8th Cir. 1991)

RECOMMENDED READING

Benjamin B. Austin, *Twenty-Sixth Annual Review of Criminal Procedure: III. Trial—Right to Jury Trial,* 85 Georgia Law Journal 1240 (1997).

Lofton, John. *Justice and the Press.* Boston: Beacon Press, 1966.

Curtis R. Reitz, *Federal Habeas Corpus: Impact of an Abortive State Proceeding,* 74 Harvard Law Review 1315 (May 1961).

Case Title: *Jacobson v. Commonwealth of Massachusetts*

Alternate Case Title: Vaccination Case

Legal Citation: 197 U.S. 11

Year of Decision: 1905

KEY ISSUES

Does a healthy adult have a constitutional right, under the Fourteenth Amendment's due process clause, to be exempted from a state law requiring vaccination to prevent the spread of a dangerous disease?

HISTORY OF THE CASE

A Massachusetts state law empowered city health boards to make mandatory vaccination laws if the need arose. Because of a local outbreak of smallpox, the city of Cambridge, Massachusetts, adopted a regulation, on February 27, 1902, that "all the inhabitants of the city who have not been successfully vaccinated since March 1, 1897, be vaccinated or revaccinated." A state law exception existed for children who had a note from a registered physician saying that they were unfit for vaccination. However, according to state law, "[w]hoever, being over twenty-one years of age and not under guardianship, refuses or neglects to comply with such requirement shall forfeit $5."

In this case, Jacobson refused to comply with the requirement. One of the reasons he gave for refusing was that he had, "when a child," been caused great and extreme suffering for a long period by a disease produced by a vaccination. The state brought charges against him. He claimed, among other things, that his constitutional right to due process was violated by the city ordinance. In a jury trial, he was found guilty of violating the regulation and sentenced to pay the $5 fine. The court ordered that he be placed in custody until he paid the fine.

Jacobson appealed to the Massachusetts Supreme Court, which sustained the action of the trial court. Jacobson then petitioned the U.S. Supreme Court.

SUMMARY OF ARGUMENTS

Jacobson argued that the city regulation violated his constitutional right to due process under the Fourteenth Amendment of the Constitution. He claimed that his inherent right to bodily integrity was invaded when the state subjected him to a fine of imprisonment for refusing to submit to vaccination. He said that the vaccination was "nothing short of an assault upon his person." Massachusetts argued that the state's police power allowed it to vaccinate people to protect their health, safety, and welfare.

DECISION

Justice Harlan delivered the opinion of the Court. While recognizing the fundamental right of every individual to care for his own body and health, the Court found that the state has a compelling interest to protect the health and safety of its citizens. The Court held that "a community has the right to protect itself against an epidemic of disease which threatens the safety of its members." Further, the Court found that the means employed by the state—mandatory vaccination—has a substantial relation to the end of protecting public health and safety.

The Court considered Jacobson's concern that arose out of his bad experience with vaccination as a child, but found that he was now "in perfect health and a fit subject of vaccination." The Court recognized the common belief that vaccination has a decided tendency to prevent the spread of smallpox and that "the legislature has the right to pass laws which, according to the common belief of the people, are adopted to prevent the spread of contagious diseases." The Court noted that this power to pass laws to protect public health and safety "is commonly called the police power—power which the state did not surrender when becoming a member of the Union under the Constitution."

The Court held that "the police power of a state, whether exercised directly by the legislature, or by a local body acting under its authority, may be exerted in such circumstances . . . as to justify the interference of the courts to prevent wrong and oppression." As summarized in an article on legislative reform of Washington's tuberculosis law, "[I]n essence, the Court held that the compulsory vaccine was not unconstitutional because even individual liberty interests are subject to the 'common good.'"

AFTERMATH

This case has not been overturned.

SIGNIFICANCE

This case is significant because it defines state police power to protect public health and safety. It is also a good example of "strict scrutiny" analysis—that is, the two-prong test the Court employs when a fundamental right is at issue:

1. Does the state have a "compelling interest" to regulate the activity?
2. Has the state employed the best means to achieve that end?

RELATED CASE

Zucht v. King, 225 S.W. 267 (Tex. Civ. App. 1920), *cert. dismissed*, 260 U.S. 174 (1922)

RECOMMENDED READING

Suzanne M. Malloy, *Comment: Mandatory HIV Screening of Newborns: A Proposition Whose Time Has Not Yet Come*, 45 American University Law Review 1185 (1996).

Paula Mindes, *Note: Tuberculosis Quarantine: A Review of Legal Issues in Ohio and Other States*, 10 Journal of Law and Health 403 (1995–96).

Rosemary G. Reilly, *Combating the Tuberculosis Epidemic: The Legality of Coercive Treatment Measures*, 27 Columbia Journal of Law and Social Problems 101 (1993).

Michael Sanzo, *Vaccines and the Law*, 19 Pepperdine Law Review 29 (1991).

Symposium on Tuberculosis: Legislative Reform of Washington's Tuberculosis Law: The Tension between Due Process and Protecting Public Health, 71 Washington Law Review 989 (1996).

Case Title: *Local 28 of the Sheet Metal Workers' International Association v. Equal Employment Opportunity Commission*

Legal Citations: 478 U.S. 421; 106 S.Ct. 3019; 92 L.Ed. 2d 344

Year of Decision: 1986

KEY ISSUES

Does Title VII of the Civil Rights Act of 1964, which prohibits employment discrimination, give a court the power to order relief that benefits individuals other than identified victims of discrimination?

HISTORY OF THE CASE

In 1971, the Equal Employment Opportunity Commission (EEOC) brought this action in the U.S. District Court for the Southern District of New York against Local 28, a labor union. It was alleged that Local 28 had engaged in discriminatory practices against minorities in union membership. The suit was based on Title VII of the Civil Rights Act. It was found that the union had a long history of racial discrimination. When court action finally began, it was found that discrimination existed. The district court ordered that steps be taken to recruit more minorities. In 1982, New York went back to court for a finding that Local 28 be held in contempt. The court ordered further remedial measures. Another hearing was held a year later with a similar result, which was upheld by the court of appeals. The court held that its findings were in response to continued discrimination and did not involve identifiable minority individuals.

SUMMARY OF ARGUMENTS

The union argued that the contempt remedies were imposed without due process and the appointment of an administrator interfered with the union's right of self-governance. The union also argued that the membership goals and the Employment, Training, Education and Recruitment Fund imposed as remedies were unconstitutional because they exceeded the scope of the available Title VII remedies in violation of the equal protection section of the Fifth Amendment due process clause.

The EEOC argued that the union was guilty of discrimination and was properly judged in contempt. The EEOC also argued that the membership goal and the fund were prohibited by Title VII because preferential relief can be given only to actual victims of unlawful discrimination.

DECISION

The Court found that the orders of the district court did not violate the due process clause of the Fifth Amendment because they furthered the government's compelling interest in remedying past discrimination.

Justice Brennan wrote the opinion for the majority, which upheld the contempt findings and approved the appointment of a supervisor to oversee the union compliance with Title VII, since there was a history of union noncompliance. There is no legislative history of Title VII section 703 that indicates that it is enacted only to identify victims of past discrimination. No quotas are required to correct an imbalance. A district court can institute racial preferences to remedy past discrimination. But this is not always proper. It was not the intent of Congress to create a racially balanced workplace.

AFTERMATH

The case upheld membership goals and timetables for achieving such goals as acceptable remedies for discrimination in the employment area.

SIGNIFICANCE

Affirmative action plans incorporating racial preferences may be used by employers to remedy past discrimination.

RELATED CASES

Firefighters Local Union No. 1784 v. Stotts, 467 U.S. 561 (1984)

Franks v. Bowman Transportation Company, 424 U.S. 727 (1976)

International Brotherhood of Teamsters v. United States, 431 U.S. 327 (1977)

RECOMMENDED READING

Kathleen E. McGrath, *Supreme Court Endorses Court-Ordered Affirmative Action for Non-victims: Local 28 v. EEOC*, 29 Boston College Law Review 266 (1987).

Eric Schnapper, *The Varieties of Numerical Remedies*, 39 Stanford Law Review 851 (1987).

Joel L. Selig, *Affirmative Action in Employment: The Legacy of a Supreme Majority*, 63 Indiana Law Review 310 (1988).

Case Title: *Lynch v. Household Finance Corporation*

Legal Citations: 405 U.S. 538; 92 S.Ct. 1113; 31 L.Ed. 2d 424

Year of Decision: 1972

KEY ISSUES

Does a court lack jurisdiction to hear a case if it involves the impairment of property rights versus the impairment of personal rights?

HISTORY OF THE CASE

Dorothy Lynch had asked her employer to deposit $10.00 from her salary into a savings account; Household Finance sued her for nonpayment of a promissory note. Before she received the complaint, her bank account was garnished. Dorothy Lynch challenged the validity of a pre-judicial garnishment statute in district court. The court dismissed the complaint on grounds that it lacked jurisdiction.

SUMMARY OF ARGUMENTS

Lynch argued that the district court's decision that it lacked jurisdiction because her complaint involved the impairment of property rights deprived indigent litigants of a forum to protect their constitutional rights. Lynch also argued that deprivation of property in violation of the Fourteenth Amendment was proper grounds to invoke the jurisdiction of the district court.

Household Finance Corporation argued that the Supreme Court lacked jurisdiction to hear the case and that Lynch's complaint was not appropriate for the Court's review.

Justice Stewart wrote the majority opinion noting that applicable federal law was intended to protect personal and property rights. Rights in property are basic civil rights, which are "basic civil rights."

> [T]he dichotomy between personal liabilities and property rights is a false one. Property does not have rights. People have rights. The right to enjoy property without unlawful deprivation, no less than the right to speak or the right to travel, is in truth a "personal" right, whether the "property" in question be a welfare check, a home, or a savings account.

Justice White dissented, writing that the constitutional question should be litigated in the state court along with the garnishment.

DECISION

The case was remanded to district court, which held the Connecticut pre-garnishment statute unconstitutional on due process grounds.

AFTERMATH

Property rights are similar to all other personal rights. This idea led to a period of debate on issues in federal criminal procedure.

SIGNIFICANCE

Justice Scalia reversed this trend. He views personal rights and property rights as separate concepts. His view strengthens property claims.

RELATED CASES

Dolan v. City of Tigard, 512 U.S. 374 (1994)

Pennsylvania v. Mahon, 260 U.S. 393 (1922)

RECOMMENDED READING

Francis S. Chlapowski, *The Constitutional Protection of Informational Privacy,* 71 Boston University Law Review 133 (1991).

Michael Collins, *Symposium: "Economic Rights," Implied Constitutional Actions and the Scope of Section 1983,* 77 Georgetown Law Review 1493 (1989).

Case Title: *Mallory v. United States*

Legal Citations: 354 U.S. 449; 77 S.Ct. 1356; 1 L.Ed. 2d 1479

Year of Decision: 1957

KEY ISSUES

Does a violation of Rule 5(a) of the Federal Rules of Criminal Procedure, which requires an arrested person be taken before a magistrate "without unnecessary delay," occur when an arrested person's appearance before a magistrate is delayed until after a confession is obtained?

HISTORY OF THE CASE

Mallory was convicted of rape and sentenced to death by a jury. At trial his confession was admitted. On the afternoon of his arrest, he had been detained at police headquarters. He was not told of his right to counsel or to a preliminary examination before a magistrate, and was not warned to keep silent. He had confessed and was taken to the magistrate the next morning.

The court of appeals affirmed the district court's judgment. The case was heard in the Supreme Court on the issue of illegal detention.

SUMMARY OF ARGUMENTS

Mallory argued that his confession was erroneously admitted into evidence. The United States argued that Mallory's confession was properly admitted into evidence.

DECISION

Justice Frankfurter wrote the opinion for the Court saying that Rule 5(a) of the Federal Rules of Criminal Procedure required arraignment be "without unnecessary delay." In order to enforce the congressional requirement of prompt arraignment, incriminating statements from defendants during a period of unlawful detention are inadmissible.

Police may not arrest on mere suspicion, only on probable cause. Arraignment must follow as quickly as possible so the suspect can be advised of his or her rights.

AFTERMATH

Congress enacted 18 U.S.C. § 3501, which limited the delay before presentation to a magistrate to six hours for a confession prior to such presentation to be admissible, in response to this case and *McNabb v. U.S.* (1943), which also dealt with the admission of confessions after delay in arraignment. The *McNabb-Mallory* doctrine was subsequently superseded by the decision in MIRANDA V. ARIZONA (1966).

SIGNIFICANCE

Mallory reinforced the decision in *McNabb* that a confession obtained during an unnecessary delay in the arraignment of an arrested person was inadmissible in a federal case.

RELATED CASES

McNabb v. U.S., 318 U.S. 332 (1943)

Rogers v. Richmond, 365 U.S. 534 (1961)

Watts v. Indiana, 338 U.S. 49 (1949)

RECOMMENDED READING

Sara Sun Beale, *Reconsidering Supervisory Power in Criminal Cases: Constitutional and Statutory Limits on the Authority of Federal Courts*, 84 Columbia Law Review 1433 (1984).

Welsh S. White, *False Confessions and the Constitution: Safeguards against Untrustworthy Confessions*, 32 Harvard Civil Rights–Civil Liberties Law Review 105 (1997).

Case Title: *Malloy v. Hogan*

Legal Citations: 378 U.S. 1; 84 S.Ct. 1489; 12 L.Ed. 2d. 653

Year of Decision: 1964

KEY ISSUES

Is the Fifth Amendment incorporated by the due process of the Fourteenth Amendment into state criminal proceedings?

HISTORY OF THE CASE

William Malloy was arrested by Patrick J. Hogan, sheriff of Hartford County, Connecticut, for taking part in an unlawful gambling operation. He was sentenced to one year in jail, but after 90 days his prison term was suspended, and he was placed on probation for two years. While he was on probation, he was called to testify at a state inquiry into gambling and other crimes possibly committed by the Mafia. The investigation was conducted by a former state supreme court justice.

Malloy was asked a number of questions regarding the events surrounding his arrest and conviction, which he refused to answer on the grounds it may incriminate him. These questions included his employment, the location where he was arrested, and questions relating to his earlier arrest, trial, and guilty plea.

Malloy was held in contempt of court and imprisoned until he was willing to answer these questions. By a unanimous decision, the Supreme Court of Errors of Connecticut found that Malloy was in contempt of court. The U.S. Supreme Court agreed to review the case on a writ of habeas corpus based on federal grounds.

SUMMARY OF ARGUMENTS

Malloy's attorney argued that since the Fourth Amendment's prohibition against unreasonable searches and seizures is enforceable against the states through the Fourteenth Amendment, and that the Fifth Amendment is intimately connected with the Fourth Amendment as complementary and equal parts of the Bill of Rights, the provisions of the Fifth Amendment protecting a person in a criminal case from testifying against himself should be extended by the Fourteenth Amendment to cover state criminal proceedings. Malloy's attorney also argued that the propriety of the questions should be determined on constitutional standards rather than the standards set by the state of Connecticut. The fact that the state of Connecticut may deem the questions harmless would not matter under federal standards, where the mere possibility of disclosure of incriminating or dangerous information to the witness would uphold the privilege.

The Office of the Attorney General of Connecticut argued that the Fifth Amendment privileges against self-incrimination did not apply in all particularities to the states. Citing the *TWINING V. NEW JERSEY* (1908) case and *ADAMSON V. CALIFORNIA* (1947), Connecticut argued that the state court had made a reasonable accommodation of Malloy's right not to convict himself. They felt Malloy did have a duty to respond to an orderly inquiry with regard to matters of legitimate importance to the state. Connecticut asserted that Malloy had no reasonable grounds to fear danger from these answers because he had already been convicted, and there was absolutely no explanation or basis to show why his possible answers to these questions might be injurious.

DECISION

In a surprising 5–4 decision, Justice William Brennan led the Court's rejection of its former view that the states were not bound to follow the due process clause of the Fourteenth Amendment. Rejecting the *Twining v. New Jersey* and *Adamson v. California* decisions, Justice Brennan found that it was appropriate for the Court to reexamine its past decisions regarding the Fourteenth Amendment's role in the preservation of basic liberties.

He found that the decisions of the Supreme Court since *Twining* and *Adamson* have "departed from the contrary view expressed in those cases."

In tracing various criminal decisions of the Court, Justice Brennan found that "the shift reflects recognition that the American system of criminal prosecution is accusatorial, not inquisitorial, and that the Fifth Amendment privilege is its essential mainstay." Thus all governments, whether state or federal, are constitutionally compelled to establish guilt by evidence, independently and freely obtained. The right of a person to remain silent, unless he chooses to speak, in the "unfettered exercise of his own free will, and to suffer no penalty" is now the law.

Justice Brennan further attacked the assertion of the state of Connecticut that the accusatorial system has become a fundamental part of our society and that a less stringent state standard based on tradition is entitled to be respected. The Court thus rejected the notion that the Fourteenth Amendment applies only to the states on a "watered-down subjective version of the individual guarantees of the Bill of Rights."

Justices John Harlan and Tom Clark dissented, stating that they would follow *Twining* and *Adamson*, so that there would be a consistent line of case authority. Justice Harlan was concerned that the Court was now using the Fourteenth Amendment as shorthand to pick and choose among the provisions of the first eight amendments to the Constitution and apply the chosen ones with their entire body of federal doctrine to the law enforcement procedures of the states. Justice Harlan found that the Court's "undiscriminating approach to the due process clause carries serious implications for the sound working of our federal system in the field of criminal law." He found that the Court ignored Connecticut's traditional approach to fundamental fairness and mechanically implied a federal standard.

Justices Byron White and Potter Stewart wrote that the Fifth Amendment safeguards were "an important complex of values," but they did not find that the privilege was properly invoked in Mr. Malloy's case. White and Stewart would at least require the defendant's lawyer to state the grounds for his asserting the privilege to questions that were seemingly irrelevant to any incriminating matters. As Malloy was immune from any prosecution for his activities, the justices categorized his refusal to

answer as something relating more to answering "distasteful questions" rather than placing him in any potentially incriminating situation.

AFTERMATH

With Justices Brennan, Black, Douglas, Goldberg, and Warren finding that the Fourteenth Amendment makes the Fifth Amendment applicable to the states, *Malloy* suddenly reversed the tide of older cases. Further, with the addition of Justices White and Stewart's dissent, which held that only the standards for judging Malloy's claim of privilege were in question, not the basic issue of the application of the privilege against self-incrimination, the Court had now incorporated the self-incrimination clause of the Fifth Amendment into all state criminal trials.

SIGNIFICANCE

With the Court's decision in *Malloy* and in GRIFFIN V. CALIFORNIA (1965), in the following year, the Supreme Court set a consistent standard of incorporating the protections of the first eight amendments of the Bill of Rights into state criminal trials.

RELATED CASES

Griffin v. California, 380 U.S. 609 (1965)
Palko v. Connecticut, 302 U.S. 319 (1937)
Twining v. New Jersey, 211 U.S. 78 (1908)

RECOMMENDED READING

Berger, Raoul. *Government by Judiciary: The Transformation of the Fourteenth Amendment.* Cambridge, Mass.: Harvard University Press, 1977.

Cortner, Richard C. *The Supreme Court and the Second Bill of Rights: The Fourteenth Amendment and the Nationalization of Civil Liberties.* Madison: University of Wisconsin Press, 1981.

Mykkeltvedt, Roald Y. *The Nationalization of the Bill of Rights: Fourteenth Amendment Due Process and Procedural Rights.* Port Washington, N.Y.: Associated Faculty Press, 1983.

Case Title: *Ex Parte McCardle*

Alternate Case Title: Habeas Corpus Case

Legal Citation: 74 U.S. 506

Year of Decision: 1868

KEY ISSUES

Is it unlawful for the Supreme Court to continue hearings in a case for writ of habeas corpus, an order commanding release of a person from unlawful imprisonment, when an act of Congress has taken away the Supreme Court's power to grant such writ?

HISTORY OF THE CASE

McCardle, a Mississippi newspaper editor, was charged by the military with disturbing the peace and other charges based on articles he wrote and published denouncing Reconstruction. Between the hearing and decision, Congress passed an act taking away the Supreme Court's power to hear habeas corpus cases. Congress was fearful that the Court would use this to strike down Reconstruction acts, post–Civil War legislation that placed the South under military rule and conditioned readmittance to the Union on the states' adoption of the Fourteenth Amendment and extension of the right to vote to blacks.

SUMMARY OF ARGUMENTS

McCardle argued that the Constitution vested judicial power in the Supreme Court and Congress could not take it away. McCardle also argued that the Supreme Court must be able to exercise its whole judicial power whether or not Congress passes legislation regarding such power and, therefore, the Court could render judgment on the merits of the case despite the congressional repeal.

The military commander holding McCardle argued that the Court had no jurisdiction to render judgment on the merits of the case because the congressional act conferring jurisdiction on the Court had been repealed.

Justice Chase wrote the opinion that the Court had no jurisdiction, as Congress had taken away the Supreme Court's power to hear habeas corpus cases. Without this power, the Supreme Court could not proceed; it could only announce the fact and dismiss the case.

DECISION

The case was dismissed for lack of jurisdiction when Congress repealed the Supreme Court's power in habeas corpus cases.

AFTERMATH

This was an attempt to limit the Court's power and certainly not the last as shown by Franklin Roosevelt's attempt to influence the power of the Supreme Court and gain support for his post-depression economic recovery legislation through judicial reforms aimed at adding justices to the bench.

SIGNIFICANCE

This is the only time in U.S. history that Congress prevented the Court from deciding a pending case by removing its jurisdiction over the subject matter of the case. Congress used Constitution Article III, section 2, clause 2, which allowed regulation of the Supreme Court's appellate jurisdiction, as a political weapon by granting and repealing the appellate jurisdiction over certain types of cases to ensure the Court's ability or inability to rule on the merits whichever would produce the outcome desired by Congress.

RELATED CASES

Coleman v. Thompson, 501 U.S. 722 (1991)

Fay v. Noia, 372 U.S. 391 (1963)

Watkins v. United States, 354 U.S. 178 (1957)

RECOMMENDED READING

Keyes, Edward and Randall K. Miller. *The Court v. Congress.* Durham, N.C.: Duke University Press, 1989.

Case Title: *Ex Parte Milligan*

Legal Citation: 71 U.S. 2

Year of Decision: 1866

KEY ISSUES

Does the Constitution give the president the power to have civilians tried in military courts when regular courts continue to function?

HISTORY OF THE CASE

This case came to the U.S. Supreme Court from the circuit court in Indiana for discharge from imprisonment. The Judiciary Act of 1789 gives courts the right to issue writs of habeas corpus, orders directing the release of a person from unlawful detention or imprisonment. In 1863, another statute gave the president the right to suspend the writ during the rebellion. The president did so in cases where by his authority, "aiders and abettors of the enemy" were active and so fell under military jurisdiction. However, President Lincoln attempted to suspend the writ of habeas corpus after the Civil War had ended and continue governing under martial law.

After the Civil War Milligan, a civilian, was arrested for disloyalty and conspiracy, and confined to military prison, then tried by a military court and found guilty and sentenced to death. He filed a petition in the circuit court stating that when he was tried civilian courts were open and available; therefore, he should have been tried in a civilian, not military, court. The case was certified to the Supreme Court for direction to the circuit court judges, who could not reach a decision.

SUMMARY OF ARGUMENTS

Lambdim P. Milligan, petitioner, argued that he was not tried by a constitutionally authorized tribunal, nor was he properly charged; therefore, the judgment and sentence of the Military Commission was void.

The United States argued the martial law granted the Military Commission its authority. Martial law is the will of the commanding officer or an armed force, and the president, as commander in chief, had full power to effectively use his armed forces in this manner.

Justice Davis wrote for the Court that it appeared that Milligan was to be hanged by presidential order. This is beyond presidential powers, which stipulate one can only be tried by law and there was no law to justify the military trial. The Constitution provides for trials of crimes to be by jury; Chief Justice Chase wrote for the dissent finding that the military tribunal was valid under the Constitution's grant of war powers. The war power is derived from congressional power to make necessary laws. Additionally, during wartime when the threat of danger is imminent, Congress can authorize the use of military tribunals for the purpose of promoting public safety.

DECISION

Military commissioners in a state not engaged in open rebellion and in which federal courts are open have no jurisdiction to try, convict, or sentence a civilian for a criminal offense.

AFTERMATH

After the Court's decision, legislation was introduced seeking to limit the appellate jurisdiction of the Court.

Years later, when President Roosevelt exercised his presidential power by issuing an executive order to exclude and relocate Japanese Americans, the Court upheld the president's use of power. However, the congressional attempt to suspend the writ of habeas corpus after World War II failed because such action was not required for public safety.

SIGNIFICANCE

Ex Parte Milligan defined the basic principles that were to govern the relationship between the civilian and military worlds in wartime and in peacetime.

Outside wartime, the president had no power to suspend the use of the writ of habeas corpus.

RELATED CASES

Hirabayashi v. United States, 320 U.S. 81 (1943)

Prize Cases, 67 U.S. 635 (1862)

Yakus v. United States, 321 U.S. 414 (1944)

RECOMMENDED READING

McCloskey, Robert G. *The American Supreme Court.* Chicago: University of Chicago Press, 1960.

tenBroek, Jacobus et al. *Prejudice, War and the Constitution.* Berkeley: University of California Press, 1968.

Lewis J. Wertheim, *The Indianapolis Treason Trials: The Election of 1864 and the Power of the Partisan Press,* 65 Indiana Magazine of History 236 (1989).

Case Title: *Miranda v. Arizona*

Legal Citations: 384 U.S. 436; 86 S.Ct. 1602

Year of Decision: 1966

KEY ISSUES

Are statements obtained from a defendant while in police custody, or otherwise deprived of his freedom of action in any significant way, admissible in court? What procedures are required to assure that the individual is accorded his privilege under the Fifth Amendment not to be compelled to incriminate himself?

HISTORY OF THE CASE

Part of the Bill of Rights added to the original Constitution to ensure its ratification by the states, the Fifth Amendment states that "[n]o person . . . shall be compelled in any criminal case to be a witness against himself" and that "the accused shall . . . have the Assistance of Counsel." Two years prior to *Miranda,* the Supreme Court held in *Escobedo v. Illinois* (1964), that the Fifth Amendment prohibits the admission at trial of a confession obtained during police interrogation of a suspect denied his request to speak to his attorney. Thus, the Court extended the reach of the Fifth Amendment beyond the courtroom to the police station.

Because admissions or confessions of the prisoner have always ranked high in the scale of incriminating evidence, the police are tempted to overbearing interrogation techniques, including browbeating, intimidation, psychological ploys, and entrapment. At its worst, police behavior toward the prisoner could include physical brutality and "third degree" interrogation techniques. In fact, the *Miranda* decision cites a 1965 New York case in which the police beat, kicked, and placed lighted cigarette butts on the back of a potential witness under interrogation for the purpose of securing a statement incriminating a third party. The Warren Court, in the midst of implementing its "criminal procedure revolution," which significantly expanded criminal defendants' procedural safeguards, saw in *Miranda* the opportunity to eradicate practices of this nature. In so doing, the Court would make clear that the Fifth Amendment privilege against self-incrimination would apply not only in the courtroom but also in police custody.

The opinion known as *Miranda* is actually the result of four separate cases combined for purposes of consideration by the Supreme Court. Each case concerned the custodial interrogation and the evils it can bring. In *Miranda v. Arizona,* the police arrested Miranda and took him to a special interrogation room, where they obtained a confession. In *Vinera v. New York,* the defendant made oral admissions to the police after interrogation in the afternoon and then signed an incriminating statement upon being questioned by an assistant district attorney later the same evening. In *Westover v. United States,* the defendant was handed over to the FBI by local authorities after they had detained and interrogated him for a lengthy period, both at night and the following morning. After some two additional hours of questioning, the federal officers obtained signed statements of guilt from Westover. Finally, in *California v. Stewart,* the local police held the defendant for five days in the station and interrogated him on nine separate occasions before they secured his incriminating statement. Demonstrating the potential for compulsion, the Court points out that Miranda was an indigent Mexican American with pronounced sexual fantasies and that Stewart was an indigent African American who had dropped out of school in the sixth grade. In none of the cases did officers undertake to afford appropriate safeguards at the outset of the interrogation to guarantee that the incriminating statements were truly the product of free choice.

SUMMARY OF ARGUMENTS

With variations depending on the specific facts of the four different cases, prosecutors argued that the confessions were voluntary, in that the circumstances of the interrogations did not amount to compulsion, and therefore that the confessions were properly admitted as evidence at trial. The defendants argued that, because they were afforded no procedural safeguards such as warnings of the right to remain silent and the right to have a lawyer present, their confessions were unconstitutionally obtained and should have been excluded from the evidence presented at trial.

DECISION

Writing for the majority, Chief Justice Earl Warren held that the prosecution may not use statements stemming from custodial interrogation of the defendant unless it demonstrates the use of procedural safeguards to secure the privilege against self-incrimination. To provide clear guidelines to police and prosecutors, Warren's opinion spells out the procedural safeguards to be employed, in language that would become known as the "Miranda warning": Prior to any questioning initiated by law enforcement officers after a person has been taken into custody, the person must be warned that (1) he has a right to remain silent, (2) anything he does say may be used as evidence against him, (3) he has a right to the presence of an attorney during the questioning, and (4) if indigent he has a right to a lawyer without charge. Unless the defendant received this fourfold warning, the court would assume any statement he made was coerced and therefore inadmissible as evidence: "The Fifth Amendment privilege is so fundamental to our system of constitutional rule and the expedient of giving an adequate warning as to the availability of the privilege so simple, we will not pause to inquire in individual cases whether the defendant was aware of his rights without a warning being given."

In three separate dissenting opinions, Justices Clark, Harlan, Stewart, and White disagreed with the majority on various constitutional and public policy grounds. In Justice Clark's words, the majority erred "in one full sweep changing the traditional rules of custodial interrogation which this Court has for so long recognized as a justifiable and proper tool in balancing individual rights against the rights of society."

AFTERMATH

The speed and ease with which the term "Miranda warning" entered everyday speech demonstrate the effect of the decision. As any viewer of American television or films knows, police nationwide adopted the warning nearly verbatim from Chief Justice Warren's opinion. Contrary to the fears of the dissenters, the procedural safeguards introduced by *Miranda* did not have a negative impact on the process of obtaining confessions, according to subsequent studies. Miranda was prosecuted and convicted again on the original charges without the use of the confession as evidence.

SIGNIFICANCE

Probably the best-known decision of the Warren Court's "criminal procedure revolution," *Miranda* also became the touchstone for public criticism of that revolution. To advocates of law enforcement and the rights of crime victims, *Miranda* seemed perversely to value the rights of suspects and, worse, to allow convicted criminals to escape punishment through "technicalities." To civil libertarians, *Miranda* wisely recognized the restraints society must observe consistent with the Constitution in prosecuting individuals for crimes. Given the political backlash—which included attempts by Congress to pass legislation overturning *Miranda* in the federal courts and which arguably led to the election of Richard Nixon as president and his appointment of more conservative justices to the Court—*Miranda* may be regarded as the zenith of the criminal procedure revolution.

RELATED CASES

Beckwith v. United States, 425 U.S. 341, 96 S.Ct. 1612 (1976)

Duckworth v. Eagan, 492 U.S. 195, 109 S.Ct. 2875 (1989)

Edwards v. Arizona, 451 U.S. 477, 101 S.Ct. 1880 (1981)

Escobedo v. Illinois, 378 U.S. 478, 84 S.Ct. 1758 (1964)

Gideon v. Wainwright, 372 U.S. 335, 83 S.Ct. 792 (1963)

Malloy v. Hogan, 378 U.S. 1, 84 S.Ct. 1489 (1964)

North Carolina v. Butler, 441 U.S. 369, 99 S.Ct. 1755 (1979)

Oregon v. Mathiason, 429 U.S. 492, 97 S.Ct. 711 (1977)

Rhode Island v. Innis, 446 U.S. 291, 100 S.Ct. 1682 (1980)

RECOMMENDED READING

Gerald Caplan, *Questioning Miranda,* 38 Vanderbilt Law Review 1417 (1985).

Fred E. Inbau, *Over-Reaction: The Mischief of* Miranda v. Arizona, 73 Journal of Criminal Law & Criminology 797 (1982).

Stephen J. Schulhofer, *Reconsidering Miranda,* 54 University of Chicago Law Review 435 (1987).

Welsh S. White, *Defending Miranda,* 39 Vanderbilt Law Review 1 (1986).

Case Title: *Moore v. Dempsey*

Legal Citations: 261 U.S. 86; 43 S.Ct. 265; 67 L.Ed. 543

Year of Decision: 1923

KEY ISSUES

Does a murder trial in state court in which the accused are rushed to conviction without regard to their rights and under mob threat violate the due process clause of the Fourteenth Amendment to the U.S. Constitution?

HISTORY OF THE CASE

This is an appeal from an order of the District Court for the Eastern District of Arkansas dismissing a writ of habeas corpus, an action seeking release from unconstitutional imprisonment. Five black men, including Frank Moore, were convicted of murder and sentenced to death by the Court of the State of Arkansas. The writ is based on grounds that the state court proceedings were not performed correctly but done only to get a conviction and execution, that they were hurried to conviction under mob dominance without regard to their rights and without due process.

The case began when a number of black people gathered at their church and were attacked by white men. In the mayhem a white man was killed. After the blacks were arrested, a mob came to lynch them. A court-appointed lawyer attempted to represent the accused, but because of fear of mob violence he could not demand a delay or call witnesses. The all-white jury brought back a verdict in five minutes.

SUMMARY OF ARGUMENTS

Appellants, including Frank Moore, argued that habeas corpus should be granted because the appellants were convicted without due process of law. In support of their argument, appellants stated that the trial was unfair, with little effort made to determine the merits of the case.

E. H. Dempsey, the keeper of the Arkansas State penitentiary and appellee in this case, argued that the appellants had been provided due process of law. In support of this argument, he stated that the prosecution was conducted according to the regular course of judicial proceedings and the jury was correctly given the law of the case.

DECISION

The petition for habeas corpus was granted and the case sent back to district court to decide the due process allegations as the state court's "corrective process" was not good enough to provide a fair trial. The federal district court would review the case to ensure that constitutional rights were protected.

Justice Holmes wrote the opinion of the Court. The requirement for a fair trial is that the state must provide an adequate corrective process and watch for an unfair trial: "But if the case is that the whole proceeding is a mask, that counsel, jury and judge were swept away to the fatal end by an irresistible wave of public passion, and that the State Courts failed to correct the wrong, neither perfection in the machinery for correction nor the possibility that the trial court and counsel saw no other way of avoiding an immediate outbreak of the mob can prevent this court from securing to the petitioners their constitutional rights."

Justice McReynolds wrote a dissent stating that if every person thought he or she could get federal review to impeach his or her trial, the courts, which are already overloaded, would react with long delays. He also saw the state courts as the best judges because they were at the scene.

AFTERMATH

The writ of habeas corpus began to be interpreted in light of constitutional due process rights and its focus was enlarged so that all federal constitutional claims could be heard, even if the state courts provided an adequate forum, on the theory that federal review was required to determine whether personal liberties had been denied.

SIGNIFICANCE

Brown v. Allen (1953), which held that habeas corpus could be used for claims of constitutional error, pointed toward the significance of *Moore* by going beyond jurisdiction and beginning to interpret the writ in light of constitutional due process claims. This marked a broad expansive role for habeas corpus.

RELATED CASES

Brown v. Allen, 344 U.S. 443 (1953)

Fay v. Noia, 372 U.S. 391 (1963)

Frank v. Magnum, 237 U.S. 309 (1915)

RECOMMENDED READING

Developments in the Law-Federal Habeas Corpus, 83 Harvard Law Review 1050 (1970).

Greenberg, Jack. *Race Relations and American Law.* New York: Columbia University Press, 1959.

Curtis R. Reitz, *Federal Habeas Corpus: Impact of an Abortive State Proceeding,* 74 Harvard Law Review 1315 (1961).

Case Title: *Munn v. Illinois*

Alternate Case Title: The Grain Elevator Case

Legal Citation: 94 U.S. 113

Year of Decision: 1876

KEY ISSUES

May the government regulate the economic use of private property?

HISTORY OF THE CASE

In 1870 the state of Illinois revised its constitution, adding requirements for the operation of public warehouses and grain elevators. At the time the new constitution was enacted, the business of grain storage was relatively new. The constitutional changes addressed the fact that the private owners of those facilities greatly affected grain distribution to a large part of the country and yet were not regulated in any way. Munn and another defendant were charged with violating the new provisions for warehousemen that required them to obtain licenses and to post bonds. They also were charged with setting storage fee rates higher than the constitutionally set limit. Munn and the other defendant were found guilty and fined $100.00. The Illinois Supreme Court affirmed the judgment. It is from the judg-

ment of the state supreme court that the U.S. Supreme Court agreed to hear the case.

SUMMARY OF ARGUMENTS

Munn argued that the new state constitutional provisions violated the third clause of Article 1, section 8 of the U.S. Constitution, which confers upon Congress the power to regulate commerce between the states. Munn believed that the federal government, and not the state, was the only appropriate party to regulate his warehouse business.

Munn also argued that the Illinois constitution's sections violated the sixth clause of Article 1, section 9, which requires that no preference shall be given by any regulation of commerce or revenue to the ports of one state over those of another. Munn felt that other cities in other states without regulation had preferential treatment.

Munn's final argument was that the new state constitutional provisions violated his right to due process and equal protection as guaranteed by the Fifth and Fourteenth Amendments to the U.S. Constitution. In Munn's opinion, the new regulations effectively deprived him of his interest in property and prevented him from capturing the full value of his private investment.

The state of Illinois argued that the new provisions were not regulations of commerce in the sense conveyed by the U.S. Constitution. The state was merely regulating internal affairs that may or may not have affected interstate commerce. The state relied on the argument that if the regulation was one of interstate commerce then it belonged within the class of powers that may be exercised by the state in the absence of any conflicting congressional legislation.

Illinois responded to Munn's Fifth and Fourteenth Amendment challenge by arguing that the warehousemen engaged in a sort of "public employment." The state argued that warehousemen operated in a position similar to common carriers, those engaged in the transportation of persons and property for money, who were themselves required to follow certain regulations in the interest of the public. The Illinois public needed some sort of certainty in the business of warehouses and grain elevators as well. The new state constitutional provisions provided the certainty and protection that was needed.

The state countered Munn's argument concerning preferential treatment of other ports with the conclusion that the constitutional provision related only to congressional action and not action of the states.

DECISION

Chief Justice Waite delivered the majority opinion of the Court, which included a lengthy historical discussion of private and public property rights in English legal history. Justice Waite found that when one devoted his property "to a use in which the public has an interest, he, in effect, grants to the public an interest in that use, and must submit to be controlled by the public for the common good, to the extent of the interest he has thus created. He may withdraw his grant by discontinuing the use; but, so long as he maintains the use, he must submit to the control." He concluded that "rights of property which have been created by the common law cannot be taken away without due process; but the law itself, as a rule of conduct, may be changed at the will, or even at the whim, of the legislature, unless prevented by constitutional limitations." In the majority's opinion, there was no limitation in the U.S. Constitution that would prevent the operation of the revised Illinois Constitution's provisions. Justice Waite did not believe that the regulation deprived Munn of property without due process or equal protection.

The Court dealt with the issue of the "commerce clause" by concluding that "it is not every thing that affects commerce that amounts to a regulation of it, within the meaning of the Constitution." As a result, the state of Illinois was well within its rights to regulate the grain industry. Congress had not acted on the issue and until such action occurred, the Court found that the state could exercise all powers of the government over the grain warehouse industry.

The Court quickly dismissed the argument proposed by Munn that the regulation gave preference to other ports. The provision of the Constitution operates only as a limitation on the powers of Congress and in no respect affects the states in the regulation of their domestic affairs.

Two dissenting justices, Field and Strong, both felt that the decision greatly hampered private property rights and opened the doors to legislative interference. In their view, the defendants "were no more public warehousemen than the merchant who sells his merchandise to the public is a public merchant . . . and it was a strange notion that by calling them so they would be brought under legislative control." The dissenters felt that if the government was given an inch it would take a mile. As a result, no individual would be safe in his private economic conduct if it so much as touched the public realm.

AFTERMATH

In the 30 years following this decision, the Court grappled with the concept of economic liberty and economic due process. In 1905, the concept of legislative regulation of private economic activity narrowed considerably. The Court entered what come to be known as the "Lochner Era, an era named after the decision in LOCHNER V. NEW YORK (1905)": From 1905 until the mid-1940s, the Court gave great leeway in the interests of individual economic pursuits striking down many government regulations regarding employment. The Court has since switched its position and resorted to different power bases to determine the validity of governmental regulation of private economic conduct: among them, the "commerce clause" in Article 1, section 8 and the due process clauses of the Fifth and Fourteenth Amendments.

SIGNIFICANCE

This case did exactly what the dissenters feared it would do: It opened the doors for the government to interfere in private economic concerns. Although it has been overshadowed by later decisions, it is the first link in a very important chain of cases affecting the economic rights of American citizens.

RELATED CASES

Lochner v. New York, 198 U.S. 45 (1905)

Shafer v. Farmers' Grain Company of Embden, 268 U.S. 189 (1925)

Swift & Company v. U.S., 196 U.S. 375 (1905)

RECOMMENDED READING

Barry Cushman, *A Stream of Legal Consciousness: The Current of Commerce Doctrine from Swift to Jones & Laughlin,* 61 Fordham Law Review 105 (1992).

Edmund W. Kitch and Clara Ann Bowler, *The Facts of Munn v. Illinois,* 1978 Supreme Court Review 313 (1978).

Case Title: *Near v. Minnesota ex rel. Olson, County Attorney*

Legal Citations: 283 U.S. 697; 51 S.Ct. 625; 75 L.Ed. 2d 1357

Year of Decision: 1931

KEY ISSUES

Does a state statute, under which the publication of printed matter could be enjoined permanently if after trial it was found to be a public nuisance, violate the First Amendment freedom of speech and the due process clause of the Fourteenth Amendment?

HISTORY OF THE CASE

Chapter 285 of the Sessions Laws of Minnesota provides for the abatement, as a public nuisance, of a "malicious, scandalous and defamatory newspaper, magazine or other periodical." Under clause "b" of this statute, the county attorney brought this action to enjoin the publication of such printed matter in the *Saturday Press,* published by the defendants. Articles in the newspaper pointed out the deficiencies of the police and public figures. One article stated that the city was run by a Jewish gangster and no one did anything about it.

Action was brought by a city official against Jay Near, the owner of the paper. The district court did not decide the whole case and instead sent it to the state supreme court. The court found that the Minnesota statute violated both the state constitution and the Fourteenth Amendment of the U.S. Constitution.

SUMMARY OF ARGUMENTS

Jay Near, the publisher of the *Saturday Press,* argued that the Minnesota law violated the due process clause of the Fourteenth Amendment.

The state argued that the law dealt with the "business of publishing defamation," not publication per se. The state also argued that the law was enacted to prevent the spread of scandal, which might lead to crime.

DECISION

The Court held that the statute was an infringement of the liberty of the press guaranteed by the Fourteenth Amendment.

Chief Justice Hughes delivered the opinion for the Court, saying that liberty of the press and of speech is guarded by the due process clause of the Fourteenth Amendment from state invasion. The effect of the statute in question is that public authorities may bring the owner before a judge on the charge of publishing scandalous and defamatory matter. This kind of censorship is not consistent with the concept of ordered liberty.

For almost 150 years before this case no one had challenged the imposition of previous restraints' prohibiting the publication of an expression before its release to the public, on publications relating to the unsatisfactory nature in which public officials carry out their jobs. Such restraints would clearly violate the Constitution.

Justice Butler wrote in his dissent that the Court's decision takes from the states the power to issue injunctions on periodicals that are malicious and defamatory and amount to a public nuisance. He said the decision gives freedom of the press a meaning "and scope not heretofore recognized and construes liberty in the Due Process Clause of the Fourteenth Amendment to put upon the states a federal restriction that is without precedent."

AFTERMATH

Prior restraint becomes the method in dealing with freedom of expression cases. An injunction postpones the publication of the protected material until after a final determination of its acceptability. *Near* incorporated the freedom of the press in the Fourteenth Amendment, making it applicable to state action.

SIGNIFICANCE

This was the first decision of the Court finding state legislation to be in violation of the First Amendment as incorporated by the Fourteenth Amendment. The decision also indicated prior restraint may be acceptable in times of war. Because of the expansion of nonprint media, actions seeking freedom of the press protection for print media have decreased.

RELATED CASES

De Jonge v. Oregon, 299 U.S. 353 (1937)

Herndon v. Lowry, 301 U.S. 242 (1937)

Stromberg v. California, 283 U.S. 359 (1931)

RECOMMENDED READING

Margaret A. Blanchard, *The Institutional Press and Its First Amendment Privileges*, 1978 Supreme Court Review 225.

Thomas I. Emerson, *The Doctrine of Prior Restraint*, 20 Law and Contemporary Problems 648 (1955).

Lofton, John. *Justice and the Press.* Boston: Beacon Press, 1966.

Note: *Previous Restraints upon Freedom of Speech*, 31 Columbia Law Review 1148 (1931).

Case Title: *O'Connor v. Donaldson*

Legal Citations: 422 U.S. 563; 95 S.Ct. 2486; 45 L.Ed. 2d 396

Year of Decision: 1975

KEY ISSUES

Does the state's confinement of a nondangerous individual who is capable of caring for himself and who has roots in the community violate such individual's due process rights to liberty?

HISTORY OF THE CASE

Kenneth Donaldson was civilly committed to a mental institution and kept there for 15 years against his will. He petitioned for release several times, claiming that he was of danger to no one, that he was not mentally ill, and in any case the hospital provided him with no treatment. Donaldson brought suit in the U.S. District Court for the Northern District of Florida, claiming the intentional denial of his liberty. The court of appeals affirmed the grant of compensatory and punitive damages. The Supreme Court agreed to review the case.

SUMMARY OF ARGUMENTS

Petitioner, Dr. J. B. O'Connor, argued that he had acted in good faith and that state law authorized Donaldson's custodial confinement even if his release would not be harmful. Therefore, O'Connor contended he was immune from liability. Respondent, Donaldson, argued that O'Connor intentionally deprived him of his constitutional right to liberty.

Justice Stewart delivered the opinion of the Court that a state cannot deny an individual's right to liberty through confinement when that person poses no danger and does not receive treatment. The court limited its holding to the particular facts of the case. The holding does not apply to involuntary treatment but only involuntary custodial confinement. Also, it does not apply to confinement of mentally ill persons who are dangerous to themselves and others, or to whether they have a right to treatment.

DECISION

A state cannot constitutionally confine a nondangerous individual who is capable of caring for himself. This is a violation of due process right to liberty.

AFTERMATH

This case has a very narrow application to involuntary custodial confinement.

SIGNIFICANCE

In its narrow application, the case does not concern itself with what facts a state must prove for commitment. It does not deal with what factors are required before a state can commit a mentally ill person. It does not deal with requirements for treatment. Its importance lies mainly in the fact that a sane person cannot be denied liberty. Moreover, a finding of mental illness, by itself, cannot justify confining a person against his or her will.

RELATED CASES

Addington v. Texas, 441 U.S. 418 (1979)

Jackson v. Indiana, 406 U.S. 715 (1972)

RECOMMENDED READING

William J. Fremouw, *A New Right to Treatment*, 2 Journal of Psychiatry and Law 7 (1974).

Louis E. Kopolow, *A Review of Major Implications of the O'Connor v. Donaldson Decision,* 133 American Journal of Psychiatry 379 (1976).

Kirsten E. Lundergan, *The Right to Be Present: Should It Apply to the Involuntary Civil Commitment Hearing,* 17 New Mexico Law Review 165 (1987).

Case Title: *Palko v. Connecticut*

Legal Citations: 302 U.S. 319; 58 S.Ct. 149; 82 L.Ed. 288

Year of Decision: 1937

KEY ISSUES

Does the Fifth Amendment's ban on double jeopardy, prosecution for an offense a defendant has already been tried on, apply to the states?

HISTORY OF THE CASE

Frank Palka, who had just been paroled on a rape conviction in New York, was convicted of breaking into a music store, stealing a radio, and shooting and killing two police officers. Palka was intoxicated at the time, and there was a question of his intent to murder the police officers. Palka escaped to Buffalo, New York. Police caught him there and he confessed to the murders. At his first trial, he was convicted of murder in the second degree. The state of Connecticut appealed and a new trial was ordered. The appeals court ordered the new trial because Palka's confession was not used in evidence. In the confession, Palka said he shot the policemen because he knew an arrest while on parole would send him back to jail. At his second trial, he was convicted of first degree murder and sentenced to death.

In an appeal to the Supreme Court of Errors of Connecticut, Palka's attorney addressed the issue of double jeopardy. Although the Fifth Amendment to the U.S. Constitution prohibits being tried twice for the same crime, they found that no such protection existed under Connecticut law. At some point in the appeal, Palka's name was misspelled as "Palko."

SUMMARY OF ARGUMENTS

Palka's attorney argued that the second conviction placed him on trial twice for the same offense. His attorney further argued that in addition to the Fifth Amendment, which provided protection from double jeopardy, the Fourteenth Amendment guaranteed Palka due process of law. Whatever would be a violation of the federal Bill of Rights and is unlawful if done by the federal government under the Fourteenth Amendment should be equally unlawful if done by the states.

The state of Connecticut argued that the Supreme Court had consistently rejected this theory, and as long as the state met its own due process standards, there was no violation of a criminal defendant's rights. The state further argued that the retrial ordered by the appeal did not interfere with any of Palka's rights as a citizen of the United States—it merely served to assure that a fair trial was held.

DECISION

Justice Benjamin Cardozo traced the history of those rights guaranteed under the federal Bill of Rights that had been required of the states. Cardozo was careful to prevent any breaking of this orderly process. Some rights are so fundamental that they must be protected against any interference, whether by the state or federal governments. These include freedom of speech, freedom of the press, free exercise of religion, right of peaceable assembly, and right of an accused to have counsel. But Cardozo found that there are other rights that can be handled in different ways and can still result in justice and fair trials, without being uniform between the states and the federal government. He found that the Connecticut system was fundamentally fair, and that Palka's basic liberty and justice had not been violated. He thus refused to totally apply the Bill of Rights to the states.

Only Justice Pierce Butler dissented, and he did write a dissenting opinion.

AFTERMATH

Not until *Benton v. Maryland* (1969) was the precise issue of double jeopardy reexamined by the Court. In *Benton,* the Court overruled *Palko* in part and applied the prohibition against double jeopardy through the Fourteenth Amendment onto the states. Palka was executed April 12, 1938, in Connecticut's electric chair.

SIGNIFICANCE

In *Palko,* the Court adopted the "selective incorporation theory," in favor of the fundamental rights test. The finding in TWINING V. NEW JERSEY (1908) that the Fourteenth Amendment did not automatically extend all of the first eight Amendments to the states was reaffirmed, and freedom from double jeopardy was not found to be a fundamental liberty.

RELATED CASES

Adamson v. California, 322 U.S. 46 (1947)

Benton v. Maryland, 395 U.S. 784 (1969)

Twining v. New Jersey, 211 U.S. 78 (1908)

RECOMMENDED READING

Berger, Raoul. *Government by Judiciary: The Transformation of the Fourteenth Amendment.* Cambridge, Mass.: Harvard University Press, 1977.

Cortner, Richard C. *The Supreme Court and the Second Bill of Rights: The Fourteenth Amendment and the Nationalization of Civil Liberties.* Madison: University of Wisconsin Press, 1981.

Levy, Leonard, Charles Forrman, and Stanley Morrison. *The Fourteenth Amendment and the Bill of Rights: The Incorporation Theory.* New York: Da Capo Press, 1970.

Case Title: *Poe v. Ullman*

Alternate Case Title: Birth Control Case

Legal Citations: 367 U.S. 497; 81 S.Ct. 1752; 6 L.Ed. 2d 989

Year of Decision: 1961

KEY ISSUES

The two issues addressed in this case are (1) whether a state can prohibit the use of contraceptives, and (2) whether a party's failure to suffer arrest under the prohibition is sufficient to provide a justiciable constitutional question.

HISTORY OF THE CASE

The case represented a consolidation of three actions brought in Connecticut state court for declaratory relief from enforcement of a state statute that prohibited the use of contraceptives. The plaintiffs in one of the actions were a married couple who had already suffered three consecutive pregnancies that resulted in infants with multiple congenital abnormalities causing death shortly after birth. The couple had consulted an obstetrician/gynecologist as a means of preventing the probable consequence of severe psychological strain that would result from another such pregnancy. The doctor was prevented from giving advice about contraceptives, the method he deemed best to prevent such occurrence, due to the Connecticut law.

The plaintiff in the second action was a 25-year-old housewife who had recently suffered a disastrous pregnancy causing a critical physical illness that left her with partial paralysis, marked impairment of speech, and emotional instability. She and her doctor, the same obstetrician/gynecologist in the first action, felt that another pregnancy would be exceedingly perilous to her life.

The third action was one by Dr. Buxton, the aforementioned obstetrician/gynecologist. He brought action for declaratory judgment so that he could counsel the other plaintiffs about their available contraceptive options. He claimed that failure to allow him this course of action constituted a deprivation of his liberty and property without due process.

The Connecticut state courts sustained summary judgments in favor of the state on the grounds that the interpretation of the statute had been before the courts before, the courts had upheld the statute and therefore, an action for declaratory judgment could not be maintained.

SUMMARY OF ARGUMENTS

The plaintiffs all claimed that the statute deprived them of due process rights. They noted the ban against contraceptives was so pervasive as to affect their marital relations—a sphere that was argued to be beyond the regulation of the state.

Connecticut argued that the statute was a permissible exercise of its police power in relationship to the morals of its citizens.

DECISION

The Court ruled 5-4 that the case was nonjusticiable, a case that does not present a controversy appropriate for judicial determination, because the plaintiffs had not actually suffered criminal prosecution under the Connecticut statute. Notwithstanding the claim from the Connecticut Attorney General's Office that it was prepared to enforce the law, the historical lack of enforcement "deprive[d] these controversies of the immediacy which is an indispensable condition of constitutional adjudication."

The importance of *Poe v. Ullman*, however, is based more upon the statements in dissent than the actual decision in the case. In particular, the statements of Justices Douglas and Harlan provided furtive ground for the expansion of fundamental rights jurisprudence under the rubric of substantive due process. Both justices noted that they would have held the case justiciable, and then would have held the law unconstitutional for its invasion of the privacy of the marital relationship. These statements formed the basis for the Court's holding four years later, in GRISWOLD V. CONNECTICUT, that the same Connecticut criminal statute was unconstitutional.

AFTERMATH

Poe v. Ullman marked the beginning of a period in which the Supreme Court more readily adjudicated controversies that delineated the fundamental rights that emanated from the Constitution's restraint of the government's control over individual rights. Four years later, in *Griswold v. Connecticut,* the Court overturned the Connecticut statute. The Court explained that the fundamental right to the use of contraceptives emanated as a "penumbra" from those rights set out in the Bill of Rights. Over the next 20 years the Court extended such protections in holding that a woman has a right to an abortion within the term of pregnancy and that a person may not be restrained from marrying an individual of the opposite sex because the other individual is of another race. Moreover, the right to use contraceptives was extended a little over a decade later to unmarried individuals.

SIGNIFICANCE

Poe v. Ullman did not represent any new ground in constitutional jurisprudence as a matter of precedence, but the pronouncements of Justices Douglas and Harlan established the theoretical underpinnings for the subsequent recognition and establishment of the fundamental liberties that concerned marital and reproductive rights.

RELATED CASES

Eisenstadt v. Baird, 405 U.S. 438 (1972)

Griswold v. Connecticut, 381 U.S. 479 (1965)

Loving v. Virginia, 388 U.S. 1 (1967)

Roe v. Wade, 410 U.S. 113 (1973)

Tileston v. Ullman, 318 U.S. 44 (1943)

RECOMMENDED READING

Bobbitt, Philip. *Constitutional Fate: Theory of the Constitution.* New York: Oxford University Press, 1982.

Henry J. Bourguignon, *The Second Mr. Justice Harlan: His Principles of Judicial Decision Making,* Supreme Court Review 251–328 (1979).

Redlich, Norman. "Are There Certain Rights . . . Retained by the People." In *The Rights Retained by the People.* Edited by Randy E. Barnett. Fairfax, Va.: George Mason University Press, 1989.

Case Title: *Powell v. Alabama*

Alternate Case Title: Scottsboro Case

Legal Citations: 287 U.S. 45; 53 S.Ct. 55; 77 L.Ed. 158

Year of Decision: 1932

KEY ISSUES

Does the denial of counsel in a capital case where the defendant is illiterate or otherwise incapable of making his own case violate the due process clause of the Fourteenth Amendment to the U.S. Constitution?

HISTORY OF THE CASE

Eight black youths were involved in a fight with white youths on a moving train. The white young women claimed they were raped. Indicted and arraigned amid threat of mob violence, the defendants were unrepresented by counsel until the morning of their trial, at which time a local attorney reluctantly agreed to represent them. The defendants were convicted and the jury imposed the death sentence on all eight. The Alabama Supreme Court affirmed the convictions. The U.S. Supreme Court agreed to hear the case.

SUMMARY OF ARGUMENTS

Ozie Powell argued that petitioners were denied the right to counsel and, therefore, due process of law. Powell also argued that petitioners were denied equal protection because they were tried by juries from which qualified members of their race were systematically excluded.

The state of Alabama argued that petitioners had been given fair and impartial trials and, therefore, were not denied due process. The state also argued that the petitioners were not denied equal protection of the laws because there were no members of their race on the jury convicting them.

DECISION

In a capital case, where the defendant is unable to employ counsel and cannot make his own defense because of ignorance, mental disability, or illiteracy, the court must assign counsel to comply with due process.

Justice Sutherland delivered the opinion of the Court. He emphasized that effective assistance of counsel is crucial to a fair criminal trial. A court's duty to assign counsel for a defendant is not fulfilled by an assignment so late in the proceedings that it prevents the effective aid of counsel in trial preparation: "During perhaps the most critical period of the proceedings against these defendants, that is to say, from the time of their arraignment until the beginning of their trial, when consultation, thoroughgoing investigation are vitally important, the defendants did not have the aid of counsel in any real sense, although they were as much entitled to such aid during that period as at the trial itself."

Justice Sutherland went on to say that the right of the accused, at least in capital cases, to have the benefit of counsel with sufficient preparation time is essential. In this case from the time of their arraignment until the beginning of the trial, when consultation, investigation, and preparation are so important, the defendants did not have counsel in any real sense. The Sixth Amendment provides that in all criminal proceedings the accused shall enjoy the right "to have the assistance of counsel for his defense." This is a right of compelling interest and therefore is covered by the due process clause of the Fourteenth Amendment.

The right to counsel in this case does not require a determination of whether it is required in other circumstances. All that is decided is that in a capital case, where defendant is incapable of making his own defense, the court must appoint representation.

Justice Butler wrote the dissent, saying that the record did not show a denial of counsel. Trial counsel did not apply for a continuance and there was no suggestion that the representation afforded the defendants was inferior.

AFTERMATH

The holding in this case is narrow and limited to the facts, but the Court for the first time recognized the existence of a constitutional right to pretrial assistance of counsel, although not beyond the first right of appeal nor to noncapital cases. This right came 30 years later.

The defendants were convicted at a second trial, but that decision was subsequently overturned upon a finding of racial discrimination during the jury selection process. Ultimately, several of the defendants were convicted. The charges against others were dropped.

SIGNIFICANCE

Powell "initiated the end of the stone age of American criminal procedure" (Yale Kamisar, 73 *Michigan Law Review* 15, 16 [1974]). The court mandated, although on a limited basis, the appointment of counsel. The holding introduced the modern law of constitutional criminal procedure.

RELATED CASES

Argersinger v. Hamlin, 407 U.S. 25 (1972)

Gideon v. Wainwright, 372 U.S. 335 (1963)

Ross v. Moffitt, 417 U.S. 600 (1974)

Recommended Reading

Yale Kamisar, *Kauper's "Judicial Examination of the Accused" Forty Years Later: Some Comments on a Remarkable Article*, 73 Michigan Law Review 15 (1974).

Mykkeltvedt, Roald Y. *The Naturalization of the Bill of Rights.* New York: Associated Faculty Press, 1983.

Case Title: *Rhode Island v. Innis*

Legal Citations: 446 U.S. 291; 64 L.Ed. 2d 297; 100 S.Ct. 1682

Year of Decision: 1980

Key Issues

Did the remarks of officers, to which suspect in custody responded with self-incriminating testimony, constitute interrogation in violation of the suspect's *Miranda* rights?

History of the Case

After the discovery of the body of a taxicab driver who had died from a shotgun blast, and after another taxicab driver who had been robbed by a man wielding a sawed-off shotgun identified his assailant on the basis of photographs in a police station, a police patrolman spotted the man whose picture had been identified in the area of a school for handicapped children. The man, Innis, who was unarmed at the time, was then arrested and advised of his rights under MIRANDA V. ARIZONA (1966). Within minutes of the arrest, other police arrived on the scene, including a police sergeant and captain, both of whom again advised the suspect of his *Miranda* rights. After the suspect stated that he understood his *Miranda* rights and wanted to speak with a lawyer, the captain directed that the suspect be placed in a police car and driven to the police station accompanied by three patrolmen.

While the police car was proceeding to its destination, two of the patrolmen conversed with each other concerning the possibility that one of the handicapped children from the nearby school might find a weapon with shells and get hurt. The suspect, overhearing the conversation, told the officers to turn the car around so that he could show them where a shotgun was located. Interrupting the trip to the police station after the car had been on the road for only a few minutes, the police returned to the scene of the arrest, where a search for the shotgun was in progress. On arrival, the suspect was again advised of his *Miranda* rights. He replied that he understood his rights, but "wanted to get the gun out of the way because of the kids in the area in the school." The man then led the police to a nearby field where he pointed out a shotgun. Subsequently, upon being indicted for the kidnapping, robbery, and murder of the deceased taxicab driver, the man was convicted of such offenses in the Superior Court of Kent County, Rhode Island, at a trial in which the shotgun and the testimony relating to its discovery had been admitted into evidence. On appeal, the Rhode Island Supreme Court set aside the conviction, holding, among other things, that the defendant had invoked his right to counsel at the time of his arrest, and that—contrary to the mandate of the *Miranda* case that, in the absence of counsel, all custodial interrogation then cease—the police officers who had carried on the conversation about a handicapped child finding a gun had interrogated the defendant without a valid waiver of his right to counsel.

Summary of Arguments

The defendant claimed that the trial judge erred in denying his motion to suppress evidence obtained in violation of his Fifth Amendment rights.

It was the plaintiff's position that the defendant had been given his *Miranda* warning and that the officers' remarks did not constitute direct questioning and did not coerce the defendant to respond. The defendant's response was voluntary and constituted a waiver of his constitutional rights.

Decision

On certiorari, the U.S. Supreme Court vacated the decision and remanded the case to the court below. In an opinion by Justice Stewart, joined by Justices White, Blackmun, Powell, and Rehnquist, it was held that procedural safeguards under the *Miranda* rule come into play whenever a person in custody is subject to either express questioning or its functional equivalent. The term "interrogation" refers not only to express questioning but also to any words or actions on the part of the police (other than those normally involved in arrest and custody) that the police should know are reasonably likely to elicit an incriminating response from the suspect—that is, any response that the prosecution may seek to introduce at trial. This definition focuses primarily upon the perception of the suspect, rather than the intent of the police. The Court also held that the defendant had not been "interrogated" in violation of his right to remain silent until after consulting with a lawyer, since there had been no express questioning of the defendant in the police car: the conversation between the officers was, at least in form, nothing more than a dialogue between the two officers. It invited no response from the defendant, and since the defendant had not been subjected to the functional equivalent of questioning, in that the record did not suggest the officers were aware that the defendant was peculiarly susceptible to concern for the safety of handicapped children, and the record contained nothing to suggest that the police knew the defendant was unusually disoriented or upset at the time of his arrest.

Aftermath

The Court continues to uphold the *Innis* interpretation of *Miranda*. In *Pennsylvania v. Muniz* (1990), the Court stressed (1) the Court's definition in *Innis* of the phrase "functional equivalent" of express questioning to include "any words or actions on the part of the police (other than those normally attendant to arrest and custody) that the police should know are reasonably likely to elicit an incriminating response from the suspect. The latter part of this definition focuses primarily upon the perceptions of the suspect, rather than the intent of the police"; and (2) the Court's holding in *Innis* that "[a]ny knowledge the police may have had concerning the unusual susceptibility of a defendant to a particular form of persuasion might be an important factor in determining" what the police reasonably should have known.

Significance

Rhode Island v. Innis represents a refinement on the decision in *Miranda v. Arizona* that the "prosecution may not use statements . . . stemming from custodial *interrogation* of the defendant" unless it demonstrates that the defendant has waived the rights specified in *Miranda* and guaranteed by the Fifth Amendment. The *Innis* majority's analysis represents a surprisingly broad construction of *Miranda*. In *Innis* the Court explicitly disavowed *Miranda*'s limited definition of "interrogation" as actual "questioning initiated by law enforcement officers" and ruled instead that in view of the purposes of *Miranda,* "interrogation" must be construed to include words or conduct that are the "functional equivalent" of direct questioning. This broad construction of *Miranda* affords suspects greater protection than that guaranteed by some lower courts before *Innis* because it is now clear that "interrogation" can take place even when the police speech is not punctuated by a question mark, nor directly addressed to the suspect. Moreover, it is also clear that "interrogation" now includes police tactics that do not even involve speech. Nevertheless, despite the Court's seemingly broad reading of *Miranda*, the *Innis* test is ambiguous. Under one interpretation, the test contains a flaw that could lead to expanded use of coercive tactics by the police.

Related Cases

Duckworth v. Eagan, 492 U.S. 195 (1989)

Illinois v. Perkins, 496 U.S. 292 (1990)

Pennsylvania v. Muniz, 496 U.S. 582 (1990)

Recommended Reading

White, Welsh S. *Life in the Balance*. Ann Arbor: University of Michigan Press, 1984.
———, *Interrogation without Questions:* Rhode Island v. Innis *and* United States v. Henry, 78 Michigan Law Review 1209 (1980).

Case Title: *Rideau v. Louisiana*

Legal Citations: 373 U.S. 723; 83 S.Ct. 1417; 10 L.Ed. 2d 663

Year of Decision: 1963

Key Issues

Does due process of law require a trial before a jury of local people who have not seen or heard the defendant's televised interview in jail with the sheriff?

HISTORY OF THE CASE

Rideau was arrested for bank robbery, kidnapping, and murder. While in the Calcasieu Parish jail in Lake Charles, Louisiana, a film was made of an "interview" between the prisoner and the sheriff, during which Rideau confessed to the reported crimes without the benefit of counsel. Later the same day, the film was televised to some 24,000 people in the community. The next day an estimated 53,000 people saw the interview. On a third showing, about 23,000 saw it. Calcasieu had a population of 150,000.

Subsequently, Rideau was arraigned and two lawyers were appointed to defend him. The lawyers promptly moved for a change of venue on the ground that no fair trial was possible in Calcasieu Parish after the three television broadcasts. The motion was denied. Three members of the jury admitted to seeing the broadcasts but stated that it would not affect their views. The Louisiana Supreme Court affirmed the judgment.

SUMMARY OF ARGUMENTS

Wilbert Rideau argued that he had no chance of receiving a fair and impartial trial because his confession was televised.

The state of Louisiana argued that Rideau had no constitutional right to be protected from publicity.

DECISION

Justice Stewart wrote the opinion for the Court that the state court had denied Rideau due process of law when it refused his request for a change of venue, since the inhabitants of Calcasieu had been repeatedly exposed to the defendant's confession: "For anyone who has ever watched television, the conclusion cannot be avoided that this spectacle, to the tens of thousands of people who saw and heard it, in a very real sense was Rideau's trial at which he pleaded guilty to murder. Any subsequent court proceedings in a community so pervasively exposed to such a spectacle could be but a hollow formality."

Justice Clark dissented, saying that no nexus was established between the televised interview and the trial almost two months later: "Unless the adverse publicity is shown by the record to have fatally infected the trial, there is simply no basis

for the Court's interference that the publicity, epitomized by the television interview, [made] petitioner's trial a meaningless formality." Clark said the Court applied no guidelines in reaching its decision, most notably those set out in *IRVIN V. DOWD* (1961), that a pattern of prejudice be shown to be present in the community.

AFTERMATH

Rideau was tried and convicted a second time, but that conviction was overturned, too. After a third trial and conviction, Rideau was sentenced to death row. Rideau's death sentence was vacated by the U.S. Supreme Court's decision in *FURMAN V. GEORGIA*, which found the death penalty unconstitutional. Rideau was resentenced to life in prison.

SIGNIFICANCE

Rideau indicated that due process requires that a defendant receive a requested change of venue when prejudicial publicity has occurred. Therefore, increased media attention has resulted in more defendant motions for a change of venue as the only way to get a fair trial.

RELATED CASES

Beck v. Washington, 369 U.S. 541 (1962)

Irvin v. Dodd, 366 U.S. 717 (1961)

Shepherd v. Florida, 341 U.S. 50 (1951)

RECOMMENDED READING

Kane, Peter E. *Murder, Courts and the Press.* Edwardsville: Southern Illinois University Press, 1986.

Case Title: *Harry Roberts v. Louisiana*

Legal Citation: 431 U.S. 633

Year of Decision: 1977

KEY ISSUES

May a state mandate the death sentence for a crime without considering mitigating circumstances?

HISTORY OF THE CASE

The Eighth Amendment to the U.S. Constitution prohibits cruel and unusual punishment. If cruel and unusual punishment is inflicted upon a person for a crime, that punishment may be considered a denial of due process.

In February 1974, two police officers responded to a disturbance call in a New Orleans, Louisiana, neighborhood. When they arrived at the scene they were directed to Roberts, who fled on foot. The officers chased Roberts in their squad car. Roberts shot several times at the car, mortally wounding one officer. The police captured Roberts later in the evening and he was identified by the surviving officer who had earlier given chase. A jury trial found Roberts guilty of first-degree murder of a police officer and sentenced him to death, as required by a state statute. The Louisiana Supreme Court affirmed the conviction and the U.S. Supreme Court agreed to hear the case.

SUMMARY OF ARGUMENTS

Roberts's attorney argued that the statute requiring the death penalty for crimes classified as first degree murder was procedurally defective in that it did not allow the jury to consider the circumstances of the offense or the character of the accused.

The state of Louisiana argued that the statute was narrow and specific. Mitigating circumstances were incorporated into the statute by its narrowness. The state held that if other mitigating circumstances were allowed to affect the sentencing then the deterrent effect of the statute would be made pointless.

DECISION

The Court overruled the conviction in a 5-4 decision. The majority held that the fundamental respect for humanity encompassed in the Eighth Amendment requires consideration of circumstances surrounding the crime before the death sentence can be imposed.

Justice Rehnquist, joined by Justice White, dissented. Both felt that under certain circumstances the crime could be so heinous that the imposition of the death sentence without further consideration would be constitutionally permissible. Rehnquist believed that some crimes are so serious that nothing can lessen their seriousness. In support of his position, Rehnquist quoted members of the present majority who had previ-ously recognized the interest of society in mandating the death penalty for certain crimes.

AFTERMATH

Roberts required that all states rewrite their death penalty statutes to include mitigating circumstances. States responded by enacting statutes that included not only mitigating circumstances but aggravating circumstances as well.

SIGNIFICANCE

Roberts injected clarity into state death penalty statutes. As a result, blanket mandatory death penalties were abolished. Capital offenses now require a showing of aggravating circumstances before the death penalty can be handed down.

RELATED CASES

Eddings v. Oklahoma, 455 U.S. 104 (1982)

Furman v. Georgia, 408 U.S. 238 (1972)

Lockett v. Ohio, 438 U.S. 586 (1978)

RECOMMENDED READING

Anthony Grosserand, *"Protecting the Foot Soldiers of an Ordered Society": An Analysis of State Statu-tory Aggravating Circumstances of Murdering a Police Officer in the Performance of His or Her Duty*, 58 University of Missouri Kansas City Law Review 675 (1990).

John W. Poulos, *The Supreme Court, Capital Punish-ment and the Substantive Criminal Law: The Rise and Fall of Mandatory Capital Punishment*, 28 Arizona Law Review 143 (1986).

Case Title: *Rochin v. California*

Legal Citations: 342 U.S. 165; 72 S.Ct 205; 96 L.Ed. 183

Year of Decision: 1952

KEY ISSUES

What limits does the due process clause of the Fourteenth Amendment to the U.S. Constitution impose on the conduct of criminal proceedings of the states?

HISTORY OF THE CASE

This case addresses bodily intrusion in the course of a search for evidence. The police, looking for narcotics, illegally broke into the bedroom of a suspect. Rochin, the defendant, quickly swallowed two capsules of morphine that were on his night stand. A violent struggle ensued as the police tried unsuccessfully to retrieve the capsules from Rochin's mouth. He was then taken to a hospital where a doctor forced a medication that induces vomiting through a tube into his stomach. Rochin vomited the capsules containing the morphine. He was convicted of unlawful possession of morphine, and the evidence used against him was the two capsules he had regurgitated.

The California Court of Appeals found that the police were "guilty of unlawfully breaking into and entering Rochin's home and were guilty of unlawfully assaulting, battering, torturing and falsely imprisoning the defendant at the hospital." They also found the police and doctor guilty of the same acts. The court upheld Rochin's conviction, however, because at that time illegally obtained evidence was admissible on a criminal charge in California.

SUMMARY OF ARGUMENTS

Antonio Pichard Rochin argued that his arrest, search, extraction of evidence, and subsequent seizure violated his rights under the Fourth, Fifth, and Fourteenth Amendments.

The state of California argued that no constitutional rights of Rochin had been violated and that the evidence obtained from Rochin was admissible in court.

DECISION

The conviction was reversed because the evidence was obtained in violation of the due process clause of the Fourteenth Amendment. Justice Frankfurter wrote the majority opinion that historically the Court subjected convictions from state courts to very narrow scrutiny authorized by the due process clause. Narrow scrutiny required the Court to give free rein so long as the convictions were brought about "by methods that offend a sense of justice." He then explained why

California had violated standards of fundamental justice: "The proceedings by which this conviction was obtained do more than offend some fastidious squeamishness or private sentimentalism about combating crime too energetically. This is conduct that shocks the conscience. Illegally breaking into the privacy of the petitioner, the struggle to open his mouth and remove what was there, the forcible extraction of his stomach's contents, this course of proceeding by agents of the government to obtain evidence is bound to offend even hardened sensibilities. They are methods too close to the rack and the screw to permit of constitutional differentiation."

Justice Black concurred, arguing that the Fifth Amendment was applicable to the states and that California had violated the amendment by forcibly taking incriminating evidence from the defendant. He criticized Frankfurter's "nebulous standards" of civil justice as a "chancellor's foot veto" over law enforcement practices of which the Court did not approve.

AFTERMATH

Justice Frankfurter thought that the due process clause incorporated none of the provisions of the Bill of Rights. Instead due process of law would be decided on a case-by-case basis. Black advocated total incorporation of the Bill of Rights. The Court ultimately decided on neither view but on one with more flexibility using some of Frankfurter's concepts.

Rochin was decided before the Fifth Amendment and the exclusionary rule against evidence obtained in violation of the Fourth Amendment had been applied to the states.

SIGNIFICANCE

This is the first case to involve bodily intrusion and unreasonable search and seizure, but this involved due process analyzed prior to certain of the Bill of Rights being incorporated in the 14th Amendment for application to the States. This case draws an analogy between forcible extraction of evidence from the body and coerced confessions. The development of modern technology makes it possible to obtain evidence from the body and so the Court in the future must balance society's interest in the crime with the individual's human dignity.

RELATED CASES

Griswold v. Connecticut, 381 U.S. 479 (1965)

Malinski v. New York, 324 U.S. 401 (1945)

Stanley v. Georgia, 394 U.S. 557 (1969)

RECOMMENDED READING

Francis A. Allen, *Due Process and State Criminal Procedure: Another Look,* 48 Northwestern University Law Review 16 (1953).

Case Title: *Ross v. Moffitt*

Legal Citations: 417 U.S. 600; 94 S.Ct. 2437; 41 L.Ed. 2d 341

Year of Decision: 1974

KEY ISSUES

Does the due process clause of the Fourteenth Amendment require states to provide counsel for an indigent on a discretionary appeal to a state supreme court?

HISTORY OF THE CASE

An indigent defendant, Claude Franklin Moffitt, represented by court-appointed counsel was convicted of forgery in state court. His conviction was upheld on appeal to the North Carolina Court of Appeals. The North Carolina Supreme Court then denied him counsel for the discretionary or nonmandatory review. Ultimately the U.S. Court of Appeals held that he was entitled to appointment of counsel both on his petition for review by the state supreme court and on his petition for certiorari, a petition asking for review by a higher court.

SUMMARY OF ARGUMENTS

Major Fred R. Ross and the state of North Carolina argued that an indigent defendant did not have a constitutional right to assistance of counsel to petition for a writ of certiorari to the North Carolina Supreme Court or to petition for a writ of certiorari to the U.S. Supreme Court.

Moffitt argued that the due process clause and equal protection clause of the Fourteenth Amendment required North Carolina to furnish indigent defendants with assistance of counsel to petition for writs of certiorari to the North Carolina Supreme Court and the U.S. Supreme Court.

Justice Rehnquist delivered the opinion of the Court, saying that a state cannot arbitrarily cut off an indigent's right of appeal while leaving open appeal rights for more affluent people. The due process clause, however, does not require a state to provide Moffitt with counsel on a discretionary appeal to the state supreme court. At the trial stage, the right of an indigent to counsel has been held fundamental. But there are significant differences between trial and appellate stages in a criminal proceeding. At the trial level the state must find a presumably innocent person guilty. This is an adversarial procedure that requires that an indigent have counsel. The contrary is true on appeal, where the defendant initiates the process: "The defendant needs an attorney on appeal not as a shield to protect him against being haled into court, but rather as a sword to upset the prior determination of guilt."

Justice Douglas wrote the dissent, arguing that the indigent defendant proceeding without counsel is at a substantial disadvantage relative to the more affluent represented by counsel when he is forced to fend for himself in seeking discretionary review.

DECISION

The due process clause is not violated when a state does not provide a defendant with counsel for a discretionary appeal.

AFTERMATH

This case is an example of what one commentator, Charles Ogletree, calls "the limiting and restricting of the equalizing principles of the Warren Court." The Court has consistently refused to extend protections for indigent defendants and at times restricted their access to the courts.

SIGNIFICANCE

State-provided assistance to indigent defendants was limited by *Ross v. Moffitt* and meeting due process requirements consisted only of provision of counsel for appeals of right or automatic appeals.

RELATED CASES

Douglas v. California, 372 U.S. 353 (1963)

Evitts v. Lucey, 469 U.S. 387 (1985)

Gagnon v. Scarpelli, 411 U.S. 778 (1973)

RECOMMENDED READING

Schwartz, Bernard. *The Ascent of Pragmatism: The Burger Court in Action.* New York: Addison-Wesley, 1990.

Case Title: *Schall v. Martin*

Legal Citation: 467 U.S. 253

Year of Decision: 1984

KEY ISSUES

Does pretrial detention of accused juvenile delinquents violate the due process clause of the Fourteenth Amendment to the U.S. Constitution?

HISTORY OF THE CASE

The Fourteenth Amendment to the U.S. Constitution guarantees the right to due process of the law. This has come to mean, generally, that a person accused of a crime shall be notified of the accusation and receive a hearing on the accusation.

The New York Family Court Act authorized the detention of accused juvenile delinquents until the time of trial if there was a serious risk that the juvenile would commit a crime before the hearing date. Three different juveniles were arrested in separate offenses including robbery, assault, and criminal possession of a weapon. The state detained the accused in accordance with the statute. While in detention, one of the juveniles brought a class action habeas corpus proceeding to determine the constitutionality of the detention procedures. The U.S. District Court for the Southern District of New York struck down the statute as a denial of due process. The U.S. Court of Appeals for the Second Circuit affirmed the decision of the district court. The U.S. Supreme Court agreed to hear the case after the Second Circuit appeal.

SUMMARY OF ARGUMENTS

Schall, the commissioner of the New York Department of Juvenile Justice, argued that the provision ensured the legitimate objective of community safety. In addition, Schall maintained that juvenile delinquency respondents received greater protection than adult criminal defendants who received all constitutionally required procedural benefits.

Appellees Gregory Martin and the other class representatives argued that the law lacked procedural protections, and that it was overly broad and unnecessary. They assured the court that the administration of the juvenile justice system would improve because under the law, too many respondents were being retained. The detentions also adversely affected the juvenile respondents' character during the proceedings, by causing juveniles to view society as hostile and oppressive and to view themselves as delinquent.

DECISION

Justice Rehnquist wrote for the majority in the 6-3 decision upholding the detention procedures and reversing the lower courts. The Court found that juveniles, unlike adults, are always in some form of custody. Children, by definition of law, are not assumed to be able to take care of themselves. As a result, the juvenile's liberty may appropriately be subordinated to the state's interest. The Court did not see the detention as punishment but rather as a legitimate regulatory scheme. The law gave ample procedural safeguards, such as notice of the charges and a hearing on the issue of detention, and allowed for the accused to be represented by counsel at the hearing. In sum, there was no denial of equal protection or due process.

Justice Marshall, joined by Justices Brennan and Stevens, dissented, finding the law and its effects tantamount to adult imprisonment. They believed that if anything, the liberty protected by the due process clause is the liberty from physical restraint. The dissenters maintained that only a very strong government interest could justify taking that liberty away and the arguments posed by the state of New York were not strong enough.

AFTERMATH

The Court resurrected a policy of "parens patriae," or governmental parenting, which effectively gives the government strong powers over the regulation of juveniles. The policy has remained virtually unchecked since this decision.

SIGNIFICANCE

The Court's decision added a significant dimension to due process law in general. The Court had never ruled on preventive detention prior to this decision. Affirming the practice greatly affected the procedural rights of all citizens regardless of age as states have adopted similar provisions for a host of criminal activities.

RELATED CASES

In re Gault, 387 U.S. 1 (1967)

U.S. v. Salerno, 481 U.S. 739 (1987)

Reno v. Flores, 507 U.S. 292 (1993)

Kansas v. Hendricks, 521 U.S. 346 (1997)

RECOMMENDED READING

Martin Guggenheim, *The Treatment of Juveniles in Our Court System*, 1 Criminal Justice 25 (1986).

John F. McCune, *Juvenile Law: Whatever Happened to In re Gault and Fundamental Fairness in Juvenile Proceedings?*, 22 Wake Forest Law Review 347 (1987).

Case Title: *Screws v. United States*

Legal Citations: 325 U.S. 91; 65 S.Ct. 1031; 89 L.Ed. 1495

Year of Decision: 1945

KEY ISSUES

Does bludgeoning a man to death in the course of an arrest violate the Federal Criminal Code, which prohibits violating a dead man's rights under the due process clause?

HISTORY OF THE CASE

M. Claude Screws, sheriff of Baker County, Georgia, and two other white law enforcement officers, Frank Edward Jones and Jim Bob Kelley, arrested Robert Hall, a black man. The arrest was made late at night at Hall's home on a warrant charging him with theft of a tire. Hall was handcuffed and taken to the courthouse, where he was beaten to death. There was evidence that Screws held a grudge against Hall.

An indictment was issued against Screws and the other officers and a trial was held in which the jury returned a guilty verdict. The Circuit Court of Appeals affirmed. The Supreme Court agreed to hear the case because of the important questions of criminal law administration.

SUMMARY OF ARGUMENTS

Screws and the other petitioners argued that the U.S. district court was without jurisdiction to try the petitioners and that Hall was not killed under state authority. Petitioners also argued that an arresting officer cannot act for the state unless such action is authorized by law.

The United States argued that Hall was killed while the petitioners were exercising a state function and exerting state power and while acting in such a capacity, deprived Hall of his Fourteenth Amendment rights.

DECISION

In a prosecution of three law enforcement officials who arrested and beat to death a black man, the conviction of willfully depriving the deceased of federal rights was reversed for a new trial. In doing so, the Court saved 18 U.S.C. 242, a civil rights law making it a crime for a person acting under legal authority to deprive a person of his or her constitutional rights based on race, from invalidity due to vagueness by imposing a high mental state requirement on the term "willfully" in the challenged statute, resulting in a strict interpretation of the provision.

Justice Douglas announced the opinion of the plurality of the Court saying that the particular section of the Federal Criminal Code was not vague. A statute's ambiguity or vagueness may be remedied if conviction under the law requires a showing of intent. Justice Douglas stated:

> [W]here the punishment imposed is only for an act knowingly done with the purpose of doing that which the statute prohibits, the accused cannot be said to suffer from lack of warning or knowledge that the act

which he does is a violation of law. The requirement that the act must be willful or purposeful may not render certain, for all purposes, a statutory definition of the crime which is in some respects uncertain. But it does relieve the statute of the objection that it punishes without warning an offense of which the accused was unaware.

So long as "willful" was strictly construed as a purpose to deprive a person of a specific constitutional right, the statute was not invalid for vagueness or indefiniteness.

Justice Rutledge, in his concurring opinion, did not think that the vagueness problem would ever assert itself. No state official whose conduct led to indictment under 18 U.S.C. 242 could deny the constitutional rights underpinning the statute.

Justice Frankfurter, who wrote for the dissent, indicated that an expansion of federal criminal jurisdiction would violate the doctrine of federalism. He thought that common crimes should be left to the states, if only to protect civil rights. If citizens turned to federal courts under the due process clause, then states would not be accountable.

AFTERMATH

The result of *Screws* was the requirement of a certain state of mind for a conviction to be upheld or "mens rea."

SIGNIFICANCE

This case was part of criminal civil rights enforcement. Because of the decision it made it more difficult for the Civil Rights Section of the Department of Justice to prosecute civil rights crimes because an intent to deprive a person of a specific constitutional right had to be shown. Further, the decision indicated that unauthorized actions by government employees could still violate the Fourteenth Amendment.

RELATED CASES

Smith v. Goguen, 415 U.S. 566 (1974)

United States v. Classic, 313 U.S. 299 (1941)

RECOMMENDED READING

Frederick M. Lawrence, *Civil Rights and Criminal Wrongs: The Mens Rea of Federal Civil Rights Crimes*, 67 Tulane Law Review 2113 (1993).

Rachael Simonoff, Ratzlal v. United States: *The Meaning of "willful" and the Demands of Due Process*, 28 Columbia Journal of Legal and Social Problems 397 (1995).

Case Title: *Smith v. Goguen*

Legal Citation: 415 U.S. 566

Year of Decision: 1974

KEY ISSUES

Does a statute that imposes criminal liability for "contemptuous" treatment of the U.S. flag violate constitutional protections?

HISTORY OF THE CASE

Valarie Goguen wore an American flag patch on his jeans. Police confronted Goguen while he was standing peaceably on a public street in Leominster, Massachusetts, and questioned him about his patch. Other people present with Goguen during the meeting with the police laughed at what seemed a silly issue. The following day, the officer swore out a complaint against Goguen under the contempt provision of the Massachusetts flag-misuse statute. The court convicted Goguen and sentenced him to six months in state prison. The Massachusetts Supreme Court affirmed the conviction. Goguen filed a writ of habeas corpus in the federal district court. The court granted the writ and ordered Goguen released. The federal court of appeals affirmed the release. The state of Massachusetts appealed to the U.S. Supreme Court. The Court agreed to hear the case because of the importance of the issues raised.

SUMMARY OF ARGUMENTS

The state of Massachusetts argued that the statute was constitutional because it gave defendants adequate notice of what actions constituted a violation. The statute dealt only with "actual flags" of the United States.

Goguen argued that the action of contempt was too broad for a reasonable person to know what conduct actually constituted a violation of the statute. Since due process requires notice, the statute could not be held valid as it is written.

DECISION

Justice Powell wrote for the majority in the 6-3 decision affirming Goguen's release. The Court did not address any First Amendment claims and instead relied on the Fourteenth Amendment's due process requirement of notice. The Court agreed with Goguen's argument and held that the statute's language was overly broad and therefore unconstitutional. Because of the virtually unlimited possibilities for a determination of contempt for the flag, no citizen could be protected adequately from arbitrary government action. The statute left the determination of contempt up to police, judges, and juries, all of which could enforce the statute on a whim. As a result, the Court affirmed the circuit court's release.

AFTERMATH

The Court has repeatedly dealt with the issue of what is constitutional treatment of the flag and what is not. The issue was virtually put to rest in 1990 when the Court determined that state flag-use statutes must serve a compelling state interest and must also be narrowly drawn to achieve that end. In response to the Court's decision, President George Bush attempted to launch a drive for an amendment to the Constitution regarding flag desecration. The U.S. Senate rejected the amendment. However, Congress passed and the president signed into law the Flag Protection Act. Immediately, protesters around the country burned flags in public places in response to the law. Police arrested a group of protesters who had burned a flag on the steps of the Capitol and charged them under the new law. The Supreme Court promptly declared the law unconstitutional.

SIGNIFICANCE

This case is one of a long line of cases dealing with the use of the American flag. Its reliance on Fourteenth Amendment rather than First Amendment principles leaves open the possibility that a statute defining in a very specific way the forbidden treatment of the flag could be constitutional.

RELATED CASES

Spence v. Washington, 418 U.S. 405 (1974)

Street v. New York, 394 U.S. 576 (1969)

Texas v. Johnson, 491 U.S. 397 (1989)

U.S. v. Eichman, 496 U.S. 310 (1990)

RECOMMENDED READING

Robert A. Brazener, *What Constitutes a Violation of Flag Desecration Statutes?*, 41 American Law Reports 502 (1972).

Case Title: *Sniadach v. Family Finance Corporation of Bay View*

Legal Citations: 395 U.S. 337; 23 L.Ed. 2d. 349; 89 S.Ct. 1820

Year of Decision: 1969

KEY ISSUES

Does the garnishment of wages by a finance corporation, without an opportunity for the alleged debtor to be heard and tender any defense he might have, constitute a taking of property without the procedural due process that is required by the Fourteenth Amendment?

HISTORY OF THE CASE

The plaintiff finance corporation, in accordance with the procedure provided by a Wisconsin statute, instituted a garnishment action in the Milwaukee County Court, Wisconsin, against the defendant and her employer, as garnishee. The complaint alleged a claim of $420 on a promissory note, and the employer in its answer stated it had wages of $63.18 under its control earned by Christine Sniadach and unpaid, and that it would pay one-half to Sniadach as a subsistence allowance and would hold the other half subject to the order of the court. Sniadach was served with summons and complaint on the same day as her employer, but moved that the garnishment proceedings be dismissed for failure to satisfy the due process requirements of the Fourteenth Amendment, as she was not given notice or opportunity to be heard before the seizure of her wages. The Wisconsin Supreme Court sustained the county court in approving the procedure.

SUMMARY OF ARGUMENTS

The plaintiff argued that the Wisconsin statutes allowing this garnishment (1) deprived her of her property without due process of law, (2) denied her due process of law because the statutes afforded her no right to an immediate hearing to challenge the validity of the garnishment, (3) gave the legislature judicial powers in violation of the Wisconsin Constitution, and (4) denied appellant equal protection of the laws because the statutes subjected wage earners to harsher summary process than other classes of debtors.

DECISION

The U.S. Supreme Court reversed the state court's decision. Justice Douglas, expressing the view of seven members of the Court, held that the Wisconsin prejudgment garnishment procedure, whereby the defendant's wages are frozen in the interim between the garnishment of the wages and the culmination of the main suit without the defendant having a chance to be heard, violates the due process clause of the Fourteenth Amendment.

AFTERMATH

In all, 17 states had permitted courts to tie up half an employee's wages without establishing proof of debt. This ruling's stance on fair debt collection invalidated numerous collection devices.

In *Fuentes v. Shevin,* 407 U.S. 67 (1972), the court found that the replevin laws, laws allowing a person to recover property wrongfully taken from his or her possession, of Florida and Pennsylvania violated the due process clause of the Fourteenth Amendment insofar as they denied the right to a hearing before property was taken from a person.

SIGNIFICANCE

Some legal scholars have interpreted *Sniadach* as resting upon the special importance of wages that, in the constitutional balance, might well deserve special protection.

RELATED CASES

Connecticut v. Doehr, 501 U.S. 1 (1991)

Pacific Mutual Life Insurance Co. v. Haslip, 499 U.S. 1 (1991)

Tulsa Pro. Collection Service Inc. v. Pope, 485 U.S. 478 (1988)

RECOMMENDED READING

The Supreme Court 1968 Term, 83 Harvard Law Review 113 (1969).

Case Title: *South Carolina v. Katzenbach*

Legal Citations: 383 U.S. 301; 86 S.Ct. 803; 15 L.Ed. 2d 769

Year of Decision: 1966

KEY ISSUES

Does the Voting Rights Act of 1965 violate the U.S. Constitution by interfering with states' rights and due process?

HISTORY OF THE CASE

Although black citizens were guaranteed the right to vote in 1870 with the ratification of the Fifteenth Amendment, many states got around this by using poll taxes and literacy tests. The federal government attempted for 100 years to combat this disenfranchisement with little success on a case-by-case basis. Finally, upset with the states' disregard for the Fifteenth Amendment, Congress passed the Voting Rights Act of 1965.

SUMMARY OF ARGUMENTS

South Carolina argued that the Voting Rights Act deprived the state and its citizens of their basic rights protected by the Constitution and its provisions were not reasonably designed to enforce the Fifteenth Amendment.

Nicholas de B. Katzenbach, the attorney general of the United States, argued that Congress had the authority to protect and enforce the right to vote free of racial discrimination and that measures suspending literacy tests and other tests were proper to accomplish the objective of enforcing the Fifteenth Amendment.

DECISION

The Court held that the Voting Rights Act of 1965 is constitutional: It does not violate the Fifteenth Amendment, states' rights, or due process.

Chief Justice Warren delivered the Court's majority opinion saying that the Voting Rights Act was "designed by Congress to banish the blight of racial discrimination in voting which has infected the electoral process in parts of our country for nearly a century." Congress's power to do this is based on the Fifteenth Amendment. The act is valid. There is no doubt that voting rights are traditionally a matter of states' rights. The act provides that "as against the reserved powers of the states, Congress may use any rational means to effectuate the constitutional prohibition of racial discrimination in voting." The Court also upheld the review provision of the act that allows the government to examine them to see if they were in compliance with the act.

Justice Black dissented from the notion of the review provisions, which he felt was a violation of federalism and due process. He believed that the southern states were treated like "conquered provinces" and that southern law officials would have to "grovel" on their knees to the federal administrators.

AFTERMATH

This case provided a way to test the proposition that Congress could do no more than forbid violations of the Fifteenth Amendment in a general way, and that only the Court had the power to devise specific remedies for particular jurisdictions.

SIGNIFICANCE

This case established the broad authority granted to Congress under the Fifteenth Amendment. This standard is still valid today. Congressional action pursuant to the Fifteenth Amendment is constitutional if the regulations are fair in relation to the prohibition of racial discrimination in voting.

RELATED CASES

Baker v. Carr, 369 U.S. 186 (1962)

Gomillion v. Lightfoot, 364 U.S. 339 (1960)

Reynolds v. Sims, 377 U.S. 533 (1964)

RECOMMENDED READING

Alexander M. Bickel, *The Voting Rights Cases*, 1966 Supreme Court Review 79 (1966).

Samuel Estreicher, *Congressional Power and Constitutional Rights: Reflections on Proposed Human Life Legislation*, 68 Virginia Law Review 333 (1982).

Schwartz, Bernard, ed. *Statutory History of the United States Civil Rights, Part II*. New York: Chelsea House Publishers, 1970.

Case Title: *Stanley v. Illinois*

Legal Citations: 405 U.S. 645; 92 S.Ct. 1208

Year of Decision: 1972

KEY ISSUES

Is an unwed father entitled to a hearing on his fitness as a parent before his children can be taken from him after the death of the children's natural mother?

HISTORY OF THE CASE

Statutory family law in Illinois provided two principal methods of removing nondelinquent children from the homes of their parents. In a dependency proceeding, the state could demonstrate that the children are wards of the state because they have no surviving parent or guardian. In a neglect proceeding, the state could show that children should be wards of the state because the present parent(s) or guardian does not provide suitable care. Parents were defined as the father and mother of a legitimate child or the natural mother of an illegitimate child. The term "parent" did not include unwed fathers. Thus, the state did not need to prove unfitness of the unwed father in a neglect proceeding; unlike an unwed mother, the unwed father was not a "parent" whose existing relationship with his children must be considered.

Peter Stanley lived with Joan Stanley intermittently for 18 years, during which time they had three children. When Joan Stanley died, Peter

Stanley lost not only her but also his children. Upon Joan Stanley's death, in a dependency proceeding instituted by the state of Illinois, Stanley's children were declared wards of the state and placed with court-appointed guardians. Stanley appealed the result of the dependency proceeding, claiming that he had never been shown to be an unfit parent. Since married fathers and unwed mothers could not be deprived of their children without a showing of unfitness, Stanley claimed that he had been deprived of the equal protection of the laws guaranteed him by the Fourteenth Amendment. The Illinois Supreme Court accepted the fact that Stanley's own unfitness had not been established but rejected the equal protection claim. The Illinois court held that Stanley could properly be separated from his children upon proof of the single fact that he and the dead mother had not been married.

SUMMARY OF ARGUMENTS

In the Supreme Court, Stanley continued to press his equal protection claim that he had unconstitutionally been treated differently from married fathers and unwed mothers in otherwise identical circumstances. The state responded that unwed fathers are legally presumed unfit to raise their children and that it is unnecessary to hold individualized hearings to determine whether particular fathers are in fact unfit parents before they are separated from their children.

DECISION

In an opinion written by Justice Byron White, the U.S. Supreme Court held that Stanley was entitled to a hearing on his fitness as a parent before his children were taken from him and that, by denying him a hearing while extending it to all other parents whose custody of their children is challenged, the state denied Stanley the equal protection of the laws guaranteed by the Fourteenth Amendment. Citing previous opinions that emphasized the importance of the family, even family relationships unlegitimized by a marriage ceremony, the Court recognized Stanley's substantial interest in retaining custody of his children. While it also recognized the state's interest in protecting the welfare of children, the Court questioned the state interest in separating children from fathers without a hearing designed to determine whether the father is unfit in a particular disputed case. Indeed, the Court demonstrated

that the state defeats its own goal of protecting children when it needlessly separates children from their family.

In the final analysis, the state gained only administrative convenience by denying Stanley a hearing; and, in the Court's words, "the Constitution recognizes higher values than speed and efficiency." To guarantee due process under the equal protection clause of the Fourteenth Amendment, the Court held that Stanley and those like him are to be accorded a hearing as to his fitness as a parent before his children are to be declared wards of the state.

In a dissenting opinion joined by Justice Blackmun, Chief Justice Burger accused the majority of overreaching its constitutional powers in fashioning its due process analysis of the issue, because the due process issue was not raised in state court. To Chief Justice Burger, the only constitutional question raised in the case was whether the Illinois statute omitting unwed fathers from the definition of "parents" violated the equal protection clause. Chief Justice Burger would have answered that question in the negative, finding that the objective of the statutory classification was not to penalize unwed parents but to further the welfare of illegitimate children.

AFTERMATH

Stanley was clear in its holding that procedural due process demanded notice and a hearing before Stanley's parental rights could be terminated. However, the opinion left open the question of Stanley's substantive rights as an unwed father—could the law treat unwed fathers differently from other parents? In the aftermath of *Stanley*, the Court decided a series of cases that addressed the constitutional rights of putative fathers. In *Quillion v. Walcott* (1978), the Court refused to give the unwed father the same veto power over the adoption of his child as enjoyed by unwed mothers, married parents, and divorced parents. The next year, in *Caban v. Mohammed* (1979), the Court invalidated a New York statute that treated unwed parents differently solely on the basis of gender. Finally, in *Lehr v. Robertson* (1983), the Court limited the unwed father's right to notice of an adoption proceeding when the father had not established a relationship with his child. The net result of the line of cases is to allow unwed fathers to be treated differently from unwed mothers. While all classes of parents have certain due process rights to notice and hearing in proceedings that may deprive them of their children, the extent of unwed fathers' rights depends on the relationship the father has previously developed with his children, whereas the relationship between a mother and a child is created solely by the biological connection between them.

SIGNIFICANCE

Apart from its specific context in family law, *Stanley* is a landmark decision among the Court's efforts in the latter half of the 20th century to delineate the scope of due process. In general, the Court established that the Constitution demands certain steps of procedural fairness—most commonly, notice and hearing—before government can deprive people of rights or property.

RELATED CASES

Bell v. Burson, 402 U.S. 535, 91 S.Ct. 1586 (1971)

Caban v. Mohammed, 441 U.S. 380, 99 S.Ct. 1760 (1979)

Carrington v. Rash, 380 U.S. 89, 85 S.Ct. 775 (1965)

Lehr v. Robertson, 463 U.S. 248, 103 S.Ct. 2985 (1983)

Quillion v. Walcott, 434 U.S. 246, 98 S.Ct. 549 (1978)

RECOMMENDED READING

Elizabeth Buchanan, *The Constitutional Rights of Unwed Fathers before and after* Lehr v. Robertson, 45 Ohio State Law Journal 313 (1984).

L. J. Eveleigh, *Certainly Not Child's Play: A Serious Game of Hide and Seek with the Rights of Unwed Fathers,* 40 Syracuse Law Review 1055 (1989).

Stacy Lynn Hill, *Putative Fathers and Parental Interests: A Search for Protection,* 65 Indiana Law Journal 939 (1990).

Shelley Weinhaus, *Substantive Rights of the Unwed Father: The Boundaries Are Defined,* 19 Journal of Family Law 445 (1981).

Case Title: *Stone v. Powell*

Legal Citation: 428 U.S. 465

Year of Decision: 1976

KEY ISSUES

When a state has provided an opportunity for full and fair litigation of a state prisoner's habeas corpus claim, does the Fourth Amendment require the federal judiciary to hear the claim as well?

HISTORY OF THE CASE

The federal habeas corpus statute mandates relief, a hearing to determine whether the prisoner should be released, to state prisoners held in custody in violation of the Constitution. Generally, convictions obtained by use of evidence gathered through a violation of the Fourth Amendment are not open to attack on habeas corpus review. Review is available, however, when the state does not provide a defendant with an opportunity for full and fair litigation of a search and seizure claim. The Supreme Court has determined that, generally, evidence obtained in an illegal search and seizure is inadmissible under a judicially constructed doctrine called the exclusionary rule.

This case is a consolidation of two similar claims. The prosecution in each case relied upon evidence obtained by searches and seizures that the defendants alleged to have been unlawful. The courts in the two states convicted both defendants. The convictions were upheld by the state courts of appeal. One federal circuit court affirmed a conviction and another reversed the other conviction. Both were brought before the U.S. Supreme Court and consolidated.

SUMMARY OF ARGUMENTS

The states argued that the violation of rights, if any, was technical and did not involve a flagrant abuse of police power. As a result, they argued that the Court should limit the scope of federal habeas corpus to whether the defendants had the opportunity to present their claims in a full and fair litigation.

The defendants argued that the Court should not overrule a long line of cases permitting habeas corpus review by state prisoners in federal court. They believed that Fourth Amendment claims were appropriate for federal review because such claims do not usually involve questions of guilt or innocence.

DECISION

Justice Powell wrote for the majority in the 6-3 decision upholding the convictions. The Court held that the exclusionary rule is not a personal constitutional right but a deterrent to police officers. The Court developed a cost-benefit analysis weighing the advantages and disadvantages of the exclusionary rule into two categories: (1) those incident to the rule's application at trial and on appeal and (2) those incident to application during collateral review at a federal habeas corpus proceeding. The Court concluded that the cost to society in applying the rule repeatedly outweighed any deterrence of Fourth Amendment violations and thus cannot be the basis for federal habeas corpus relief.

AFTERMATH

The Court narrowed the opportunities for prisoners to get relief in the federal courts under habeas corpus claims over the course of the years following the *Stone* decision. Virtually every case since *Stone* provided the Court the opportunity to implement procedural hurdles for prisoner relief. Presently, the restraints on habeas corpus actions are very tightly construed.

SIGNIFICANCE

The Court severely limited the ability of state prisoners to get relief under the federal habeas corpus statute. *Stone* marks the beginning of the Court's disinterest in preserving the rights of criminals.

RELATED CASES

Herrera v. Collins, 506 U.S. 390 (1993)

Schneckloth v. Bustamonte, 412 U.S. 218 (1973)

Withrow v. Williams, 507 U.S. 680 (1993)

Wright v. West, 505 U.S. 277 (1992)

RECOMMENDED READING

Comment, Stone v. Powell *and the Effective Assistance of Counsel*, 80 Michigan Law Review 1326 (1982).

Erwin Chemerinsky, *Thinking about Habeas Corpus*, 37 Case Western Reserve Law Review 748 (1987).

Philip Halpern, *Federal Habeas Corpus and the Mapp Exclusionary Rule after* Stone v. Powell, 82 Columbia Law Review 1 (1982).

Case Title: *Tison v. Arizona*

Alternate Case Title: The Felony Accomplice to Murder Case

Legal Citation: 481 U.S. 137

Year of Decision: 1987

KEY ISSUES

May a state under a felony-murder statute execute a person who, although he did not commit murder, played a major role in the underlying felony and demonstrated a reckless indifference to human life?

HISTORY OF THE CASE

Ricky and Raymond Tison were the sons of Gary Tison, a convicted murderer who was serving a life sentence as the result of a prison escape in which he had killed a guard. Several years after the first escape, Ricky and Raymond entered their father's prison with an ice chest full of guns and helped him to escape again. When the family's getaway vehicle broke down, they stopped a passing motorist, kidnapping him and his family. Gary Tison eventually murdered the motorist and his family in a brutal shotgun execution. Tison's sons, then ages 19 and 20, did nothing to stop Tison and continued to assist him until his subsequent death following an armed confrontation with the police. Raymond and Ricky were charged with murder under Arizona's felony-murder statute, which made it a crime punishable by death to take part in any robbery or kidnapping in which a murder is committed; under the statute each participant in the robbery or kidnapping is legally responsible for the acts of his accomplices. The brothers were convicted and sentenced to death; their case later reached the U.S. Supreme Court on appeal.

SUMMARY OF ARGUMENTS

The Tisons argued that they were accomplices only to the kidnapping, not the murder. They contended that because they lacked the intent to kill, the death penalty would be gravely disproportional to the gravity of their crime and therefore unconstitutional.

Arizona argued that its felony-murder statute was constitutional as applied because the Tison brothers were deeply involved in the crime and displayed a reckless indifference to human life.

DECISION

The Supreme Court, in an opinion written by Justice O'Connor, held that although the Tisons lacked any specific intent to kill, their death sentences were permissible if the district court found that they were recklessly indifferent to human life. The case was remanded to the district court on that basis.

Justice O'Connor noted that the two justifications for the death penalty, deterrence and retribution, were both furthered by its application in this case. She contended that imposing the death penalty for felony murder would deter criminals from being indifferent to the value of life. It also comports with the retributive justification, which suggests that the defendant's punishment should not exceed his culpability for any given crime. Justice O'Connor argued that a person who was recklessly indifferent to life could be more culpable for a given crime than one who kills a specific person intentionally.

In this case, the Tison brothers' participation in the crime was "major," and the evidence suggested that they "subjectively appreciated that their acts were likely to result in the taking of human life." Consequently, there was no constitutional barrier to their execution. Justice O'Connor found support for this view in the fact that "the majority of American jurisdictions clearly authorize capital punishment" where the defendant plays a significant role in the underlying crime and is recklessly indifferent to human life.

Justice Brennan wrote a dissent, joined by three other justices. He argued that the death penalty would be cruel and unusual punishment for the Tisons because they had only committed the crime of kidnapping. He found it untenable that two men who neither killed nor intended to kill should be put to death, and he noted that few civilized nations applied the felony-murder rule in such situations.

AFTERMATH

The factors contained in the *Tison* decision became a new standard for evaluating the imposition of the death penalty.

SIGNIFICANCE

Tison indicated that accomplices could be subject to capital punishment if the nature and extent of their participation was sufficient.

RELATED CASES

Enmund v. Florida, 458 U.S. 782 (1982)

Gregg v. Georgia, 428 U.S. 153 (1976)

RECOMMENDED READING

David H. Ganz, *The Supreme Court and* Tison v. Arizona: *A Capital Example of Judicial Unsoundness*, 29 Boston College Law Review 969 (1988).

Lynn Wittenbrink, *Overstepping Precedent:* Tison v. Arizona *Imposes the Death Penalty on Felony Murder Accomplices*, 66 North Carolina Law Review 817 (1988).

Case Title: *Tollett v. Henderson*

Legal Citations: 411 U.S. 258; 93 S.Ct. 1602; 36 L.Ed. 2d 235

Year of Decision: 1973

KEY ISSUES

May a state prisoner, pleading guilty on the advice of counsel, obtain release through a habeas corpus petition by proving that he was indicted by an unconstitutionally selected grand jury?

HISTORY OF THE CASE

Henderson, a black man, and two others were arrested by Tennessee authorities for the robbery of a liquor store, which resulted in the death of an employee. The grand jury returned a murder indictment and Henderson signed a confession admitting his involvement in the robbery and shooting.

Twenty-five years later, Henderson filed a petition for a writ of habeas corpus in federal court. He contended that his confession was coerced and that he had been denied effective assistance of counsel. The district court denied these claims. Henderson then sought state habeas corpus alleging for the first time that he was denied his constitutional rights because blacks were excluded from the jury.

SUMMARY OF ARGUMENTS

Petitioner argued that respondent had waived his Fourteenth Amendment right to be indicted by a constitutionally selected grand jury because he pled guilty to the offense charged.

Respondent argued that he was denied his constitutional rights because blacks were excluded from serving on the grand jury. Further, the respondent argued that he had not waived his constitutional rights because he was unaware blacks were being systematically excluded from the grand jury.

DECISION

Justice Rehnquist delivered the majority opinion, extending the then existing law to include situations in which neither the client nor the attorney knew the facts that led to the constitutional claim: "[J]ust as it is not sufficient for the criminal defendant seeking to set aside such a plea to show that his counsel in retrospect may not have correctly appraised the constitutional significance of certain historical facts . . . it is likewise not sufficient that he show that if counsel had pursued a certain factual inquiry such a pursuit would have uncovered a possible constitutional infirmity in the proceedings."

Justice Marshall, dissenting, noted that counsel's ability to bind a client "should be limited narrowly to situations in which practical realities bar consultations, as often may happen during the course of the trial."

A state prisoner pleading guilty with the advise of counsel may not later obtain release through a federal habeas corpus petition by proving only that the indictment was returned by an unconstitutionally selected grand jury.

AFTERMATH

This case came three years after *Brady v. United States, McMann v. Richardson,* and *Parker v. North Carolina. Tollett* added another exclusion to the habeas corpus qualifications.

SIGNIFICANCE

This case represents a continuing tightening of the right to use habeas corpus as a means of relief from confinement. Entering a guilty plea can bar a defendant from collaterally attacking a conviction through a habeas corpus proceeding.

RELATED CASES

Brady v. United States, 397 U.S. 742 (1970)

McMann v. Richardson, 397 U.S. 759 (1970)

Parker v. North Carolina, 397 U.S. 790 (1970)

RECOMMENDED READING

Bradley Jay Butwin, *Federal Habeas Corpus Review of State Forfeitures Resulting from Assigned Counsel's Refusal to Raise Issues on Appeal.* 52 Fordham Review 850 (1984).

Vivian O. Burger, *The Supreme Court and Defense Counsel: Old Roads, New Paths, A Dead End?,* 86 Columbia Law Review 9 (1986).

Case Title: *Twining v. State of New Jersey*

Legal Citations: 211 U.S. 78; 29 S.Ct. 14; 53 L.Ed. 97

Year of Decision: 1908

KEY ISSUES

May a judge bring to the jury's attention the defendant's failure to testify in his own defense?

HISTORY OF THE CASE

Albert Twining and David Cornell were indicted by a grand jury in New Jersey for knowingly exhibiting false records to a bank examiner with the intent to deceive him as to the condition of the Monmouth Trust and Safe Deposit Company. Under the law of New Jersey, such an act was a high misdemeanor. The defendants were found guilty by a jury verdict and sentenced to prison. The sentence was affirmed by the New Jersey Supreme Court and then by the New Jersey Court of Errors and Appeals. Five directors of the bank signed the paper in question. One of the directors, S. A. Patterson, testified at the trial that the paper was false. Twining and Cornell did not testify.

After the conclusion of the trial and before the jury's deliberation, the trial judge in his charge to the jury remarked that both Twining and Cornell were seated in the courtroom, heard the testimony of Patterson, and did not deny it. The judge called upon the jury to consider why neither of them took the stand to deny the allegations against them.

SUMMARY OF ARGUMENTS

The attorneys for Twining and Cornell argued that the comments by the trial court judge were a denial of the right to a fair trial, in violation of the due process clause of the Fourteenth Amendment to the U.S. Constitution. While the New Jersey statute giving the defendants the right to call witnesses or testify themselves may appear harmless, with regard to comments by the court, the attorneys argued that it was systematically enforced to violate the fundamental rights of those accused of a crime who failed or refused to testify. The judge's comment upon the failure of the accused to testify violated their privileges as citizens of the United States. Twining and Cornell's attorneys argued that the privilege was a fundamental right and that the judge's comments were the equivalent of physical or mental torture.

The attorney general of the state of New Jersey, Robert McCarter, argued that there was no fundamental right guaranteed to the defendants because the powers of the state differ from the powers of the federal government. Federal citizenship is independent of state rights and is not equipped with common law protections; rather, such protections are formed from the words of the federal Constitution. Twining and Cornell possessed two citizenships whose rights were not necessarily identical. Thus, although the Fifth and Fourteenth Amendments may create rights for U.S. citizens, they are not necessarily guaranteed to citizens of the various states. The attorney general argued that New Jersey courts had long established that inferences may be raised concerning the failure of defendants to deny a direct criminal accusation, and this was not a violation of the privilege against self-incrimination.

DECISION

Justice William Moody wrote for eight of the justices, who agreed that state law permitted such an inference to be drawn. He noted that all the states of the Union have included some form of protection against self-incrimination in their state constitutions with the exception of New Jersey and Iowa, and those states found that the right existed under their common law.

Justice Moody rejected the idea that the Fourteenth Amendment automatically extended all of the first eight amendments of the Bill of Rights to the states. He had no trouble agreeing with the attorney general of New Jersey that there is a citizenship of the United States and a separate citizenship of the state.

Justice Moody was concerned that the authority and independence of the states would be reduced by subjecting all of their legislative and judicial acts to review by federal courts if such a sweeping view of the Fourteenth Amendment was adopted.

Justice Moody further went on to state that certain privileges of national citizenship were recognized as being superior to all others. These included the right to travel freely from state to state, the right to petition Congress, the right to vote for national officers, the right to enter and own public land of the United States, and the right to be protected while in the custody of a U.S. marshall. The process of law provided by New Jersey was well settled before either the U.S. Constitution or the Fourteenth Amendment was adopted, and, indeed, New Jersey ratified the Constitution without proposing any amendments to it. Only four of the original 13 states had a privilege against self-incrimination in their respective constitutions. Moody found that New Jersey had guarded the privilege against self-incrimination to the satisfaction of its citizens up to the time of the adoption of the Fourteenth Amendment in 1868, and there was no reason they could not continue to do so: "If the people of New Jersey are not content with the laws as declared in repeated decisions of their courts, the remedy is in their hands."

Justice John Harlan dissented, arguing that state action must be found objectionable when it violates the privileges of national citizenship that substantially affect life, liberty, or property. He found it repugnant that what he considered to be a fundamental principle of Anglo-American liberty had been violated by the courts of New Jersey in their encroachment on the privileges of their citizens:

Is it conceivable that a privilege or immunity of such a priceless character, one expressly recognized in the Supreme Law of the Land, one thoroughly interwoven with the history of Anglo-American liberty, was not in the mind of the country when it declared in the Fourteenth Amendment, that no state shall abridge the privileges or immunities of citizens of the United States? The Fourteenth Amendment would have been disapproved by every state in the Union if it had saved or recognized the right of a State to compel one accused of crime, in its courts, to be a witness against himself. We state the matter in this way because it is common knowledge that the compelling of a person to criminate himself shocks or ought to shock the sense of right and justice of every one who loves liberty. Indeed, this court has not hesitated thus to characterize the Star Chamber method of compelling an accused to be a witness against himself.

Harlan concluded that the trial court had violated Twining and Cornell's rights and found that any of the privileges or immunities of national citizenship are binding on the citizens of every state.

AFTERMATH

It was not until *MALLOY V. HOGAN* in 1964 that the Supreme Court reversed the *Twining* decision. The Court, however, did begin to struggle with the question of whether the protections of the federal Bill of Rights applied to the citizens of the states.

SIGNIFICANCE

Justice John Harlan's dissent was a strong vote in favor of total incorporation of the Bill of Rights onto all the states. His view has never been adopted and, in subsequent cases, the theory of selective incorporation has been applied to most of the rights set out in the first eight amendments.

RELATED CASES

Malloy v. Hogan, 378 U.S. 1 (1964)

Adamson v. California, 332 U.S. 46 (1947)

Palko v. Connecticut, 302 U.S. 319 (1937)

RECOMMENDED READING

Berger, Raoul. *Government by Judiciary: The Transformation of the Fourteenth Amendment.* Cambridge, Mass.: Harvard University Press, 1977.

Cortner, Richard C. *The Supreme Court and the Second Bill of Rights: The Fourteenth Amendment and the Nationalization of Civil Liberties.* Madison: University of Wisconsin Press, 1981.

Mykkeltvedt, Roald Y. *The Nationalization of the Bill of Rights: Fourteenth Amendment Due Process and Procedural Rights.* Port Washington, N.Y.: Associated Faculty Press, 1983.

Case Title: *Washington v. Glucksberg*

Alternate Case Title: Right to Die Case

Legal Citation 521 U.S. 702

Year of Decision: 1997

KEY ISSUES

Is a state statute that bans assisted suicide unconstitutional as a violation of the due process clause?

HISTORY OF THE CASE

The state of Washington had a statute that made it a felony to knowingly cause or aid another person to attempt suicide. Four physicians, including Harold Glucksberg, M.D., a nonprofit organization, Compassion in Dying, and three gravely ill persons brought suit against the state alleging the statute was unconstitutional. The federal district court found the assisted suicide ban unconstitutional as an undue burden on a protected liberty interest. The Ninth Circuit Court of Appeals affirmed the district court's decision and the U.S. Supreme Court granted review.

SUMMARY OF ARGUMENTS

The state of Washington argued that its interest in the preservation of human life and the protection of the integrity of the medical profession, among others, was rationally related to prohibiting assisted suicide. The state also argued that the interest asserted by the respondents was not deeply rooted in national history or tradition and it would be difficult to confine the right to terminally ill persons.

Harold Glucksberg and the other respondents argued the ban on assisting suicide was an unconstitutional violation of a liberty interest, the right to die or to control one's final days, protected by the Fourteenth Amendment due process clause.

DECISION

Chief Justice Rehnquist gave the opinion of the Court, finding that the issues before the Court were whether the liberties protected by the due process clause included a right to commit suicide and thus, a right to assistance in committing suicide. The Court found that the statute was rationally related to a legitimate state interest, therefore, the statute did not violate the due process clause.

Justice Rehnquist first examined the legal traditions and practices with respect to assisted suicide and found that it was a crime in almost every state to assist an individual in committing suicide. Moreover, suicide and assisted suicide had been punished for over 700 years. Justice Rehnquist next examined the due process clause, finding that it provided protection for certain fundamental rights and liberty interests against governmental intrusion. When performing a substantive due process analysis, only fundamental rights and liberties that were deeply rooted in national history and tradition received protection and such fundamental rights and liberties must be carefully described. Justice Rehnquist determined that history and tradition rejected the asserted "right to die." Justice Rehnquist also reviewed the decisions of the Court in *Planned Parenthood of Southeastern Pa. v. Casey* (1992) and *Cruzan v. Director, Missouri Dept. of Health* (1990), finding the right in Cruzan to have life sustaining treatment withheld was consistent with national history and tradition and had not been formed out of personal autonomy concepts. Thus, Justice Rehnquist found that the right to assisted suicide was not a fundamental liberty interest that was protected by the due process clause. Justice Rehnquist also reviewed the state's interest in having a ban on assisted suicide and concluded that the statute was rationally related to the state's interest.

Justice O'Connor concurred, finding that there was no general right to commit suicide and the state's interest justified a prohibition on assisted suicide. Justice O'Connor found it unnecessary to address whether suffering patients had an interest in obtaining relief, as these patients had the opportunity to obtain medicines that would hasten death.

Justice Stevens also concurred indicating that there might be some situations in which the Washington statute would be invalid, although history and tradition weighed in favor of refusing to find a fundamental right to commit suicide. Justice Stevens felt the *Cruzan* decision was an authorization of conduct that would hasten death, though the source of that authorization was the right to refuse medical treatment and an interest in dignity. Stevens felt that the gravely ill plaintiffs, who later died, may have had a liberty interest even stronger than Nancy Cruzan had, that of avoiding indignity and intolerable pain. Therefore, Justice Stevens found the state's interest in banning assisted suicide did not have the same force in all cases. Justice Stevens concluded that little distinction existed between the terminally ill patient who removes life support and the patient who seeks physician assistance in committing suicide.

Justice Souter wrote a separate concurrence reviewing the history of substantive due process law and determining that the Washington statute may prevent a doctor from exercising his or her best professional judgment. Justice Souter found substantive due process decisions were directly tied to how the statements of competing interests between state and individual were framed and analogized the right to die decision to the decision to choose to have an abortion.

AFTERMATH

Since *Washington v. Glucksberg*, no state has enacted legislation legalizing physician-assisted suicide. Oregon remains the only state to enact a statute permitting physician-assisted suicide, the Death with Dignity Act. However, in 2003, Arizona, Hawaii, and Vermont introduced legislation to legalized physician-assisted suicide.

SIGNIFICANCE

While the Court has recognized the due process clause included the rights to marry, have children, have an abortion, use contraception, direct the education and upbringing of one's children, and secure marital privacy, the Court refused to recognize a right to die; therefore, affirmative assistance to a person attempting suicide may still be punished.

RELATED CASES

Planned Parenthood of Southeastern Pa. v. Casey, 505 U.S. 833 (1992)

Cruzan v. Director, Missouri Dept. of Health, 497 U.S. 261 (1990)

RECOMMENDED READING

Colby, William H. *Long Goodbye: The Deaths of Nancy Cruzan.* Carlsbad, Calif.: Hay House, 2002.

Fireside, Bryna J. Cruzan v. Missouri: *The Right to Die Case.* Berkeley Heights, N.J.: Enslow Publishers, 1999.

Lois L. Shepherd, *Dignity and Autonomy after* Washington v. Glucksberg: *An Essay about Abortion, Death and Crime,* 7 Cornell Journal of Law and Public Policy 431 (1998).

Case Title: *Washington v. Texas*

Alternate Case Title: Willing Witness Case

Legal Citation: 388 U.S. 14

Year of Decision: 1967

KEY ISSUES

Does a defendant in a state criminal trial have a right to obtain witnesses in his favor?

HISTORY OF THE CASE

Washington was convicted of murder in connection with a fatal shooting. His accomplice, Fuller, had been convicted earlier and was willing to give testimony at Washington's trial that was "vital" to Washington's defense. Nonetheless, he was barred from doing so by a Texas statute that prevented persons charged with or convicted of the same crime from testifying for one another, although they could testify for the prosecution. Washington appealed to the Texas Court of Criminal Appeals on the grounds that, by depriving him of Fuller's testimony, Texas had denied him the due process of law. The Texas Court of Crim-

inal Appeals upheld the conviction, and Washington appealed to the U.S. Supreme Court.

SUMMARY OF ARGUMENTS

Washington's attorney argued that the Texas statute deprived him of compulsory process for obtaining witnesses, thus violating his Fourteenth Amendment right to the due process of law.

Texas argued that its statute was a permissible means of reducing the opportunity for perjury in criminal trials.

DECISION

Chief Justice Warren, writing for a unanimous Court, reversed the conviction. The opinion held that the right of a criminal defendant to compulsory process for obtaining favorable witnesses, guaranteed in federal courts by the Sixth Amendment, also applied to state criminal trials because it was incorporated in the Fourteenth Amendment's notion of "due process." Chief Justice Warren argued that the right to compel the attendance of witnesses "is in plain terms the right to present a defense. . . . This right is a fundamental element of due process of law." By making Fuller's testimony inadmissible in Washington's defense, the Texas statute clearly deprived Washington of this right. The chief justice also noted that the statute could not be justified as a means of preventing perjury because it allowed for a person in Fuller's position to testify *against* the defendant.

Concurring in the result by writing a separate opinion, Justice Harlan disagreed with the Court's reliance on the Sixth Amendment to justify its decision. He noted that "the Due Process clause is not a series of isolated points [*i.e.,* clauses drawn from other amendments], but is rather a rational continuum which, broadly speaking, includes a freedom from all substantial arbitrary impositions and purposeless restraints." In this case, Texas barred the defendant's use of admittedly relevant testimony, and Justice Harlan felt that this was unconstitutional.

AFTERMATH

After *Washington v. Texas,* the compulsory process clause applied to state proceedings, though federal rules of evidence determined whom a defendant could call as a witness.

SIGNIFICANCE

The decision incorporated the right to compulsory process, obtaining witnesses favorable to defendant's position, into the Fourteenth Amendment.

RELATED CASES

Gideon v. Wainwright, 372 U.S. 335 (1963)

Duncan v. Louisiana, 391 U.S. 145 (1968)

RECOMMENDED READING

Jerold H. Israel, *Foreword: Selective Incorporation Revisited,* 71 Georgia Law Journal 253 (1982).

Case Title: *Williams v. State of Florida*

Legal Citations: 399 U.S. 78; 26 L.Ed. 2d. 446; 90 S.Ct. 1893

Year of Decision: 1970

KEY ISSUES

Did Florida statutes requiring that a defendant give the names of alibi witnesses to the prosecution in advance of trial, and that the court impanel a jury of only six members, violate the defendant's constitutional rights?

HISTORY OF THE CASE

Before a Florida robbery trial, the defendant, Johnny Williams, filed two motions. The first sought a protective order excusing him from the requirements, under a Florida rule of criminal procedure, that he furnish the prosecuting attorney in advance of trial with the names and addresses of any alibi witnesses and information about the place he was claiming to have been. He objected to the disclosure requirements on the ground that the rule compelled him to be a witness against himself in violation of his Fifth and Fourteenth Amendment rights. His second motion sought to impanel a 12-person jury instead of the six-person jury provided by Florida statute in all but capital cases. Both motions were denied. The defendant was convicted as charged and was sen-

tenced to life imprisonment. The Florida District Court of Appeals affirmed, rejecting the defendant's claims that his Fifth and Sixth Amendment rights had been violated.

SUMMARY OF ARGUMENTS

The appellant argued (1) that the Florida statute violated his privilege against self-incrimination, as provided by the Fifth and Fourteenth Amendments of the U.S. Constitution, and (2) that his constitutional rights were violated when the trial court denied his request for a trial by a jury of 12 instead of six. The state of Florida argued that the alibi disclosure did not violate the due process clause of the Fourteenth Amendment nor the Fifth Amendment privilege against self-incrimination. Further, the state of Florida argued that having 12 jurors was not essential to fulfilling the jury's purpose.

DECISION

The U.S. Supreme Court affirmed the state court's decision. An opinion by Justice White, expressing the view of six members of the court, held in Part I that the notice-of-alibi rule was constitutional. The Court also held, in Part II, expressing the view of seven members of the Court, that the six-person jury was constitutional.

AFTERMATH

After this decision, many states began using smaller juries. Only two years later, in *Apodaca v. Oregon* and *Johnson v. Louisiana,* a closely divided Court further diluted the Sixth Amendment guarantee to a trial by jury and temporarily, at least, appeared to disincorporate that procedural safeguard. The Court upheld Oregon and Louisiana statutes that allowed a less-than-unanimous jury verdict to convict defendants of a felony.

SIGNIFICANCE

White found the common law requirement of a 12-member jury, arising in the 18th century, to be merely an historical accident, and that a six-member jury could fulfill the same functions as a 12-member jury.

RELATED CASES

Collins v. Youngblood, 497 U.S. 37 (1990)

McKoy v. North Carolina, 494 U.S. 433 (1990)

Payne v. Tennessee, 501 U.S. 808 (1991)

RECOMMENDED READING

Eric D. Blumenson, *Constitutional Limitations on Prosecutorial Discovery,* 18 Harvard Civil Rights–Civil Liberties Law Review 123 (winter 1983).

Mykkeltvedt, Roald Y. *The Nationalization of the Bill of Rights.* New York: Associated Faculty Press, 1983.

Case Title: *Wolf v. Colorado*

Legal Citations: 388 U.S. 25; 69 S.Ct. 1359

Year of Decision: 1949

KEY ISSUES

Is the Fourth Amendment's prohibition against unreasonable searches and seizures applicable to state-level investigations?

HISTORY OF THE CASE

The first 10 amendments to the Constitution, collectively called the Bill of Rights, originally were applicable only to actions taken by the federal government against citizens. Over the years, the Court has "incorporated" the amendments into the Fourteenth Amendment so that they not only apply to the federal government but to state governments as well. When a federal policing agency violated the Fourth Amendment, any evidence was held inadmissible under a judicially constructed doctrine called the exclusionary rule. This doctrine had not been examined as it would apply to the states until this case.

Julius Wolf was convicted in state court of conspiring with others to commit abortions. The prosecution offered evidence obtained by a search and seizure that the U.S. Supreme Court had held unreasonable and in violation of the Fourth Amendment. Since the exclusionary rule applied only to federal searches and seizures, the Court admitted the evidence. The Colorado Supreme Court affirmed the conviction. The U.S. Supreme Court agreed to hear the case because of the importance of the issue presented.

SUMMARY OF ARGUMENTS

Wolf argued that the evidence was illegally obtained and therefore should have been excluded from trial. He maintained that the harm caused was the same and should therefore be protected the same way.

The state of Colorado argued that since the Fourth Amendment had not been incorporated to apply to state police searches, the evidence was properly admitted by the state court.

DECISION

Justice Frankfurter wrote the majority opinion in the 6-3 decision affirming Wolf's conviction. The Court held that the due process clause of the Fourteenth Amendment encompassed a large part of the Fourth Amendment but not the amendment's full protection. Subsequently, the Court found that the Fourth Amendment remedy of excluding illegally seized evidence was not required by due process. The Court reviewed practices in American and British jurisdictions and concluded that the exclusionary rule was not necessary to the implementation of the right of privacy. The exclusionary rule is not part and parcel of the Fourth Amendment. The rule is a judicially created remedy available only in federal courts. As a result, the Court believed that the evidence in Wolf's trial was properly admitted.

AFTERMATH

The decision in *Wolf* effectively incorporated the Fourth Amendment into the Fourteenth Amendment, making it applicable to the states. However, the Court found that the exclusionary rule was not mandatory and was not included in the incorporation. However, the Court overruled its treatment of the exclusionary rule in MAPP V. OHIO.

SIGNIFICANCE

Wolf stands out as a reminder of the frailty of assumed constitutional protections. The Court realizes that the exclusionary rule is not absolute and that the Fourth Amendment is a deterrent for police misconduct and not a safeguard for individual privacy.

RELATED CASES

Mapp v. Ohio, 367 U.S. 643 (1961)

Stone v. Powell, 428 U.S. 465 (1976)

Weeks v. U.S., 232 U.S. 383 (1914)

RECOMMENDED READING

Francis A. Allen, *The* Wolf *Case: Search and Seizure, Federalism, and Civil Liberties*, 45 Illinois Law Review 1 (1950).

———, *Federalism and the Fourth Amendment: A Requiem for* Wolf, 1961 Supreme Court Review 1 (1961).

Yale Kamisar, Wolf *and* Lustig *Ten Years Later: Illegal State Evidence in State and Federal Courts*, 43 Minnesota Law Review 1084 (1959).

Case Title: *Woodson v. North Carolina*

Legal Citations: 428 U.S. 280; 49 L.Ed. 2d. 944; 96 S.Ct. 2978

Year of Decision: 1976

KEY ISSUES

Did North Carolina, in enacting a mandatory death penalty law for first-degree murder, allow adequate procedural due process?

HISTORY OF THE CASE

After the U.S. Supreme Court's decision in *Furman v. Georgia* in 1972—which held that the imposition of the death sentence under certain state statutes constituted cruel and unusual punishment in violation of the Eighth and Fourteenth Amendments because under such statutes the juries had untrammeled discretion to impose or withhold the death penalty—the North Carolina Supreme Court held unconstitutional the provision of the North Carolina death penalty statute that gave the jury unbridled discretion to return a verdict of guilty of first-degree murder without capital punishment, but held further that such provision was severable so that the statute survived as a mandatory death penalty law. Thereafter, the North Carolina legislature enacted a new law that made the death penalty mandatory

for first-degree murder, which includes any willful, deliberate, and premeditated killing and any murder committed in perpetrating or attempting to perpetrate a felony. Upon a jury trial in a North Carolina state court under the new statute, two defendants were convicted of first-degree murder for their participation in an armed robbery and were sentenced to death. The North Carolina Supreme Court affirmed.

SUMMARY OF ARGUMENTS

The petitioners argued that the imposition of the death penalty under any circumstances was cruel and unusual punishment in violation of the Eighth and Fourteenth Amendments. The petitioners contended that their sentences were imposed in violation of the Constitution because North Carolina had failed to eliminate discretion, use of judgment based on the circumstances, from all phases of its procedure for imposing capital punishment.

The state argued that the legislation sought to remove any sentencing discretion in the imposition of capital punishment and thus was not in violation of the Eighth Amendment. Specifically, the state argued that the legislation fixed the problems in the death penalty statute that were found to be unconstitutional in *FURMAN V. GEORGIA* (1972).

DECISION

The U.S. Supreme Court reversed the judgment of the Supreme Court of North Carolina and sent the case back to the Supreme Court of North Carolina for further proceeding guided by the court's decision. Although unable to agree on an opinion, five members of the court agreed that the imposition of the mandatory death sentence under the North Carolina statute violated the prohibition against the infliction of cruel and unusual punishment under the Eighth and Fourteenth Amendments.

Justices Powell and Stevens announced the judgment of the court and filed an opinion, delivered by Justice Stewart, expressing the view that (1) the imposition of the death penalty did not, under all circumstances, constitute cruel and unusual punishment, (2) the purpose of the Eighth Amendment was to assure that the state's power to punish was exercised within the limits of civilized standards, thus requiring a determination of contemporary standards regarding the infliction of capital punishment, (3) although the mandatory death penalty for specified offenses was uniformly followed by the states at the time the Eighth Amendment was adopted, almost from the outset jurors reacted unfavorably to the harshness of mandatory death sentences, resulting in frequent refusals to convict in order to avoid subjecting defendants to automatic death sentences, and thus most state legislatures eventually replaced automatic death penalty statutes with discretionary jury sentencing, (4) the North Carolina mandatory death penalty statute was unconstitutional as being inconsistent with contemporary standards rejecting automatic imposition of the death sentence upon every person convicted of a specified offense, (5) the North Carolina statute did not provide a constitutionally tolerable response to the *Furman* decision's rejection of unbridled jury discretion in the imposition of capital sentences, since it was reasonable to assume that many juries under mandatory statutes would continue to consider the grave consequences of a conviction in reaching a verdict, and North Carolina's statute provided no standards to guide the jury in its inevitable exercise of the power to determine which first-degree murderers should live and which should die, and no meaningful appellate review of the jury's decision, and (6) the North Carolina statute was also unconstitutional on the ground that, in capital cases, the fundamental respect for humanity underlying the Eighth Amendment required consideration of the character and record of the individual offender and the circumstances of the particular offense as a constitutionally indispensable part of the process of inflicting the death penalty.

AFTERMATH

In 1976, the Court upheld three statutes that allowed for the discretionary imposition of the death penalty where there are objective standards and rules to control the discretion of those charged with imposing the penalty (*Proffitt v. Florida*, 428 U.S. 242; *Jurek v. Texas*, 428 U.S. 262; *Gregg v. Georgia*, 428 U.S. 153). The court struck down statutes that had mandatory death

sentences for certain crimes (*Woodson v. North Carolina*; ROBERTS V. LOUISIANA, 428 U.S. 325).

These cases were not decided with a majority opinion. Justices Brennan and Marshall voted to strike down the death penalty under the Eighth Amendment prohibition against cruel and unusual punishment. Chief Justice Burger and Justices White, Blackmun, and Rehnquist voted to uphold the use of the death penalty in all five cases. Justices Stewart, Powell, and Stevens voted to allow the discretionary systems in the first three cases but to invalidate the mandatory systems. It was these three swing votes that accounted for the differing results.

The Court has not required that a jury rather than judge determine whether the death penalty should be imposed after the defendant has been found guilty of an offense that may be punished by death. A state may have a death penalty system that allows a judge to disregard a jury's recommendation of life imprisonment and instead impose a capital sentence on the defendant if the system is otherwise procedurally fair (*Spaziano v. Florida*, 468 U.S. 447 [1984]).

SIGNIFICANCE

The Supreme Court has held that the government may impose the death penalty on persons for certain crimes without violating either the due process clause of the Fourteenth Amendment or the Eighth Amendment prohibition of cruel and unusual punishment.

RELATED CASES

Delo v. Lashley, 507 U.S. 272 (1993)

Graham v. Collins, 506 U.S. 461 (1993)

Sawyer v. Whitley, 505 U.S. 333 (1992)

RECOMMENDED READING

Stephen Gilers, *Deciding Who Dies*, 129 University of Pennsylvania Law Review 1 (November 1980).

Sheleff, Leon Shaskolsky. *Ultimate Penalties.* Columbus: Ohio State University Press, 1987.

The Supreme Court, 1975 Term, 90 Harvard Law Review 63 (November 1976).

EXECUTIVE PRIVILEGE

Case Title: *Haig v. Agee*

Legal Citation: 453 U.S. 280

Year of Decision: 1981

KEY ISSUES

May the president, consistent with the First and Fifth Amendments of the U.S. Constitution and acting through the secretary of state, revoke the passport of an American citizen on the ground that the holder's activity in foreign countries has caused or is likely to cause damage to the foreign policy or national security of the United States?

HISTORY OF THE CASE

Philip Agee was an American citizen who had been employed by the Central Intelligence Agency (CIA). While at the CIA he was trained in clandestine operations, including the ways to identify and protect intelligence officers overseas. He announced a campaign to expose the officers in the CIA and agents working in foreign countries. In addition, he announced that he would expose them and drive them out of the countries in which they were operating. His actions resulted in several CIA agents being exposed. In response to these activities the secretary of state, Alexander Haig, revoked Agee's passport while he was living in West Germany. Haig sent a notice to Agee in which he explained that his action was based on a regulation that authorized the revocation of passport when the secretary determined an American citizen's activities abroad "are causing or likely to cause serious damage to the national security or the foreign policy of the United States." The notice that Agee received advised him of his right to a post-revocation hearing.

Agee responded by filing suit against Haig in federal district court. He alleged that the regulation relied on by Haig had not been authorized by Congress and was impermissibly overbroad. As a result, the statute violated his First Amendment right to criticize the policies of the U.S. government. In addition, he argued that the failure to provide him with a pre-revocation hearing violated his right to procedural due process

established by the Fifth Amendment of the U.S. Constitution.

The federal district court granted summary judgment for Agee and ordered Haig to return his passport. The court reasoned the statute exceeded the secretary's powers under the Passport Act of 1926, which authorized the secretary to "grant and issue passports, and cause passport to be granted, issued and verified in foreign countries by diplomatic representatives of the United States under such rules as the President shall designate and prescribe." The court of appeals affirmed this decision and held that Haig was required to show that Congress had authorized the regulation by express delegation or implied such by "substantial and consistent" administrative practice.

SUMMARY OF ARGUMENTS

Agee argued that Haig, acting on behalf of the president, violated his rights under the First and Fifth Amendments. His First Amendment argument was that by revoking his passport, Haig infringed on his right to criticize the government. His Fifth Amendment argument was that Haig denied him procedural due process by not providing him with a pre-revocation hearing.

Haig argued that the statute and the 1926 act provided him with the authority as secretary of state to revoke Agee's passport because Agee violated both provisions. Agee's acting contrary to the interest of the U.S. government and to the detriment of its instruments required the secretary to revoke his passport to protect the safety of the CIA agents and the national security.

DECISION

Justice Burger wrote for the majority. He held that the 1926 Passport Act authorized the revocation of Agee's passport. He reasoned that the challenged regulation was exercised in a "sufficient, substantial and consistent" manner and therefore justified the conclusion that Congress intended to approve it. In addition, he reasoned that as applied, the regulation was constitutional.

Justice Burger held that the Passport Act did not explicitly give the secretary the power to revoke a passport, but that the authority Haig exercised was consistent with the "broad rule making authority granted in the [1926] Act." He noted matters of foreign policy are of such a nature that they rarely are subject to judicial intervention, particularly because of their close relation to national security.

He went on to note that the nature of a passport is that of a letter of introduction from the host country, and it vouches for the bearer. The only means by which an American citizen may leave and reenter the country is with a passport. It is a travel control document that vouches for allegiance of the bearer to the United States.

He traced the history of regulation of passport to support the argument that passports historically had been subject to withdrawal by executive authority on the basis of national security and foreign policy. The first Passport Act of 1856 gave the secretary the authority to grant and issue passports under rules and regulations established by the president. The president and secretary construed the broad language of the statute to allow them to withhold passports for reasons of national security and foreign policy. In 1918 Congress enacted the first travel control statute. The statute prevented the international travel of citizens if it would be contrary to national security. The legislative history of the act revealed that the statute was designed to prevent renegade Americans traveling abroad and transferring information about military information to persons not entitled to it. The 1926 Passport Act was enacted with this background and Justice Burger found that "[t]here is no evidence of any intent to repudiate the long-standing administrative construction." Justice Burger stated that absent showing that Congress intended a different construction he would follow the administrative construction established by the 1856 statute.

Justice Burger also noted that the history of executive orders relating to this issue established that potential damage to national security was the single most important variable used by the president and the secretary of state in deciding to revoke a passport. The president's promulgation of executive orders and the Department of State's submission of reports continually presented to Congress the history of the Passport Act's administrative construction.

The Court refuted Agee's argument that the secretary could establish implicit congressional approval only through consistent and long-standing enforcement of the claimed power. Justice Burger held that such a reading was inaccurate. The frequency with which a statute is enforced does not determine how viable the statute is; a regulation's validity does not depend on the number of situations it applies to or how often it is enforced. Burger explained that the secretary of state rarely had been forced to exercise this power to protect national security, but although the power was not used often it was used consistently.

Justice Burger went on to contend that the protection accorded beliefs is different from the protection afforded actions. Though Agee had the right to express his views, which were critical of the United States, he could not act in such a manner that was detrimental to national security: "Revocation of passports undeniably curtails travel, but the freedom to travel abroad with a 'letter of introduction' in the form of a passport issued by the sovereign is subordinate to national security and foreign policy considerations; as such, it is subject to reasonable government regulation." The protection of foreign policy is a government interest of great importance: "Measures to protect the secrecy of our Government's foreign intelligence operations plainly serve these interests." Justice Burger concluded that Agee had acted in a manner not only to compromise the security of the United States but also to endanger the interest of other countries. He concluded that restricting Agee's travel was the government's only mechanism to limit his activities.

Justice Burger refuted Agee's First Amendment argument on the grounds that the Constitution does not protect speech whose aim is to interfere with and obstruct intelligence operations. This conduct was beyond the reach of law. He concluded that "[t]o the extent the revocation of his passport operates to inhibit Agee, it is an inhibition of action, rather than of speech" (quoting *Zemel v. Rusk* [1965]).

Based on the facts, the Court held that the government was not required to hold a pre-revocation hearing. The substantial likelihood of serious damage resulting from Agee's actions justified the immediate revocation to ensure that "the holder may not exploit the sponsorship of his travels by the United States." The Constitution required only a statement of reasons and the opportunity for a prompt post-revocation hearing.

Justice Blackmun concurred. He stated that the Court should have explicitly overruled *Zemel v. Rusk* (1965) and *Kent v. Dulles* (1958), inasmuch as they suggest long-standing executive policy and construction is not probative of the fact the secretary and the president do have the authority to revoke passports. In that he felt that the Court had in effect done just that, he joined the opinion.

Justice Brennan, who was joined by Justice Marshall, dissented on the grounds that the Court's reliance of previous decisions to support its decision was misplaced. He asserted that what the Court had in fact done was depart from the holdings in those cases. He noted that neither the *Kent* nor the *Zemel* case supported the contention that long-standing executive policy or construction is sufficient proof that Congress implicitly authorized the action of the secretary of state. He noted that the point the Court should make is that the authority of the executive to revoke passports involves important constitutional rights, and the Court should narrowly construe this power of the executive so that these constitutional rights are not diluted or curtailed: "The point that *Kent* and *Zemel* make, and that today's opinion should make, is that the Executive's authority to revoke passports touches an area fraught with important constitutional rights, and that the Court should therefore 'construe narrowly all delegated powers that curtail or dilute them.'" The presumption is that the secretary must be granted the authority by Congress to revoke passports before he may act on such authority. To overcome this presumption the government must prove implied delegation by "administrative practice sufficiently substantial and consistent." He argued that only in this way may the government satisfy to the Court that Congress has implicitly approved the exercise of such authority.

He concluded that the Court had overruled the case history on this issue. Congress has lawmaking authority within our system, and the Court's decision ignored that.

AFTERMATH

The Court has continued to extend the authority of the executive in areas where the Congress has not expressly prohibited the granting of such authority. In *Dames & Moore v. Regan* (1981), the Court held that the president in a national emergency has broad power to resolve private claims against foreign countries through executive agreement. Among these powers are the powers to freeze a foreign country's assets, transfer the assets from the United States, and nullify any licensed attachments against those assets.

In 1982 Congress passed the Intelligence Identities Protection Act, designed to prohibit the disclosure of the identities of U.S. foreign intelligence operatives by making such revelations criminal. This legislation reflected the concern that exposure of such agents could threaten their personal safety and affect the efficiency of intelligence operations abroad.

Agee moved to Cuba and in 2000, in conjunction with his protest against the U.S. trade embargo, began a web-based travel business to bring Americans to Cuba.

SIGNIFICANCE

The Court expanded the authority of the executive in foreign affairs. Where the executive was formerly required to meet the requirement set out in *Zemel* and *Kent*—to demonstrate that in the absence of express grant of authority, Congress implied authorization—this case rejected the notion that the exercise of authority must be a substantial and consistent practice for it to be deemed implicitly accepted by Congress. In holding that the "substantial" exercise was no longer required, the Court held that the lack of opportunity to exercise authority did not render it unacceptable. Rather, the consistency in application is what should be considered.

The Court also expounded on the doctrine of seditious libel in ruling that the type of speech Agee exercised was not protected by the First Amendment. Seditious libel is criticism that causes injury to the government. It has its roots in English common law. It became an enforceable offense in England in the early 17th century, where it was designed to combat armed rebellion by prohibiting the publication of scandalous opinions about the Crown, its policies, and its officers. In America the issue of sedition was addressed by the Sedition Act of 1798, which punished criticism of Congress or the president. After the act expired, the issue of sedition was not addressed in any significant way until the Civil War, when President Lincoln tried to use this principle to protect national security. After World War II, the issue of seditious libel once again rose to a level of national significance, this time targeting communism. During those periods the government used the concept to weed out controversial views that it felt were threatening to national security.

RELATED CASES

Dames & Moore v. Regan, 453 U.S. 654 (1981)

Kent v. Dulles, 357 U.S. 116 (1958)

United States v. The Progressive, Inc., 467 F. Supp. 990 (1979)

Zemel v. Rusk, 381 U.S. 1 (1965)

RECOMMENDED READING

Susan D. Charkes, *The Constitutionality of the Intelligence Identities Protection Act,* 83 Columbia Law Review 727 (1983).

William P. Hovell, Brian M. Mueller, and Kirk S. Schumacher, *Separation of Powers—Congressional Acquiescence to Executive Discretion in Foreign Affairs,* 57 The Notre Dame Lawyer 868 (1982).

Judith Schenck Koffler and Bennett L. Gershman, *The New Seditious Libel,* 69 Cornell Law Review 816 (1984).

Case Title: *Schick v. Reed*

Legal Citation: 419 U.S. 256

Year of Decision: 1974

KEY ISSUES

Is it within the president's pardoning power as defined in the Constitution to change a federal prisoner's death sentence to life imprisonment?

HISTORY OF THE CASE

In 1954, Army Master Sergeant Maurice Schick was stationed in Japan and tried for the brutal murder of an eight-year-old girl. Schick admitted the crime, yet he contended that he was insane when he did it. Defense experts testified that the soldier could not distinguish between right and wrong. Prosecution psychiatrists, on the other hand, testified that Schick exhibited nonpsychotic behavioral disorders and was mentally aware of,

and able to control, his actions. The U.S. Army court-martialed Schick for the murder under the Uniform Code of Military Justice (UCMJ). The court sentenced Schick to death—a penalty upheld, first, by the Army Board of Review, and second, by the Court of Military Appeals. For final review, the case was forwarded to President Eisenhower. On March 25, 1965, the president commuted the sentence to dishonorable discharge, forfeiture of all pay and allowances, and confinement at hard labor for the term of Schick's life. The president's action substituted a life sentence for the death sentence imposed in 1954 subject to certain described conditions.

In 1971, Schick filed suit against George Reed, chairman of the U.S. Board of Parole, demanding the board grant him parole. The district court granted the board's motion for summary judgment. The court of appeals affirmed, unanimously upholding the president's power to commute a sentence upon condition that the prisoner not be paroled.

SUMMARY OF ARGUMENTS

Schick argued that the presidential conditions attached to his sentence, which gave him life in prison without parole, put him in a worse position than he would have been in had he contested his death sentence. He contended that if he had beaten the death sentence penalty, and remained alive, he would have since been eligible for parole. In sum, the defendant complained that President Eisenhower exceeded his constitutional powers by imposing a condition not expressly authorized by the statutory UCMJ.

To the contrary, the government argued that President Eisenhower's pardon of Schick's death sentence, with its attached condition, was within his constitutional discretion, and therefore, lawful.

DECISION

After summarizing the facts and delving into the historical origin of the executive power to substitute lesser sentences for more severe ones, the Court majority addressed two questions: Was the conditional commutation of Schick's death sentence lawful? And, if it was lawful, did prior case law retroactively void such conditions?

Article II, section 2 of the Constitution provides that "The President . . . shall have Power to grant Reprieves and Pardons for Offenses against the United States, except in Cases of Impeachment." This prerogative is the source of the president's commutation power. The ruling emphasized that the only limits that can be imposed on the presidential pardon power are those in the Constitution itself.

The majority opinion acknowledged that the commuted sentence was not one for which the statutory UCMJ expressly provided. Nevertheless, it cited previous Supreme Court cases that consistently read the Constitution as authorizing the president to deal with individual cases by granting conditional pardons. In fact, the Court found that treating each case individually is the "very essence of the pardoning power." Additionally, "considerations of public policy and humanitarian impulses support an interpretation of that power" which lawfully allow conditions that are constitutionally unobjectionable to be attached.

Regardless of the legality of applying conditions to sentences, the Court examined whether a particular earlier decision could retroactively nullify their application. The majority considered the case of FURMAN V. GEORGIA, which invalidated the imposition and carrying out of discretionary death sentences. The *Schick* decision did not decide whether *Furman* applied to the military. However, it did rule that even if *Furman* applied to the military, it could not apply retroactively. *Furman* did not alter the conditional commutation granted 12 years earlier in Master Sergeant Schick's case.

In its 11-page dissent, the minority argues that the no-parole condition is constitutionally defective. The opinion stresses the extralegal nature of the executive action and the appropriate retrospective application of *Furman*. It concludes that Schick be resentenced to life with the opportunity for parole.

AFTERMATH

The conditions placed on Schick's revised sentence were upheld. The presidential pardon power as interpreted is only limited by the Constitution itself. Congress cannot limit this power.

SIGNIFICANCE

Schick continued the Supreme Court's historical trend of extending the president's power to pardon, perhaps beyond its originally intended boundaries. One of the few major limitations under Article II, section 2 is that which the major-

ity recognized, namely, the "President may not aggravate punishment."

RELATED CASES

Ex parte Garland, 4 Wall. 333, 18 L.Ed. 366 (1867)

Ex parte Grossman, 267 U.S. 87 (1925)

Ex parte Wells, 18 How. 307, 15 L.Ed. 421 (1856)

Furman v. Georgia, 408 U.S. 238 (1972)

United States v. Wilson, 7 Pet. 150, 8 L.Ed. 640 (1833)

RECOMMENDED READING

Hamilton, Alexander. *The Federalist No. 74*. Edited by J. Cooke. Middletown, Conn.: Wesleyan University Press, 1961.

The Supreme Court, 1974 Term, 89 Harvard Law Review (1975).

Case Title: *United States v. Nixon*

Alternate Case Title: The Watergate Tapes Case

Legal Citation: 418 U.S. 683

Year of Decision: 1974

KEY ISSUES

Does the president have an absolute executive privilege from being forced to provide evidence relevant to the prosecution of a criminal trial?

HISTORY OF THE CASE

Seven men involved in the Watergate break-in, a break-in of the Democratic National Committee's headquarters located in the Watergate complex, were indicted by a federal grand jury. President Richard Nixon was named by the grand jury as an unindicted co-conspirator. Archibald Cox, who had been appointed as special prosecutor to investigate the Watergate affair, obtained a subpoena that required President Nixon to deliver to the district court tape recordings of his meetings with various assistants. The president released certain edited versions of the tapes to the public, but refused to yield the full transcripts to the district court. Both Cox and the president filed special petitions to have the issue heard immediately by the U.S. Supreme Court.

SUMMARY OF ARGUMENTS

President Nixon argued that the courts lacked the power to compel production of the tapes. He asserted that because the dispute was between the president and the special prosecutor, it was purely an executive branch conflict not subject to judicial resolution. He also argued that it was for the president, not the courts, to ascertain the scope of the executive privilege. Finally, President Nixon contended that even if the Court were the proper branch to decide the scope of the privilege, the need for executive confidentiality justified the application of the privilege in this case.

The government contended that even if the Court were to acknowledge the existence of an executive privilege, the need for evidence in this criminal trial outweighed that privilege.

DECISION

The Supreme Court, in an opinion written by Chief Justice Burger, held that the tapes had to be turned over to the district court for an in-chambers inspection by the judge. Chief Justice Burger argued that this controversy was appropriately before the Court, rather than within the president's discretion, because "it is the duty of the courts to say what the law is." Here, the position of special prosecutor had been intended to be highly independent, thus the Court was justified in resolving the conflict between Cox and the president. Chief Justice Burger asserted that the executive privilege flows from the Constitution and the Court is the ultimate interpreter of that Constitution; consequently, it was for the Court and not the president to define the scope of the privilege. He then determined that the privilege was merely presumptive, rather than absolute; thus, it might be overcome in certain cases by the "legitimate needs of the judicial process." Chief Justice Burger then proceeded to balance the interests of the president and the prosecution.

He began by noting that the president's right to secrecy was different from that of an ordinary individual: "A President and those who assist him must be free to explore alternatives in the process of shaping policies and making decisions and to do so in a way many would be unwilling to express except privately." Nonetheless, Cox had proven that the tapes were relevant to the government's case and "[t]he need to develop all relevant facts in the adversary system is both fundamental and comprehensive." Chief Justice Burger asserted that the claim of privilege did not rest on the ground that the tapes contained military or diplomatic secrets; thus, it was appropriate to subordinate the privilege to the search for truth in a criminal trial. He was quick to note that this decision was based on a unique set of facts. The president had asserted only a "generalized interest in confidentiality," while the specific need for relevant evidence in a criminal trial is a requirement of the Fifth Amendment's guarantee of due process.

Chief Justice Burger noted that in conducting the inspection of the president's tapes, "the District Court has a very heavy responsibility to see to it that Presidential conversations . . . are accorded that high degree of respect due the President of the United States." Even under the circumstances, President Nixon's communications were to receive "the greatest protection consistent with the fair administration of justice."

AFTERMATH

Twelve days after the decision, the president made an abridged transcript of the tapes available to the public. Fifteen days after the decision, President Nixon resigned.

SIGNIFICANCE

While the outcome of the case was unfavorable to President Nixon, *United States v. Nixon* expanded the power of the presidency. This was the first time the Supreme Court acknowledged that an executive privilege exists; the decision thus resolved decades of controversy over the constitutionality of that privilege.

RELATED CASES

Nixon v. Fitzgerald, 457 U.S. 731 (1982)

Youngstown Sheet & Tube Co. v. Sawyer, 343 U.S. 579 (1952)

RECOMMENDED READING

Kurland, Philip B. *Watergate and the Constitution.* Chicago: University of Chicago Press, 1978.

Westin, Alan. U.S. v. Nixon: *The President Before the Supreme Court.* New York: Chelsea House Publishers, 1974.

Case Title: *Wiener v. United States*

Alternate Case Title: The Executive Power-to-Remove Case

Legal Citation: 357 U.S. 349

Year of Decision: 1958

KEY ISSUES

May the president remove a member of an independent adjudicatory body, without cause, in the absence of a congressional grant of such removal power?

HISTORY OF THE CASE

Congress created the War Claims Commission to adjudicate claims for personal injury or property damage suffered at the hands of the enemy during World War II. The commission was composed of three members and was to wind up affairs three years after the final date for submission of claims, which was set as 1952. The tenure of the commissioners was defined as the duration of the commission, and Congress made no provision for the removal of a commissioner. Myron Wiener was appointed as a commissioner by President Harry S. Truman, but was removed by President Dwight D. Eisenhower in 1953 because the president "regard[ed] it as in the national interest to complete the administration of the War Claims Act . . . with personnel of [his] own selection." Wiener later filed suit to recover his salary as a commissioner from the time of his removal until the last day of the commission's existence. He was unsuccessful in the court of claims, and appealed to the U.S. Supreme Court.

SUMMARY OF ARGUMENTS

Wiener argued that his removal was an unconstitutional exercise of the president's removal power, because that power extended only to the executive branch and he was a nonexecutive official.

The government argued that the president possessed broad and complete removal power over such officials so that he could exercise his "constitutional duty of seeing that the laws be faithfully executed."

DECISION

Justice Frankfurter, writing for a unanimous Court, held that Wiener's removal had been unconstitutional. He argued that President Eisenhower's reliance upon the *Myers* case, in which the Court held that the president possesses plenary removal power over *executive* officials, was misplaced. In this case, Wiener was not an executive official but a member of a quasi-judicial body; thus, "the versatility of circumstances often mocks a natural desire for definitiveness." Justice Frankfurter held that for nonexecutive officials, the president's removal power exists only to the extent conferred by Congress. In his opinion, the rule rested on the sound reasoning that "one who holds his office only during the pleasure of another, cannot be depended upon to maintain an attitude of independence against the latter's will." Justice Frankfurter then found, after a discussion of the history surrounding the commission's creation and the express language of the act, that Congress had not intended to confer any removal power upon the president.

AFTERMATH

The president's removal power was limited by *Wiener,* prohibiting the president from exercising his removal power within agencies that had an adjudicatory purpose.

SIGNIFICANCE

Wiener is one of the early cases recognizing a congressional power to create independent agencies, such as the Federal Trade Commission, which are free from presidential removal power.

RELATED CASES

Buckley v. Valeo, 424 U.S. 1 (1976)

Humphrey's Executor v. United States, 295 U.S. 602 (1935)

RECOMMENDED READING

Nathan D. Grundstein, *Presidential Power, Administration and Administrative Law,* 18 George Washington Law Review 285 (1950).

Geoffrey P. Miller, *Independent Agencies,* 1986 Supreme Court Review 41.

INTERSTATE COMMERCE

Case Title: *Carter v. Carter Coal Co.*

Alternate Case Title: The "Coal Mining Regulation" Case

Legal Citations: 298 U.S. 238; 56 S.Ct. 855

Year of Decision: 1936

KEY ISSUES

Was the Bituminous Coal Conservation Act within the power of the federal government to regulate commerce and did it violate the due process clause of the Fifth Amendment to the U.S. Constitution?

HISTORY OF THE CASE

The Bituminous Coal Conservation Act of 1935 was intended to stabilize the coal industry during a period of sustained industrial crisis. The act contained provisions to control the wages, hours, and working conditions of the miners engaged in the production of coal and sought to guarantee their right of collective bargaining in labor disputes. A stockholder in Carter Coal, James Walter Carter, sued to stop the company from complying with the act. The lower courts sustained the act and the stockholder sought review from the U.S. Supreme Court.

SUMMARY OF ARGUMENTS

Carter argued that the act was unconstitutional and void whether considered as a whole or in its several regulatory provisions. He further argued that Congress may only exercise the powers specifically enumerated in the Constitution and in this case, Congress had no power under either the commerce clause or the taxation clause of the Constitution to regulate production of bituminous coal because coal mining was a local activity. The commerce clause grants Congress the exclusive power to regulate interstate commerce, which is commerce with foreign nations, among the states, and with Indian tribes, and the taxation clause grants Congress the power to "lay and collect taxes" for the general welfare of the United States.

The government argued that wages affected cost and cost controlled price, that they are a principal factor in price-cutting and are behind unfair competition, so they may be subjected to federal control and regulation. The government also argued that the act was a valid exercise of the congressional power to regulate commerce since the provisions of the act on collective bargaining had a direct effect on interstate commerce.

DECISION

Justice Sutherland wrote the opinion for the court holding that the provisions of the act were beyond the powers of Congress. Justice Sutherland also found that the regulations in the act were compulsory, thus the regulations delegating the power to fix wages and hours to an arbitrary and unofficial body of coal producers violated the Fifth Amendment right to due process. He also believed that the price-fixing provisions were not separate from the labor provisions and therefore could not stand independently. He did not consider the constitutionality of the price-fixing provisions.

Justice Sutherland reiterated the established principle that the general government may exercise only those powers expressly stated in the Constitution, or those implied powers as were "necessary and proper" to carry out the enumerated powers. He then stated the importance of distinguishing between the powers a general government may exercise and the means that body may use. He reasoned that governmental powers were limited to the Constitution's enumerations, but the means by which they were carried out were not restricted as long as they were consistent with and not prohibited by the Constitution.

Justice Sutherland then reviewed the nature of national and state governments under the Constitution and found that because the states existed prior to the drafting of the Constitution, their legislative powers also existed prior to the Constitution. As such, Justice Sutherland believed that the framers carved from those state powers only portions they felt it wise to confer upon the federal government. The result was that those powers not included in the Constitution were vested in the states. He then argued that every addition to federal powers decreases states' power, and to preserve the balance intended by the Constitution, it was important not to extend the powers of the general government too far beyond the express terms of the Constitution. He recognized the danger of the national government gaining so much power that the states could become little more than "geographical subdivisions of the national domain." He then turned the inquiry to whether the act was a regulation of interstate commerce, believing that the validity of the act was dependent on this finding.

Justice Sutherland did not view the mining of coal and duties leading up to it as commerce once he defined "commerce" as "intercourse for the purposes of trade." He felt that these duties of fixing wages, hours, working conditions, and the bargaining thereof were for the purposes of production, not trade. He added that production was a purely local activity, and that the problems that occurred between employers and employees over wages and working conditions were also local matters, local conditions, and local controversies. He maintained that their only effect on interstate commerce was secondary and indirect. Justice Sutherland concluded by stating that the federal government could not regulate where there was no interstate commerce intercourse.

Chief Justice Hughes wrote a separate opinion stressing that although the act's labor provisions were invalid, the act could be sustained because Congress has the power, limited by the due process clause of the Constitution, to fix prices of commodities sold in interstate commerce.

Justice Cardozo wrote a dissenting opinion, joined by Justices Brandeis and Stone. He concluded that the price-fixing provisions was severable from the labor provisions. He believed that the challenge to the labor provisions was premature because there had not been any enforcement of the provisions at the time of the suit. As such, he did not address the constitutionality of the labor provisions. He then asked whether the regulation of prices came within the commerce power as applied to intrastate sales where interstate prices were directly affected. He found that they did. He urged against using the terms "direct" and "indirect" in relation to the effect on interstate commerce too narrowly and found that the prices for interstate sales of coal had a very close relation to interstate sales, justifying the regulation of both.

Once he came to the conclusion that the commerce clause was a sufficient source of power, he asked whether the power was used within the

confines of the Fifth Amendment. He then recounted previous times in the coal industry when the prices and profits were very low due to overproduction, and the strikes spread far and were very violent. These counts led Justice Cardozo to conclude that only through a system of regulated prices could the industry be stabilized and that this goal was within the Fifth Amendment. He believed that because an evil existed, and the lawmakers had the power to correct it, that they could use any means that they chose.

AFTERMATH

After *Carter,* the Court maintained an "affecting commerce" doctrine in which Congress was allowed to regulate intrastate activities such as manufacturing and mining. It was the prolonged and persistent popular support of regulatory administration that eventually won out, fundamentally altering the constitutional system.

SIGNIFICANCE

Carter was the last case in which the Court invalidated a statute because it exceeded Congress's power under the interstate commerce clause until *National League of Cities* (1976), which held that, under the commerce clause, Congress could not enforce certain provisions of the Fair Labor Standards Act against the states "in areas of traditional government functions." However, *Garcia v. San Antonio Metro. Transit Auth.*, 469 U.S. 528 (1985) overruled *National League,* finding the "traditional government functions" test to be unworkable. The Court also found in *United States v. Lopez,* 115 S.Ct. 1624 (1995) that the commerce clause did not give Congress the power to make it a federal offense to possess a firearm in a school zone. Other recent decisions involving the commerce power have reaffirmed the Court's power to protect the federal balance by way of enforcing the Tenth Amendment, which reserves for the states the powers not delegated to the federal government (*New York v. United States,* 505 U.S. 144 [1992]).

RELATED CASES

A. L. A. Schechter Poultry Corp. v. United States, 295 U.S. 495 (1935)

NLRB v. Jones & Laughlin Steel Corp., 301 U.S. 1 (1937)

RECOMMENDED READING

Richard A. Epstein, *The Proper Scope of the Commerce Power*, 73 Virginia Law Review 1387 (1987).

Case Title: *Champion v. Ames*

Alternate Case Title: The Lottery Case

Legal Citations: 188 U.S. 321; 47 L.Ed. 492; 23 S.Ct. 321

Year of Decision: 1903

KEY ISSUES

Does Congress have the power under the U.S. Constitution to suppress lotteries by prohibiting lottery tickets to be carried from one state to another?

HISTORY OF THE CASE

The Federal Lottery Act of 1895 prohibited the interstate transportation of foreign lottery tickets. It contained three separate features of anti-lottery legislation: (1) use of the United States mails, (2) importations from abroad, and (3) causing lottery tickets to be carried from one state to another by any means other than the mails. The appellant, Charles Champion, was indicted for shipping a box of Paraguayan lottery tickets from Texas to California. He was ordered to give a bond for his appearance at trial and, upon failing to provide one, was taken into custody. He brought suit against the appellee, John Ames, a U.S. marshal seeking a writ of habeas corpus, which is essentially an order issued by the court removing a person from custody. The circuit court rejected his challenge that the act was unconstitutional. He appealed to the U.S. Supreme Court.

SUMMARY OF ARGUMENTS

Champion argued that the act of 1895 was void under the Constitution of the United States and that carrying lottery tickets from one state to another does not constitute commerce among the states. Consequently, Congress cannot make it an offense to cause such tickets to be carried between the states.

The government contended that express companies engaged in the business of transportation from one state to another, for hire, are instruments of commerce among the states. The carrying of lottery tickets from one state to another, therefore, is commerce that Congress regulates, and Congress may make it an offense against the United States to cause lottery tickets to be carried from one state to another.

DECISION

Justice Harlan delivered the opinion for the Court that lottery tickets were subjects of traffic among those who sold or bought them; the carriage of them among the states by independent carriers was interstate commerce; Congress, subject to the limitations of the Constitution, has the authority to regulate such commerce; and legislation to that end is consistent with any limitation upon the exercise of the powers granted to Congress.

Justice Harlan stated that the carrying of lottery tickets from one state to another, by independent carriers, which entitled the holder to money, constituted commerce among the states just as the carrying of "things or commodities" which were ordinary subjects of traffic and had a recognized monetary value constituted interstate commerce. He also stated that the regulation of such commerce was within the power of Congress under the Constitution.

Justice Harlan believed that if Congress had the power to regulate the shipment of goods between the states, it made little sense that Congress must allow the interstate shipment of goods it deemed intolerable and detrimental to the public welfare. He concluded that if the states could prohibit the sale of lottery tickets they deemed harmful to their citizens, then certainly Congress, in the interest of protecting commerce between the states, could prohibit the interstate shipment of lottery tickets. He even found that such a regulation could take the form of a prohibition and remain constitutional. He cautioned, however, that the power of Congress to regulate among the states could not be arbitrary and was subject to the limitations of the Constitution. Therefore, he argued that the power could not be used to infringe upon rights protected by the Constitution. Justice Harlan dismissed the Tenth Amendment issue because "the power to regulate commerce among the [s]tates had been expressly delegated to Congress."

Chief Justice Fuller wrote a dissenting opinion joined by Justices Brewer, Shiras, and Peckham. He maintained that the issue was whether the prohibition of carrying lottery tickets between the states by means other that the mails was within the powers vested in Congress by the Constitution. He argued that the power to preserve and promote the public health was a power originally belonging to the states, not Congress. He then reasoned that the suppression of lotteries as a harmful business fell within the state's police powers.

Chief Justice Fuller reasoned that carrying lottery tickets from one state to another was not interstate commerce. He saw lottery tickets as contracts, and a means of enforcing contractual rights. He felt that the simple act of carrying the tickets between the states did not make them articles of commerce. He feared that such a holding would result in wiping away all state lines, creating a centralized government. He also did not believe that the constitutional grant to Congress to regulate interstate commerce also conferred the absolute power to prohibit it.

AFTERMATH

Champion had a profound influence upon the subsequent development of the national police power and has been regarded as establishing a doctrine regarding the power of Congress to prohibit various kinds of interstate commerce that was far more than the Court proposed to sanction. In 1918, with the passage of the Eighteenth Amendment, which prohibited the manufacture, sale, and transportation of intoxicating liquor, there was a flood of federal prosecutions until the amendment was repealed in 1933. Then, during the New Deal, a period of social reform and economic recovery support by programs and policies introduced by President Franklin Roosevelt, Congress provided for a wide range of civil and criminal penalties in a range of social and economic initiatives. The next major surge in federal criminal jurisdiction came in 1971, when the Court upheld federal regulation of an overinclusive class of activities (see *United States v. Perez*).

After *Champion*, the Court upheld the seizure of a shipment of eggs that violated the Pure Food and Drugs Act of 1906, in *Hipolite Egg Co. v. United States* 45 (1911), holding that the power to seize after arrival at destination was an "appropriate means" to preventing their interstate shipment. The Court then upheld the Mann Act's prohibition of transportation of women in commerce for immoral purposes in *Hoke v. United States* (1913), stating that "Congress had complete power over interstate commerce and could develop means that had the quality of police regulation."

SIGNIFICANCE

Some consider the decision in *Champion v. Ames* to be the source of the determination to use the commerce power for criminal jurisdiction purposes.

RELATED CASES

Gibbons v. Ogden, 9 Wheat. 1 (1824)

Hipolite Egg Co. v. United States, 220 U.S. 45 (1911)

Hoke v. United States, 227 U.S. 308 (1913)

Reid v. Colorado, 187 U.S. 137 (1902)

RECOMMENDED READING

Robert E. Cushman, *The National Police Power under the Commerce Clause of the Constitution,* 3 Minnesota Law Review 289 (1903).

Case Title: *Cooley v. Board of Port Wardens*

Alternate Case Title: The "Dormant Commerce Clause" Case

Legal Citation: 53 U.S. 299

Year of Decision: 1851

KEY ISSUES

Does the commerce clause, the constitutional provision granting Congress the power to regulate commerce with foreign nations, among the states, and with Indian tribes, deprive the states of the power to regulate pilots?

HISTORY OF THE CASE

A Pennsylvania law adopted in 1803 required all ships entering or leaving the port of Philadelphia to use a local pilot or pay a fine into a fund to support retired pilots and their dependents. The board of wardens, which was established to regulate pilots, brought an action against Aaron Cooley, the person shipping goods, for pilot compensation because Cooley sailed a vessel from Philadelphia without a pilot, when one could have been secured. This occurred twice, and both actions were combined in this case. The magistrate gave judgment for the warden, and Cooley appealed to the Court of Common Pleas. The Court of Common Pleas held for the city and the county of Philadelphia. The case was carried to the Pennsylvania Supreme Court, which affirmed the judgment for the city and county of Philadelphia upholding the act and the board of wardens. Cooley then brought the case to the U.S. Supreme Court.

SUMMARY OF ARGUMENTS

The appellant argued that the Pennsylvania statute was unconstitutional and void since it was repugnant to various parts of the Constitution. Specifically, the appellant claimed the Pennsylvania statute violated the commerce clause and the power of Congress to lay and collect taxes, duties, imposts, and excises uniformly throughout the United States, which restricted the ability of states to lay imposts or duties on imports or exports without the consent of Congress.

The appellee argued that the Pennsylvania statute did not violate any provision of the Constitution.

DECISION

Justice Curtis wrote the opinion for the Court upholding the statute and agreeing that the regulation of pilots was a regulation of interstate commerce even though pilots stayed with the ships for only brief periods. Justice Curtis also held that the commerce clause itself preempted an entire field from state regulation when the differences in individual state laws would make it difficult to move goods between states. Justice Curtis also held that the states could regulate those aspects of interstate commerce, such as pilotage, for which local differences necessitated different regulations. On the other hand, the national government could regulate those aspects of interstate commerce that required uniformity of treatment. Thus, the dormant commerce clause was held to restrict state regulation of those aspects of interstate commerce that were "so national in character as to require uniformity in character."

Justice Curtis first found that the state statute constituted a regulation of commerce. The first step of Justice Curtis's analysis was to enumerate a test to resolve whether the power of Congress under the commerce clause was exclusive or concurrent with the states. He then concluded that the Constitution granted concurrent powers to the states and the federal government regarding the regulation of pilots. Justice Curtis then held that the Pennsylvania law was valid because it did not conflict with the two relevant acts of Congress.

Justice Curtis referred to a federal statute adopted in 1789 providing that "all pilots [shall be] regulated in conformity with [such] laws as the States may respectively hereafter enact for the purpose, until further legislative provision shall be made by Congress." By referring to that 1789 statute, he rejected the argument that Congress was granted exclusive power to regulate commerce. He maintained that if the Constitution stripped the states of all power to regulate commerce, then Congress could not delegate such power to the states. Justice Curtis argued that since the 1789 act sanctioned such state statutes, there was "necessarily implie[d] a constitutional power to legislate" on the part of the states. Justice Curtis then argued that the mere grant of such power to Congress impliedly prohibited the states from exercising the same power. He believed that the exercise of that power by Congress is what was incompatible with the exercise of the same power by the states. He maintained, however, that the states could legislate in the absence of congressional regulations.

Justice Curtis wanted to view the power to regulate in terms of the subject being regulated. He stated that the Court must determine whether a "subject" is of a "nature" requiring uniform national regulation or diverse local regulation. He stated that some matters of local concern involve interstate commerce, such as pilotage, but can never be fully dealt with by Congress due to their local character. Thus, Justice Curtis based his decision on whether the statute should be upheld on its distinction between "local" and "national." He believed that the Pennsylvania statute regulating commerce fell into the diversity or local category. He stated that "the nature of the subject [before the Court] is not such as to require exclusive legislation." Justice Curtis concluded that when commercial matters are of national interest, a state may not individually regulate that field. He also reemphasized the Court's adoption of the narrow, "selective" approach to questions concerning the regulation of interstate commerce, rationalizing that the Court's opinion was confined to the precise question before it.

Justice McLean wrote a dissenting opinion stating that the state did not have the power to pass the law. He argued that Congress had the power over the subject of pilotage and should have adopted the law of the state. He was also against allowing the states to regulate an area until such regulation is annulled by Congress. Justice Daniel wrote a concurring and dissenting opinion agreeing with the majority in affirming the lower courts' decisions, but disagreeing with its analysis. He argued that the power to regulate pilots was an original and inherent power in the states that should not have been held subject to the sanction of the federal government.

AFTERMATH

The Court's decision, while simple in theory, was difficult in application. The Court used the test for a long period, but later abandoned it in favor of a balancing test. In the 1977 case *Complete Auto Transit, Inc. v. Brady,* the Court introduced the four-part "economic-realities" test that has since dominated dormant commerce clause jurisprudence. As such, the attempt to classify the subject matter of regulation as either local or national has largely been abandoned. However, *Cooley's* underlying theme still maintains some continuing vitality.

SIGNIFICANCE

The negative, or dormant, commerce clause was first developed in *Cooley,* which greatly expanded the commerce clause, making the nature of the regulated activity determine whether state regulation violated the commerce clause. It was also the first time the Court held that the commerce clause limited state action that burdened interstate commerce even in areas where Congress had not spo-

ken. *Cooley* has been characterized as the "bridge" to modern commerce clause analysis due to its practical approach of distinguishing between commerce activities that can be regulated at the local level and those that need national regulation to ensure equal treatment across the United States.

RELATED CASES

Brown v. Maryland, 25 U.S. 419 (1827)

Gibbons v. Ogden, 22 U.S. (9 Wheat.) 1 (1824)

RECOMMENDED READING

William Cohen, *Congressional Power to Validate Unconstitutional State Laws: A Forgotten Solution to an Old Enigma,* 35 Stanford Law Review 387 (1983).

Martin H. Redish and Shane V. Nugent, *The Dormant Commerce Clause and the Constitutional Balance of Federalism,* Duke Law Journal 569 (1987).

Case Title: *Edwards v. California*

Legal Citation: 314 U.S. 160

Year of Decision: 1941

KEY ISSUES

Whether a state statute that prohibited any person from "bringing into the State any indigent person who is not a resident of the State" passes constitutional muster.

HISTORY OF THE CASE

Many cases have involved state regulations that, either intentionally or otherwise, place barriers upon the importing of goods into the state. As a general rule, the Court has held that the test to which these regulations will be subjected depends on the nature of the state interest being served. The Court has long recognized a constitutional right to travel, even though the precise source of the right remains somewhat obscure. In *Crandall v. Nevada* (1868), the Court invalidated a state law imposing a tax of one dollar on "every person leaving the state by any [vehicle engaged] in the business of transporting passengers for hire." The Court explained: "For all the great purposes for which the Federal Government was formed we are one people, with one common country [and] as members of the same community must have the right to pass and repass through every part of it without interruption."

California had a law that made it a misdemeanor to bring into the state an indigent nonresident. The law was aimed at stemming the flow of "Okies," agricultural workers from Oklahoma and other states hurt by drought and dust storms during the Dust Bowl years. Edwards was a citizen of the United States and a resident of California. In December 1939, he left his home in California for Texas, with the intention of bringing back to California his wife's brother, a Texas resident. Edwards knew that his wife's brother was an indigent person. Edwards and the brother agreed that Edwards should transport the brother to California in Edwards's car. Edwards was convicted and sentenced to six months' imprisonment in the county jail. The superior court upheld the statute as a valid exercise of the police power of the state of California.

SUMMARY OF ARGUMENTS

The state of California argued that each community should care for its own indigent, and that relief is solely the responsibility of local governments. California's argument was based on the problems a huge influx of migrants into California caused in health, morals, and especially finance, the proportions of which were staggering.

Edwards argued that the California law's purpose and effect was to prohibit the transportation of indigent persons across the California border and that the indigent nonresidents who were the real victims of the statute were deprived of the opportunity to exert political pressure upon the California legislature in order to obtain a change in policy.

DECISION

The Court invalidated the law on the grounds that it was an unconstitutional burden on commerce. Justice Byrnes's opinion in *Edwards* quoted the national common market theory advanced by Cardozo in *Baldwin v. G. A. F. Seelig, Inc.* (1941)

as support for the principle that just as a state cannot shut its gates to the influx of competitive commodities, it also is prohibited from thwarting the influx of indigents. Justice Byrnes stated that the Constitution "was framed upon the theory that the people of the several states must sink or swim together." Although the "huge influx of migrants into California in recent years has resulted in problems of health, morals and especially finance, the proportions of which are staggering," no state can "isolate itself from difficulties common to all of them by restraining the transportation of persons and property across its borders."

Justice Byrnes also emphasized that in order to maintain the existence of a national entity, the guarantee of unrestricted personal mobility must be equivalent, if not superior to, the guarantee afforded commercial products. The Court rejected the contention that such state legislation could be justified as a valid exercise of the police power, noting that the statute's sole purpose was to burden interstate commerce by impeding the movement of people across state lines.

Although the Court relied solely on the commerce clause to invalidate the statute, it suggested in passing that it would not accept stereotypical judgments about the poor as justifications for laws disadvantaging them: "Whatever may have been the [previously prevailing] notion, we do not think that it will now be seriously contended that because a person is without employment and without funds he constitutes a 'moral pestilence.'"

Concurring separately, Justice Douglas urged that ultimately the right of personal mobility could be diluted by relying on the commerce clause for its efficacy. Douglas, joined by Justices Murphy and Black, reiterated Miller's statement in the *Crandall* case recognizing that the right of persons to move from state to state is a fundamental right implicit in national citizenship.

AFTERMATH

Subsequent personal mobility decisions have incorporated both the majority's reluctance to enlarge the scope of the privileges and immunities doctrine that equalizes the treatment of citizens from different states, and the concern expressed by Justice Douglas of relegating the protection of the right to travel to the commerce clause provision. Consequently, equal protection increasingly has been invoked as a preferential ground for challenging state legislation that impinges the right to travel.

SIGNIFICANCE

Edwards is frequently cited to support the proposition that the right of interstate travel is a privilege of national citizenship.

RELATED CASES

Baldwin v. G. A. F. Seelig, Inc., 294 U.S. 160 (1941)

Crandall v. Nevada, 73 U.S. 35 (1868)

Shapiro v. Thompson, 394 U.S. 618 (1969)

RECOMMENDED READING

Benson, Paul R., Jr. *The Supreme Court and the Commerce Clause, 1937–1970.* New York: Dunellen, 1970.

Katheryn D. Katz, *More Equal than Others: The Burger Court and the Newly Arrived State Resident*, 19 New Mexico Law Review 329 (1989).

Case Title: *Gibbons v. Ogden*

Legal Citation: 22 U.S. 1

Year of Decision: 1824

KEY ISSUES

Does the commerce clause give Congress or the states the power to regulate interstate commerce?

HISTORY OF THE CASE

The New York legislature granted Robert R. Livingston and Robert Fulton exclusive right to operate steamboats in New York waters. Aaron Ogden obtained permission from Livingston and Fulton to operate his ships between New York and New Jersey. Thomas Gibbons was also operating boats between these two states. He had obtained his license under federal laws on coasting trade. Ogden obtained an injunction to prohibit Gibbons from operating his ships between the points where Ogden received an exclusive right to operate his own ships.

SUMMARY OF ARGUMENTS

Ogden argued that the states, through the Tenth Amendment's reservation of powers, had retained power by which they could regulate commerce within their state; that the federal government did not have exclusive jurisdiction over commerce; and that the grant of exclusive right to operate his ship concerned only intrastate commerce.

Gibbons argued that under Article I, section 8, clause 3, only Congress could regulate interstate commerce and that New York State had illegitimately attempted to regulate interstate commerce by granting exclusive rights and enforcing them with an injunction.

DECISION

Justice Marshall wrote the opinion of the Court, in which he reasoned that any state law that conflicts with a congressional act regulating commerce is void and the congressional act is controlling. He stated that Congress has the power to regulate navigation within the limits of every state and the regulations passed by Congress controlling navigation within New York borders were valid.

The Court rejected Ogden's Tenth Amendment argument and held that Congress was given all power necessary to regulate interstate commerce. He noted, however, that the states may pass regulations that affect some activity related to interstate commerce, as long as the power is from a source other than commerce power.

The Court dismissed Ogden's suit.

AFTERMATH

It was not until later in the 19th century that controversy arose again over the proper interpretation of the commerce clause. During that time Congress began to exercise its power to respond to post–Civil War developments. In the first two decades of the 20th century, congressional attempts to address the negative consequences of industrialism were bolstered. During the New Deal era Congress regulated many areas of everyday life under the guise of the commerce clause. Among many other things, Congress established the 40-hour work week and the first minimum wage. Initially, the Supreme Court was hostile to such legislation, but after President Roosevelt threatened to pack the Court with judges who would support the New Deal legislation, its position began to change rapidly.

Since 1937 the Supreme Court has upheld, with few exceptions, congressional regulations that involve all areas of everyday life. The Court had adopted what is regarded as a realist approach, which allows for regulation in cases in which the activity exerts a "substantial economic effect" on interstate commerce. In the last four decades the commerce clause has been used as conduit through which to effect social change. The Court has deemed congressional legislation constitutional as long as there is a remote connection to interstate commerce.

In a break from its previous decisions, the Court in *National League of Cities v. Usery* invalidated provisions of the Fair Labor Standards Act on the grounds that they exceeded Congress's power under the commerce clause. However, nine years later in *Garcia v. San Antonio Metropolitan Transit Authority,* the Court returned to its realistic approach to regulation under the commerce clause. The Court reasoned that absent "compelling" constitutional reasons such regulations would be upheld. In *United States v. Lopez,* the Court held that Congress may regulate three broad categories of activities under the commerce clause: those in which interstate commercial channels were used, actual instruments of interstate commerce, and those activities having a substantial relationship to interstate commerce.

SIGNIFICANCE

Gibbons was the first case to interpret the scope of Congress's power under the commerce clause. The rule of law set out by Marshall in this case—that any state law affecting interstate commerce that conflicts with federal law is void—is still the rule applied in laws regarding interstate commerce. In addition, the Court still follows the doctrine that the power to regulate commerce is not exclusive and that a state may indirectly regulate interstate commerce.

RELATED CASES

Garcia v. San Antonio Metropolitan Transit Authority, 469 U.S. 528 (1985)

Hammer v. Dagenhart, 247 U.S. 251 (1918)

Heart of Atlanta Motel v. United States, 379 U.S. 241 (1964)

Katzenbaum v. McClung, 379 U.S. 294 (1964)

National Labor Relations Board v. Jones & Laughlin Steel Corporation, 301 U.S. 1 (1937)

National League of Cities v. Usery, 426 U.S. 833 (1976)

United States v. Lopez, 115 S.Ct. 1624 (1995)

RECOMMENDED READING

Richard A. Epstein, *The Proper Scope of the Commerce Power,* 73 Virginia Law Review (1987).

Larry E. Gee, *Federalism Revisited: The Supreme Court Resurrects the Notion of Enumerated Powers by Limiting Congress's Attempt to Federalize Crime,* 27 St. Mary's Law Journal 151 (1995).

Tribe, Laurence H. *American Constitutional Law.* Mineola, N.Y.: Foundation Press, 1978.

———. *Constitutional Choices.* Cambridge, Mass.: Harvard University Press, 1985.

Case Title: *Hammer v. Dagenhart*

Alternate Case Title: Child Labor Decision

Legal Citations: 247 U.S. 251; 38 S.Ct. 529; 62 L.Ed. 1101

Year of Decision: 1918

KEY ISSUES

Does Congress have the right to prohibit the shipment in interstate commerce of products made by minor children?

HISTORY OF THE CASE

Roland Dagenhart had two minor sons, Reuben and John, who both worked in a cotton mill in Charlotte, North Carolina. John was 15 when the suit was filed, and his brother Reuben was under the age of 14. In 1916, Congress passed the Keating-Owen Child Labor Law, which stated that products from mines or factories that were manufactured by children under the age of 14 or children between the ages of 14 and 16 who worked more than eight hours a day or more than six days in a week could not be shipped in interstate commerce. The boys' father obtained an injunction in the U.S. District Court for the Western District of North Carolina to prohibit the enforcement of the law. The injunction was appealed to the U.S. Supreme Court. W. C. Hammer was the U.S. attorney for the Western District of North Carolina.

SUMMARY OF ARGUMENTS

The solicitor general of the United States, John W. Davis, argued that the act was both a regulation of interstate and foreign commerce and totally appropriate under the U.S. Constitution. Further, he argued that the law was a legitimate exercise for the protection of the public health, specifically the health of youth. The extension of laws prohibiting child labor in all factories and mines was reasonable, given that many states had already adopted laws to prevent the employment of children. North Carolina prohibited labor by children under 12. The federal law would encourage uniformity among the states.

The attorneys for the Dagenharts argued that Congress had exceeded its police power because every article or item or person of which it does not approve may for all practical purposes be regulated as having an effect on interstate commerce. In order for Congress to validly exercise its police power, there must be a real evil or injury involved with or related to the product itself. Dagenhart's attorneys further argued that Congress may not impose its will on manufacturers in the various states because there is no real evil accomplished by the commerce itself. The case was argued on April 15 and 16 and decided on June 3, 1918.

DECISION

Justice William Rufus Day wrote the majority opinion for the Court. By a vote of 5–4, the Court declared that the 1916 law was unconstitutional. Justice Day ruled that the Congress had the right to use the commerce clause to regulate transportation when it would prevent harmful results. Thus, it was appropriate for Congress to regulate the shipment of liquor, lottery tickets, or even women who might be sold into debauchery, but in the present case, there was nothing harmful about cotton goods manufactured by youth. The goods themselves were "harmless." Justice Day con-

cluded that merely because goods were made by children, Congress does not have the authority to set a uniform standard for the states as to the age of employment. There is no right to exercise police power over local trade and manufacture. Justice Day noted that every state had some law regarding the employment of children in mines and factories and that in North Carolina, children under the age of 12 were not permitted to work. While he noted that it may be desirable that such laws be uniform among the states, the Constitution gives that principle to state and local government and not to Congress.

Justice Oliver Wendell Holmes wrote the dissenting opinion for Justices McKenna, Brandeis, and Clarke. Holmes's thundering dissent clearly stated that the power to regulate means the power to prohibit. Justice Holmes did not mince words about opinions in McCray v. United States (1904) regarding the manufacturer of oleomargarine, and he left little doubt that he believed the majority's opposition to the child labor law was personal in nature: "It is enough that in the opinion of Congress, the transportation encourages the evil." Justice Holmes compared child labor to adulterated food and white slavery, which all agreed were well within the prerogative of Congress to regulate. The evil of premature and excessive child labor was something he found to be understood in all civilized countries. Holmes said that he was able to keep his own moral concepts to himself, and he advised the majority that Congress can validly use its feelings of morality when making law.

AFTERMATH

The congressional efforts to reverse *Hammer v. Dagenhart* were unsuccessful. Congress tried to pass a tax law to discourage the use of child labor but, in 1922, the Court held that act to be unconstitutional. It was not until 1941 in the case of *U.S. v. Darby Lumber* that the Court overturned its own ruling. In 1923, Reuben Dagenhart, who was then 20, gave an interview to *Labor Magazine* in which he was asked what benefit he received from the suit. "We got some automobile rides with them big lawyers from the North was down here. Oh yes, and they bought both of us a Coca Cola! That's all we got out of it. . . . Oh, John [Reuben's younger brother] and me never was in court, just Pa was there. John and me was just little kids in short pants. I guess we wouldn't of looked like much in court. . . . We were working in the mill while the case was going on."

SIGNIFICANCE

Dagenhart continued to have an effect on labor law, both on working ages and a minimum federal wage. The Court ruled that Congress could not pass a 10 percent tax on the net profits of any company that employed children under a minimum age because the child labor tax was a penalty to force employers to end the use of child labor. In 1941, the Supreme Court unanimously reversed *Hammer v. Dagenhart* and said that the decision was "a departure from the principles which have prevailed in the interpretation of the Commerce clause."

Justice Holmes's dissent was almost immediately recognized as brilliant. In *U.S. v. Darby,* a case addressing the interstate shipment of goods produced by employees paid less than the minimum wage or who worked more than the maximum number of hours, Justice Harlan Stone praised it as "classic."

RELATED CASES

Bailey v. Drexel Furniture Co., 259 U.S. 20 (1922)

U.S. v. Darby Lumber Co., 312 U.S. 100 (1941)

RECOMMENDED READING

Clopper, Edward. *Child Labor in City Streets.* New York: Macmillan, 1912.

Wood, Stephen. *Constitutional Politics in the Progressive Era: Child Labor and the Law.* Chicago: University of Chicago Press, 1968.

Zelizer, Viviana. *Pricing the Priceless Child: The Changing Social Value of Children.* New York: Basic Books, 1985.

Case Title: *Heart of Atlanta Motel v. United States*

Legal Citation: 379 U.S. 241

Year of Decision: 1964

KEY ISSUES

Does Title II of the Civil Rights Act of 1964 violate the U.S. Constitution?

HISTORY OF THE CASE

The 216-room motel, located in downtown Atlanta, sought a declaratory judgment that Title II of the Civil Rights Acts was unconstitutional.

Title II of the Civil Rights Act was passed in January 1964. The act was intended to prohibit discrimination in voting, employment, federally secured programs, and in places of accommodation and public facilities. Title II had three parts. Section 201 (a) provided that "all persons shall be entitled to full and equal enjoyment of goods, services, facilities, privileges, advantages, and accommodations of any place of public accommodation . . . without discrimination or segregation on the ground of race, color, religion, or national origin. Section 201 (b) listed four classes of businesses that serve the public and are places of public accommodation. They include "any inn, hotel, motel, or other establishment which provides lodging to transient guests, other than an establishment located within a building which contains not more than five rooms for rent or hire which is actually occupied by the proprietor of such establishment as his residence." Section 201 (c) defined the phrase "affect commerce": it declared that any of the above listed establishments that provided lodging to transients affects commerce per se.

SUMMARY OF ARGUMENTS

The motel owner argued that the business of the motel was of a local character (although 75 percent of the guests were from out-of-state) and therefore did not affect interstate commerce. In addition, it was argued that by requiring the motel to accommodate African Americans, the act worked unconstitutionally to deprive the owner of liberty and property in violation of the Fifth Amendment. Last, the motel owner argued that the act exceeded the powers of Congress under the commerce clause in that interstate travel was not affected by the operation of the motel.

The United States argued that the motel affected interstate commerce per se as stated by the act, and that the act was within the power of Congress.

DECISION

Justice Clark wrote the opinion of the Court that racial discrimination had a disruptive effect on interstate commerce, and this burden empowered Congress to enact the legislation at issue. In refuting the contention of the motel owner that the business was of a local character and thus did not affect interstate commerce, he reasoned that all that was required for Congress to act was that the local business affect, even in a minimal way, interstate commerce: "Thus the power of Congress to promote interstate commerce also includes the power to regulate the local incidents thereof, including local activities in both the States of origin and destination, which might have a substantial and harmful effect upon that commerce."

He also refuted the contention that the act deprived the motel owner of liberty or property under the Fifth Amendment. He reasoned that the power invoked by Congress in this case was authorized by the Constitution. The power is specific and plenary, requiring only that Congress has a rational basis for finding racial discrimination and that the means selected to eliminate the evil is reasonable and appropriate. If Congress meets these requirements then the motel owner has no "right" to select its guests free from governmental regulation. Justice Clark continued that it was doubtful the motel owner would suffer an economic loss from having to cease its discriminatory practices. However, Clark reasoned that in any case, suffering an economic loss was not sufficient to bar such legislation. Citing *Bowles v. Willingham* (1944), which upheld rent control legislation, he reasoned "that fact that a member of the class which is regulated may suffer economic losses not shared by others . . . has never been a barrier to such legislation."

He concluded that the act served interstate travelers and was within the power granted the legislature by the commerce clause of the Constitution. That the Congress might have pursued other means to eradicating racial discrimination is a policy question within Congress's discretion. The only restriction on this choice of appropriate policy is that it must be reasonably adapted to the permissible constitutional end.

Justice Douglas wrote a separate opinion in which he agreed with the Court's conclusion, but he expressed reservation with basing the holding solely on the commerce clause because he believed the interstate movement of people warranted more protection than the movement of goods.

Justices Black and Goldberg filed concurring opinions.

AFTERMATH

The commerce clause was extended by this case to address the evil of racial discrimination that affected interstate commerce. The clause has been used since to criminalize interstate travel with the purpose of inciting a riot, prohibiting interstate shipments as a means to enforce local laws, and criminalize conduct that does not directly affect federal interest and that is not tied to interstate movement.

In *Perez v. United States* (1971), Perez challenged the constitutionality of Title II of the Consumer Protection Act, which was enacted pursuant to Congress's power under the commerce clause. The Court in upholding the act held that the commerce clause reaches principally three categories of problems: (1) the use of interstate commerce for purposes that Congress deems as misuse; (2) protection of instrumentalities of interstate commerce, such as aircraft or trucks; and (3) activities affecting commerce. In upholding the constitutionality of the act the Court held that it fell within the last category. The Court reemphasized the deference that should be given to a congressional determination if it is rationally based and is tailored to meet a legitimate government interest.

In *Garcia v. San Antonio Metropolitan Transit Authority* (1985), the Court held that the hour and wage provisions of the Fair Labor Standards Act apply to employees of the San Antonio Metropolitan Transit Authority and that the act did not overextend the power of Congress under the commerce clause. The Court reasoned that the most significant restraint of the states on the power of Congress to act under this power is their participation in the federal government. Such participation, reasoned the Court, will ensure that laws which unduly and negatively affect states will not be passed.

SIGNIFICANCE

This case was argued with *Katzenbach v. McClung* (1964). Both cases are prime examples of Congress extending its powers under the commerce clause to address the problem of racial discrimination. They also were tests cases for the newly enacted civil rights legislation. The issues that arose out of the case address the motivation of the enactment of the statute, which was more to address the evil of racial discrimination than to prevent an adverse affect on interstate commerce.

Previously the Court had extended the commerce clause to prohibit the transportation via interstate commerce of lottery tickets, stolen vehicles, and women for immoral purposes.

RELATED CASES

Brooks v. United States, 267 U.S. 432 (1925)

Carimenetti v. United States, 242 U.S. 470 (1917)

Garcia v. San Antonio Metropolitan Transit Authority, 468 U.S. 528 (1985)

Gibbons v. Ogden, 9 Wheat 1, 195 (1824)

Katzenbach v. McClung, 379 U.S. 294 (1964)

Lottery Case (Champion v. Ames), 188 U.S. 321 (1903)

Perez v. United States, 402 U.S. 146 (1971)

United States v. Darby, 312 U.S. 100 (1941)

RECOMMENDED READING

Paul Brest, *The Conscientious Legislator's Guide to Constitutional Interpretation,* 27 Stanford Law Review 585 (1975).

Robert L. Stern, *The Commerce Clause Revisited—The Federalization of Intrastate Crime,* 15 Arizona Law Review 271 (1973).

Case Title: *Maryland v. Wirtz*

Legal Citations: 392 U.S. 183; 88 S.Ct. 2017; 20 L.Ed. 2d 1020

Year of Decision: 1968

KEY ISSUES

Do the 1966 amendments to the Fair Labor Standards Act, insofar as they apply to state employees, constitute an impermissible use of Congress's power under the commerce clause?

HISTORY OF THE CASE

The state of Maryland and 27 other states sought a declaration that the 1966 amendments to the Fair Labor Standards Act as they apply to employees of states are unconstitutional. The U.S. District Court for the District of Maryland held that the extension of coverage to state institutions was within Congress's power.

As originally enacted, the Fair Labor Standards Act of 1938 required every employer to pay his or her employees who were engaged in commerce a minimum hourly wage and to pay a higher wage for overtime. The term "employer" excluded the United States or any other state. In 1961, Congress changed the coverage to add all employees of any business engaged in interstate commerce and included employees of hospitals and schools.

SUMMARY OF ARGUMENTS

Maryland not only stated that this statute violated the commerce clause but that it also violated sovereign immunity granted by the Eleventh Amendment.

DECISION

The Court upheld the two amendments to the Fair Labor Standards Act that resulted in the expansion of the federal minimum wage and maximum hour statute to cover not just employees engaged in commerce or in the production of goods for commerce but also all employers of a business that has employees engaged in interstate commerce. The Court also upheld the act's coverage of nonprofessional, nonadministrative employees of state hospitals and public schools.

Justice Harlan wrote the majority opinion, which brought employees of state-owned enterprises into the scope of the commerce clause. The Court stated that Congress had interfered with state functions only to the point of subjecting the state to the same limitation as other employers whose activities affected commerce. The Court held that Congress could make state schools and hospitals comply with the regulations if the government could regulate the same economic activities engaged in by a private person. The questions of sovereign immunity as well as whether the employees of particular institutions handle interstate commerce would be considered at a later time.

Justice Stewart wrote the dissent, asserting that "what is done here is . . . such a serious invasion of state sovereignty protected by the Tenth Amendment that it is in my view not consistent with our constitutional federalism."

AFTERMATH

This case touches on issues that helped shape the "Rehnquist era," the period beginning in 1986 and presently continuing during which William Rehnquist has served as chief justice of the Supreme Court. The themes of state sovereignty and federalism expressed in the dissenting opinion of this case were later picked up and employed by the current chief justice.

SIGNIFICANCE

Justice Rehnquist was instrumental in reversing *Wirtz*. In *National League of Cities v. Usery* (1976), the Court held that the Fair Labor Standards Act was inapplicable to state employees engaged in traditional governmental functions. This overruled the section of *Wirtz* applicable to employees of public schools and hospitals. In 1985, *Garcia v. San Antonio Metropolitan Transit Authority* overruled *Usery* holding that the Fair Labor Standards Act is applicable to municipal mass-transit employees.

RELATED CASES

National League of Cities v. Usery, 426 U.S. 833 (1976)

Garcia v. San Antonio Metropolitan Transit Authority, 469 U.S. 528 (1985)

Hodel v. Virginia Surface Mining & Reclamation Association, Inc., 452 U.S. 264 (1981)

RECOMMENDED READING

Rosemarie E. Delmonte, Garcia v. San Antonio Metropolitan Transit Authority: *And the States Stand Alone,* 19 Creighton Law Review 105 (1986).

Case Title: *National Labor Relations Board v. Jones & Laughlin Steel Corporation*

Legal Citations: 301 U.S. 1; 57 S.Ct. 615; 81 L.Ed. 893

Year of Decision: 1937

KEY ISSUES

Does the National Labor Relations Act of July 5, 1935, which empowers the National Labor Relations Board to prevent a person from engaging in unfair labor practices that affect commerce, violate the commerce clause and the Tenth Amendment?

HISTORY OF THE CASE

In a hearing under the National Labor Relations Act of 1935, the National Labor Relations Board (NLRB) found the Jones & Laughlin Steel Corporation had violated the act by engaging in unfair labor practices. The NLRB found that Jones & Laughlin discriminated against union members with regard to hiring and tenure and was coercing and intimidating its employees not to join a union. Certain employees were fired. The NLRB ordered the corporation to stop its intimidation, to reinstate the fired employees, and to give them back pay. The corporation refused to do so and the board appealed to the court of appeals. The court denied the petition and the U.S. Supreme Court granted certiorari.

SUMMARY OF ARGUMENTS

The petitioner, the National Labor Relations Board, argued that the National Labor Relations Act was a valid exercise of the congressional commerce power.

The respondent, Jones & Laughlin Steel Corporation, argued that the National Labor Relations Act did not apply to its transactions with its employees and the act's provisions violated Article III, section 2 of the Constitution and the Fifth and Seventh Amendments.

Chief Justice Hughes delivered the opinion of the Court stating that the labor board found that the corporation interacted with many different states. It received raw materials from Michigan, Minnesota, West Virginia, and Pennsylvania. They transformed the materials and transferred them to all parts of the nation. The employees who were fired were all active union members, which was the obvious reason they were discharged.

The NLRB was challenged as not being a proper regulatory body for commerce. Opponents said its main purpose was to allow the federal government to regulate all industrial labor relations within the nation. The Supreme Court, on the other hand, found that the NLRB's authority to regulate commerce was limited by state action. The Court acknowledged the distinction between commerce among the states and commerce within the state, stating "that distinction between what is national and what is local in commerce is vital to the maintenance of our federal system." In this case, the unfair labor practices of Jones & Laughlin affected interstate commerce and were therefore within the power of Congress to regulate.

DECISION

The Court upheld the validity of the National Labor Relations Act and validated the use of the commerce clause as a source of power for the NLRB. The Court recognized the limitation on the NLRB's power to reach only what is deemed to obstruct interstate commerce.

AFTERMATH

The National Labor Relations Act was upheld as a constitutionally valid exercise of congressional commerce powers. State sovereignty could not be used as a basis for invalidating federal laws. Federal commerce power reaches local industrial facilities that affect interstate commerce.

SIGNIFICANCE

This case signifies an expansion of Congress's ability to regulate local business activities under the power of the commerce clause.

RELATED CASES

Carter v. Carter Coal Co., 298 U.S. 238 (1936)

United States v. Darby, 312 U.S. 100 (1941)

Wickard v. Filburn, 317 U.S. 111 (1942)

RECOMMENDED READING

Cox, Archibald. *The Court and the Constitution.* Boston: Houghton Mifflin, 1987.

Richard M. Fischl, *Self, Others, and Section 7: Mutualism and Protected Protest Activities under the National Labor Relations Act,* 89 Columbia Law Review 789 (1989).

Case Title: *Railway Express Agency, Inc. v. New York*

Legal Citation: 336 U.S. 106

Year of Decision: 1949

KEY ISSUES

Does banning paid advertising on vehicles, with the exception of self-advertising, violate the equal protection clause of the U.S. Constitution?

HISTORY OF THE CASE

A New York City traffic regulation prohibited vehicles to display advertising unless the owner of the vehicle was advertising his own products. An express company that sold advertising space on the sides of its trucks was fined for violating the ordinance. The court of special sessions and court of appeals affirmed the conviction. It was then appealed to the U.S. Supreme Court.

SUMMARY OF ARGUMENTS

The Railway Express Agency argued that the statute violated its Fourteenth Amendment rights of due process and equal protection. It contended that much more distracting advertising was allowed on owners' vehicles as well as around the city in general, such as the displays in Times Square. The agency also contended that the statute burdened interstate commerce, violating Article I, section 8, clause 8 of the Constitution.

New York contended that the statute applied equally to everyone in a permissible classification because it prohibited everyone from selling advertising. New York argued that it would not eliminate all advertising, but it would eliminate paid advertising, thereby reducing the hazard sought to be controlled, distractions to vehicle drivers and pedestrians affecting public safety.

DECISION

The Court, per Justice Douglas, did not weigh evidence on the due process issue in order to determine the validity of the statute. The Court held that the statute did not violate the equal protection clause and that equal protection did not require that "all evils of the same genus be eradicated or none at all." Additionally, the Court dismissed the interstate commerce claim, saying that great leeway was granted to authorities where the use and control of the highways was involved.

A concurrence from Justice Jackson contended that the statute should be upheld because those it protected were using the signs for their self-interest. He found a difference between this and selling advertising space on the vehicles. Justice Jackson stated, however, that the Court's rationale could lead to purely arbitrary decisions on who would be regulated.

AFTERMATH

The Court has continued to presume statutes to be constitutional so long as there is a plausible reason for the statute. The exceptions have been statutes involving racism or other serious discrimination problems.

SIGNIFICANCE

Legislation dealing with mainly economic problems will be looked at with a presumption of constitutionality and will not be invalidated because only a part of a larger problem is confronted.

RELATED CASES

Daniel v. Family Security Life Ins. Co., 336 U.S. 220 (1949)

McDonald v. Board of Election, 394 U.S. 802 (1969)

McGinnis v. Royster, 410 U.S. 263 (1973)

U.S. Railroad Retirement Bd. v. Fritz, 449 U.S. 166 (1980)

RECOMMENDED READING

Raffi S. Baroutjian, *The Advent of the Multifactor, Sliding-Scale Standard of Equal Protection Review:* *Out with the Traditional Three-Tier Method of Analysis, in with* Romer v. Evans, 30 Loyola of Los Angeles Law Review 1277 (1997).

Richard E. Levy, *Escaping Lochner's Shadow: Toward a Coherent Jurisprudence of Economic Rights,* 73 North Carolina Law Review 329 (1995).

Case Title: *A.L.A. Schechter Poultry Corp. v. United States*

Alternate Case Title: The Sick Chicken Case

Legal Citations: 295 U.S. 495; 55 S.Ct. 837; 79 L.Ed. 1570

Year of Decision: 1935

KEY ISSUES

The issues addressed in this case are (1) whether Congress impermissibly delegated its legislative power to the president in enacting the National Industrial Recovery Act (NIRA) and (2) whether the code of fair competition for the live poultry industry of the metropolitan area in and about the city of New York, which was promulgated under the act, unconstitutionally regulated intrastate activity.

HISTORY OF THE CASE

Congress enacted the NIRA as part of the New Deal legislation that was meant to bring the country out of the Great Depression. Since the scope of its undertaking was vast, Congress relied upon a general delegation of power to various administrative agencies and authorities to make regulations, and indirectly therefore to the president, as a means of implementing specifically stated public policy goals. The administrative authorities promulgated the "Live Poultry Code" as part of this delegation of power.

Schechter was a corporation engaged in the business of performing slaughterhouse services in New York City. Representatives of the corporation would purchase live poultry at markets in New York City as these creatures arrived in the city from various destinations around the United States. The corporation would then perform the slaughtering services and resell the meat to retail poultry dealers and butchers.

A.L.A. Schechter Poultry Corp. had been indicted and convicted on 18 counts for violations of the "Live Poultry Code." Two charges concerned the corporation's violation of the code's minimum wage and maximum hour (work week) provisions, and others dealt with the corporation's methods of slaughtering the poultry and numerous specific violations. The convictions were handed down by the U.S. District Court for the Eastern District of New York. On appeal to the Second Circuit Court of Appeals, the convictions for all but the minimum wage and maximum hour violations were upheld. Both Schechter and the government appealed this decision to the Supreme Court.

Summary of Arguments

Schechter argued that the "Live Poultry Code" was part of an impermissible delegation of legislative authority, the ability to make laws, as part of the NIRA. It also argued that the minimum wage and maximum hour provisions were beyond the power of Congress to regulate since the provisions involved solely intrastate commerce.

The government argued that the congressional delegation of legislative authority was necessary in light of the extraordinary conditions that the Great Depression imposed upon any proposed legislative scheme. The government further argued that Schechter's activities affected interstate commerce due to its role as a slaughterhouse in New York City—the largest live poultry market in the United States.

Decision

In a unanimous decision, the Supreme Court held that the NIRA impermissibly delegated legislative authority, and that the minimum wage and maximum hour provisions were beyond the scope of Congress's commerce clause power.

In determining that the NIRA contained too general a delegation of authority to administrative bodies, the Court held that the broad statement of providing "fair competition" was too general and undefined to contain a permissible basis for the delegation. The intent that each industry be permitted to deem what is fair for each industry was found to be too speculative to comprise a legislative act. The Court showed concern that such a delegation would empower industry representatives to actually make the law. Moreover, the ultimate delegation to the president to either approve or prescribe the resulting regulations was likewise held to leave too much discretion in his hands as to the substance of the law.

Schechter's intrastate slaughtering and marketing activity was found to cause too indirect an effect on interstate commerce for it to be subject to federal minimum wage and maximum hour restrictions.

Aftermath

Although the *Schechter* decision represented a setback in President Franklin Delano Roosevelt's New Deal program for bringing the country out of the Great Depression, the effects of the decision were short-lived. The government proceeded with the program, enforcing new laws as they were challenged on their constitutionality and creating new schemes as the old ones were found unconstitutional. Furthermore, the Supreme Court underwent a fundamental shift a mere two years later when the Court adopted a new stance toward the Congress's commerce clause power, which allowed most governmental regulation. Once the shift was complete, the Court regularly, and without exception for decades, upheld Congress's power to regulate the economy through its commerce clause power.

Significance

The Court dealt an immense blow to Roosevelt's New Deal strategy by holding the NIRA as an invalid delegation of legislative authority to administrative bodies. *Schechter* represented one of the last cases in which federalism concerns prevented Congress from validly using its commerce clause power to regulate the U.S. economy.

Related Cases

Lochner v. United States, 198 U.S. 45 (1905)

N.L.R.B. v. Jones, 301 U.S. 1 (1937)

United States v. Lopez, 115 S.Ct. 1624 (1995)

West Coast Hotel Co. v. Parrish, 300 U.S. 379 (1937)

Wickard v. Filburn, 317 U.S. 111 (1942)

RECOMMENDED READING

Benson, Paul R., Jr. *The Supreme Court and the Commerce Clause, 1937–1970.* New York: Dunellen Publishing Co., 1970.

Bigel, Alan I. *The Supreme Court on Emerging Powers, Foreign Affairs and Protection of Civil Liberties, 1935–1975.* New York: University Press of America, 1986.

Bork, Robert H. *The Tempting of America: The Political Seduction of the Law.* New York: Free Press, 1990.

Case Title: *South Dakota v. Dole*

Legal Citations: 483 U.S. 203; 97 L.Ed. 2d 17; 107 S.Ct. 2793

Year of Decision: 1987

KEY ISSUES

May Congress condition a state's receipt of federal highway funds on that state's adherence to a minimum legal drinking age of 21?

HISTORY OF THE CASE

Congress, in order to reduce the interstate dangers and problems created by differing state drinking ages, passed a statute that directed the secretary of transportation to withhold a percentage of federal highway funds from states permitting the purchase or public possession of any alcoholic beverage by a person under the age of 21.

South Dakota allowed persons 19 years of age or older to purchase beer containing up to 3.2 percent alcohol. South Dakota sued in U.S. District Court seeking a declaratory judgment that the federal statute violated the constitutional limitations on congressional spending power and the Twenty-first Amendment. South Dakota argued that the setting of the drinking age is a "core power" reserved to the states under section 2 of the Twenty-first Amendment, which provides: "The transportation or importation into any State, or possession of the United States for delivery or use therein of intoxicating liquors, in viola-

tion of the laws thereof, is hereby prohibited." The district court rejected the state's claims, and the Court of Appeals for the Eighth Circuit affirmed.

SUMMARY OF ARGUMENTS

South Dakota claimed that the statute's conditional spending impermissibly interfered with its exclusive powers under the Tenth and Twenty-first Amendments. The Tenth Amendment reserves to the states the powers not delegated to the federal government by the Constitution. South Dakota also argued that because the Twenty-first Amendment directly reserves the regulation of drinking ages to the states, the federal statute falls outside of Congress's power to regulate commerce.

Respondent Elizabeth Dole argued that Congress may conditionally allocate federal funds based on a national objective so long as the inducement of the state action is not in and of itself unconstitutional. Additionally, respondent argued that this indirect inducement does not violate the Twenty-first Amendment, which "confirms the States' broad power to impose restrictions on the sale and distribution of alcoholic beverages but does not confer on them any power to *permit* sales that Congress seeks to *prohibit*."

DECISION

Chief Justice Rehnquist, joined by Justices White, Marshall, Blackmun, Powell, Stevens, and Scalia, held that objectives that appear to be outside the scope of "enumerated legislative fields" nevertheless may be achieved through the use of the spending power and the conditional grant of federal funds. The Court also held that the conditional spending did not violate any limitations on the spending power because (1) the expenditure was for the general welfare, (2) the conditions were unambiguously stated, (3) the conditions were reasonably related to the purpose of the expenditure, and (4) the legislation did not violate any independent constitutional prohibition. The Court deferred to Congress's findings that "the differing drinking ages in the States created particular incentives for young persons to combine their desire to drink with their ability to drive, and that this interstate problem required a national solution." Finally, the Court stated that the conditional spending program was not exceedingly coercive "to the point at which 'pressure turns into compulsion.'" Also, because the states still *in fact* retain the power to enact their own drinking ages, Congress's "mild encouragement" to the states to enact higher drinking ages did not invade the state's sovereignty.

Justice Brennan dissented because he believed the Twenty-first Amendment reserved to the states the power to regulate the minimum age of purchasing liquor. Thus, he reasoned that Congress cannot condition a federal grant in a manner that abridges this right. In addition to agreeing with Justice Brennan, Justice O'Connor dissented on the grounds that Congress's condition that a state must raise its drinking age to 21 was not reasonably related to the expenditure of funds for highway construction. She believed that the condition was too attenuated, and that "[t]here is a clear place at which the Court can draw the line between permissible and impermissible conditions on federal grants."

AFTERMATH

Federal funds could be withheld from states that failed to enact statutes increasing the age to purchase alcohol to 21. The Court reaffirmed *Dole*'s holding in *New York v. U.S.* (1992). The Court implicitly stated that Congress had the power to achieve otherwise impermissible regulation of the states through conditional offers of federal funds. In essence, Congress can indirectly coerce a policy change that it could not directly implement on its own.

SIGNIFICANCE

The Court made it clear that conditions on federal grants-in-aid represented a constitutional tool for regulating state behavior, thereby giving Congress an additional incentive to spend. Thus, *Dole* made it clear that Congress has broad powers to attach conditions to spending. The Court, in *Dole*, also endorsed the proposition that Congress is not limited in its goals by the Constitution's enumeration of its powers.

Since *Dole*, many commentators have criticized the Court's granting to Congress seemingly absolute power to bargain with the states. First, many argue that previous constitutional limitations on Congress's regulatory powers can now be evaded through combined use of the taxing and

spending power because Congress can coerce states to implement policies it could not under its regulatory powers by threatening to withhold funding or threatening to implement a tax. Second, scholars have questioned the states' ability to protect themselves from federal conditional spending. These scholars argue that the limitations on the process have been "unworkable as they can easily be evaded." Also, because the states attach great importance to a continued high level of federal financial assistance, they are often left in an undesirable position of campaigning against the perceived objectionable conditions.

RELATED CASES

Fullilove v. Klutznick, 448 U.S. 448 (1980)

Harris v. McRae, 448 U.S. 297 (1980)

Massachusetts v. United States, 435 U.S. 444 (1978)

New York v. United States, 505 U.S. 144 (1992)

RECOMMENDED READING

James V. Corbelli, *Tower of Power:* South Dakota v. Dole *and the Strength of the Spending Power,* 49 University of Pittsburgh Law Review 1097 (1988).

Thomas R. McCoy and Barry Friedman, *Conditional Spending: Federalism's Trojan Horse,* 1988 Supreme Court Review 85 (1988).

Patrick H. Wood III, *Constitutional Law: National Minimum Drinking Age,* 11 Harvard Journal of Law and Public Policy 569 (1988).

Case Title: *Southern Pacific Co. v. Arizona*

Legal Citations: 325 U.S. 761; 65 S.Ct. 1515; 89 L.Ed. 1915

Year of Decision: 1945

KEY ISSUES

Does Congress have the right to restrict the power of the states to regulate the length of interstate trains as a safety measure?

HISTORY OF THE CASE

The state of Arizona brought suit against the Southern Pacific railroad for penalties incurred while operating two interstate trains within the state. The Arizona Train Limit Law made it unlawful to operate a train in Arizona of more than 14 passenger cars and a freight train of more than 70 cars. Southern Pacific argued that the Arizona statute violated the interstate commerce clause and the Fourteenth Amendment and conflicted with federal legislation. The Arizona Superior Court gave judgment for the company and was reversed on appeal.

SUMMARY OF ARGUMENTS

Appellant, Southern Pacific, argued that the train limit law invaded a field of regulation that was exclusive to the federal government and that the law obstructed interstate commerce. Southern Pacific also argued that the law deprived it of its property without due process of law.

The state of Arizona argued that the train limit law did not invade a field of legislation exclusive to the federal government and was not unconstitutional.

Justice Stone, writing for the majority, reversed the Arizona Supreme Court and held that the proper inquiry was not "whether there is basis for the conclusion . . . that the prohibited conduct had an adverse impact upon safety of operation." Rather, the decisive question was whether "the total effect of the law as a safety measure in reducing accidents and casualties was so slight or problematical as not to outweigh the national interest in keeping interstate commerce free from interference which seriously impeded it."

DECISION

The Court held that the Arizona law was unconstitutional. In weighing the statute's effect on the safety of Arizona citizens against the burden imposed on interstate commerce, the Court decided that the obstruction of the free flow of commerce among the states was greater. The law controlled the operations of railroads both within and without the state. Only the federal government may enact such regulation.

Justice Stone then went on to review the trial court findings and concluded "that the Arizona Train Limit Law, viewed as a safety measure, affords at most slight and dubious advantage, if any, over unregulated train lengths."

Justice Douglas, one of two dissenters, wrote that courts should intervene only when state legislation contradicts congressional enactments. As of this case, Congress had not acted in this area.

AFTERMATH

The Court abandoned its attempts to distinguish between national and local activities as a means to determine whether federal or state law was applicable. Instead, the Court adopted a balancing test.

SIGNIFICANCE

This case replaced the direct/indirect test with a balancing test. This approach advanced the Court's ability to decide whether state regulations were permissible based on fact and not label. The balancing approach is alive and well today, as the Court continues to weigh state benefits against the burden on interstate commerce on a case-by-case basis.

RELATED CASES

Buck v. Kuykendall, 267 U.S. 307 (1925)

George W. Bush & Sons v. Mallory, 267 U.S. 317 (1925)

Raymond Motor Transportation, Inc. v. Rice, 434 U.S. 429 (1978)

RECOMMENDED READING

David M. Forman, *The Dormant Commerce Clause and the Massachusetts Landfill Moratorium: Are National Market Principles Adequately Served*, 24 Boston College Environmental Affairs Law Review 425 (1997).

Earl M. Maltz, *How Much Regulation Is Too Much—An Examination of Commerce Clause Jurisprudence*, 50 George Washington Law Review 47 (1981).

Donald H. Regan, *The Supreme Court and State Protectionism: Making Sense of the Dormant Commerce Clause*, 84 Michigan Law Review 1091 (1986).

Case Title: *United States v. Carolene Products Co.*

Alternate Case Title: The Filled Milk Case

Legal Citation: 304 U.S. 144

Year of Decision: 1938

KEY ISSUES

May Congress prohibit the shipment in interstate commerce of properly labeled filled milk?

HISTORY OF THE CASE

The defendant, Carolene Products Co., was indicted for shipping from one state to another certain packages of Milnut, a brand of filled milk, in violation of the Filled Milk Act. Filled milk is milk in which the milkfat is removed and replaced with coconut oil; the result is that the milk tastes the same and costs less, but lacks many of the nutrients contained in regular milk. The Filled Milk Act prohibited the shipment of filled milk in interstate commerce on the grounds that such milk was "injurious to the public health."

SUMMARY OF ARGUMENTS

The defendant argued that the act was beyond Congress's power over interstate commerce, that the act violated the equal protection clause of the U.S. Constitution, and that the act deprived the defendant of property without due process of law.

Congress contended that the act was a reasonable use of its commerce power to protect public safety.

DECISION

The Supreme Court, in an opinion written by Justice Stone, held that the act was constitutional. Justice Stone argued that "Congress is free to exclude from interstate commerce articles whose use . . . may be injurious to the public health, morals or welfare." Nor did the act violate the equal protection clause by failing to ban the shipment of certain other adulterated products because a legislature is free to address one problem without tackling another. Justice Stone asserted that regulatory legislation affecting commercial legislation is presumptively valid, and can be attacked only by proof that it lacks any rational basis. In this case, Congress had based its decision on extensive investigation and studies which revealed that filled milk deprived consumers of essential nutrients contained in ordinary milk. Consequently, Justice Stone held that the act had not deprived the defendant of its right to due process of law.

In what has been called "the most celebrated footnote in constitutional law," Justice Stone in footnote 4 of the opinion discussed some caveats to the general rule of judicial deference toward legislative judgment indicating that while the Court presumes most laws are constitutional, if it is shown that a law infringes on individual rights or liberties, the burden of proof shifts to the government. He argued that "statutes directed at particular religious, . . . national . . . or racial minorities . . . may call for a correspondingly more searching judicial inquiry." He justified this heightened scrutiny on the grounds that "prejudice against discrete and insular minorities may be a special condition, which tends seriously to curtail the operation of those political processes ordinarily relied upon to protect minorities."

AFTERMATH

Later studies demonstrated that filled milk was in fact healthier than canned whole milk; research has shown that the Filled Milk Act was a pure example of partisan politics, with such companies as Borden using Congress to eliminate competition. In the 1970s, various federal district courts held the Filled Milk Act unconstitutional as an arbitrary exercise of power.

SIGNIFICANCE

Footnote 4 has served as the fountainhead for the representation-reinforcement theory of constitutional law, a theory that has been used to support affirmative action and antidiscrimination laws against constitutional challenges. The footnote also presaged the era of bilevel review, giving "personal" liberties Court protection while leaving "economic" liberties to the vicissitudes of the legislature.

RELATED CASES

Washington v. Seattle School Dist. No. 1, 458 U.S. 457 (1982)

Williamson v. Lee Optical of Oklahoma, 348 U.S. 483 (1955)

RECOMMENDED READING

Ely, John. *Democracy and Distrust: A Theory of Judicial Review.* Cambridge, Mass.: Harvard University Press, 1980.

Geoffrey P. Miller, *The True Story of Carolene Products,* Supreme Court Review 397 (1987).

Case Title: *Wickard v. Filburn*

Alternate Case Title: The Wheat Case

Legal Citation: 317 U.S. 111

Year of Decision: 1942

KEY ISSUES

May Congress regulate a farmer's personal consumption of wheat he has grown on his own farm?

HISTORY OF THE CASE

Filburn was charged a penalty under 1941 amendments to the Agricultural Adjustment Act of 1938 because he produced an amount of wheat in excess of quotas set by Wickard, the secretary of agriculture. Filburn consumed most of the excess wheat on his own farm, either as feed for livestock or food for the home; he sold a small portion. The act also provided subsidies to wheat farmers so that the U.S. price per barrel of wheat was $1.16, whereas the world market price was only 40 cents. Filburn filed suit in federal district court, and the court issued an injunction against the enforcement of the act. Wickard appealed to the U.S. Supreme Court.

SUMMARY OF ARGUMENTS

Filburn argued that the act violated his Fifth Amendment right to the due process of law by penalizing him for planting wheat and disposing of his crop as he saw fit. He also contended that the act was not a permissible use of Congress's power, under Article I, section 8, clause 3 of the Constitution, to regulate interstate commerce.

Wickard argued that because personal consumption of wheat by farmers as a whole had a substantial effect on interstate demand and, therefore, commerce between the states, it was within the power of Congress to regulate that consumption.

DECISION

Justice Jackson, writing for a unanimous Court, held that the penalties assessed under the act were constitutional. He quickly dispensed with Filburn's claim that the home consumption of wheat had, at best, an "indirect" effect on interstate commerce. Justice Jackson argued that the issue was not whether the effect was direct or indirect, but whether the home consumption of wheat "in a substantial way" interferes with Congress's ability to regulate interstate commerce in that product. He held that it did, because such consumption, if undertaken by all similarly situated farmers, would defeat the act's purpose of increasing demand for wheat. In Justice Jackson's opinion, Filburn was attempting to benefit (through his partial sale of the wheat) from the subsidized price while avoiding having to pay that price for the wheat he consumed.

As to Filburn's argument that the act deprived him of due process, Justice Jackson succinctly disagreed: "It is hardly lack of due process for the Government to regulate that which it subsidizes."

AFTERMATH

The Court's far-reaching interpretation of the commerce clause made all intrastate activity vulnerable to regulation by the federal government.

SIGNIFICANCE

This case established that even activities that seem wholly local are within Congress's regulatory power under the commerce clause. Consequently, much of the expansive New Deal and Great Society legislation was enacted pursuant to this power.

RELATED CASES

United States v. Darby, 312 U.S. 100 (1941)

United States v. Lopez, 115 S.Ct. 1624 (1995)

RECOMMENDED READING

Benson, Paul R., Jr. *The Supreme Court and the Commerce Clause, 1937–1970.* New York: Dunellen Publishing, 1970.

Bork, Robert H. *The Tempting of America: The Political Seduction of the Law.* New York: Free Press, 1990.

LABOR UNIONS

Case Title: *Adair v. United States*

Alternate Case Title: The "Yellow-dog" Contracts Case

Legal Citations: 208 U.S. 161; 28 S.Ct. 277

Year of Decision: 1908

KEY ISSUES

May Congress make it a criminal offense against the United States for the authorized agent or officer of an interstate carrier, which is generally defined as one engaging in the transportation of persons or property between states or between a state and a foreign nation by rail or water, to discharge an employee from service simply because of his membership in a labor organization?

HISTORY OF THE CASE

This case involves the constitutionality of section 10 of the Erdman Act, an act of Congress concerning carriers engaged in interstate commerce passed June 1, 1898 (c. 370, 30 Stat. 424). The purpose of the Erdman Act was to regulate the resolution of disputes between interstate carriers and their employees. Section 10 prohibited employers governed by the Erdman Act from (1) requiring employees to enter into an agreement either not to join a labor organization or not to remain a member of a labor organization, and (2) discharging or threatening discharge because of an employee's labor organization membership. Defendant William Adair was an agent and employee of Louisville and Nashville Railroad Company. Louisville and Nashville Railroad Company was a common carrier of interstate commerce, and an employer subject to the provisions of the Erdman Act. O. B. Coppage was an employee of the same railroad carrier and a member of the Order of Locomotive Firemen, a labor organization, which defendant William Adair allegedly knew about. Defendant Adair fired Coppage because of his membership in the labor organization.

The first count of the indictment charged that William Adair unlawfully and unjustly discriminated against O. B. Coppage, an employee of a common carrier, by discharging him merely because of his membership in the labor organization, contrary to the forms of the statute, and against the peace and dignity of the United States. The second count charged that William Adair unlawfully threatened O. B. Coppage with loss of employment because of his membership in the labor organization, contrary to the forms of the statute and against the peace and dignity of the United States.

The accused Adair demurred to the indictment, admitting the facts it contained, but alleging that the facts were insufficient to support the action against him. The demurrer was overruled. The district court for the Eastern District of Kentucky held that section 10 of the act of Congress was constitutional (152 Fed. Rep. 737). The defendant pleaded not guilty on the first count. After the trial, a verdict of guilty was returned on the first count and a judgment rendered that Adair pay $100.00 fine to the United States. The Supreme Court considered only the first count of the indictment.

SUMMARY OF ARGUMENTS

Defendant Adair argued that section 10 of the Erdman Act was unconstitutional since it only affected commerce remotely and indirectly and it laid down no rule or regulation to which the carrier was required to conform, nor any rules as to traffic or transportation. Adair further argued that section 10 violated the Fifth Amendment by impairing the property right of contract. He also argued that section 10 was unconstitutional class legislation because it separated persons into classes based on arbitrary and unreasonable principles.

The attorney general and William R. Harr, special assistant to the attorney general, argued that section 10 of the act had a clear and direct relation to interstate commerce. They argued that section 10 should not be considered separately from the other provisions of the act and that Congress has the constitutional authority to regulate the business of a common carrier engaged in interstate commerce as adequately to protect and safeguard the interests of such commerce. They also claimed that the right of individuals or corporations to make contracts and do business is at all times subservient to the power of Congress to regulate interstate commerce. Further, when the business of the carrier is interstate, the power of the state to control the conduct of the business is subject to the paramount right of Congress, which may displace all state regulations by legislation of its own.

DECISION

Justice Harlan, writing for the Court, held that section 10 constituted an invasion of the personal liberty, as well as the right of property, guaranteed by the Fifth Amendment. He stated that under the Fifth Amendment, Adair had the right to prescribe the terms upon which the services of Coppage would be accepted. Likewise, Coppage had the right to become, or not become, an employee of the railroad company upon the terms offered to him. Justice Harlan relied upon LOCHNER V. NEW YORK (1905)—a case involving a state regulation of the number of hours for labor in bakeries—in support of these general rights to contract in relation to one's business. He asserted that a state cannot deprive a person of life, liberty, or property without due process of law, unless there are circumstances that exclude the right. He stated that the test for determining whether the exception exists is whether the state legislation is a fair, reasonable, and appropriate exercise of the police power of the state.

Justice Harlan concluded that it was the legal right of Adair to discharge Coppage because of his membership in the labor organization, as it was the legal right of Coppage to quit the service in which he engaged because Adair employed persons who were not members of a labor organization. Justice Harlan also stated that the parties can contract to fix the period of service and method of termination. But in the absence of such a contract, an employer is not under any obligation, against his will, to retain an employee in his personal service, any more than an employee can be compelled, against his will, to remain in the personal service of another.

In this case, since there was not a contract controlling the conduct of the parties toward each other, Justice Harlan argued that Congress could not make it a crime against the United States to discharge the employee because of his membership in a labor organization and remain consistent with the Fifth Amendment. Justice Harlan then engaged in a secondary analysis led by the assertion that the act can fall within the power of Congress to regulate interstate commerce, without regard to

personal liberty or right of property arising under the Fifth Amendment. He stated that the only way for this to occur is if the statute in question is, within the meaning of the Constitution, a regulation of commerce among the states.

Justice Harlan defined the type of commerce that Congress has the power to regulate, pointed out Congress's large discretion to select the means to regulate such commerce, and reviewed several cases in which this Court sustained the authority of Congress, under its power to regulate interstate commerce. This led to his articulation of a standard that "any rule prescribed for the conduct of interstate commerce, in order to be within the competency of Congress under its power to regulate commerce among the States, must have some real or substantial relation to or connection with the commerce regulated."

Justice Harlan found that the general purpose of labor organizations is to improve the conditions of their members, and has nothing to do with interstate commerce. In addition, the fitness of an employee neither depends on nor is related to his membership in such an organization. Looking solely to the words of the statute, Justice Harlan held that there is no such connection between interstate commerce and membership in a labor organization that authorizes Congress to make it a crime against the United States for an agent of an interstate carrier to discharge an employee because of his membership in such an organization. Thus, he believed that section 10 arbitrarily sanctioned an illegal invasion of the personal liberty as well as the right of property of Adair, and was therefore invalid.

Justice McKenna and Justice Holmes wrote separate dissenting opinions. Justice McKenna briefly summarized the provisions of the Erdman Act, arguing that when read as a whole, the justification for including section 10 in the act was apparent. Congress was recognizing the existence of labor organizations and their influence on the dispute resolution process. He argued that the liberty guaranteed by the Fifth Amendment was not free from all restraints and limitations. Thus, the proper standard to judge legislation that imposed restraints and limitations was to ask, "what is their purpose and is the purpose within one of the powers of government?"

To answer this inquiry, Justice McKenna looked to the Employer's Liability Cases, 207 U.S.

463, which allowed Congress to regulate the relationship between master and servant. McKenna agreed with the majority on their definition of interstate commerce, but disagreed with their opinion on what qualifies as a regulation of it. Justice McKenna also noted other examples of the liberty of contract, and of forming business relations, that were forced to give way to the power of Congress: *Northern Securities Company v. United States*, 193 U.S. 197 (1904); *United States v. Joint Traffic Association*, 171 U.S. 571 (1898); GIBBONS V. OGDEN 1 (1824); and *Lottery Case*, 188 U.S. 321 (1903). Each time, the power of Congress to regulate commerce was pronounced paramount over the railroad's liberty to contract, and it was not subservient to or controlled by the provisions of the Fifth Amendment.

Justice McKenna then used historical arguments, stating that a prior act—25 Stat. 501, c. 1063—failed to recognize labor associations, or to distinguish between them, and could not avert the 1894 strike of the Pullman Company, a railroad car maker in Chicago. The Pullman strike was initiated in response to wage cuts and soon extended nationwide due to the involvement of a labor organization. He also mentioned the report sent by the Committee on Labor and a letter from the secretary of the Interstate Commerce Commission, both urging passage of the act to reduce labor strikes, which affect interstate commerce. He ended with a comparison of the Adair case to that of *Johnson v. Railroad*, 196 U.S. 17 (1904), the latter being upheld as within the power of Congress since the primary objective "was to promote the public welfare by securing the safety of employers and travelers." He agreed that some rights may not be disturbed or limited when exercised in a private business, but that rights exercised in a quasi-public business are subject to control in the interest of the public.

In a dissenting opinion, Justice Holmes found the statute constitutional since labor unions had a direct influence upon the terms and employment in that business. He noted that some of the relations of railroads with unions of railroad employees were connected with commerce closely enough to justify regulation by Congress. He believed that the majority incorrectly relied on the Fifth Amendment to argue that rights were infringed. Instead, he saw section 10 as no more than a limited interference with the freedom of contract. He

thought that the section merely prohibited the more powerful party from unjustly discriminating on certain grounds against those already employed. He emphasized that Congress can restrain the rights to contract freely where there is an important ground of public policy. He further added that preventing strikes and fostering a scheme of arbitration might be deemed by Congress an important point of public policy.

AFTERMATH

The "at will" rule governing *Adair,* under which either employer or employee could terminate the employment relationship at any time, has since suffered substantial erosion—a direct result of unionization, the increase in government employees, and large amounts of New Deal legislation passed in the 1930s that changed the government's posture toward labor-management relations. All of these worked to increase job security and decrease instances of arbitrary dismissal.

SIGNIFICANCE

This case is an example of the quest for contractual freedom that formed part of the historical movement by which the modern market economy grew. *Adair* occurred three years after *Lochner v. New York* (198 U.S. 45 [1905]) was decided and provides perhaps the most famous example of Lochnerian content neutrality, an effort by the Court to ensure legislation was reasonable in content and in application. It also served as precedent to strike down similar state laws that protected labor unions.

RELATED CASES

Coppage v. Kansas, 236 U.S. 1 (1915)

Gibbons v. Ogden, 9 Wheat (1824)

Lochner v. New York, 198 U.S. 45 (1905)

NLRB v. Jones & Laughlin Steel Corp., 301 U.S. 1 (1937)

RECOMMENDED READING

William E. Forbath, *The Shaping of the American Labor Movement,* 102 Harvard Law Review 1109, 1237–1248 (1989).

Tribe, L. *American Constitutional Law.* 2d ed. Mineola, N.Y.: Foundation Press, 1988.

Case Title: *Coppage v. Kansas*

Alternate Case Title: The "Kansas Yellow-dog Contract" Case

Legal Citations: 236 U.S. 1; 35 S.Ct. 240

Year of Decision: 1915

KEY ISSUES

Can a statute make it a criminal offense, punishable with a fine or imprisonment, for any employer or his agent to prohibit an employee from joining or remaining a member of any labor organization if the employee remains free to exercise a voluntary choice, not subject to incapacity or disability?

HISTORY OF THE CASE

Coppage was a superintendent of the St. Louis & San Francisco Railway Company. He requested employee Hedges to sign an agreement to withdraw from the Switchman's Union as a condition of his continued employment. Hedges refused. As a result, Coppage fired Hedges and Hedges brought suit charging Coppage with a violation of an act of the legislature of the state of Kansas that made it unlawful for an employer to coerce, require, demand, or influence any person or persons to enter into any agreement as a condition of securing employment. Coppage was found guilty and adjudged to pay a fine, with imprisonment as the alternative, in a local court. The judgment was affirmed by the supreme court of the state. The case was brought to the U.S. Supreme Court on the ground that the statute, as applied and construed in this case, was unconstitutional.

SUMMARY OF ARGUMENTS

Coppage argued that the statute was in conflict with the Fourteenth Amendment of the Constitution of the United States, which declares that no state shall deprive a person of liberty or property without due process of law.

Kansas argued that employees were not financially able to be as independent in making contracts for the sale of their labor as employers were in making contracts for the purchase of it, and therefore the statute was necessary to protect employees from the effects of inequalities of bargaining power. The state argued that the statute actually furthered the Fourteenth Amendment by better protecting the privileges and immunities of citizens of the United States.

DECISION

Justice Pitney wrote the opinion for the Court holding that the Kansas act of March 13, 1903, as construed and applied—punishing with fine or imprisonment any employer who required that an employee agree not to remain or become a member of any labor organization—was repugnant to the "due process" of the 14th Amendment. He began his analysis by considering whether Coppage "coerced" Hedges in any way, and found nothing to show that Hedges was subject to any pressure or influence.

Justice Pitney referred to *ADAIR V. UNITED STATES* (1908), which dealt with a question similar to the one in this case. He quoted the Court's holding in *Adair,* which stated that the employee and employer had equality of right, which no legislation could disturb without arbitrarily interfering with the liberty of contract. The Court, in *Adair,* added that it was the legal right of an employer to fire an employee because of the employee's membership in a labor organization. Justice Pitney found it unconstitutional for a state to punish an employer for requiring his employee, as a condition of securing employment, to agree not to become or remain a member of an organization while employed there. He argued that yellow dog contracts—contracts that require employees to agree not to join a union as a condition of employment—were not indistinguishable from ordinary exchanges between individuals in the market. He felt that the employee's right to refuse employment was equivalent to the employer's right to hire; prohibiting the parties to agree to these terms interfered with their freedom of contract.

Justice Pitney upheld *Adair*'s basic principle that the right to make contracts for the acquisition of property is included in the basic right of personal liberty and property. He stated that most important among such contracts is that of personal employment. He added that if this right was arbitrarily interfered with, it substantially impaired liberty and thus was unsupportable as a reasonable exercise of the state's police power. He recognized that some inequalities of fortune would result from the exercise of the freedom of contract and freedom of private property, but he believed that reducing economic inequality was not an appropriate state end. Justice Pitney concluded that the Kansas act was void.

Justice Holmes wrote a dissenting opinion agreeing with the state of Kansas that the statute was necessary to establish an equality of position between the contracting parties and pressed for the Court to overrule *Adair*. Justice Day also wrote a dissenting opinion showing concern for the far reach of the Court's decision. He also asserted that although the right of contract was guaranteed and could not be arbitrarily interfered with, it was also subject to limitation and restraints within the limits of public health, safety, and welfare. He believed that the Kansas statute promoted parity between the employer and employee and did not go beyond the legitimate exercise of the police power of the state.

AFTERMATH

Continuing societal changes forced the Court to abandon its laissez-faire principles (freedom of choice and freedom of contract) and contractual formalism (the idea that the employment relationship is a voluntary contractual relation) seen in *Coppage*. The Court began to limit the power of employers to freely discharge employees. In *NLRB V. JONES & LAUGHLIN STEEL CORP.* (1937) the Court upheld the National Labor Relations Act, which protected employees' right to unionize free from employer harassment and intimidation.

SIGNIFICANCE

The Court prohibited states from banning "yellow-dog" contracts that preconditioned employment on employees' promises not to join a union. The Court's decision extended the protection of the employment at-will doctrine, the doctrine providing that either employee or employer may terminate the employment relationship at any time for any reason, to states, and protected from any state or federal regulation an employer's absolute power to discharge employees.

RELATED CASES

Adair v. United States, 208 U.S. 161 (1908)

Allegeyer v. Louisiana, 165 U.S. 578 (1897)

Lochner v. New York, 198 U.S. 45 (1905)

NLRB v. Jones & Laughlin Steel Corp., 301 U.S. 1 (1937)

RECOMMENDED READING

Atleson, James B. *Values and Assumptions in American Labor Law*. Amherst: University of Massachusetts Press, 1983.

Roscoe Pound, *Liberty of Contract*, 18 Yale Law Journal 454 (1908).

J. Peter Shapiro, and James F. Tune, *Implied Contract Rights to Job Security*, 26 Stanford Law Review 335 (1974).

Case Title: *Lincoln Federal Labor Union v. Northwestern Iron & Metal Co.*

Legal Citations: 335 U.S. 525; 69 S.Ct. 251; 93 L.Ed. 212

Year of Decision: 1949

KEY ISSUES

Do state laws of Nebraska and North Carolina against the denial of employment because the job candidate is not a member of a union violate the Constitution? May employers refuse to hire a person because he or she is or is not a union member?

HISTORY OF THE CASE

North Carolina and Nebraska both had constitutional amendments providing that no person shall be denied the opportunity to obtain or retain employment because of his status as a union or nonunion member. Additionally, employers in these states were forbidden to enter contracts that obligated them to exclude persons from employment because of their union or nonunion status. These state laws were challenged on many grounds; however, the North Carolina and

Nebraska Supreme Courts rejected such contentions. The state supreme court decisions were appealed and heard together by the U.S. Supreme Court.

SUMMARY OF ARGUMENTS

Lincoln Federal Labor Union argued that the state amendment violated the First and Fourteenth Amendments. The union also argued that the state amendment was arbitrary, discriminatory, and without rational basis.

Northwestern Iron and Metal Company argued that the political or economic wisdom or soundness of a state constitutional amendment was not within the province of the U.S. Supreme Court. Northwestern also argued that the amendment was within the state's police power and did not violate the U.S. Constitution. Finally, Northwestern argued that the amendment was not arbitrary and capricious.

DECISION

Legislative protection can be afforded nonunion workers just as it does union workers. There is no due process violation.

Justice Black wrote the opinion for the Court that employers may not enter into agreements to exclude prospective employees because they are or are not labor union members. The laws forbid employers and unions to restrict employment to union members. The state laws protect union members equally with nonunion workers. There is no denial of equal protection but a grant of nondiscrimination.

This case is one of a number of cases that rejected the due process philosophy of *Adair-Coppage*, which favored employers and was used to strike down minimum wage and maximum hour legislation and uphold discrimination based on union or nonunion membership. The Court found that states have the power to legislate as long as such statutes do not harm the public and violate the Constitution.

AFTERMATH

The Court repudiated the *Lochner* doctrine, a substantive due process doctrine favoring employers and permitting the invalidation of minimum wage and maximum hour laws, so that the Court was no longer caught between the state legislatures and business. Business no longer used the Fourteenth Amendment to challenge state law.

SIGNIFICANCE

After 1960 corporations revived *Lochner* by challenging government under the Bill of Rights rather than the Fourteenth Amendment. Where the latter was useful in the 19th century to protect business from state regulation, the Bill of Rights helps in fighting the more difficult modern federal regulation.

RELATED CASES

Olson v. Nebraska, 313 U.S. 236 (1941)

Williamson v. Lee Optical Co., 348 U.S. 483 (1955)

Nebbia v. New York, 291 U.S. 502 (1934)

RECOMMENDED READING

Charles A. Bieneman, Book Review. *American Legal History: Judicial Power and Reform Politics: The Anatomy of* Lochner v. New York, 89 Michigan Law Review 1712 (1990).

G. Sidney Buchanan, *A Very Rational Court*, 30 Houston Law Review 1509 (1993).

Carl J. Mayer, *Personalizing the Impersonal: Corporations and the Bill of Rights*, 41 Hastings Law Journal 577 (1990).

FREEDOM OF THE PRESS

Case Title: *Branzburg v. Hayes*

Alternate Case Titles: The Newsmen Immunity Case, Right to Gather News Case

Legal Citation: 408 U.S. 665

Year of Decision: 1972

KEY ISSUES

Does requiring reporters to appear and testify before state or federal grand juries abridge the freedom of speech and press guaranteed by the First Amendment?

HISTORY OF THE CASE

Petitioner Branzburg was a newspaper reporter who published several articles describing unlawful drug activities in Kentucky. As a result, Branzburg was subpoenaed by the Jefferson and Franklin County grand juries. He appeared but refused to identify the individuals he had seen using or possessing marijuana, or the persons he had seen making hashish. He sought protection from the Kentucky reporter's privilege statute, the First Amendment of the U.S. Constitution, and sections 1, 2, and 8 of the Kentucky Constitution.

In both cases, the Kentucky Court of Appeals rejected Branzburg's First Amendment arguments and maintained a construction of the Kentucky Constitution that it does not permit a reporter to refuse to testify about events he had observed personally, including the identities of the persons he observed. Branzburg appealed to the U.S. Supreme Court to review both judgments of the Kentucky Court of Appeals.

SUMMARY OF ARGUMENTS

Branzburg claimed that forcing him to go before a grand jury or to answer questions regarding the identity of the informants would damage his effectiveness as a reporter. He maintained that his ability to gather news would be destroyed and that these requirements violated his rights under the First Amendment, the Kentucky Constitution, and the Kentucky reporter's privilege statute.

The respondents, the state trial court judges that ordered Branzburg to testify, argued that neither the First Amendment, the Kentucky Constitution nor the Kentucky reporter's privilege statute authorized Branzburg's refusal to answer.

DECISION

Justice White wrote the opinion for the Court holding that requiring newsmen to appear and testify before state or federal grand juries did not abridge the freedom of press and speech guaranteed by the First Amendment. Justice White noted the common-law and constitutional rule that the First Amendment did not guarantee the press a constitutional right of special access to information not available to the public generally. He added that even though news gathering may be hampered, the press was regularly excluded from grand jury proceedings, meetings of private organizations, crime scenes, and other occurrences from which the public is excluded. Justice White believed that the public interest in law enforcement and ensuring effective grand jury proceedings was sufficient to override the consequential burden on news gathering that petitioners contended resulted from forcing them, like other citizens, to respond to relevant questions asked of them in a regular grand jury investigation or criminal trial. Justice White was not convinced that the flow of information to the public would be greatly constrained by reporters having to answer to grand juries. However, he stated that newsgathering had some First Amendment protections, and grand juries must operate within the limits of the First Amendment: They cannot harass a reporter, for example, simply to disrupt the reporter's relationship with his news sources.

Justice Powell, in a concurring opinion, stressed the limited nature of the Court's holding. He reiterated that the Court would not tolerate harassment of newsmen and that newsmen had remedies—motions to quash and protective orders—for grand jury investigations conducted in other than good faith. He tried to strike a balance between freedom of the press and the obligation of all citizens to give relevant testimony with respect to criminal conduct. He insisted that where there are legitimate First Amendment interests that require protection, newsmen would have the availability of the courts.

Justice Douglas, in his dissenting opinion, asserted that the Court's decision would impede the dissemination of information of ideas and counterthought that the free press fostered and protected. He believed the flow of information is essential to the success of intelligent government and would not mandate the disclosure of a reporter's confidential source of information upon which he based a story.

Justice Stewart also wrote a dissenting opinion joined by Justice Brennan and Justice Marshall. He argued that the Court showed great insensitivity to the critical role of an independent press in our society. He believed that the promise of confidentiality was often necessary to a productive relationship between a reporter and his informant.

Justice Stewart contended that the proper test to determine whether there has been a constitutional infringement was not showing empirical evidence of the deterrent effects of such a law. Rather, he urged that the question should be whether there was a rational connection between the cause and the effect, and whether the effect would occur with some regularity. For example, Stewart thought the question should be whether it was likely that compelling reporters to testify before grand juries about informants would deter those informants from providing information on a regular basis rather than exactly how many informants would be deterred. Moreover, he asserted that evidence and plain common sense showed the deterrent effect of a loss of confidentiality. He also asserted that the rule the Court relied on was not absolute and had been limited by the Fifth Amendment, the Fourth Amendment, and the evidentiary privileges of common law. Instead, Justice Stewart would apply the safeguards developed in performing government investigations, when an investigation impinges on First Amendment rights, to grand jury inquiries in these cases. He argued that this would require some delicate judgment by the courts, but he believed this was within their duties.

AFTERMATH

After the decision, Branzburg was approached again by prosecutors trying to get information. As before Branzburg declined. He was found in contempt of court, but never served his sentence. Since *Branzburg*, a majority of states have enacted some form of "shield" law to protect the confidentiality of press sources. Currently, the law still does not grant special protection to newsgathering under the First Amendment.

SIGNIFICANCE

The Court has never directly addressed whether courts should recognize a First Amendment defense for criminal charges arising out of newsgathering. In *Branzburg*, however, the Court implicitly rejected this defense by denying journalists a general privilege under the First Amendment.

RELATED CASES

Caldwell v. United States, 434 F.2d 1081 (1970)

Zemel v. Rusk, 381 U.S. 1 (1965)

RECOMMENDED READING

Anthony Lewis, *A Preferred Position for Journalism?*, 7 Hofstra Law Review 595, 616, 617 (1979).

Potter Stewart, *Or of the Press*, 26 Hastings Law Review 631, 635 (1975).

Case Title: *Gannett Co., Inc. v. Daniel DePasquale*

Alternate Case Title: Public Trial Case

Legal Citation: 443 U.S. 368

Year of Decision: 1979

KEY ISSUES

Does the exclusion of public and press from a pretrial suppression hearing in a murder case violate the Sixth Amendment guarantee of a speedy and public trial by an impartial jury and the First Amendment right of freedom of the press?

HISTORY OF THE CASE

Newspaper owner Gannett brought a proceeding to vacate and prohibit enforcement of two trial count orders that excluded the public and press from a pretrial suppression hearing in a murder prosecution. The New York Supreme Court, Appellate Division, Fourth Department vacated the orders and appeal was made. The New York Court of Appeals upheld the exclusion of press and public from the pretrial proceedings.

Two accused murderers were tried in district court. The facts of the case caused a sensation and the press made the most of this. Motions were filed to suppress evidence and allegedly involuntary confessions. Judge DePasquale heard the case. The defense argued for an exclusion of public and press. A reporter was present and made no objection. The motion was granted but the next day the press wrote the judge asking to cover the trial and for access to the transcript. The judge denied the motions. The newspaper moved to set aside the exclusionary order. The judge ruled that the interest of press and public does not outweigh defendants' right to a fair trial. The New York Supreme Court vacated the order holding that public interest in this case had been unlawfully restrained. The New York Court of Appeals upheld the order.

SUMMARY OF ARGUMENTS

Appellant, Gannett Co., Inc., argued that the trial court's order excluding the public during pretrial proceedings violated the First, Sixth, and Fourteenth Amendments because the public and press had a constitutional right to attend criminal trials and the free flow of information may not be cut off without meeting prior restraint standards.

Appellee, the trial court judge, argued that the Sixth Amendment right to a public trial was personal to the accused and that his actions were consistent with appellant's First and Fourteenth Amendment right to access.

DECISION

Closure of a preliminary hearing with the agreement of the prosecution and the defense does not violate the Sixth Amendment guarantee of a public trial.

Justice Stewart wrote for the majority, holding that members of the public had no constitutional right under the Sixth and Fourteenth Amendments to attend criminal trials. Any First and Fourteenth Amendment right of the press to attend criminal trials was not violated by orders excluding public and press from pretrial suppression hearings nor from access to the transcript.

Both orders were necessary to assure defendants' rights to a fair trial.

Justice Blackmun in his opinion stated that Sixth Amendment rights are personal to the accused. All participants are subject to scrutiny to guard against a miscarriage of justice, but it is the judge who decides when, in the interest of the accused, publicity must be curtailed.

AFTERMATH

The attempt to close preliminary hearings to minimize pretrial publicity did not last. Later decisions minimized the impact of *Gannett* by guaranteeing press and public access to jury selection proceedings in criminal trials and preliminary hearings. No single case has expressly overruled these precedents, but some think the combination of *Richmond Newspapers v. Virginia* (1980) and *Waller v. Georgia* (1984) have come close.

SIGNIFICANCE

It is not so much that the impact of Gannett has been minimized as that protections have evolved through the courts enabling the press to better do its job of bringing news to the public. Nothing stops the presses. *Gannett* effectively denied the public and press access to pretrial hearings to uphold defendants' rights to a fair trial.

RELATED CASES

Richmond Newspapers v. Virginia, 448 U.S. 555 (1980)

Nebraska Press Association v. Stuart, 423 U.S. 1319 (1975)

Waller v. Georgia, 467 U.S. 39 (1984)

RECOMMENDED READING

Kane, Peter E. *Courts and the Press: Issues in Free Press/Free Trial.* Carbondale: Southern Illinois University Press, 1986.

Arthur J. Keefe, *The Boner Called* Gannett, 66 ABA Journal 227 (1980).

David E. Kendall, Book Review. *News of Crime: Courts and Press in Conflict,* J. Edward Gerald, 37 Vanderbilt Law Review 647, 660 (1984).

Anthony Lewis, *A Public Right to Know about Public Institutions: The First Amendment as a Sword,* 1980 Supreme Court Review 1.

Schwartz, Bernard. *The Ascent of Pragmatism: The Burger Court in Action.* New York: Addison-Wesley Publishing, 1990.

Case Title: *Miami Herald Publishing Co., Division of Knight Newspapers, Inc. v. Tornillo*

Legal Citations: 418 U.S. 241; 94 S.Ct. 2831; 41 L.Ed. 2d 730

Year of Decision: 1974

KEY ISSUES

Does a state statute granting a political candidate equal space to reply to criticism and attacks on his record by a newspaper violate the guarantees of a free press?

HISTORY OF THE CASE

After the *Miami Herald* newspaper had refused to print Pat Tornillo's replies to editorials critical of his candidacy for state office, Tornillo brought suit in Florida's circuit court seeking injunctive and declaratory relief and damages, based on Florida's "right of reply" statute. This statute grants a political candidate a right to equal space to answer criticism and attacks on his record by a newspaper, and makes it a misdemeanor for the newspaper to fail to comply. The circuit court held the statute unconstitutional as infringing on the freedom of the press and dismissed the action. The Florida Supreme Court reversed, holding that the statute did not violate constitutional guarantees, and that civil remedies, including damages, were available, and remanded to the trial court for further proceedings.

SUMMARY OF ARGUMENTS

Appellant contended the statute was void on its face because it purported to regulate the content of a newspaper in violation of the First Amendment. Another argument faulted the statute for vagueness, since no editor could know exactly what words would call the statute into operation. The statute also failed to distinguish between critical comment that is and is not defamatory.

The appellee and supporting advocates of an enforceable right of access to the press vigorously argued that government has an obligation to ensure that a wide variety of views reach the public. Access advocates submitted that although newspapers of the present are superficially similar to those of 1791, the press of today is in reality very different from that known in the nation's early years. Most large cities no longer have competing newspapers, and there is a concentration of control of the media, with a single interest owning, for example, a newspaper, a television station, a radio station. The result is that the power to inform the American people and shape public opinion is concentrated, with little opportunity for the public to contribute in a meaningful way to debate.

DECISION

Chief Justice Burger wrote the opinion for a unanimous court that the statute violated the First Amendment's guarantee of a free press, on the following grounds: (a) Governmental compulsion on a newspaper to publish that which "reason" tells it should not be published is unconstitutional. (b) The statute operates as a command by a state in the same sense as a statute or regulation forbidding appellant to publish specified matter. (c) The statute exacts a penalty on the basis of the content of a newspaper by imposing additional printing, composing, and materials costs and by taking up space that could be devoted to other material the newspaper may have preferred to print. (d) Even if a newspaper would face no additional costs to comply with the statute and would not be forced to forgo publication of news or opinion by the inclusion of a reply, the statute still fails to clear the First Amendment's barriers because of its intrusion into the function of editors in choosing what material goes into a newspaper, and in deciding on the size and content of the paper and the treatment of public issues and officials.

The court acknowledged the monopoly position of newspapers, but finds the dangers of government regulation to be more serious.

In a concurrence, Justice Brennan, joined by Justice Rehnquist, noted that the decision seemed to address only "right of reply" statutes, and did not address the constitutionality of "retraction" statutes, which would enable plaintiffs able to prove defamatory falsehoods a statutory action to require publication of a retraction.

In a concurrence, Justice White noted that to allow "right of reply" statutes would be to dictate editorial content, which should not be allowed.

But he went on to note that while newspapers may publish without government censorship, they have never been free from liability for what they choose to print. He criticized the NEW YORK TIMES CO. V. SULLIVAN (1964) and its progeny, such as *Gertz v. Robert Welch, Inc.,* (1974), a companion case to the case at issue, because they trivialized a private citizen's interest in reputation and removed virtually all the protection the law has always afforded by increasing the burden of proving liability and making it more difficult to prove damages.

AFTERMATH

Since *Miami,* the Court has continued to demonstrate in its decisions that the state may not constitutionally require an individual to participate in the dissemination of an ideological message.

SIGNIFICANCE

The case applies to "right of reply" statutes arguments given in *New York Times Co. v. Sullivan* (1964)—that there is "a profound national commitment to the principle that debate on public issues should be uninhibited, robust, and wide-open," and that government-enforced right of access inescapably "dampens the vigor and limits the variety of public debate."

RELATED CASES

Abood v. Detroit Bd. of Educ., 431 U.S. 209, 232–237 (1977)

Hurley v. Irish-American Gay, Lesbian & Bisexual Group, 115 S.Ct. 2338, 2350–51 (1995)

Pacific Gas & Elec. Co. v. Public Util. Comm'n, 475 U.S. 1, 12–17 (1986)

Wooley v. Maynard, 430 U.S. 705 (1977)

RECOMMENDED READING

Henry Geller, *Does Red Lion Square with* Tornillo, 29 University of Miami Law Review 477–481 (spring 1975).

Abbott B. Lipsky, Jr., *Reconciling Red Lion and Tornillo: A Consistent Theory of Media Regulation.* 28 Stanford Law Review 563 (1979).

L. A. Power, Jr., *Tornillo,* 1987 Supreme Court Review 345–396 (1987).

Schmidt, Benno C., Jr. *Freedom of the Press vs. Public Access.* New York: Praeger Publishers, 1976.

Case Title: *Nebraska Press Association v. Stuart*

Legal Citations: 427 U.S. 539; 49 L.Ed. 2d 683; 96 S.Ct. 2791

Year of Decision: 1976

KEY ISSUES

Is a prior restraint on pretrial publicity, intended to ensure the fairness of a criminal defendant's trial, subject to a lesser standard of review than prior restraints generally?

HISTORY OF THE CASE

The respondent, a Nebraska state trial judge, in anticipation of a trial for a multiple murder that had attracted widespread news coverage, entered an order which, as modified by the Nebraska Supreme Court, restrained petitioner newspapers, broadcasters, journalists, news media associations, and national newswire services from publishing or broadcasting accounts of confessions or admissions made by the accused to law enforcement officers or anyone else, except members of the press, and other facts "strongly implicative" of the accused. The modification of the order had occurred in the course of an action by the petitioners, who had sought a stay of the trial court's original order and in which the accused and the state of Nebraska intervened. The Supreme Court agreed to determine whether the order violated the constitutional guarantee of freedom of the press. The order expired by its own terms when the jury was impaneled. Respondent was convicted; his appeal was pending in the Nebraska Supreme Court.

SUMMARY OF ARGUMENTS

The Nebraska Press Association, the petitioner, argued that the court's imposition of a prior restraint on criminal reporting violated the First Amendment. Further, the petitioner argued that a defendant's Sixth Amendment rights may be fully protected without a prior restraint being imposed upon the press.

Hugh Stuart, the judge of the district court of Lincoln County and the respondent in this case, argued that under certain circumstances a defendant's Sixth Amendment rights could be denied because of pretrial publicity and a temporary restraint on First Amendment freedoms could be imposed in such a situation if no other alternative exists to protect the defendant.

The Sixth Amendment guarantees "trial, by an impartial jury" in federal criminal prosecutions. Because "trial by jury in criminal cases is fundamental to the American scheme of justice," the due process clause of the Fourteenth Amendment guarantees the same right in state criminal prosecutions. In the overwhelming majority of criminal trials, pretrial publicity presents few unmanageable threats to this important right. But when the case is a "sensational" one, tensions develop between the right of the accused to trial by an impartial jury and the rights guaranteed others by the First Amendment. The respondent argued that a restraint on pretrial publicity was justified in such a situation.

Decision

Chief Justice Burger delivered the opinion of the Court, in which Justices White, Blackmun, Powell, and Rehnquist joined.

While the guarantees of freedom of expression are not an absolute prohibition under all circumstances, the barriers to prior restraint remain high and the presumption against its use continues intact. Although it is unnecessary to establish a priority between First Amendment rights and the Sixth Amendment right to a fair trial under all circumstances, as the authors of the Bill of Rights declined to do, the protection against prior restraint should have particular force as applied to reporting of criminal proceedings.

The Court held that the heavy burden imposed as a condition to securing a prior restraint was not met in this case, for the following reasons:

(a) On the pretrial record the trial judge was justified in concluding that there would be intense and pervasive pretrial publicity concerning the case, and he could also reasonably conclude, based on common human experience, that publicity might impair the accused's right to a fair trial. His conclusion about the impact was of necessity speculative, however, dealing as he was with factors unknown and unknowable.

(b) There is no finding that measures short of prior restraint on the press and speech would not have protected the accused's right; the Nebraska Supreme Court no more than implied that alternative measures might not suffice, and the record lacks evidence that would support such a finding.

(c) It is not clear that prior restraint on publication would have effectively protected the accused's rights, in view of such practical problems as the limited territorial jurisdiction of the trial court issuing the restraining order, the difficulties inherent in predicting what information will in fact undermine the jurors' impartiality, the problem of drafting an order that will effectively keep prejudicial information from prospective jurors, and the fact that in this case the events occurred in a small community where rumors would travel swiftly by word of mouth.

(d) To the extent that the order prohibited the reporting of evidence adduced at the open preliminary hearing held to determine whether the accused should be bound over for trial, it violated the settled principle that "there is nothing that proscribes the press from reporting events that transpire in the courtroom" (*Sheppard v. Maxwell* [1966]), and the portion of the order restraining publication of other facts "strongly implicative" of the accused is too vague and too broad to survive the scrutiny given to restraints on First Amendment rights.

Justice Brennan, joined by Justices Stewart and Marshall, concurred in the judgment only: "I would hold . . . that resort to prior restraints on the freedom of the press is a constitutionally impermissible method for enforcing [the right to a fair trial]; judges have at their disposal a broad spectrum of devices for insuring that fundamental fairness is accorded the accused without necessitating so drastic an incursion on the equally fundamental . . . constitutional mandate that discussion of public affairs in a free society cannot depend on the preliminary grace of judicial censors."

AFTERMATH

Perhaps the most important practical result of the *Nebraska Press Association* case may be the increase of restraining orders upon the parties under the trial court's control: the attorneys, the police, and witnesses. But such "silence orders" usually will not be upheld in lower courts, if there is the absence of any showing of imminent peril to an unprejudiced trial. Such orders will perhaps prove more effective than in the past due to the holding in *Branzburg v. Hayes* (1972), that supports the power of the courts to compel reporters to reveal the source of their information.

SIGNIFICANCE

Nebraska Press probably presents the strongest case imaginable for a gag order furthering the right of fair trial. Therefore, the result of the decision is that such orders will virtually never be constitutional, at least as long as the press acquires its information without violating the law.

RELATED CASES

Austin v. Michigan Chamber of Commerce, 494 U.S. 652 (1990)

Branzburg v. Hayes, 408 U.S. 665 (1972)

Gentile v. State Bar of Nevada, 501 U.S. 1030 (1991)

Mu'Min v. Virginia, 500 U.S. 415 (1991)

Sheppard v. Maxwell, 384 U.S. 333 (1966)

Simon & Schuster, Inc. v. Members of the New York Crime Victims Board, 502 U.S. 105 (1991)

RECOMMENDED READING

Kane, Peter E. *Murder, Courts and the Press*. Carbondale: Southern Illinois University Press, 1986.

Case Title: *New York Times Co. v. Sullivan*

Alternate Case Title: The Freedom of the Press Case

Legal Citations: 376 U.S. 254; 84 S.Ct. 710; 11 L.Ed. 2d. 686

Year of Decision: 1964

KEY ISSUES

To what degree does the First Amendment protect the freedom of speech and press by limiting damage awards in libel actions brought by public officials against those who have criticized their official conduct?

HISTORY OF THE CASE

On Tuesday, March 29, 1960, the *New York Times* ran a full-page advertisement paid for by the Committee to Defend Martin Luther King and the Struggle for Freedom in the South. The advertisement listed the names of prominent Americans, southern clergy, and civil rights activists who supported the movement, and it summarized instances in which the civil rights of blacks had been abused. Two paragraphs described events that had taken place in Montgomery, Alabama. The first of these paragraphs read as follows:

> In Montgomery, Alabama, after students sang "My Country, 'Tis of Thee" on the State Capitol steps, their leaders were expelled from school, and truckloads of police armed with shotguns and tear-gas ringed the Alabama State College Campus. When the entire student body protested to state authorities by refusing to re-register, their dining hall was padlocked in an attempt to starve them into submission.

Three paragraphs later, the advertisement continued:

> Again and again the Southern violators have answered Dr. King's peaceful protests with intimidation and violence. They have bombed his home, almost killing his wife and child. They have assaulted his person. They have arrested him seven times—for "speeding," "loitering" and similar "offenses." And now they have charged him with "perjury"—a felony under which they could imprison him for ten years.

Many of these statements were inaccurate. Although students had been expelled from the college, they had not been expelled for demonstrating on the capitol steps but for demanding service at a segregated lunch counter. Part of the student body, not the entire student body, had protested the expulsions, and had protested not by refusing to register for classes, but instead by boycotting classes on a single day. Furthermore, the campus dining hall had never been padlocked, and Martin Luther King Jr. had been arrested four times, not seven times as stated in the advertisement.

L. B. Sullivan was the city commissioner who oversaw the police department of Montgomery, Alabama. Sullivan brought a libel action in the circuit court of Montgomery County, arguing that he had been defamed by the untrue statements in the advertisement because it used the term "police." He argued that because he was in charge of the police in Montgomery, he was the one the article accused of "ringing" the college campus and of arresting Dr. King.

The state trial judge submitted the case to the jury, instructing them that "because the statements were libelous per se, 'the law . . . implies legal injury from the bare fact of publication itself,' 'falsity and malice are presumed,' and 'punitive damages may be awarded by the jury even though the amount of actual damages is neither found nor shown.'" The jury found in favor of Sullivan and awarded him $500,000 in damages, an unprecedented recovery for the time.

The *New York Times* appealed the verdict, contending that the trial court's rulings abridged the freedoms of speech and press guaranteed by the First and Fourteenth Amendments. The Alabama Supreme Court upheld the court's instruction to the jury, stating that this was "libel per se" and that it was actionable without "proof of pecuniary injury" since such injury was implied. Alabama's high court also approved the jury's finding, stating: "We think it common knowledge that the average person knows that municipal agents, such as police and firemen, and others, are under the control and direction of the city governing body, and more particularly under the direction and control of a single commissioner. In measuring the performance or deficiencies of such groups, praise or criticism is usually attached to the official in complete control of the body."

The state supreme court rejected the newspaper's constitutional challenges, asserting that "[t]he First Amendment of the U.S. Constitution does not protect libelous publications" and "[t]he Fourteenth Amendment is directed against States action and not private action."

DECISION

The U.S. Supreme Court unanimously reversed the Alabama decision, in an opinion written by Justice William J. Brennan, Jr.

The Court based its decision on "[t]he general proposition that freedom of expression upon public questions is secured by the First Amendment." Even if a statement is erroneous, "it must be protected if the freedoms of expression are to have the 'breathing space' that they 'need . . . to survive.'" Justice Brennan continued: "The constitutional guarantees require, we think, a federal rule that prohibits a public official from recovering damages for a defamatory falsehood relating to his official conduct unless he proves that the statement was made with 'actual malice'—that is, with knowledge that it was false or reckless disregard of whether it was false or not."

The Court held that Alabama's libel law did not meet this standard because it raised "the possibility that a good-faith critic of government will be penalized for his criticism." Discussion of the functioning of government would be discouraged by the threat of lawsuits.

The Court then held that "the Constitution delimits a State's power to award damages for libel in actions brought by public officials against critics of their official conduct." The Alabama libel law permitted public officials to recover for libel without showing that the statements made with actual malice violated the constitutional limitation. It allowed Sullivan to recover by "presuming" damages rather than by proving he had actually been harmed.

Justice Brennan also rejected Sullivan's claim that the statements had been directed against him. To treat legitimate criticism of government action as "libel of an official responsible for those operations . . . strikes at the very center of the constitutionally protected area of free speech."

Justices Black and Goldberg wrote concurring opinions, supporting the reversal of the Alabama decision, but for reasons other than those given by Justice Brennan. Justice Black took a more extreme position than Justice Brennan, arguing that the states could never constitutionally allow recovery for libel "for merely discussing public affairs and criticizing public officials." The power of the federal and state governments to permit recovery against public officials, in Black's words, was "precisely nil." "We would . . . more faithfully interpret the First Amendment by holding that at the very least it leaves the people and the press free to criticize officials and discuss public affairs with impunity."

Justice Goldberg expressed similar views in his concurrence: "I strongly believe that the Constitution accords citizens and press an unconditional freedom to criticize official conduct." Thus, according to both Justice Black and Justice Goldberg, no one who criticizes governmental action should ever be subject to libel suits.

AFTERMATH

Given the only slight connection of the advertisement to Mr. Sullivan, and the lack of evidence of damage suffered by him, the libel action was dismissed by the state court after the U.S. Supreme Court had made its decision.

SIGNIFICANCE

This was the first of a number of Supreme Court cases that, to a large degree, abolished state defamation law. Prior to *New York Times*, defamation law had been determined exclusively by state courts. Now, however, the First Amendment's protections struck down much of the common law of defamation. This has given the news media more freedom to report stories without the fear of lawsuits.

RELATED CASES

Dun & Bradstreet, Inc. v. Greenmoss Builders, Inc., 472 U.S. 749 (1985)

Gertz v. Robert Welch, Inc., 418 U.S. 323 (1974)

RECOMMENDED READING

David Anderson, *Libel and Press Self-Censorship*, 53 Texas Law Review 422 (1975).

Alexander D. Del Russo, *Freedom of the Press and Defamation: Attacking the Bastion of* New York Times Co. v. Sullivan, 25 St. Louis University Law Journal 501 (1981).

W. Page Keeton, *Defamation and Freedom of the Press*, 54 Texas Law Review 1221 (1976).

Case Title: *Pell v. Procunier*

Legal Citation: 417 U.S. 843

Year of Decision: 1974

KEY ISSUES

Does the press have the right to interview inmates?

HISTORY OF THE CASE

Various reporters, including Eve Pell, requested permission from the appropriate corrections officials to interview inmates. The editors of a magazine requested to visit another inmate to discuss publishing his writings and to talk to him about the conditions of the prison. These requests were denied pursuant to a California statute that stated that the press will not be permitted to interview specific individual inmates. The reporters and the inmates sued Raymond K. Procunier, the director of the California Department of Corrections, and several other subordinate corrections officers. The district court granted the inmates summary judgment, saying that their First and Fourteenth Amendment rights had been infringed. The district court granted the defendants' motion to dismiss the media plaintiffs' case because the media still had the right to enter prisons and interview at random. Additionally, the district court said the ruling for the prisoners in this case granted the reporters even broader access. The media plaintiffs and the corrections director appealed to the U.S. Supreme Court.

SUMMARY OF ARGUMENTS

The inmate plaintiffs contended that the California statute violated their First Amendment right of free speech applied to the states through the Fourteenth Amendment. The media plaintiffs contended that the statute infringed their right under the First and Fourteenth Amendments of the freedom of the press.

The defendants argued that before the statute was enacted, the press could interview certain specific inmates, and that resulted in a small group of inmates becoming virtual public figures, gaining a disproportionate amount of notoriety and influence among other inmates. Because of this, they became severe disciplinary problems, impairing the purposes of the penal system.

DECISION

Justice Stewart delivered the opinion of the Court, which held that the statute did not violate the inmates' rights of free speech. The inmates inevitably lost some privileges when they became incarcerated. As long as the limitation was neutral, without regard to the content, and the prisoners still had alternative channels of communication, the statute was held to be constitutional and a restriction to which prisoners are necessarily subjected in order to carry out the objectives of the corrections system.

The Court likewise held that the media plaintiffs' right to the freedom of the press was not violated. The Court stated that the press does not have a constitutional right to information that is not available to the public generally. This, coupled with the fact that the press had greater access than the public to prisons through their ability to enter prisons, speak to prisoners, and interview prisoners at random, was enough to convince the Court that no right had been violated.

Justice Powell dissented by stating that the ban of prisoner-press interviews restrains the press from performing its constitutionally protected duty of informing the people of the government's conduct.

Justices Douglas, Brennan, and Marshall dissented, stating that the prisoners' First Amendment rights are extremely important and are not outweighed by the state's interest in this case. They argued that the prison could still carry out its duties effectively if the inmates were allowed to give interviews. They also dissented as to the media, stating that their job is to inform the public, and this restriction harms the public's access to information.

AFTERMATH

The Court has continued to hold that the press has no right of prison access greater than that of the general public in cases such as *Houchins v. KQED, Inc.* (1978).

SIGNIFICANCE

While the Court held that the First Amendment rights were not violated by this statute, the strong

dissent followed by four justices may one day turn out to be the majority with a different Supreme Court. The *Pell* decision indicated that the availability access to prisons was equal among the public and the media.

RELATED CASES

Gannett Co. v. DePasquale, 443 U.S. 368 (1979)

Houchins v. KQED, Inc., 438 U.S. 1 (1978)

Richmond Newspapers, Inc. v. Virginia, 448 U.S. 555 (1980)

Saxbe v. Washington Post Co., 417 U.S. 843 (1974)

RECOMMENDED READING

Margaret A. Blanchard, *The Institutional Press and Its First Amendment Privileges,* Supreme Court Review 225–296 (1978).

Joseph C. Hutchinson, *Analyzing the Religious Free Exercise Rights of the Inmates: The Significance of Pell, Jones* and *Wolfish,* 11 NYU Review of Law and Social Change 413–440 (1982–1983).

Case Title: *Time, Inc. v. Firestone*

Alternate Case Title: The Responsible Press Case

Legal Citation: 424 U.S. 448

Year of Decision: 1976

KEY ISSUES

Is the press subject to a libel action based upon an erroneous report of the contents of a judicial proceeding?

HISTORY OF THE CASE

Mary Alice Firestone was the wife of Russell Firestone, scion of the wealthy industrial family. She filed an action seeking support and maintenance, and he counterclaimed for divorce on the grounds of mental cruelty and adultery. In a highly publicized trial in Palm Beach, Florida, the court held in favor of Russell. In the court's judgment, the implication from the trial testimony was that the "extramarital escapades of [Mary Alice Firestone] were bizarre and of an amatory nature which would have made Dr. Freud's hair curl." Other testimony had suggested that Russell Firestone "was guilty of bounding from one bedpartner to another with the erotic zest of a satyr." *Time* magazine ran an item in its "Milestones" section, which stated that the divorce had been granted on grounds of extreme cruelty and adultery. In fact, the court had not stated clearly its specific grounds for granting the divorce.

Mrs. Firestone demanded that *Time* retract the item, but *Time* refused to do so. Firestone then filed a libel suit in a Florida court. She won a jury verdict of $100,000, and the judgment was affirmed by both the Florida District Court of Appeals and the Florida Supreme Court.

SUMMARY OF ARGUMENTS

Firestone argued that *Time* had published a false statement about her, and because she was not a public figure she was entitled to damages.

Time argued that it had published a report about a judicial proceeding; thus, under Supreme Court precedent the magazine could be subjected to a libel action only if it had published the material with actual malice toward Firestone, which clearly was not the case here.

DECISION

The Supreme Court, in an opinion written by Justice Rehnquist, held that *Time* could be required to pay damages, but only upon a showing of fault. The Court remanded the case to the Florida courts to determine whether *Time* had been negligent in publishing the item. Justice Rehnquist argued that the requirement of actual malice on the part of *Time* presented in NEW YORK TIMES V. SULLIVAN (1964) was inapplicable here because Firestone was not a "public figure" for First Amendment purposes. He asserted that a public figure assumes "any role of especial prominence in the affairs of society" or thrusts "herself to the forefront of [a] particular public controversy in order to influence the resolution of the issues involved in it." Mrs. Firestone had done neither. Justice Rehnquist also rejected *Time*'s argument that judicial proceedings were of sufficient importance to implicate the actual malice requirement. He first noted that the inquiry as to whether a person is a public figure will often determine the significance of the public's interest in the courtroom proceeding; he then stated, "The details of many, if not most, courtroom battles would add almost nothing toward advancing the uninhibited debate on public issues thought to provide principal support for the decision in *New York Times*."

Justice Rehnquist argued that once it was determined that Firestone was not a public figure, the only constitutional barrier to her libel verdict would be a finding that *Time* had erroneously published the item without fault. Because the record suggested a strong possibility that *Time* was negligent, the Court remanded the case so the lower court could answer that question.

AFTERMATH

Interest in the socially elite or rich and famous does not convert those types of people into public figures for libel issues.

SIGNIFICANCE

This decision distinguished between two classes of persons and two standards of liability for the purpose of deciding libel issues. Specifically, the court distinguished persons in the public eye from public figures and found that only negligence was required for liability regarding persons in the public eye whereas actual malice was required for public figures.

RELATED CASES

Gertz v. Robert Welch Inc., 418 U.S. 323 (1974)

New York Times v. Sullivan, 376 U.S. 254 (1964)

RECOMMENDED READING

Margaret A. Blanchard, *The Institutional Press and Its First Amendment Privileges,* Supreme Court Review 225 (1978).

Case Title: *Time, Inc. v. Hill*

Legal Citations: 385 U.S. 374; 17 L.Ed. 2d 456; 87 S.Ct. 534

Year of Decision: 1967

KEY ISSUES

Do citizens' right to privacy preclude the presentation of fictionalized accounts of events in their lives when those events are matters of legitimate public concern?

HISTORY OF THE CASE

The plaintiff, James Hill, brought the action in a New York state court, under a New York statute protecting the right of privacy, for damages. The plaintiff alleged an article in *Life* magazine falsely reported that a new play portrayed an experience suffered by plaintiff and his family when held hostage by escaped convicts in the plaintiff's home. The trial court failed to instruct the jury that a verdict of liability could be predicated only on a finding of knowing or reckless falsity in the publication of the article; the jury awarded the plaintiff compensatory and punitive damages. On appeal, the Appellate Division of the New York Supreme Court ordered a new trial on damages but sustained the jury verdict of liability. At the new trial on damages, a jury was waived and the court awarded compensatory damages without punitive damages. The New York Court of Appeals affirmed. On appeal, the U.S. Supreme Court set aside the judgment of the court of appeals and remanded the case for further proceedings.

SUMMARY OF ARGUMENTS

The complaint sought damages under a New York statute on allegations that the *Life* article was intended to, and did, give the impression that the play mirrored the Hill family's experience, which, to the knowledge of the defendant, "was false and untrue." Appellant's defense was that the article was "a subject of legitimate news interest," "a subject of general interest and of value and concern to the public" at the time of publication, and that it was "published in good faith without any malice whatsoever."

DECISION

In his opinion, Justice Brennan, joined by five of the other justices, held that (1) the First Amendment precluded the statute's application to false reports of matters of public interest in the absence of proof that defendant published the report knowing it was false or recklessly disregarding the truth, (2) the proof would support either a jury finding of innocence or mere negligence or a finding of actual knowledge of falsity or reckless disregard of truth, and (3) the trial court's failure to use the correct standard of liability in its instructions required a new trial.

AFTERMATH

Although the Court applied the NEW YORK TIMES V. SULLIVAN standard, a standard requiring the plaintiff to show statements were made with actual malice, to the Hills' privacy action, it left open the question of whether the same standard of liability should be applicable in a libel action to persons voluntarily and involuntarily thrust into the public limelight. Four years later the Court offered a tentative answer to this question in *Rosenbloom v. Metromedia*, a fragmented plurality decision containing five separate opinions. The Court ruled, in a decision that did not attract even a bare majority of the justices, that the *New York Times* standard must apply to private citizens caught up in events of public interest—whether voluntarily or involuntarily so involved. But this concept ended as abruptly as it appeared, as the Court found private figures may recover by showing the defendant was negligent in making the statement.

SIGNIFICANCE

Time, Inc. v. Hill indicated that the "actual malice" requirement applied to private individuals bringing libel actions. However, it is not at all clear that *Time v. Hill* remains good law following the *Gertz v. Welch* (1974) decision, a decision finding that private persons only need to show that defamatory statements were made negligently. Since *Gertz* represents the majority's repudiation of the view that the *New York Times* standard must apply to *all* defamation actions arising out of a matter of "public interest," even ones brought by private figures, it can be plausibly argued that the reasoning of *Gertz* also applies to "false light" actions brought by private persons.

RELATED CASES

Dun & Bradstreet Inc. v. Greenmoss Builders Inc., 472 U.S. 749 (1985)

Florida Star v. B.J.F., 491 U.S. 524 (1989)

Hustler Magazine v. Falwell, 485 U.S. 46 (1988)

RECOMMENDED READING

Melville B. Nimmer, *The Right to Speak from Times to Time: First Amendment Theory Applied to Libel and Misapplied to Privacy*, 56 California Law Review 935–967 (August 1968).

Don R. Pember and Dwight L. Teeter, Jr., *Privacy and the Press since* Time Inc. v. Hill, 50 Washington Law Review 57–91 (1974).

Case Title: *Zurcher v. Stanford Daily*

Alternate Case Title: The "Third Party" Search Newspaper Case

Legal Citation: 436 U.S. 547

Year of Decision: 1978

KEY ISSUES

May police obtain a warrant to search the premises of a newspaper for evidence where neither the newspaper nor its staff is implicated in the crime in question?

HISTORY OF THE CASE

The *Stanford Daily* newspaper published a special edition that carried articles and photographs pertaining to a violent clash between police and demonstrators at the university hospital. Several police officers were injured in the confrontation. The police obtained a warrant to search the *Daily* newsroom for negatives and photographs revealing the identity of the demonstrators involved in the assault. The *Daily* and its staff were not involved in the unlawful acts. They brought a civil action under the federal civil rights statute against the district attorney and the police officers who conducted the search, alleging violations, under state law, of their rights under the First, Fourth, and Fourteenth Amendments to the U.S. Constitution. The *Daily* and its staff won both in the dis-

trict court and in the Ninth Circuit Court of Appeals, and the defendants appealed to the U.S. Supreme Court.

SUMMARY OF ARGUMENTS

The *Daily* argued that where the innocent third party being searched is a newspaper, a warrant should be issued only in rare circumstances due to First Amendment considerations. It asserted that "searches of newspaper offices for evidence of crime . . . will seriously threaten the ability of the press to gather, analyze, and disseminate news." This would occur through a chilling effect upon the editorial process, disruptions of publication, and a decrease in access to confidential sources of information.

The police argued that the only constitutional requirement for obtaining a warrant, even from an innocent third party, was that they have probable cause to believe that the items to be seized would be found on the property or person being searched. They contended that any First Amendment concerns of the press were adequately protected by the procedure for obtaining the warrant.

DECISION

Justice White, writing for five of the justices, held that the procedures for obtaining search warrants offered sufficient protections to make third-party searches of newspaper offices constitutional. Justice White emphasized that the innocence of the person whose property is being searched is not the key factor in the issuance of a warrant. Rather, the emphasis is on whether the police had a reasonable belief that fruits, instrumentalities or evidence of a crime, would be found on the person or property in question. Justice White then noted that the conflict between the government and the press had played a significant role in the history of the Fourth Amendment. He observed that the government might use search warrants in order to stifle liberty of expression, but he argued that this concern could be addressed by requiring magistrates to apply warrant preconditions such as probable cause, reasonableness, and the requirement that items to be searched for be listed specifically, with "particular exactitude" when there were potential dangers to First Amendment interests. As to the possible decrease in availability of confidential sources, Justice White stated that any potential effect in that regard "does not make a constitutional difference."

Justice Powell, in a concurring opinion, argued that the press was not entitled to a special procedure when government authorities required evidence in its possession. He construed the Court's opinion as requiring a magistrate to "take cognizance of the independent values protected by the First Amendment" when considering whether to issue a warrant for a search involving the press.

Justice Stewart, in a dissent joined by Justice Marshall, argued that in third-party search situations involving the press, the search should be constitutionally permissible only where there has been a clear showing that (1) important materials would be destroyed; and (2) a restraining order would be futile. Otherwise, the police should be required to serve the newspaper with a subpoena that would require it to deliver any listed items to the police without a search of the premises. Justice Stewart disagreed with the majority on the impact police searches have upon press access to confidential sources. He stated that since those searches "prevent a newsman from being able to promise confidentiality to his potential sources, it seems obvious to me that a journalist's access to information, and thus the public's, will thereby be impaired."

Justice Stevens, in a lone dissent, avoided the First Amendment question by arguing that the search warrant in this case was unconstitutional under the Fourth Amendment. Justice Stevens asserted that the search was impermissible because the *Daily* was not implicated in the crime and there was no danger that any evidence would be lost through the use of a subpoena; the fact that the press was involved was not relevant to his analysis.

AFTERMATH

After tremendous criticism of the decision by the news media, Congress responded with the Privacy Protection Act of 1980. This act prohibited government searches of the press unless there is probable cause to believe that the person or office being searched is involved in the crime being investigated or there is reason to believe that giving notice by subpoena would result in the loss of the evidence.

SIGNIFICANCE

The *Zurcher* case was one of the most significant in a line of Burger Court decisions that address the First Amendment rights of the press. These cases suggest that any rights created by the First Amendment apply equally to the press and private citizens; thus, the constitutional test for free speech in press cases is what any member of the public can say in a given situation.

RELATED CASES

Branzburg v. Hayes, 408 U.S. 665 (1972)

Stanford v. Texas, 379 U.S. 476 (1965)

RECOMMENDED READING

Margaret A. Blanchard, *The Institutional Press and Its First Amendment Privileges,* Supreme Court Review 225 (1978).

First Amendment Symposium, 16 Harvard Civil Rights–Civil Liberties Law Review (fall 1981).

PRIVACY

Case Title: *Bowers v. Hardwick*

Alternate Case Title: Sodomy Laws Case

Legal Citation: 478 U.S. 186

Year of Decision: 1986

KEY ISSUES

What are the constitutional limits within which a state may regulate adult sexual activity?

HISTORY OF THE CASE

Hardwick was arrested in his bedroom for violating a Georgia statute prohibiting sodomy, the performance or submission to sexual acts "involving the sex organs of one person and the mouth or anus of another." Police went to Hardwick's home on a matter unrelated to this case, were let in by a houseguest, and allegedly discovered Hardwick committing sodomy with another adult male. He brought this action because he regularly engaged in private homosexual acts with consenting adults. The district court dismissed his suit, but he appealed and won in the Eleventh Circuit Court of Appeals. The court held that Hardwick's sexual activities were beyond state control.

SUMMARY OF ARGUMENTS

Bowers, the attorney general of Georgia, argued that this case was similar to a lower court ruling upheld by the Supreme Court that a Virginia sodomy statute was constitutional: *Doe v. Commonwealth's Attorney for City of Richmond,* 425 U.S. 901 (1976). Sodomy is not protected, as are marriage and child rearing, because it was proscribed in biblical times. Bowers argued that upholding moral values is a legitimate state function, and that sodomy enjoys no protection because it is immoral.

Hardwick argued that the Constitution safeguards the home and when intimate conduct takes place there, it must be protected. Criminal laws on sexual activity at home do not criminalize commercial prostitution or rape.

DECISION

This case gave the Supreme Court the opportunity to clarify the constitutional limits that a state may set to regulate adult sexual intimacy. Justice White wrote the opinion of the Court. The Court held the statute constitutional, saying that the Constitution does not confer a right on homosexuals to engage in sodomy. The Court found that the statute had a rational basis in Georgia where the electorate felt that homosexual sodomy was immoral and unacceptable. This was the rational basis for the statute.

Chief Justice Burger concurred, reemphasizing the majority's position that there is no such thing as a fundamental right to commit homosexual sodomy, by summarizing the history of the condemnation of sodomy. Justice Powell also concurred, agreeing that a fundamental right to commit homosexual sodomy did not exist, but asserting that the prison sentence for sodomy might create an Eighth Amendment issue. However, Powell indicated that the Eighth Amendment issue was not before the Court because Hardwick was not tried, convicted, or sentenced under the sodomy statute, nor had Hardwick raised the issue in the courts below.

Justice Blackmun wrote a dissent joined by Justices Brennan, Marshall, and Stevens. In his dissent, Blackmun disagreed with the majority on what issue was raised by the case, stating that the case was about the right to be left alone, not the fundamental right to engage in homosexual sodomy. Blackmun felt the majority ignored the broad language of the sodomy statute and Hardwick's complaint when making its decision and was obsessed with narrowly focusing on homosexual activity. Contrary to the majority view, Blackmun felt the sex and status of the person engaged in the prohibited act and the Court's familiarity with upholding sodomy statutes were irrelevant to deciding the constitutionality of the statute. Blackmun also disagreed with the majority's refusal to consider whether the sodomy statute violated the Eighth Amendment, Ninth Amendment, or the Fourteenth Amendment. He indicated that consideration of these potential violations was required since the case was before them on a motion to dismiss, and the standard for determining whether an action should be dismissed was whether any relief was possible on any theory. Blackmun thought Hardwick had stated a claim indicating the sodomy statute interfered with his protected privacy interests and his freedom of intimate association and found Bowers's justifications of "adverse consequences to public health and welfare" and "interference with the maintenance of a decent society" to be insufficient to support dismissal of Hardwick's claim.

Finally, Justice Stevens also wrote a dissent, in which Justices Brennan and Marshall joined. Stevens posed and answered two questions: could a state totally prohibit conduct with a neutral law that applied to all persons and, if not, could the state save its law by enforcing it only against homosexuals? Stevens answered no to his first question, finding intimate sexual contact between both heterosexuals and homosexuals to be a protected form of liberty. Stevens also answered no to his second question, finding no sufficient justification was presented for selective application of the sodomy law.

AFTERMATH

The decision went against cases such as GRISWOLD V. CONNECTICUT (1965) by applying a lower standard than compelling state interest, saying that the Court's previous right-to-privacy cases did not include homosexual conduct. The result is an uncertainty in the right-to-privacy area, breaking with judicial precedent. In this case the Court held that government intrusion in the bedroom is constitutional if the conduct taking place there is immoral. Hardwick died of AIDS several years after the case was decided.

SIGNIFICANCE

This decision was a setback to gay rights, encouraging discrimination against homosexuals in employment, child custody, and housing. In December 2003 the Supreme Court heard the case of *Lawrence and Garner v. Texas,* which dealt with the 1998 arrest of two men under a Texas law that made same-sex intercourse a crime. The court found that the law and others like it violated the due process clause of the Fourteenth Amendment. This ruling effectively reverses the Supreme Court's decision in *Bowers v. Hardwick.*

RELATED CASES

Griswold v. Connecticut, 381 U.S. 479 (1965)

Loving v. Virginia, 388 U.S. 1 (1967)

Roe v. Wade, 410 U.S. 113 (1973)

RECOMMENDED READING

Anne B. Goldstein, *History, Homosexuality, and Political Values: Searching for Hidden Determinants of* Bowers v. Hardwick, 97 Yale Law Journal 1073–1104 (May 1988).

Jed Rubenfeld, *The Right of Privacy,* 102 Harvard Law Review 737–807 (February 1989).

Norman Vieira, *Hardwick and the Right of Privacy,* 55 University of Chicago Law Review 1181–1191 (fall 1988).

Case Title: *Carey v. Population Services Int'l.*

Alternate Case Title: The Contraceptive Advertising Case

Legal Citations: 431 U.S. 678; 97 S.Ct. 2010; 52 L.Ed. 2d 675

Year of Decision: 1977

KEY ISSUES

Was the district court correct in invalidating the provisions of a state law prohibiting the distribution of nonmedical contraceptives?

HISTORY OF THE CASE

Population Planning Associates (PPA) was a corporation that made mail-order sales of nonmedical contraceptive devices from its North Carolina offices and regularly advertised its products in New York periodicals. This corporation also filled mail orders from New York City residents without limiting availability of the products to persons of any particular age. Section 6811 (8) of the New York Education Law made it a crime (1) for any person to sell or distribute any contraceptive to a minor under 16; (2) for anyone other than a licensed pharmacist to distribute contraceptives to persons 16 or over; and (3) for anyone, including pharmacists, to advertise or display contraceptives.

PPA challenged the constitutionality of section 6811(8). A three-judge district court declared the statute unconstitutional in its entirety under the First and Fourteenth Amendments insofar as it applied to nonprescription contraceptives. State officials including Hugh Carey, the governor of New York, sought review by the U.S. Supreme Court.

SUMMARY OF ARGUMENTS

The state argued that the "right of access to contraceptives" was not a fundamental aspect of personal liberty. It also argued that section 6811(8) furthered that state interests that young people not sell contraceptives, protected the varying products against tampering, and furthered other provisions of the statute. Lastly, they argued it served the state interests by restricting access to contraceptives and so discouraging increased sexual activity.

PPA argued that the state's policy to discourage sexual activity of minors was itself unconstitutional because the right of privacy comprehends a right of minors as well as adults to engage in private consensual sexual behavior.

DECISION

In a plurality opinion written by Justice Brennan, the New York law prohibiting any person other than a licensed pharmacist to distribute contraceptives was held invalid. Justice Brennan found regulations that imposed a burden on a decision as fundamental as whether to bear or beget a child could be justified only by a compelling state interest, and that the law must be narrowly drawn to express only those interests. He then found that the state provision burdened the right of individuals to use contraceptives if they so desired. Justice Brennan argued that the provision served no compelling state interest because it could not be justified as protecting health nor by a concern that young people not sell contraceptives. He further contended that it was not designed to serve as a quality control device or to further enforcement of the other provisions of the statute.

Justice Brennan reasoned that the prohibition of advertisements or displays of contraceptives could not be justified on the grounds that advertising these products would offend or embarrass people exposed to them. Neither could the argument that permitting advertisements or displays would legitimize sexual activity of young people be used as a justification. Justice Brennan concluded that these were all invalid justifications for suppressing expression protected by the First Amendment. He asserted that the expressions in this case merely

stated the availability of products, which were entirely legal and protected by the Constitution.

Justice White concurred in the opinion and emphasized that the "legality of state laws forbidding premarital intercourse is not at issue here." He believed that the state did not demonstrate that the prohibition against distribution of contraceptives to minors measurably contributed to the deterrent purposes that the state advanced.

Justice Powell also wrote a concurring opinion. He believed that the challenged statute was defective because it prohibited parents from distributing contraceptives to their children. He argued that this was a restriction that unjustifiably interfered with parental interests in rearing their children. He added that the Constitution may allow a state to require "prior parental consultation" as a condition for minors to obtain contraceptives.

In a concurring opinion, Justice Stevens argued that the prohibition against distribution of contraceptives to persons under 16 denied them and their parents a choice that could reduce exposure to venereal disease or unwanted pregnancy. He also believed that the prohibition could not be justified as a means of discouraging sexual activity by minors. Chief Justice Burger and Justice Rehnquist dissented.

AFTERMATH

After *Carey,* the Court established that a state cannot prevent individuals from deciding whether or when they wish to procreate.

SIGNIFICANCE

In *Carey,* the Court secured the right to reproductive autonomy and identified this right, rather than the existence of a marital relationship or an equal protection violation, as the deciding factor in creating the zone of privacy.

RELATED CASES

Bolger v. Youngs Drug Products Corp., 463 U.S. 60 (1983)

Virginia Pharmacy Bd. v. Virginia Citizens Consumer Council, 425 U.S. 748 (1976)

RECOMMENDED READING

Richards, D. *Toleration and the Constitution.* New York: Oxford University Press, 1986.

Case Title: *Eisenstadt v. Baird*

Alternate Case Title: The "Contraception for Unmarried Persons" Case

Legal Citations: 405 U.S. 438; 92 S.Ct. 1029

Year of Decision: 1972

KEY ISSUES

Is a Massachusetts statute permitting married persons to obtain contraceptives but prohibiting distribution of contraceptives to single persons constitutional?

HISTORY OF THE CASE

The Massachusetts General Laws Ann., c. 272, s 21 made it a felony for anyone, other than a registered physician or pharmacist, to dispense any article with the intention that it be used for the prevention of conception. Appellee, William Baird, was convicted at a bench trial in the Massachusetts Superior Court of violating a Massachusetts law for exhibiting contraceptive articles in the course of delivering a lecture on contraception to a group of students at Boston University, and for giving a woman contraceptive foam at the close of his lecture.

The Massachusetts Supreme Judicial Court set aside the conviction for exhibiting contraceptives on the ground that it violated appellee's First Amendment rights, but upheld the conviction for giving away the foam. The appellee subsequently filed a petition for writ of habeas corpus, which the district court dismissed. On appeal, the Court of Appeals for the First Circuit vacated the dismissal and remanded the action. The sheriff of Suffolk County appealed to the U.S. Supreme Court.

SUMMARY OF ARGUMENTS

The appellant, the sheriff of Suffolk County, Massachusetts, argued that Baird lacked standing to assert the rights of unmarried persons who were denied access to contraceptives. The appellant stated that the purpose of the Massachusetts statute regulating the distribution of contraceptives was to "promote marital fidelity and discourage premarital sex." Appellant also argued that only Baird's conduct was at issue; therefore, the statute did not violate Baird's First Amendment rights.

Baird argued that the Massachusetts statute's different treatment for married and unmarried persons violated the equal protection clause of the Fourteenth Amendment.

DECISION

Justice Brennan wrote the opinion for the Court holding that the Massachusetts statute permitting married persons to obtain contraceptives to prevent pregnancy but prohibiting distribution of contraceptives to single persons for that purpose violated the rights of single persons under the equal protection clause of the Fourteenth Amendment. Justice Brennan, agreeing with the Massachusetts Court of Appeals, stated that the goals of deterring premarital sex and regulating the distribution of potentially harmful objects could not reasonably be regarded as the legislative aim of the law. Justice Brennan, in applying a traditional rational basis review, which looks for a reasonable basis for the statute's enactment and a reasonable relationship to a legitimate government interest, held that none of the interests asserted in defense of the statute were sufficient to justify the challenged classification.

First, Justice Brennan concluded that the deterrence of premarital sex could not be reasonably regarded as the purpose of the law. He came to this conclusion after finding that (a) the statute did not prohibit the distribution of contraceptives to prevent the "spread of disease," and thus was "so riddled with exceptions" that its effect did not have a strong relationship to the stated objective, and (b) it was unreasonable to believe Massachusetts prescribed pregnancy as the punishment for fornication—a misdemeanor under Massachusetts law.

Justice Brennan also rejected the appellant's contention that the classification was designed to serve the health needs of the community by regulating what they perceived to be "potentially harmful articles." He found that not all contraceptives were potentially harmful, and that rationale did not serve to distinguish between married and unmarried persons. In coming to this conclusion, Justice Brennan redefined personal privacy to include "the right of the individual . . . to be free from unwarranted government intrusion into matters so fundamentally affecting a person as the decision whether to bear or beget a child." Justice Brennan declared procreation a matter of individual choice that did not implicate the state.

Justice Brennan then rejected the moral arguments for sustaining the statute and prohibiting contraception. He stated that the rights must be the same for the married and unmarried, whatever those rights to access to contraceptives may be. He looked to GRISWOLD V. CONNECTICUT (1965), which ruled that even if a state prohibited the distribution of contraceptives, the state could not outlaw distribution to unmarried, but not married persons and remain within the confines of the equal protection clause.

Justice Douglas wrote a concurring opinion on a narrower ground. He believed the instant case to be a First Amendment concern, arguing that appellee had the right to give the lecture on birth control and that there was no proof or finding that he intended the young woman to whom he handed the foam to keep it. Baird was not advocating views on contraception that would incite lawless action. Therefore, the test for denying First Amendment protection laid out in *Brandenburg v. Ohio*, which turned on whether advocacy incited violence, was not met.

Chief Justice Burger wrote a dissenting opinion and Justice Powell and Justice Rehnquist took no part in the decision.

AFTERMATH

The Court still has declined to locate the right to privacy in any specific constitutional provision. Instead, it has held that the right inheres in the First, Fourth, Fifth, and Ninth Amendments. Decisions after *Eisenstadt* made it clear that the rights articulated in *Griswold* and *Eisenstadt* apply equally to married and unmarried persons. See *Carey v. Population Services Int'l*, 431 U.S. 678 (1977). It should be noted that *Eisenstadt* was one case in a line of cases seeking reproductive freedom. In fact the Court decided ROE V. WADE (1973), the decision regarding abortion, the year following its decision in *Eisenstadt*.

SIGNIFICANCE

In *Griswold v. Connecticut*, the right to privacy inhered in the marital relationship. *Eisenstadt* specifically extended the zone of privacy beyond marriage. It supports the view that the individual's right to control her decisions about procreation does not come from the marital relationship, but instead flows from each individual's interest in autonomy.

RELATED CASES

Griswold v. Connecticut, 381 U.S. 479 (1965)

Roe v. Wade, 410 U.S. 113 (1973)

Skinner v. Oklahoma, 316 U.S. 535 (1942)

RECOMMENDED READING

Cass R. Sunstein, *Six Theses on Interpretation*, 6 Constitutional Commentary 91 (1989).

Harry Wellington, *Common Law Rules and Constitutional Double Standards: Some Notes on Adjudication*, 83 Yale Law Journal 221 (1973).

Case Title: *Griswold v. Connecticut*

Legal Citation: 381 U.S. 479

Year of Decision: 1965

KEY ISSUES

Does a state statute that prohibits the use and the provision of assistance or counseling about contraceptives violate the right of marital privacy as protected by the First, Third, Fourth, Fifth, Ninth, and Fourteenth Amendments to the U.S. Constitution?

HISTORY OF THE CASE

Estelle Griswold was the executive director of Planned Parenthood League of Connecticut. She was joined in this suit by C. Lee Buxton, who was a licensed physician and the medical director at the Yale Medical School. They both gave information, instruction, and medical advice to married persons regarding the availability of contraceptives to prevent conception. They examined and prescribed contraceptive devices for use by women.

Two state statutes regulated such conduct. The first statute prohibited the use of any device to prevent conception. The second statute provided that anyone who "assists, abets, causes, hires, or commands another to commit any offense may be prosecuted and punished as if he were the principal offender."

Griswold and Buxton were convicted of violating the statutes by acting as accessories. They were fined $100 each. The Appellate Division of the Circuit Court affirmed these convictions. The state's Supreme Court of Errors also affirmed this judgment.

SUMMARY OF ARGUMENTS

Griswold and Buxton argued that the statutes violated the right to marital privacy, which is protected by the Constitution. They asserted case history established that certain basic rights involved with procreation, marriage, and family life may not be infringed upon by the government, except where the state demonstrates a compelling state interest and achieves that end through a narrowly tailored mechanism.

The state of Connecticut argued that as long as the statute served a legitimate state interest it was within the state's discretion to determine what legislation is appropriate. They argued that the statute served the legitimate state purpose of preventing marital infidelity. The purpose of the act was not to infringe the right of marital privacy, but rather to exercise legitimate state police powers to circumscribe the conduct of persons who are married.

DECISION

Justice Douglas wrote the opinion of the Court. As to the preliminary matter of whether Griswold and Buxton had standing to assert the claim, he held that they did by nature of their professional relationship with married people. He reasoned that in a circumstance where the person taking action and the person assisting with the action are both punished, the person assisting should have the right to challenge the statute that ascribes culpability to the commission of the act.

In addressing the merits of the case, Justice Douglas held that the law was unconstitutional because it infringed on the relationship of a married couple and their physician. He noted that the Court was not infringing on the right to legislate in areas of economics, business affairs, or social conditions; however, in circumstances in which the legislature infringes on the right of association, the Court may invalidate the law. Though

not explicitly stated in the Bill of Rights or the Constitution, the right of association has been construed as protected by the First Amendment. The state may not, consistent with the First Amendment, designate the spectrum of available knowledge. Justice Douglas thus reaffirmed the holdings in *Pierce v. Society of Sisters* (1925) and *Meyer v. the State of Nebraska* (1923).

Justice Stewart held that there is a right to marital privacy created by several constitutional guarantees: "Various guarantees create zones of privacy. The right of association contained in the penumbra of the First Amendment is one. . . . The Third Amendment in its prohibition against the quartering of soldiers 'in any house' in time of peace without the consent of the owner is another facet of that privacy. The Fourth Amendment explicitly affirms the 'right of the people to be secure in their persons, houses, papers, and effects, against unreasonable searches and seizures. The Fifth Amendment in its self-incrimination clause enables the citizen to create a zone of privacy which government may not force him to surrender to his detriment. The Ninth Amendment provides: 'The enumeration in the Constitution, of certain rights, shall not be construed to deny or disparage others retained by the people.'"

In invalidating the statute, Justice Stewart also relied on previous decisions. In *Boyd v. United States* it was held that the Fourth and Fifth Amendments were "protection against all government invasions 'of the sanctity of a man's home and the privacy of life.'" In MAPP V. OHIO the Court held that the Fourth Amendment created a right of privacy equal in importance to other rights reserved to people. The statute at issue had a destructive impact on marital privacy. Marital infidelity could be prevented through regulating the manufacture or sale of contraceptives in the state. He concluded that the state may not accomplish a legitimate state end in an unnecessarily broad manner that invades the area of protected freedoms.

Justice Goldberg wrote a concurring opinion in which the chief justice and Justice Brennan joined. He agreed that the statute was unconstitutional because it unnecessarily intruded in the area of marital privacy. He added that the Ninth Amendment had relevance to the Court's holding. The Ninth Amendment states: "the enumeration in the Constitution, of certain rights, shall not be construed to deny or disparage others retained by the people." He contended that since 1791 the Ninth Amendment has been a basic part of the Constitution and the possibility of the invasion of the right of marital privacy provided the opportunity to use this amendment: "To hold that a right so basic and fundamental and so deep-rooted in our society as the right of privacy in marriage may be infringed because that right is not guaranteed in so many words by the first eight amendments to the Constitution is to ignore the Ninth Amendment and to give it no effect whatsoever." He concluded that this right lent support to the contention of Griswold and Buxton that the right of marital privacy, though not an enumerated, constitutionally protected right, still is protected under the general right to privacy established by various amendments and judicial decisions.

He continued that the purpose of the Constitution made the right to marital privacy of comparable magnitude to the fundamental rights that are constitutionally protected. The fact that no provision of the Constitution "explicitly forbids the State from disrupting the traditional relation of the family—a relation as old and as fundamental as our entire civilization—surely does not show that the Government was meant to have the power to do so." Rather, as the Ninth Amendment expressly recognizes, fundamental personal rights such as this one are protected from abridgment by the government though not specifically mentioned in the Constitution. The purpose of the statute at issue was not to advance a compelling state interest and thus did not justify the encroachment of the statute on a fundamental right.

Justice Harlan concurred in judgment only. He stated that the majority's opinion implied that the incorporation doctrine, which makes certain portions of the Bill of Rights applicable to the states, may be used to restrict the due process clause of the Fourteenth Amendment, which he found a constitutionally unacceptable position. He felt that the appropriate constitutional inquiry was whether the statute violated "basic values implicit in the concept of ordered liberty."

Justice White concurred in judgment. He argued that the Connecticut statute worked to deprive married couples of liberty without due process of law. He noted that the statute addressed a substantive segment of the marital relationship. Case law had established that where a state law encroaches in such a significant way

the state must show that it does so for a compelling reason: "Where there is a significant encroachment upon personal liberty only upon showing a subordinating interest which is compelling." In that the state did not show such an interest in this case, he thought the statute was unconstitutional: "It is purely fanciful to believe that the broad proscription on use facilitates discovery of use by persons engaging in a prohibited relationship or for some other reason makes such use more unlikely and thus can be supported by any sort of administrative consideration."

Justice Black dissented; Justice Stewart joined this opinion. Black noted that the First Amendment does not protect the conduct that the defendants, Griswold and Buxton, were engaged in simply because speech was involved. For this reason the First Amendment argument offered by Justice Douglas was not compelling. In addition, he felt that the Court presented the right to privacy as absolute. He noted that the right to privacy has been proscribed by certain constitutional provisions for certain places and times and was not as all-encompassing as presented by the concurring justices.

He also refuted the arguments that the right to marital privacy was established by either the due process clause or the Ninth Amendment. He felt to extend these provisions to invalidate the statute by creating a right to marital privacy was illegitimate: "I think that is properly construed neither the due process clause nor the Ninth Amendment, nor both together, could under any circumstances be a proper basis for invalidating the Connecticut law."

In addition, he argued that legislatures do not enact statutes that they believe are irrational or unjustifiable. Though the Court may not agree with the statute, it does not automatically make it unconstitutional. He noted that the concurring opinion's reliance on *Pierce* and *Meyer* was misplaced, as the holding in these cases had later been repudiated. He noted that the Court in this situation misused its power to find laws unconstitutional because no provision in the Constitution supported the finding that Connecticut law at issue was unconstitutional. He concluded that the Court instead had based its finding on its feeling that the statute was unwise. While the feeling may be legitimate, a Court decision based on this impulse was not. Not only was it illegitimate, it threatened the separation of powers in the federal system and among the federal government and the states:

> My point is that there is no provision of the Constitution which either expressly or impliedly vests the power in this Court to sit as a supervisory agency over acts of duly constituted legislative bodies and set aside their laws because of the Court's belief that the legislative policies adopted are unreasonable, unwise, arbitrary, capricious or irrational. The adoption of such a loose, flexible, uncontrolled standard for holding laws unconstitutional, if ever it is finally achieved will amount to a great unconstitutional shift of power to the courts which I believe and am constrained to say will be bad for courts and worse for the country. Subjecting federal and state laws to such an unrestrained judicial control [would], I fear, jeopardize the separation of powers that the Framers set up and at the same time threaten to take away much of the power of States to govern themselves which the Constitution plainly intended them to have.

The doctrine that the courts have the power to invalidate those laws that it finds unreasonable, that prevailed in the *Lochner* and *Burns* cases, had long since been abandoned by the Court.

Justice Stewart dissented and Justice Black joined his dissent. Stewart reasoned that he was unable to find the law unconstitutional. He found nothing in the First, Third, Fourth, and Fifth Amendments to support the contention that the Connecticut law was invalid. He refuted the contention that the Ninth Amendment was at all applicable to this case and further held that such an interpretation misconstrued the amendment. He continued that there was a general right to privacy established in the Constitution that the Court could have relied on to support its holding in this case. He concluded that if the law at issue does not conform with the prevailing community standard, it should be overturned through legislative action rather than through judicial intervention.

Aftermath

Seven years after this decision, in *EISENSTADT V. BAIRD*, the Court held that a Massachusetts statute that prohibited the distribution of contraceptive devices or medicines to any unmarried person violated the equal protection clause of the Constitution. The Court reasoned that the justifications offered by the state for the classifications was insufficient.

In *CAREY V. POPULATION SERVICES INTERNATIONAL* (1977) the Court held that a New York statute that allowed only licensed pharmacists to distribute contraceptives was invalid. The reasoning of the decision was that "*Griswold* may no longer be read as holding only that a State may not prohibit a married couple's use of contraceptives. Read in light of its progeny, the teaching of *Griswold* is that the Constitution protects individual decisions in matters of childbearing from unjustified intrusion by the State." In that the New York statute represented such an unjustified intrusion, it was invalid. The Court held that the restriction of contraceptives infringed on the right to make decisions regarding childbearing.

In *ROE V. WADE* (1973) the Court held that there is a constitutional right of privacy which encompasses a woman's right to choose whether to terminate a pregnancy.

Griswold was a landmark case in the area of reproductive rights and expanded the area of privacy protected by the Court. It set the stage for further challenges to state regulations in the area of privacy. The Court has been unwilling to extend the right of privacy to the area of sexual activity between same-sex couples, however. In *BOWERS V. HARDWICK* the Court rejected the contention that a statute that prohibited sodomy violated the constitutionally protected right of the plaintiff to privacy. The Court reasoned to invalidate the statute would invalidate many state criminal statutes prohibiting sodomy, and such an idea ran counter to Judeo-Christian moral and ethical standards.

Significance

Griswold was the first in a series of constitutional cases dealing with the rights of privacy and to abortion, which set the stage for debate over fundamental rights jurisprudence. As a result of this decision the Court was criticized for its protection of rights not explicitly granted by the Constitution as fundamental rights. This case demonstrated that in the proper context the Court was willing to go beyond the text in protecting what is established by the Constitution as fundamental. It viewed the Constitution as a living document, for adaptation when the needs of society change and its technology advances.

Griswold became a precedent for protection of individual decisions in the area of contraception and family planning. Justice Brennan's statement that "if the right of privacy means anything, it is the right of the individual, married or single, to be free from unwarranted governmental intrusion into matters so fundamentally affecting a person as the decision whether to bear or beget a child" has become the principle for which *Griswold* has come to stand.

In addition, this decision was significant for establishing marital right of privacy and attempting to interpret the Ninth Amendment.

RELATED CASES

Bowers v. Hardwick, 478 U.S. 186 (1986)

Carey v. Population Services International, 431 U.S. 678 (1977)

Eisenstadt v. Baird, 405 U.S. 438 (1972)

Meyer v. State of Nebraska, 2626 U.S. 390 (1923)

Pierce v. Society of Sisters, 268 U.S. 510 (1925)

Roe v. Wade, 410 U.S. 113 (1973)

RECOMMENDED READING

John Hart Ely, *The Wages of Crying Wolf: A Comment on* Roe v. Wade, 82 Yale Law Journal 920 (1973).

Louis Henkin, *Privacy and Autonomy,* 74 Columbia Law Review 1410 (1974).

Paul G. Kauper, *Penumbras, Peripheries, Emanations, Things Fundamental and Things Forgotten: The Griswold Case,* 64 Michigan Law Review 235 (1965).

Jed Rubenfeld, *The Right to Privacy,* 102 Harvard Law Review 737 (1989).

Mark John Kappelhoff, Bowers v. Hardwick: *Is There a Right to Privacy?* 37 American University Law Review 487 (1988).

Case Title: *Stenberg v. Carhart*

Alternate Case Title: "Partial-Birth Abortion" Case

Legal Citation: 530 U.S. 914

Year of Decision: 2000

KEY ISSUES

Does a Nebraska statute that bans partial-birth abortions, abortions performed by partially delivering the fetus, terminating the life of the fetus, and then completing the delivery of the fetus, violate the U.S. Constitution?

HISTORY OF THE CASE

Two types of abortion procedures were used to perform abortions after the 13th week of pregnancy, dilation and evacuation (D & E) and dilation and extraction (D & X). As the case exhibits, there was controversy about whether these procedures are sufficiently similar or different. The state of Nebraska had enacted a law stating "[n]o partial birth abortion shall be performed in this state, unless such procedure is necessary to save the life of the mother whose life is endangered by a physical disorder, physical illness, or physical injury, including a life-endangering physical condition caused by or arising from the pregnancy itself." The statute went on to define partial-birth abortion as a procedure during which an unborn child was partially delivered, then killed before the delivery was completed. The statute also further defined the "partial delivery" language to mean the delivery of a substantial part of the child. Violation of the statute was a felony and carried a penalty of a prison term of up to 20 years and up to a $25,000 fine, as well as automatic revocation of a doctor's license to practice in the state of Nebraska.

Dr. Leroy Carhart, a Nebraska physician who performed abortions, filed a lawsuit against the state of Nebraska alleging that the statute violated the U.S. Constitution and seeking an order stopping its enforcement. The district court found the Nebraska statute unconstitutional and the Eighth Circuit Court of Appeals affirmed the district court's decision. The Supreme Court granted certiorari to review the case.

SUMMARY OF ARGUMENTS

Don Stenberg, the attorney general of the state of Nebraska, argued that the Nebraska statute did not encompass the more common D & E abortion procedure and that the purpose of enacting the statute was to ban the D & X procedure. Stenberg further argued that constitutional principles required this interpretation. Finally, Stenberg argued that the statute did not place an undue burden on a woman's right to seek an abortion.

Dr. Carhart argued that the Nebraska statute prohibited most abortions and could not be narrowed to limit its scope. Additionally, Dr. Carhart argued that even if the statute was rewritten, it would still violate a woman's right to privacy, imposing an undue burden on a woman's right to seek an abortion and lacking an exception for ill and dying women.

Decision

Justice Breyer gave the opinion of the Court and was joined by Justices Stevens, O'Connor, Souter, and Ginsberg. As an initial matter, Justice Breyer cited the controversial nature of the topic at hand and went through a lengthy technical discussion of the methods of performing abortions, stating that the D & E and D & X procedures were sufficiently similar. Justice Breyer applied the legal principles of the Court's decisions in ROE V. WADE (1973) and *Planned Parenthood of Southeastern Pa. v. Casey* (1992) to the facts of the case. Justice Breyer stated those legal principles as (1) a woman has a right to choose to terminate her pregnancy before viability, the point at which the child could survive outside the womb; (2) state laws to further a state's interest imposing an undue burden on a woman's choice to seek a pre-viability abortion are unconstitutional; and (3) after viability, a state may regulate and even prohibit abortion to further its interest in human life except where abortion would be necessary to preserve the mother's life or health. Justice Breyer found that the Nebraska statute violated the U.S. Constitution because the statute lacked an exception to preserve the mother's life or health and the statute imposed an undue burden on the woman's right to choose an abortion by burdening her ability to choose the D & E procedure.

Justice Breyer found the Nebraska statute to apply to both pre- and post-viability abortions and found that it did not further the state's interest in human life as it regulated only "a method of performing abortion." Because in the Court's prior decisions it had found that a "State may

promote but not endanger a woman's health when it regulates the methods of abortion," Breyer found a health exception was necessary, rejecting the state's arguments that there was no need for a health exception because other safe alternatives were available. Further, because the statute covered a broad category of abortion procedures, and did not differentiate between types of procedures, it placed an undue burden on a woman's right to terminate her pregnancy pre-viability. Justice Breyer declined to adopt a narrowing construction of the statute finding that the statutory interpretation of the attorney general of Nebraska that the statute did differentiate between procedures was not binding on the Court. Therefore, the Court found the statute to be unconstitutional.

Justices Stevens and Ginsburg concurred stating that just because the description of the procedures involved in partial birth abortions may be unpleasant, such unpleasantry did not provide a reason to uphold the statute.

Justice O'Connor concurred separately emphasizing that the statute failed to provide the health preservation exception required by *Casey* and that the statute's breadth imposed an undue burden on a woman's right to choose a pre-viability abortion. Justice O'Connor indicated that other states had enacted similar statutes that were tailored more narrowly so as to proscribe only the D & X procedure and, if Nebraska had so limited its statute, the result may have been different.

Chief Justice Rehnquist wrote a brief separate dissent indicating that he thought *Casey* was wrongly decided.

Justice Scalia dissented acknowledging his revulsion at the descriptions of the abortion methodology and stating that the Court's decision was the "predictable consequence" of the Court's decision in *Casey*, a decision that Scalia believed created a "hopelessly unworkable" standard, the undue burden standard. Scalia stated that he did not agree with the Court's definition of undue burden, indicating that how one defines undue burden is a value judgment, thus the decision of the Court is no more than a policy judgment with which Scalia disagreed. Scalia further disagreed with the Court's application of constitutional interpretation principles, finding that ambiguous statute should be interpreted to make them constitutional if at all possible.

Justice Kennedy, joined by the chief justice, dissented in finding that the Nebraska statute placed no undue burden on a woman's right to choose. Kennedy believed the Court disregarded the state's interest in prohibiting partial-birth abortion in making its decision and found that it was not the Court's place to determine whether the Nebraska statute differentiated between procedures, but rather Nebraska should make that interpretation. Further, Justice Kennedy found that *Casey* supported the state's interests as legitimate. Justice Kennedy also found the majority misapplied statutory construction doctrines when interpreting the statute's terms.

Finally, Justice Thomas dissented, joined by Chief Justice Rehnquist and Justice Scalia. Justice Thomas also indicated that he believed the majority was imposing its value judgment on the state and that the *Casey* standard of undue burden reflected this value judgment. Thomas likened partial-birth abortion to infanticide and found that the majority misapplied *Casey*'s undue burden standard and constitutional construction principles.

AFTERMATH

The decision in *Stenberg* voided the partial-birth abortion statutes of at least 28 states. In November 2003 President George W. Bush signed into law a bill outlawing a procedure used in partial-birth abortions. This legislation is being challenged, though, in courtrooms in California, Nebraska, and New York.

SIGNIFICANCE

Any state legislation enacted to restrict abortion must be narrowly tailored and contain a health exception allowing abortion when "necessary, in the appropriate medical judgment, for the preservation of the life or health of the mother."

RELATED CASES

Planned Parenthood of Southeastern Pa. v. Casey, 505 U.S. 833 (1992)

Roe v. Wade, 410 U.S. 113 (1973)

RECOMMENDED READING

Aimee M. Gauthier, Stenberg v. Carhart: *Have the States Lost Their Power to Regulate Abortion?*, 36 New England Law Review 625 (2002).

Stephanie D. Schmutz, *Infanticide Civil Rights for Women: Did the Supreme Court Go Too Far in Stenberg v. Carhart?*, 39 Houston Law Review 529 (2002).

Case Title: *Whalen v. Roe*

Legal Citations: 429 U.S. 590; 97 S.Ct. 869; 51 L.Ed. 2d 64

Year of Decision: 1977

KEY ISSUES

Does a New York statute requiring that the state be provided with a copy of prescriptions for certain drugs unconstitutionally violate a patient's right to privacy?

HISTORY OF THE CASE

The New York legislature passed a law in 1972 that sought to stop legally prescribed drugs from being diverted to unlawful uses. The statute required that prescriptions for the most dangerous legitimate (Schedule II) drugs be prepared on an official triplicate form. This form included the doctor's name, the dispensing pharmacy, the drug and dosage, and the patient's name, address, and age. The law mandated that one copy be retained each by the prescribing physician and the dispensing pharmacy. The State Health Department received the third copy. The statute provided that the Health Department keep this information for five years in its computer files. The department restricted access to the locked and alarm-protected file room to a limited number of investigatory personnel.

Richard Roe and appellees, patients using Schedule II drugs, sued New York Commissioner of Health Robert P. Whalen, challenging the law as an unconstitutional infringement on their federal right to privacy. They also alleged specific New York statutory rights violations. The district court agreed and enjoined statute enforcement. The state of New York appealed in Whalen's name. The Supreme Court accepted the case and held that the statutes were a reasonable exercise of the state's broad police power.

SUMMARY OF ARGUMENTS

Roe contended that the statute invaded a constitutionally protected "zone of privacy," and that a variety of provisions in the Bill of Rights and previous opinions of the Court or its individual justices justified this position. Roe argued that two different privacy interests exist under a constitutional "penumbra." This undefined right to privacy forms an independent source of constitutional protection. In one way, an individual has an interest in avoiding disclosure of personal matters. In a second respect, he has another interest in independence in making certain kinds of important decisions. Roe asserted that the law makes some patients reluctant to use, and some doctors reluctant to prescribe, the regulated drugs for fear that the information will become publicly known. By putting the statute-required information in a readily available form, Roe and appellees argued that the New York statute impaired both of these penumbral privacy rights.

The state argued against both assertions and claimed that the state legislature reasonably exercised its legitimate police power in regulating the drugs.

DECISION

The justices agreed with Whalen and the state of New York, reversed the trial court injunction, and identified three holdings. First, the Court found the patient-identification procedure a reasonable exercise of the state's police power. Second, it concluded that neither the perceived nor the real impact of the patient-identification requirement constituted any patient constitutional invasion. The opinion dismissed four supporting arguments on this point. Finally, the Court ruled that the statute did not interfere with a physician's right to practice medicine free from unwarranted state interference.

On the first issue, the Court determined that "an orderly and rational" process governed the legislative decision to deal with the unlawful drug diversion problem. This "rational relationship" test allowed the Court to defer to legislative wisdom in creating the law on three conditions. There had to be a legitimate state objective—almost any health, safety, or general welfare goal would be considered legitimate—and this state aim must minimally relate to the law. Additionally, the proposed legislation must not impair any fundamental constitutional right. Justice Stevens

wrote that the state had a "vital interest in controlling the distribution of dangerous drugs," and this, at the very least, supported the new legislation. Indeed, regulation going to lawful health, safety, or general welfare goals could take a variety of valid forms.

On the "zone of privacy" question, the Court discerned no Fourteenth Amendment violation. The opinion identifies four scenarios in which statute violation might occur, discounting all as not violating Roe's privacy right. In the first scenario, Justice Stevens wrote that the possibility that a doctor or pharmacist would willingly violate the new statute existed under prior law. Therefore, this point did not relate to the computerized data bank specified in the new law. In the second case, the justice found no support for assuming the state would improperly administer the law's security provisions. The Court referred to the Health Commission's own investigation into the California and Illinois central filing systems—a system emulated by the New York statute. That inquiry showed that not a single patient's privacy was invaded. Roe argued that a third situation, involving the judiciary, might also compromise an individual's privacy. The Court, however, considered the possibility of poor judicial supervision over patient-identifying evidence as too remote. It deemed this reason insufficient for invalidating the entire patient-identification program. In the fourth circumstance, Roe suggested that concern about mandatory disclosure might deter patients from receiving needed medication. Justice Stevens's opinion, however, pointed out that state-licensed doctors and pharmacists filed about 100,000 prescriptions for Schedule II drugs each month before the trial court's injunction. This, the Justice wrote, clearly showed that the statute did not deprive the public of access to the drugs. The Court concluded that Roe and patients in similar circumstances suffered no Fourteenth Amendment right or liberty invasion.

The Court's third point answered the constitutional question of whether the statute infringed on doctor's right to practice medicine free of unwarranted state interference. To the extent that this claim raised patient disclosure concerns that might inhibit doctors from prescribing the Schedule II drugs, the Court ruled this claim derives from the patients. The Court found this argument similar to the one alleging that some patients might decline medication for fear of "publicity." As the Court dismissed this worry, it similarly dispatched with the like contention relating to physicians.

In sum, the *Whalen* opinion held that New York reasonably asserted its police power to legislate in a recognized matter of health, safety, or general welfare. The Court also found the law reasonable in its limitations on the use and distribution of the collected data. Following from this, no basis existed for finding the program invalid. The legislation infringed no patient or physician constitutional privacy.

AFTERMATH

The highly deferential rational relationship review standard most commonly applies to cases involving economic regulation. *Whalen* demonstrates the Court's willingness to apply the same liberal formula to social regulation as well. Since *Whalen*, the Supreme Court has confronted the propriety of government data collection only in terms of the Fourth Amendment right to be free from unreasonable searches and seizures, and the Fifth Amendment prohibition against compelling persons to incriminate themselves.

SIGNIFICANCE

Because the Constitution does not specifically mention privacy, one can only make a theoretical argument that the Constitution protects an individual's privacy against having the government gather information about oneself, or in the alternative, in not having the government release this information. The ruling in GRISWOLD V. CONNECTICUT (1965) might support such a position. The Supreme Court, though, has not granted particular weight to any such general interest in nondisclosure. As found in *Whalen*, a state's interest in gathering data on health, safety, and general welfare—matters within its police power purview—will, for now, always outweigh the individual's privacy interest to the contrary.

RELATED CASES

Griswold v. Connecticut, 381 U.S. 479 (1965)

New State Ice Co. v. Liebmann, 285 U.S. 262 (1932)

Planned Parenthood of SE Pennsylvania v. Casey, 505 U.S. 833 (1992)

Roe v. Wade, 410 U.S. 113 (1973)

Stanley v. Georgia, 394 U.S. 557 (1969)

United States Dept. of Justice v. Reporters Committee for Freedom of the Press, 489 U.S. 749 (1989)

RECOMMENDED READING

Wendy Parment, *Public Health Protection and the Privacy of Medical Records*, 16 Harvard Civil Rights–Civil Liberties Law Review 270 (1981).

FREEDOM OF RELIGION

Case Title: *School District of Abington Township, Pennsylvania v. Schempp*

Alternate Case Title: Bible-Reading Case

Legal Citation: 374 U.S. 203

Year of Decision: 1963

KEY ISSUES

May public schools require that the Bible be read in the classroom?

HISTORY OF THE CASE

This case arose from two related disputes. The first involved a suit by parents in Pennsylvania trying to prevent the enforcement of a state law that provided that the Bible would be read at the opening of school. The second case involved an action brought by Madalyn Murray, a well-known atheist, objecting to the requirement in the Baltimore city schools that the opening of school begin with the reading of the Bible or the recitation of the Lord's Prayer. In the Pennsylvania case, the parents won, and in the Baltimore case, Ms. Murray lost. An appeal was taken to the Supreme Court directly in the Pennsylvania case, and, in the Baltimore case, to the Court of Appeals of Maryland, which ruled in favor of the school board. The cases were consolidated before the U.S. Supreme Court.

SUMMARY OF ARGUMENTS

The attorney general of Pennsylvania argued that the students had not been deprived of any constitutional right because they had not been compelled to believe, disbelieve, participate in, or attend these Bible reading exercises. Further, no measurable tax burden was created by the reading. Eighteen other attorneys general joined with the Maryland attorney general in arguing that the required Bible reading did no harm, since it was done without comment.

The attorneys for the parents argued that the mere requirement of the reading constituted the establishment of religion and also violated the Fourteenth Amendment because it was done under a state law.

DECISION

Justice Tom Clark, writing for eight of the justices, held that the practice of Bible reading was unconstitutional under the establishment of religion clause of the First Amendment.

Justice Clark found that the recitation of the Lord's Prayer over an intercom system or by a homeroom teacher and/or the reading of the Bible, whether in the King James or Douay or Revised Standard versions, or from the Jewish scriptures, interfered with the neutrality mandated by the federal Constitution. In a discussion of the First Amendment, Justice Clark reviewed the historical reasons for the refusal of either the state or the federal government to endorse a particular religion and the reason for the prohibition of the establishment of religion. The other clause of the First Amendment, otherwise known as the free exercise clause, does recognize the value of religious training and the right of every person to freely choose his or her own religion, free of compulsion from the state. Justice Clark recognized that the two clauses may overlap.

The test he put forth in the decision was that the purpose and primary effect of the act must be examined. If advancement or inhibition of religion is the purpose of the legislation, then it is prohibited. If, however, the purpose is secular, and the primary effect neither advances nor inhibits religion, the use may be permitted. The study of the Bible in a nondevotional use would be plainly accepted. Further, discussions could be held about the differences between religious sects in classes dealing with literature, history, or philosophy.

Justice Clark noted the argument that, unless religious exercises were permitted, a "religion of secularism" would be established in the schools. He stated that the government may not establish any kind of religion, whether secular or religious in a traditional sense. The majority cannot use its power to enforce the practice of its beliefs. Justice Clark stated that the place of religion is exalted in our culture and was achieved through a long tradition of study in the home and church and in the individual heart and mind, but the role of the state must be a firm commitment to neutrality.

Justice Douglas wrote a concurring opinion, as did Justice Brennan, who went to great lengths to trace the historical and legal trends in the interpretation of the First Amendment. In particular, he looked at Sunday closing laws and religious exercises in schools. He noted that Boston had required the use of prayer and the reading of the scriptures in its schools since 1789. In tracing the development of the requirement of the use of scriptures in schools, he noted that as American culture became more diverse, there was a greater movement to accommodate those of different religious backgrounds. In 1875, President Ulysses Grant had made a statement that matters of religion should be removed from the school and left to the "family, altar, the church, and the private school, supported entirely by private contributions." President Theodore Roosevelt declared that the schools should be "absolutely nonsectarian" and that it was "not our business to have the Protestant Bible or the Catholic Vulgate or the Talmud read in those schools." Justice Brennan found that there were many activities which may have had a religious origin but have ceased to have a religious meaning, and that there was nothing novel or radical about the decision of the court in outlawing prayer or Bible reading in school.

Justice Goldberg and Justice Harlan filed another concurring opinion.

In the only dissent, Justice Stewart (who also dissented in ENGEL V. VITALE) argued that the cases were "fundamentally deficient" and felt that it was a tremendous oversimplification of the act of merely requiring the reading of scripture. He could not connect the Court's reasoning in the majority decisions with the fact that the U.S. government provided chaplains for Armed Forces personnel. He felt that the Court's decision restricted religious liberty. He felt that none of the parties presented any evidence that there was any coercion or psychological compulsion to participate in these required readings. He felt that school boards had enough inventiveness to accommodate in some way those who wished to worship and those who did not wish to worship.

AFTERMATH

As a result of this case, Madalyn Murray became a national celebrity. The decision was widely criticized, and, in view of the fact that it followed *Engel v. Vitale* by about one year, the tenor of much of the earlier outcry was rekindled by the fear that religion was being destroyed through these decisions.

SIGNIFICANCE

Abington Township was considered by many to be the Supreme Court decision that kicked the Bible out of public schools. On the contrary, the decision did not totally eliminate the Bible from public schools, but rather eliminated the Bible's use when it was required to be read for an underlying religious purpose. Despite a movement to "impeach Earl Warren" and to condemn Madalyn Murray, after *Abington Township* the question of Bible reading in school began to abate. Ultimately, the *Abington Township* decision provided the basis from which the current test for determining establishment clause violations evolved.

RELATED CASES

Engel v. Vitale, 370 U.S. 421 (1962)

Lee v. Weisman, 112 S.Ct. 2649, 129 L.Ed. 2d. 467 (1992)

Wisconsin v. Yoder, 406 U.S. 205 (1972)

RECOMMENDED READING

Cord, Robert. *Separation of Church and State.* New York: Lambeth Press, 1982.

Freund, Paul, and Robert Ulrich. *Religion and the Public Schools.* Cambridge, Mass.: Harvard University Press, 1965.

Pfeffer, Leo. *Church, State and Freedom.* Boston: Beacon Press, 1967.

Case Title: *Braunfeld v. Brown*

Alternate Case Title: The "Sunday Closing" Case

Legal Citations: 366 U.S. 599; 81 S.Ct. 1144; 6 L.Ed. 2d 563

Year of Decision: 1961

KEY ISSUES

Does a statute that prohibits the Sunday retail sale of certain commodities interfere with the free exercise of religion?

HISTORY OF THE CASE

Jacob Braunfeld and the other appellants were merchants in Philadelphia who sold clothing and home furnishings. They were also members of the Orthodox Jewish faith, which requires the closing of their places of business and total abstention from all manner of work from Friday night until Saturday night. They brought suit to enjoin enforcement of the 1959 Pennsylvania criminal statute, which does not allow retail sale of certain specified commodities on Sundays.

SUMMARY OF ARGUMENTS

Appellants claimed that the statute violated the equal protection clause of the Fourteenth Amendment. They further claimed that the statute constituted a law respecting an establishment of religion and that it interfered with the free exercise of their religion by imposing serious economic disadvantages upon them. They argued that the law would operate to hinder the Orthodox Jewish faith's ability to get new members.

Appellees Brown, the Philadelphia police commissioner, and the state of Pennsylvania argued that although Sunday closing laws took their origins in religious practice, their modern function is constitutional because it provides a common day of rest on which family and friends might come together.

DECISION

Chief Justice Warren wrote the decision for the Court in which Justices Black, Clark, and Whittaker concurred. He held that the Pennsylvania statute did not violate the equal protection clause of the Fourteenth Amendment, nor did it constitute a law respecting an establishment of religion. Moreover, it did not prohibit the free exercise of appellant's religion within the meaning of the First Amendment, made applicable to states by the Fourteenth Amendment.

Chief Justice Warren looked at the history of Sunday closing laws, which were supposedly important for the health, safety, morals, and general well-being of the citizens. He knew that the statute would hurt appellants economically since their religion would not allow work on Saturdays, but he turned the inquiry to whether, under these circumstances, the First and Fourteenth Amendments forbade application of the law to appellants.

Chief Justice Warren then noted that the "freedom to hold religious beliefs and opinions" was absolute, but the "freedom to act" was not totally free from legislative restrictions. He reasoned that this case was about the freedom to act in accord with one's religious convictions, which could be regulated if found to be in "violation of important social duties or subversive of good order," even if the actions were demanded by one's religion.

Chief Justice Warren, adopting the reasoning in *Reynolds v. United States* (1879), stated that the indirect burden placed on Orthodox Jews was constitutionally permissible. He contended that the criminal statute did not curtail the freedom to hold religious views, but simply made religious practice more expensive. He added that the statute did not inconvenience all Orthodox Jews, but only those wishing to work on Sunday. Chief Justice Warren saw the statute in question as legislation that caused only an indirect burden on the exercise of religion when he stated that government infringement on religious conduct must withstand "the most critical scrutiny" or it would radically restrict the operating latitude of the legislature.

Chief Justice Warren then developed a standard for legislation that does not violate the First Amendment's freedom of religion: a statute is valid if the state regulates conduct by enacting a general law within its power, and if the purpose and effect of it is to advance its secular goals. Relying on *McGowan v. Maryland* (1961), Chief Justice Warren found that the "family day of rest" purpose was valid. He admitted that although there were other tenable solutions, the Court's concern was not with the wisdom of the legislation, but with its constitutionality. He also noted that allowing Orthodox Jews to do business on Sundays would give them an economic advantage over those forced to rest on Sundays. The economic advantage would cause them to complain that their religions were being discriminated against. He added that exempt employers would have to hire employees who themselves qualified for the exemption, hurting a state's ability to prohibit religious discrimination in hiring.

Justice Frankfurter, joined by Justice Harlan, submitted a long concurring opinion, agreeing substantially with the plurality analysis. Justice Brennan wrote a concurring and dissenting opinion.

He agreed that there was no merit to appellant's establishment and equal protection claims. However, he disagreed with the Court's finding that Pennsylvania had not prohibited the free exercise of appellant's religion. Justice Brennan believed the issue presented was whether a state may put an individual to a choice between his business and his religion. He found that the state cannot put an individual to this choice. Justice Brennan described the state's interest as "the mere convenience of having everyone rest on the same day" and called the plurality's concern about a system allowing exemptions "fanciful." He further stated that this "[elevates] administrative convenience to a constitutional level high enough to justify making one religion economically disadvantageous."

Justice Stewart also wrote a dissenting opinion agreeing with most of Justice Brennan's concurring and dissenting opinion. He believed that the state cannot constitutionally make a person choose between his religion and his economic survival. He added that this was a cruel choice, and that the impact on appellants grossly violated their constitutional right to the free exercise of their religion. Justice Douglas also dissented.

Aftermath

In *Braunfeld,* the Court rejected the free exercise claim by the Orthodox Jews. However, it strongly hinted that even indirect pressures that impede religious observance may require a free exercise exemption. The Court did not squarely hold that the free exercise clause protects religious beliefs differently or more extensively than the free speech clause protects political beliefs until 1963 in *SHERBERT V. VERNER* (1963).

Significance

The *Braunfeld* case is the first of a string of cases in which the Court began to apply the free exercise clause to religion, imposing a stringent requirement of justification upon the State for harm that it inflicts upon religiously motivated action.

Related Cases

McGowan v. Maryland, 366 U.S. 420 (1961)

Reynolds v. United States, 98 U.S. 145 (1879)

Sherbert v. Verner, 374 U.S. 398 (1963)

Recommended Reading

Richard A. Epstein, *Unconstitutional Conditions, State Power, and the Limits of Consent,* 102 Harvard Law Review 4, 83–85 (1988).

Ira C. Lupu, *Where Rights Begin: The Problem of Burdens on the Free Exercise of Religion,* 102 Harvard Law Review 933, 935, 966, 973–976 (1988).

Case Title: *Cantwell v. Connecticut*

Alternate Case Title: The "Breach of the Peace" Case

Legal Citations: 310 U.S. 296; 60 S.Ct. 900; 84 L.Ed. 1213

Year of Decision: 1940

Key Issues

Can the conviction of a man who peacefully expressed religious views that tended to incite animosity stand under a statute that generally makes "breach of the peace" a punishable offense?

History of the Case

Newton Cantwell and his two sons, Jesse and Russell, were members of a group known as Jehovah's Witnesses and claimed to be ordained ministers. On Cassius Street in New Haven, Connecticut—a thickly populated neighborhood where about 90 percent of the residents are Roman Catholic—they played a phonograph record that sharply attacked the Roman Catholic religion to persons they encountered on the street in an effort to advertise their religion and solicit contributions. Each was charged with various statutory and common law offenses. The Court of Common Pleas of New Haven convicted them on the third count, which charged a violation of section 6294 of the General Statutes of Connecticut, which generally prohibited solicitation of money for religious causes unless approved by the secretary of the public welfare council. They were also convicted on the fifth count, which charged commission of the common law offense of inciting a breach of the peace. On appeal, the state supreme court affirmed the conviction of all three on the third count. The conviction of Jesse on the fifth count was affirmed, but the conviction of Newton and Russell on that count was reversed and a new trial ordered. The Cantwells sought review from the U.S. Supreme Court.

SUMMARY OF ARGUMENTS

The Cantwells argued that the statute under which the third count was drawn was offensive to the due process clause of the Fourteenth Amendment because it denied them freedom of speech and prohibited their free exercise of religion. They further argued that requiring them to obtain a certificate to solicit support for their views amounted to a prior restraint on the exercise of their religion within the meaning of the Constitution.

The State argued that the act, as construed by the Supreme Court of Connecticut, imposed no previous restraint upon the dissemination of religious views or teaching but merely safeguarded against the perpetration of frauds under the cloak of religion.

DECISION

Justice Roberts wrote the opinion for the Court that the Cantwell conviction of the common law offense of breach of the peace violated constitutional guarantees of religious liberty and freedom of speech.

Justice Roberts saw the statute as general and undefined, with "breach of the peace" embracing a variety of conduct. Justice Roberts found it obvious that the state had the power to punish immediate threats to public safety, peace, or order. He also believed it obvious that a state could not unduly suppress communication of views, whether they were religious or other under a guise of promoting desirable conditions. He did not believe, however, that this particular case bore such characteristics.

Justice Roberts stressed that even though Cantwell's communications had a negative effect on the hearers, Cantwell's conduct did not amount to a breach of the peace. He found that Cantwell did not intend to "insult or affront the hearers" nor direct "profane, indecent, or abusive remarks" to them. He believed that Cantwell merely made an effort to persuade a willing listener to buy a book or to contribute money. Justice Roberts concluded that although the contents of the record aroused animosity, Cantwell was on a public street where he had a right to peacefully impart his views, invading no right or interest of the public. Justice Roberts believed that the statute should have been narrowly tailored to define and punish the specific conduct that constituted a clear and present danger to a substantial interest of the state. He found that Cantwell's communication raised no such clear and present danger to public peace and order as to render him liable to the common law conviction.

AFTERMATH

In *Cantwell*, the Court undermined the belief-action distinction (separating religious beliefs from religious actions) and recognized that the First Amendment "embraces two concepts—freedom to believe and freedom to act." The distinction remains today only insofar as freedom of belief is regarded as absolute while freedom of action is subject to limitation when the state demonstrates compelling interests.

SIGNIFICANCE

Cantwell signifies the first time that the Court applied the free exercise clause, the language of the First Amendment providing that Congress shall make no law prohibiting the free exercise of a religion, to the states through the Fourteenth Amendment. This case is also a classic early articulation of the view that the Constitution supports a world of debate "that transcends the bounds and perspectives of any particular community."

RELATED CASES

Feiner v. New York, 340 U.S. 315 (1951)

Murdock v. Pennsylvania, 319 U.S. 105 (1943)

Terminiello v. Chicago, 337 U.S. 1 (1949)

RECOMMENDED READING

Thomas M. Scanlon, *A Theory of Freedom of Expression,* 1 Philosophy & Public Affairs 204 (1972).

Geoffrey R. Stone, *Content Regulation and the First Amendment,* 25 William and Mary Law Review 189, 207–217 (1983).

Case Title: *Engel v. Vitale*

Alternate Case Title: School Prayer Decision

Legal Citation: 370 U.S. 421

Year of Decision: 1962

KEY ISSUES

Do public schools have the right to require the use of prayer?

HISTORY OF THE CASE

This controversy began when the parents of 10 children enrolled in a school in New York State brought suit against the school board and the state Board of Regents for requiring the use of a prayer as part of the opening ceremonies at the beginning of each school day. The procedure was adopted by the state Board of Regents, which was the government agency created by the New York State Constitution to oversee the state's public schools. The prayer was to be optional both for the local school boards and for the individual students, but the school district in question made no provision for excusing children from the classroom who did not wish to participate in the prayer.

The parents who brought the suit were of a variety of religious beliefs: Some were Jewish, some were Unitarians, and some were agnostic.

The parents lost their case in the trial court of New York and that decision was affirmed by both the Appellate Division and the Court of Appeals of New York. New York's highest court felt that the First Amendment was not intended to prohibit the "mere profession of belief in God," but rather only to "prohibit the official adoption of a religion."

SUMMARY OF ARGUMENTS

Mr. Engel and the parents were represented by William Butler, who argued before the Court that any act of the state or of local officials that requires prayer is a legal statement that there is a belief in the existence of God. This practice thus confers on theism the preference of the state. A required prayer tries to bridge, in the guise of education, the separation of church and state, which the authors of the Constitution so carefully framed. To introduce religion under the civil authority of the schools and the use of public funds for its observance is a clear violation of the First and Fourteenth Amendments to the Constitution.

The school board president, Mr. Vitale, and the Board of Regents argued through various attorneys that the intent of the First Amendment was to prohibit the establishment of a state religion, not to inhibit the growth of a religious state. B. D. Daiker argued that the Constitution does not discriminate against religion; it merely states that denominational religion is to be put in its place outside of public support. Daiker further argued that one's views of a creator are separate from a particular form of worship and belief as to his being, character, or will. Twenty-two attorneys general joined with Daiker and the other attorneys for the school board and Board of Regents in urging that the conduct of the public schools be left to those in charge of running them, not the courts.

DECISION

Justice Hugo Black held that the New York Regents' prayer, a 22-word nondenominational invocation, was a religious activity. Further, he found that the use of a public school system to encourage the recital of a prayer was a practice totally inconsistent with the First Amendment, even though pupils were not required to participate in such a prayer. The Court voted 6-1 to reverse the New York Court of Appeals, with only Justice Potter Stewart dissenting. Justices Frankfurter and White did not decide the case.

Justice Black traced the history of established religion in England and the background of the First Amendment. Particular scrutiny was given to the establishment of the tax-supported Church of England, which was the legally recognized church in at least five colonies (Maryland, Virginia, North Carolina, South Carolina, and Georgia). Additionally, the Church of England may have been officially established in New York and New Jersey, but there is no doubt that it did receive tax support in those two states. In Massachusetts, New Hampshire, and Connecticut, the Congregationalist Church was officially established. In Pennsylvania and Delaware, all Christian sects were treated equally, but the Roman Catholic Church was discriminated against. In Rhode

Island, all Protestants enjoyed equal privileges, but it appears that Catholics were not allowed to vote. Thus, with this strong historical precedent of churches being supported by governments, the framers of the First Amendment were keenly aware of the political opposition by minority religious groups to these established churches. Justice Black further noted that James Madison and Thomas Jefferson were not members of any religious groups, and they opposed all religious establishments on principle.

Justice Black found that, although this particular prayer may be denominationally neutral and its observance may appear to be voluntary, nothing prevents the coercion of individual students by the use of such a prayer. When the power and prestige of the government is placed behind a religious belief, there is clear pressure to conform to the prevailing officially approved view. Justice Black wrote that the First Amendment was written to put an end to the government's control of religion and prayer, not to destroy either. To those who thought that because the prayer was so short and general as to not be a danger, he observed that, in the words of James Madison, "it is proper to take alarm at the first experiment on our liberties."

In his dissent, Justice Stewart felt that the Court missed the mark by concerning itself with the establishment of the Church of England. He felt that the history of religious traditions in America, including the opening of each session of the Supreme Court, the employment by the U.S. Senate and House of Representatives of a chaplain, and the requirement that the presidents of the United States take their oath of office under an oath for the help of God, indicated that the Constitution was not hostile to religion.

AFTERMATH

Public outcry at the decision was intense. In many places, the decision was ignored. It was publicly criticized by former president Eisenhower and, not unexpectedly, by church leaders. There were many attempts to amend the Constitution to overturn the *Engel* decision.

SIGNIFICANCE

Engel was the first case regarding prayer in public school to come before the Supreme Court. In the years following *Engel*, the Supreme Court heard a number of "prayer-in-school" cases, addressing and striking down prayer in school in a number of

different circumstances, including graduation ceremonies (*Lee v. Weisman*, 1992) and pre-game activities (*Santa Fe Independent School District v. Doe*, 2000).

However, despite the efforts to overturn *Engel*, interest in the question of prayer in schools has declined for most Americans. The recognition that prayer properly belongs in a church or home setting has also encouraged the growth of private denominational schools. The Ninth Circuit's decision in *Newdow v. U.S. Congress* (2002), striking down the use of the pledge of allegiance as unconstitutional, may create a new resurgence of interest in church and state related issues.

RELATED CASES

Lee v. Weisman, 112 S.Ct. 2649, 120 L.Ed. 2d. 467 (1992)

McCollum v. Board of Education, 333 U.S. 203 (1948)

School District of Abington Township v. Schempp, 374 U.S. 203 (1963)

Wisconsin v. Yoder, 406 U.S. 205 (1972)

RECOMMENDED READING

Cord, Robert. *Separation of Church and State*. New York: Lambeth Press, 1982.

Freund, Paul, and Robert Ulich. *Religion and the Public Schools*. Cambridge, Mass.: Harvard University Press, 1965.

Pfeffer, Leo. *Church, State and Freedom*. Boston: Beacon Press, 1967.

Case Title: *Epperson v. Arkansas*

Alternate Case Title: The "Teaching Evolution in School" Case

Legal Citations: 393 U.S. 97; 89 S.Ct. 266

Year of Decision: 1968

KEY ISSUES

Is the state of Arkansas's "anti-evolution" statute, which prohibits the teaching in its public schools and universities of the theory that men evolved from other species of life, constitutional?

HISTORY OF THE CASE

In 1928, Arkansas enacted a statute prohibiting "the teaching in its public schools and universities of the theory that man evolved from other species of life." Susan Epperson, a tenth-grade biology teacher in a school in Arkansas, was given a new textbook to use for classroom instruction, which contained a chapter on the theory of evolution. Consequently, she brought an action to declare that Arkansas anti-evolution statutes were void and to enjoin her dismissal for violation of the statute. The Arkansas Chancery Court rendered judgment in favor of the teacher holding that the statute violated the Fourteenth Amendment of the U.S. Constitution. The Arkansas Supreme Court reversed and the teacher appealed to the U.S. Supreme Court.

SUMMARY OF ARGUMENTS

Appellant argued that the statute was vague and uncertain and therefore within the condemnation of the Fourteenth Amendment.

The state made what Justice Black referred to as an "unenthusiastic" defense of the Arkansas statute. The state clarified the opinion of the Supreme Court stating that it should be interpreted as finding that teaching the mere existence of an evolutionary theory would result in dismissal. The state also argued that a state had a right to prescribe the curriculum for its public schools. Finally, the state indicated that it would make no attempt to enforce the statute as written.

DECISION

Justice Fortas wrote the opinion for the Court that Arkansas statutes forbidding the teaching of evolution in public schools and in colleges and universities, supported in whole or in part by public funds, were contrary to the freedom of religion mandate of the First Amendment and in violation of the Fourteenth Amendment. Justice Fortas based the decision on the First Amendment's establishment and free exercise clauses. These clauses prohibit the passage of laws respecting an establishment of religion or prohibiting the free exercise of religion. Laws giving preference to a certain religion and laws promoting belief or disbelief of a certain religion are prohibited under these clauses. He stated

that regardless of the vagueness of the statute, it could not stand because Arkansas's sole reason for the statute was a particular religious doctrine based upon the interpretation of the book of Genesis by a particular religious group.

Justice Fortas insisted that government must remain neutral in matters of religious doctrine and theory. He added that the government cannot be hostile to, nor favor any religious group or doctrine, or lack of religion as demanded by the First Amendment. He also did not believe it the proper role of courts to intervene in conflicts that arose in the daily operation of school systems unless they implicated "basic constitutional values." The Court relied on its history of using the due process clause to condemn "arbitrary" restrictions on the freedoms of teachers to teach and students to learn, neither of which could be tailored to the principles of "any religious sect or dogma."

Justice Fortas stated that even though a state had a right to proscribe the curriculum for its public schools, the First Amendment did not allow a state to prohibit the teaching of a scientific theory or doctrine, if that prohibition was based upon reasons that violated the First Amendment. Then he maintained that in the instant case, the state of Arkansas prevented its teachers from discussing the theory of evolution solely due to its conflict with the religious views of some of its citizens, and not based on any state policy. Since the Arkansas law could not stand as an act of religious neutrality, like prohibiting all discussion of the origin of man, it was contrary to the mandate of the First and in violation of the Fourteenth Amendment to the Constitution. Therefore, the Court found that the statute created an unconstitutional establishment of religion, and the teaching of evolution in Arkansas schools was permitted.

Justice Stewart concurred in the result, noting that prohibiting student's exposure to this knowledge "impinged upon the guarantees of free communication contained in the First Amendment" by denying access to an "entire system of respected human thought." Justice Black, concurring, supported distinguishing *Epperson* from a state law "prohibiting all teaching of human development." He believed, however, that the statute should have been struck down for no other reason than its vagueness. Justice Harlan also wrote a concurring opinion criticizing the statute's vagueness.

AFTERMATH

Following *Epperson,* the Court reviewed a similar case and added a new twist by applying the "Lemon test" to review school curricular decisions that were believed to affect student's beliefs. Under the Lemon test (*LEMON V. KURTZMAN,* 403 U.S. 602 [1971]), government action regarding religion is unconstitutional unless the court is convinced that the challenged action has a secular purpose, and has a primarily secular effect, and does not excessively entangle the government with religion.

SIGNIFICANCE

Epperson set the principle that the establishment clause of the First Amendment mandates that government "be neutral on matters of religious theory, doctrine, and practice," and "not aid, foster, or promote one religion or religious theory against another." It also established the proposition that there is no valid secular reason for prohibiting the teaching of evolution in the public schools.

RELATED CASES

Edwards v. Aguillard, 482 U.S. 578 (1987)

McLean v. Arkansas Board of Education, 529 F. Supp. 1255 (E.D. Ark. 1982)

Stone v. Graham, 449 U.S. 39 (1980)

Wallace v. Jaffree, 472 U.S. 38 (1985)

RECOMMENDED READING

Ginger, Ray. *Six Days or Forever?* New York: Oxford University Press, 1958.

Sarason, Seymour. *The Culture of the School and the Problem of Change.* 2d ed. Boston: Allyn and Bacon, 1982.

Weissberg, Robert. *Political Learning, Political Choice, and Democratic Citizenship.* Englewood Cliffs, N.J.: Prentice Hall, 1974.

Case Title: *Gallagher v. Crown Kosher Supermarket of Massachusetts, Inc.*

Alternate Case Title: Blue Law Case

Legal Citation: 366 U.S. 617

Year of Decision: 1961

KEY ISSUES

Do the Massachusetts Sunday closing laws, also known as "blue laws," violate the equal protection, establishment of religion, or the prohibition of its free exercise clauses of the U.S. Constitution?

HISTORY OF THE CASE

Patrons of a kosher meat market in Massachusetts and the officers of the market sued the state for an injunction preventing the enforcement of the blue laws against the market. Blue laws regulated certain activities, including work and commerce, on Sundays. The patrons argued that because their religious beliefs forbid their shopping on the Jewish Sabbath, the effect of the statute would deprive them from Friday afternoon until Monday of the opportunity to buy kosher food.

SUMMARY OF ARGUMENTS

Appellant, the chief of police of Springfield, Massachusetts, argued that the Massachusetts Sunday closing laws did not violate the equal protection clause because the classifications of what could be sold and done on Sunday were reasonable. Appellant also argued that the statutes were not religious, but were to provide a day of "rest and quiet."

Appellees, the Crown Kosher Market, members of the Orthodox Jewish faith, and a group of Orthodox Jewish rabbis, argued that the Massachusetts Sunday closing laws violated the equal protection clause of the Fourteenth Amendment and the free exercise clause of the First Amendment.

DECISION

Sunday closing laws for retailers do not violate the establishment clause nor free exercise claims.

Chief Justice Warren, writing for the majority, found that the consequences of the statute were grave, but not as grave as in *BRAUNFELD V. BROWN* (1961), in which these laws were upheld. The statute in question did not have as its purpose any unlawful religious discrimination.

Justice Douglas dissented, writing that the establishment clause protects citizens from any religion singled out by the government whose observance resulted in fines and imprisonment.

AFTERMATH

This is one of four cases upholding the validity of Sunday closing laws.

SIGNIFICANCE

Gallagher indicated the Court would uphold laws with clear religious origins if it was determined the law had evolved to the point where secular purposes predominated. Justice Douglas's dissent was ultimately adopted by Justice O'Connor and the Court in *Allegheny v. ACLU,* 492 U.S. 573 (1983), which disallowed the practice of displaying a nativity scene at the county courthouse.

RELATED CASES

Braunfeld v. Brown, 366 U.S. 599 (1961)

McGowan v. Maryland, 366 U.S. 420 (1961)

Two Guys from Harristown-Allentown, Inc. v. McGinley, 366 U.S. 582 (1962)

RECOMMENDED READING

Laband, David N., and Deborah Hendry Heinbuch. *Blue Laws: The History, Economics and Politics of Sunday Closing Laws.* Lexington, Mass.: Lexington Books, 1987.

The Supreme Court, 1960 Term, 75 Harvard Law Review 150 (1961).

Case Title: *Girouard v. United States*

Legal Citation: 328 U.S. 61

Year of Decision: 1946

KEY ISSUES

Is an act that requires an alien conscientious objector to take an oath that he or she will take up arms to defend the United States as a condition of being granted citizenship constitutional?

HISTORY OF THE CASE

In 1942 Girouard, a Canada native, filed a petition for naturalization. He noted on his application that he understood the principles of government and was willing to take the oath of allegiance. Part of the oath of allegiance reads "that I will support and defend the Constitution and laws of the United States of America against all enemies, foreign and domestic." His application included a question regarding his willingness to take up arms to defend the country. To this question, Girouard responded that he was unwilling to take up arms to defend the country because of his religious beliefs as a Seventh-Day Adventist. He explained before the examiner that he was a Seventh-Day Adventist and the tenets of his faith prohibited him from engaging in combative behavior. Before the Selective Service Board he did not claim exemption from all military service, but only combatant positions.

At a hearing in the district court he testified that he was a Seventh-Day Adventist and that he would serve in the military, but he would not bear arms. At that time of his hearing there were approximately 10,000 Seventh-Day Adventists serving in the U.S. military as noncombatants. The district court admitted him to citizenship. The U.S. Circuit Court of Appeals reversed that decision based on *United States v. Schwimmer* (1929), *United States v. Macintosh* (1931), and *United States v. Bland* (1931). Those cases stand for the general rule that an alien who refuses to bear arms will not be admitted to citizenship.

SUMMARY OF ARGUMENTS

Girouard argued that the tenets of his faith required that he not engage in combative positions. He argued that his willingness to serve in noncombatant positions should allow him to obtain citizenship, as he was not opposed to serving in the military but only serving in combatant positions.

The United States argued that the case history established that an alien would not be admitted a citizen unless he took the oath that he would bear arms in defense of the United States. Girouard's case was factually identical to the cases in which the Court proscribed this rule. Therefore, Girouard should be denied citizenship.

DECISION

Justice Douglas, in writing the majority opinion, overruled the *Schwimmer, Macintosh,* and *Bland* cases, and held that Girouard should be admitted for citizenship. He argued that this was a case involving statutory construction and that previous cases' holdings construed the Naturalization Act and the oath of allegiance as requiring that an alien must agree to bear arms, where this was not a literal requirement of either: "The oath required of aliens does not in terms require that they promise to bear arms. Nor has Congress expressly made any such finding a prerequisite to citizenship. To hold that it is required is to read into the Act by implication." He went on to conclude that the Court should not do so, especially when doing so represents a departure from tradition.

He noted that a person's religious scruples would not disqualify him or her from serving in Congress or holding public office. He found the suggestion that a higher standard was required of aliens seeking citizenship not plausible. He went on to note that Congress in various draft laws has recognized religious scruples against bearing arms: "Congress has thus recognized that one may adequately discharge his obligations as a citizen by rendering non-combatant as well as combatant services." He concluded that this recognition by Congress over the years is evidence of the meaning of the oath: "It is recognition by Congress that even in time of war one may truly support and defend our institutions though he stops short of using weapons of war."

Lastly, he noted that the silence of Congress in the aftermath of the Court's interpretation of the Naturalization Act did not legitimize the Court's interpretation or forbid its reevaluation. In fact, he argued that in light of the legislative history the Court should not place its error of interpretation on the shoulders of Congress.

Justice Jackson did not participate in the decision.

Justice Stone dissented and argued that the lower court's decision should be affirmed, as it applied the controlling provisions of the naturalization statutes and applied them in the manner previously construed by the Court. He argued that the reenactment of the Naturalization Act of 1906, which created the Bureau of Immigration and Naturalization and standardized naturalization procedures and the incorporation of the oath into the act, was evidence of the purpose and will of Congress regarding these acts. The legislative history, he argued, made clear that Congress did not intend to relax the requirements of the oath of allegiance. Justices Reed and Frankfurter joined this dissenting opinion.

AFTERMATH

In 1950 Congress amended the naturalization oath to allow conscientious objectors the option of performing noncombatant service in the armed forces or to do nonmilitary work of national significance when required by law, instead of promising to bear arms. To qualify for this option, the person has to show by clear and convincing evidence that he or she is opposed to bearing arms for religious reasons.

The larger issue in question is government infringement on the free exercise of religion that is protected by the First Amendment of the Constitution. In 1963 the Court decided *SHERBERT V. VERNER* and developed a standard, the Sherbert test, to gauge the constitutionality of a government infringement challenged on the grounds that it violated the free exercise clause of the First Amendment. The Sherbert test balances the government interest in regulation against the religious exercise interests of an objecting party. To prevail, the government must demonstrate a compelling state interest that could not be accomplished in a less restrictive way than by burdening the objector's religious behavior.

SIGNIFICANCE

This case supports the contention that respect for conscience and religion, as established in the First Amendment to the Constitution, requires that in certain circumstances a person is exempted from certain generally applicable government proscriptions. This decision is consistent with those decisions in which the Court held that a public school could not require a student who conscientiously refused to salute the flag and recite the Pledge of Allegiance; that schools could allow religious students to be released early to attend religious instruction; and that government agents could not force one conscientiously opposed to swear before a flag to receive citizenship status.

RELATED CASES

Sherbert v. Verner, 374 U.S. 398 (1963)

United States v. Macintosh, 283 U.S. 605 (1931)

United States v. Bland, 283 U.S. 636 (1931)

United States v. Schwimmer, 279 U.S. 644 (1929)

RECOMMENDED READING

Spencer E. Davis, Jr., *Constitutional Right or Legislative Grace? The Status of Conscientious Objection Exemptions,* 19 Florida State University Law Review 191 (1991).

Ronald B. Flowers, *Government Accommodation of Religious-Based Conscientious Objection,* 24 Seton Hall Law Review 695 (1993).

John Witte, Jr., *The Essential Rights and Liberties of Religion in the American Constitutional Experiment,* Notre Dame Law Review 371 (1996).

Case Title: *Goldman v. Weinberger*

Legal Citation: 475 U.S. 503

Year of Decision: 1986

KEY ISSUES

Does a military regulation that prevents a person from wearing a yarmulke while on duty and in uniform infringe upon the First Amendment freedom to exercise one's religious beliefs?

HISTORY OF THE CASE

Goldman was an Orthodox Jew and an ordained rabbi. He was ordered not to wear his yarmulke while on duty and in uniform as a commissioned officer in the U.S. Air Force. An air force regulation stated that military headgear may be worn out of doors, but headgear may not be worn indoors. The only exception was for the armed security police in the performance of their duties.

Until 1981 Goldman was not prevented from wearing his yarmulke on the base. He avoided controversy by remaining close to his duty station, the military hospital, and wearing his service cap over his yarmulke when out of doors. In 1981 he testified at a court-martial hearing wearing his yarmulke but not his service cap. A complaint was lodged by counsel at the hearing that Goldman's practice constituted a violation of air force regulations. Goldman was informed that wearing the yarmulke violated U.S. Air Force policy and he was ordered not to violate the regulation outside

of the military hospital. He refused to comply with the order. Later the order was revised to prohibit Goldman from wearing the yarmulke even in the hospital. He received a letter of reprimand and was warned that his failure to comply with the regulation could subject him to court-martial.

Goldman sued Weinberger, who was the secretary of defense, and others, claiming that the application of the regulation preventing him from wearing his yarmulke infringed upon his First Amendment freedom to exercise his religious beliefs. The district court permanently enjoined the air force from enforcing the regulations against Goldman. The court of appeals reversed.

SUMMARY OF ARGUMENTS

Goldman argued that the free exercise clause of the First Amendment permits him to wear a yarmulke while in uniform, notwithstanding the air force regulation mandating the uniform dress of personnel. He contended that the free exercise clause required the air force to make an exception to its uniform dress requirement for religious apparel, unless such exceptions created a danger of undermining discipline. He argued that the air force failed to prove that wearing a yarmulke threatened discipline.

Weinberger argued that the goal of fostering discipline within the personnel justified the strict enforcement of the uniform dress requirement. He argued that the professional judgment of the air force was that the traditional uniformity in presentation of its personnel encourages the subordination of personal preferences and identities in favor of the group identity. Uniforms encourage a sense of hierarchy, as the only distinguishing characteristics are those that identify personnel by rank, rather than as individuals.

DECISION

Arguing that the military is a specialized part of society, Justice Rehnquist, writing for the Court, held that the military, because of its special function within society, was entitled to deferential constitutional review, meaning the military did not have to tolerate as broad a spectrum of expression as civilian society of the challenged regulation. The Court noted that an intrinsic part of the military's effectiveness comes from its insistence upon respect for duty and discipline: "The military need not encourage debate or tolerate protest to the extent that such tolerance is required of the civilian state by the First Amendment; to accomplish its mission the military must foster instinctive obedience, unity, commitment, and esprit de corps."

Justice Rehnquist went on to note that the military community does not allow the same level of individual autonomy as in the civilian community. The appropriate standard by which to gauge the validity of the regulation is the appropriate military officials in their official judgment. The military is under no obligation to abandon their professional judgment. He concluded that the First Amendment does not require that the military accommodate the wearing of a yarmulke to the extent that it detracted from the uniformity of dress sought. To the extent that the regulation fosters uniformity and discipline within the military, it is a valid regulation: "The First Amendment therefore does not prohibit them from being applied to petitioner even though their effects is to restrict the wearing of the headgear require by his religious beliefs."

Justice Steven concurred, and he was joined by Justices White and Powell. He argued that the regulation should be tested against not only Goldman and his religious beliefs but all service personnel whose religious beliefs may conflict with military commands. In so doing, he felt that the uniformity could be justified as uniformity in restriction against all religious faiths. He noted that the rule was neutral and was not motivated with any prejudice toward the groups to which Goldman belonged. To allow an exception for Goldman would depart from the uniformity in application that supported the rule.

Justice Brennan dissented and Justice Marshall joined his dissent. Brennan argued that the Court had abandoned its duty to protect individual liberties in showing undue deference to the military's unsupported assertions of military necessity. He argued that the First Amendment restricted the ability of the government to prevent Goldman from wearing a yarmulke, much less punish him for it. He also argued that the Court unpersuasively attempted to minimize the effect of negating Goldman's religious freedom rights.

While agreeing that a deferential standard should be applied, he contended that this deference should not be to such a degree that the Court

affirms regulations that defy common sense: "When a military service burdens the free exercise rights of its members in the name of necessity, it must provide, as an initial matter and at a minimum, a credible explanation of how the contested practice is likely to interfere with the proffered military interest."

Justice Blackmun dissented on the grounds that the free exercise clause of the First Amendment means an individual's choice to follow one's faith is not merely a matter of personal preference to be accommodated by the government when it is convenient. He contended previous cases had established that claims of free exercise of religion could only be overridden in circumstances in which the government had a substantial interest. He refuted the conclusion of the majority that free exercise must be compromised because the military says so. He argued that the Air Force had not shown why they feared that a significant number of enlisted men would request exemptions, and if this did occur, how it would impair the overall image of the service.

Justice O'Connor, joined by Justice Marshall, dissented on the grounds that the Court did not even attempt to weigh Goldman's interest in exercising his right under the First Amendment and the interest of the air force in uniformity of dress within the military hospital. She noted the Court precedent in this area established two consistent themes. One is that the government must show an "unusually important interest is at stake" when it attempts to infringe upon rights protected under the free exercise clause of the First Amendment. The second theme is that when an exemption is requested from such a regulation, the government must show that granting the request will do substantial harm to the interest it seeks to protect. It can do so by showing that it is employing the least restrictive means to protecting the interest or that the interest will not otherwise be served. She concluded that these requirements were applicable to the *Goldman* case. In applying these requirements she agreed that the need for military discipline and esprit de corps is an important government interest. However, she found that the government did not establish with convincing proof the assertion that granting an exemption to Goldman would substantially harm military discipline.

AFTERMATH

In response to this decision, in 1988 Congress included a religious apparel accommodation provision in the defense authorization bill. The religious apparel provision directed the Department of Defense to enact directives to maintain the neat and conservative appearance of the military, while accommodating religious dress in situations in which it is both fair and reasonable.

SIGNIFICANCE

The Goldman case was the first in which the Court considered the free exercise claim of a service member. The case exemplified the Court's most deferential attitude in application of the military necessity doctrine, which was established in 1953 in *Orloff v. Willoughby* (1953) and *Burns v. Wilson* (1953).

RELATED CASES

Burns v. Wilson, 346 U.S. 140 (1953).

Orloff v. Willoughby, 345 U.S. 83 (1953).

Parker v. Levy, 417 U.S. 733 (1955).

RECOMMENDED READING

C. Thomas Dienes, *When the First Amendment Is Not Preferred: The Military and Other "Special Contexts,"* 56 University of Cincinnati Law Review 779 (1988).

John Nelson Ohlweiler, *The Principle of Deference: Facial Constitutional Challenges to Military Regulations,* 10 Journal of Law & Politics 147 (1993).

Dwight H. Sullivan, *The Congressional Response to Goldman v. Weinberger,* 121 Military Law Review 125 (1988).

Case Title: *Lemon v. Kurtzman*

Legal Citations: 403 U.S. 602; 91 S.Ct. 2105; 29 L.Ed. 2d 745

Year of Decision: 1971

KEY ISSUES

Does aid to parochial schools violate the establishment clause of the First Amendment?

HISTORY OF THE CASE

This case was the first in a series to struggle with state grants to religious schools. A Pennsylvania statute allowed public schools to purchase "secular educational services" from nonpublic schools and reimburse the nonpublic schools. However, these reimbursements were limited by requirements that the reimbursements could be paid only for secular subjects and that all materials must be approved by the superintendent. Challenges to similar provisions in other states were consolidated with this appeal. It was the states' need to monitor the teachers that resulted in an entanglement between government and religion.

SUMMARY OF ARGUMENTS

Alton J. Lemon and others argued that the Pennsylvania act violated the First and Fourteenth Amendments.

David H. Kurtzman, the superintendent of public instruction of Pennsylvania, and others argued that the Pennsylvania act did not violate the free exercise and establishment clauses of the First Amendment. Kurtzman also argued that no appellant had standing to challenge the act under the Fourteenth Amendment.

DECISION

The court held that aid to parochial schools violates the establishment clause of the First Amendment. Chief Justice Burger wrote for the Court that in education at the below college level "religion was so enmeshed that it would be impossible to separate them without unconstitutionally entangling the state and religious bodies." A three-part test for determining if a state violated the establishment clause was put into effect:

1. It must have a secular purpose.
2. Its principal effect must not advance nor inhibit religion.
3. It must not foster "an excessive governmental entanglement with religion."

This test, which came to be known as the *Lemon* test, is based on the principle that religion is not government business. The test prohibits any practice that entangles government with religious institutions.

AFTERMATH

Religion cases have been decided without the three-part test and without setting objective standards against which government action is to be judged.

SIGNIFICANCE

The *Lemon v. Kurtzman* decision became the standard by which all subsequent statutes involving a church-state interaction were judged. However, the Court's inconsistency in the manner in which the *Lemon* test was applied resulted in varied decisions and critics have questioned whether the *Lemon* test is useful.

RELATED CASES

Everson v. Board of Education, 330 U.S. 1 (1947)

Kiryas Joel v. Grumet, 512 U.S. 687 (1994)

Tilton v. Richardson, 403 U.S. 672 (1971)

RECOMMENDED READING

Giannella, Donald A. "Lemon and Tilton." In *Church and State.* Edited by Philip B. Kurland. Chicago: University of Chicago Press, 1975.

Pfeffer, Leo. *Religion, State and the Burger Court.* Buffalo, N.Y.: Prometheus Books, 1984.

Weber, Paul J., and Dennis A. Gilbert. *Private Churches and Public Money.* Westport, Conn.: Greenwood Press, 1981.

Case Title: *Lynch v. Donnelly*

Legal Citation: 465 U.S. 668

Year of Decision: 1984

KEY ISSUES

Does a crèche or nativity scene as part of an annual Christmas display by a municipality violate the establishment clause of the First Amendment?

HISTORY OF THE CASE

An action was brought in federal district court alleging that the inclusion of a crèche in an annual display in Pawtucket, Rhode Island, violated the establishment clause. The district court enjoined the city from including the crèche in the display and the court of appeals affirmed.

SUMMARY OF ARGUMENTS

Dennis Lynch, the mayor of Pawtucket, and others argued that the city's display of the nativity scene did not constitute an establishment of religion because it was part of a dominantly secular Christmas celebration.

Daniel Donnelly and others argued that the display of a public nativity scene violated the establishment clause of the First Amendment because it did not advance a secular purpose, had the primary effect of advancing religion, and fostered an excessive entanglement between the government and religion.

DECISION

The Court found a publicly sponsored display of a nativity scene not in violation of the establishment clause.

Chief Justice Burger wrote the majority opinion stating that complete separation of church and state is not required by the Constitution. Only accommodation is necessary; hostility to any religion is what is forbidden. The crèche is merely a part of the Christmas season; as such it has a legitimate secular purpose.

Justice Brennan wrote a dissent, saying that Pawtucket's display constituted a life-size replica of the biblical description of Christ's birth; as such, it is an impermissible governmental endorsement of a particular faith and therefore unconstitutional. The result is that a religious minority is made to feel like a stranger in the political community.

SIGNIFICANCE

In this ruling the Court rejected the three-part *Lemon* test (effect of legislation on religion, intent of the legislature when enacting it, and impact between church and state) and used the status quo in judging its constitutionality.

With no standard to judge religion and government, the Court displayed inconsistencies in religious-based cases; it has been called the growth of "civil religion."

RELATED CASES

Lemon v. Kurtzman, 403 U.S. 602 (1971)

Marsh v. Chambers, 463 U.S. 783 (1983)

Zorach v. Clausen, 343 U.S. 306 (1952)

RECOMMENDED READING

Pfeffer, Leo. *Religion, State and the Burger Court.* Buffalo, N.Y.: Prometheus Books, 1984.

Sidney Miles Rogers, Lynch v. Donnelly: *Our Christmas Will Be Merry Still,* 36 Mercer Law Review 409 (1984).

Swanson, Wayne R. *The Christ Child Goes to Court.* Philadelphia: Temple University Press. 1990.

William Van Alstyne, *Trends in the Supreme Court: Mr. Jefferson's Crumbling Wall: A Comment on* Lynch v. Donnelly, 1984 Duke Law Journal 770 (1984).

Leading Cases of the 1983 Term, 98 Harvard Law Review 174 (1984).

Case Title: *Marsh v. Chambers*

Legal Citations: 463 U.S. 783; 103 S.Ct. 3330; 77 L.Ed. 2d 1019

Year of Decision: 1983

KEY ISSUES

Does the practice of opening each daily session of a state legislature with a prayer by a state-paid chaplain violate the First Amendment?

HISTORY OF THE CASE

Since 1855, the Nebraska legislature has retained a legislative chaplain to open each daily session with a prayer. In 1965 the Executive Board of the Legislative Council appointed and allocated public funds for a Presbyterian minister to perform the opening prayer. Members of the legislature were not required to attend the prayer. On three occasions in the late 1970s, compilations of the prayers were printed and distributed to the state legislators and the public at state expense.

Ernest Chambers, a Nebraska legislator, brought suit in U.S. District Court challenging the Nebraska practice as a violation of the First Amendment's establishment clause, which prohibits any law "respecting an establishment of religion." The district court judge found that the prayers did not violate the establishment clause, but that paying the chaplain with public funds did. On appeal, the Court of Appeals for the Eighth Circuit held that the practice as a whole was an unconstitutional establishment of religion. The Supreme Court granted review in order to review this holding.

SUMMARY OF ARGUMENTS

Petitioner Frank Marsh, the Nebraska state treasurer, argued that the chaplain's opening prayer was not a religious observance. Instead, he contended that the practice was merely a ceremonial one that served the secular purpose of bringing the legislature to order.

Mr. Chambers contended that the Nebraska practice impermissibly established religion in violation of the First Amendment. He believed that any direct state aid to an overtly religious activity could not be justified as advancing a secular purpose. He added that the mere historical use of an opening prayer could not justify a practice that violates the establishment clause.

DECISION

Chief Justice Burger delivered the 6-3 majority opinion for the Court. The Court held that the Nebraska practice did not violate the establishment clause. Burger based his opinion almost entirely on the theory that such practices have deep historical roots, dating back to the first Congress. He explained that the challenged practices were not viewed as a threat to the establishment clause by the original draftsmen of the First Amendment. Burger did stress that historical practices, standing alone, cannot justify contemporary violations of constitutional guarantees.

Justice Brennan, joined by Justice Marshall, questioned the majority's emphasis on the intent of the members of the first Congress. He argued that the Constitution is not a "static document," and that practices which may have been unacceptable to no one in the time of Jefferson and Madison may today be highly offensive to many persons. Justice Stevens filed a separate dissent, arguing that the Nebraska legislature's choice of a Presbyterian to hold the position of chaplain for

16 years constituted an impermissible preference of one religion over another. He believed that such a preference was a direct violation of the establishment clause.

AFTERMATH

In 1992 the Court held in *Lee v. Weisman* that the use of completely nondenominational prayer in a state-sponsored graduation ceremony violated the establishment clause. *Marsh* was distinguished in *Lee* because the atmosphere at a state legislature's opening, where adults are free to enter and leave, "cannot compare with the constraining potential of the one school event most important for the student to attend." Although *Marsh* remains good law, the Court's reliance on history and the specific intent of the framers of the Constitution is rarely used to justify potential violations of the establishment clause.

SIGNIFICANCE

Marsh suggested that references to religious themes in public settings will be upheld when the reference is part of a long-standing tradition or historical practice. For example, the Pledge of Allegiance ("One nation, under God . . .") and the words on the dollar bill ("In God We Trust") would likely not be a violation of the establishment clause because of their historic roots.

RELATED CASES

Allegheny County v. ACLU, 492 U.S. 573 (1989)

Capitol Square Review Bd. v. Pinette, 115 S.Ct. 2440 (1995)

Lee v. Weisman, 505 U.S. 577 (1992)

Walz v. Tax Comm'n, 397 U.S. 664 (1970)

RECOMMENDED READING

Donald L. Drakeman, *Antidisestablishmentarianism: The Latest (and Longest) Word From the Supreme Court,* 5 Cardozo Law Review 153–182 (fall 1983).

Pfeffer, Leo. *Religion, State and the Burger Court.* Buffalo, New York: Prometheus Books, 1984.

Diane L. Walker, Marsh v. Chambers: *The Supreme Court Takes a New Look at the Establishment Clause,* 11 Pepperdine Law Review 591–611 (1984).

Case Title: *Illinois ex rel. McCollum v. Board of Education of School District No. 17, Champaign County, Illinois et al.*

Legal Citations: 333 U.S. 203; 68 S.Ct. 461; 92 L.Ed. 649

Year of Decision: 1948

KEY ISSUES

Does the state's use of its tax-supported public school system to further religious instruction violate the First and Fourteenth Amendments?

HISTORY OF THE CASE

The Board of Education agreed under its supervisory powers over public school buildings to give religious instruction once a week to students whose parents so agreed. Other students were not released from their studies. They had to take their books and go to another area of the school. Religious classes were conducted in the school's classrooms. Attendance was taken.

A resident and taxpayer whose child attended school in the district sued in a state court for a writ of mandamus, an order of the court commanding a person or entity to take a certain action, requiring the Board of Education to terminate this practice.

SUMMARY OF ARGUMENTS

The taxpayer argued that the practice of the Board of Education was an impermissible government sanction of religion under the establishment clause of the Constitution.

DECISION

Justice Black wrote the opinion for the Court, saying that the use of tax-supported property for religious instruction and the close cooperation between school and religious authorities aids religious groups and falls directly under the "ban" of the First Amendment.

Justice Frankfurter, in his concurring opinion, wrote that the pressure on students to attend religious class is great. Conformity is a part of society, and no child wants to be stigmatized. The result is that he or she will go to the religious classes even if they are not his or her own sect. This will bring dissension at home. School should be a training ground for community values, not divisiveness. He further stated that conflicts will arise in a country with a variety of religions whether government so involves itself or not.

Justice Reed, in his dissent, wrote that religious classes foster tolerance, not intolerance. He found that religious instruction of public school children during school hours was now prohibited, and this was not within his interpretation of the First Amendment: "For the First Amendment rests upon the premise that both religion and government can best work to achieve their lofty aims if each is left free from the other within its respective sphere."

AFTERMATH

Current federal guidelines say that public schools may teach religion but neither promote nor inhibit its practice. As agents of the government, public schools have the difficult task of maintaining the separation of church and state while still respecting the value of religious practice as a vital aspect of students' lives. This tension is embodied in the very language of the First Amendment: "Congress shall make no law respecting an establishment of religion, or prohibiting the free exercise thereof." One example of recent respect for religious freedom was seen in Florida, where public school children can observe Rosh Hashanah, the Jewish New Year, without an attendance demerit.

A highly divisive political issue in this area has been the recent push for school voucher programs, in which families of qualified students can divert property taxes used to fund public schools to help offset the cost of sending their children to private or parochial schools. Carol Schields, the president of People for the American Way, an organization that fights for constitutionally guaranteed freedoms, recently chastised the backers of such school voucher programs: "It is outrageous that the Radical Right has usurped the language of the civil rights movement in their efforts to sell school vouchers. Abandoning our public schools is far from a civil rights issue—it is indeed counter to the civil rights movement's commitment to quality education for all."

SIGNIFICANCE

Using state-funded public schools and the state's mechanism for compulsory public school attendance to allow sectarian groups to give religious instruction to students in public school rooms violates the First Amendment, made applicable to the states through the Fourteenth Amendment. This case was an early test of the religion–public school education debate and was a foundation for the many cases that would follow involving school prayer and Bible readings, among others. Additionally, it found "released time," time during which students are released from their secular studies for religious instruction, to be unconstitutional.

RELATED CASES

Engel v. Vitale, 370 U.S. 421 (1962)

Lemon v. Kurtzman, 403 U.S. 602 (1971)

Zorach v. Clauson, 343 U.S. 306 (1952)

RECOMMENDED READING

Samuel A. Alioto, *The Released Time Cases Revisited,* 83 Yale Law Journal 1202 (1974).

Elkins, Rita. "Jewish Students Can Celebrate Rosh Hashanah without Penalty: Sawyer Pledges Better Awareness of Religious Practices in Schools," *Florida Today,* October 1, 1997, at 3-B.

Johnson, Alvin W., and Frank H. Yost. *Separation of Church and State in the United States.* Minneapolis: University of Minneapolis Press, 1948.

Kauper, Paul G. *Religion and the Constitution.* Baton Rouge: Louisiana State University Press, 1960.

"NAACP: NAACP, People for the American Way Oppose Vouchers for the District of Columbia." *M2 PRESSWIRE,* September 29, 1997.

Case Title: *Pierce v. Society of Sisters*

Alternate Case Titles: Private Religious Schooling, Compulsory School Law Case

Legal Citations: 268 U.S. 510; 45 S.Ct. 571; 69 L.Ed. 1070

Year of Decision: 1925

KEY ISSUES

Does a state have the right to require all of its school-aged children to attend public schools?

HISTORY OF THE CASE

The Society of the Sisters of the Holy Names of Jesus and Mary organized a corporation in 1880 with power to care for orphans, educate and instruct youth, establish and maintain academies or schools, and acquire real or personal property necessary for these endeavors. The Hill Military Academy was incorporated in 1908 under the laws of Oregon to own, operate, and conduct for profit an elementary college-preparatory and military training school for boys between the ages of five and 21.

In 1922, the voters of Oregon adopted an initiative requiring that virtually every parent send children between eight and 16 to public schools. The amendment of the compulsory education act made minor exemptions for children physically unable to attend school, children who had finished the eighth grade, and children who lived more than three miles by the nearest travelled road from a public school. Supporters of the initiative appear to have been primarily organized by the Ku Klux Klan, which inflamed fears arising from World War I. Anti-Catholicism was also a major theme in the initiative.[1]

A federal district court declared the initiative invalid, in violation of the due process clause of the Fourteenth Amendment, and issued an injunction stopping the enforcement of the law. Governor Walter Pierce of Oregon appealed to the Supreme Court.

SUMMARY OF ARGUMENTS

Willis Moore, assistant attorney general of Oregon, argued that any provision of a corporation charter and any law pursuant to which a corporation has entered into contracts are subject to modification and annulment under the state's police power. He further argued that the American people have determined that there will be an absolute and unequivocable division of church and state, and that public schools shall be maintained and conducted free from the influence of any religious organization. In that sense, he argued that the statute did not interfere with the religious liberty of anyone.

The attorneys for the Society of Sisters argued that the conducting of schools is a useful occupation protected by the Fourteenth Amendment. Further, the compulsory school law deprives the society of its right to conduct its schools and it violates the right of parents to control their children. Further, the compulsory school law cannot be upheld as a legitimate police power of the state. The attorneys for the military academy argued that the legislature had no power to interfere with the liberty or property of individuals unless for the purpose of correcting an evil or promoting some competent purpose. There was no effort to improve or promote the public welfare by denying individuals the right to have a private education. The ownership and operation of a private school is clearly a useful and legitimate business.

DECISION

Justice James McReynolds wrote the opinion for the unanimous Court that the act would destroy all private primary schools for normal children within the state of Oregon. Further, he found that there was nothing inherently harmful in the operation of private schools. Rather, they had been always regarded as useful and meritorious. No one has suggested that either of the schools failed to properly instruct their pupils or that there was any emergency or extraordinary condition which would require them to be closed. In short, the Court found that there was no reasonable relation of the state's police power to this law: "The child is not the mere creature of the state; those who nurture him and direct his destiny have the right, coupled with the high duty, to recognize and prepare him for additional obligations."

AFTERMATH

The *Pierce* decision clearly stated that states may compel attendance at a school, but that parents have the right to choose between public and private schools. *Pierce* has never been overruled and is cited often with favor.

SIGNIFICANCE

The *Pierce* decision emphasized fundamental rights not expressly stated in the Constitution and was one of the first cases to find a privacy right

---

[1]*Oxford Companion to the Supreme Court of the United States.* New York: Oxford University Press, 1992, p. 634.

that could be protected by the Court, in this case, the private decision of a family as to the schooling of its children.

RELATED CASES

Board of Education v. Allen, 392 U.S. 236 (1968)

Cantwell v. Connecticut, 310 U.S. 296 (1940)

RECOMMENDED READING

Dwight Tompkins, *An Argument for Privacy in Support of the Choice of Home Education by Parents,* 20 Journal of Law and Education 301 (1991).

Barbara Woodhouse, *"Who Owns the Child":* Meyer *and* Pierce *and the Child as Property,* 33 William and Mary Law Review 995 (1992).

Mark Yudof, *When Governments Speak: Toward a Theory of Government Expression and the First Amendment,* 57 Texas Law Review 863 (1979).

Case Title: *Sherbert v. Verner*

Legal Citations: 374 U.S. 398; 83 S.Ct. 1790; 10 L.Ed. 2d 965

Year of Decision: 1963

KEY ISSUES

May a state deny unemployment compensation benefits to an otherwise eligible recipient whose failure to meet all the requirements is based on a religious belief?

HISTORY OF THE CASE

Adell H. Sherbert was a member of the Seventh-Day Adventist Church. This religion prohibits its members from working on Saturday, its Sabbath day. In 1959, Sherbert's South Carolina employer fired her because she could not work on Saturday. After her discharge, she found no suitable five-day work that would conform to her religious scruples.

Sherbert later applied for unemployment compensation benefits under the South Carolina Unemployment Compensation Act. The Employment Security Commission denied Sherbert bene-

fits because the law required that employment seekers could reject jobs only with "good cause." Thereafter, Sherbert appealed to the Court of Common Pleas, which sustained the commission's finding. The South Carolina Supreme Court also affirmed, finding no infringement on Sherbert's constitutional free exercise of religious liberty.

SUMMARY OF ARGUMENTS

Sherbert argued that the state's denial of benefits based on her refusal to work on Saturday impermissibly interfered with her First Amendment right to the free exercise of religion. The First Amendment bars the government from making any law "prohibiting the free exercise" of religion.

South Carolina maintained that the granting to Sherbert of unemployment compensation benefits would clash with the First Amendment's prohibition of any law "respecting an establishment of religion." The state contended that the government would be impermissibly respecting the Seventh-day Adventist religion by granting religious groups an exception to the general rule.

DECISION

Justice Brennan delivered the 7-2 majority opinion of the Court. The Court held that denying unemployment benefits constituted an unconstitutional burden on Sherbert's free exercise of religion. The Court believed that South Carolina, in effect, forced Sherbert to choose between receiving the benefits and following her religion. The justices reasoned that placing such a choice on her would be equivalent to imposing a direct fine upon her for her Saturday worship practice. The Court also noted a discriminatory element in South Carolina's policy, since Sunday worshippers were not faced with the dilemma that confronts Saturday worshippers. Most important, however, the Court found no *substantial* state interest justifying the policy. The state did not convince the Court that an exemption for Saturday worshippers would prevent the state from achieving its objective of assuring that benefits flowed only to those involuntarily unemployed.

In his dissent, Justice Harlan held that the majority's holding violated the state's constitutional obligation of neutrality toward religion. He reasoned that a state would have to single out financial assistance for religiously motivated groups, even though it denies assistance to others whose identical behavior (the inability to work on Saturdays) is not religiously motivated. Harlan also maintained that the overall effect of South Carolina's policy on religion was "indirect, remote, and insubstantial." Thus, he believed this case did not fall within the area in which the Constitution requires special treatment for religion.

AFTERMATH

The ruling and rationale of *Sherbert* as applied to unemployment benefits remains good law. The Court has remained divided, however, on whether *Sherbert*'s rationale should be extended to generally applied criminal laws. In 1990, in *Employment Division v. Smith,* the Court ruled that the government does not have to prove a compelling interest to criminalize Native Americans' right to possess and ingest peyote, an illegal hallucinogenic drug, as part of their religious rites. In response to the *Smith* ruling, Congress passed the Religious Freedom Restoration Act (RFRA) in an attempt to return the standard of review in free exercise cases to *Sherbert*'s compelling interest test. However, in 1997, the Supreme Court invalidated RFRA as an unconstitutional exercise of congressional power.

SIGNIFICANCE

The *Sherbert* case makes the government prove a compelling interest whenever state regulations have the unintended effect of burdening religious beliefs. The Court will uphold such laws when they are the least restrictive means of accomplishing that objective. For example, the Court ruled in *United States v. Lee* (1982) that the federal government's refusal to grant Amish employers an exemption from paying social security taxes on wages paid did not violate the First Amendment's free exercise clause. As noted earlier, however, the Court has refused to extend this strict review standard to generally applicable criminal laws.

RELATED CASES

Braunfeld v. Brown, 366 U.S. 599 (1961)

City of Boerne v. Flores, 521 U.S. 507 (1997)

Employment Division v. Smith, 494 U.S. 872 (1990)

Hobbie v. Unemployment Appeals Comm'n of Fla., 480 U.S. 136 (1987)

Frazee v. Illinois Dept. of Employment Security, 489 U.S. 829 (1989)

United States v. Lee, 455 U.S. 252 (1982)

Wisconsin v. Yoder, 406 U.S. 205 (1972)

RECOMMENDED READING

Kenneth Marin, Employment Division v. Smith: *The Supreme Court Alters the State of Free Exercise Doctrine,* 40 American University Law Review 1431–1471 (summer 1991).

David E. Steinberg, *Rejecting the Case against the Free Exercise Exemption: A Critical Assessment,* 75 Boston University Law Review 241–306 (1995).

Clare Zerangue, *Sabbath Observance and the Workplace: Religion Clause Analysis and Title VII's Reasonable Accommodation Rule,* 46 Louisiana Law Review 1265–1288 (1986).

Case Title: *Stone v. Graham*

Legal Citation: 449 U.S. 39

Year of Decision: 1982

KEY ISSUES

Does displaying the Ten Commandments on a public school wall violate the establishment clause?

HISTORY OF THE CASE

Kentucky passed a statute in 1978 that said, in part, that a copy of the Ten Commandments was to be displayed on the wall of every public classroom in the state. The copy was to be funded by private contributions, and was to contain a statement of its secular purpose at the bottom of the document. Stone and others brought an action against Graham, the superintendent of public instruction of Kentucky, seeking an injunction against the enforcement of the statute. The statute was upheld in the trial court as well as in the Kentucky Supreme Court.

SUMMARY OF ARGUMENTS

The petitioners contended that the display violated the establishment clause of the First Amendment, which states, in part, that Congress shall make no law respecting an establishment of religion. This is applied to the states through the Fourteenth Amendment. The respondents contended that there was a secular purpose for the display, which was to show the model for the legal code and common law of the United States, and that this purpose was stated at the bottom of the display.

DECISION

The Court used the *Lemon* test in invalidating the statute. The test, established in *LEMON V. KURTZMAN* (1971), held that a statute must satisfy three criteria in order to be free from establishment clause violations: (1) It must have a secular legislative purpose; (2) its primary effect cannot advance nor inhibit religion; (3) it must not create an excessive entanglement with government and religion. The Court held that the statute violated the first prong, and it was therefore unconstitutional. The Court gave no weight to the secular purpose offered by the respondents, nor to the fact that it was privately funded; instead, it held that the display was obviously religious in nature.

Justice Blackmun and Chief Justice Rehnquist dissented, stating that sometimes government and religion are inseparable, and the display of a document with such secular significance would stand up to the first prong of the *Lemon* test.

Justice Stewart dissented to the summary reversal of the Kentucky courts who appeared to use the constitutional criteria correctly in coming to their decisions.

AFTERMATH

Other cases that dealt with religion in schools were treated similarly; there was very little tolerance for anything that could be construed as state support of religion.

SIGNIFICANCE

The Court established with this case that it would look into the true purpose of legislation, not just the purpose stated by the legislature, to determine whether its purpose was religious or secular. The justices were intent on separating sham secular purposes from true secular purposes.

RELATED CASES

School District of *Abington Township, Pennsylvania v. Schempp,* 374 U.S. 203 (1963)

Edwards v. Aguillard, 482 U.S. 578 (1987)

Lemon v. Kurtzman, 403 U.S. 602 (1971)

Wallace v. Jaffree, 472 U.S. 38 (1985)

RECOMMENDED READING

Russell E. Hinds, *Constitutional Law—Statute Requiring That the Ten Commandments Be Posted in Classrooms Held Unconstitutional,* 12 Cumberland Law Review 197 (1982).

Pfeffer, Leo. *Religion, State and the Burger Court.* Buffalo, N.Y.: Prometheus Books, 1984.

Swanson, Wayne R. *The Christ Child Goes to Court.* Philadelphia: Temple University Press, 1990.

Case Title: *Thomas v. Review Board*

Alternate Case Title: The Termination and Religion Case

Legal Citation: 450 U.S. 707

Year of Decision: 1981

KEY ISSUES

Can a state deny unemployment compensation benefits to a person who quits his job because of his religious beliefs?

HISTORY OF THE CASE

Thomas, a Jehovah's Witness, quit his job at an industrial company when he was transferred from the foundry to a department that produced turrets for tanks. He believed that producing the turrets was contrary to the dictates of his religion, and he was unable to transfer to any part of the company that was not producing military materials. Thomas applied for unemployment compensation, but the review board refused to grant him benefits because it found that his religious beliefs did not meet the statutory requirement of "just cause" for quitting his job. He was successful in the state court of appeals, but the Indiana Supreme Court reversed and denied him any benefits.

SUMMARY OF ARGUMENTS

Thomas argued that by withholding benefits from those who quit their jobs because of their religious beliefs, Indiana was denying them their First Amendment right to the free exercise of religion.

Indiana argued that its denial of benefits was only a slight burden on Thomas's religious beliefs, and that this burden was justified by the state's interest in maintaining the integrity of its unemployment compensation fund.

DECISION

The Supreme Court, in an opinion written by Chief Justice Burger, held that the state's denial of benefits had violated Thomas's rights under the First Amendment, which applies to the states through the due process clause of the Fourteenth Amendment. Chief Justice Burger noted that this case did not involve the "difficult and delicate task" of deciding what constitutes a religious belief, because the Indiana Review Board had conceded that Thomas quit his job because of his religion. In Chief Justice Burger's opinion, it was "coercive" for the state to withhold benefits from Thomas unless he was willing to work in violation of his religious faith. He argued that it was unconstitutional for the state to force a person "to choose between the exercise of a First Amendment right and participation in an otherwise available public program." Chief Justice Burger found no state interest sufficiently compelling to justify the impingement of Thomas's rights; he contended that it was highly unlikely that the unemployment fund would face many claims similar to those presented by Thomas. Nor did Chief Justice Burger accept the view that, by compelling benefit payments to Thomas because of his religious beliefs, the Court was forcing Indiana to "establish" religion in violation of the First Amendment's establishment clause. The Court was simply forcing Indiana to be neutral in the face of religious differences.

Justice Rehnquist wrote the lone dissent. He noted the tension between the free exercise clause and the establishment clause in this case. He attributed this to several factors: First, the First Amendment was originally intended to apply only to the federal government (the Court had made it applicable to the states through the Fourteenth Amendment); second, the increased government involvement in people's lives through social wel-

fare legislation; and third, the overly expansive interpretation each clause had been given by the Court. Justice Rehnquist argued that the free exercise clause should apply only when government prohibits religion, not merely makes it costly to have a religious belief. He dissented from what he saw as the Court's holding: "[T]hat the State of Indiana is constitutionally required to provide direct financial assistance to a person solely on the basis of his religious beliefs."

AFTERMATH

Thomas affirmed the Court's decision in SHERBERT V. VERNER (1963) and prohibited deprivation of unemployment benefits because of work limitations based on religious beliefs.

SIGNIFICANCE

Thomas was one of only a couple of major decisions involving Jehovah's Witnesses and prohibited a state's refusal to grant unemployment benefits when such refusal was based on an employee's work limits caused by religious beliefs.

RELATED CASES

Sherbert v. Verner, 374 U.S. 398 (1963)

Everson v. Board of Education, 330 U.S. 1 (1947)

RECOMMENDED READING

Donald S. Stefanski, *Religious Discrimination in the Workplace: A Comparison of* Thomas v. Review Board *and Title VII Cases,* 33 Syracuse Law Review 843 (1982).

Case Title: *Tilton v. Richardson*

Legal Citation: 403 U.S. 672

Year of Decision: 1971

KEY ISSUES

Is a 20-year limit on the federal government's supervision of grant money given to colleges a subtle endorsement of religion?

HISTORY OF THE CASE

The Higher Education Facilities Act of 1963 provided funds for private colleges and universities for the construction of academic facilities. The money was not to be used for facilities that would have religious purposes. After 20 years, however, the government would no longer supervise how the facilities were used. A group of taxpayers brought an action in district court seeking an injunction to halt the funding. The district court refused the injunction and dismissed the case. The U.S. Supreme Court agreed to hear the case.

SUMMARY OF ARGUMENTS

The taxpayers argued that the schools were parochial and religious in character and should therefore not receive any funds from federal sources. They further urged that the 20-year supervisory period would enable the recipients to later convert publicly funded facilities to religious facilities.

The Department of Health, Education, and Welfare argued that the funding was not intended for religious purposes and that the government's supervision over the expenditures was sufficient to prevent sectarian use of the funds.

DECISION

Chief Justice Burger held for the majority that the act did not violate the religion clauses of the First Amendment. The Court reasoned that college-level education was significantly different from church-related elementary and secondary schools. There was a higher degree of intellectual liberty at the college level than at lower levels of education. The Court also believed that college students were less likely to fall victim to religious indoctrination. The state could fund these types of colleges and universities without endangering the integrity of the First Amendment.

AFTERMATH

The Court constantly looks at religious intermingling in education. Several cases have come to the Court and virtually all have been decided on a fact-by-fact analysis. The test formulated in LEMON V. KURTZMAN (1971) permeates the decisions, however: For an act to be valid, it must have a secular purpose, it must not have the primary effect of advancing or inhibiting religion, and it must not foster excessive government entanglement. The *Tilton* decision was used as a basis for the Court's subsequent decision in *Roemer v. Board of Public Works of Maryland* (1976).

SIGNIFICANCE

Tilton decided on the same day as *Lemon v. Kurtzman* illustrates that there is no clear, definitive rule governing establishment clause jurisprudence. By considering the purpose and overall effect of the 20-year supervisory limit on oversight of state subsidies to private colleges, the Court determined that the funding in question did not constitute an impermissible establishment of religion. The difference in the same-day decisions of *Tilton* and *Lemon* indicated that aid to higher educational facilities can more readily meet constitutionality tests than aid to elementary and high schools.

RELATED CASES

Bradfield v. Rogers, 175 U.S. 291 (1899)

Everson v. Board of Education, 330 U.S. 1 (1947)

Lemon v. Kurtzman, 403 U.S. 602 (1971)

Witters v. Washington Department of Services for the Blind, 474 U.S. 481 (1986)

Zobrest v. Catalina Foothills School District, 506 U.S. 813 (1992)

RECOMMENDED READING

Giannella, Donald A. *Lemon* and *Tilton*. In *Church and State*. Edited by Philip B. Kurland. Chicago: University of Chicago Press, 1975.

Pfeffer, Leo. *Religion, State and the Burger Court*. Buffalo, N.Y.: Prometheus Books, 1984.

Weber, Paul J., and Dennis A. Gilbert. *Private Churches and Public Money*. Westport, Conn.: Greenwood Press, 1971.

Case Title: *Torcaso v. Watkins*

Alternate Case Title: The Test Oath Case

Legal Citation: 367 U.S. 488

Year of Decision: 1961

KEY ISSUES

May the state condition public employment upon affirmation of the employee's belief in God?

HISTORY OF THE CASE

Roy R. Torcaso was appointed to the office of Notary Public, but he was denied his commission because he refused to affirm his belief in God as required by the Maryland Constitution. He sued in state court to compel the issuance of his commission, but he was unsuccessful.

SUMMARY OF ARGUMENTS

Torcaso argued that the required oath violated his right to freedom of religion under the First and Fourteenth Amendments to the Constitution.

Maryland argued that the test oath did not violate Torcaso's rights because he was not being compelled to hold public office.

DECISION

The Supreme Court, in a unanimous opinion written by Justice Black, held the test oath unconstitutional. Justice Black noted that Article VI of the Constitution explicitly forbids test oaths in federal employment, while the First Amendment creates a total "wall of separation between church and state." He contended that the Fourteenth Amendment had extended the reach of this wall to the state governments; consequently, "neither a State nor the Federal Government can constitutionally force a person to profess a belief or disbelief in any religion." In the Court's opinion, the fact that Torcaso was not compelled to become a notary did not mean that Maryland could use constitutionally impermissible criteria to bar him from office.

AFTERMATH

Persons who do not hold religious beliefs now have their disbelief protected by the First Amendment.

SIGNIFICANCE

A person's religious beliefs are not the government's business. Furthermore, the belief or disbelief in a religion or deity cannot be a qualification to hold public office. Torcaso proved that the First Amendment protects both freedom of religion and freedom from religion.

RELATED CASES

Everson v. Board of Education, 330 U.S. 1 (1947)

Zorach v. Clauson, 343 U.S. 306 (1952)

RECOMMENDED READING

Note, *Toward a Constitutional Definition of Religion*, 91 Harvard Law Review 1056 (1978).

Case Title: *West Virginia State Board of Education v. Barnette*

Legal Citation: 319 U.S. 624

Year of Decision: 1943

KEY ISSUES

Does a state regulation requiring all school children to salute the U.S. flag violate the Constitution's guarantee of freedom of speech or freedom of religion?

HISTORY OF THE CASE

The West Virginia state legislature passed laws requiring all schools in the state to teach courses in history, civics, and the Constitution of the United States "for the purpose of teaching, fostering and perpetuating the ideals, principles and spirit of Americanism, and increasing the knowledge of the organization and machinery of the government." The state Board of Education adopted a resolution ordering a regular salute to the U.S. flag to further the legislature's goal of fostering Americanism.

Children, including Marie and Gathie Barnette, who were Jehovah's Witnesses, were expelled from school for refusing to salute the U.S. flag. Their religion incorporated a body of teaching in which the obligations imposed by God were superior to the obligation imposed by the government. Parents of the expelled children had been prosecuted for causing the failure to salute the flag. The district court refused to enforce the regulation, and the Board of Education brought the case to the U.S. Supreme Court.

SUMMARY OF ARGUMENTS

The plaintiffs argued that the regulation was an unconstitutional denial of religious freedom and freedom of speech, and violated the Fourteenth Amendment's equal protection and due process clauses. The defendants argued that the regulation was not unconstitutional. They cited a similar prior Supreme Court decision that had not invalidated Pennsylvania's regulation requiring school children to salute the U.S. flag at school.

DECISION

The majority of the Court found that the regulation requiring students to salute the national flag violated the plaintiffs' right to freedom of religion. In order not to confine the issue to one of freedom of religion, the Supreme Court also decided that the regulation was unconstitutional because it violated the right to free speech. They reasoned that the state had no power to force individuals to believe or confess particular political views.

AFTERMATH

This case has not been overruled and has been cited frequently to support freedom of expression.

SIGNIFICANCE

This was one of the first cases outlining the right *not* to speak. It emphasized the importance of freedom of thought, which includes freedom of religion and expression.

RELATED CASES

Prince v. Commonwealth of Massachusetts, 321 U.S. 158 (1944)

U.S. v. Ballard, 322 U.S. 78 (1944)

RECOMMENDED READING

Johnson, Alvin W., and Frank H. Yost. *Separation of Church and State in the United States.* Minneapolis: University of Minnesota Press, 1948.

Louis H. Pollak, *The Supreme Court, 1962 Term. Foreword: Public Prayer in Public Schools,* 77 Harvard Law Review (1962).

Stevens, Leonard A. *Salute!* New York: Coward, McCann and Geoghegan, 1973.

Mark G. Yudof, *When Government Speaks: Toward a Theory of Government Expression and the First Amendment,* 57 Texas Law Review 863 (August 1979).

Case Title: *Wisconsin v. Yoder*

Alternate Case Title: The Case of the Amish Children

Legal Citation: 406 U.S. 205

Year of Decision: 1972

KEY ISSUES

May the state compel Amish children to attend public school until they are 16, when doing so is contrary to Amish religious beliefs?

HISTORY OF THE CASE

Yoder was a member of the Amish religion and the father of two children, ages 14 and 15. He was convicted of violating Wisconsin's mandatory school attendance law by declining to send the children to public or private school through the age of 16. He declined to do so because he believed sending the children to school would expose them to a culture that values materialism, competition, and technology, thereby endangering the Amish faith, which values community, farm labor, and practical wisdom. The children received an informal vocational education, which prepared them for life in the Amish community; the state conceded that Amish people who emerge from this process are exceptionally self-sufficient and law-abiding citizens. Yoder challenged his conviction in the Wisconsin Supreme Court, alleging a violation of his rights under the free exercise of religion clause of the First Amendment, which is made applicable to the states by the Fourteenth Amendment. The Wisconsin Supreme Court overturned the convictions, and the state appealed to the U.S. Supreme Court.

SUMMARY OF ARGUMENTS

Yoder argued that by endangering the future of the Amish faith, the compulsory education law violated his right to the free exercise of his religion.

Wisconsin argued that Yoder's right to exercise his religion should be subordinate to the state's compelling interest in universal compulsory education. It asserted that education is vital because it prepares citizens to participate in the political life of the community and enables them to be self-sufficient.

DECISION

The Court, in an opinion written by Chief Justice Burger, held Yoder's convictions invalid under the First Amendment, finding that the state had violated the free exercise clause. Chief Justice Burger was extremely careful in noting that the outcome of the case turned heavily upon its facts. He made numerous references to the sincerity of Yoder's religious beliefs, the long-standing tradition of the Amish faith, and the fact the children involved would receive an education that on the whole fulfilled all the interests which the state law was intended to protect. The Court acknowledged that providing public education was a significant state interest; thus, the case was resolved by balancing the state's interest against Yoder's fundamental right to the free exercise of religion. This balance was tipped in Yoder's favor by the fact that the additional two years of schooling could no better prepare them to participate in society than the Amish's long-standing program of vocational education. Chief Justice Burger emphasized that the Amish's "long history as a successful and self-sufficient segment of American society" and "the adequacy of their alternative mode of continuing informal vocational education . . ." were showings "that probably few other religious groups or sects could make."

Justice White wrote a concurring opinion joined by Justices Brennan and Stewart. He sought to emphasize that under normal circumstances the state interest in public education would take precedence over even First Amendment rights, and that the result in this case occurred because the deviation from the state law was "relatively slight."

Justice Douglas dissented. He was unwilling to accede to Yoder's First Amendment claim when there was a possibility that the children might have wanted to attend the public schools. The majority had taken note of the significance of this issue but did not consider it because the children's views were not in the record. Justice Douglas also disagreed with the Court's narrow definition of religion for First Amendment purposes. Whereas the Court had suggested that, as an example, Henry David Thoreau's philosophical objection to society was not entitled to constitutional protection, Justice Douglas would have given equal dignity to such an "exalted view of 'religion.'"

AFTERMATH

Since *Wisconsin v. Yoder,* the Court has not had many opportunities to address the free exercise clause.

SIGNIFICANCE

The decision in *Wisconsin v. Yoder* made it impossible for states to have an absolute right to implement statutes requiring compulsory high school education.

RELATED CASES

Sherbert v. Verner, 374 U.S. 398 (1963)

United States v. Lee, 455 U.S. 252 (1982)

RECOMMENDED READING

Pfeffer, Leo. *Religion, State and the Burger Court.* Buffalo, N.Y.: Prometheus Books, 1984.

David A. J. Richards, *The Individual, the Family and the Constitution: A Jurisprudential Perspective,* 55 New York University Law Review 1 (1980).

Case Title: *Zelman v. Simmons-Harris*

Alternate Case Title: School Voucher Case

Legal Citation: U.S. 122 S.Ct. 2460

Year of Decision: 2002

KEY ISSUES

Does a state statute that provides educational funds to low-income families for use at the school of their choice violate the establishment clause if most of the families choose to have the funds applied to education provided by private religious schools?

HISTORY OF THE CASE

The Cleveland City School District had some of the worst-performing public schools in the United States. Less than one-third of the students in these schools graduated from high school. In response to this situation, the state of Ohio enacted a Pilot Scholarship Program (the "Program") that gave financial assistance to families in Ohio school districts that were under supervision by the state superintendent. The Program provided tuition aid for children in elementary grades to attend a participating public or private school chosen by the child's parents. The Program also provided tutorial aid for students whose parents chose to keep them in public school. In 1996, respondents, a group of Ohio taxpayers, brought suit challenging the Program. The Ohio Supreme Court found the Program in violation of Ohio constitutional procedure requirements. These problems were subsequently corrected by the state legislature. The respondents then filed an action in the federal district court alleging the Program violated the establishment clause. The district court found in favor of the respondents and the court of appeals affirmed its decision. The Supreme Court granted certiorari to review the case.

SUMMARY OF ARGUMENTS

Petitioner Susan Tave Zelman, the superintendent of public instruction of Ohio, argued that the Program was constitutional because it was religiously neutral and parents had a choice as to where their children attended school.

The respondents, including Doris Simmons-Harris, argued the Program violated the establishment clause because it allowed the state to finance religious education. Further, respondents argued that the Program created an incentive for parents to choose a private religious school for their child's education and created a public perception that the state was supporting religion.

DECISION

The Supreme Court reversed the court of appeals and held that the Program did not violate the establishment clause. Chief Justice Rehnquist, joined by Justices O'Connor, Scalia, Kennedy, and Thomas, gave the opinion of the Court. The chief justice distinguished between government programs providing aid directly to private religious schools and government programs providing for private choice, programs under which state funds reached private religious schools because of an individual's choice to apply them to the institution. After making this distinction, the chief justice affirmed the Court's previous decisions in which challenges to private choice legislation were rejected as not in violation of the establishment clause. The chief justice held that the Program was constitutional because it was a program of true private choice and any benefit to religious institutions was indirect. The chief justice further found the Program created a disincentive for families to choose religious schools as they would not receive as much assistance as if their child attended one of the other available institutions, focusing on the fact that parents could choose from private nonreligious schools, private religious schools, public schools, magnet schools, or community schools.

Justice O'Connor concurred separately, specifically identifying the figures and statistics that indicated the funds flowing to private religious institutions were less than those going to community and magnet schools. Justice O'Connor also pointed to the fact that the amount of money flowing to these religious schools was small when compared to what the government currently provided to religious institutions through tax exemptions, tax credits, tax deductions, public health programs, and grants for higher education. While Justice O'Connor indicated this did not justify the Program, it did put the Program in perspective.

Justice Thomas also concurred, questioning whether the establishment clause test of whether an activity had a secular purpose and a primary effect of advancing or inhibiting religion, should even be applied to the states as the establishment clause states "Congress shall make no law respecting an establishment of religion." Regardless of whether the establishment clause should be applicable, Justice Thomas found that the Program was not forcing religious education onto individuals, but gave parents a choice as to how to educate their children.

Justice Stevens dissented finding the crisis faced by the Cleveland City School District, the educational choices available within the public school system, and the private choice to choose religious education to be irrelevant to the issue of constitutionality.

Justice Souter, joined by Justices Stevens, Ginsburg, and Breyer, dissented as well. Justice Souter found that the majority improperly addressed the neutrality and choice elements of the Program. Justice Souter found the Program not to be neutral, but skewed to favor a religious direction. Additionally, he thought parents did not really have a choice as to where to spend the funds as there were more participating private schools that were religious than those that were nonreligious.

Finally, Justice Breyer, joined by Justices Stevens and Souter, dissented separately to emphasize the risk of social conflict he felt was created by this and other such programs that could not be remedied by parental choice. Because of the religious diversity of our nation, Justice Breyer found that only creating clear lines separating church and state could avoid conflict between the various religious groups as it would be impossible to grant the various groups an equal opportunity to introduce their religious beliefs and practices into public schools.

AFTERMATH

In the wake of *Zelman*, lawsuits have been filed in several states seeking to remove obstacles to public funding of religious education. Currently, only Florida, Ohio, and Wisconsin provide state funds to families for education in private schools.

SIGNIFICANCE

Reaction to *Zelman* was mixed, ranging from "the most important educational decision since BROWN V. BOARD OF EDUCATION" to "devastating to public school systems." In addition, the decision was considered by some to be a serious blow to the separation of church and state.

RELATED CASES

Everson v. Board of Ed. of Ewing, 330 U.S. 1 (1947)

Mitchell v. Helms, 530 U.S. 793 (2000)

Mueller v. Allen, 463 U.S. 388 (1983)

Winters v. Washington Dept. of Servs. for Blind, 474 U.S. 481 (1986)

Zobrest v. Catalina Foothills School Dist., 509 U.S. 1 (1993)

RECOMMENDED READING

Bolick, Clint. *Voucher Wars: Waging the Battle over School Choice*. Washington, D.C.: Cato Institute, 2003.

Moffit, Robert E., Jennifer J. Garrett, and Janice A. Smith. *School Choice 2001: What's Happening in the States*. Washington, D.C.: Heritage Foundation, 2001.

Case Title: *Zorach v. Clauson*

Alternate Case Title: The Religion in School Case

Legal Citation: 343 U.S. 306

Year of Decision: 1952

KEY ISSUES

May a public school create a program that allows students to leave school if they attend off-campus religious exercises, while requiring nonparticipants to remain in school?

HISTORY OF THE CASE

New York City had a "released time" program that permitted public schools to release students upon the written request of their parents so that the students could attend religious instruction or devotional exercises. The instruction did not occur in the schools and involved no public expenditures. Students not released were required to stay in the classrooms, and the churches reported to the schools the names of those students who were released but failed to attend the devotional services. The parents of certain schoolchildren challenged the law on the grounds that it involved an establishment of religion in violation of the First and Fourteenth Amendments. The New York Court of Appeals sustained the constitutionality of the law, and the parents appealed to the U.S. Supreme Court.

SUMMARY OF ARGUMENTS

The parents argued that the state had put its weight behind a program of religious instruction, and that the program constituted a subtle form of coercion which allowed only those who would attend religious training to leave the classroom during school hours.

The city responded that the program was voluntary and was paid for entirely by the religious organizations; thus, it involved no establishment of religion.

DECISION

Justice Douglas delivered the opinion for a majority of six justices. The Court held that New York City's released time program was constitutional. Justice Douglas accepted the view that with respect to an establishment of religion, the separation of church and state must be unequivocal. He contended, however, that in other areas the two need not be alien to each other. Justice Douglas pointed to prayers in legislative halls and municipal fire and police protection of churches as examples of government respecting religious diversity without favoring any particular sect. In Justice Douglas's words, "We are a religious people whose institutions presuppose a Supreme Being." Consequently, an accommodation of public institutions to the religious needs of the people was within the intent of the Founding Fathers, reflecting the fact that government was not to be hostile toward religion.

Justice Douglas distinguished the landmark case of MCCOLLUM V. BOARD OF EDUCATION (1948), which held an Illinois released time program unconstitutional, on the grounds that in McCollum the public school classrooms were actually used for religious instruction.

Justice Black, in a vehement dissent, argued that this case was substantially similar to McCollum. He contended that the crucial element in McCollum was not the use of public classrooms for religious instruction, but the fact Illinois had "manipulate[d] the compelled classroom hours of its compulsory school machinery so as to channel children into sectarian classes." Because in this case New York was manipulating its compulsory education laws to help religious sects get pupils, this law clearly failed to heed the wall of separation between church and state that had been mandated by McCollum. In Justice Black's view, requiring the state to be neutral insured that it would not use its power to favor one religious group over another, thus promoting true religious freedom.

Justice Jackson wrote a dissenting opinion in which he broke the released time program down into two stages: "[F]irst, that the State compel each student to yield a large part of his time for public secular education; and, second, that some of it be 'released' to him on the condition that he devote it to sectarian religious purposes." In his opinion this amounted to achieving an unconstitutional result by indirection. Rather than giving all students time off, the school restricted their freedom by requiring their attendance, then made church attendance one of the two permissible uses of their time. Justice Jackson took note of the potential implications of the Court's decision: "The day that this country ceases to be free for irreligion it will cease to be free for religion—except for the sect that can win political power."

Justice Frankfurter also dissented.

AFTERMATH

The controversial "released time" program was upheld indicating that the government can accommodate religious practices and beliefs.

SIGNIFICANCE

Zorach is the Court's initial articulation of governmental accommodation of religion.

RELATED CASES

McCollum v. Board of Education, 333 U.S. 203 (1948)

Stone v. Graham, 449 U.S. 39 (1980) (per curiam)

RECOMMENDED READING

Cord, Robert L. *Separation of Church and State: Historical Fact and Current Fiction.* New York: Lambeth Press, 1982.

Michael W. McConnell, *Accommodation of Religion,* Supreme Court Review 1 (1985).

SEARCH AND SEIZURE

Case Title: *Bivens v. Six Unknown Named Agents of Federal Bureau of Narcotics*

Alternate Case Title: The Unreasonable Search by Federal Agents Case

Legal Citations: 403 U.S. 388; 91 S.Ct. 1999; 29 L.Ed. 619

Year of Decision: 1971

KEY ISSUES

Does a warrantless search and arrest by federal officials violate the Fourth Amendment prohibition against unreasonable search and seizure and entitle the person to money damages?

HISTORY OF THE CASE

On November 26, 1965, agents of the Federal Bureau of Narcotics, acting under claim of federal authority, entered Mr. Bivens's apartment and arrested him for alleged narcotics violations. The agents took Mr. Bivens to the federal courthouse where he was questioned, booked, and subjected to a visual strip search. Believing that the agents entered his apartment without a warrant, searched the apartment, and arrested him on narcotics charges, all without probable cause, Bivens brought suit on July 7, 1967, in federal district court. He also asserted that unreasonable force was used in making the arrest in front of his wife and children. He claimed to have endured great humiliation, embarrassment, and mental suffering as a result of the agents' actions and sought $15,000 from each of them in damages.

The district court dismissed the complaint on the ground that it failed to state facts entitling Bivens to judicial relief and that the agents were immune from suit by virtue of their official position. The court of appeals affirmed the decision. The U.S. Supreme Court agreed to review the case.

SUMMARY OF ARGUMENTS

Bivens argued that his arrest was "done unlawfully, unreasonably and contrary to law." He also argued that the search was without "cause, consent or warrant," in violation of the Fourth Amendment.

The Federal Bureau of Narcotics argued that Bivens could obtain money damages to redress invasion of his Fourth Amendment rights only by commencing a state law tort action, an action for civil wrong or injury committed against another's person or property, in state court. They urged the Supreme Court to uphold the dismissal of his complaint in federal court, and remit him to filing an action in state courts in order that the case could properly be removed to the federal courts for decision on the basis of state law.

DECISION

Justice Brennan, writing for the Court, held that Bivens was entitled to recover money damages for any injuries he suffered as a result of the agents' violation of the Fourth Amendment. Justice Brennan found that the Fourth Amendment limited the exercise of federal power and guaranteed to citizens of the United States the absolute right to be free from unreasonable searches and seizures carried out by virtue of federal authority. He rejected the agents' argument that the Fourth Amendment served only as a limitation on federal defenses to a state law claim, and not as an independent limitation upon the exercise of federal power.

Justice Brennan pointed out the difference between unlawful trespass by private citizens and by officers of the government. He reasoned that for a trespass by a private citizen, one could have resorted to the local police or barred the door against the unwanted entry. For one demanding admission under a claim of federal authority, however, there were no police protections, nor alternative means for the protection of privacy. A person's only remedy was in the protection of the judicial tribunals. Thus, he believed that the interests protected by the state laws regulating trespass and the invasion of privacy, and those protected by the Fourth Amendment's guarantee against unreasonable search and seizure, may be inconsistent.

Justice Brennan noted that historically, money damages were regarded as the ordinary remedy for invasion of personal interests. He found that although the Fourth Amendment does not specifically provide for money damages, there was no congressional declaration that persons injured by a federal officer's violation of the

Fourth Amendment may not recover money damages from the agents. (Justice Brennan did not address the immunity question, which was not passed on by the court of appeals.)

Justice Harlan wrote a concurring opinion in the judgment. He agreed with Justice Brennan that the court of appeals was incorrect in dismissing the complaint and joined in the judgment of reversal. He found that the interest which Bivens claimed—to be free from official conduct in contravention of the Fourth Amendment—was a federally protected interest. Therefore, Bivens's entitlement to be free from the type of official conduct prohibited by the Fourth Amendment does not depend on a decision by the state in which he resides to accord him a remedy.

Justice Harlan then compared the federal courts' power to grant equitable relief with its power to grant compensatory relief. He concluded that the statute that empowered a federal court to grant equitable relief also empowered it to grant traditional legal remedies. Harlan found that compensatory relief was "necessary" and "appropriate" to vindicate the interests asserted, stating that damages of some form was the only possible remedy for someone in Bivens's alleged position. Harlan dismissed the idea that providing a damage remedy would increase the number of frivolous claims filed or would have limited usage due to jury hostility and the limited individual resources of government officials. He concluded that a damage remedy should be afforded to litigants alleging the most flagrant police misconduct, even if the remedy was not ultimately chosen.

Chief Justice Burger and Justice Blackmun wrote dissenting opinions. Justice Burger believed that the damage remedy given by the majority was judicially created, and was not provided for in the Constitution nor enacted by Congress. He saw this as a separation of powers issue and found that Congress, and not the judiciary, was responsible for making legislation. Justice Burger gave several reasons that the exclusionary rule did not work and recognized that the majority was trying to fill in the gaps left by the suppression doctrine. He felt, however, that they did so by impinging on the legislative and policy functions that the Constitution has vested in Congress. He also criticized the length of time taken to find better ways to

deter government officials from violating Fourth Amendment rights when making searches and seizures. He concluded that an entirely different remedy was necessary, but it was beyond the judicial power, as was the step the majority took in this case.

Justice Burger laid out a statutory scheme that would provide a remedy for innocent persons hurt by illegal police conduct. It allowed for an awarding of damages, recorded the conduct in the officer's personnel file, and made appellate judicial review available. Finally, he made a plea to Congress to review the suppression doctrine which requires illegally obtained evidence to be excluded from consideration. Burger believed the suppression doctrine was poorly designed and he hoped that a congressional review would result in the formation of a policy that afforded appropriate redress to innocent victims and that did not let criminals go free.

In Justice Black's dissenting opinion, he indicated Congress had the ability to pass legislation that made it possible for persons meeting a certain set of facts to recover damages for unreasonable searches violating the Fourth Amendment, but had chosen not to do so. Black believed the majority was creating "judicial" legislation by providing a damage remedy and acting outside its scope of power.

Justice Blackmun also dissented from the majority opinion, referring to Chief Justice Lombard's opinion for the court of appeals that stated, among other things, a belief that the Fourth Amendment framers had not contemplated wholly new federal actions based directly on the amendment. He added that the majority created an opportunity for an "avalanche" of new federal cases, as their decision could prompt those who suspect a Fourth Amendment violation to immediately sue in federal court. Justice Blackmun felt other adequate remedies were available, and if not, Congress, not the Supreme Court, should act.

AFTERMATH

After the decision, federal courts expanded the *Bivens* doctrine to protect other constitutional rights, thereby creating a damages remedy for all individuals whose constitutional rights were violated by federal officials. Since 1980, however, the Court has become considerably more reluctant to imply *Bivens* actions. For example, in *United States v. Stanley,* 107 S.Ct. 3054 (1982). The Court refused to allow a damages remedy for the violation of a serviceman's constitutional rights when the violation resulted from activity incident to military service and in *Bush v. Lucas,* 462 U.S. 367 (1983) the Court disallowed Bivens's action for the violation of a civil servant's First Amendment rights.

SIGNIFICANCE

This landmark decision permitted actions for damages when federal authorities violated certain constitutional rights. The Court was able to limit the discretion of police, at a time when police misconduct was rampant, by requiring a warrant and by extending the remedy of excluding evidence illegally obtained. This is a judicially created remedy for those victims of police overreaching who were unlikely to win a jury's sympathy in light of the pressing concerns of the day. Prior to *Bivens,* there was no available action against federal officials to recover damages for the violation of constitutional rights. The decision in *Bivens* created such an action.

RELATED CASE

Monell v. Department of Social Services, 436 U.S. 658 (1978)

Case Title: *California v. Ciraolo*

Alternate Case Title: The "Home-grown Marijuana" Case

Legal Citations: 476 U.S. 207; 106 S.Ct. 1809; 90 L.Ed. 2d 210

Year of Decision: 1986

KEY ISSUES

Does aerial surveillance of a person's fenced backyard constitute an illegal search in violation of the Fourth Amendment?

HISTORY OF THE CASE

Police in Santa Clara, California, flew a plane over Ciraolo's home to confirm an anonymous tip that he was growing marijuana in his fenced backyard. The police, who were trained in marijuana identification, secured a private airplane, observed a plot of marijuana from the plane, and on the basis of this observation obtained a warrant to conduct a ground search of Ciraolo's property. Police seized 73 marijuana plants during the subsequent search. After the trial court denied a motion to suppress the evidence, Ciraolo pled guilty to cultivation of marijuana. The California Court of Appeals overturned the conviction, holding that the initial aerial observation was an unauthorized search under KATZ V. UNITED STATES (1967), and rendered the subsequent search warrant invalid. *Katz* held that if a person has a justifiable expectation of privacy that person is protected by the Fourth Amendment from illegal search and seizure. The *Katz* test for "expectation of privacy" has two parts: (1) did the individual's conduct manifest an actual expectation of privacy, and (2) is society willing to recognize the person's expectation as reasonable.

SUMMARY OF ARGUMENTS

The state argued that Ciraolo knowingly exposed his backyard to aerial observation because all that was seen was visible to the naked eye from any aircraft flying overhead.

Ciraolo argued that he did all that he reasonably could do to tell the world that he wished to maintain the privacy of his garden without covering his yard. He argued that he did not "knowingly" expose himself to aerial views and because his yard was part of his home, no governmental aerial observation was permissible under the Fourth Amendment without a warrant.

DECISION

Chief Justice Burger wrote the 5-4 split decision for the Court holding that a naked-eye aerial observation of Ciraolo's backyard did not violate the Fourth Amendment. The Court assumed that Ciraolo had a subjective expectation of privacy. The Court also assumed that Ciraolo's backyard was within the boundaries of his home, "where privacy expectations are most heightened." Nonetheless, the Court concluded that the aerial observation did not constitute a Fourth Amendment search because Ciraolo's subjective expectation that his backyard activities would be shielded from aerial observation was unreasonable and "not an expectation that society was prepared to honor." The Court acknowledged that the 10-foot fence surrounding the yard adequately manifested an intent to preserve privacy from ground-level observations, but the Court questioned whether the fence indicated that Ciraolo expected privacy from the air.

The Court relied almost entirely on the assertion that Ciraolo had waived his expectations of privacy by knowingly exposing his backyard to the public. Chief Justice Burger cited *Katz* for the proposition that objects and activities exposed to the "plain view" of outsiders do not receive protection under the Fourth Amendment. The Chief Justice then argued that because air travel is "routine," and because air travelers who pass above Ciraolo's home could look down into his yard, Ciraolo had knowingly exposed his marijuana within the meaning of the "plain view" doctrine. The Court rejected all arguments to the contrary; it was irrelevant that the police officers were trained to recognize marijuana and had conducted a focused observation. Chief Justice Burger also dismissed objections that the majority was insensitive to the dangers posed by intrusive, modern technology that inspired the Court in *Katz*.

In Justice Powell's dissent, joined by Justices Brennan, Marshall, and Blackmun, he criticized the majority for determining the reasonableness of expectations by examining the manner of police surveillance rather than the "personal and societal values protected by the Fourth Amendment." Justice Powell further argued that Ciraolo's expectation of privacy was reasonable because his yard was within the boundaries of his home where an individual's expectation of privacy "virtually always will be legitimate." Justice Powell dismissed the "plain view" doctrine as inapplicable because the activity took place in the "private area immediately adjacent to a home" and because the actual danger to privacy posed by passengers on commercial airliners was "virtually nonexistent" and "too trivial to protect against."

AFTERMATH

Ciraolo's redefinition of what could be considered a "private" area made the inside of a person's home seem like the only truly private place, but with the use of thermal imaging, even that might be subject to police surveillance.

SIGNIFICANCE

The Court in *Ciraolo* cut back on the general reach of Fourth Amendment protection by sharply limiting the situations in which an individual could reasonably expect privacy from warrentless governmental intrusion.

RELATED CASES

California v. Greenwood, 108 S.Ct. 1625 (1988)

Dow Chemical Co. v. United States, 106 S.Ct. 1819 (1986)

Katz v. United States, 389 U.S. 347 (1967)

RECOMMENDED READING

Cheryl Corrada, *Comment:* Dow Chemical *and* Ciraolo: *For Government Investigators the Sky's No Limit,* 36 Catholic University Law Review 667 (1987).

Jonathan T. Laba, *If You Can't Stand the Heat, Get Out of the Drug Business: Thermal Imagers, Emerging Technologies, and the Fourth Amendment,* 84 California Law Review 1437 (1996).

Case Title: *Chimel v. California*

Alternate Case Title: The "Search Incident to an Arrest" Case

Legal Citations: 395 U.S. 752; 89 S.Ct. 2034

Year of Decision: 1969

KEY ISSUES

Is a warrantless search of a person's entire house constitutionally justified as related to the person's constitutionally valid arrest?

HISTORY OF THE CASE

Police officers went to the home of Ted Chimel, a burglary suspect, to execute a warrant for his arrest. They did not have a search warrant. The officers arrested Chimel and then proceeded to search his entire house, attic, and garage. They directed his wife to open drawers and move the contents around so that they could view potential evidence. The police seized various items in their search, which lasted close to an hour. The seized items were admitted into evidence at Chimel's subsequent state trial, over his objection that they had been seized unconstitutionally. He was convicted, and the judgments of conviction were affirmed by both the California Court of Appeal and the California Supreme Court. Chimel sought relief from the U.S. Supreme Court.

SUMMARY OF ARGUMENTS

Chimel argued that the warrantless search violated the Fourth and Fourteenth Amendments; therefore, the evidence obtained from the search should have been suppressed. Chimel also pointed out that the Supreme Court's previous holdings allowing broad searches incident to arrest gave law enforcement officers the opportunity to engage in searches without probable cause if they arranged to arrest a suspect at home rather than somewhere else.

The state argued that the search of Chimel's house did not violate the Fourth and Fourteenth Amendments and that the search of a person's house was reasonable when a person was arrested there. The state relied on a previous decision of the Supreme Court in *United States v. Rabinowitz*, 339 U.S. 56 (1950), which stood for the proposition that warrantless searches incident to arrest can extend to areas in possession or under control of the arrested person.

DECISION

Justice Stewart wrote the opinion for the Court holding that the warrantless search of defendant's entire house at the time of his arrest in his house on a burglary charge was unreasonable because it extended beyond the defendant's person and area from which he might have obtained either a weapon or something else that could have been used as evidence against him.

After reviewing the history of search and seizure case law, Justice Stewart discredited the case relied upon by the state of California, *United States v. Rabinowitz,* and found it based on an impeachable line of authority that could be dis-puted because of its lack of consistency. He also felt that the rationale that the state relied upon to justify the search of Chimel's house was unsupported by the background and purpose of the Fourth Amendment. He then stated that police officers must obtain advance judicial approval of searches and seizures through the warrant procedure to perform a search. He added that the burden was on those who sought to dispense with the search warrant to prove the need for an exemption to that general rule.

Justice Stewart then recounted the "search incident to arrest" principle, which allows an officer to search a person being placed under arrest, and the area within his immediate control, in order to remove any weapons that the arrestee might use to resist arrest, or to grab evidentiary evidence. He believed these searches were justified for the safety and protection of the arresting officer. Justice Stewart could not find justification for the routine search of any room outside of the room in which the arrest took place, or of the desk drawers or other concealed or closed areas in the room itself. He overruled the parts of *United States v. Rabinowitz* (1950) and *Harris v. United States* (1947) that were inconsistent with the principles expounded above. Justice Stewart stated that the only way to constitutionally extend a search beyond the immediate area of the arrest was through a search warrant.

Justice Harlan wrote a concurring opinion stressing the importance of the administrative effect on states that resulted from expansion of situations in which a warrant would be required that the majority opinion created. Justice White, joined by Justice Black, wrote a dissenting opinion stating that he would have upheld the search in this case since there was probable cause for the search and the arrest.

AFTERMATH

As discovered in the subsequent decision of *New York v. Belton* (1981), *Chimel* failed to establish a workable definition of what exactly should be considered the area within the immediate control of an arrestee in situations that are not house arrests. Here, the Supreme Court rewrote its search-incident-to-arrest exception to the Fourth Amendment protection against unreasonable search and seizure. Subsequently, the state courts rejected this change.

SIGNIFICANCE

In *Chimel*, the Court settled on the proper scope of a search incident to a lawful arrest—severely restricting it without a search warrant—and clearly set forth the rationale behind the exception. The *Chimel* decision provided a mechanism by which courts could measure the reasonableness of a search. The Court, however, did not abolish altogether the authority to conduct a warrantless search for evidence.

RELATED CASES

New York v. Belton, 453 U.S. 454 (1981)

United States v. Robinson, 414 U.S. 218 (1973)

RECOMMENDED READING

Hall, John. *Search and Seizures.* Rochester, N.Y.: Lawyer's Co-operative Publishing, 1982.

Lafave, Wayne R. *Search and Seizure: A Treatise on the Fourth Amendment.* St. Paul: West Publishing, 1978.

J. Robert Nelson, Note, Chimel v. California: *A Potential Roadblock to Vehicle Searches*, 17 UCLA Law Review 626 (1970).

Case Title: *Katz v. United States*

Alternate Case Title: Wiretapping Case

Legal Citation: 389 U.S. 347

Year of Decision: 1967

KEY ISSUES

Does wiretapping a public phone to tape a private conversation violate the Fourth Amendment's prohibition against unreasonable searches and seizures?

HISTORY OF THE CASE

FBI agents arrested and convicted Charles Katz for violation of a federal statute that outlawed interstate transmission of bets or wagers by wire communication. The agents obtained evidence by attaching an electronic listening and recording device to the outside of a public telephone booth where the agents suspected that Katz had been making the illegal transactions.

SUMMARY OF ARGUMENTS

Katz argued that a public telephone booth was a constitutionally protected area so that evidence obtained from attaching an electronic listening and recording device to the booth violated the right of privacy and was inadmissible at trial. He argued that the FBI officers who tapped the phone booth violated the Fourth Amendment's prohibition against unreasonable searches and seizures.

The government argued that the telephone booth was not a constitutionally protected area and that the activities of the FBI agents should not be tested by the Fourth Amendment because the agents did not physically penetrate the telephone booth. The government also argued that the agents' actions complied with constitutional standards. Finally, the government argued that the telephone booth surveillance should have been exempted from the requirement of advanced authorization by a magistrate upon a showing of probable cause.

DECISION

Justice Stewart delivered the opinion of the Court, which held that the FBI violated the Fourth Amendment. Although judging in favor of Katz, the Court noted that he misconstrued the issues. Justice Stewart stated, "[T]he Fourth Amendment protects people, not places." Katz's argument about a "constitutionally protected area" did not persuade the Court. Justice Stewart noted, "[I]ndeed, we have expressly held that the Fourth Amendment governs not only seizure of tangible items, but extends as well to the recording of oral statements overheard without any 'technical trespass under . . . local property law.'" Recognizing that the Fourth Amendment was not limited only to physical searches and seizures, the Court held that "[t]he Government's activities in electronically listening to and recording the petitioner's words violated the privacy upon which he justifiably relied while using the telephone booth and thus constituted a 'search and seizure' within the meaning of the Fourth Amendment."

Next, the Court found that the electronic search and seizure employed in this case was unreasonable. The general rule is that searches conducted without a warrant are unlawful, subject to only a few narrow exceptions. The Court found that the facts of this case did not fit any of the exceptions to the general rule. In this case, the FBI agents "ignored 'the procedure of antecedent justification . . . that is central to the Fourth Amendment,' a procedure that we hold to be a constitutional precondition of the kind of electronic surveillance involved in this case." In other words, warrantless eavesdropping by government officials violates the Fourth Amendment.

In a widely quoted concurring opinion, Justice Harlan presented a two-part test to determine the privacy interests that the Fourth Amendment protects: (1) "a person [must] have exhibited an actual (subjective) expectation of privacy"; and (2) this "expectation [must] be one that society is prepared to recognize as 'reasonable.'"

Aftermath

Since *Katz,* many federal courts have considered whether the use without a warrant of binoculars or telescopes to view private activity and objects violates the Fourth Amendment. Although the Supreme Court has never squarely addressed the issue, the scholar Lawrence K. Marks suggests that, under the reasonable expectation of privacy standard, the Court would exclude such evidence: "The development of the reasonable expectation of privacy standard since *Katz,* and a comparison of telescope and binocular surveillance to electronic wiretapping, supports this conclusion." Nevertheless, a number of federal courts have admitted evidence obtained by such long-range surveillance.

Significance

The Court soundly rejected the proposition that the Fourth Amendment protection against warrantless searches and seizures extends only to physical trespass into constitutionally protected areas.

Related Cases

Boyd v. United States, 116 U.S. 616 (1886)

Olmstead v. United States, 277 U.S. 438 (1928)

United States v. Donovan, 429 U.S. 413 (1977)

United States v. Giordano, 416 U.S. 505 (1974)

United States v. Kim, 415 F. Supp. 1252 (D. Hawaii 1976)

United States v. Taborda, 653 F.2d 131 (2d Cir. 1980)

Recommended Reading

Edmund W. Kitch, *Katz v. United States: The Limits of the Fourth Amendment,* Supreme Court Review 133–152 (1968).

Lawrence Kaiser Marks, *Telescopes, Binoculars and the Fourth Amendment,* 67 Cornell Law Review 379–395 (January 1982).

Miller, Frank W. et al. *The Police Function.* New York: Foundation Press, 1986.

Mark Rahdert, *Tracking Katz: Beepers, Privacy and the Fourth Amendment,* 86 Yale Law Journal 1461–1508 (1977).

Case Title: *Ker v. State of California*

Legal Citation: 374 U.S. 23

Year of Decision: 1963

Key Issues

Does California's "hot pursuit" exception, which allows police officers to enter the home of a suspect without knocking and announcing their presence and purpose, to the general requirement of a warrant or lawful arrest for a legal search and seizure violate the Fourth Amendment of the U.S. Constitution?

History of the Case

During a narcotics investigation, police officers witnessed a transaction from a considerable distance that they had good reason to believe was a marijuana purchase. The officers then followed a car involved in the transaction that they later discovered was registered in George Ker's name. The officer's lost Ker's trail when he made a U-turn, but when they learned the name of the registered owner and that he was strongly suspected of narcotics violations, they drove to his apartment. The police obtained a master key from the apartment manager and proceeded to enter Ker's apartment under cover of stealth. After entering the apartment unannounced, testimony conflicted about whether the officers then made their intentions clear or simply arrested Ker as he sat peacefully in his living room. Ker's wife, Diane, emerged from the kitchen. An officer then went to the entrance to the kitchen and there observed a small scale atop the kitchen sink, upon which lay what appeared to be a "brick" of marijuana. George Ker and his wife denied any knowledge of the contents of the package and failed to answer questions about ownership. George and Diane Ker were then arrested for possession of narcotics.

Subsequent to the arrest, the officers, proceeding without search warrants, found a half-ounce package of marijuana in the kitchen cupboard and another atop the bedroom dresser. The following day, an officer without a warrant searched a car registered to Diane Ker, finding marijuana and marijuana seeds in the glove compartment and under the rear seat. The marijuana found on the kitchen scale, that found in the kitchen cupboard and in the bedroom, and that found in Diane Ker's car were all introduced into evidence against the two Kers. The Kers were subsequently convicted of possession of narcotics.

SUMMARY OF ARGUMENTS

The conviction was challenged on the ground that the marijuana had been seized as a result of an unlawful search and could not properly be admitted into evidence in the rule established in MAPP V. OHIO (1961). Mapp held that the Fourth Amendment's prohibition of unlawful searches and seizures is enforceable against the states through the Fourteenth Amendment. Since the officers had no search warrant, in order for the evidence to be admissible in court, it must have been the product of a search incident to a lawful arrest. The lawfulness of the arrest without a warrant, in turn, must be based upon probable cause.

The Kers argued that the unannounced entry and subsequent arrest were unlawful. California law requires that police officers must announce their purpose and authority before breaking into an individual's home. In California, however, this requirement is qualified by a narrow exception in very limited circumstances, when the facts surrounding the particular entry support a finding

that those within actually knew or must have known of the officer's presence and purpose to seek admission. Ker argued that the officers' unannounced entry did not fit into this narrow exception.

California argued that under the Fourteenth Amendment it is able to enforce its own reasonable search and seizure rules. California also argued that it did not violate the Kers' rights under the Fourteenth Amendment because the officers had probable cause, they lawfully entered the Kers' apartment, and the marijuana was lawfully seized.

DECISION

Justice Clark delivered the opinion of the Court. In a 5 to 4 decision, the Court held that the unannounced entry and subsequent arrest was lawful. Justice Clark found that this case fell within the judicially created exception to the requirement that police officers without a warrant must demand admittance and explain their purpose before breaking into an individual's home. Justice Clark found that "justification for the officers' failure to give notice is uniquely present." He found such justification in the experience of the arresting officers that narcotics are often disposed of during an attempted arrest and in Ker's apparent effort to elude the police shortly before the arrest. Justice Clark stated, "We therefore hold that in the particular circumstances of this case the officers' method of entry, sanctioned by the laws of California, was not unreasonable under the standards of the Fourth Amendment as applied to the States through the Fourteenth Amendment."

In sharp contrast, Justice Brennan, who wrote the dissenting opinion of the Court, found that the exception to the California statute "patently violates the Fourth Amendment." He argued that the officers were not in "fresh pursuit" of the suspects and therefore violated the requirement of an announced entry. Justice Brennan stated, "More convincing evidence of the complete unawareness of an imminent police visit can hardly be imagined. Indeed, even the conjecture that the Kers 'might well have been expecting the police' has no support in the record." He continued, dramatically, "[I]f police experience in pursuing other narcotics suspects justified an unannounced police intrusion to a home, the Fourth Amendment would afford no protection at all."

AFTERMATH

This case has not been overturned.

SIGNIFICANCE

The decision in this case established that unannounced entry without a warrant is not necessarily illegal and that it was not unreasonable on the facts of this case.

RELATED CASES

Boyd v. United States, 116 U.S. 616 (1886)

Mapp v. Ohio, 367 U.S. 643 (1961)

Miller v. United States, 357 U.S. 301 (1958)

People v. Maddox, 46 Cal. 2d 301, 294 P. 2d 6, cert. denied, 352 U.S. 858 (1956)

RECOMMENDED READING

The Supreme Court, 1962 Term, 77 Harvard Law Review 113–119 (November 1963).

Case Title: *Mapp v. Ohio*

Legal Citations: 367 U.S. 643; 81 S.Ct. 1684

Year of Decision: 1961

KEY ISSUES

The Fourth Amendment guarantees protection against unreasonable searches and seizures by the police, and the Fifth Amendment bans compelled self-incrimination. Taken together, the two amendments led the Court to decide in *Weeks v. United States* (1914), that unconstitutionally seized evidence must be excluded from evidence presented in trials in federal courts. The issue in *Mapp* is whether such evidence must be similarly excluded from trials in state courts.

HISTORY OF THE CASE

As recently as 1949, the Court had held that "in a prosecution in a State court for a State crime the Fourteenth Amendment does not forbid the admission of evidence obtained by an unreason-able search and seizure" (*Wolf v. Colorado* (1949)). In other words, because the Bill of Rights, including the Fourth and Fifth Amendments, applied only to the federal government, there was no prohibition on state prosecutors using unconstitutionally seized evidence against criminal defendants in state courts. Since most criminal laws operate not on the federal but on the state level, the practical effect was to leave the majority of criminal defendants without judicial protection from unlawful police behavior, such as conducting searches without search warrants, seizing evidence found in those searches, and using the evidence against the defendants at trial.

In this case, three Cleveland police officers acting on a tip from an informant arrived at Dolly Mapp's home seeking a person wanted for questioning in connection with a recent bombing. Mapp refused to admit the officers without a search warrant. More officers were called to the house, which the police then forcibly entered. During the ensuing search of the house, the police found obscene materials for possession, of which Mapp was ultimately convicted. At the trial no search warrant was produced by the prosecution, nor was the failure to produce one explained. On appeal, the Ohio Supreme Court upheld Mapp's conviction. Mapp asked the U.S. Supreme Court to rule that the evidence should have been excluded from her trial because it was unconstitutionally seized.

SUMMARY OF ARGUMENTS

The state of Ohio argued that even if the search were made without a warrant, or otherwise unreasonably, the state was not prevented from using the unconstitutionally seized evidence at trial. Mapp asked the Court to review its holding in the 1949 *Wolf* case that such evidence could be used in state courts.

DECISION

In a decision written by Justice Tom Clark, the Court held for Mapp that evidence obtained by unconstitutional search was inadmissible, and reversed her conviction: "We hold that all evidence obtained by searches and seizures in violation of the Constitution is, by that same authority, inadmissible in a state court." In Clark's reasoning, the Fourth and Fifth Amendment protections were "incorporated" by the due process clause of the Fourteenth Amendment as enforceable against the states. To give the protections against unreasonable searches and coerced confessions practical effect, it is necessary to exclude illegally seized evidence from trial. Thus, Justice Clark found the exclusionary rule an essential part of both the Fourth and Fourteenth Amendments.

Justice Harlan, in a dissent joined by Justices Frankfurter and Whittaker, wrote that the Court ignored judicial restraint and did not abide by previously decided cases in overruling *Wolf*. The dissenters would have continued to let the individual states decide whether to impose the exclusionary rule in their respective courts.

AFTERMATH

As a former prosecutor himself, Justice Clark understood clearly the practical effect of differing standards for evidence in the federal and state courts: "Presently, a federal prosecutor may make no use of evidence illegally seized, but a State's attorney across the street may, although he supposedly is operating under the enforceable prohibitions of the same Amendment." In the aftermath of *Mapp*, criminal suspects were protected in both federal and state courts from illegal police searches, and prosecutors were not allowed to use unconstitutionally seized evidence to convict defendants.

SIGNIFICANCE

Mapp v. Ohio is a keystone in the Warren Court's "criminal procedure revolution" during which the Court significantly expanded criminal defendants' procedural safeguards. Other cases held the remainder of the Bill of Rights applicable to proceedings in state courts. Consequently, police departments and prosecutors became very sensitive to following strict procedural guidelines for search warrants, *Mapp* exclusionary rules, warnings set by MIRANDA V. ARIZONA (1966), and other protections for subjects of criminal investigations. In the inevitable public backlash, the courts were accused of coddling criminals and neglecting victims' rights. But the exclusionary rule announced in *Mapp* stands, and perhaps it is fitting to let Justice Clark have the last word: "There is no war between the Constitution and common sense."

RELATED CASES

Boyd v. United States, 116 U.S. 616, 6 S.Ct. 524 (1886)

United States v. Calandra, 414 U.S. 338, 94 S.Ct. 613 (1974)

Weeks v. United States, 34 S.Ct. 341 (1914)

Wolf v. Colorado, 338 U.S. 25, 69 S.Ct. 1359 (1949)

RECOMMENDED READING

Francis A. Allen, *Federalism and the Fourth Amendment: A Requiem for* Wolf, Supreme Court Review 1 (1961).

Robert B. McKay, Mapp v. Ohio: *The Exclusionary Rule and the Right of Privacy*, 15 Arizona Law Review 327 (1973).

Stevens, Leonard A. *Trespass: The People's Privacy vs. the Power of the Police.* New York: Coward, McCann and Geoghegan, 1977.

Case Title: *New Jersey v. T.L.O.*

Legal Citation: 469 U.S. 325

Year of Decision: 1985

KEY ISSUES

Do school authorities conducting searches of schoolchildren and their belongings need "probable cause" before performing the search?

HISTORY OF THE CASE

Fourteen-year-old freshman T.L.O. was caught smoking cigarettes in the lavatory at her New Jersey high school. When questioned by a vice principal about this violation of school rules, T.L.O. denied she smoked at all. The vice principal demanded to see her purse. His search revealed cigarettes, a small portion of marijuana, rolling papers, plastic baggies, a list of students who owed T.L.O. money, and a wad of dollar bills, among other things. The state brought delinquency charges.

The juvenile court refused to suppress the evidence acquired by the purse search as a violation of T.L.O.'s Fourth Amendment rights, and the intermediate state appellate court affirmed. The

New Jersey Supreme Court reversed, holding the search to be unreasonable. The U.S. Supreme Court agreed to review the case. The initial question posed was whether the exclusionary rule, a rule barring illegally obtained evidence from being used at trial, existed as an appropriate remedy to bar consideration of evidence in juvenile proceedings when inappropriately seized by public school authorities. The Court ordered reargument, however, on the broader question of what limits, if any, the Fourth Amendment places on the activities of school authorities. This latter issue is the one decided.

SUMMARY OF ARGUMENTS

The state of New Jersey argued that the Fourth Amendment was intended to regulate only searches and seizures by law enforcement officers. While conceding that public school officials are state agents for purposes of the Fourteenth Amendment, the state argued that the Fourth Amendment creates no rights enforceable against school authorities in this student-school official context. In dealings with students, teachers and school administrators act *in loco parentis:* their authority is that of the parents, not the state, and is therefore not subject to Fourth Amendment constraints.

T.L.O. argued that the Constitution intends to protect all members in our society from government intrusions, and, therefore, must be applied with equal force to children in the public schools.

DECISION

The Court handed down three rulings. First, the Court held that the Fourth Amendment, which prohibits unreasonable searches and seizures by state officers, is not limited to law enforcement authorities. The Court expressly decided for the first time that public school authorities are also state officials to whom the Fourth Amendment applies. The Fourth Amendment, therefore, prohibits school officers from unduly interfering in students' privacy and protects students from school official encroachment. Prior to this decision, courts generally viewed school representatives as exerting their authority *in loco parentis,* a position potentially subjecting the student to severe violations of reasonable, and protected, privacy expectations.

Second, schoolchildren have legitimate expectations of privacy that society recognizes and that the law will protect. On the other hand, schools have equally legitimate expectations for maintaining order in an environment conducive to education. The Court sought to balance these needs.

Ordinarily, state officials must have "probable cause" to search an individual—a state officer must have a reason to believe that a violation of the law probably has occurred. The Court found that the legality of a student search should depend on the reasonableness, under all the circumstances, of the search. Two factors make up what constitutes "reasonableness under all the circumstances": (1) whether the search was justified at its inception, and (2) whether the search was reasonably related in scope to the circumstances that justified the interference in the first place.

Third, the Court ruled that the assistant vice principal's search of T.L.O.'s purse was not unreasonable for Fourth Amendment purposes because it met this test.

AFTERMATH

Many critics have argued against the *T.L.O.* decision. Some believe that the enunciated legal standard for student searches is inconsistent with precedent, will increase unjustified student searches and elevated confusion among school administrators and courts, and will decrease exclusionary rule application. This group believes the decision is contrary to the time-tested probable cause standard, a standard considering the facts and circumstances in determining whether a search is warranted, which was workable, effective, and allowed for flexibility in maintaining a safe school environment while protecting students' privacy interests. Others point out that the decision merely loosened the probable cause standard, pointing out that *T.L.O.*'s reasonable grounds were left undefined by the Court. Certainly, in some contexts, as in student strip searches, *T.L.O.* did little to clarify the constitutionality of such actions.

SIGNIFICANCE

The decision is significant on two levels. First, the majority opinion clearly states that the Fourth Amendment applies to public school officials. In so ruling, the Court sounds the death knell for the *in loco parentis* doctrine and establishes the proper standard to govern student searches in public schools. Second, the minority opinion by Justice Stevens addresses the dangers of arbitrarily interpreting the Constitution. He writes that doing so runs counter to the principle of "liberty and justice for all."

RELATED CASES

Goss v. Lopez, 419 U.S. 565 (1975)

Mapp v. Ohio, 367 U.S. 643 (1961)

Terry v. Ohio, 392 U.S. 1 (1967)

United States v. Leon, 468 U.S. 897 (1984)

Vernonia School Dist. v. Acton, 515 U.S. 646, 115 S.Ct. 2386 (1995)

RECOMMENDED READING

Charles W. Hardin, Jr., *Searching Public Schools:* T.L.O. *and the Exclusionary Rule,* 47 Ohio State Law Journal 1099–1114 (fall 1986).

Gerald S. Reamey, N.J. v. T.L.O.: *The Supreme Court's Lesson on School Searches,* 16 St. Mary's Law Review 933–949 (1985).

Dale Edward F. T. Zane, *School Searches under the Fourth Amendment,* 72 Cornell Law Review 368–396 (January 1987).

Case Title: *Olmstead v. United States*

Alternate Case Title: The Wiretapping Case

Legal Citations: 277 U.S. 438; 48 S.Ct. 564; 72 L.Ed. 944

Year of Decision: 1928

KEY ISSUES

Can evidence obtained by wiretapping a criminal defendant's telephone lines, without a search warrant, be used against the defendant in his criminal trial?

HISTORY OF THE CASE

The Eighteenth Amendment to the U.S. Constitution prohibited the manufacture, sale, transportation, and importation of alcoholic beverages. As the law of supply and demand would predict, violating the Eighteenth Amendment—or prohibition, as it came to be known—became a thriving business. Roy Olmstead was one of these illicit entrepreneurs. Olmstead's "bootlegging" operation, based in Seattle, Washington, "involved the employment of not less than fifty persons, of two seagoing vessels for the transportation of liquor," smaller vessels for coastal operations, a central office to coordinate his operation, and a large ranch on the outskirts of Seattle. In the words of Chief Justice Taft, "[i]n a bad month sales amounted to $176,000."

Four federal prohibition officers obtained evidence of the operation by wiretapping the telephone lines of Olmstead's central office and several of his employees' homes. While the telephone lines were tapped without trespassing on the property of the defendants, wiretapping itself was illegal under a Washington statute. As a result of evidence gathered by the federal agents listening to the tapped telephone lines over a several-month period, nearly 80 persons were charged with and convicted of conspiracy to violate the National Prohibition Act in the District Court for the Western District of Washington.

Olmstead and his fellow defendants challenged their conviction, first in the Ninth Circuit Court of Appeals, and later before the U.S. Supreme Court, arguing that the evidence gathered through use of the wiretaps should have been excluded at their trials. The defendants argued that both their Fourth and Fifth Amendment rights had been violated. They argued that the tapping of the phone lines was an illegal search in violation of the Fourth Amendment: "The right to the exclusive enjoyment of a telephone free of interference from anybody, is a right of privacy." To wiretap an individual's phone line was just as unconstitutional as "to raise the curtain and peek through another's window." Merely because the telephone conversations were electronic rather than written could not mean that the Fourth Amendment would not protect them, the defendants argued: "It is not the paper which is protected by the constitutional inhibitions, but it is the message contained in the letter."

The defendants argued that their Fifth Amendment rights were violated because the wiretapping "compelled the defendants to give evidence just as effectively as if they had been forced to take the witness stand and themselves testify as to the messages sent over the telephone." Also, the Fifth Amendment had been violated by admitting evidence gathered by means that violated the Constitution, namely, a search that violated the Fourth Amendment.

The United States argued that the Fourth Amendment should be interpreted literally. The Fourth Amendment was adopted as a reaction to two abusive practices by the English government during colonial times: the use of general warrants and the use of writs of assistance, which gave agents of the Crown almost unlimited authority in conducting searches and seizures. While conceding that there were benefits to construing the Constitution liberally, the United States asserted that there were limits: "By no liberality of construction can a conversation passing over a telephone wire become a 'house,' no more can it become a 'person,' a 'paper,' or an 'effect.'" Similarly, the Fifth Amendment was not applicable because the defendants had not been forced to talk about their criminal activities over the phone.

In addition to the briefs submitted by the parties to the suit, an amicus curiae (friend of the court) brief was filed by several telephone companies, among them the Pacific Telephone and Telegraph Company and American Telephone and Telegraph Company, because of their interest in the outcome of the case. The telephone companies argued that the purpose of the telephone was "to enable any two persons at a distance to converse privately with each other as they might do if both were personally present in the privacy of the home or office of either one. When the lines of the two 'parties' are connected at the central office, they are intended to be devoted to their exclusive use, and in that sense to be turned over to their exclusive possession." Therefore, any third party tapping the lines "violates the property rights of both persons then using the telephone, and of the telephone company as well." The brief for the telephone companies argued that wiretapping should be treated the same as an unauthorized physical search, considering the former was worse than the latter "because the citizen is utterly helpless to detect the espionage to which he is subjected."

The Ninth Circuit Court of Appeals affirmed the convictions of the defendants, rejecting their arguments, and construing the Fourth and Fifth Amendments narrowly.

DECISION

Five members of the Supreme Court, in an opinion written by Chief Justice William Taft, affirmed the decision of the court of appeals. The Court cursorily rejected the defendants' argument that their Fifth Amendment rights had been violated in that they had been forced to testify against themselves when the phone lines were tapped: "There is no room in the present case for applying the Fifth Amendment unless the Fourth Amendment was first violated. There was no evidence of compulsion to induce the defendants to talk over their many telephones."

The Court went on to reject the defendants' claims based on the Fourth Amendment, declining to interpret the amendment expansively, beyond its literal terms: "The Amendment itself shows that the search is to be of material things—the persons, the house, his papers or his effects." Although the advent of the telephone expanded the reach and speed of communication, the Fourth Amendment could not similarly be expanded: "The language of the Amendment cannot be extended and expanded to include telephone wires reaching to the whole world from the defendant's house or office. The intervening wires are not part of his house or office any more than are the highways along which they are stretched." The Court conceded that "the Fifth Amendment and the Fourth Amendment were to be liberally construed to effect the purpose of the framers of the Constitution in the interest of liberty. But that can not justify enlargement of the language employed beyond the possible practical meaning of houses, persons, papers, and effects, or so to apply the words search and seizure as to forbid hearing or sight."

Additionally, the Court did not consider the Washington statute that made wiretapping a misdemeanor to be relevant to whether evidence gathered by wiretapping was admissible in court: "Whether the State of Washington may prosecute and punish federal officers violating this law and those whose messages were intercepted may sue them civilly is not before us. But clearly a statute, passed twenty years after the admission of the State into the Union can not affect the rules of evidence applicable in the courts of the United States in criminal cases."

Four of the nine justices who heard the case believed that the defendants' convictions should have been overturned, considering that the evidence gathered by wiretapping violated their Fourth Amendment rights and therefore should have been excluded. Justice Louis Brandeis's dissent was the most thorough: "When the Fourth and Fifth Amendment were adopted, 'the form that evil had therefore taken,' had been necessarily simple." Justice Brandeis viewed invasions of privacy as the evil that the amendments were intended to prevent.

[The amendments] sought to protect Americans in their beliefs, their thoughts, their emotions and their sensations. They conferred, as against the Government, the right to be let alone—the most comprehensive of rights and the right most valued by civilized men. To protect that right, every unjustifiable intrusion by the Government upon the privacy of the individual, whatever the means employed, must be deemed a violation of the Fourth Amendment.

Justice Brandeis believed that the Fourth and Fifth Amendments prohibited any governmental action that invaded the privacy of the individual. Justice Brandeis was a strong advocate of "a right to privacy," and in fact while still in private practice had written a very influential law review article that argued that the right to privacy was based in the common law.

Justice Brandeis also would have reversed the convictions "[i]ndependently of the constitutional question." Justice Brandeis believed that the evidence could not be used in the defendants' criminal trial because a federal officer had violated Washington state law to obtain it. The following is Justice Brandeis's eloquent commentary stating that the rule of law is dangerously undermined when government agents break the law while purporting to enforce it:

Decency, security and liberty alike demand that government officials shall be subjected to the same rules of conduct that are commands to the citizen. In a government of laws, existence of the government will be imperilled if it fails to observe the law scrupulously. Our Government is the potent,

the omnipresent teacher. For good or for ill, it teaches the whole people by its example. Crime is contagious. If the Government becomes a lawbreaker, it breeds contempt for law; it invites every man to become a law unto himself; it invites anarchy. To declare that in the administration of the criminal law the end justifies the means—to declare that the Government may commit crimes in order to secure the conviction of a private criminal—would bring terrible retribution. Against that pernicious doctrine this Court should resolutely set its face.

Justice Brandeis thus thought the convictions should have been reversed based on two separate grounds: the federal officers' violation of the defendants' Fourth and Fifth Amendment rights, and the federal officers' violation of the laws of the state of Washington.

Justice Oliver Wendell Holmes also wrote a dissenting opinion. He did not dissent for quite the same reasons as Justice Brandeis, however:

While I do not deny it, I am not prepared to say that the penumbra of the Fourth and Fifth Amendments covers the defendant, although I fully agree that Courts are apt to err by sticking too closely to the words of a law where those words import a policy that goes beyond them.

Instead, Justice Holmes viewed the case as a conflict between two competing interests:

[W]e must consider the two objects of desire, both of which we cannot have, and make up our minds which to choose. It is desirable that criminals should be detected, and to that end that all available evidence should be used. It also is desirable that the Government should not itself foster and pay for crimes, when they are the means by which the evidence is to be obtained.

Justice Holmes viewed the latter interest, that of not permitting the government to use criminal means to obtain its ends, as the stronger: "[F]or my part I think it a less evil that some criminals should escape than that the Government should play an ignoble role."

Justice Owen J. Roberts also dissented, seemingly influenced in part by the arguments made by the telephone companies in their amicus brief:

> Telephones are used generally for transmission of messages concerning official, social, business and personal affairs including communications that are private and privileged—those between physician and patient, lawyer and client, parent and child, husband and wife. The contracts between telephone companies and users contemplate the private use of the facilities employed in the service. The communications belong to the parties between whom they pass.

Because Justice Roberts believed that conversations carried on telephone lines were privileged communications, belonging to the people using the telephones, the conversations were under the ambit of the Fourth Amendment's protection. He believed the majority erred with its overly literal reading of the Constitution.

Justice Harlan F. Stone also dissented, and in a paragraph-long opinion, he agreed with the viewpoints of Holmes and Brandeis, and with all of Roberts's opinion but for a single jurisdictional point.

AFTERMATH

The defendants' conviction was affirmed, and for some time after, the Fourth and Fifth Amendments were read narrowly by the U.S. Supreme Court.

SIGNIFICANCE

This is the first case in which the U.S. Supreme Court addressed arguments that there is a constitutional right to privacy. The Court held that there is such a right in *Griswold v. Connecticut* (1965), a case upon which the controversial ROE V. WADE 410 U.S. 113 (1973) was based.

RELATED CASES

Goldman v. United States, 316 U.S. 129 (1942)

Griswold v. Connecticut, 381 U.S. 479 (1965)

Katz v. United States, 389 U.S. 347 (1967)

Poe v. Ullman, 367 U.S. 497 (1961)

Silverman v. United States, 365 U.S. 505 (1961)

RECOMMENDED READING

Louis D. Brandeis and S. D. Warren, *The Right to Privacy*, 4 Harvard Law Review 193 (1890).

Cederbaums, Juris. *Wiretapping and Electronic Eavesdropping: The Law and Its Implications; A Comparative Study*. New York: Criminal Law & Research Center, 1969.

Ernst, Morris L., and Alan U. Schwartz. *Privacy: The Right to Be Left Alone*. New York: Macmillan, 1962.

Case Title: *Payton v. New York*

Legal Citation: 445 U.S. 573

Year of Decision: 1980

KEY ISSUES

Does the Fourth Amendment prohibit searches and seizures after a warrantless entry into a suspect's home where there is no immediate danger or threat to safety?

HISTORY OF THE CASE

The Fourth Amendment provides that the right of the people to be secure in their persons, houses, papers, and effects shall not be violated by unreasonable searches and seizures. Generally, a warrantless search and seizure must involve a fear of imminent destruction of evidence, immediate threats to the safety of the public or the law enforcement officers, fires or other emergencies, or hot pursuit.

New York police assembled enough evidence to give them probable cause to believe that Theodore Payton had murdered a gas station manager. Six officers went to Payton's Bronx apartment, intending to arrest him. They did not obtain a warrant. After knocking on his door and waiting for about 30 minutes for a response, they forced the door open with a crowbar and entered the apartment. Nobody was in the apartment, but there was a .30-caliber shell casing in plain view. The shell casing was later admitted into evidence at Payton's trial. Payton eventually surrendered, was indicted for murder, and moved to suppress the evidence taken from his apartment. The trial judge upheld the warrantless search and seizure, holding that there were compelling circumstances that justified the officers' failure to announce their purpose before entering. The appellate division affirmed the trial court.

In a related case, Obie Riddick was arrested for robbery after police went to his house without a warrant. Riddick's young son answered the door and the police saw Riddick in bed. After entering Riddick's home without his consent, they opened a chest of drawers and found narcotics and related paraphernalia. The court refused to suppress the evidence in Riddick's narcotics trial. The court of appeals affirmed the trial court.

The U.S. Supreme Court consolidated the two appeals because of the similarity of the issues presented.

DECISION

Justice Stevens wrote for the majority in the 6–3 decision reversing the lower courts. The Court believed that a search and seizure in connection with a warrantless arrest of a person must be reasonable, like any other search and seizure. The Court looked to the history of warrantless arrests in the home and found virtually no uniformity. At the time of this decision, 24 states allowed the warrantless entry, 15 prohibited it, and 11 states did not have any position on it. The Court struggled with the disjointed approaches of the various states and concluded that the highest interest protected by the Fourth Amendment is the overriding respect for the sanctity of the home. An entry to arrest and an entry to search and seize implicate the same privacy interests and must adhere to the same level of constitutional protection. As a result, without a warrant based on probable cause, law enforcement officers cannot force themselves into a private residence unless they have an immediate pressing need. Because no arrest warrant was obtained, the "fruit" of the subsequent searches was inadmissible.

AFTERMATH

After the Supreme Court decided *Payton*, every state was required either to adopt, change, or affirm its law on warrantless entry.

SIGNIFICANCE

Payton attempted to create uniformity in the states concerning searches and seizures. After *Pay-*

ton police were required to obtain an arrest warrant to enter a persons home without consent and make an arrest. Surprisingly, Fourth Amendment law has not fully developed after more than 200 years.

RELATED CASES

N.Y. v. Harris, 495 U.S. 14 (1990)

U.S. v. Watson, 423 U.S. 411 (1976)

RECOMMENDED READING

Jeffrey L. Evans, *Constitutional Restraints on Residential Warrantless Arrest Entries: More Protection for Privacy Interests in the Home*, 10 American Journal of Criminal Law 1 (1982).

Joseph D. Harbaugh and Nancy L. Faust, *Knock on Any Door: Home Arrests after* Payton *and* Steagald, 86 Dickinson Law Review 191 (1982).

Walter V. Schaefer, *Prospective Rulings: Two Perspectives*, Supreme Court Review 1 (1982).

Alan C. Yarcusko, Brown *to* Payton *to* Harris: *A Fourth Amendment Double Play by the Supreme Court*, 43 Case Western Reserve Law Review 253 (1992).

Case Title: *Schmerber v. California*

Legal Citation: 384 U.S. 757

Year of Decision: 1966

KEY ISSUES

Is taking a blood sample without consent unconstitutional?

HISTORY OF THE CASE

Schmerber was involved in an automobile accident in which he was injured. A police officer noticed signs of drunkenness at the accident scene, including the scent of alcohol on Schmerber's breath. The officer placed Schmerber under arrest at the hospital and had the hospital draw a blood sample for testing. This was done without Schmerber's consent on the advice of his attorney. The results showed that Schmerber was intoxicated, and he was convicted of driving under the influence of intoxicating liquor. The Appellate Department of the California Superior Court affirmed the conviction, and the U.S. Supreme Court agreed to review the case.

SUMMARY OF ARGUMENTS

Schmerber contended that taking the blood sample without his consent violated his due process rights under the Fourteenth Amendment, his privilege against self-incrimination under the Fifth Amendment, his right to counsel under the Sixth Amendment, and his right not to be subjected to unreasonable searches and seizures under the Fourth Amendment.

California denied these allegations and asserted that the officer had probable cause and authority to order the blood test.

DECISION

Justice Brennan delivered the opinion of the Court, which affirmed the conviction. The Court found that Schmerber's due process rights were not violated because his blood was taken in a hospital by a physician in a simple, medically acceptable manner. His privilege against self-incrimination was not violated because the withdrawal of blood to be used against him did not compel him to testify against himself. His right to counsel was not violated because he had consulted with his lawyer. He was not allowed to follow his lawyer's advice, but this does not mean that he was denied counsel. Finally, the Court found that Schmerber was not subject to an unlawful search and seizure because the officer had probable cause (Schmerber's signs of intoxication), and the blood test was a reasonable method of ascertaining whether Schmerber was intoxicated or not.

Justices Harlan and Stewart concurred, adding that the Fifth Amendment's privilege against self-incrimination was not even an issue because the case did not involve testimonial compulsion.

Chief Justice Warren, joined by Justice Douglas, dissented on the basis that Schmerber's rights of due process and privacy were violated.

Justices Black and Fortas also dissented, arguing that the state compelled Schmerber to submit to a process that would uncover evidence used to convict him, which amounted to a viola-tion of his Fifth Amendment privilege against self-incrimination.

AFTERMATH

Schmerber is still followed today in allowing the taking of blood or breath samples when someone is suspected of intoxication. Some argue that advances in technology, however, such as cellular phones, now enable officers to obtain search warrants prior to taking blood tests.

SIGNIFICANCE

The consent of a person is not necessary in order to test the person's blood-alcohol level when the procedure is reasonable and the officer has probable cause to do so. Furthermore, the taking of blood in a normal medical procedure is not testimonial-type evidence protected by the Fifth Amendment.

RELATED CASES

Breithaupt v. Abram, 352 U.S. 432 (1957)

Escobedo v. Illinois, 378 U.S. 478 (1964)

Skinner v. Railway Labor Executive's Ass'n, 489 U.S. 602 (1989)

RECOMMENDED READING

E. Jon Wherry, Jr., *Vampire or Dinosaur: A Time to Revisit* Schmerber v. California?, 19 American Journal of Trial Advocacy 503 (1996).

Case Title: *Schneckloth v. Bustamonte*

Legal Citation: 412 U.S. 218

Year of Decision: 1973

KEY ISSUES

Is a person's knowledge of the right to refuse consent to a search mandatory for that search to be constitutional?

HISTORY OF THE CASE

Bustamonte was in a car with five other men when it was stopped by a police officer for having a burned-out headlight and license plate light. Neither the driver nor four of the other men had a driver's license. Alcala, the brother of the car's owner, was the only person who had a license. The police officer asked Alcala if he could search the car, and Alcala consented. The officer found three checks underneath the rear seat that had been stolen from a car wash. Bustamonte was convicted of possessing a check with intent to defraud. The California Court of Appeals affirmed the conviction, and the California Supreme Court denied review. Bustamonte then sought a writ of habeas corpus in a federal district court, which was denied. The Ninth Circuit Court of Appeals decided that Bustamonte was entitled to know that he was free to deny consent, and remanded the case to the district court while vacating the district court's order denying the writ of habeas corpus. The Supreme Court agreed to review the case.

SUMMARY OF ARGUMENTS

Bustamonte contended that he did not know of his right to refuse consent, and therefore his consent was invalid, thereby violating his Fourth Amendment right against an unlawful search and seizure.

Schneckloth, the superintendent of the California Conservation Center, the facility where Bustamonte was held, argued that Bustamonte's consent was voluntary, which gave the officer the right to search the car.

DECISION

Justice Stewart delivered the opinion of the Court that when a subject is not in custody, voluntary consent is required to conduct a search, but the subject's knowledge of a right to refuse is not mandatory in establishing that voluntary consent. The consent cannot be coerced and there must be a legitimate need for such searches. The Court mentioned the need for officers to conduct valid consent searches in certain instances in which the probable cause needed to arrest someone is lacking, but the officer has some evidence of illegal activity. Additionally, the Court feared that the requirement of the knowledge to refuse consent would enable defendants to unduly prevent the introduction of evidence simply by testifying that they did not know they could refuse consent; it

would place an insurmountable burden on the prosecution.

Justice Powell, joined by Justice Rehnquist and Chief Justice Burger, concurred, stating that the Court's review extended the writ of habeas corpus beyond its traditional purpose and placed form in front of substance. The concurrence placed the emphasis on the guilt or innocence of the accused party, not whether a piece of evidence should be excluded because of a question of the right to refuse consent.

Justice Blackmun concurred, agreeing with Justice Powell, but decided it was not necessary to consider those issues in the present case.

Justices Douglas and Brennan dissented, stating that knowledge of the right to refuse consent was necessary in forming a voluntary consent.

Justice Marshall also dissented, going further than Douglas and Brennan by adding that someone who gives consent because an officer, correctly or incorrectly, claims the authority to conduct a search invalidates the consent. This is not really a voluntary consent because the accused does not know of his right to refuse.

AFTERMATH

Knowledge of the right to refuse consent is still not necessary in order to show voluntary consent. Some critics believe that it should be required because of the public's tendency to obey authority figures.

SIGNIFICANCE

Schneckloth made voluntary consent the only requirement for a search without the constitutionally required search warrant and probable cause. The knowledge of the right to refuse consent also is not necessary in establishing voluntary consent.

RELATED CASES

Schmerber v. California, 384 U.S. 757 (1966)

Thompson v. Louisiana, 469 U.S. 17 (1985)

United States v. Watson, 423 U.S. 411 (1976)

RECOMMENDED READING

Adrian J. Barrio, *Rethinking* Schneckloth v. Bustamonte: *Incorporating Obedience Theory into the Supreme Court's Conception of Voluntary Consent*, 97 University of Illinois Law Review 215 (1997).

Case Title: *Smith v. Maryland*

Legal Citations: 442 U.S. 735; 99 S.Ct. 2577; 61 L.Ed. 2d 220

Year of Decision: 1979

KEY ISSUES

Does a police examination of a pen register, a device used by the telephone company to record the phone numbers dialed from one's home, constitute a "search" within the meaning of the Fourth Amendment?

HISTORY OF THE CASE

Michael Lee Smith was suspected of robbing a woman and thereafter making threatening and obscene phone calls to her. At police request, the telephone company installed a pen register at its central office to record the numbers dialed from Smith's telephone line. The police did not get a warrant or court order prior to the installation of the pen register. After the register revealed that Smith was calling the robbery victim's line, the police used this and other evidence to obtain a warrant to search Smith's residence. Soon after, Smith was indicted in the Criminal Court of Baltimore for robbery. The pen register record was admitted into evidence at trial, and Smith was subsequently convicted of robbery.

On appeal, the Court of Appeals of Maryland considered whether the pen register evidence had been properly admitted at Smith's trial. The court of appeals affirmed the judgment of conviction, holding that the pen register did not constitute a "search" within the meaning of the Fourth Amendment. The Supreme Court agreed to review the case.

SUMMARY OF ARGUMENTS

Smith argued that the failure of the police to secure a warrant prior to the pen register's installation violated the Fourth Amendment, which protects "the right of the people to be secure . . . against unreasonable searches and seizures[.]" Smith claimed that the use of the pen register by the state infringed a "legitimate expectation of privacy."

The state argued, among other things, that the pen register does not invade one's legitimate expectation of privacy because the device is not used to listen to actual conversations. Instead, the pen register simply provides a list of the calls one makes. Because telephone users are aware that the phone company keeps such lists, a police examination of this list is not an unreasonable search under the Fourth Amendment.

DECISION

In a 5-3 decision delivered by Justice Blackmun, the Supreme Court held that the use of a pen register to record numbers dialed from a particular phone did not invade one's reasonable expectation of privacy. First, the Court rejected Smith's contention that he had a subjective expectation of privacy in the phone numbers he dialed. The Court reasoned that since telephone subscribers receive a list of their calls on their monthly bills and know that the telephone company can help track down obscene callers, they are aware that the numbers they dial will not remain secret. Second, the Court held that a person has no legitimate expectation of privacy in information he voluntarily turns over to third parties. Thus, when Smith "exposed" the numbers he dialed to the telephone company, he assumed the risk that the company would disclose to the police the numbers he dialed.

The dissenters, Justices Stewart, Brennan, and Marshall, argued that the mere fact that a telephone company transmits the call does not mean that the caller yields an expectation of privacy in the phone numbers dialed. The justices maintained that when a person discloses limited information to a phone company or a bank, he or she does not expect that information to be freely distributed to the police. Instead, this information is disclosed for a "limited business purpose" under the assumption that the information will not be released for any other purposes.

AFTERMATH

The Court's holding in *Smith* that a person using a telephone does not have a "legitimate expectation of privacy" in the dialed phone numbers has been expanded to other situations in subsequent cases. For example, in 1988 the Court held that individuals do not have a reasonable expectation of privacy in garbage that they place outside their house for collection by a trash collector. Thus, a warrantless search and seizure of the garbage was permissible.

After *Smith*, some state courts have adopted the Court's reasoning and held that the use of pen registers fails to activate Fourth Amendment protections. Other state courts, however, have given more expansive protection under their state constitutional privacy provisions and concluded that the use of a pen register is a search requiring probable cause.

SIGNIFICANCE

The *Smith* case ruled that the police do not need a warrant, "probable cause," or any cause whatsoever to use a pen register to track the phone calls one makes. Thus, the Court held there is no constitutional privacy interest attached to the numbers dialed on a telephone. This holding could become increasingly significant as courts are confronted with the constitutionality of new surveillance or detection devices.

RELATED CASES

California v. Greenwood, 486 U.S. 135 (1988)

Katz v. United States, 389 U.S. 347 (1967)

United States v. Knotts, 442 U.S. 735 (1983)

United States v. New York Telephone Co., 434 U.S. 159 (1977)

RECOMMENDED READING

John Applegate and Amy Grossman, *Pen Registers after Smith v. Maryland*, 15 Harvard Civil Rights–Civil Liberties Law Review 753–778 (winter 1980).

Gregory J. DeMars, *Criminal Procedure—Pen Registers Not Subject to the Requirements of the Fourth Amendment*, 27 Wayne Law Review 393–403 (fall 1980).

Philip H. Marcus, *A Fourth Amendment Gag Order— Upholding Third Party Searches at the Expense of First Amendment Freedom of Association Guarantees*, 47 University of Pittsburgh Law Review 275–293 (fall 1985).

Case Title: *Terry v. Ohio*

Alternate Case Title: The Cause to Search Case

Legal Citation: 392 U.S. 1

Year of Decision: 1968

KEY ISSUES

May a police officer conduct a frisk search without "probable cause"?

HISTORY OF THE CASE

A Cleveland detective observed John W. Terry and two other men walking back and forth in front of a store window in the middle of the afternoon. The detective began to suspect that the men were "casing" the store in preparation for a robbery. After they had repeated this routine 24 times, the detective approached the three men and asked their names. He then spun Terry around, patted down his outside clothing, and discovered that he had a pistol. A similar search revealed that one of the other men was carrying a revolver. Terry eventually was convicted of carrying a concealed weapon, and his conviction was affirmed by the Ohio Supreme Court.

SUMMARY OF ARGUMENTS

Terry argued that the weapons were inadmissible as evidence because they were obtained through a search and seizure conducted without probable cause in violation of the Fourth Amendment.

The state argued that the frisk search conducted by the detective was permissible because he reasonably perceived that the frisk was necessary to avoid the possibility that the person searched might use a gun on him.

DECISION

Chief Justice Warren delivered the opinion of the Court. He noted that this case involved the tension between the public interest in safety and the individual's right of privacy. Chief Justice Warren added: "Nothing we say today is to be taken as indicating approval of police conduct outside the legitimate investigative sphere." On the other hand, if the Court found the search unconstitutional Terry would go free because the exclusionary rule makes evidence obtained through unconstitutional means inadmissible in a criminal trial. Chief Justice Warren resolved the issue by holding that the Fourth Amendment did apply to the detective's actions, but those actions were constitutional in this case. He argued that the frisk search is a "serious intrusion upon the sanctity of the person." Thus, the constitutional test was whether the search without a warrant was "justified at its inception, and whether it was reasonably related in scope to the circumstances which justified the interference in the first place." Nonetheless, Chief Justice Warren viewed the Court's test as roughly analogous to the requirements for a warrant.

Chief Justice Warren argued that the initial approach made by the detective was justified by the government's generalized interest in crime prevention; the frisk search itself was justified by the detective's own interest in self-protection. The difference between this case and the warrant process is that here, the detective did not need to have probable cause to arrest Terry in order to search him for weapons. Chief Justice Warren contended that this reduced burden on the detective was reasonable because the weapons search is less extensive than a general evidentiary search such as those done at crime scenes. He stated, "A perfectly reasonable apprehension of danger may arise long before the officer is possessed of adequate information to justify taking a person into custody."

The thrust of the Court's holding was that a limited search for hidden weapons is constitutional when an officer reasonably believes that he is dealing with an armed and dangerous individual. Here, the detective had approached the three men based upon a reasonable suspicion that they were contemplating criminal activity and he conducted a search limited in scope to the discovery of weapons. Chief Justice Warren found that under these facts the weapons were admissable evidence.

Justice Douglas wrote a dissenting opinion. He argued that if probable cause was the requirement for a magistrate to issue a search warrant, it was improper to allow police to conduct warrantless searches without at least that level of justification. Justice Douglas asserted that "[t]o give the police greater power than a magistrate is to take a long step down the totalitarian path . . . if it is taken, it should be the deliberate choice of the people through a constitutional amendment." He would have reversed Terry's conviction because he found no reasonable basis for the detective to con-

clude that Terry was committing the crime of carrying a concealed weapon.

AFTERMATH

After the *Terry* decision, the Court has continued to address similar search and seizure issues. The most frequent issue addressed is what constitutes sufficient cause to "stop and frisk" a person.

SIGNIFICANCE

The *Terry* decision allowed law enforcement personnel to detain a suspect based upon less than probable cause, a significant development in the law of criminal procedure. After *Terry*, such "stop and frisk" situations are commonly referred to as "Terry stops."

RELATED CASES

Beck v. Ohio, 379 U.S. 89 (1964)

Elkins v. United States, 364 U.S. 206 (1960)

RECOMMENDED READING

John A. MacKintosh, Jr., *Constitutional Law*—Terry v. Ohio, 47 Texas Law Review 138 (1968).

Case Title: *U.S. v. U.S. District Court for the Eastern District of Michigan Southern Division et al; Lawrence Robert "Pun" Plamondon et al., Real Parties in Interest*

Legal Citation: 407 U.S. 297

Year of Decision: 1972

KEY ISSUES

May the president order an investigative agency to conduct electronic surveillance without a search warrant?

HISTORY OF THE CASE

Robert Plamondon and others were charged with destruction of government property and conspiracy to destroy government property. In a pretrial motion, the defense requested disclosure of electronic surveillance information gathered by the federal government. The government responded that the surveillance was gathered under national security measures and should therefore not be fully disclosed. The district court ruled that the searches violated the Fourth Amendment's protection against warrantless searches and ordered the surveillance surrendered to the defense. The government appealed and lost. The U.S. Supreme Court agreed to hear the case because of the importance of the issue presented.

SUMMARY OF ARGUMENTS

The government argued that the surveillance was lawful, albeit warrantless, because it was a reasonable exercise of the president's power under 18 U.S.C. § 2511(3), which states that nothing limits the president's constitutional power to protect against the overthrow of the government or other clear and present danger to government. The government maintained that the importance of national security mandated that, in certain circumstances, no warrant is necessary to gather information.

The district court maintained that the operative statute did not enlarge the president's powers and consequently did not authorize him to conduct warrantless searches.

DECISION

Justice Powell delivered the opinion of the Court in the unanimous decision affirming the district court's decision ordering the release of the surveillance. The Court found although the president has a constitutionally mandated duty to protect the nation from actual or potential hostile attack, he must still abide by the provisions of the Fourth Amendment. The act under which the government claimed to have conducted the surveillance at the president's request did not limit or increase the president's executive powers under the Constitution. As a result, the surveillance violated the Fourth Amendment and was ordered released.

AFTERMATH

This case is virtually unique as it deals with a very narrow issue in a very specific law. This case has not been overruled.

SIGNIFICANCE

This case is a reminder of the limited power of the president. The president is not an all-powerful head of state. Were the Court to have found otherwise, the nature of threats to the national security would be entirely at the discretion of the chief executive.

RELATED CASES

Katz v. United States, 389 U.S. 347 (1967)

United States v. Rabinowitz, 339 U.S. 56 (1950)

RECOMMENDED READING

Bigel, Alan I. *The Supreme Court on Emergency Powers, Foreign Affairs and Protection of Civil Liberties, 1935–1975.* New York: University Press of America, 1986.

Fisher, Louis. *The Constitution between Friends.* New York: St. Martin's Press, 1978.

Case Title: *Wilson v. Layne*

Alternate Case Title: Media Ride-Along Case

Legal Citation: 526 U.S. 603

Year of Decision: 1999

KEY ISSUES

Is it a violation of the Fourth Amendment for media personnel to accompany law enforcement officers into a private home during the execution of an arrest warrant?

HISTORY OF THE CASE

In 1992, as part of an operation to apprehend dangerous criminals, U.S. marshals and Montgomery County police officers obtained arrest warrants for Dominic Wilson. At the time the law enforcement officers went to arrest Wilson, a reporter and photographer from the *Washington Post* were with the officers as part of a media "ride-along." The reporter and the photographer accompanied the officers when they entered what they believed was the suspect's home. The home turned out to be that of Wilson's parents, Charles and Geraldine Wilson. While the officers searched the house, the photographer took pictures. These pictures were never published.

The Wilsons brought a suit against the officers alleging the violation of their Fourth Amendment rights because of the presence of the media during the execution of the warrants. The district court found in favor of the Wilsons; however, the court of appeals reversed finding the officers were entitled to qualified immunity, a defense that protects public officials from the imposition of damages. The Supreme Court granted certiorari.

SUMMARY OF ARGUMENTS

Petitioners Charles and Geraldine Wilson, argued that the officers violated their Fourth Amendment rights by allowing the media to enter their home during the execution of the arrest warrants.

Respondents, law enforcement officers including Harry Layne, a deputy U.S. marshal, argued that the presence of the media served legitimate law enforcement purposes such as publicizing the government's effort to fight crime, to ensure accurate reporting of law enforcement activities, and to protect suspects from police abuses.

DECISION

Chief Justice Rehnquist wrote the opinion on behalf of a unanimous Court. The Court identified the steps in evaluating a claim of qualified immunity as (1) determining whether the plaintiff had been deprived of a constitutional right, and (2) determining whether the constitutional right was clearly established at the time of the violation. The Court found the officers were entitled to enter the Wilson's home because they had obtained an arrest warrant. However, the actions of the officers had to be related to the objective authorized by the warrant in order to comply with the Fourth Amendment and the presence of the media was not related to the officers' objectives on this occasion. Therefore, the Court found it violated the Fourth Amendment for police to bring the media inside a home during the execution of a warrant if their presence was not aiding the execution of the warrant.

The Court then addressed whether the petitioners' right to be free from the media's intrusion was clearly established at the time of the incident's occurrence. The Court defined "clearly estab-

lished" as it pertained to qualified immunity to mean that the right was sufficiently clear so that a reasonable officer would understand he is violating the right. The Court found that it was not unreasonable for officers to believe it was lawful to have media along during the execution of a warrant at the time of the incident because the constitutional question had not been definitively determined.

Justice Stevens agreed that the presence of the media violated the Fourth Amendment, but he disagreed with the Court on whether the petitioners' right was clearly established. Justice Stevens found that the petitioners' right was clearly established prior to the incident because police action during the execution of a warrant was "strictly limited to the objectives of the authorized intrusion" and it was obvious that the presence of the media exceeded the authorized objective. Moreover, the fact the Court unanimously agreed the action was a violation of the Fourth Amendment clearly indicated the constitutional right was clearly established.

AFTERMATH

Media coverage of law enforcement activities has been significantly limited by this decision and subsequent media ride-alongs will have a narrower scope, though they have not been completely banned. Law enforcement officers who allow media personnel to accompany them into private homes in the future will not be granted qualified immunity.

SIGNIFICANCE

It is now unconstitutional for media personnel to accompany law enforcement officers into a private home to execute a warrant.

RELATED CASES

Arizona v. Hicks, 480 U.S. 321 (1987)

Bivens v. Six Unknown Fed. Narcotics Agents, 403 U.S. 388 (1971)

Hanlon v. Berger, 526 U.S. 808 (1999)

RECOMMENDED READING

Kathy A. Brown, Wilson v. Layne: *Bans Press with Police in Home, but Leaves Media Ride-Along Intact,* 102 West Virginia Law Review 895 (2000).

Greenhalgh, William W. *The Fourth Amendment Handbook: A Chronological Survey of Supreme Court Decisions.* Chicago: Criminal Justice Section, American Bar Association, 2002.

FREEDOM OF SPEECH
AND ASSEMBLY

Case Title: *Abrams v. United States*

Alternate Case Title: The "Anti-American Circulars" Case

Legal Citations: 250 U.S. 616; 40 S.Ct. 17

Year of Decision: 1919

KEY ISSUES

Are circulars, intended to provoke and encourage resistance to the United States in the war with Germany, and inciting and advocating a general strike of workers in ammunition factories for the purpose of curtailing production, sufficient evidence to sustain a conviction of conspiracy to violate the Espionage Act?

HISTORY OF THE CASE

Five defendants were convicted of conspiring to violate provisions of the Espionage Act of Congress (§ 3, Title I, of Act approved June 15, 1917, as amended May 16, 1918, 40 Stat. 553). The Espionage Act was a federal law that punished spying and transmitting national defense information with the intent to harm the United States or to benefit a foreign nation. The defendants printed and distributed circulars in the city of New York. Each of the defendants was born in Russia, but at the time of arrest had lived in the United States for terms varying from five to 10 years. None of the defendants had applied for naturalization during that time.

The defendants met in New York City in rooms rented under an assumed name by defendant Abrams. There, the defendants discussed printing and distributing the circulars about two weeks before they were arrested. They admitted at trial that they united for this very purpose. Defendant Abrams then purchased a printing outfit with which the circulars were printed on July 27, 1918, and installed it in a basement room. On or about August 22, 1918, the defendants printed and distributed about 5,000 circulars by throwing some out of a window where one of the defendants worked, and distributing the others secretly. The defendants pleaded "not guilty" to four counts charged against them. The conspiracy and the overt acts were largely admitted and fully established at trial.

SUMMARY OF ARGUMENTS

The defendants argued that the acts charged against them were lawful because they were within the protection of the freedom of speech and of the press guaranteed by the First Amendment to the Constitution of the United States. They alleged that the Espionage Act is unconstitutional because it is in conflict with that amendment. The defendants further argued that there was no substantial evidence in the record to support the judgment upon the verdict of guilty and that the motion of the defendants for an instructed verdict was erroneously denied.

The government argued that the "judge-made" or common law regarding written communications advocating governmental change through the use of unlawful means, also known as seditious libel, remained in force despite the enactment of the First Amendment.

DECISION

Justice Clarke wrote the majority opinion for seven of the justices. Justice Brandeis concurred and Justice Holmes wrote a dissenting opinion. Justice Clarke affirmed the judgment and convictions of the district court. He found that the language of the circulars was intended to provoke and encourage resistance to the United States in the war.

Justice Clarke looked to the plain language of the circulars to determine the intent of the defendants in writing them. Some of that language was as follows: "The Russian Revolution cries: Workers of the World! Awake! Rise! Put down your enemy and mine!" He noted that the defendants also criticized the government of the United States as their "hypocritical," "cowardly," and "capitalistic" enemy. Based upon this language, Justice Clarke found that the purpose was to throw the United States into a state of revolution if possible and to thereby frustrate the military program of the government.

Justice Clarke also found that the defendants urged and advocated a resort to a general strike of workers in ammunition factories for the purpose of curtailing the production of ordinance and munitions necessary and essential to the prosecution of war as charged in the fourth count. He again came to this conclusion based upon the writing in the circulars themselves, which stated: "Workers, our reply to the barbaric intervention has to be a general strike! Any open challenge only will let the government know that not only the Russian worker fights for freedom, but also here in America lives the spirit of the revolution." The plain language in the circulars led Justice Clarke to conclude that there was enough evidence tending to prove that the defendants were guilty as charged in both the third and fourth counts of the indictment.

Justice Clarke dismissed the argument that the defendants only intended to prevent injury to the Russian cause. He stated that men have to be held to, and be accountable for, the effects that their acts were likely to produce. Thus, Justice Clarke concluded that even if the defendants' primary purpose was to aid the cause of the Russian Revolution, their plan of action could have had the effect of defeating the war program of the United States by persuading those addressed in the circulars not to aid government loans nor work in ammunitions factories.

In his dissent, Justice Holmes also argued that the language in the circulars in no way attacked the form of government of the United States. Justice Holmes then conceded that the circulars advocated a general strike. He also conceded that they may have curtailed production of things necessary to the prosecution of war within the meaning of the act, in violation of the fourth charge. However, he insisted that there was no intent to cripple or hinder the United States in the prosecution of war, as required by the act to make the conduct criminal. Justice Holmes believed that the only objective of the circulars was to help Russia and stop the American intervention there, not to impede the United States in the war it was waging. Justice Holmes argued that this was not the requisite intent needed to bring the circulars within the scope of the law and to be punishable.

He then turned to a free speech argument, stating that the theory of our Constitution is based on the belief that the best test of truth is the power of the thought to get itself accepted in the competition of the market. Therefore, he believed that we should not hinder the expression of ideas that we loathe, unless they imminently threaten immediate interference with the lawful and press-

ing purpose of the law and the immediate suppression of those ideas is required to save the country.

Justice Holmes finally argued that the United States has shown its repentance for the Sedition Act of 1798, stressing that "Congress shall make no law . . . abridging the freedom of speech." He did not believe that the common law as to seditious libel was still in force. Justice Holmes concluded that the defendants were denied their rights under the Constitution of the United States in their conviction.

AFTERMATH

Justice Holmes's spirited dissent increased his reputation as a champion of First Amendment free speech rights. His visions of the First Amendment gained popularity and resulted in a First Amendment jurisprudence that places great weight on freedom from government regulation of speech. Today, the ideas of defending speech have been greatly expanded, and the "clear and present danger" test, a test used to determine when speech is unprotected by the First Amendment, has been limited to expression that is directed to and is likely to produce imminent lawless action.

SIGNIFICANCE

Justice Holmes was steadfast in his demand for fundamentality in the First Amendment at a time when the Supreme Court, and dominant legal opinion, were willing to justify virtually all legislative restrictions on unpopular speech. His dissent represents one of the finest expressions of pragmatism in free speech doctrine with his fear that the Sedition Act would inhibit free speech and the search for the truth. Few American judicial figures have aroused as much interest and controversy in both popular and legal circles as Justice Holmes. His theories continue to affect discourse decades after he first articulated them, and they still form the basis of many contemporary legal debates.

RELATED CASES

Debs v. United States, 249 U.S. 211 (1919)

Lochner v. New York, 198 U.S. 45 (1905)

Schenck v. United States, 249 U.S. 47 (1919)

RECOMMENDED READING

Kalven, Harry, Jr. *A Worthy Tradition: Freedom of Speech in America.* New York: Harper and Row, 1988.

Mill, J. "Essay On Liberty." In *On Liberty and Considerations on Representative Government, 1859.* 1, 13–48 Ed. R. McCallum. New York: Macmillan, 1946.

Polenberg, R. *Fighting Faiths: The* Abrams *Case, the Supreme Court, and Free Speech.* New York: Viking, 1987.

Case Title: *Barenblatt v. United States*

Alternate Case Title: The "Communism in Education" Case

Legal Citations: 360 U.S. 109; 79 S.Ct. 1081

Year of Decision: 1959

KEY ISSUES

Can the United States convict a defendant of contempt for refusing to answer questions about his participation in or knowledge of alleged Communist Party activities at educational institutions in this country?

HISTORY OF THE CASE

On June 28, 1954, Barenblatt, an instructor at Vassar College, was subpoenaed and appeared as a witness before the House Un-American Activities Committee during an inquiry into the field of education. After answering a few general questions, he refused to answer five specific questions about his "political" and "religious" beliefs or any "other personal and private affairs" or "associational activities." As a result of his refusal, he was convicted of contempt of Congress.

This case came before the U.S. Supreme Court twice. Barenblatt's conviction was originally affirmed in 1957 by a unanimous panel of the court of appeals (100 U.S. App. D.C. 13, 240 F.2d 875). The Supreme Court vacated the judg-ment of the court of appeals and remanded the case to that Court for further consideration in light of *Watkins v. United States,* 354 U.S. 178 (1957). In *Watkins,* the Supreme Court reversed a contempt of Congress conviction. The Supreme Court again agreed to consider Barenblatt's statutory and constitutional challenges to his conviction. Particularly, the Supreme Court wanted to consider his claim that the previous judgment could not stand under their decision in the *Watkins* case.

SUMMARY OF ARGUMENTS

Barenblatt argued that the compelling of testimony by the subcommittee was too vague to be legislatively authorized or constitutionally permissible. Barenblatt further alleged that he was not told why the subcommittee's questions were pertinent to the subject matter of the inquiry. He also believed that the questions the subcommittee asked infringed his First Amendment rights.

The United States argued that the committee was authorized to conduct an investigation of communism in education by compelling Barenblatt's attendance for questioning. The United States also argued that Barenblatt had no First Amendment right to refuse to tell the committee whether he was a member of the Communist Party and Barenblatt had no foundation for his claim that he was not sufficiently informed of the pertinency of the questions.

DECISION

Justice Harlan wrote the opinion for the Court upholding Barenblatt's conviction for contempt of Congress. Justice Harlan's decision that the conviction did not violate the First Amendment addressed the conflict between constitutional claims of congressional power and Barenblatt's rights to resist its exercise. Harlan found that based on historical precedent, Congress has the legislative authority to investigate communist activities in this country in pursuance of its "legislative concerns in the domain of national security." He added that Rule XI, the congressional rule that chartered the committee, does not exclude the field of education from the committee's compulsory authority. Justice Harlan then found that the record showed Barenblatt was adequately made aware of the pertinence of the subcommittee's questions.

In striking a balance between the individual and governmental interests at stake, Justice Harlan found in favor of the government. The subcommittee's inquiries about Barenblatt's past or present membership in the Communist Party were related to a valid legislative purpose, since Congress has wide power to legislate in the field of communist activity in this country and to conduct appropriate investigations to aid in this endeavor. Justice Harlan stated that the Court would not deny Congress investigatory power in this domain solely because the field of education was involved. Justice Harlan found that Congress did not inquire into the content of the lectures or discussions at Vassar, nor was its true purpose merely "exposure." Harlan also failed to find other factors on the record that might have indicated the individual interests at issue outweighed the government interests.

Justice Harlan concluded by stating that the balance between the individual and the governmental interests in this case must be struck in favor of the government, and that therefore the provisions of the First Amendment had not been offended.

Justice Black and Justice Brennan wrote dissenting opinions. Justice Black argued that the Supreme Court should not sanction the use of the contempt power to enforce questioning by congressional committees in the realm of speech and association. He believed that the questions the subcommittee asked Barenblatt and the resolution establishing the House Un-American Activities Committee violated the Constitution in many respects. Justice Black found Rule XI and the term "un-American" too vague to give guidance to a witness and too vague to support a conviction for a refusal to testify. He also believed that laws directly abridging First Amendment freedoms could not be justified by a congressional balancing process. Although he agreed with cases involving the right of a city to control its streets, even where this power might affect speech, he argued that Rule XI attempted to inquire into beliefs, not actions or conduct, and therefore it abridged freedom of speech, press, and association.

Justice Black further concluded that the conviction violates the Constitution because the chief aim, purpose, and practice of the House Un-American Activities Committee is to try to punish witnesses because they are or have been Communists, or refuse to admit to communist affiliations. Justice Black criticized the committee's efforts to expose and punish any suspected "un-American" activities that it reports cannot be reached by legislation, administrative action, or by any other agency of government, including courts. He argued that Congress cannot perform these tasks under the Constitution. Punishment is to be left to the courts and a jury, after a trial with all judicial safeguards.

Justice Brennan also dissented, stating that he completely agreed with Justice Black's dissent that the whole purpose of the subcommittee's investigation was exposure, purely for the sake of exposure. This is an invalid purpose for which Barenblatt's First Amendment rights can be subordinated, and is therefore unconstitutional.

AFTERMATH

Congress's investigative powers were strengthened by the Court's decision to require persons to answer questions regarding their involvement with the Communist Party. The decision also indicated that when the government's interest in national security was balanced against an individual's interest in keeping silent about his or her political activities, the government's interest would be favored.

SIGNIFICANCE

In *Barenblatt*, the Court retreated from its prior holding in *Watkins v. United States* (1957), which limited the scope of congressional investigations and permitted inquiry into political beliefs and associations by ignoring First Amendment concerns.

RELATED CASES

Gibson v. Florida Legislative Investigating Committee, 372 U.S. 539 (1963)

Uphaus v. Wyman, 360 U.S. 72 (1959)

RECOMMENDED READING

Emerson, T. *The System of Freedom of Expression.* New York: Random House, 1970.

Harry Kalven Jr., *Meiklejohn and the* Barenblatt *Opinion,* 27 University of Chicago Law Review 315, 325–326 (1960).

Case Title: *Beauharnais v. Illinois*

Alternate Case Title: Group Case Libel

Legal Citations: 343 U.S. 250; 72 S.Ct. 725; 96 L.Ed. 919

Year of Decision: 1952

KEY ISSUES

May an individual be found guilty of libeling an entire group of people by publishing a flyer?

HISTORY OF THE CASE

Under an Illinois statute, it was illegal to publish or present in any public place a publication or exhibition that portrayed "depravity, criminality, unchastity, or lack of virtue" in a class of citizens of any race, color, creed, or religion, or that exposed the citizens of such groups to contempt or derision or that produced a breach of the peace or riots. The law was passed in 1917 when the state of Illinois was struggling to deal with race riots, which had occurred in East St. Louis. In the summer of 1919, the city of Chicago was the scene of a race riot that lasted for seven days. The legislature of Illinois, in the face of these extreme episodes of racial violence, reenacted the law.

Joseph Beauharnais was the leader of an organization called the White Circle League of America, which was headquartered in Chicago. Beauharnais prepared a petition on a leaflet with the large headline "Preserve and protect white neighborhoods! from the constant and continuous invasion, harassment, and encroachment by the Negroes. We want two million signatures of white men and women." The flyer went on to say that the white people of Chicago must unite to prevent the Negro from spreading "rapes, robberies, knives, guns and marijuana" into white neighborhoods. On January 7, 1950, Beauharnais held a meeting to gain members for his White Circle League and passed out these leaflets to those assembled, with instructions that they be distributed throughout the city of Chicago.

Beauharnais was charged with violating the criminal statute discussed above, on the theory that the intent of the leaflet was to disturb the peace. The case was tried before a jury, which found Beauharnais guilty as charged and fined him the maximum sum under the statute. Beauharnais brought a direct appeal to the Illinois Supreme Court challenging the constitutionality of the statute. Beauharnais always admitted that he was the founder, president, and director of the White Circle League, and that he prepared the literature and had given specific instructions on how to distribute it on the streets of Chicago.

Beauharnais argued that his rights were violated because he was deprived of the freedom of speech, the due process of law, the right of assembly, and the right to petition the government.

In a unanimous decision, the Illinois Supreme Court found that the state had the right to regulate "fighting words" that were liable to cause violence and disorder between the races: "Any ordinary person could only conclude from the libelous character of the language that a clash and riots would eventually result between the members of the White Circle League of America and the Negro race" *People v. Beauharnais*, 97 NE 2d 343, 346 (1949). Beauharnais argued that there was truth in all of his allegations and offered evidence attempting to show that crime rates in the white areas of Chicago were lower than in districts populated by blacks. He further offered testimony that when black families moved into a block, real estate values went down. The Illinois Supreme Court ruled that the trial court had properly refused to admit Beauharnais's evidence and affirmed the jury's verdict, stating that Beauharnais's language was so inflammatory and of such a character that it was not entitled to the protection of freedom of speech.

SUMMARY OF ARGUMENTS

Beauharnais's attorneys argued that there had never been any clear and present danger of riots or other civil disturbance as a result of the language. His attorneys further stated that the definition of libel developed through judicial decisions became vague when it was applied to a group, making it unclear what would constitute a punishable offense. They further argued that Beauharnais had a right to speak, regardless of the social value of his views, and that his pamphlet contained no fighting words.

The state of Illinois argued that the pamphlet was indeed full of fighting words and that the common law certainly understood the tendency of such words to cause a breach of the peace.

DECISION

The Supreme Court upheld the conviction of Beauharnais by a vote of 5 to 4. Justice Felix Frankfurter wrote the majority opinion that the flyer did indeed contain fighting words that could cause a breach of the peace and lead to civil disturbances, and met the test of a clear danger necessary for conviction for libel at common law. Justice Frankfurter stated that libel against an individual was a common law crime in all 48 states. Although all of the laws dealing with libel were directed at designated individuals, rather than toward a group, Justice Frankfurter found that it was well within the power of the state legislature to deal with matters of social science, and that the U.S. Supreme Court had long ago recognized the economic rights of groups, such as unions and other bargaining organizations. While questions could be raised regarding the efficiency or effectiveness of Illinois law, Frankfurter found no problem with the state legislature's authority to make a legislative judgment. He felt that no fundamental liberty was jeopardized by such conviction of Mr. Beauharnais.

Justice Hugo Black and Justice William Douglas dissented. They found that Mr. Beauharnais's speech was a genuine effort to petition his elected representatives. They further felt that the First Amendment freedoms should not be subject to any test, but should be absolute: there should be no legislative control over speech.

Justice Stanley Reed also dissented.

Justice Robert Jackson felt that the conviction violated Beauharnais's due process rights, as he had no opportunity to prove the truth of his opinions. Jackson found no record that the flyer had disturbed the peace and found no basis at all to suppress Beauharnais's speech.

AFTERMATH

With the conviction upheld, the name of Beauharnais became established as a test of First Amendment rights with regard to group defamation.

SIGNIFICANCE

This was the first and only time the Court directly addressed group libel. The Supreme Court found that the First Amendment did prohibit group defamation when the slight value of truth was outweighed by social interest. The cries of censorship were immediate. However, some states retained their group libel laws, but without enforcement.

RELATED CASES

Cantwell v. Connecticut, 310 U.S. 296 (1940)

Chaplinsky v. New Hampshire, 315 U.S. 568 (1942)

R.A.V. v. St. Paul, 60 U.S.L.W. 4667; 112 S.Ct. 2538; 120 L.Fd. 2d 305 (1992)

RECOMMENDED READING

Lillian R. Bevier, *The First Amendment and Political Speech,* 30 Stanford Law Review 299 (1979).

William J. Brennan, Jr., *The Supreme Court and the Meikeljohn Interpretation of the First Amendment,* 79 Harvard Law Review 1 (1965).

Case Title: *Boy Scouts of America v. Dale*

Alternate Case Title: Homosexual Exclusion Case

Legal Citations: 530 U.S. 640; 120 S.Ct. 2446

Year of Decision: 2000

KEY ISSUES

Does the application of a state antidiscrimination law, which prohibits discriminatory behavior in public places, violate an association's First Amendment right to express its viewpoint by excluding certain persons from its membership?

HISTORY OF THE CASE

James Dale, a Boy Scout from the age of 12, applied for a scoutmaster position in the Boy Scouts of America. The Boy Scouts accepted

Dale's application. Shortly thereafter, Dale openly acknowledged that he was gay and began participating in a gay activist group on his college campus. Newspaper coverage of a seminar addressing gay issues featured a picture of Dale and noted Dale's involvement in a gay rights group. Not long after the newspaper article was published, Dale received a letter revoking his membership in the Boy Scouts. When asked for an explanation, the Boy Scouts stated the revocation was based on Dale's sexual orientation. Dale brought an action against the Boy Scouts in the New Jersey state court, alleging violation of the state's public accommodation law, a law that prohibits discrimination in public places on the basis of sexual orientation, and the state's common law, law made by judicial decisions. The trial court upheld the Boy Scouts' revocation, dismissing both of Dale's claims. The appellate division reversed the dismissal of the public accommodation law claim and the New Jersey Supreme Court agreed, stating the Boy Scouts' action violated the public accommodation law. The New Jersey Supreme Court also found that the application of the public accommodation did not violate the Boy Scouts' constitutional rights. The Boy Scouts sought review of the decision by the U.S. Supreme Court.

SUMMARY OF ARGUMENTS

Dale argued that the Boy Scouts violated a New Jersey law prohibiting discrimination based on sexual orientation in public places when it revoked his membership. The Boy Scouts argued that Dale's homosexuality was inconsistent with its expressed values and that the application of the New Jersey public accommodation law violated its First Amendment rights.

DECISION

The Court upheld the Boy Scouts' revocation of Dale's membership. Chief Justice Rehnquist wrote the majority opinion. In reaching his conclusion, Rehnquist first determined that the Boy Scouts engaged in expressive association joining together to transfer ideas and viewpoints because it engaged in a form of expression through its transmittal of values from adult members to youth. Next, Rehnquist examined the Boy Scouts' view on homosexuality to determine whether forcing the Boy Scouts to include Dale in its membership affected the Boy Scouts' ability to advocate its

viewpoint on homosexuality. The examination revealed that the Boy Scouts viewed homosexuality to be inconsistent with the values found in its Scout oath and Scout laws, specifically, its "morally straight" and "clean" values. The Boy Scouts stated that it did not want to promote homosexuality as legitimate behavior. Nowhere in the listed Boy Scout values was sexual orientation mentioned. However, Chief Justice Rehnquist noted that the Court believed the Boy Scouts sincerely held its viewpoint on homosexuality, and that it was not the Court's role to reject an expressed value because the Court disagreed with it or found it inconsistent with other values held by the Boy Scouts as an organization.

In light of the Boy Scouts' expressed viewpoint, Chief Justice Rehnquist stated Dale's presence would significantly burden the Boy Scouts' ability to promote its viewpoint. Specifically, Dale's presence would interfere with the Boy Scouts' choice and force it to convey a certain message regarding the legitimacy of homosexual behavior. Rehnquist stated that the First Amendment protected the Boy Scouts' viewpoint even if all of its members did not agree with the viewpoint expressed.

Finally, Rehnquist examined whether the New Jersey public accommodations law violated the Boy Scouts' freedom of expressive association. Noting that the Court had found that states had a compelling interest in eliminating discrimination against women in public places in ROBERTS V. UNITED STATES JAYCEES (1984) and *Board of Directors of Rotary Int'l v. Rotary Club of Duarte* (1987), the chief justice stated that the enforcement of the state antidiscrimination statutes in those cases did not materially interfere with the expressions of the organizations in question. After balancing New Jersey's interests and the Boy Scouts' interests, Rehnquist determined the broad state law infringed on the Boy Scouts' First Amendment rights. The chief justice specifically indicated the Court's decision was not based on its view of whether the Boy Scouts' antihomosexuality policy was correct.

Justices Stevens and Souter wrote dissenting opinions. Justice Stevens took issue with the Boy Scouts' lack of clear expression of its viewpoint and the Court's deference to the Boy Scouts' assertion of what would constitute impairment of its viewpoint. Justice Stevens also stated that the Boy Scouts' view on homosexual behavior was inconsistent with its view on religion. Specifically, the Boy Scouts adopted no single position on religion, yet some religions do not hold the same view on homosexuality as the Boy Scouts. Stevens also pointed out that the Boy Scouts presented no evidence that Dale intended to use his position as a scoutmaster to promote homosexual behavior; Dale held a view indistinguishable from a religious or political view. Political and religious views would not have been challenged by the Boy Scouts as long as a scoutmaster complied with the Boy Scout policies regarding those views. Finally, Stevens noted that American society had become more accepting of homosexual behavior, and he cautioned against making a habit of enforcing an unfavorable opinion of homosexuality without additional analysis. Justice Souter, joined by Justices Ginsburg and Breyer, agreed with Justice Stevens's dissent, but also pointed out that the move toward societal acceptance of homosexual behavior should not control the Court's decision on the case.

AFTERMATH

In the months following the Court's decision, a number of public and private schools and civic organizations withdrew support and funding of the Boy Scouts, citing compliance with antidiscrimination policies. Gay rights organizations encouraged such withdrawals of support. Protest rallies were held seeking to end the Boy Scouts' discrimination, and men returned previously earned Boy Scout badges in protest. One congressional representative sought to have the Boy Scouts' Congressional Charter revoked.

However, the Boy Scouts announced that even after the decision its membership was increasing. Some groups sought to protect the Boy Scouts from the backlash of the decision through legislative and monetary support. The Boy Scouts itself published responses to questions regarding its membership standards after the decision. Included in these key messages were statements that indicated the Boy Scouts' intention to hold its ground regarding homosexuality: "Boy Scouts of America is committed to the concept that sexual intimacy is the sole providence of a man and a woman within the bonds of marriage" and "[a]lthough the [Boy Scouts] makes no effort to discover the sexual orientation of any person, the [Boy Scouts] believes an avowed homosexual is

not a role model for the faith-based values espoused in the Scout Oath and Law."

SIGNIFICANCE

The Court's determination in *Boy Scouts of America* that Dale's mere presence could be expressive, even though Dale was not promoting homosexuality in the Boy Scouts, has serious First Amendment implications. In addition, the Court's determination affects how state public accommodation law will be applied to the use of public spaces by associations with discriminatory memberships, like the Boy Scouts. Moreover, the Court's unquestioning deference to what an association claims its viewpoint to be and who or what might impair the expression of that viewpoint gives wide latitude to associations to maintain exclusionary membership practices.

RELATED CASES

Board of Directors of Rotary Int'l v. Rotary Club of Duarte, 481 U.S. 537 (1987)

Hurley v. Irish-American Gay, Lesbian and Bisexual Group of Boston, Inc., 515 U.S. 557 (1995)

Roberts v. United States Jaycees, 468 U.S. 609 (1984)

RECOMMENDED READING

Arthur S. Leonard, *Boy Scouts of America v. Dale:* The "Gay Rights Activist" as Constitutional Pariah, 12:1 Stanford Law & Policy Review (2001).

Case Title: *Brandenburg v. Ohio*

Alternate Case Titles: The Restraint of Speech Case, the Ku Klux Klan Rally Case

Legal Citations: 395 U.S. 444; 89 S.Ct. 1827; 23 L.Ed. 430

Year of Decision: 1969

KEY ISSUES

At what point can free speech be restrained?

HISTORY OF THE CASE

Speech that advocates illegal activities became a major concern in the United States as early as 1901, when President William McKinley was assassinated by a professed anarchist. Many states enacted criminal anarchy or "syndicalism" laws, which made it a felony for anyone to advocate criminal anarchy by speech or print and distribution. The Supreme Court originally upheld the constitutionality of these statutes, but by the late 1930s, convictions under these statutes were often reversed because the Court held that either the statutes were too broad or the person advocating the criminal activity did not pose an immediate threat to the government. The rule then used by the Court in the GITLOW V. NEW YORK (1925) line of cases was the "bad tendency" rule, which gave states the right and duty to protect the public from speech that *might* lead to substantial public welfare dangers such as corrupting public morals, inciting criminal behavior, or disturbing the peace. The dissent, consisting of Justices Holmes and Brandeis, advocated the use of the "clear and present danger" rule to protected speech at the state level when the speech did not pose a clear and present danger to society. However, even in 1951, the Court in DENNIS V. UNITED STATES still held that speech *tending* to lead to violent revolution may be punished without constitutional violations when the gravity of the situation dictates.

In *Brandenburg v. Ohio,* the Court once again faced the question of speech restraint in a different time, one of civil unrest. Clarence Brandenburg, the leader of a Ku Klux Klan group, declared in a speech that revenge may be taken if the president, Congress, and Supreme Court continued to suppress the Caucasian race. Brandenburg invited a news reporter and photographer to film the event, and a clip from the rally was broadcast later locally and nationally. Brandenburg was then convicted of violating the Ohio Criminal Syndicalism statute for "advocat[ing] . . . the duty, necessity, or propriety of crime, sabotage, violence, or unlawful methods of terrorism as a means of accomplishing industrial or political reform" and for "voluntarily assembl[ing] with any society, group or assemblage of persons formed to teach or advocate the doctrines of criminal syndicalism." The Court took this opportunity both to reconsider the changes that have occurred and to clarify the rule that would apply in speech cases in the future.

SUMMARY OF ARGUMENTS

Brandenburg challenged the constitutionality of the Ohio Criminal Syndicalism statute under the First and Fourteenth Amendments to the U.S. Constitution. The state, however, centered its arguments on the violation of the law, using evidence such as the film and testimony identifying Brandenburg as the person who communicated with the reporter and who spoke at the rally. The state introduced into evidence several articles appearing in the film, including a pistol, a rifle, a shotgun, ammunition, a Bible, and a red hood worn by the speaker in the films. Because the Ohio statute was so similar to the California statute that was upheld by the Court in WHITNEY V. CALIFORNIA (1927), the state also relied on the value of this precedent under the rationale that "advocating" violent means to effect political and economic change involved such danger to the security of the state that the state may outlaw it.

DECISION

The Court unanimously held that freedoms of speech and press given under the First and Fourteenth Amendments did not permit a state to forbid advocacy of the use of force or of law violation except where such advocacy was directed to inciting or producing imminent lawless action and was likely to incite or produce such action. Because the Ohio Criminal Syndicalism statute would punish mere advocacy, the Court held that the statute fell under the condemnation of the First and Fourteenth Amendments.

With this decision, the Court also overruled *Whitney v. California.* Therefore, the Brandenburg conviction was overturned.

AFTERMATH

The Court's position regarding free speech in the political context was clarified by its decision to protect politically relevant speech. The Court's distinction between speech that imparted ideas and speech that incited lawless action further reinforced its position in this area. Not surprisingly, the standards developed by the Court in *Brandenburg* are still the test used in the area today.

SIGNIFICANCE

The *Brandenburg* case expanded the First Amendment freedoms and signified the final step in the development of a constitutional test for speech advocating illegal actions. In distinguishing between the advocacy of illegal action and the advocacy of political ideas, the Court only restricted speech that was likely to incite illegal action and to result in imminent danger. Because the test required findings of actual imminent harm, the result of this opinion is that state governments may restrict speech only in unusual circumstances.

RELATED CASES

Dennis v. U.S., 341 U.S. 494 (1951)

Gitlow v. New York, 268 U.S. 652 (1925)

Whitney v. California, 274 U.S. 357 (1927)

RECOMMENDED READING

Gerald Gunther, *Learned Hand and the Origins of Modern First Amendment Doctrine: Some Fragments of History,* 27 Stanford Law Review 719 (1975).

Bernard Schwartz, *Holmes versus Hand: Clear and Present Danger or Advocacy of Unlawful Action?,* Supreme Court Review 209 (1994).

Case Title: *Buckley v. Valeo*

Alternate Case Title: The Limitation on Campaign Contributions Case

Legal Citations: 424 U.S. 1; 96 S.Ct. 612; 46 L.Ed. 2d 659

Year of Decision: 1976

KEY ISSUES

Whether the Federal Election Commission Act limitations on contributions and expenditures of money and on reporting and disclosure violate the First Amendment and whether the composition and powers of the Federal Election Commission violate Article Two of the Constitution.

HISTORY OF THE CASE

The Federal Election Campaign Act of 1971 was a piece of election reform legislation that placed restrictions on political contributions and expenditures and set up the Federal Elections Commission.

The appellants, Senator James Buckley and other individuals and groups involved in the political election process, challenged the constitutionality of the act and related provisions of the Internal Revenue Code of 1954, all as amended in 1974. Their suit was originally filed in the U.S. District Court for the District of Columbia. Appellants requested the convocation of a three-judge district court as to all matters and also requested certification of constitutional questions to the court of appeals. The district judge denied the application for a three-judge court and directed that the case be transmitted to the court of appeals. The court of appeals remanded the case back to the district court. On remand, the district judge entered a memorandum order adopting the augmented record back to the court of appeals. The court of appeals upheld all but one of the statutory provisions rejecting most of appellant's constitutional attacks. The appellants sought review by the U.S. Supreme Court.

SUMMARY OF ARGUMENTS

Appellants argued that limiting the use of money for political purposes restricts communication in violation of the First Amendment. Further, they argued that the reporting and disclosure provisions of the act unconstitutionally impinged on their right to freedom of association. They also viewed the federal subsidy provisions of subtitle H as violations of the general welfare clause, and as inconsistent with the First and Fifth Amendments. Finally, they argued against the commission's composition and powers.

The appellees, Francis Valeo, the secretary of the Senate, the Federal Election Commission, and others argued that the act regulated conduct and only incidentally affected speech and association. The appellees also contended that the government's interest in preventing corruption from large financial contributions, equalizing citizens' ability to affect election outcomes, and halting the increasing cost of political campaigns justified the act's restrictions on contributions.

DECISION

The Court unanimously upheld the constitutionality of individual contribution limits, the disclosure and reporting provisions, and the public financing scheme. The Court invalidated the composition of the Federal Election Commission and the limitations on expenditures.

The Court stated that the act's contribution and expenditure limitations operated in an area of the most fundamental First Amendment activities, the discussion of political ideas to bring about social and political change. However, unlike the court of appeals, the Court did not share the view that the act's contribution and expenditure limitations were comparable to restrictions on conduct as seen in *UNITED STATES V. O'BRIEN*, 391 U.S. 367 (1968)—which ruled that the destruction of a draft card was not protected as a freedom of speech or expression—since spending money is not like destroying a draft card.

The Court next compared the act's contribution and expenditure limitations to the "time, place and manner" cases such as *COX V. LOUISIANA* 379 U.S. 559 (1965), *Adderly v. Florida* 385 U.S. 39 (1966), and *Kovacs v. Cooper* 336 U.S. 77 (1949). The Court stated that the act was different since it imposed direct quantity restrictions on political communication and association by persons, groups, candidates, and political parties in addition to any reasonable time, place, and manner regulations otherwise imposed. The Court found that a restriction on the amount of money a person or group could spend on political communication during a campaign reduced the quantity of expression since virtually every means of communication required the expenditure of money. However, the Court argued that it entailed only a marginal restriction upon the contributor's ability to engage in free communication—as opposed to limitations on expenditure for political expression. The Court stated that the contribution limits were constitutional for federal elected offices because they were narrowly tailored to the goal of limiting corruption and the appearance of corruption. (The corruption could be spawned by the real or imagined coercive influence of large financial contributions on candidates' positions and on their actions if elected to office.) The Court cautioned that if the contribution limits were too low, the limits could also be unconstitutional.

The Court invalidated the act's independent expenditure ceilings as imposing significantly more restrictions on protected freedoms of political expression and association than did its limitations on financial contributions.

The Federal Election Campaign Act created an eight-member federal Election Commission to oversee federal elections with two members of the commission appointed by the president pro tempore of the Senate, two by the Speaker of the House, and two by the president. The Court held that vesting a commission whose members were appointed in this manner with some of these functions violated the appointments clause of Article Two of the Constitution.

The Federal Election Campaign Act of 1971 also required political candidates and "political committees" to maintain records of the names and addresses of all persons who contribute more than $10 in a calendar year and to make such records available for inspection by the commission, the public, and for copying. The Court upheld these provisions because they provided the electorate with information about where campaign money comes from, aiding voters in evaluating those who seek election. Second, the disclosure deterred actual corruption and avoided the appearance of corruption by exposing contributors. Third, the requirements were essential for the gathering of data necessary to detect violations of the contribution limitations. Thus, the Court found that the disclosure requirements directly served substantial governmental interests.

The Court also considered the constitutionality of subtitle H of the Internal Revenue Code, which established a scheme of campaign "subsidies" to equalize the financial resources of political candidates. The Court upheld the public financing provisions, stating that Subtitle H was a congressional effort to use public money to facilitate and enlarge public discussion and participation in the electoral process. Thus, it furthered, not abridged, pertinent First Amendment values.

Chief Justice Burger wrote a concurring and dissenting opinion. He argued that contributions and expenditures are two sides of the same coin and limiting one effectively limited the other. Thus, he argued that the contribution limits were unconstitutional, as were the expenditure limits. He added that such a restraint can be justified only, if at all, by the very strongest of state interests.

Justice White also wrote a concurring and dissenting opinion. He did not think that the expenditure limits violated the First Amendment. He believed that limiting the importance of personal wealth, by limiting the amount of money a candidate can spend on a campaign, helped to assure that only those with a little support would be viable candidates. He argued that this may discourage the notion that the outcome of elections is only a function of money. Justice White also believed that the limitation also equalized access to the political arena. He insisted that the First Amendment did not prohibit Congress from determining that personal wealth ought to play less of a role in political campaigns.

Justice Marshall wrote a decision concurring in part and dissenting in part. He did not agree that the section of the act limiting personal and familial spending violated a candidate's First Amendment rights. He argued that the belief that personal wealth wins elections discouraged candidates without a lot of money from running for office and undermined public confidence in the integrity of the electoral process. Justice Marshall added that this concern was heightened by the Court's decision to limit campaign contributions since access to large contributions was important for a candidate without substantial personal wealth to spend on his campaign. He argued that large contributions are their only means of countering a wealthy candidate's immediate access to large sums of money. Justice Blackmun also concurred in part and dissented in part, and he was not persuaded by the Court's distinction between contribution limits and expenditure limits.

AFTERMATH

Since *Buckley,* the Court has struggled to define the First Amendment interests implicated by political spending and to delineate the circumstances in which those interests may be abridged. In *McIntyre v. Ohio Elections Commission* (1995), *Buckley* was undermined by minimizing the informational interest at stake in the electoral context. It also raised doubt about whether a state can ever assert that informing the electorate is a compelling interest sufficient to uphold a statute that limits political speech.

SIGNIFICANCE

The landmark decision of *Buckley v. Valeo* established that legislative limitations on spending in support of political candidates may violate the First Amendment right to freedom of speech. It set the standard that campaign contributions are protected speech, even if subject to restriction. Additionally, with the decision in *Buckley* that the powers given to the Federal Elections Commission under the act violated the separation of powers in Article Two of the Constitution, the Burger court began to revive the legal discussion and analysis of the separation of powers.

RELATED CASES

Austin v. Michigan Chamber of Commerce, 110 S.Ct. 1391 (1990)

First National Bank v. Bellotti, 435 U.S. 765 (1978)

McIntyre v. Ohio Elections Commission, 115 S.Ct. 1511 (1995)

RECOMMENDED READING

Daniel D. Polsby, Buckley v. Valeo: *The Special Nature of Political Speech,* Supreme Court Review 1, 26–41 (1976).

Case Title: *Chaplinsky v. New Hampshire*

Alternate Case Title: The "Fighting Words" Case

Legal Citations: 315 U.S. 568; 62 S.Ct. 766; 86 L.Ed. 1031

Year of Decision: 1942

KEY ISSUES

Is a statute that criminalized offensive language against individuals in public places a violation of the Fourteenth Amendment of the U.S. Constitution?

HISTORY OF THE CASE

Chaplinsky, a member of the religious sect known as Jehovah's Witnesses, was distributing the literature of his sect on the streets of Rochester, New Hampshire, on a Saturday afternoon. Members of the local citizenry complained to the city marshall, Bowering, that Chaplinsky was denouncing all religion as a "racket." Bowering told the complainers that Chaplinsky was lawfully engaged, and warned Chaplinsky that the crowd was growing restless. Some time later, a disturbance occurred. Chaplinsky was taken to a police station and charged with violation of chapter 378, section 2, of the public laws of New Hampshire, which proscribed the use of offensive language against individuals in public places.

Chaplinsky was found guilty in the municipal court, and in the superior court on appeal. He was found guilty and the judgment of conviction was affirmed by the New Hampshire Supreme Court. He appealed to the U.S. Supreme Court, challenging the constitutionality of the statute.

SUMMARY OF ARGUMENTS

Chaplinsky argued that the statute violated the Fourteenth Amendment of the Constitution of the United States because it placed an unreasonable restraint on freedom of speech, freedom of the press, and freedom of worship, and was vague and indefinite.

New Hampshire argued that the statute was a proper subject for the exercise of the state's police powers and, as applied to Chaplinsky, did not create an unconstitutional standard in violation of due process. New Hampshire also argued that the statute did not deprive Chaplinsky of his right of freedom of speech.

DECISION

Justice Murphy wrote the decision for the Court and held that the challenged statute, on its face and as applied, did not violate the Fourteenth Amendment. Justice Murphy, backed by a united court, immediately dismissed Chaplinsky's attacks relating to his First Amendment rights to freedom of the press and freedom of worship. In addressing his free speech claims, Justice Murphy said that "the right to free speech is not absolute at all times and under all circumstances." He articulated limited classes of speech that can be prohibited within the confines of the Constitution, including "lewd and obscene, the profane, the libelous, and the insulting or 'fighting' words." He then defined "fighting words" as "those which by their very utterance inflict injury or tend to incite an immediate breach of the peace." Justice Murphy reasoned that such words lacked significance to the exposition of ideas and have little social value, so any benefit from the speech was clearly outweighed by the harm to society.

Justice Murphy relied upon the authority of earlier decisions and declared that the statute's purpose was to preserve the public peace. He then stated that because the statute was narrowly drawn and limited to specific conduct within the domain of the state power, it did not violate the Constitution. He found that the phrases "damned racketeer" and "damned fascist" were epithets likely to provoke retaliation in the average person, causing a breach of the peace. Thus, he concluded that the statute did not unreasonably impinge upon the privilege of free speech when applied to the facts of the case.

AFTERMATH

Only seven years after *Chaplinsky* in 1949, the Court refined the "fighting words" doctrine in *Terminiello v. Chicago*, stating that mere offensiveness did not make words proscribable under the *Chaplinsky* doctrine. However, the Court never changed its definition of fighting words, leaving open the possibility of its finding that some words alone may be "words that wound." Additionally, the courts have adjusted the scope of insulting or fighting words. New categories have been added, such as the graphic description of sexual conduct by children, and other categories have been significantly narrowed, such as libelous speech. (See *New York v. Ferber*, 458 U.S. 747 [1982] and *New York Times v. Sullivan*, 376 U.S. 254 [1964]).

SIGNIFICANCE

The Court in *Chaplinsky* first articulated what would later be called "the two-level" theory of speech by Professor Harry Kalven, a University of Chicago law professor: speech is either "protected" or "unprotected" by the First Amendment according to the Court's assessment of its relative "value" at the time.

RELATED CASES

Beauharnais v. Illinois, 343 U.S. 250 (1952)

Roth v. United States, 354 U.S. 476 (1957)

RECOMMENDED READING

Greenwalt, Kent. *Fighting Words: Individuals, Communities and Liberties of Speech.* Princeton, N.J.: Princeton University Press, 1995.

Harry Kalven, Jr., *The Metaphysics of the Law of Obscenity,* Supreme Court Review 1, 10 (1960).

Matsuda, Mari et al. *Words That Wound: Critical Race Theory, Assaultive Speech, and the First Amendment.* Boulder, Colo.: Westview Press, 1993.

Case Title: *Cohen v. California*

Alternate Case Title: The "Fuck the Draft" Jacket Case

Legal Citations: 403 U.S. 15; 91 S.Ct. 1780; 29 L.Ed. 2d 284

Year of Decision: 1971

KEY ISSUES

Do vulgar words on clothing constitute obscenity?

HISTORY OF THE CASE

On April 26, 1968, Paul Robert Cohen wore a jacket bearing the words "Fuck the Draft" while walking down a hallway in the Los Angeles County Courthouse. Women and children were in the corridor. When Mr. Cohen was arrested he testified that he wore the jacket knowing that there were words on it and that the words were meant to inform the public of his strong feelings against the Vietnam War and the draft. He was accused of maliciously and willfully disturbing the peace and quiet of the neighborhood by offensive conduct, was subsequently convicted, and given a 30-day jail sentence. His sentence was affirmed by the California Court of Appeals. The California Supreme Court declined to review the case.

SUMMARY OF ARGUMENTS

Cohen's attorneys argued that the action of merely wearing clothing had no tendency to cause others to commit violence. Just because the words may be hostile or offensive to others does not deprive Cohen of his right of free speech. Although political speech may be profane, the First Amendment applies equally to offensive and nonoffensive speech.

The state of California argued that the Supreme Court did not have jurisdiction because this was solely a state concern. They further argued that persons who want to protest or promote a view have a right to do so but it must be balanced against other public interests. Freedom of speech is not abridged by legislation making certain conduct illegal. They further argued that the state has an interest to protect the welfare of children and see to it that they are safeguarded from abuses.

DECISION

In a 5 to 4 vote, Justices John Harlan, William Brennan, Potter Stewart, William O. Douglas, and Thurgood Marshall reversed Cohen's conviction. Justice Blackmun, Chief Justice Burger, Justice Black, and Justice White dissented. Justice Harlan wrote that while Cohen's jacket may be vulgar, it clearly used words to convey a message to the public. There was no conduct involved; he was convicted solely for speaking in a constitutionally protected way. Justice Harlan wrote that the fact Cohen was arrested in the courthouse had no bearing on the decision. The statute made no distinction between locations. Additionally, Harlan found that in order for the state to have some power to prohibit an obscene expression, the expression must be in some way erotic. The words on his jacket, while perhaps offensive to members of the Selective Service System, could hardly be considered a stimulant. Further, Justice Harlan wrote that the words were not addressed to anyone in particular and were not likely to provoke any violent reaction. There was no personal insult intended. The jacket may have been distasteful, but people could simply avert their eyes to avoid looking at his jacket: "One cannot lose sight of the fact that in what otherwise might seem a trifling and annoying instance of individual distasteful abuse of a privilege, these fundamental societal values are truly implicated." While the particular four-letter word being litigated here is distasteful, it is nevertheless true that one man's vulgarity is another man's lyric. The Court cannot overlook the fact that words convey ideas and that ideas also contain emotions. Words are chosen for their emotion as well as their intellectual force. Simply banning certain words is unconstitutional because that would lead to the banning of the expression of unpopular opinions.

Justice Blackmun wrote the dissent, which was joined by Chief Justice Burger, Justice Hugo Black, and Justice Byron White. The dissent may be summarized as viewing Cohen's jacket as immature conduct and not as speech.

AFTERMATH

Cohen expanded the constitutional protection for provocative thoughts. The Court subsequently invalidated a number of breach of peace statutes.

SIGNIFICANCE

By this decision the Court expanded the definition of free speech and found that language can be considered obscene only when it is linked with sex.

RELATED CASES

Whitney v. California, 274 U.S. 357 (1927)

Tinker v. Des Moines Independent Community School District, 393 U.S. 503 (1969)

Roth v. U.S., 354 U.S. 476 (1957)

RECOMMENDED READING

William Cohen, *A Look Back at Cohen v. California*, 34 UCLA Law Review 1595 (1987).

Daniel A. Farber, *Civilizing Public Discourse: An Essay on Professor Bickel, Justice Harlan, and the Enduring Significance of Cohen v. California*, Duke Law Journal 283 (1980).

Wind, Wabun. *The People's Lawyers*. New York: Holt, Reinhart and Winston, 1973.

Case Title: *Cole v. Richardson*

Alternate Case Title: The "Loyalty Oath" Case

Legal Citation: 405 U.S. 676

Year of Decision: 1971

KEY ISSUES

Is a Massachusetts statute that requires public employees to take an oath that they will uphold the state and federal constitutions, and oppose the overthrow of the government, constitutionally permissible?

HISTORY OF THE CASE

Lucretia Richardson was hired as a research sociologist by the Boston State Hospital. Dr. Jonathan Cole was a superintendent at the hospital. Richardson was asked to take the oath required of all public employees in Massachusetts. A Massachusetts statute required all public employees to swear, "I will uphold and defend the Constitution of the United States of America and the Constitution of the Commonwealth of Massachusetts [and] oppose the overthrow of the government of the United States of America or of this Commonwealth by force, violence or any illegal or unconstitutional method."

Richardson refused to take the oath due to a belief that it violated the U.S. Constitution. She was released from employment at the hospital until she subscribed to the oath. She subsequently filed a complaint in the U.S. District Court for the District of Massachusetts, which upheld the first part of the oath but struck down the "oppose and overthrow" language as vague, because it could be interpreted as requiring an undefined action in the face of a revolution. Appellants appealed to the U.S. Supreme Court.

SUMMARY OF ARGUMENTS

Richardson argued that the statute was void for vagueness, its provisions were inconsistent with the First Amendment, and it did not provide for a hearing prior to the determination not to hire a person based on the refusal to take the oath.

Cole argued that the provisions of the oath were not inconsistent with the First Amendment and did not violate due process.

DECISION

Justice Burger wrote the 4-3 opinion for the Court joined by Justices White, Blackmun, and Stewart.

He held that the Massachusetts oath was constitutionally permissible and sufficiently clear. Justice Burger also held that the "uphold and defend" clause was permissible as a paraphrase of the constitutional oath. He stated that it was not necessary for an oath to have the same language as that in the Constitution and that the "uphold and defend" language was indistinguishable from the "preserve, protect and defend" language Article II, section 1, clause 8 of the U.S. Constitution.

Regarding the "oppose the overthrow" language, Justice Burger found that it was not designed to require specific action in defense of the government and did not deprive an oath taker of any constitutional right. Instead, he believed its purpose was to assure that those in positions of public trust would commit themselves to live by the government's constitutional processes. In disagreeing with the lower court, Justice Burger found that the "oppose and overthrow" language meant nothing more than the first part of the oath: It was a promise not to participate in the violent overthrow of the government.

Justice Burger further declared that the oath was not void for vagueness and that the only punishment in the statute was perjury, which required a knowing and willful falsehood. He argued that the danger of punishment without fair notice, or by mere prosecution, was removed. He added that there had not been a prosecution under the statute since 1948—the statute's date of enactment—and that there were no threats or possibilities of prosecution under the statute.

Although Justice Burger acknowledged that "neither federal nor state government could condition employment on taking oaths that impinged on rights guaranteed by the First and Fourteenth Amendments," he found that since the Massachusetts statute did not ask prospective employees about their own opinions, it did not interfere with their freedom of political views. Finally, Justice Burger maintained that there was no constitutionally protected right to overthrow a government by force, violence, or illegal or unconstitutional means. Therefore, there was no requirement that a person refusing to take the Massachusetts oath be granted a hearing for the determination of other facts before being released from employment.

A concurring opinion by Justice Stewart and White considered whether the oath impinged upon conscience or belief and concluded that it did not. Justice Douglas wrote a dissenting opinion. Citing *Board of Education v. Barnette* (1943), he expressed a general opposition to loyalty oaths. He characterized them as "tools of the tyranny" aimed at "coercing and controlling the minds of men" and therefore "odious to a free people." He stated that the oath required that appellee "oppose" that which she had a constitutional right to advocate.

Justice Marshall also wrote a dissenting opinion, which was joined by Justice Brennan. He agreed with Justice Douglas's belief concerning the evils of loyalty oaths and the relationship between a constitutionally patterned support oath and expanded loyalty oaths. Justice Marshall drew a careful line between the two and stated that minimal oaths were tolerated as an expression of the idea that public employees would abide by the law in the performance of their duties. On the other hand, Justice Marshall felt that more expansive oaths were highly suspect and were justified only in an emergency. He saw the oaths as possible instruments "of thought control and a means of enforcing complete political conformity," and believed that the government had only limited power to "force its citizens to perform symbolic gestures of loyalty."

AFTERMATH

In *Cole*, the Court for the first time clearly distinguished between the permissible sort of support oath, and unconstitutional oaths that conditioned employment on the relinquishment of rights to political beliefs and associations secured by the First Amendment.

SIGNIFICANCE

The Court developed several tests in *Cole* that an oath requirement must meet. An employer could not condition employment upon taking oaths that impinge upon rights guaranteed by the First and Fourteenth Amendments; the oath could not contain a promise that one had not engaged in or would not engage in protected speech activities or associations, and it could not be so vague that "men of common intelligence must necessarily guess at its meaning and differ as to its application." In the 1960s, the Court often invalidated state and federal loyalty programs on the grounds of vagueness or overbreadth.

RELATED CASES

Connell v. Richardson, 405 U.S. 676 (1972)

Knight v. Board of Regents, 390 U.S. 36 (1968)

Wieman v. Updegraff, 344 U.S. 183 (1952)

RECOMMENDED READING

Anthony G. Amsterdam, *The Void-for-Vagueness Doctrine in the Supreme Court*, 109 University of Pennsylvania Law Review 67 (1960).

Note, *The First Amendment Overbreadth Doctrine*, 83 Harvard Law Review 844 (1970).

※

Case Title: *Cox v. Louisiana*

Alternate Case Title: The "Courthouse Protest of Segregated Lunch Counters" Case

Legal Citation: 379 U.S. 536

Year of Decision: 1965

∼

KEY ISSUES

Can a state convict a demonstrator for breach of the peace for leading a large group of students to a courthouse singing, clapping, and cheering, but otherwise remaining peaceful? Does a state have the right to regulate the use of city streets and other facilities to assure the safety and convenience of the people of free speech and assembly?

HISTORY OF THE CASE

Cox was an ordained minister and field secretary of the Congress of Racial Equality. He led approximately 2,000 black students in a peaceful civil rights protest of segregation generally, and more specifically, of the recent arrest of 23 black students who had picketed stores that maintained segregated lunch counters. The protest occurred across the street from the local courthouse, which contained the jail holding the 23 previously arrested students. The sheriff deemed statements made by Cox to "go eat at the segregated lunch counters" as "inflammatory" and ordered the demonstrators to disperse. The protestors ignored

the police. The police responded by firing tear gas, which caused the demonstrators to leave. Cox was arrested the next day and later convicted of breach of the peace, obstructing public passageways, and picketing before a courthouse. The Louisiana Supreme Court affirmed the convictions.

SUMMARY OF ARGUMENTS

Cox invoked the "clear and present danger" doctrine, which states that speech inciting unlawful action falls outside the First Amendment's protection to support his argument that the Louisiana disturbing the peace statute could not constitutionally be applied to his conduct. Cox invoked the "clear and present danger" doctrine to support his argument that the Louisiana disturbing the peace statute could not constitutionally be applied to his conduct. The disturbing the peace statute provided that if a person intended to cause a breach of the peace or the circumstances were such that a breach would occur and the person congregated with others in or upon a public place and refused to move when ordered to so, the person violated the law. He also argued that the statute concerning obstructing public passages was an unconstitutional infringement on freedom of speech and assembly. The obstructing public passages statute made it a violation to obstruct a public way by restraining traffic.

The state argued that the demonstrators' singing and cheering converted a peaceful demonstration into a riotous one in violation of its constitutional "disturbing the peace" statute. The state also argued that the conviction of the demonstrators should have been upheld because the demonstration may have attracted violence.

DECISION

Justice Goldberg wrote the unanimous opinion for the Court, which overturned Cox's conviction for breach of the peace. Goldberg held that Louisiana deprived Cox of his rights of free speech and free assembly in violation of the First and Fourteenth Amendments in arresting and convicting him under the circumstances disclosed by the record. He further held that the breach of peace statute was unconstitutionally vague, and that Baton Rouge's practice of giving local officials complete discretion in regulating the streets for parades and meetings abridged Cox's freedom of speech and assembly in violation of the First and Fourteenth Amendments.

Justice Goldberg observed at the onset that the Court was required to independently examine the record, as in EDWARDS V. SOUTH CAROLINA. He did not want to be bound completely by state court factual determinations on essential issues because of the constitutional rights at stake and the fear of hindering federal law by distorted state fact finding. Justice Goldberg then found that Cox's call for the demonstrators to "sit in" did not change the demonstration from its protected character, nor was there any conduct that the state could have prohibited as a breach of the peace.

Justice Goldberg rejected the state's contention that the convictions were valid since "violence was about to erupt." He did not find any indication that the demonstrators themselves were violent or threatened violence, nor were they "hostile, aggressive, or unfriendly." He also argued that there was no indication from the white onlookers across the street that they threatened violence, and, in any event, there was adequate police protection to handle the crowd.

The Court rejected the notion that the First and Fourteenth Amendments afforded the same kind of freedom to those who communicated via marching and picketing as those who communicated their ideas through "pure speech" in addressing the public forum issue. The Court stated that it did not violate the First or Fourteenth Amendments for officials to make conduct, carried out through language, illegal. However, the Court concluded that because the record disclosed that city officials had allowed other "meetings" and "parades" to take place that had obstructed traffic, the Court had no occasion to consider the uniform and nondiscriminatory application of the statute, which forbade access to public streets and buildings for parades and meetings. The Court actually invalidated the statute under the doctrine of Lovell v. Griffin, overturning the conviction on technical grounds, although the Court suggested that the statute was constitutional both on its face and as applied. Justice Goldberg stated that the state had a legitimate interest in protecting its judicial system from the pressures that picketing near it could create. He did not feel that the statute infringed upon constitutionally protected free speech or assembly and as stated above, he saw the instant issue as "expression mixed [with] conduct," not "a pure form of expression such as a newspaper comment." Thus, Justice Goldberg concluded that the facts of Cox were very similar to Edwards, in which demonstrators sang, clapped their hands, and stomped their feet, and a very far cry from FEINER VS. NEW YORK, in which derogatory comments were made about the President and local political officials and an attempt was made to arouse the blacks against the whites.

Justices Black, Clark, and White filed separate opinions concurring in the Court's disposition of the breach of the peace conviction.

AFTERMATH

Later decisions did not stick to Cox's distinction between speech and conduct. In Grayned v. Rockford, 408 U.S. 104 (1972), for example, the Court ruled that peaceful demonstrations in public places are protected by the First Amendment, subject to reasonable time, place, and manner regulations. In Grayned, the Court focused on whether the expression was incompatible with the normal activity of a particular place, rather than whether an expression was conduct or pure speech.

SIGNIFICANCE

Cox is an example of the Court's distinction between communicative "conduct" and "pure speech," with the Court reversing a breach of peace conviction of a civil rights demonstrator who refused to obey a police order to disperse despite the potential for a disturbance involving onlookers.

RELATED CASES

Edwards v. South Carolina, 372 U.S. 229 (1963)

Feiner v. New York, 340 U.S. 315 (1951)

RECOMMENDED READING

Bollinger, Lee. The Tolerant Society: Freedom of Speech and Extremist Speech in America. New York: Oxford University Press, 1986.

Emerson, Thomas. The System of Freedom of Expression. New York: Random House, 1970.

Case Title: De Jonge v. Oregon

Alternate Case Title: The "Right of Petition Clause" Case

Legal Citations: 299 U.S. 353; 57 S.Ct. 255

Year of Decision: 1937

KEY ISSUES

Does a state statute prohibiting criminal syndicalism, the advocation of the use of crime or violence or sabotage to effect change in government or industry, violate the right of peaceable assembly protected by the First Amendment?

HISTORY OF THE CASE

The appellant, Dirk De Jonge, assisted in conducting a meeting held under the auspices of the Communist Party. The meeting was open to the public and was concerned primarily with a continuing maritime strike, allegedly unlawful raids on workers' halls and homes, and the shooting of a striking longshoreman by local police. No one at the meeting advocated criminal syndicalism or any other unlawful conduct. Defendant was convicted under a provision of Oregon's Criminal Syndicalism Law declaring it unlawful for any person to assist "in conducting a meeting" of any organization that advocates criminal syndicalism. The state courts sustained De Jonge's conviction after finding that the Communist Party had advocated criminal syndicalism at other times and places. De Jonge appealed to the U.S. Supreme Court.

SUMMARY OF ARGUMENTS

De Jonge argued that the Oregon statute, as applied to him, for merely assisting at a meeting called by the Communist Party at which nothing unlawful was done or advocated, violated the due process clause of the Fourteenth Amendment.

The state of Oregon argued that the Communist Party was an organization that advocated criminal syndicalism in general and that general advocacy made De Jonge's participation in a meeting held by the Communist Party a criminal act.

DECISION

The Court invalidated De Jonge's conviction. Chief Justice Hughes wrote the opinion for the Court that the right to peacefully assemble was guaranteed by the Fourteenth Amendment. He stated that the legislature could intervene against abusive speech only by dealing with the abusive speech itself. The state could not make the peaceful assembly of persons for lawful discussion criminal, nor prohibit such meetings, and persons helping with the conduct of such meetings could not be made criminals for doing so.

Chief Justice Hughes wanted to direct the inquiry to the purpose of the meeting, not the guise under which the meeting was held. He insisted that the Court decide whether the speech went beyond that which was protected by the Constitution, not concern itself with the relations of the speakers. He argued that a right could be protected by more than one constitutional provision. Chief Justice Hughes concluded that the state could not use the mere participation in a peaceful assembly and lawful public discussion as the basis for a criminal charge.

AFTERMATH

The same year, a divided Court also ruled in favor of a black communist organizer in Georgia who had been convicted in 1933 of "attempting to incite to insurrection" under Georgia law (See *Herndon v. Lowry* [1937]). The Court would later use a "clear and present danger" test as the appropriate test for a variety of First Amendment issues.

SIGNIFICANCE

By implication, *De Jonge* overruled *United States v. Cruikshank*, 92 U.S. 542 (1875), which found that First Amendment right to assembly and the Second Amendment right to bear arms were not protected by the Fourteenth Amendment. However, *De Jonge* did more to muddle than clarify the law governing subversive advocacy. While *De Jonge* proclaimed the right to assemble and peaceably discuss political issues was protected, it also indicated that the right to assemble could be abused. However, the Court did not identify where the line would be drawn between protected speech and assembly and speech and assembly that transcended the bounds of the First Amendment, allowing legislative intervention. This was the first time that the freedom to assemble was made applicable to the states by means of the due process clause of the Fourteenth Amendment.

RELATED CASES

Herndon v. Lowry, 301 U.S. 242 (1937)

Terminiello v. Chicago, 337 U.S. 1 (1949)

RECOMMENDED READING

Glenn S. Howard, *Comment, Patronage Dismissals: Constitutional Limits and Political Justifications,* 41 Chicago Law Review 297 (1974).

Sunstein, Cass R. *Democracy and the Problem of Free Speech.* New York: The Free Press, 1993.

Case Title: *Dennis v. United States*

Alternate Case Title: Communist Conspiracy Case

Legal Citation: 341 U.S. 494

Year of Decision: 1951

KEY ISSUES

Does the application of the Smith Act, an act punishing the advocacy of the overthrow of the U.S. government by force or violence, violate the First and Fifth Amendments?

HISTORY OF THE CASE

The petitioners, members of the Communist Party, were found guilty in federal district court of advocating "a successful overthrow of the existing order by force and violence and intended to initiate a violent revolution whenever the propitious occasion appeared." The Second Circuit Court of Appeals affirmed and the case went to the Supreme Court.

SUMMARY OF ARGUMENTS

The appellants, leaders of the Communist Party in the United States, argued that the provisions of the Smith Act violated the First and Fifth Amendments of the Constitution by impairing the right to free speech and by insufficiently advising persons of the limitations on advocacy activities. The appellants contended that the statute was invalid because it prohibited academic discussion and that they had the right to advocate a particular political theory as long as the advocacy did not create immediate dangers.

The appellee, the United States, argued that the government had a right to safeguard the security of the United States and the Smith Act did not violate the First and Fifth Amendments.

DECISION

The Smith Act requires as proof of criminal purpose an intent to overthrow the government by force and violence. Government is protected not from change by "peaceable, lawful and constitutional means," but from change by violence, revolution, and terrorism. The Court held that the Communist Party is an organization of conspiracy with sufficient "evil" that Congress has a right to prevent it and justify the application of the Smith Act under the First and Fifth Amendments.

Chief Justice Vinson wrote for the majority, finding the Smith Act "directed at advocacy, not discussion. Peaceful discussions were valid being of no threat to the community." Justice Frankfurter concurred, stressing the need to balance conflicting interests.

Justice Black wrote in dissent that the act could be considered limited to the Communist Party, and that a person should be punished for his actions, not his beliefs.

AFTERMATH

Dennis went to prison in 1951, but upon his release, he resumed his participation in Communist Party activities. This case exemplifies the Court's deference to Congress in the area of speech, the real fear of the communist threat in the 1950s, and a limited approach to the First Amendment, allowing government to restrict speech to avoid danger.

SIGNIFICANCE

Dennis upheld the constitutionality of the Smith Act thereby allowing a number of conspiracy convictions. It was thought that the supposed communist threat touched the heart of our system of freedom of speech and for a time blocked the growth of the prevailing "clear and present danger" test for evaluating laws regulating political speech. *Dennis* also helped the government justify its power to investigate the Communist Party.

RELATED CASES

Brandenberg v. Ohio, 395 U.S. 444 (1969)

Scales v. United States, 367 U.S. 203 (1961)

Yates v. United States, 354 U.S. 298 (1957)

RECOMMENDED READING

Belknap, Michael R. *Cold War Political Justice.* Westport, Conn.: Greenwood Press, 1977.

Berns, Walter F. *Freedom, Virtue and the First Amendment.* Chicago: Gateway Editions, 1963.

Emerson, Thomas I. *The System of Freedom of Expression.* New York: Random House, 1970.

Wallace Mendelson. *"Clear and Present Danger"—From* Schenck *to* Dennis, 52 Columbia Law Review 313–333 (1952).

❧

Case Title: *Edwards v. South Carolina*

Alternate Case Title: The "Anti-Segregation Protest–Peaceful Breach of the Peace" Case

Legal Citations: 372 U.S. 229; 83 S.Ct. 680

Year of Decision: 1963

❧

KEY ISSUES

Does arresting and convicting a group of people for marching peacefully on a sidewalk to protest discrimination violate their constitutionally protected rights of free speech, free assembly, and freedom to petition?

HISTORY OF THE CASE

A group of 187 black high school and college students met at the Zion Baptist Church in Columbia, South Carolina. At about noon, they walked in an orderly manner to the South Carolina State House in groups of 15, carrying placards with such messages as "I am proud to be a Negro" to protest discrimination. Subsequently, a crowd of about 300 onlookers gathered, none of whom caused or threatened any trouble. The protest did not interfere significantly with vehicular or pedestrian traffic and there was adequate police protection at the scene at all times. Police warned the students to disperse within 15 minutes. When they did not, and instead sang religious songs while clapping their hands and stamping their feet, they were arrested. They were convicted in a magistrate's court in Columbia, South Carolina, for breaching the peace. Their convictions were affirmed by the South Carolina Supreme Court. The U.S. Supreme Court agreed to consider the claim that these convictions could not be squared with the Fourteenth Amendment of the U.S. Constitution.

SUMMARY OF ARGUMENTS

The petitioners, 187 black students including Edwards, contended that there was a complete absence of any evidence of the commission of breach of the peace, and that they were thus denied one of the most basic elements of due process of law. They also argued that their arrest, conviction, and punishment violated their rights of free speech, assembly, and right to petition.

The state argued that by failing to disperse after being warned, the petitioners violated the common law offense of breach of the peace.

DECISION

Justice Stewart wrote the decision for the Court holding that the arrest, conviction, and punishment of the students for breach of the peace by marching peacefully to publicize their dissatisfaction with discriminatory actions against African Americans infringed their constitutionally protected rights of free speech, free assembly, and freedom to petition for redress of their grievances.

After making "an independent examination" of the record, the Court found that the petitioners had exercised their basic constitutional rights in their "most pristine and classic form." The Court, in comparing the instant case to *FEINER V. NEW YORK* (1951), where a speaker attempted to get the blacks to fight with the whites and the crowd was unruly, noted that here there was no violence nor threat of violence either by the petitioners or the crowd. The Court also recognized the sufficient police protection in case of disorder. Therefore, the Court believed that given the facts of the case, petitioners had been convicted based upon the content of their expressions, which were against the views of the majority of the community and which attracted a crowd necessitating police protection. The Court then stated that the Constitution did not permit a state to make the peaceful expression of unpopular views criminal.

Justice Stewart concluded that the South Carolina courts defined a criminal offense so as to permit conviction if one's speech "stirred people to anger, invited public dispute, or brought about a condition of unrest." These grounds, Justice Stewart stated, were insufficient to sustain the petitioners' conviction.

Justice Clark was the sole dissenter. He rejected the Court's distinction of *Feiner,* and insisted that the demonstration created a much greater danger of violence and disorder. He believed that the town official's actions may have prevented a catastrophe. He saw the police officers' actions as reasonable, even if they overestimated the imminence of danger, to avoid a public fight. Justice Clark felt that the petitioners' response to the officer's "reasonable" requests were defiant and uncooperative. He opposed making police officers wait until a riot erupts before being able to act.

AFTERMATH

Many critics felt that *Edwards v. South Carolina* was the height of the "speech-protective" phase of the forum doctrine in which the Court raised its level of scrutiny for speech occurring in traditional public forums. However, speech protective public forum doctrine was greatly restricted beginning with *Perry Education Ass'n v. Perry Local Educator's Ass'n* (1983), in which the Court focused on the nature of the forum in which the expression occurred, instead of the type of regulation involved. The Court identified three levels of public forums in *Perry:* traditional public forums such as streets and parks, public forums designated by the state, and public forums that were not traditional or designated. Speech in areas not classified as traditional public forums received more restrictive treatment.

SIGNIFICANCE

Edwards v. South Carolina effectively overruled *Feiner v. New York,* 340 U.S. 315 (1951), in which the Court assumed that the police could restrain the speaker instead of protecting the speaker from the hostile audience. After *Edwards,* the assumption was that the police had a constitutionally imposed duty to protect the speaker from the hostile audience.

RELATED CASES

Cox v. Louisiana, 379 U.S. 536 (1965)

Gregory v. City of Chicago, 394 U.S. 111 (1969)

Terminiello v. Chicago, 337 U.S. 1 (1949)

RECOMMENDED READING

Kalven, Harry. *The Negro and the First Amendment.* Columbus: Ohio State University Press, 1965.

Thomas Scanlon, *A Theory of Freedom of Expression,* 1 Philosophy & Public Affairs 204 (1972).

Case Title: *Federal Communications Commission v. League of Women Voters*

Legal Citation: 468 U.S. 364

Year of Decision: 1984

KEY ISSUES

Does an act that bans television and radio stations from "editorializing" infringe on the First Amendment right of free speech?

HISTORY OF THE CASE

The Public Broadcasting Act of 1967 was a part of Congress's program to create an alternative to commercial broadcast programming. The act established the Corporation for Public Broadcasting, a nonprofit corporation authorized to disburse federal funds in support of noncommercial television and radio stations that offer educational programming. A section of the act forbade any noncommercial station that received federal funds from the Corporation for Public Broadcasting from "engaging in editorializing." The constitutionality of this section was challenged by Pacifica Foundation (a nonprofit corporation that owned several stations that received funds from the Corporation for Public Broadcasting), the League of Women Voters of California, and a congressman.

SUMMARY OF ARGUMENTS

The Federal Communications Commission (FCC) argued that the ban was necessary to protect noncommercial educational broadcasting stations from being coerced into serving as vehicles for government propaganda because they receive government funds, and to prevent the stations from being controlled by interest groups wishing to express their viewpoints.

The League of Women voters argued that the act infringed upon the fundamental right protected by the First Amendment—freedom of speech. In addition they argued that the act was aimed at suppressing in these venues a specific type of speech, with the aim of shaping the public debate and limiting the discussion of controversial topics.

DECISION

Justice Brennan, writing for five of the justices, held that the act was invalid because the state interest cited to support the infringement of First Amendment rights was "not sufficiently substantial or are not served in a sufficiently limited manner to justify the substantial abridgment of important journalistic freedoms which the First Amendment jealously protects." He reached the conclusion by applying heightened scrutiny to analyze the act in question.

Under heightened scrutiny, the act would be constitutional only if it served a compelling state interest, an interest a state is obliged to protect, and the means of achieving this interest were narrowly tailored. Brennan noted that because of unique considerations that are involved in broadcast regulation, the Court had held in previous cases that the state interest does not necessarily have to be compelling, but the means of regulation be narrowly tailored to advance the government's interest.

The Court held that the ban in this case was invalid because it prohibited the type of speech that the Court had deemed to be the most in need of protection. The ban targeted editorial speech, which largely addresses issues of public concern, and which Brennan stated was "at the heart of First Amendment protection." In addition, the act banned speech based solely on its content. To determine whether the content was "editorial" in nature the management would have to screen the content of all messages and programs to be conveyed over the air. To that end, management would control views that were expressed to the public and control and shape the debate on issues of public concern. Brennan cited *Consolidated Edison Co. v. Public Service Commission* (1980), a decision in which struck down the regulation of

the content of utility bill inserts, as authoritative on this issue: "a regulation of speech that is motivated by nothing more than a desire to curtail expression of a particular point of view on controversial issues of general interest is the purest example of a 'law . . . abridging the freedom of speech, or of the press.'" Brennan noted that the section of the act in question "singles out noncommercial broadcasters and denies them the right to address their chosen audience on matters of public importance." In addition, Brennan said the ban was not tailored sufficiently to protect against the harms that the government stated it was trying to prevent.

There were two dissenting opinions in this case. Justice Rehnquist, joined by Justices Burger and White, stated that the noncommercial broadcasters had agreed to the conditions set forth in the act, including the prohibition of "editorial" speech, when they accepted the payment from the Corporation for Public Broadcasting. In addition, he felt that the act in question codified a rational decision on the part of Congress not to let managers "promulgate [their] own views on the air at the taxpayers' expense."

Justice Stevens in his dissent argued that the legislators of the act had a legitimate concern to protect and prohibit the government from exercising control over what is broadcast. In that the act guarded against the grave evil of governmental interference, he would have found the statute valid.

AFTERMATH

The doctrine established in this case—where there is a compelling interest to infringe on First Amendment rights, the means to accomplish this goal must be narrowly tailored—has been used to challenge other overbroad and vague restrictions on journalistic freedom. This decision has given stations the ability to editorialize without the fear of sanction; has allowed noncommercial stations to be more straightforward in the expression of editorial opinions; and has allowed stations to make ideological perspectives a source of programming. In practice, broadcasters state that editorials represent the opinion of management, and they must provide equal time to individuals who disagree.

SIGNIFICANCE

This was one in a line of decisions that loosened regulations imposed on public broadcasters. The

Court held that the public interest to be informed was not well served by restricting the right to editorialize because it diminished rather than increased the ability to broadcast controversial issues.

In addition, this decision sets the standard for the review of cases involving infringement of First Amendment rights. It rejects the notion that Congress needs only a rational basis and benign purpose to place restrictions on free speech as a condition of federal funding. The Court affirmed the notion that all content-based restrictions of expression are suspect and subject to heightened judicial scrutiny.

RELATED CASES

Buckley v. Valeo, 424 U.S. 1, 90 (1976)

Columbia Broadcasting System, Inc. v. FCC., 453 U.S. 367 (1981)

Consolidated Edison Co. v. Public Service Comm'n of N.Y., 447 U.S. 530 (1980)

New York Times v. Sullivan, 376 U.S. 254 (1964)

Regan v. Taxation with Representation, 461 U.S. 540 (1983)

Red Lion Broadcasting Co. v. F.C.C., 395 U.S. 367 (1969)

RECOMMENDED READING

L. Allyn Dixon, Jr., *Broadcasters' First Amendment Rights: A New Approach?,* 39 Vanderbilt Law Review 323 (1986).

Kathy Gregolet, *FCC v. League of Women Voters: Freedom of Public Broadcasters to Editorialize,* 39 University of Miami Law Review 573 (1985).

Rocio de Lourdes Cordoba, *To Air or Not to Err: The Threat of Conditioned Federal Funds for Indecent Programming on Public Broadcasting,* 42 Hastings Law Journal 635 (1991).

Benjamin Marcus, *FCC v. League of Women Voters: Conditions on Federal Funding That Inhibit Speech and Subject Matters Restrictions on Speech,* 71 Cornell Law Review 453 (1986).

Murray J. Rossini, *The Spectrum Scarcity Doctrine: A Constitutional Anachronism,* 39 Southwestern Law Journal 827 (1985).

The Supreme Court, 1983 Term: 2. Restrictions on Public Broadcasters' Rights to Editorialize, 98 Harvard Law Review 205 (November 1984).

Case Title: *Feiner v. New York*

Legal Citation: 340 U.S. 315

Year of Decision: 1951

KEY ISSUES

May a speaker be arrested because of the reaction engendered by his speech?

HISTORY OF THE CASE

Feiner made a speech on a street corner. A large crowd, which spilled into the street, gathered around to listen to his speech. During his speech, the purpose of which was to publicize a meeting of the Young Progressives of America and protest the revocation of a permit to hold this meeting in a public school, he used words with negative connotations to describe the president of the United States, the American Legion, the mayor of Syracuse, New York, and other political figures. He also made the statement, "The Negroes don't have equal rights; they should rise up in arms and fight for them." These statements excited several members of the gathered crowd. According to the police, the crowd became hostile and started pushing. After requesting twice that Feiner stop speaking, the police arrested him. He was convicted of disorderly conduct.

SUMMARY OF ARGUMENTS

Feiner argued that the arrest by the police for disorderly conduct infringed upon his First Amendment right of freedom of speech. He reasoned that the government, through the police as its agent, censored his speech. He argued that instead of arresting him, the police should have arrested the members of the crowd who were exhibiting excited behavior. To arrest him was to censor him and make him responsible for the actions of others. It also was an unlawful use of the police to censor views, according to the ruling in *Cantwell v. State of Connecticut* (1940).

The government argued the police had the responsibility to protect the peace, and the police officers acted to prevent disorder when it was clear the speech given by Feiner was likely to cause such a breach of the peace. Feiner was not arrested for the content of the speech or for making a speech, but rather for the reaction that this speech actually engendered.

DECISION

Justice Vinson, writing for six of the justices, reasoned that, based on *Cantwell v. State of Connecticut,* the arrest of Feiner was appropriate. He focused on the reasoning in *Cantwell,* which stated that "when clear and present danger of riot, disorder, interference with traffic upon the public streets, or other immediate threat to public safety, peace or order, appears, the power of the State to prevent or punish is obvious." The Court held that the conditions at the speech that Feiner was making was such that the conditions described in *Cantwell* were present and the police should have acted as they did.

The Court refuted Feiner's contention that the arrest was a mechanism to suppress his right to speak, in violation of the First Amendment. The Court found that, instead of merely expressing his views, Feiner was using his speech to incite a riot. In doing so the Court placed greater emphasis on preventing breaches of peace than on freedom of speech: "It is one thing to say that the police cannot be used as an instrument for the suppression of unpopular views, and another to say that, when as here the speaker passes the bounds of argument or persuasion and undertakes incitement to riot, they are powerless to prevent a breach of the peace."

Justice Black in his dissent argued that Feiner had in fact been sentenced to the penitentiary for lawfully expressing unpopular views. He argued that the Court should have reexamined the evidence presented at trial, to determine for itself the truth or falsity of the assertions and also to determine whether the Court was protecting constitutional guarantees. He said the majority's decision "makes a mockery of the free speech guarantees of the First and Fourteenth Amendments. The end result of affirmance here is to approve a simple and readily available technique by which cities and states can with impunity subject all speeches, political or otherwise, on streets or elsewhere, to the supervision and censorship of the local police."

In reconsidering the evidence presented at trial, Justice Black found that the asserted finding of an ensuing riot was exaggerated. He further argued that the responsibility of the police officers was to protect Feiner's right to speak. The police erred by shirking this responsibility when they arrested Feiner.

Justices Douglas and Minton dissented in a separate opinion. Justice Douglas reassessed the evidence presented at the trial and came to the same conclusion that Justice Black did: that there was no eminent danger of a riot starting because of Feiner's speech. In addition, he found that the right of speech is one of the fundamental rights in this society, which the police should work arduously to protect: "Public assemblies and public speech occupy an important role in American life. One high function of the police is to protect these lawful gatherings so that the speakers may exercise their constitutional rights."

AFTERMATH

The "fighting words" standard developed in CHAPLINSKY V. NEW HAMPSHIRE (1942) was transformed to a new standard: that the government may act to control or ban speech when it will cause a breach of the peace. The cases that followed *Feiner* have narrowed the "fighting words" doctrine to make government control over speech legitimate only when the words that are uttered will have a direct tendency to cause acts of violence by the person to whom, individually, the remark is directed. The Court now relies heavily on the circumstances surrounding the utterance to determine whether they were in fact "fighting words."

SIGNIFICANCE

This holding expanded on the fighting words doctrine established in *Chaplinsky v. New Hampshire,* in which the Court held that it was constitutional to ban works that ordinary people know are likely to cause a breach of the peace. By holding Feiner responsible for the reactions caused by his speech, the Court reaffirmed the ruling in *Chaplinsky* that words or speeches that cause hostile reaction are not protected by the First Amendment.

RELATED CASES

Cantwell v. State of Connecticut, 310 U.S. 296 (1940)

Chaplinsky v. New Hampshire, 315 U.S. 568 (1942)

Cohen v. California, 403 U.S. 15 (1971)

Edwards v. South Carolina, 372 U.S. 229 (1963)

Kunz v. People of State of New York, 340 U.S. 290 (1951)

Niemotko v. State of Maryland, 340 U.S. 268 (1951)

Sellers v. Johnson, 163 F.2d 877 (8th Cir. 1947)

RECOMMENDED READING

David G. Barnum, *Freedom of Assembly and the Hostile Audience in Anglo-American Law*, 29 American Journal of Comparative Law 59 (1981).

The Demise of the Chaplinsky Fighting Words Doctrine: An Argument for Its Interment, 106 Harvard Law Review 1129 (1993).

Franklyn S. Haiman, *How Much of Speech Is Free?*, The Civil Liberties Review 111 (winter 1975).

———. *Speech and Law in Free Society*. Chicago: University of Chicago Press, 1981.

Carlton L. Parhms, *Fighting Words and* R.A.V. v. City of St. Paul, Minnesota, 19 Southern University Law Review 461 (1992).

Martin Redish, *The Value of Free Speech*, 130 University of Pennsylvania Law Review 591 (1982).

Eve H. Lewin Wagner, *Heckling: A Protected Right or Disorderly Conduct?*, 60 Southern California Law Review 215 (1986).

Case Title: *First National Bank of Boston v. Bellotti*

Legal Citation: 435 U.S. 765

Year of Decision: 1978

KEY ISSUES

Is it a violation of the First Amendment and Fourteenth Amendments for a state to prohibit corporate expenditures to support the expression of views on an issue?

HISTORY OF THE CASE

Massachusetts had a statute that made it a criminal act, punishable by fine or imprisonment, for a corporation to make a contribution or expenditure "for the purpose of . . . influencing or affecting the vote on any question submitted to the voters, other than one materially affecting any of the property, business or assets of the corporation." The First National Bank of Boston, two national banking associations, and three business corporations wanted to spend money to support the publicizing of views opposing a referendum proposal to amend the Massachusetts Constitution. Francis Bellotti, the attorney general for the state of Massachusetts, threatened to prosecute the appellants under the statute if they did so. The subject of the referendum was a graduated personal income tax. The banks and corporations opposed the graduated personal income tax because they believed it would have a significant effect on their business. Specifically, the banks and corporations thought the tax would discourage executives and other business personnel from working and settling in Massachusetts and would discourage corporations from settling in Massachusetts. It was thought that this would adversely affect bank loans and deposits. The action involved the challenge by these various groups to the constitutionality of the criminal statute.

The case was submitted to a single justice of the Supreme Judicial Court of Massachusetts upon agreed facts. The issue for resolution was the effect that the proposed statute would have on the appellants' businesses. The judgment was reserved and the case was submitted to the full state supreme court. The state court held that the statute was constitutional because it acted in an area of fundamental First Amendment activities. The state court held that the rights of a corporation are limited to those that affect its business, property, or costs. The state court then rejected the claim of the First National Bank of Boston, et al. that the statute abridged their right to freedom of speech in violation of the First and Fourteenth Amendments.

SUMMARY OF ARGUMENTS

First National Bank of Boston, the national banking associations, and the business corporations involved argued that the statute violated their right to freedom of speech, their due process rights, and their equal protection rights. They argued that the statute violated the First Amendment by prohibiting the expression of views on an issue of public importance: the state not only prohibited speech but also targeted these specific groups to screen out certain positions from the public debate. In addition, they argued that their speech should not be excluded from First Amendment protection merely because of their status as corporations. They argued that the statute was unconstitutional on its face and as it would be applied to their proposed expenditures.

Bellotti, in his capacity as the attorney general for the state of Massachusetts, argued the right to freedom of speech is a personal right that does not apply to corporations. In addition, he argued that the particular statute at issue in no way adversely affected the interests of these entities because it prohibits contributions only in situations where the interests of these entities are not affected. Moreover, the state presented two reasons it regarded as compelling and supportive of restraint on corporate expenditures in this area: (1) the statute encouraged individuals to participate in government, which would avoid corruption and maintain public confidence in the electoral process; (2) the statute protected shareholders whose views may differ from those of the managers of the corporation.

DECISION

The first issue to be resolved by the Court was whether the action, by virtue of the referendum having been voted on, was no longer an issue. The Court held, relying on the case of *Southern Pacific Terminal Co. v. FCC*, that this was the type of action "capable of repetition, yet evading review." Under this standard the issue presented was in need of review.

The Court then turned to the issues and held that there was no support in the Constitution for the proposition stated by the Massachusetts Supreme Court that the First Amendment protection of expression of views of public importance does not extend from individuals to corporations, because a corporation cannot prove the effect such a prohibition will have on its interests. Using the logic employed by the Court in BUCKLEY V. VALEO, which indicated that a restriction on the amount of money one could spend on a political

communication during a campaign reduced expression, the Court found that the statute's restriction on corporate free speech infringed upon the First Amendment rights of corporations. The Court held that the expression of views of public importance "is the type of speech indispensable to decision making in a democracy, and this is no less true because the speech comes from a corporation rather than an individual. The inherent worth of the speech in terms of its capacity for informing the public does not depend upon the identity of the source." The Court went on to state that the legislature did not have authority to dictate the subject on which a person may speak and who may address a public issue.

The Court next noted that infringements on First Amendment protected rights are subject to strict scrutiny and to pass constitutional muster must be narrowly tailored to serve a legitimate government end. The Court held that the state does have a compelling interest in ballot measures to preserve the integrity of the process and prevent corruption; the corruption applicable to ballot measure campaigns could be proven by showing that the corporate advocacy threatened the democratic process by overwhelming the electorate and threatening the confidence of the citizenry in the government. If these criteria were met then the advocacy could be prevented. The Court in examining the facts found that this threat had not been presented by these corporations and that the political process was intact.

Last, the Court struck down the statute on the ground that it was both over- and underinclusive. It was overinclusive because it prohibited a corporation from supporting or opposing a measure even if the shareholders were in complete agreement with such actions; it was underinclusive in that it prohibited only corporate fund expenditure when the public issue became the subject of a referendum.

Justice Burger filed a concurring opinion.

Justice White, joined by Justices Brennan and Marshall, dissented. They argued that the statute was designed to protect First Amendment rights by preventing institutions who have amassed wealth from acquiring an unfair advantage in the political process, especially where there is a material connection between the statute at issue and the business of the corporation. In addition they argued that the statute protects the overriding interests of shareholders not to have to support the exposition of view by the managers of the corporation with which they may not agree.

Justice Rehnquist in his dissent argued that it was not required by the Fourteenth Amendment that a corporation be given the power of political speech.

AFTERMATH

The 1970s marked a change in the judicial perception of state statutory restrictions on corporate spending in ballot measure campaigns. This decision, with its sweeping language, allowed for the growth of corporate influence in the political process, most noticeably in the formation of political action committees whose agenda is to affect the views of others. The personification of the corporation and the simultaneous granting of the personal right to freedom of speech have led to the expanded involvement of corporations in the political process, restricted only in cases where this involvement poses an imminent danger to the democratic system.

Recent decisions of the Court have limited the sweeping language of the *Bellotti* decision and given legislatures more control over how corporations may influence politics through money.

SIGNIFICANCE

The Bellotti Court allowed for the expenditure of money by corporations on ballot measures and in the political process in line with the newly adopted theory that the democratic principles of unrestrained debate and the importance of a well-informed citizenry require such freedom of expression for corporation as well as individuals, and statutes that prohibit corporate political messages are impermissible means of restricting political expression.

RELATED CASES

Austin v. Michigan Chamber of Commerce, 110 S.Ct. 1391 (1990)

Buckley v. Valeo, 424 U.S. 1 (1976)

F.E.C. v. National Right to Work Committee, 459 U.S. 197 (1982)

F.E.C. v. Massachusetts Citizens for Life, 107 S.Ct. 616 (1986)

RECOMMENDED READING

Nicole Bremner Cásarez, *Corruption, Corrosion, and Corporate Political Speech*, 70 Nebraska Law Review 689 (1991).

Michael J. Garrison, *Corporate Political Speech, Campaign Spending, and First Amendment Doctrine*, 27 American Business Law Journal 163 (1989).

Paul Lansing and Gerald M. Sherman, *The "Evolution" of the Supreme Court's Political Spending Doctrine: Restricting Corporate Contributions to Ballot Measure Campaigns after* Citizens against Rent Control v. City of Berkeley, California, 8 Journal of Corporation Law 79 (1982).

Steven A. Mogck, *Constitutional Law—Substance Prevails over Form in Corporate Political Speech:* Austin v. Michigan Chamber of Commerce, 16 Journal of Corporation Law 341 (1991).

Case Title: *Gertz v. Robert Welch, Inc.*

Legal Citation: 418 U.S. 323

Year of Decision: 1974

KEY ISSUES

May a plaintiff recover damages from a media defendant who negligently publishes libelous statements? Do private individuals have to prove that a media defendant acted with actual malice? What types of damages can be recovered by a private individual from a media defendant when libelous statements are made?

HISTORY OF THE CASE

Robert Welch, Inc., published a periodical, *American Opinion*, which was described by the court to be "a monthly outlet for the views of the John Birch Society." *American Opinion* published an article that stated, among other statements, that Elmer Gertz, an attorney, was a "Communist-fronter," a "Leninist," a member of the "Intercollegiate Socialists Society," and a member of the "Marxist League for Industrial Democracy." Gertz filed a libel action against *American Opinion* seeking damages.

SUMMARY OF ARGUMENTS

Gertz argued that his right of privacy was wrongfully destroyed by Robert Welch, Inc. and that attorneys are specifically entitled to protection in their representation of clients. Gertz also argued that Robert Welch, Inc. acted with actual malice. Finally, Gertz argued that he was denied due process and a fair trial.

Robert Welch, Inc. argued that Gertz was a person covered by the *New York Times v. Sullivan* libel standard because he was a public official and a public figure. Robert Welch, Inc. further argued that the subject of its article was a matter of public interest. Robert Welch, Inc. denied that it acted with malice and argued that Gertz's right to privacy had not been destroyed, nor had Gertz been denied due process. Moreover, Robert Welch, Inc. argued that attorneys were not entitled to special protection.

The majority made a distinction between plaintiffs who were public individuals and those who were private individuals. The Court stated that public figures had to prove that a media defendant acted with actual malice in order to recover damages. The Court reasoned that since public figures, as opposed to private individuals, have greater access to mass media, they are able to quickly rebut any defamatory statements made against them. Additionally, public individuals have implicitly consented to the risk of having false statements made about them. They assume the burden of extreme public scrutiny, and actual malice must be proven in order for them to recover damages in any litigation. Conversely, private figures have not agreed to be in the center of the public attention and are not required to meet the more demanding standard of actual malice.

Various dissenting judges disagreed. One dissenting judge argued that strict liability should be imposed in these circumstances to protect the interest of private individuals. Another argued for absolute immunity for media defendants for any "discussion of public affairs." A final dissenting judge argued that actual malice should be proved by private and public individuals when the media published information of public or general interest.

DECISION

States may determine the appropriate standard of liability for a media defendant as long as they don't impose a strict liability standard. In other words, private individuals may recover damages from a media defendant who acts negligently, and they do not have to prove that a media defendant acted with actual malice. The Court stated that there is a "strong and legitimate state interest in compensating private individuals for injury to reputation." However, the Court also noted that states may allow damages only to compensate for the actual injury suffered by the plaintiff. Presumed and punitive damages are not allowed unless the plaintiff demonstrates that the media defendant acted with actual malice.

AFTERMATH

Gertz never conclusively solved whether a public individual has to prove actual malice in a defamation suit against any defendant or only against a defendant involved in the media. Language in the *Gertz* decision leads to the assumption that actual malice applies only to media defendants. Subsequent courts have split regarding whether the actual malice standard applies to nonmedia defendants.

SIGNIFICANCE

The *Gertz* decision established that public individuals must prove by clear and convincing evidence that the defendant acted with actual malice. Private individuals have a lower standard of proof.

The *Gertz* decision also overruled the Supreme Court's prior decision in *Rosenbloom v. Metromedia, Inc.*, 403 U.S. 29 (1971), which held that the actual malice standard extended to private citizens who were somewhat involved in matters of public interest. The *Gertz* decision turned the focus away from whether the alleged defamation or libel was a matter of public interest to the question of whether the citizen harmed was a private or public individual.

RELATED CASES

New York Times v. Sullivan, 376 U.S. 254 (1964)

Time, Inc. v. Hill, 385 U.S. 374 (1967)

Time, Inc. v. Firestone, 424 U.S. 448 (1976)

RECOMMENDED READING

Erik L. Collins, and J. Douglas Drushal. *The Reaction of the State Courts to* Gertz v. Robert Welch, Inc.,

28 Case Western Reserve Law Review 306–343 (1978).

Joel D. Eaton, *The American Law of Defamation through* Gertz v. Robert Welch, Inc. and Beyond: *An Analytic Primer,* 61 Virginia Law Review 1351–1451 (November 1975).

Stanley Godofsky, *Protection of the Press from Prior Restraint and Harassment under Libel Laws,* 29 University of Miami Law Review 462–476 (spring 1975).

Harry W. Stonecipher, and Robert Trager, *The Impact of* Gertz *on the Law of Libel,* 5 Journalism Quarterly 609–618 (winter 1976).

Case Title: *Ginsberg v. State of New York*

Legal Citation: 390 U.S. 629

Year of Decision: 1968

Key Issues

Does a New York criminal obscenity statute, which prohibits the sale to juveniles of material defined to be obscene on the basis of its appeal to them, violate the First Amendment right to expression of juveniles?

History of the Case

Ginsberg and his wife operated a luncheonette in which they sold stationery and magazines. Ginsberg was convicted of personally selling two "girlie" magazines to a 16-year-old boy on two days. New York Penal Law 484-h made it an offense "knowingly to sell . . . to" a minor under 17 "(a) any picture . . . which depicts nudity . . . and which is harmful to minors," and "(b) any . . . magazine which contains [such pictures] and which, taken as a whole, is harmful to minors." Ginsberg was tried and found guilty on both counts. The judge found that the magazines contained pictures that were harmful to minors because the quality of the representation was of the type that would appeal to the "prurient, shameful or morbid interest of minors" and was offensive to the prevailing standards within the adult community in terms of what is suitable for minors. He held that both sales constituted a violation of the New York statute.

The Supreme Court of Appeals affirmed his conviction and the New York Court of Appeals denied him leave to appeal.

Summary of Arguments

Ginsberg challenged the statute's constitutionality on several grounds. His primary argument was that the state did not have the power to define the material's obscenity on the basis of its appeal to minors and to exclude material defined in this way from the area of protected expression. Ginsberg argued that the constitutional freedom of expression granted to a citizen to read or see material concerned with sex cannot be made to depend on the age of the person.

The state argued that it had an interest in preventing the distribution of objectionable material to minors and that under its powers to protect the health, safety, and morals of the community it could bar the distribution to minors of material deemed suitable for adults. The state contended that two interests justified the statute. The first interest was based on the fact that the Constitution had been interpreted to recognize a parent's claim to authority in their household to direct the rearing of children as basic within the structure of society. The state went on to conclude that it is within the legislature's authority to support the parents by enacting laws designed to aid in the discharge of their responsibility to their children. The second interest is the state's independent interest in the well-being of minors in the state. To the extent that this is a valid interest, the only question that remains is whether the statute is rationally related to the type of material that is restricted.

Decision

Justice Brennan wrote the majority opinion and upheld the conviction of Ginsberg. He first noted that material which is protected for distribution to adults is not necessarily protected for minors: "The concept of obscenity or of unprotected matter may vary according to the group to whom the questionable material is directed or from whom it is quarantined." He went on to say that the state had an "exigent interest" in protecting minors from exposure to objectionable material:

"Because of the State's exigent interest in preventing distribution to children of objectionable material, it can exercise its power to protect the health, safety, welfare and morals of its community by barring the distribution to children of books recognized to be suitable for adults."

The Court rejected Ginsberg's argument that the state's regulation was an invasion of minors' constitutional freedoms. He noted that the statute at issue reflected the reality of the sexual interests of minors. Brennan concluded that it was clearly within the state's power to construct legislation in that manner: "That the State has power to make that adjustment seems clear, for we have recognized that even where there is an invasion of protected freedoms, the power of the state to control the conduct of children reaches beyond the scope of authority over adults."

Although Brennan noted that the legislature's conclusion that the prohibited literature "is a basic factor in impairing the ethical and moral development of our youth and a clear and present danger to the people of the state" is not an accepted scientific fact, it can be suppressed because obscenity is not protected expression. Brennan noted that the Court had to conclude only that it was not irrational to pass the statute at issue. He then concluded that it was not irrational to state that there is a relation between prohibiting the obscene material and fulfilling the objective of safeguarding minors.

Justice Stewart wrote a concurring opinion in which he stated that if one were to apply the First Amendment to this case without looking at the purpose of the amendment, then the statute would have to be nullified. He noted that the First Amendment is designed to protect free choice to read, see, and listen to whatever one wishes. He went on to reason that this presupposes the capacity of members to choose. When the expression occurs in a setting where the ability to choose is absent—where there is a captive audience—then a legislature may permissibly prohibit people from imposing their opinions on others. To the extent that the state may act in this manner, then he argued that they should likewise be able to regulate what children may be exposed to, as they too lack full capacity to choose: "I think a State may permissibly determine that, at least in some precisely delineated areas, a child—like someone in a captive audience—is not possessed of that full capacity for individual choice which is the presupposition of First Amendment guarantees." Based on this reasoning he concluded the statute did not on its face violate the First and Fourteenth Amendments.

Justice Douglas, with whom Justice Black concurred, dissented on the grounds that under the First Amendment that statute should be nullified. He stated that the First Amendment was designed to keep the state from becoming involved in censoring what material would be published and distributed, and that the statute at issue conflicted with this purpose. He went on to state the Court was not in the position to sit as censors and moreover not qualified to determine what qualifies as obscene material. He concluded that, short of a constitutional amendment that allowed the state to censor certain material, statutes such as the one at issue were unconstitutional.

Justice Fortas dissented on the grounds that the Court sidestepped its duty to define exactly what constituted obscene material for minors. He felt that in sidestepping this duty the Court avoided resolving whether Ginsberg was unfairly convicted: "By so doing the Court avoids the essence of the problem; for if the State's power to censor freed from the prohibitions of the First Amendment depends upon obscenity, and if obscenity turns on the specific content of the publication, how can we sustain the conviction here without deciding whether the particular magazines in question are obscene?"

He concluded that to apply a principle that a certain type of material is obscene and its distribution to minors must be regulated, the Court must first define the principle it is applying. While he agreed that the state may in the exercise of its police power differentiate between adults and children, it may not do so in an "arbitrary, freewheeling basis." He noted that Ginsberg, because of the lack of clarity about what constitutes obscenity in this case, was convicted without proof of fault and the result was a serious invasion of freedom.

AFTERMATH

A standard for what constitutes obscenity for minors has yet to be clearly defined. The Court has conflated the definition of obscenity established in *Ginsberg* with the standard for indecency, upholding prohibitions on the dissemination of merely indecent material to minors.

In the aftermath of this decision many states regulated material that would be exposed to minors under the notion that it would be "harmful to minors" and therefore could be regulated by the state under its power to regulate the safety and morals of its community. However, these statutes did not regulate display of materials harmful to minors. As a result states had to amend their statutes to capture not only the sale of these materials but also their display. Many constitutional challenges were brought against these amended statutes because of their overbreadth and vagueness.

SIGNIFICANCE

This case was in the progeny of ROTH V. UNITED STATES, in which the Court held that obscenity did not fall within the purview of the First Amendment protections of freedom of the press and speech. This is the first case in which the Court recognized the concept of variable obscenity. Using a variable obscenity standard, material is judged by its appeal and effect upon its primary audience. Under this theory material is not inherently obscene, but rather the determination of its obscenity varies with the circumstances of its dissemination. The concept of variable obscenity, because of its ambiguity, has not been used by the Supreme Court in recent years.

RELATED CASES

Board of Education, Island Trees Union Free School District No. 26 v. Pico, 457 U.S. 853 (1982)

Butler v. Michigan, 352 U.S. 380 (1957)

Erznoznik v. City of Jacksonville, 422 U.S. 205 (1975)

Roth v. United States, 354 U.S. 476 (1957)

RECOMMENDED READING

Anne L. Clark, *"As Nasty As They Wanna Be": Popular Music on Trial,* 65 New York University Law Review 1481 (1990).

Thomas Emerson, *Toward a General Theory of the First Amendment,* 72 Yale Law Journal 877 (1963).

Marion D. Hefner, *"Roast Pigs" and Miller-Light: Variable Obscenity in the Nineties,* University of Illinois Law Review 843 (1996).

Christopher W. Weller, *See No Evil: The Divisive Issue of Minors' Access Laws,* 18 Cumberland Law Review 141 (1987–1988).

Case Title: *Gitlow v. People of the State of New York*

Alternate Case Title: *Gitlow v. New York*

Legal Citation: 268 U.S. 652

Year of Decision: 1925

KEY ISSUES

Does a statute that defines and prohibits the advocacy of criminal anarchy violate the First Amendment guarantees of freedom of speech and press and the Fourteenth Amendment?

HISTORY OF THE CASE

Benjamin Gitlow was convicted with three others of the statutory crime of criminal anarchy. He was tried separately, convicted, and sentenced to imprisonment. He was indicted on two counts. The first charge was that he "advocated, advised and taught the duty, necessity and propriety of overthrowing and overturning organized government by force, violence and unlawful means." The second charge was that he had "printed, published and knowingly circulated and distributed a certain paper called 'The Revolutionary Age,' containing the writings set forth in the first count." His judgment was affirmed by both the appellate division and the court of appeals.

The statute at issue defined criminal anarchy as "the doctrine that organized government should be overthrown by force or violence, or by assassination of the executive head or of any executive officials of government of such doctrine either by word of mouth or writing." The statute prohibiting advocacy of criminal anarchy defined the criminal act as the advocacy, with writings or by word of mouth, of the duty, the necessity, or propriety of overthrowing or overturning organized government by force or violence. It also made

Freedom of Speech and Assembly ■ 393

it a crime to print, publish, edit, issue or knowingly circulate, sell, distribute, or publicly display any such book, paper, document, or written or printed matter in any form, containing or advocating the doctrine that organized government should be overthrown.

At trial no evidence was presented regarding the effect of the distribution of this material.

SUMMARY OF ARGUMENTS

Gitlow argued that the statute by its terms and as applied to his case violated the due process clause of the Fourteenth Amendment. He argued that as a matter of law the publication at issue did not contravene the statute. His primary argument rested upon two propositions: (1) that the liberty protected by the Fourteenth Amendment includes liberty of speech and the press; and (2) that liberty of expression, though not an absolute right, may be restricted only in circumstances in which there is necessary causal connection between the proscribed behavior and method of the restraint, thus the restraint must be justified by the circumstances surrounding the expression.

The state argued that the material disseminated by Gitlow and which he actively advocated violated the statute at issue. They further argued that it is within the legislative powers of the state to determine which utterances are inimical to the general welfare and involve danger to such a degree to justify the exercise of its police powers. In addition, they argued that this determination must be shown deference by the Court. It was established in *Mulger v. Kansas* (1887) that issues of the validity or constitutionality of a statute are to be decided presuming the statute's validity, which must be disproved by the plaintiffs. They argued that it is well established that cases should be decided on the principle that the state is the best judge of which regulations are in the best interest of public safety and welfare. Finally, they argued that they cannot reasonably be expected to wait until the peace has been breached until they may act to prevent certain behavior.

DECISION

Justice Sanford, writing for the majority, affirmed Gitlow's conviction, noting that the only issue litigated was "whether the statute, as construed and applied in this case, by the State courts, deprived the defendant of his liberty of expression in viola-

tion of the due process clause of the Fourteenth Amendment." To this issue he responded that the statue at issue was not a vague proscription of the general right of expression, but rather aimed at that speech which had the quality of inciting concrete action: "The statute does not penalize the utterance or publication of abstract 'doctrine' or academic discussion having no quality of incitement to any concrete action. . . . What it prohibits is language advocating, advising or teaching the overthrow of organized government by unlawful means. These words imply urging action."

He noted that the trial court applied this analysis and correctly found that material which advocates the violent overthrow of government qualifies as the type of speech that the state legitimately may proscribe: "The Manifesto, plainly, is neither the statement of abstract doctrine. . . . It advocates and urges in fervent language mass action which shall progressively foment industrial disturbances and through political mass strikes and revolutionary mass action overthrow and destroy organized parliamentary government." He reasoned that the document, which in some of its more controversial areas noted "the necessity of accomplishing the 'Communist Revolution' through militant and 'revolutionary Socialism,' based on 'the class struggle' and mobilizing the 'power of the proletariat in action,' through mass industrial revolts developing into mass political strikes and 'revolutionary mass action,' for the purpose of conquering and destroying the parliamentary state and establishing in its place . . . the system of Communist socialism," had the purpose of direct incitement.

Though the freedom of speech and the press has long been recognized as fundamental, it is not an absolute right. Justice Sanford noted that the state may, in the exercise of its police powers, punish those who abuse this right. This is especially true in those circumstances when the speech may "corrupt public morals, incite crime, or disturb the public peace."

The right of the state to exercise this power against those who advocate direct attacks on the state through force and violence is legitimate in situations that endanger the general welfare and involve danger of "substantive evil." Justice Sanford further argued that the state's use of police power should only be deemed illegitimate in circumstances when it is arbitrary and unreasonable.

This was not such a situation, as a publication that advocates the violent overthrow of the U.S. government "present[s] a sufficient danger of substantive evil to bring their punishment within the range of legislative direction."

Justice Sanford refuted Gitlow's assertion that the state should be forced to wait until the threat of danger is realized. He contended that if that were the accepted method, the right to proscribe behavior would come into effect simultaneously with the overthrow of government, in which neither the prosecution nor enforcement of the laws would be effective: "We cannot hold that the present statute is an arbitrary or unreasonable exercise of the police power of the State, unwarrantable infringing the freedom of speech or press; and we must and do sustain its constitutionality." Under this principle any utterance that in any way has a tendency to jeopardize public welfare and safety can be prohibited by the statute—no utterance is too trivial: "When the legislative body has determined generally, in the constitutional exercise of its discretion, that utterances of a certain kind involve such a danger of substantive evil that they may be punished, the question whether any specific utterance coming within the prohibited class is likely, in and of itself, to bring about the substantive evil, is not open to consideration. It is sufficient that the statute itself be constitutional and that the use of the language comes within the prohibition."

Justice Holmes wrote a dissenting opinion, which Justice Brandeis joined. He contended that the principle of free speech is included within the meaning of the Fourteenth Amendment as indicated by the use of the word "liberty." He argued that the "clear and present danger" test, established in SCHENCK V. UNITED STATES, should be applied. Under that test only words "of such a nature as to create a clear and present danger that they will bring about the substantive evils that [the State] has a right to prevent" can be regulated by the state. Under the *Schenck* test it was clear that Gitlow's advocacy and publication did not reach the level that allowed for proscription. Justice Holmes refuted the contention of the majority that the manifesto was more than a theory, and asserted that under the majority's definition every idea could be considered incitement. He concluded that Gitlow was indicted for the publication of this material and not for its propensity to produce a certain harm. He reasoned that Git-

low's publication merely presented a belief with fervor and the constitutionality of statements contained therein should not be judged by the fervency of their presentation: "If in the long run the beliefs expressed in proletarian dictatorship are destined to be accepted by the dominant forces of the community, the only meaning of free speech is that they should be given their chance and have their way."

AFTERMATH

The Court's treatment of state proscription of speech that the state seeks to regulate has varied. In the subversive advocacy context advocation of the overthrow of the government, the speech was suppressed because of its ability to effectively persuade the audience to act in a manner that the state considers "undesirable." The prohibition of certain viewpoints in the *Gitlow* case was absolute. In cases involving hostile audiences the limitations have been more limited in scope.

In later decisions the Court adopted the "clear and present danger" standard to gauge the appropriateness of state restrictions in various first amendment contexts. In BRANDENBURG V. OHIO (1969), the Court established the current rule regarding the validity of state restrictions on the right of free speech: a state may not restrict free speech of the press except where the expression of certain views is directed at inciting or producing imminent lawless and is likely to incite or produce such action.

SIGNIFICANCE

This law was used to prosecute Gitlow, a radical socialist, in response to the assassination of President McKinley and was intended for use against social anarchists.

Gitlow was the first case to address the extent to which First Amendment rights are incorporated within the fundamental rights and liberties protected by the due process clause of the Fourteenth Amendment. Justice Holmes's dissent in this case provided the mechanisms for establishing national standards for state and private behavior. It now serves as the mechanism by which citizens protect their rights against coercive state and private action.

RELATED CASES

Abrams v. United States, 250 U.S. 616 (1919)

Brandenburg v. Ohio, 395 U.S. 444 (1969)

Debs v. United States, 249 U.S. 211 (1919)

Frohwerk v. United States, 249 U.S. 204 (1919)

Great Northern Ry. v. Clara City, 246 U.S. 434 (1918)

Mulger v. Kansas, 123 U.S. 623 (1887)

Schenck v. United States, 249 U.S. 47 (1919)

Whitney v. California, 274 U.S. 357 (1927)

RECOMMENDED READING

Thomas C. Mackey, *"They Are Positively Dangerous Men": The Lost Court Documents of Benjamin Gitlow and James Larkin Before the New York City Magistrates' Court, 1919,* 69 New York University Law Review 421 (1994).

William G. Ross, *A Judicial Janus: Meyer v. Nebraska in Historical Perspective,* 57 University of Cincinnati Law Review 125 (1988).

Geoffrey R. Stone, *Reflections of the First Amendment: The Evolution of the American Jurisprudence of Free Expression,* 131 Journal of American Philosophical Society 251 (1987).

Case Title: *Good News Club v. Milford Central School*

Alternate Case Title: Limited Public Forum Case

Legal Citation: 533 U.S. 98

Year of Decision: 2001

KEY ISSUES

Is the exclusion of a Christian organization from using a public school's facilities that have been opened for school district residents' use for education and meetings a violation of First Amendment free speech rights? If so, is the violation justified because granting such permission would violate the establishment clause?

HISTORY OF THE CASE

Milford Central School (the "School") adopted a policy that allowed school district residents to use the School for "'instruction in any branch of education, learning or the arts,'" and for "'social, civic and recreational meetings and entertainment events, and other uses pertaining to the welfare of the community, provided that such uses shall be non-exclusive and shall be opened to the general public.'" The Good News Club (the "Club"), a Christian organization, requested permission to hold weekly meetings at the School. The Club's request was denied as being the same as a religious worship service. The Club brought an action against the School in the district court alleging a violation of the Club's right of free speech under the First and Fourteenth Amendments, its right to equal protection under the Fourteenth Amendment, and alleging a violation of the Club's right to religious freedom under the Religious Freedom Restoration Act of 1993. The district court dismissed the Club's claim under the Religious Freedom Restoration Act because the act had been declared unconstitutional by the Supreme Court in *City of Boerne v. Flores,* 521 U.S. 507 (1997). The district court also granted an injunction that ordered the School to allow the Club to use its facilities. Later, the district court rescinded this order and found in favor of the School because the subject matter of the Club's meetings was religious, not a discussion of secular issues from a religious perspective. The Court of Appeals affirmed the decisions of the district court. The Supreme Court granted certiorari to review the issue.

SUMMARY OF ARGUMENTS

The Good News Club argued that the School's exclusion of the Club from using the School facilities was not viewpoint neutral, stating that the School had created a limited public forum and had excluded the Club from use of that forum based upon its viewpoint. Further, the Club argued that its exclusion was unreasonable and the School could not show that it had a compelling reason to suppress the Club's viewpoint.

The School also argued that the School was a limited public forum and that the Club was conducting a religious worship during its meetings; therefore, the School was required to exclude the

Club's activities to avoid a violation of the establishment clause.

DECISION

Justice Thomas gave the opinion of the Court and was joined in the opinion by Chief Justice Rehnquist and Justices O'Connor, Scalia, and Kennedy. Justice Thomas acknowledged the parties' agreement that the School was a limited public forum and pointed out that this designation allowed the School to restrict speech, but not to discriminate against certain types of speech based on their viewpoint. The Court compared the case to its prior decisions in *Lamb's Chapel v. Center Moriches Union Free School Dist.* (1993) and *Rosenberger v. Rector and Visitors of Univ. of Va.* (1995) and found that the exclusion of the Club constituted viewpoint discrimination. Therefore, the Court did not need to address whether the restrictions imposed by the School were unreasonable.

The Court determined that the Club promoted "moral and character development" of children as permitted by the School's policy, but did so from a religious viewpoint. Justice Thomas stated that the Court found no difference between a foundation of Christianity for lessons and a foundation of teamwork or loyalty. Additionally, the Court found the School could not defend its exclusion as an attempt to avoid an establishment clause violation. The Court rejected the School's argument that allowing the Club access to the School would compromise its neutrality toward religion, stating that the Club was requesting to be treated neutrally and teach the same lessons of morals and good character as other groups; therefore, the Club's inclusion would actually ensure neutrality toward religion. The Court also dismissed arguments by the School alleging the kids would think the School was endorsing religion if the Club was allowed to use the School's facilities. As a result, the Court held the School had violated the First Amendment's free speech clause by excluding the Club from using its facilities and the Club had not advanced a valid establishment clause claim.

Justice Scalia concurred with the Court's decision, agreeing that the School engaged in viewpoint discrimination and addressing the majority's disagreement with the dissenting members of the Court over the part of the Club's meetings that were not purely the teaching of morals and character from a religious viewpoint. Justice Scalia found that the inclusion of the persuasive aspects of the Club's message did not transform its meetings into religious services.

Justice Breyer also concurred, agreeing that the government's neutrality toward religion should be considered when determining whether the establishment clause has been violated, stating the belief or disbelief of the kids that the School was endorsing religion was important to the establishment clause question and finding that due to the procedure the case had followed to get to the Supreme Court, the Court could not fully resolve the establishment clause issue without giving the parties an opportunity to supplement the record.

Justice Stevens dissented, distinguishing among three types of speech for religious purposes: (1) speech about a topic from a religious point of view; (2) religious speech that rises to the level of worship; and (3) speech that promotes a belief in a particular religious faith. Justice Stevens found the Club's speech to be in category number three. Stevens indicated that access to a limited public forum could be regulated as long as the regulation was viewpoint neutral and was in furtherance of the purpose of the forum. However, Stevens found that the Club was in essence "recruiting" members for its faith and not just teaching certain topics from a religious viewpoint and this type of activity could properly be excluded from the School's limited public forum.

Justice Souter was joined by Justice Ginsburg in his dissent, which found that the main part of the Club meetings was the "invitation" to join the religious faith and the use of the School in this manner was properly prohibited. Justice Souter also took issue with the Court's review and decision on the School's claim that it would have violated the establishment clause if it allowed the Club to use the School. Justice Souter thought the Court improperly acted as a trial court rather than a court of review when making this determination.

AFTERMATH

In the wake of *Good News Clubs*, some schools banned all clubs from using school facilities for their meetings rather than be forced to allow religious groups to be admitted. Other clubs that were viewed as "undesirable" or "extreme" now had equal access to use of limited public forums if they could show they merely were espousing topics from a different viewpoint.

SIGNIFICANCE

Limited public forums created by schools or other public facilities may not exclude religious groups from using the facilities if the purpose of the group is to perform permitted activities from a religious viewpoint.

RELATED CASES

Lamb's Chapel v. Center Moriches Union Free School Dist., 508 U.S. 384 (1993)

Rosenberger v. Rector and Visitors of Univ. of Va., 515 U.S. 819 (1995)

RECOMMENDED READING

Chris Brown, *Good News? Supreme Court Overlooks the Impressionability of Elementary-Aged Students in Finding a Parental Permission Slip Sufficient to Avoid an Establishment Clause Violation.* Good News Club v. Milford Central School, 121 S.Ct. 2093 (2001), 27 *University of Dayton Law Review* 269 (2002).

❧

Case Title: *Jacobellis v. Ohio*

Alternate Case Title: The "I Know It When I See It" Case

Legal Citations: 378 U.S. 184; 84 S.Ct. 1676; 12 L.Ed. 2d 793

Year of Decision: 1964

~

KEY ISSUES

What is the standard for judging hard-core pornography in a motion picture?

HISTORY OF THE CASE

Nico Jacobellis, a theater manager, was convicted in Cleveland, Ohio, of exhibiting an obscene motion picture, *Les Amants* (The Lovers). He was found guilty by the trial court and ordered to pay a fine of $2,500. The Court of Appeals of Ohio affirmed the judgment. Another appeal was taken to the Ohio Supreme Court (179 N.E.2d 777), where the court attempted to apply the *ROTH V. UNITED STATES* (1957) test to this film. This test determined material was obscene if, to the average person, applying community standards, the dominant theme appealed to the prurient interest. The Ohio Supreme Court found that the obscenity statute gave adequate warning of the conduct that was prohibited and marked the boundaries sufficiently for application by judges and juries. Further, the court found that one who sells hard-core pornography is presumed to know what he is selling and that he cannot profess ignorance. He must either stop selling or displaying it or destroy it; otherwise, he is guilty of selling obscene material.

The Ohio Supreme Court reviewed the findings of facts in the lower court. In the trial court, three judges found the film obscene. The Court of Appeals ruled on the weight of the evidence and upheld the verdict. The Ohio Supreme Court felt it was necessary to view the film. In the words of Justice Radcliff, "This court viewed *Les Amants.* The film ran for ninety minutes. To me, it was 87 minutes of boredom induced by the vapid drivel appearing on the screen and three minutes of complete revulsion during the showing of an act of perverted obscenity. *Les Amants* was not hard-core pornography, that is, filth for filth's sake. It was worse. It was filth for money's sake."

Mr. Jacobellis filed an appeal to the U.S. Supreme Court.

SUMMARY OF ARGUMENTS

The attorneys for the theater manager argued that the statute violated the constitutional right of freedom of communication. They further argued that he was denied due process because on its face the state law of Ohio denied him freedom of the press and should be declared void as unconstitutional. They further argued that seeking economic gain for the sale or distribution of a communication does not affect one's right to protection under the Constitution.

The state of Ohio argued that the statute was constitutional, and that it was not applied in the abstract. The statute did not involve federal constitutional guarantees in that it was the decision of a state court on question of state law.

DECISION

On appeal, six justices of the Supreme Court voted to reverse, but they were unable to agree upon a single opinion in support of their decision. Justice William Brennan, joined by Justice Arthur Goldberg, felt that it was time to reexamine *Roth* in light of its seven-year history. Brennan, the author of the *Roth* decision, reaffirmed the view that obscenity is excluded from constitutional protection because it is utterly without redeeming social importance. Brennan said there had been many suggestions that the community standard language in *Roth* implied a determination based on particular local communities from which each case arose. He felt that this was an incorrect reading. He rejected the concept of a local community standard and found that it would take a very brave person to risk showing a particular film in one locality, where it might not be held obscene, and then showing it in another community, where it might be held obscene. Brennan found this result would be to restrict the public's access and stated that the constitutional status of an allegedly obscene film must be determined on the basis of a national standard: "It is, after all, a national Constitution we are expounding."

Brennan went on to suggest that state and local authorities might want to consider passing laws aimed at preventing the distribution of obscene material to children rather than trying to prohibit its distribution in general. The Court stated that it had reviewed the film, which involved a woman who abandoned her husband and family to have an affair with a young archaeologist. While there is an explicit love scene in the final minutes of the film, the film was favorably reviewed in a number of national publications. The film was widely shown throughout the United States. The six justices in the majority did not find that the film was obscene.

Justice Byron White joined in this decision.

Justice Hugo Black and Justice William O. Douglas entered a separate opinion, based on their arguments in *Roth,* namely, that anyone convicted of exhibiting an obscene motion picture has had his or her freedom under the First Amendment restricted.

In the most famous language of the decision, Justice Potter Stewart wrote that while he agreed that hard-core pornography is not protected by the First Amendment, he could not attempt to define the kinds of material that are included within that term: "perhaps I could never succeed in intelligibly doing so. But I know it when I see it, and the motion picture involved in this case is not that." Justice Arthur Goldberg wrote an additional concurring opinion, which stressed that the basic principles of freedom of speech and the press should be favored over any decision to restrict the liberty of expression.

Chief Justice Earl Warren and Justice Tom Clark dissented, saying that they agreed with the obscenity test set forth by Justice Brennan both in *Roth* and in this decision, but that the test was based on a local community standard. They further argued that in applying Brennan's new standard, the Court would become a "super-censor" and its proper role is to limit itself to considering whether or not there is evidence in the record to find obscenity under the *Roth* standards.

Justice John Harlan dissented on the ground that the states were not prohibited from banning materials that in state judicial proceedings were found to be offensive, as long as rational criteria were established for judging such material.

AFTERMATH

This case broadened the "community standards" term of the obscenity test in *Roth.* The Supreme Court now determined that community standards referred to national, not local, standards.

SIGNIFICANCE

Jacobellis became a landmark for revealing that the *Roth* definition was so ambiguous that each justice was forced to follow his own conscience. The decision in *Jacobellis* lasted only nine years, until MILLER V. CALIFORNIA (1973) created yet another test for obscenity.

RELATED CASES

Miller v. California, 413 U.S. 1519 (1973)

Roth v. United States, 354 U.S. 476 (1957)

RECOMMENDED READING

Bosmajian, Haiga. *Obscenity and Freedom of Expression.* New York: B. Franklin, 1976.

DeGrazia, Edward. *Censorship Landmarks.* New York: Bowker, 1969.

Friedman, Leon. *Obscenity: The Complete Oral Arguments before the Supreme Court in the Major Obscenity Cases.* New York: Chelsea House, 1970.

Case Title: *Keyishian v. Board of Regents*

Legal Citation: 385 U.S. 589

Year of Decision: 1967

KEY ISSUES

Can a public university require employees to certify that they are not members of subversive organizations?

HISTORY OF THE CASE

Teachers in the New York public university system were terminated or threatened with termination when they refused to certify that they were not and had never been communists. They also had to certify that they had not been members of any other group that advocated the forceful overthrow of the government. New York's law also stated that teachers who advocated or were involved with the distribution of written materials that promoted the forceful overthrow of the government would be discharged. The teachers challenged these laws. The Supreme Court decided to hear the case.

SUMMARY OF ARGUMENTS

The teachers argued that the laws, as written, were too vague. The law stated that "treasonable or seditious" utterances or acts were grounds for dismissal. However, the law never defined "seditious" or "treasonable." They also asserted that the laws stifled academic freedom in a university setting.

The Board of Regents argued that the law was not vague, and that this type of law had been constitutionally upheld by the Supreme Court in the past.

DECISION

Justice Brennan delivered the opinion of the Court. In a 5 to 4 decision, the Court ruled that the law was too vague because a teacher had no way of knowing what types of statements or activities were forbidden. They noted that academic freedom was of special concern under the

First Amendment. The law, as written, required teachers to forgo some of their constitutional rights to freedom of expression in order to obtain employment. The Supreme Court also noted that mere membership in an organization that was perceived as subversive without direct knowledge that the member had a specific intent to further the unlawful aims of the organization was not an adequate reason to condition employment on the surrender of constitutional rights.

Justice Clark, Justice Harlan, Justice Stewart, and Justice White dissented. Justice Clark argued "that the majority has by its broadside swept away one of our most precious rights, namely, the right of self-preservation." He bemoaned the bad effects the Court's decision would have on the "public education system" and the "minds of our youth," which "will determine the future of our land." He felt that the law was not vague, but covered a very narrow and important issue: whether those who advocate overthrow of the government should be disqualified from teaching in a state university. He exclaimed, "My answer, in keeping with all of our cases up until today, is 'Yes.'"

AFTERMATH

This case has not been overruled. Subsequent decisions have had little impact on the law controlling the government's ability to discharge workers because of their speech or associations.

SIGNIFICANCE

This case demonstrated the Supreme Court's commitment to academic freedom and the freedom of expression as protected by the First Amendment.

RELATED CASES

Connell v. Higginbotham, 403 U.S. 207 (1971)

United States v. Robel, 389 U.S. 258 (1967)

RECOMMENDED READING

Bolmeier, Edward C. *Landmark Supreme Court Decisions on Public School Issues*. Charlottesville, Va.: The Michie Co., 1973.

Malcolm Stewart, *The First Amendment, the Public Schools and the Inculcation of Community Values*, 18 Journal of Law and Education 23–92 (1989).

Case Title: *Kingsley Int'l Pictures Corp. v. Regents of University of New York State*

Legal Citation: 360 U.S. 684

Year of Decision: 1959

KEY ISSUES

Does a state law that restricts the expression of unconventional or immoral ideas violate the U.S. Constitution?

HISTORY OF THE CASE

A New York statute made it unlawful to exhibit, sell, lease, or lend for exhibition any motion picture without a valid license or permit from the State Education Department. The Education Department was required to grant a license or permit unless any part of a film was, among other things, obscene, immoral, or indecent. Immoral was defined as "of such a character that its exhibition would tend to corrupt morals" or a film in which the "dominant purpose or effect [was] erotic or pornographic; or which portray[ed] acts of sexual immorality, perversion, or lewdness, or which expressly or impliedly present[ed] such acts as desirable, acceptable or proper patterns of behavior."

A motion picture distributor wanted to obtain a license from the Education Department for *Lady Chatterley's Lover*. The Education Department determined that three scenes in the movie were immoral and refused to issue a license. The distributor appealed to the regents of the University of the State of New York, who upheld the ruling of the Education Department on a broader ground. They determined that the theme of the movie was immoral because it portrayed adultery as acceptable, desirable, and proper behavior. The distributor appealed to the appellate division, which overturned the two lower decisions. However, the court of appeals reversed the appellate division and upheld the decision to refuse a license. The court found that the film was immoral because it "portray[ed]

adultery as proper behavior." The case was appealed to the U.S. Supreme Court.

SUMMARY OF ARGUMENTS

Kingsley argued that the New York statute violated the First and Fourteenth Amendments because it suppressed speech and deprived Kingsley of its property without due process of law. Kingsley also argued that the suppression of the film was unwarranted.

The Regents argued that New York could constitutionally bar films that depicted sexual immorality as proper behavior.

DECISION

The Supreme Court ruled that the New York law violated the First Amendment's guarantee of free speech and was, therefore, unconstitutional.

The Court noted that the New York law required the denial of a license for a film portraying adulterous relationships. The Supreme Court also acknowledged that the theme of the film, *Lady Chatterley's Lover*, could be characterized as portraying adultery as proper behavior in certain circumstances. However, the Court determined that the effect of the New York law was to prevent exhibition of films that advocated an "idea," which violated the First Amendment because the First Amendment's "basic guarantee is of freedom to advocate ideas." The Court stated that the law "struck at the very heart of constitutionally protected liberty" and pointed out that the Constitution was not a device to guarantee only the expressions of the majority of the population but was a guarantee for the unconventional or unpopular expressions of the minority.

AFTERMATH

This case has not been overruled. It is still impermissible for states to regulate the expression of ideas in this manner.

SIGNIFICANCE

Although entertainment provided in theaters may be erotic or involve immorality, this brand of expression is fully protected from unjustified governmental interference by the First and Fourteenth Amendments to the U.S. Constitution. Though this case specifically dealt with motion pictures, its holding can be applied to other forms of expression including literature.

RELATED CASES

Joseph Burstyn, Inc. v. Wilson, 343 U.S. 495 (1952)

Eisenstadt v. Baird, 405 U.S. 438, 459 (1972)

Jenkins v. Georgia, 418 U.S. 153 (1974)

NAACP v. Button, 371 U.S. 415, 444–45 (1963)

RECOMMENDED READING

Harry Kalven, Jr., *The Metaphysics of the Law of Obscenity,* Supreme Court Review 1–45 (1960).

Lockhart, William B., and Robert C. McClure. *Obscenity Censorship: The Core Constitutional Issue— What Is Obscene. Commentaries on Obscenity.* Edited by Donald Sharp. Metuchen, N.J.: Scarecrow Press, 1970.

Case Title: *Konigsberg v. State Bar of California*

Alternate Case Title: Konigsberg I

Legal Citation: 353 U.S. 252

Year of Decision: 1957

KEY ISSUES

Can a state's committee of bar examiners refuse to admit a candidate to the state bar solely because the candidate refuses to answer questions about past membership in the Communist Party?

HISTORY OF THE CASE

After successfully completing law school and passing the bar exam, Raphael Konigsberg applied for admission to the state bar of California. The State Committee of Bar Examiners, after several hearings, refused to certify him to practice law on the grounds that he had failed to prove (1) that he was of good moral character and (2) that he did not advocate the overthrow of the government by force or violence. Konigsberg appealed to the California Supreme Court. The court denied his petition for review by a narrow margin. He then appealed to the U.S. Supreme Court.

SUMMARY OF ARGUMENTS

Raphael Konigsberg argued that the State Bar Committee's action refusing to certify him to practice law on the grounds that he had failed to prove that he was of good moral character and that he did not advocate forcible overthrow of the government denied him due process and equal protection of the law under the Fourteenth Amendment.

The State Committee of Bar Examiners argued that substantial doubts were raised about his character by (1) the testimony of an ex-Communist that Konigsberg had attended meetings of a Communist Party unit in 1941; (2) his criticism of certain public officials and their policies; and (3) his refusal to answer certain questions about his political associations and beliefs. The committee also found that Konigsberg had failed to prove that he did not advocate the overthrow of the government of the United States or California by force or violence.

DECISION

Justice Black delivered the opinion of the Court that the evidence did not rationally support the only two grounds upon which the committee relied in rejecting Konigsberg's application for admission to the California bar. Addressing the issue of "good moral character," the Court noted that the term is "unusually ambiguous" and that "[s]uch a vague qualification . . . can be a dangerous instrument for arbitrary and discriminatory denial of the right to practice law." The Court considered the evidence of Konigsberg's moral character, noting that "forty-two individuals who had known Konigsberg at different times during the past twenty years attested to his excellent character. . . . Included among them were a Catholic priest, a Jewish rabbi, lawyers, doctors, professors, businessmen and social workers." The Court noted that "not a single person has testified that his character was bad or questionable in any way."

The Court also looked at Konigsberg's background, which "furnished strong proof that his life had always been honest and upright." After graduating from Ohio State University in 1931, he taught history and literature for a time in a Cleveland high school. In 1943 he was given a scholarship to Ohio State University and received a master of arts degree in social administration. He then worked as a supervisor in the District of Columbia Department of Health. In 1936 he went to California, where he worked as the direct supervisor for the California State Relief Administration. With U.S. entry into World War II, he volunteered for the army and was commissioned a second lieutenant. He was promoted to captain and, while in Germany, was made orientation officer for the entire Seventh Army. After an honorable discharge in 1946 he resumed his career in social work. In 1950, at the age of 39, Konigsberg entered the law school of the University of Southern California and was graduated in 1953. The Court found that "[t]here is no criticism in the record of his professional work, his military service, or his performance at the law school."

With respect to the testimony of the ex-Communist, the Court held, "Even if it be assumed that Konigsberg was a member of the Communist Party in 1941, the mere fact of membership would not support an inference that he did not have good moral character." As for the criticism of public officials, the Court held, "Because of the very nature of our democracy such expressions of political views must be permitted. Citizens have a right under our constitutional system to criticize government officials and agencies." On the issue of Konigsberg's refusal to answer questions, the Court held, "On the record before us, it is our judgment that the inferences of bad moral character which the committee attempted to draw from Konigsberg's refusal to answer questions about his political affiliations and opinions are unwarranted."

The Court also addressed the committee's finding that Konigsberg failed to prove that he did not advocate the overthrow of the government by force. The Court found that "Konigsberg repeatedly testified under oath before the committee that he did not believe in nor advocate the overthrow of any government in this country by any unconstitutional means." The Court noted that he emphatically denied advocating the overthrow of the government by force when questioned by the committee on the matter. He declared, "I answer specifically that I do not, I never did or never will."

Justice Frankfurter wrote one of the dissenting opinions and argued that the question of Konigsberg's fitness for the California bar was essentially a state matter. He argued that the record did not clearly indicate that a constitutional violation was at issue. Therefore, the Court had no authority to decide the case.

Justice Harlan also wrote a dissenting opinion. He agreed with the jurisdictional concerns of Justice Frankfurter, stating, "For me, today's decision represents an unacceptable intrusion into a matter of state concern." He also took issue with the Court's ruling and argued that Konigsberg's refusal to answer questions about his alleged membership in the Communist Party were sufficient grounds to deny his application to the state bar of California.

AFTERMATH

Konigsberg was subjected to a second hearing before the Committee of Bar Examiners. Again he refused to answer any questions relating to his membership in the Communist Party. As a result, the committee declined to certify him on the ground that his refusal to answer had "obstructed a full investigation into his qualifications." Again, he appealed to the U.S. Supreme Court. This time, however, the Court sustained the action of the committee in a 5-to-4 decision. The Court held that his refusal to answer the questions of the committee, and not his alleged membership in the Communist Party, was a sufficient ground for denying his admission to the California bar. In a dissenting opinion, Justice Black, joined by Chief Justice Warren and Justice Douglas, insisted that Konigsberg had in fact been rejected because the committee suspected that he had once been a Communist Party member.

SIGNIFICANCE

Under the First Amendment's protection of freedom of expression, a person's political associations or beliefs cannot be grounds for nonadmission to a state-sponsored professional guild.

RELATED CASES

Konigsberg v. State Bar of California, 366 U.S. 36 (1961) (Konigsberg II)

Schware v. Board of Bar Examiners, 353 U.S. 232 (1957)

RECOMMENDED READING

Emerson, Thomas I. *The System of Freedom of Expression.* New York: Random House, 1970.

Alexander Meiklejohn, *The First Amendment Is Absolute*, Supreme Court Review 245–266 (1961).

***

Case Title: *Laird v. Tatum*

Legal Citation: 408 U.S. 1

Year of Decision: 1972

KEY ISSUES

Does the mere existence of a governmental data-gathering system over civilian political activity with the potential for domestic unrest inhibit the exercise of First Amendment rights and thereby provide for a justiciable controversy?

HISTORY OF THE CASE

The president is authorized by the U.S. Constitution to make use of the armed forces to quell insurrection and other domestic violence if and when certain conditions occur within one of the states. President Johnson ordered federal troops to assist local authorities at the time of the civil disorders in Detroit, Michigan, in the summer of 1967 and during the disturbances that followed the assassination of Martin Luther King, Jr. Prior to the Detroit disorders, the army had a general contingency plan for providing such assistance to local authorities, but the 1967 experience led army authorities to believe that more attention should be given to such preparatory planning. A data-gathering system was established in connection with the development of detailed and specific contingency planning and was designed to permit the army, when called upon to assist local authorities, to respond effectively with a minimum of force.

The system put into operation as a result of the army's 1967 experience consisted essentially of the collection of information about public activities that were thought to have at least some potential for civil disorder, the reporting of that information to army intelligence headquarters at Fort Holabird, Maryland; the dissemination of these reports from headquarters to major army

posts around the country; and the storage of the reported information in a computer data bank located at Fort Holabird. The principal sources of information were the news media and publications in general circulation, although some of the information came from army intelligence agents who attended meetings that were open to the public and from civilian law enforcement agencies.

In 1970 Congress had become concerned with the scope of the army's domestic surveillance system, and hearings were held before the Subcommittee on Constitutional Rights of the Senate Committee on the Judiciary. Respondents, Tatum and others, brought a class action in the district court of the District of Columbia claiming that their rights were being invaded by the army's surveillance system. The district court granted Secretary of Defense Laird's motion to dismiss, holding that there was no justiciable claim. A divided court of appeals reversed and ordered the case remanded for further proceedings. It was that judgment that was under review by the U.S. Supreme Court.

SUMMARY OF ARGUMENTS

The petitioners, Secretary of Defense Laird and others, argued that nothing detrimental to respondents had been done, that nothing was contemplated to have been done, and that even if some action by the army against respondents were possibly foreseeable, this possibility did not present a controversy that could presently be heard and decided by the Court.

The respondents, Tatum et al., contended that the system of gathering and distributing information constituted an impermissible burden on them and others similarly situated, which exercised a present inhibiting effect on their full expression and use of their First Amendment rights. Respondents argued that although there was no specific action against them, the surveillance could possibly lead to misuse of the information against them.

DECISION

In a 5-4 decision, Chief Justice Burger recognized for the majority that there are cases where constitutional violations have resulted from the deterrent, or "chilling," effect of governmental regulations that fall short of a direct prohibition against the exercise of First Amendment rights. In none of those cases, however, did the chilling effect arise merely from the individual's knowledge that a government agency was engaged in certain activities or from the individual's fear that, armed with the fruits of those activities, the agency might in the future take some other and additional action detrimental to that individual. Chief Justice Burger quoted *Ex parte Levitt* (1937) in stating that those decisions have not eroded the "established principle that to entitle a private individual to invoke the judicial power to determine the validity of executive or legislative action he must show that he has sustained or is immediately in danger of sustaining a direct injury as the result of that action." Allegations of a subjective chill are not an adequate substitute for a claim of specific present objective harm or a threat of specific future harm. As a result, respondents had not presented a case capable of resolution by the courts.

The dissent by Justice Douglas argued that no law expressly authorized surveillance over civilians and that the Constitution does not give the government any such authority. What the law at issue did do, however, was give procedural standards for the government in the regulation of the land and naval forces. Justice Douglas found it difficult to imagine how those powers could be extended to military surveillance over civilian affairs. The armed forces, he argued, are not regulatory agencies or bureaus that may be created as Congress desires. Even when "martial law" is declared, its appropriateness is subject to judicial review. He further argued that the tradition in the United States has been one of civilian supremacy and subordination of military power. Justice Douglas believed that the framers of the Constitution expressly recognized a necessity to prevent military overreaching by enacting the Second and Third Amendments, specifically authorizing a decentralized militia, guaranteeing the right of the people to keep and bear arms, and prohibiting the quartering of troops in any house in time of peace without the consent of the owner. In sum, Justice Douglas believed that turning the armies loose on surveillance of civilians was a gross repudiation of the nation's traditions.

On the issue of ripeness, whether an actual, present controversy exists, Justice Douglas felt that the withholding of standing to the respondents practically immunized all surveillance activity from judicial scrutiny. Quoting an earlier Supreme Court case, Justice Douglas thought that the issue was indeed capable of resolve: the gist of the standing issue is whether the party seeking relief has "alleged such a personal stake in the outcome of the controversy as to assure that concrete adverseness which sharpens the presentation of issues upon which the court so largely depends on illumination of difficult Constitutional questions." Justice Douglas believed that the First Amendment was designed to allow rebellion to remain as our national heritage, the Constitution designed to keep the government off of the backs of the people, and the Bill of Rights added to keep the precincts of belief and expression, of the press, of political and social activities free from surveillance. He concluded strongly that there can be no influence more paralyzing of those objectives than army surveillance, which would tend to liken the American government to the government of the former Soviet Union.

Justices Brennan, Stewart, and Marshall dissented, agreeing with the court of appeals that the record showed that most if not all of the respondents and/or organizations of which they were members had been the subject of army surveillance reports and their names had appeared in the army's records. The three justices felt that since that was precisely the injury of which they complained, they had standing to seek redress for that alleged injury in court. The justices concluded that although the respondents may or may not have been able to prove the case they alleged, they were at least entitled to try.

AFTERMATH

The Court left the door open for challenges concerning political intelligence gathering by governmental entities. The apparent political discretion exercised by the Court in refusing to answer the constitutionally based challenges may have quelled discontent and mistrust of the government to an extent, yet it gave no real meaning to First Amendment rights in the context of which the case was decided.

SIGNIFICANCE

Political intelligence gathering by the government has not always been circumscribed to legitimate criminal and national security investigations. Intelligence operations have been directed toward lawful activity without regard to constitutional liberties in the past. Political surveillance of civilians is a government activity that has emerged periodically in response to the mere perception that social order is threatened. If large groups of citizens again assert their right to object openly to government policy, as was the case in the late 1960s and early 1970s, government officials may again perceive a threat to the stability of the nation and again pursue operations such as those at issue in *Laird v. Tatum*. The case did not provide any test to determine the constitutionality of the surveillance and, as a result, leaves the public exposed to clandestine domestic military operations.

RELATED CASES

Alliance to End Repression v. Rochford, 407 F. Supp. 115 (N.D. Ill. 1975)

Baggett v. Bullitt, 377 U.S. 360 (1964)

Baird v. State Bar of Arizona, 401 U.S. 1 (1971)

Handschu v. Special Services Division, 349 F. Supp. 766 (S.D.N.Y. 1972)

Keyishian v. Board of Regents, 385 U.S. 589 (1967)

Lamont v. Postmaster General, 381 U.S. 301 (1965)

Philadelphia Yearly Meeting of the Religious Society of Friends v. Tate, 519 F.2d 1335 (3d. Cir. 1975)

RECOMMENDED READING

Eric Ladiere, *Justiciability and Constitutionality of Political Intelligence Gathering*, 30 UCLA Law Review 976 (1983).

Jeffrey W. Stempel, *Rehnquist, Recusal and Reform*, 53 Brooklyn Law Review 589 (1987).

Case Title: *Lamont v. Postmaster General*

Legal Citations: 381 U.S. 301; 85 S.Ct. 1493; 14 L.Ed. 2d 398

Year of Decision: 1965

KEY ISSUES

Does the Postal Service and Federal Employees Salary Act of 1962 violate the First Amendment?

HISTORY OF THE CASE

A section of the Postal Service and Federal Employees Salary Act of 1962 required the postmaster general to detain and deliver (on the addressee's request) any unsealed foreign mailings of "communist political propaganda." Under the act, the Post Office would send the addressee a card that must be returned to have the mailing delivered. Dr. Corliss Lamont, who published and distributed pamphlets, sued to enjoin enforcement of the statute.

SUMMARY OF ARGUMENTS

Lamont argued that the act's provision requiring the Post Office to hold certain mail until its delivery was approved by the addressee violated his rights under the First and Fifth Amendments.

The postmaster general argued that the act's provision was only an inconvenience and not an abridgement of First Amendment rights. The postmaster also argued that the justification for the provision was that the publications to be held were those that were often offensive to recipients.

DECISION

Justice Douglas wrote the majority opinion and held the postal law unconstitutional "[b]ecause it required an official act (returning the reply card) as a limitation on the unfettered exercise of the addressee's First Amendment rights." The Court's opinion rested on the ground that the government could not place such an affirmative action on an individual, especially when that obligation would have a detrimental effect. Here, even though the concerns involved foreign affairs, the governmental interests were insufficient to outweigh individual rights.

The act violates the First Amendment "as it imposes on the addressee an affirmative obligation that amounts to an unconstitutional limitation of rights under the First Amendment."

AFTERMATH

The Court slowly begins to ensure the proper protection of First Amendment freedoms. Dr. Corliss

Lamont went on to teach a humanism course at Columbia University.

SIGNIFICANCE

The case established that the right to receive information from whatever source is protected by the Constitution.

RELATED CASES

Blount v. Rizzi, 400 U.S. 410 (1971)

Hannegan v. Esquire, Inc., 327 U.S. 146 (146)

RECOMMENDED READING

Cable, John L. *Decisive Decisions of United States Citizenship.* Charlottesville, Va.: The Michie Co., 1965.

William E. Lee, *The Supreme Court and the Right to Receive Expression,* Supreme Court Review 303–344 (1987).

Case Title: *Lloyd Corp., Ltd. v. Tanner et al.*

Legal Citations: 407 U.S. 551; 92 S.Ct. 2219; 33 L.Ed. 2d 131

Year of Decision: 1972

KEY ISSUES

Does a privately owned shopping center have the right to prohibit the distribution of handbills on its property when the handbills have no relation to the shopping center's activities?

HISTORY OF THE CASE

Tanner and his associates tried to distribute handbills inside a privately owned shopping mall that had a strictly enforced rule against handbills. The mall security guards asked Tanner to stop under threat of arrest and suggested that he and his associates resume this activity outside the mall, which they did. Tanner claimed that the restriction violated First Amendment rights. The district court held that the mall was open to the public and that the policy of prohibiting handbills within the mall

violated Tanner's First Amendment rights. The court of appeals affirmed.

SUMMARY OF ARGUMENTS

Lloyd Corporation argued that it had the right to regulate how First Amendment activity was conducted on its premises. Lloyd Corporation also argued that the decision of the lower courts that Tanner and his associates had a First Amendment right to distribute handbills in its mall violated its rights of private property protected by the Fifth and Fourteenth Amendments.

Donald Tanner, Betsy Wheeler, and Susan Roberts argued that they had a First Amendment right to distribute handbills in the mall. They also argued that because the mall was open to the public, Lloyd Corporation could not enforce its restriction against handbilling on the premises.

DECISION

Where handbilling is unrelated to any activity within the center (unlike Logan Valley, where the activity involved labor picketing and so was related to the business of the plaza) and where Tanner "had adequate alternative means of communication," the rights of the private owner were upheld and did not violate the First Amendment.

Justice Powell wrote the decision of the Court. He said that the case called into question the right of private owners to prohibit the distribution of handbills on its property when the handbills were unrelated to the business of the mall. Lloyd owned the mall, parking facilities, stairways and escalators, and so forth. There are 12 uniformed security guards for shoplifting and general security. They are employed and report to Lloyd. Distribution of handbills has been strictly enforced without exception. The activity is considered an annoyance to shoppers, creates litter, and is incompatible with the purpose of the mall.

Tanner's handbills invited people to an anti–Vietnam War rally, an activity in no way related to the business of the mall. It was noted that previously politicians, as well as various veterans groups, were invited to speak at the mall. However, the main purpose of the mall is for the public to shop, and only activities related to that purpose can be promoted. The handbilling is unrelated to Lloyd's business, and Tanner had alternative means of communication.

Justice Marshall wrote the dissent. He felt that ownership of a mall did not come with the privilege to determine whether or not it will be used as a public area. He saw a comparison with this case and *Amalgamated Food Employees Union v. Logan Valley Plaza* (1968) as both the mall and the Logan business district were the equivalent of public premises. Speakers were invited, and if the mall were open to First Amendment activities then Tanner and his handbills could not be excluded. There is a need to balance First Amendment rights with the freedom of the private property owner to control his or her property.

AFTERMATH

State legislation reclassified malls as public forums, interpreting the role of mall owner as fulfilling a state function.

SIGNIFICANCE

Justice Marshall predicted that government would rely more and more on private enterprise and that public property would decrease in favor of privately owned property. Then it would be harder for people to find ways to communicate and free speech would be hindered.

RELATED CASES

Amalgamated Food Employees Union v. Logan Valley Plaza, 391 U.S. 308 (1968)

Marsh v. Alabama, 326 U.S. 501 (1946)

PruneYard Shopping Center v. Robins, 447 U.S. 74 (1980)

RECOMMENDED READING

Laurence M. Cohen, PruneYard Shopping Center v. Robins: *Past, Present and Future,* 57 Chicago-Kent Law Review 373 (1981).

Michele Cortese, *Property Rights and Human Values: A Right of Access to Private Property for Tenant Organizers,* 17 Columbia Human Rights Law Journal 257 (1986).

Supreme Court, 1971 Term, 86 Harvard Law Review 122 (1972).

Case Title: *A Book Named "John Cleland's Memoirs of a Woman of Pleasure" v. Massachusetts*

Alternate Case Titles: *Memoirs v. Massachusetts,* The "Fanny Hill" Case

Legal Citations: 383 U.S. 413; 86 S.Ct. 975; 16 L.Ed. 2d 1

Year of Decision: 1966

KEY ISSUES

What is the standard for judging the obscenity of a book?

HISTORY OF THE CASE

Under a statute of Massachusetts, the attorney general brought suit to suppress the publication of a novel commonly known as *Fanny Hill,* the adventures of a young girl who became a prostitute in London. The same book had been the subject of an obscenity trial in 1821, also in the state of Massachusetts (*Commonwealth v. Holmes,* 17 Mass. 336).

John Cleland had written the book in 1749 in London, and it had appeared in various editions over the years. Some of these editions were illustrated and some were not. The book consists of two long letters from "Fanny" in which she retells her life story in London. It concentrates on her sexual experiences, which were quite varied. G. P. Putnam's Sons was the copyright holder on the book. In 1963, Putnam's had undertaken to republish the memoirs without illustration. An unusually large number of orders were placed, including many by college and university libraries. Additionally, the Library of Congress had requested the right to translate the book into Braille (383 U.S. 413 at 426). The attorney general of the Commonwealth of Massachusetts brought suit to have the book declared obscene, and the trial judge entered an order finding that *Fanny Hill* was obscene and not entitled "to the protection of the First and Fourteenth Amendments." The Massachusetts Supreme Judicial Court affirmed the decree.

SUMMARY OF ARGUMENTS

The attorney for Putnam's argued that under the Supreme Court decision of ROTH V. UNITED STATES (1957), material could be declared obscene only if the average person applying contemporary community standards would find that the book appealed to the prurient interest. Putnam's attorney also argued that the book at issue had a presence that is elegant and an absence of truly offensive material. Therefore, under the second part of the *Roth* test—namely, that the book be utterly without redeeming social importance—the book should not be considered obscene. In addition, Putnam's attorney claimed that the book occupied a significant place in the development of the novel. It depicted a social trend toward a freer attitude about life and built upon themes developed by Henry Fielding in his famous novel *Tom Jones* and, to a lesser extent, by Samuel Richardson in the novels *Pamela* and *Clarissa*. Putnam's attorney also argued that the book provided a social history for anyone interested in understanding the battle going on between "puritan" ethics and those who advocated a more open, generous attitude toward life. Additionally, he argued that the book had redeeming qualities because Fanny's reaction to her life and experiences was portrayed in anger, disgust, and horror. She ultimately married one of her clients and found redemption through married love.

The attorney general's office of Massachusetts argued that the book was utterly without any redeeming social values and importance. It further argued that the book was patently offensive and was an affront to anyone's standards of decency. The state argued that the book was entirely sex-oriented and lacked any idea or other element that warranted constitutional protection.

In addition to the publisher and the state, a group called Citizens for Decent Literature filed a brief, urging that the book be censored. Among the attorneys representing the Citizens for Decent Literature was Charles H. Keating, Jr., later to become president of the Lincoln Savings and Loan.

DECISION

Six members of the Court voted for reversal; that is, they found that Cleland's book was not obscene. There were three dissenting justices. Justice William Brennan wrote the main opinion, joined by Chief Justice Earl Warren and Justice Abe Fortas. Justice Brennan wrote that if a book is found to have any literary or other value, then it cannot be obscene. Therefore, "obscene" was a status reserved for worthless trash. A new obscen-

ity test was created, which consisted of three parts: "(1) The dominant theme of the material taken as a whole must appeal to a prurient interest in sex. (2) The material is patently offensive because it affronts contemporary community standards relating to the description or representation of sexual matters. (3) The material is utterly without redeeming social value." Justice Brennan felt that the first two tests clearly were stated in *Roth,* and that the third test had been defined in subsequent cases.

Justice Hugo Black concurred on the grounds he stated in *Roth:* that the Court is without constitutional power to censor speech or the press, regardless of the subject discussed.

Justice William Douglas concurred on the ground that the federal government has no power over the expression of ideas. Justice Douglas was very impressed that professors of English at Williams College, Harvard College, Boston University, the Massachusetts Institute of Technology, and Brandeis University all found that the book had literary merit. He felt that as a judge and not as a literary expert, his thoughts had no greater weight than those of any adult citizen. Justice Douglas felt that the function of a judge was not to be a censor. The First Amendment is absolute and deprives the government of any power to pass laws on the value, propriety, or morality of any expression.

Justice Potter Stewart reaffirmed his opinion in *Roth:* that the Constitution protects all but hard-core pornography.

Three justices wrote dissenting opinions. Justice Tom Clark claimed that even though he was not a "shrinking violet—this book is too much, even for me." He went on to describe the book's contents, which he said caused him embarrassment. He would not quote directly from the book, because he did not want to debase his opinion. He found that the expert testimony was of no substance and that the book was not a work of art. He felt that the book was designed solely to appeal to sexual interests and was written solely for profit.

Justice John Harlan dissented on the grounds that the Constitution does not bind the states and the federal government in precisely the same way. He felt that the Massachusetts court had a right to regulate obscene material, and that the statute and the decision of the Massachusetts court reasonably did this.

Justice Byron White agreed that the First Amendment allowed state legislatures to forbid the sale of obscene material.

AFTERMATH

This ruling authorized the publication of *Fanny Hill*. The Supreme Court had made the social value test a part of its obscenity standard.

SIGNIFICANCE

The *Fanny Hill* case became a landmark in unraveling the old standards of obscenity. The decision lasted only seven years, until MILLER V. CALIFORNIA was decided and reworked the obscenity standard. In *Miller,* the Court redefined the community standards test and modified the social value test from "utterly without redeeming social value" to "lacks serious literary, artistic, political, or scientific value."

RELATED CASES

Jacobellis v. Ohio, 378 U.S. 184 (1964)

Miller v. California, 413 U.S. 15 (1973)

Roth v. United States, 354 U.S. 476 (1957)

RECOMMENDED READING

Oboler, Eli. *The Fear of the Word: Censorship and Sex.* Metuchen, N.J.: Scarecrow Press, 1964.

Randall, Richard. *Freedom and Taboo: Pornography and the Politics of a Self Divided.* Berkeley: University of California Press, 1989.

Rembar, Charles. *The End of Obscenity: The Trials of Lady Chatterley, Tropic of Cancer, and* Fanny Hill. New York: Random House, 1968.

Case Title: *Meyer v. Nebraska*

Legal Citation: 262 U.S. 390

Year of Decision: 1923

KEY ISSUES

May a state prohibit schools from teaching foreign languages or prohibit educators from teaching in a language other than English?

HISTORY OF THE CASE

Nebraska approved statutes in 1919 that prohibited teachers in private, public, denominational, and parochial schools from teaching any subject in a language other than English unless the student had passed the eighth grade. A person guilty of teaching in another language was subject to a fine or imprisonment. Robert Meyer, a teacher, was tried and convicted of teaching a child who had not passed the eighth grade the subject of reading in the German language.

The Nebraska Supreme Court affirmed the conviction, holding that the statute was a valid exercise of a state's police power that did not violate the Fourteenth Amendment.

SUMMARY OF ARGUMENTS

Meyer argued that the Fourteenth Amendment protects the right to choose and pursue a profession and the Nebraska statute prohibited pursuit of Meyer's chosen profession. Meyer also argued that the Nebraska statute was an illegitimate exercise of Nebraska's police power and that the statute denied him equal protection of the law.

Nebraska argued that the Nebraska statute was a legitimate exercise of its police powers and did not unlawfully interfere with Meyer's profession. Nebraska also argued that the Nebraska statute did not deny Meyer equal protection of the law.

DECISION

The Supreme Court ruled that the state statute was an unconstitutional infringement on the Constitution's guarantee of liberty. They held that a teacher's right to teach "and the right of parents to engage him so to instruct their children" are within the Fourteenth Amendment's guarantee of liberty. The Constitution applies to all, including those who speak languages other than English.

The majority argued that the state statute unreasonably interfered with the liberty guaranteed by the Fourteenth Amendment. They noted that liberty stood for more than freedom from bodily restraint. It also denoted, "the right of the individual to contract, to engage in any of the common occupations of life, to acquire useful knowledge, to marry, establish a home and bring up children, to worship God according to the dictates of his own conscience, and generally to enjoy those privileges long recognized at common law as essential to the orderly pursuit of happiness by free men."

The majority recognized the state's reason for enacting such a statute, that the English language should become the primary language of all children raised in the United States. However, the majority argued that liberty could not be "interfered with, under the guise of protecting the public interest, by legislative action which is arbitrary or without reasonable relation to some purpose within the competency of the State to effect."

Two Supreme Court justices dissented from the majority without opinion.

AFTERMATH

This case has not been overruled. The year that the Court decided this case, a congressman introduced a bill proposing to make "American" the official language in the United States. The bill did not pass. Some states have made English the official language in their state.

SIGNIFICANCE

This decision makes it clear that states may not prohibit teaching a subject in a foreign language or the teaching of foreign language itself. However, the decision applies only to private, not public schools. The decision does not prevent a state from encouraging the use of English, nor does the decision prevent a state from requiring that English be taught in all schools. According to the Court in *Meyer,* a state still has the power to "make reasonable regulations for all schools, including the requirement that they shall give instruction in English."

RELATED CASES

Keyes v. School District No. 1, 413 U.S. 189 (1973)

Yu Cong Eng v. Trinidad, 271 U.S. 500 (1926)

RECOMMENDED READING

Bolmeier, Edward C. *Landmark Supreme Court Decisions on Public School Issues.* Charlottesville, Va.: The Michie Co., 1973.

David A. J. Richards, *The Individual, the Family and the Constitution: A Jurisprudential Perspective,* 55 NYU Law Review 1–62 (1980).

───※───

Case Title: *Miller v. California*

Alternate Case Title: The Community Standards Case

Legal Citations: 413 U.S. 15; 93 S.Ct. 2d 607; 37 L.Ed. 2d 419

Year of Decision: 1973 (Decided on same day as *Paris Adult Theater I v. Slaton.*)

───

KEY ISSUES

After the Supreme Court in *Jacobellis* found that the community standards language applied on a national basis, was the *Roth* test still intact?

HISTORY OF THE CASE

Marvin Miller operated an adult bookstore that mailed unsolicited brochures containing pictures and drawings of an explicitly sexual nature to residents of California. On five separate occasions, he mailed brochures to a restaurant in Newport Beach, California. The envelopes were opened by the manager of the restaurant and his mother. They had not requested the brochures, and filed a complaint with the police.

Miller was tried and convicted for violating a California statute that made it a misdemeanor to distribute obscene material. On appeal, the appellate department of the Superior Court of California affirmed the decision.

SUMMARY OF ARGUMENTS

Miller's attorney argued that the California statute mandated a statewide standard rather than a national standard to measure and establish whether printed material was an affront to community standards. Miller's attorney further argued that both the ROTH V. UNITED STATES (1957) decision and the statute interfered with the free flow of commerce throughout the United States. Thus, they argued that federal law must allow for the determination of contemporary local community standards for the purpose of establishing obscenity.

The state of California argued that it and not the federal government had the right to regulate sexual morality. The state further argued that it could easily identify hard-core pornography, and that the pretense of artistic value did not cause undue difficulty in enforcing the law in question.

DECISION

Chief Justice Warren Burger wrote for a five-justice majority in a decision that resummarized obscenity standards. The chief justice reviewed the struggle of the Court to define obscenity since the 1950s and the confusion that had arisen from the Court's definitions of obscenity in the *Roth v. United States* (1957) and MEMOIRS V. MASSACHU-SETTS (1966) decisions, as well as in the JACOBEL-LIS V. OHIO (1964) decision. The Court had undergone a significant change in its membership, and since the *Memoirs* case had been decided, Chief Justice Earl Warren had been replaced by Chief Justice Warren Burger. Harry A. Blackmun, Lewis F. Powell, and William Rehnquist now replaced Justices Abe Fortas, Hugo Black, and John Harlan. Burger traced the development of the decisions in the above-mentioned cases and found that the *Roth* definition was essentially still workable with some fine tuning.

The Court thus held that (1) obscene material was not protected by the First Amendment; (2) the proper First Amendment standard to be applied by the states in determining whether particular material was obscene and subject to regulation is (A) whether the average person, applying contemporary community standards, would find that the work, taken as a whole, appealed to a prurient interest, (B) whether the work depicted or described, in a patently offensive way, sexual conduct that specifically is defined in state law as written by the legislature or authoritatively construed by the courts, and (C) whether the work, taken as a whole, lacks serious literary, artistic, political, or scientific value; (3) there is no longer a requirement that the material must be shown to be "utterly without redeeming social value"; (4) the state laws that specifically define sexual conduct must provide a fair notice to the public about what would bring prosecution; (5) obscenity was not to be determined by applying national standards, but rather by applying "contemporary community standards."

Chief Justice Burger emphasized that it was not the Court's purpose to provide regulatory schemes for the states and that the Court would await legislative efforts to determine what can or cannot be sold within their boundaries.

Chief Justice Burger stressed that it was not realistic to think that there could be a national standard because the people in Maine and Mississippi have different ideas of what is acceptable conduct when compared to those in Las Vegas or New York City.

Justice William Douglas wrote a dissent, saying that the Court had worked long and hard to define obscenity and had repeatedly failed. While he felt that the decision of Chief Justice Burger was sincere and well intentioned, he had difficulty with any form of censorship being permitted under the First Amendment: "What causes one person to boil up in rage over one pamphlet or movie may reflect only his neurosis, not shared by others. We deal here with a regime of censorship which, if adopted, should be done by constitutional amendment after full debate by the people." Justice Douglas went on to say that obscenity cases generate too many emotional outbursts from the public, which do not belong in the courts. They should be debated properly and resolved in a constitutional amendment. Justice Douglas felt that the First Amendment was not supposed to be a tranquilizer for the people. Its main function was to keep debate open, and that may include offensive as well as staid debate.

Justices Brennan, Stewart, and Marshall dissented as well, stating that they felt the states had the power only to regulate the distribution of sexually oriented materials to juveniles or the exposure of such materials to nonconsenting adults.

AFTERMATH

The *Miller* decision shifted the burden of the responsibility of determining whether each part of the obscenity standard has been met to criminal juries in local communities.

SIGNIFICANCE

The *Miller* standard has stood for more than 20 years as the test of obscenity.

RELATED CASES

A Book Named John Cleland's Memoirs of a Woman of Pleasure v. Massachusetts, 383 U.S. 413 (1966)

Jacobellis v. Ohio, 378 U.S. 184 (1974)

Roth v. United States, 354 U.S. 476 (1957)

RECOMMENDED READING

Heather C. Beatty, *Enough Already to the Obscene Results of* Miller v. California, 11 Loyola Entertainment Law Journal 623 (1991).

Downs, Robert B., and Ralph E. McCoy, eds. *The First Freedom Today: Critical Issues Relating to Censorship and Intellectual Freedom.* Chicago: American Library Association, 1984.

Middleton, Kent, and Lori M. Mersky. *Freedom of Expression: A Collection of Best Writings.* Buffalo, N.Y.: Hein, 1981.

Case Title: *National Association for the Advancement of Colored People v. Alabama*

Legal Citation: 357 U.S. 449

Year of Decision: 1958

KEY ISSUES

May a state require that a corporation disclose the names and addresses of its members?

HISTORY OF THE CASE

The National Association for the Advancement of Colored People (NAACP), a nonprofit membership corporation, had chartered affiliates that opened an office in Alabama. The affiliates did not comply with an Alabama statute that required out-of-state corporations to qualify before doing business in the state by filing a corporate charter and designating a place of business and an agent to whom legal complaints should be delivered. Alabama brought an equity suit in state court to enjoin the NAACP from doing business until it had complied with the statute. The state court issued a restraining order preventing the NAACP from engaging in activities as well as from taking steps to qualify. The NAACP fought the restraining order, and upon motion by Alabama, the state court ordered the association to produce many documents, including membership lists. The NAACP complied with everything except the request for membership lists. It was found in contempt and fined $100,000. The NAACP appealed

and the Alabama State Supreme Court refused the case. The U.S. Supreme Court agreed to review it.

SUMMARY OF ARGUMENTS

Alabama contended that the NAACP was irreparably harming the property and civil rights of the residents and citizens of Alabama by doing business without complying with the qualification statute.

The NAACP contended that its activities did not subject it to the state's qualification requirements and that the request for membership lists would violate its members' freedom of speech and assembly guaranteed under the Fourteenth Amendment of the U.S. Constitution.

DECISION

Justice Harlan delivered the opinion of the Court, which reversed the state court's decision. The Court held that the right to engage in association to further beliefs and ideas is protected by the due process clause of the Fourteenth Amendment, which embraces the First Amendment's freedom of speech. The request for membership lists would put a substantial restraint on this freedom of association. The state could overcome this only by showing a compelling state interest that could not be met by less restrictive means. This test is called strict scrutiny. The Court held that Alabama did not have a compelling interest because the NAACP had complied with all of the requests except for the membership lists, which were not deemed necessary for the qualifying statute.

AFTERMATH

The Court has continued to use the strict scrutiny standard for all questions involving restraints on the freedom of association or expression.

SIGNIFICANCE

This case made the freedom of association, which was implied in the First Amendment, a right on equal footing with the enumerated rights of press, speech, assembly, and petition. Only the strict scrutiny test can determine if a state may impair one's freedom of association.

RELATED CASES

Buckley v. Valeo, 424 U.S. 1 (1976)

NAACP v. Button, 371 U.S. 415 (1963)

Schware v. Board of Bar Examiners, 353 U.S. 232 (1957)

Shelton v. Tucker, 364 U.S. 479 (1960)

RECOMMENDED READING

Bork, Robert H. *The Tempting of America: The Political Seduction of the Law.* New York: Free Press, 1990.

Emerson, Thomas I. *The System of Freedom of Expression.* New York: Random House, 1970.

Marsha Rockey Schermer, *Freedom of Association: N.A.A.C.P. v. Alabama?,* 41 Ohio State Law Journal 823 (1980).

Case Title: *National Association for the Advancement of Colored People v. Button, Atty. General of Virginia*

Legal Citations: 371 U.S. 415; 83 S.Ct. 328; 9 L.Ed. 2d 405

Year of Decision: 1963

KEY ISSUES

Does a state statute, which bans "the improper solicitation of any legal or professional business," violate the Fourteenth Amendment and the NAACP's right to freedom of speech?

HISTORY OF THE CASE

The National Association for the Advancement of Colored People (NAACP) is a nonprofit organization with several branches in Virginia. Its purpose is to eliminate racial discrimination, to which it devotes extensive time to litigation through its own attorneys. NAACP defrays all expenses.

Chapter 33, passed by the Virginia legislature, amended existing statutes regarding attorney malpractice to expand the definition of solicitation of legal business, by including the acceptance of a case from a person not a party to the lawsuit.

The case was first brought by the NAACP in the U.S. District Court for the Eastern District of Virginia on the grounds that the statute violated the Fourteenth Amendment. The court did not pass on the constitutionality of Chapter 33. The circuit court of appeals did, however, and found it constitutional.

SUMMARY OF ARGUMENTS

The NAACP argued that Chapter 33 violated the First and Fourteenth Amendments.

Button, the attorney general of Virginia, argued that the solicitation of legal business was not protected by the First Amendment. Button also argued that Chapter 33 was a valid exercise of the state's power to regulate the legal profession.

DECISION

The Court held that the activities of the NAACP, its affiliates, and legal staff are modes of expression and association protected by the First and Fourteenth Amendments. Therefore, Virginia may not prohibit, under its power to regulate the legal profession, as improper the solicitation of legal business that does not violate the Canon of Professional Ethics.

Justice Brennan, writing for the majority of the Court, held the Virginia statutes were unconstitutional. He stated that the activities of the NAACP were protected by the First Amendment. The Court found that the statutes did not advance any state interest. The Court concluded that the NAACP, its affiliates, and legal staff are modes of expression and association protected by the First and Fourteenth Amendments and that Virginia, in its attempt to regulate the legal profession, may not prohibit the solicitation of legal business.

Justice Harlan wrote the dissenting opinion, stating his belief that the invalidation of a Virginia statute contradicts constitutional doctrine in the domain of state regulatory power over the legal profession. Justice Harlan expressed concern that the Court's determination that litigation was a type of political expression only caused more problems, because other organizations may believe this finding is applicable to them.

AFTERMATH

With this case, the Supreme Court began to address cases concerning First Amendment rights for commercial speech and professional solicitation.

SIGNIFICANCE

This decision affirmed the use of solicitation and subsequent litigation as a means to address political grievances and as expression and association protected by the First Amendment.

RELATED CASES

American Communications Association v. Douds, 339 U.S. 382 (1950)

Stromberg v. California, 283 U.S. 242 (1931)

Thomas v. Collins, 323 U.S. 516 (1945)

RECOMMENDED READING

Emerson, Thomas I. *The System of Freedom of Expression.* New York: Random House, 1970.

The Supreme Court, 1977 Term, 92 Harvard Law Review 166 (1978).

The Supreme Court, 1962 Term, 77 Harvard Law Review 122 (1963).

Case Title: *New York Times Co. v. United States*

Alternate Case Title: The Pentagon Papers Case

Legal Citations: 403 U.S. 713; 91 S.Ct. 2140; 29 L.Ed. 2d 822

Year of Decision: 1971

KEY ISSUES

May the government prevent the publication of sensitive government documents?

HISTORY OF THE CASE

Two newspapers, the *New York Times* and the *Washington Post,* began publishing a series of articles based on and containing excerpts from a secret Defense Department study. The study involved the origins of the war then intensifying in Vietnam. The newspapers received the information from a former Defense Department analyst and member of the National Security Council who had previously been given the documents in confidence. Because the government believed that public exposure of this material would be prejudicial to America's defense and foreign policy interests, it sought an injunction for prior restraint, preventing the newspapers from further publication.

SUMMARY OF ARGUMENTS

The government argued that it has an inherent power to protect its secrets. It also argued that the president, through his constitutional power over the conduct of foreign affairs and his authority as commander in chief, should be able to decide what may threaten the country's security. In addition, the government argued that publication would violate various provisions of the Espionage Act.

The newspapers argued, among other things, that the drafters of the First Amendment aimed to forbid all governmental action that seeks to prevent expression from occurring. They argued that allowing such prior restraints would cause a "chilling effect" on the exercise of First Amendment rights. They also noted that the most recent events described in the study were more than three years old at the time of publication, and that several of the articles were based on information from the public domain. Thus, they reasoned, there was no threat to current military or diplomatic affairs.

DECISION

The Court held that the government was not entitled to the injunction. Citing prior case law, the Court noted that there is a heavy presumption against the constitutionality of denying the use of a public forum before any expression occurs. However, all nine justices filed separate opinions, three of which would have dissented and have upheld the granting of the preliminary injunction pending a speedy trial on the facts and elements of the case.

Six justices thought that prior restraints were inappropriate. Although Justices Black and Douglas wrote separate opinions, each joined the opinion of the other. They both believed that the First Amendment requires an absolute prohibition against prior restraints, not just a "heavy presumption" against their constitutionality. Justice White opined that prior restraints could occur in extraordinary circumstances, but added that this "heavy presumption" does not prohibit the government from seeking a criminal conviction that the published information violates the Espionage Act. Justice Marshall noted that Congress had not authorized suits enjoining the publication of security secrets. Thus, he reasoned, it would be impermissible for the Court to issue an injunction against conduct that Congress specifically declined to prohibit.

The three dissenters, Chief Justice Burger and Justices Blackmun and Harlan, each stressed the unfortunate speed in which the litigation had been conducted. Although Burger and Blackmun recognized a heavy presumption against prior restraints, they rejected the idea that the First Amendment absolutely barred prior restraints. Both Justices favored remand in order to permit further development of the evidence. Justice Harlan believed that the injunction should be upheld if the subject matter of the dispute fell within the proper scope of the president's power over foreign relations, and the appropriate executive department official determined that disclosure would irreparably impair the national security. Any other inquiry, Harlan believed, would be a violation of separation of powers principles.

AFTERMATH

The newspapers proceeded to finish publishing the excerpts of the Pentagon Papers. The government never showed or claimed that the publication subsequently caused "the death of soldiers, the destruction of alliances, the greatly increased difficulty of negotiation with our enemies, the inability of our diplomats to negotiate" (Blackmun's dissent at 763). Although the government did not criminally prosecute the newspapers subsequent to the Pentagon Papers decision, it did prosecute Daniel Ellsberg, the former government employee who leaked the papers. The trial judge acquitted Ellsberg, however, due to various prosecution improprieties. Today, the test described in Justice Harlan's dissent controls the majority of the Court.

SIGNIFICANCE

The Pentagon Papers case established that the governmental classification of a document does not automatically entitle the government to an injunction prohibiting its publication. The government must prove that the document is highly inappropriate for public examination in order to override the First Amendment's hostility toward prior restraints.

RELATED CASES

Near v. Minnesota, 283 U.S. 697 (1931)

Nebraska Press Assoc. v. Stuart, 427 U.S. 539 (1976)

Snepp v. United States, 376 U.S. 301 (1980)

RECOMMENDED READING

Margaret A. Blanchard, *The Institutional Press and Its First Amendment Privileges,* Supreme Court Review 225 (1978).

Stanley Godofsky, *Protection of the Press from Prior Restraint and Harassment under Libel Laws,* 29 University of Miami Law Review 462 (spring 1975).

Louis Henkin, *The Right to Know and the Duty to Withhold: The Case of the Pentagon Papers,* 120 University of Pennsylvania Law Review 271 (1971).

Case Title: *Paris Adult Theater I v. Slaton*

Alternate Case Title: The Consenting Adult Case

Legal Citations: 413 U.S. 49; 93 S.Ct. 2628; 37 L.Ed. 2d 446

Year of Decision: 1973 (Decided on same day as *Miller v. California.*)

KEY ISSUES

May an individual commercially exhibit obscene material to consenting adults?

HISTORY OF THE CASE

Investigators for the Atlanta district attorney's office paid their admission and attended two movies, *Magic Mirror* and *It All Comes Out in the End,* at the adult theater known as the Paris

Adult Theater in downtown Atlanta. After viewing the films, the Atlanta district attorney brought complaints that the theater was exhibiting obscene films and asked for a restraining order to prohibit the theater from showing the films. The owner of the theater produced the movies to the trial court, where they were shown to a judge. Additionally, photographs of the outside of the theater were shown, indicating that on the door of the theater was a sign saying "Adult Theater: You must be 21 and able to prove it. If viewing the nude body offends you, please do not enter." No evidence was ever presented that minors had ever entered the theater. The trial centered on whether the owner of the theater had made any effort to indicate the full nature of what was shown in the movies. In particular, the question was raised as to whether certain sexual acts that were depicted in the movie had been advertised. The trial court dismissed the complaint and felt that there was adequate notice to the public, and that showing such movies was permissible.

On appeal, the Georgia Supreme Court reversed unanimously. They found that a full warning to the public of the nature of the films shown must be given. They felt that the films constituted hard-core pornography and that their showing should be prohibited.

SUMMARY OF ARGUMENTS

The owners argued that, at best, these were borderline films and were entitled to full constitutional protection as protected speech. There was no evidence that minors had ever seen the movies or that there was any attempt to intrude on the privacy of any individual who preferred to avoid this kind of material. Further, the attorneys for the theater argued that the censor has the duty to have evidence of the elements of obscenity, and they maintained that the state had failed to prove any encroachment on the rights of individuals by this showing of these two movies in what was clearly marked as an adult theater.

The attorneys for the state argued that the films themselves were the best evidence of what they contain. They stated that the materials were hard-core pornography and, in spite of the fact that they were displayed in a sexually oriented commercial theater, there was no notice displayed as to the contents of the film. They further argued that obscene materials are not treated as protected expression under the First Amendment, regardless of whether they are shown to consenting adults or not.

DECISION

The same 5-4 split as in *Miller v. California* enabled Chief Justice Warren Burger to write the opinion of the majority of the justices in this case as well. Chief Justice Burger rejected the argument that there was privacy for consenting adults in a commercial setting. In an effort to avoid reopening the controversy in STANLEY V. GEORGIA (1969), which held that individuals have the absolute right to view obscene materials in their homes, Chief Justice Burger focused on the fact that there are state interests in controlling the commercial showing of obscenity. These include the total quality of community life and the tone of commerce for the city and possibly public safety. He found that there was no comparison to a private home or even a marital bedroom on behalf of a commercial venture.

Chief Justice Burger used *Paris Adult Theater I* as another link in the chain from *Roth* to MILLER V. CALIFORNIA (1973).

Justice William O. Douglas again dissented. While he noted that he would personally find many books and movies offensive that are brought before the Court, he had yet to be trapped into seeing or reading something that was offensive. As a parent, priest, or teacher, he felt he could steer his children away from such books and movies, but not as a judge making decisions on behalf of the police power of the United States.

Justice William Brennan also dissented. In a review of earlier cases, he found that the lesson of *Roth* was that the outright suppression of obscenity cannot be reconciled with the principles of the First and Fourteenth Amendments. He felt that the Court had failed to come up with a standard that distinguishes protected from unprotected speech and that the Court had obscured the rationale in its decisions. Because of the hopeless confusion that these decisions had created, he found it was impossible to define obscenity with enough precision to warrant the arrest and conviction of anyone for displaying or selling obscene material. Thus one cannot say with any certainty what is obscene until at least five members of the Supreme Court apply an obscure standard and pronounce the material to be obscene. Therefore, because of the lack of notice, there is a chill on expression and a stress imposed on the state and federal courts in trying to enforce obscenity laws.

Justice Brennan suggested that "apart from the interest of juveniles and unconsenting adults . . . I am compelled to conclude that these interests [the states' regulation of obscenity] cannot justify the substantial damage to the constitutional rights and to this nation's judicial machinery that inevitably results from state efforts to bar the distribution even of unprotected material to consenting adults."

AFTERMATH

The *Paris* decision was handed down the same day as *Miller v. California*. Both decisions shifted the regulation of obscene material from the national to the local level. In response, many towns enacted obscenity laws that reflected their community's values.

SIGNIFICANCE

Paris Adult Theater I v. Slaton effectively removed the U.S. Supreme Court from the business of deciding obscenity cases, as the Court indicated it would defer to the judgments of state legislatures as to the effects of obscenity.

RELATED CASES

Jacobellis v. Ohio, 378 U.S. 184 (1964)

Miller v. California, 413 U.S. 15 (1973)

Stanley v. Georgia, 394 U.S. 557 (1969)

RECOMMENDED READING

Joel E. Friedlander, *Constitution and Kulture Kampf: A Reading of the Shadow Theology of Justice Brennan,* 140 University of Pennsylvania Law Review 1049 (1992).

Schauer, F. *The Law of Obscenity.* Washington: Bureau of National Affairs, 1976.

Darlene Sordillo, *Emasculating the Defense in Obscenity Cases: The Exclusion of Expert Testimony and Survey Evidence on Community Standards,* 10 Loyola Entertainment Law Journal 619 (1990).

Case Title: *Board of Regents, University of Wisconsin System v. Southworth*

Alternate Case Title: Wisconsin Student Fee Case

Legal Citation: 120 S.Ct. 1346

Year of Decision: 2000

KEY ISSUES

Can public colleges and universities use money from mandatory student activities fees to finance student groups that engage in political speech that some students find objectionable?

HISTORY OF THE CASE

The University of Wisconsin is a public corporation of the state of Wisconsin and ranks among the nation's largest institutions of higher learning. Since its founding, the university has required full-time students enrolled at its Madison campus to pay a nonrefundable activity fee. The fee is separate and segregated from the university's tuition charge. A large majority of the fee income is used by the university to cover expenses such as student health services, intramural sports, debt service, and the upkeep and operations of the student union facilities. Approximately 20 percent of the fee income supports extracurricular endeavors pursued by the university's registered student organizations. The activities undertaken by registered student organizations are diverse in range and content, from displaying posters and circulating newspapers throughout the campus to hosting campus debates and guest speakers to political lobbying. The university publishes guidelines for regulating the conduct and activities of registered student organizations.

In 1996 some university students filed suit in federal court, alleging that imposition of the activity fee violated their right of free speech under the First Amendment. The students contended that the university must grant them the choice not to fund student organizations that engage in political and ideological expression offensive to their personal beliefs.

The federal trial court ruled in favor of the complaining students, deciding that the fee program compelled students to support political and ideological activity with which they disagree in violation of their First Amendment rights. The court of appeals agreed, reasoning that the students have a First Amendment interest in not being compelled to contribute to an organization whose expressive activities conflict with the students' own personal beliefs.

Because of the importance of the issue, and because other courts considering First Amendment challenges to similar student fee programs had reached conflicting results, the U.S. Supreme Court agreed to hear the case.

SUMMARY OF ARGUMENTS

Relying on case precedents that protect members of unions and bar associations from being required to pay fees used for speech the members find objectionable, the students argued that the mandatory student fee is unconstitutional under the First Amendment.

The university argued that its mandatory student activity fee and the speech it supports are appropriate to further its educational mission.

DECISION

The Court decided unanimously in favor of the university, holding that the First Amendment permits a public university to charge its students an activity fee used to fund a program to facilitate extracurricular speech, provided that allocation of funding support is viewpoint neutral. The main hurdle for the Court was to draw a distinction between this case and the precedents involving members of unions and bar associations. In his opinion for the Court, Justice Kennedy demonstrated that the rule in the earlier cases limited the required subsidy to speech relevant to the purposes of the union or bar association. Relevancy is an unattainable standard in the public university setting, particularly where that state undertakes to stimulate the whole universe of speech and ideas. According to Justice Kennedy's opinion, it is not for the Court to say what is or is not relevant to the ideas to be pursued in an institution of higher learning.

To assure some protection for students' First Amendment rights, the Court emphasized the requirement of viewpoint neutrality in the allocation of funding support. In other words, when a university requires its students to pay fees to support the extracurricular speech of other students, all in the interest of open discussion, it may not prefer some viewpoints to others.

AFTERMATH

The complaining students and the university agreed in court (or "stipulated," in legal jargon) that the program for student organizations respects the principle of viewpoint neutrality. Accordingly, the existing program may remain in place as long as it continues to treat all viewpoints equally. Most colleges divide up fees in a similar manner, which has now been approved by the Court.

SIGNIFICANCE

After two decades of increasing controversy and confrontation, speech on campus was an explosive issue by the time this case reached the Supreme Court. The decision suggests that the Court will continue to see a robust exchange of speech and ideas as the best guarantee of First Amendment rights. Viewpoint neutrality is the tool endorsed by the Court to assure that minority views are treated with the same respect as are majority views.

RELATED CASES

Abood v. Detroit Board of Education, 431 U.S. 209 (1977)

Keller v. State Bar of California, 496 U.S. 1 (1990)

Rosenberger v. Rector and Visitors of University of Virginia, 515 U.S. 819 (1995)

RECOMMENDED READING

Travis Crabtree, Southworth v. Grebe: *The Inquisition of the First Amendment,* 36 Houston Law Review (1999).

David G. Savage, *Freedom from Forced Fees: University Students Reject the Notion of Subsidizing Campus Groups Whose Views They Don't Share,* 85 ABA Journal 38 (November 1999).

Case Title: *Red Lion Broadcasting Co. v. FCC v. Radio Television News Directors Association*

Legal Citation: 385 U.S. 367

Year of Decision: 1969

KEY ISSUES

Does a requirement that radio stations give reply time to answer personal or political attacks violate the First Amendment guarantee of freedom of speech?

HISTORY OF THE CASE

The Federal Communications Commission (FCC) imposed a requirement on radio and television broadcasters that discussion of public issues be presented and that each side of those issues be given fair coverage. The requirement was known as the fairness doctrine. A Pennsylvania radio station carried a 15-minute broadcast as part of a "Christian Crusade" by the Reverend Billy James Hargis. Hargis accused the author of a book on Barry Goldwater of working for a communist-affiliated publication and of defending Alger Hiss. Hargis claimed that the book was written in an attempt to "smear and destroy" Barry Goldwater. The author of the book claimed that he had been personally attacked and demanded free reply time pursuant to FCC regulations and the fairness doctrine. The station refused to give the author reply time. The FCC concluded that the broadcast was indeed a personal attack and ordered the radio station to give the author free reply time. In a consolidated case, the Radio Television News Directors Association challenged the FCC's political and editorializing rules. The court of appeals for the D.C. circuit upheld the FCC's position requiring the free reply time. The Seventh Circuit Court of Appeals held that the rules compromised freedom of speech and freedom of the press. The Supreme Court granted certiorari and consolidated the two cases.

SUMMARY OF ARGUMENTS

Red Lion Broadcasting and the Radio Television News Directors Association argued that the fairness doctrine as carried out by the FCC substantially impaired their ability to broadcast as they chose and therefore violated First Amendment guarantees of freedom of speech and freedom of the press. They made the analogy that since no person could be required to give equal weight to opposing views in what he or she publishes or speaks, then broadcasters must have the same latitude and protection.

The FCC argued that given the unique nature of radio and television broadcasting, the different mediums were subject to different First Amendment standards. The FCC argued that, because of the limited frequencies available to broadcasters, not everyone could access the radio or television. Since the excluded parties should be given a voice in those mediums, the regulations and the fairness doctrine were constitutionally permissible.

DECISION

Justice White delivered the 8-0 decision of the Court upholding the fairness doctrine. Justice Douglas did not participate in the decision. The Court reasoned that broadcasters are not owners of frequencies but merely temporarily privileged license holders. The Court traced the history of broadcasting back to the days before regulation when virtual chaos existed on the airwaves. The Court concluded that if there is to be any effective communication by radio or television, it must be regulated in the public interest. As a result, the government cannot allow monopolization of the market. The fairness doctrine was a reasonable and feasible solution in the Court's opinion. The Court held that the rights of the viewers and listeners is paramount over the rights of the broadcasters. Since the First Amendment preserves an uninhibited marketplace of ideas, the lopsided broadcasting could not be permitted in the public interest.

AFTERMATH

The Court's decision established the constitutionality of regulations requiring access rights in broadcast media. In 1981, the Court upheld a requirement that broadcasters give "reasonable and good faith attention" to federal candidates for political office when they seek air time. The decision did not constitute an unlimited right to access, but attempted to balance the competing interests of the First Amendment, the public, and the broadcasters themselves.

SIGNIFICANCE

Given the boom in information technology and the recent move to consolidate cyberspace and television media, the fairness doctrine and access rights will inevitably resurface in American jurisprudence. *Red Lion* was the first case to rule on this issue on constitutional grounds and will no doubt become a pivotal decision in any future litigation concerning access rights and the First Amendment.

RELATED CASES

Columbia Broadcasting System v. Democratic National Committee, 412 U.S. 94 (1973)

Miami Herald Publishing Co. v. Tornillo, 418 U.S. 241 (1974)

National Broadcasting Co., Inc. v. U.S., 319 U.S. 190 (1943)

RECOMMENDED READING

John C. Barrett and Mary Louise Frampton, *From the FCC's Fairness Doctrine to* Red Lion*'s Fiduciary Principle,* 5 Harvard Civil Rights–Civil Liberties Law Review 89 (January 1970).

Abbott B. Lipsky, Jr., *Reconciling* Red Lion *and* Tornillo: *A Consistent Theory of Media Regulation,* 28 Stanford Law Review 563 (1979).

Richard D. Marks, *Broadcasting and Censorship: First Amendment Theory after* Red Lion, 38 George Washington Law Review 974 (1970).

Schmidt, Benno C., Jr. *Freedom of the Press vs. Public Access.* New York: Praeger Publishers, 1976.

Case Title: *Reno v. American Civil Liberties Union*

Alternate Case Title: Communications Decency Act Case

Legal Citation: 521 U.S. 844

Year of Decision: 1997

KEY ISSUES

Are two provisions of the Communications Decency Act of 1996, enacted to protect minors from "indecent" and "patently offensive" communications on the Internet, unconstitutional in abridging the freedom of speech protected by the First Amendment?

HISTORY OF THE CASE

The Internet is an international network of interconnected computers. Since the early 1990s, the Internet has experienced extraordinary growth. The number of "host" computers—those that store information and relay communications—was approximately 9,400,000 by 1996, when the Communications Decency Act was passed by Congress. The best-known category of communication over the Internet is the World Wide Web, which allows users to search for and retrieve information stored in remote computers, as well as, in some cases, to communicate back to designated sites. The Web is comparable from the users' viewpoint to both a vast library including millions of readily available and indexed publications and a sprawling mall offering goods and services.

Any person or organization with a computer connected to the Internet can "publish" information. Publishers include government agencies, educational institutions, commercial entities, advocacy groups, and individuals. From the publishers' point of view, the Web constitutes a vast platform from which to address and hear from a worldwide audience of millions of researchers, readers, viewers, and buyers. Publishers may either make their material available to the entire pool of Internet users or confine access to a select group, such as those willing to pay for the privilege. No single organization controls any membership in the Web, nor is there any single centralized point from which individual websites or services can be blocked from the Web.

Sexually explicit material on the Internet includes text, pictures, and interactive chat. These files are created, named, and posted in the same manner as material that is not sexually explicit and may be accessed either deliberately or unintentionally during a search. However, unlike communications received by radio or television, the receipt of information on the Internet requires a series of affirmative steps more deliberate and directed than merely turning a dial. A child would need some sophistication and some ability to retrieve material and thereby to use the Internet unattended. Systems have been developed to help parents control the material that may be available on a home computer with Internet access and to block material that parents may consider inappropriate for their children.

The Communications Decency Act of 1996 contained two provisions addressing the perceived availability to minors of sexually explicit material through the Internet. The first, informally described as the "indecent transmission" provision, prohibited the knowing transmission of obscene or indecent messages to any recipient under 18 years of age. The second, the "patently offensive display" provision, prohibited the knowing, sending, or displaying of patently offensive messages in a manner that is available to a person under 18 years of age.

In ruling on a lawsuit brought by the American Civil Liberties Union and several other interested organizations, a federal district court prohibited the government from enforcing the two provisions described above. According to the district court, the terms "patently offensive" and "indecent" were so inherently vague that criminal enforcement of either provision would violate constitutional protections of the First and Fifth Amendments.

SUMMARY OF ARGUMENTS

In the U.S. Supreme Court, the American Civil Liberties Union argued that the Communications Decency Act was so overbroad and vague that it chilled adults' right to the freedom of expression guaranteed by the First Amendment. The government argued that the challenged provisions of the act were neither overbroad nor vague and that the act was plainly constitutional in light of relevant Supreme Court precedents.

DECISION

The Supreme Court held that the "indecent transmission" and "patently offensive display" provisions of the Communications Decency Act abridge the freedom of speech protected by the First Amendment. In its opinion written by Justice Stevens, the Court explained that the act's broad coverage is wholly unprecedented. The scope of the Communications Decency Act is not limited to commercial speech or commercial entities. Its open-ended prohibitions embrace all nonprofit entities and individuals posting indecent messages or displaying them on their own computers in the presence of minors. The general, undefined terms "indecent" and "patently offensive" cover large amounts of nonpornographic material with serious educational or other value.

Moreover, as explained in Justice Stevens's opinion, the act poses a special burden in the context of the Internet. Under relevant precedents, "indecent" and "patently offensive" materials would be evaluated under "community standards." Applying the "community standards" criterion to the Internet would mean that any communication available to a nationwide audience would be judged by the standards of the community most likely to be offended by the message.

AFTERMATH

The growth of the Internet has been and continues to be phenomenal. In the absence of governmental censorship, industry has been encouraged to develop and improve filtering software that provides concerned parents with a measure of control over the material that is available to children through the Internet.

SIGNIFICANCE

The decision in this case represents an early effort by the Court to address legal issues in the context of the Internet age. Entire fields of law—intellectual property, banking and other forms of electronic commerce, privacy, communications, and many others—may be recast in response to technological developments. Faced with the prospect of regulating virtual communities without political or geographic boundaries, lawmaking bodies have a range of choices. At one end of the spectrum, Congress could adopt a hands-off attitude toward the Internet; at the other end, it could attempt to replicate the existing legal structure in cyberspace. *Reno v. American Civil Liberties Union* suggests that, at least in these relatively young days of the Internet, the Court is reluctant to support governmental regulation of electronic communications.

RELATED CASES

FCC v. Pacifica Foundation, 438 U.S. 726 (1978)

Ginsberg v. New York, 390 U.S. 629 (1968)

Renton v. Playtime Theatres, Inc., 475 U.S. 41 (1986)

Sable Communications of Cal., Inc. v. FCC, 492 U.S. 115 (1989)

RECOMMENDED READING

James V. Dobeus, *Rating Internet Content and the Spectre of Government Regulation,* 16 John Marshall Journal of Computer & Information Law 625 (1998).

Praveen Goyal, *Congress Fumbles with the Internet,* 21 Harvard Journal of Law & Public Policy 637 (1998).

Mark S. Kende, *The Supreme Court's Approach to the First Amendment in Cyberspace: Free Speech as Technology's Hand-Maiden,* 14 Constitutional Commentary 465 (1997).

Eugene Volokh, *Freedom of Speech, Shielding Children, and Transcending Balancing,* Supreme Court Review 141 (1997).

Case Title: *Richmond Newspapers, Inc. v. Virginia*

Legal Citations: 448 U.S. 555; 100 S.Ct. 2814; 65 L.Ed. 2d 973

Year of Decision: 1980

KEY ISSUES

Does a court order that bars the public and press from the right of access to a murder trial violate the First Amendment right to freedom of speech, press, and association and the Fourteenth Amendment?

HISTORY OF THE CASE

Stevenson was indicted for the murder of a hotel manager who was found stabbed to death. Stevenson was found guilty, but the Virginia Supreme Court reversed because a bloodstained shirt was not admitted to evidence properly. There were two other trials, and both ended in mistrials.

The trial judge who had presided over two of the three previous trials of Stevenson excluded the public and press from the fourth trial. This was on motion of the Stevenson's counsel to which the prosecution, the public, and the press did not object. The judge granted the motion to close the trial, all under the legitimacy of a state statute.

Later that same day, a newspaper and its two reporters sought a hearing on a motion to vacate the closure order, stating that the court should first determine that the rights of the defendant to a fair trial could be protected in no other way. The court allowed the hearing but denied the motion. On appeal, the Virginia Supreme Court upheld the trial court. The Supreme Court agreed to hear the case.

SUMMARY OF ARGUMENTS

The newspaper argued that it had the right to attend a criminal trial under the First and Fourteenth Amendments.

The state of Virginia argued that neither the Constitution nor the Bill of Rights guaranteed the public the right to attend criminal trials and, therefore, such a right was not protected.

DECISION

Chief Justice Burger delivered the Court's opinion that the First and Fourteenth Amendments guarantee the public's right to attend criminal trials. Without an overriding interest based on findings, a criminal trial must be open to the public. In this case the trial judge had made no findings to support closure, no inquiry into alternative measures to ensure fairness, and no recognition of any constitutional right for the public or the press to attend the trial. This was the first time the Court had to distinguish between a trial and pretrial. Justice Burger found historical evidence between open society and open trials: "We are bound to conclude that a presumption of openness adheres in the very nature of a criminal trial under our system of justice."

Justice Stevens, concurring separately, called it a "watershed" case: "The Court unequivocally holds that an arbitrary interference with access to important information is an abridgment of the freedoms of speech and of the press protected by the First Amendment."

Justice Rehnquist was the sole dissenter. He felt that reviewing closure orders of state trial judges was not within the power of the federal judicial system. These judges, he wrote, "are making the same effort as we to uphold the Constitution."

Criminal trials are open to the public under the First Amendment. A court order closing a murder trial to the public and the press violates the right of access granted by the First and Fourteenth Amendments.

AFTERMATH

The holding brought about a flurry of activity to keep criminal trials open to the public. This decision applied only to criminal proceedings, however, not to civil ones.

In subsequent criminal cases, the Supreme Court reaffirmed that a presumption in favor of an open and public proceeding exists.

SIGNIFICANCE

This case was one of first impression for the Supreme Court and its decision marked the first time that the Court had found that acquiring newsworthy material was constitutionally protected.

RELATED CASES

First National Bank of Boston v. Bellotti, 435 U.S. 765 (1978)

Gannett Co. v. DePasquale, 443 U.S. 368 (1979)

Nebraska Press Association v. Stuart, 427 U.S. 539 (1976)

RECOMMENDED READING

Kane, Peter. *Murder, Courts and the Press.* Edwardsville: Southern Illinois University Press, 1986.

Roy V. Leeper, *Richmond Newspapers, Inc. v. Virginia and the Emerging Right of Access*, 61 Journalism Quarterly 615 (1984).

Anthony Lewis, *A Public Right to Know about Public Institutions: The First Amendment as a Sword*, Supreme Court Review 1 (1980).

Case Title: *Roberts v. United States Jaycees*

Legal Citations: 468 U.S. 609; 104 S.Ct. 3244; 82 L.Ed. 2d 462

Year of Decision: 1984

KEY ISSUES

Does the freedom of association allow a group to discriminate based on sex?

HISTORY OF THE CASE

The United States Jaycees is a nonprofit corporation whose objective is to promote the growth and development of young men's civic organizations. The Jaycees limited their memberships to men between the ages of 18 and 35. Women could join as associate members, but could not vote or hold office.

Two Minnesota local chapters of the Jaycees admitted women as full members, thereby violating Jaycees by-laws. The national office began to consider revoking the charters of the local chapters. Consequently, members of both chapters filed complaints with the Minnesota Department of Human Rights, claiming that the Jaycees discriminated against women in violation of the Minnesota Human Rights Act. Before a hearing took place with respect to the state charge, the Jaycees filed a suit in federal court. The federal district court certified the question of whether the application of the Minnesota Human Rights Act would violate the male Jaycees' freedom of association. The federal district court certifies a question to place an issue before the Supreme Court for instruction on how to resolve the issue. The state supreme court answered that it would be violative. The U.S. Court of Appeals disagreed.

DECISION

The acting commissioner of the Minnesota Department of Human Rights, Kathryn R. Roberts, argued that the exclusion of women from full membership in the Jaycees violated the Minnesota Human Rights Act.

The United States Jaycees argued that requiring the Jaycees to accept women as regular voting members would violate the male members' rights of free speech and association under the First and Fourteenth Amendments. The Jaycees also argued that the interpretation of the Minnesota Human Rights Act by the Minnesota Supreme Court made the act unconstitutionally vague and overbroad.

The U.S. Supreme Court rejected the claims of the Jaycees. The Court pointed out that there are two types of associational freedoms: (1) the freedom of intimate association, and (2) the freedom of expressive association, the right to associate for the purpose of participating in First Amendment–protected activities. While expressive association concerns activities protected by the First Amendment such as speech, assembly, and religion, intimate association stems from the right of the individual to define her own identity "that is central to the concept of ordered liberty." Because of the large size and generally unselective nature of the group, the Jaycees did not fall within the realm of intimate associations. Consequently, the issue before the Court became whether the application of the Minnesota Human Rights Act would violate the right to expressive association. That right is not absolute, explained the Court, and may be justified by compelling state interests, unrelated to the suppression of ideas. The Court noted that the Minnesota Human Rights Act, like the Civil Rights Act, was meant to prohibit the stigmatization and economic harms that arise in cases of discrimination in places of public accommodation. Consequently, the Court found that the state had a compelling state interest in prohibiting sex discrimination unrelated to the expression of the ideas. Therefore, the Court found that application of the Minnesota Human Rights Act would not violate the rights of the Jaycees to freely associate.

AFTERMATH

In 1984, the Jaycees amended their bylaws to admit women as full and regular members.

In *Board of Directors of Rotary Internat'l v. Rotary Club,* 481 U.S. 537 (1987), the Supreme Court applied the *Roberts* ruling to find that a California antidiscrimination law that prohibited the exclusion of women from local Rotary clubs did not deny the freedom of association.

SIGNIFICANCE

In *Roberts,* the Court established a structure to allow the Court to analyze claims of freedom of association. Further, the case forced the Court to address the tension between equality and association.

The application of antidiscrimination statutes to large clubs generally does not violate any freedom of association.

RELATED CASES

Rotary International v. Rotary Club of Duarte, 481 U.S. 537 (1987)

N.Y. State Club Ass'n v. New York, 487 U.S. 1 (1988)

RECOMMENDED READING

Gold, Susan Dudley. Roberts v. U.S. Jaycees (1984): *Women's Rights.* New York: Twenty-First Century Books, 1995.

Douglas O. Linder, *Comment: Freedom of Association after* Roberts v. United States Jaycees, 82 Michigan Law Review 1878 (1984).

Case Title: *Roemer v. Board of Public Works of Maryland*

Legal Citations: 426 U.S. 736; 96 S.Ct. 2337; 49 L.Ed. 2d 179

Year of Decision: 1976

KEY ISSUES

Does a Maryland program that provides aid to private higher educational institutions for religious purposes violate the First Amendment?

HISTORY OF THE CASE

In 1971, Maryland enacted a statute that authorized the payment of state funds to private institutions of higher learning within the state. The schools had to meet certain criteria and refrain from awarding religiously oriented degrees. The grants could not be used by institutions for sectarian purposes. The assistance program was administered by the Maryland Council for Higher Education, which determined eligibility, oversaw that the funds were not used for sectarian purposes, and demanded an annual accounting.

Four Maryland taxpayers, including John C. Roemer, brought this suit in district court, claiming that this statute violated the establishment clause of the First Amendment. The district court applied the three-prong *Lemon* test, formulated in *Lemon v. Kurtzman* (1971): State aid such as this must have a secular purpose, a primary effect other than the advancement of religion, and no tendency to entangle the state in church affairs. The court upheld the statute finding that despite its grant of aid to a college with a Catholic affiliation, it was not "pervasively sectarian" because the aid extended to "the sectarian side." The court also found that "there is no necessity for state officials to investigate the conduct of particular classes of educational programs to determine whether a school is attempting to indoctrinate its students under the guise of secular education."

SUMMARY OF ARGUMENTS

The appellants, John C. Roemer III and three other Maryland citizens and taxpayers, argued that the grants provided under the Maryland statute violated the establishment clause of the First Amendment.

Appellees, the Maryland Board of Public Works, four Roman Catholic universities, and others, argued that the grants did not violate the establishment clause of the First Amendment.

DECISION

The Court found that a program of annual non-categorical grants to private colleges does not violate the First Amendment, regardless of whether or not the colleges have a religious affiliation and whether or not the funds are used for sectarian purposes.

Justice Blackmun wrote the majority opinion for the Court affirming the district court holding. The Maryland statute met the requirements of the Lemon test. The aid provided did not have the advancement of religion as its primary effect, and there was no government entanglement since it was extended to all private colleges, most of which do not have any religious affiliation.

Justice Brennan wrote a dissenting opinion that this statute simply used taxpayer money to subsidize religion and to further the interests of a religion at sectarian institutions.

AFTERMATH

This case demonstrates a weakening of the Lemon test because aid to a religious school was upheld. It also clearly shows that the Court draws a distinction between higher and lower education for the purposes of public aid.

SIGNIFICANCE

Roemer affirmed *TILTON V. RICHARDSON* (1971), finding that aid to higher educational facilities was constitutional. Since this case, the Court has been inconsistent in striking down statutes that subsidize religion. It was 10 years before the Supreme Court heard another case involving aid to private educational institutions.

RELATED CASES

Bowen v. Kendrick, 487 U.S. 589 (1988)

Lemon v. Kurtzman, 403 U.S. 602 (1988)

Marsh v. Chambers, 463 U.S. 783 (1983)

Tilton v. Richardson, 403 U.S. 672 (1971)

RECOMMENDED READING

James C. Kirby, *Everson to Meek and Roemer,* 55 North Carolina Law Review 563 (1977).

Pfeffer, Leo. *Religion, State and the Burger Court.* Buffalo, N.Y.: Prometheus Books, 1984.

The Supreme Court, 1975 Term, 90 Harvard Law Review 133 (1976).

Case Title: *Roth v. United States*

Alternate Case Title: The Community Standards Case

Legal Citations: 354 U.S. 476; 77 S.Ct. 1304; 1 L.Ed. 2d 1498

Year of Decision: 1957

KEY ISSUES

What is the standard for judging obscenity of material that is mailed through the postal system?

HISTORY OF THE CASE

Under a federal law known as the Comstock Act, it was illegal to mail obscene material through the U.S. Postal Service. Samuel Roth, a Polish immigrant, conducted a business in New York State that published and sold magazines, photographs, and books such as *Photo and Body* and *The American Aphrodite.* To solicit sales, he sent various advertising circulars to individuals on purchased mailing lists, several of whom complained to the Post Office. The postal inspectors established false names and addresses and placed orders with Roth. In a companion case, David Alberts was convicted of violating an obscenity statute in the California Penal Code in his conduct of a mail order business from Los Angeles. Both men were convicted by trial courts and had their convictions affirmed by appellate courts. The issue raised in both cases was whether obscenity fell within the area of protected speech and freedom of the press.

SUMMARY OF ARGUMENTS

The attorneys for Roth argued that the federal obscenity statute did not provide a reasonably ascertainable standard of guilt. They argued that the statute should be held invalid because no one could reasonably decipher its requirements. Because a First Amendment right was involved, the standards must be particularly clear and precise. Further, the government must show that there is a substantive evil, so dangerous that clear and immediate harm would occur unless the publications in question were suppressed.

The United States argued that the material was worthless speech and that there was no social interest in protecting it. Indeed, society had an interest in public morality and in keeping such publications out of the marketplace. The preservation of public morality is of fundamental importance and would be seriously affected if the material Roth sought to sell was allowed to be distributed by the mails.

The United States argued that every state had some law regulating obscenity and that there were various international agreements regulating the distribution of obscene books and writings between countries.

Alberts's attorneys attacked the California statute as vesting broad powers of censorship in the government when the laws against obscene materials were vague and undefined. The attorney general of California argued that the states have a right to regulate morals under their police powers and that there is a framework of community values that gives these statutes sufficient meaning to protect society from the evils of censorship. (The Post Office was not involved in the Alberts case.)

The Authors League of America intervened as a friend of the court, and their attorneys argued that there were three kinds of speech: (1) Seditious or treasonous words, which the government does have the power to abridge; (2) merchandising words, which the government has a right to regulate in order to promote a fair marketplace; and (3) pure ideas, which the government may not abridge because they deal with the pure freedom of speech. Morris L. Ernst argued that neither the commerce power, the postal power, nor the Constitution gave any right to the federal government to use the Post Office as a censor. Abe Fortas, later to become a Supreme Court justice, filed a friend of the court brief for two publishing companies, also arguing that the federal statute was unworkable and provided no meaningful standard for administration.

The American Book Publishers Council also filed a brief in which it asserted that freedom of speech must be given a preferred place in our system of liberties and that protection extends to all types of writing regardless of their literary worth. Since no one had ever established a connection between obscene publications and any evil, the restrictions on the freedom of the press could not be justified.

The American Civil Liberties Union also intervened, saying that the statutes did not meet the due process test of the Fourteenth Amendment.

DECISION

Justice William Brennan wrote the majority opinion. Justices William O. Douglas, Hugo Black, and John Harlan dissented. Justice Brennan's majority opinion reviewed the history of the idea of obscenity from colonial days, through the Continental Congress, and up until the adoption of the Bill of Rights. Brennan found that it is implicit in the history of the First Amendment that obscenity, matter that is utterly without redeeming social importance, should be restrained. Loud and obscene utterances are not an essential part of the transmission of ideas and are of such a slight social value as steps toward truth that any benefit from them is clearly outweighed by society's interest in order and morality.

Justice Brennan found that sex and obscenity were not identical. The portrayal of sex in art, literature, and scientific work is not universally sufficient to allow blanket protection. Sex itself is a vital problem of human interest and public concern. Justice Brennan then stated that the proper test should be "whether to the average person, applying contemporary community standards, the dominant theme of the material taken as a whole appeals to prurient interest." Books, pictures, and magazines must be judged in their entire context and not in detached or isolated portions.

In his dissent, Justice John Harlan felt that obscenity statutes should be entrusted to the care of the states, not the federal government. He felt that Congress had no substantial power over sexual morality. He raised the example of the D. H. Lawrence novel *Lady Chatterley's Lover*. Supposing one state found it offensive and banned it, the states adjoining it remained free to make their own choices. There would not be a uniform standard. Thus there would be 48 separate choices, none of which would constitute a blanket ban on a book.

Justices William O. Douglas and Hugo Black also dissented, stating that there was no scientific basis to determine what material was obscene. They felt that obscene literature is an insignificant fact in influencing behavior in a community. In the absence of dependable information on the effect of obscene literature, they would be leery of any decision that would intrude on the freedom of speech.

AFTERMATH

The convictions of both Roth and Alberts were affirmed. The Supreme Court had now made community standards a critical test in the definition of obscenity.

SIGNIFICANCE

Roth remains important because it clearly established that obscenity was not protected speech. The importance of *Roth* stems from Justice Brennan's efforts to define obscenity. The Court continued to struggle with a workable definition, and it was not until *MILLER V. CALIFORNIA* (1973) that the Court produced any sort of lasting guidelines.

RELATED CASES

Memoirs v. Massachusetts, 383 U.S. 413 (1966)

Miller v. California, 413 U.S. 15 (1973)

Shenck v. U.S., 249 U.S. 47 (1919)

RECOMMENDED READING

William J. Brennan, Jr., *The Supreme Court and the Meikeljohn Interpretation of the First Amendment*, 79 Harvard Law Review 1 (1965).

Freidman, Leon. *Obscenity: The Complete Oral Arguments before the Supreme Court in the Major*

Obscenity Cases. New York: Chelsea House Publishers, 1970.

Eric Hoffman, *Feminism, Pornography and Law*, 133 University of Pennsylvania Law Review 497 (1985).

Rembar, Charles. *The End of Obscenity: The Trials of Lady Chatterley, Tropic of Cancer and Fanny Hill*. New York: Random House, 1968.

Simon Roberts, *The Obscenity Exemption: Abusing the First Amendment*, 10 Cardozo Law Review 677 (1989).

Case Title: *Saia v. New York*

Legal Citations: 334 U.S. 558; 68 S.Ct. 1148; 92 L.Ed. 1574

Year of Decision: 1948

KEY ISSUES

Do city ordinances prohibiting the use of sound amplification devices without a permit in cases of news, matters of public concern, and athletic activities violate the First Amendment right to free speech?

HISTORY OF THE CASE

Saia, a Jehovah's Witness minister, was convicted of violating a municipal ordinance prohibiting the use of amplification devices that project sound onto streets and public places for the purpose of attracting the attention of the passing public or advertising. Saia obtained permission from the chief of police to amplify lectures on religious subjects in a public park on Sundays. When the permit expired, he was refused another one because complaints had been made. He continued to use his amplification equipment in the park without a permit. The court of Niagara County affirmed the defendant's conviction in police court. The New York Court of Appeals affirmed the county court decision. The Supreme Court agreed to review the case.

SUMMARY OF ARGUMENTS

Saia argued that the ordinance forbidding the use of sound amplification devices except with the permission of the chief of police violated the First Amendment right to free speech.

New York argued that the ordinance did not violate the Constitution.

DECISION

Justice Douglas delivered the opinion of the Court. In a 5-4 decision, the Court held that part of the ordinance was unconstitutional because the use of amplification devices was subject to the police chief's uncontrolled discretion. It established a previous restraint on the right to free speech in violation of the First Amendment, which is protected by the Fourteenth Amendment against state action. There were no standards established for the use of the police chief's discretion. The Court noted that noise could be controlled by regulating decibels and the hours and place of public discussion, but a city could not allow an official uncontrolled discretion to ban loudspeakers, because it would sanction a device for suppression of a free communication of ideas.

Three dissenting justices argued that the right of Saia to use loudspeakers, effectively forcing his message on the public, did not outweigh the public's right to quiet and privacy. They noted that municipalities have to try to make city life endurable in light of the new problems sound equipment creates. They argued that the right of the public to put their mind and attention to their own use should not be denied, and that there was no constitutional right to force unwilling people to listen to a broadcast from loudspeakers in a public place.

The last dissenter, Justice Jackson, noted that Saia parked his car mounted with speakers in the park in an area not open to other vehicles and strung electric wires across a sidewalk. He also placed microphones in other areas of the park away from his vehicle. He asserted that Saia was convicted of setting up this system of microphones and wires, not for speaking. A municipality can police and control erection of equipment in its public parks as a precaution against annoyance or injury. Because Saia was not denied the right to use the park to speak or invite assemblage, Justice Jackson argued that this was not a free speech issue.

AFTERMATH

The courts have continued to follow the holding in *Saia*. Although uncontrolled administrative dis-

cretion of loudspeakers is not permitted, regulation of such amplification devices is allowed.

SIGNIFICANCE

Saia's decision is important and "amplified" as the Court has only been presented with the loudspeaker issue on a couple of occasions. While Saia is still good law, it was a 5-4 decision, which implies that it could be overruled in the future.

RELATED CASES

Kovacs v. Cooper, 336 U.S. 77 (1949)

Public Utilities Comm'n v. Pollak, 343 U.S. 451 (1952)

RECOMMENDED READING

Berns, Walter. *Freedom, Virtue and the First Amendment.* Baton Rouge: Louisiana State University Press, 1957.

Richard A. Posner, *The Uncertain Protection of Privacy by the Supreme Court,* 1979 Supreme Court Review 173–216 (1979).

Case Title: *Scales v. United States*

Legal Citations: 367 U.S. 203; 81 S.Ct. 1469; 6 L.Ed. 2d 782

Year of Decision: 1961

KEY ISSUES

Does the membership clause of the Smith Act, which makes it a felony to join any organization that advocates the violent overthrow of the government, violate the Constitution?

HISTORY OF THE CASE

Junius Irving Scales was convicted of violating the membership clause of the Smith Act, which makes membership in an organization that advocates the overthrow of the government by force or violence illegal. It was alleged that the Communist Party was such an organization, of which Scales was a member with knowledge of the party's illegal purpose and specific intent to overthrow the government. The jury in the District Court for the Middle District of North Carolina considered whether Scales was an "active" member of the party or an inactive member with knowledge of the illegal advocacy with a specific intent to overthrow the government.

SUMMARY OF ARGUMENTS

Scales argued that the membership clause of the Smith Act was unconstitutional under the First, Fifth, and Sixth Amendments to the U.S. Constitution.

The United States argued that the membership clause of the Smith Act was constitutional.

DECISION

In a rare decision, the Supreme Court affirmed Scales's lower court conviction. Justice Harlan delivered the opinion of the Court, interpreting the Smith Act to require "specific intent to accomplish violent overthrow" and "active" membership in a proscribed organization. He noted that the distinction between active and nominal is well known. The active member is the one who will likely engage in the prohibited activity. The nominal, or passive, member is not likely to do so. The Smith Act allows conviction based on membership in the Communist Party where the defendant had the specific intent to carry out the party's aims by illegal means. Mere passive membership is not actionable. If Congress intended to punish passive membership, it would be a First Amendment violation.

Justice Brennan wrote the dissent, finding that Scales was not charged with a single illegal act. The essence of the crime is belief in the proletariat revolution, belief in the communist creed. The case was not saved by showing that Scales was an active member because none of his activity was a crime: He recruited, directed a school, taught, and handed out leaflets. According to Justice Brennan, none of these had an illegal element.

AFTERMATH

After Scales began serving a six-year sentence, President Kennedy commuted the sentence. Scales died in 2002.

SIGNIFICANCE

This case represents the only time the Supreme Court upheld the criminal conviction of a citizen solely for membership in a political organization. The decision in DENNIS V. UNITED STATES (1950) required that the government show a connection between advocacy and action. This ended most Smith Act prosecutions because no longer could mere membership in the Communist Party support a conviction. There were not many convictions under the act.

RELATED CASES

Aptheker v. Secretary of State, 378 U.S. 500 (1964)

Dennis v. United States, 339 U.S. 162 (1950)

Yates v. United States, 354 U.S. 298 (1957)

RECOMMENDED READING

Emerson, Thomas I. *The System of Freedom of Expression.* New York: Random House, 1970.

The Supreme Court, 1960 Term, 75 Harvard Law Review 111 (1961).

Case Title: *Charles T. Schenck v. United States*

Alternate Case Titles: Clear and Present Danger Case, Shouting Fire in a Crowded Theater Case

Legal Citations: 249 U.S. 47; 63 L.Ed. 470; 30 S.Ct. 247

Year of Decision: 1919

KEY ISSUES

May freedom of speech be restricted during wartime?

HISTORY OF THE CASE

Charles T. Schenck was the general secretary of the Socialist Party. When the United States entered World War I against Germany, the Congress passed the Espionage Act of 1917, which made it illegal to cause insubordination in the military forces of the United States, to obstruct recruiting and enlistment into the armed services of the

United States, or to convey false information that would interfere with U.S. military operations. The Socialist Party met in Philadelphia in August 1917 and voted to send 15,000 leaflets to men who had recently been drafted. Schenck had personally attended to the printing of the pamphlets and was involved in addressing envelopes. The pamphlet in question contained the idea that conscription was little better than forced servitude. It compared those conscripted to those convicted of crimes in violation of the Thirteenth Amendment to the U.S. Constitution, which outlawed slavery. It further urged that those conscripted assert their rights and refuse to be drafted. The pamphlet further went on to state that the Socialist Party felt the draft interfered with the citizen's individual rights as well as his freedom of religion. The pamphlet urged people to stop by the Socialist offices and sign a petition. Several people complained. The Philadelphia postal inspectors raided the Socialist Party offices on August 28, 1917, and seized records and files, all without a search warrant.

SUMMARY OF ARGUMENTS

Attorneys Henry John Nelson and Henry J. Gibbons argued for Schenck that unless citizens are able to have a full and free discussion about whether a war is just or unjust, they cannot reach a decision. They argued that Schenck and the Socialist Party were guaranteed the constitutional right of free speech and had the sincere purpose to communicate their honest opinions and beliefs, whether or not it masks an intent to incite action against the government. Schenck's attorneys further argued that the issue of conspiracy and the seizure of the Socialist Party papers violated other constitutional protections. Finally, they argued that the case was a political issue.

John O'Brian, special assistant to the attorney general for war work, and Alfred Bettman, special assistant to the attorney general, responded for the United States. They argued that there was ample evidence that Schenck had conspired to violate the Espionage Act, a federal law that punished spying and other crimes, and that there was a clear basis during wartime for the U.S. Congress to pass such a law as a way of dealing with wartime fears.

DECISION

In a unanimous ruling, Justice Oliver Wendell Holmes, Jr., quickly dismissed any concerns raised by Schenck regarding the legality of the evidence seized. Further, Justice Holmes found that the pamphlet had the intent and certainly a tendency to obstruct the draft. Whether or not it did so was not important. Justice Holmes further went on to state that obstructing the draft went beyond the interference with conscripted soldiers because it also affected voluntary efforts to recruit fresh troops. In the most important portion of the opinion, Justice Holmes spoke of the protection of free speech and the appropriate legal restraints during wartime: "The most stringent protection of free speech would not protect a man in falsely shouting 'Fire!' in a theater, and causing a panic." Justice Holmes stated that the question in every case is whether Congress has a right to protect words of such a nature as to create a "clear and present danger." Clearly, wartime circumstances differ from peaceful settings, and Congress has the right to prevent and punish obstructions and conspiracies to obstruct the raising of troops during war.

AFTERMATH

Justice Holmes's decision upheld the Espionage Act and the large number of cases generated under it.

SIGNIFICANCE

Justice Holmes's "clear and present danger" test became the line between legal and illegal free speech. Holmes's decision found that as long as there was an intent to break the law, it did not matter if there was a successful result. In *ABRAMS V. UNITED STATES* (1919), Holmes had occasion to refine the test stating that "only the present danger of immediate evil or the intent to bring it about warrants Congress in setting a limit to the expression of opinion where private rights are not concerned."

RELATED CASES

Abrams v. United States, 250 U.S. 616 (1919)

Debs v. United States, 249 U.S. 211 (1919)

RECOMMENDED READING

Edward J. Bloustein, *Criminal Attempts and the "Clear and Present Danger" Theory of the First Amendment,* 74 Cornell Law Review 1116 (1989).

Chamberlin, Bill F., and Charlene J. Brown, eds. *The First Amendment Reconsidered: New Perspectives on the Meaning of Speech and Press.* New York: Longman, 1982.

Martin H. Redish, *Advocacy of Unlawful Conduct and the First Amendment: In Defense of Clear and Present Danger,* 70 California Law Review 1159 (1982).

Worton, Stanley N. *Freedom of Speech and Press.* Rochelle Park, N.J.: Hayden Book Co., 1975.

Case Title: *Schneider v. Irvington*

Legal Citation: 308 U.S. 147

Year of Decision: 1939

KEY ISSUES

May a municipality completely ban the distribution of leaflets in the city to prevent littering?

HISTORY OF THE CASE

Four different cities completely banned the distribution of information leaflets. The cities mainly argued that the ban was to prevent littering. State courts upheld convictions under the municipal ordinances regulating or forbidding the distribution of literature in public places or the streets. The Supreme Court took two of the cases through certiorari, and two went to the Supreme Court through appeal.

SUMMARY OF ARGUMENTS

The plaintiffs argued that the ordinance violated the right to free speech as guaranteed by the First Amendment.

The cities argued that keeping the streets clean was a substantial interest that outweighed an individual's right to be on a public street handing out literature.

DECISION

Justice Roberts delivered the opinion of the Court. The Supreme Court invalidated the ordinances forbidding the distribution of leaflets because they violated the constitutional protection of the freedom of speech and press. The Court stated that the purpose of keeping the streets clean was not a good enough reason to

deny a person the right to free expression through literature. The Court also noted that the street was a natural place to disseminate information and opinion. Litter control could be managed by punishing those who actually threw the leaflets on the ground, not by punishing those who handed out the literature.

AFTERMATH

Schneider has not been overruled and is still cited as good law.

SIGNIFICANCE

Schneider has played a role in keeping a public forum open for communication through the distribution of information on the street. The right to use the streets as a public forum cannot be banned completely, and can be regulated only if there are weighty reasons.

RELATED CASES

Hague v. CIO, 307 U.S. 496 (1939)

Jamison v. Texas, 318 U.S. 413 (1943)

RECOMMENDED READING

Stephen Durden and David Ray, *Litter or Literature: Does the First Amendment Protect Littering of Neighborhoods,* 26 Stetson Law Review 837 (spring 1997).

Michael S. Wichman, *Cyberia: The Chilling Effect of Online Free Speech by the Communications Decency Act,* 3 U.C.L.A. Entertainment Law Review 427 (1996).

Case Title: *Stanley v. Georgia*

Legal Citations: 394 U.S. 557; 89 S.Ct. 1243

Year of Decision: 1969

KEY ISSUES

Can the mere private possession of obscene material constitutionally be made a crime?

HISTORY OF THE CASE

Earlier cases, most notably *ROTH V. UNITED STATES* (1957), held that obscenity is not within the area of constitutionally protected speech or press. Typical state statutes forbidding commercial sales of obscene material were therefore constitutional. Georgia, however, passed a statute that extended the reach of the criminal law to any person "who shall knowingly have possession of . . . any obscene matter."

Federal and state agents investigated Robert Eli Stanley for alleged bookmaking activities. In the course of the investigation, the agents obtained a search warrant for Stanley's home. Under authority of the warrant, agents entered Stanley's house and found little evidence of bookmaking activity—but three reels of eight-millimeter film were discovered in an upstairs bedroom. The agents concluded that the films were obscene, seized the films, and placed Stanley under arrest. Stanley was tried before a jury and convicted. His conviction was upheld by the Georgia Supreme Court.

SUMMARY OF ARGUMENTS

Stanley argued that the Georgia obscenity statute, insofar as it punished mere private possession of obscene materials, violated the First Amendment, as made applicable to the states by the Fourteenth Amendment. The state of Georgia argued that, because obscenity is not within the area of constitutionally protected speech or press under the First Amendment, the state is free to deal with obscenity in any way deemed necessary. If the state can protect the body of a citizen, argued Georgia, may it not protect his mind?

DECISION

In an opinion written by Justice Thurgood Marshall, the Court held that the First and Fourteenth Amendments prohibit making mere possession of obscene material a crime. Marshall's opinion begins with the recognition that obscenity is not protected by the First Amendment. However, *Roth* and subsequent cases dealt for the most part with use of the mails to distribute objectionable material or with some form of public distribution or dissemination. Prior to *Stanley,* the Supreme Court had not considered the legality of simple private possession of obscene materials. Confronted with that question, Justice Marshall concludes for the Court that the fact of obscenity is insufficient justification for the state to undertake a drastic invasion of personal liberties guaranteed by the First and Fourteenth Amendments: "If the First Amendment means anything, it means that a State has no business telling a man, sitting alone in his own house, what books he may read or what films he may watch." While the opinion affirms that states retain broad power to regulate obscenity, it draws the line at simple possession by the individual in the privacy of his own home.

No justice dissented from the majority decision, but some justices reached their conclusion by different reasoning. Justice Black, who (along with Justice Douglas) held an absolutist view of the mandates of the First Amendment, wrote a short concurring opinion. Justices Stewart, Brennan, and White concurred in the result of the reversal of Stanley's conviction, but would not have reached the issue decided by the majority opinion. Those three justices, in an opinion by Justice Stewart, maintained that the seizure of the obscene films violated the Fourth Amendment, because the police were acting under a warrant to search for evidence of illegal bookmaking activities, not obscene materials. Seized in violation of the Fourth and Fourteenth Amendments, the films should have been ruled inadmissible in evidence at Stanley's trial.

AFTERMATH

Without explicitly overruling the earlier case, the Court's decision in *Stanley* weakened the viability of *Roth v. United States*. By placing an emphasis on the private sanctity of Stanley's home where the films were seized, the Court tipped the scales against the broad statement in *Roth* that obscenity is not within the area of constitutionally protected speech or press. In the aftermath of *Stanley,* obscene materials in a private home would be cloaked with constitutional protection, unless the state could demonstrate that the materials were intended for distribution to minors or an unwilling audience.

SIGNIFICANCE

Together with *GRISWOLD V. CONNECTICUT* (1965), in which the Court found the state's interest in preventing the use of contraceptives an insufficient justification for invading the bedroom sanctuary, *Stanley* demonstrates how the Warren Court fashioned a right of privacy that is not explicit in the text of the Constitution. The Court established a comprehensive right of citizens to be let alone by the government: "[F]undamental is the right to be free, except in very limited circumstances, from unwanted governmental intrusions into one's privacy."

RELATED CASES

Ginsberg v. New York, 390 U.S. 629, 88 S.Ct. 1274 (1968)

Griswold v. Connecticut, 381 U.S. 479, 85 S.Ct. 1678 (1965)

Jacobellis v. Ohio, 378 U.S. 184, 84 S.Ct. 1676 (1964)

Redrup v. New York, 386 U.S. 767, 87 S.Ct. 1414 (1967)

Roth v. United States, 354 U.S. 476, 77 S.Ct. 1304 (1957)

Smith v. California, 361 U.S. 147, 80 S.Ct. 215 (1959)

RECOMMENDED READING

Al Katz, *Privacy and Pornography:* Stanley v. Georgia, Supreme Court Review 203 (1969).

Simon Roberts, *The Obscenity Exception: Abusing the First Amendment,* 10 Cardozo Law Review 677 (1989).

Claudia Tuchman, *Does Privacy Have Four Walls? Salvaging* Stanley v. Georgia, 94 Columbia Law Review 2267 (1994).

Case Title: *Terminiello v. City of Chicago*

Legal Citation: 337 U.S. 1

Year of Decision: 1949

KEY ISSUES

Is a municipal ordinance which prohibits speech that "stirs people to anger, invites public dispute or brings about a condition of unrest" an unconstitutional restriction on the freedom of speech?

HISTORY OF THE CASE

Terminiello gave a speech in front of a crowd of about 400 people. A crowd of about 1,000 protesters gathered outside the hall where he was speaking. Terminiello called the protesters "scum" and continued in his incendiary speech about communists and "Zionist Jews." The crowd outside lost control and began to throw rocks, bottles, and bricks at the assembly hall. Police were unable to adequately control the crowd. The city of Chicago charged Terminiello with violating a city ordinance regarding breach of the peace. The municipal court found Terminiello guilty. The appellate court and the state supreme court affirmed. The U.S. Supreme Court agreed to hear the case because of the importance of the issue presented.

SUMMARY OF ARGUMENTS

Terminiello argued that the municipal ordinance was a violation of his First Amendment rights, as it was overly broad.

The city of Chicago argued that the ordinance prohibited "fighting words" and was therefore constitutionally permissible.

DECISION

Justice Douglas delivered the majority opinion in the 5-4 decision vacating the conviction of Terminiello. *Terminiello* was the first case to test the "fighting words" doctrine since the adoption of the doctrine seven years earlier. Under CHAPLINSKY V. STATE OF NEW HAMPSHIRE (1942), fighting words were made an exception to the First Amendment's freedom of speech guarantee and could therefore be regulated. However, the Court found that the ordinance under which Terminiello was convicted was overly broad, as it not only included speech that the state could regulate but also included speech that could not be regulated. The Court could not hold that the lower courts convicted Terminiello under the permissible parts of the ordinance rather than the impermissible parts because the reasons for the conviction were not made clear by the record.

AFTERMATH

The Court further developed the concept of "fighting words" in the years following *Terminiello*. The various nuances involved in regulating speech now include whether the speech is inherently likely to provoke a violent reaction, personal provocation directed at an actual addressee, and the likelihood of an imminent lawless action.

SIGNIFICANCE

Terminiello is the first case to apply the "fighting words" doctrine after its creation. Some commentators see it as an early attempt to prevent government regulation of speech in a political context. The case has not been overruled and still provides a model for determining First Amendment rights.

RELATED CASES

Brandenburg v. Ohio, 395 U.S. 444 (1969)

Chaplinsky v. New Hampshire, 315 U.S. 568 (1942)

Cohen v. California, 403 U.S. 15 (1971)

R.A.V. v. City of St. Paul, 505 U.S. 377 (1992)

RECOMMENDED READING

Berns, Walter. *Freedom, Virtue, and the First Amendment.* Baton Rouge: Louisiana State University Press, 1957.

Aviva O. Wertheimer, *The First Amendment Distinction between Conduct and Content: A Conceptual Framework for Understanding Fighting Words Jurisprudence*, 63 Fordham Law Review 793 (1994).

Case Title: *Texas v. Johnson*

Alternate Case Title: Flag Burning Case

Legal Citations: 491 U.S. 397; 109 S.Ct. 2533; 105 L.Ed. 2d 342

Year of Decision: 1989

KEY ISSUES

Is the public burning of an American flag as a means of political protest protected by the right to free speech as set forth in the First Amendment?

HISTORY OF THE CASE

Symbolic speech, defined as the conveyance of a message without the use of words, similar to the use of a visual aid, is protected by the First Amendment provision that "Congress shall make no law . . . abridging the freedom of speech, or of the press." The Supreme Court has attempted to balance this guarantee of free expression against governmental interests in a series of flag desecration cases, of which *Johnson* is one.

Flag desecration statutes exist in most jurisdictions. They usually limit the use of words or acts that show disrespect for the flag as a symbol of national power. In previous cases, the Court held that legislation requiring a person to show respect by saluting the flag is unconstitutional (see *WEST VIRGINIA BOARD OF EDUCATION V. BARNETTE* (1943).

Furthermore, a state cannot forbid disrespect unless there is a legitimate interest at stake. Such was the holding in *U.S. V. O'BRIEN* (1968), which set a precedent for the subsequent flag burning cases. That case dealt with the burning of a draft card in protest against the Vietnam conflict. The Supreme Court held that the efficient operation of the Selective Service Board justified this imposition on free speech. However, when a protestor burned a flag upon hearing of the death of a noted civil rights leader in *Street v. New York* (1969), or wore a flag on the seat of his jeans in *SMITH V. GOGUEN* (1974), the actions were found to be constitutionally protected free speech because no state interest was impaired. A similar holding was the result in *Spence v. Washington* (1974), where a peace symbol had been taped to the flag displayed from Spence's window.

In this case, during the 1984 Republican National Convention in Dallas, Johnson burned the American flag in the course of a political demonstration. He was protesting the policies of the Reagan administration and some Dallas-based corporations. No one was hurt, although some witnesses were offended by the act. Johnson was found to have violated a Texas criminal statute that prohibited the desecration of a state or national flag in a manner that would seriously offend observers. The Texas Court of Criminal Appeals reversed the conviction, holding that Johnson's conduct was symbolic speech protected by the First Amendment and that the state could not designate flag desecration a crime in order to preserve the flag as a symbol of national unity. The state appealed to the Supreme Court, which agreed to hear the case.

SUMMARY OF ARGUMENTS

The case was argued on March 21, 1989, with Kathi Alyce Drew representing the state of Texas and William M. Kunstler representing Gregory Johnson. Kunstler stressed the political nature of the flag burning, as the demonstration was in conjunction with the renomination of Ronald Reagan as president. He argued that the action was protected by the First Amendment and the state did not have any right to legislate in this area.

Texas argued that preserving the flag as a national symbol is a compelling state interest because every flag burning by its nature is offensive conduct, possessing the potential for violence. This follows from the fact that the flag has special symbolic value.

DECISION

Justice Brennan read the majority opinion for the Court. He stated that Johnson's conduct of burning the flag was legitimate political expression protected by the First Amendment because the conduct was politically motivated. Furthermore, there was no compelling governmental interest asserted by the state in limiting the conduct on the basis of preventing breaches of the peace. Only if the flag burning actually sought to cause "imminent lawless action" could the government take preventive measures. Freedom of expression, Justice Brennan explained, is more important than an interest in preserving the flag as a symbol of "nationhood and national unity." The government cannot dictate what a symbol such as the flag represents by "prohibiting the expression of an idea simply because society finds the idea itself offensive or disagreeable." The flag cannot be used to represent an idea. It is a "potent political symbol" whose use cannot be limited because of differing opinions.

AFTERMATH

Political uproar was set off by the *Johnson* decision as members of Congress rushed to introduce legislation that would outlaw flag burning. The Flag Protection Act of 1989 was subsequently passed, making physical abuse of the flag a criminal act. In 1990, the Supreme Court's decision in *U.S. v. Eichman*, 496 U.S. 310 (1990) found prosecution under the Flag Protection Act to be unconstitutional.

SIGNIFICANCE

This case clarified and expanded the First Amendment free expression protections. It established that the government cannot enact laws prohibiting political expression relating to the flag without a legitimate governmental interest. Because of the Constitution's commitment to individual freedoms, the flag as a symbol can be used for political discourse regardless of a given act's offensiveness.

RELATED CASES

Smith v. Goguen, 415 U.S. 566, 94 S.Ct. 1242, 39 L.Ed. 2d 605 (1974)

Spence v. Washington, 418 U.S. 405, 94 S.Ct. 2727, 41 L.Ed. 2d 842 (1974)

Street v. New York, 394 U.S. 576, 89 S.Ct. 1354, 22 L.Ed. 2d 572 (1969)

U.S. v. O'Brien, 319 U.S. 367, 88 S.Ct. 1673, 20 L.Ed. 2d 842 (1968)

West Virginia Board of Education v. Barnette, 319 U.S. 624, 63 S.Ct. 1178, 87 L.Ed. 1628 (1943)

RECOMMENDED READING

Robert A. Brazener, *What Constitutes Violation of Flag Desecration Statutes*, 41 American Law Reports 3d 502 (1972).

❧

Case Title: *Thornhill v. Alabama*

Legal Citation: 310 U.S. 88

Year of Decision: 1940

KEY ISSUES

Alabama passed a statute prohibiting people from picketing in front of a business in order to impede, interfere, or injure business. The statute applied only to scenes of labor disputes. The statute also prohibited loitering in front of a place of business in order to persuade people not to buy from, deal with, or work for such places. Byron Thornhill was charged with violating this Alabama statute. Thornhill challenged the statute as a violation of the right to free speech as protected by the Constitution.

HISTORY OF THE CASE

Thornhill worked for a company whose union had ordered a strike. A picket line formed outside the company on company property. Thornhill, who was picketing, approached someone who reported to work and told the worker that the union did not want employees to work. Thornhill was convicted of a misdemeanor under the Alabama statute prohibiting picketing during a labor dispute. The court of appeals considered the constitutional issue and affirmed the judgment. The Alabama Supreme Court refused to hear the case. The U.S. Supreme Court agreed to hear the case because of the important constitutional question presented.

SUMMARY OF ARGUMENTS

Thornhill argued that the Alabama statute violated the Constitution by depriving him of his right of peaceful assembly, his right to free speech, and his right to petition for redress. The state of Alabama argued that the purpose of the statute was to protect the community from violence and breaches of peace that occurred during labor disputes. They argued that the statute was needed to keep peace.

DECISION

The Supreme Court ruled that the Alabama statute violated the First Amendment's guarantee of free speech and press. They stated that a penal statute covering such a large number of activities lent itself to discriminatory enforcement by local officials against groups they did not favor. This resulted in a continuous restraint on the freedom of discussion. The Court ruled that labor matters were a public concern, and that the "freedom of speech and of the press" guaranteed in the First Amendment embraced the liberty to publicly and truthfully discuss all matters of public concern without restraint or fear of punishment.

The Court did not agree with Alabama that a breach of peace was imminent whenever labor matters were discussed during a labor dispute. They stated that a restraint on free speech or free press would impair opportunities for education and were essential for the "effective exercise of the power of correcting error through processes of popular government."

AFTERMATH

This case has not been overruled and is cited frequently when the courts look at free speech issues.

SIGNIFICANCE

This case developed the idea that a law can be unconstitutionally overbroad. Because the statute in this case prohibited all forms of picketing, even peaceful picketing, the Court ruled that the statute was too broad. Today, laws can be rejected for the same reason.

Picketing has not been protected if it furthers illegal activities, although, courts continue to uphold the idea that only through the free exchange of ideas and free debate can a government respond to public will.

RELATED CASES

Arnett v. Kennedy, 416 U.S. 134 (1974)

Lovell v. Griffin, 303 U.S. 444 (1938)

Milk Wagon Drivers Union of Chicago, Local 753 v. Meadowmoor Dairies, Inc., 312 U.S. 287 (1941)

RECOMMENDED READING

Jenson, Carol E. *The Network of Control.* Westport, Conn.: Greenwood Press, 1982.

Case Title: *Tinker v. Des Moines School District*

Alternate Case Title: The Black Armband Case

Legal Citation: 393 U.S. 503

Year of Decision: 1969

KEY ISSUES

May a school board prohibit students from wearing black armbands where the students are not otherwise disruptive of school discipline or decorum?

HISTORY OF THE CASE

Tinker and other students at an Iowa high school wore black armbands to school in protest of the U.S. involvement in the Vietnam War. Aside from wearing the armband, Tinker and the others had been passive and nondisruptive. They were nonetheless suspended for violating a regulation that prohibited the wearing of armbands at school. The regulation was upheld by both the district court and the Court of Appeals for the Eighth Circuit.

SUMMARY OF ARGUMENTS

Tinker argued that the regulation violated his right to freedom of speech under the First and Fourteenth Amendments because the wearing of the armbands was a form of symbolic speech.

The state argued that the regulation was a reasonable exercise of its power to preserve order in the classroom and that its purpose was to prevent disruption, not suppress expression.

DECISION

The Supreme Court, in an opinion written by Justice Fortas, held that the regulation violated Tinker's constitutional rights. Justice Fortas found that students and teachers do not "shed their constitutional rights to freedom of speech or expression at the schoolhouse gate." He acknowledged the state's interest in preserving order in the classroom, but in this case there was no intrusion upon the work of the school or the rights of other students. Justice Fortas asserted that while "[a]ny departure from absolute regimentation may cause trouble," such openness is "the basis of our national strength and of the independence and vigor of Americans who grow up and live in this relatively permissive, often disputatious, society." In the absence of a substantial interference with the operation of the school, Justice Fortas found the regulation offensive to the constitutional guarantee of freedom of speech.

In a brief concurrence, Justice Stewart noted that while he found the regulation unconstitutional, previous Supreme Court opinions did not support Justice Fortas's assertion that the First Amendment rights of children were equal to those of adults.

Justice Black wrote a dissent in which he excoriated the majority for substituting its own judgment for that of the school board. He argued that the Constitution does not grant each citizen "the right to give speeches or engage in demonstrations where he pleases and when he pleases." The state had the right to regulate in order to ensure that students' minds were focused on their classwork rather than being disrupted by other subjects. Justice Black contended that the school board might reasonably have perceived that the wearing of armbands could distract other students. He noted that the *Meyers* case, relied upon by the majority, had long been discredited as an example of the Court striking down a law merely because it thought the law unwise. Justice Black argued that it would "be a sad day for the country" when the Court returned to the notion that "due process" was synonymous with the value preferences of a Supreme Court majority. Because Iowa's schools "are operated to give students an opportunity to learn, not to talk politics," Justice Black would have upheld the anti-armband regulation.

AFTERMATH

Six years later the Court ruled that schools may suspend a student for misconduct only after providing some fair procedures for determining whether the misconduct actually occurred. For the 10-day suspension imposed in *Goss v. Lopez* (1975), the Court said the student had to be given notice of the charges and an opportunity to explain his version of the story.

Three decisions in the 1980s indicated the Court's shift toward even greater deference to school authorities.

In *New Jersey v. T.L.O.* (1985) the Court refused to require school authorities to obtain a warrant to search a student's locker. The Court said a search was constitutional when there were reasonable grounds for suspecting that it would turn up evidence and when the search itself was not "excessively intrusive."

One year later the Court upheld the right of school officials to suspend a student for a lewd speech given in a student assembly (*Bethel School District No. 43 v. Fraser* [1986]). In 1988 the Court held that school officials could censor student articles in a school newspaper if the paper was published as part of the school's curriculum (*Hazelwood School District v. Kuhlmeier*).

SIGNIFICANCE

The students' right to free expression was upheld. The Court in *Tinker* explicitly declined to deal with the constitutionality of school regulations dealing with hair length, clothing type, and other aspects of personal appearance, which arguably have an expressive content.

RELATED CASES

Board of Educ. of Westside Community Schools v. Mergers, 496 U.S. 226 (1990)

Board of Trustees of Univ. of N.Y. v. Fox, 492 U.S. 469 (1989)

United States v. Kokinda, 497 U.S. 720 (1990)

RECOMMENDED READING

John Hart Ely, *Flag Desecration: A Case Study in the Roles of Categorization and Balancing in First Amendment Analysis*, 88 Harvard Law Review 1482–1508 (1975).

Sheldon H. Nahmod, *Beyond Tinker: The High School as an Educational Public Forum*, 5 Harvard Civil Rights–Civil Liberties Law Review 278 (January 1970).

The Supreme Court 1968 Term, 83 Harvard Law Review 154 (November 1969).

Case Title: *United Public Workers v. Mitchell*

Legal Citation: 330 U.S. 75

Year of Decision: 1947

KEY ISSUES

A group of federal employees brought suit to restrain the Civil Service Commission from enforcing a ban against their participation in political activities. The issue in this case is whether these employees have a concrete claim or controversy that can be addressed in federal court.

HISTORY OF THE CASE

The Hatch Act of 1940 prohibits federal employees in the executive branch from participating in political campaigns or political management. All but one of the federal employees in this case had not participated in political activity, but sought to restrain the Civil Service Commission from enforcing the ban against such participation. The lower court dismissed the claim.

SUMMARY OF ARGUMENTS

Because all but one of the federal employees had not participated in political activity and therefore had not been punished, the defendants, Harry B. Mitchell, Lucille Foster McMillin, and Arthur S. Fleming, argued that the complaint of the employees should be dismissed because there was not an actual controversy.

The plaintiffs argued that the ban on political activity in the Hatch Act was unconstitutional and violated rights to free speech.

DECISION

Pertaining to the individuals who had not participated in political activity, the Supreme Court decided that the issue was not sufficiently concrete to be worth adjudicating. The plaintiffs' claims were too general. The fact that they had a personal interest in the possible threat of interference by the Civil Service Commission upon participation in political activity did not make this a case or controversy worthy of decision. The Supreme Court characterized the plaintiff's claim as seeking an advisory opinion, a nonbinding interpretation of the law, which the Court does not give.

AFTERMATH

The Court in *Mitchell* relied on the legislative judgment that restrictions on a federal government employee's First Amendment rights of freedom of expression were necessary for the smooth operation of government. The Court also gave deference to the legislature's idea that working for the federal government was a privilege, not a right. Though Mitchell has not yet been overruled, both of these ideas have been attacked in subsequent decisions.

More recent cases seem to indicate that the Court may intervene to protect freedoms of association and expression especially where criminal sanctions, the threat of loss of job, or other penalties are involved.

SIGNIFICANCE

Mitchell is a good example of the doctrine of justiciability. Before a federal court can even hear a case, the claims must be sufficiently concrete to be worthy of adjudication. A case that is not sufficiently concrete is said to be not "ripe."

RELATED CASES

Adler v. Board of Education, 32 U.S. 485 (1952)

Mancuso v. Taft, 476 F. 2d 187 (1973)

U.S. v. Congress of Ind. Org., 335 U.S. 106 (1948)

RECOMMENDED READING

Radcliff, James E. *The Case or Controversy Problem.* University Park: Pennsylvania State University Press, 1978.

Case Title: *United States v. O'Brien*

Alternate Case Title: The Draft Card Burning Case

Legal Citation: 391 U.S. 367

Year of Decision: 1968

KEY ISSUES

Does a law prohibiting the destruction of a draft card violate one's constitutional right to freedom of speech?

HISTORY OF THE CASE

O'Brien burned his draft card in front of a large crowd in an attempt to influence others to adopt his antiwar beliefs. He was arrested and charged with violating a 1965 amendment to the Uniform Military Training and Service Act, which made it a crime to "knowingly destroy, knowingly mutilate or in any manner change" one's draft certificate. Before the amendment, the act had already made it a crime for a registered man to fail to keep his registration certificate in his "personal possession at all times." O'Brien was convicted of violating the amended act by the U.S. District Court. He then appealed to the First Circuit Court of Appeals, which reversed and held that the amendment was unconstitutional because it could have been intended only to punish speech in the form of draft card burning protests. The court of appeals nonetheless upheld O'Brien's conviction on the grounds that, by destroying his card, he had also violated the clearly constitutional nonpossession portion of the act. Both O'Brien and the government appealed to the U.S. Supreme Court.

SUMMARY OF ARGUMENTS

O'Brien argued that because the act already punished nonpossession, the amendment could only have been intended as a means of prohibiting public destruction of draft cards; thus, the amendment was an unconstitutional abridgment of O'Brien's right to engage in symbolic speech in the form of protest. He then contended that his conviction for destroying the draft card was not enough to support a conviction under the nonpossession part of the act, because destruction was not necessarily equivalent to nonpossession.

The government argued that the amendment was a legitimate use of its constitutional power to raise and support armies because the destruction of draft cards hampered the efficiency of the selective service system.

DECISION

Chief Justice Warren, writing for a seven-justice majority, held the amendment to the act constitutional. He acknowledged that O'Brien's destruction of the draft certificate might have been a form of constitutionally protected speech, but he argued that when speech and nonspeech elements are combined in conduct, Congress may regulate that conduct in order to further a substantial governmental interest. Here, Congress had implemented the draft pursuant to its constitutional power to raise and support armies. It had used a registration certificate as a means to ensure the efficient operation of the selective service system; and it prohibited the destruction of those certificates to preserve the system's effectiveness. Because the government's interest in raising armies was unrelated to the suppression of free expression, and because the amendment's restriction on First Amendment freedoms was no greater than necessary to preserve the government's interest, O'Brien's conduct was subject to the act and its amendments.

Chief Justice Warren argued that O'Brien's conviction was thus justified by the fact that the noncommunicative element of his conduct had interfered with the government's important interest in preserving the certificates. The fact that this interest was already protected by the act's non-possession regulation was not controlling: Congress may provide "alternative statutory avenues of prosecution to assure the effective protection of one and the same interest." Given the adequacy of the government interest and the narrow means chosen to fulfill that interest, Chief Justice Warren was unwilling to examine Congress's motives in adding the amendment to the act.

Justice Douglas dissented. He argued that the Court had ignored a question which undermined the rest of its analysis: whether Congress could implement a draft when the nation was not in an official state of war. Justice Douglas asserted that if Congress lacked the power to implement a draft, then the government's interest in the certificates was nullified and O'Brien's right to free speech would be sufficient to justify overturning his conviction.

AFTERMATH

The Supreme Court heard several other cases regarding draft card destruction following *O'Brien*. The draft card issue was ultimately extinguished in 1973 when an all-volunteer system for military participation was adopted.

SIGNIFICANCE

Not all forms of conduct can be considered speech and be protected by the First Amendment.

Further, limits on an individual's First Amendment rights may be justified when conduct is being regulated.

RELATED CASES

Schacht v. United States, 398 U.S. 58 (1970)

Wayte v. United States, 470 U.S. 598 (1985)

RECOMMENDED READING

Dean Alfange, Jr., *Free Speech and Symbolic Conduct: The Draft-Card Burning Case,* Supreme Court Review 1 (1968).

Emerson, Thomas I. *The System of Freedom of Expression.* New York: Random House, 1970.

Melville B. Nimmer, *The Meaning of Symbolic Speech under the First Amendment,* 21 UCLA Law Review 29 (1973).

Case Title: *Valentine v. Chrestensen*

Legal Citations: 316 U.S. 52; 62 S.Ct. 920; 86 L.Ed. 1262

Year of Decision: 1942

KEY ISSUES

Does the Constitution impose any restraint on government regulation of purely commercial advertising?

HISTORY OF THE CASE

After mooring his former U.S. Navy submarine to a state-owned pier, F. J. Chrestensen began distributing handbills in the city streets, which advertised tours of the boat for a stated fee. The police commissioner advised Chrestensen that his commercial advertising violated the city's sanitary code, and that he could only distribute handbills solely devoted to "information or a public protest." In response to the commissioner's advice, Chrestensen prepared a double-sided handbill. One side contained the advertisement of the boat, with the admission fee deleted, and the other a protest against the City Dock Department for its refusal to grant Chrestensen wharf facilities. After being restrained by the police, Chrestensen sought an injunction preventing the police from interfering with his newly printed advertisements. The district court granted a permanent injunction, and the Second Circuit Court of Appeals affirmed.

SUMMARY OF ARGUMENTS

Chrestensen contended that by adding the political protest to the handbill, he was engaging in the distribution of matter appropriate for public examination. This matter, he argued, is protected by the First Amendment's guarantee of free speech.

Valentine, the police commissioner, argued that Chrestensen's sole purpose in distributing the handbills was to gain private profit, which is not protected by the First Amendment. He contended that the government, in regulating commercial and business advertising on the public streets, appropriately determined that the distribution of handbills on public streets undesirably interfered with their appropriate use.

DECISION

Justice Roberts, writing a unanimous decision for the Court, held that the New York City officials could prevent distribution of the handbills without violating the First Amendment. The Court, in stating what has become known as the "commercial speech" doctrine, held that the Constitution imposes no restraint on government concerning purely commercial advertising. The Court distinguished between the freedom to express political views on the public streets, which is protected by the First Amendment, and the freedom to advertise a commercial enterprise, which is not. The Court also believed that Chrestensen's inclusion of the political protest to the back of handbills was for the purpose of evading the prohibition of the sanitary code. The Court noted that condoning such an overt attempt to evade the ordinance would allow every merchant who desires to broadcast advertising leaflets in the street to simply append a political protest or opinion to them.

AFTERMATH

The *Chrestensen* rule has suffered extensive criticism since its inception. Subsequent cases have held that "purely commercial" speech is entitled to First Amendment protection. It has been argued that such speech often contains a high informational value that outweighs a weak state interest in suppressing the advertising. In 1980, the Court proposed a four-part test to determine whether a given regulation of commercial speech violates the First Amendment. First, all commercial speech receives at least partial protection except for (1) speech that is misleading; and (2) speech that concerns illegal activity. Second, the governmental interest in regulating the speech must be *substantial*. Third, the regulation must directly advance the governmental interest. Finally, the speech must be regulated in a way that is "reasonably tailored" to the governmental objective. Thus, the state can issue time, place, and manner regulations of commercial speech.

SIGNIFICANCE

The *Chrestensen* case represents the Court's initial position that commercial speech should be excluded from the coverage of the First Amendment. Today, commercial speech receives extensive First Amendment protection, albeit at a lower level than political speech.

RELATED CASES

Bigelow v. Virginia, 421 U.S. 809 (1975)

Capitol Broadcasting Co. v. Mitchell, 333 F. Supp 582 (D.D.C. 1971)

Central Hudson Gas v. Public Services Comm'n, 447 U.S. 557 (1980)

Rubin v. Coors Brewing Co., 514 U.S. 476 (1995)

Virginia Pharmacy Bd. v. Virginia Consumer Council, 425 U.S. 748 (1976)

RECOMMENDED READING

Mary B. Nutt, *Trends in First Amendment Protection of Commercial Speech*, 41 Vanderbilt Law Review 173 (1988).

Case Title: *Watkins v. United States*

Legal Citations: 354 U.S. 178; 1 L.Ed. 2d. 1273; 77 S.Ct. 1173

Year of Decision: 1957

~&

KEY ISSUES

Can a witness before a congressional committee refuse to answer questions regarding past political activities during an investigation of citizens' current political affiliations?

HISTORY OF THE CASE

John Watkins, a union officer, appearing as a witness before a subcommittee of the House Committee on Un-American Activities, refused to answer questions about past Communist Party membership of certain persons because he believed the questions were not pertinent to the subject under inquiry by the subcommittee. In a prosecution in the U.S. District Court for the District of Columbia, he was convicted of violating the statute providing for criminal punishment of witnesses before congressional committees who refuse to answer any question pertinent to the question under inquiry, and the conviction was affirmed by the U.S. Court of Appeals for the District of Columbia Circuit.

SUMMARY OF ARGUMENTS

Petitioner argued that the subcommittee was engaged in a program of exposure for the sake of exposure.

Petitioner also argued that the questions asked by the committee were outside the scope of its activities and no public purpose was served by the interrogation.

The government argued that its questioning was based on protecting the public interest because Congress must be informed of subversive activity in order to enact legislative safeguards.

DECISION

On certiorari, the U.S. Supreme Court reversed the conviction. Chief Justice Warren, speaking for five members of the Court, ruled that to support a conviction under the statute, a congressional investigating committee must, upon objection of a witness on the grounds of pertinence, state for the record the subject under inquiry at that time and the manner in which the propounded questions are pertinent thereto. In the instant case, it was said, the evidence failed to show that the question under investigative inquiry at the time of the questioning was ever made known to the witness.

AFTERMATH

In June 1959, two years after *Watkins,* the case of *Barenblatt v. United States* reached the Court. *Barenblatt* involved the same committee (the House Un-American Activities Committee), the same year (1954), and the same general topic of Communist affiliations of the witness. In *Barenblatt,* however, the witness refused to testify not only about others but also about himself, and the Court upheld his conviction. The two cases set precedents for the powers of congressional committees.

SIGNIFICANCE

The decision, while reinforcing that Congress could conduct investigations, appeared to shift the balance of power back toward the witness because the witness only had to testify if the questions were pertinent to the investigation's purpose and the witness had been told of the purpose.

RELATED CASES

Eastland v. United States Servicemen's Fund, 421 U.S. 491 (1975)

Michigan v. Tucker, 417 U.S. 433 (1974)

Nixon v. Administrator of General Services, 433 U.S. 425 (1977)

RECOMMENDED READING

Belknap, Michael R. *Cold War Political Justice.* Westport, Conn.: Greenwood Press, 1977.

Fisher, Louis. *The Constitution between Friends.* New York: St. Martin's Press, 1978.

Harry Klavan, Jr., *Mr. Alexander Meiklejohn and the Barenblatt Opinion,* 27 University of Chicago Law Review 315 (1960).

Case Title: *Wayte v. United States*

Alternate Case Title: The Selective Prosecution Case

Legal Citation: 470 U.S. 598

Year of Decision: 1985

KEY ISSUES

May the government, under the Selective Service Act, prosecute only those people who reported themselves as having failed to register for the draft or who are reported by others?

HISTORY OF THE CASE

In 1980, President Ronald Reagan issued a proclamation requiring most adult male citizens to register with the Selective Service system (the military draft). Wayte, an eligible male, not only failed to register but also wrote letters to the president and other government officials indicating his refusal to do so. The Selective Service put Wayte's name in a file with the names of other men who had announced their failure to register or had been reported by others as having failed to do so. Under its so-called beg policy, the service then made an additional attempt to convince these men, including offers to forgo prosecution in exchange for their registration. Wayte again refused.

After the service had given nonregistered men a third notice it implemented its passive enforcement policy, under which it prosecuted only those men who had been in the original file and had subsequently refused to register. Thus, out of the 286 men whose names were originally in the file (who were themselves only a small portion of the approximately 674,000 nonregistrants nationwide), only 13 were indicted. The Selective Service adopted this passive policy, which did not provide for the prosecution of nonregistered men who were not in the original file, because it was not considered feasible to investigate and prosecute all nonregistered men.

The indictment against Wayte was dismissed by the Federal District Court for the Central District of California, on the grounds that Wayte was being selectively prosecuted because of his exercise of his First Amendment rights. The government appealed, and the Court of Appeals for the Ninth Circuit reversed the district court's decision.

SUMMARY OF ARGUMENTS

Wayte argued that the passive enforcement plan was unconstitutional because he had been selectively prosecuted for exercising, by virtue of his vocal opposition to registration, his First Amend-

ment rights. He also alleged that the selectivity of the enforcement scheme violated his right to the equal protection of the laws under the Fifth Amendment.

The government replied that any restrictions on Wayte's right to freedom of speech were "incidental"; the passive scheme was a reasonable use of its limited prosecutorial resources and the registration was a valid exercise of its constitutional power to raise and support armies.

DECISION

The Supreme Court affirmed the decision of the Court of Appeals and restored the indictment against Wayte. Justice Powell, writing for a majority of seven justices, argued that the Court was ill-suited to second-guess the government's decision as to whom to prosecute. Applying traditional equal protection analysis, the burden was upon Wayte to "show both that the passive enforcement system had a discriminatory effect and that it was motivated by a discriminatory purpose." Because the government had not prosecuted those who initially reported themselves but later registered, or those who protested registration but were not in the service's file, Wayte could not demonstrate that vocal nonregistrants had been subjected to any special burden, nor had Wayte shown that he was prosecuted *because of* his protest activities, instead of his failure to register.

Justice Powell also disagreed with Wayte's contention that the passive enforcement policy was directly offensive to the First Amendment. Noting that Wayte's protest and nonregistration involved both "speech" and "nonspeech" conduct, the Court analyzed the regulation under the test it had set forth earlier in *UNITED STATES V. O'BRIEN* (1968). Under this test, the government must show that the regulation "furthers an important governmental interest . . . the governmental interest is unrelated to the suppression of the freedom of expression and . . . the incidental restriction on alleged First Amendment freedoms is no greater than is essential to the furtherance of that interest." Here, the service's policy was a means of ensuring national security, an important interest clearly unrelated to suppressing freedom of expression. Justice Powell reasoned that by prosecuting vocal nonregistrants, the government was avoiding the high cost of investigating other potential nonregistrants. Further, convicting those who had vocally protested would be relatively easy and would send a powerful deterrent message to potential nonregistrants. Powell concluded that because the passive enforcement scheme was the only interim solution available to carry out registration policy, it was constitutional.

In dissent, Justice Marshall, joined by Justice Brennan, argued that Wayte had not been given adequate access to important government documents relevant to his defense of selective prosecution. Thus the Court could not properly decide to restore Wayte's indictment unless it reviewed *all* of the evidence, which it could not have done in this case.

RELATED CASE

United States v. O'Brien, 391 U.S. 367 (1968)

RECOMMENDED READING

Barry Lynn Creech, *And Justice for All: The Defense of Selective Prosecution*, 64 North Carolina Law Review 385 (1986).

Norma Vieira, *Registration, Protest and the Rationale of* Wayte v. United States, 40 Arkansas Law Review 841 (1987).

Case Title: *Whitney v. California*

Alternate Case Title: The Criminal Syndicate Case

Legal Citation: 274 U.S. 357

Year of Decision: 1927

KEY ISSUES

May the state make it a crime for a person to join a group that has been organized to commit "criminal syndicalism," regardless of that person's role in the group?

HISTORY OF THE CASE

Charlotte Anita Whitney attended a convention for the purpose of establishing a California branch of the Communist Labor Party. She spon-

sored a resolution calling for the achievement of the party's goals through the political process, but the convention adopted a more militant platform. Nonetheless, she remained at the convention and thereafter continued her membership in the party. She was later convicted of violating the California Criminal Syndicalism Act, which made it a crime to organize or knowingly become a member of a group organized to advocate criminal syndicalism, defined as "any doctrine . . . advocating . . . the commission of crime, sabotage or acts of force or violence . . . as a means of accomplishing a change in industrial ownership or control, or affecting any political change." Her petition to have the case heard by the California Supreme Court was denied, but the case reached the U.S. Supreme Court on a writ of error from the California Court of Appeal.

SUMMARY OF ARGUMENTS

Whitney argued that because she had not intended that the party become an instrument of violence or lawlessness, the act as applied violated her Fourteenth Amendment due process right to freedom of assembly.

California argued that the Syndicalism Act was a reasonable use of its police power in response to a perceived danger to the public peace.

DECISION

The Court, in an opinion delivered by Justice Sanford, held that the Syndicalism Act was a constitutional exercise of the state's police power. Justice Sanford argued that Whitney's claim to a lack of knowledge concerning the eventual disposition of the party was a factual issue that the jury had resolved against her on the basis of evidence such as her continued membership in the party. The act, as an exercise of the state's police power, was to be upheld unless capricious or arbitrary. In Justice Sanford's opinion, the danger posed by criminal syndicalism was not only a sufficient basis for the act but also served to override any constitutional free speech or assembly interest that Whitney could assert.

Justice Brandeis, joined by Justice Holmes, wrote a powerful concurring opinion. He agreed with the judgment of the Court only because Whitney had not raised her First Amendment argument for consideration by the district court judge and jury; under procedural rules, this barred the Supreme Court from reviewing that issue. Nonetheless, Justice Brandeis argued cogently that the act did infringe upon Whitney's right to freedom of assembly. In his opinion, the state could justify the act only by demonstrating that it was a response to a "clear and present danger" of a serious evil. Justice Brandeis asserted that this higher standard of review comported with the framers' intent that we "not exalt order at the cost of liberty." in Brandeis's words: "To courageous, self-reliant men, with confidence in the power of free and fearless reasoning through the processes of popular government, no danger flowing from speech can be deemed clear and present, unless the incidence of evil apprehended is so imminent that it may befall before there is opportunity for full discussion." Justice Brandeis argued that, had the issue been up for review, the state's justification for the act would have been subjected to a far more exacting examination than the one conducted by the Court in the case.

AFTERMATH

This decision made mere membership in a group involved in subversive activity punishable. However, Whitney was pardoned by the governor several months after her conviction was upheld by the Court.

SIGNIFICANCE

Brandeis's continued use of the "clear and present danger" standard secured its role in First Amendment analysis. His view that free speech is valuable because of its role in the deliberative process is arguably the progenitor of the representation-reinforcement theory, a theory that suggests the federal government prevents any state or group of people from acting contrary to the whole, used in subsequent cases concerning due process.

RELATED CASES

Fiske v. Kansas, 274 U.S. 380 (1927)

Gitlow v. New York, 268 U.S. 652 (1925)

RECOMMENDED READING

Vincent Blasi, *The First Amendment and the Ideal of Civic Courage: The Brandeis Opinion in* Whitney v. California, 29 William Mary & Law Review 653 (1988).

Jenson, Carol E. *The Network of Control.* Westport, Conn.: Greenwood Press, 1982.

Case Title: *Wieman v. Updegraf*

Alternate Case Title: The Public Employee-Member Case

Legal Citation: 344 U.S. 183

Year of Decision: 1952

KEY ISSUES

May a state deny someone a job solely because he fails to take an oath affirming lack of affiliation with communist or subversive organizations?

HISTORY OF THE CASE

An Oklahoma statute required each state employee to take a "loyalty oath" stating that he was not, and had not been for the preceding five years, a member of any group listed by the attorney general of the United States as "subversive" or a "communist front." Wieman, a professor at an Oklahoma college, refused to subscribe to this oath, and the state enjoined payment of his salary. He attacked the validity of the statute on the grounds that it violated the due process clause of the Fourteenth Amendment. On appeal, the Oklahoma Supreme Court held that the statute was constitutional.

SUMMARY OF ARGUMENTS

Wieman argued that by excluding him from government employment solely on the basis of his membership in an organization, the act violated his Fourteenth Amendment right to freedom of association.

Oklahoma argued that the statute was a constitutional means of insuring loyalty in its employees.

DECISION

Justice Clark, writing for a unanimous Court, held the required oath unconstitutional. The

Oklahoma Supreme Court had held by implication that Wieman's knowledge, or lack thereof, of his organization's status was irrelevant to the operation of the statute. Justice Clark argued that by refusing to consider whether Wieman knew that his organization was on the attorney general's list, the state had created a conclusive presumption of disloyalty. He quickly dispensed with the validity of the statute: "Indiscriminate classification of innocent with knowing activity must fall as an assertion of arbitrary power." Thus, had the statute required that Wieman be aware of the status of any group he had joined, it might have been less arbitrary and therefore constitutional.

Justice Black wrote a concurring opinion in which he stated that "test oaths are notorious tools of tyranny" and are therefore "unspeakably odious to a free people."

Justice Frankfurter also concurred. He noted that "[s]olid threats . . . may be met by preventive measures . . .," but argued that the overly restrictive statute in this case infringed upon Wieman's right to freedom of inquiry, a right of particular importance in the teaching profession.

AFTERMATH

Teacher fitness tests based on guilt by association with certain organizations were abolished.

SIGNIFICANCE

The decision precluded public employers from firing employees based on their refusal to acknowledge whether they had been a member of a subversive organization.

RELATED CASES

Adler v. Board of Education, 342 U.S. 485 (1952)

Garner v. Board of Public Works, 341 U.S. 716 (1951)

RECOMMENDED READING

Emerson, Thomas I. *The System of Freedom of Expression.* New York: Random House, 1970.

Case Title: *Wooley v. Maynard*

Alternate Case Title: The "Live Free or Die" Case

Legal Citation: 430 U.S. 705

Year of Decision: 1977

KEY ISSUES

Can the state force an individual to display an ideological message on private property so that it can be read by the public?

HISTORY OF THE CASE

George Maynard was a Jehovah's Witness who covered up New Hampshire's "Live Free or Die" motto on his license plates because the motto offended his moral, religious, and political beliefs. He was convicted of a misdemeanor statute, which required that all license plates carry the motto. Maynard then sought an injunction in the federal district court to prevent the enforcement of the statute, on the grounds that it violated his rights under the First Amendment of the U.S. Constitution.

SUMMARY OF ARGUMENTS

Maynard argued that the statute violated his right to hold an intellectual point of view different from that of the majority. He also claimed that covering up the motto was "symbolic speech"; thus, the statute was an unconstitutional infringement on his right to freedom of speech.

New Hampshire, with future Supreme Court justice David Souter in the office of attorney general, argued that the statute was constitutional because it served two compelling government interests: (1) the efficient identification of passenger vehicles; and (2) the appreciation of history, individualism, and state pride.

DECISION

In an opinion written by Chief Justice Burger, the Court held that the statute was an unconstitutional infringement on Maynard's First Amendment rights. Chief Justice Burger argued that "the right of freedom of thought protected by the First Amendment against state action includes the right to speak freely and the right to refrain from speaking at all." Thus the statute, by forcing Maynard to display the state's motto in public, was also forcing him to speak in order to implement the state's ideological message. Chief Justice

Burger dismissed the state's two proffered interests. There were numerous less restrictive ways to design license plates for easy identification, and promoting history and pride was not a sufficient state interest to override Maynard's First Amendment rights. The Court rejected Maynard's claim that covering up the motto was a form of symbolic speech because he had conceded that he would be willing to accept a license plate without the motto.

Justice Rehnquist, joined by Justice Blackmun, dissented. He argued forcefully that the statute did not require Maynard to say anything, and in the absence of speech there is no First Amendment issue. In Justice Rehnquist's opinion, free speech issues do not arise until a citizen is required to affirm a belief or be prevented from speaking. He noted that Maynard could easily have used a bumper sticker to dispel any question as to his beliefs. Justice Rehnquist argued that a state could clearly tax citizens such as Maynard in order to erect "Live Free or Die" billboards, even though that route would also make Maynard an instrument in the implementation of the state's message. He concluded by asking whether the Court's decision invalidated a statute that makes it a crime to deface U.S. currency; Justice Rehnquist thought it would, because the state places the religious mottoes "In God We Trust" and "*E pluribus unum*" on that currency.

AFTERMATH

George Maynard could not be required to display the New Hampshire state motto on his license plate.

SIGNIFICANCE

Displays of words are symbolic speech that receives First Amendment protection; however, First Amendment protection for symbolic speech is not as broad as that for pure speech.

RELATED CASE

Board of Education v. Barnette, 319 U.S. 624 (1943)

RECOMMENDED READING

Mark G. Yudof, *When the Government Speaks: Toward a Theory of Government Expression and the First Amendment*, 57 Texas Law Review 863 (1979).

Case Title: *Yates v. United States*

Alternate Case Title: The Call to Overthrow Case

Legal Citation: 354 U.S. 298

Year of Decision: 1957

KEY ISSUES

Is the advocacy of the violent overthrow of the government as abstract doctrine, as opposed to advocacy aimed at inciting action to that effect, protected by the First Amendment?

HISTORY OF THE CASE

Fourteen members of the Communist Party of the United States were convicted of conspiracy to violate the Smith Act, which makes it a crime to (1) knowingly advocate the duty or necessity of overthrowing the government by force or violence, or (2) organize any group of persons who advocate the overthrow of the government by force or violence. The Ninth Circuit Court of Appeals affirmed the convictions, and the members appealed to the Supreme Court.

SUMMARY OF ARGUMENTS

The defendants argued that they founded the Communist Party in 1945, and thus the indictments for "organizing" the party (which occurred in 1951) were barred by the three-year statute of limitations. They also claimed that the Smith Act's use of the word "advocate" required advocacy "of a kind calculated to 'incite' persons to action for the forcible overthrow of the government."

The government asserted that the term "organize" includes recruitment and continuous restructuring as opposed to the founding period alone; thus, the statute of limitations would not bar the indictments. It also argued that all advocacy was within the grasp of the Smith Act, while the First Amendment protects only "discussion or exposition of violent overthrow as an abstract theory."

DECISION

The Court, in an opinion written by Justice Harlan, acquitted five of the defendants and remanded the other nine for retrial. Because there was no evidence of what Congress had intended regarding the question, he applied traditional rules of interpretation to read the Smith Act narrowly. Thus the Court accepted the defendants' version of the term "organize" and held that claims on that count were barred by the statute of limitations.

The most significant portion of Justice Harlan's opinion was his distinction between advocacy of doctrine and advocacy intended to incite action. Only the former was entitled to constitutional free speech protection. While the "indoctrination of a group in preparation for future violent action" would likely have violated the act, merely advocating the idea of violence in this case was protected by the First Amendment.

Justice Clark delivered the lone dissent. He disagreed with the Court's construction of the word "organize." In Justice Clark's opinion, the main congressional purpose behind the Smith Act was to curb the growth of the Communist Party. He argued that the Court's interpretation of the act's first clause meant that it ceased to have effect three years after the party was founded, which was clearly not the intent of Congress. Justice Clark also found the Court's distinction between advocacy of doctrine and advocacy of action "too subtle to grasp." In his view, even advocacy of the doctrine of violent overthrow of the government had as its ultimate purpose the incitement of action toward that end.

AFTERMATH

Once the nine defendants were remanded for a new trial, the government dropped its charges on the grounds that proving advocacy of action would be too difficult.

SIGNIFICANCE

Proof of advocacy of a specific violent action to overthrow the government is necessary to support a conviction under the Smith Act. This standard of proof deterred prosecution of expression under the Smith Act.

RELATED CASES

Brandenburg v. Ohio, 395 U.S. 444 (1969)

Dennis v. United States, 341 U.S. 494 (1951)

RECOMMENDED READING

Emerson, Thomas I. *The System of Freedom of Expression.* New York: Random House, 1970.

The Supreme Court, 1960 Term, 75 Harvard Law Review 113 (1961).

Case Title: *Young v. American Mini Theatres*

Legal Citations: 427 U.S. 50; 96 S.Ct. 2440; L.Ed. 2d 310

Year of Decision: 1976

KEY ISSUES

Does a zoning ordinance that limits the places where adult bookstores and adult movie theaters may be located (1) violate the First Amendment's protection of free speech and (2) meet the requirements of equal protection in zoning classifications?

HISTORY OF THE CASE

From 1969 to 1972, Detroit sustained a rapid expansion in the number of adult bookstores, adult theaters, and topless cabarets. Because several residents complained that some of these adult businesses were located too close to their neighborhoods, the city adopted two zoning ordinances that amended an "Anti-Skid Row Ordinance" adopted 10 years earlier. The new ordinances regulated the location of such adult businesses, which were defined as those that emphasized "specified sexual activity" or that depicted "specified anatomical areas" in the films it showed or the publications it sold or displayed. One ordinance provided that no more than two of the "regulated uses" (including adult book stores, cabarets, bars, taxi, dance hotels, and hotels) may be located within 1,000 feet of each other unless a special waiver was obtained. The other ordinance prohibited the locating of an adult business within 500 feet of a residential area. The purposes of the zoning were to prevent the emergence of "skid row" areas caused by the concentration of the regulated uses and to protect the residential areas from adverse effects such as the "blighting or downgrading of the surrounding neighborhood."

One established adult theater was notified that it was in violation of the zoning ordinance because it was located within 1,000 feet of two other regulated uses. Another adult theater was denied a certificate of occupancy because of its location within 500 feet of a residential area. The theaters filed suit in U.S. District Court for the Eastern District of Michigan against appropriate city officials, seeking a declaratory judgment that they had a constitutional right to continue their business free from interference from the city and seeking an injunction against the enforcement of the zoning ordinances. The district court granted summary judgment in favor of the city. The theaters appealed, and the Court of Appeals for the Sixth Circuit held the new ordinances unconstitutional.

SUMMARY OF ARGUMENTS

The city of Detroit argued that the ordinances are a legitimate exercise of the power to control land use in order to promote important values for the community. The city contended that the ordinances do not prevent the establishment of adult business but merely regulate the "time, place, and manner" of making adult materials available to the public. It was also argued that the city had a compelling interest in singling out adult businesses for special regulation in order to preserve neighborhood values as well as other aesthetic, social, and economic values. These values were said to be in jeopardy from the concentration of the adult establishments, which could depress property values and increase criminal activity.

The theaters argued that the ordinances were in violation of the First Amendment's protection of free speech because they focused on the content of the publications or films offered as adult materials. They maintained that Detroit was attempting to censor the content of materials considered to be merely offensive or controversial, but not obscene. The theaters also contended that the ordinances were not written with adequate precision to pass constitutional tests for regulations affecting First Amendment rights. Because of this vagueness, the theaters argued that businesses will reluctantly suppress materials considered protected by the First Amendment out of fear of being prosecuted.

DECISION

The Court upheld the "Anti-Skid Row" ordinance restricting the locations of the adult businesses. Justice Stevens, writing for a plurality, stated "[t]he question whether speech is, or is not, protected by the First Amendment often depends on the content of the speech." Stevens contended that adult movies, because of their injurious impact on the quality of urban life, contain a lesser value than other types of speech, especially political debate. He maintained that "there is surely a less vital interest in the uninhibited exhibition of material that is on the borderline between pornography and artistic expression than in the free dissemination of ideas of social and political significance." Stevens agreed that the evils Detroit sought to prevent were sufficiently plausible and imminent to justify the ordinance's limited invasion on expression interests. He stressed that although sexually explicit materials could not be completely suppressed, they could be regulated to an extent to which political speech could not.

Justices Stewart, joined by Justices Blackmun, Marshall, and Brennan, objected to the plurality's contention that certain forms of speech, which arguably contain a lesser value, ought not be equally scrutinized. In response to the the plurality's argument that "few of us would march our sons and daughters off to war to preserve the citizen's right to see 'Specified Sexual Activities' exhibited in the theaters[,]" the dissent urged that the right to free expression should not be defined and circumscribed by current popular opinion. Stevens maintained that the guarantees of the Bill of Rights were designed to protect "such majoritarian limitations on individual liberty." The dissenters further argued that content-based restrictions—those premised on expression's "offensiveness"—should be permissible only in the "limited context of a captive or juvenile audience," an exception not applicable to these facts.

Justice Powell's separate concurrence was the "swing vote" that ultimately upheld the ordinance. While Powell did not join Stevens's "lesser value" theory, he believed that the ordinance's effect was "incidental and minimal." Using a four-part test, Powell believed that (1) the regulation was within the constitutional power of the Detroit Common Council to enact; (2) it furthered an important or substantial governmental interest; (3) the governmental interest was unrelated to the suppression of free expression; (4) the incidental restriction on First Amendment freedoms was no greater than what is necessary in furtherance of that interest. Powell praised the city's efforts to preserve "stable neighborhoods" through an "innovative, land-use regulation." He also believed that there was no indication that the ordinance would suppress production of or restrict access to adult films. He maintained that the governmental interest prompting the inclusion in the ordinance of adult businesses was wholly unrelated to any suppression of free expression.

Aftermath

Since *Young,* the Court has remained deeply divided over the issue of content discrimination. The Court has increasingly upheld content-based restrictions in the areas of commercial and sexually explicit speech. However, attempts to completely ban all forms of adult businesses supplying nonobscene, sexually explicit forms of entertainment in a municipality or town have been struck down by the Court. For example, in the 1981 case of *Schad v. Mount Ephraim,* the Court held that the total ban was a significant limitation on communicative activity, and the fact that the adult entertainment was available in a nearby town was irrelevant. The *Young* case was distinguished in *Schad* because the adult businesses were "merely dispersed," not wholly suppressed.

Significance

Although sexually explicit materials cannot be regulated solely on account of their internal qualities and negative impact upon women, the Supreme Court has approved regulations of pornographic expression based upon the harmful secondary effects it has on the surrounding community. Consequently, legislatures have passed several zoning regulations focusing on these secondary effects of adult-oriented businesses. If a regulation is aimed at the secondary effects of the speech and not the speech itself, it has a much greater chance of being upheld. Also, later cases have followed Powell's analysis in *Young* by ruling that if a particular regulation has only minor or incidental burdens on First Amendment concerns, the Court will not strictly scrutinize the regulation but will determine if the police power had a "rational basis" for the regulation.

Related Cases

Arcara v. Cloud Books, Inc., 478 U.S. 697 (1986)

Chicago Police Dept. v. Mosley, 408 U.S. 92 (1972)

City of Renton v. Playtime Theaters, Inc., 475 U.S. 41, 48 (1986)

Schad v. Borough of Mt. Ephraim, 452 U.S. 61 (1981)

Recommended Reading

John J. Costonis, *Law and Aesthetics: A Critique and a Reformulation of the Dilemmas,* 80 Michigan Law Review 451 (1982).

Note, *Content Regulation and the Dimension of Free Expression,* Harvard Law Review 1854 (1983).

Note or comment, *The Supreme Court—1975 Term,* 90 Harvard Law Review 196 (1976).

TAXATION

Case Title: *Breedlove v. Suttles, Tax Collector*

Alternate Case Title: The Right to Vote/Poll Tax Case

Legal Citations: 302 U.S. 277; 58 S.Ct. 205; 82 L.Ed. 252

Year of Decision: 1937

KEY ISSUES

Does a statute requiring persons between the ages of 21 and 60 with the exclusion of blind persons and women not registered to vote, to pay poll taxes, as a prerequisite of voting for federal and state officials, deny equal protection under the Fourteenth Amendment or privileges and immunities protected by the Nineteenth Amendment's guarantee of a right to vote?

HISTORY OF THE CASE

The state of Georgia had a statute that required the levying and collection of poll taxes of one dollar each year from every inhabitant of the state between the ages of 21 and 60, with the exception of the blind or females who did not register to vote. The statute also required that a person have paid all poll taxes to be entitled to register and vote at any election. The statute did not allow tax collectors to register a person for voting unless he paid the required poll taxes.

Nolen R. Breedlove was a white 28-year-old male citizen who applied to T. Earl Suttles to register to vote for federal and state officers at primary and general elections. He had not made poll tax returns nor paid any poll taxes. He demanded that Suttles administer the oath, omit the part declaring payment of poll taxes, and allow him to register. Suttles refused and Breedlove brought suit in the superior court of Fulton County to have the poll-tax clause of the statute declared repugnant to the U.S. Constitution, and to compel Suttles to register him to vote without payment of the poll taxes.

SUMMARY OF ARGUMENTS

Breedlove argued that the privilege of voting for federal officials is one to which he is entitled, unrestricted by a tax unreasonably imposed. He contended that the provisions in question were repugnant to the equal protection clause and the privileges and immunities clause of the Fourteenth and Nineteenth Amendments.

Suttles argued that the right to vote did not arise by virtue of the Constitution and that state regulations defining voter qualifications were not prohibited by the privileges and immunities clause. Suttles also argued that the Georgia laws did not deny U.S. citizens, living in Georgia, a republican form of government, nor did the Georgia law withhold any right guaranteed by the First or Fifteenth Amendment.

DECISION

Justice Butler wrote the unanimous opinion for the Court. He held that a payment of poll taxes as a prerequisite of voting did not deny privileges and immunities protected by the Fourteenth Amendment. He further held that the poll tax did not violate the Nineteenth Amendment since the right to vote was neither denied nor abridged on account of sex. The Court upheld the Georgia statute requiring the payment of a one dollar poll tax as a precondition for voting.

Justice Butler proposed that the equal protection clause did not require absolute equality. He then stated why it would be unreasonable to request payment of a poll tax from minors, non-registered women, and men over 60 years old since such a tax would be considered harsh and unjust for minors, and an extra burden on men to levy the tax on their unregistered wives since the men are the heads of their households. He added that different exemptions for men over 60 were commonplace, reasoning that the tax was laid only upon those within the defined class, and served to aid the collection from electors desiring to vote. He found that such a use of the state's power was not exempted by the federal Constitution.

Justice Butler contended that the privilege of voting does not come from the United States; rather, it is conferred by the state. As such, the state could condition suffrage as it deemed appropriate. The privileges and immunities protected by the Fourteenth Amendment were only those arising from the Constitution and laws of the United States, and therefore Justice Butler felt that no violation of the Fourteenth Amendment occurred. He also stated that the payment of poll taxes as a prerequisite of voting was a "familiar and reasonable regulation" with a long history in many of the states. Further, because the right to vote was neither denied nor abridged on account of sex, the challenged enactment did not violate the Nineteenth Amendment.

AFTERMATH

The Court followed the reasoning in *Breedlove* until the 1960s. In REYNOLDS V. SIMS (1964) and five companion cases, the Court changed directions, making the right to vote a fundamental matter. This holding opened the door to a more active judicial scrutiny of voter qualifications. The Court then overruled *Breedlove* in *Harper v. Virginia State Board of Elections* (1966) by invalidating a Virginia Law requiring the payment of a poll tax as a precondition for voting as a violation of the equal protection clause.

SIGNIFICANCE

The original Constitution left it to the states to determine the qualifications for voting in both state and federal elections. The *Breedlove* case was important for determining that it was constitutional for states to set the qualifications for voting, except where a particular qualification was expressly prohibited by a specific amendment, even if it resulted in many individuals being unable to participate in the elections.

RELATED CASES

Harper v. Virginia State Board of Elections, 383 U.S. 663 (1966)

Lassiter v. Northhampton County Board of Elections, 360 U.S. 45 (1959)

Reynolds v. Sims, 377 U.S. 533 (1964)

RECOMMENDED READING

Bickel, Alexander. *The Supreme Court and the Idea of Progress.* New York: Harper and Row, 1970.

Ely, John. *Democracy and Distrust: A Theory of Judicial Review.* Cambridge, Mass.: Harvard University Press, 1980.

Shapiro, Martin. *Law and Politics in the Supreme Court.* New York: Free Press of Glencoe, 1964.

William Van Alstyne, *The Fourteenth Amendment, the "Right" to Vote, and the Understanding of the Thirty-ninth Congress,* Supreme Court Review 33 (1965).

Case Title: *Everson v. Board of Education of the Township of Ewing et al.*

Alternate Case Title: Everson Case

Legal Citation: 303 U.S. 1

Year of Decision: 1947

KEY ISSUES

Do a state statute and school board resolution violate the First and Fourteenth Amendments when they authorize bus fare reimbursements to parents of children attending public and Catholic parochial schools?

HISTORY OF THE CASE

A New Jersey statute authorized district boards of education to make rules and contracts for the transportation of children to and from school, other than private schools operated for profit. A board of education passed a resolution authorizing reimbursement of parents for fares paid by children attending public and Catholic schools where religious instruction was part of the curriculum. A taxpayer challenged the statute and resolution saying that the school board had no power to reimburse parents for bus fares incurred for transportation of children to schools other than public schools.

This is an appeal from the Court of Errors and Appeals of New Jersey. The New Jersey Supreme Court held that the state legislature did not have the power under the state constitution to authorize reimbursement to parents of bus fares for transporting their children to schools other than public schools. The New Jersey Court of Errors and Appeals reversed. Neither statute nor resolution violated the federal or state constitutions.

SUMMARY OF ARGUMENTS

Appellant, a taxpayer, argued that the statute allowing for the reimbursement of transportation expenses violated the First and Fourteenth Amendments of the U.S. Constitution. Appellant argued that the statute authorized the state to take property from some and give it to others in violation of the due process clause of the Fourteenth Amendment. Appellant also argued that the statute violated the First Amendment as incorporated by the Fourteenth Amendment because the statute forced persons to pay taxes to support religious schools.

Appellee, the Ewing Township Board of Education, argued that the statute did not violate the U.S. Constitution as it did not support religion, but instead supported education.

DECISION

Justice Black wrote for the majority finding the establishment clause of the First Amendment, which states "Congress shall make no law respecting an establishment of religion," to prohibit "laws which aid one religion, and all religions, or prefer one religion over another. No tax in any amount, large or small, can be levied to support any religious activities or institutions . . . In the words of Jefferson the establishment clause was intended to erect 'a wall of separation between church and state.'" The reimbursement is valid for the welfare of all the children in the district. It is not unconstitutional because the First Amendment requires neutrality, not hostility.

Justice Rutledge and Justice Frankfurter wrote the dissent asking for very strict separation of church and state and found this case to be public aid to religious institutions, thus violating the establishment clause. The expenditure of public funds for a public purpose did not violate the due process clause of the Fourteenth Amendment and the statute and resolution did not violate the First Amendment prohibiting any "law respecting an establishment of religion."

AFTERMATH

The holding drew criticism from all over; commentators liked it. It did influence the decisions in other Supreme Court cases. *Everson* has served as the foundation for determining other disputes regarding public funds and parochial schools, including the more recent school voucher cases.

SIGNIFICANCE

This case represented the first contemporary controversy concerning the meaning of the establishment clause. *Everson* applied the First Amendment

establishment clause to the states and presented a lengthy definition of the establishment clause, which would have future precedential value.

RELATED CASES

Cochran v. Louisiana State Board of Education, 286 U.S. 370 (1930)

Illinois ex rel. McCollum v. Board of Education, 333 U.S. 203 (1948)

Zorach v. Clauson, 343 U.S. 306 (1952)

RECOMMENDED READING

Samuel A. Alito, "The Released Time Cases Revisited, 83 Yale Law Journal 1202 (1974).

James C. Kirby, *Everson to Meek to Roemer,* 55 North Carolina Law Review 563 (1977).

Pfeffer, Leo. *Religion, State and the Burger Court.* Buffalo, N.Y.: Prometheus Books, 1984.

Rodney K. Smith, *Getting off on the Wrong Foot,* 20 Wake Forest Law Review 569 (1984).

Case Title: *Flast v. Cohen*

Legal Citation: 392 U.S. 83

Year of Decision: 1968

KEY ISSUES

Can federal taxpayers challenge the constitutionality of a federal statute that they allege violates the First Amendment of the Constitution?

HISTORY OF THE CASE

This action was brought by federal taxpayers who challenged the use of federal funds to purchase instruction material and textbooks for use in parochial schools. The rule established by *Frothingham v. Mellon* was that a federal taxpayer was without standing to challenge the constitutionality of a federal statute. The preliminary question faced by the Court was whether the *Frothingham* standard was still appropriate.

Article III, section 2 of the Constitution gives the Supreme Court jurisdiction only over cases and controversies, as defined in that article. The article had been interpreted to limit the Court's authority to prevent it from issuing merely advisory opinions, deciding political questions or questions in which the Court had a stake. The act served as a means of judicial restraint.

SUMMARY OF ARGUMENTS

The taxpayers argued that the statute that allowed for the expenditure of federal funds to purchase textbooks and instructional materials for parochial schools violated both the establishment clause and the free exercise clause. They argued that the statute, which allowed such expenditures, violated the prohibition against laws that respect the establishment of religion and prohibited the free exercise of religion on the part of the taxpayers because it constituted compulsory taxation for religious purposes.

Cohen, secretary of health, education, and welfare, argued for the government that the taxpayers under the *Frothingham* standard lacked authority to bring this claim. In addition, the government contended that the Supreme Court lacked jurisdiction to consider the claim on direct appeal from the district court because, under 28 U.S.C. 1283, direct appeal to the Supreme Court from the district court is permissible only "from an order granting or denying . . . an interlocutory or permanent injunction in any civil action, suit or proceeding required by any Act of Congress to be heard and determined by a district court of three judges." The government in connection with this contention argued the taxpayers only challenged the constitutionality of the local programs and did not seek to enjoin the operation of the broader federal program in which the program operated; only if the latter were true would a three-judge panel have been appropriate to consider the claim.

DECISION

As to the preliminary questions of standing and jurisdiction, the Court held that the taxpayers had standing to sue and that the Court had jurisdiction over the case. The Court went on to reverse the holding of the district court that the taxpayers were without standing to sue, stating that the applicable standard for judging whether the claim was a case or controversy of the type which the Court could assert jurisdiction was whether there is "a logical nexus between the status asserted and the claim

thought to be adjudicated." In addition, the Court held that because the relief sought by the taxpayers would have to be applied evenly to all federal programs and the claim involved constitutional as well as nonconstitutional issues, the issue was properly before the Court. Justice Douglas concurred in the opinion but stated that the ruling would lead to the erosion of the *Frothingham* standard.

Justice Stewart concurred in the opinion. He felt that this case was distinguishable from *Frothingham* in that "the taxpayer did not rely on an explicit constitutional prohibition but instead questioned the scope of the powers delegated on the national legislature" and therefore the issue of whether the decision erodes that doctrine is moot.

Justice Fortas concurred stating that the decision should be limited to stand for the proposition that a taxpayer has standing to bring an action to challenge the constitutionality of a federal expenditure that is viewed as violating the establishment clause of the Constitution.

Justice Harlan dissented on the grounds that the *Frothingham* standard was still controlling.

AFTERMATH

This case established the taxpayer standing doctrine, which is a two-part test that determines whether a taxpayer has standing to sue. The *Flast* test required the Court to assess whether the party had a personal stake in the outcome of the controversy and whether there was an official action that violated a legally protected interest.

However, this doctrine has been limited in subsequent opinions, notably *Valley Forge Christian College v. Americans United for Separation of Church and State, Inc., Scheslinger v. Reservists Comm. to Stop the War,* and *United States v. Richardson.* These cases exemplify the Court's more recent attempts to limit the doctrine of taxpayer standing by interpreting literally the decision in *Flast* and not applying the principle underlying the decision, which is that when there is an official abridgment of a legally protected interest, the taxpayer should have standing to sue. In these later decisions the Court has held the abridgment of a legally protected right does not provide standing unless the claimant can show that he or she actually was injured by the official action. The Court has come to require more than generalized grievances, abstract injuries, and assertion of "personal" constitutional rights.

SIGNIFICANCE

The *Flast* decision provided a vehicle for the taxpayers to challenge how their taxes were being spent. As long as the taxpayer's claim met the requirements of challenging the use of congressional taxing and spending as violating a constitutional prohibition, the taxpayer had standing. The requirements have increasingly been criticized by the courts and by legal scholars who feel certain cases that should be heard and resolved on the merits are precluded from such a decision by the law of standing.

To date, *Flast* serves as the most expansive reading of the establishment clause. More recent cases such as *Valley Forge* (see Related Cases, below) have read the two requirements for standing set out in *Flast* strictly and therefore have severely limited the doctrine established by the case. The current trend is toward a general limitation on taxpayer standing.

RELATED CASE

Valley Forge Christian College v. Americans United for Separation of Church and State, Inc., 454 U.S. 464 (1982)

RECOMMENDED READING

Robert L. Kahan, *Federal Taxpayers and Standing:* Flast v. Cohen, 16 University of California–Los Angeles Law Review 444 (1969).

Case Title: *McCray v. United States*

Alternate Case Title: Oleomargarine Case

Legal Citations: 195 U.S. 27; 24 S.Ct. 769; 49 L.Ed. 78

Year of Decision: 1904

KEY ISSUES

Does the taxation of artificially colored oleomargarine at a higher rate than oleomargarine without color violate the due process clause?

HISTORY OF THE CASE

Congress imposed a high tax on all retailers of artificially colored oleomargarine, effectively rendering the product too expensive to compete with natural butter. McCray, a licensed retailer of yellow oleomargarine, brought suit in federal district court alleging that the discriminatory tax was unconstitutional.

SUMMARY OF ARGUMENTS

McCray objected to the fact that Congress "arbitrarily" chose to impose a far lower tax on noncolored oleomargarine, whereas colored natural butter was not taxed at all. He argued that the tax violated his constitutional right of due process before being deprived of property.

DECISION

Justice White wrote for the Court upholding the constitutionality of the tax, stating that it was within congressional taxing power. Operating on the assumption that the primary objective of the statute was to raise money, Congress had exercised its power within constitutional limits. The Court did not determine whether the tax was unwise or inquire into Congress's motive in passing it. The Court held that the taxation of artificially colored oleomargarine at a higher rate than oleomargarine without color does not violate the due process clause.

AFTERMATH

The Court left open the option to examine future tax schemes despite the fact that it shied away from examining motive and injury in this case.

SIGNIFICANCE

McCray upholds Congress's use of taxation as a regulatory power. Additionally, the Court clearly held that as long as a tax was within the congressional grant of power, it would not be invalidated because its effect was to limit or prohibit an activity.

RELATED CASES

Champion v. Ames, 186 U.S. 321 (1903)

Gibbons v. Ogden, 22 U.S. 1 (1824)

Spencer v. Merchant, 126 U.S. 345 (1888)

RECOMMENDED READING

McCloskey, Robert G. *The American Supreme Court.* Chicago: University of Chicago Press, 1960.

Case Title: *Mueller v. Allen*

Legal Citations: 463 U.S. 388; 77 L.Ed. 2d 721; 103 S.Ct. 3062

Year of Decision: 1983

KEY ISSUES

Does a statute allowing state taxpayers to claim a deduction for expenses incurred in educating their children in public or private schools establish religion in violation of the First Amendment?

HISTORY OF THE CASE

Since 1955, Minnesota allowed an income tax deduction for tuition, textbooks, and transportation expenses paid by the parent or guardian of a child attending elementary or secondary schools. The maximum deduction ranged from $500 to $700, depending on the child's level of education.

In 1980 Minnesota taxpayers brought suit in federal court complaining that the deductions violated the establishment clause of the First Amendment. The establishment clause prohibits any law "respecting an establishment of religion," and its main purpose is to prohibit government from endorsing or supporting religion. The taxpayers complained, among other things, that only parents of children in parochial schools benefited significantly from the available deductions. The district court entered summary judgment against the taxpayers. The Court of Appeals for the Eighth Circuit affirmed.

SUMMARY OF ARGUMENTS

The plaintiffs argued that a tax deduction for private school tuition is the equivalent of a direct subsidy. They contended that 96 percent of children in private schools attend parochial schools, and that because tuition was a much larger expense than the other deductible expenses under the plan, parents of private-school children disproportionately benefited from the deduction for tuition. The plaintiffs further argued that a deduction for textbooks that can be used for religious instruction is a subsidy for such materials and thus impermissibly establishes religion.

The defendants argued that because the tax deductions available benefit both parents of public and private school children, the plan has a neutral purpose and effect toward religion. The defendants added that a tax deduction is a passive form of aid and thus is less suspect than a direct subsidy.

DECISION

The Court, in a 5-4 decision written by Justice Rehnquist, held that the Minnesota statute did not violate the establishment clause by providing financial assistance to parochial schools. The Court stressed that the primary effect of the program was secular because (1) the tax deduction was only one among many deductions—such as those for medical expenses and charitable contributions—and that the Minnesota legislature is entitled to substantial deference in attempting to "achieve an equitable distribution of the tax burden"; (2) the deduction was available to all parents, including those whose children attended public schools and those whose children attended nonsectarian or sectarian private schools, thereby having a neutral quality; and (3) the assistance was available to the parents, not directly to the parochial schools, thus preventing any "imprimatur of state approval" from being given to any particular religion. The majority also remarked that the program could fairly be regarded as a rough return for the benefits provided to the state and all the taxpayers by parents sending their children to private schools.

Justice Marshall, joined by Justices Brennan, Blackmun, and Stevens, dissented on the grounds that the provision had the direct and immediate effect of advancing religion. In the dissenting view, the deductions available to parents who send their children to public school were insignificant compared to those of parents who send their children to private schools. The dissent reasoned that tuition, an expense not paid by those attending public schools, was the overwhelmingly largest expense deductible under the Minnesota statute. The dissent supported their argument that the primary effect of the statute was nonsecular in noting that over 90 percent of the private school students in Minnesota attended parochial schools. The dissenters also objected on the grounds that because the textbooks and other instructional materials were "subsidized by the Minnesota tax deduction," they "plainly may be used to inculcate religious values and belief." Thus they concluded that the state of Minnesota provided substantial aid to the education function of parochial schools in violation of the First Amendment.

AFTERMATH

The Court continued to uphold state financial aid to religious institutions when the scheme was facially neutral. For example, the Court held by 5-4 that a public university could fund student-run religious publications without violating the establishment clause. In *Rosenberger v. Univ of Virginia* (1995), the Court observed that (1) the funds were also given to nonreligious publications, and (2) the funds were not given directly to the religious publication, but to a "neutral" third party, a printing service.

SIGNIFICANCE

The *Mueller* decision continued the Court's trend of allowing more contacts between church and state. The case demonstrates greater tolerance for financial assistance to parochial schools than the Court had shown in previous decisions. A tax relief program, which is on its face available to parents who send their children to public schools, may be upheld even if the majority of the benefits flow to parents who send their children to sectarian institutions. Therefore, if parents increasingly choose private school education for their children, the quality of public education could erode. This erosion would theoretically occur because if the majority of parents of children attending public schools were of the low-income bracket, they would have less political power to ensure adequate funding for their schools.

RELATED CASES

Comm. for Public Ed. v. Nyquist, 413 U.S. 756 (1973)

Roemer v. Maryland Public Works Bd., 426 U.S. 736 (1976)

Rosenberger v. Univ. of Virginia, 115 S.Ct. 2510 (1995)

Walz v. Tax Comm'n, 397 U.S. 664 (1970)

Witters v. Wash. Dept. of Svcs. for the Blind, 474 U.S. 481 (1986)

RECOMMENDED READING

Carla R. Ambrose, Mueller v. Allen, 19 New England Law Review 459 (1984).

Martin L. Nussbaum, Mueller v. Allen, Harvard Journal of Law and Public Policy 551 (1984).

Pfeffer, Leo. *Religion, State and the Burger Court.* Buffalo, N.Y.: Prometheus Books, 1984.

Case Title: *Pollock v. Farmers' Loan and Trust Company*

Legal Citations: 158 U.S. 601; 15 S.Ct. 912; 39 L.Ed. 1108

Year of Decision: 1895

KEY ISSUES

Do the provisions of the Tariff Act of August 15, 1894, imposing a tax on incomes violate Article 1, section 9 of the Constitution, which provides that direct taxes must be apportioned among the states?

HISTORY OF THE CASE

The Tariff Act imposed a tax of 2 percent on a citizen's gains, profits, and income and imposed a 2 percent tax on the net profits of a corporation. The Circuit Court of the United States for the Southern District of New York held that the Tariff Act was unconstitutional if it imposed a tax on rent from real estate and income from municipal bonds. The court did not give an opinion whether an income tax itself was unconstitutional nor whether an unconstitutional provision within the act made the entire act unconstitutional.

SUMMARY OF ARGUMENTS

The appellant, Charles Pollock, argued that the taxes imposed violated the constitutional requirement of uniformity and, therefore, were invalid. Further, the government could not enforce an unequal tax law because it violated the due process provisions of the Fifth Amendment.

The appellee, the Farmers' Loan and Trust Company, did not argue the constitutionality or unconstitutionality of the tax law, but merely asked the Court to render a judgment on Pollock's issues so that they would know what their duty was under the law and could comply with it.

DECISION

Chief Justice Fuller delivered the opinion of the Court that the Constitution gave the states the power of absolute taxation. The federal government received the power of the same taxation if it was apportioned among the states. If an income tax is a direct tax, it is unconstitutional if it is unapportioned (not based on population).

Justice Harlan dissented, writing that "the primary object of all taxation by the general government is to pay the debts and to provide for the common defense and general welfare of the United States." Why, he argued, should this purpose be thwarted by distinctions between direct and indirect tax?

The provisions in question of the Tariff Act of 1894 concerning tax on income are unconstitutional because they are not apportioned according to representation within the meaning of the Constitution.

AFTERMATH

The 1894 act proved to be one of the most important statutes in the history of income tax. Not only is it a peacetime income tax, but Congress later incorporated its language into the Revenue Act of 1913. The 1894 act was clearly a product of a conservative time as the Court protected the "privilege of unburdened accumulation of wealth."

SIGNIFICANCE

This case was overruled by the Sixteenth Amendment, which was ratified in 1913. It states "The Congress shall have the power to lay and collect taxes on incomes, from whatever source derived, without apportionment among the several states, and without regard to any census or enumeration." The Revenue Act of 1913 followed the ratification of the amendment.

RELATED CASES

Chicago, Milwaukee, & St. Paul Ry. Co. v. Minnesota, 134 U.S. 418 (1890)

Coppage v. Kansas, 236 U.S. 1 (1915)

Block v. Hirsh, 256 U.S. 135 (1921)

RECOMMENDED READING

Andrzej Rapaczynski, *From Sovereignty to Process: The Jurisprudence of Federalism after Garcia*, Supreme Court Review 341 (1985).

Semonche, John E. *Charting the Future: The Supreme Court Responds to a Changing Society, 1890–1920.* Westport, Conn.: Greenwood Press, 1978.

JURISDICTION

Case Title: *Erie Railroad Company v. Tompkins*

Legal Citation: 304 U.S. 64

Year of Decision: 1938

KEY ISSUES

Does federal or state law apply in a case before a federal court where jurisdiction is based on diversity of citizenship, the situation in which the plaintiff and defendant are citizens of different states?

HISTORY OF THE CASE

Tompkins, a Pennsylvania citizen, was injured by a passing freight train of the Erie Railroad while walking along its right of way at night. He claimed the accident occurred through the negligence of the train company. He filed an action in the Federal Court of the Southern District of New York, which had jurisdiction of the case because the railroad was incorporated in that state. Erie insisted that it owed no duty to Tompkins because he was a trespasser; it also contended that its liability should be determined by Pennsylvania law.

SUMMARY OF ARGUMENTS

Appellant, Erie Railroad, argued that its duty to Tompkins should have been determined by Pennsylvania state law as determined by the state's highest court.

Appellee, Tompkins, argued that general law, law not restricted to a certain locality, applied to the issues of negligence and contributory negligence.

DECISION

With the exception of issues governed by the federal Constitution or acts of Congress, the law to be applied in this case is the law of the state where the accident occurred. Justice Brandeis delivered the majority opinion, noting that except for matters governed by the federal Constitution or by acts of Congress, the applicable law in any case is the law of the state, including its written laws and case law. Therefore this case depends, in the absence of a federal or state statute, on the unwritten law of the state where the accident occurred.

AFTERMATH

Erie overrules *SWIFT V. TYSON* (1842). *Tyson* held that only state statutory law could be applied in federal diversity of citizenship cases. State common law, including judicial interpretation of state statutes, was inapplicable under *Tyson*. *Erie*, however, made this law applicable to diversity cases.

SIGNIFICANCE

This marked the beginning of the importance of diversity actions. While diversity actions may have started out as more protective of state prerogatives where application of state law would generate a different law than if the federal law was applied, later diversity exemplified the relationship between the states and federal government, with the presumption in favor of federal law.

RELATED CASES

Bryd v. Blue Ridge Rural Electric Cooperative, Inc. 356 U.S. 525 (1958)

Hanna v. Plummer, 380 U.S. 460 (1965)

Swift v. Tyson, 41 U.S. 1 (1842)

RECOMMENDED READING

Charles E. Clark, *State Law in the Federal: The Brooding Omnipotence of* Erie v. Tompkins, 55 Yale Law Journal 265–296 (1946).

John Hart Ely, *The Irrepressible Myth of* Erie, 87 Harvard Law Review 693 (1974).

Freyer, Tony. *Harmony and Dissonance.* New York: New York University Press, 1981.

Philip B. Kurland, *Mr. Justice Frankfurter, the Supreme Court and the Erie Doctrine in Diversity Cases,* 67 Yale Law Journal 187 (1957).

Case Title: *Kinsella v. Krueger*

Alternate Case Title: *Reid v. Covert*

Legal Citations: 354 U.S. 1; 77 S.Ct. 1222

Year of Decision: 1957

≈

KEY ISSUES

Can Congress pass regulations that authorize the court-martial of civilians for capital crimes?

HISTORY OF THE CASE

This case consolidates two factually similar cases. In the first one, Covert, a civilian, killed her husband, a sergeant in the U.S. Air Force stationed at an airbase in England. The military asserted jurisdiction over her under the Uniform Code of Military Justice (UCMJ), tried her by court-martial, found her guilty of murder, and sentenced her to life imprisonment. The Air Force Board of Review affirmed, but the court of military appeals reversed because of prejudicial errors concerning her insanity defense. She filed a writ of habeas corpus in the federal district court. The court granted the writ, setting her free. The government appealed to the Supreme Court.

In the second case, Smith, a civilian, killed her army officer husband while he was posted in Japan. She, too, was tried by court-martial, found guilty despite considerable evidence showing she was insane at the time of the crime, and sentenced to life imprisonment. The Army Board of Review approved the judgment, as did the court of military appeals. Mrs. Smith's father, Krueger, also filed a habeas corpus petition in federal district court. The court refused the petition and the father appealed to the court of appeals.

After the two cases were initially joined and argued before the Supreme Court, the justices ruled that under the Constitution Article 1, section 8, clause 14, Congress could command military trial of civilians. Later, however, the Court granted a petition for rehearing and chose to hear arguments on both cases once again. What follows is the summary of arguments for that proceeding.

SUMMARY OF ARGUMENTS

The civilian families simply argued that the Constitution did not allow civilians to be tried by military courts.

The government argued two points. First, it pointed out that U.S. armed forces were stationed in other countries by virtue of international agreement. Given this, under the treaty provision of Article 6, agreements between the United States

and other nations were the "supreme Law of the Land." Second, the government claimed that when taken together, Article 1, section 8, clauses 14 (empowering Congress "to make Rules for the Government and Regulation of the land and naval Forces") and 18 (the "Necessary and Proper" clause), allow Congress to authorize civilian trials by military tribunals. The UCMJ was just such an authorization, the government said.

DECISION

In a well-organized and clearly expressed opinion, the 6-2 majority (Justice Charles E. Whittaker did not take part in these cases) ruled that Covert and Smith be released from custody. Justice Hugo Black wrote the Court's majority opinion; Justices Felix Frankfurter and John Marshall Harlan concurred in separate opinions; Tom C. Clark and Harold H. Burton dissented.

Justice Black first reviewed certain constitutional provisions that expressly guarantee a citizen's right to jury trial in criminal matters. He described Article 3, section 2 ("The Trial of all Crimes, except in Cases of Impeachment, shall be by Jury . . .") as being designed to restrict the government in its criminal prosecutions. He wrote that section 2 is clearly intended to apply to criminal trials outside the United States, as well as here at home. The Fifth Amendment similarly declares that "no person shall be held to answer for a capital" crime without a grand jury indictment. The Sixth Amendment reaffirms this right to trial by jury in criminal cases. Black cited historical arguments as further evidence that "the Constitution and the Bill of Rights . . . [guarantee] that trial before a civilian judge and by an independent jury picked from the common citizenry is . . . a fundamental right."

The majority opinion continued to find nothing in Article 6 that alludes to the idea that treaties, and the laws passed to enact them, do not have to comply with other constitutional provisions. Justice Black cited the history of constitutional drafting and ratification to reinforce this point: treaties and laws must follow the Constitution.

He proceeded next to discuss how the Court had earlier and mistakenly supported its previous related rulings. The majority opinion explained that prior decisions upholding military courts-martial of civilians "rested, at least in substantial part, on a fundamental misconception" that the Constitution has no application abroad. Contrary to the government's argument, Justice Black concluded that "the Constitution in its entirety applied to the trials of Mrs. Smith and Mrs. Covert." This includes all its protections in criminal trials.

The justice concluded that a natural reading of the two section 8 clauses demonstrates the extent of the power granted to Congress. Certainly, Congress can make all rules necessary and proper to govern those persons in the "land and naval forces," but this cannot extend military jurisdiction to civilians, whether associated with the military or not: "Under the grand design of the Constitution[,] civilian courts are the normal repositories of power to try persons charged with crimes against the United States." Article 3 and the Fifth and Sixth Amendment prove this.

The concurring opinions emphasized the narrowness of the Court's holding, stressing the civilian's capital offense and the armed forces' alleged jurisdiction.

The dissent argued several points. It felt that the Court should adhere to its earlier cases and pointed out that the UCMJ was a reasonable enactment of the power of Congress to govern the military. Furthermore, history showed that "the military has always exercised jurisdiction by court-martial over civilians accompanying armies in time of war" and argued for the same now in peacetime.

The Constitution does not allow Congress to pass regulations that allow the military to court-martial a civilian. To do so would be to deprive an individual of all the safeguards of the Constitution and Bill of Rights, as well as the protections of civil laws and procedures.

AFTERMATH

Three years later, the Court ruled that civilian court-martials for noncapital crimes were also unconstitutional. *Covert* and its progeny unequivocally strike down military jurisdiction over civilian crimes against the United States.

SIGNIFICANCE

The *Covert* line of cases struck down military jurisdiction over civilian dependents of military forces for all crimes against the United States. From this point on, the Constitution was to be interpreted as granting and ensuring that the Bill of Rights would protect all U.S. citizens accused of crimes no matter where those crimes occurred.

RELATED CASES

Kinsella v. United States ex rel. Singleton, 361 U.S. 234, 80 S.Ct. 297 (1960)

United States ex rel. Toth v. Quarles, 350 U.S. 11, 76 S.Ct. 1, 100 L.Ed. 8 (1955)

RECOMMENDED READING

Bigel, Alan I. *The Supreme Court on Emergency Powers, Foreign Affairs and Protection of Civil Liberties, 1935–1975.* Lanham, Md.: University Press of America, 1986.

Gregory A. McClelland, *The Problem of Jurisdiction over Civilians Accompanying the Forces Overseas—Still with Us,* 117 Military Law Review 153 (1987).

Case Title: *Kinsella v. United States ex rel. Singleton*

Legal Citations: 361 U.S. 234; 80 S.Ct. 297

Year of Decision: 1960

KEY ISSUES

Can Congress pass regulations that authorize the court-martial of civilians for noncapital crimes?

HISTORY OF THE CASE

Joanna S. Dial was the wife of a tank battalion U.S. Army soldier. Husband and wife and their three children were stationed in Germany. When one of the children was found dead, the Dials were charged with unpremeditated murder under the Uniform Code of Military Justice (UCMJ). At the court-martial in Germany, the two pled guilty to the lesser offense of involuntary manslaughter. They were tried and convicted. The court of military appeals upheld the convictions.

This case appeared before the Supreme Court because Mrs. Dial's mother, Alberta Singleton, filed a habeas corpus petition in U.S. District Court challenging the jurisdiction of the court-martial proceeding over the civilian Mrs. Dial. The trial court granted the petition, freeing Mrs. Dial from prison. Kinsella, the prison warden, appealed to the Supreme Court.

SUMMARY OF ARGUMENTS

In pursuing the appeal, Kinsella sought to overcome a previous and related Supreme Court decision. The 1957 case of *Reid v. Covert* declared Article 2(11) of the Uniform Code of Military Justice, which provided for the court-martial of "all persons . . . accompanying the armed forces" in foreign countries, unconstitutional when applied to civilian dependents charged with capital offenses. Kinsella attempted to distinguish the *Covert* case from the present one on two main grounds.

First, Kinsella argued that the *Covert* decision should be followed only in capital offense situations. Since this case involved a "significantly different" noncapital crime, the Court need not follow its earlier decision. Kinsella argued a number of compelling considerations for prosecuting civilian dependents within court-martial jurisdiction. Second, the government asserted that military legal history shows a well-established practice of court-martialing civilians who accompany the armed forces.

From these arguments, it concluded that civilian dependents may be included as a necessary and proper incident to the congressional power "To make Rules for Government and Regulation of the land and naval Forces," as granted in the U.S. Constitution, Article 1, section 8, clause 14.

Singleton, on the other hand, argued that the Court had it right in *Covert* and should follow that decision. She pointed out that Article 2(11) doesn't distinguish between capital and noncapital crimes. Given that the Court previously decided that civilian dependent capital offenders are not subject to the UCMJ, she argued that other civilian dependents of military personnel should also be immune to the UCMJ for noncapital crimes as well. Mrs. Singleton contended that when the Court decided the *Covert* case, it effectively decided the issue for the entire class of civilian dependents, regardless of the nature of the crimes. Since the Court already decided the UCMJ did not apply to civilian dependents in capital crimes, she concluded consistency demanded a similar decision in her noncapital case.

DECISION

The Court affirmed the trial court decision, holding that it is unconstitutional to court-martial civilian dependents of military personnel for non-capital crimes.

Justice Tom C. Clark wrote the 7-2 majority opinion. After summarizing the facts, Justice Clark discussed Article 2(11) of the UCMJ—the basis for court-martialing Mrs. Dial. The constitutionality of Article 2(11) as it applies to civilian dependents charged with noncapital crimes was the sole issue decided by the Court.

The majority then addressed the government's first argument. Contrary to the government's position, the Court found these arguments "about the same as those asserted in capital cases." As the *Covert* court found them an unreasonable basis for military prosecution of a civilian, so did the majority here. Additionally, the Court declined to include civilian dependents in the term "land and naval Forces," as described in clause 14. The Court pointed out that the necessary and proper clause does not grant Congress specific power, but instead declares that Congress possesses all the means to carry out its constitutionally granted powers. As such, it cannot expand clause 14 to include prosecution of civilian dependents for noncapital offenses. Moreover, other portions of the Constitution, which grant affirmative rights to citizens regarding trials, further limit the government's power to make military trial of civilians.

With respect to the government's second position that sought to justify prosecution based on history, the Court found this argument illogical: "Its application today . . . would free from military prosecution a civilian . . . who committed a capital offense, while the same civilian [dependent] could be prosecuted by the military for a noncapital crime."

AFTERMATH

As a result of *Kinsella* and its predecessors, it is clear that the Constitution imposes substantive constraints on the federal government, even when it operates abroad.

SIGNIFICANCE

In *Covert,* the Supreme Court struck down court-martial jurisdiction over civilians in capital crime trials. *Kinsella* continued that trend by disallowing military trials of civilians for noncapital offenses. The result was to eliminate U.S. extraterritorial jurisdiction over civilians accompanying its forces overseas.

RELATED CASES

Reid v. Covert (Kinsella v. Krueger), 354 U.S. 1, 77 S.Ct. 1222, 1 L.Ed. 2d 1148 (1957)

United States ex rel. Toth v. Quarles, 350 U.S. 11, 76 S.Ct. 1, 100 L.Ed. 8 (1955)

RECOMMENDED READING

Bigel, Alan I. *The Supreme Court on Emergency Powers, Foreign Affairs and Protection of Civil Liberties, 1935–1975.* Lanham, Md.: University Press of America, 1986.

Gregory A. McClelland, *The Problem of Jurisdiction over Civilians Accompanying the Forces Overseas—Still with Us,* 117 Military Law Review 153 (1987).

Case Title: *Marbury v. Madison*

Legal Citations: 5 U.S. 137; 2 L.Ed. 60

Year of Decision: 1803

KEY ISSUES

Does the Constitution give the Supreme Court the authority to review acts of Congress and declare them, if repugnant to the Constitution, to be void?

HISTORY OF THE CASE

This landmark constitutional case arose from a political dispute in the aftermath of the bitter presidential election of 1800. Republican Thomas Jefferson defeated incumbent Federalist John Adams for the presidency. Adams, in his final days in office, attempted to entrench Federalists in the judiciary by appointing 16 new circuit judges and 42 new justices of the peace for the District of Columbia. Commissions for four of the new justices of the peace, including William Marbury, were not delivered before Adams's last day in office.

When President Jefferson's secretary of state, James Madison, refused to give the four men their commissions, Marbury asked the Supreme Court to issue a writ of mandamus ordering him to do so. The case presented a dilemma for Chief Justice Marshall, a committed Federalist whom Adams had named chief justice immediately after his electoral defeat. If the Supreme Court issued the order, Madison might refuse, and the Court had no means to enforce compliance. If the Court did not issue the writ, it risked surrendering judicial power to Jefferson and the Republicans.

SUMMARY OF ARGUMENTS

Marshall noted that the question of whether a federal statute contrary to constitutional provisions could be the law of the land was "not of an intricacy proportioned to its interest." The basis for this ruling was the concept that the people of the nation had the right to establish binding principles for the governing of society, which had the effect of enforceable law. While the people might have established a government of general powers, they chose instead to create one of defined and limited powers.

Marshall reasoned that there could be no middle ground between these types of government. That left, in his opinion, the choices of either declaring the Constitution to be the superior and binding law or allowing the legislature to be an entity of unlimited powers. The fact that the nation had sought to establish a *written* Constitution with fundamental principles to bind it in the future was evidence that the Constitution should be the superior and binding law. If the Constitution was the superior law, then an act repugnant to it must be invalid.

DECISION

Marbury's action was discharged because the Court did not have original jurisdiction. The Judiciary Act was unconstitutional. The Court found that the construction of the Constitution, when given its plain meaning, specifically enumerated the types of cases over which the Court had original and appellate jurisdiction. The Court also found that a mandamus action, an action seeking an order from the Court commanding a person to take a certain action, sought to invoke the original, not the appellate, jurisdiction of the Court. Since such an action was not enumerated in the Constitution as an action coming under the Court's original jurisdiction, the Judiciary Act enacted by Congress, which gave the Court the power to issue a writ of mandamus, was contrary to the Constitution and void. In arriving at this conclusion, the Court found that the review of laws to judge their conformity with the Constitution was the essence of the Court's judiciary duty. The Constitution is superior to any ordinary legislative act; therefore, it must govern a case to which both apply. The supremacy clause (Article 6, section 2) declares that the Constitution and those acts of Congress made in pursuance thereof shall be the supreme law of the land. Thus, the Court must determine when such acts are actually made in pursuance of the Constitution. The power of judicial review is implicit in the Constitution.

AFTERMATH

In more recent times, the Court has asserted a broad judicial review power, claiming the responsibility of being the ultimate interpreter of the Constitution. Once a law is declared unconstitutional, the courts simply decline to enforce it.

SIGNIFICANCE

Judicial review of legislative acts was a controversial subject even before the Constitution was ratified and adopted. Alexander Hamilton upheld the theory of judicial review in the *Federalist Papers*. He argued that the judiciary, being the most vulnerable branch of the government, was designed to be an intermediary between the people and the legislature. Since the interpretation of laws was the responsibility of the judiciary, and the Constitution the supreme law of the land, any conflict between legislative acts and the Constitution were to be resolved by the Court in favor of the Constitution. But other authorities have attacked this position. In the case of *Eakin v. Raub* (1825), Justice Gibson dissented, stating that the judiciary's function was limited to interpreting the laws and should not extend to scrutinizing the legislature's authority to enact them. Judge Learned Hand felt that judicial review was inconsistent with the separation of powers. But history has supported the authority of judicial review of legislative acts. The United States survives on a tripartite government. Theoretically, the three branches should be strong enough to check and balance one another. To limit the judiciary to the passive task of interpretation would be to limit its strength in the tripartite structure. *Marbury* served to buttress the judiciary branch, making it equal to the executive and legislative branches.

RELATED CASES

Franklin v. Massachusetts, 505 U.S. 788 (1992)

Lujan v. Defenders of Wildlife, 504 U.S. 555 (1992)

Planned Parenthood of Southeastern Pennsylvania v. Casey, 505 U.S. 833 (1992)

RECOMMENDED READING

Bickel, Alexander M. *The Least Dangerous Branch.* New Haven, Conn.: Yale University Press, 1962.

Currie, David P. *The Constitution in the Supreme Court, 1789–1888.* Chicago: University of Chicago Press, 1985.

Fisher, Louis. *The Constitution between Friends.* New York: St. Martin's Press, 1978.

Thomas C. Grey, *Do We Have an Unwritten Constitution,* 27 Stanford Law Review 703 (February 1975).

Keynes, Edward, with Randall K. Miller. *The Court vs. Congress.* Durham, N.C.: Duke University Press, 1989.

McCloskey, Robert G. *The American Supreme Court.* Chicago: University of Chicago Press, 1960.

Case Title: *Martin v. Hunter's Lessee*

Legal Citations: 14 U.S. 304; 4 L.Ed. 97

Year of Decision: 1816

KEY ISSUES

Does the U.S. Supreme Court have appellate jurisdiction over the highest state courts on issues involving the federal Constitution, laws, and treaties?

HISTORY OF THE CASE

Defendant Denny Martin, a British subject, was heir to the Virginia estates of Lord Fairfax, who died in England in 1781. Through state legislation confiscating the property of British loyalists, Virginia had conveyed title to David Hunter, a Virginia citizen. Hunter's lessee brought an action of ejectment, an action to regain possession of land and recover damages. Martin defended his title by virtue of two treaties between the United States and Britain that protected such British-owned property. The Virginia Court of Appeals sustained the plaintiff's claim but was reversed by the U.S. Supreme Court. The Virginia court refused to comply with the reversal, and Martin again appealed.

SUMMARY OF ARGUMENTS

Martin's representatives based their claim to the land on the anticonfiscation clauses of treaties between the United States and Great Britain. Hunter, and the state of Virginia, claimed that title had vested in Virginia, making Virginia the absolute owner of the property, prior to these treaties so that they were not applicable to his title.

DECISION

The Virginia court was required to obey the U.S. Supreme Court's rulings on the following grounds: (1) The Judiciary Act of 1789, section 25, provided for review by the U.S. Supreme Court of final state court decisions rejecting claims under the federal Constitution and laws. The outcome of this case depends on the constitutionality of that section. (2) Appellate jurisdiction is given by the Constitution to the Supreme Court in all cases in which it does not have original jurisdiction, subject to congressional regulations. (3) All cases involving the Constitution, laws, and treaties of the United States are included in the judicial power granted by the Constitution to the Supreme Court; hence, all such cases are properly subject to that Court's appellate jurisdiction, and section 25 of the Judiciary Act is valid. (4) Such power is necessary for uniformity of decisions throughout the whole United States, upon all subjects within the purview of the Constitution.

AFTERMATH

In *Cohens v. Virginia*, 19 U.S. 264 (1821), a case involving the illegal sale in Virginia of lottery tickets issued with congressional authority in the District of Columbia, the Court extended the *Martin* decision to permit review of state court criminal judgments.

The Supreme Court now holds the state and federal governments to identical standards when reviewing their acts under any constitutional guarantee applicable to both. This position is based on two principles: first, the constitutional meaning that the judiciary is bound to respect and enforce is the same whether applied to the states or the federal government, and second, the federal judiciary is a nondemocratic institution when reviewing the legislative acts both of the states and of the federal government.

SIGNIFICANCE

Justice Story ruled that the people of the nation, when they set up the central government, chose to limit state sovereignty when they established a Constitution, specifically restricting state acts in a variety of ways, such as those included in Article 1.

The supremacy clause of Article 6 of the U.S. Constitution makes state law subordinate to the federal treaties and laws, as well as the Constitution. That provision charges state court judges with the duty of following the Constitution of the United States as opposed to state law whenever the two conflict. The framers would have taken an incomprehensible, inconsistent position if they had intended to have state judges review the constitutionality of state acts under the U.S. Constitution while denying a similar power to the Supreme Court in the appellate jurisdiction granted to it. If nothing else, the supremacy clause strengthens the Court's claim to review state laws as a necessary way of declaring uniform principles of constitutional law. If each of the states is free to go its own way in matters of constitutional interpretation, the Constitution would have little impact as a national law.

These arguments, as well as those made in the early cases concerning the review of state laws, have found almost universal acceptance among the justices and scholars. Thus, even Justice Holmes, who was opposed to active review of federal laws, found that the review of state acts was a necessary part of the federal judicial function.

RELATED CASES

American Trucking Associations Inc. v. Smith, 496 U.S. 167 (1990)

Howlett v. Rose, 496 U.S. 356 (1990)

New York v. United States, 504 U.S. 144 (1992)

RECOMMENDED READING

Currie, David P. *The Constitution in the Supreme Court, 1789–1888.* Chicago: University of Chicago Press, 1985.

McCloskey, Robert G. *The American Supreme Court.* Chicago: University of Chicago Press, 1960.

Thorton F. Miller, John Marshall v. Spencer Roance: *A Reevaluation of* Martin v. Hunter's Lessee, 96 Virginia Magazine of History and Biography 297–314 (July 1988).

Case Title: *National League of Cities v. Usery*

Legal Citation: 426 U.S. 833

Year of Decision: 1976

KEY ISSUES

May Congress regulate certain state operations, such as the wages and hours of state employees?

HISTORY OF THE CASE

Congress passed the Fair Labor Standards Act of 1938 pursuant to their power to regulate interstate commerce under Article I, section 8 of the Constitution. The act required employers to comply with child labor standards as well as minimum wage and overtime pay requirements. In 1974, the act was amended to include coverage of nonsupervisory state and municipal employees, such as firefighters and police officers.

In 1974, the National League of Cities, along with several other states and municipalities, brought suit against the secretary of labor seeking a declaratory judgment that the 1974 amend-ments were beyond Congress's power to regulate interstate commerce. Additionally, they sought an injunction against enforcing the amendments. The district court dismissed the case, and the plaintiffs appealed directly to the Supreme Court.

SUMMARY OF ARGUMENTS

The National League of Cities contended that the 1974 amendments allowed Congress to regulate virtually all state and local employees, thereby allowing Congress to overstep its bounds. They argued that Congress had the power to regulate interstate commerce, but not state and local governmental matters. National League of Cities also cited MARYLAND V. WIRTZ (1968), which held that the 1966 amendment to the act, extending coverage to hospitals and schools, was constitutional because the Court did not want to distinguish between state and private employers that affected commerce in essentially the same way: the regulation applied only to state and local employers who were in competition with private commercial activity.

The secretary of labor contended that the ruling in *Wirtz* applied to this case as well because both cases were not based on competition with private enterprises, but instead on the substantial amount of interstate commerce involved.

DECISION

The Court overturned *Wirtz* and held that Congress has no right to regulate matters that deal with the integral operations of traditional governmental functions of the states. The commerce clause gives Congress great authority, but it has its limits, such as the Tenth Amendment, which gives states the powers not reserved to Congress and prohibits Congress impairing the ability of states to function. The Court decided that states are on a different footing from private individuals or corporations, and that to allow the *Wirtz* rule would be to allow the federal government to usurp state sovereignty.

Justice Blackmun concurred on the basis that the Court's opinion seemed to be a balancing approach and would not prohibit federal regulation where the federal interest is greater than the state interest and compliance by the states would be necessary.

Justice Brennan, joined by Justices White and Marshall, dissented on the basis that the commerce power gave Congress the right to pass the amendments. Additionally, they believed that *Wirtz* was wrongly overturned and should have been the authority under stare decisis.

Justice Stevens dissented because although he believed the amendments were valid, he thought there were instances where it would be unwise for the federal government to interfere with state activities.

AFTERMATH

In cases similar to this one, the Court has not decided the same way. The justices have been more willing to hold that the federal government can regulate, drawing distinctions between regulation of private persons and regulation of states. The Court also has had trouble agreeing on the definition of "integral operations of traditional governmental functions."

In decisions following *National League of Cities,* the Court has upheld congressional power under the commerce clause by distinguishing *National League of Cities.*

SIGNIFICANCE

This was the first case in several decades in which the Court held unconstitutional an act of Congress under the power of interstate commerce.

The Court showed that the regulatory power of Congress under the commerce clause did have limits, although these limits were short-lived, and the holding was essentially overruled in *Garcia v. San Antonio Metropolitan Transit Authority* (1985), which afforded municipal transit employees the protection of the Fair Labor Standards Act wage and hour provisions.

RELATED CASES

Equal Employment Opportunities Comm'n v. Wyoming, 460 U.S. 226 (1983)

Federal Energy Regulatory Comm'n v. Mississippi, 456 U.S. 742 (1982)

Garcia v. San Antonio Metro. Transit Auth., 469 U.S. 528 (1985)

Hodel v. Virginia Surface Mining & Reclamation Ass'n, 452 U.S. 264 (1981)

Maryland v. Wirtz, 392 U.S. 183 (1968)

New York v. United States, 505 U.S. 144 (1992)

United Transp. Union v. Long Island R. R. Co., 455 U.S. 678

RECOMMENDED READING

Calvin R. Massey, *State Sovereignty and the Tenth and Eleventh Amendments,* 1978 Supreme Court Review 225 (1978).

Frank I. Michelman, *States' Rights and States' Roles: Permutations of "Sovereignty" in* National League of Cities v. Usery, 86 Yale Law Journal 1165 (1977).

Robert F. Nagel, *Federalism as a Fundamental Value:* National League of Cities *in Perspective,* 1981 Supreme Court Review 81 (1981).

Schwartz, Bernard. *The Ascent of Pragmatism: The Burger Court in Action.* New York: Addison-Wesley Publishing, 1990.

Laurence H. Tribe, *Unravelling* National League of Cities: *The New Federalism and Affirmative Rights to Essential Government Services,* 90 Harvard Law Review 1065 (1977).

Case Title: *Scheuer v. Rhodes*

Alternate Case Title: Kent State Massacre Case

Legal Citation: 416 U.S. 232

Year of Decision: 1974

KEY ISSUES

When a state officer acts in a manner that may violate the U.S. Constitution, is that official afforded immunity from suit in federal court?

HISTORY OF THE CASE

The Eleventh Amendment to the U.S. Constitution states that the judicial power of the United States shall not be construed to extend to any suit commenced against one of the states by citizens of another state. This means that a federal court does not have jurisdiction to hear and decide a case brought by citizens of one state against another state.

In 1970, students at Kent State University protested the Vietnam War. There was a general state of disorder, and the governor of Ohio, Rhodes, called in the National Guard to help control and contain the protesters. During a confrontation with the National Guard, four students were shot by guardsmen. The representatives of the estates of three of the students, including Scheuer, brought an action in federal district court against the governor, the adjutant general of the Ohio National Guard, various guard members, and the university president alleging that the students' civil rights were violated by the unnecessary use of force by the troops. The district court dismissed the claim for want of jurisdiction because of the Eleventh Amendment. The court of appeals affirmed and concluded that the common-law doctrine of executive immunity, a doctrine precluding suit against a member of the executive branch of government, was absolute and therefore barred the action against the state officials in addition to the Eleventh Amendment prohibitions. The Supreme Court agreed to hear the case because of the importance of the issues presented.

SUMMARY OF ARGUMENTS

The representatives of the deceased students argued that the use of force violated 42 U.S.C. § 1983, a law governing civil actions for deprivation of rights.

The governor, National Guard, and university president argued that since they were acting in their official capacity, they were not only barred from suit in federal court because of the Eleventh Amendment but because of absolute executive immunity, a doctrine precluding suit against a member of the executive branch of government as well.

DECISION

Justice Burger delivered the opinion of the unanimous court reversing the lower courts and allowing the case to proceed. The Court held that there was no such thing as absolute immunity in all cases and, as a result, narrowed the concept considerably. The Court developed a qualified immunity test, which gave immunity when the official had reasonable grounds to believe his actions were constitutional and when he acted in good faith. Without qualified immunity, citizens would have virtually no recourse for their injuries. The

Court also felt that some protection for government officials was necessary to permit them to exercise their discretion without undue fear of liability for mistakes.

The Court dealt with the Eleventh Amendment argument by concluding that the Eleventh Amendment is not absolute: it does not provide a shield for a state official confronted by a claim that he had deprived another of a federal right under the color of state law.

AFTERMATH

The Court continued to examine the doctrines of absolute and qualified immunity over the course of the following decades. The Court has all but done away with absolute immunity and has revised its view of qualified immunity. Qualified immunity is now afforded an official when he or she acted within the scope of his or her discretionary duties unless the conduct violates clearly established constitutional rights of which a reasonable person would have known. The Court since *Scheuer* eliminated the subjective good faith prong of the qualified immunity test.

SIGNIFICANCE

Scheuer opened the door for suits against not only government officials but also against states in federal court. By making the Courts more accessible to citizens who have been wronged, the Court bolstered the egalitarian basis of the U.S. government.

RELATED CASES

Anderson v. Creighton, 483 U.S. 635 (1987)

Clinton v. Jones, 117 S.Ct. 1636 (1997)

Ex parte Young, 209 U.S. 123 (1908)

Harlow v. Fitzgerald, 457 U.S. 800 (1982)

Mitchell v. Forsyth, 472 U.S. 511 (1985)

Pierson v. Ray, 386 U.S. 547 (1967)

RECOMMENDED READING

Mitchell Green, *Qualified Immunity for Public Officials under Section 1983 in the Fifth Circuit,* 60 Texas Law Review 127 (1981).

Harold S. Lewis, *Reshaping Section 1983's Asymmetry,* 140 University of Pennsylvania Law Review 755 (1992).

Laura Oren, *Immunity and Accountability in Civil Rights Litigation: Who Should Pay?*, 50 University of Pittsburgh Law Review 935 (1989).

⚜

Case Title: *Sierra Club v. Morton*

Legal Citations: 405 U.S. 727; 92 S.Ct. 1361; 31 L.Ed. 2d 636

Year of Decision: 1972

KEY ISSUES

Can an organization with a special interest in protecting the environment allege an injury as a representative of the public?

HISTORY OF THE CASE

The Mineral King Valley, located in the Sierra Nevada mountains in northern California, was a wilderness area largely free from the products of civilization. In January 1969, the U.S. Forest Service approved a $35 million plan by Walt Disney Enterprises, Inc., to construct a complex of motels, restaurants, swimming pools, parking lots, and other structures over 80 acres of the valley. Ski lifts, ski trails, a cog-assisted railway, and utility installations were to be constructed in the mountain slopes and in other parts of the valley. Also, the state of California proposed to construct a highway 20 miles long through the adjacent Sequoia National Park to provide access to the estimated 14,400 daily visitors.

The Sierra Club, a membership corporation with a "special interest in the conservation and sound maintenance of the national parks, game refuges, and forests of the country," brought suit in the U.S. District Court for the Northern District of California seeking a declaratory judgment that the Disney plan violated various federal laws and regulations, and also seeking injunctions to restrain federal officials from their involvement with the project. The district court granted the preliminary injunctions. However, the Court of Appeals for the Ninth Circuit reversed, holding that the Sierra Club did not have a sufficient

stake in the claim other than that the proposal was "personally displeasing or distasteful." Thus, the court of appeals held that the Sierra Club had no legal standing to challenge the government action in federal court. The Supreme Court granted certiorari.

SUMMARY OF ARGUMENTS

Regarding the standing issues, Sierra Club relied on section 10 of the Administrative Procedure Act, 5 U.S.C. § 702, which provides:

> A person suffering a *legal wrong* because of agency action, or adversely affected or aggrieved by agency action within the meaning of a relevant statute, is entitled to judicial review [emphasis added].

In addition, Sierra Club argued that development would injure the ecology of the area and prevent aesthetic enjoyment for future generations.

The respondents argued that Sierra Club's complaint was outside the scope of Article 3 of the Constitution, which limits federal court jurisdiction to cases and controversies. They argued that Sierra Club did not demonstrate an adequate personal stake in the outcome of the controversy. Therefore, they contended that if the Supreme Court reviewed the case on its merits, it would be rendering an illegal advisory opinion.

DECISION

Justice Stewart, joined by Justices Burger, White, and Marshall, held in a 4-3 decision that Sierra Club lacked standing to sue. Stewart explained that an organization needs more than "injury to a cognizable interest" to prove standing. He found that Sierra Club did not show an individualized harm or concrete injury because the organization failed to complain that the development of the ski lodge in the Sierra Nevada would adversely affect it or its members. The Court did note, however, that noneconomic harm, such as recreational or aesthetic harm, could invoke proper standing if (1) the individual has suffered actual or threatened injury as a result of the alleged violation, (2) the injury is fairly traceable to the violation, and (3) the injury is redressable by a favorable court decision.

Justices Douglas, Brennan, and Blackmun filed dissenting opinions. Justice Douglas proposed that the Mineral King Valley should be allowed to be the nominal plaintiff to ensure that "the voice of the existing beneficiaries of these environmental wonders . . . be heard." Justice Blackmun, joined by Justice Brennan, argued for a more "imaginative expansion of our traditional concepts of standing" where organizations with "pertinent, bona fide, and well recognized attributes and purposes in the area of the environment" could litigate environmental issues.

AFTERMATH

After the Court's standing decision, the Sierra Club amended its complaint to allege that some of its members used the forest and would be injured by the construction. Thus, the Sierra Club corrected the problem by representing specific persons, and not the overall public. Later cases have decided that the injury in fact must be "actual or imminent." Therefore, if the threatened harm will occur too far into the future or is too speculative, no standing will be found. Walt Disney Enterprises ultimately terminated the project.

SIGNIFICANCE

While the Court in *Sierra Club* broadened the scope of standing in acknowledging aesthetic and recreational as well as economic interests, the Court reinforced the limit of standing to parties whose interests have been or will be affected. Thus, environmental groups must submit evidence that they or their members have already suffered or will directly suffer harm.

RELATED CASES

Hunt v. Washington Apple Advertising Comm., 432 U.S. 333 (1977)

Lujan v. Defenders of Wildlife, 504 U.S. 555 (1992)

United States v. SCRAP, 412 U.S. 669 (1973)

RECOMMENDED READING

Jeanne A. Compitello, *Organizational Standing in Environmental Litigation,* 6 Touro Law Review 295 (1990).

Kathleen Zimmerman, *Life after* Lujan: *Standing and Ripeness in the Environmental Lawsuits of the Nineties,* 4 Tulane Environmental Law Journal 157 (1990).

Case Title: *Swift v. Tyson*

Legal Citation: 41 U.S. 1

Year of Decision: 1842

KEY ISSUES

Which laws shall apply in commercial cases before the Supreme Court: state or federal?

HISTORY OF THE CASE

Swift brought a case in New York involving a negotiable instrument, a written promise or order to pay money, such as a check, from Maine. The New York court held that the laws of New York would apply. Under that view, Swift lost. Therefore, there was disagreement as to what law should be applied to the facts of the case. The Supreme Court agreed to hear the case because of the importance of the issue presented.

SUMMARY OF ARGUMENTS

Swift argued that general commercial principles should apply, as the transaction did not entirely occur within New York.

Tyson argued that the laws of New York governed because the contract at issue was agreed upon in New York. He relied upon legal principles of the state courts and the Judiciary Act of 1789, which allowed for states to govern their own actions.

DECISION

Justice Story wrote the majority opinion reversing the New York courts. The Court felt that the laws of the commercial world and not the laws of any particular state should govern. As a result, the general common law was in Swift's favor. New York was merely an exception to the general rules of law accepted in the rest of the country. In holding that the commercial laws of the states must comport to generally accepted standards, the Court ruled in the interest of interstate commerce.

AFTERMATH

The Supreme Court overruled *Swift v. Tyson* almost 100 years later in *ERIE RAILROAD V. TOMPKINS* (1938). The Court determined that there was no generally accepted "federal common law." As a result, only statutes and regulations enacted by Congress and signed into law by the president were to be the law of the land.

SIGNIFICANCE

Swift held that there was a federal common law or unwritten legal principles that could be applied by the federal government in the absence of any specific state legislation. The case serves as a significant reminder of the relatively new nature of much of the U.S. government's lawmaking in 1842. Today, there is no law on the federal level that is not first passed through the regular channels of legislation.

RELATED CASES

Chapman & Cole v. Itel Container Intern, 865 F.2d 676 (1989)

Erie R. Co. v. Tompkins, 304 U.S. 64 (1938)

RECOMMENDED READING

David P. Currie, *The Constitution in the Supreme Court: Article IV and the Federal Powers, 1836–1864*, 1983 Duke Law Journal 695 (1983).

William A. Fletcher, *The General Common Law and Section 34 of the Judiciary Act of 1789: The Example of Marine Insurance*, 97 Harvard Law Review 1513 (1984).

Freyer, Tony. *Harmony and Dissonance: The* Swift *and* Erie *Cases in American Federalism*. New York: New York University Press, 1981.

Horowitz, Morton J. *The Transformation of American Law, 1780–1860*. Cambridge, Mass.: Harvard University Press, 1977.

Case Title: *Wayman v. Southard*

Legal Citation: 23 U.S. 1

Year of Decision: 1825

KEY ISSUES

Do the federal courts have to apply the laws followed in their respective state courts? May Congress delegate rule-making authority to federal courts?

HISTORY OF THE CASE

Congress authorized the federal courts to adopt state common law writs, state judicial orders, that existed in 1789. The federal courts were authorized to modify the writs or to adopt additional writs by making new court rules. The state of Kentucky enacted a statute after 1789 that limited the state judicial orders that could be used to execute judgments within the state. A federal magistrate executed a judicial order without following the Kentucky statute.

SUMMARY OF ARGUMENTS

The defendants insisted that the Constitution did not allow Congress to grant power to the judicial branch. They also argued that Congress did not have the power to make laws governing proceedings in suits between private individuals.

The plaintiffs argued that the necessary and proper clause gave Congress the ability to grant federal courts the power to make laws necessary to conduct trials in their courts.

DECISION

The Court upheld the delegation of power to the federal courts using the necessary and proper clause and allowed Congress to convey power to the courts. The Supreme Court limited the ability of Congress to convey power to the courts by stating that they could not convey such power if it was exclusively legislative in nature. The Court emphasized that Congress has the authority to establish federal courts and regulate their proceedings in the United States.

AFTERMATH

This case has not been overruled, and the Supreme Court continues to acknowledge Congress's authority to grant power to the federal courts to regulate their matters of practice. Since this case, however, the Supreme Court has withdrawn from some of its broad statements in

Wayman concerning the ability to grant power to other branches of government.

SIGNIFICANCE

This case outlines the ability of Congress to grant power to the judicial branch to regulate matters of substance and procedure within their courts.

RELATED CASES

Hanna v. Plumer, 380 U.S. 460 (1965)

Marshall Field & Co. v. Clark, 143 U.S. 649 (1892)

RECOMMENDED READING

Bigel, Alan I. *The Supreme Court on Emergency Powers, Foreign Affairs and Protection of Civil Liberties, 1935–1975.* Lanham, Md.: University Press of America, 1986.

Currie, David P. *The Constitution in the Supreme Court, 1888–1986.* Chicago: University of Chicago Press, 1985.

ADDITIONAL CASES

Case Title: *Atkins v. Virginia*

Alternate Case Title: Mentally Retarded Execution Case

Legal Citation: 122 S.Ct. 2242

Year of Decision: 2002

KEY ISSUES

Is the death penalty cruel and unusual punishment in violation of the Eighth Amendment when imposed upon a mentally retarded individual?

HISTORY OF THE CASE

Daryl Renard Atkins was convicted of abducting, robbing, and murdering Eric Nesbitt. At Atkins's sentencing hearing, evidence was presented that Atkins was mentally retarded. The jury sentenced Atkins to death. A second sentencing hearing was ordered by the Virginia Supreme Court based on a misleading jury form. After the second hearing, Atkins was again given the death penalty and the Virginia Supreme Court affirmed his sentence, though two judges dissented. The U.S. Supreme Court granted certiorari to review the case.

SUMMARY OF ARGUMENTS

Daryl Renard Atkins, petitioner, argued that procedures allowing the death penalty to be inflicted upon mentally retarded individuals, despite their diminished culpability, violated the Eighth Amendment. Atkins further argued that executing mentally retarded individuals offended standards of decency and such a sentence was excessive and disproportionate.

The state of Virginia argued that any person who was found criminally responsible could be executed even if the person is mentally retarded, though mental retardation could be considered a mitigating factor at sentencing.

DECISION

Justice Stevens gave the opinion for the majority of the Court, which found the imposition of the death penalty upon mentally retarded defendants to be cruel and unusual punishment in violation of the Eighth Amendment. Justice Stevens stated that the standard for punishments was that a punishment must be proportionate to the crime. Whether a punishment was excessive was to be determined by contemporary standards. Justice Stevens found the most objective evidence of contemporary standards was legislation enacted by the states. However, Justice Stevens indicated that after a review of state legislation, the Court could apply its own judgment and agree or disagree with the legislatures.

Justice Stevens found that a consensus existed in favor of prohibiting the execution of mentally retarded individuals, but more important, according to Justice Stevens, was the direction of the change in legislation toward such a prohibition. Finally, Justice Stevens found the prohibition of the death penalty was consistent with death penalty jurisprudence. Justifications for the death penalty, retribution and deterrence, would not necessarily apply to mentally retarded persons and the risk of the imposition of such a penalty in spite of mitigating factors was high because such persons would likely be poor witnesses and be unable to assist their counsel. Therefore, the imposition of the death penalty would not be proper.

Chief Justice Rehnquist dissented, joined by Justices Scalia and Thomas, contesting the Court's reliance on foreign laws, professional and religious group opinions, and opinion polls in determining that a consensus existed in favor of prohibiting the death penalty for mentally retarded persons. Rehnquist found that sentencing jury statistics were also significant in determining contemporary values and that such statistics and state legislations should be the sole factors to determine these values.

Justice Scalia also dissented, joined by Justices Rehnquist and Thomas, finding that the Court had manufactured a consensus and followed their personal feelings in deciding the case. Scalia found the statistics failed to support the existence of a consensus and he found that state legislation prohibiting execution of mentally retarded individuals to be still in its infancy. Scalia further stated that the symptoms of mental retardation could be easily faked, pointing out that even while the case was pending petitions were being filed by persons on death row claiming mental retardation. Ultimately, Scalia found that mentally retarded individuals should not be immune from the death penalty, but their background could be considered as a mitigating factor in sentencing.

AFTERMATH

States that still allowed the execution of mentally retarded individuals were forced to adjust their statutes in light of the Atkins decision. Additionally, an increased number of "mental retardation" claims were expected as a means to avoid the death penalty.

SIGNIFICANCE

Individuals arrested and convicted on murder charges will be able to avoid the death penalty if they can prove mental retardation.

RELATED CASES

Frothingham v. Mellon, 262 U.S. 447 (1923)

Furman v. Georgia, 408 U.S. 238 (1972)

Penry v. Lynaugh, 492 U.S. 302 (1989)

Schlesinger v. Reservists Comm. to Stop the War, 418 U.S. 208 (1974)

United States v. Richardson, 418 U.S. 166 (1974)

RECOMMENDED READING

Bedau, Hugo Adam. *Death Is Different: Studies in the Morality, Law, and Politics of Capital Punishment.* Boston: Northeastern University Press, 1987.

Donald L. Doernberg, *"We the People": John Locke, Collective Constitutional Rights, and Standing to Challenge Government Action,* 73 California Law Review 52 (1985).

David A. Logan, *Standing to Sue: A Proposed Separation of Powers Analysis,* Wisconsin Law Review 37 (1984).

William P. Marshall, and Maripat Flood, *Establishment Clause Standing: The Not Very Revolutionary Decision at Valley Forge,* 11 Hofstra Law Review 63 (1982).

Victor L. Streib, *Adolescence, Mental Retardation, and the Death Penalty: The Siren Call of* Atkins v. Virginia, 33 New Mexico Law Review (2003) (in press).

The Supreme Court, 1981 Term 1. Citizen and Taxpayer Standing, 96 Harvard Law Review 196 (1982).

Case Title: *Bowsher v. Synar*

Alternate Case Title: Gramm-Rudman Case

Legal Citation: 478 U.S. 714

Year of Decision: 1986

KEY ISSUES

The case deals with three issues. The first involves the separation of powers between the executive and legislative branches; the second deals with the power of the president to fire officers of the United States; the third discusses Congress's power to delegate legislative functions to nonlegislative officers.

HISTORY OF THE CASE

The fundamental principle of separation of power is strengthened by the system of checks and balances. This allows each of the three branches to remain independent, free from intrusions. Congress enacted the Balanced Budget and Emergency Deficit Control Act of 1985, sponsored by Senators Phil Gramm, Warren Rudman, and Ernest Hollings and, therefore, also known as the Gramm-Rudman-Hollings Act. The act set out a maximum amount for federal spending from 1986 to 1991 to reduce the deficit to zero and placed responsibility in the hands of the comptroller general subject to legislative removal.

This case is a constitutional challenge to the Balanced Budget and Emergency Deficit Control Act. The U.S. District Court for the District of Columbia held the reporting provisions invalid. On appeal, the Supreme Court held that the powers vested in the comptroller general violated the separation of powers. Congress may not execute laws.

SUMMARY OF ARGUMENTS

Bowsher, the comptroller general of the United States, argued that the comptroller general was not part of the legislative branch because he performed his duties independently of Congress and was not subservient to Congress. Bowsher also claimed that the comptroller general's duties were ministerial and did not constitute executing or putting the act into effect. However, if the Court found the act unconstitutional, Bowsher sought nullification of the provision authorizing Congress's removal of the comptroller general rather than invalidation of the act, alleging that Congress would prefer that remedy.

Synar and the other appellees did not seek nullification of Congress's authority to remove the comptroller general, but argued the executive powers granted to the comptroller could only be exercised by officers removable by the president at will. Appellees alleged Congress's intent on how to handle the act if its provisions were constitutionally challenged was found in the language of the act.

DECISION

The Court held that powers vested by the comptroller general under the act violated the doctrine of separation of powers; Congress's right to remove this person signifies an enforcement of the law, an executive act.

Chief Justice Burger delivered the Court's opinion that placing responsibility for carrying out the act in the comptroller general and not the president, as well as in the hands of someone subject to removal by Congress, was an attempt by Congress to intrude on the executive function. Justice Blackmun dissented, stating that if the act is unconstitutional on removal grounds, it can be remedied by preserving the duties of the comptroller general and vesting the removal power in the president.

AFTERMATH

Separation of powers between the executive and legislative branches was preserved, and so, of course, was the deficit.

SIGNIFICANCE

The case protects and strengthens the three branches of government. Congress cannot appoint or remove officers with executive authority.

RELATED CASES

Humphrey's Executor v. United States, 295 U.S. 602 (1935)

Myers v. United States, 272 U.S. 52 (1926)

RECOMMENDED READING

David P. Currie, *The Distribution of Powers After* Bowsher, Supreme Court Review 19–40 (1986).

Daniel J. Gifford, *The Separation of Powers Doctrine and the Regulatory Agencies after* Bowsher v. Synar, 55 George Washington Law Review 441–481 (March 1987).

Schwartz, Bernard. *Ascent of Pragmatism: The Burger Court in Action.* New York: Addison-Wesley, 1990.

Peter L. Strauss, *Formal and Functional Approaches to Separation of Powers Questions: A Foolish Inconsistency?*, 72 Cornell Law Review 488–526 (March 1987).

Case Title: *Chisolm v. Georgia*

Alternate Case Title: The "Suits against States" Case

Legal Citation: 2 U.S. 419

Year of Decision: 1793

KEY ISSUES

May a state be sued by an individual of another state under the U.S. Constitution?

HISTORY OF THE CASE

Chisolm, the executor of the estate of a South Carolina merchant, sued the state of Georgia to recover Revolutionary War debts owed by the state of Georgia to the merchant's estate. He brought his suit pursuant to Article 3's grant of federal jurisdiction over suits in federal court between "a State and Citizens of another State." The action was instituted in the U.S. Supreme Court in the August term 1792 when Edmond Randolph, attorney general of the United States, as counsel for the plaintiff, moved for a court order that unless the state of Georgia made an appearance on behalf of the state, judgment be entered for the plaintiff awarding a writ of inquiry, which allowed review of the plaintiff's demands and assessed his damages. The Court held the case under advisement from February 5 to February 18, then delivered the opinion seriatim (in a series).

SUMMARY OF ARGUMENTS

Attorney General Edmond Randolph argued that Article 3 was a self-executing, mandatory grant of the judicial power of the United States to the federal courts. He argued that "the Constitution vested a jurisdiction in the Supreme Court over a State as a defendant, at the suit of a private citizen of another State."

The state of Georgia argued that it was a sovereign state, and therefore was not liable to such actions.

DECISION

The Court held that a state may be sued, in the Supreme Court, by an individual citizen of another state. It further stated that in such suit judgment may be entered in default of an appearance.

The Court held that under Article 3, the individual states had waived their sovereign immunity regarding citizens of other states, and the South Carolina merchant could bring a suit against the state of Georgia. The Court also held it had jurisdiction of the case and that unless Georgia could present timely defenses to Chisolm's claim, a default judgment would be entered against the state. Finally, it found that a service of a summons on the governor and attorney general was a competent service because the Georgia Constitution made the governor the "channel" to the legislature, bound to defend it, and the attorney general was the instrument of defense.

The Court came to its conclusions based upon the "explicit" language in, and the spirit of the Constitution and stated that "the Constitution vests a jurisdiction in the Supreme Court over a state, as a defendant, at the suit of a private citizen of another State." It argued against an interpretation that the Constitution allowed suits between states and citizens only when the state was a plaintiff and believed that the Constitution "strongly intended" to include states as defendants. The Court described the different actions that a state cannot take, such as pass a bill of attainder, emit bills of credit, or confiscate the estate of a citizen, and argued that they could not be redressed unless the states could be made

defendants. The Court argued that certain unconstitutional undertakings by states could be corrected only by a suit against the state itself.

The Court further supported its findings by looking to the intentions of the framers, the relation of the states to the federal government, the precedents from other sovereignties, the judicial act and process act, the power of forming executions, and upon the inference that states' sovereignty would not be degraded by their having to submit to a Supreme Judiciary of the United States. Then the Court, after acknowledging the sovereignty of the states, and asserting that a state could be sued, insisted that this rule did not apply to the U.S. government, which still could not be sued.

The Court maintained that the Judicial Act recognize the jurisdiction over states since it used the words "where a State shall be a party" and deduced that "party" included plaintiff and defendant. The Court then conceded that the judicial act did not expressly address how such jurisdiction should be carried out. However, it reasoned that no one questioned whether the Court had jurisdiction in suits between two states and this also was not expressly stated; therefore, the lack of express execution was not a problem. The Court asked if the Supreme Court could make a mode of execution for a state defeated at law by another state, then why could the Court not use the same means where an individual was successful against a State?

The Court stated that although a state was suable in some situations, it was not suable in all situations but that a suit in assumpsit, an action for damages for the breach of a contract, was "most free from cavil" (concerning the issue of whether an action of assumpsit would lie against a state). Finally, the Court assured the states that they need not fear increased power by the federal government since the people and legislatures had various powers that they could hold over "almost every movement of the National Government."

In Justice Iredell's dissenting opinion, he argued that the action in assumpsit could not be legally maintained before the U.S. Supreme Court. He believed that first, the action had to be in virtue of the Constitution of the United States, and of some law of Congress. He then looked at the Constitution and found Article 3, section 2 as the part of the Constitution concerning this power and the judicial act as the act of Congress. Justice Iredell found that only the legislature, by acts of appointing courts and prescribing their methods of operation, could carry the Constitution into effect in regard to judicial authority. He also found that Congress had not made a new law in regard to the instant case. He argued that Congress only referred the Court to precedent, and that neither precedent nor analogy to it authorized the suit in this case.

Justice Iredell stated that a citizen of another state should not be able to hale a state into court. He insisted that even if the Constitution allowed such a suit, a new law was necessary to carry it out, and none of the existing law applied. Justice Iredell contended that it was not the intention to create new and unheard of remedies, by subjecting sovereign states to actions at the suit of individuals. Rather, it was to invest the federal courts with jurisdiction to hear and determine controversies and cases, between the parties designated, that were properly susceptible of litigation in courts. Justice Iredell was against any construction of the Constitution that allowed a compulsive suit against a state.

AFTERMATH

In the February term of 1794, judgment was rendered for the plaintiff and a writ of inquiry awarded. However, the writ was never sued and executed. Therefore, this case, and other suits against states, were removed from the records of the Court by the Eleventh Amendment. The Eleventh Amendment was at once proposed and adopted to reverse the Court's holding, since the decision created such a surprise. Congress passed a resolution to create an amendment to protect state sovereign immunity one day after the *Chisolm* decision and the Eleventh Amendment was ratified by the states less than one year later.

SIGNIFICANCE

Chisolm created tremendous congressional concern over the erosion of state sovereignty and independence within the federal system. It was a very controversial ruling in which Justice Iredell's dissenting opinion stated the leading principles of what later became known as the "States' Rights Doctrine." In subsequent decisions, the Supreme Court looked to Justice Iredell's dissent as the guide for how the amendment should be interpreted.

RELATED CASES

Hans v. Louisiana, 134 U.S. 1 (1890)

Hollingsworth v. Virginia, 3 Dall. 378 (1798)

RECOMMENDED READING

Hurwitz, Leon. *The State as Defendant: Governmental Accountability and the Redress of Grievances.* Westport, Conn.: Greenwood Press, 1981.

Powell, H. Jefferson. *Languages of Power: A Source Book of Early American Constitutional History.* Durham, N.C.: Carolina Academic Press, 1991.

Street, H. *Governmental Liability: A Comparative Study.* Cambridge: Cambridge University Press, 1953.

Case Title: *Frothingham v. Mellon*

Alternate Case Title: Frothingham Case

Legal Citation: 262 U.S. 447

Year of Decision: 1924

KEY ISSUES

Does the Maternity Act of November 23, 1921, violate the Tenth Amendment, and does this action violate the constitutional provision, that judicial power extends to controversies between states?

HISTORY OF THE CASE

This case challenges the constitutionality of the Maternity Act, which provided funds to participating states to reduce maternal and infant mortality. The case consolidated two cases, one brought by the Commonwealth of Massachusetts, the other by a taxpayer, Frothingham. Both cases had been brought against the secretary of the treasury, Mellon.

SUMMARY OF ARGUMENTS

The Commonwealth of Massachusetts argued that the Maternity Act was an attempt by Congress to legislate outside its constitutional powers and intrude upon the powers reserved to the state in violation of the Tenth Amendment. Frothingham argued that the Maternity Act would increase her taxes and, therefore, take her property without due process of law.

Mellon argued that neither appellant had presented a justiciable case or controversy and, therefore, lacked standing.

DECISION

This case was disposed of for lack of jurisdiction because the state has no justifiable controversy and no interest in the subject matter. No appropriate injury was threatened.

Justice Sutherland delivered the opinion of the Court. He reviewed the act and its purpose, in the appellant's view, an attempt by Congress to usurp state powers, and found that there is no justifiable controversy and therefore no subject matter interest. State powers, he wrote, are not invaded since the act does not impose an obligation, only an option. Nothing can be done without a state's consent under the act. Therefore the issue is political, not judicial; further, the interest of a taxpayer in federal moneys is too indirect for standing to challenge the constitutionality of federal appropriations.

AFTERMATH

A taxpayer has no standing to sue on the constitutionality of federal appropriations because the interest is too remote.

The *Frothingham* decision barred taxpayer actions for approximately 40 years until, in 1968, the Court revised the *Frothingham* standard in *FLAST V. COHEN.*

SIGNIFICANCE

The standing requirement makes it very difficult for taxpayers to challenge congressional spending on the basis that such provision is a waste of taxpayer dollars. Therefore, the standing requirements insulate Congress and allow it to enact legislation without general taxpayer backlash.

RELATED CASES

Baker v. Carr, 369 U.S. 186 (1962)

Flast v. Cohen, 392 U.S. 83 (1968)

United States et al. v. Richardson, 418 U.S. 166 (1974)

RECOMMENDED READING

Note, *Constitutional Law-Higher Education Facilities Act—Constitutionality of Federal Aid to Church Related Colleges,* 77 Harvard Law Review 1353 (1964).

Pfeffer, Leo. *Religion, State and the Burger Court.* Buffalo, N.Y.: Prometheus Books, 1984.

Ratcliffe, James E. *The Case or Controversy Provision.* University Park: Pennsylvania State University Press, 1978.

Case Title: *Garcia v. San Antonio Metropolitan Transit Authority (SAMTA)*

Alternate Case Title: Fair Labor Standards Act Case

Legal Citation: 469 U.S. 528

Year of Decision: 1985

KEY ISSUES

Does the "extension of the FLSA to the wages and hours of employees of a city-owned transit system unconstitutionally impinge on fundamental state sovereignty" in violation of the Tenth Amendment?

HISTORICAL BACKGROUND

Suit was filed in federal district court for declaratory relief against SAMTA. The court held that the operation of a mass transit system is exempt from federal obligations imposed by FLSA. Appeal was made to the U.S. Supreme Court.

HISTORY OF THE CASE

Public transportation in San Antonio has a similar history to other states: It was originally provided on a private basis. In 1959, the city bought the privately owned San Antonio Transit Co. and made it public; then in 1970, it applied for federal funding to prevent it from becoming an inferior system.

SUMMARY OF ARGUMENTS

Joe G. Garcia argued that the Tenth Amendment did not preclude Congress from requiring SAMTA to comply with the Fair Labor Standards Act provisions.

SAMTA argued that transit systems were exempt from application of the Fair Labor Standards Act provisions under *NATIONAL LEAGUE OF CITIES V. USERY* (1976) because SAMTA's provision of street maintenance and public transportation was a traditional state activity. SAMTA also argued that the Fair Labor Standards Act could not apply to state or local government employees without a constitutional amendment.

DECISION

The Tenth Amendment does not immunize states from the requirements of FLSA. Justice Brennan wrote the opinion for the majority abandoning his case-by-case approach for an across-the-board rule. In previous cases addressing alleged congressional violations of the Tenth Amendment, the Court applied the test laid out in *National League of Cities v. Usery,* which distinguished between traditional and nontraditional areas of government function. However, since no specific definition of "traditional government function" was given, the Court made this determination on a case-by-case basis. Brennan determined that there was no test that would satisfactorily determine what constituted a "traditional government function." He felt that it was impossible to draw boundaries of state regulatory immunity in terms of "traditional government function" and nontraditional government function. He also wrote that state interests were better protected by federal procedural safeguards than judicially created limitations on federal power.

Justice Powell, in the dissent, wrote that the view that the federal government will protect the states is inconsistent with political reality and the Tenth Amendment is reduced to meaningless rhetoric when congressional action involves the states.

AFTERMATH

This case overruled *National League of Cities v. Usery.* It altered the state of the separation of powers and federalism as the courts allowed the legislature more power over the states by removing the identification and definition of limits on Congress's commerce power as it affects state sovereignty.

SIGNIFICANCE

The case opened the door to direct federal regulation of state government labor forces after over 200 years of state sovereignty in this area. The Tenth Amendment was no longer a judicial protection for state powers.

RELATED CASES

Maryland v. Wirtz, 392 U.S. 183 (1968)

National League of Cities v. Usery, 426 U.S. 833 (1976)

Transportation Union v. Long Island Railroad, 455 U.S. 678 (1982)

RECOMMENDED READING

Rosemarie E. Delmonte, Garcia v. San Antonio: *And the State Stands Alone,* 19 Creighton Law Review 105 (1986).

Calvin R. Massey, *State Sovereignty and the Tenth and Eleventh Amendments,* 56 University of Chicago Law Review 61 (1989).

Andrzej Rapaczynski, *From Sovereignty to Process: The Jurisprudence of Federalism after* Garcia, 1985 Supreme Court Review 341.

Schwartz, Bernard. *The Ascent of Pragmatism: The Burger Court in Action.* New York: Addison-Wesley, 1990.

Case Title: *Hawaii Housing Authority v. Midkiff*

Legal Citation: 467 U.S. 229

Year of Decision: 1984

KEY ISSUES

Is the use of a state's eminent domain power to redistribute private property an unconstitutional taking that violates the Fifth Amendment's public use clause?

HISTORY OF THE CASE

Property in Hawaii had been controlled by the Hawaiian monarchy. An attempt was made in the 1800s to divide the property, but it was discovered in the 1960s that 47 percent of the land in the state was controlled by 72 people. The Hawaiian legislature enacted the Land Act of 1967 to address this concentration of land. The Housing Authority stated that the act "created a mechanism for condemning residential tracts and for transferring ownership of the condemned fees simple to existing lessees. By condemning the land in question, the Hawaii Legislature intended to make the land sales involuntary, thereby making the federal tax consequences less severe while still facilitating the redistribution of fees simple." The act was an attempt to get around the landowners' excuse for not selling—that the federal taxes would be too high. Tenants living on single-family lots were entitled to ask the Hawaiian Housing Authority to condemn the property on which they lived. "When 25 eligible tenants, or tenants on half the lots in the tract, whichever is less, file appropriate applications, the Act authorizes HHA to hold a public hearing to determine whether acquisition by the State [will] effectuate the public purposes of the Act." HHA was authorized to acquire the former fee owner's title and interest in the land and after HHA determined that a public purpose would be served by the land's acquisition. After compensation has been set by either a condemnation trial or through negotiations between the lessor an lessee, HHA could sell the land titles to those who applied for fee simple ownership for the land.

The property owners brought a suit to challenge the constitutionality of the act on the grounds that it constituted an illegal taking of property on the part of the state. The court of appeals struck down the act; it reasoned that it was "a naked attempt on the part of the state of Hawaii to take the private property of A and transfer it to B solely for B's private use and benefit."

SUMMARY OF ARGUMENTS

Appellant, the Hawaii Housing Authority, argued that the district court should have abstained from hearing the case because questions of state law must first be resolved and the federal questions could have been presented in state proceedings concerning state interests. The Hawaii Housing Authority also argued that the act did not violate the public use requirement of the Fifth and Fourteenth Amendments.

Appellees, the landowners, argued that the act violated the public use requirement of the Fifth and Fourteenth Amendments. The landowners also argued that the act violated due process by allowing the lessees to initiate the "taking" process. Finally, the landowners argued that the exercise of the state's power of eminent domain violated the contracts clause.

DECISION

The Court unanimously upheld the act in an opinion written by Justice O'Connor. She reasoned that the Court's decision in *Berman v. Parker* (1954) was controlling in this situation. In that case the Court upheld the District of Columbia Redevelopment Act of 1945, which allowed both for the comprehensive use of eminent domain power and for the sale and lease of the condemned lands to private interest. The Court in that case reasoned that the act was constitutional because it was a use of police powers that are to be determined by the legislature—as it was in this case. Citing *Berman,* the Court reasoned that "subject to specific constitutional limitation, when the legislature has spoken, the public interest has been declared in terms well-nigh conclusive. In such cases the legislature, not the judiciary, is the main guardian of the public needs to be served by social legislation, whether it be Congress legislating concerning the District of Columbia . . . or the States legislating concerning local affairs. . . . This principle admits of no exception merely because the power of eminent domain is involved." The Court held that the "public use" requirement, which is a condition to a government taking defined by the facts of each case, is within the scope of the police powers. Once the legislature has determined that something is a public use, it may use its power to effect that end.

In addition, Justice O'Connor argued that the legislative history suggests the Court should not replace the judgment of the legislature with its own judgment of what constitutes public use, except in those circumstances in which the state's determination is without reasonable foundation. Though case history suggests that a person's property should not be taken from him without a justifiable public purpose, even in cases where the person is being compensated, in situations where eminent domain power is rationally related to a public purpose the Court has never held that a compensated taking violated the Public Use Clause. Based on this, the Court concluded that the Hawaii act was constitutional. Through the legislature the people of Hawaii determined that they would redistribute the land traceable to the island's oligarchy. The legislature determined that such oligarchy created deterrents to the natural operations and transfer of land. Regulations directed at oligarchies and the consequent evils, such as forcing Hawaiians to lease rather than buy land, have historically been the subject of the state's police powers: "When the legislature's purpose is legitimate and its means are not irrational, our cases make clear that empirical debates over the wisdom of takings—no less than debates over the wisdom of other kinds of socioeconomic legislation—are not to be carried out in the federal courts." The redistribution of land held in fee simple, which means the owner is entitled to the entire property, is a legitimate exercise of state authority and therefore the act passed the scrutiny of the Public Use Clause.

AFTERMATH

The Court adopted a deferential approach to analyzing the state's use of its police power to exercise a taking under the eminent domain power. This deferential, less stringent, approach has become the approach currently used by the Court in analyzing similar acts.

SIGNIFICANCE

This case reinforced the public use requirement. The eminent domain clause required that for "takings there be compensation and the taking be for public use." This requirement was initially construed strictly such that any taking that did not go to public use was prohibited, whether it generally benefited the public or not. The Court eventually took a less stringent view and allowed taking in situations in which the public would benefit. *Midkiff* represents the less stringent approach of the Court. This expansion of the notion of public use has been paralleled by the expansion of police powers.

RELATED CASE

Berman v. Parker, 348 U.S. 26 (1954)

RECOMMENDED READING

Allison Dunham, Griggs v. Allegheny County *in Perspective: Thirty Years of Supreme Court Expropriation Law,* Supreme Court Review 63 (1962).

Epstein, Richard. *Takings: Private Property and the Power of Eminent Domain.* Cambridge, Mass.: Harvard University Press, 1985.

Scot Powe, *Reality, Not Theory,* 3 Constitutional Commentary (summer 1986).

The Public Use Limitation on Eminent Domain: An Advance Requiem, 58 Yale Law Journal 599 (1949).

Case Title: *Humphrey's Executor v. United States*

Legal Citation: 295 U.S. 602

Year of Decision: 1935

KEY ISSUES

May Congress restrict the president's right to remove federal officials from their positions?

HISTORY OF THE CASE

William E. Humphrey was nominated by President Herbert Hoover to be a member of the Federal Trade Commission. President Franklin D. Roosevelt, who succeeded Hoover, later asked him to resign for policy reasons. After Humphrey refused to resign, Roosevelt removed him from office. The Federal Trade Commission Act passed by Congress listed situations in which a president could remove an officer from his position with the Federal Trade Commission. These included "inefficiency, neglect of duty, or malfeasance in office." Humphrey was not removed for one of these reasons. After Humphrey's death, his estate sued the United States for Humphrey's lost wages, alleging that the president did not have the power to remove Humphrey from office.

SUMMARY OF ARGUMENTS

Humphrey's executor argued that the president's power to remove commissioners under the Federal Trade Commission Act was limited to certain specific causes and this limitation did not violate the Constitution.

The government argued that the president's removal power under the Federal Trade Commission Act was not limited and if it was limited, the limitation was unconstitutional.

DECISION

The Court held that Congress can limit the president's power to remove officials if the duties of the position involve quasi-judicial or quasi-legislative duties, even if the officials hold office through presidential appointment. The president still has absolute power to remove officials whose duties are purely executive.

The Court looked at the nature of Humphrey's position with the Federal Trade Commission and found that the duties were not purely executive in nature but were quasi-judicial and quasi-legislative duties. The Court noted that regulatory agencies such as the Federal Trade Commission should be nonpartisan and act without bias. The Court acknowledged that the activities of the Federal Trade Commission would be curtailed if the president had absolute power to remove officers.

There were no dissenting judges.

AFTERMATH

This case has not been overruled. The president still has the power to remove purely executive officers, but not officers whose positions entail quasi-judicial and quasi-legislative duties.

SIGNIFICANCE

Humphrey's slightly limited an earlier Supreme Court decision, *Myers v. United States* (1926), which held that a president had absolute power to remove officers of governmental agencies and departments where the president had the power to appoint such officers. *Humphrey's Executor* limited the president's exclusive power to remove to only purely executive officers.

RELATED CASES

Myers v. United States, 272 U.S. 52 (1926)

Weiner v. United States, 357 U.S. 349 (1958)

RECOMMENDED READING

Dry, Murray. "The Congressional Veto and the Constitutional Separation of Powers." In *The Presidency in the Constitutional Order*. Edited by Joseph M. Bessette and Jeffrey Tulis. Baton Rouge: Louisiana State University Press, 1981.

Fisher, Louis. *The Constitution between Friends*. New York: St. Martin's Press, 1978.

Geoffrey P. Miller, *Independent Agencies*, Supreme Court Review 41–97 (1986).

Schwartz, Bernard. *The Ascent of Pragmatism: The Burger Court in Action*. New York: Addison-Wesley, 1990.

Case Title: *Hutchinson v. Proxmire*

Legal Citation: 443 U.S. 111

Year of Decision: 1979

KEY ISSUES

Are words uttered by members of Congress outside of the chambers of Congress protected by the speech or debate clause of the Constitution (Article I, section 6, paragraph 1) or the Constitution's First Amendment free speech clause?

HISTORY OF THE CASE

Hutchinson, a research behavioral scientist, received federal grant money from various federal agencies to study emotional behavior. He tried to measure aggression, concentrating primarily on behavior patterns of animals. One test included the study of the jaw-clenching tendency of monkeys when exposed to various stressful or aggravating stimuli. The research was intended to help federal agencies address problems associated with the confinement of humans in undersea and space exploration.

Senator William Proxmire (D.-Wisc.) initiated the "Golden Fleece of the Month Award" and granted the award to the government agency with the most wasteful spending. In a speech written by one of Proxmire's assistants, Proxmire declared that the spending on Hutchinson's research made "a monkey out of the American taxpayer." He included portions of his speech in a newsletter sent to his constituents, and also mentioned the award on a television program.

Hutchinson filed suit claiming that the remarks made by Proxmire were defamatory and caused him lost income and humiliation. The district court ruled that Proxmire's newsletter and speech were privileged because they were protected under the speech or debate clause of the Constitution, which protects the speech and debate of members of Congress during legislative activities. The U.S. Supreme Court decided to hear the case.

SUMMARY OF ARGUMENTS

Proxmire asserted that his utterances and acts were protected by the speech or debate clause and that his criticisms of federal spending was privileged under the free speech clause of the First Amendment. Proxmire also argued that Hutchinson was a public figure, so he could not charge Proxmire with libel unless he could prove Proxmire acted with "actual malice."

Hutchinson argued that he was not a public figure and that Proxmire's statements were not protected under the speech or debate clause or the free speech clause of the First Amendment. Because the statements were not protected, the utterances made by Proxmire were defamatory. Hutchinson alleged that they led to loss of income, humiliation, physical illness, and mental anguish, and a loss in ability to earn future income.

DECISION

The Supreme Court ruled that neither the speech or debate clause nor the free speech clause of the Constitution provided absolute immunity from liability for defamatory statements made outside the legislative chamber. They did note that statements made on the Senate or House floor, committee reports, and committee hearings were protected. Newsletters and press releases are not protected by the Constitution because these activities are not necessary to or part of the legislative function or process. The Supreme Court noted that congressional privilege is limited only to legislative actions such as the preparation of internal reports, voting, and debate. Therefore, the Court found the publication of Proxmire's statements to be unprotected by the speech and debate clause.

AFTERMATH

This case has not been overruled. Under the present interpretation of the speech or debate clause, members of Congress and their legislative aides are not liable for defamatory speech if their actions are directly and essentially related to the legislative process.

SIGNIFICANCE

This case exemplifies the idea that congressional statements made through the press, mail, or electronic media are not protected by the free speech clause of the First Amendment or the speech or debate clause.

RELATED CASES

New York Times v. Sullivan, 376 U.S. 254 (1964)

Time, Inc. v. Firestone, 424 U.S. 448 (1976)

Wolsten v. Reader's Digest Ass'n, 443 U.S. 157 (1979)

RECOMMENDED READING

Bradden C. Backer, *Constitutional Protection of Critical Speech and the Public Figure Doctrine: Retreat by Reaffirmation*—Hutchinson v. Proxmire, Wisconsin Law Review 568–595 (1980).

Bruce Jones, *Qualified Immunity for Federal Officials: A Proposed Standard for Defamation Cases*, 58 Texas Law Review 789–807 (April 1980).

Jeff Turner, *Legislative Immunity and Congressional Necessity*, 68 Georgetown Law Review 783–805 (February 1980).

Case Title: *I.N.S. v. Chadha*

Legal Citation: 462 U.S. 919

Year of Decision: 1983

KEY ISSUES

Does the use of the legislative veto in Congress violate the Constitution's procedures for the exercise of legislative power?

History of the Case

An East Indian, Jagdish Rai Chadha, entered the United States lawfully on a nonimmigrant student visa. He stayed in the United States after his visa expired. The Immigration and Naturalization Service held a deportation hearing in which Chadha requested to have his deportation suspended under the Immigration and Nationality Act of 1952, which is the organization and codification of United States immigration laws that regulate among other things, citizenship, deportation, and employment authorization. The immigration judge suspended Chadha's deportation. The attorney general conveyed the recommendation for suspension to Congress as required by law. In the immigration act, Congress had granted the attorney general the authority to approve immigration decisions, but either house of Congress had the power to veto the attorney general's determination. The House of Representatives passed a resolution against the suspension of Chadha's deportation. This resolution was not treated as a legislative act, and, therefore, was not submitted to the Senate for a vote or presented to the president for his approval.

After the vote by the House of Representatives, the immigration judge reopened Chadha's deportation hearing in order to deport him. Chadha moved to terminate the proceedings, arguing that the immigration act was unconstitutional. The Court of Appeals for the Ninth Circuit ruled that the act violated the constitutional doctrine of separation of powers. The Supreme Court decided to hear the case.

Summary of Arguments

Chadha argued that the act violated the Constitution because it allowed only one House of Congress (the legislative branch) to veto a decision by the attorney general (the executive branch). The Constitution provides that every bill or resolution be passed by both houses and presented to the president for approval. This procedure supports the idea of separation of powers. Chadha argued that the resolution passed by the House of Representatives in his case was actually legislation, and, as such, should have been passed by both houses of Congress and presented to the president.

The United States argued that the procedure outlined in the act was more "efficient, convenient, and useful in facilitating functions of govern-ment." They argued that since the president assented to the bill, it should be upheld. They also argued that the action taken by the House of Representatives was not legislation, and, therefore, did not require a vote by both houses or presentation to the president.

Decision

The Supreme Court ruled that the paragraph of the Immigration and Nationality Act that authorized one House of Congress, by resolution, to invalidate a decision by the executive branch (the attorney general) was unconstitutional. They ruled that the action taken by the House of Representatives was essentially legislation and subject to constitutional requirements of passage by both Houses of Congress and presentation to the president.

Aftermath

This case has not been overruled. Congress may amend and repeal statutes, but only if passed by both houses and presented to the president for approval as the Constitution requires. Congress is not allowed to alter the rights of the executive or judicial branch without observing the constitutional requirements.

Significance

This case emphasizes the importance of separation of powers as designed in the Constitution. The Constitution outlines four instances when either house of Congress may act alone: ratification of treaties, impeachment, trials after impeachment, and confirmations of presidential appointments. The Supreme Court did not allow Congress to create a new situation in which they could act separately.

Related Cases

Metropolitan Washington Airports Authority v. Citizens for the Abatement of Aircraft Noise, Inc., 501 U.S. 252 (1991)

Recommended Reading

Craig, Barbara Hinkson. *Chadha*. New York: Oxford University Press, 1988.

Dry, Murray. "The Congressional Veto and the Constitutional Separation of Powers." In *The Presidency in the Constitutional Order*. Edited by Joseph M. Bessette and Jeffrey Tulis. Baton Rouge: Louisiana State University Press, 1981.

E. Donald Elliott, INS v. Chadha: *The Administrative Constitution, the Constitution and the Legislative Veto,* Supreme Court Review 125–176 (1983).

Schwartz, Bernard. *The Ascent of Pragmatism: The Burger Court in Action.* New York: Addison-Wesley, 1990.

Case Title: *Karcher v. Daggett*

Legal Citation: 462 U.S. 725

Year of Decision: 1983

KEY ISSUES

Does a congressional apportionment design, which is the way in which the population is divided into legislative districts, have to represent a good faith effort to attain population equality under the Constitution?

HISTORY OF THE CASE

After the 1980 census, the governor of New Jersey was notified that the number of U.S. Representatives to which the state was entitled had decreased from 15 to 14. Therefore, the New Jersey legislature had to reapportion the districts in 1982 in response to the reduction in representatives. The new districts had an average population of 526,059. The largest district had a population of 527,472, and the smallest district had a population of 523,798. The difference between the largest and smallest district was 3,674 people, or 0.6984 percent.

A group of individuals filed suit claiming that the apportionment violated Article I, section 2 of the Constitution, which requires that "Representatives . . . shall be apportioned among the several states which may be included within the Union, according to their respective numbers."

The district court held that the population variances in the redistricting plan were not "unavoidable." The plaintiffs had the burden of showing that the differences in population size could have been avoided and were not the result of a good faith effort to achieve equality. If the plaintiffs succeeded in meeting their burden of

proof, the defendants then had to prove that the variance was necessary to achieve a consistent, nondiscriminatory policy. The district court ruled that the defendants did not prove that the inequality was necessary to further a legitimate policy. The Supreme Court decided to hear the case.

SUMMARY OF ARGUMENTS

Appellants, including Karcher, the speaker of the New Jersey Assembly, argued that the apportionment plan was the product of a good faith effort to achieve population equality because the maximum deviation between congressional districts was lower than the deviation in the census numbers. Appellants also argued that the apportionment plan was justified as an effort to preserve the voting strength of racial minority groups.

Appellees, a group of individuals including the incumbent Republican New Jersey members of Congress, argued that the congressional districts, as reapportioned, were not functionally equal noting that other plans had been presented that had lower population deviations. Appellees also argued that the configuration of the congressional districts was bizarre and, therefore, demonstrated that the reapportionment plan was not adopted in good faith.

DECISION

Justice Brennan delivered the opinion of the Court. In a 5 to 4 decision, the Court agreed with the district court and noted that even though exact mathematical equality may be impossible, districts must be apportioned to achieve population equality as nearly as possible. Justice Brennan also noted situations that could justify a difference in populations, such as preserving the cores of prior districts, avoiding contests between incumbents, making districts compact, and respecting municipal boundaries. The Court held that the defendants did not meet their burden of proof because they did not show that there was a justification for the variance in population.

Justice Stevens, writing a concurring opinion, noted that the shapes of the districts should be considered as well as the mathematical equality of the populations in each district.

Justice White dissented, joined by Chief Justice Burger, Justice Powell, and Justice Rehnquist. White believed the majority was unreasonable to expect perfect equality when apportioning congressional districts. He felt that small deviations in population size should not constitute an automatic constitutional violation.

AFTERMATH

This case has not been overruled. Legislatures must aspire to exact mathematical equality in the population of each congressional district in order to comply with the Constitution.

SIGNIFICANCE

This case exemplifies the length to which the Supreme Court will go to ensure that each individual's vote weighs equally.

RELATED CASES

Kirkpatrick v. Preisler, 394 U.S. 526 (1969)

Reynolds v. Sims, 377 U.S. 533 (1964)

RECOMMENDED READING

Richard H. Bagger, *The Supreme Court and Congressional Apportionment: Slippery Slope to Equal Representation Gerrymandering,* 38 Rutgers Law Review 109–137 (fall 1985).

Richard G. Niemi, *The Relationship Between Votes and Seats: The Ultimate Question in Political Gerrymandering,* 33 UCLA Law Review 185–212 (October 1985).

Case Title: *Katzenbach v. McClung*

Legal Citation: 379 U.S. 294

Year of Decision: 1964

KEY ISSUES

May Congress regulate local businesses through its power under the commerce clause?

HISTORY OF THE CASE

A restaurant in Alabama located 11 blocks from an interstate highway allowed table service for whites only, with a take-out service for African Americans. Nearly half the food the restaurant bought came from out of state. The Civil Rights Act of 1964 contained a provision, Title II, which made it illegal to discriminate on the basis of race if a restaurant obtained food through interstate commerce or served or offered to serve interstate travelers. The restaurant continued to discriminate after the Civil Rights Act of 1964 was passed.

The owner of the restaurant, McClung, challenged Title II of the Civil Rights Act. The district court granted an injunction against enforcement of this part of the Civil Rights Act. The district court found that there was no connection between food purchased from out of state and the conclusion of Congress that discrimination in restaurants affected commerce. Without a close relation between local activities and interstate commerce, the district court argued that Congress cannot control the local activity to protect interstate commerce. The appellate court held that the law was unconstitutional. The Supreme Court agreed to hear the case.

SUMMARY OF ARGUMENTS

The government argued that there was a sufficiently close, connection between interstate commerce and discrimination. The government argued that racial discrimination at restaurants that serve food received from out of state imposed a commercial burden nationally on interstate commerce. The government asserted that restaurants served less food when they discriminated because they served fewer people. This affected commerce because the restaurant did not buy as much food as it could. Also, the government asserted that discrimination hindered interstate travel by African Americans because it was hard for them to find prepared food while on trips.

McClung argued that no connection existed. He argued that Congress arbitrarily presumed all restaurants that discriminated and ordered food from out of state affected commerce.

DECISION

The Supreme Court decided that Congress can regulate local business if any part of the business affects interstate commerce. They agreed with the government that discrimination in restaurants did affect interstate commerce.

AFTERMATH

This case has not been overruled and is still cited to support the idea that Congress has great power to regulate local activities that affect interstate commerce.

SIGNIFICANCE

This case illustrates the Supreme Court's broad interpretation of the commerce clause, giving Congress great authority to regulate local activity. This power has only recently been questioned by the Court (*U.S. v. Lopez,* 1995) (*U.S. v. Morrison,* 2000).

RELATED CASES

Daniel v. Paul, 395 U.S. 298 (1969)

Heart of Atlanta Motel v. U.S., 379 U.S. 241 (1964)

RECOMMENDED READING

Benson, Paul R., Jr. *The Supreme Court and the Commerce Clause 1937–1970.* New York: Dunellen Publishing, 1970.

❧

Case Title: *Kent v. Dulles*

Legal Citations: 357 U.S. 116; 78 S.Ct. 1113; 2 L.Ed. 2d 1204

Year of Decision: 1958

❧

KEY ISSUES

Under certain broad, generalized powers, may the government prohibit a U.S. citizen, who is a known or suspected communist, from obtaining a passport?

HISTORY OF THE CASE

Rockwell Kent wanted to travel to Helsinki, Finland, to attend a "World Council of Peace" meeting. To do so, he needed to obtain a U.S. passport. The secretary of state, John Foster Dulles, denied him one because of Kent's communist political beliefs. The secretary claimed additional legal justification for this denial on the basis of a federal regulation that had not yet gone into effect.

Kent sued in federal district court. The court ruled for the secretary, and the appellate court affirmed. Mr. Kent sought a hearing in the Supreme Court, and the Court granted his petition.

SUMMARY OF ARGUMENTS

Kent argued that he had a constitutional right to travel, therefore, he had a right to a passport. Kent also argued that the secretary of state did not have the authority to issue the regulations under which he was denied a passport. Finally, Kent argued that the application of the regulations violated his First Amendment and due process rights.

Dulles argued that the secretary of state had the authorization to use his discretion in the denial of passports based on past or present membership in the Communist Party and his refusal to issue Kent a passport did not violate Kent's constitutional rights.

DECISION

The Supreme Court ruled 5-4 that the secretary of state did not have authority to promulgate regulations denying passports to communists.

Justice William O. Douglas wrote the majority opinion of the Court. Justice Douglas first discussed the history of passports in the United States. He noted that, except in certain situations (usually wartime), "a passport was not a condition to entry or exit." A passport had other diplomatic purposes and established the holder to reenter the United States.

He next found that "[t]he right to travel is a part of the liberty of which the citizen cannot be deprived without the due process of the law under the Fifth Amendment." The freedom to travel is an important aspect of the citizen's liberty, and therefore deserves constitutional protection.

Justice Douglas further held that if this constitutional liberty is to be regulated, it must be pursuant to the lawmaking functions of Congress. The Court will construe narrowly all delegated powers that curtail or dilute such liberties. When Congress delegated passport granting or withholding power to the secretary, it did so on two broad grounds. The first relates to citizenship or allegiance to the country, and the second to criminal or unlawful conduct. Neither was present here. The majority opinion went on to find that it doubted Congress intended to grant the secretary unbridled discretion in granting or withholding a passport from a citizen. In the absence of this authority, the majority refused to "trench so heavily on the rights of citizens."

Justice Tom C. Clark authored the minority opinion of the Court. His opinion stressed the legislative history of statutes granting the secretary authority to issue or refuse to issue passports. After extensive discussion on this point, the minority concluded "[t]he implication is unmistakable that the Secretary was intended to exercise his traditional passport function" to protect the country's internal security. This is true in times of peace and war.

The minority pointed out communist philosophical goals of "world conquest" and emphasized the implied threat to the United States's security. In light of this and the tense, post–World War II international political climate, the secretary was justified in denying Kent a passport.

AFTERMATH

Later decisions on the right to travel tended to follow the *Kent* concept. Specifically, the Court would allow the secretary of state to refuse to issue a passport only as long as the regulations abridging the right to travel were explicitly and narrowly defined.

SIGNIFICANCE

Kent's importance stems not from its constitutional interpretation, but rather from its broad extrajudicial commentary. The decision specifically states that it "do[es] not reach the question of constitutionality." Instead, when Congress does not explicitly provide the grounds which the secretary may employ in granting or denying passports, loosely defined powers will not be allowed to infringe a citizen's constitutional rights. The Court accepted that governmental power may, in certain circumstances, overcome an individual's right to travel internationally. However, when the government's power is broad and ill-defined, the constitutional right to travel must not be impinged.

RELATED CASES

Aptheker v. Secretary of State, 378 U.S. 500; 84 S.Ct. 1659; 12 L.Ed.2d 992 (1964)

Dayton v. Dulles, 357 U.S. 144; 78 S.Ct. 1127 (1964)

Zemel v. Rusk, 381 U.S. 1; 85 S.Ct. 1271; 14 L.Ed.2d 179 (1964)

RECOMMENDED READING

Lonnie E. Griffith, Jr., *Passports*, 59A American Jurisprudence 2d 1015 (1987).

The Supreme Court, 1980 Term, "The Right to Travel," 95 Harvard Law Review 91 (1981).

Case Title: *Keyes v. School District No. 1 of Denver, CO*

Legal Citation: 413 U.S. 189

Year of Decision: 1973

KEY ISSUES

Does proof of deliberate segregation in a section of a school district raise a presumption that other segregation in the school district is intentional?

HISTORY OF THE CASE

Parents of Denver schoolchildren brought suit alleging that the Denver School Board maintained racially or ethnically segregated schools in the Park Hill area of the city. The district court ordered the board to desegregate the schools in the Park Hill area but did not order desegregation for the rest of the city. The court concluded that its finding of racial segregation in the Park Hill area did not mean that the school board had to desegregate the rest of the city. The district court did rule, however, that the inner-city schools were inferior to other schools and that the board did have to offer equal educational opportunities to all students. The board appealed, and the court of appeals agreed with the district court that the board had engaged in systematic segregation in the Park Hill area. The court of appeals decided that the intentional segregation of other parts of the Denver school district was not proven by the fact that Park Hill was intentionally segregated. The Supreme Court decided to hear the case.

SUMMARY OF ARGUMENTS

The parents argued that Denver's inner-city schools were inferior to other schools and that the school board had to offer equal educational opportunities to all students. The school board argued that the intentional segregation of other parts of the Denver school district was not proven by the fact that Park Hill was intentionally segregated.

DECISION

Justice Brennan delivered the opinion of the Court, which held that proof of intentional segregation in one area of the city raises a presumption that there has been deliberate segregation in other area of the city.

The Court decided that the district court should have considered the placement of blacks and Hispanics in the same category for the purposes of defining a segregated core city school. Additionally, it found that the correct legal standard was not followed for deciding whether deliberate segregation had occurred. The majority held that finding intentional segregation of a substantial portion of the district would support a finding of a dual system of the whole district, which could only be rebutted by showing that the segregated part was a separate, unrelated area. Even if the district was found to be separated into unrelated areas, the intent to segregate in one area (Park Hill) would create a presumption that the whole area was segregated intentionally. This could be rebutted by showing that intent was not the motivation behind the segregation or that past acts of segregation did not produce the current segregation.

Justice Powell, who wrote a concurring opinion, agreed with the result but disfavored the emphasis on intent. He believed that all school districts should make an affirmative effort to desegregate schools regardless of whether the segregation occurred as a result of intent, coincidence, or residential patterns.

Justice Rehnquist dissented, stating that the intentional segregation of Park Hill should not have been considered as a presumption that other areas were also intentionally segregated. He also believed that the history of how blacks and Hispanics moved throughout the course of the previous two decades showed that the segregation was a natural result and not intentional.

AFTERMATH

The Court still follows *Keyes,* and later went on to decide in *Dayton Board of Education v.*

Brinkman (1979) that where intentional segregation was in place in schools in 1954, a prima facie case, one in which there is sufficient evidence to proceed, can be made that current segregation was a result of past segregation.

SIGNIFICANCE

Keyes was the first case to confront racial segregation in schools outside of the South. It also established the presumption and prima facie case for intentional segregation in certain circumstances in which there has been intentional segregation in a small part of a larger district.

RELATED CASES

Columbus Board of Education v. Penick, 443 U.S. 449 (1979)

Dayton Board of Education v. Brinkman, 443 U.S. 526 (1979)

Milliken v. Bradley, 418 U.S. 717 (1974)

RECOMMENDED READING

Graglia, Lino A. *Disaster by Decree.* Ithaca, N.Y.: Cornell University Press, 1976.

Christina B. Whitman, *Individual and Community: An Appreciation of Mr. Justice Powell,* 68 Virginia Law Review 303–332 (February 1982).

Case Title: *Kirby v. Illinois*

Legal Citation: 406 U.S. 682

Year of Decision: 1972

KEY ISSUES

Does a person have a Sixth Amendment right to counsel during a pre-indictment identification at a police station?

HISTORY OF THE CASE

On February 21, 1968, a man named Willie Shard reported to the Chicago police that the previous day two men had robbed him on a Chicago street of a wallet containing, among other things, traveler's checks and a Social Security card. On February 22, two police officers stopped Thomas Kirby and a companion, Ralph Bean, on West Madison Street in Chicago. The officers stopped Kirby because they thought he was a man named Hampton, who was wanted on an unrelated criminal offense. When asked for identification, Kirby produced a wallet that contained three traveler's checks and a Social Security card, all bearing the name of Willie Shard. Papers with Shard's name on them were also found in Bean's possession. The officers then arrested Kirby and Bean and took them to the police station.

Only after arriving at the police station, and checking the records there, did the arresting officers learn of the Shard robbery. A police car was then dispatched to Shard's place of employment, where it picked up Shard and brought him to the police station. Immediately upon entering the room in the police station where Kirby and Bean were seated at a table, Shard positively identified them as the men who had robbed him two days earlier. No lawyer was present in the room, and neither Kirby nor Bean had been asked whether he wanted legal assistance or advised of any right to the presence of counsel.

More than six weeks later, Kirby and Bean were indicted for the robbery of Willie Shard. Upon arraignment, counsel was appointed to represent them, and they pleaded not guilty. A pretrial motion to suppress Shard's testimony was denied, and at the trial Shard testified as a witness for the prosecution. In his testimony he described his identification of the two men at the police station on February 22, and identified them again in the courtroom as the men who had robbed him on February 20. He was cross-examined at length regarding the circumstances of his identification of the two defendants. The jury found both defendants guilty, and the petitioner's conviction was confirmed on appeal.

SUMMARY OF ARGUMENTS

Kirby argued that he was denied his Sixth Amendment right to counsel during the pre-indictment identification. Kirby argued that the Sixth Amendment, as applied to the states through the Fourteenth Amendment, required that an accused person be allowed counsel at all critical stages of the criminal process and that a pre-indictment confrontation was a critical stage.

Illinois argued that the right to counsel was only applicable to post-indictment confrontations.

DECISION

Justice Stewart announced the judgment of the Court that the Sixth Amendment right to assistance of counsel does not commence until a person has been formally charged with a crime: "In a line of constitutional cases . . . stemming back to the Court's landmark opinion in *Powell v. Alabama,* it has been firmly established that a person's Sixth and Fourteenth Amendment right to counsel attaches only after the time that adversary judicial proceedings have been initiated against him." Such adversary proceedings do not begin, Justice Stewart held, until criminal charges have been filed—"whether by way of formal charge, preliminary hearing, indictment, information, or arraignment."

Justice Brennan wrote a dissenting opinion in which Justices Douglas and Marshall joined. He argued that the Court misread its own precedent on the coverage of the Sixth Amendment right to counsel. He argued that "'the initiation of adversary judicial criminal proceedings' . . . is completely irrelevant to whether counsel is necessary at a pretrial confrontation for identification in order to safeguard the accused's constitutional rights to confrontation and the effective assistance of counsel at trial." He contended that the starting point of the whole system of criminal justice is at the arrest, not the indictment. Justice Brennan relied heavily on the case of *United States v. Wade,* in which the Court held that a criminal defendant had a right to assistance of counsel at a post-indictment lineup. He argued that the Sixth Amendment guarantee articulated in *Wade,* which "encompasses counsel's assistance whenever necessary to assure a meaningful defense," applied equally to the pre-indictment identification in the present case.

AFTERMATH

This case has not been overturned.

SIGNIFICANCE

This case limits the scope of the Sixth Amendment right to effective assistance of counsel to the time after formal criminal charges have been filed. This case also demonstrates the narrower reading of the Constitution that distinguished the Supreme

Court under Chief Justice Burger from the Court's emphasis on individual rights under Chief Justice Warren during the 1960s.

RELATED CASES

Gideon v. Wainwright, 372 U.S. 335 (1963)

Gilbert v. California, 388 U.S. 263 (1967)

Powell v. Alabama, 287 U.S. 45 (1932)

United States v. Wade, 388 U.S. 218 (1967)

RECOMMENDED READING

Schwartz, Bernard. *The Ascent of Pragmatism: The Burger Court in Action.* New York: Addison-Wesley, 1990.

The Supreme Court, 1971 Term, 86 Harvard Law Review 157–164 (1972).

Case Title: *Kirkpatrick v. Preisler*

Legal Citation: 394 U.S. 526

Year of Decision: 1969

KEY ISSUES

Does the 1967 Missouri congressional redistricting statute violate the rule in *Wesberry v. Sanders* (1964) that "as nearly as practicable one man's vote in a congressional election is to be worth as much as another's"?

HISTORY OF THE CASE

After several unsuccessful attempts to enact a congressional redistricting statute that complied with the Supreme Court's decision in *Wesberry v. Sanders,* the General Assembly of the Missouri legislature enacted another such statute in 1967. The District Court for the Western District of Missouri held that "the 1967 Act did not meet the constitutional standard of equal representation for equal numbers of the people 'as nearly as practicable,' and that the State had failed to make any acceptable justification for the variances." The state supreme court agreed.

SUMMARY OF ARGUMENTS

Missouri argued that the population variances among the districts created by the 1967 Act were so small that they should be considered de minimis (trivial) and, for that reason, should satisfy the "as nearly as practicable" limitation without independent justification. However, Missouri also offered six independent justifications for the population variances among the 10 congressional districts.

DECISION

Justice Brennan delivered the opinion of the Court. The Court rejected Missouri's argument that the percentage population variance was small enough to be considered trivial. Justice Brennan stated, "We can see no nonarbitrary way to pick a cutoff point at which population variances suddenly become de minimis." He continued:

> [T]he command of Art. I, s 2, that States create congressional districts which provide equal representation for equal numbers of people permits only the limited population variances which are unavoidable despite a good-faith effort to achieve *absolute equality,* or for which justification is shown. (emphasis added)

In this case an average variance among districts of 1.6 percent was too high because the variance did not come as close to equality as it could have. The most populous district was 3.13 percent above the mathematical ideal, and the least populous was 2.84 percent below.

The Court also rejected each of the six justifications offered by Missouri for its congressional redistricting statute. Justice Brennan stated, "We agree with the District Court that Missouri has not satisfactorily justified the population variances among the districts." Thus, the Missouri redistricting Act of 1967 was found to be unconstitutional as a violation of the "as nearly as practicable" rule laid down in *Wesberry v. Sanders.*

AFTERMATH

The most extreme illustration of this rule came in *KARCHER V. DAGGETT* (1983), where by a 5-4 vote the Court rejected a New Jersey apportionment scheme that had a maximum variance of about

0.7 percent. The majority was unwilling to recognize an exception even for de minimis variations, unless a state showed why greater precision could not be achieved by use of the "best available census data."

SIGNIFICANCE

In congressional redistricting, states must make a "good faith effort to achieve precise mathematical equality." The Court's decision in *Kirkpatrick* has made it clear that there is no fixed numerical percentage that will explicitly be considered "as nearly as practicable" to equality. The Court has made it clear that variances will be judged on a case-by-case basis and must be justified, no matter how small.

RELATED CASES

Karcher v. Daggett, 462 U.S. 725 (1983)

Reynolds v. Sims, 377 U.S. 533 (1964)

RECOMMENDED READING

Bushnell, Eleanore, ed. *The Court Steps In: Impact of Reapportionment on the Thirteen Western States.* Salt Lake City: University of Utah Press, 1970.

Case Title: *Luther v. Borden*

Legal Citation: 48 U.S. 1

Year of Decision: 1849

KEY ISSUES

May the Supreme Court decide what form of government is the established one in a state?

HISTORY OF THE CASE

Rhode Island did not make a new constitution at the time of the American Revolution, as the other states did. Instead, it kept the form of government established by the charter of the English king Charles II. In 1841, a convention was elected to form a new state constitution to be submitted to the people. The constitution was written and rat-

ified by the people. A governor, legislature, and other officers were elected according to the new constitution. The charter government refused to recognize this new government, however. The state of Rhode Island, as well as the president of the United States, recognized the charter government as the official government. The charter government declared a state of martial law in order to defend the state against the new government, which they saw as trying to overthrow the official government.

On June 29, 1842, a group of officers entered the home of the plaintiffs, Martin and Rachel Luther, under military orders authorized by the charter government because they believed that the Luthers were members of the new government trying to overthrow the established charter government. The Luthers sued the officers for trespass, and the Circuit Court of the United States for the District of Rhode Island found for the defendants. The case for the Luthers went to the Supreme Court.

SUMMARY OF ARGUMENTS

The Luthers sued for trespass. They contended that the defendants were guilty of breaking and entering, that they had no authorization or consent to enter their home, and that the new government under the new constitution was legal and authorized by the people of Rhode Island.

Luther M. Borden and other citizens of Rhode Island admitted that they had entered the Luther's house without consent, but they contended that they had authorization and justification to do so. They argued that they were under orders to defend the state under martial law against an insurrection of men who were trying to overthrow the government. They were officers who were ordered to enter the Luthers' home, arrest Martin Luther (whom they contended was engaged in the insurrection), and search his house while doing as little damage as possible.

DECISION

Chief Justice Taney delivered the opinion of the Court that the decision on which government is the established government is not for the Court to make. It was labeled as a political question, and therefore, nonjusticiable. According to Article 4, section 4, of the Constitution, the Congress or president (when the Congress cannot be convened) are the branches to be applied to when invoking the republican form of government guarantee.

Because the charter government had been recognized by the state, the U.S. courts must also recognize it as the established government. The Court also held that a state may declare martial law to fight an armed insurrection if the civil authority cannot handle it, and officers during this martial law may arrest those whom they reasonably believe to be a part of the armed insurrection. Because of this and the nonjusticiable political question, the Court affirmed the Circuit Court's finding for the defendants.

AFTERMATH

Luther is seen by some to be a starting point for reduced participation in politics because the Court would not defend political rights. Courts later used the term "lack of judicially discoverable and manageable standards" as a reason for declaring political questions nonjusticiable.

SIGNIFICANCE

The Court still abides by the political question rule regarding the guarantee clause, but gets around it by using the equal protection clause, as illustrated in the case of BAKER V. CARR (1962).

RELATED CASES

Baker v. Carr, 369 U.S. 186 (1962)

East Lake v. Forest City Enter., Inc., 426 U.S. 668 (1976)

Hunter v. Erikson, 393 U.S. 385 (1969)

Pacific States Tel. & Tel. Co. v. Oregon, 223 U.S. 118 (1912)

RECOMMENDED READING

David P. Currie, *The Constitution in the Supreme Court: Article IV and Federal Powers, 1836–1864*, Duke Law Journal 695 (1983).

———. *The Constitution in the Supreme Court, 1789–1888*. Chicago: University of Chicago Press, 1985.

Elliot, Ward E. Y. *The Rise of Guardian Democracy*. Cambridge, Mass.: Harvard University Press, 1974.

Note, *Political Rights as Political Questions: The Paradox of* Luther v. Borden, 100 Harvard Law Review 1125 (1987).

Wiecek, William M. *The Guarantee Clause of the Constitution*. Ithaca, N.Y.: Cornell University Press, 1972.

Case Title: *McCulloch v. Maryland*

Legal Citations: 17 U.S. 316; 4 L.Ed. 579

Year of Decision: 1819

KEY ISSUES

Even though the Constitution does not expressly grant Congress the power to incorporate a bank, can it do so under a doctrine of implied powers?

HISTORY OF THE CASE

The state of Maryland, plaintiff, imposed a tax requiring all banks chartered outside the state to print their banknotes on stamped paper if they established any branch or office within Maryland's boundaries. The tax was similar to those passed in other states during a period of strong state sentiment against the Bank of the United States. The taxes were aimed at excluding the Bank of the United States from operating branches within those states. The bank fell within the statutory definition but issued notes on unstamped paper. Accordingly, Maryland brought an action for debt collection against McCulloch, the cashier of the Baltimore branch of the Bank of the United States. The state courts imposed penalties on the defendant, from which he appealed.

SUMMARY OF ARGUMENTS

Chief Justice Marshall began by examining the general basis of authority for the federal government and the Constitution. This designation of the people as the source of authority for the new nation was the theoretical basis for federal supremacy over "states' rights." The states had claimed that the Constitution emanated from their independent sovereignties and that the exercise of the federal power could not predominate over the states' claims to power. Marshall rejected this theory by stating that the federal government emanates from the people and not from the states. Because the power is not derived from the states, they cannot limit grants of power to Congress.

The second major part of the opinion dealt with the breadth of the powers that can be exercised by the federal government. Flexibility being essential, Marshall defined the broad standards within which federal laws must fall. Here he interpreted the grant of powers to Congress as allowing for the full effectuation of national goals. The necessary and proper clause, when combined with the specific grants of powers, evidenced the granting of generalized powers to Congress.

Justice Marshall gave what has become the classic test for the existence of federal power: "Let the end be legitimate, let it be within the scope of the constitution, and all means which are appropriate, which are plainly adapted to that end, which are not prohibited, but consist with the letter and spirit of the constitution, are constitutional." Under this test federal acts were valid so long as they bore a reasonable relationship to an enumerated power of the government. Hence, the second Bank of the United States was allowed because a connection could be found between it and the powers granted to "lay and collect taxes; to borrow money; to regulate commerce; to declare and conduct a war; and to raise and support armies and navies."

The existence of such powers also could be derived from the necessary and proper clause. According to Marshall, this clause did not require Congress to use only means which were absolutely necessary to pursue an enumerated federal power. He found that the framers did not use the word "necessary" in this restrictive way and that it would be illogical to establish a nation with only very restricted powers. Instead, this clause authorized the federal government to select any reasonable means to achieve its ends. All such forms of legislation would be reasonably necessary and proper to the exercise of the enumerated powers. Whether a law met this test was a question of degree, which the Congress was better suited to answer. Thus, the Court would not void the law unless it was clear that it was designed for "the accomplishment of objects not intrusted to the government."

In the third major portion of the opinion, Marshall held that the Maryland tax had to be stricken because it interfered with the exercise of

a valid federal action. In all cases of conflict between federal and state laws, the supremacy of federal law was established by the Constitution. From this principle it was found that the states could not possess incompatible powers that might be hostile to the federal actions.

DECISION

The Court found that Congress has the power to incorporate a bank. (1) Under the necessary and proper clause, an appropriate means that Congress uses to attain legitimate ends that are within the scope of the Constitution and not prohibited by it, but are consistent with the letter and spirit of the Constitution, are constitutional. (2) The federal government is one of the enumerated powers, which are found in the Constitution. However, the Constitution cannot contain an accurate detail of all the subdivisions of governmental powers and of all the means by which they may be carried into execution. Otherwise, the Constitution would become nothing more than a legal code. The government must have the ability to execute the powers entrusted to it through the best available means. (3) Any means that directly executes a power enumerated in the Constitution may be considered incidental to the enumerated power. The word "necessary" in the necessary and proper clause does not limit Congress to indispensable means; rather, the term enlarges the powers vested in the federal government. Congress has discretion in choosing the best means to perform its duties in the manner most beneficial to the people. (4) The creation of a corporation is one of those powers that can be implied as incidental to other powers or used as a means of executing them. The incorporation of the Bank of the United States is a convenient, useful, and essential instrument in the performance of the fiscal operations of the federal government. The United States is a sovereign entity and thus has the power to create a corporation.

AFTERMATH

In 1832 Congress extended the charter of the bank, but President Andrew Jackson vetoed the legislation. Among other things, he objected to the windfall that the original private stockholders would have received upon extension of the charter. He also objected that many of these stockholders were foreigners. He found insufficient precedent to sustain the act because Congress had been inconsistent over the years in its support and because the states were primarily against it. The Supreme Court's opinion was not determinative; President Jackson felt that each branch of the government had to determine for itself the constitutionality of a proposal, and he did not view the bank as necessary and proper.

SIGNIFICANCE

This case is one of the most important in the history of the Court because it established the doctrine of implied powers and emphatically articulated the supremacy of the federal government. The opinion went far beyond the needs of the specific case to promote a powerful federal government. Many commentators at the time disagreed with the Court's decision, saying that the idea of the nation as a union of sovereign states was being undermined. Instead of giving Congress only those additional powers that were needful or indispensable, the necessary and proper clause was now a grant of discretionary power. However, exercise of this discretion must be based on powers granted by the Constitution.

RELATED CASES

Cipollone v. Liggett Group, 505 U.S. 504 (1992)

National Railroad Passenger Corp. v. Boston and Maine Corp., 503 U.S. 407 (1992)

New York v. United States, 505 U.S. 144 (1992)

RECOMMENDED READING

Bickel, Alexander M. *The Least Dangerous Branch.* New Haven, Conn.: Yale University Press, 1962.

Currie, David P. *The Constitution in the Supreme Court, 1789–1888.* Chicago: University of Chicago Press, 1985.

Keynes, Edward, with Randall K. Miller. *The Court vs. Congress.* Durham, N.C.: Duke University Press, 1989.

McCloskey, Robert G. *The American Supreme Court.* Chicago: University of Chicago Press, 1960.

Case Title: *McGowan v. State of Maryland*

Legal Citation: 366 U.S. 420

Year of Decision: 1961

KEY ISSUES

The issues in this case involve the validity of Maryland's Sunday closing laws, also known as the "blue laws," which generally prohibit all labor, business, and other commercial activities on Sunday. The questions presented are whether (1) the classifications within the statutes bring about a denial of equal protection of the law; (2) whether the laws are too vague to give reasonable notice of the forbidden conduct and therefore violate due process; and (3) whether the statutes harm the state's neutrality toward religion, as required by the First Amendment.

HISTORY OF THE CASE

Seven employees of a large discount store, including McGowan, were indicted for selling merchandise on Sunday in violation of Maryland's statute. The pertinent provisions of the statute prohibit several forms of commercial and recreational activities on Sunday. The employees were eventually convicted and fined five dollars and the costs of trial. After an unsuccessful appeal to the Maryland Court of Appeals, the employees appealed to the U.S. Supreme Court.

SUMMARY OF ARGUMENTS

Appellants argued that the Maryland statute violated the equal protection clause of the Fourteenth Amendment because its classifications were without rational basis. Appellants also argued that the Maryland statute was unconstitutionally vague and violated the establishment and free exercise clauses of the First Amendment, made applicable to the states by the Fourteenth Amendment.

Appellee, the state of Maryland, argued that the Maryland statute did not violate constitutional guarantees of religious freedom and was not arbitrary, capricious, or unconstitutionally vague.

The majority, in an opinion by Chief Justice Warren, recognized that states have a wide scope of discretion in enacting laws that affect some groups of citizens more than others. Because this case involved purely economic legislation, the classifications made by the blue laws meet constitutional scrutiny so long as they have a rational relation to a legitimate state end. The majority held that the goal of the blue laws, to provide a uniform day of rest, is a legitimate government interest, just as any other state law regulating the hours and conditions of labor.

The question as to whether these laws violated the establishment clause received the most attention in the majority opinion. Warren wrote that the "purpose and effect" of these laws was not religious, even though the original enactment of these laws may have been "motivated by religious forces." Crucial to the majority's determination was the fact that the history of the laws showed that the laws have become nonreligious over the years. Thus, even though the blue laws coincided with religious tenets, the state legislature was free to regulate the general welfare through such laws.

The vagueness question was easily disposed of in the opinion. The majority found that business persons of ordinary intelligence—such as the appellants—could understand the requirements and exceptions to the blue laws.

In a concurring opinion, Justice Frankfurter, joined by Justice Harlan, focused on the history of Sunday labor laws, dating back to the laws in England before America was colonized. American colonies, and thereafter states, adopted these labor laws. Although these laws originated out of religious belief, at some point in history the legislatures recognized that these laws served to provide workers with a needed "Day of Rest." This day of rest serves as a substantial governmental interest, and such that the establishment clause is not offended.

The dissenting opinion by Justice Douglas expressed concern for the enforcement of laws that have a Christian origin on non-Christians believers. Douglas felt such state action flew in the face of the First Amendment.

AFTERMATH

Although Maryland's blue laws were held to be constitutional, the Court stated that in the future if similar laws were enacted for the purpose of advancing religion, they would be unconstitutional, even if they had the secular effect of a day of rest (See *EPPERSON V. ARKANSAS*, 1968).

The Court also has held that a state law affording Sabbatarians an absolute right not to work on the Sabbath had the primary effect of advancing religion, thus violating the establishment clause (See *Estate of Thornton v. Clador*, 1985).

SIGNIFICANCE

The legacy of this case is that state regulations that merely coincide with religious tenets do not violate the establishment clause as long as the present "purpose and effect" of these laws is secular. The *McGowan* decision also upholds the principle that states have a wide degree of latitude in regulating commercial activities. Such regulations will be upheld under due process and equal protection grounds if they are related to a legitimate state end.

The *McGowan* holding—along with many other establishment clause cases with respect to the proper test to determine establishment clause violations—was later refined in *LEMON V. KURTZMAN* (1972).

RELATED CASES

Corporation of Presiding Bishop of the Church of Jesus Christ of Latter-Day Saints v. Amos 483 U.S. 327 (1987)

Epperson v. Arkansas 393 U.S. 97 (1968)

Estate of Thornton v. Caldor, Inc. 472 U.S. 703 (1985)

Lemon v. Kurtzman 403 U.S. 602 (1972)

RECOMMENDED READING

Frederick Mark Gedicks, *Motivation, Rationality, and Secular Purpose in Establishment Review*, 1985 Arizona State Law Journal 677–726 (summer 1985).

Michael E. Smith, *The Special Place of Religion in the Constitution*, 1983 Supreme Court Review 83–123 (1983).

Constitutional Law—Higher Education Facilities Act—Constitutionality of Federal Financial Aid to Church Related Colleges, 77 Harvard Law Review 1353–1360 (March 1964).

Case Title: *McGrain v. Daugherty*

Legal Citation: 273 U.S. 135

Year of Decision: 1927

Key Issues

May either house of Congress compel a private individual to give testimony needed to enable Congress to exercise its legislative function provided for under the Constitution?

History of the Case

The Senate was investigating actions by the attorney general, the executive official in charge of running the Department of Justice. The committee of senators in charge of the investigation summoned Mally Daugherty, who was the brother of the attorney general and the president of a bank, to testify before the committee. After the witness ignored the subpoena, a warrant was issued for his arrest. The witness was eventually taken into custody by John J. McGrain, the deputy sergeant at arms for the U.S. Senate, with the purpose of bringing him before the investigating committee. After being arrested, the witness petitioned a federal district court for a writ of habeas corpus, an order commanding his release from unlawful detention.

Summary of Arguments

The appellant, John J. McGrain, argued that the houses of Congress had the power to investigate to aid their legislative function. He argued that compelling witness testimony and the production of evidence was part of this investigatory power. Specifically, appellant argued that this particular investigation was legislative in character and thus the investigation was lawful.

Mally S. Daugherty, the appellee, argued that the investigation was judicial in character, not legislative, and Congress only has the power to try a person in impeachment proceedings. Further, Daugherty argued that when Congress is acting in its legislative capacity, it lacks the power to arrest persons and compel testimony.

The Court—no dissenting opinion—recognizes that there is no provision in the Constitution which expressly grants Congress (House and Senate) the power to make investigations and exact testimony. The Court finds, however, that the power to secure needed information is so far incidental to the power to legislate as to be an implied power of a legislature. Historically, this implied power has been used in the British Parliament,

the pre–American Revolution colonies, the post-Revolution Congress, and state legislatures.

Decision

Either the House of Representatives, the Senate, or committees from each house have the power to hold a witness in contempt for ignoring its summons or refusing to answer its inquiries.

Aftermath

The Court later acknowledged the importance of investigatory powers in the legislative process.

Significance

The Court's decision in McGrain confirmed the ability of Congress to conduct investigations and it indicated that the Court would not find fault with inquiries into subjects upon which Congress may properly legislate.

Related Cases

Kilbourn v. Thompson, 103 U.S. 168 (1880)

Watkins v. United States, 354 U.S. 178 (1957)

Recommended Reading

Barth, Alan. *When Congress Investigates*. New York: Public Affairs Committee, 1955.

Eberling, Ernest J. *Congressional Investigations: A Study of the Origin and Development of the Power of Congress to Investigate and Punish for Contempt*. New York: Octagon Books, 1973.

Case Title: *Missouri v. Holland*

Legal Citations: 252 U.S. 416; 40 S.Ct. 382; 64 L.Ed. 641

Year of Decision: 1920

Key Issues

May the federal government override a state's authority to regulate activities within its boundaries under the guise of the treaty power granted in the Constitution?

HISTORY OF THE CASE

The United States and Great Britain proclaimed a treaty on December 8, 1916, for the protection of migratory birds as they traveled between the United States and Canada. The Migratory Bird Treaty Act was enacted on July 3, 1918, to give effect to the treaty. The act prohibited the killing, capturing, or selling of the migratory birds included in the terms of the treaty except as permitted by regulations compatible with those terms.

Missouri sought to prevent the U.S. game warden, Ray P. Holland, from enforcing the Act. The U.S. District Court for the Western District of Missouri dismissed the action on the ground that the act was constitutional.

SUMMARY OF ARGUMENTS

The United States argued that Article 2, section 2 of the U.S. Constitution delegated to the federal government the express power to make treaties and that Article 6 made such treaties, along with the Constitution and laws in pursuance thereof, the supreme law of the land.

Missouri argued that the act infringed upon its sovereign rights under the Tenth Amendment to the Constitution. Missouri also argued that the federal government should not be allowed to legislate, under the guise of the treaty power, what it could not legislate directly. Missouri also argued that its exclusive authority to regulate the killing and selling of the migratory birds derived from its ownership of those birds.

DECISION

Justice Holmes wrote the opinion of the Court that the Migratory Bird Treaty Act was a permissible exercise of federal authority. The Court noted that a prior act of Congress that attempted to regulate the killing of migratory birds, but which did not conform to a treaty entered into by the United States, had been held unconstitutional. Nevertheless, the Court declared that acts of Congress are the supreme law of the land when they conformed to the Constitution and that treaties are such law when made under the authority of the United States. The Court observed that "there may be matters of the sharpest exigency for the national well-being that an act of Congress could not deal with but that a treaty followed by such an act could; and it is not lightly to be assumed

that, in matters requiring national action, 'a power which must belong to and somewhere reside in every civilized government' is not to be found." Thus, the treaty and correlative act were "binding within the territorial limits of the States as [it was] elsewhere throughout the dominion of the United States."

The Court further observed that, while the state may regulate the killing and sale of birds by its inhabitants, wild birds are not anyone's possession. The transitory nature of the migratory birds at issue provided the basis for the transnational protection of the birds in the first place.

AFTERMATH

Holland helped to delineate the lines of federal authority with regard to international relations. Subsequent cases have continuously recognized the expanded authority of the federal government when dealing with questions of international importance.

SIGNIFICANCE

The *Holland* decision widened the scope of authority for the federal government. Justice Holmes's opinion particularly addressed the ability of the federal government to deal with issues of international importance that the government would be unable to legislate and regulate in the absence of a treaty.

RELATED CASES

Dames & Moore v. Regan, 453 U.S. 654 (1981)

Reid v. Covert, 354 U.S. 1 (1957)

Santovincenzo v. Egan, 284 U.S. 30 (1931)

United States v. Belmont, 301 U.S. 324 (1937)

RECOMMENDED READING

Charles A. Lofgren, Missouri v. Holland *in Historical Perspective*, Supreme Court Review 77 (1975).

Case Title: *Perez v. Brownell*

Legal Citation: 356 U.S. 44

Year of Decision: 1958

KEY ISSUES

May Congress repeal a person's U.S. citizenship under the foreign affairs power for voting in another country?

HISTORY OF THE CASE

Perez was born in Texas in 1909, moved to Mexico about 10 years later with his parents, and lived there until 1943. In 1928 he was informed that he was born in Texas. During World War II, he knew that male U.S. citizens were under an obligation to register for the draft, but he did not register. He came to the United States in 1943 and 1944 as an alien railroad laborer. Then, in 1947, he applied for admission to the United States as a citizen. He was not allowed in on the grounds that he had expatriated himself by evading military service and by voting in Mexico. He entered the United States in 1952 claiming to be a native-born Mexican, and he was later deported in 1953 for being an illegal alien. He sued the attorney general in 1954 in a U.S. district court. The court found that Perez had lost his U.S. citizenship through the Nationality Act of 1940, which stated that a U.S. citizen would lose his citizenship by voting in a political election in a foreign state. The Ninth Circuit Court of Appeals affirmed, and the Supreme Court agreed to review the case.

SUMMARY OF ARGUMENTS

Perez argued that he was born in the United States, which made him a U.S. citizen under the Fourteenth Amendment, and that Congress was overstepping its power by passing the law that took away his citizenship.

The attorney general argued that Congress, under its implied power over foreign affairs, was authorized to pass the law.

DECISION

Justice Frankfurter delivered the opinion of the Court that Congress did have the authority to pass the Nationality Act of 1940. While the powers of Congress are largely enumerated ones, it does have an implied power over foreign affairs. This power is derived from the power over foreign commerce (Article 1, section 8, clause 8) and the necessary and proper clause (Article 1, section 8, clause 18) of the Constitution. These two clauses give Congress the power to deal with foreign relations with the purpose of avoiding embarrassment in that capacity. The Court looked at whether there was a reasonable relationship between the means and the end. The Court found that Congress was justified because the withdrawal of citizenship for voting in a foreign nation is an acceptable means for carrying out its foreign relations power and avoiding embarrassment.

Chief Justice Warren and Justices Black and Douglas dissented on the ground that a citizen's intent to relinquish citizenship should have been the determinative factor of whether citizenship should be removed. The majority had said that the action had to be voluntary, but intent did not matter. The dissent pointed out the strong rights guaranteeing citizenship and protecting it from government power under the Fourteenth Amendment and stated that citizenship should not be taken away without intent by the actor.

AFTERMATH

Perez was overruled in 1967 by *Afroyim v. Rusk*, which held that a U.S. citizen had to have the intent to relinquish his citizenship in order to lose it. Congress had neither express nor implied power to take away the citizenship of people guaranteed to them through the Fourteenth Amendment.

SIGNIFICANCE

Perez upheld the divestiture of citizenship based on the conduct of voting in a foreign election. Chief Justice Warren's dissent sparked the change in the view of denationalizing citizens.

While *Afroyim* is still good law, it was a 5-4 decision of the Court. Whether intent is a necessary element to relinquish U.S. citizenship may be a question that the Court may decide differently in the future.

RELATED CASES

Afroyim v. Rusk, 387 U.S. 253 (1967)

Zschernig v. Miller, 389 U.S. 429 (1968)

RECOMMENDED READING

Cable, John L. *Decisive Decisions of United States Citizenship.* Charlottesville, Va.: The Michie Co., 1967.

Philip B. Kurland, *The Supreme Court, 1963 Term: Forward—Equal in Origin and Equal in Title to the*

Legislative and Executive Branches of the Government, 78 Harvard Law Review 143–176 (November 1964).

Case Title: *Powell v. McCormack*

Legal Citations: 395 U.S. 486; 89 S.Ct. 144; 23 L.Ed. 2d 491

Year of Decision: 1969

KEY ISSUES

May the House of Representatives refuse to seat a member of Congress who meets all requirements but who has committed other infractions?

HISTORY OF THE CASE

Adam Clayton Powell, Jr., an elected congressman from the Harlem neighborhood of New York City, challenged the House's refusal to seat him. The refusal came after one of its committees found that Powell had dodged the process of the New York courts, had wrongfully diverted House funds, and made false reports to a House committee. Powell sued for a declaratory judgment that the refusal to seat him was unconstitutional; the House defense was on the ground that Article 1, section 5 of the U.S. Constitution gave the House the sole right to determine what qualifications are required for membership. Powell argued that the clause gives the House only the right to determine whether a person possesses the "standing" qualifications of age, citizenship, and residency as set out in Article 1, section 2 of the Constitution.

SUMMARY OF ARGUMENTS

The petitioner, Adam Clayton Powell, Jr., argued that it was a violation of the Constitution to exclude him from membership in the House of Representatives when he met the membership qualifications and had been duly elected. Specifically, Powell argued that his exclusion violated the constitutional provision prohibiting bills of attainder and ex post facto laws and violated the due process clause of the Fifth Amendment.

The respondent, John W. McCormack, argued that the federal courts lacked jurisdiction to review the House of Representatives' exclusion of Powell and the action taken by the House of Representatives was a proper exercise of its power to determine its members' qualifications.

The case was not moot even though Powell was seated in a subsequent session of Congress. Therefore, the federal courts had jurisdiction and the suit was not "nonjusticable."

Chief Justice Warren delivered the opinion for the Court, saying Article 1, section 5 was a grant to Congress of the right only to determine the three standing qualifications for membership in the House of Representatives as set out by the Constitution were met. Congress had not been given the right to impose additional qualifications for membership. Powell met the qualifications for membership; therefore, the issue of the court's ability to review is still not resolved. The Court found the House was without power to exclude Powell as he was elected by the voters and was not disqualified by any provision in the constitution.

AFTERMATH

The public became concerned about the impeachment process (criminal proceedings against public officers). The feeling was that Congress and the courts could not deal with misconduct.

SIGNIFICANCE

The decision affirms that Congress cannot alter the qualifications for serving in Congress found in the Constitution.

RELATED CASES

United States v. Nixon, 418 U.S. 683 (1974)

Alcee Hastings v. United States Senate, 492 U.S. 930 (1989)

RECOMMENDED READING

Berger, Raoul. *Executive Privilege: A Constitutional Myth.* Cambridge, Mass.: Harvard University Press, 1974.

Lewis Donald Asper, et al., *Comments on* Powell v. McCormack, 17 UCLA Law Review 1 (1969).

Case Title: *Profitt v. Florida*

Legal Citations: 428 U.S. 242; 96 S.Ct. 2960; 49 L.Ed. 2d 913

Year of Decision: 1976

KEY ISSUES

Does the imposition of the death sentence for the crime of murder under Florida law violate the Eighth and Fourteenth Amendments?

HISTORY OF THE CASE

Mr. and Mrs. Joel Ronnie Medgebow went to a party, returned to their apartment, and went to bed. Mrs. Medgebow woke up to her husband's moaning and found a knife in his chest. A man on that side of the bed hit her and fled. She removed the knife from her husband's chest and called the police.

Charles Profitt was indicted and tried for the murder of Joel Medgebow. At trial, a witness testified that she heard Profitt tell his wife that he killed a man while committing a burglary. Profitt was convicted by a jury of first degree murder and sentenced to death. The sentence and conviction were unanimously affirmed by the Florida Supreme Court.

Florida law provides for two separate hearings in capital felonies. After deciding guilt or innocence, the jury determines whether the imposition of the death penalty is supported by aggravated circumstances that outweigh any mitigating circumstances. This is a nonbinding verdict, as the judge also weighs these same issues and then decides whether or not to impose the death penalty. After a sentence of death, an appeal to the Florida Supreme Court is automatic.

SUMMARY OF ARGUMENTS

Profitt argued that the death penalty was cruel and unusual punishment under any circumstance and it violated the Eighth and Fourteenth Amendments. Profitt also argued that the Florida sentencing procedures were arbitrary and capricious and the statutory aggravating and mitigating factors were vague and overbroad. Finally, Profitt argued that the Florida Supreme Court's review of death sentences was subjective and unpredictable.

The state of Florida argued that the capital sentencing procedures gave trial judges specific guidance to determine whether the death penalty should be imposed and death penalty decisions were reviewed to ensure consistency.

DECISION

Justice Stewart concluded that the imposition of the death sentence is not cruel and unusual punishment in violation of the Eighth and Fourteenth Amendments. He found the Florida procedures for the imposition of the death penalty to be constitutional. Florida judges were given specific guidelines to adhere to in imposing either the death sentence or life imprisonment. These guidelines are clear and do not lack merit. The penalty is not unconstitutional because it provides for discretion, judicial judgment based on the circumstances. The terms of the sentencing process are not broad.

Florida's law for imposing the death sentence by providing for a bifurcated sentencing hearing and the weighing of mitigating and aggravating circumstances with an advisory finding from the jury does not violate the Eighth and Fourteenth Amendments.

AFTERMATH

The Supreme Court reviewed the capital punishment statutes of four other states the same day it decided *Profitt*. The Court found three of the five state statutes to be constitutional. Many state legislatures attempted to comply with the direction given by the Court in FURMAN V. GEORGIA (1972), a case in which the Court found the imposition of the death penalty to be in violation of the Eighth Amendment due to the arbitrariness of its application, to make their capital punishment procedures comply with the Eighth Amendment.

SIGNIFICANCE

The *Profitt* decision indicated that a sentence imposing the death penalty must be arrived at through the application of factors used to direct a court's discretion and reduce the possibility of an arbitrary action.

RELATED CASES

Godfrey v. Georgia, 446 U.S. 420 (1980)

Gregg v. Georgia, 428 U.S. 153 (1976)

Jurek v. Texas, 428 U.S. 262 (1976)

RECOMMENDED READING

The Supreme Court, 1975 Term, 90 Harvard Law Review 63 (1976).

Case Title: *Prune Yard Shopping Center v. Robins*

Legal Citation: 447 U.S. 74

Year of Decision: 1980

KEY ISSUES

Do state constitutional provisions that permit individuals to collect petition signatures on private property that is open to the public violate the owner's property rights under the Fifth and Fourteenth Amendments? Does the state constitution violate the property owner's free speech rights under the First and Fourteenth Amendments?

HISTORY OF THE CASE

In 1974, a group of Campbell, California, high school students opposed a particular United Nations resolution condemning Zionism as a form of racism and discrimination. The students traveled to the local Prune Yard shopping center. In the corner of a parking lot, the students set up a card table and handed out leaflets and collected signatures for a petition they intended to send to the president and members of Congress. Their actions were peaceful and orderly and did not offend the Prune Yard's patrons. Nevertheless, the Prune Yard did not permit such activity. A security guard informed the students that their conduct violated center regulations, and the group left the premises. They filed this lawsuit seeking to stop the center from denying them access to circulate their petitions.

The state trial court ruled that neither California nor U.S. law entitled due students to exercise their asserted free speech rights on the shopping center owner's private property. The appellate court affirmed this decision. The California Supreme Court reversed, holding that the California Constitution protects "speech and petitioning, reasonably exercised, in shopping centers even when the centers are privately owned." The court's ruling allowed the students to carry on their activity. The Prune Yard owner appealed to the U.S. Supreme Court.

SUMMARY OF ARGUMENTS

Prune Yard argued three principles to the Supreme Court. First, it asserted that previous Court decisions prevented states from requiring a private shopping center owner to provide access to persons exercising their state-guaranteed free speech and petition rights when adequate alternatives were available. Second, the Prune Yard argued that a property owner's rights are rooted in the Fifth Amendment guarantee against the taking of property without just compensation. The Fourteenth Amendment guarantee against taking property without due process of law further incorporates this right. Forcing a property owner to grant access to others amounts to taking the owner's property without compensating him for it, the Prune Yard reasoned. Finally, the Prune Yard argued that the state cannot compel a property owner to use his property as a forum for the speech of others without violating the owner's First Amendment right.

The students, on the other hand, argued that their First Amendment rights to free speech and association allowed them access to circulate petitions and materials on Prune Yard property.

DECISION

The Court rejected all three Prune Yard arguments that the students' actions violated the shopping center's private property and free speech rights. With regard to the first argument, the Court reiterated and clarified its 1972 *LLOYD CORP. V. TANNER* decision. Justice Rehnquist, delivering the Court's opinion, repeated *Lloyd's* finding that property does not lose its private character merely because its owner invites the public to use it. Justice Rehnquist continued, however, that this decision does not on its own force limit a state's police power to adopt reasonable—that is, constitutional—restrictions on private property. Furthermore, *Lloyd* does not restrict a state from adopting in its own constitution individual liberties more expansive than those conferred by the U.S. Constitution. This reasoning, the Justice wrote, supports upholding the California Constitution's guarantee to "freely speak, write and publish" one's opinions. The same reasoning also supports the right of the students to "petition [their] government for redress of grievances."

On Prune Yard's second contention, the majority opinion agreed that an essential stick in the bundle of property rights is the right to exclude others from one's property. However, the Court ruled that for a property owner to make a successful charge that state laws allow the taking of property without just compensation and without due process, the owner must prove that the laws "force some people alone to bear public burdens which, in all fairness and justice, should be borne by the public as a whole." In examining the California free speech provision, the Court found no infringement of property rights at the shopping center. It determined that the students' activities did not interfere with the value or use of shopping center property. The Court also decided that the Prune Yard owner could reasonably restrict the activities to prevent interference with the normal commercial functions of the center. Concluding that no property rights are absolute and construing California's constitutional guarantees as lawful, the Court found little merit in Prune Yard's Fifth and Fourteenth Amendment arguments that it had been denied its property without due process of law.

The Court also dispensed with the Prune Yard's third argued point, that the California Supreme Court's ruling essentially forced the Prune Yard owner to use its property as a forum for others' speech. It did so by distinguishing the earlier cases upon which Prune Yard based these arguments. In *Wooley v. Maynard* (1977), the government itself prescribed the message, required it to be displayed openly on the owner's personal and daily used property, and refused to permit him to take any measures to cover up the message. To the contrary, in the Prune Yard situation, there existed neither a specific state-dictated message nor solely private, "as part of . . . daily

life" property, nor edict that the owner not disclaim the message expressed by the students. In this case, the speech conveyed was personal to the students, and the property on which the message was expressed though private was generally open to the public. Additionally, the property owner could expressly disavow any connection or sponsorship of the students' views by simply posting a sign in the area where the speakers or handbillers stand. The Rehnquist opinion concluded that no First Amendment infringement existed.

AFTERMATH

The present rule is clear: the First Amendment grants no citizen the right to express him- or herself in shopping centers over that property owner's objection. Although there is no federally guaranteed right to access to privately owned property, states themselves may broaden the federal free speech guarantee and allow such activity. It is not clear whether the same rule applies to the business district of a modern-day company town or to other types of privately owned communities.

SIGNIFICANCE

Prune Yard's result left it to the individual state supreme courts to resolve future conflicts between free speech rights and property rights. State supreme courts subsequently have arrived at different decisions. Some courts hold that shopping centers can deny access, whereas other courts hold that they cannot. Abortion clinics, office complexes, private universities, residential complexes, and migrant labor camps provide additional and analogous situations for courts to weigh rights of private property and public expression.

RELATED CASES

Lloyd Corp. v. Tanner, 407 U.S. 551 (1972)

Pacific Gas & Elec. Co. v. P.U.C. of California, 475 U.S. 1 (1986)

Wooley v. Maynard, 430 U.S. 705 (1977)

RECOMMENDED READING

Laurence M. Cohen, *Pruneyard Shopping Center v. Robins: Past, Present and Future,* 57 Chicago-Kent Law Review 373 (1981).

Richard A. Epstein, *Takings, Exclusivity and Speech: The Legacy of* Pruneyard v. Robins, 64 University of Chicago Law Review 21 (1997).

Maurice F. Kirchofer III, *Constitutional Law–Freedom of Speech–New Jersey State Constitution Requires Privately Owned Shopping Malls to Allow Access for Expressional Leafletting Subject to the Owner's Reasonable Time, Place and Manner Restrictions*—New Jersey Coalition against War in the Middle East v. J. M. B. Realty Corp., 138 N. J. 326, 650 A. 2d 757 (1994), Note, 27 Seton Hall Law Review 289 (1996).

James M. McCauley, *Transforming the Privately Owned Shopping Center into a Public Forum*: Pruneyard Shopping Center v. Robins, 15 University of Richmond Law Review 699 (1981).

Ian J. McPheron, *From the Ground to the Sky: The Continuing Conflict between Private Property Rights and Free Speech Rights on the Shopping Center Front Seventeen Years after* Pruneyard, 16 Northern Illinois University Law Review 717 (1996).

Cordelia S. Munroe, *Constitutional Law–Free Speech–Granting Access to Private Shopping Center Property for Free Speech Purposes on the Basis of a State Constitutional Provision Does Not Violate the Shopping Center Owner's Federal Constitutional Property Rights or First Amendment Free Speech Rights*, Pruneyard Shopping Center v. Robins, *100 S.Ct. 2035*, 64 Marquette Law Review 507 (1981).

Stephen G. Opperwall, *Shopping for a Public Forum*: Pruneyard Shopping Center v. Robins, *Publicly Used Private Property, and Constitutionally Protected Speech*, 21 Santa Clara Law Review 801 (1981).

Case Title: *Pulley v. Harris*

Legal Citation: 465 U.S. 37

Year of Decision: 1984

KEY ISSUES

Must the highest court of each state that has capital punishment review each death sentence to ascertain whether it is proportionate against the background of other capital sentences?

HISTORY OF THE CASE

Harris, on parole from a homicide conviction, decided to rob a bank with his younger brother and steal a car to escape from the robbery scene. They kidnapped two 16-year-old boys from the parking lot of a hamburger stand and made them drive to a secluded area. Harris then shot the two teens to prevent them from being witnesses and ate their hamburgers. Harris and his brother then used the car to rob the bank, but they were followed and apprehended.

Harris was convicted of two counts of murder and was sentenced to death after the jury found special circumstances legitimating consideration of the death penalty (either the fact that the victims were killed because they were potential witnesses or the fact that they were killed during a kidnapping). The California Supreme Court affirmed the convictions and capital sentences. Harris petitioned a federal district court for habeas corpus on several grounds, including proportionality, but was denied. However, the Ninth Circuit stayed Harris's execution while it reviewed his arguments, and ordered the writ of habeas corpus to be granted unless the California Supreme Court conducted a proportionality review: a review of the proportion of death penalty punishments imposed on others convicted of similar crimes.

SUMMARY OF ARGUMENTS

The state of California and Warden Pulley argued that the Supreme Court had never required proportionality review, and that California state law did not provide for it. Additionally, they argued that the Eighth Amendment, which prohibits cruel and unusual punishment, does not require a review of proportionality.

Harris argued that proportionality should be a key element in appellate review of capital sentences to protect against arbitrary and capricious sentences. He also argued that because California gives juries and courts broad discretion in applying the death penalty, a proportionality review should be constitutionally mandated.

DECISION

Justice White delivered the opinion of the Court, which held that proportionality was not mandatory in order to comply with the Eighth Amendment. While mandatory appellate review was deemed necessary to assure that the sentence was not arbitrary or capricious, a proportionality review was not the only means of coming to that conclusion. Also, the Court held that the writ of habeas corpus was improperly granted because it is supposed to be used only when someone is imprisoned against the Constitution or the laws or treaties of the United States, not on a perceived error of state law.

Justice Stevens concurred, stating that meaningful appellate review of capital sentences was necessary, but proportionality did not necessarily have to be a part of that review.

Justices Brennan and Marshall dissented, stating that case law demonstrated that proportionality review was a way to eliminate irrationality in capital sentences. Their view was that the death penalty was cruel and unusual punishment in every circumstance, but in the event that a state adopts capital punishment, proportionality should be used to guard against an arbitrary decision.

AFTERMATH

The Court has continued to follow its holding that proportionality is not a mandatory element in the appellate review of death penalty cases. This has propelled some states, such as New Jersey, to amend their capital sentencing statutes. New Jersey's old statute made a proportionality review mandatory; it was amended to include a proportionality review only if insisted upon by the defendant.

SIGNIFICANCE

The Court, in deciding that the Eighth Amendment did not mandate a proportionality review, gave considerable discretion to the states to set their own standards in capital sentence appeals.

RELATED CASES

Coker v. Georgia, 433 U.S. 584 (1977)

Emmund v. Florida, 458 U.S. 782 (1982)

Furman v. Georgia, 408 U.S. 238 (1972)

Gregg v. Georgia, 428 U.S. 153 (1976)

Jurek v. Texas, 428 U.S. 262 (1976)

Proffitt v. Florida, 428 U.S. 242 (1976)

Solem v. Helm, 463 U.S. 277 (1983)

Zant v. Stevens, 462 U.S. 862 (1983)

RECOMMENDED READING

Cheryl Cook, *Does the Crime Fit the Punishment,* 6 Criminal Justice Journal 333–343 (spring 1983).

Case Title: *Ex Parte Quirin*

Legal Citation: 317 U.S. 1

Year of Decision: 1942

KEY ISSUES

Does the president have the power under the Constitution to order enemies captured on American soil to be tried by a military tribunal without the protection of the Fifth and Sixth Amendments to the U.S. Constitution?

HISTORY OF THE CASE

All the petitioners in this case (totaling seven) were born in Germany; all had lived in the United States, but returned to Germany between 1933 and 1941. All but one of them became citizens of the German Reich, with which the United States was at war. The government found that the one who was not a citizen of the German Reich had elected to maintain his German allegiance and by his conduct renounced or abandoned his U.S. citizenship.

After the declaration of war between the United States and the German Reich, petitioners received training at a sabotage school near Berlin, Germany, where they were instructed on the use of explosives and in methods of secret writing. Thereafter, petitioners proceeded from Germany to a seaport in occupied France where they boarded two German submarines. One submarine carried three of them across the Atlantic to Long Island, New York; the other took four of them to Ponte Vedra Beach, Florida. They all came ashore during the hours of darkness, carrying with them a supply of explosives, fuses, and incendiary and timing devices. They all wore German marine infantry uniforms or parts of such uniforms, which they immediately buried on arrival. The two groups then proceeded in civilian dress to Jacksonville, Florida, and then to various places in the United States. All were taken into custody in New York or Chicago by agents of the Federal Bureau of Investigation. All had received instructions in Germany from an officer of the German High Command to destroy war industries and war facilities in the United States.

SUMMARY OF ARGUMENTS

The petitioner's main contention was that the president had no statutory or constitutional authority to order them tried by military tribunal for the offenses with which they were charged. They argued that they were entitled to be tried in the civil courts with the safeguards, including trial by jury, that the Fifth and Sixth Amendments guarantee to all persons charged in such courts with criminal offenses. Respondent argued that the military commission had jurisdiction over the prisoners and the determination of the president regarding necessity of trial by military tribunal should not be lightly disregarded.

DECISION

Chief Justice Stone delivered the opinion of the Court, which began its analysis by declaring that "Congress and the President, like the courts, possess no power not derived from the Constitution." In other words, if the Constitution does not give Congress or the president a certain power, then no such power exists. The Court then provided an overview of Congress and the president's power with respect to war. Under Article 1 of the Constitution, Congress has the power to provide for the common defense, to raise and support armies, to declare war, and to define and punish offenses against the law of nations. The Constitution authorizes Congress: "To make all Laws which shall be necessary and proper for carrying into Execution" these enumerated powers. Under Article 2 of the Constitution, the president is granted the "executive power" and has the duty to "take Care that the Laws be faithfully executed." Article 2 also makes the president "Commander in Chief of the Army and Navy" and empowers him (or her) to appoint and commission officers of the United States.

On July 2, 1942, the president appointed a Military Commission to try the petitioners in this case for offenses against the law of war and the articles of war. On the same day, the president also made a proclamation that gave the military tribunals jurisdiction to try the case and closed the petitioners' access to the civil courts.

The Court held that the president's action was constitutionally authorized. The power was given to him by Congress through the articles of war and by the President's role as the commander in chief of the military. The Court held that the Fifth and Sixth Amendments do not apply to military tribunals. Therefore, the petitioners were not entitled to their protection.

AFTERMATH

The drama of the Nazi saboteurs that began in Germany ended in the electric chair at the District of Columbia jail. A new drama ensued: Although the case was a victory for the war effort against the Axis powers, the Court's decision put individual liberties in great jeopardy. This threat was realized in 1942 when the Court stood by as the army removed loyal Japanese Americans from their homes on the West Coast and hauled them off to inland concentration camps. Edward S. Corwin, an authority on U.S. constitutional law and theory, described these cases as "the most dramatic invasion of the rights of citizens of the United States by their own government . . . in the history of our nation."

Another such invasion of individual liberties under the banner of war—this time the cold war—occurred in 1951 when the Court upheld the conviction of 11 of the top leaders of the Communist Party of the United States. According to Professor Michael R. Belknap, "[F]or more than a decade after the summer of 1942 the judicial attitudes that led to the decision in *Ex Parte Quirin* continued to dominate the Supreme Court and to endanger the constitutional rights of the American people." It was not until Chief Justice Warren took charge in 1952 that the Supreme Court "shook off its total war mentality and displayed an invigorated concern for civil liberties."

SIGNIFICANCE

This case demonstrates the broad powers that the Constitution grants to Congress and the president during a time of war. The Supreme Court decided that the claims of a government waging total war outweighed the individual rights of the Nazi saboteurs.

RELATED CASES

Dennis v. United States, 341 U.S. 494 (1951)

Ex Parte Milligan, 4 Wall. 2, 18 L.Ed. 281 (1884)

Hirabayashi v. United States, 320 U.S. 81 (1943)

Korematsu v. United States, 323 U.S. 214 (1944)

RECOMMENDED READING

Michael R. Belknap, *The Supreme Court Goes to War: The Meanings and Implications of the Nazi Saboteur Case,* 89 Military Law Review 59–95 (summer 1980).

Robert Cushman, *The Nazi Saboteur Case,* 28 Cornell Law Quarterly 54–65 (1942).

Case Title: *Scott v. Illinois*

Legal Citations: 440 U.S. 367; 99 S.Ct. 1158; 59 L.Ed. 2d 383

Year of Decision: 1979

KEY ISSUES

Does a criminal defendant have the right to assistance of appointed counsel in his defense whenever imprisonment is an *authorized* penalty?

HISTORY OF THE CASE

Aubrey Scott was convicted of shoplifting merchandise valued at less than $150. The applicable Illinois statute set the maximum penalty for this offense at a $500 fine, one year in jail, or both. After the bench trial, Scott was fined $50 but was not sentenced to prison.

Scott ultimately appealed to the Illinois Supreme Court, however, claiming he had a right to a state-appointed counsel under the Sixth and Fourteenth Amendments. The Sixth Amendment provides that in all criminal prosecutions, the accused shall have the assistance of counsel for his defense. The Fourteenth Amendment provides that no person shall be denied liberty without due process of law. The Illinois Supreme Court rejected Scott's contention, concluding that the Constitution does not require a state trial court to appoint counsel for a criminal defendant when imprisonment is an authorized penalty. The U.S. Supreme Court agreed to resolve this issue.

SUMMARY OF ARGUMENTS

Scott's attorney relied on a 1972 Supreme Court case (*Arbersinger v. Hamlin*) that extended the constitutional right to counsel in misdemeanor cases if imprisonment is *imposed.* He contended that this case left open the issue of whether a constitutional right to counsel exists where imprisonment is authorized, but not necessarily imposed.

The State argued that *Arbersinger* turned on whether a criminal defendant would suffer a "loss of liberty," not upon the classification of the offense and its attendant penalties. Thus, the state maintained that a criminal defendant has a constitutional right to a state-appointed counsel only where actual, not merely authorized, imprisonment occurs.

DECISION

The Court held, in a 5-4 decision, that Scott was not entitled to appointed counsel. They believed that the Sixth Amendment, as to misdemeanor charges, requires only that no indigent criminal defendant be *sentenced* to imprisonment unless the state has afforded him the right to assistance of appointed counsel. Thus, where there is no imprisonment, the right to counsel does not attach in misdemeanor cases. The Court noted that the "actual imprisonment standard" had proved reasonably workable, and that any change would create confusion and unpredictable results in the 50 states.

The dissenters argued that the plain language of the Sixth Amendment and the Court's precedents compel the conclusion that Scott's conviction violated the Sixth and Fourteenth Amendments. They reasoned that the Sixth Amendment, by its terms, applied to all criminal prosecutions, regardless of whether a loss of liberty resulted. Additionally, they noted that authorized, not actual, penalties have been used consistently by the Court as the true measure of the seriousness of offenses.

AFTERMATH

Subsequent due process opinions referred to the loss of liberty as the most significant element in establishing a due process right to appointed counsel. Thus, the Court has continued to use the actual imprisonment standard to assess the right to state-appointed counsel. However, states have the option of providing appointed counsel for all misdemeanor defendants. At least where the misdemeanors are not punishable only by fine, many states exercise that option.

SIGNIFICANCE

Practical problems of providing counsel for all misdemeanor charges certainly influenced the Court's holding. Typically, misdemeanor cases carry a caseload 10 times as large as felony cases. It appears that when a judge decides against appointing counsel to a misdemeanor defendant under the belief that he will receive only a fine, the judge may not later sentence him to prison without committing reversible error.

RELATED CASES

Argersinger v. Hamlin, 407 U.S. 25 (1972)

Gideon v. Wainwright, 372 U.S. 335 (1963)

Nichols v. United States, 511 U.S. 738 (1994)

RECOMMENDED READING

Paul H. Abramson, *Constitutional Right to Counsel: Another Anachronism When Handed down,* 31 University of Florida Law Review 786–798 (summer 1979).

Ralph Ruebner et al., *Shaking the Foundation of* Gideon: *A Critique of Nichols in Overruling* Baldasar v. Illinois, 25 Hofstra Law Review 507–560 (winter 1996).

***

Case Title: *Selective Service System v. Minn. Public Interest Research Group*

Legal Citation: 468 U.S. 841

Year of Decision: 1984

KEY ISSUES

Does the denial of federal higher education assistance to male students who have failed to register for the draft as required by law violate the Constitution?

HISTORY OF THE CASE

The Military Selective Service Act allows the president to require the registration of every male citizen and resident alien between the ages of 18 and 26 for the purposes of conscription. The act also imposes a criminal penalty for failing to register. The Department of Defense Authorization Act of 1983 became law in 1982. Section 1113 of the act provided that men who failed to register for the draft as required by law would be ineligible for any form of higher education assistance. It also provided that in order to qualify for federal financial aid, men had to file a statement of compliance with the Military Selective Service Act with their university or college.

The validity of this statute was challenged in two ways. First, the plaintiffs claimed section 1113 was a bill of attainder, which is prohibited by Article 1 of the Constitution. A bill of attainder is a law that determines guilt and inflicts punishment on an identifiable individual without the protections of a judicial trial. Second, the plaintiffs claimed that the act violated the Fifth Amendment. They argued that the requirement that men file a statement of compliance with the Military Selective Service Act in order to receive financial aid would force them to incriminate themselves. The district court concluded that the statute was an unconstitutional bill of attainder. They also ruled that the statute violated the constitutional privilege against compelled self-incrimination as outlined in the Fifth Amendment of the Constitution.

SUMMARY OF ARGUMENTS

The Selective Service System argued that section 1113 was not a bill of attainder because it did not refer specifically to past conduct, which an easily identifiable person could have engaged in and would be powerless to change, but instead regulated present and future conduct. They also argued that section 1113 was not a bill of attainder because the purpose of section 1113 was not to punish individuals nor dispense with the judicial process in any case that required a judicial hearing. Selective Service System argued that section 1113 did not compel self-incrimination in violation of the Fifth Amendment because if students do not wish to supply registration information, they need not apply for aid.

The Minnesota Public Interest Research Group argued that the statute was a bill of attainder because it determined guilt of an identifiable person and punished without the benefit of a judicial trial. They also argued that the statue violated the Fifth Amendment because students who needed financial aid but had not registered for the draft as required by law were compelled to disclose the fact that they had not registered in order to qualify for financial aid.

DECISION

The Supreme Court ruled that the statute was not a bill of attainder because the statute clearly gave students 30 days after receiving notice that they were ineligible for financial aid to register for the draft and qualify for aid. The statute did not single out people and make them ineligible for financial aid based on past conduct. The statute's purpose was to encourage registration by those who were required to register but had not. The section also did not inflict punishment for failure to register with the draft. It did not even deprive appellees of the financial aid benefits permanently, since the statute left open perpetually the possibility of qualifying for aid upon registration with Selective Service. Conditioning receipt of financial aid was a rational means to improve compliance with the Selective Service registration requirements.

The Court also held that section 1113 did not violate the Fifth Amendment privilege against compelled self-incrimination. Students were aware that they would be denied financial aid if they applied for it without having registered for the draft. They were not compelled to seek aid. Also, students were not required to list the date of their draft registration on their application for financial aid. The fact that they would have to reveal to Selective Service that they had not registered on time did not violate the Fifth Amendment. The students were not denied the opportunity to register for the draft and were not disqualified for financial aid because of asserting a constitutional privilege.

AFTERMATH

This case has not been overruled and is often cited as support for the resolution of issues involving bills of attainder.

SIGNIFICANCE

This decision provided an analytical framework for resolving issues involving bills of attainder.

RELATED CASES

Plaut v. Spendthrift Farm, Inc., 115 S.Ct. 1447 (1995)

Wayte v. U.S., 470 U.S. 598 (1985)

RECOMMENDED READING

Leading Cases of the 1983 Term, 98 Harvard Law Review 87–97 (November 1984).

Pfeffer, Leo. *Religion, State and the Burger Court*. Buffalo, N.Y.: Prometheus Books, 1984.

Rowland L. Young, *Court Upholds Tie between Draft Registration and Aid*, 70 American Bar Association Journal 132–133 (September 1984).

Case Title: *Solem v. Helm*

Legal Citation: 463 U.S. 277

Year of Decision: 1983

KEY ISSUES

Does a mandatory sentence of life without parole imposed against a persistent nonviolent felony offender violate the Eighth Amendment prohibition against cruel and unusual punishment?

HISTORY OF THE CASE

South Dakota had a "three strikes, you're out" provision that required mandatory life in prison with no parole upon conviction of three or more felonies. Jerry Helm pleaded guilty to a felony of passing a forged no-account check in the amount of $100. He had been previously convicted three times for third-degree burglary and one time each for driving while intoxicated, grand larceny, and obtaining money under false pretenses. Helm was sentenced to life in prison without parole. The South Dakota Supreme Court affirmed the sentence. Helm applied for federal habeas corpus relief release from an unlawful imprisonment, which the district court denied. The Eighth Circuit reversed and ordered that the writ be granted unless the court resentenced Helm. The Supreme Court agreed to hear the case because of the importance of the issue.

SUMMARY OF ARGUMENTS

Solem, warden of the South Dakota State Penitentiary, argued that the sentencing law did not fall within the narrow concept of extremely disproportionate punishment because it covers only crimes that are properly punishable as felonies. He also argued that Helm's sentence was not disproportionate in light of his lengthy record and likelihood of recidivism following release.

Helm argued that the Eighth Amendment requires that a life sentence without parole must bear some relationship to the gravity of the crime. The punishment Helm received was as severe as that for murder, first-degree manslaughter, first-degree arson, and kidnapping. The sentence was more severe than that for first-degree rape or robbery. As a result, the punishment could not reasonably contribute to acceptable goals of punishment and was therefore disproportionate and violative of the Eighth Amendment.

DECISION

Justice Powell wrote the majority opinion for the 5-4 decision affirming the Court of Appeals. The Court concluded that some sort of balancing test was required in Eighth Amendment cases involving cruel and unusual punishment. The Court had decided cases in the past using a proportionality approach to the crime and subsequent punishment. If the punishment was disproportionate to the crime, the Eighth Amendment prohibition against cruel and unusual punishment would be violated. The Court found that mandatory life sentences without possibility of parole based on repeated nonviolent felonies indeed violated the Eighth Amendment.

AFTERMATH

After *Solem v. Helm,* punishments must fit the crime or risk being found in violation of the Eighth Amendment.

The Court continues to struggle with the cruel and unusual punishment prohibition of the Eighth Amendment. Several cases have modified the position of the Court yet none seems to be dominant.

SIGNIFICANCE

If a sentence is disproportionate to the crime, it violates the Eighth Amendment.

By requiring a comparison approach to cruel and unusual punishment, the Court leaves itself open to challenges under the Eighth Amendment. This uncertainty, however, makes every sentence in itself constitutional unless decided otherwise.

RELATED CASES

Harmelin v. Michigan, 501 U.S. 957 (1991)

Hutto v. Davis, 454 U.S. 370 (1982)

Rummel v. Estelle, 445 U.S. 263 (1980)

Weems v. U.S., 217 U.S. 349 (1910)

RECOMMENDED READING

Lyndon F. Bittle, *Punitive Damages and the Eighth Amendment: An Analytical Framework for Determining Excessiveness,* 75 California Law Review 1433 (1987).

Steven Grossman, *Proportionality in Non-capital Sentencing: The Supreme Court's Tortured Approach to Cruel and Unusual Punishment,* 84 Kentucky Law Journal 107 (1995).

J. Drew Page, *Cruel and Unusual Punishment and Sodomy Statutes: The Breakdown of the* Solem v. Helm *Test,* 56 University of Chicago Law Review 367 (1989).

Case Title: *Steward Machine Co. v. Davis, Collector of Internal Revenue*

Legal Citations: 301 U.S. 548; 57 S.Ct. 883; 81 L.Ed. 1279

Year of Decision: 1937

KEY ISSUES

Does federal unemployment insurance tax violate the Constitution?

HISTORY OF THE CASE

Based on wages paid, the Social Security Act imposes an tax on employers of eight or more employees. The proceeds go into the General Treasury; however, if a taxpayer has made contributions to a state unemployment fund, that money can be credited against the federal tax, provided state law has satisfied certain criteria. From 1929 to 1936, during the Great Depression, unemployment was extremely high, and the states were unable to give adequately to the indigent. Steward Machine Co. paid the federal tax according to the statute and filed for a refund, asserting that the Social Security Act is unconstitutional.

SUMMARY OF ARGUMENTS

Chas. C. Steward Machine Company, petitioner, argued that the Social Security Act was an invasion of the reserved powers of the states, a denial of due process, and was unreasonable and arbitrary, among other things.

Harwell G. Davis, respondent, argued that the act was a valid exercise of congressional power and the tax imposed was not in violation of the Fifth or Tenth Amendments.

DECISION

A federal unemployment insurance tax statute, which provides for credit for contributions made to state unemployment funds, is valid since Congress enacted it to safeguard its own treasury.

Justice Cardozo wrote for the majority, upholding the Social Security Act. In times of crisis, the use of the nation's monies to help the unemployed and their dependents promotes the general welfare. When Congress passed the Social Security Act in 1935, the unemployment situation was so severe that states could not help their needy citizens. The act was passed to place the states on equal footing as to unemployment insurance, since some states did not provide for it. The funds were not earmarked for a special group but went into the General Treasury. Also, the states did not have to give up any of their sovereignty. The condition that state laws meet Social Security criteria assured that those who need protection will receive it.

Justice Sutherland in his dissent wrote that the act contemplates a surrender by the states to the federal government of state power to administer their own unemployment laws.

AFTERMATH

The Court's decision to uphold the constitutionality of the Social Security Act marked a reversal of the Court's position on New Deal laws, which it had previously struck down.

SIGNIFICANCE

The decision indicated that the Court would allow Congress to coerce states to enact programs benefiting its citizens by threatening to tax or withhold funding.

RELATED CASES

Helvering v. Davis, 301 U.S. 619 (1937)

United States v. Butler, 297 U.S. 1 (1936)

RECOMMENDED READING

Evan H. Caminker, *State Sovereignty and Subordinacy: May Congress Commandeer State Officers to Implement Federal Law?* 95 Columbia Law Review 1001 (1995).

Benjamin Andrew Zelermyer, *Benjamin N. Cardozo: A Directive Force in Legal Science,* 69 Boston University Law Review 213 (1989).

Case Title: *Tileston v. Ullman*

Legal Citations: 318 U.S. 44; 63 S.Ct. 493; 87 L.Ed. 603

Year of Decision: 1943

KEY ISSUES

May a doctor attack the constitutionality of a state anticontraceptive statute on the ground that it prevents him from giving professional advice to his patients?

HISTORY OF THE CASE

A Connecticut doctor challenged a state statute that prohibited giving advice to married women about the use of contraceptives. Specifically, the doctor had three patients whose lives would be endangered by childbearing. Thus, the doctor believed the statute deprived his patients of their due process rights under the Fourteenth Amendment, which provides that "[n]o . . . State shall deprive any person of their life, liberty, or property, without due process of law[.]" The Connecticut Supreme Court eventually sustained the statute. Thereafter, Dr. Tileston appealed to the U.S. Supreme Court, seeking judgment that the statute was unconstitutional.

SUMMARY OF ARGUMENTS

Dr. Tileston described to the Court that the health of three of his patients would be dramatically impaired by pregnancy. He explained that the medical consensus was that the safest way doctors could aid patients for whom pregnancy was life-threatening was to prescribe contraceptives. He argued that the statute, by preventing him from counseling these married women on the use of contraceptives, denied the women their rights under the Fourteenth Amendment.

The state argued that the legislature determined that abstention from intercourse was the most positive and certain method to prevent the unfortunate consequences that the women would suffer from pregnancy. Also, the state contended that Dr. Tileston lacked standing because he did not demonstrate that he had been or would be injured by enforcement of the statute.

DECISION

In a short per curiam decision, an opinion by the whole Court, the Court unanimously dismissed the doctor's appeal on the ground that he had no standing to litigate this constitutional question. The Court explained that the doctor gave no allegation or proof that his own life, liberty, or property would be endangered by the enforcement of the statute. Instead, the doctor asserted that his patients were being denied their due process rights. Therefore, because his patients were not parties to this proceeding, the Court held that the doctor could not allege an injury on their behalf. Since the doctor had no standing, the Court declined to discuss the merits of the case.

AFTERMATH

Eighteen years later, the same vexing statute was again before the Court. Once again an appeal of right was dismissed for lack of standing. However, the Court eventually struck down the Con-

necticut statute by a 7-2 vote in *GRISWOLD V. CONNECTICUT,* 381 U.S. 479 (1965). In that case the Court held that the statute was unconstitutional since the right of married persons to use contraceptives falls within a protected zone of privacy. In *Griswold* the plaintiffs had standing because they had actually been *convicted* of counseling married persons to use the contraceptives.

SIGNIFICANCE

This case illustrates the concept of third-party standing. Generally, a litigant may not assert the constitutional rights of persons not before the Court. There are certain exceptions, however, to this general rule. For example, if there is a "special relationship" between the litigant and the third party, such that the litigant's interest is so closely related to the third party's interest, the courts may deem that litigant an "effective proponent."

RELATED CASES

Barrows v. Jackson, 346 U.S. 249 (1953)

New York State Club Ass'n, Inc. v. New York, 487 U.S. 1 (1988)

Singleton v. Wulff, 428 U.S. 106 (1976)

RECOMMENDED READING

Radcliffe, James E. *The Case or Controversy Provision.* University Park: Pennsylvania State University Press, 1978.

Case Title: *United Jewish Organization v. Carey*

Legal Citations: 430 U.S. 144; 97 S.Ct. 996; 51 L.Ed. 2d 229

Year of Decision: 1977

KEY ISSUES

Is it constitutional for a state to consciously take the race of voters into account when drawing lines for state legislative districts for the purpose of giving nonwhite voters a majority of voters in the districts?

HISTORY OF THE CASE

Three counties in New York were subject to the terms of the Voting Rights Act of 1965. The act was implemented to alleviate the effects of past discrimination against minorities. Additionally, the act provides that new "voting regulations" such as redistricting must be approved by the U.S. attorney general's office or upheld by a special three-judge panel in the District of Columbia.

In 1974 New York passed a redistricting plan that aspired to create more Senate and Assembly districts with substantial nonwhite majorities. The attorney general subsequently approved this plan. One effect of the plan was that a Hasidic Jewish community would be dispersed throughout the concentrated nonwhite districts. Thus, a suit was brought on behalf of the Jewish community to prohibit implementation of the plan. The U.S. District Court for the Eastern District of New York dismissed the suit. The court of appeals affirmed, concluding that New York could constitutionally use racial lines in drawing electoral districts.

SUMMARY OF ARGUMENTS

The Hasidic community argued that drawing lines based on race is never justified. They also complained that there was no proof that the New York legislature had ever discriminated against nonwhites. Thus, they reasoned, race-conscious lines were inappropriate in this matter.

The respondents maintained that the Hasidic community had no constitutional right to preserve ethnic community unity in single Senate and Assembly districts. They also urged that the use of racial considerations in drawing district lines was a valid remedial procedure under the Voting Rights Act of 1965. They contended that the act does not require the showing of specific evidence of past discrimination to trigger its remedial provisions. They concluded that the race-conscious line drawing was an appropriate measure since it would strengthen minorities' chances of electing representatives in proportion to their voting strength.

DECISION

The Court upheld the redistricting plan in a 7-1 decision, although no majority could agree on a decisive rationale. Some justices stressed that the New York legislators did not intend to injure white voters. Instead, they argued, the legislators were merely intending to aid African-American voters. Rejecting one of the United Jewish Organization's contentions, they firmly believed that racial awareness in legislative apportionment is not unconstitutional per se. Other justices believed the new plan created no discriminatory effect. After the redistricting plan, 70 percent of the newly created districts were left with white majorities, and only 65 percent of the countywide population was white.

The lone dissenter, Chief Justice Burger, maintained that the drawing of political boundary lines with the sole, explicit objective of reaching a predetermined racial result cannot be squared with the Constitution. He felt that although reference to racial composition may serve as a starting point in the shaping of a remedy, it may not be the only criterion used in drawing district lines.

AFTERMATH

Today, it appears that a plaintiff group rarely prevails in complaining that its voting strength has been diluted. It appears that such plaintiffs must prove both that the legislature intended to disadvantage their group and that the districting plan had the effect of disadvantaging that group in terms of the entire political process.

Nonetheless, in 1993 the Court ruled, 5-4, that white voters can use the equal protection clause to challenge a district that is "highly irregular" in shape and drawn to "segregate voters by race." The challenged district was proven to be irrational because of its bizarre, snakelike shape. The majority also believed that allowing such districts would send an undesirable message to the elected officials to represent only the members of the racially dominant group.

SIGNIFICANCE

At the time the case was handed down, *Carey* was the only case in which the Court had addressed the issue, namely, what equal protection requires concerning affirmative action. Specifically, the view that racial criteria are permitted in legislative districting despite no showing of prior intentional discrimination paved the way for the numerous affirmative action cases that followed over the next two decades.

RELATED CASES

Allen v. State Board of Elections, 393 U.S. 544 (1969)

Beer v. United States, 425 U.S. 130 (1976)

Gomillion v. Lightfoot, 364 U.S. 339 (1960)

Richmond v. J. A. Croson Co., 448 U.S. 469 (1989)

Shaw v. Reno, 509 U.S. 630 (1993)

South Carolina v. Katzenbach, 383 U.S. 301 (1966)

RECOMMENDED READING

Bork, Robert H. *The Tempting of America: The Political Seduction of the Law.* New York: Free Press, 1990.

Thomas Goldstein, *Unpacking and Applying* Shaw v. Reno, 43 American University Law Review 1135–1196 (spring 1994).

Roy E. Paul, *An Answer to the Other Half of* Reynolds v. Sims, 14 Georgia Law Review 823–880 (summer 1980).

Case Title: *United States v. Butler*

Legal Citation: 297 U.S. 1

Year of Decision: 1936

KEY ISSUES

For what purposes may Congress tax and spend?

HISTORY OF THE CASE

Because farm prices collapsed during the Great Depression, Congress passed the Agricultural Adjustment Act of 1933. The Agricultural Adjustment Act levied a tax on certain agricultural processors in order to pay for a subsidy to farmers who reduced their crop output voluntarily. The goal was to reduce the supply of farm products in order to raise prices. Congress used the taxing and spending power granted in the Constitution.

SUMMARY OF ARGUMENTS

Butler argued that the Constitution did not give Congress the power to spend money for farm subsidies. The United States asserted that spending money for farm subsidies was allowed because Article I, section 8 of the Constitution did authorize spending for the general welfare.

DECISION

The Court concluded that Congress did have the power to "tax and spend for the general welfare," and that this power was separate and distinct from other powers granted in Article I, section 8 of the Constitution. However, Congress did not have the power to regulate for the general welfare. The phrase in the Constitution "to provide for the general welfare" was not an independent provision giving Congress the power to provide for the general welfare through general means. Instead, it qualified the term "to lay and collect taxes." Therefore, the Court decided that providing for the general welfare could be accomplished only through taxing and spending.

The Supreme Court decided that the Agricultural Adjustment Act violated the Constitution because Congress could not regulate local businesses nor tax them, as it would usurp the powers of the states. The Court declined to decide the precise scope of the taxing and spending power. They found that regulating the quality and quantity of agricultural production was a state power, and the Tenth Amendment prohibits the federal government from asserting powers that belong to the states.

AFTERMATH

Since the *Butler* decision, courts have been able to reach matters traditionally belonging to the states through the commerce clause. The Tenth Amendment is no longer a limitation on federal spending power or federal commerce power.

SIGNIFICANCE

The most important idea from *Butler* that is relevant today is that Congress has power to tax and spend for the general welfare, but Congress has no power to regulate in order to provide for the general welfare.

RELATED CASES

Lehigh Valley Coop. Farmers v. U.S., 370 U.S. 76 (1962)

Fullilove v. Klutznick, 448 U.S. 448 (1980)

RECOMMENDED READING

Bork, Robert H. *The Tempting of America: The Political Seduction of the Law.* New York: Free Press, 1990.

Thomas R. McCoy and Barry Freidman, *Conditional Spending: Federalism's Trojan Horse,* Supreme Court Review 85–127 (1988).

Albert J. Rosenthal, *Conditional Federal Spending and the Constitution,* 39 Stanford Law Review 1103–1164 (1987).

Case Title: *United States v. Ursery*

Alternate Case Title: Asset Forfeiture Case

Legal Citation: 518 U.S. 267

Year of Decision: 1996

KEY ISSUES

Does the double jeopardy clause of the Fifth Amendment prohibit the government from both punishing a defendant for a criminal offense and forfeiting his property for that same offense in a separate civil proceeding?

HISTORY OF THE CASE

The double jeopardy clause of the Fifth Amendment states: "[N]or shall any person be subject for the same offense to be twice put in jeopardy of life or limb."

Michigan police found marijuana growing adjacent to Guy Ursery's house and discovered marijuana seeds, stems, stalks, and a grow light within the house. The United States instituted civil forfeiture proceedings against the house, alleging that the property was subject to forfeiture because it had been used for several years to facilitate the unlawful processing and distribution of a controlled substance. Ursery ultimately paid the United States $13,250 to settle the forfeiture claim in full. Shortly before the settlement was completed, Ursery was indicted for manufacturing marijuana. A jury found him guilty, and he was sentenced to 63 months in prison. The court of appeals reversed Ursery's criminal conviction, holding that the conviction violated the double jeopardy clause. In the appellate court's view, Ursery had been punished in the forfeiture proceeding against his house and could not be subsequently tried in a criminal proceeding for the same offense.

SUMMARY OF ARGUMENTS

Ursery argued that the civil forfeiture proceeding against his house constituted punishment and that the separate criminal proceeding against him was therefore subject to the prohibition of the double jeopardy clause.

The government challenged Ursery's characterization of the forfeiture, arguing that the court of appeals was wrong to conclude that civil forfeitures are punitive for double jeopardy purposes.

DECISION

By a large majority, the Supreme Court held that civil forfeitures are neither "punishment" nor criminal proceedings for purposes of the double jeopardy clause. Chief Justice Rehnquist, in his opinion for the majority, recited at length the history of cases recognizing civil forfeiture not as an additional penalty for the commission of a criminal act, but rather as a separate civil sanction, remedial in nature.

In dissent, Justice Stevens pointed to the different situations covered by the numerous federal statutes authorizing forfeiture. While he agreed with the majority that forfeiture is appropriate for property that is contraband or proceeds from a crime, Justice Stevens noted that Ursery's house was not purchased with the proceeds of unlawful activity, and the house itself was surely not contraband. Therefore, Justice Stevens concluded that the confiscation of Ursery's home was punitive and his prosecution thus violated the double jeopardy clause.

AFTERMATH

In declining to recognize the kind of distinction urged by Justice Stevens, the Court appears to have given Congress the freedom to enact broad civil forfeiture laws.

SIGNIFICANCE

After nearly three decades of a federal "war on drugs," both Congress and the state legislatures have armed their law enforcement agencies with new powers to forfeit property that vastly exceed their traditional tools. The statute at issue in *Ursery* subjects to forfeiture all real property that is used, or intended to be used, in the commission or even the facilitation of a federal drug offense. Arguably, the statute is so broad that it differs not only in degree but also in kind from its historical antecedents. In concluding that a homeowner is not punished by the loss of his residence, the Court has provided an unnerving example of the tension between the war on drugs and the protections of the Bill of Rights. In Justice Stevens's words, "Consider how drastic the remedy would have been if Congress in 1931 had authorized the forfeiture of every home in which alcoholic beverages were consumed."

RELATED CASES

Austin v. United States, 509 U.S. 602 (1993)

Department of Revenue of Montana v. Kurth Ranch, 511 U.S. 767 (1994)

United States v. Halper, 490 U.S. 435 (1989)

Various Items of Personal Property v. United States, 282 U.S. 577 (1931)

RECOMMENDED READING

Rachael L. Brand, *Civil Forfeiture as Jeopardy,* 20 Harvard Journal of Law & Public Policy 292 (1996).

Matthew Costigan, *Go Directly to Jail, Do Not Pass Go, Do Not Keep House,* 87 Journal of Criminal Law and Criminology 719 (1997).

Ryan H. Stuart, *Penalties and Taxes May Break My Bones, but Forfeitures Will Never Punish Me: A Critical Examination of the Double Jeopardy Clause after* United States v. Ursery, 41 Saint Louis University Law Journal 1367 (1997).

Sarah Jean Watterson, *Putting the* Halper *Genie Back in the Bottle: Examining* United States v. Ursery *in Light of* Halper, Austin, *and* Kurth Ranch, 1997 Brigham Young University Law Review 235 (1997).

Case Title: *Waller v. Florida*

Legal Citation: 397 U.S. 387

Year of Decision: 1970

KEY ISSUES

Is a municipality a separate government entity for purposes of criminal prosecutions?

HISTORY OF THE CASE

The city of St. Petersburg, Florida, convicted Waller of violating two city ordinances: destruction of city property and disorderly breach of the peace. The state of Florida then convicted Waller of grand larceny arising out of the same acts. The district court of appeals affirmed the convictions. The Florida Supreme Court refused to hear the case. The U.S. Supreme Court agreed to hear the case because of the very narrow issue presented and its importance in national jurisprudence.

SUMMARY OF ARGUMENTS

Waller argued that because the convictions resulted from the same acts, he was put in double jeopardy in violation of the Constitution.

The state of Florida argued that the municipality was a separate sovereign entity and was therefore allowed to try and convict separately from the state.

DECISION

Chief Justice Burger delivered the opinion of the Court in the unanimous decision vacating the second conviction. The Court concluded that the municipal and state courts were merely parts of the same "sovereign." As a result, the separate sovereign entity argument was a falsity.

AFTERMATH

The Court has virtually set in stone the requirements for successive punishments for the same acts. The separate sovereignty argument is virtually the only exception to the double jeopardy prohibition. For all intents and purposes, however, there are no separate sovereignties in the

United States with the exception of state and federal governments, and even that dichotomy is not absolute.

SIGNIFICANCE

Waller is a potentially hobbling case for prosecutors. In eliminating the difference between municipality and state for purposes of double jeopardy, the Supreme Court requires prosecutors to choose under what laws they wish to prosecute. The result may be weaker punishment under municipal laws that may be easier to prove or a stronger punishment under state laws that are more difficult to prove.

RELATED CASES

Blockburger v. U.S., 284 U.S. 299 (1932)

Green v. U.S., 355 U.S. 184 (1957)

U.S. v. Wheeler, 435 U.S. 313 (1978)

RECOMMENDED READING

Nancy J. King, *Portioning Punishment: Constitutional Limits on Successive and Excessive Penalties*, 144 University of Pennsylvania Law Review 101 (1995).

Note, *The Supreme Court, 1969 Term*, 84 Harvard Law Review 140 (1970).

APPENDIXES

Appendix I
CASES BY TITLE

Appendix II
CHRONOLOGICAL LIST
OF CASES

1793	*Chisolm v. Georgia*		1891	*Cooley v. Board of Wardens of the Port of Philadelphia*
1798	*Calder v. Bull*			
1803	*Marbury v. Madison*		1895	*Pollock v. Farmers' Loan and Trust Co.*
1816	*Martin v. Hunter's Lessee*			
1819	*Dartmouth College v. Woodward*			*United States v. E. C. Knight*
	McCulloch v. Maryland			*Wayte v. United States*
1824	*Gibbons v. Ogden*		1896	*Plessy v. Ferguson*
1825	*Wayman v. Southard*		1903	*Champion v. Ames*
1837	*Charles River Bridge Co. v. Warren Bridge Co.*		1904	*McCray v. United States*
			1905	*Jacobson v. Massachusetts*
1842	*Swift v. Tyson*			*Lochner v. New York*
1849	*Luther v. Borden*			*Swift and Co. v. United States*
1857	*Dred Scott v. Sandford*		1908	*Adair v. United States*
1866	Ex parte *Milligan*			*Muller v. Oregon*
1869	Ex parte *McCardle*			*Twining v. New Jersey*
1872	*Butcher's Benevolent Association (Slaughterhouse Cases)*		1910	*Fletcher v. Peck*
			1911	*Coppage v. Kansas*
1873	*Slaughterhouse Cases*			*Standard Oil of New Jersey v. United States*
1877	*Munn v. Illinois*			
1880	*Stone v. Mississippi*		1914	*Weeks v. United States*
	Strauder v. West Virginia		1918	*Hammer v. Dagenhart*
1884	*Hurtado v. California*		1919	*Abrams v. United States*
1886	*Yick Wo v. Hopkins*			*Schenck v. United States*

1920	Missouri v. Holland		In re Quirin
1923	Frothingham v. Mellon		Skinner v. Oklahoma
	Meyer v. Nebraska		Valentine v. Chrestensen
	Moore v. Dempsey		Wickard v. Filburn
1925	Gitlow v. New York	1943	Tileston v. Ullman
	Pierce v. Society of Sisters		West Virginia v. Barnette
1927	McGrain v. Daugherty	1944	Korematsu v. United States
	Whitney v. California		Smith v. Allwright
1928	Olmstead v. United States	1945	Screws v. United States
1931	Near v. Minnesota		Southern Pacific Railroad Co. v. Arizona
	New York Times v. United States	1946	Colegrove v. Green
1932	Powell v. Alabama		Girouard v. United States
1934	Home Building and Loan Association v. Blaisdell	1947	Adamson v. California
	Nebbia v. New York		Everson v. Board of Education
1935	Humphrey's Executor v. United States		United Public Workers v. Mitchell
		1948	McCollom v. Board of Education
	Schecter Poultry Corp. v. United States		Saia v. New York
1936	Carter v. Carter Coal Co.		Shelley v. Kramer
	United States v. Butler	1949	Lincoln Federal Labor Union v. Northwestern Iron Co.
1937	Breedlove v. Suttles		Railway Express Agency v. New York
	DeJonge v. Oregon		
	National Labor Relations Board v. Jones & Laughlin		Terminiello v. Chicago
	Palko v. Connecticut		Wolf v. Colorado
	Steward Machine Co. v. Davis	1950	Sweatt v. Painter
	West Coast Hotel Co. v. Parrish	1951	Dennis v. United States
1938	Erie Railroad Co. v. Tompkins		Feiner v. New York
	Missouri ex rel. Gaines v. Canada	1952	Beauharnais v. Illinois
	United States v. Carolene Products Co.		Rochin v. California
1939	Lane v. Wilson		Wieman v. Updegraff
	Schneider v. Irvington		Zorach v. Clauson
	Thornhill v. Alabama	1953	Terry v. Adams
1940	Cantwell v. Connecticut	1954	Bolling v. Sharp
1941	Edwards v. California		Brown v. Board of Education
1942	Betts v. Brady	1957	Kinsella v. Krueger
	Chaplinsky v. New Hampshire		Konigsberg v. State Bar of California
			Mallory v. United States

GLOSSARY*

❦

acquittal   The verdict in a criminal trial in which the defendant is found not guilty.

act   An alternative name for statutory law. When introduced into the first house of the legislature, a piece of proposed legislation is known as a bill. When passed to the next house, it may then be referred to as an act. After enactment, the terms law and act may be used interchangeably. An act has the same legislative force as a joint resolution but is technically distinguishable, being of a different form and introduced with the words *be it enacted* instead of *be it resolved*.

action   The formal legal demand of one's rights from another person brought in court.

adjudication   The formal pronouncing or recording of a judgment or decree by a court.

administrative agency   A governmental authority, other than a legislature or court that issues rules and regulations or adjudicates disputes arising under its statutes and regulations. Administrative agencies usually act under authority delegated by the legislature.

administrative law   A law that affects private parties, promulgated by governmental agencies other than courts or legislative bodies. These administrative agencies derive their power from

legislative enactments and are subject to judicial review.

advance sheets   Current pamphlets containing the most recently reported opinions of a court or the courts of several jurisdictions. The volume and page numbers usually are the same as in the subsequently bound volumes of the series, which cover several numbers of the advance sheets.

advisory opinion   An opinion rendered by a court at the request of the government or an interested party that indicates how the court would rule on a matter should adversary litigation develop. An advisory opinion is thus an interpretation of the law without binding effect. The International Court of Justice and some state courts will render advisory opinions; the Supreme Court of the United States will not.

affidavit   A written statement or declaration of facts sworn to by the maker, taken before a person officially permitted by law to administer oaths.

alternative dispute resolution   The process of resolving disputes through such means as mediation or arbitration rather than through litigation.

ALWD citation manual   A manual of legal citation form prepared by the Association of Legal Writing Directors.

amicus curiae   Literally "friend of the court," a party with strong interest in or views on the subject matter of the dispute will petition the court

*This glossary is excerpted from *Fundamentals of Legal Research*, 8th ed. (Foundation Press, 2002), by Roy M. Mersky and Donald J. Dunn. It has been revised by Fred R. Shapiro of Yale Law School. Additional terms have been provided by Cindy Tate Slarinski.

for permission to file a brief, ostensibly on behalf of a party but actually to suggest a rationale consistent with its own views.

annotations (1) Statutory: brief summaries of the law and facts of cases interpreting statutes passed by Congress or state legislatures that are included in codes; or (2) Textual: expository essays of varying length on significant legal topics chosen from selected cases published with the essays.

answer The pleading filed by the defendant in response to plaintiff's complaint.

appeal papers The briefs and transcripts of records on appeal filed by attorneys with courts in connection with litigation.

appellant The party who requests that a higher court review the actions of a lower court. Compare with APPELLEE.

appellee The party against whom an appeal is taken (usually, but not always, the winner in the lower court). It should be noted that a party's status as appellant or appellee bears no relation to his or her status as plaintiff or defendant in the lower court.

arbitration The hearing and settlement of a dispute between opposing parties by a third party. This decision is often binding by prior agreement of the parties.

assault An unlawful, intentional show of force or an attempt to do physical harm to another person. Assault can constitute the basis of a civil or criminal action. See also BATTERY.

assault and battery See BATTERY.

attorney general opinion An opinion issued by the government's chief counsel at the request of some governmental body interpreting the law for the requesting agency in the same manner as a private attorney would for his or her client. The opinion is not binding on the court but is usually accorded some degree of persuasive authority.

authority That which can bind or influence a court. Case law, legislation, constitutions, admin-istrative regulations, and writings about the law are all legal authority. See PRIMARY AUTHORITY; MANDATORY AUTHORITY; PERSUASIVE AUTHORITY.

bail Security given, in the form of a bail bond or cash, as a guarantee that released prisoners will present themselves for trial. This security may be lost if the released person does not appear in court at the appointed time.

battery An unlawful use of force against another person resulting in physical contact (a tort); it is commonly used in the phrase "assault and battery," assault being the threat of force, and battery the actual use of force. See also ASSAULT.

bill A legislative proposal introduced in the legislature. The term distinguishes unfinished legislation from enacted law.

black letter law An informal term indicating the basic principles of law generally accepted by the courts and/or embodied in the statutes of a particular jurisdiction.

Bluebook A manual of legal citation form published by the *Harvard Law Review, Yale Law Journal, Columbia Law Review,* and *University of Pennsylvania Law Review.*

Boolean logic A form of search strategy used in databases, such as Westlaw and LexisNexis. In a Boolean search, connectors such as AND, OR, and NOT are used to construct a complex search command. The command "fungible and gasoline" for example, retrieves documents in which the term "fungible" and the term "gasoline" both appear. Compare with NATURAL LANGUAGE.

breach of contract The failure to perform any of the terms of an agreement.

brief (1) In American law practice, a written statement prepared by the counsel arguing a case in court. It contains a summary of the facts of the case, the pertinent laws, and an argument of how the law applies to the facts supporting counsel's position; (2) a summary of a published opinion of a case prepared for studying the opinion in law school.

briefs and records   See APPEAL PAPERS.

calendar   Usually, the order in which cases are to be heard during a term of court. *Martindale-Hubbell Law Directory* contains calendars for state and federal courts, and includes the name of the court, the name of the judge, and the date of the term's beginning.

CALR   An acronym for Computer-Assisted Legal Research. Westlaw and LexisNexis are CALR systems.

caption   See STYLE OF A CASE.

casebook   A textbook used to instruct law students in a particular area of law. The text consists of a collection of court opinions, usually from appellate courts, and notes by the author(s).

case in point   A judicial opinion that deals with a fact situation similar to the one being researched and substantiates a point of law to be asserted. (Also called *case on all fours*.)

case law   The law of reported judicial opinions as distinguished from statutes or administrative law.

cause of action   A claim in law and in fact sufficient to bring the case to court; the grounds of an action. (Example: breach of contract.)

CD-ROM   An abbreviation for "compact disk–read-only memory." A compact disk is a disk approximately four inches in diameter on which data are coded to be scanned by a laser beam and transmitted to a computer monitor. A large volume of data can be stored on such a disk.

certiorari   A writ issued by a superior to an inferior court requiring the latter to produce the records of a particular case tried therein. It is most commonly used to refer to the Supreme Court of the United States, which uses the writ of certiorari as a discretionary device to choose the cases it wishes to hear. The term's origin is Latin, meaning to be informed of.

charter   A document issued by a governmental entity that gives a corporation legal existence.

chattel   Any article of personal property, as opposed to real property. It may refer to animate as well as inanimate property.

chose   Any article of personal property. See PROPERTY.

citation   The reference to authority necessary to substantiate the validity of one's argument or position. Citation to authority and supporting references is both important and extensive in any form of legal writing. Citation form is also given emphasis in legal writing, and early familiarity with *The Bluebook: A Uniform System of Citation* will stand the law student in good stead.

citators   A set of books and online sources that provide the subsequent judicial history and interpretation of reported cases or lists of cases and legislative enactments construing, applying, or affecting statutes. In America, the most widely used citators are Shepard's Citations and KeyCite.

cited case   A case that is referred to by other cases.

citing case   The case that refers to the cited case.

civil law   (1) Roman law embodied in the Code of Justinian, which presently prevails in most countries of western Europe other than Great Britain and that is the foundation of Louisiana law; (2) the law concerning noncriminal matters in a common law jurisdiction.

claim   (1) The assertion of a right, as to money or property; or (2) the accumulation of facts that give rise to a right enforceable in court.

class action   A lawsuit brought by a representative party on behalf of a group, all of whose members have the same or a similar grievance against the defendant.

code   In popular usage, a compilation of statutes. Technically, in a code, the laws in force and judicial decrees having the force of law are rewritten and arranged in classified order. Repealed and temporary acts are eliminated and the revision is reenacted.

codification   The process of collecting and arranging systematically, usually by subject, the laws of a state or country.

commerce clause   A provision found in Article I of the Constitution that gives Congress the power to regulate interstate commerce (commerce between the states and foreign nations).

common law   The origin of the Anglo-American legal systems, English common law was largely customary law and unwritten, until discovered, applied, and reported by the courts of law. In theory, the common law courts did not create law but rather discovered it in the customs and habits of the English people. The strength of the judicial system in preparliamentary days is one reason for the continued emphasis in common law systems on case law. In a narrow sense, common law is the phrase still used to distinguish case law from statutory law.

compiled statutes   In popular usage, a code. Technically, it is a compilation of acts printed verbatim as originally enacted but in a new classified order. The text is not modified; however, repealed and temporary acts are omitted.

complaint   A plaintiff's initial pleading. Under Federal Rules of Civil Procedure, it is no longer full of the technicalities demanded by the common law. A complaint need only contain a short and plain statement of the claim upon which relief is sought, an indication of the type of relief requested, and an indication that the court has jurisdiction to hear the case.

connector   See BOOLEAN LOGIC.

consideration   Something to be done, or abstained from, by one party to a contract in order to induce another party to enter into a contract.

consolidated statutes   In popular usage, a code. Technically, it is a compilation of acts rewritten, arranged in classified order, and reenacted. Repealed and temporary acts are eliminated.

constitution   The system of fundamental principles by which a political body or organization

governs itself. Most national constitutions are written; the English and Israeli constitutions are unwritten.

contracts clause   A clause in Article I of the Constitution that prohibits states from passing laws that impair contract obligations.

conversion   The wrongful appropriation to oneself of the personal property of another.

conveyance   The transfer of title to property from one person to another.

count   A separate and independent claim. A civil petition or a criminal indictment may contain several counts.

counterclaim   A claim made by the defendant against the plaintiff in a civil lawsuit; it constitutes a separate cause of action.

court decision   The disposition of the case by the court. See OPINION.

court rules   Rules of procedure promulgated to govern civil and criminal practice before the courts.

damages   Monetary compensation awarded by a court for an injury caused by the act of another. Damages may be actual or compensatory (equal to the amount of loss shown), exemplary or punitive (in excess of the actual loss given to punish the person for the malicious conduct that caused the injury), or nominal (a trivial amount given because the injury is slight or because the exact amount of injury has not been determined satisfactorily).

database   A collection of information organized for rapid retrieval by computer. In legal research, it usually refers to a commercial service searched online. A full-text database provides the complete text of documents such as court cases or newspaper articles. Westlaw and LexisNexis are full-text databases. A bibliographic database provides citations or abstracts of articles, books, reports, or patents.

decision   See COURT DECISION.

declaratory relief A judicial ruling that determines the legal rights and duties of the parties.

decree A determination by a court of the rights and duties of the parties before it. Formerly, decrees were issued by courts of equity and distinguished from judgments, which were issued by courts of law. See EQUITY.

defendant The person against whom a civil or criminal action is brought.

demurrer A means of objecting to the sufficiency in law of a pleading by admitting the actual allegations made, but disputing that they frame an adequate legal claim.

dictum See OBITER DICTUM.

digest An index to reported cases, providing brief, unconnected statements of court holdings on points of law, which are arranged by subject and subdivided by jurisdiction and courts.

docket number A number, sequentially assigned by the clerk at the outset to a lawsuit brought to a court for adjudication.

due care The legal duty one owes to another according to the circumstances of a particular case.

due process of law A term found in the Fifth and Fourteenth Amendments of the U.S. Constitution and also in the constitutions of many states. Its exact meaning varies from one situation to another and from one era to the next, but basically it is concerned with the guarantee of every person's enjoyment of his or her rights (e.g., the right to a fair hearing in any legal dispute).

en banc A session in which the entire bench of the court will participate in the decision rather than the regular quorum. In other countries it is common for a court to have more members than are usually necessary to hear an appeal. In the United States, the Circuit Courts of Appeals usually sit in groups of three judges but for important cases may expand the bench to nine members, when they are said to be sitting en banc.

encyclopedia A work containing expository statements on principles of law, topically arranged, with supporting footnote references to cases in point.

equal protection clause A provision of the Fourteenth Amendment that prohibits a state from denying any individual equal protection of the law; requires a state to treat people in similar circumstances with the same benefits and protections of the law.

equity Justice administered according to fairness as contrasted with the strictly formulated rules of common law. It is based on a system of rules and principles that originated in England as an alternative to the harsh rules of common law and that were based on what was fair in a particular situation. One sought relief under this system in courts of equity rather than in courts of law.

establishment clause A provision in the First Amendment that prohibits the state and federal governments from passing laws that support or prefer a particular religion or religious affiliation or that require the belief or disbelief in a religion.

estate (1) The interest or right one has in real or personal property; or (2) the property itself in which one has an interest or right.

executive agreement An international agreement, not a treaty, concluded by the president without senatorial consent on the president's authority as commander in chief and director of foreign relations. The distinction between treaty and executive agreement is complicated and often of questionable constitutionality, but the import of such agreements as that of Yalta or Potsdam is unquestionably great.

executive order An order issued by the president under specific authority granted to the president by Congress. There is no precise distinction between a presidential proclamation and an executive order; however, a proclamation generally cover matters of widespread interest, and an executive order often relates to the conduct of government business or to organization of the executive department. Every act of the president authorizing or directing the performance of an act, in its general context, is an executive order. See PRESIDEN-TIAL PROCLAMATION.

fiche See MICROFICHE.

FindLaw A portal on the World Wide Web (http://www.findlaw.com) providing links to a wide range of law-related information. FindLaw is owned by West Group, but access is free of charge.

form books Sample instruments that are helpful in drafting legal documents.

forms of action These governed common law pleadings and were the procedural devices used to give expression to the theories of liability recognized by the common law. Failure to analyze the cause of the action properly, to select the proper theory of liability and to choose the appropriate procedural mechanism or forms of action could easily result in being thrown out of court. A plaintiff had to elect his or her remedy in advance and could not subsequently amend the pleadings to conform to his or her proof or to the court's choice of another theory of liability. According to the relief sought, actions have been divided into three categories: real actions were brought for the recovery of real property; mixed actions were brought to recover real property and damages for injury to it; personal actions were brought to recover debts or personal property, or for injuries to personal, property, or contractual rights. The common law actions are usually considered to be 11 in number: trespass, trespass on the case, trover, ejectment, detinue, replevin, debt, covenant, account, special assumpsit, and general assumpsit.

fraud A deception that causes a person to part with his or her property or a legal right.

full text See DATABASE.

grand jury A jury of six to 23 persons that sits permanently for a specified period and that hears criminal accusations and evidence, and then determines whether indictments should be made. Compare with PETIT JURY.

guarantee clause A provision in Article IV of the Constitution that guarantees states a government consisting of representatives chosen by the people.

headnote A brief summary of a legal rule or significant facts in a case that precedes the printed opinion in reports.

hearings Proceedings extensively employed by both legislative and administrative agencies. Adjudicative hearings of administrative agencies can be appealed in a court of law. Investigative hearings are often held by congressional committees prior to enactment of legislation, and are important sources of legislative history.

Hein-On-Line A database containing page images and searchable text of retrospective legal journals and other legal materials. Hein-On-Line is provided by the William S. Hein & Co., Inc.

holding The declaration of the conclusion of law reached by the court as to the legal effect of the facts of the case.

holograph or olograph A will, deed, or other legal document that is entirely in the handwriting of the signer.

hornbook The popular reference to a series of treatises published by West Group each of which reviews a certain field of law in summary, textual form, as opposed to a casebook that is designed as a teaching tool and includes many reprints of court opinions.

indemnity A contractual arrangement whereby one party agrees to reimburse another for losses of a particular type.

indictment A formal accusation of a crime made by a grand jury at the request of a prosecuting attorney.

information An accusation based not on the action of a grand jury but rather on the affirmation of a public official.

injunction A judge's order that a person do or, more commonly, refrain from doing, a certain act. An injunction may be preliminary or temporary, pending trial of the issue presented, or it may be final if the issue has already been decided in court.

Internet A worldwide system of interconnected computer networks using the TCP/IP protocols.

The Internet facilitates various data communication services.

intestate   The condition of not having a valid will.

judgment   See COURT DECISION.

jurisdiction   The power given to a court by a constitution or a legislative body to make legally binding decisions over certain persons or property, or the geographical area in which a court's decisions or legislative enactments are binding.

jurisprudence   (1) The science or philosophy of law; (2) a collective term for case law as opposed to legislation.

key number   A building block of the major indexing system devised for American case law, developed by West Group. The key number is a permanent number given to a specific point of this case law.

law review or law journal   A legal periodical. The term "law review" usually describes a scholarly periodical edited by students at a law school.

legislative history   That information embodied in legislative documents that provides the meanings and interpretations (intent) of statutes. Citations and dates of legislative enactments, amendments, and repeals of statutes are sometimes imprecisely identified as legislative histories. More accurate designations of these citations of legislative changes, as included in codes, are historical notes or amendatory histories.

LexisNexis   LexisNexis is a database providing the full text of court decisions, statutes, administrative materials, ALR annotations, law review articles, reporter services, Supreme Court briefs, and other items. Keyword searches, natural-language searches, segment searches, and citator searches are available.

liability   The condition of being responsible either for damages resulting from an injurious act or for discharging an obligation or debt.

libel   (1) Written defamation of a person's character. Compare with SLANDER; (2) in an admiralty court, the plaintiff's statement of the cause of action and the relief sought.

lien   A claim against property as security for a debt, under which the property may be seized and sold to satisfy the debt.

litigate   To bring a civil action in court.

Loislaw   Loislaw is a database providing the full text of court decisions, statutes, administrative materials, and other sources.

looseleaf services and reporters   These contain federal and state administrative regulations and decisions or subject treatment of a legal topic. They consist of separate, perforated pages or pamphlet-sized inserts in special binders, simplifying frequent insertion or substitution of new material.

malpractice   Professional misconduct or unreasonable lack of skill. This term is usually applied to such conduct by doctors, lawyers, and accountants.

mandatory authority   Authority that a given court is bound to follow. Mandatory authority is found in constitutional provisions, legislation, and court cases. Compare with PERSUASIVE AUTHORITY.

memorandum   (1) An informal record; (2) a written document that may be used to prove that a contract exists; (3) an exposition of all the points of law pertaining to a particular case (referred to as a memorandum of law); or (4) an informal written discussion of the merits of a matter pending in a lawyer's office, usually written by a law clerk or junior associate for a senior associate or partner (referred to as an office memorandum).

microfiche   A sheet of film, usually 4 × 6 inches or 3 × 5 inches in size, containing miniaturized photographic images of printed text. The term "fiche" is synonymous with microfiche. Ultrafiche is a type of microfiche containing images that are reduced by a factor of 90 or more.

microfilm A film containing miniatured photographic images of printed text. This is usually in a reel, but may also be in a cartridge or cassette form.

microform A general term describing miniatured reproduction of printed text on film or paper. Microfilm and microfiche are specific types of microform.

model codes Codes formulated by various groups or institutions to serve as model laws for legislatures, intended to improve existing laws or unify diverse state legislation.

moot point A point that is no longer a subject of contention and that is raised only for the purpose of discussion or hypothesis. Many law schools conduct moot courts where students gain practice by arguing hypothetical or moot cases.

motion A formal request made to a judge pertaining to any issue arising during the pendency of a lawsuit.

National Reporter System The network of reporters published by West Group, which attempts to publish and digest all cases of precedential value from all state and federal courts.

natural language An on-line database search strategy using normal English-language sentences or phrases instead of Boolean commands. See BOOLEAN LOGIC.

necessary and proper clause A provision in Article I of the Constitution that gives Congress the power to make any laws necessary to carry out the other powers granted to it in the Constitution.

negligence The failure to exercise due care.

Nexis The general and business news database of LexisNexis, a subsidiary of Reed Elsevier PLC. Nexis provides the full text of newspaper, magazine and newsletter articles, wire-service stories, and other items.

nisi prius Generally, a court where a case is first tried, as distinguished from an appellate court.

noter-up (1) The term used in the British Commonwealth countries for a citator; or (2) the name

of the updating service for Fundamentals of Legal Research and Legal Research Illustrated.

obiter dictum An incidental comment, not necessary to the formulation of the decision, made by the judge in his or her opinion. Such comments are not binding as precedent.

official reports Court reports directed by statute. Compare with UNOFFICIAL REPORTS.

opinion An expression of the reasons why a certain decision (the judgment) was reached in a case. A majority opinion is usually written by one judge and represents the principles of law that a majority of his or her colleagues on the court deem operative in a given decision; it has more precedential value than any of the following. A separate opinion may be written by one or more judges in which he, she, or they concur in or dissent from the majority opinion. A concurring opinion agrees with the result reached by the majority, but disagrees with the precise reasoning leading to that result. A dissenting opinion disagrees with the result reached by the majority and thus disagrees with the reasoning and/or the principles of law used by the majority in deciding the case. A plurality opinion (called a judgment by the Supreme Court) is agreed to by less than a majority as to the reasoning of the decision, but is agreed to by a majority as to the result. A per curiam opinion is an opinion by the court that expresses its decision in the case but whose author is not identified. A memorandum opinion is a holding of the whole court in which the opinion is very concise.

oral argument A spoken presentation of reasons for a desired decision directed to an appellate court by attorneys for the parties.

ordinance The equivalent of a municipal statute, passed by the city council and governing matters not already covered by federal or state law.

pamphlet supplement A paperbound supplement to a larger bound volume, usually intended to be discarded eventually.

parallel citation A citation reference to the same case printed in two or more different reports.

per curiam Literally, by the court. Usually a short opinion written on behalf of the majority of the court. It may be accompanied by concurring or dissenting opinions.

periodical A publication appearing at regular intervals. Legal periodicals include law school publications, bar association publications, commercially published journals, and legal newspapers.

permanent law An act that continues in force for an indefinite time.

personal property See PROPERTY.

persuasive authority That law or reasoning that a given court may, but is not bound to, follow. For example, decisions from one jurisdiction may be persuasive authority in the courts of another jurisdiction. Compare with MANDATORY AUTHORITY.

petition A formal, written application to a court requesting judicial action on a certain matter.

petit jury A group of six, nine, or 12 persons that decides questions of fact in civil and criminal trials. Compare with GRAND JURY.

petitioner The person presenting a petition to a court, officer, or legislative body; the one who starts an equity proceeding or the one who takes an appeal from a judgment.

plaintiff The person or other entity who brings a lawsuit against another.

plea bargaining The process whereby the accused and the prosecutor in a criminal case work out a mutually satisfactory disposition of the case. It usually involves the defendant's pleading guilty to a lesser offense or to only one or some of the counts of a multi-count indictment in return for a lighter sentence than that possible for the graver charge.

pleadings Technical means by which parties to a dispute frame the issue for the court. The plaintiff's complaint or declaration is followed by the defendant's answer; subsequent papers may be filed as needed.

pocket supplement or pocket part A paperbound supplement to a book, inserted in the book through a slit in its back cover. Depending on the type of publication, it may have textual, case, or statutory references keyed to the original publication.

popular name table A table listing popular names by which some cases and statutes have become known, and identifying for each popular name the official name and citation of the case or statute.

portal A starting site for users of the World Wide Web.

power of attorney A document authorizing a person to act as another's agent.

precedent See STARE DECISIS.

preliminary prints The name given to the advance sheets of the official United States Reports.

presentment In criminal law, a written accusation made by the grand jury without the consent or participation of a prosecutor.

presidential proclamations A declaration issued under specific authority granted to the president by Congress. Generally, it relates to matters of widespread interest. Some proclamations have no legal effect but merely are appeals to the public, e.g., the observance of American Education Week. See EXECUTIVE ORDER.

primary authority Constitutions, statutes, administrative regulations issued pursuant to enabling legislation, and case law. Primary authority may be either mandatory or persuasive. All other legal writings are secondary authority and are never binding on courts. See AUTHORITY; MANDATORY AUTHORITY; PERSUASIVE AUTHORITY.

prior restraint A prohibition on expression before it actually takes place; for example, prohibiting an article from being published before the publication has been distributed to the public.

private law An act that relates to a specific person.

probable cause A reasonable belief that certain facts exist and justify a governmental action, such as the search of an individual or an arrest.

procedural law That law that governs the operation of the legal system, including court rules and rules of procedure, as distinguished from substantive law.

property Ownership or that which is owned. Real property refers to land; personal property refers to movable things or chattels; chose in action refers to a right to personal property of which the owner does not presently have possession but instead has a right to sue to gain possession (e.g., a right to recover a debt, demand, or damages in a contractual action or for a tort or omission of a duty).

public law An act that relates to the public as a whole. It may be (1) general (applies to all persons within the jurisdiction); (2) local (applies to a geographical area); or (3) special (relates to an organization that is charged with a public interest).

ratio decidendi The point in a case that determines the result—the basis of the decision.

rational basis The least stringent standard of constitutional review; requires legislation to be rationally related to a legitimate government interest.

real property See PROPERTY.

record The documentation, prepared for an appeal, of the trial court proceedings (pleadings, motions, transcript of examination of witnesses, objections to evidence, rulings, jury instructions, opinion, etc.).

records and briefs See APPEAL PAPERS.

regional reporter A unit of the National Reporter System that reports state court cases from a defined geographical area.

regulations Rules or orders issued by various governmental departments to carry out the intent of the law. Agencies issue regulations to guide the activity of their employees and to ensure uniform application of the law. Regulations are not the work of the legislature and do not have the effect of law in theory. In practice, however, because of the intricacies of judicial review of administrative action, regulations can have an important effect in determining the outcome of cases involving regulatory activity. U.S. government regulations appear first in the *Federal Register,* published five days a week, and are subsequently arranged by subject in the *Code of Federal Regulations.*

relief The remedy or redress sought by a complainant from the court.

remand To send back for further proceedings, as when a higher court sends back to a lower court.

reports (1) Court reports—published judicial cases arranged according to some grouping, such as jurisdiction, court, period of time, subject matter, or case significance; and (2) administrative reports or decisions—published decisions of an administrative agency.

resolution A formal expression of the opinion of a rule-making body adopted by the vote of that body.

respondent The party who makes an answer to a bill in an equity proceeding or who contends against an appeal.

restatements of the law Systematic restatements of the existing common law in certain areas, published by the American Law Institute since 1923. The Restatements are valuable secondary research sources, but are not binding as law.

revised statutes In popular usage, a code. Technically, it is a compilation of statutes in the order and wording originally passed by the legislature, with temporary and repealed acts deleted.

rules of court The rules regulating practice and procedure before the various courts. In most jurisdictions, these rules are issued by the individual courts or by the highest court in that jurisdiction.

sanction (1) to assent to another's actions; (2) a penalty for violating a law.

scope note a notation appearing below a topic heading in a publication that delimits and identifies the content of the topic.

search engine Software used to search data for specific information. On the Internet, a search engine is a coordinated set of programs that seeks out the World Wide Web pages, indexes them, and enables searches for indexed pages to be run.

secondary authority See PRIMARY AUTHORITY.

section line The subject of a key number in West's Key Number Digests, printed after the key number.

selective incorporation The theory under which certain constitutional amendments contained in the Bill of Rights are made applicable to actions by the states.

session laws Laws enacted by a legislature that are published in bound or pamphlet volumes after adjournment of each regular or special session.

shepardized A trademark of Shepard's Citations, Inc., descriptive of the general use of its publications.

slander Oral defamation of a person's character. Compare with LIBEL.

slip law A legislative enactment published in pamphlet or single-sheet form immediately after its passage.

slip opinion An individual court case published separately soon after it is decided.

squib A very brief rendition of a single case or a single point of law from a case. Compare with HEADNOTE.

stare decisis The doctrine of English and American law that states that when a court has formulated a principle of law as applicable to a given set of facts, it will follow that principle and apply it in future cases where the facts are substantially the same. It connotes the decision of present cases on the basis of past precedent.

star pagination A scheme in reprint editions of court reports used to show where the pages of the text of the official edition begin and end.

status table A document detailing the current status of a bill or court decision.

statutes Acts of a legislature. Depending upon its context in usage, a statute may mean a single act of a legislature or a body of acts that are collected and arranged according to a scheme or for a session of a legislature or parliament.

statutes at large The official compilation of acts passed by the U.S. Congress. The arrangement is currently by Public Law number, and by chapter number in pre-1951 volumes. This is the official print of the law for citation purposes where titles of the United States Code have not been enacted into positive law.

statutes of limitations Laws setting time limits after which a dispute cannot be taken to court.

statutory instruments English administrative regulations and orders. The term applies especially to the administrative rules published since 1939, supplementing the English administrative code, Statutory Rules and Orders.

Statutory Rules and Orders English administrative regulations and orders.

strict scrutiny A standard for determining whether equal protection rights and fundamental rights have been violated; the standard is generally applied to classifications based on race, national origin, and alienage; under this standard, the government must prove that the law it has made is substantially related to a compelling government interest.

style of a case The parties to a lawsuit as they are written in the heading at the beginning of a written case. Also known as the caption of a case.

subpoena A court order compelling a witness to appear and testify in a certain proceeding.

substantive law That law which establishes rights and obligations, as distinguished from procedural law, which is concerned with rules for establishing their judicial enforcement.

summary judgment   A judgment entered prior to litigation on the merits of a case if there is no dispute as to the facts and only a question of law must be decided. A summary judgment may be entered to dispose of a single issue in a case or the entire case.

summons   A notice delivered by a sheriff or other authorized person informing a person that he or she is the defendant in a civil action, and specifying a time and place to appear in court to answer to the plaintiff.

supersede   To displace or to supplant one publication or its segment with another.

supreme court   (1) the court of last resort in the federal judicial system (the Supreme Court of the United States also has original jurisdiction in some cases); (2) in state judicial systems, except New York and Massachusetts, the highest appellate court or court of last resort.

suspect classification   A classification based on race, national origin, alienage, or other trait that seems to go against constitutional principles; suspect classifications are subject to strict scrutiny.

syllabus   See HEADNOTE.

table of cases   A list of cases, arranged alphabetically by case names, with citations and references to the body of the publication where the cases are found or treated.

table of statutes   A list of statutes with references to the body of the publication where the statutes are treated or construed.

temporary law   An act that continues in force for a limited period of time.

term of court   Signifies the space of time prescribed by law during which a court holds session. The court's session may actually extend beyond the term. The October Term of the Supreme Court of the United States is now the only term during which the Court sits, and lasts from October to June or July.

Tenth Amendment   Constitutional provision that reserves powers not specifically given to the federal government for the states and citizens of the United States.

Thirteenth Amendment   The constitutional amendment abolishing slavery.

tort   A civil wrong that does not involve a contractual relationship. The elements of a tort are a duty owed, a breach of that duty, and the resultant harm to the one to whom the duty was owed.

transcript of record   The printed record as made up in each case of the proceedings and pleadings necessary for the appellate court to review the history of the case.

treatise   An exposition, which may be critical, evaluative, interpretative, or informative, on case law or legislation. Usually it is more exhaustive than an encyclopedia article, but less detailed and critical than a law review article.

treaty   An agreement between two or more sovereign nations.

trespass   An unlawful interference with one's person, property, or rights. At common law, trespass was a form of action brought to recover damages for any injury to one's person or property or relationship with another.

ultrafiche   See MICROFICHE.

uniform laws   Statutes drafted for adoption by the several states in the interest of uniformity. A considerable number of uniform laws on various subjects have been approved by the National Conference of Commissioners on Uniform State Laws, and have been adopted in one or more jurisdictions in the United States and its possessions. The Uniform Commercial Code is now the law in 49 states.

uniform system of citation   See BLUEBOOK.

unofficial reports   Court reports published without statutory direction. They are not distinguished from official reports on grounds of varying quality or accuracy of reporting.

URL An abbreviation for Uniform Resource Locator. A URL is a standard address for a resource or site on the Internet. A URL such as http://www.tiddlywinks.com describes the access method used (http) and the location of the server hosting the site (www.tiddlywinks.com). The most common use of a URL is to enter into a World Wide Web browser program such as Internet Explorer or Netscape.

venue The particular geographical area where a court with jurisdiction may try a case.

waiver The voluntary relinquishment of a known right.

Web See WORLD WIDE WEB.

Westlaw The computerized legal research system of West Group. Westlaw provides the full text of court decisions, statutes, administrative materials, ALR annotations, law review articles, reporter services, Supreme Court briefs, and other items. Keyword searches, natural language searches, field searches, and citator searches are available.

World Wide Web (Web) A subset of the Internet using hypertext links and mixing text, graphics, sound files, multimedia. The Web has become the major medium for publishing information on the Internet.

writ A written order, of which there are many types, issued by a court and directed to an official or party, commanding the performance of some act.

wrongful death A type of lawsuit brought by or on behalf of a deceased person's beneficiaries, alleging that the death was attributable to the willful or negligent act of another.

SOURCES BY CASE

Abrams v. United States, 250 U.S. 616 (1919)

Beschle, Donald L. "An Absolutism That Works: Reviving the Original 'Clear and Present Danger' Test." *Southern Illinois University Law Journal* (1983): 127–160.

Cox, Archibald. *The Court and the Constitution.* Boston: Houghton Mifflin, 1987.

Emerson, Thomas I. *Toward a General Theory of the First Amendment.* New York: Random House, 1962.

Semonche, John E. *Charting the Future: The Supreme Court Responds to a Changing Society, 1890–1920.* Westport, Conn.: Greenwood Press, 1978.

Adair v. United States, 208 U.S. 161 (1908)

"The Adamson Case: A Study in Constitutional Technique." *Yale Law Review* 58 (1949): 268.

Cox, Archibald. *The Court and the Constitution.* Boston: Houghton Mifflin, 1987.

Semonche, John E. *Charting the Future: The Supreme Court Responds to a Changing Society, 1890–1920.* Westport, Conn.: Greenwood Press, 1978.

Adamson v. California, 332 U.S. 46 (1947)

Cohen, William. "Justices Black and Douglas and the 'Natural Due Process' Formula." *U.C. Davis Law Review* 20 (winter): 381.

Mykkeltvedt, Roald Y. *The Naturalization of the Bill of Rights.* New York: Associated Faculty Press, 1983.

Baker v. Carr, 369 U.S. 186 (1962)

Ball, Howard. *The Warren Court's Conceptions of Democracy.* New Jersey: Fairleigh Dickinson University Press, 1971.

Cortner, Richard C. *The Apportionment Cases.* Knoxville: University of Tennessee Press, 1970.

Elliott, Ward E. Y. *The Rise of Guardian Democracy.* Cambridge, Mass.: Harvard University Press, 1974.

Emerson, Thomas I. "Malapportionment and Judicial Power." *Yale Law Journal* 72 (1962): 64–80.

Graham, Gene. *One Man, One Vote.* Boston: Little, Brown, 1972.

McCloskey, Robert G. "The Supreme Court 1961 Term. Forward: The Reapportionment Case." *Harvard Law Review* (1974): 1–74.

Neal, Phil C. "*Baker v. Carr*: Politics in Search of Law." *Supreme Court Review* (1962): 252–327.

Wiecek, William M. *The Guarantee Clause of the U.S. Constitution.* Ithaca, N.Y.: Cornell University Press, (1972).

Barenblatt v. United States, 360 U.S. 109 (1960)

Emerson, Thomas I. *The System of Freedom of Expression.* New York: Random House, 1970.

Kalvan, Harry, Jr. "Mr. Alexander Meiklejohn and the Barenblatt Opinion." *University of Chicago Law Review* 27 (1960): 315–328.

Meiklejohn, Alexander. "The Barenblatt Opinion." *University of Chicago Law Review* 27 (1960) 329–340.

Batson v. Kentucky, 476 U.S. 79 (1986)

Alschuler, Albert W. "The Supreme Court and the Jury: voir dire, peremptory challenges and the review of jury verdicts." *University of Chicago Law Review* 56 (winter 1989): 329–340.

Cassidy, Helen, and Poppy Northcutt. "Holy Moly, Batson." Houston *Lawyer* 27 (January/February 1990): 30–38.

Goldwasser, Katherine. "Limiting a Criminal Defendant's Use of Peremptory Challenges: On Symmetry and the Jury in a Criminal Trial." *Harvard Law Review* 102 (February 1989): 808–840.

Kavanaugh, Brett M. "Defense Presence and Participation: A Procedural Minimun for *Batson v. Kentucky* Hearings." *Yale Law Journal* 99 (October 1989): 187–207.

Pizzi, William T. "*Batson v. Kentucky*: Curing the Disease but Killing the Patient." *Supreme Court Review* (1987): 97–156.

Beauharnais v. Illinois, 343 U.S. 250 (1952)

Arkes, Hadley. "Civility and the Restriction of Speech: Rediscovering the Defamation of Groups." *Supreme Court Review* (1974): 281–335.

Berns, Walter F. *Freedom, Virtue and the First Amendment*. Chicago: Gateway Editions, 1965.

Kalvan, Harry, Jr. "The Metaphysics of the Law of Obscenity." *Supreme Court Review* 1 (1960): 3–4.

Betts v. Brady, 316 U.S. 455 (1942)

Lusky, Louis. "Minority Rights and Public Interest." *Yale Law Review* 52 (December 1942): 1–42.

Vetter, Harold J., and Clifford E. Simonsen. *Criminal Justice in America*. Philadelphia: W. B. Saunders, 1976, pp. 197–200.

Bivens v. Six Unknown Agents, 403 U.S. 388 (1971)

"Fourth Amendment Does Not Establish a Federal Cause of Action for Damages Caused by an Unreasonable Search and Seizure." *Harvard Law Review* 83 (1970): 684–690.

Posner, Richard A. "Rethinking the Fourth Amendment." *Supreme Court Review* (1981): 49–79.

Schwartz, Bernard. *The Ascent of Pragmatism: The Burger Court in Action*. New York: Addison-Wesley, 1990.

Bolling v. Sharp, 347 U.S. 497 (1954)

Kluger, Richard. *Simple Justice: The History of Brown v. Board of Education and Black America's Struggle for Equality*. New York: Knopf, 1976.

Bowers v. Hardwick, 478 U.S. 186 (1986)

Goldstein, Anne B. "History, Homosexuality, and Political Values: Searching for Hidden Determinants of *Bowers v. Hardwick*." 97 *Yale Law Journal* (May 1988): 1073–1104.

Rubenfeld, Jed. "The Right of Privacy." *Harvard Law Review* 102 (February 1989): 737–807.

Vieira, Norman. *Hardwick and the Right of Privacy*. University of Chicago Law Review 55 (fall 1988): 1181–1191.

Bowsher v. Synar, 478 U.S. 714 (1986)

Currie, David P. "The Distribution of Powers after Bowsher." *Supreme Court Review* (1986): 19–40.

Gifford, Daniel J. "The Separation of Powers Doctrine and the Regulatory Agencies after *Bowsher v. Synar*." *George Washington Law Review* 55 (March 1987): 441–481.

Schwartz, Bernard. *The Ascent of Pragmatism: The Burger Court in Action*. New York: Addison-Wesley, 1990.

Strauss, Peter L. "Formal and Functional Approaches to Separation of Powers Questions: A Foolish Inconsistency?" *Cornell Law Review* 72 (March 1987): 488–526.

Brandenburg v. Ohio, 395 U.S. 444 (1969)

Beschle, Donald L. "An Absolutism That Works: Reviving the Original 'clear and present danger' test." *Southern Illinois University Law Journal* (1983): 127–159.

Gottesman, Lawrence P. "The Intelligence Identities Protection Act of 1982: An Assessment of the Constitutionality of Section 601(c)." *Brooklyn Law Review* 49 (spring 1983): 479–516.

Jenson, Carol E. *The Network of Control*. Westport, Conn.: Greenwood Press, 1982.

Branzburg v. Hayes, 408 U.S. 665 (1972)

Blanchard, Margaret A. "The Institutional Press and Its First Amendment Privileges." *Supreme Court Review* (1978): 225–296.

Goodale, James C. "Branzburg and the Protection of Reporters' Sources." *University of Miami Law Review* 29 (spring 1975): 456–458.

Kane, Peter E. *Murder, Courts and the Press*. Edwardsville: Southern Illinois University Press, 1986.

Mejelski, Paul, and Kurt Finsterbusch. "The Prosecutor and the Researcher: Present and Prospective Variations in the Supreme Court's *Branzburg* Decision." *Social Problems* 21 (summer 1973): 3–20.

Braunfeld v. Brown, 366 U.S. 599 (1961)

Giannella, Donald A. "Religious Liberty: Non-establishment and Doctrinal Development." *Harvard Law Review* 80 (May 1967): 1,381–1,431.

Katz, Wilber G. *Religion and American Constitutions.* Evanston, Ill.: Northwestern University Press, 1964.

Kauper, Paul G. *Religion and the Constitution.* Baton Rouge: Louisiana State University Press, 1964.

Breedlove v. Suttles, 302 U.S. 277 (1937)

Bork, Robert H. *The Tempting of America: The Political Seduction of the Law.* New York: Free Press, 1990.

Brown v. Board of Education of Topeka, 349 U.S. 294 (1954)

Cohen, David K. "Segregation, Desegregation and *Brown:* A Twenty-Year Retrospective." *Society* 12 (November/December 1974): 34–40.

Gewirtz, Paul. "Remedies and Resistance." *Yale Law Journal* 92 (March 1983): 585–681.

Graglia, Lino A. *Disaster by Decree.* Ithaca, N.Y.: Cornell University Press, 1976.

Kluger, Richard. *Simple Justice: The History of* Brown v. Board of Education *and Black America's Struggle for Equality.* New York: Knopf, 1976.

Rodgers, Harrell R., Jr., and Charles S. Bullock. *Law and Social Change: Civil Rights Laws and Their Consequences.* New York: McGraw Hill, 1972.

Buckley v. Valeo, 424 U.S. 1 (1976)

Dry, Murray. "The Constitutional Veto and the Constitutional Separation of Powers." In *The Presidency in the Constitutional Order,* Joseph M. Bessette and Jeffrey Tulis, eds. Baton Rouge: Louisiana State University Press, 1981.

Fisher, Louis. *The Constitution between Friends.* New York: St. Martin's Press, 1978.

Schwartz, Bernard. *The Ascent of Pragmatism: the Burger Court in Action.* New York: Addison-Wesley, 1990.

Caban v. Mohammed, 441 U.S. 380 (1979)

Doyle, Gerald P. "Voluntary Legitimization Rights of Unwed Fathers in Texas." *Houston Law Review* 20 (July 1983): 1,157–1,178.

Klein, Rona. "Punative Fathers: Unwed but No Longer Unprotected." *Hofstra Law* Review 8 (winter 1980): 425–449.

Radford, Mary F. "New York Statute Requiring Consent of Mothers." *Emory Law Journal* 29 (summer 1980): 833–858.

Calder v. Bull, 3 U.S. 386 (1798)

Currie, David P. *The Constitution in the Supreme Court 1789–1888.* Chicago: University of Chicago Press, 1985.

Wiecek, William M. *The Guarantee Clause of the United States Constitution.* Ithaca, N.Y.: Cornell University Press, 1972.

Bork, Robert H. *The Tempting of America: The Political Seduction of the Law.* New York: Free Press, 1990.

California v. Ciraola, 476 U.S. 207 (1986)

Nelms, William G. "Aerial Surveillance and the Fourth Amendment." *Arizona Law Review* 30 (spring 1988): 361–370.

Schwartz, Bernard. *The Ascent of Pragmatism: The Burger Court in Action.* New York: Addison-Wesley, 1990.

Cantwell v. Connecticut, 310 U.S. 296 (1940)

Emerson, Thomas I. *The System of Freedom of Expression.* New York: Random House, 1970.

Johnson, Alvin W., and Frank H. Yost. *The Separation of Church and State in the United States.* Minneapolis: University of Minnesota Press, 1948.

Lusky, Louis. "Minority Rights and Public Interest." *Yale Law Review* 52 (December 1942): 1–42.

Recent Decisions. *Columbia Law Review* 40 (June 1940): 1,067.

Carey v. Population Services, International, 431 U.S. 678 (1977)

Pfeffer, Leo. *Religion, State and the Burger Court.* New York: Prometheus Books, 1984.

Richards, David A. J. "The Individual, the Family, and the Constitution: A Jurisprudential Perspective." *N.Y.U. Law Review* 55 (spring 1980): 1–62.

Siliciano, John. "The Minor's Right to Privacy: Limitations on State Action after *Danforth* and *Carey.*" *Columbia Law Review* 77 (December 1977): 1,216.

Carter v. Carter Coal Co., 298 U.S. 238 (1936)

Benson, Paul R., Jr. *The Supreme Court and the Commerce Clause, 1937–1970.* New York: Dunellen Publishing, 1970.

Champion v. Ames, 188 U.S. 321 (1903)

Benson, Paul R., Jr. *The Supreme Court and the Commerce Clause, 1937–1970.* New York: Dunellen Publishing, 1970.

Chaplinsky v. New Hampshire, 315 U.S. 568 (1942)

Arkes, Hadley. "Civility and the Restriction of Speech: Rediscovering the Defamation of Groups." *Supreme Court Review* (1974): 281–335.

Tilton, Robert P. "Constitutional Law: Limitation on the Freedom of Speech." *Boston University Law Review* 22 (July 1942): 446–449.

Wright, George R. "A Rationale from J. S. Mill for the Free Speech Clause." *Supreme Court Review* (1985): 149–178.

Charles River Bridge Co. v. Warren Bridge Co., 36 U.S. 420 (1837)

Currie, David P. *The Constitution in the Supreme Court 1789–1888.* Chicago: University of Chicago Press, 1985.

———. "The Constitution in the Supreme Court: Article IV and Federal Powers 1836–1864." *Duke Law Journal* (September 1983): 695–747.

Horwitz, Morton J. *The Transformation of American Law, 1780–1860.* Cambridge, Mass.: Harvard University Press, 1977.

Merrill, Thomas W. "Public Contracts and the Transformation of the Constitutional Order." *Case Western Reserve Law Review* 37 (summer): 597–630.

Chimel v. California, 395 U.S. 752 (1969)

"The Supreme Court 1968 Term." *Harvard Law Review* 83 (November 1969): 154.

Chisolm v. Georgia, 2 U.S. 419 (1793)

Currie, David P. *The Constitution in the Supreme Court, 1789–1888.* Chicago: University of Chicago Press, 1985.

Keynes, Edward, with Randall K. Miller. *The Court v. Congress: Prayer, Busing and Abortion.* Durham, N.C.: Duke University Press, 1989.

McCloskey, Robert G. *The American Supreme Court.* Chicago: University of Chicago Press, 1960.

Cohen v. California, 403 U.S. 15 (1971)

Cox, Archibald. *The Role of the Supreme Court in American Government.* New York: Oxford University Press, 1976.

Posner, Richard A. "The Uncertain Protection of Privacy by the Supreme Court." *Supreme Court Review* (1979): 173–213.

Stone, Geoffrey R. "Fora Americana: Speech in Public Places." *Supreme Court Review* (1974): 233–280.

Wright, George R. "A Rationale from J. S. Mill for the Free Speech Clause." *Supreme Court Review* (1985): 149–178.

Cole v. Richardson, 405 U.S. 676 (1971)

Colegrove v. Green, 328 U.S. 549 (1946)

Ball, Howard. *The Warren Court's Conceptions of Democracy.* East Rutherford, N.J.: Fairleigh Dickinson University Press, 1971.

Bickel, Alexander. "The Durability of *Colegrove v. Green.*" *Yale Law Journal* 72 (1962): 39–45.

Bushnell, Eleanore. The Court Steps In. *Impact of Reapportionment on the Thirteen Western States.* Eleanore Bushnell, ed. Salt Lake City: University of Utah Press, 1970.

Cooley v. Board of Wardens of the Port of Philadelphia, 53 U.S. 299 (1891)

Benson, Paul R., Jr. *The Supreme Court and the Commerce Clause, 1937–1970.* New York: Dunellen Publishing, 1970.

Cox, Archibald. *The Court and the Constitution.* Boston: Houghton Mufflin, 1987.

Currie, David P. *The Constitution in the Supreme Court, 1789–1888.* Chicago, Ill.: University of Chicago Press, 1985.

Cooper v. Aaron, 358 U.S. 1 (1963)

Bolmeier, Edward C. *Landmark Supreme Court Decisions on Public School Issues.* Charlottesville, Va.: The Michie Co., 1973.

Gewirtz, Paul. "Remedies and Resistance." *Yale Law Journal* 92 (March 1983): 585–681.

Keynes, Edward, with Randall K. Miller. *The Court vs. Congress: Prayer, Busing and Abortion.* Durham, N.C.: Duke University Press, 1989.

Coppage v. Kansas, 236 U.S. 1 (1911)

Casebeer, Kenneth M. "Teaching an Old Dog Old Tricks: *Coppage v. Kansas* and At Will Employment Revisited." *Cardozo Law Review* 6 (summer 1985): 765–791.

Semonche, John E. *Charting the Future: The Supreme Court Responds to a Changing Society, 1890–1920.* Westport, Conn.: Greenwood Press, 1978.

Tushnet, Mark. "The Newer Property: Suggestion for the Revival of Substantive Due Process." *Supreme Court Review* (1975): 261–288.

Cox v. Louisiana, 379 U.S. 536 (1965)

Emerson, Thomas I. *The System of Freedom of Expression.* New York: Random House, 1970.

Kalven, Harry, Jr. "The Concept of the Public Forum: *Cox v. Louisiana.*" *Supreme Court Review* (1965): 1–32.

Stephan, Paul B., III. "The First Amendment and Content Discrimination." *Virginia Law Review* 68 (February 1982): 203–251.

Craig v. Borden, 429 U.S. 190 (1976)

Kanowitz, Leo. "'Benign' Sex Discrimination: Its Troubles and Their Cure." *Hastings Law Journal* 31 (1980): 1,379–1,431.

Kirp, Donald L. et al. *Gender Justice.* Chicago: University of Chicago Press, 1986.

Roberts, John C. "Gender Based Draft Registration: Congressional Policy and Equal Protection." *Wayne Law Review* 27 (fall 1980): 35–93.

Dandridge v. Williams, 397 U.S. 254 (1970)

Cox, Archibald. *The Court and the Constitution.* Boston: Houghton Mufflin, 1987.

"The Equal Protection Clause and Exclusionary Zoning after *Valtierra* and *Dandridge.*" *Yale Law Journal* 81 (1971): 61–86.

Schwartz, Bernard. *The Ascent of Pragmatism: The Burger Court in Action.* New York: Addison-Wesley, 1990.

Dartmouth College v. Woodward, 17 U.S. 518 (1819)

Campbell, B. A. "John Marshall, the Virginia Political Economy, and the Dartmouth College Decision." *American Journal of Legal History* 19 (1975): 40.

Friendly, Henry J. *The Dartmouth College Case and the Public-Private Penumbra.* Austin, Texas: University of Texas Press, 1968.

Hunting, Warren B. *The Obligations of the Contract Clause of the United States Constitution.* Westport, Conn.: Greenwood Press, 1919.

Stites, Francis N. *Private Interest and Public Gain: The Dartmouth College Case, 1819.* Amherst: University of Massachusetts Press, 1972.

DeJonge v. Oregon, 299 U.S. 353 (1937)

Emerson, Thomas I. *The System of Freedom of Expression.* New York: Random House, 1970.

Fellman, David. "Constitutional Rights of Association." *Supreme Court Review* (1961): 74–134.

Jenson, Carol E. *The Network of Control.* Westport, Conn.: Greenwood Press, 1982.

Dennis v. New York, 341 U.S. 494 (1951)

Belknap, Michael R. *Cold War Political Justice.* Westport, Conn.: Greenwood Press, 1977.

Berns, Walter F. *Freedom, Virtue and the First Amendment.* Chicago: Gateway Editions, 1963.

Emerson, Thomas I. *The System of Freedom of Expression.* New York: Random House, 1970.

Mendelson, Wallace. "'Clear and Present Danger'—From *Schenck* to *Dennis.*" *Columbia Law Review* 52 (1952): 313–333.

Dred Scott v. Sandford, 60 U.S. 393 (1857)

Cable, John L. *Decisive Decisions of United States Citizenship.* Charlottesville, Va.: The Michie Co., 1967.

Cox, Archibald. *The Court and the Constitution.* Boston: Houghton Mufflin, 1987.

Currie, David P. *The Constitution in the Supreme Court, 1789–1888.* Chicago: University of Chicago Press, 1985.

Meyer, Howard N. *The Amendment That Refused to Die.* Radnor, Pa.: Chilton Books, 1973.

Vishneski, John S., III. "What the Court Decided in *Dred Scott v. Sandford.*" *American Journal of Legal History* 32 (October 1988): 373–390.

Duncan v. Louisiana, 391 U.S. 145 (1968)

Gillers, Stephen. "Deciding Who Dies." *University of Pennsylvania Law Review* 129 (November 1980): 1–124.

Schultz, Marjorie S. "The Jury Redefined: A Review of the Burger Court Decisions." *Law and Contemporary Problems* 43 (autumn 1980): 8–23.

Edwards v. California, 314 U.S. 160 (1941)

Benson, Paul R., Jr. *The Supreme Court and the Commerce Clause, 1937–1970.* New York: Dunellen Publishing, 1970.

Katz, Katheryn D. "More Equal Than Others: The Burger Court and the Newly Arrived State Residents." *New Mexico Law Review* 19 (spring 1989): 329–376.

Edwards v. South Carolina, 372 U.S. 229 (1963)

EEOC v. Wyoming, 460 U.S. 226 (1983)

Alfange, Dean, Jr. "Congressional Regulation of the 'States Qua States': From *National League of*

Cities to EEOC v. Wyoming." *Supreme Court Review* (1983): 215–281.

Keynes, Edward, with Randall K. Miller. *The Court vs. Congress: Prayer, Busing and Abortion.* Durham, N.C.: Duke University Press, 1989.

Eisenstadt v. Baird, 405 U.S. 438 (1972)

Keynes, Edward, with Randall K. Miller. *The Court vs. Congress: Prayer, Busing and Abortion.* Durham, N.C.: Duke University Press, 1989.

"On Privacy: Constitutional Protection for Personal Liberty." *NYU Law Review* 48 (1973): 670.

Schwartz, Bernard. *The Ascent of Pragmatism: The Burger Court in Action.* New York: Addison-Wesley, 1990.

Engle v. Vitale, 370 U.S. 421 (1962)

Bobbitt, Philip. *Constitutional Fate: Theory of the Constitution.* New York: Oxford University Press, 1982.

Kurland, Philip B. "The School Prayer Cases." In *The Wall between Church and States.* Dallin H. Oaks and Robert F. Drinan, eds. Chicago: University of Chicago Press, 1963.

———. "The Regent's Prayer Case." In *Church and State.* Philip B. Kurland, ed. Chicago: University of Chicago Press, 1975.

Pfeffer, Louis. "The New York Regent's Prayer Case." *Journal of Church and State* 4 (November 1962): 150–158.

Pollak, Louis H. "The Supreme Court, 1962 Term. Foreword: Public Prayers in Public Schools." *Harvard Law Review* 77 (November 1963): 62–78.

Epperson v. Arkansas, 393 U.S. 97 (1968)

Bolmeier, Edward C. *Landmark Supreme Court Decisions on Public School Issues.* Charlottesville, Va.: The Michie Co., 1973.

Erie Railroad Co. v. Tompkins, 304 U.S. 64 (1983)

Clark, Charles E. "State Law in the Federal Courts: The Brooding Omnipresence of *Erie v. Tompkins.*" *Yale Law Journal* 55 (February 1946): 265–296.

Ely, John Hart. "The Irrepressible Myth of Erie." *Harvard Law Review* 87 (1974): 693–740.

Freyer, Tony. *Harmony and Dissonance.* New York: New York University Press, 1981.

Kurland, Philip B. "Mr. Justice Frankfurter, the Supreme Court and the Erie Doctrine in Diversity Cases." *Yale Law Review* 67 (1957): 187–218.

Escobedo v. Illinois, 378 U.S. 478 (1964)

Dripps, Donald. "Supreme Court Review-Forward: Against Police Interrogation." *Journal of Criminal Law and Criminology* 78 (winter 1988): 699–734.

Michaux, Roy H., Jr. "Notes and Comments—Constitutional Law—Right to Retained Counsel at Time of Arrest." *North Carolina Law Review* 43 (1964): 187–199.

"The Supreme Court, 1963 Term." *Harvard Law Review* 78 (November 1964): 218–223.

Everson v. Board of Education, 330 U.S. 1 (1947)

Alito, Samuel A. "The Released Time Cases Revisited." *Yale Law Journal* 83 (May 1974): 1,202–1,236.

Kirby, James C. "Everson to Meek and Roemer." *North Carolina Law Review* 55 (1977): 563–75.

Pfeffer, Leo. *Religion, State and the Burger Court.* Buffalo, N.Y.: Prometheus Books, 1984.

Smith, Rodney K. "Getting Off on the Wrong Food." *Wake Forest Law Review* 20 (fall 1984): 569–642.

Swanson, Wayne R. *The Christ Child Goes to Court.* Philadelphia, Pa.: Temple University Press, 1990.

Ex Parte McCardle, 74 U.S. 506 (1869)

Keyes, Edward, with Randall K. Miller. *The Court vs. Congress.* Durham, N.C.: Duke University Press, 1989.

Ex Parte Milligan, 71 U.S. 2 (1866)

McCloskey, Robert G. *The American Supreme Court.* Chicago: University of Chicago Press, 1960.

tenBroek, Jacobus, et al. *Prejudice, War and the Constitution.* Berkeley: University of California Press, 1968.

Wertheim, Lewis J. "The Indianapolis Treason Trials: The Election of 1864 and the Power of the Partisan Press." *Indiana Magazine of History* 85 (September 1989): 236–260.

F.C.C. v. League of Women Voters, 104 S.Ct. 3106 (1984)

Hixson, Richard F. *Mass Media and the Constitution.* New York: Garland Publishing, 1989.

"Leading Cases of the 1983 Term." *Harvard Law Review* 98 (November 1984): 205.

"The Supreme Court Strikes Down the Public Broadcasting Editorial Ban: *F.C.C. v. League of Women Voters.*" *Pepperdine Law Review* 12 (1985): 699.

Fay v. Noia, 372 U.S. 391 (1963)

Bourguignon, Henry J. "The Second Mr. Justice Harlan: His Principles of Judicial Decision Making." *Supreme Court Review* (1979): 251–328.

Chemerinsky, Erwin. "Thinking About Habeas Corpus." *Case Western Reserve Law Review* 37 (summer 1987): 748–793.

Sallet, Jonathan B., and Saul B. Goodman. "Closing the Door to Federal Habeas Corpus." *American Criminal Law Review* 20 (1983): 465–483.

"The Supreme Court, 1962 Term." *Harvard Law Review* 77 (1963): 140–149.

Feiner v. New York, 340 U.S. 315 (1951)

Emerson, Thomas I. *The System of Freedom of Expression.* New York: Random House, 1970.

Fellman, David. "Constitutional Rights of Association." *Supreme Court Review* (1961): 74–134.

Ferguson v. Skrupa, 372 U.S. 726 (1963)

Schwartz, Bernard. *A Commentary on the Constitution of the United States.* Part II *The Rights of Property.* New York: Macmillan, 1965.

First National Bank of Boston v. Bellotti, 435 U.S. 765 (1978)

Prentice, R. A. "Consolidated Edison and Bellotti: First Amendment Protection of Corporate Political Speech." *Tulsa Law Journal* 16 (1981): 598.

"The Supreme Court, 1977 Term." *Harvard Law Review* 92 (November 1978.): 163.

Flast v. Cohen, 392 U.S. 83 (1968)

Davis, Kenneth Culp. "Standing: Taxpayers and Others." *University of Chicago Law Review* 35 (1968): 601–636.

Pfeffer, Leo. *Religion, State and the Burger Court.* New York: Prometheus Books, 1984.

Velvel, Laurence R. *Undeclared War and Civil Disobedience.* New York: Dunellen Co., 1970.

Fletcher v. Peck, 10 U.S. 87 (1910)

Magrath, C. Peter. *Yazoo: Law and Politics in the New Republic: The Case of* Fletcher v. Peck. Providence, R.I.: Brown University Press, 1966.

McCloskey, Robert G. *The American Supreme Court.* Chicago: University of Chicago Press, 1960.

Palmer, Robert C. "Obligations of Contracts: Intent and Distortion." *Case Western Reserve Law Review* 37 (summer 1987): 631–673.

Wiecek, William M. *The Guarantee Clause of the United States Constitution.* Ithaca, N.Y.: Cornell University Press, 1972.

Foley v. Connelie, 435 U.S. 291 (1978)

Casad, Steven J. "Alienage and Public Employment: The Need for an Intermediate Standard in Equal Protection." *Hastings Law Journal* 32 (September 1980): 163–199.

"A Dual Standard for State Discrimination Against Aliens." *Harvard Law Review* 92 (1979): 1,516–1,537.

Schwartz, Bernard. *The Ascent of Pragmatism: The Burger Court in Action.* New York: Addison-Wesley, 1990.

Frontiero v. Richardson, 411 U.S. 677 (1973)

Cox, Archibald. *The Court and the Constitution.* Boston: Houghton Mifflin, 1987.

Johnston, John D., Jr. "Sex Discrimination and the Supreme Court 1971–1974." *NYU Law Review* 49 (November 1974): 617–692.

Kirp, David L. *Gender Justice.* Chicago: University of Chicago Press, 1986.

Schwartz, Bernard. *The Ascent of Pragmatism: The Burger Court in Action.* New York: Addison-Wesley, 1990.

Frothingham v. Mellon, 262 U.S. 447 (1923)

"Constitutional Law–Higher Education Facilities Act–Constitutionality of Federal Financial Aid to Church Related Colleges." *Harvard Law Review* 77 (March 1964): 1,353–1,360.

Pfeffer, Leo. *Religion, State and the Burger Court.* Buffalo, N.Y.: Prometheus Books, 1984.

Radcliffe, James E. *The Case or Controversy Provision.* University Park: Pennsylvania State University Press, 1978.

Furman v. Georgia, 408 U.S. 283 (1972)

Baldus, David C. et al. "Identifying Comparatively Excessive Standards of Death: A Quantitative Approach." *Stanford Law review* 33 (November 1980): 1–74.

Sheleff, Leon Shaskolsky. *Ultimate Penalties.* Columbus: Ohio State University Press, 1987, pp. 82–87.

White, Welsh S. *Life in a Balance.* Ann Arbor: University of Michigan Press, 1984.

Gallagher v. Crown Kosher Supermarket, 366 U.S. 617 (1961)

Laband, David N., and Deborah Hendry Heinbuch. *Blue Laws: The History, Economics and Politics of*

Sunday Closing Laws. Lexington, Mass: Lexington Books, 1987.

"The Supreme Court, 1960 Term." *Harvard Law Review* 75 (1961): 150.

Gannett v. DiPasquale, 443 U.S. 368 (1979)

Kane, Peter E. *Murder, Courts and the Press: Issues in Free Press/Free Trial.* Carbondale: Southern Illinois University Press, 1986.

Keefe, Arthur J. "The Boner Called Gannett." *ABA Journal* 66 (1980): 227–230.

Lewis, Anthony. "A Public Right to Know about Public Institutions: The First Amendment as a Sword." *Supreme Court Review* (1980): 1–26.

Schwartz, Bernard. "The Ascent of Pragmatism: The Burger Court in Action." New York: Addison-Wesley, 1990.

Garcia v. San Antonio, 469 U.S. 528 (1985)

Delmonte, Rosemarie E. "*Garcia v. San Antonio:* And the State Stands Alone." *Creighton Law Review* (fall 1986): 105–131.

Massey, Calvin R. "State Sovereignty and the Tenth and Eleventh Amendments." *University of Chicago Law Review* 56 (winter 1989): 61–152.

Rapaczynski, Andrzej. "From Sovereignity to Process: The Jurisprudence of Federalism after *Garcia.*" *Supreme Court Review* (1985) 341–420.

Schwartz, Bernard. *The Ascent of Pragmatism: The Burger Court in Action.* New York: Addison-Wesley, 1990.

Gertz v. Robert Welch, Inc. 418 U.S. 323 (1974)

Eaton, Joel D. "The American Law of Defamation through *Gertz v. Robert Welch, Inc.* and Beyond: An Analytic Primer." *Virginia Law Review* 61 (November 1975): 1,351–1,451.

Collins, Erik L., and J. Douglas Drushal. "The Reaction of the State Courts to *Gertz v. Robert Welch, Inc.*" *Case Western Reserve Law Review* 28 (1978): 306–343.

Godofsky, Stanley. "Protection of the Press from Prior Restraint and Harassment under Libel Laws." *University of Miami Law Review* 29 (spring 1975): 462–476.

Stonecipher, Harry W., and Robert Trager. "The Impact of Gertz on the Law of Libel." *Journalism Quarterly* 5 (winter 1976): 609–618.

Gibbons v. Ogden, 22 U.S. 1 (1824)

Baxter, Maurice G. *The Steamboat Monopoly,* Gibbons v. Ogden, *1824.* New York: Knopf, 1972.

Benson, Paul R., Jr. *The Supreme Court and the Commerce Clause 1937–1970.* New York: Dunellen Publishing, 1970.

Currie, David P. *The Constitution in the Supreme Court 1789–1888.* Chicago: University of Chicago Press, 1985.

Frankfurter, Felix. *The Commerce Clause under Marshall, Taney and Waite.* Chicago: Quadangle Books, 1964.

McCloskey, Robert G. *The American Supreme Court.* Chicago: University of Chicago Press, 1960.

Morrison, Fred L. "The Right to Fish for Seacoast Products: *Gibbons v. Ogden* Resurrected." *Supreme Court Review* (1977): 239–256.

Gideon v. Wainwright, 372 U.S. 335 (1963)

Israel, Jerold H. "*Gideon v. Wainwright:* The Art of Overruling." *Supreme Court Review* (1963): 211–277.

Lewis, Anthony. *Gideon's Trumpet.* New York: Random House, 1964.

"The Supreme Court, 1962 Term." *Harvard Law Review* 77 (November 1963): 103–105.

Ginsberg v. New York, 390 U.S. 629 (1968)

Coulter, Ann H. " Restricting Adult Access to Material Obscene as to Juveniles." *Michigan Law Review* 85 (June 1987): 1,681–1,898.

Emerson, Thomas I. *The System of Freedom of Expression.* New York: Random House, 1970.

Krislov, Samuel. "From *Ginzburg* to *Ginsberg:* The Unhurried Children's Hour in Obscenity Litigation." *Supreme Court Review* (1968): 153–197.

Weller, Christopher W. "See No Evil: The Decisive Issue of Minors' Access Laws." *Cumberland Law Review* 16 (winter 1988): 141–179.

Girouard v. United States, 328 U.S. 61 (1946)

Cable, John L. *Decisive Decisions on United States Citizenship.* Charlottesville, Va.: The Michie Co., 1967.

Gitlow v. New York, 268 U.S. 652 (1925)

Blanchard, Margaret A. "The Institutional Press and Its First Amendment Privileges." *Supreme Court Review* (1978) 225–296.

Emerson, Thomas I. *The System of Freedom of Expression.* New York: Random House, 1970.

Jenson, Carol E. *The Network of Control.* Westport, Conn.: Greenwood Press, 1982.

Goldman v. Weinburger, 475 U.S. 503 (1986)

"Constitutional Law—The Clash between the Free Exercise of Religion and the Military's Uniform Regulations." *Temple Law Quarterly* 58 (spring 1985): 195–219.

Schwartz, Bernard. *The Ascent of Pragmatism: The Burger Court in Action.* New York: Addison-Wesley, 1990.

Gomillion v. Lightfoot, 364 U.S. 339 (1960)

Elliot, Ward E. Y. *The Rise of Guardian Democracy.* Cambridge, Mass.: Harvard University Press, 1974.

Lucas, J. D. "Dragon in the Thicket: A Perusal of *Gomillion v. Lightfoot.*" *Supreme Court Review* (1961): 194–244.

"The Supreme Court, 1960 Term." *Harvard Law Review* 75 (1961): 136–138.

Goss v. Lopez, 419 U.S. 565 (1975)

Richards, David A. J. "The Individual, the Family, and the Constitution: A Jurisprudential Perspective." *NYU Law Review* 55 (April 1980): 1–62.

Wilkinson, J. Harvie, III. "*Goss v. Lopez: The Supreme Court as School Superintendent.*" *Supreme Court Review* (1975): 25–76.

Graham v. Richardson, 403 U.S. 365 (1971)

"A Dual Standard for State Discrimination against Aliens." *Harvard Law Review* 92 (1979): 1,516–1,537.

Casad, Steven J. "Alienage and Public Employment: The Need for an Intermediate Standard in Equal Protection." *Hastings Law Review* 32 (September 1980): 163–199.

Levi, David F. "The Equal Treatment of Aliens: Preemption or Equal Protection." *Stanford Law Review* 31 (July 1979): 1,069–1,091.

Rosberg, Gerald M. "The Protection of Aliens from Discriminatory Treatment by the National Government." *Supreme Court Review* (1977): 275–339.

Griffin v. Breckenridge, 403 U.S. 88 (1971)

"The Supreme Court, 1970 Term." *Harvard Law Review* 85 (November 1971): 95–104.

Griffin v. California, 308 U.S. 609 (1965)

Bradley, Craig M. "*Griffin v. California:* Still Viable after All These Years." *Michigan Law Review* 79 (May 1981): 1,290–1,298.

Griswold v. Connecticut, 381 U.S. 479 (1965)

Bork, Robert. "Neutral Principles and Some First Amendment Problems." *Indiana Law Journal* 47 (1971): 7–11.

Dixon, Robert G. "The Griswold Penumbra: Constitutional Charter for an Expanded Law of Privacy." *Michigan Law Review* 64 (December 1965): 197–218.

Ely, John Hart. "The Ninth Amendment." In *The Rights Retained by the People,* Randy E. Barrett, ed. Fairfax, Va.: George Mason University Press, 1989.

"On Privacy: Constitutional Protection for Personal Liberty." *NYU Law Review* 48 (1973): 670.

Schwartz, Bernard. *The Ascent of Pragmatism: The Burger Court in Action.* New York: Addison-Wesley, 1990.

Van Loan, Eugene M., III. "Natural Rights and the Ninth Amendment." In *The Rights Retained by the People.* Randy E. Barrett, ed. Fairfax, Va.: George Mason University Press, 1989.

Haig v. Agee, 453 U.S. 280 (1981)

Farber, Daniel A. "National Security, the Right to Travel and the Court." *Supreme Court Review* (1981): 263–290.

Schwartz, Bernard. *The Ascent of Pragmatism: The Burger Court in Action.* New York: Addison-Wesley, 1990.

"The Supreme Court: 1980 Term. Executive Branch Power." *Harvard Law Review* 95 (November 1981): 191–211.

Hammer v. Dagenhart, 247 U.S. 251 (1918)

Benson, Paul R., Jr. *The Supreme Court and the Commerce Clause, 1937–1970.* New York: Dunellen Publishing, 1970.

Semonche, John E. *Charting the Future: The Supreme Court Responds to a Changing Society 1890–1920.* Westport, Conn.: Greenwood Press, 1978.

Hampton v. Mow Sun Wong, 426 U.S. 88 (1976)

Levi, David F. "The Equal Treatment of Aliens: Preemption or Equal Protection." *Stanford Law Review* 31 (July 1979): 1,069–1,091.

Maltz, Earl M. "The Burger Court and Alienage Classifications." *Oklahoma Law Review* 31 (1978): 671–691.

Rosberg, Gerald M. "The Protection of Aliens from Discriminatory Treatment by the National

Government." *Supreme Court Review* (1977): 275–339.

Harper v. Virginia State Board of Elections, 383 U.S. 663 (1966)

Bickel, Alexander. "The Voting Rights Cases." *Supreme Court Review* (1966): 79–102.

Bobbitt, Philip. *Constitutional Fate: Theory of the Constitution.* New York: Oxford University Press, 1982.

Bork, Robert H. *The Tempting of America: The Political Seduction of the Law.* New York: Free Press, 1990.

Harris v. McRae, 448 U.S. 297 (1980)

Appleton, Susan Frelich. "Beyond the Limits of Reproductive Choice: The Contributions of the Abortion Funding Cases to Fundamental Rights Analysis and to the Welfare Rights Thesis." *Columbia Law Review* 81 (May 1981): 721–758.

Hardy, David T. "*Harris v. McRae*: Clash of a Nonenumerated Right with Legislative Control of the Purse." *Case Western Law Review* 31 (spring 1981): 465–508.

Keynes, Edward, and Randall K. Miller. *The Court vs. Congress: Prayer, Busing and Abortion.* Durham, N.C.: Duke University Press, 1989.

Nixon, George Cameron. "*Harris v. McRae*: Cutting Back Abortion Rights." *Columbia Human Rights Law Review* 12 (spring/summer 1980): 113–136.

Harris v. New York, 401 U.S. 222 (1971)

Dershowitz, Alan, and John Hart Ely. "*Harris v. New York*: Some Anxious Observations on the Candor and Logic of the Emerging Nixon Majority." *Yale Law Journal* 80 (1971): 1,198.

Hawaii Housing Authority v. Midkiff, 467 U.S. 229 (1984)

"Leading Cases of the 1983 Term." *Harvard Law Review* 98 (1984): 225.

Heart of Atlanta Motel v. United States, 379 U.S. 241 (1964)

Benson, Paul R., Jr. *The Supreme Court and the Commerce Clause 1937–1970.* New York: Dunellen Publishing, 1970.

Schwartz, Bernard, ed. *Statutory History of the United States: Part II. Civil Rights.* New York: Chelsea House, 1970.

Home Building and Loan Association v. Blaisdell, 290 U.S. 398 (1934)

Keynes, Edward, with Randall K. Miller. *The Court vs. Congress: Prayer, Busing and Abortion.* Durham, N.C.: Duke University Press, 1989.

Palmer, Robert C. "Obligations of Contracts: Intent and Distortion." *Case Western Reserve Law Review* 37 (summer 1987): 631–673.

Humphrey's Executor v. United States, 295 U.S. 602 (1935)

Dry, Murray. "The Congressional Veto and the Constitutional Separation of Powers." In *The Presidency in the Constitutional Order*, Joseph M. Bessette and Jeffrey Tulis, eds. Baton Rouge: Louisiana State University Press, 1981.

Fisher, Louis. *The Constitution between Friends.* New York: St. Martin's Press, 1978.

Miller, Geoffrey P. "Independent Agencies." *Supreme Court Review* (1986): 41–97.

Schwartz, Bernard. *The Ascent of Pragmatism: The Burger Court in Action.* New York: Addison-Wesley, 1990.

Hurtado v. California, 110 U.S. 516 (1884)

Acker, James R. "Grand Jury and Capital Punishment." *Pacific Law Journal* 21 (1989): 31–118.

Hutchinson v. Proxmire, 443 U.S. 111 (1979)

Backer, Bradden C. "Constitutional Protection of Critical Speech and the Public Figure Doctrine: Retreat by Reaffirmation—*Hutchinson v. Proxmire*." *Wisconsin Law Review* (1980): 568–595.

Jones, Bruce. "Qualified Immunity for Federal Officials: A Proposed Standard for Defamation Cases." *Texas Law Review* 58 (April 1980): 789–807.

Turner, Jeff. "Legislative Immunity and Congressional Necessity." *Georgetown Law Review* 68 (February 1980): 783–805.

In re Gault, 387 U.S. 1 (1967)

Clark, Glen W. "Procedural Rights in the Juvenile Court: Incorporation or Due Process." *Pepperdine Law Review* 7 (spring 1980): 865–896.

Dorsen, Norma, and Daniel A. Rezneck. "In re *Gault* and the Future of Juvenile Law." *Family Law Quarterly* 1 (December 1967): 1–47.

Lefstein, Norman et al. "In Search of Juvenile Justice." In *Impact of Supreme Court Decisions: Empirical Studies.* 2d. ed. Theodore L. Becker and Malcolm

M. Feeley, eds. New York: Oxford University Press, 1973.

Paulsen, Monrad G. "The Constitutional Domestication of the Juvenile Court." *Supreme Court Review* (1967): 233–266.

In re Quirin, 317 U.S. 1 (1942)

Belknap, Michael R. "The Supreme Court Goes to War: The Meanings and Implications of the Nazi Saboteur Case." *Military Law Review* 89 (summer 1980): 59–95.

Cushman, Robert. "The Nazi Saboteur Case." *Cornell Law Quarterly* 28 (1942): 54–65.

INS v. Chadha, 462 U.S. 919 (1983)

Craig, Barbara Hinkson. *Chadha.* New York: Oxford University Press, 1988.

Dry, Murray. "The Congressional Veto and the Constitutional Separation of Power." In *The Presidency in the Constitutional Order,* Joseph M. Bessette and Jeffrey Tulis, eds. Baton Rouge: Louisiana State University Press, 1981.

Elliott, E. Donald. "*INS v. Chadha:* The Administrative Constitution, the Constitution and the Legislative Veto." *Supreme Court Review* (1983): 125–176.

Schwartz, Bernard. *The Ascent of Pragmatism: The Burger Court in Action.* New York: Addison-Wesley, 1990.

Irvin v. Doud, 366 U.S. 717 (1961)

Lofton, John. *Justice and the Press.* Boston: Beacon Press, 1966.

Reitz, Curtis R. "Federal Habeas Corpus: Impact of an Abortive State Proceeding." *Harvard Law Review* 74 (May 1961): 1,315.

Jacobellis v. Ohio 378 U.S. 184 (1964)

Emerson, Thomas I. *The System of Freedom of Expression.* New York: Random House, 1970.

Melott, Robert A. "Constitutional Law—Obscenity—Notes and Comments." *North Carolina Law Review* 43 (1964): 172–187.

"The Supreme Court, 1963 Term." *Harvard Law Review* 78 (November 1964): 207–210.

Jacobson v. Massachusetts, 197 U.S. 11 (1905)

James v. Valtierra, 402 U.S. 137 (1971)

"The Equal Protection Clause and Exclusionary Zoning after *Valtierra* and *Dandridge.*" *Yale Law Journal* 89 (1971): 61–86.

"The Supreme Court, 1970 Term." *Harvard Law Review* 85 (November 1971): 122–134.

Johnson v. Transportation Agency, Santa Clara County, 480 U.S. 616 (1987)

Bork, Robert H. *The Tempting of America: The Political Seduction of the Law.* New York: Free Press, 1990.

Meyer, David D. "Finding a 'Manifest Inbalance': The Case for a Unified Statistical Test for Voluntary Affirmative Action under Title VII." *Michigan Law Review* 87 (June 1989): 1,986–2,025.

Karcher v. Daggett, 462 U.S. 725 (1983)

Bagger, Richard H. "The Supreme Court and Congressional Apportionment: Slippery Slope to Equal Representation Gerrymandering." *Rutgers Law Review* 38 (fall 1985): 109–137.

Niemi, Richard G. "The Relationship between Votes and Seats: The Ultimate Question in Political Gerrymandering." *UCLA Law Review* 33 (October 1985): 185–212.

Powers, William B. "*Karcher v. Daggett:* The Supreme Court Draws the Line on Malapportionment and Gerrymandering in Congressional Redistricting." *Indiana Law Review* 17 (September 1984): 651–686.

Katz v. United States, 389 U.S. 347 (1967)

Kitch, Edmund W. "*Katz v. United States:* The Limits of the Fourth Amendment." *Supreme Court Review* (1968): 133–152.

Marks, Laurence Kaiser. "Telescopes, Binoculars and the Fourth Amendment." *Cornell Law Review* 67 (January 1982): 379–395.

Miller, Frank W. et al. *The Police Function.* New York: Foundation Press, 1986.

"Tracking Katz: Beepers, Privacy and the Fourth Amendment." *Yale Law Journal* 86 (1977): 1,461–1,508.

Katzenbach v. McClung, 379 U.S. 294 (1964)

Benson, Paul R., Jr. "The Supreme Court and the Commerce Clause 1937–1970." New York: Dunellen Publishing, 1970.

Katzenbach v. Morgan, 384 U.S. 641 (1966)

Bickel, Alexander M. "The Voting Rights Cases." *Supreme Court Review* (1966): 79–102.

Burt, Robert A. "Miranda and Title II: A Morganatic Marriage." *Supreme Court Review* (1969): 81–134.

Carter, Stephen L. "The Morgan 'Power' and the Forced Reconsideration of Constitutional Decisions." *University of Chicago Law Review* 53 (1986): 819–863.

Keynes, Edward, with Randall K. Miller. *The Courts vs. Congress.* Durham, N.C.: Duke University Press, 1989.

Leffell, Daniel J. "Congressional Power to Enforce Due Process Rights." Columbia *Law Review* 80 (October 1980): 1,265–1,295.

Kent v. Dulles, 357 U.S. 116 (1958)

Farber, Daniel A. "National Security: The Right to Travel and the Court." *Supreme Court Review* (1981): 263–290.

Ker v. California, 374 U.S. 23 (1963)

"*The Supreme Court, 1962 Term.*" *Harvard Law Review* 77 (November 1963): 113–119.

Keyes v. School District #1 of Denver, 413 U.S. 189 (1973)

Graglia, Lino A. "Disaster by Decree." Ithaca, N.Y.: Cornell University Press, 1976.

Whitman, Christina B. "Individual and Community: An Appreciation of Mr. Justice Powell." *Virginia Law Review* 68 (February 1982): 303–332.

Keyishian v. Board of Regents, 385 U.S. 589 (1967)

Bolmeier, Edward C. *Landmark Supreme Court Decisions on Public School Issues.* Charlottesville, Va.: The Michie Co., 1973.

Stewart, Malcolm. "The First Amendment, the Public Schools and the Inculcation of Community Values." *Journal of Law and Education* 18 (1989): 23–92.

Kingsley International Pictures Corp. v. Regents of University of New York State, 360 U.S. 684 (1959)

Kalven, Harry, Jr. "The Metaphysics of the Law of Obscenity." *Supreme Court Review* (1960): 1–45.

Lockhart, William B., and Robert C. McClure. "Obscenity Censorship: The Core Constitutional Issue—What Is Obscene." In *Commentaries on Obscenity.* Donald Sharp, ed. Metuchen, N.J.: Scarecrow Press, 1970.

Kinsella v. Krueger, 354 U.S. 1 (1957)

Bigel, Alan I. *The Supreme Court on Emergency Powers, Foreign Affairs and Protection of Civil Liber-ties 1935–1975.* New York: University Press of America, 1986.

McClelland, Gregory A. "The Problem of Jurisdiction over Civilians Accompanying the Forces Overseas–Still With Us." *Military Law Review* 117 (summer 1987): 153–217.

Kinsella v. U.S. ex rel. Singleton, 361 U.S. 234 (1960)

Bigel, Alan I. *The Supreme Court on Emergency Powers, Foreign Affairs and Protection of Civil Liberties 1935–1975.* New York: University Press of America, 1986.

Schwartz, Bernard. *A Commentary on the Constitution of the United States.* Part I. *The Powers of Government.* New York: Macmillan, 1963.

Kirby v. Illinois, 406 U.S. 682 (1972)

Schwartz, Bernard. *The Ascent of Pragmatism: The Burger Court in Action.* New York: Addison-Wesley, 1990.

"The Supreme Court, 1971 Term." *Harvard Law Review* 86 (1972): 157–164.

Kirchberg v. Feenstra, 450 U.S. 455 (1981)

Kirp, Donald et al. *Gender Justice.* Chicago: University of Chicago Press, 1986.

Kirkpatrick v. Preisler, 394 U.S. 526 (1969)

Eleanore Bushnell, ed. *The Court Steps In. Impact of Reapportionment of the Thirteen Western States.* Salt Lake City: University of Utah Press, 1970.

Konigsberg v. State Bar of California, 353 U.S. 252 (1957)

Emerson, Thomas I. *The System of Freedom of Expression.* New York: Random House, 1970.

Meiklejohn, Alexander. "The First Amendment Is Absolute." *Supreme Court Review* (1961): 245–266.

Korematsu v. United States, 323 U.S. 214 (1944)

Dembitz, Nanette. "Racial Discrimination and the Military Judgment: The Supreme Court's Korematsu Endo Decisions." *Columbia Law Review* 45 (1945): 175.

Rostow, Eugene V. "The Japanese American Cases—A Disaster." *Yale Law Review* 54 (1945): 489.

Ten Broek, Jacobus et al. *Prejudice, War and the Constitution.* Berkeley: University Press of California, 1968.

Kramer v. Union Free School District No. 15, 395 U.S. 621 (1969)

"The Supreme Court, 1968 Term." *Harvard Law Review* 83 (1969): 77–83.

Laird v. Tatum, 408 U.S. 1, 1972.

Ladiere, Eric. "The Justiciability and Constitutionality of Political Intelligence Gathering." *UCLA Law Review* 30 (June 1983): 976–1051.

Stempel, Jeffrey W. "Rehnquist, Recusal and Reform." *Brooklyn Law Review* 53 (fall 1987): 589–667.

Lamont v. Postmaster-General, 381 U.S. 301 (1965)

Cable, John L. *Decisive Decisions of United States Citizenship.* Charlottesville, Va: The Michie Co., 1967.

Lee, William E. "The Supreme Court and the Right to Receive Expression." *Supreme Court Review* (1987): 303–344.

Lane v. Wilson, 307 U.S. 268 (1939)

Lau v. Nichols, 414 U.S. 563 (1974)

Haft, Jonathan D. "Assuring Equal Educational Opportunities for Language Minority Students: Bilingual Education and the Equal Educational Opportunity Act of 1974." *Columbia Journal of Law and Social Positions* 18 (spring 1983): 209–293.

"Intent or Impact: Proving Discrimination under Title VI of the Civil Rights Act of 1964." *Michigan Law Review* 80 (April 1982): 1095–1110.

Levin, Betsy. "An Analysis of the Federal Attempt to Regulate Bilingual Education: Protecting Civil Rights or Controlling Curriculum. *Journal of Law and Education* 12 (January 1983): 29–60.

Lemon v. Kurtzman, 403 U.S. 602 (1971)

Weber, Paul J., and Dennis A. Gilbert. *Private Churches and Public Money.* Westport, Conn.: Greenwood Press, 1981.

Pfeffer, Leo. *Religion, State and the Burger Court.* Buffalo, N.Y.: Prometheus Books, 1984, pp. 115–167.

Giannella, Donald A. "Lemon and Tilton." In *Church and State,* Philip B. Kurland, ed. Chicago: University of Chicago Press, 1975.

Lincoln Federal Labor Union v. Northwestern Iron Co., 335 U.S. 525 (1949)

Lloyd Corp. v. Tanner, 407 U.S. 551 (1972)

Cohen, Laurence M. "*Pruneyard Shopping Center v. Robins:* Past, Present and Future." *Chicago-Kent Law Review* 57 (spring 1981): 373–395.

Cortese, Michele. "Property Rights and Human Values: A Right of Access to Private Property for Tenant Organizers. 17 *Columbia Human Rights Law Journal* 17 (spring/summer 1986): 257–282.

"Supreme Court, 1971 Term." *Harvard Law Review* 86 (1972): 122–130.

Local 28 of the Sheetmetal Workers' International Association v. EEOC, 478 U.S. 421 (1986)

McGrath, Kathleen E. "Supreme Court Endorses Court-Ordered Affirmative Action for Non-Victims: *Local 28 v. EEOC. Boston College Law Review* 29 (December 1987): 266–276.

Schnapper, Eric. "The Varieties of Numerical Remedies." *Stanford Law Review* 39 (1987): 851–916.

Selig, Joel L. "Affirmative Action in Employment: The Legacy of a Supreme Court Majority." *Indiana Law Review* 63 (spring 1988): 310–368.

Lochner v. New York, 198 U.S. 45, 1905.

Bork, Robert H. *The Tempting of America: The Political Seduction of the law.* New York: Macmillan, 1990.

Cox, Archibald. *The Court and the Constitution.* Boston: Houghton Mifflin, 1987.

Rubenfeld, Jed. "Right of Privacy." *Harvard Law Review* 102 (February 1989): 737–807.

Semonche, John E. *Charting the Future: The Supreme Court Responds to a Changing Society, 1890–1920.* Westport, Conn.: Greenwood Press, 1978.

Loving v. Virginia, 388 U.S. 1 (1967)

Lombardo, Paul A. "Miscegenation, Eugenics and Racism: Historical Footnotes to *Loving v. Virginia. U.C. Davis Law Review* 21 (winter 1988): 421–452.

Sickels, Robert J. *Race, Marriage and the Law.* Albuquerque: University of New Mexico Press, 1972.

Wadlington, Walter. "The Loving Case: Virginia's Antimiscegenation Statute in Historical Perspective." *Virginia Law Review* 52 (1966): 1,189–1,123.

Luther v. Borden, 48 U.S. 1 (1849)

Currie, David P. "The Constitution in the Supreme Court: Article IV and Federal Powers,

1836–1864." *Duke Law Journal* (September 1983): 695–747.

———. *The Constitution in the Supreme Court, 1789–1888*. Chicago: University of Chicago Press, 1985.

Elliott, Ward E. Y. *The Rise of Guardian Democracy*. Cambridge, Mass: Harvard University Press, 1974.

"Political Rights as Political Questions: The Paradox of *Luther v. Borden*." *Harvard Law Review* 100 (March 1987): 1,125–1,145.

Wiecek, William M. *The Guarantee Clause of the U.S. Constitution*. Ithaca, N.Y.: Cornell University Press, 1972.

Lynch v. Donnelly, 465 U.S. 668 (1984)

"Leading Cases of the 1983 Term." *Harvard Law Review* 98 (November 1984): 174.

Pfeffer, Leo. *Religion, State and the Burger Court*. Buffalo, N.Y.: Prometheus Books, 1984.

Rogers, Sidney Miles. "*Lynch v. Donnelly*: Our Christmas Will Be Merry Still." *Mercer Law Review* 36 (February 1984): 409–420.

Swanson, Wayne R. The Christ Child Goes to Court. Philadelphia, Pa.: Temple University Press, 1990.

Van Alstyne, William. "Trends in the Supreme Court: Mr. Jefferson's Crumbling Wall: A Comment on *Lynch v. Donnelly*." *Duke Law Journal* (1984): 770.

Lynch v. Household Finance Corp., 405 U.S. 538 (1972)

"The Supreme Court, 1971 Term." *Harvard Law Review* 86 (1972): 201–208.

Maher v. Roe, 432 U.S. 464 (1977)

Bobbitt, Philip. *Constitutional Fate: Theory of the Constitution*. New York: Oxford University Press, 1982.

Estreicher, Samuel. "Congressional Power and Constitutional Rights: Reflections on Proposed 'Human Life' Legislation." *Virginia Law Review* 68 (1982): 333–458.

Mallory v. United States, 354 U.S. 449 (1957)

Malloy v. Hogan, 378 U.S. 1 (1964)

Craver, Comann P., Jr. "Notes and Comments—Constitutional Law–Extension of the Privilege against Self-Incrimination." *North Carolina Law Review* 43 (1964): 161–172.

McKay, Robert B. "Self-Incrimination and the New Privacy." *Supreme Court Review* (1967): 193–232.

"The Supreme Court, 1963 Term." *Harvard Law Review* 78 (November 1964): 224–227.

Mapp v. Ohio, 367 U.S. 643 (1961)

Fine, Ralph. *Escape of the Guilty*. New York: Dodd, Mead, 1986.

Knowlton, R. E. "Supreme Court, *Mapp v. Ohio*, and Due Process of Law." *Iowa Law Review* 49 (1963): 14.

Stevens, Leonard A. *Trespass!* New York: Coward, McCann and Geoghegan, 1977.

Wingo, Harvey. "Rewriting *Mapp* and *Miranda*: A Preference for Due Process." *University of Kansas Law* 31 (winter 1983): 219–244.

Marbury v. Madison, 5 U.S. 137 (1803)

Bickel, Alexander M. *The Least Dangerous Branch*. New Haven, Conn.: Yale University Press, 1962.

Currie, David P. *The Constitution in the Supreme Court, 1789–1888*. Chicago: University of Chicago Press, 1985.

Fisher, Louis. *The Constitution between Friends*. New York: St. Martin's Press, 1978.

Grey, Thomas C. "Do We Have an Unwritten Constitution?" *Stanford Law Review* 27 (February 1975): 703.

Keynes, Edward, with Randall K. Miller. *The Court vs. Congress*. Durham, N.C.: Duke University Press, 1989.

McCloskey, Robert G. *The American Supreme Court*. Chicago: University of Chicago Press, 1960.

Marsh v. Chambers, 463 U.S. 783 (1983)

Drakeman, Donald L. "Antidisestablishmentarianism: The Latest (and Longest) Word from the Supreme Court." *Cardozo Law Review* 5 (fall 1983): 153–182.

Pfeffer, Leo. *Religion, State and the Burger Court*. Buffalo, N.Y.: Prometheus Books, 1984.

Walker, Diane L. "*Marsh v. Chambers*: The Supreme Court Takes a New Look at the Establishment Clause." *Pepperdine Law Review* 11 (1984): 591–611.

Martin v. Hunter's Lessee, 14 U.S. 304 (1816)

Currie, David P. *The Constitution in the Supreme Court 1789–1888*. Chicago: University of Chicago Press, 1985.

McCloskey, Robert G. *The American Supreme Court*. Chicago: Chicago University Press, 1960.

Miller, Thornton F. "John Marshall v. Spencer Roane: A Reevaluation of *Martin v. Hunter*'s Lessee." *Vir-*

ginia *Magazine of History and Biography* 96 (July 1988): 297–314.

Maryland v. Wirtz, 392 U.S. 183 (1967)

Delmonte, Rosemarie E. "*Garcia v. S.A. Metropolitan Transit Authority:* And the States Stand Alone." *Creighton Law Review* 19 (fall 1986): 105–131.

McCollom v. Board of Education, 333 U.S. 203 (1948)

Alioto, Samual A. "The Released Time Cases Revisited." *Yale Law Journal* 83 (1974): 1,202–1,236.

Johnson, Alvin W., and Frank H. Yost. *Separation of Church and State in the United States.* Minneapolis: University of Minneapolis Press, 1948.

Kauper, Paul G. *Religion and the Constitution.* Baton Rouge: Louisiana State University Press, 1964.

McCray v. United States, 195 U.S. 27 (1904)

McCloskey, Robert G. *The American Supreme Court.* Chicago: University of Chicago Press, 1960.

McCulloch v. Maryland, 17 U.S. 316 (1819)

Bickel, Alexander M. *The Least Dangerous Branch.* 2d ed. New Haven, Conn.: Yale University Press, 1962.

Currie, David P. *The Constitution in the Supreme Court, 1789–1888.* Chicago: University of Chicago Press, 1985.

Keynes, Edward, with Randall K. Miller. *The Court vs. Congress.* Durham: N.C.: Duke University Press, 1989.

McCloskey, Robert G. *The American Supreme Court.* Chicago: University of Chicago Press, 1960.

McGowan v. Maryland, 366 U.S. 420 (1961)

"Constitutional Law: Higher Education Facilities Act—Constitutionality of Federal Financial Aid to Church Related Colleges." *Harvard Law Review* 77 (March 1964): 1,353–1,360.

Gedicks, Frederick Mark. "Motivation, Rationality, and Secular Purpose in Establishment Review." *Arizona State Law Journal* (summer 1985): 677–726.

Smith, Michael E. "The Special Place of Religion in the Constitution." 1983 *Supreme Court Review* (1983): 83–123.

McGrain v. Daugherty, 273 U.S. 135 (1927)

Berger, Raoul. *Executive Privilege: A Constitutional Myth.* Cambridge, Mass.: Harvard University Press, 1974.

Fisher, Louis. *The Constitution between Friends.* New York: St. Martin's Press, 1978.

Memoirs of a Woman of Pleasure v. Massachusetts, 383 U.S. 413 (1966)

Monaghan, Henry P. "Obscenity." In *Commentaries on Obscenity,* Donald B. Sharp, ed. Metuchen, N.J.: Scarecrow Press, 1970.

Rembar, Charles. *The End of Obscenity.* New York: Random House, 1968.

"The Supreme Court, 1965 Term." *Harvard Law Review* 80 (November 1966): 186.

Meyer v. Nebraska, 262 U.S. 390 (1923)

Bolmeier, Edward C. *Landmark Supreme Court Decisions on Public School Issues.* Charlottesville, Va.: The Michie Co, 1973.

Richards, David A. J. "The Individual, the Family and the Constitution: A Jurisprudential Perspective." *NYU Law Review* 55 (1980): 1–62.

Miami Herald Publishing Co. v. Tornillo, 418 U.S. 241 (1974)

Geller, Henry. "Does *Red Lion* Square with *Tornillo.*" *University of Miami Law Review* 29 (spring 1975): 477–481.

Lipsky, Abbott B., Jr. "Reconciling *Red Lion* and *Tornillo:* A Consistent Theory of Media Regulation." *Stanford Law Review* 28 (1979): 563.

Power, L. A., Jr. "*Tornillo.*" *Supreme Court Review* (1987): 345–396.

Schmidt, Benno C., Jr. *Freedom of the Press vs. Public Access.* New York: Praeger Publishers, 1976.

Michael M. v. Superior Court of Sonoma County, 450 U.S. 464 (1981)

"Gender Based Statutory Rape Law Does Not Violate the Equal Protection Clause." *Cornell Law Review* 67 (August 1982): 1,109–1,127.

Kirp, Donald L. *Gender Justice.* Chicago: University of Chicago Press, 1986.

Olsen, Frances. "Statutory Rape: A Feminist Critique of Rights Analysis. *Texas Law Review* 63 (November 1984): 387–432.

Miller v. California, 413 U.S. 15 (1973)

Leventhal, Harold. "An Empirical Inquiry into the Effects of *Miller v. California* on the Control of Obscenity." *NYU Law Review* 52 (1977): 810.

Milliken v. Bradley, 418 U.S. 717 (1974)

Gewirtz, Paul. "Remedies and Resistance." *Yale Law Journal* 92 (March 1983): 585–681.

Graglia, Lino A. *Disaster by Decree.* Ithaca, N.Y.: Cornell University Press, 1976.

Miranda v. Arizona, 384 U.S. 436 (1966)

Baker, Liva. Miranda: *Crime, Law and Politics.* New York: Atheneum Press, 1983.

Berger, Mark. "Compromise and Continuity: Miranda Waivers, Confession Admissibility, and the Retention of Interrogation Protections." *University of Pittsburgh Law Review* 49 (summer 1988): 1,007–1,064.

Hallworth, G. L. "Myth of the Jury Trial: Analysis of the *Miranda v. Arizona* Decision." *Commonweal* 90 (April 25, 1969): 161–164.

Kamisar, Yale. "A Dissent from the Miranda Dissents: Some Comments on the 'New' Fifth Amendment and the Old 'Voluntariness' Test." *Michigan Law Review* 65 (1966): 59–104.

Medalie, Richard J. et al. "Custodial Police Interrogation." In *The Impact of Supreme Court Decisions.* 2d ed. Theodore L. Becker and Malcolm M. Feeley, eds. New York: Oxford University Press, 1973.

Nappi, Paul A. "Miranda and the Rehnquist Court: Has the Pendulum Swung Too Far? *Boston College Law Review* 30 (March 1989): 523–571.

White, Welsh S. *Life in a Balance.* Ann Arbor: University of Michigan Press, 1984.

Wingo, Harvey. "Rewriting *Mapp* and *Miranda*: A Preference for Due process." *University of Kansas Law Review* 31 (winter 1983): 219–244.

Mississippi University of Women v. Hogan, 458 U.S. 718 (1982)

Kirp, Donald L. et al. *Gender Justice.* Chicago: University of Chicago Press, 1986.

Keynes, Edward, with Randall K. Miller. *The Court vs. Congress: Prayer, Busing and Abortion.* Durham, N.C.: Duke University Press, 1989.

Shull, Mary Ellen. "Reinforcement of Middle-Level Review Regarding Gender Classification." *Pepperdine Law Review* 11 (1984): 421–440.

Missouri Ex rel. Gaines v. Canada, 305 U.S. 337 (1938)

Lusky, Louis. *By What Right?* Charlottesville, Va.: The Michie Co., 1975.

Lusky, Louis. "Minority Rights and the Public Interest." *Yale Law Journal* 52 (December 1942): 1–42.

Missouri v. Holland, 252 U.S. 416 (1920)

Lofgren, Charles A. "*Missouri v. Holland* in Historical Perspective." *Supreme Court Review* (1975): 77–122.

City of Mobile v. Bolden, 446 U.S. 55 (1980)

Binion, Gayle. "'Intent' and Equal Protection: A Reconsideration." Supreme Court Review (1983): 397–457.

Thernstrom, Abigail M. *Whose Vote Counts?* Cambridge, Mass.: Harvard University Press, 1987.

"Making the Violation Fit the Remedy: The Intent Standard and Equal Protection Law." *Yale Law Journal* 92 (December 1982): 328–351.

Moore v. Dempsey, 261 U.S. 86 (1923)

"Developments in the Law—Federal Habeas Corpus." *Harvard Law Review* 83 (March 1970): 1,050–1,121.

"Federal Habeas Corpus: Impact of an Abortive State Proceeding." *Harvard Law Review* 74 (1961): 1,315.

Greenberg, Jack. *Race Relations and American Law.* New York: Columbia University Press, 1959, p. 331.

Moose Lodge No. 107 v. Irvis, 407 U.S. 163 (1972)

Burns, Michael M. "The Exclusion of Women from Influential Men's Clubs and the Inner Sanctum and the Myth of Full Equality." *Harvard Civil Rights and Civil Liberties Law Review* 18 (1983): 321–408.

Hollingsworth, Lucretia I. "Sex Discrimination in Private Clubs." *Hastings Law Journal* 29 (November 1977): 421–449.

"The Supreme Court, 1971 Term." *Harvard Law Review* 86 (November 1972): 70–75.

Mueller and Noyes v. Allen, 463 U.S. 388 (1983)

Ambrose, Carla R. "*Mueller v. Allen.*" *New England Law Review* 19 (fall 1984): 459–486.

Nussbaum, Martin L. "*Mueller v. Allen.*" *Harvard Journal of Law and Public Policy* 7 (fall 1984): 551–580.

Pfeffer, Leo. *Religion, State and the Burger Court.* Buffalo: Prometheus Books, 1984.

Muller v. Oregon, 208 U.S. 412 (1908)

Collins, Ronald K. L., II, and Jennifer Frieser. "Looking Back on *Muller v. Oregon.*" Parts I and II. *ABA Journal* 69 (March 1983): 294–298; 472–477.

Semonche, John E. *Charting the Future: The Supreme Court Responds to a Changing Society, 1890–1920.* Westport, Conn.: Greenwood Press, 1978.

Munn v. Illinois, 94 U.S. 113 (1877)

Kitch, Edmund W., and Clara Ann Bowler. "The Facts of *Munn v. Illinois.*" *Supreme Court Review* (1978): 313–344.

Magrath, C. Peter. *Morrison R. Waite: The Triumph of Character.* New York: Macmillan, 1963.

Mykkeltvedt, Roald Y. *The Naturalization of the Bill of Rights.* New York: Associated Faculty Press, 1983.

N.A.A.C.P. v. Alabama, 357 U.S. 449 (1958)

Bork, Robert H. *The Tempting of America: The Political Seduction of the Law.* New York: Free Press, 1990.

Emerson, Thomas I. *The System of Freedom of Expression.* New York: Random House, 1970.

Schermer, Marsha Rockey. "Freedom of Association: *N.A.A.C.P. v. Alabama*" *Ohio State Law Journal* 41 (summer 1980): 823–857.

N.A.A.C.P. v. Button, 371 U.S. 415 (1963)

Emerson, Thomas I. *The System of Freedom of Expression.* New York: Random House, 1970.

"The Supreme Court, 1977 Term." *Harvard Law Review* 92 (November 1978): 166.

"The Supreme Court 1962 Term." Harvard Law Review 77 (November 1963): 122–124.

National League of Cities v. Usery, 426 U.S. 833 (1976)

Massey, Calvin R. "State Sovereignty and the Tenth and Eleventh Amendments." *Supreme Court Review* (1978): 225–296.

Michelman, Frank I. "States' Rights and States' Roles: Permutations of 'Sovereignty' in *National League of Cities v. Usery.*" *Yale Law Journal* 86 (May 1977): 1,165–1,195.

Nagel, Robert F. "Federalism as a Fundamental Value: National League of Cities in Perspective." *Supreme Court Review* (1981): 81–110.

Schwartz, Bernard. *The Ascent of Pragmatism: The Burger Court in Action.* New York: Addison-Wesley, 1990.

Tribe, Laurence H. "Unravelling *National League of Cities:* The New Federalism and Affirmative Rights to Essential Government Services." *Harvard Law Review* 90 (April 1977): 1,065–1,104.

Near v. Minnesota, 283 U.S. 697 (1931)

Blanchard, Margaret A. "The Institutional Press and Its First Amendment Privileges." *Supreme Court Review* (1978): 225–296.

Emerson, Thomas I. "The Doctrine of Prior Restraint." *Law and Contemporary Problems* 20 (1955): 648–671.

Lofton, John. *Justice and the Press.* Boston: Beacon Press, 1966.

"Previous Restraints on Speech." *Columbia Law Review* 31 (1931): 1,148–1,152.

Nebbia v. New York, 291 U.S. 502 (1934)

Bork, Robert H. *The Tempting of America: The Political Seduction of the Law.* New York: Free Press, 1990.

Schwartz, Bernard. *A Commentary on the Constitution of the United States.* Part II. *The Rights of Property.* New York: Macmillan, 1985, pp. 104–111.

Nebraska Press Association v. Stuart, 427 U.S. 539 (1976)

"First Amendment Protection of Criminal Defense Attorney's Extrajudicial Statements in the Decade since *Nebraska Press Association v. Stuart.*" *Whittier Law Review* (1987): 1,021.

Kane, Peter E. *Murder, Courts and the Press.* Carbondale: Southern Illinois University Press, 1986.

New Jersey v. T.L.O., 469 U.S. 325 (1985)

Hardin, Charles W., Jr. "Searching Public Schools: T.L.O. and the Exclusionary Rule." *Ohio State Law Journal* 47 (fall 1986): 1,099–1,114.

Reamey, Gerald S. "*N.J. v. T.L.O.:* The Supreme Court's Lesson on School Searches." *St. Mary's Law Review* 16 (1985): 933–949.

Zane, Dale Edward F. T. "School Searches under the Fourth Amendment." *Cornell Law Review* 72 (January 1987): 368–396.

New York Times v. Sullivan, 376 U.S. 254 (1964)

"Clear and Convincing." *Yale Law Journal* 92 (December 1982): 520–543.

Kalven, Harry, Jr. "The *New York Times* Case: A Note on the Central Meaning of the First Amendment." *Supreme Court Review* (1964): 191.

Nimmer, Melville G. "The Right to Speak from Times to Time: The First Amendment Theory Applied to Libel and Misapplied to Privacy." *California Law Review* 56 (August 1968): 935–967.

Schmidt, Benno C., Jr. *Freedom of the Press v. Public Access.* New York: Praeger, 1976.

New York Times v. United States, 403 U.S. 697 (1971)

Blanchard, Margaret A. "The Institutional Press and Its First Amendment Privileges." *Supreme Court Review* (1978): 225–296.

Godofsky, Stanley. "Protection of the Press from Prior Restraint and Harassment under Libel Laws." *University of Miami Law Review* 29 (spring 1975): 462–477.

Henkin, Louis. "The Right to Know and the Duty to Withhold: The Case of the Pentagon Papers." *University of Pennsylvania Law Review* 120 (1971): 271.

NLRB v. Jones, 301 U.S. 1 (1937)

Cox, Archibald. *The Court and the Constitution.* Boston: Houghton Mifflin, 1987.

O'Connor v. Donaldson, 422 U.S. 563 (1975)

Fremouw, William J. A New Right to Treatment. *Journal of Psychiatry and Law* 2 (spring 1974) 7–32.

Kopolow, Louis E. "A Review of Major Implications of the *O'Connor v. Donaldson* Decision." *American Journal of Psychiatry* 133 (April 1976): 379–383.

Lundergan, E. Kirsten. "The Right to Be Present: Should It Apply to the Involuntary Civil Commitment Hearing." *New Mexico Law Review* 17 (winter 1987): 165–187.

Olmstead v. United States, 277 U.S. 438, 1928.

Posner, Richard A. "The Uncertain Protection of Privacy of the Supreme Court." *Supreme Court Review* (1979): 173–216.

Oregon v. Mitchell, 400 U.S. 112 (1970)

Estreicher, Samuel. "Congressional Power and Constitutional Rights: Reflections on Proposed 'Human life' Legislation." *Virginia Law Review* 68 (February 1982): 333–458.

Orr v. Orr, 440 U.S. 268 (1979)

Becker, Mary E. "Prince Charming: Abstract Equality." *Supreme Court Review* (1987): 201–247.

Gilson, Gary D. "Alimony Awards and Middle-Tier Equal Protection Scrutiny." *Nebraska Law Review* 59 (winter 1980): 172–189.

Signoracci, Diane M. "A Husband's Constitutional Right Not to Pay Alimony." *Ohio State Law Journal* 41 (winter 1980): 1,061–1,086.

Palko v. Connecticut, 302 U.S. 319 (1937)

Bork, Robert H. *The Tempting of America: The Political Seduction of the Law.* New York: Free Press 1990.

Cox, Archibald. *The Court and the Constitution.* 1987. Boston: Houghton Mifflin Co.

Henkin, Louis. "Selective Incorporation in the Fourteenth Amendment." *Yale Law Journal* 73 (1963): 74–88.

Paris Adult Theatre I v. Slaton, 413 U.S. 49 (1973)

"On Privacy: Constitutional Protection for Personal Liberty." *NYU Law Review* 48 (1963) 670.

"The Supreme Court, 1972 Term." *Harvard Law Review* 87 (1973): 160–175.

Payton v. New York, 445 U.S. 573 (1980)

Evans, Jeffrey L. "Constitutional Restraints on Residential Warrantless Arrest Entries: More Protection for Privacy Interests in the Home." *American Journal of Criminal Law* 10 (March 1982): 1–27.

Harbaugh, Joseph D., and Nancy Lesse Faust. "Knock on Any Door: Home Arrests after *Payton* and *Steagald.*" *Dickinson Law Review* 86 (winter 1982): 191–238.

Schaefer, Walter V. "Prospective Rulings: Two Perspectives." *Supreme Court Review* (1982): 1–24.

"The Supreme Court, 1979 Term." *Harvard Law Review* 94 (1980): 178–187.

Pell v. Procunier, 417 U.S. 817 (1974)

Blanchard, Margaret A. "The Institutional Press and Its First Amendment Privileges." *Supreme Court Review* (1979): 225–296.

Hutchinson, Joseph C. "Analyzing the Religious Free Exercise Rights of the Inmates: The Significance of *Pell, Jones* and *Wolfish.*" *NYU Review of Law and Social Change* 11 (1982–1983): 413–440.

Perez v. Brownell, 356 U.S. 44 (1958)

Cable, John L. *Decisive Decisions of United States Citizenship.* Charlottesville, Va.: The Michie Co., 1967.

Kurland, Philip B. "The Supreme Court, 1963 Term. Forward: Equal in Origin and Equal in Title to the Legislative and Executive Branches of the Government." *Harvard Law Review* 78 (November 1964): 143–176.

Personnel Administrator v. Feeney, 442 U.S. 256, 1983.

Binion, Gayle. "'Intent' and Equal Protection: A Reconsideration." *Supreme Court Review* (1983): 397–457.

Kanowitz, Leo. "'Benign' Sex Discrimination: Its Troubles and Their Cure." *Hastings Law Review* 31 (July 1980): 1,379–1,431.

Rosenblum, Bruce E. "Discriminatory Purpose and Disproportionate Impact: An Assessment after Feeney." *Columbia Law Review* 79 (1979): 1,376–1,413.

Pierce v. Society of Sisters, 268 U.S. 510 (1925)

Johnson, Alvin W., and Frank H. Yost. *Separation of Church and State in the United States.* Minneapolis: University of Minnesota Press, 1948.

Pfeffer, Leo. *Religion, State and the Burger Court.* Buffalo, N.Y.: Prometheus Books, 1984.

Richards, David A. J. "The Individual, the Family and the Constitution: A Jurisprudential Perspective." *NYU Law Review* 55 (1980): 1–62.

Yudof, Mark G. "When the Government Speaks: Toward a Theory of Government Expression in the First Amendment. *Texas Law Review* 57 (August 1979): 863.

Planned Parenthood of Central Missouri v. Danforth, 428 U.S. 52, 1976.

Keynes, Edward, with Randall K. Miller. *The Courts vs. Congress: Prayer, Busing and Abortion.* Durham, N.C.: Duke University Press, 1989.

Richards, David A. J. "The Individual, the Family and the Constitution: A Jurisprudential Perspective." *NYU Law Review* 55 (April 1980): 1–62.

Siliciano, John. "The Minor's Right to Privacy: Limitations on State Action after *Danforth* and *Carey.*" *Columbia Law Review* 77 (December 1977): 1,216.

Plessy v. Ferguson, 163 U.S. 537 (1896)

Kluger, Richard. *Simple Justice: The History of* Brown v. Board of Education *and Black America's Struggle for Equality.* New York: Knopf, 1976.

Lofgren, Charles A. *The Plessy Case.* New York: Oxford University Press, 1987.

Maidment, Richard A. "*Plessy v. Ferguson* Re-examined." *Journal of American Studies* 7 (August 1973): 125–132.

Poe v. Ullman, 367 U.S. 497 (1961)

Bobbitt, Philip. *Constitutional Fate: Theory of the Constitution.* New York: Oxford University Press, 1982.

Bourguignon, Henry J. "The Second Mr. Justice Harlan: His Principles of Judicial Decision Making." *Supreme Court Review* (1979): 251–328.

Redlich, Norman. "Are There Certain Rights . . . Retained by the People." In *The Rights Retained by the People,* Randy E. Barnett, ed. Fairfax, Va.: George Mason University Press, 1989.

Pollock v. Farmers' Loan and Trust Co., 158 U.S. 601 (1895)

Rapaczynski, Andrzej. "From Sovereignty to Process: The Jurisprudence of Federalism after Garcia." *Supreme Court Review* (1985): 341–420.

Semonche, John E. "Charting the Future: The Supreme Court Responds to a Changing Society, 1890–1920." Westport, Conn.: Greenwood Press, 1978.

Powell v. Alabama, 287 U.S. 45 (1932)

Lusky, Louis. "Minority Rights and the Public Interest." *Yale Law Journal* 52 (December 1942): 1–42.

Mykkeltvedt, Roald Y. *The Naturalization of the Bill of Rights.* New York: Associated Faculty Press, 1983, pp. 42–50.

Powell v. McCormack, 395 U.S. 486 (1969)

Berger, Raoul. *Executive Privilege: A Constitutional Myth.* Cambridge, Mass.: Harvard University Press, 1974.

"Comments on *Powell v. McCormack.*" *U.C.L.A. Law Review* 17 (1969): 1–41.

Profitt v. Florida, 428 U.S. 242 (1976)

"The Supreme Court, 1975 Term." *Harvard Law Review* 90 (November 1976): 63–76.

Pruneyard Shopping Center v. Robins, 447 U.S. 74 (1980)

Cohen, Laurence M. "Pruneyard Shopping Center v. Robins: Past, Present and Future." *Chicago-Kent Law Review* 57 (spring 1981): 373–395.

McCauley, James M. "Comments: Transferring the Privately Owned Shopping Center into a Public Forum." *University of Richmond Law Review* 15 (spring 1981): 699.

Munroe, Cordelia S. "Notes—Constitutional Law." *Marquette Law Review* 64 (spring 1970): 507.

Pulley v. Harris. 465 U.S. 37 (1984)

Cook, Cheryl. "Does the Crime Fit the Punishment." *Criminal Justice Journal* 6 (spring 1983): 333–343.

Railway Express Agency v. New York,
336 U.S. 106 (1949)

Red Lion Broadcasting Co. v. F.C.C.,
395 U.S. 367 (1969)

Barrett, John C., and Mary Louise Frampton. "From the F.C.C.'s Fairness Doctrine to *Red Lion's* Fiduciary Principle." *Harvard Civil Liberties Law Review* 5 (January 1970): 89.

Lipsky, Abbott B., Jr. "Reconciling *Red Lion* and *Tornillo:* A Consistent Theory of Media Regulation." *Stanford Law Review* 28 (1979): 563.

Marks, Richard D. "Broadcasting and Censorship: First Amendment Theory after *Red Lion.*" *George Washington Law Review* 38 (July 1970): 974.

Schmidt, Benno C., Jr. *Freedom of the Press vs. Public Access.* New York: Praeger, 1976.

Reed v. Reed, 404 U.S. 71 (1971)

Johnston, John D., Jr. "Sex Discrimination and the Supreme Court, 1971–1974." *NYU Law Review* 49 (November 1974): 617–692.

Kirp, David L., et al. *Gender Justice.* Chicago: University of Chicago Press, 1986.

Schwartz, Bernard. *The Ascent of Pragmatism: The Burger Court in Action.* New York: Addison-Wesley, 1990.

Regents of the University of California v. Bakke,
438 U.S. 265 (1978)

Dreyfuss, Joel, and Charles Lawrence, III. *The* Bakke *Case: The Politics of Inequality.* New York: Harcourt Brace Jovanovich, 1979.

Lofgren, Charles A. *The* Plessy *Case.* New York: Oxford University Press, 1987.

Schwartz, Bernard. *Behind Bakke: Affirmative Action and the Supreme Court.* New York: New York University Press, 1988.

Stone, Julius. "Justice in the Slough of Equality." *Hastings Law Review* (May 1978): 995–1,024.

Reynolds v. Sims, 377 U.S. 533 (1964)

Ball, Howard. *The Warren Court's Conceptions of Democracy.* East Rutherford, N.J.: Fairleigh Dickinson University Press, 1971.

Bushnell, Eleanore. "The Court Steps In." In *Impact of Reapportionment on the Thirteen Western States,* Eleanore Bushnell, ed. Salt Lake City: University of Utah Press, 1970.

Cortner, Richard C. *The Apportionment Cases.* Knoxville: University of Tennessee Press, 1970.

Kurland, Philip B. "The Supreme Court, 1963 Term. Forward: Equal in Origin and Equal in Title to the Legislative and Executive Branches of the Government." *Harvard Law Review* 78 (November 1964): 143–176.

Rhode Island v. Innes, 446 U.S. 291 (1980)

White, Welsh S. *Life in the Balance.* Ann Arbor: University of Michigan Press, 1984.

———. "Interrogation without Questions: *Rhode Island v. Innes* and *United States v. Henry.*" *Michigan Law Review* 78 (1980): 1209.

Richmond Newspapers, Inc. v. Virginia,
448 U.S. 555 (1980)

Kane, Peter E. *Murder, Courts and the Press.* Edwardsville: South Illinois University Press, 1986.

Leeper, Roy V. "*Richmond Newspapers, Inc. v. Virginia* and the Emerging Right of Access." *Journalism Quarterly* 61 (autumn 1984): 615.

Lewis, Anthony. "A Public Right to Know about Public Institutions: The First Amendment as a Sword." *Supreme Court Review* (1980): 1–26.

Rideau v. Louisiana, 373 U.S. 723 (1963)

Kane, Peter E. *Murder, Courts and the Press.* Edwardsville: Southern Illinois University Press, 1986.

Roberts v. Louisiana, 431 U.S. 633 (1977)

"Leading Cases of the 1983 Term." *Harvard Law Review* 98 (November 1984): 195.

"The Supreme Court, 1975 Term." *Harvard Law Review* 90 (November 1975): 63–67.

Roberts v. U.S. Jaycees, 468 U.S. 609 (1984)

Sheleff, Leon Shaskolsky. *Ultimate Penalties.* Columbus: Ohio State University, 1987, p. 88.

Rochin v. California, 342 U.S. 165 (1952)

Allen, Francis A. "Due Process and State Criminal Procedure: Another Look." *Northwestern University Law Review* 48 (1953): 16–35.

Roe v. Wade, 410 U.S. 113 (1973)

Ely, John Hart. "The Wages of Crying Wolf: A Comment on *Roe v. Wade.*" *Yale Law Journal* 82 (April–July 1973): 920–949.

Faux, Marian. *Roe v. Wade.* New York: Macmillan, 1980.

Glendon, Mary Ann. *Abortion and Divorce in Western Law.* Cambridge, Mass: Harvard University Press, 1987.

Horan, Dennis et al., eds. *Abortion and the Constitution: Reversing* Roe v. Wade *through the Courts.* Washington, D.C.: Georgetown University Press, 1987.

Keynes, Edward, with Randall K. Miller. *The Court vs. Congress: Prayer, Busing and Abortion.* Durham, N.C.: Duke University Press, 1989.

Rabin, Eva R. *Abortion, Politics and the Courts:* Roe v. Wade *and Its Aftermath.* Rev. ed. New York: Greenwood Press, 1987.

Schwartz, Bernard. *The Ascent of Pragmatism: the Burger Court in Action.* New York: Addison-Wesley, 1990.

Roemer v. Board of Public Works, 426 U.S. 736 (1976)

Kirby, James C. "*Everson* to *Meek* and *Roemer.*" *North Carolina Law Review* 55 (1977): 563–575.

Pfeffer, Leo. *Religion, State and the Burger Court.* Buffalo, N.Y.: Prometheus Books, 1984.

"The Supreme Court, 1975 Term." *Harvard Law Review* 90 (1976): 133–142.

Rogers v. Lodge, 458 U.S. 613 (1982)

O'Rourke, Timothy G. "Constitutional and Statutory Challenges to Local At-Large Elections." *University of Richmond Law Review* 17 (fall 1982): 39–98.

"The Supreme Court, 1981 Term." *Harvard Law Review* 96 (November 1982): 106–110.

Ross v. Moffitt, 417 U.S. 600 (1974)

Schwartz, Bernard. *The Ascent of Pragmatism: The Burger Court in Action.* New York: Addison-Wesley, 1990.

Rostker v. Goldberg, 453 U.S. 57 (1981)

"Equal Protection, the Supreme Court, 1980 Term." *Harvard Law Review* 95 (November 1981): 162–181.

Kirp, Donald L., et al. *Gender Justice.* Chicago: University of Chicago Press, 1986.

"Males Only Draft Registration Does Not Violate Equal Protection Component of the Fifth Amendment." *Washington University Law Quarterly* 59 (winter 1982): 1,371–1,392.

Roth v. United States, 354 U.S. 476 (1957)

Henkin, Louis. "Morals and the Constitution: The Sin of Obscenity." In *Commentaries on Obscenity,* Donald B. Sharp, ed. Metuchen, N.J.: Scarecrow Press, 1970.

Monaghan, Henry P. "Obscenity 1966: The Marriage of Obscenity Per Se and Obscenity Per Quod." In *Commentaries on Obscenity,* Donald B. Sharp, ed. Metuchen, N.J.: Scarecrow Press, 1970.

Sharp, Donald B. "Obscenity Law and the Intransigent Threat of *Ginzburg.*" In *Commentaries on Obscenity,* Donald B. Sharp, ed. Metuchen, N.J.: Scarecrow Press, 1970.

Runyon v. McCray, 427 U.S. 160 (1976)

Kaczorowski, Robert J. "The Enforcement Provisions of the Civil Rights Act of 1866: A Legislative History in Light of *Runyon v. McCrary.*" *Yale Law Journal* 98 (January 1989): 565–595.

McClellan, James. "The Foibles and Fables of Runyon." *Washington University Law Quarterly* 67 (winter 1989): 13–45.

Tushnet, Mark. "Patterson and the Politics of the Judicial Process." *Supreme Court Review* (1988) 43–60.

Saia v. New York, 334 U.S. 558 (1948)

Berns, Walter. *Freedom, Virtue and the First Amendment.* Baton Rouge: Louisiana State University Press, 1957.

Scales v. United States, 367 U.S. 203 (1961)

Emerson, Thomas I. *The System of Freedom of Expression.* New York: Random House, 1970.

"The Supreme Court, 1960 Term." *Harvard Law Review* 75 (1961): 111–117.

Schall v. Martin, 467 U.S. 253 (1984)

Guggenheim, Martin. "The Treatment of Juveniles in Our Court System." *Criminal Justice* 1 (spring 1986): 25–27.

McCune, John Foster. "Juvenile Law: Whatever Happened to In Re *Gault* and Fundamental Fairness in Juvenile Delinquency Proceedings?" *Wake Forest Law Review* 22 (summer 1987): 347–366.

Schecter Poultry Corp. v. United States, 295 U.S. 495 (1935)

Benson, Paul R., Jr. *The Supreme Court and the Commerce Clause, 1937–1970.* New York: Dunellen, 1970.

Bigel, Alan I. *The Supreme Court on Emerging Powers, Foreign Affairs and Protection of Civil Liberties, 1935–1975.* Lanham, Md.: University Press of America, Inc., 1986.

Bork, Robert H. *The Tempting of America: The Political Seduction of the Law.* New York: Free Press, 1990.

Schenck v. United States, 249 U.S. 47 (1919)

Mendelson, Wallace. "Clear and Present Danger—From *Schenck* to *Dennis*." *Columbia Law Review* 52 (1952): 313.

Redish, Martin H. "Advocacy of Unlawful Conduct and the First Amendment: In Defense of Clear and Present Danger." *California Law Review* 70 (September 1982): 1,159–1,200.

Strong, Frank R. "Fifty Years of 'Clear and Present Danger': From *Schenck* to *Brandenburg* and Beyond." *Supreme Court Review* (1969): 41–80.

Scheuer v. Rhodes, 416 U.S. 232 (1974)

Schick v. Reed, 419 U.S. 256 (1974)

"The Supreme Court, 1974 Term." *Harvard Law Review* 89 (1975): 59–67.

Schlesinger v. Ballard, 419 U.S. 498 (1975)

"The Supreme Court, 1974 Term." *Harvard Law Review* 89 (1975): 97–103.

Schmerber v. California, 384 U.S. 757 (1966)

Hardy, Julie A. "The Admissibility of Mental State Observations Obtained during Unlawful Custodial Interrogation: Drawing the Line on the Red or Physical Evidence Distinction." *Boston College Law Review* 30 (1989): 1,029–1,069.

Mell, Christina Louise. "Employee Drug Testing: Guilty until Proven Innocent." *Missouri Law Review* 52 (summer 1987): 625–646.

Miller, Frank W. *The Police Function.* 4th ed. New York: Foundation Press, 1986.

Schneckloth v. Bustamonte, 412 U.S. 218 (1973)

White, Welsh S. *Life in a Balance.* Ann Arbor: University of Michigan Press, 1984.

Schneider v. Irvington, 308 U.S. 367 (1979)

School District of Abington Township v. Schempp, 374 U.S. 203 (1963)

Becker, Theodore L., and Malcolm M. Feeley. *The Impact of Supreme Court Decisions.* 2d ed. New York: Oxford University Press, 1973.

Bobbitt, Philip. *Constitutional Fate: Theory of the Constitution.* New York: Oxford University Press, 1982.

Katz, Wilbert G. *Religion and American Constitutions.* Evanston, Ill.: Northwestern University Press, 1964.

Keynes, Edward, with Randall K. Miller. *The Court vs. Congress: Prayer, Busing and Abortion.* Durham, N.C.: Duke University Press, 1989.

Kurland, Philip B. "The School Prayer Cases." In *The Wall between Church and State,* Dallin H. Oaks and Robert F. Drinan, eds. Chicago: University of Chicago Press, 1963.

Scott v. Illinois, 440 U.S. 367 (1979)

Abramson, Paul H. "Constitutional Law—Right to Counsel: Another Anachronism When Handed Down." *University of Florida Law Review,* 31 (summer 1979): 786–798.

Screws v. United States, 325 U.S. 91 (1945)

Selective Service System v. Minnesota Public Interest Research Group, 468 U.S. 841 (1984)

"Leading Cases of the 1983 Term" *Harvard Law Review* 98 (November 1984): 87–97.

Pfeffer, Leo. *Religion, State and the Burger Court.* Buffalo, N.Y.: Prometheus Books, 1984.

Young, Rowland L. "Court Upholds Tie between Draft Registration and Aid." *American Bar Association Journal* 70 (September 1984): 132–133.

Shapiro v. Thompson, 394 U.S. 618 (1969)

Keynes, Edward, with Randall K. Miller. *The Court vs. Congress.* Durham, N.C.: Duke University Press, 1989.

Lusky, Louis. *By What Right.* Charlottesville, Va.: The Michie Co., 1975.

BIBLIOGRAPHY

Abernathy, M. Glenn. *Civil Liberties Under the Constitution.* 5th ed. Columbia: University of South Carolina Press, 1989.

Bigel, Alan I. *The Supreme Court on Emergency Powers, Foreign Affairs, and Protection of Civil Liberties 1935–1975.* Lanham, Md.: University Press of America, 1986.

Bodenhamer, David J. *Fair Trial: Rights of the Accused in American History.* New York: Oxford University Press, 1992.

Cortner, Richard C. *The Supreme Court and the Second Bill of Rights.* Madison: University of Wisconsin Press, 1981.

Currie, David P. *The Constitution in the Supreme Court: The Second Century 1888–1986.* Chicago: University of Chicago Press, 1990.

Epstein, Lee, and Thomas G. Walker. *Constitutional Law for a Changing America.* 4th ed. Washington, D.C.: CQ Press, 2001.

Finkelman, Paul. *Religion and American Law: An Encyclopedia.* New York: Garland Publishing, 2000.

Hemmer, Joseph J., Jr. *The Supreme Court and the First Amendment.* New York: Praeger Publishers, 1986.

Keynes, Edward. *Court v. Congress: Prayer, Busing, and Abortion.* Durham, N.C.: Duke University Press, 1989.

LaFave, Wayne R. *Search and Seizure: A Treatise on the Fourth Amendment.* 2d ed. St. Paul, Minn.: West Publishing, 1987.

Lee, Rex E. *A Lawyer Looks at the Equal Rights Amendment.* Provo, Utah: Brigham Young University Press, 1980.

Lieberman, Jethro K. *A Practical Companion to the Constitution: How the Supreme Court Has Ruled on Issues from Abortion to Zoning.* Berkeley: University of California Press, 1999.

Marks, Thomas C., Jr., and J. Tim Reilly. *Constitutional Criminal Procedure.* North Scituate, Mass.: Duxbury Press, 1979.

McWhirter, Darien A. *Equal Protection.* Phoenix, Ariz.: Oryx Press, 1995.

Morgan, Richard E. *The Law and Politics of Civil Rights and Liberties.* New York: Alfred A. Knopf, 1985.

Nelson, William E. *The Fourteenth Amendment: From Political Principle to Judicial Doctrine.* Cambridge, Mass.: Harvard University Press, 1988.

Pfeffer, Leo. *Religious Freedoms.* Skokie, Ill.: National Textbook Co., 1977.

Phillips, Michael J. *The Lochner Court, Myth and Reality: Substantive Due Process from the 1890s to the 1930s.* Westport, Conn.: Praeger Publishers, 2001.

Strong, Frank R. *Substantive Due Process of Law: A Dichotomy of Sense and Nonsense.* Durham, N.C.: Carolina Academic Press, 1986.

Taylor, Telford. *Grand Inquest: The Story of Congressional Investigations.* New York: Da Capo Press, 1974.

Tedford, Thomas L. *Freedom of Speech in the United States.* New York: Random House, 1985.

Urofsky, Melvin I. *Affirmative Action on Trial: Sex Discrimination in* Johnson v. Santa Clara. Lawrence: University Press of Kansas, 1997.

Van Alstyne, William W. *Interpretations of the First Amendment.* Durham, N.C.: Duke University Press, 1984.

Warsoff, Louis A. *Equality and the Law.* New York: Liveright Publishing, 1938.

Wright, Benjamin Fletcher, Jr. *The Contracts Clause of the Constitution.* Westport, Conn.: Greenwood Press, 1982.

INDEX

❦